A Concise Dictionary

of Minnesota Ojibwe

The University of Minnesota Press
gratefully acknowledges
the generous assistance provided
for publication of this book
by
the Mille Lacs Band of Ojibwe Indians
and
Grand Casino, Inc.

A Concise Dictionary
of Minnesota Ojibwe

John D. Nichols and Earl Nyholm

Illustrations by Earl Nyholm

University of Minnesota Press

Minneapolis

London

Published by the University of Minnesota Press
111 Third Avenue South, Suite 290, Minneapolis, MN 55401-2520
Printed in the United States of America on acid-free paper

Library of Congress Cataloging-in-Publication Data

Nichols, John (John D.)
    A concise dictionary of Minnesota Ojibwe / John D. Nichols and
Earl Nyholm.
        p.   cm.
    Includes index.
    Rev., expanded ed. of: Ojibwewi-Ikidowinan. 1979.
    ISBN 0-8166-2427-5 (acid-free paper).—ISBN 0-8166-2428-3 (pbk. :
acid-free paper)
    1. Ojibwa language—Dictionaries—English. 2. English language—
Dictionaries—Ojibwa. I. Nyholm, Earl. II. Ojibwewi-Ikidowinan.
III. Title.
PM853.N53   1995
497'.3—dc20   94-35219

Contents

Preface

This dictionary of Anishinaabemowin, the Ojibwe or Chippewa language, can be used by all interested in the linguistic and cultural heritage of the Anishinaabe. It is intended primarily for students of Ojibwe as a second language, and for speakers wishing models for spelling in a standardized orthography. Although, with just over seven thousand words, it contains but a small part of the language's total vocabulary, the words included have been selected to be representative of the everyday language of conversation and of narration. To these have been added a rich sample of traditional cultural vocabulary.

Anishinaabemowin is not spoken in a single standard form but varies from place to place in sounds, vocabulary, and grammar. The words in this dictionary represent the speech of several individuals belonging to the Mille Lacs Band of Ojibwe at Mille Lacs Lake, near Onamia, Minnesota. Other forms of the same words used there and elsewhere are equally valid. Teachers will want to supplement the words listed here with those prevalent in their home communities.

This book is an expansion and complete revision of *Ojibwewi-Ikidowinan: An Ojibwe Word Resource Book* published in 1979. We have long felt the need to revise that book and wish to thank Kent Smith, Director of Indian Studies at Bemidji State University, for his encouragement and support for the necessary editorial meetings. The Social Sciences and Humanities Research Council of Canada supported the data collection and analysis by John Nichols that underlies this book. The Mille Lacs Band of Ojibwe provided technical support for database processing and manuscript preparation. Richard Rhodes's superb *Eastern Ojibwa-Chippewa-Ottawa Dictionary* (1985), covering several of the more easterly dialects of Anishinaabemowin, introduced a number of new conventions for Ojibwe dictionaries, some of which we have adopted here.

The words are drawn largely from the stories and conversations of Maude Kegg (b. 1904) and the late Jim Littlewolf (b. 1895), among others. Many words were originally supplied by the late Selam Ross of Cass Lake for the first student word list prepared at Bemidji State University, or by Earl Nyholm. Others at Mille Lacs have supplied words or helped to determine meanings, among them Mildred Benjamin, James Clark, Jessie Clark, Lucy Clark, Loretta Kalk, Betty Kegg, Darrell Kegg, Donald Kegg, Ernest Kegg, Herman Kegg, Jesse Kegg, Matt Kegg, Batiste Sam, Frances Sam, and Frank Sam. The language lessons of Rose Barstow, Angeline Northbird, and Timothy Dunnigan (1977–80) of the University of Minnesota, Mildred Benjamin (1991) of Neyashing School at Mille Lacs, and Richard Gresczyk and James Clark (1992) of Minneapolis suggested many new words to include. The total database from which the words were selected has over 25,000 words. This will serve as the basis for a future reference dictionary. Nearly all of the words have been rechecked with Maude Kegg, to whom we owe the greatest debt.

John D. Nichols
Department of Native Studies/
    Department of Linguistics
University of Manitoba
Winnipeg, Manitoba

Earl Nyholm
Department of Modern
    Languages
Bemidji State University
Bemidji, Minnesota

Key to Entries

General Form of Entries

Each entry in the Ojibwe-English section begins with a **head word**, printed in boldface, and is sequenced according to the position of this head word in the Ojibwe alphabetical order:

a, aa, b, c, d, e, g, h, ', i, ii, j, k, m, n, o, oo, p, s, t, w, y, z

The head word is often only one of many inflected word forms sharing a common **word stem**. The word stem carries the basic meaning of a word. Inflections are prefixes, suffixes, or sound changes, applied to the core word stem, which express grammatical ideas such as 'plural' or 'first person'. The actual number of inflected word forms that share a stem can be large; for example, the stem *ganawaabam-* ('looks at someone') can occur in well over a thousand inflected forms, of which the following are only a few examples:

inganawaabamaa 'I look at someone'
giganawaabamaasiwaanaanig 'we don't look at them'
oganawaabamaawaan 'they look at someone'
inganawaabamigonaadog 'someone must be looking at us'
ganawaabamagiban 'had I looked at someone'
genawaabamajig 'the ones you look at'

The addition of prefixes called **preverbs** to indicate secondary ideas such as time and direction creates thousands more possible word forms for each word stem. A few examples related to the first of the examples above are as follows:

ingii-kanawaabamaa 'I looked at someone'
ingii-pi-ganawaabamaa 'I came here to look at someone'
inga-ganawaabamaa 'I will look at someone'
niwii-kanawaabamaa 'I want to look at someone'
inga-gagwe-ganawaabamaa 'I will try to look at someone'

Since the number of actual forms of a given word stem is too large for all of them to be in a dictionary, a single word form is selected as the head word to stand in for all of the inflected forms sharing the stem.

The head word is followed by a **class code**, printed in italics, identifying the kind of word the head word is, and a **gloss**, suggesting possible translations of the head word. The following illustrates a complete entry for a simple word:

HEAD WORD   CLASS CODE   GLOSS

biindig *pc* indoors, inside

Other kinds of information may be given in an entry. The following sample entry contains additional **forms** of the head word and a **reference** to an alternate form of the head word or to a similar word in another local variety of the language. These are printed in boldface. The **labels** that identify the forms and introduce a reference word are printed in italics, as are any other notes on the structure or use of the word:

HEAD WORD   CLASS CODE   GLOSS   PLURAL FORM

babiigomakakii *na* toad; *pl* **babiigomakakiig**;

dim **babiigomakakiins**; *also* **obiigomakakii**

DIMINUTIVE FORM   REFERENCE

Head words or reference words followed by an asterisk identify word forms not used at Mille Lacs by the contributors, but which are known to be used by others or in adjacent varieties of the language. For example, the equivalent of 'those' (when referring to animates) in Mille Lacs Ojibwe is *ingiw*, but two forms of the same word used in other varieties of Ojibwe are also given and marked with the asterisk as *igiw*⋆ and *agiw*⋆.

Some entries present the **word stem** after the head word when the form of the stem cannot be determined by inspection of the head word. It appears in boldface and between slashes as a warning that it is not necessarily a complete word by itself without inflections:

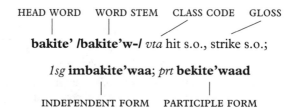

HEAD WORD   WORD STEM   CLASS CODE   GLOSS

bakite' /**bakite'w-**/ *vta* hit s.o., strike s.o.;

1sg **imbakite'waa;** *prt* **bekite'waad**

INDEPENDENT FORM   PARTICIPLE FORM

In the English-Ojibwe Index, the words are grouped under English **keys**, sequenced in English alphabetical order. The keys are important words or phrases occurring in the gloss of one or more Anishinaabemowin words in the dictionary. The keys are printed in capitals flush to the left margin. Under each key appear one or more **secondary keys**, printed in small capitals and indented from the left margin. These are English words or phrases incorporating the key, but usually giving additional words to narrow down the range of meaning of the target word. Anishinaabemowin words whose gloss incorporates the meaning of the secondary key follow one by one, with a **gloss** for each (unless it is the same as an immediately preceding secondary key or the gloss for the previous word), a **word stem** or **plural ending** for some entries, then the **head word** in boldface, and a **class code** in italics:

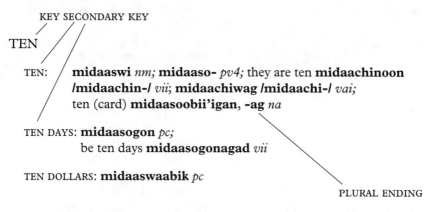

KEY   SECONDARY KEY

TEN

TEN: **midaaswi** *nm;* **midaaso-** *pv4;* they are ten **midaachinoon** /**midaachin-**/ *vii;* **midaachiwag** /**midaachi-**/ *vai;* ten (card) **midaasoobii'igan, -ag** *na*

TEN DAYS: **midaasogon** *pc;* be ten days **midaasogonagad** *vii*

TEN DOLLARS: **midaaswaabik** *pc*

PLURAL ENDING

Entries for the Different Word Classes

The major classes of words in Anishinaabemowin are verbs, nouns, pronouns, and particles. The verbs and nouns occur in a number of subclasses, each coded differently and using a particular set of inflections. Several kinds of pronouns exist, some with inflected forms. Particles are uninflected words and can be divided into many sub-classes depending on their structure and the way they are used in sentences. Major word-building prefixes called **preverbs** are given separate entries although the head of each entry is not a separate word by itself. The major forms of the inflec-

Table I. Class Codes

Code	Word class	Description
na	animate noun	noun of the animate gender that is not obligatorily possessed
nad	dependent animate noun	noun of the animate gender that is obligatorily possessed
na-pt	animate participle	participle form of a verb functioning as a noun of the animate gender
ni	inanimate noun	noun of the inanimate gender that is not obligatorily possessed
nid	dependent inanimate noun	noun of the inanimate gender that is obligatorily possessed
ni-pt	inanimate participle	participle form of a verb functioning as a noun of the inanimate gender
nm	number	uninflectable number particle
pc	particle	uninflectable particle (adverb, conjunction, exclamation, etc.)
pf	prefix	personal prefix appearing on nouns and verbs
pn	prenoun	lexical prefix forming a particle from a noun stem
pr	pronoun	pronoun (demonstrative, dubitative, indefinite, interrogative, pausal, or personal)
pv1	preverb of class 1	tense, aspect, mood, or syntactic prefix appearing on verbs
pv2	preverb of class 2	directional prefix occurring on verbs
pv3	preverb of class 3	relative prefix occurring on verbs (and on some nouns and particles)
pv4	preverb of class 4	lexical prefix occurring on verbs, nouns, or particles
vai	animate intransitive verb	verb with an intransitive stem, an animate subject, and no object
vai2	class 2 animate intransitive verb	verb with a transitive stem (as for an inanimate object), an animate subject, and no object; inflected as intransitive
vai + o	animate intransitive verb with object	verb with an intransitive stem, an animate subject, and an object
vii	inanimate intransitive verb	verb with an intransitive stem, an inanimate subject, and no object
vta	transitive animate verb	verb with a transitive stem and an animate object

Table I. Class Codes (cont.)

Code	Word class	Description
vti	transitive inanimate verb	verb with a transitive stem, and an inanimate object, and a characteristic set of inflections
vti2	class 2 transitive inanimate verb	verb with an inanimate object but with a different characteristic set of inflections
vti3	class 3 transitive inanimate verb	verb with an inanimate object but with a different characteristic set of inflections

tional personal prefixes are also given entries of their own. The class codes for words are interpreted in Table 1.

Entries for Nouns. The typical noun entry has the singular form of the noun as the head word. The class codes identify the **gender** of the noun: *na* for animate nouns and *ni* for **inanimate** nouns. Nouns in the animate gender include a number of non-living things (e.g., mitts, nets, and playing cards) as well as words identifying humans, animals, trees, and spirits. Other words referring to nouns agree with them in gender.

The full **plural** form of a noun, labelled *pl*, is given in noun entries in the Ojibwe-English section of the dictionary. A plural noun form contains the noun stem and a plural suffix, and reveals the gender: plurals ending in *g* are animate and those ending in *n* are inanimate. Although the stem of a noun is abstract and not necessarily identical to the singular form, it is convenient to view the plural form of most nouns as consisting of the singular form to which a plural ending is added. In the English-Ojibwe Index, the singular form of the noun is followed by this plural ending, cited with an initial hyphen.

In the Ojibwe-English section, certain other important inflected forms are provided to help students, although they are usually predictable from a comparison of the singular and plural forms, or from the abstract stem. The **locative** form, labelled *loc*, is an adverbial form of a noun stem indicating location 'in, at, to, from, etc.' or comparison. The locative forms of nouns naming living things and abstractions are omitted here; although possible, they are relatively uncommon. All the locative forms end in *-ng*. The **diminutive** form, labelled *dim*, indicates relative small size: 'a small one (small for the kind of thing named), a baby one'. The diminutive forms are omitted for nouns naming abstractions and for others where a diminutive seems to be uncommon. All of the productive diminutives cited end in a long nasalized vowel followed by *s*, indicated in the orthography with the long vowel followed by *ns*.

The following is a typical entry for a noun:

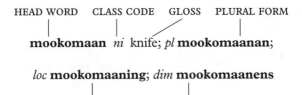

HEAD WORD   CLASS CODE   GLOSS   PLURAL FORM

mookomaan *ni* knife; *pl* **mookomaanan**;

loc **mookomaaning**; *dim* **mookomaanens**

LOCATIVE FORM   DIMINUTIVE FORM

The head word of a typical entry for a **dependent** noun, an obligatorily possessed noun always having a personal prefix before its stem, is a singular form with a first-person possessor shown by the personal prefix. The class codes also indicate gender: *nad* for animate dependent nouns and *nid* for inanimate dependent nouns. The underlying stem, to which other personal prefixes may be attached, is given between slashes and with preceding and trailing hyphens:

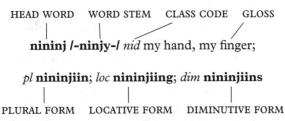

HEAD WORD   WORD STEM   CLASS CODE   GLOSS

nininj /-ninjy-/ *nid* my hand, my finger;

pl **nininjiin**; *loc* **nininjiing**; *dim* **nininjiins**

PLURAL FORM   LOCATIVE FORM   DIMINUTIVE FORM

The stem of a noun is given for dependent nouns and for those nouns commonly occurring only in the plural form, which is then used as the head word of the entry. The stem in such entries is given with a trailing hyphen and between slashes, following the head word. The stem of other nouns may be determined from the singular form and the plural form.

Entries for Verbs. The form of the inflected word selected as the head word in entries for verbs varies according to the class of the verb. The classes are distinguished on the basis of the stem class, reflecting transitivity and gender, and the paradigm class of inflections used. Because of grammatical differences between Anishinaabemowin and English, it is convenient to use certain **gloss codes** in the glosses for special types of verb objects. Table 2 gives definitions of such codes.

Several additional inflected forms are supplied. Entries for the verbs most likely to have a first-person subject are supplied with an **independent**

Table 2. Gloss codes

Code	Expansion	Description
s.o.	someone	the object is animate, either human or non-human
s.t.	something	the object is inanimate
(s.t.)	(something)	optional second object of either gender

form (also called form A) word inflected for a first-person subject. Forms using the independent or A order (paradigm) of inflections occur primarily in main clauses. All verb entries also give a **participle** form inflected for a third-person subject. A participle is a nominalized verb form similar to the **conjunct** form (also called form B) of verbs appearing primarily in subordinate clauses. Both share the conjunct or B order (paradigm) of inflections to which participles may add noun-like plural or other inflections. The participles occur in a variety of grammatical constructions including relative clauses and who and what questions. The participle forms characteristically show the ablaut process called **initial change,** which alters the first syllable of the stem by a change in sounds, the insertion of a syllable, or the addition of a prefix. Initial change may also appear on certain other conjunct verb forms. The most common expressions of this process of initial change are presented in Table 3.

    Entries for Animate Intransitive Verbs (*vai* and *vai2*). These are verbs that typically take an animate subject and make no inflectional reference to an object. The head word for an animate intransitive verb is a third-person singular subject form in the independent or A (main clause) order of inflections, meaning 'he, she, or it (something animate) is X, does X, is doing X'. If the stem differs from the head word, it is given between slashes and with a trailing hyphen. The class code and a gloss follow. The glosses are given as English infinitives but without the 'to'. The independent form, labelled *1sg*, is given for the verbs most likely to have a first-person singular subject. It means 'I am X, do X, am doing X'. The participle, labelled *prt*,

Table 3. Initial change

Initial change is a process that affects the first syllable of a preverb or verb stem in a conjunct verb or participle. In the regular process of initial change the first vowel of the preverb or stem is replaced as follows:

Unchanged	Changed
a	e
aa	ayaa
e	aye
i	e
ii	aa
o	we
oo	waa

Certain stems beginning in *dan, dazh, das, dash,* or *daa* do not undergo regular initial change but rather prefix *en.* The main other irregular form is the change of the direction prefix *bi-* 'here, hither' to *ba-*.

has a third-person singular subject and means 'one who is X, does X, is doing X'. The following is a typical entry for such a verb:

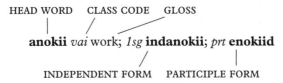

HEAD WORD   CLASS CODE   GLOSS

anokii *vai* work; *1sg* **indanokii**; *prt* **enokiid**

INDEPENDENT FORM   PARTICIPLE FORM

For verbs most commonly used in a plural form, the head word is a third-person plural independent form and the gloss may include a plural pronoun. Many of these are **reciprocal** verbs, the reciprocal or mutual action of which is typically expressed by translations such as 'they see each other', and 'we run out together'. Other inflected forms in these entries are also plural: the independent form labelled *1pl* means 'we are X, do X, are doing X', and the participle means 'the ones who are X, do X, are doing X'. The word stem, stripped of all inflections, is presented with a trailing hyphen and between slashes following the plural head word. The following is a typical entry for such a verb:

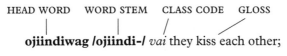

HEAD WORD   WORD STEM   CLASS CODE   GLOSS

ojiindiwag /ojiindi-/ *vai* they kiss each other;

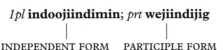

1pl **indoojiindimin**; *prt* **wejiindijig**

INDEPENDENT FORM   PARTICIPLE FORM

For some verbs commonly used in an impersonal form, the head word is such a form with the ending *-m*. The stem follows.

Entries for Animate Intransitive Verbs with Objects (*vai* + *o*). Although the animate intransitive (*vai*) verbs typically occur without objects, many of them may take objects and some often do. The later are labelled *vai* + *o* here. Their independent inflections may then be somewhat different from those used when no object is present. The gloss in the entry for one of these verbs includes the code (s.t.) to indicate an object may be present. The form of the entry follows that of the animate intransitive verbs, but two first-person singular subject independent forms are given, the first used without an object and the second with an inanimate object and meaning 'I do X to it, I am doing X to it'.

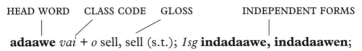

HEAD WORD   CLASS CODE   GLOSS   INDEPENDENT FORMS

adaawe *vai* + *o* sell, sell (s.t.); *1sg* **indadaawe, indadaawen**;

prt **edaawed**

|

PARTICIPLE FORM

Entries for Inanimate Intransitive Verbs (*vii*). These verbs take an inanimate or impersonal subject, but no object. The head word is a singular subject independent order verb form, generally the same as the stem. The gloss, following the class code, omits the English subject pronoun 'it' when the subject is singular. Since the subject of such a verb is always inanimate and thus third person, there are no first-person forms. The singular participle form follows the gloss. Inanimate intransitive stems, especially those ending in a long vowel, may occur with an augment -*magad* with no apparent change in meaning. For the long vowel-final stems, the augmented singular subject independent form is given after the label *aug*, followed by the participle of the augment, labelled as *prt aug:*

HEAD WORD   CLASS CODE   GLOSS   PARTICIPLE FORM

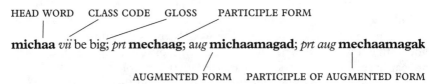

michaa *vii* be big; *prt* **mechaag**; *aug* **michaamagad**; *prt aug* **mechaamagak**

AUGMENTED FORM   PARTICIPLE OF AUGMENTED FORM

Where the verb is most commonly used in the plural, the head word is given in the plural subject independent order form with the stem following. The other forms are also given with plural subjects:

HEAD WORD   WORD STEM   CLASS CODE   GLOSS   PARTICIPLE FORM

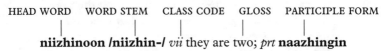

niizhinoon /**niizhin-**/ *vii* they are two; *prt* **naazhingin**

The stem is also given for verbs of this class that have a stem ending in a short vowel, but that generally add an augment *n* in the head word form:

HEAD WORD   WORD STEM   CLASS CODE   GLOSS   PARTICIPLE FORM

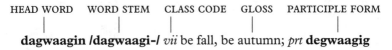

dagwaagin /**dagwaagi-**/ *vii* be fall, be autumn; *prt* **degwaagig**

Entries for Transitive Inanimate Verbs (*vti, vti2, vti3*). These verbs typically take an animate subject and an inanimate object. The head word is a second-person singular subject on inanimate singular object form in the **imperative** (command) order of inflections: '(you) do X to it!' The class code and gloss follow. The position of the inanimate object is shown in the gloss by the gloss code s.t., standing for 'something'. The first-person singular subject on inanimate singular object independent form, labelled *1sg*, means 'I do X to it, am doing X to it'. The participle form has a third-person singular subject and an inanimate singular object and means 'one who does X to it, is doing X to it':

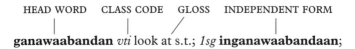

HEAD WORD   CLASS CODE   GLOSS   INDEPENDENT FORM

ganawaabandan *vti* look at s.t.; *1sg* **inganawaabandaan;**

prt **genawaabandang**

PARTICIPLE FORM

The underlying stem of each type of transitive inanimate verb can be found by stripping the inflectional ending from the head word. For the *vti*, the ending to remove is *an*; for the *vti2*, it is *oon*, and for most of the others it is *n*. Thus the stem of the preceding example is /ganawaaband-/ found by removing the ending -*an* from the head word.

Entries for Transitive Animate Verbs (*vta*). Transitive animate verbs take animate objects. The typical head word is a second-person singular subject on animate singular object form in the imperative (command) order of inflections: '(you) do X to her, him, or it (animate thing)'. Where this form is not identical to the stem, the word stem is given between slashes and with a trailing hyphen. Three special symbols using capital letters may appear in such word stems. They are explained in Table 4.

The class code and gloss follow. The position of the animate object in the gloss is marked by the gloss code s.o., standing for 'someone', meaning here 'him, her, or it (animate thing)'. This code indicates that the object is grammatically animate, not that it is necessarily human or a living being. Thus it stands for any animate noun object, including the non-living ones (e.g., mitts, nets, and playing cards), as well as humans and animals. The first-person singular subject on animate singular object independent form follows, labelled *1sg* and meaning 'I do X to her, him, or it (animate thing); I am doing X to her, him, or it (animate thing)'. All entries are given with a third-person subject on animate singular object participle meaning 'one who does X to him, her, or it (animate thing); one who is doing X to him, her, or it (animate thing)'.

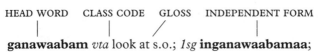

HEAD WORD   CLASS CODE   GLOSS   INDEPENDENT FORM

ganawaabam *vta* look at s.o.; *1sg* **inganawaabamaa;**

prt **genawaabamaad**

PARTICIPLE FORM

Some **double-object** verbs allow a second object of either gender in addition to the primary animate object (often the recipient or benefici-ary). This second object is indicated in the glosses with (s.t.), here indicat-

Table 4. Special symbols in word stems

Symbol	Meaning
N	The stem shows an alternation between *n* in certain inflected forms and *zh* in others, e.g., /miiN-/ in *nimiinaa* 'I give it to someone' and *miizh* 'give it to someone!'
S	The stem shows an alternation between *s* in certain inflected forms and *sh* in others, e.g., /mawadiS-/ in *nimawadisaa* 'I visit someone' and *mawadishishin* 'visit me!'
nN	The stem shows an alternation between *n* in certain inflected forms and *nzh* in others, e.g., /wiinN-/ in *wiinaad* 'that he names him' and *wiinzh* 'name someone!'

ing a noun of either gender. No inflectional reference is made to this second object.

miizh /miiN-/ give (s.t.) to s.o.; *1sg* **nimiinaa;** *prt* **maanaad**

A few verbs of this class commonly do not occur in the imperative forms chosen as the head word. In these cases the head word is replaced by an underlying stem, indicated as such by a trailing hyphen.

Reduplication on Verb Stems. Verb stems may be extended by a process of reduplication in which a copy of all or part of the first syllable of the stem, sometimes altered, is added to the front of the stem. A reduplicated stem may carry meanings of extension, distribution, or repetition in time or space, or plurality, such as 'keep doing X', 'do X here and there', 'do X off and on', 'do X to or for each (of several)'. For example, the verb stem /niimi-/ 'dance' has a reduplicated form /naaniimi-/ as in *naaniimi* 'he/she keeps dancing, dances here and there, dances off and on'. On stative verbs it is commonly used by older speakers when the subject is plural: *ginwaa* 'it is long', *gagaanwaawan* 'they (inanimate) are long'. The most common regular strategies for reduplication are suggested in Table 5. However, there are many stems that use an irregular pattern of reduplication. It has not been possible to check all of the verbs in this dictionary with enough different speakers to establish all of the possible reduplicated forms of each stem. To help those looking up Ojibwe words here, some irregular reduplication strategies are shown in the Ojibwe-English section by cross-reference entries, with the head of the entry being the start of an irregular reduplicated stem followed by a reference to the unreduplicated form. For example, the entry indicating that stems beginning with *gagaanw-* (with the final *w* of such entries to be treated also as *o*, so also *gagaano-*) may be based on a stem beginning with *ginw-* (or *gino-*):

gagaanw= < ginw=

Table 5. Regular verb reduplication strategies

Reduplication is a process that prefixes a copy or partial copy of the first syllable of a word stem to that stem, generally adding meanings of extension, repetition, distribution, or plurality. While verb stems can be reduplicated with a regular reduplication strategy as suggested here, other stems require different strategies. Still others seem to allow the use of more than one strategy, with the resulting forms, perhaps, differing in meaning. In general, in the regular strategies, the length of the initial syllable is preserved and repeated in the prefixed element. Except for initial syllables with the vowel *e* the vowel of the prefixed element is *a*, or, if the vowel of the initial syllable is long, *aa*. Initial *o* is treated as if initial *wi-* or *wo-*, apparently in free variation. The cover symbol C stands for any initial consonant.

Unreduplicated initial sound	Reduplicated as
a=	aya=
aa=	aayaa=
e=	eye=
i=	ayi=
o=	wawo= or wawi=
Ca=	CaCa=
Caa=	CaaCaa=
Ce=	CeCe=
Ci=	CaCi=
Cii=	CaaCii=
Co=	CaCo=
Coo=	CaaCoo=

Some stems in initial *Cw-* retain the *w* in the prefixed element and others do not. Stems that prefix *en-* in initial change may add a prefix *in-* before undergoing regular reduplication. In irregular reduplication strategies, the vowel of the initial syllable of the stem, the vowel of the prefixed element, or both may change in ways other than those described above. The initial consonant may become fortis or appear as the second member of a consonant cluster when the prefixed element is added.

In a few cases full entries are given for stems that have reduplication, either regular or irregular. Several stems show a kind of frozen reduplication that is not the result of the productive application of a reduplication strategy. The common reduplicated forms of some of the particles are also given separate entries.

Entries for Pronouns (*pr*), Particles (*pc*), Numbers (*nm*), and Preverbs (*pv*). The entries for pronouns, particles, numbers, and preverbs contain the **head word** (not actually a full word in the case of preverbs), the **class code**, the **gloss**, and, in some entries, a note in italics providing some explanation of the classification or use of the word:

HEAD WORD   CLASS CODE   GLOSS   GLOSS NOTE

niin *pr* I, me *first-person singular personal pronoun*

Entries for Prefixes (*pf*). The entries for personal prefixes begin with a prefix given with a trailing equal sign, indicating that the prefix is a word part, not a word. When written in a full word, the personal prefix (or other item so marked) is written without the equal sign and attached directly to the rest of the word in which it occurs.

Notes on Glosses

The glosses for verbs may include qualifying words, sometimes enclosed within parentheses, that indicate the nature or quality of the being or thing described. For example, the gloss for the head word *miskwaabikad* is 'be red (as something mineral)', showing that this verb is normally used only to describe things made of mineral substances such as metal, rock, or glass. Other classifying phrases may limit the usual application of a verb to something stick- or woodlike (sticks, trees, people, etc.), sheetlike (cloth, clothing, bark, paper, etc.), or stringlike (rope, lines, snakes, etc.), among others. There is usually a general verb for each meaning that is not limiting in this way, and this is the one preferred by younger apeakers. In translating from Ojibwe to English, such classifying phrases are not needed, but in translating from English to Ojibwe it is necessary to take these phrases into account to make sure the appropriate verb for the material described is used, unless the general form is preferred. In the traditional language, figurative use of such classifying verbs will also be found.

There are few single-word equivalents in English for Ojibwe verbs of motion. Most types of motion are represented in Ojibwe not by a general verb but by a word part, which combines with another word part or parts having directional or descriptive meaning. For example, there is no general word equivalent to English 'run' but rather a set of verb stems describing specific ways of running, all containing a common word part meaning 'run', as in *biijibatoo* 'run here', *gizhiikaabatoo* 'run fast', and *maajiibatoo* 'start off running'. The closest equivalents to English general motion verbs are forms with initial *bim(i)=* meaning 'along, by' as in *bimibatoo* 'run along, run by'.

Verb stems ending in *=bizo* (*vai*) or *=bide* (*vii*) are often translated here by phrases including English verbs such as 'drive, fly, operate, run, speed'. The basic meaning of such verb stems is that the action is one of rapid motion or operation, and the selection of the appropriate English equivalents requires the subject and situation to be taken into account. Similarly, verb stems ending in *=(i)se* (but not *=ose*) may be translated with a wide range of English words indicating smooth, rapid, and, often, uncontrolled or self-initiated movement or action such as 'fly, fall, happen, pass (as time)'. Again the subject and situation must be considered before the appropriate translation can be selected.

The glosses for transitive verbs may include indications of the means or instrument of execution of the action, or other qualifying words. For example, the gloss for the head word *bookoshkan* is 'break s.t. in two by foot or body', indicating the use of this verb is generally restricted to breaking done by the body (as in sitting on or bumping against something) or by the feet (as in kicking or stamping on something). Other common instrumental phrases are 'by hand' (which might also indicate some abstract means), 'with the hands' or 'by pulling', 'by heat', 'by hitting', 'by throwing or dropping' or 'in impact', and 'using something' (i.e., some tool). In translating from Ojibwe to English it may not be necessary to include such qualifying words, but in translating from English to Ojibwe it is necessary to look at the full gloss to make sure the correct verb for a given means or instrument is used.

Glosses containing the word 'certain' in phrases such as 'to a certain place', 'from a certain place', or 'a certain number' translate words or per-verbs containing (or acting as if they contained) word parts called **relative roots**. Within a word these hold a place usually reserved for a part that specifies location, direction, manner, extent, shape, size, number, or some other adverbial idea. The relative roots classify the relative kind of specification required but leave its exact nature open. They just tell that some direction, way, extent, degree, amount, or number is to be specified. In sentences they are used to point to some word or phrase (or even a gesture) that specifies the adverbial idea more exactly. For example, the verb stem *izhaa* 'go to a certain place' contains the relative root *izh=* (sometimes turning up in other stems as *in=*), which points to some place or direction. In a statement this place or direction is specified with a separate word or phrase. The word *oodenaang* 'to town' serves as the specifier in this example: *Oodenaang ingii-izhaa* 'I went to town'. The relative root may also point to a question word asking for the exact specification, as in this example with *aandi* 'where?': *Aandi gaa-izhaayan?* "Where did you go?"

Sounds and Orthography

There is no standard orthography shared by all of the local varieties of Anishinaabemowin. Some speakers write in a kind of English folk phonetics. Many speakers in Northern Canada write with the special characters of the shorthand-based Northern Algonquian syllabary. The roman orthography used in the book is only one of many possible writing systems that have been recently developed for Anishinaabemowin. Devised by Charles Fiero, it has won wide acceptance among language teachers in the United States and Canada. The main principles underlying it are that the letters or combinations of letters, although drawn from the same alphabet used to write English, stand for Ojibwe sounds, not English sounds, and that only the basic sounds (phonemes) of the language are written, not the predictable phonetic variants of them.

As most speakers of Ojibwe familiar with this writing system are literate in English, they often adopt English capitalization and punctuation conventions. In this dictionary, however, capitalization is generally restricted to place-names and personal names. Writers of Ojibwe should feel free to follow English conventions of capitalization (and so capitalize names of nationalities, days of the week, months, spirits and deities, etc.) and punctuation if they find them helpful.

In the brief description of Ojibwe sounds and orthography given in this section, some English words containing equivalents for Ojibwe sounds are listed. These are only approximations as each language has its own system of sounds and pronunciations. The actual pronunciation of a speaker of Minnesota Ojibwe should be followed.

Ojibwe Alphabetical Order

In this dictionary Ojibwe words are alphabetized in the following order:

a, aa, b, c, d, e, g, h, ', i, ii, j, k, m, n, o, oo, p, s, t, w, y, z

Note that the double vowels are treated as standing for unit sounds and are alphabetized after the corresponding single vowels. The digraphs *ch, sh,* and *zh,* although standing for unit sounds, are alphabetized as sequences of two letters. The character ' stands for a glottal stop, which is a significant speech sound in Minnesota Ojibwe.

Vowels

Basic Vowels. There are three short vowels: a, i, and o.

Table 6. Short Vowels

	Short Vowels	
	Front	Back
High	i	o
Low	a	

The four long vowels take more time to say than the short vowels. Three of them are paired with corresponding short vowels and so are written double: *aa, ii, oo.* The fourth long vowel is not paired with any short vowel and so it is written without doubling: *e.*

Table 7. Long Vowels

	Long Vowels	
	Front	Back
High	ii	oo
Low	e	aa

Each basic vowel is given below along with a phonetic transcription, Ojibwe words containing it, and one or more English words containing roughly equivalent sounds. The letters standing for the sounds focused on are given in boldface in the examples.

	Phonetic	Ojibwe examples		English equivalents
a	[ə]~[ʌ]	*agim*	'count someone!'	**a**bout
		namadabi	'sits down'	
		baashkizigan	'gun'	
aa	[aː]	*aagim*	'snowshoe'	f**a**ther
		maajaa	'goes away'	

e	[e:]~[ɛ:]	*emikwaan* 'spoon'	café
		awenen 'who'	
		anishinaabe 'person, Indian, Ojibwe'	
i	[I]	*inini* 'man'	pin
		mawi 'cries'	
ii	[i:]	*niin* 'I'	seen
		googii 'dives'	
o	[o]~[U]	*ozid* 'someone's foot'	obey, book
		anokii 'works'	
		nibo 'dies, is dead'	
oo	[o:]~[u:]	*oodena* 'town'	boat, boot
		anookii 'hires'	
		goon 'snow'	
		bimibatoo 'runs along'	

Nasal Vowels. Nasal vowels are indicated by writing the appropriate basic vowel followed by *nh*. Before a *y* or a glottal stop ' the *h* may be omitted in writing. In some earlier versions of this orthography, they were written with a hook underneath or underlined. There are no direct English equivalents:

aanh	[ã:]	*banajaanh* 'nestling'
enh	[ẽ:]~[ɛ̃:]	*nisayenh* 'my younger sister or brother'
iinh	[ĩ:]	*awesiinh* 'wild animal'
		agaashiinyi, agaashiinhyi '(someone) is big'
oonh	[õ:]~[ũ:]	*giigoonh* 'fish'

Nasalized Vowels. Vowels are nasalized before *ns, nz,* and *nzh.* The *n* is then omitted in pronunciation. A few examples are:

> *gaawiin ingikendanziin* 'I don't know it'
> *jiimaanens* 'small boat'
> *oshkanzhiin* 'someone's fingernail(s)'

Long vowels after a nasal consonant *m* or *n* are often nasalized, especially before *s, sh, z,* or *zh*. It is often difficult to decide whether to write these as nasalized vowels or not. For example, while we write the word for 'moose' without indicating the phonetic nasalization, many prefer to write it with an *n*:

> *mooz* or *moonz* 'moose'

Consonants and Other Sounds

The non-nasal consonants occur in pairs with one member of the pair a strong or **fortis** consonant and the other member of the pair a weak or **lenis** consonant. The strong consonants do not occur at the beginning of words (unless a vowel is left off), may sound long or double, and are voiceless. The weak consonants can occur at the beginning of words and are often voiced, especially in the middle of words.

Table 8. Consonants and other sounds

		Labial	Aveolar	Palatal	Velar	Glottal
Stops and Affricates	Strong	p	t	ch	k	
	Weak	b	d	j	g	
Sibilants	Strong		s	sh		
	Weak		z	zh		
Nasals		m	n			
Other sounds		w		y		h, '

	Phonetic	Ojibwe examples	English equivalents
b	[b]~[p]	*bakade* 'is hungry' *nibi* 'water' *gigizheb* 'in the morning'	**b**ig, s**p**in
ch	[č:]	*michaa* 'it is big' *miigwech* 'thanks'	sti**tch**
d	[d]~[t]	*debwe* 'tells the truth' *biidoon* 'bring it!' *waagaakwad* 'ax'	**d**o, s**t**op
g	[g]~[k]	*giin* 'you' *waagosh* 'fox' *ikwewag* 'women'	**g**eese, s**k**i
h	[h]	*hay'*	**h**i
'	[ʔ]	*bakite'an* 'hit it!' *ode'* 'someone's heart'	

j	[j]~[č]	*jiimaan* 'boat, canoe'	jump
		ajina 'a little while'	
		ingiikaj 'I'm cold'	
k	[k:]	*makizin* 'moccasin, shoe'	pick
		amik 'beaver'	
m	[m]	*miinan* 'blueberries'	man
		jiimaan 'boat, canoe'	
		miijim 'food'	
n	[n]	*naanan* 'five'	name
	[ε] before *g, k*	*bangii* 'a little bit'	hunger
p	[p:]	*opin* 'potato'	rip
		imbaap 'I laugh'	
s	[s:]	*asin* 'stone, rock'	miss
		wiiyaas 'meat'	
sh	[š:]	*ashigan* 'bass'	bush
		animosh 'dog'	
t	[t:]	*ate* '(something) is there'	pit
		anit 'fish spear'	
w	[w]	*waabang* 'tomorrow'	way
		giiwe 'goes home'	
		bizindaw 'listen to someone!'	
y	[y]	*wiiyaw* 'someone's body'	yellow
		inday 'my dog'	
z	[z]~[s]	*ziibi* 'river'	zebra
		ozid 'someone's foot'	
		indaakoz 'I am sick'	
zh	[ž]~[š]	*zhaabonigan* 'needle'	measure
		azhigan 'sock'	
		biizh 'bring someone!'	

Consonant Clusters

The following consonant clusters occur:

sk	[sk]	*miskozi* 'is red'
shp	[šp]	*ishpiming* 'up above, in heaven'

sht	[št]	*nishtigwaan* 'my head'
shk	[šk]	*ishkode* 'fire'
		gayaashk 'gull'
mb	[mb]	*wiimbaa* 'is hollow'
nd	[nd]	*aandi* 'where'
		aanind 'some'
nj	[nj]	*biinjise* 'flies in'
		nininj 'my hand'
ng	[ɛg]	*bangii* 'a little bit'
		waabang 'tomorrow'

A single consonant (except *w*, *h*, and *y*) or a consonant cluster may be followed by *w* before a vowel. A few examples are **bw**aan 'Dakota', *o***pw**aa-gan 'pipe', **gw**iiwizens 'boy', *ami***kw**ag 'beavers', *nis***w**i 'three', *bagi-da'***w**aa 'sets a net', *mis***kw**i 'blood', and *bi***ngw**i 'sand, ashes'.

Part I

Ojibwe–English

A

abanzh *ni* lodge pole, rafter; *pl* **abanzhiin;** *loc*
abanzhiing; *dim* **abanzhiins**
abashkwebiigininjiishin *vai* get a blister on one's
hand; *1sg* **indabashkwebiigininjiishin;** *prt*
ebashkwebiigininjiishing
abashkwebiigizi *vai* have a blister; *1sg*
indabashkwebiigiz; *prt* **ebashkwebiigizid**
abashkwebiigizideshin *vai* get a blister on one's
foot; *1sg* **indabashkwebiigizideshin;** *prt*
ebashkwebiigizideshing
abaabas /abaabasw-/ *vta* cense s.o.; *1sg*
indabaabaswaa; *prt* **ebaabaswaad**
abaabasan *vti* cense s.t.; *1sg* **indabaabasaan;** *prt*
ebaabasang
abaabaso *vai* cense oneself; *1sg* **indabaabas;** *prt*
ebaabasod
abaagamide *vii* be warm (as a liquid); *prt*
ebaagamideg; *aug* **abaagamidemagad;** *prt*
aug **ebaagamidemagak**
abaagamizan *vti* warm s.t. (as a liquid); *1sg*
indabaagamizaan; *prt* **ebaagamizang**
abaasandeke *vai* bask in the sun; *1sg*
indabaasandeke; *prt* **ebaasandeked**
abaaso *vai* warm up in the sun; *1sg* **indabaas;** *prt*
ebaasod
abaate *vii* warm up (of the weather); *prt* **ebaateg;**
aug **abaatemagad;** *prt aug* **ebaatemagak**
abaawiganezo *vai* warm one's back; *1sg*
indabaawiganez; *prt* **ebaawiganezod**
abi *vai* be at home, be in a certain place, sit in a
certain place; *1sg* **indab;** *prt* **ebid**
abininjiizo *vai* warm one's hands; *1sg*
indabininjiiz; *prt* **ebininjiizod**
abinoojiinh *na* child; *pl* **abinoojiinyag;** *dim*
abinoojiiyens, abinoojiins
abinoojiinh-biizikaagan *ni* item of children's
clothing; *pl* **abinoojiinh-biizikaaganan;** *loc*
abinoojiinh-biizikaaganing; *dim* **abinoojiinh-
biizikaagaans**
abinoojiinyikaazo *vai* pretend to be a child; *1sg*
indabinoojiinyikaaz; *prt* **ebinoojiinyikaazod**
abinoojiinyiwi *vai* be a child; *1sg*
indabinoojiinyiw; *prt* **ebinoojiinyiwid**
abinoojiiyens *na* baby; *pl* **abinoojiiyensag;** *also*
abinoojiins
abiwin *ni* room, living room; *pl* **abiwinan;** *loc*
abiwining; *dim* **abiwinens**
abiz /abizw-/ *vta* warm s.o. at the fire; *1sg*
indabizwaa; *prt* **ebizwaad**
abizamaw *vta* warm (s.t.) for s.o. at the fire; *1sg*
indabizamawaa; *prt* **ebizamawaad**
abizan *vti* warm s.t. at the fire; *1sg* **indabizaan;** *prt*
ebizang
abizidezo *vai* warm one's feet; *1sg* **indabizidez;** *prt*
ebizidezod
abiichigaade *vii* be occupied; *prt* **ebiichigaadeg;**
aug **abiichigaademagad;** *prt aug*
ebiichigaademagak
abiitan *vti* live in s.t., occupy s.t.; *1sg* **indabiitaan;**
prt **ebiitang**

abiitaw *vta* sit up with s.o. (e.g., the deceased at a
wake); *1sg* **indabiitawaa;** *prt* **ebiitawaad**
abiiwigamig *ni* living room; *pl* **abiiwigamigoon;**
loc **abiiwigamigong;** *dim* **abiiwigamigoons**
abwaadan *vti* roast s.t., cook s.t. over a fire; *1sg*
indabwaadaan; *prt* **ebwaadang**
abwaajigan *na* bread cooked over an open fire; *pl*
abwaajiganag; *loc* **abwaajiganing;** *dim*
abwaajigaans
abwaajigan *ni* roasted meat, roasted fish; *pl*
abwaajiganan; *dim* **abwaajigaans**
abwaajige *vai* roast things; *1sg* **indabwaajige;** *prt*
ebwaajiged
abwaanaak *ni* drying rack for strips of meat over a
fire; *pl* **abwaanaakoon;** *loc* **abwaanaakong;**
dim **abwaanaakoons**
abwaazh /abwaaN-/ *vta* roast s.o., cook s.o. over a
fire; *1sg* **indabwaanaa;** *prt* **ebwaanaad**
abwe *vai+o* roast (s.t.), cook (s.t.) over a fire; *1sg*
indabwe, indabwen; *prt* **ebwed**
abweninjii *vai* have a sweaty hand; *1sg*
indabweninjii; *prt* **ebweninjiid**
abwewas /abwewasw-/ *vta* cure s.o. over a fire; *1sg*
indabwewaswaa; *prt* **ebwewaswaad**
abwewasan *vti* cure s.t. over a fire; *1sg*
indabwewasaan; *prt* **ebwewasang**
abwewasigan *ni* fire-cured meat or fish; *pl*
abwewasiganan; *loc* **abwewasiganing;** *dim*
abwewasigaans
abwewasige *vai* cure things over a fire; *1sg*
indabwewasige; *prt* **ebwewasiged**
abwewin *ni* frying pan; *pl* **abwewinan;** *loc*
abwewining; *dim* **abwewinens**
abwezide *vai* have a sweaty foot; *1sg*
indabwezide; *prt* **ebwezided**
abwezo *vai* sweat; *1sg* **indabwez;** *prt* **ebwezod**
abwi *ni* paddle; *pl* **abwiin;** *loc* **abwiing;** *dim* **abwiins**
achaab *ni* bowstring; *pl* **achaabiin;** *loc* **achaabiing;**
dim **achaabiins**
achigaade *vii* be put in a certain place; *prt*
echigaadeg; *aug* **achigaademagad;** *prt aug*
echigaademagak
achigaazo *vai* be put in a certain place; *prt*
echigaazod
achige *vai* put things in a certain place, place a bet;
1sg **indachige;** *prt* **echiged**
adaam *vta* buy (s.t.) from s.o.; *1sg* **indadaamaa;**
prt **edaamaad**
adaawam *vta* borrow (s.t.) from s.o., rent (s.t.)
from s.o.; *1sg* **indadaawamaa;** *prt*
edaawamaad
adaawange *vai+o* borrow (s.t.) from people, rent
(s.t.) from people; *1sg* **indadaawange,**
indadaawangen; *prt* **edaawanged**
adaawaagan *ni* fur for trade; *pl* **adaawaaganan;** *loc*
adaawaaganing; *dim* **adaawaagaans**
adaawaage *vai+o* sell (s.t.); *1sg* **indadaawaage,**
indadaawaagen; *prt* **edaawaaged**
adaawe *vai+o* buy (s.t.); *1sg* **indadaawe,**
indadaawen; *prt* **edaawed**
adaawetamaw *vta* buy (s.t.) for s.o.; *1sg*
indadaawetamawaa; *prt* **edaawetamawaad**
adaawetamaazo *vai* buy (s.t.) for oneself; *1sg*
indadaawetamaaz; *prt* **edaawetamaazod**

adaawewigamig *ni* store; *pl* adaawewigamigoon;
loc adaawewigamigong; *dim*
adaawewigamigoons
adaawewinini *na* store clerk, trader; *pl*
adaawewininiwag
adaawewininiikwe *na* store clerk (female), trader
(female); *pl* adaawewininiikweg
adik *na* caribou, reindeer; *pl* adikwag; *dim*
adikoons
adikameg *na* whitefish; *pl* adikamegwag; *dim*
adikamegoons
adim *vta* catch up to s.o., overtake s.o.; *1sg*
indadimaa; *prt* edimaad
adima' /adima'w-/ *vta* catch up to s.o. in a boat,
overtake s.o. in a boat; *1sg* indadima'waa; *prt*
edima'waad
adindan *vti* catch up to s.t., overtake s.t.; *1sg*
indadindaan; *prt* edindang
adoopowin *ni* table; *pl* adoopowinan; *loc*
adoopowining; *dim* adoopowinens
adoopowiniigin *ni* table cloth; *pl*
adoopowiniiginoon; *loc* adoopowiniiginong;
dim adoopowiniiginoons
agadendam *vai2* be ashamed, feel shy; *1sg*
indagadendam; *prt* egadendang
agadendan *vti* be ashamed of s.t.; *1sg*
indagadendaan; *prt* egadendang
agadendaagozi *vai* be ashamed, be embarrassed;
1sg indagadendaagoz; *prt* egadendaagozid
agadendaagwad *vii* be shameful, be embarrassing;
prt egadendaagwak
agadenim *vta* be ashamed of s.o., be embarrassed
by s.o.; *1sg* indagadenimaa; *prt* egadenimaad
agaji *vai* be bashful, be shy; *1sg* indagaj; *prt* egajid
agaji' *vta* make s.o. ashamed, embarrass s.o.; *1sg*
indagaji'aa; *prt* egaji'aad
agajishki *vai* be a shy person; *1sg* indagajishk; *prt*
egajishkid
agajiitaw *vta* be shy in front of s.o., be ashamed
before s.o.; *1sg* indagajiitawaa; *prt*
egajiitawaad
agamiing *pc* on the shore, at the water, at the lake
agawaate'on *ni* umbrella; *pl* agawaate'onan; *loc*
agawaate'oning; *dim* agawaate'onens
agawaatese *vai* cast a shadow flying; *prt*
egawaatesed
agawaatese *vii* cast a shadow flying; *prt*
egawaateseg; *aug* agawaatesemagad; *prt aug*
egawaatesemagak
agawaateshin *vai* be in shade, be in shadow; *1sg*
indagawaateshin; *prt* egawaateshing
agawaateshkan *vti* shade s.t., cast a shadow on
s.t.; *1sg* indagawaateshkaan; *prt*
egawaateshkang
agawaateshkaw *vta* shade s.o., cast a shadow on
s.o.; *1sg* indagawaateshkawaa; *prt*
egawaateshkawaad
agawaatesin *vii* be in shade, be in shadow; *prt*
egawaatesing
agawaateyaa *vii* there is shadow, there is shade;
prt egawaateyaag; *aug* agawaateyaamagad;
prt aug egawaateyaamagak
agazom *vta* embarrass s.o. by speech; *1sg*
indagazomaa; *prt* egazomaad
agaamakiing *pc* overseas, in Europe

agaamashkosiw *pc* on the other side of the
meadow
agaamayi'ii *pc* on the other side of it, across it
agaamaakwaa *pc* on the other side of the clearing
agaami- *pn* on the other side of, across
agaamikana *pc* on the other side of the road or
trail, across the road or trail
agaamindesi *pc* other side of the lodge
agaamindesing *pc* on the other side of the lodge
agaaming *pc* on the other side of the lake, across
the lake
agaamishkode *pc* on the other side of the fire
agaasade' *vta* make s.o. narrow; *1sg*
indagaasade'aa; *prt* egaasade'aad
agaasademon /agaasademo-/ *vii* be narrow (as a
road or trail); *prt* egaasademog
agaasadengwe *vai* have a narrow face; *1sg*
indagaasadengwe; *prt* egaasadengwed
agaasadetigweyaa *vii* be narrow (as a river); *prt*
egaasadetigweyaag; *aug*
agaasadetigweyaamagad; *prt aug*
egaasadetigweyaamagak
agaasadetoon *vti2* make s.t. narrow; *1sg*
indagaasadetoon; *prt* egaasadetood
agaasadeyaa *vii* be narrow; *prt* egaasadeyaag; *aug*
agaasadeyaamagad; *prt aug*
egaasadeyaamagak
agaasadeyaabikad *vii* be narrow (as something
mineral); *prt* egaasadeyaabikak
agaasadeyaabikizi *vai* be narrow (as something
mineral); *prt* egaasadeyaabikizid
agaasadeyaabiigad *vii* be narrow (as something
string-like); *prt* egaasadeyaabiigak
agaasadeyaabiigizi *vai* be narrow (as something
string-like); *prt* egaasadeyaabiigizid
agaasadeyiigad *vii* be narrow (as something sheet-
like); *prt* egaasadeyiigak
agaasadeyiigizi *vai* be narrow (as something sheet-
like); *prt* egaasadeyiigizid
agaasadeyoonagad *vii* be narrow (as a boat); *prt*
egaasadeyoonagak
agaasadezi *vai* be narrow; *prt* egaasadezid
agaasadinaa *vii* there is a small hill; *prt*
egaasadinaag; *aug* egaasadinaamagad; *prt*
aug egaasadinaamagak
agaasate *vii* be small (as a room or house); *prt*
egaasateg; *aug* agaasatemagad; *prt aug*
egaasatemagak
agaasaa *vii* be small; *prt* egaasaag; *aug*
agaasaamagad; *prt aug* egaasaamagak
agaasaabaminaagozi *vai* appear small, look small;
prt egaasaabaminaagozid
agaasaabaminaagwad *vii* appear small, look
small; *prt* egaasaabaminaagwak
agaasaabikad *vii* be small (as something mineral);
prt egaasaabikak
agaasaabikizi *vai* be small (as something mineral);
prt egaasaabikizid
agaasaabiigad *vii* be small (as something string-
like), be fine (as something string-like); *prt*
egaasaabiigak
agaasaabiigizi *vai* be small (as something string-
like), be fine (as something string-like); *prt*
egaasaabiigizid

agaasaakozi *vai* be small (as something stick- or wood-like); *prt* **egaasaakozid**
agaasaakwad *vii* be small (as something stick- or wood-like); *prt* **egaasaakwak**
agaasaatoon *vti2* make s.t. small; *1sg* **indagaasaatoon**; *prt* **egaasaatood**
agaasendan *vti* think little of s.t., consider s.t. insignificant; *1sg* **indagaasendaan**; *prt* **egaasendang**
agaasendaagozi *vai* be considered insignificant; *1sg* **indagaasendaagoz**; *prt* **egaasendaagozid**
agaasendaagwad *vii* be considered insignificant; *prt* **egaasendaagwak**
agaasenim *vta* think little of s.o., consider s.o. insignificant; *1sg* **indagaasenimaa**; *prt* **egaasenimaad**
agaashiinyi *vai* be small; *1sg* **indagaashiinh**; *prt* **egaashiinyid**
agaasi' *vta* make s.o. small; *1sg* **indagaasi'aa**; *prt* **egaasi'aad**
agaasiminagad *vii* be small (as something ball-like); *prt* **egaasiminagak**
agaasiminagizi *vai* be small (as something ball-like); *prt* **egaasiminagizid**
agaasiigad *vii* be small (as something sheet-like); *prt* **egaasiigak**
agaasiigizi *vai* be small (as something sheet-like); *prt* **egaasiigizid**
agaawaa *pc* hardly, barely
agaawaadan *vti* wish for s.t., desire s.t.; *1sg* **indagaawaadaan**; *prt* **egaawaadang**
agaawaazh /**agaawaaN-**/ *vta* wish for s.o., desire s.o.; *1sg* **indagaawaanaa**; *prt* **egaawaanaad**
agidajiw *pc* on top of a mountain; *also* **ogidajiw***, **wagidajiw**
agidakamig *pc* on top of the ground; *also* **ogidakamig***, **wagidakamig**
agidasin *pc* on top of a rock; *also* **ogidasin***, **wagidasin**
agidaabik *pc* on something mineral (e.g., metal, glass, rock); *also* **ogidaabik***, **wagidaabik**
agidaajiwan *pc* upstream; *also* **ogidaajiwan***, **wagidaajiwan**
agidaaki *pc* on top of a hill; *also* **ogidaaki***, **wagidaaki**
agidaakiiwe *vai* go uphill; *1sg* **indagidaakiiwe**; *prt* **egidaakiiwed**
agidaakiiwebatoo *vai* run uphill; *1sg* **indagidaakiiwebatoo**; *prt* **egidaakiiwebatood**
agidibiig *pc* on top of the water; *also* **ogidibiig***, **wagidibiig**
agidigamig *pc* on top of the house; *also* **ogidigamig***, **wagidigamig**
agidiskwam *pc* on top of the ice; *also* **ogidiskwam***, **wagidiskwam**
agig *na* phlegm
agigokaa *vai* have a cold; *1sg* **indagigokaa**; *prt* **egigokaad**
agijayi'ii *pc* on top of it; *also* **ogijayi'ii***, **wagijayi'ii**
agiji- *pn* on top of; *also* **ogiji-***, **wagiji-**
agim *vta* count s.o.; *1sg* **indagimaa**; *prt* **egimaad**
agindamaw *vta* count (s.t.) for s.o., read (s.t.) for s.o.; *1sg* **indagindamawaa**; *prt* **egindamawaad**

agindamaage *vai* count (s.t.) for people, read (s.t.) for people; *1sg* **indagindamaage**; *prt* **egindamaaged**
agindan *vti* count s.t., read s.t.; *1sg* **indagindaan**; *prt* **egindang**
agindaaso *vai* count, read; *1sg* **indagindaas**; *prt* **egindaasod**
agindaasoowigamig *ni* library; *pl* **agindaasoowigamigoon**; *loc* **agindaasoowigamigong**; *dim* **agindaasoowigamigoons**
aginjigaade *vii* be counted, be read; *prt* **eginjigaadeg**; *aug* **aginjigaademagad**; *prt aug* **eginjigaademagak**
aginjigaazo *vai* be counted; *prt* **eginjigaazod**
aginzo *vai* be counted, belong to a group; *1sg* **indaginz**; *prt* **eginzod**
agiw* *pr* those *animate plural demonstrative; also* **ingiw, igiw***
agogwaadan *vti* sew s.t. on; *1sg* **indagogwaadaan**; *prt* **egogwaadang**
agogwaajigan *ni* appliqué piece, trim; *pl* **agogwaajiganan**; *loc* **agogwaajiganing**; *dim* **agogwaajigaans**
agogwaaso *vai* sew something on; *1sg* **indagogwaas**; *prt* **egogwaasod**
agogwaazh /**agogwaaN-**/ *vta* sew s.o. on; *1sg* **indagogwaanaa**; *prt* **egogwaanaad**
agokadoon *vti2* stick s.t. on; *1sg* **indagokadoon**; *prt* **egokadood**
agokazh /**agokaN-**/ *vta* stick s.o. on; *1sg* **indagokanaa**; *prt* **egokanaad**
agoke *vai* stick on, adhere; *1sg* **indagoke**; *prt* **egoked**
agoke *vii* stick on, adhere; *prt* **egokeg**; *aug* **agokemagad**; *prt aug* **egokemagak**
agokiwas /**agokiwasw-**/ *vta* glue s.o., paste something on s.o.; *1sg* **indagokiwaswaa**; *prt* **egokiwaswaad**
agokiwasan *vti* glue s.t., paste something on s.t.; *1sg* **indagokiwasaan**; *prt* **egokiwasang**
agokiwasigan *ni* glue, paste; *pl* **agokiwasiganan**; *loc* **agokiwasiganing**; *dim* **agokiwasigaans**
agokiwaso *vai* be glued, be pasted on; *1sg* **indagokiwas**; *prt* **egokiwasod**
agokiwate *vii* be glued, be pasted on; *prt* **egokiwateg**; *aug* **agokiwatemagad**; *prt aug* **egokiwatemagak**
agomo *vai* float, be suspended in water; *1sg* **indagom**; *prt* **egomod**
agon *vta* hold s.o. up against; *1sg* **indagonaa**; *prt* **egonaad**
agonan *vti* hold s.t. up against; *1sg* **indagonaan**; *prt* **egonang**
agonde *vii* float, be suspended in water; *prt* **egondeg**
agongos *na* chipmunk, Scandinavian; *pl* **agongosag**; *dim* **agongosens**
agongosimo *vai* speak a Scandinavian language; *1sg* **indagongosim**; *prt* **egongosimod**
agonjidoon *vti2* soak s.t., put s.t. in to soak; *1sg* **indagonjidoon**; *prt* **egonjidood**
agonjijigaade *vii* be put in to soak; *prt* **egonjijigaadeg**; *aug* **agonjijigaademagad**; *prt aug* **egonjijigaademagak**

agonjijigaazo *vai* be put in to soak; *prt*
egonjijigaazod
agonjim *vta* soak s.o., put s.o. in to soak; *1sg*
indagonjimaa; *prt* **egonjimaad**
agonjoonaagan *ni* net float; *pl* **agonjoonaaganan**;
loc **agonjoonaaganing**; *dim* **agonjoonaagaans**
agoodakikwaan *ni* kettle hanger; *pl*
agoodakikwaanan; *loc* **agoodakikwaaning**;
dim **agoodakikwaanens**
agoodasabii *vai* hang up a net; *1sg*
indagoodasabii; *prt* **egoodasabiid**
agoodaw *vta* hang (s.t.) for s.o., set a snare for
s.o.; *1sg* **indagoodawaa**; *prt* **egoodawaad**
agoode *vii* hang; *prt* **egoodeg**; *aug* **agoodemagad**;
prt aug **egoodemagak**
agoodoo *vai* set a snare; *1sg* **indagoodoo**; *prt*
egoodood
agoodoon *vti2* hang s.t.; *1sg* **indagoodoon**; *prt*
egoodood
agoodwaagan *ni* snare; *pl* **agoodwaaganan**; *loc*
agoodwaaganing; *dim* **agoodwaagaans**
agoodwaaganeyaab *ni* snare wire; *pl*
agoodwaaganeyaabiin; *loc*
agoodwaaganeyaabiing; *dim*
agoodwaaganeyaabiins
agoojiganaatig *ni* clothesline pole; *pl*
agoojiganaatigoon; *loc* **agoojiganaatigong**;
dim **agoojiganaatigoons**
agoojiganeyaab *ni* clothesline; *pl*
agoojiganeyaabiin; *loc* **agoojiganeyaabiing**;
dim **agoojiganeyaabiins**
agoojige *vai* hang things, hang up laundry; *1sg*
indagoojige; *prt* **egoojiged**
agoojin *vai* hang, be in the sky (e.g., a star, the
sun, or the moon); *1sg* **indagoojin**; *prt*
egoojing
agoojiwanaanaak *ni* hanging rack for food drying;
pl **agoojiwanaanaakoon**; *loc*
agoojiwanaanaakong; *dim*
agoojiwanaanaakoons
agoozh /**agooN-**/ *vta* hang s.o.; *1sg* **indagoonaa**;
prt **egoonaad**
agoozi *vai* be perched up on something; *1sg*
indagoozi; *prt* **egoozid**
agwadaashi *na* sunfish; *pl* **agwadaashiwag**; *dim*
agwadaashiins
agwajiing *pc* outside, outdoors
agwanem *vta* put s.o. in one's mouth, hold s.o. in
one's mouth; *1sg* **indagwanemaa**; *prt*
egwanemaad
agwanendan *vti* put s.t. in one's mouth, hold s.t.
in one's mouth; *1sg* **indagwanendaan**; *prt*
egwanendang
agwanenjige *vai* put things in one's mouth, hold
things in one's mouth, chew tobacco; *1sg*
indagwanenjige; *prt* **egwanenjiged**
agwanogaan *ni* canopy; *pl* **agwanogaanan**; *loc*
agwanogaaning; *dim* **agwanogaanens**
agwapidoon *vti2* tie s.t. on something; *1sg*
indagwapidoon; *prt* **egwapidood**
agwapijigaade *vii* be tied on, be hitched on; *prt*
egwapijigaadeg; *aug* **agwapijigaademagad**;
prt aug **egwapijigaademagak**
agwapijigaazo *vai* be tied on, be hitched on; *prt*
egwapijigaazod

agwapizh /**agwapiN-**/ *vta* tie s.o. on something;
1sg **indagwapinaa**; *prt* **egwapinaad**
agwazhe *vai* be covered with blankets; *1sg*
indagwazhe; *prt* **egwazhed**
agwazhe' *vta* cover s.o. with blankets; *1sg*
indagwazhe'aa; *prt* **egwazhe'aad**
agwazhe'on *ni* blanket, covering; *pl*
agwazhe'onan; *loc* **agwazhe'oning**; *dim*
agwazhe'onens
agwaabatoo *vai* run ashore; *1sg* **indagwaabatoo**;
prt **egwaabatood**
agwaabidoon *vti2* pull s.t. ashore, pull s.t. from
the water; *1sg* **indagwaabidoon**; *prt*
egwaabidood
agwaabikide *vii* burn to the pan; *prt*
egwaabikideg; *aug* **agwaabikidemagad**; *prt*
aug **egwaabikidemagak**
agwaabikiz /**agwaabikizw-**/ *vta* burn s.o. to the
pan; *1sg* **indagwaabikizwaa**; *prt*
egwaabikizwaad
agwaabikizan *vti* burn s.t. to the pan; *1sg*
indagwaabikizaan; *prt* **egwaabikizang**
agwaabikizo *vai* burn to the pan; *prt*
egwaabikizod
agwaabizh /**agwaabiN-**/ *vta* pull s.o. ashore, pull
s.o. from the water; *1sg* **indagwaabinaa**; *prt*
egwaabinaad
agwaabiiga' /**agwaabiiga'w-**/ *vta* take s.o. off the
water using something; *1sg*
indagwaabiiga'waa; *prt* **egwaabiiga'waad**
agwaabiiga'amaw *vta* take s.t. (s.t.) off the water
using something for s.o.; *1sg*
indagwaabiiga'amawaa; *prt*
egwaabiiga'amawaad
agwaabiiga'an *vti* take s.t. off the water using
something; *1sg* **indagwaabiiga'aan**; *prt*
egwaabiiga'ang
agwaabiigin *vta* take s.o. off the water, take s.o. off
the fire; *1sg* **indagwaabiiginaa**; *prt*
egwaabiiginaad
agwaabiiginan *vti* take s.t. off the water, take s.t.
off the fire; *1sg* **indagwaabiiginaa**; *prt*
egwaabiiginaad
agwaadaabaadan *vti* drag s.t. ashore; *1sg*
indagwaadaabaadaan; *prt* **egwaadaabaadang**
agwaadaabaazh /**agwaadaabaaN-**/ *vta* drag s.o.
ashore; *1sg* **indagwaadaabaanaa**; *prt*
egwaadaabaanaad
agwaadaabii *vai* drag something ashore; *1sg*
indagwaadaabii; *prt* **egwaadaabiid**
agwaagoshi *vai* be moldy; *prt* **egwaagoshid**
agwaagosin *vii* be moldy; *prt* **egwaagosing**
agwaagwaabikad *vii* be rusty; *prt*
egwaagwaabikak
agwaagwaabikishin *vai* turn rusty; *prt*
egwaagwaabikishing
agwaagwaabikisin *vii* turn rusty; *prt*
egwaagwaabikising
agwaagwaabikizi *vai* be rusty; *prt*
egwaagwaabikizid
agwaa'o *vai* land, come ashore in a boat; *1sg*
indagwaa'; *prt* **egwaa'od**; *also* **agwaa'am**
agwaa'oodoon *vti2* take s.t. ashore by boat; *1sg*
indagwaa'oodoon; *prt* **egwaa'oodood**

agwaakwa'an *vti* nail s.t. up against the wall, post
s.t. up; *1sg* indagwaakwa'aan; *prt*
egwaakwa'ang
agwaakwa'igan *ni* sign, notice, poster; *pl*
agwaakwa'iganan; *loc* agwaakwa'iganing; *dim*
agwaakwa'igaans
agwaanaaso *vai* unload a boat; *1sg* indagwaanaas;
prt egwaanaasod
agwaashim *vta* take s.o. ashore, take s.o. off the
fire; *1sg* indagwaashimaa; *prt* egwaashimaad
agwaasidoon *vti2* take s.t. ashore, take s.t. off the
fire; *1sg* indagwaasidoon; *prt* egwaasidood
agwaasijigaade *vii* be taken ashore, be taken off
the fire; *prt* egwaasijigaadeg; *aug*
agwaasijigaademagad; *prt aug*
egwaasijigaademagak
agwaasijigaazo *vai* be taken ashore, be taken off
the fire; *prt* egwaasijigaazod
agwaataa *vai* go ashore, come ashore; *1sg*
indagwaataa; *prt* egwaataad
agwaawebin *vta* throw s.o. out of the water; *1sg*
indagwaawebinaa; *prt* egwaawebinaad
agwaawebinamaw *vta* throw (s.t.) out of the
water for s.o.; *1sg* indagwaawebinamawaa; *prt*
egwaawebinamawaad
agwaawebinan *vti* throw s.t. out of the water; *1sg*
indagwaawebinaan; *prt* egwaawebinang
agwaayaadagaa *vai* swim ashore; *1sg*
indagwaayaadagaa; *prt* egwaayaadagaad
agwaayaashi *vai* be blown ashore, sail ashore; *1sg*
indagwaayaash; *prt* egwaayaashid
agwaayaasin *vii* be blown ashore; *prt*
egwaayaasing
a'aw *pr* that *animate singular demonstrative*; *also* aw,
'aw, 'a
a'awedi *pr* that over there *animate singular
demonstrative*; *also* awedi
ajidagoode *vii* hang upside down; *prt*
ejidagoodeg; *aug* ajidagoodemagad; *prt aug*
ejidagoodemagak
ajidagoodoon *vti2* hang s.t. upside down; *1sg*
indajidagoodoon; *prt* ejidagoodood
ajidagoojin *vai* hang upside down; *prt*
ejidagoojing
ajidagoozh /ajidagooN-/ *vta* hang s.o. upside
down; *1sg* indajidagoonaa; *prt* ejidagoonaad
ajidamoo *na* red squirrel; *pl* ajidamoog; *dim*
ajidamoons
ajidin *vta* hold s.o. upside down; *1sg* indajidinaa;
prt ejidinaad
ajidinan *vti* hold s.t. upside down; *1sg*
indajidinaan; *prt* ejidinang
ajijaak *na* sandhill crane; *pl* ajijaakwag; *dim*
ajijaakoons
ajijibizo *vai* fall head first; *1sg* indajijibiz; *prt*
ejijibizod
ajijiingwese *vai* fall on one's face; *1sg*
indajijiingwese; *prt* ejijiingwesed
ajina *pc* a little while
akakanzhe *ni* charcoal, coals, coal; *loc*
akakanzheng; *dim* akakanzhens
akakanzhebwe *vai+o* cook (s.t.) on the coals, grill
(s.t.); *1sg* indakakanzhebwe,
indakakanzhebwen; *prt* ekakanzhebwed

akakanzhekaa *vii* be coals, be hot ashes; *prt*
ekakanzhekaag; *aug* akakanzhekaamagad;
prt aug ekakanzhekaamagak
akakojiish *na* woodchuck; *pl* akakojiishag; *dim*
akakojiishens
akamaw *vta* lie in wait for s.o.; *1sg* indakamawaa;
prt ekamawaad
akandoo *vai* lie in wait for game, use a blind; *1sg*
indakandoo; *prt* ekandood
akandoowin *ni* hunting blind; *pl* akandoowinan;
loc akandoowining; *dim* akandoowinens
akawaabam *vta* wait in watch for s.o., expect s.o.
to come; *1sg* indakawaabamaa; *prt*
ekawaabamaad
akawaabandan *vti* wait in watch for s.t., expect s.t.
to come; *1sg* indakawaabandaan; *prt*
ekawaabandang
akawaabi *vai* wait in watch, expect; *1sg*
indakawaab; *prt* ekawaabid
akawe *pc* first (in a time sequence), first of all; *also*
kawe
akeyaa *pc* in the direction of; *also* gakeyaa,
nakakeyaa*
aki *ni* earth, land, ground, country; *pl* akiin; *loc*
akiing; *dim* akiins
akik *na* kettle, pail, pot, pan; *pl* akikoog; *loc*
akikong; *dim* akikoons
akikoons *na* outboard motor; *pl* akikoonsag; *loc*
akikoonsing
akina *pc* all, every; *also* kina, gakina
akina gegoo *pr* everything; *also* kina gegoo,
gakina gegoo
akiwenzii *na* old man; *pl* akiwenziiyag
akiwenziiyiwi *vai* be an old man; *1sg*
indakiwenziiyiw; *prt* ekiwenziiyiwid
akii-mazina'igan *ni* map; *pl* akii-mazina'iganan;
loc akii-mazina'iganing; *dim* akii-
mazina'igaans
akiiwan *vii* be the earth; *prt* ekiiwang
akiiwe-wiigiwaam *ni* earth lodge; *pl* akiiwe-
wiigiwaaman; *loc* akiiwe-wiigiwaaming; *dim*
akiiwe-wiigiwaamens
akiiwigamig *ni* sod house, root house; *pl*
akiiwigamigoon; *loc* akiiwigamigong; *dim*
akiiwigamigoons
ako- *pv3* since, a certain length, as long as, as far as
akoo' *vta* make s.o. a certain length, make s.o. so
long; *1sg* indakoo'aa; *prt* ekoo'aad
akootoon *vti2* make s.t. a certain length, make s.t.
so long; *1sg* indakootoon; *prt* ekootood
akoozi *vai* be a certain length, be a certain height,
be so long, be so tall; *1sg* indakooz; *prt*
ekoozid
akwa'waa *vai* fish through the ice with spear; *1sg*
indakwa'waa; *prt* ekwa'waad
akwa'wewigamig *ni* fish house for spearing; *pl*
akwa'wewigamigoon; *loc*
akwa'wewigamigong; *dim*
akwa'wewigamigoons
akwanaamo *vai* be short of breath, take short
breaths; *1sg* indakwanaam; *prt* ekwanaamod
akwaa *vii* be a certain length, be a certain height,
be so long, be so tall; *prt* ekwaag; *aug*
akwaamagad; *prt aug* ekwaamagak

akwaabikad *vii* be a certain length (as something mineral), be so long (as something mineral); *prt* **ekwaabikak**

akwaabikizi *vai* be a certain length (as something mineral), be so long (as something mineral); *prt* **ekwaabikizid**

akwaabiigad *vii* be a certain length (as something string-like), be so long (as something string-like); *prt* **ekwaabiigak**

akwaabiigizi *vai* be a certain length (as something string-like), be so long (as something string-like); *prt* **ekwaabiigizid**

akwaakozi *vai* be a certain height, be a certain length (as something stick- or wood-like); *1sg* **indakwaakoz**; *prt* **ekwaakozid**

akwaakwad *vii* be a certain height, be a certain length (as something stick- or wood-like); *prt* **ekwaakwak**

akwaakwaa *vii* woods go a certain distance; *prt* **ekwaakwaag**; *aug* **akwaakwaamagad**; *prt aug* **ekwaakwaamagak**

akwaandawaagan *ni* stairway, ladder, elevator; *pl* **akwaandawaaganan**; *loc* **akwaandawaaganing**; *dim* **akwaandawaagaans**

akwaandawe *vai* climb up, go upstairs; *1sg* **indakwaandawe**; *prt* **ekwaandawed**

akwaandawebatoo *vai* climb up fast; *1sg* **indakwaandawebatoo**; *prt* **ekwaandawebatood**

akwaandawebizo *vai* climb up fast (e.g., in an elevator); *1sg* **indakwaandawebiz**; *prt* **ekwaandawebizod**

akwaandawebizon *ni* elevator; *pl* **akwaandawebizonan**; *loc* **akwaandawebizoning**; *dim* **akwaandawebizonens**

akwegad *vii* be a certain length (as something sheet-like), be so long (as something sheet-like); *prt* **ekwegak**

akwegizi *vai* be a certain length (as something sheet-like), be so long (as something sheet-like); *prt* **ekwegizid**

akwiindimaa *vii* be deep to a certain extent; *prt* **ekwiindimaag**; *aug* **akwiindimaamagad**; *prt aug* **ekwiindimaamagak**

amadaji *vai* wake from being cold; *1sg* **indamadaj**; *prt* **emadajid**

amadin *vta* wake s.o.; *1sg* **indamadinaa**; *prt* **emadinaad**

amajim *vta* wake s.o. by vocal noise; *1sg* **indamajimaa**; *prt* **emajimaad**

amajine *vai* wake from pain; *1sg* **indamajine**; *prt* **emajined**

amajise *vai* come awake; *1sg* **indamajise**; *prt* **emajised**

amajwebin *vta* shake s.o. awake; *1sg* **indamajwebinaa**; *prt* **emajwebinaad**

amaniso *vai* be alarmed; *1sg* **indamanis**; *prt* **emanisod**

amanisodaw *vta* be alarmed by s.o.; *1sg* **indamanisodawaa**; *prt* **emanisodawaad**

amanj *pc* I don't know how, I wonder how *dubitative*; *also* **amanj iidog, namanj*, namanj iidog***

amanj apii *pc* I don't know when, I wonder when *dubitative*

amanj igo *pc* however *dubitative*

amanj igo apii *pc* whenever, anytime *dubitative*

ambe *pc* come on!, let's go!, attention!

amik *na* beaver; *pl* **amikwag**; *dim* **amikoons**

amikwayaan *na* beaver hide; *pl* **amikwayaanag**; *dim* **amikwayaanens**

amikwiish *ni* beaver lodge; *pl* **amikwiishan**; *loc* **amikwiishing**; *dim* **amikwiishens**

amo /amw-/ *vta* eat s.o.; *1sg* **indamwaa**; *prt* **emwaad**

ana'o *vai* choke on something stuck in one's throat; *1sg* **indana'**; *prt* **ena'od**

anama'e- *pv4* Christian; *also* **aname-**

anama'e-giizhigad *vii* be Sunday; *prt* **enama'e-giizhigak**; *also* **aname-giizhigad**

anama'e-mazina'igan *ni* prayer book; *pl* **anama'e-mazina'iganan**; *loc* **anama'e-mazina'iganing**; *dim* **anama'e-mazina'igaans**

anama'eminensag *na* rosary *plural*

anama'e-nagamon *ni* hymn; *pl* **anama'e-nagamonan**

anama'etaw *vta* pray for s.o.; *1sg* **indanama'etawaa**; *prt* **enama'etawaad**

anama'ewigamig *ni* church; *pl* **anama'ewigamigoon**; *loc* **anama'ewigamigong**; *dim* **anama'ewigamigoons**; *also* **anamewigamig**

anama'ewikwe *na* nun; *pl* **anama'ewikweg**; *dim* **anama'ewikwens**

anami'aa *vai* pray, be Christian; *1sg* **indanami'aa**; *prt* **enami'aad**

anamikaw *vta* greet s.o.; *1sg* **indanamikawaa**; *prt* **enamikawaad**

anamikaadiwag /anamikaadi-/ *vai* they greet each other; *1pl* **indanamikaadimin**; *prt* **enamikaadijig**

anamikaage *vai* greet people; *1sg* **indanamikaage**; *prt* **enamikaaged**

anang *na* star; *pl* **anangoog**; *loc* **anangong**; *dim* **anangoons**

anaakan *ni* woven mat, rug; *pl* **anaakanan**; *loc* **anaakaning**; *dim* **anaakanens**

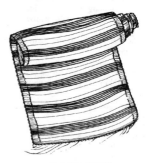

anaakan (mat)

anaakanashk *ni* reed, rush; *pl* **anaakanashkoon**; *loc* **anaakanashkong**; *dim* **anaakanashkoons**

anaamakamig *pc* under the ground

anaamaki *pc* underground
anaamayi'ii *pc* under it
anaamaagon *pc* under the snow; *also* **anaamaagonag**
anaamaatig *pc* under wood (e.g., a tree or stick)
anaamendan *vti* suspect s.t.; *1sg* **indanaamendaan**; *prt* **enaamendang**
anaamenim *vta* suspect s.o.; *1sg* **indanaamenimaa**; *prt* **enaamenimaad**
anaami- *pn* under
anaamibiig *pc* underwater
anaamim *vta* blame s.o. (in speech), accuse s.o.; *1sg* **indanaamimaa**; *prt* **enaamimaad**
anaamindiwag /anaamindi-/ *vai* they blame each other; *1pl* **indanaamindimin**; *prt* **enaamindijig**
anaamindizo *vai* blame oneself; *1sg* **indanaamindiz**; *prt* **enaamindizod**
anaaminge *vai* blame people; *1sg* **indanaaminge**; *prt* **enaaminged**
anaamisag *pc* under the floor, in the basement
anaamisagadaweshiinh *na* wren; *pl* **anaamisagadaweshiinyag**
anaamiskwam *pc* under the ice
anaamiindim *pc* in the depths of a body of water
anaamoonag *pc* under a boat
angobide *vii* wear out in operation; *prt* **engobideg**; *aug* **angobidemagad**; *prt aug* **engobidemagak**
angobizo *vai* wear out in operation; *prt* **engobizod**
ango' *vta* reduce s.o. to nothing; *1sg* **indango'aa**; *prt* **engo'aad**
angoshkan *vti* wear s.t. out with foot or body; *1sg* **indangoshkaan**; *prt* **engoshkang**
angoshkaw *vta* wear s.o. out with foot or body (e.g., pants); *1sg* **indangoshkawaa**; *prt* **engoshkawaad**
angotoon *vti2* reduce s.t. to nothing; *1sg* **indangotoon**; *prt* **engotood**
ani- *pv2* going away, going along, in progress, on the way, coming up to in time; *also* **ni-**
anijiiminan /anijiimin-/ *ni* peas *plural*
anijiiminaaboo *ni* pea soup; *loc* **anijiiminaaboong**
anikamaanan /anikamaan-/ *ni* suspenders *plural*
anima'adoo *vai* follow a trail away; *1sg* **indanima'adoo**; *prt* **enima'adood**
anima'adoon *vti2* follow s.t. away as a trail; *1sg* **indanima'adoon**; *prt* **enima'adood**
anima'amaazo *vai* go away singing; *1sg* **indanima'amaaz**; *prt* **enima'amaazod**
anima'azh /anima'aN-/ *vta* follow s.o.'s trail away; *1sg* **indanima'anaa**; *prt* **enima'anaad**
anima'oodoon *vti2* take s.t. away by boat; *1sg* **indanima'oodoon**; *prt* **enima'oodood**
anima'oozh /anima'ooN-/ *vta* take s.o. away by boat; *1sg* **indanima'oonaa**; *prt* **enima'oonaad**
animaabogo *vai* float away, drift away; *1sg* **indanimaabog**; *prt* **enimaabogod**
animaaboode *vii* float away, drift away; *prt* **enimaaboodeg**; *aug* **animaaboodemagad**; *prt aug* **enimaaboodemagak**
animaadagaa *vai* swim away; *1sg* **indanimaadagaa**; *prt* **enimaadagaad**
animaadagaako *vai* go away on the ice; *1sg* **indanimaadagaak**; *prt* **enimaadagaakod**
animaadagaazii *vai* wade away; *1sg* **indanimaadagaazii**; *prt* **enimaadagaaziid**

animaada'e *vai* skate away; *1sg* **indanimaada'e**; *prt* **enimaada'ed**
animaa'an *vii* drift away on the waves; *prt* **enimaa'ang**
animaa'ogo *vai* drift away on the waves; *1sg* **indanimaa'og**; *prt* **enimaa'ogod**
animaanakwad *vii* clouds go away; *prt* **enimaanakwak**
animaapi *vai* go away laughing; *1sg* **indanimaap**; *prt* **enimaapid**
animaashi *vai* be blown away, sail away; *1sg* **indanimaash**; *prt* **enimaashid**
animaasin *vii* be blown away, sail away; *prt* **enimaasing**
animaazakonenjige *vai* go away with a light; *1sg* **indanimaazakonenjige**; *prt* **enimaazakonenjiged**
animaazakonenjigebizo *vai* drive away with a light; *1sg* **indanimaazakonenjigebiz**; *prt* **enimaazakonenjigebizod**
animiba'idiwag /animiba'idi-/ *vai* they run away (in the other direction) together; *1pl* **indanimiba'idimin**; *prt* **enimiba'idijig**
animiba'igo *vai* drive away with horses; *1sg* **indanimiba'ig**; *prt* **enimiba'igod**
animibatoo *vai* run away; *1sg* **indanimibatoo**; *prt* **enimibatood**
animibatwaadan *vti* run away (in the other direction) with s.t.; *1sg* **indanimibatwaadaan**; *prt* **enimibatwaadang**
animibatwaazh /animibatwaaN-/ *vta* run away (in the other direction) with s.o.; *1sg* **indanimibatwaanaa**; *prt* **enimibatwaanaad**
animibide *vii* speed away, drive away, fly away; *prt* **enimibideg**; *aug* **animibidemagad**; *prt aug* **enimibidemagak**
animibizo *vai* speed away, drive away, fly away; *1sg* **indanimibiz**; *prt* **enimibizod**
animibizoni' *vta* drive away with s.o. (e.g., a car); *1sg* **indanimibizoni'aa**; *prt* **enimibizoni'aad**
animibizonitoon *vti2* drive away with s.t.; *1sg* **indanimibizonitoon**; *prt* **enimibizonitood**
animibiisaa *vii* rain goes away; *prt* **enimibiisaag**; *aug* **animibiisaamagad**; *prt aug* **enimibiisaamagak**
animidaabii *vai* drag away; *1sg* **indanimidaabii**; *prt* **enimidaabiid**
animidaabii'iwe *vai* drive away; *1sg* **indanimidaabii'iwe**; *prt* **enimidaabii'iwed**
animigidaazo *vai* go away mad; *1sg* **indanimigidaaz**; *prt* **enimigidaazod**
animijiwan *vii* flow away; *prt* **enimijiwang**
animikawe *vai* leave tracks going away; *1sg* **indanimikawe**; *prt* **enimikawed**
animikii *na* thunderbird, thunderer; *pl* **animikiig**; *dim* **animikiins**
animikiikaa *vii* there is thunder; *prt* **enimikiikaag**; *aug* **animikiikaamagad**; *prt aug* **enimikiikaamagak**
animikogaabawi *vai* stand with the back out; *1sg* **indanimikogaabaw**; *prt* **enimikogaabawid**
animikon *vta* turn s.o. face down, turn s.o. to face backwards; *1sg* **indanimikonaa**; *prt* **enimikonaad**

animikonan *vti* turn s.t. face down, turn s.t. to
face backwards; *1sg* indanimikonaan; *prt*
enimikonang
animikonigaade *vii* be turned face down, be
turned to face backwards; *prt*
enimikonigaadeg; *aug*
animikonigaademagad; *prt aug*
enimikonigaademagak
animikonigaazo *vai* be turned face down, be
turned to face backwards; *prt*
enimikonigaazod
animikose *vai* fall face down; *prt* enimikosed
animikose *vii* fall face down; *prt* enimikoseg; *aug*
animikosemagad; *prt aug* enimikosemagak
animikoshim *vta* lay s.o. face down; *1sg*
indanimikoshimaa; *prt* enimikoshimaad
animikoshin *vai* lie face down; *1sg*
indanimikoshin; *prt* enimikoshing
animikosidoon *vti2* lay s.t. face down; *1sg*
indanimikosidoon; *prt* enimikosidood
animikosin *vii* lie face down; *prt* enimikosing
animikwabi *vai* sit facing backwards; *1sg*
indanimikwab; *prt* enimikwabid
animikwabiitaw *vta* sit with back to s.o.; *1sg*
indanimikwabiitawaa; *prt*
enimikwabiitawaad
animinizhimo *vai* run away scared; *1sg*
indaniminizhim; *prt* eniminizhimod
animise *vai* fly away; *1sg* indanimise; *prt* enimised
animise *vii* fly away; *prt* enimiseg; *aug*
animisemagad; *prt aug* enimisemagak
animishimo *vai* dance away; *1sg* indanimishim;
prt enimishimod
animishkaa *vai* paddle away, go away in a canoe;
1sg indanimishkaa; *prt* enimishkaad
animiwidoon *vti2* take s.t. away, carry s.t. away;
1sg indanimiwidoon; *prt* enimiwidood
animiwizh /animiwiN-/ *vta* take s.o. away, carry
s.o. away; *1sg* indanimiwinaa; *prt*
enimiwinaad
animose *vai* walk away; *1sg* indanimose; *prt*
enimosed
animosh *na* dog; *pl* animoshag; *dim* animoons;
also inday
animoode *vai* crawl away; *1sg* indanimoode; *prt*
enimooded
animoom *vta* carry s.o. away on one's back; *1sg*
indanimoomaa; *prt* enimoomaad
animoomigo *vai* ride away on horseback; *1sg*
indanimoomig; *prt* enimoomigod
animoondan *vti* carry s.t. away on one's back; *1sg*
indanimoondaan; *prt* enimoomdang
animoons *na* puppy; *pl* animoonsag
animwewebatoo *vai* run away making noise; *1sg*
indanimwewebatoo; *prt* enimwewebatood
animwewebide *vii* speed away making noise, drive
away making noise, fly away making noise; *prt*
enimwewebideg; *aug* animwewebidemagad;
prt aug enimwewebidemagak
animwewebizo *vai* speed away making noise,
drive away making noise, fly away making
noise; *1sg* indanimwewebiz; *prt*
enimwewebizod
animwewetoo *vai* walk away making noise; *1sg*
indanimwewetoo; *prt* enimwewetood

animwewidam *vai2* go away speaking; *1sg*
indanimwewidam; *prt* enimwewidang
ani-naagozi *vai* go out of sight; *1sg* indani-naagoz;
prt eni-naagozid
ani-naagwad *vii* go out of sight; *prt* eni-naagwak
aninaatig *na* maple; *pl* aninaatigoog; *loc*
aninaatigong; *dim* aninaatigoons; *also*
ininaatig
anishaa *pc* just for nothing, without purpose, just
for fun, not really
anishinaabe *na* person, human (in contrast to non-
human beings), Indian (in contrast to non-
Indians), Ojibwe; *pl* anishinaabeg; *dim*
anishinaabens
anishinaabe-bimaadizi *vai* live the Indian way; *1sg*
indanishinaabe-bimaadiz; *prt* enishinaabe-
bimaadizid
anishinaabe-gaagiigido *vai* speak in an Indian
language (especially in Ojibwe); *1sg*
indanishinaabe-gaagiigid; *prt* enishinaabe-
gaagiigidod
anishinaabekaa *vii* there are many people, there
are many Indians; *prt* enishinaabekaag
anishinaabekwe *na* Indian woman; *pl*
anishinaabekweg; *dim* anishinaabekwens
anishinaabekwewi *vai* be an Indian woman; *1sg*
indanishinaabekwew; *prt* enishinaabekwewid
anishinaabe-maawanjii'idiiwigamig *ni* Indian
center; *pl* anishinaabe-
maawanjii'idiiwigamigoon; *loc* anishinaabe-
maawanjii'idiiwigamigong
anishinaabemo *vai* speak an Indian language
(especially Ojibwe); *1sg* indanishinaabem; *prt*
enishinaabemod
anishinaabemotaw *vta* speak an Indian language
(Ojibwe) to s.o.; *1sg* indanishinaabemotawaa;
prt enishinaabemotawaad
anishinaabemowin *ni* Indian language (especially
Ojibwe); *pl* anishinaabemowinan
anishinaabewaki *ni* Indian country; *loc*
anishinaabewakiing
anishinaabewi *vai* be human (in contrast to non-
human beings), be Indian (in contrast to non-
Indians), be Ojibwe; *1sg* indanishinaabew; *prt*
enishinaabewid
anishinaabewibii'amaw *vta* write (s.t.) in Indian
(Ojibwe) to s.o.; *1sg*
indanishinaabewibii'amawaa; *prt*
enishinaabewibii'amawaad
anishinaabewibii'an *vti* write s.t. in Indian
(Ojibwe); *1sg* indanishinaabewibii'aan; *prt*
enishinaabewibii'ang
anishinaabewibii'igan *ni* Indian (Ojibwe) writing,
something written in Indian (Ojibwe); *pl*
anishinaabewibii'iganan
anishinaabewibii'igaade *vii* be written in Indian
(Ojibwe); *prt* enishinaabewibii'igaadeg; *aug*
anishinaabewibii'igaademagad; *prt aug*
enishinaabewibii'igaademagak
anishinaabewibii'ige *vai* write in Indian (Ojibwe);
1sg indanishinaabewibii'ige; *prt*
enishinaabewibii'iged
anishinaabewinikaadan *vti* call s.t. in Indian
(Ojibwe); *1sg* indanishinaabewinikaadaan; *prt*
enishinaabewinikaadang

anishinaabewinikaade *vii* be called in Indian (Ojibwe); *prt* **enishinaabewinikaadeg**; *aug* **anishinaabewinikaademagad**; *prt aug* **enishinaabewinikaademagak** /**anishinaabewinikaaN-**/ *vta* call s.o. in Indian (Ojibwe); *1sg* **indanishinaabewinikaanaa**; *prt* **enishinaabewinikaanaad**

anishinaabewinikaazo *vai* be called in Indian (Ojibwe); *1sg* **indanishinaabewinikaaz**; *prt* **enishinaabewinikaazod**

anishinaabewisidoon *vti2* write s.t. in Indian (Ojibwe) (e.g., a book); *1sg* **indanishinaabewisidoon**; *prt* **enishinaabewisidood**

anishinaabewisin *vii* be written in Indian (Ojibwe) (e.g., a book or document); *prt* **enishinaabewising**

anishinaabe-ziinzibaakwad *ni* maple sugar; *loc* **anishinaabe-ziinzibaakwadong**

anit *ni* fish spear; *pl* **anitiin**; *loc* **anitiing**; *dim* **anitiins**

aniw* *pr* those *inanimate plural demonstrative*, that, those *obviative demonstrative*; *also* **iniw**

aniib *na* elm; *pl* **aniibiig**; *loc* **aniibiing**; *dim* **aniibiins**

aniibiimin *ni* highbush cranberry; *pl* **aniibiiminan**; *dim* **aniibiiminens**

aniibiiminagaawanzh *na* highbush cranberry bush; *pl* **aniibiiminagaawanzhiig**; *loc* **aniibiiminagaawanzhiing**; *dim* **aniibiiminagaawanzhiins**

aniibiish *ni* leaf, tea; *pl* **aniibiishan**; *loc* **aniibiishing**; *dim* **aniibiishens**

aniibiishakik *na* teakettle; *pl* **aniibiishakikoog**; *loc* **aniibiishakikong**; *dim* **aniibiishakikoons**

aniibiishaaboo *ni* tea; *loc* **aniibiishaaboong**; *also* **aniibiish**

aniibiishaabooke *vai* make tea; *1sg* **indaniibiishaabooke**; *prt* **eniibiishaabooked**

aniibiishaabookewinini *na* Chinese, Oriental; *pl* **aniibiishaabookewininiwag**

aniibiishaabookewininiiwi *vai* be Chinese, be Oriental; *1sg* **indaniibiishaabookewininiiw**; *prt* **eniibiishaabookewininiiwid**

aniibiishibag *ni* leaf; *pl* **aniibiishibagoon**; *loc* **aniibiishibagong**; *dim* **aniibiishibagoons**; *also* **aniibiish**

aniibiishikaa *vii* there are many leaves; *prt* **eniibiishikaag**; *aug* **aniibiishikaamagad**; *prt aug* **eniibiishikaamagak**

aniibiishike *vai* make tea; *1sg* **indaniibiishike**; *prt* **eniibiishiked**

anjiko *vai* be pregnant; *1sg* **indanjik**; *prt* **enjikod**

anokaadan *vti* work at s.t.; *1sg* **indanokaadaan**; *prt* **enokaadang**

anokaajigan *ni* manufacture, craft, something worked on, project; *pl* **anokaajiganan**; *loc* **anokaajiganing**; *dim* **anokaajigaans**

anokaazh /**anokaaN-**/ *vta* work at s.o.; *1sg* **indanokaanaa**; *prt* **enokaanaad**

anokii *vai* work; *1sg* **indanokii**; *prt* **enokiid**

anokii' *vta* make s.o. work; *1sg* **indanokii'aa**; *prt* **enokii'aad**

anokiikaazo *vai* pretend to work; *1sg* **indanokiikaaz**; *prt* **enokiikaazod**

anokiitaw *vta* work for s.o.; *1sg* **indanokiitawaa**; *prt* **enokiitawaad**

anokiitaage *vai* work for people; *1sg* **indanokiitaage**; *prt* **enokiitaaged**

anokiitaazo *vai* work for oneself; *1sg* **indanokiitaaz**; *prt* **enokiitaazod**

anokiiwigamig *ni* factory, workshop; *pl* **anokiiwigamigoon**; *loc* **anokiiwigamigong**

anokiiwikwe *na* worker (female); *pl* **anokiiwikweg**

anokiiwin *ni* work, job; *pl* **anokiiwinan**

anokiiwinini *na* worker; *pl* **anokiiwininiwag**

anooj *pc* various, all kinds

anooj gegoo *pr* a variety of things, various things; *also* **anooji-gegoo**

anookii *vai* hire, give an order, commission; *1sg* **indanookii**; *prt* **enookiid**

anoozh /**anooN-**/ *vta* hire s.o., give an order to s.o., commission s.o.; *1sg* **indanoonaa**; *prt* **enoonaad**

anwaataa *vai* finish (in work or an activity); *1sg* **indanwaataa**; *prt* **enwaataad**

anwaatin *vii* be calm weather; *prt* **enwaating**

anwebi *vai* rest; *1sg* **indanweb**; *prt* **enwebid**

anweshin *vai* rest lying down; *1sg* **indanweshin**; *prt* **enweshing**

anwi *ni* bullet, shotgun shell; *pl* **anwiin**; *loc* **anwiing**; *dim* **anwiins**

anwii-baashkizigan *ni* shotgun; *pl* **anwii-baashkiziganan**; *loc* **anwii-baashkiziganing**; *dim* **anwii-baashkizigaans**

anwiins *ni* twenty-two bullet; *pl* **anwiinsan**

apabiwin *ni* chair; *pl* **apabiwinan**; *loc* **apabiwining**; *dim* **apabiwinens**

apagajinaazhikamaw *vta* drive game for s.o.; *1sg* **indapagajinaazhikamawaa**; *prt* **epagajinaazhikamawaad**

apagajinaazhikaw *vta* drive s.o. as game; *1sg* **indapagajinaazhikawaa**; *prt* **epagajinaazhikawaad**

apagajinaazhikaage *vai* drive game; *1sg* **indapagajinaazhikaage**; *prt* **epagajinaazhikaaged**

apagidan *vti* throw s.t.; *1sg* **indapagidaan**; *prt* **epagidang**; *also* **apagidoon**

apagidaw *vta* throw (s.t.) at s.o.; *1sg* **indapagidawaa**; *prt* **epagidawaad**

apagidaadiwag /**apagidaadi-**/ *vai* they throw (s.t.) at each other; *1pl* **indapagidaadimin**; *prt* **epagidaadijig**

apagidoon *vti2* throw s.t.; *1sg* **indapagidoon**; *prt* **epagidood**; *also* **apagidan**

apagijige *vai* throw things; *1sg* **indapagijige**; *prt* **epagijiged**

apagijigewinini *na* pitcher (in baseball); *pl* **apagijigewininiwag**

apagizh /**apagiN-**/ *vta* throw s.o.; *1sg* **indapaginaa**; *prt* **epaginaad**

apagizo *vai* throw self down against something; *1sg* **indapagiz**; *prt* **epagizod**

apa' *vta* run with s.o. to a certain place; *1sg* **indapa'aa**; *prt* **epa'aad**

apa'idiwag /**apa'idi-**/ *vai* they run to a certain place together; *1pl* **indapa'idimin**; *prt* **epa'idijig**

apa'igo *vai* ride to a certain place with horses; *1sg* **indapa'ig**; *prt* **epa'igod**

apa'iwe *vai* run away from people to a certain place; *1sg* indapa'iwe; *prt* epa'iwed

apakwaan *ni* roofing; *pl* apakwaanan; *loc* apakwaaning; *dim* apakwaanens

apakwe *vai* put on a roof; *1sg* indapakwe; *prt* epakwed

apakweshkway *na* cattail mat, cattail; *pl* apakweshkwayag

apane *pc* always, all the time, continually

apangishin *vai* fall down against; *1sg* indapangishin; *prt* epangishing

apangisin *vii* fall down against; *prt* epangising

apanjige *vai* eat things with something else (e.g., butter with bread); *1sg* indapanjige; *prt* epanjiged

apatoo *vai* run to a certain place, run in a certain way; *1sg* indapatoo; *prt* epatood

apaabikinigan *ni* potholder; *pl* apaabikiniganan; *loc* apaabikiniganing; *dim* apaabikinigaans

apaabowe *vai+o* flavor (s.t.), season (s.t.); *1sg* indapaabowe, indapaabowen; *prt* epaabowed

apaakozigan *ni* kinnikinnick (tobacco and bark smoking mixture)

apaakozige *vai* make kinnikinnick; *1sg* indapaakozige; *prt* epaakoziged

apegish *pc* I wish that ...; *also* ambegish*, ambesh*

apenimo *vai+o* rely on (s.t.), depend on (s.t.); *1sg* indapenim, indapenimon; *prt* epenimod

apenimonodan *vti* depend on s.t.; *1sg* indapenimonodaan; *prt* epenimonodang

apenimonodaw *vta* depend on s.o.; *1sg* indapenimonodawaa; *prt* epenimonodawaad; *also* apenimodaw

apibii'igan *ni* desk, writing surface; *pl* apibii'iganan; *loc* apibii'iganing; *dim* apibii'igaans

apibii'ige *vai* write on something; *1sg* indapibii'ige; *prt* epibii'iged

apiganegwaajigan *ni* moccasin cuff; *pl* apiganegwaajiganan; *loc* apiganegwaajiganing; *dim* apiganegwaajigaans; *also* apigwanegwaason

apigwayawegwaajigan *ni* collar; *pl* apigwayawegwaajiganan; *loc* apigwayawegwaajiganing; *dim* apigwayawegwaajigaans

apikan *ni* strap, harness; *pl* apikanan; *loc* apikaning; *dim* apikaans

apikaans *ni* fan belt; *pl* apikaansan

apikweshimo *vai* lie with head on something; *1sg* indapikweshim; *prt* epikweshimod

apikweshimon *ni* pillow; *pl* apikweshimonan; *loc* apikweshimoning; *dim* apikweshimonens

apikweshimoniigin *ni* pillowcase; *pl* apikweshimoniiginoon; *loc* apikweshimoniiginong; *dim* apikweshimoniiginoons

apishimo *vai* lie on something; *1sg* indapishim; *prt* epishimod

apishimon *ni* mattress, bed (made on the floor or ground); *pl* apishimonan; *loc* apishimoning; *dim* apishimonens

apishimonike *vai* make a bed (as in camp); *1sg* indapishimonike; *prt* epishimoniked

apishimoniigin *ni* sheet; *pl* apishimoniiginoon; *loc* apishimoniiginong; *dim* apishimoniiginoos

apishin *vai* lie as padding; *prt* epishing

apishkaamon *ni* mat on bottom of canoe; *pl* apishkaamonan; *loc* apishkaamoning; *dim* apishkaamonens

apisidaagan *na* floor piece of canoe; *pl* apisidaaganag; *loc* apisidaaganing; *dim* apisidaagaans

apisidoon *vti2* lay something on or under s.t. for protection; *1sg* indapisidoon; *prt* episidood

apisijigan *ni* protective mat, cushion; *pl* apisijiganan; *loc* apisijiganing; *dim* apisijigaans

apisin *vii* lie as padding; *prt* epising

apizideshinowin *ni* footstool; *pl* apizideshinowinan; *loc* apizideshinowining; *dim* apizideshinowinens

apizideyaakwa'igan *ni* cradle board footrest; *pl* apizideyaakwa'iganan

apii *pc* when, then, at the time

apiichaa *vii* be a certain distance; *prt* epiichaag; *aug* apiichaamagad; *prt aug* epiichaamagak

apiichi- *pv3* a certain extent, as much as

apiichibatoo *vai* run at a certain speed; *1sg* indapiichibatoo; *prt* epiichibatood

apiichibide *vii* drive at a certain speed, fly at a certain speed, run at a certain speed (e.g., a machine); *prt* epiichibideg; *aug* apiichibidemagad; *prt aug* epiichibidemagak

apiichibizo *vai* drive at a certain speed, fly at a certain speed, run at a certain speed (e.g., a machine); *1sg* indapiichibiz; *prt* epiichibizod

apiichigi *vai* grow up a certain extent, grow at a certain speed; *prt* epiichigid

apiichigidaazo *vai* be angry to a certain extent; *1sg* indapiichigidaaz; *prt* epiichigidaazod

apiichigin *vii* grow up a certain extent, grow at a certain speed; *prt* epiichiging

apiichi-giizhigad *vii* be so late in the day; *prt* epiichi-giizhigak

apiichishin *vai* lie to a certain depth; *prt* epiichishing

apiichisin *vii* lie to a certain depth; *prt* epiichising

apiichitaa *vai* be engaged in an activity to a certain extent, be so far along in an activity; *1sg* indapiichitaa; *prt* epiichitaad

apiingwe'igan *ni* moccasin vamp; *pl* apiingwe'iganan; *loc* apiingwe'iganing; *dim* apiingwe'igaans

apiitagim *vta* set a price of a certain height on s.o.; *1sg* indapiitagimaa; *prt* epiitagimaad

apiitagindan *vti* set a price of a certain height on s.t.; *1sg* indapiitagindaan; *prt* epiitagindang

apiitaginde *vii* have a price of a certain height; *prt* epiitagindeg; *aug* apiitagindemagad; *prt aug* epiitagindemagak

apiitaginzo *vai* have a price of a certain height; *prt* epiitaginzod

apiitaa *vii* be a certain height, be a certain thickness; *prt* epiitaag; *aug* apiitaamagad; *aug* epiitaamagak

apiitaanimad *vii* the wind has a certain speed; *prt* epiitaanimak

apiitendan vti be proud of s.t. to a certain extent, regard s.t. to a certain degree; 1sg indapiitendaan; prt epiitendang
apiitendaagozi vai be valued to a certain extent, be at a certain rank; 1sg indapiitendaagoz; prt epiitendaagozid
apiitendaagwad vii be valued to a certain extent, be at a certain rank; prt epiitendaagwak
apiitendi vai be absent a certain length of time, be gone a certain length of time; 1sg indapiitend; prt epiitendid
apiitenim vta be proud of s.o. to a certain extent, feel about s.o. to a certain extent; 1sg indapiitenimaa; prt epiitenimaad
apiitenimo vai be proud of oneself; 1sg indapiitenim; prt epiitenimod
apiitinigozi vai weigh a certain amount, be so heavy; 1sg indapiitinigoz; prt epiitinigozid
apiitinigwad vii weigh a certain amount, be so heavy; prt epiitinigwak
apiitizi vai be a certain age, have a certain thickness, have a certain extent; 1sg indapiitiz; prt epiitizid
apiizikaa vai go a certain speed, go as fast as possible; 1sg indapiizikaa; prt epiizikaad
asab na net; pl asabiig; loc asabiing; dim asabiins
asabaab ni thread; pl asabaabiin; loc asabaabiing; dim asabaabiins
asabaabiiwaatig ni spool (for thread); pl asabaabiiwaatigoon; loc asabaabiiwaatigong; dim asabaabiiwaatigoons
asabike vai make nets; 1sg indasabike; prt esabiked
asabikeshiinh na spider; pl asabikeshiinyag
Asabikone-zaaga'iganiing place Nett Lake Reservation; also Asabikonaye-zaaga'iganiing
asanjigo vai+o cache (s.t.); 1sg indasanjig, indasanjigon; prt esanjigod
asanjigoowigamig ni storage lodge; pl asanjigoowigamigoon; loc asanjigoowigamigong; dim asanjigoowigamigoons
asanjigoowin ni cache; pl asanjigoowinan; loc asanjigoowining; dim asanjigoowinens
asasawemin ni chokecherry; pl asasaweminan
asasaweminagaawanzh na chokecherry bush; pl asasaweminagaawanzhiig; loc asasaweminagaawanzhiing; dim asasaweminagaawanzhiins
asaawe na perch; pl asaaweg; dim asaawens
asekaan na tanned hide; pl asekaanag; loc asekaaning; dim asekaanens
asekaazh /asekaaN-/ vta tan s.o. (e.g., a hide); 1sg indasekaanaa; prt esekaanaad
aseke vai tan hides; 1sg indaseke; prt eseked
asekewin ni tanning
asemaa na tobacco; loc asemaang; dim asemaans
asemaawipwaagaans na cigarette; pl asemaawipwaagaansag; also asemaa-opwaagaans
asham vta feed (s.t.) to s.o.; 1sg indashamaa; prt eshamaad
ashandiwin ni commodity food, rations; pl ashandiwinan

ashange vai feed people, serve food to people; 1sg indashange; prt eshanged
ashangewigamig ni welfare office, commodity store; pl ashangewigamigoon; loc ashangewigamigong; dim ashangewigamigoons
ashangewikwe na social worker (female), welfare worker (female); pl ashangewikweg
ashangewinini na social worker, welfare worker; pl ashangewininiwag
ashaweshk ni sword; pl ashaweshkoon; loc ashaweshkong; dim ashaweshkoons
ashaageshiinh na crayfish, crab; pl ashaageshiinyag
ashi /aS-/ vta put s.o. in a certain place; 1sg indasaa; prt esaad
ashi-aabita nm and a half
ashi-bezhig nm and one, eleven
ashi-bezhigo- pv4 and one, eleven
ashi-bezhigo-diba'iganed vii be eleven o'clock; prt eshi-bezhigo-diba'iganek
ashidin vta hold s.o. against; 1sg indashidinaa; prt eshidinaad
ashidinan vti hold s.t. against; 1sg indashidinaan; prt eshidinang
ashigan na largemouth bass; pl ashiganag
ashi-ingodwaaso- pv4 and six; also ashi-ningodwaaso-*
ashi-ingodwaaswi nm and six, sixteen; also ashi-ningodwaaswi*
ashi-ishwaaso- pv4 and eight; also ashi-nishwaaso-*
ashi-ishwaaswi nm and eight, eighteen; also ashi-nishwaaswi*
ashi-naanan nm and five, fifteen
ashi-naano- pv4 and five
ashi-ningodwaaso-* pv4 and six; also ashi-ingodwaaso-
ashi-ningodwaaswi* nm and six, sixteen; also ashi-ingodwaaswi
ashi-nishwaaso-* pv4 and eight; also ashi-ishwaaso-
ashi-nishwaaswi* nm and eight, eighteen; also ashi-ishwaaswi
ashi-niso- pv4 and three
ashi-niswi nm and three, thirteen
ashi-niiwin nm and four, fourteen
ashi-niiwo- pv4 and four; also ashi-niiyo-
ashi-niiyo- pv4 and four; also ashi-niiwo-
ashi-niizh nm and two, twelve
ashi-niizho- pv4 and two
ashi-niizho-diba'iganed vii be twelve o'clock; prt eshi-niizho-diba'iganek
ashi-niizhwaaso- pv4 and seven
ashi-niizhwaaswi nm and seven, seventeen
ashiwaa vii be dull; prt eshiwaag; aug ashiwaamagad; prt aug eshiwaamagak
ashi-zhaangaso- pv4 and nine
ashi-zhaangaswi nm and nine, nineteen
ashki- pv4 raw
ashkibagaa vii there are green leaves; prt eshkibagaag; aug ashkibagaamagad; prt aug eshkibagaamagak
ashkibagong inaande vii be leaf-green; prt ashkibagong enaandeg; aug ashkibagong

inaandemagad; *prt aug* ashkibagong
enaandemagak
ashkibagong inaanzo *vai* be leaf-green; *prt*
ashkibagong enaanzod
ashkide *vii* be incompletely cooked; *prt* eshkideg;
aug ashkidemagad; *prt aug* eshkidemagak
ashkikomaan *ni* lead (metal); *loc* ashkikomaaning
ashkin *vii* be raw (as meat); *prt* eshking
ashkini *vai* be raw (as meat); *prt* eshkinid
ashkizo *vai* be incompletely cooked; *1sg*
indashkiz; *prt* eshkizod
asho-wiidige *vai* be engaged; *1sg* indasho-wiidige;
prt esho-wiidiged
asho-wiidigendiwag /asho-wiidigendi-/ *vai* they
are engaged to each other; *1pl* indasho-
wiidigendimin; *prt* esho-wiidigendijig
asigagim *vta* add s.o. together (e.g., money); *1sg*
indasigagimaa; *prt* esigagimaad
asigagindan *vti* add s.t. together; *1sg*
indasigagindaan; *prt* esigagindang
asigagindaaso *vai* add together, total up; *1sg*
indasigagindaas; *prt* esigagindaasod
asigibii'igan *ni* number; *pl* asigibii'iganan; *loc*
asigibii'iganing; *dim* asigibii'igaans
asigibii'ige *vai* write numbers; *1sg* indasigibii'ige;
prt esigibii'iged
asigin *vta* gather s.o. up, collect s.o.; *1sg*
indasiginaa; *prt* esiginaad
asiginan *vti* gather s.t. up, collect s.t.; *1sg*
indasiginaan; *prt* esiginang
asiginaak *na* blackbird; *pl* asiginaakwag; *dim*
asiginaakoons
asiginigaade *vii* be gathered up; *prt* esiginigaadeg;
aug asiginigaademagad; *prt aug*
esiginigaademagak
asiginigaazo *vai* be gathered up; *prt* esiginigaazod
asigizhooniyaawe *vai* collect money as a donation;
1sg indasigizhooniyaawe; *prt*
esigizhooniyaawed
asigobaan *ni* processed basswood bark fiber
asigobaani-mazinichigan *na* doll of processed
basswood bark fiber; *pl* asigobaani-
mazinichiganag; *dim* asigobaani-
mazinichigaans
asin *na* stone, rock; *pl* asiniig; *loc* asiniing; *dim*
asiniins
asinaab *na* net sinker; *pl* asinaabiig; *loc*
asinaabiing; *dim* asinaabiins
asinii-bwaan *na* Assiniboin; *pl* asinii-bwaanag
asiniikaa *vii* there are many rocks, there are many
stones; *prt* esiniikaag; *aug* asiniikaamagad; *prt*
aug esiniikaamagak
asinii-miikana *ni* concrete road; *pl* asinii-
miikanan; *loc* asinii-miikanaang; *dim* asinii-
miikanaans
asinii-opwaagan *na* stone pipe; *loc* asinii-
opwaaganing; *dim* asinii-opwaagaans
asiniiwan *vii* be of stone, be of rock; *prt* esiniiwang
ataw *vta* put (s.t.) in a certain place for s.o., play
cards with s.o., bet with s.o.; *1sg* indatawaa;
prt etawaad
ataadiwag /ataadi-/ *vai* they gamble with each
other, they bet with each other; *1pl*
indataadimin; *prt* etaadijig

ataadiwin *na* playing card; *pl* ataadiwinag; *loc*
ataadiwining; *dim* ataadiwinens
ataage *vai* bet, gamble; *1sg* indataage; *prt*
etaaged
ataagib *ni* algae; *loc* ataagibiing
ataaso *vai+o* store something, store (s.t.); *1sg*
indataas, indataason; *prt* etaasod
ataasowin *ni* cupboard, closet; *pl* ataasowinan; *loc*
ataasowining; *dim* ataasowinens
ataasoowigamig *ni* storage lodge, shed; *pl*
ataasoowigamigoon; *loc*
ataasoowigamigong; *dim*
ataasoowigamigoons
ate *vii* be in a certain place; *prt* eteg; *aug*
atemagad; *prt aug* etemagak
atis /atisw-/ *vta* dye s.o.; *1sg* indatiswaa; *prt*
etiswaad; *also* adis
atisan *vti* dye s.t.; *1sg* indatisaan; *prt* etisang; *also*
adisan
atisigan *ni* dye; *pl* atisiganan; *also* adisigan
atisige *vai* dye things; *1sg* indatisige; *prt* etisiged;
also adisige
atiso *vai* be ripe; *prt* etisod; *also* adiso
atite *vii* be ripe; *prt* etiteg; *aug* atitemagad; *prt*
aug etitemagak; *also* adite
atoobaan *ni* trough, tank; *pl* atoobaanan; *loc*
atoobaaning
atoon *vti2* put s.t. in a certain place; *1sg* indatoon;
prt etood
atoono *vai* make a canoe; *1sg* indatoon; *prt*
etoonod
aw *pr* that *animate singular demonstrative*; *also* a'aw,
'aw, 'a
awakaan *na* domestic animal, slave; *pl* awakaanag
awakaanigamig *ni* barn; *pl* awakaanigamigoon;
loc awakaanigamigong; *dim*
awakaanigamigoons
awan *vii* be foggy, there is a fog; *prt* ewang
awanibiisaa *vii* be sprinkling rain, be misty; *prt*
ewanibiisaag; *aug* awanibiisaamagad; *prt aug*
ewanibiisaamagak
awanjish *pc* persistently, stubbornly, even though
awas *pc* go away!
awasagaam *pc* over across the water
awasajiw *pc* beyond the mountain, over across the
mountain
awasayi'ii *pc* beyond it, over across it
awasaakwaa *pc* beyond the woods, over across the
woods
awas-biboonong *pc* winter before last
awas-dagwaagong *pc* fall before last
awashime *pc* much more
awashtoyaa *na* blacksmith; *pl* awashtoyaag; *also*
awishtoyaa
awasi- *pn* beyond, over across
awasishkode *pc* beyond the fire, over across the
fire
awas-niibinong *pc* summer before last
awasonaago *pc* day before yesterday
awas-waabang *pc* day after tomorrow
awas-ziigwanong *pc* spring before last
awazo *vai* warm oneself by the fire; *1sg* indawaz;
prt ewazod
awazowin *ni* heater; *pl* awazowinan; *loc*
awazowining; *dim* awazowinens

awaazisii *na* bullhead; *pl* **awaazisiig**; *dim*
  awaazisiins; *also* **owaazisii, wawaazisii**
awedi *pr* that over there *animate singular*
  demonstrative; also **a'awedi**
awegonen *pr* what *inanimate interrogative; pl*
  awegonenan; *also* **wegonen**
awegwen *pr* I don't know who *animate dubitative*, I
  wonder who *animate dubitative; pl* **awegwenag**
awegwen igo *pr* whoever *animate dubitative*
awenen *pr* who *animate interrogative; pl*
  awegnenag
awenesh *pr* who, who then *animate interrogative*
awesiinh *na* wild animal; *pl* **awesiinyag**; *dim*
  awesiins
awi- *pv2* go over to; *after a personal prefix:* **a'o-**; *also*
  'o-
awibaa *vii* be calm, be windless; *prt* **ewibaag**; *aug*
  awibaamagad; *prt aug* **ewibaamagak**
awi' *vta* lend (s.t.) to s.o.; *1sg* **indawi'aa**; *prt*
  ewi'aad
awi'iwe *vai* lend (s.t.) to people, rent (s.t.) to
  people; *1sg* **indawi'iwe**; *prt* **ewi'iwed**
awiya *pr* somebody *animate indefinite*, anybody
  animate indefinite; also **awiiya**
aya'aa *pr* a being, someone, I don't remember who
ayaa *vai* be (in a certain place), *with a pv4* be in a
  certain state, *with a pv4* move a certain way; *1sg*
  indayaa; *prt* **eyaad**
ayaa *vii* be (in a certain place), *with a pv4* be in a
  certain state, *with a pv4* move a certain way; *prt*
  eyaag; *aug* **ayaamagad**; *prt aug* **eyaamagak**
ayaabe *na* buck; *pl* **ayaabeg**; *dim* **ayaabens**
ayaakw= < **akw=**
ayaan *vti3* have s.t., own s.t.; *1sg* **indayaaan**; *prt*
  eyaang
ayaangodinong *pc* sometimes, occasionally; *also*
  aangodinong
ayaangwaamim *vta* warn s.o., caution s.o.; *1sg*
  indayaangwaamimaa; *prt*
  eyaangwaamimaad
ayaangwaamizi *vai* be careful, be cautious; *1sg*
  indayaangwaamiz; *prt* **eyaangwaamizid**
ayaanig= < **inig=**
ayaanigokw= < **inigokw=**
ayaapiich= < **apiich=**
ayaapiit= < **apiit=**
ayaapiiz= < **apiiz=**
ayaaw *vta* have s.o., own s.o.; *1sg* **indayaawaa**; *prt*
  eyaawaad
ayeko' *vta* make s.o. tired; *1sg* **indayeko'aa**; *prt*
  eyeko'aad
ayekozi *vai* be tired; *1sg* **indayekoz**; *prt* **eyekozid**
ayekwamanji'o *vai* feel tired; *1sg*
  indayekwamanji'; *prt* **eyekwamanji'od**
ayi'ii *pr* thing, something, I don't remember what
ayindan= < **dan=**
ayindap= < **dap=**
ayindas= < **das=**
ayindash= < **dash=**
ayindazh= < **dazh=**
ayindaa= < **daa=**
ayindood= < **dood=**
azaadi *na* poplar; *pl* **azaadiwag**; *loc* **azaadiing**; *dim*
  azaadiins
azhashki *ni* mud; *loc* **azhashkiing**

azhashkiikaa *vii* there is much mud; *prt*
  ezhashkiikaag; *aug* **azhashkiikaamagad**; *prt*
  aug **ezhashkiikaamagak**
azhashkiiwan *vii* be muddy; *prt* **ezhashkiiwang**
azhashkiiwizide *vai* have muddy feet; *1sg*
  indazhashkiiwizide; *prt* **ezhashkiiwizided**
azhe- *pv4* go back
azhebidoon *vti2* pull s.t. back; *1sg*
  indazhebidoon; *prt* **ezhebidood**
azhebizh /**azhebiN-**/ *vta* pull s.o. back; *1sg*
  indazhebinaa; *prt* **ezhebinaad**
azhebizo *vai* back up a vehicle; *1sg* **indazhebiz**; *prt*
  ezhebizod
azheboyaanaak *ni* oar; *pl* **azheboyaanaakoon**; *loc*
  azheboyaanaakong; *dim* **azheboyaanaakoons**
azheboye *vai* row (a boat); *1sg* **indazheboye**; *prt*
  ezheboyed
azhegaabawi *vai* stand back; *1sg* **indazhegaabaw**;
  prt **ezhegaabawid**
azhegiiwe *vai* go back, return; *1sg* **indazhegiiwe**;
  prt **ezhegiiwed**
azhe'o *vai* paddle backwards; *1sg* **indazhe'**; *prt*
  ezhe'od
azhen *vta* return s.o., take s.o. back, hand s.o.
  back; *1sg* **indazhenaa**; *prt* **ezhenaad**
azhenamaw *vta* return (s.t.) to s.o., take (s.t.)
  back to s.o.; *1sg* **indazhenamawaa**; *prt*
  ezhenamawaad
azhenamaage *vai* return (s.t.) to people; *1sg*
  indazhenamaage; *prt* **ezhenamaaged**
azhenan *vti* return s.t., take s.t. back, hand s.t.
  back; *1sg* **indazhenaan**; *prt* **ezhenang**
azheshkaa *vai* go backwards; *1sg* **indazheshkaa**;
  prt **ezheshkaad**
azhetaa *vai* go backwards, back up; *1sg*
  indazhetaa; *prt* **ezhetaad**
azhigan *ni* sock; *pl* **azhiganan**; *loc* **azhiganing**; *dim*
  azhigaans
azhigwa *pc* now, at this time, already, then; *also*
  zhigwa, zhigo
aabadad *vii* be useful, be used; *prt* **ayaabadak**
aabadizi *vai* be useful, be used; *1sg* **indaabadiz**; *prt*
  ayaabadizid
aaba' /**aaba'w-**/ *vta* undo s.o., untie s.o.; *1sg*
  indaaba'waa; *prt* **ayaaba'waad**
aaba'amaw *vta* undo (s.t.) for s.o., untie (s.t.) for
  s.o.; *1sg* **indaaba'amawaa**; *prt*
  ayaaba'amawaad
aaba'an *vti* undo s.t., untie s.t.; *1sg* **indaaba'aan**;
  prt **ayaaba'ang**
aaba'igaade *vii* be undone, be untied; *prt*
  ayaaba'igaadeg; *aug* **aaba'igaademagad**; *prt*
  aug **ayaaba'igaademagak**
aaba'igaazo *vai* be undone, be untied; *prt*
  ayaaba'igaazod
aaba'oodoo *vai* untie wild rice; *1sg*
  indaaba'oodoo; *prt* **ayaaba'oodood**
aaba'oodoon *vti2* untie s.t.; *1sg* **indaaba'oodoon**;
  prt **ayaaba'oodood**
aabajichigan *ni* tool; *pl* **aabajichiganan**; *loc*
  aabajichiganing; *dim* **aabajichigaans**
aabaji' *vta* use s.o.; *1sg* **indaabaji'aa**; *prt*
  ayaabaji'aad
aabajitoon *vti2* use s.t.; *1sg* **indaabajitoon**; *prt*
  ayaabajitood

aabanaabam *vta* turn and look back at s.o.; *1sg* **indaabanaabamaa**; *prt* **ayaabanaabamaad**
aabanaabandan *vti* turn and look back at s.t.; *1sg* **indaabanaabandaan**; *prt* **ayaabanaabandang**
aabanaabi *vai* turn and look back; *1sg* **indaabanaab**; *prt* **ayaabanaabid**
aabawaa *vii* be warm weather, be mild weather; *prt* **ayaabawaag**; *aug* **aabawaamagad**; *prt aug* **ayaabawaamagak**
aabaabika' /**aabaabika'w-**/ *vta* unlock s.o.; *1sg* **indaabaabika'waa**; *prt* **ayaabaabika'waad**
aabaabika'amaw *vta* unlock (s.t.) for s.o.; *1sg* **indaabaabika'amawaa**; *prt* **ayaabaabika'amawaad**
aabaabika'an *vti* unlock s.t.; *1sg* **indaabaabika'aan**; *prt* **ayaabaabika'ang**
aabaabika'igan *ni* key; *pl* **aabaabika'iganan**; *loc* **aabaabika'iganing**; *dim* **aabaabika'igaans**
aabaabika'igaade *vii* be unlocked; *prt* **ayaabaabika'igaadeg**; *aug* **aabaabika'igaademagad**; *prt aug* **ayaabaabika'igaademagak**
aabaabiigin *vta* unwind s.o. (as something string-like), unravel s.o. (as something string-like); *1sg* **indaabaabiiginaa**; *prt* **ayaabaabiiginaad**
aabaabiiginan *vti* unwind s.t. (as something string-like), unravel s.t. (as something string-like); *1sg* **indaabaabiiginaan**; *prt* **ayaabaabiiginang**
aabaakawad *vii* revive, clear off after a storm; *prt* **ayaabaakawak**
aabaakawi' *vta* revive s.o.; *1sg* **indaabaakawi'aa**; *prt* **ayaabaakawi'aad**
aabaakawizi *vai* revive, come to; *1sg* **indaabaakawiz**; *prt* **ayaabaakawizid**
aabibidoon *vti2* rip s.t. open; *1sg* **indaabibidoon**; *prt* **ayaabibidood**
aabibizh /**aabibiN-**/ *vta* rip s.o. open; *1sg* **indaabibinaa**; *prt* **ayaabibinaad**
aabidanokii *vai* work without stopping; *1sg* **indaabidanokii**; *prt* **ayaabidanokiid**
aabidaanagidoon *vai* talk without stopping; *1sg* **indaabidaanagidoon**; *prt* **ayaabidaanagidoong**
aabiding *pc* once, at one time
aabiji- *pv4* continually
aabijiibaa *vai* revive, come alive; *1sg* **indaabijiibaa**; *prt* **ayaabijiibaad**
aabiskon *vta* undo s.o. by hand; *1sg* **indaabiskonaa**; *prt* **ayaabiskonaad**
aabiskonan *vti* undo s.t. by hand; *1sg* **indaabiskonaan**; *prt* **ayaabiskonang**
aabiskose *vai* come undone, unravel; *prt* **ayaabiskosed**
aabiskose *vii* come undone, unravel; *prt* **ayaabiskoseg**; *aug* **aabiskosemagad**; *prt aug* **ayaabiskosemagak**
aabiskwegin *vta* unfold s.o. (as something sheet-like); *1sg* **indaabiskweginaa**; *prt* **ayaabiskweginaad**
aabiskweginan *vti* unfold s.t. (as something sheet-like); *1sg* **indaabiskweginaan**; *prt* **ayaabiskweginang**
aabita *pc* half
aabita- *pv4* half
aabita-niibino-giizis *na* July

aabitawayi'ii *pc* halfway along it
aabitawaabik *na* half-dollar
aabitawaabikizi *vai* be half (as something mineral, e.g., the moon); *prt* **ayaabitawaabikizid**
aabita-zhooniyaans *na* nickel (coin); *pl* **aabita-zhooniyaansag**
aabitaa-dibikad *vii* be midnight; *prt* **ayaabitaa-dibikak**
aabitoobadoon *vti2* fill s.t. half full (of liquid); *1sg* **indaabitoobadoon**; *prt* **ayaabitoobadood**
aabitoobazh /**aabitoobaN-**/ *vta* fill s.o. half full (of liquid); *1sg* **indaabitoobanaa**; *prt* **ayaabitoobanaad**
aabitoobii *vai* be half full (of liquid); *prt* **ayaabitoobiid**
aabitoobii *vii* be half full (of liquid); *prt* **ayaabitoobiig**; *aug* **aabitoobiimagad**; *prt aug* **ayaabitoobiimagak**
aabitoose *vii* be Wednesday; *prt* **ayaabitooseg**; *aug* **aabitoosemagad**; *prt aug* **ayaabitoosemagak**
aabitooshkin *pc* half a bag
aabitooshkinadoon *vti2* fill s.t. half full; *1sg* **indaabitooshkinadoon**; *prt* **ayaabitooshkinadood**
aabitooshkina' *vta* fill s.o. half full (of solids); *1sg* **indaabitooshkina'aa**; *prt* **ayaabitooshkina'aad**
aabitooshkine *vai* be half full (of solids); *prt* **ayaabitooshkined**
aabitooshkine *vii* be half full (of solids); *prt* **ayaabitooshkineg**; *aug* **aabitooshkinemagad**; *prt aug* **ayaabitooshkinemagak**
aaboodin *vta* turn s.o. inside out; *1sg* **indaaboodinaa**; *prt* **ayaaboodinaad**
aaboodinan *vti* turn s.t. inside out; *1sg* **indaaboodinaan**; *prt* **ayaaboodinang**
aaboozikan *vti* wear s.t. inside out; *1sg* **indaaboozikaan**; *prt* **ayaaboozikang**
aaboozikaw *vta* wear s.o. inside out; *1sg* **indaaboozikawaa**; *prt* **ayaaboozikawaad**
aaboozikaa *vai* turn inside out; *prt* **ayaaboozikaad**
aaboozikaa *vii* turn inside out; *prt* **ayaaboozikaag**; *aug* **aaboozikaamagad**; *prt aug* **ayaaboozikaamagak**
aadawa'am *vta* go with s.o. in a boat; *1sg* **indaadawa'amaa**; *prt* **ayaadawa'amaad**
aadizookaw *vta* tell a legend to s.o., tell a myth to s.o.; *1sg* **indaadizookawaa**; *prt* **ayaadizookawaad**
aadizookaan *na* traditional story, legend, myth, character of a legend or myth; *pl* **aadizookaanag**; *dim* **aadizookaanens**
aadizooke *vai* tell a traditional story, tell a legend, tell a myth; *1sg* **indaadizooke**; *prt* **ayaadizooked**
aadizookewinini *na* storyteller; *pl* **aadizookewininiwag**
aadodan *vti* tell a story of s.t.; *1sg* **indaadodaan**; *prt* **ayaadodang**
aagade *vai* burp; *1sg* **indaagade**; *prt* **ayaagaded**
aagask *na* prairie chicken; *pl* **aagaskwag**; *dim* **aagaskoons**
aagawe *vai* go out of sight (as around a corner); *1sg* **indaagawe**; *prt* **egaagawed**

aagim *na* snowshoe; *pl* **aagimag**; *loc* **aagiming**; *dim* **aagimens**

aagimaak *na* black ash (tree); *pl* **aagimaakwag**; *loc* **aagimaakong**; *dim* **aagimaakoons**

aagimose *vai* snowshoe; *1sg* **indaagimose**; *prt* **ayaagimosed**

aagonwetam *vai2* deny, contradict; *1sg* **indaagonwetam**; *prt* **ayaagonwetang**

aagonwetan *vti* deny s.t., contradict s.t., not believe s.t. said; *1sg* **indaagonwetaan**; *prt* **ayaagonwetang**

aagonwetaw *vta* deny what s.o. says, contradict s.o., not believe what s.o. says; *1sg* **indaagonwetawaa**; *prt* **ayaagonwetawaad**

aagonweyenim *vta* disbelieve s.o.; *1sg* **indaagonweyenimaa**; *prt* **ayaagonweyenimaad**

aajigade *na* coot, mud hen; *pl* **aajigadeg**; *dim* **aajigadens**

aajikode *vii* be notched; *prt* **ayaajikodeg**; *aug* **aajikodemagad**; *prt aug* **ayaajikodemagak**

aajim *vta* tell a story of s.o.; *1sg* **indaajimaa**; *prt* **ayaajimaad**

aajiningwa'on *ni* crutch; *pl* **aajiningwa'onan**; *loc* **aajiningwa'oning**; *dim* **aajiningwa'onens**

aajisag *pc* in the next room

aakoshkade *vai* have a stomachache; *1sg* **indaakoshkade**; *prt* **ayaakoshkaded**

aakoshkadekaw- *vta* give s.o. a stomachache; *in inverse forms: 1sg* **indaakoshkadekaagon**; *prt* **ayaakoshkadekaagod**

aakozi *vai+o* be sick, be sick (in s.t.), be ill; *1sg* **indaakoz, indaakozin**; *prt* **ayaakozid**

aakoziwin *ni* sickness, disease; *pl* **aakoziwinan**

aakoziwinikaa *vii* there is much sickness; *prt* **ayaakoziwinikaag**; *aug* **aakoziwinikaamagad**; *prt aug* **ayaakoziwinikaamagak**

aakoziikaazo *vai* pretend to be sick; *1sg* **indaakoziikaaz**; *prt* **ayaakoziikaazod**

aakoziishkaw- *vta* make s.o. sick (especially of a substance consumed); *in inverse forms: 1sg* **indaakoziishkaagon**; *prt* **ayaakoziishkaagod**

aakoziiwendaagozi *vai* be considered sickly; *1sg* **ayaakoziiwendaagozid**

aakoziiwidaabaan *na* ambulance; *pl* **aakoziiwidaabaanag**; *loc* **aakoziiwidaabaaning**; *dim* **aakoziiwidaabaanens**

aakoziiwigamig *ni* hospital; *pl* **aakoziiwigamigoon**; *loc* **aakoziiwigamigong**; *dim* **aakoziiwigamigoons**

aakoziiwinaagozi *vai* look sick; *1sg* **indaakoziiwinaagoz**; *prt* **ayaakoziiwinaagozid**

aakwaadizi *vai* be fierce; *1sg* **indaakwaadiz**; *prt* **ayaakwaadizid**

aakwendam *vai2* have intense feelings or desires; *1sg* **indaakwendam**; *prt* **ayaakwendang**

aamiwag /**aami-**/ *vai* they spawn; *prt* **ayaamijig**

aamoo *na* bee, wasp; *pl* **aamoog**; *dim* **aamoons**

aamoo-wadiswan *ni* beehive, wasp nest; *pl* **aamoo-wadiswanan**; *loc* **aamoo-wadiswaning**

aamoo-ziinzibaakwad *ni* honey

aanakwad *ni* cloud; *pl* **aanakwadoon**; *loc* **aanakwadong**; *dim* **aanakwadoons**

aanapii *pc* when? *interrogative; also* **aanapiish, aaniin apii, aaniin iw apii**

aanapiish *pc* when? *interrogative; also* **aanapii, aaniin apii, aaniin iw apii**

aanawendan *vti* dislike s.t., reject s.t., find s.t. unsatisfactory; *1sg* **indaanawendaan**; *prt* **ayaanawendang**

aanawendaagozi *vai* be disliked, be rejected, be found unsatisfactory; *1sg* **indaanawendaagoz**; *prt* **ayaanawendaagozid**

aanawendaagwad *vii* be disliked, be rejected, be found unsatisfactory; *prt* **ayaanawendaagwak**

aanawenim *vta* dislike s.o., reject s.o., find s.o. unsatisfactory; *1sg* **indaanawenimaa**; *prt* **ayaanawenimaad**

aanawenjige *vai* dislike things, reject things, find things unsatisfactory; *1sg* **indaanawenjige**; *prt* **ayaanawenjiged**

aanawewizi *vai* be inadequate, be ineffective, do in vain; *1sg* **indaanawewiz**; *prt* **ayaanawewizid**

aanawi *pc* anyhow, although, despite, but

aandabi *vai* change seat; *1sg* **indaandab**; *prt* **ayaandabid**

aandagim *vta* count s.o. over; *1sg* **indaandagimaa**; *prt* **ayaandagimaad**

aandagindan *vti c* count s.t. over; *1sg* **indaandagindaan**; *prt* **ayaandaginang**

aandaginzo *vai* count over; *1sg* **indaandaginz**; *prt* **ayaandaginzod**

aandagoode *vai* change one's dress; *1sg* **indaandagoode**; *prt* **ayaandagoodeg**

aandakii *vai* live somewhere else, change countries; *1sg* **indaandakii**; *prt* **ayaandakiid**

aandaabikinigan *ni* gearshift; *pl* **aandaabikiniganan**; *loc* **aandaabikiniganing**; *dim* **aandaabikinigaans**

aandaabikinige *vai* shift gears; *1sg* **indaandaabikinige**; *prt* **ayaandaabikiniged**

aandaakonige *vai* change plans, change laws; *1sg* **indaandaakonige**; *prt* **ayaandaakoniged**

aandeg *na* crow; *pl* **aandegwag**; *dim* **aandegoons**

aandi *pc* where? *interrogative; also* **aandish, aaniindi**

aangodinong *pc* sometimes, occasionally; *also* **aaningodinong**

aanikanootan *vti* translate s.t., interpret s.t.; *1sg* **indaanikanootaan**; *prt* **ayaanikanootang**

aanikanootaw *vta* translate s.o., interpret s.o.; *1sg* **indaanikanootawaa**; *prt* **ayaanikanootawaad**

aanikanootaage *vai* translate for people, interpret for people; *1sg* **indaanikanootaage**; *prt* **ayaanikanootaaged**

aanikanootaagewinini *na* speaker (for others), interpreter, translator; *pl* **aanikanootaagewininiwag**

aanikanootaagozi *vai* be interpreted; *1sg* **indaanikanootaagoz**; *prt* **ayaanikanootaagozid**

aanikegamaa *vii* be a chain of lakes; *prt* **ayaanikegamaag**; *aug* **aanikegamaamagad**; *prt aug* **ayaanikegamaamagak**

aanike-ogimaa *na* someone next in succession to the leader (e.g., a vice president); *pl* **aanike-ogimaag**; *dim* **aanike-ogimaans**

aanikeshkaw *vta* stand in place of s.o., follow in s.o.'s steps, be next to s.o.; *1sg* **indaanikeshkawaa**; *prt* **ayaanikeshkawaad**
aanikeshkodaadiwag /**aanikeshkodaadi-**/ *vai* they are next to each other; *1pl* **indaanikeshkodaadimin**; *prt* **ayaanikeshkodaadijig**
aanikoobijigan *na* ancestor, great-grandparent, great-grandchild; *pl* **aanikoobijiganag**; *loc* **aanikoobijiganing**; *dim* **aanikoobijigaans**
aanikooshim *vta* lay s.o. joining something else; *1sg* **indaanikooshimaa**; *prt* **ayaanikooshimaad**
aanikooshin *vai* lie joining something else; *prt* **ayaanikooshing**
aanikoosidoon *vti2* lay s.t. joining something else; *1sg* **indaanikoosidoon**; *prt* **ayaanikoosidood**
aanikoosin *vii* lie joining something else; *prt* **ayaanikoosing**
aanimad *vii* wind blows wildly, be a disturbance, be danger; *prt* **ayaanimak**
aanimendam *vai2* suffer mentally, suffer emotionally; *1sg* **indaanimendam**; *prt* **ayaanimendang**
aanimi' *vta* abuse s.o., make s.o. suffer, cause s.o. trouble; *1sg* **indaanimi'aa**; *prt* **ayaanimi'aad**
aanimim *vta* reprimand s.o.; *1sg* **inaanimimaa**; *prt* **ayaanimimaad**
aanimitoon *vti2* abuse s.t.; *1sg* **indaanimitoon**; *prt* **ayaanimitood**
aanimizi *vai* be seriously ill, be very sick, suffer, be in distress; *1sg* **indaanimiz**; *prt* **ayaanimizid**
aanind *pc* some
aanish *pc* well, well then
aanishim *vta* discourage s.o.; *1sg* **indaanishimaa**; *prt* **ayaanishimaad**
aanizhiitam *vai2* change one's mind, quit working, decide against, give up; *1sg* **indaanizhiitam**; *prt* **ayaanizhiitang**
aaniin *pc* how?, why?, in what way? *interrogative*
aaniin *pc* hello!, greetings!
aaniin apii *pc* when? *interrogative*; *also* **aanapii, aanapiish, aaniin iw apii, aaniinwapii**
aaniin dash *pc* why? *interrogative*
aaniindi *pc* where? *interrogative*; *also* **aandi**
aaniin iwapii *pc* when? *interrogative*; *also* **aanapii, aanapiish, aaniin apii**
aaniin minik *pc* how many?, how much?
aaniin danaa *pc* well how?, well why?, why not?
aaniish *pc* how?, why?, in what way? *interrogative*, well now, you see
aaniish apii *pc* when? *interrogative*; *also* **anapii, aanin apii, aanapiish, aaniin iw apii**
aaniish naa *pc* well now, you see
aanji- *pv4* change
aanji-bimaadizi *vai* change one's life; *1sg* **indaanji-bimaadiz**; *prt* **ayaanji-bimaadizid**
aanjibii'an *vti* write s.t. over; *1sg* **indaanjibii'aan**; *prt* **ayaanjibii'ang**
aanji-gozi *vai* move to a new residence; *1sg* **indaanji-goz**; *prt* **ayaanji-gozid**
aanji' *vta* change s.o., make s.o. over; *1sg* **indaanji'aa**; *prt* **ayaanji'aad**
aanjitoon *vti2* change s.t., make s.t. over; *1sg* **indaanjitoon**; *prt* **ayaanjitood**

aano- *pv1* in vain, without result
aanzikan *vti* change s.t. with foot or body (e.g., clothes); *1sg* **indaanzikaan**; *prt* **ayaanzikang**
aanzikaw *vta* change s.o. with foot or body (e.g., clothes); *1sg* **indaanzikawaa**; *prt* **ayaanzikawaad**
aanzikonaye *vai* change one's clothes; *1sg* **indaanzikonaye**; *prt* **ayaanzikonayed**
aanzikonaye' *vta* change s.o.'s clothes; *1sg* **indaanzikonaye'aa**; *prt* **ayaanzikonaye'aad**
aanzinaago' *vta* change s.o.'s appearance, transform s.o.; *1sg* **indaanzinaago'aa**; *prt* **ayaanzinaago'aad**
aanzinaago'idizo *vai* change one's own appearance, transform oneself; *1sg* **indaanzinaago'idiz**; *prt* **ayaanzinaago'idizod**
aanzinaagotoon *vti2* change s.t.'s appearance, transform s.t.; *1sg* **indaanzinaagotoon**; *prt* **ayaanzinaagotood**
aanzinaagozi *vai* look changed; *1sg* **indaanzinaagoz**; *prt* **ayaanzinaagozid**
aanzinaagwad *vii* look changed; *prt* **ayaanzinaagwak**
aanziyaan *ni* man's apron (traditional dress), breech clout, diaper; *pl* **aanziyaanan**; *loc* **aanziyaaning**; *dim* **aanziyaanens**
aapidaanagidoon *vai* talk without stopping; *1sg* **indaapidaanagidoon**; *prt* **ayaapidaanagidoong**
aapideg *pc* without a doubt, certainly
aapidendi *vai* go and not return, be gone forever; *1sg* **indaapidend**; *prt* **ayaapidendid**
aapiji *pc* very, quite
aapijibatoo *vai* run away for good; *1sg* **indaapijibatoo**; *prt* **ayaapijibatood**
aapijinazh /**aapijinaN-**/ *vta* finally and completely kill s.o.; *1sg* **indaapijinaa**; *prt* **ayaapijinaad**
aapijinizhimo *vai* flee for good; *1sg* **indaapijinizhim**; *prt* **ayaapijinizhimod**
aapijishin *vai* have a bad fall, die from a fall; *1sg* **indaapijishin**; *prt* **ayaapijishing**
aapiji-wiidige *vai* be legally married; *1sg* **indaapiji-wiidige**; *prt* **ayaapiji-wiidiged**
aapiji-wiidige-mazina'igan *ni* marriage license; *pl* **aapiji-wiidige-mazina'iganan**
aas *ni* legging; *pl* **aasan**
aasamisag *ni* wall; *pl* **aasamisagoon**; *loc* **aasamisagong**
aasaakamig *ni* moss; *pl* **aasaakamigoon**
aasodoodooshimebizon *ni* brassiere; *pl* **aasodoodooshimebizonan**; *loc* **aasodoodooshimebizoning**; *dim* **aasodoodooshimebizonens**
aatayaa *pc* man's expression of mild displeasure or disdain; *also* **taayaa**
aate *vii* be extinguished; *prt* **ayaateg**; *aug* **aatemagad**; *prt* *aug* **ayaatemagak**
aatebidoon *vti2* turn s.t. out (e.g., stove or lamp); *1sg* **indaatebidoon**; *prt* **ayaatebidood**
aatebizh /**aatebiN-**/ *vta* put out a fire on s.o. with hands; *1sg* **indaatebinaa**; *prt* **ayaatebinaad**
aatebii *vai* sober up; *1sg* **indaatebii**; *prt* **ayaatebiid**
aate'an *vti* put s.t. out (e.g., fire or light), extinguish s.t.; *1sg* **indaate'aan**; *prt* **ayaate'ang**

aate'igan *ni* fire extinguisher; *pl* aate'iganan; *loc*
aate'iganing; *dim* aate'igaans
aate'ishkodawewidaabaan *na* fire truck; *loc*
aate'ishkodawewidaabaaning; *dim*
aate'ishkodawewidaabaanens
aate'ishkodawewinini *na* fireman; *pl*
aate'ishkodawewininiwag; *dim*
aate'ishkodawewininiins
aatenaagozi *vai* appear to be extinguished (e.g.,
the moon or sun in an eclipse); *prt*
ayaatenaagozid
aatewebinan *vti* put s.t. out quickly (e.g., fire or
light); *1sg* indaatewebinaan; *prt*
ayaatewebinang
aateyaabikishin *vai* be darkened (e.g. the moon or
sun in an eclipse); *prt* ayaateyaabikishing
aatwaakogaabawi *vai* stand leaning against
something; *1sg* indaatwaakogaabaw; *prt*
ayaatwaakogaabawid
aatwaakoshim *vta* lean s.o. against (as something
stick- or wood-like); *1sg* indaatwaakoshimaa;
prt ayaatwaakoshimaad
aatwaakoshin *vai* lean against (as something stick-
or wood-like); *1sg* indaatwaakoshin; *prt*
ayaatwaakoshing
aatwaakosidoon *vti2* lean s.t. against (as
something stick- or wood-like); *1sg*
indaatwaakosidoon; *prt* ayaatwaakosidood
aatwaakosin *vii* lean against (as something stick-
or wood-like); *prt* ayaatwaakosing
aatwaakowebin *vta* throw s.o. up against (as
something stick- or wood-like); *1sg*
indaatwaakowebinaa; *prt*
ayaatwaakowebinaad
aatwaakowebinan *vti* throw s.t. up against (as
something stick- or wood-like); *1sg*
indaatwaakowebinaan; *prt*
ayaatwaakowebinang
aawadaw *vta* haul (s.t.) for s.o.; *1sg*
indaawadawaa; *prt* ayaawadawaad
aawadaaso *vai* haul something; *1sg* indaawadaas;
prt ayaawadaasod
aawadaasoowidaabaan *na* truck; *pl*
aawadaasoowidaabaanag; *loc*
aawadaasoowidaabaaning; *dim*
aawadaasoowidaabaanens
aawadoon *vti2* haul s.t.; *1sg* indaawadoon; *prt*
ayaawadood
aawajimine *vai* haul wild rice; *1sg* indaawajimine;
prt ayaawajimined
aawajinigaadan *vti* haul s.t. on one's shoulder; *1sg*
indaawajinigaadaan; *prt* ayaawajinigaadang
aawajinigaazh /aawajinigaaN-/ *vta* haul s.o. on
one's shoulder; *1sg* indaawajinigaanaa; *prt*
ayaawajinigaanaad
aawajinige *vai* haul things on one's shoulder; *1sg*
indaawajinige; *prt* ayaawajiniged
aawan *vii* be a certain thing; *prt* ayaawang
aawazh /aawaN-/ *vta* haul s.o.; *1sg* indaawanaa;
prt ayaawanaad
aawazhiwe *vai* haul people; *1sg* indaawazhiwe; *prt*
ayaawazhiwed
aawazhiwewidaabaan *na* van; *pl*
aawazhiwewidaabaanag; *loc*

aawazhiwewidaabaaning; *dim*
aawazhiwewidaabaanens
aawekaazh /aawekaaN-/ *vta* recognize s.o.; *1sg*
indaawekaanaa; *prt* ayaawekaanaad
aawenan *vti* recognize s.t. by sight, identify s.t. by
sight; *1sg* indaawenaan; *prt* ayaawenang
aawenaw *vta* recognize s.o. by sight, identify s.o.
by sight; *1sg* indaawenawaa; *prt*
ayaawenawaad
aawendan *vti* recognize s.t., identify s.t.; *1sg*
indaawendaan; *prt* ayaawendang
aawenim *vta* recognize s.o., identify s.o.; *1sg*
indaawenimaa; *prt* ayaawenimaad
aawetan *vti* recognize s.t. by sound, identify s.t. by
sound; *1sg* indaawetaan; *prt* ayaawetang
aawetaw *vta* recognize s.o. by sound, identify s.o.
by sound; *1sg* indaawetawaa; *prt*
ayaawetawaad
aawi *vai* be a certain thing or being; *1sg* indaaw;
prt ayaawid
aayaapii *pc* every once in a while
aazhawagaazii *vai* wade across; *1sg*
indaazhawagaazii; *prt* ayaazhawagaaziid
aazhawagaaziibatoo *vai* run across wading; *1sg*
indaazhawagaaziibatoo; *prt*
ayaazhawagaaziibatood
aazhawa'am *vai2* go across by boat; *1sg*
indaazhawa'am; *prt* ayaazhawa'ang; *also*
aazhawa'o
aazhawa'o *vai* go across by boat; *1sg*
indaazhawa'; *prt* ayaazhawa'od; *also*
aazhawa'am
aazhawa'oodoon *vti2* take s.t. across by boat,
ferry s.t. across; *1sg* indaazhawa'oodoon; *prt*
ayaazhawa'oodood
aazhawa'oozh /aazhawa'ooN-/ *vta* take s.o.
across by boat, ferry s.o. across; *1sg*
indaazhawa'oonaa; *prt* ayaazhawa'oonaad
aazhawayi'ii *pc* on the other side of it
aazhawaadagaa *vai* swim across; *1sg*
indaazhawaadagaa; *prt* ayaazhawaadagaad
aazhawaakoshim *vta* lay s.o. across (as something
stick- or wood-like); *1sg*
indaazhawaakoshimaa; *prt*
ayaazhawaakoshimaad
aazhawaakoshin *vai* lie across (as something stick-
or wood-like); *1sg* indaazhawaakoshin; *prt*
ayaazhawaakoshing
aazhawaakosidoon *vti2* lay s.t. across (as
something stick- or wood-like); *1sg*
indaazhawaakosidoon; *prt*
ayaazhawaakosidood
aazhawaakosin *vii* lie across (as something stick-
or wood-like); *prt* ayaazhawaakosing
aazhawaandawaagan *ni* foot bridge; *pl*
aazhawaandawaaganan; *loc*
aazhawaandawaaganing; *dim*
aazhawaandawaagaans
aazhawaandawe *vai* climb across; *1sg*
indaazhawaandawe; *prt* ayaazhawaandawed
aazhawibatoo *vai* run across; *1sg*
indaazhawibatoo; *prt* ayaazhawibatood; *also*
aazhoobatoo

aazhawigwaashkwani *vai* jump across; *1sg*
indaazhawigwaashkwan; *prt*
ayaazhawigwaashkwanid
aazhibik *ni* rock cliff; *pl* **aazhibikoon;** *loc*
aazhibikong; *dim* **aazhibikoons**
aazhidem *vta* talk back to s.o.; *answer* back to s.o.;
1sg **indaazhidemaa;** *prt* **ayaazhidemaad**
aazhideyaatig *na* cross; *pl* **aazhideyaatigoog;** *loc*
aazhideyaatigong; *dim* **aazhideyaatigoons**
aazhigidwebin *vta* throw s.o. over backwards; *1sg*
indaazhigidwebinaa; *prt* **ayaazhigidwebinaad**
aazhigidwebinan *vti* throw s.t. over backwards; *1sg*
indaazhigidwebinaan; *prt*
ayaazhigidwebinang
aazhigijise *vai* turn over backwards, turn face up;
1sg **indaazhigijise;** *prt* **ayaazhigijised**
aazhigijise *vii* turn over backwards, turn face up;
prt **ayaazhigijiseg;** *aug* **aazhigijisemagad;** *prt*
aug **ayaazhigijisemagak**
aazhigijishim *vta* lay s.o. over backwards, lay s.o.
face up; *1sg* **indaazhigijishimaa;** *prt*
ayaazhigijishimaad
aazhigijishin *vai* fall over backwards, lie face up;
1sg **indaazhigijishin;** *prt* **ayaazhigijishing**
aazhigijisidoon *vti2* lay s.t. over backwards, lay s.t.
face up; *1sg* **indaazhigijisidoon;** *prt*
ayaazhigijisidood
aazhigijisin *vii* fall over backwards, lie face up; *prt*
ayaazhigijising
aazhikwe *vai* scream; *1sg* **indaazhikwe;** *prt*
ayaazhikwed
aazhogan *ni* bridge; *pl* **aazhoganan;** *loc*
aazhoganing; *dim* **aazhogaans**
aazhoge *vai* go across water; *1sg* **indaazhoge;** *prt*
ayaazhoged
aazhogeba'idiwag /aazhogeba'idi-/ *vai* they run
across together; *1pl* **indaazhogeba'idimin;** *prt*
ayaazhogeba'idijig
aazhogebizo *vai* drive across; *1sg* **indaazhogebiz;**
prt **ayaazhogebizod**
aazhogedaabii'iwe *vai* drive across; *1sg*
indaazhogedaabii'iwe; *prt*
ayaazhogedaabii'iwed
aazhogewidoon *vti2* carry s.t. across, take s.t.
across; *1sg* **indaazhogewidoon;** *prt*
ayaazhogewidood
aazhogewizh /aazhogewiN-/ *vta* carry s.o. across,
take s.o. across; *1sg* **indaazhogewinaa;** *prt*
ayaazhogewinaad
aazhooba'idiwag /aazhooba'idi-/ *vai* they run
across together; *1pl* **indaazhooba'idimin;** *prt*
ayaazhooba'idijig
aazhoobatoo *vai* run across; *1sg* **indaazhoobatoo;**
prt **ayaazhoobatood;** *also* **aazhawibatoo**
aazhoodamon /aazhoodamo-/ *vii* go across (as a
road or trail); *prt* **ayaazhoodamog**
aazhoodaabii'iwe *vai* drive across; *1sg*
indaazhoodaabii'iwe; *prt*
ayaazhoodaabii'iwed
aazhoogaadebi *vai* sit with legs crossed; *1sg*
indaazhoogaadeb; *prt* **ayaazhoogaadebid**
aazhookoodin *vta* infect s.o. with something; *1sg*
indaazhookoodinaa; *prt* **ayaazhookoodinaad**

aazhooningwa'an *vti* wear s.t. across the shoulder;
1sg **indaazhooningwa'aan;** *prt*
ayaazhooningwa'ang
aazhooningwa'igan *na* bandolier bag; *pl*
aazhooningwa'iganag; *dim*
aazhooningwa'igaans; *also* **aazhooningwa'on;**
the usual Mille Lacs term is **gashkibidaagan**
aazhooshkaa *vai* go across; *1sg* **indaazhooshkaa;**
prt **ayaazhooshkaad**

B

ba- *pv2* toward the speaker, this way, here, hither
changed form of: **bi-**
babagiwayaan *ni* shirt; *pl* **babagiwayaanan;** *loc*
babagiwayaaning; *dim* **babagiwayaanens;** *also*
bagiwayaan
babagiwayaanegamig *ni* tent; *pl*
babagiwayaanegamigoon; *loc*
babagiwayaanegamigong; *dim*
babagiwayaanegamigoons; *also*
bagiwayaanegamig
babagiwayaanegamigwegin *ni* canvas; *pl*
babagiwayaanegamigweginoon
babagiwayaanekizin *ni* tennis shoe, canvas shoe;
pl **babagiwayaanekizinan;** *loc*
babagiwayaanekizining; *dim*
babagiwayaanekizinens; *also*
bagiwayaanekizin
babagiwayaaniigin *ni* cloth, cotton cloth; *pl*
babagiwayaaniiginoon; *loc*
babagiwayaaniiginong; *dim*
babagiwayaaniiginoons; *also* **bagiwayaaniigin**
babaa- *pv2* going about
babaa-ayaa *vai* be around, wander about; *1sg*
imbabaa-ayaa; *prt* **bebaa-ayaad**
babaabag= < bibag=
babaadagw= < badagw=
babaamadaawe *vai* go about trading, be a
peddler; *1sg* **imbabaamadaawe;** *prt*
bebaamadaawed
babaamadaawewinini *na* peddler; *pl*
babaamadaawewininiwag; *also*
babaamadaawaagewinini
babaamademo *vai* go about crying; *1sg*
imbabaamadem; *prt* **bebaamademod**
babaamaadagaa *vai* swim about; *1sg*
imbabaamaadagaa; *prt* **bebaamaadagaad**
babaamaadagaako *vai* go about on the ice; *1sg*
imbabaamaadagaak; *prt* **bebaamaadagaakod**
babaamaadagaazii *vai* wade about; *1sg*
imbabaamaadagaazii; *prt*
bebaamaadagaaziid
babaamaada'e *vai* skate about; *1sg*
imbabaamaada'e; *prt* **bebaamaada'ed**
babaamaadizi *vai* live about, travel about; *1sg*
imbabaamaadiz; *prt* **bebaamaadizid**

babaamaadizii-makak *ni* suitcase; *pl*
  babaamaadizii-makakoon; *loc*
  babaamaadizii-makakong; *dim*
  babaamaadizii-makakoons
babaamaajimo *vai* spread the news about; *1sg*
  imbabaamaajim; *prt* **bebaamaajimod**
babaamaajimoo-mazina'igan *ni* newspaper; *pl*
  babaamaajimoo-mazina'iganan; *loc*
  babaamaajimoo-mazina'iganing; *dim*
  babaamaajimoo-mazina'igaans
babaamaanakwad *vii* clouds move about; *prt*
  bebaamaanakwak
babaamaashi *vai* be blown about, sail about; *1sg*
  imbabaamaash; *prt* **bebaamaashid**
babaamaasin *vii* be blown about, sail about; *prt*
  bebaamaasing
babaamendam *vai2* pay attention, worry; *1sg*
  imbabaamendam; *prt* **bebaamendang**
babaamendan *vti* pay attention to s.t., worry
  about s.t., bother s.t.; *1sg* **imbabaamendaan;**
  prt **bebaamendang**
babaamenim *vta* pay attention to s.o., worry
  about s.o., bother s.o.; *1sg* **imbabaamenimaa;**
  prt **bebaamenimaad**
babaamiba'idiwag /babaamiba'idi-/ *vai* they run
  about together; *1pl* **imbabaamiba'idimin;** *prt*
  bebaamiba'idijig
babaamibatoo *vai* run about; *1sg*
  imbabaamibatoo; *prt* **bebaamibatood**
babaamibide *vii* speed about, drive about, fly
  about; *prt* **bebaamibideg;** *aug*
  babaamibidemagad; *prt aug*
  bebaamibidemagak
babaamibizo *vai* speed about, drive about, fly
  about; *1sg* **imbabaamibiz;** *prt* **bebaamibizod**
babaamidaabii'iwe *vai* drive about; *1sg*
  imbabaamidaabii'iwe; *prt*
  bebaamidaabii'iwed
babaamigozi *vai* move one's residence about; *1sg*
  imbabaamigoz; *prt* **bebaamigozid**
babaaminizha' /babaaminizha'w-/ *vta* chase s.o.
  about; *1sg* **imbabaaminizha'waa;** *prt*
  bebaaminizha'waad
babaaminizha'an *vti* chase s.t. about; *1sg*
  imbabaaminizha'aan; *prt* **bebaaminizha'ang**
babaaminizha'ige *vai* chase things about; *1sg*
  imbabaaminizha'ige; *prt* **bebaaminizha'iged**
babaamise *vai* fly about; *1sg* **imbabaamise;** *prt*
  bebaamised
babaamise *vii* fly about; *prt* **bebaamiseg;** *aug*
  babaamisemagad; *prt aug* **bebaamisemagak**
babaamishimo *vai* dance about; *1sg*
  imbabaamishim; *prt* **bebaamishimod**
babaamishkaa *vai* paddle about, go about in a
  boat; *1sg* **imbabaamishkaa;** *prt*
  bebaamishkaad
babaamiwidoon *vti2* take s.t. about, carry s.t.
  about; *1sg* **imbabaamiwidoon;** *prt*
  bebaamiwidood
babaamiwizh /babaamiwiN-/ *vta* take s.o. about,
  carry s.o. about, guide s.o. about; *1sg*
  imbabaamiwinaa; *prt* **bebaamiwinaad**
babaamizi *vai* do business, go about on one's
  business; *1sg* **imbabaamiz;** *prt* **bebaamizid**

babaamose *vai* walk about; *1sg* **imbabaamose;** *prt*
  bebaamosed
babaamoode *vai* crawl about; *1sg*
  imbabaamoode; *prt* **bebaamooded**
babaamoomigo *vai* ride about on horseback; *1sg*
  imbabaamoomig; *prt* **bebaamoomigod**
babaazagw= < bazagw=
babig *na* flea; *pl* **babigwag;** *dim* **babigoons**
babimose *vai* walk about, take a stroll; *1sg*
  imbabimose; *prt* **bebimosed**
babiich= < bich=
babiichii *vai* put on one's shoes, put on one's
  moccasins; *1sg* **imbabiichii;** *prt* **bebiichiid**
babiigomakakii *na* toad; *pl* **babiigomakakiig;** *dim*
  babiigomakakiins
babiikw= < bikw=
babiinzikawaagan *ni* coat, jacket; *pl*
  babiinzikawaaganan; *loc*
  babiinzikawaaganing; *dim*
  babiinzikawaagaans
babiishag= < bishag=
babiiwaawan /babiiwaa-/ *vii* they are tiny; *prt*
  bebiiwaagin
babiiwiminagadoon /babiiwiminagad-/ *vii* they
  are tiny (as something ball-like); *prt*
  bebiiwiminagakin
babiiwiminagiziwag /babiiwiminagizi-/ *vai* they
  are tiny (as something ball-like); *prt*
  bebiiwiminagizijig
babiiwizhiiniyiwag /babiiwizhiinyi-/ *vai* they are
  tiny *plural*; *1pl* **imbabiiwizhiinyimin;** *prt*
  bebiiwizhiinyijig
babiizigaakiz /babiizigaakizw-/ *vta* curl s.o.'s hair
  by heat; *1sg* **imbabiizigaakizwaa;** *prt*
  bebiizigaakizwaad
babiizigindibe *vai* have curly hair; *1sg*
  imbabiizigindibe; *prt* **bebiizigindibed**
babiizoge= < bizoge=
badagoshkan *vti* cover s.t. with body, lie
  protectively on s.t.; *1sg* **imbadagoshkaan;** *prt*
  bedagoshkang
badagoshkaw *vta* cover s.o. with body, lie protectively on s.o.; *1sg* **imbadagoshkawaa;** *prt*
  bedagoshkawaad
badagwana' /badagwana'w-/ *vta* cover s.o.; *1sg*
  imbadagwana'waa; *prt* **bedagwana'waad**
badagwana'an *vti* cover s.t.; *1sg*
  imbadagwana'aan; *prt* **bedagwana'ang**
badagwana'igaade *vii* be covered; *prt*
  bedagwana'igaadeg; *aug*
  badagwana'igaademagad; *prt aug*
  bedagwana'igaademagak
badagwana'igaazo *vai* be covered; *prt*
  bedagwana'igaazod
badagwana'ige *vai* cover things; *1sg*
  imbadagwana'ige; *prt* **bedagwana'iged**
badagwiingweshin *vai* lie with one's face covered;
  1sg **imbadagwiingweshin;** *prt*
  bedagwiingweshing
badaka' /badaka'w-/ *vta* stick something in s.o.,
  prick s.o., use a fork on s.o.; *1sg*
  imbadaka'waa; *prt* **bedaka'waad**
badaka'an *vti* stick something in s.t., prick s.t.,
  spear s.t., use a fork on s.t.; *1sg* **imbadaka'aan;**
  prt **bedaka'ang**

badaka'igan *ni* fork; *pl* **badaka'iganan;** *loc*
badaka'iganing; *dim* **badaka'igaans**
badaka'ige *vai* stick something in things, prick
things, spear; *1sg* **imbadaka'ige;** *prt*
bedaka'iged
badakijin *vai* get pricked; *1sg* **imbadakijin;** *prt*
bedakijing
badakibine'o *vai* stick a feather in one's hair or
hat; *1sg* **imbadakibine';** *prt* **bedakibine'od**
badakide *vii* stand up from a surface, be planted
in; *prt* **bedakideg;** *aug* **badakidemagad;** *prt*
aug **bedakidemagak**
badakidoon *vti2* stick s.t. in, plant s.t.; *1sg*
imbadakidoon; *prt* **bedakidood**
badakise *vai* stick in a surface; *prt* **bedakised**
badakise *vii* stick in a surface; *prt* **bedakiseg;** *aug*
badakisemagad; *prt aug* **bedakisemagak**
badakishim *vta* stick s.o. in, set s.o. in the ground;
1sg **imbadakishimaa;** *prt* **bedakishimaad**
badakisidoon *vti2* stick s.t. in, set s.t. in the
ground; *1sg* **imbadakisidoon;** *prt*
bedakisidood
badakisijige *vai* stick things in, set things in the
ground; *1sg* **imbadakisijige;** *prt* **bedakisijiged**
badakizh /badakiN-/ *vta* stick s.o. in, plant s.o. in;
1sg **imbadakinaa;** *prt* **bedakinaad**
badakizo *vai* stand up from a surface, be planted
in; *1sg* **imbadakiz;** *prt* **bedakizod**
bagakaabam *vta* see s.o. clearly; *1sg*
imbagakaabamaa; *prt* **begakaabamaad**
bagakaabandan *vti* see s.t. clearly; *1sg*
imbagakaabandaan; *prt* **begakaabandang**
bagakaabi *vai* see clearly; *1sg* **imbagakaab;** *prt*
begakaabid
bagamaadagaa *vai* arrive swimming; *1sg*
imbagamaadagaa; *prt* **begamaadagaad**
bagamaagan *ni* war club; *pl* **bagamaaganan;** *loc*
bagamaaganing; *dim* **bagamaagaans**

bagamaagan (war club)

bagamaajimo *vai* arrive with news; *1sg*
imbagamaajim; *prt* **begamaajimod**
bagamaanimad *vii* wind comes in hard; *prt*
begamaanimak

bagamaapi *vai* arrive laughing; *1sg* **imbagamaap;**
prt **begamaapid**
bagamaashi *vai* be blown in, sail in; *1sg*
imbagamaash; *prt* **begamaashid**
bagamaasin *vii* be blown in, sail in; *prt*
begamaasing
bagami- *pv4* arriving
bagami-ayaa *vai* arrive; *1sg* **imbagami-ayaa;** *prt*
begami-ayaad
bagami-ayaa *vii* arrive, come to be, come to pass;
prt **begami-ayaag;** *aug* **bagami-ayaamagad;**
prt aug **begami-ayaamagak**
bagamiba'idiwag /bagamiba'idi-/ *vai* they arrive
on the run together; *1pl* **imbagamiba'idimin;**
prt **begamiba'idijig**
bagamiba'iwe *vai* arrive fleeing from people; *1sg*
imbagamiba'iwe; *prt* **begamiba'iwed**
bagamibatoo *vai* arrive on the run; *1sg*
imbagamibatoo; *prt* **begamibatood**
bagamibide *vii* arrive speeding, arrive driving,
arrive flying; *prt* **begamibideg;** *aug*
bagamibidemagad; *prt aug*
begamibidemagak
bagamibizo *vai* arrive speeding, arrive driving,
arrive flying; *1sg* **imbagamibiz;** *prt*
begamibizod
bagamibiisaa *vii* rain is on the way; *prt*
begamibiisaag; *aug* **bagamibiisaamagad;** *prt*
aug **begamibiisaamagak**
bagamidaabii'iwe *vai* arrive driving; *1sg*
imbagamidaabii'iwe; *prt* **begamidaabii'iwed**
bagamigidaazo *vai* arrive mad; *1sg*
imbagamigidaaz; *prt* **begamigidaazod**
bagamise *vai* arrive flying; *1sg* **imbagamise;** *prt*
begamised
bagamise *vii* arrive flying; *prt* **begamiseg;** *aug*
bagamisemagad; *prt aug* **begamisemagak**
bagamishkaa *vai* arrive paddling, arrive by boat;
1sg **imbagamishkaa;** *prt* **begamishkaad**
bagamiwidoon *vti2* arrive carrying s.t.; *1sg*
imbagamiwidoon; *prt* **begamiwidood**
bagamiwizh /bagamiwiN-/ *vta* arrive carrying s.o.;
1sg **imbagamiwinaa;** *prt* **begamiwinaad**
bagamose *vai* arrive walking; *1sg* **imbagamose;**
prt **begamosed**
bagamoode *vai* arrive crawling; *1sg*
imbagamoode; *prt* **begamooded**
bagamoomigo *vai* arrive on horseback; *1sg*
imbagamoomig; *prt* **begamoomigod**
bagandizi *vai* be lazy, be shiftless, be incompetent;
1sg **imbagandiz;** *prt* **begandizid**
bagaan *na* nut, hazelnut, peanut; *pl* **bagaanag;** *loc*
bagaaning; *dim* **bagaanens**
bagaani-bimide *ni* peanut butter; *also* **bagaanensi-
bimide**
bagaaniminzh *na* hazelnut bush; *pl*
bagaaniminzhiig; *loc* **bagaaniminzhiing;** *dim*
bagaaniminzhiins
bagesaan *na* plum; *pl* **bagesaanag;** *loc*
bagesaaning; *dim* **bagesaanens**
bagesaanaatig *na* plum tree; *pl*
bagesaanaatigoog; *loc* **bagesaanaatigong;** *dim*
bagesaanaatigoons
bagesaaniminagaawanzh *na* plum bush; *pl*
bagesaaniminagaawanzhiig; *loc*

bagesaaniminagaawanzhiing; *dim*
bagesaaniminagaawanzhiins
bagese *vai* play the dish game; *1sg* **imbagese;** *prt*
begesed
bagida'waa *vai* fish with a net, set a net; *1sg*
imbagida'waa; *prt* **begida'waad**
bagidam *vta* let s.o. drop from one's mouth; *1sg*
imbagidamaa; *prt* **begidamaad**
bagidanaamo *vai* breathe, exhale; *1sg*
imbagidanaam; *prt* **begidanaamod**
bagidandan *vti* let s.t. drop from one's mouth; *1sg*
imbagidandaan; *prt* **begidandang**
bagidaabii *vai* fish with set lines; *1sg* **imbagidaabii;**
prt **begidaabiid**
bagidendan *vti* release s.t. from one's mind; *1sg*
imbagidendaan; *prt* **begidendang**
bagidenim *vta* release s.o. from one's mind, bury
s.o., complete mourning for s.o.; *1sg*
imbagidenimaa; *prt* **begidenimaad**
bagidenjigaazo *vai* be buried; *prt*
begidenjigaazod
bagidenjige *vai* release things from one's mind,
hold a funeral; *1sg* **imbagidenjige;** *prt*
begidenjiged
bagidin *vta* set s.o. down, offer s.o., release s.o., let
s.o. go, allow s.o.; *1sg* **imbagidinaa;** *prt*
begidinaad
bagidinamaw *vta* set (s.t.) down for s.o., offer
(s.t.) to s.o., release (s.t.) to s.o., allow (s.t.) to
s.o.; *1sg* **imbagidinamawaa;** *prt*
begidinamawaad
bagidinan *vti* set s.t. down, offer s.t., release s.t.,
let s.t. go, allow s.t.; *1sg* **imbagidinaan;** *prt*
begidinang
bagidinigaade *vii* be set down, be offered, be
released, be let go, be allowed; *prt*
begidinigaadeg; *aug* **bagidinigaademagad;** *prt*
aug **begidinigaademagak**
bagidinigaazo *vai* be set down, be offered, be
released, be let go, be allowed; *prt*
begidinigaazod
bagidinige *vai* set things down, offer things, release things, let things go, allow things, plant
things in; *1sg* **imbagidinige;** *prt* **begidiniged**
bagidinise *vai* put wood on the fire; *1sg*
imbagidinise; *prt* **begidinised**
bagidoom *vta* set s.o. down off one's back; *1sg*
imbagidoomaa; *prt* **begidoomaad**
bagidoondan *vti* set s.t. down off one's back; *1sg*
imbagidoondaan; *prt* **begidoondang**
bagijigan *ni* offering; *pl* **bagijiganan;** *dim*
bagijigaans
bagijige *vai* make an offering; *1sg* **imbagijige;** *prt*
begijiged
bagijiwane *vai* set down one's pack; *1sg*
imbagijiwane; *prt* **begijiwaned**
bagijwebin *vta* release s.o. quickly, throw s.o.
down quickly; *1sg* **imbagijwebinaa;** *prt*
begijwebinaad
bagijwebinan *vti* release s.t. quickly, throw s.t.
down quickly; *1sg* **imbagijwebinaan;** *prt*
begijwebinang
bagiwayaan *ni* shirt, piece of cloth; *pl*
bagiwayaanan; *loc* **bagiwayaaning;** *dim*
bagiwayaanens; *also* **babagiwayaan**

bagiwayaanegamig *ni* tent; *pl*
bagiwayaanegamigoon; *loc*
bagiwayaanegamigong; *dim*
bagiwayaanegamigoons; *also*
babagiwayaanegamig
bagiwayaaneshkimod *ni* cloth bag; *pl*
bagiwayaaneshkimodan; *loc*
bagiwayaaneshkimodaang; *dim*
bagiwayaaneshkimodens
bagiwayaanish *ni* cloth, rag; *pl* **bagiwayaanishan;**
loc **bagiwayaanishing;** *dim* **bagiwayaanishens;**
also **babagiwayaanish**
bagizo *vai* bathe, go swimming; *1sg* **imbagiz;** *prt*
begizod
bagizowin *ni* bathtub; *pl* **bagizowinan;** *loc*
bagizowining; *dim* **bagizowinens**
bagojiin *vta* gut s.o.; *1sg* **imbagojiinaa;** *prt*
begojiinaad
bagone' /bagone'w-/ *vta* drill s.o., make a hole in
s.o. using something; *1sg* **imbagone'waa;** *prt*
begone'waad
bagone'an *vti* drill s.t., make a hole in s.t. using
something; *1sg* **imbagone'aan;** *prt* **begone'ang**
bagone'igan *ni* drill; *pl* **bagone'iganan;** *loc*
bagone'iganing; *dim* **bagone'igaans**
bagoneyaa *vii* have a hole; *prt* **begoneyaag;** *aug*
bagoneyaamagad; *prt aug* **begoneyaamagak**
bagonezi *vai* have a hole; *prt* **begonezid**
bagosendam *vai2* wish, hope; *1sg*
imbagosendam; *prt* **begosendang**
bagosendan *vti* wish for s.t., hope for s.t.; *1sg*
imbagosendaan; *prt* **begosendang**
bagosenim *vta* wish of s.o., hope for s.o., have
hope for s.o.; *1sg* **imbagosenimaa;** *prt*
begosenimaad
bagoshkaa *vai* get a hole; *prt* **begoshkaad**
bagoshkaa *vii* get a hole; *prt* **begoshkaag;** *aug*
bagoshkaamagad; *prt aug* **begoshkaamagak**
bagwa' /bagwa'w-/ *vta* patch s.o.; *1sg*
imbagwa'waa; *prt* **begwa'waad**
bagwa'amaw *vta* patch (s.t.) for s.o.; *1sg*
imbagwa'amawaa; *prt* **begwa'amawaad**
bagwa'an *vti* patch s.t.; *1sg* **imbagwa'aan;** *prt*
begwa'ang
bagwa'igan *ni* patch; *pl* **bagwa'iganan;** *loc*
bagwa'iganing; *dim* **bagwa'igaans**
bagwa'igaade *vii* be patched; *prt* **begwa'igaadeg;**
aug **bagwa'igaademagad;** *prt aug*
begwa'igaademagak
bagwa'igaazo *vai* be patched, wear patches; *prt*
begwa'igaazod
bagwa'ige *vai* patch things; *1sg* **imbagwa'ige;** *prt*
begwa'iged
bagwaj *pc* in the wilderness
bagwaji- *pv4* wild
bagwajipin *na* wild potato; *pl* **bagwajipiniig;** *loc*
bagwajipiniing; *dim* **bagwajipiniins;** *also*
bagwaji-opin
bagwana *pc* at random, anyhow
bagwanawizi *vai* be ignorant, be dumb; *1sg*
imbagwanawiz; *prt* **begwanawizid**
bagwaakide *vii* have a hole burned in; *prt*
begwaakideg; *aug* **bagwaakidemagad;** *prt aug*
begwaakidemagak

bagwaakiz /bagwaakizw-/ *vta* burn a hole in s.o.; *1sg* **imbagwaakizwaa**; *prt* **begwaakizwaad**
bagwaakizan *vti* burn a hole in s.t.; *1sg* **imbagwaakizaan**; *prt* **begwaakizang**
bagwaakizo *vai* have a hole burned in; *prt* **begwaakizod**
bajiishka'ogaan *ni* tipi, lodge with pointed top; *pl* **bajiishka'ogaanan**; *loc* **bajiishka'ogaaning**; *dim* **bajiishka'ogaanens**

bajiishka'ogaan (tipi, lodge with pointed top)

bajiishkaa *vii* be pointed; *prt* **bejiishkaag**; *aug* **bajiishkaamagad**; *prt aug* **bejiishkaamagak**
bajiishkiga' /bajiishkiga'w-/ *vta* chop s.o. pointed; *1sg* **imbajiishkiga'waa**; *prt* **bejiishkiga'waad**
bajiishkiga'an *vti* chop s.t. pointed; *1sg* **imbajiishkiga'aan**; *prt* **bejiishkiga'ang**
bajiishkizi *vai* be pointed; *prt* **bejiishkizid**
bakade *vai* be hungry; *1sg* **imbakade**; *prt* **bekaded**
bakadekaazo *vai* pretend to be hungry; *1sg* **imbakadekaaz**; *prt* **bekadekaazod**
bakam *vta* bite s.o. through (e.g., something string-like); *1sg* **imbakamaa**; *prt* **bekamaad**
bakandan *vti* bite s.t. through (e.g., something string-like); *1sg* **imbakandaan**; *prt* **bekandang**
bakazhaawe *vai* clean a fish; *1sg* **imbakazhaawe**; *prt* **bekazhaawed**
bakaakadozo *vai* be thin (of a person), be skinny; *1sg* **imbakaakadoz**; *prt* **bekaakadozod**
bakaan *pc* different
bakaanad *vii* be different; *prt* **bekaanak**
bakaanige *vai* be secluded at first menses; *1sg* **imbakaanige**; *prt* **bekaaniged**
bakaanizi *vai* be different; *1sg* **imbakaaniz**; *prt* **bekaanizid**
bake *vai* go off to the side; *1sg* **imbake**; *prt* **beked**
bakebatoo *vai* run off to the side; *1sg* **imbakebatoo**; *prt* **bekebatood**
bakebide *vii* speed off to the side, drive off to the side; *prt* **bekebideg**; *aug* **bakebidemagad**; *prt aug* **bekebidemagak**
bakebizo *vai* speed off to the side, drive off to the side; *1sg* **imbakebiz**; *prt* **bekebizod**
bakegamaa *vii* lake goes off from another; *prt* **bekegamaag**; *aug* **bakegamaamagad**; *prt aug* **bekegamaamagak**

bakekazh /bakekaN-/ *vta* bypass s.o.; *1sg* **imbakekanaa**; *prt* **bekekanaad**
bakekazhiwe *vai* bypass people; *1sg* **imbakekazhiwe**; *prt* **bekekazhiwed**
bakemon /bakemo-/ *vii* go off to the side (as a road or trail); *prt* **bekemog**
baketigweyaa *vii* divide (as a river), branch (as a river); *prt* **beketigweyaag**; *aug* **baketigweyaamagad**; *prt aug* **beketigweyaamagak**
bakibidoon *vti2* snap s.t. off (e.g., something string-like), break s.t. off (e.g., something string-like); *1sg* **imbakibidoon**; *prt* **bekibidood**
bakibizh /bakibiN-/ *vta* snap s.o. off (e.g., something string-like), break s.o. off (e.g., something string-like); *1sg* **imbakibinaa**; *prt* **bekibinaad**
bakiboode *vii* break apart from rubbing (e.g., something string-like); *prt* **bekiboodeg**; *aug* **bakiboodemagad**; *prt aug* **bekiboodemagak**
bakiboozo *vai* break apart from rubbing (e.g., something string-like); *1sg* **imbakibooz**; *prt* **bekiboozod**
bakinaw *vta* win over s.o., beat s.o. in a contest; *1sg* **imbakinawaa**; *prt* **bekinawaad**
bakinaage *vai* win over people, beat people in a contest; *1sg* **imbakinaage**; *prt* **bekinaaged**
bakise *vai* part, break apart (e.g., something string-like); *prt* **bekised**
bakise *vii* part, break apart (e.g., something string-like); *aug* **bakisemagad**; *prt aug* **bekisemagak**
bakishkan *vti* snap s.t. off with foot or body (e.g., something string-like); *1sg* **imbakishkaan**; *prt* **bekishkang**
bakishkaw *vta* snap s.o. off with foot or body (e.g., something string-like); *1sg* **imbakishkawaa**; *prt* **bekishkawaad**
bakite' /bakite'w-/ *vta* hit s.o., strike s.o.; *1sg* **imbakite'waa**; *prt* **bekite'waad**
bakite'an *vti* hit s.t., strike s.t.; *1sg* **imbakite'aan**; *prt* **bekite'ang**
bakite'ibii'igan *ni* typewriter; *pl* **bakite'ibii'iganan**; *loc* **bakite'ibii'iganing**; *dim* **bakite'ibii'igaans**
bakite'igan *ni* hammer; *pl* **bakite'iganan**; *loc* **bakite'iganing**; *dim* **bakite'igaans**; *also* **bakite'igaans**
bakite'iganaak *ni* hammer handle; *pl* **bakite'iganaakoon**; *loc* **bakite'iganaakong**; *dim* **bakite'iganaakoons**
bakite'igaade *vii* be hit, be struck; *prt* **bakite'igaadeg**; *aug* **bakite'igaademagad**; *aug* **bekite'igaademagak**
bakite'igaans *ni* hand hammer; *pl* **bakite'igaansan**
bakite'igaazo *vai* be hit, be struck; *prt* **bakite'igaazod**
bakite'ige *vai* hit things, strike things; *1sg* **imbakite'ige**; *prt* **bekite'iged**
bakite'odiwag /bakite'odi-/ *vai* they hit each other, they strike each other; *1pl* **imbakite'odimin**; *prt* **bekite'odijig**
bakitejii'iganaak *ni* baseball bat; *pl* **bakitejii'iganaakoon**; *loc* **bakitejii'iganaakong**; *dim* **bakitejii'iganaakoons**

bakitejii'ige *vai* play baseball; *1sg* **imbakitejii'ige**; *prt* **bekitejii'iged**
bakitejii'igewinini *na* baseball player; *pl* **bakitejii'igewininiwag**
bakiteshin *vai* fall down hard; *1sg* **imbakiteshin**; *prt* **bekiteshing**
bakiteshka'ige *vai* thresh field crops; *1sg* **imbakiteshka'ige**; *prt* **bekiteshka'iged**
bakizh /**bakizhw-**/ *vta* snip s.o. off (e.g., something string-like); *1sg* **imbakizhwaa**; *prt* **bekizhwaad**
bakizhan *vti* snip s.t. off (e.g., something string-like); *1sg* **imbakizhaan**; *prt* **bekizhang**
bakobii *vai* go down into the water; *1sg* **imbakobii**; *prt* **bekobiid**
bakobiibatoo *vai* run into the water; *1sg* **imbakobiibatoo**; *prt* **bekobiibatood**
bakobiidaabaadan *vti* drag s.t. into the water; *1sg* **imbakobiidaabaadaan**; *prt* **bekobiidaabaadang**
bakobiidaabaazh /**bakobiidaabaaN-**/ *vta* drag s.o. into the water; *1sg* **imbakobiidaabaanaa**; *prt* **bekobiidaabaanaad**
bakobiigwaashkwani *vai* jump into the water; *1sg* **imbakobiigwaashkwan**; *prt* **bekobiigwaashkwanid**
bakobiise *vai* fall into the water; *1sg* **imbakobiise**; *prt* **bekobiised**
bakobiise *vii* fall into the water; *prt* **bekobiiseg**; *aug* **bakobiisemagad**; *prt aug* **bekobiisemagak**
bakobiiwebin *vta* throw s.o. into the water; *1sg* **imbakobiiwebinaa**; *prt* **bekobiiwebinaad**
bakobiiwebinan *vti* throw s.t. into the water; *1sg* **imbakobiiwebinaan**; *prt* **bekobiiwebinang**
bakobiiyaashi *vai* be blown into the water; *1sg* **imbakobiiyaash**; *prt* **bekobiiyaashid**
bakobiiyaasin *vii* be blown into the water; *prt* **bekobiiyaasing**
bakon *vta* skin s.o.; *1sg* **imbakonaa**; *prt* **bekonaad**
bakonige *vai* skin things; *1sg* **imbakonige**; *prt* **bekoniged**
bakwajibidoon *vti2* pull s.t. up, pluck s.t.; *1sg* **imbakwajibidoon**; *prt* **bekwajibidood**
bakwebidoon *vti2* tear a piece off of s.t.; *1sg* **imbakwebidoon**; *prt* **bekwebidood**
bakwebizh /**bakwebiN-**/ *vta* tear a piece off of s.o.; *1sg* **imbakwebinaa**; *prt* **bekwebinaad**
bakwega' /**bakwega'w-**/ *vta* chop a piece off s.o. (as something of wood); *1sg* **imbakwega'waa**; *prt* **bekwega'waad**
bakwega'an *vti* chop a piece off s.t. (as something of wood); *1sg* **imbakwega'aan**; *prt* **bekwega'ang**
bakwe' *vta* take a piece off s.o. using something; *1sg* **imbakwe'aa**; *prt* **bekwe'aad**
bakwe'an *vti* take a piece off s.t. using something; *1sg* **imbakwe'aan**; *prt* **bekwe'ang**
bakwem *vta* bite a piece off s.o.; *1sg* **imbakwemaa**; *prt* **bekwemaad**
bakwen *vta* take a piece off s.o. by hand; *1sg* **imbakwenaa**; *prt* **bekwenaad**
bakwenan *vti* take a piece off s.t. by hand; *1sg* **imbakwenaan**; *prt* **bekwenang**
bakwendan *vti* bite a piece off s.t.; *1sg* **imbakwendaan**; *prt* **bekwendang**

bakwene *vii* smoke, be smoky; *prt* **bekweneg**; *aug* **bakwenemagad**; *prt aug* **bekwenemagak**
bakwenibii *vai* choke while drinking; *1sg* **imbakwenibii**; *prt* **bekwenibiid**
bakwenige *vai* cut cards; *1sg* **imbakwenige**; *prt* **bekweniged**
bakwenishkaago *vai* choke on food; *1sg* **imbakwenishkaag**; *prt* **bekwenishkaagod**
bakweshkaa *vii* come off in pieces; *prt* **bekweshkaag**; *aug* **bakweshkaamagad**; *prt aug* **bekweshkaamagak**
bakwezh /**bakwezhw-**/ *vta* cut a piece off s.o.; *1sg* **imbakwezhwaa**; *prt* **bekwezhwaad**
bakwezhan *vti* cut a piece off s.t.; *1sg* **imbakwezhaan**; *prt* **bekwezhang**
bakwezhigan *na* bread, flour; *pl* **bakwezhiganag**; *loc* **bakwezhiganing**; *dim* **bakwezhigaans**
bakwezhiganaaboo *ni* gravy
bakwezhiganike *vai* make bread; *1sg* **imbakwezhiganike**; *prt* **bekwezhiganiked**
bakwezhiganikewigamig *ni* bakery; *pl* **bakwezhiganikewigamigoon**; *loc* **bakwezhiganikewigamigong**
bakwezhiganikewikwe *na* baker (female); *pl* **bakwezhiganikewikweg**
bakwezhiganikewinini *na* baker; *pl* **bakwezhiganikewininiwag**
bakwezhigani-makak *ni* flour box, bread box; *pl* **bakwezhigani-makakoon**; *loc* **bakwezhigani-makakong**; *dim* **bakwezhigani-makakoons**
bakwezhigaans *na* cookie, cracker, roll; *pl* **bakwezhigaansag**; *loc* **bakwezhigaansing**
bamendan *vti* care for s.t.; *1sg* **imbamendaan**; *prt* **bemendang**
bamenim *vta* care for s.o.; *1sg* **imbamenimaa**; *prt* **bemenimaad**
bami' *vta* support s.o., adopt s.o.; *1sg* **imbami'aa**; *prt* **bemi'aad**
bami'aagan *na* supported one, adopted one; *pl* **bami'aaganag**; *dim* **bami'aagaans**
bami'aagaans *na* pet; *pl* **bami'aagaansag**
bamoozhe *vai* take care of a child, baby-sit; *1sg* **imbamoozhe**; *prt* **bemoozhed**
bana' /**bana'w-**/ *vta* miss s.o. using something; *1sg* **imbana'waa**; *prt* **bena'waad**
bana'an *vti* miss s.t. using something; *1sg* **imbana'aan**; *prt* **bena'ang**
banajaanh *na* baby bird, nestling; *pl* **banajaanyag**
banaadad *vii* be spoiled, be damaged; *prt* **benaadak**
banaadendam *vai2* despair; *1sg* **imbanaadendam**; *prt* **benaadendang**
banaadendan *vti* despair of s.t., lose hope in s.t.; *1sg* **imbanaadendaan**; *prt* **benaadendang**
banaadenim *vta* despair of s.o., lose hope in s.o.; *1sg* **imbanaadenimaa**; *prt* **benaadenimaad**
banaadizi *vai* be spoiled, be damaged; *1sg* **imbanaadiz**; *prt* **benaadizid**
banaajibidoon *vti2* damage s.t. with hands; *1sg* **imbanaajibidoon**; *prt* **benaajibidood**
banaajibizh /**banaajibiN-**/ *vta* damage s.o. with hands; *1sg* **imbanaajibinaa**; *prt* **benaajibinaad**
banaaji' *vta* spoil s.o., damage s.o.; *1sg* **imbanaaji'aa**; *prt* **benaaji'aad**

banaajishin *vai* spoil; *1sg* **imbanaajishin**; *prt* **benaajishing**
banaajisin *vii* spoil; *prt* **benaajising**
banaajitoon *vti2* spoil s.t., damage s.t.; *1sg* **imbanaajitoon**; *prt* **benaajitood**
bande *vii* be singed; *prt* **bendeg**; *aug* **bandemagad**; *prt aug* **bendemagak**
bangan *vii* be peaceful, be quiet; *prt* **bengang**
bangate *vii* be a quiet house; *prt* **bengateg**; *aug* **bangatemagad**; *prt aug* **bengatemagak**
bangigaa *vii* drip down; *prt* **bengigaag**; *aug* **bangigaamagad**; *prt aug* **bengigaamagak**
bangishim *vta* drop s.o.; *1sg* **imbangishimaa**; *prt* **bengishimaad**
bangishimon /bangishimo-/ *vii* set as the sun; *conjunct* **bangishimog** in the west; *prt* **bengishimog**
bangishin *vai* fall; *1sg* **imbangishin**; *prt* **bengishing**
bangisidoon *vti2* drop s.t.; *1sg* **imbangisidoon**; *prt* **bengisidood**
bangisin *vii* fall; *prt* **bengising**
bangii *pc* a little, a little bit, few
bangiishenh *pc* a very little bit, just a little
bangiishenhwagad *vii* be a very little bit, be very few; *prt* **bengiishenhwagak**
bangiishenhwagizi *vai* be a very little bit, be very few; *prt* **bengiishenhwagizid**
bangiiwagad *vii* be a little bit, be few; *prt* **bengiiwagak**
bangiiwagizi *vai* be a little bit, be few; *prt* **bengiiwagizid**
banin *vta* let s.o. drop; *1sg* **imbaninaa**; *prt* **beninaad**
baninan *vti* let s.t. drop; *1sg* **imbaninaan**; *prt* **beninang**
banitan *vti* mishear s.t.; *1sg* **imbanitaan**; *prt* **benitang**
banitaw *vta* mishear s.o.; *1sg* **imbanitawaa**; *prt* **benitawaad**
banizi *vai* miss out; *1sg* **imbaniz**; *prt* **benizid**
banoomigo *vai* fall off a horse; *1sg* **imbanoomig**; *prt* **benoomigod**
banzan *vti* singe s.t.; *1sg* **imbanzaan**; *prt* **benzang**
banzo *vai* be singed; *1sg* **imbanz**; *prt* **benzod**
banzo /banzw-/ *vta* singe s.o.; *1sg* **imbanzwaa**; *prt* **benzwaad**
bapagone= < **bagone=**
bapagw= < **bagw=**
bapajiishk= < **bajiishk=**
bapak= < **bak=**
bapakine *na* grasshopper; *pl* **bapakineg**; *dim* **bapakinens**
bapakite= < **bakite=**
bapakwe= < **bakwe=**
bapakwaanaajiinh *na* bat; *pl* **bapakwaanaajiinyag**; *also* **apakwaanaajiinh**
bapan= < **ban=**
bapang= < **bang=**
bapas= < **bas=**
bapasangw= < **basangw=**
bapashanzhe= < **bashanzhe=**
bapashkw= < **bashkw=**
bapasidiye' /bapasidiye'w-/ *vta* spank s.o.; *1sg* **imbapasidiye'waa**; *prt* **bepasidiye'waad**

bapasikawe *vai* play shinny; *1sg* **imbapasikawe**; *prt* **bepasikawed**
bapasininjii'odizo *vai* clap one's hands; *1sg* **imbapasininjii'odiz**; *prt* **bepasininjii'odizod**
bapaw= < **baw=**
bapawaangeni *vai* shake one's wings; *1sg* **imbapawaangen**; *prt* **bepawaangenid**
bapazhib= < **bazhib=**
bapaadak= < **badak=**
bapaakwa'am *vai2* come out of the woods; *1sg* **imbapaakwa'am**; *prt* **bepaakwa'ang**
bapiimw= < **bimw=**
bapiin= < **ban=**
basadinaa *vii* be a valley; *prt* **besadinaag**; *aug* **basadinaamagad**; *prt aug* **besadinaamagak**
basangwaabapijigan *ni* blindfold; *pl* **basangwaabapijiganan**; *loc* **basangwaabapijiganing**; *dim* **basangwaabapijigaans**
basangwaabapizh /basangwaabapiN-/ *vta* blindfold s.o.; *1sg* **imbasangwaabapinaa**; *prt* **besangwaabapinaad**
basangwaabapizo *vai* be blindfolded; *1sg* **imbasangwaabapiz**; *prt* **besangwaabapizod**
basangwaabi *vai* shut one's eyes; *1sg* **imbasangwaab**; *prt* **besangwaabid**
bashanzhe' /bashanzhe'w-/ *vta* whip s.o.; *1sg* **imbashanzhe'waa**; *prt* **beshanzhe'waad**
bashanzhe'igan *ni* whip; *pl* **bashanzhe'iganan**; *loc* **bashanzhe'iganing**; *dim* **bashanzhe'igaans**
bashanzhe'ige *vai* whip; *1sg* **imbashanzhe'ige**; *prt* **beshanzhe'iged**
bashkobizh /bashkobiN-/ *vta* pluck s.o. (e.g., a bird); *1sg* **imbashkobinaa**; *prt* **beshkobinaad**
bashkwanige *vai* be toothless; *1sg* **imbashkwanige**; *prt* **beshkwaniged**
bashkwashkibidoon *vti2* pluck s.t. (as a plant), weed s.t.; *1sg* **imbashkwashkibidoon**; *prt* **beshkwashkibidood**
bashkwashkibijige *vai* weed things; *1sg* **imbashkwashkibijige**; *prt* **beshkwashkibijiged**
bashkwegin *ni* leather, hide; *pl* **bashkweginoon**; *loc* **bashkweginong**; *dim* **bashkweginoons**
bashkweginagooday *ni* buckskin dress; *pl* **bashkweginagoodayan**
bashkweginowayaan *ni* leather; *pl* **bashkweginowayaanan**
bashkweginwakizin *ni* hide moccasin; *pl* **bashkweginwakizinan**; *loc* **bashkweginwakizining**; *dim* **bashkweginwakizinens**; *also* **bashkwegino-makizin**
basidiye' /basidiye'w-/ *vta* slap s.o. on the rear; *1sg* **imbasidiye'waa**; *prt* **besidiye'waad**
basidiyeshkaw *vta* kick s.o. in the rear; *1sg* **imbasidiyeshkawaa**; *prt* **besidiyeshkawaad**
basikawaadan *vti* kick s.t.; *1sg* **imbasikawaadaan**; *prt* **besikawaadang**
basikawaazh /basikawaaN-/ *vta* kick s.o.; *1sg* **imbasikawaanaa**; *prt* **besikawaanaad**
basikwebizon *ni* headband; *pl* **basikwebizonan**; *loc* **basikwebizoning**; *dim* **basikwebizonens**
basindibe' /basindibe'w-/ *vta* slap s.o. on the head; *1sg* **imbasindibe'waa**; *prt* **besindibe'waad**

basiingwe' /basiingwe'w-/ *vta* slap s.o. on the face; *1sg* imbasiingwe'waa; *prt* besiingwe'waad
baswewe *vai* echo, resound; *1sg* imbaswewe; *prt* beswewed
baswewe *vii* echo, resound; *prt* besweweg; *aug* baswewemagad; *prt aug* beswewemagak
bawa'am *vai2* harvest wild rice, knock wild rice; *1sg* imbawa'am; *prt* bewa'ang
bawa'iganaak *na* rice knocker (stick for wild rice harvesting); *pl* bawa'iganaakoog; *loc* bawa'iganaakong; *dim* bawa'iganaakoons

bawa'iganaakoog (rice knockers)

bawa'iminagaawanzh *na* pincherry bush; *pl* bawa'iminagaawanzhiig; *loc* bawa'iminagaawanzhiing; *dim* bawa'iminagaawanzhiins
bawa'iminaan *ni* pincherry; *pl* bawa'iminaanan
bawaadan *vti* dream of s.t.; *1sg* imbawaadaan; *prt* bewaadang
bawaagone' /bawaagone'w-/ *vta* brush snow off s.o. using something; *1sg* imbawaagone'waa; *prt* bewaagone'waad
bawaagone'an *vti* brush snow off s.t. using something; *1sg* imbawaagone'aan; *prt* bewaagone'ang
bawaagonen *vta* brush snow off s.o. by hand; *1sg* imbawaagonenaa; *prt* bewaagonenaad
bawaagonenan *vti* brush snow off s.t. by hand; *1sg* imbawaagonenaan; *prt* bewaagonenang
bawaajige *vai* have dreams; *1sg* imbawaajige; *prt* bewaajiged
bawaazh /bawaaN-/ *vta* dream of s.o.; *1sg* imbawaanaa; *prt* bewaanaad
bawega' /bawega'w-/ *vta* brush s.o. using something (as something sheet-like); *1sg* imbawega'waa; *prt* bewega'waad
bawega'an *vti* brush s.t. using something (as something sheet-like); *1sg* imbawega'aan; *prt* bewega'ang
bawegin *vta* shake s.o. out (as something sheet-like); *1sg* imbaweginaa; *prt* beweginaad
baweginan *vti* shake s.t. out (as something sheet-like); *1sg* imbaweginaan; *prt* beweginang
bawin *vta* shake s.o.; *1sg* imbawinaa; *prt* bewinaad
bawinan *vti* shake s.t.; *1sg* imbawinaan; *prt* bewinang
bazagokadoon *vti2* glue s.t.; *1sg* imbazagokadoon; *prt* bezagokadood

bazagokazh /bazagokaN-/ *vta* glue s.o.; *1sg* imbazagokanaa; *prt* bezagokanaad
bazagoke *vai* stick, adhere; *prt* bezagoked
bazagoke *vii* stick, adhere; *prt* bezagokeg; *aug* bazagokemagad; *prt aug* bezagokemagak
bazagozi *vai* be sticky; *1sg* imbazagoz; *prt* bezagozid
bazagwaa *vii* be sticky; *prt* bezagwaag; *aug* bazagwaamagad; *prt aug* bezagwaamagak
bazhiba' /bazhiba'w-/ *vta* stab s.o.; *1sg* imbazhiba'waa; *prt* bezhiba'waad
bazhiba'an *vti* stab s.t.; *1sg* imbazhiba'aan; *prt* bezhiba'ang
bazhiba'ige *vai* spear things; *1sg* imbazhiba'ige; *prt* bezhiba'iged
bazhidebii *vii* overflow (as a liquid); *prt* bezhidebiig; *aug* bazhidebiimagad; *prt aug* bezhidebiimagak
bazigonjise *vai* stand up suddenly; *1sg* imbazigonjise; *prt* bezigonjised
bazigwii *vai* stand up; *1sg* imbazigwii; *prt* bezigwiid
bazikwa'o *vai* take off into the air; *1sg* imbazikwa'; *prt* bezikwa'od
baa- *pv2* about a place (locally distributed)
baabii' *vta* keep waiting for s.o.; *1sg* imbaabii'aa; *prt* bayaabii'aad
baabii'o *vai* keep waiting; *1sg* imbaabii'; *prt* bayaabii'od
baabiitoon *vti2* keep waiting for s.t.; *1sg* imbaabiitoon; *prt* bayaabiitood
baaboonaw= < bwaanaw=
baaga'adowaan *ni* lacrosse stick; *pl* baaga'adowaanan
baaga'adowe *vai* play lacrosse; *1sg* imbaaga'adowe; *prt* bayaaga'adowed
baaga'akokwaan *ni* drumstick for hand drum; *pl* baaga'akokwaanan; *dim* baaga'akokwaanens
baaga'akokwe *vai* pound on drum; *1sg* imbaaga'akokwe; *prt* bayaaga'akokwed
baagijaane *vai* have a swollen nose; *1sg* imbaagijaane; *prt* bayaagijaaned
baagijigaade *vii* be struck by lightning; *prt* bayaagijigaadeg; *aug* baagijigaademagad; *prt aug* bayaagijigaademagak
baagijigaazo *vai* be struck by lightning; *prt* bayaagijigaazod
baagininjii *vai* have a swollen hand; *1sg* imbaagininjii; *prt* bayaagininjiid
baaginiishkwe *vai* have a swollen gland (lymph node); *1sg* imbaaginiishkwe; *prt* bayaaginiishkwed
baagishi *vai* be swollen; *1sg* imbaagish; *prt* bayaagishid
baagishkiinzhigwe *vai* have swollen eyes; *1sg* imbaagishkiinzhigwe; *prt* bayaagishkiinzhigwed
baagisin *vii* be swollen; *prt* bayaagising
baagizide *vai* have a swollen foot; *1sg* imbaagizide; *prt* bayaagizided
baagiingwe *vai* have a swollen face; *1sg* imbaagiingwe; *prt* bayaagiingwed
baagwaa *vii* be shallow; *prt* bayaagwaag; *aug* baagwaamagad; *prt aug* bayaagwaamagak

baaka'aakwenh *na* chicken; *pl* baaka'aakwenyag; *dim* baaka'aakwens
baaka'aakwenhwaaboo *ni* chicken soup; *loc* baaka'aakwenhwaaboong
baaka'aakwenhwigamig *ni* chicken coop; *pl* baaka'aakwenhwigamigoon; *loc* baaka'aakwenhwigamigong; *dim* baaka'aakwenhwigamigoons
baakaakonamaw *vta* open (s.t.) for s.o. (as something stick- or wood-like, e.g., a door); *1sg* imbaakaakonamawaa; *prt* bayaakaakonamawaad
baakaakonan *vti* open s.t. (as something stick- or wood-like, e.g., a door); *1sg* imbaakaakonaan; *prt* bayaakaakonang
baakaakonigaade *vii* be opened (as something stick- or wood-like, e.g., a door); *prt* bayaakaakonigaadeg; *aug* baakaakonigaademagad; *prt aug* bayaakaakonigaademagak
baakaakose *vii* fly open (as something stick- or wood-like, e.g., a door); *prt* bayaakaakoseg; *aug* baakaakosemagad; *prt aug* bayaakaakosemagak
baakaakosin *vii* be open (as something stick- or wood-like, e.g., a door); *prt* bayaakaakosing
baakaakowebinan *vti* fling s.t. open (as something stick- or wood-like, e.g., a door); *1sg* imbaakaakowebinaan; *prt* bayaakaakowebinang
baakaakozhigan *ni* can opener; *pl* baakaakozhiganan; *loc* baakaakozhiganing; *dim* baakaakozhigaans
baakibii'an *vii* ice clears off the lake; *prt* bayaakibii'ang
baakin *vta* uncover s.o., open s.o. up; *1sg* imbaakinaa; *prt* bayaakinaad
baakinamaw *vta* uncover (s.t.) for s.o.; *1sg* imbaakinamawaa; *prt* bayaakinamawaad
baakinan *vti* uncover s.t., open s.t. up; *1sg* imbaakinaan; *prt* bayaakinang
baakinige *vai* uncover things, open things up; *1sg* imbaakinige; *prt* bayaakiniged
baakise *vai* come uncovered, come open, fly open; *prt* bayaakised
baakise *vii* come uncovered, come open, fly open; *prt* bayaakiseg; *aug* baakisemagad; *prt aug* bayaakisemagak
baakishin *vai* lie uncovered, be open; *prt* bayaakishing
baakisin *vii* lie uncovered, be open; *prt* bayaakising
baakoshim *vta* leave s.o. uncovered; *1sg* imbaakoshimaa; *prt* bayaakoshimaad
baakosidoon *vti2* leave s.t. uncovered; *1sg* imbaakosidoon; *prt* bayaakosidood
baamaa *pc* later; *also* baanimaa
baamaapii *pc* later, after a while; *also* baanimaa apii, baanimaapii
baanimaa *pc* later, after a while; *also* baamaa
baanimaa apii *pc* later, after a while; *also* baanimaapii, baamaapii

baanizhan *vti* cut s.t. into strips; *1sg* imbaanizhaan; *prt* bayaanizhang
baanizhaawe *vai* cut meat into strips for preservation; *1sg* imbaanizhaawe; *prt* bayaanizhaawed
baapagishkaa *vai* tremble, shake; *1sg* imbaapagishkaa; *prt* bayaapagishkaad
baapagishkaa *vii* tremble, shake; *prt* bayaapagishkaag; *aug* baapagishkaamagad; *prt aug* bayaapagishkaamagak
baapaagaakwa' /baapaagaakwa'w-/ *vta* knock on s.o. (as something stick- or wood-like); *1sg* imbaapaagaakwa'waa; *prt* bayaapaagaakwa'wang
baapaagaakwa'an *vti* knock on s.t. (as something stick- or wood-like, e.g., a door); *1sg* imbaapaagaakwa'aan; *prt* bayaapaagaakwa'ang
baapaagaakwa'ige *vai* knock on things (as something stick- or wood-like, e.g., a door); *1sg* imbaapaagaakwa'ige; *prt* bayaapaagaakwa'iged
baapaagimaak *na* white ash (tree); *pl* baapaagimaakwag; *loc* baapaagimaakong; *dim* baapaagimaakoons
baapaagokozh /baapaagokoN-/ *vta* give s.o. a haircut; *1sg* imbaapaagokonaa; *prt* bayaapaagokonaad
baapaagokozhiwewigamig *ni* barber shop, hairdressing salon; *pl* baapaagokozhiwewigamigoon; *loc* baapaagokozhiwewigamigong
baapaagokozhiwewikwe *na* hairdresser (female); *pl* baapaagokozhiwewikweg
baapaagokozhiwenini *na* barber, hairdresser (male); *pl* baapaagokozhiwewininiwag
baapaagokozo *vai* get a haircut; *1sg* imbaapaagokoz; *prt* bayaapaagokozod
baapaas= < baas=
baapaase *na* woodpecker; *pl* baapaaseg; *dim* baapaasens
baapaashk= < baashk=
baapaashkizige-giizhigad *vii* be the Fourth of July; *prt* bayaapaashkizige-giizhigak
baapaashkizige-giizis *na* July
baapaaw= < baw=
baapaawin *vta* hold and shake s.o. out; *1sg* imbaapaawinaa; *prt* bayaapaawinaad
baapaawinan *vti* hold and shake s.t. out; *1sg* imbaapaawinaan; *prt* bayaapaawinang
baapaazhid= < baazhid=
baapi *vai* laugh; *1sg* imbaap; *prt* bayaapid
baapi' *vta* laugh at s.o.; *1sg* imbaapi'aa; *prt* bayaapi'aad
baapinakamigad *vii* there are festivities; *prt* bayaapinakamigak
baapinakamigizi *vai* be excited; *1sg* imbaapinakamigiz; *prt* bayaapinakamigizid
baapiniziwaagan *pc* beware! (a warning based on a premonition)
baapinodaw *vta* mock s.o. disrespectfully, show disrespect for s.o.; *1sg* imbaapinodawaa; *prt* bayaapinodawaad

baapitoon *vti2* laugh at s.t.; *1sg* **imbaapitoon**; *prt* **bayaapitood**
baas /**baasw-**/ *vta* dry s.o.; *1sg* **imbaaswaa**; *prt* **bayaaswaad**
baasa' /**baasa'w-**/ *vta* crack s.o. using something, shatter s.o. using something; *1sg* **imbaasa'waa**; *prt* **bayaasa'waad**
baasa'an *vti* crack s.t. using something, shatter s.t. using something; *1sg* **imbaasa'aan**; *prt* **bayaasa'ang**
baasa'ige *vai* crack things using something, shatter things using something; *1sg* **imbaasa'ige**; *prt* **bayaasa'iged**
baasan *vti* dry s.t.; *1sg* **imbaasaan**; *prt* **bayaasang**
baasaabikiz /**baasaabikizw-**/ *vta* blast s.o.; *1sg* **imbaasaabikizwaa**; *prt* **bayaasaabikizwaad**
baasaabikizan *vti* blast s.t.; *1sg* **imbaasaabikizaan**; *prt* **bayaasaabikizang**
baasaabikizigan *ni* dynamite; *pl* **baasaabikiziganan**; *loc* **baasaabikiziganing**; *dim* **baasaabikizigaans**
baasaabikizige *vai* blast things; *1sg* **imbaasaabikizige**; *prt* **bayaasaabikiziged**
baashka' /**baashka'w-**/ *vta* burst s.o. using something; *1sg* **imbaashka'waa**; *prt* **bayaashka'waad**
baashka'an *vti* burst s.t. using something; *1sg* **imbaashka'aan**; *prt* **bayaashka'ang**
baashkakwa'am *vai2* make a thunderclap (of the thunderers); *prt* **bayaashkakwa'ang**
baashkaabigwanii *vii* blossom, bloom; *prt* **bayaashkaabigwaniig**; *aug* **baashkaabigwaniimagad**; *prt aug* **bayaashkaabigwaniimagak**
baashkaapi *vai* burst out laughing; *1sg* **imbaashkaap**; *prt* **bayaashkaapid**
baashkaawe'am *vai2* hatch; *prt* **bayaashkaawe'ang**; *also* **baashkaawe'o**
baashkaawe'o *vai* hatch; *prt* **bayaashkaawe'od**; *also* **baashkaawe'am**
baashkide *vii* explode, blow up; *prt* **bayaashkideg**; *aug* **baashkidemagad**; *prt aug* **bayaashkidemagak**
baashkijii' /**baashkijii'w-**/ *vta* burst s.o. open using something; *1sg* **imbaashkijii'waa**; *prt* **bayaashkijii'aad**
baashkijii'an *vti* burst s.t. open using something; *1sg* **imbaashkijii'aan**; *prt* **bayaashkijii'ang**
baashkijiisijige *vai* have a blowout; *prt* **bayaashkijiisijiged**
baashkiminasigan *ni* jam, preserves; *pl* **baashkiminasiganan**; *loc* **baashkiminasiganing**; *dim* **baashkiminasigaans**
baashkinede *vii* steam; *prt* **bayaashkinedeg**; *aug* **baashkinedemagad**; *prt aug* **bayaashkinedemagak**
baashkinezo *vai* steam; *prt* **bayaashkinezod**
baashkishim *vta* burst s.o. on impact; *1sg* **imbaashkishimaa**; *prt* **bayaashkishimaad**
baashkisidoon *vti2* burst s.t. on impact; *1sg* **imbaashkisidoon**; *prt* **bayaashkisidood**

baashkiz /**baashkizw-**/ *vta* shoot s.o.; *1sg* **imbaashkizwaa**; *prt* **bayaashkizwaad**
baashkizan *vti* shoot s.t.; *1sg* **imbaashkizaan**; *prt* **bayaashkizang**
baashkizigan *ni* gun; *pl* **baashkiziganan**; *loc* **baashkiziganing**; *dim* **baashkizigaans**
baashkizige *vai* shoot things, ejaculate; *1sg* **imbaashkizige**; *prt* **bayaashkiziged**
baashkizo *vai* explode, blow up; *prt* **bayaashkizod**
baashkizodizo *vai* shoot oneself; *1sg* **imbaashkizodiz**; *prt* **bayaashkizodizod**
baaside *vii* shatter from heat, crack from heat; *prt* **bayaasideg**; *aug* **baasidemagad**; *prt aug* **bayaasidemagak**
baasiga' /**baasiga'w-**/ *vta* chop s.o. into small pieces (as something of wood); *1sg* **imbaasiga'waa**; *prt* **bayaasiga'waad**
baasiga'an *vti* chop s.t. into small pieces (as something of wood); *1sg* **imbaasiga'aan**; *prt* **bayaasiga'ang**
baasigaade *vii* be dried; *prt* **bayaasigaadeg**; *aug* **baasigaademagad**; *prt aug* **bayaasigaademagak**
baasigaazo *vai* be dried; *prt* **bayaasigaazod**
baasikan *vti* shatter s.t. with foot or body; *1sg* **imbaasikaan**; *prt* **bayaasikang**
baasikaw *vta* shatter s.o. with foot or body; *1sg* **imbaasikawaa**; *prt* **bayaasikawaad**
baasikaa *vii* shatter (e.g., glass or china), crack (e.g., glass or china); *prt* **baasikaamagad**; *prt aug* **bayaasikaamagak**
baasindibeshin *vai* fall and crack one's head; *1sg* **imbaasindibeshin**; *prt* **bayaasindibeshing**
baasinigo *vai* be bloated; *1sg* **imbaasinig**; *prt* **bayaasinigod**
baasishim *vta* shatter s.o., crack s.o.; *1sg* **imbaasishimaa**; *prt* **bayaasishimaad**
baasishin *vai* shatter on impact, crack on impact; *1sg* **imbaasishin**; *prt* **bayaasishing**
baasisidoon *vti2* shatter s.t., crack s.t.; *1sg* **imbaasisidoon**; *prt* **bayaasisidood**
baasisin *vii* shatter on impact, crack on impact; *prt* **bayaasising**
baasiz /**baasizw-**/ *vta* shatter s.o. by heat, crack s.o. by heat; *1sg* **imbaasizwaa**; *prt* **bayaasizwaad**
baasizan *vti* shatter s.t. by heat, crack s.t. by heat; *1sg* **imbaasizaan**; *prt* **bayaasizang**
baasizo *vai* shatter from heat, crack from heat; *prt* **bayaasizod**
baaso *vai* be dry; *prt* **bayaasod**
baatayiinad *vii* be much, be many; *prt* **bayaatayiinak**
baatayiinatoon *vti2* have much of s.t., have many of s.t.; *1sg* **imbaatayiinatoon**; *prt* **bayaatayiinatood**
baatayiino *vai* be much, be many; *prt* **bayaatayiinod**; *also* **baatayiini**
baatayiino' *vta* have much of s.o., have many of s.o.; *1sg* **imbaatayiino'aa**; *prt* **bayaatayiino'aad**
baataam *vta* tell on s.o., testify against s.o.; *1sg* **imbaataamaa**; *prt* **bayaataamaad**

baataase *vai* get stuck; *1sg* imbaataase; *prt*
 bayaataased
baataase *vii* get stuck; bayaataaseg; *aug*
 baataasemagad; *prt aug* bayaatesemagak
baataashin *vai* be stuck; *1sg* imbaataashin; *prt*
 bayaataashing
baataasin *vii* be stuck; *prt* bayaataasing
baate *vii* be dry; *prt* bayaateg; *aug* baatemagad;
 prt aug bayaatemagak
baate- *pv4* dried
baazagobizh /baazagobiN-/ *vta* scratch s.o.; *1sg*
 imbaazagobinaa; *prt* bayaazagobinaad
baazhida' /baazhida'w-/ *vta* step over s.o.; *1sg*
 imbaazhida'waa; *prt* bayaazhida'waad
baazhida'an *vti* step over s.t.; *1sg* imbaazhida'aan;
 prt bayaazhida'ang
baazhidaandawe *vai* climb over; *1sg*
 imbaazhidaandawe; *prt* bayaazhidaandawed
baazhijigwaashkwani *vai* jump over; *1sg*
 imbaazhijigwaashkwani; *prt*
 bayaazhijigwaashkwanid
baazhijiwebin *vta* throw s.o. over; *1sg*
 imbaazhijiwebinaa; *prt* bayaazhijiwebinaad
baazhijiwebinan *vti* throw s.t. over; *1sg*
 imbaazhijiwebinaan; *prt* bayaazhijiwebinang
bebakaan= < bakaan=
bebakaan *pc* all different
bebangii *pc* a little bit each
bebangiiwag= < bangiiwag=
bebaamaadizid *na-pt* traveller, tourist; *pl*
 bebaamaadizijig
bebezhig *nm* one-by-one
bebezhigooganzhii *na* horse; *pl*
 bebezhigooganzhiig; *dim*
 bebezhigooganzhiins; *also* mishtadim*,
 mashtadim*
bebinezid bakwezhigan *na* flour
bebiikominagak *ni-pt* pill; *pl* bebiikominagakin
bedose *vai* walk slowly; *1sg* imbedose; *prt*
 bayedosed
bedowe *vai* have a soft voice; *1sg* imbedowe; *prt*
 bayedowed
bejibatoo *vai* run slowly; *1sg* imbejibatoo; *prt*
 bayejibatood
bejibide *vii* move slowly, drive slowly; *prt*
 bayejibideg; *aug* bejibidemagad; *prt aug*
 bayejibidemagak
bejibizo *vai* move slowly, drive slowly; *1sg*
 imbejibiz; *prt* bayejibizod
bekaa *pc* wait!, slow down!, hold on!
bekaadizi *vai* be quiet, be easygoing; *1sg*
 imbekaadiz; *prt* bayekaadizid
bekish *pc* at the same time
bekwaawigang *na-pt* camel; *pl* bekwaawigangig
bemaadizid *na-pt* person; *pl* bemaadizijig
bemisemagak *ni-pt* airplane; *pl* bemisemagakin
bengozi *vai* be dry; *prt* bayengozid
bengwa' /bengwa'w-/ *vta* dry s.o. using something; *1sg* imbengwa'waa; *prt* bayengwa'waad
bengwa'an *vti* dry s.t. using something; *1sg*
 imbengwa'aan; *prt* bayengwa'ang
bengwan *vii* be dry; *prt* bayengwang
bepesh= < besh=

beshaa *vii* have a line, have a stripe; *prt*
 bayeshaag; *aug* beshaamagad; *prt aug*
 bayeshaamagak
beshibii' /beshibii'w-/ *vta* mark s.o. with a stripe;
 1sg imbeshibii'waa; *prt* bayeshibii'waad
beshibii'an *vti* mark s.t.; *1sg*
 imbeshibii'aan; *prt* bayeshibii'ang
beshibii'ige *vai* mark things with a stripe; *1sg*
 imbeshibii'ige; *prt* bayeshibii'iged
beshizh /beshizhw-/ *vta* make a cut on s.o.; *1sg*
 imbeshizhwaa; *prt* bayeshizhwaad
beshizhan *vti* make a cut on s.t.; *1sg*
 imbeshizhaan; *prt* bayeshizhang
beshizi *vai* have a line, have a stripe; *1sg* imbeshiz;
 prt bayeshizid
besho *pc* near, close
beshonaagozi *vai* appear to be close; *prt*
 bayeshonaagozid
beshonaagwad *vii* appear to be close; *prt*
 bayeshonaagwak
beshowad *vii* be near, be close; *prt* bayeshowak
beshwaji' *vta* be close friends with s.o.; *1sg*
 imbeshwaji'aa; *prt* bayeshwaji'aad
beshwendan *vti* think s.t. to be close; *1sg*
 imbeshwendaan; *prt* bayeshwendang
beshwendaagozi *vai* be thought near; *prt*
 bayeshwendaagozid
beshwendaagwad *vii* be thought near; *prt*
 bayeshwendaagwak
bezhig *nm* one
bezhigo *vai* be alone, be the only one; *1sg*
 imbezhig; *prt* bayezhigod
bezhigo- *pv4* one
bezhigoobii'igan *na* ace (card); *pl*
 bezhigoobii'iganag
bezhigwan *vii* be, be the only one, be the
 same; *prt* bayezhigwang
bezhigwanong *pc* one place, in one place
bezhigwaabik *pc* one dollar
bezhizhooniyaans *na* dime; *pl*
 bezhizhooniyaansag
bezikaa *vai* move slowly; *1sg* imbezikaa; *prt*
 bayezikaad
bezikaabatoo *vai* run slowly; *1sg*
 imbezikaabatoo; *prt* bayezikaabatood
bi- *pv2* toward the speaker, this way, here, hither
bibagaa *vii* be thin; *prt* bebagaag; *aug*
 bibagaamagad; *prt aug* bebagaamagak
bibagaabikaad *vii* be thin (as something mineral);
 prt bebagaabikaak
bibagaabikizi *vai* be thin (as something mineral);
 prt bebagaabikizid
bibagaakwadin *vii* be frozen thin; *prt*
 bebagaakwading
bibagaakwaji *vai* be frozen thin; *prt*
 bebagaakwajid
bibagikodan *vti* slice s.t. thin; *1sg*
 imbibagikodaan; *prt* bebagikodang
bibagikozh /bibagikoN-/ *vta* slice s.o. thin; *1sg*
 imbibagikonaa; *prt* bebagikonaad
bibagishin *vai* lie in a thin layer; *prt* bebagishing
bibagisin *vii* lie in a thin layer; *prt* bebagising
bibagizi *vai* be thin; *prt* bebagizid
bibagiigad *vii* be thin (as something sheet-like); *prt*
 bebagiigak

bibagiigizi *vai* be thin (as something sheet-like); *prt*
bebagiigizid
bibigwan *ni* flute; *pl* bibigwanan

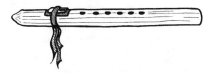

bibigwan (flute)

bibigwe *vai* play the flute; *1sg* imbibigwe; *prt*
bebigwed
bibine-bakwezhigan *na* flour
bibine-ziinzibaakwad *ni* granulated sugar
biboon *vii* be winter; *prt* beboong
biboonagad *vii* be a winter, a year passes; *prt*
beboonagak
biboonishi *vai* spend the winter somewhere; *1sg*
imbiboonish; *prt* beboonishid
biboonodaabaan *na* sleigh; *pl*
biboonodaabaanag; *loc* biboonodaabaaning;
dim biboonodaabaanens
biboonodaabaanens *na* sled; *pl*
biboonodaabaanensag
biboonong *pc* last winter
bichi- *pv4* by mistake, accidentally
bichinan *vti* shoot s.t. accidentally; *1sg*
imbichinaan; *prt* bechinang
bichinaw *vta* shoot s.o. accidentally; *1sg*
imbichinawaa; *prt* bechinawaad
bichinaadizo *vai* shoot oneself accidentally; *1sg*
imbichinaadiz; *prt* bechinaadizod
bichinaage *vai* shoot things accidentally; *1sg*
imbichinaage; *prt* bechinaaged
bigishkanad *vii* be rotten, fall to pieces; *prt*
begishkanak
bigishkanani *vai* be rotten, fall to pieces; *prt*
begishkananid
bigishkibidoon *vti2* tear s.t. to pieces; *1sg*
imbigishkibidoon; *prt* begishkibidood
bigishkibizh /bigishkibiN-/ *vta* tear s.o. to pieces;
1sg imbigishkibinaa; *prt* begishkibinaad
bigishkise *vai* go to pieces; *prt* begishkiseg
bigishkise *vii* go to pieces; *prt* begishkiseg; *aug*
bigishkisemagad; *prt aug* begishkisemagak
bigishkizh /bigishkizhw-/ *vta* cut s.o. to pieces; *1sg*
imbigishkizhwaa; *prt* begishkizhwaad
bigishkizhan *vti* cut s.t. to pieces; *1sg*
imbigishkizhaan; *prt* begishkizhang
bigishki-zhooniyaans *na* loose change; *pl* bigishki-
zhooniyaans
bigiw *ni* pitch, tar; *dim* bigiins
bigiwizigan *ni* maple taffy
bigiwizige *vai* make taffy; *1sg* imbigiwizige; *prt*
begiwiziged
bigiikaadan *vti* apply pitch to s.t. (e.g., a canoe),
putty s.t., tar s.t.; *1sg* imbigiikaadaan; *prt*
begiikaadang
bigiike *vai* apply pitch, putty, tar; *1sg* imbigiike;
prt begiiked

bigii-miikana *ni* asphalt road; *pl* bigii-miikanan;
loc bigii-miikanaang
bigiins *na* chewing gum; *pl* bigiinsag
bi-izhaa *vai* come; *1sg* imbi-izhaa; *prt* ba-izhaad
bijiinag *pc* after a while, recently, just now
bijiinaago *pc* yesterday
bikonagizhii *vai* have a potbelly; *1sg*
imbikonagizhii; *prt* bekonagizhiid
bikoojaan *ni* ball of twine or yarn; *pl* bikoojaanan;
loc bikoojaaning; *dim* bikoojaanens
bikwadinaa *vii* be a knoll, be a small hill; *prt*
bekwadinaag; *aug* bikwadinaamagad; *prt aug*
bekwadinaamagak
bikwak *ni* arrow; *pl* bikwakoon; *loc* bikwakong;
dim bikwakoons
bikwaakoganaan *ni* ankle joint; *pl*
bikwaakoganaanan; *loc* bikwaakoganaaning;
dim bikwaakoganaanens
bikwaakwad *ni* ball; *pl* bikwaakwadoon; *loc*
bikwaakwadong; *dim* bikwaakwadoons
bikwaakwado-bagamaagan *ni* ball-headed club;
pl bikwaakwado-bagamaaganan; *dim*
bikwaakwado-bagamaagaans
bimademo *vai* cry walking along; *1sg*
imbimadem; *prt* bemademod
bima'adoo *vai* follow a trail along; *1sg*
imbima'adoo; *prt* bema'adood
bima'adoon *vti2* follow s.t. along as a trail; *1sg*
imbima'adoon; *prt* bema'adood
bima'amaazo *vai* go along singing; *1sg*
imbima'amaaz; *prt* bema'amaazod
bima'an *vti* skim s.t.; *1sg* imbima'aan; *prt*
bema'ang
bima'azh /bima'aN-/ *vta* follow s.o.'s trail along;
1sg imbima'anaa; *prt* bema'anaad
bima'ige *vai* skim things along; *1sg* imbima'ige; *prt*
bema'iged
bima'oodoo *vai* pole a boat along; *1sg*
imbima'oodoo; *prt* bema'oodood
bima'oodoon *vti2* take s.t. along in a boat, pole
s.t. along in a boat; *1sg* imbima'oodoon; *prt*
bema'oodood
bima'ookii *vai* pole a boat along; *1sg*
imbima'ookii; *prt* bema'ookiid
bima'oozh /bima'ooN-/ *vta* take s.o. along in a
boat, pole s.o. along in a boat; *1sg*
imbima'oonaa; *prt* bema'oonaad
bimakwazhiwe *vai* paddle along, swim along (as a
fish); *1sg* imbimakwazhiwe; *prt*
bemakwazhiwed
bimamon /bimamo-/ *vii* lead along (as a road or
trail); *prt* bemamog; *aug* bimamoomagad; *prt*
aug bemamoomagak
bimaabiigamon /bimaabiigamo-/ *vii* lead along
(as something string-like); *prt* bemaabiigamog
bimaabiigin *vta* string s.o. along; *1sg*
imbimaabiiginaa; *prt* bemaabiiginaad
bimaabiiginan *vti* string s.t. along; *1sg*
imbimaabiiginaan; *prt* bemaabiiginang
bimaaboode *vii* drift along on current; *prt*
bemaaboodeg; *aug* bimaaboodemagad; *prt*
aug bemaaboodemagak
bimaaboono *vai* drift along on current; *prt*
bemaaboonod

bimaadagaa *vai* swim along; *1sg* **imbimaadagaa**; *prt* **bemaadagaad**
bimaadagaako *vai* walk along on the ice; *1sg* **imbimaadagaak**; *prt* **bemaadagaakod**
bimaadagaazii *vai* wade along; *1sg* **imbimaadagaazii**; *prt* **bemaadagaaziid**
bimaada'e *vai* skate along; *1sg* **imbimaada'e**; *prt* **bemaada'ed**
bimaadizi *vai* live, be alive; *1sg* **imbimaadiz**; *prt* **bemaadizid**
bimaaji' *vta* save the life of s.o.; *1sg* **imbimaaji'aa**; *prt* **bemaaji'aad**
bimaakoshim *vta* put s.o. along (as something stick- or wood-like); *1sg* **imbimaakoshimaa**; *prt* **bemaakoshimaad**
bimaakoshin *vai* lie along (as something stick- or wood-like); *1sg* **imbimaakoshin**; *prt* **bemaakoshing**
bimaakosidoon *vti2* put s.t. along (as something stick- or wood-like); *1sg* **imbimaakosidoon**; *prt* **bemaakosidood**
bimaakosin *vii* lie along (as something stick- or wood-like); *prt* **bemaakosing**
bimaanakwad *vii* clouds go along; *prt* **bemaanakwak**
bimaandawe *vai* climb along; *1sg* **imbimaandawe**; *prt* **bemaandawed**
bimaashi *vai* be blown along, sail along; *1sg* **imbimaash**; *prt* **bemaashid**
bimaasin *vii* be blown along, sail along; *prt* **bemaasing**
bimaawadaaso *vai* travel along in a group (as a school of fish); *prt* **bemaawadaasod**
bimaazakonenjige *vai* go along with a light; *1sg* **imbimaazakonenjige**; *prt* **bemaazakonenjiged**
bimaazhagaame *vai* go along the edge, go along the shore; *1sg* **imbimaazhagaame**; *prt* **bemaazhagaamed**
bimi- *pv2* along, going along, going by, going past, on the way
bimi-ayaa *vai* go along, travel along; *1sg* **imbimi-ayaa**; *prt* **bemi-ayaad**
bimiba'idiwag /**bimiba'idi-**/ *vai* they run along together; *1pl* **imbimiba'idimin**; *prt* **bemiba'idijig**
bimiba'igo *vai* ride along drawn by horses; *1sg* **imbimiba'ig**; *prt* **bemiba'igod**
bimiba'iwe *vai* run along in flight from someone; *1sg* **imbimiba'iwe**; *prt* **bemiba'iwed**
bimibatoo *vai* run along; *1sg* **imbimibatoo**; *prt* **bemibatood**
bimibide *vii* speed along, drive along, fly along; *prt* **bemibideg**; *aug* **bimibidemagad**; *prt aug* **bemibidemagak**
bimibizo *vai* speed along, drive along, fly along; *1sg* **imbimibiz**; *prt* **bemibizod**
bimibizoni' *vta* drive s.o. along, take s.o. along for a ride; *1sg* **imbimibizoni'aa**; *prt* **bemibizoni'aad**
bimibizonitoon *vti2* drive s.t. along; *1sg* **imbimibizonitoon**; *prt* **bemibizonitood**
bimibiisaa *vii* rain goes along; *prt* **bemibiisaag**; *aug* **bimibiisaamagad**; *prt aug* **bemibiisaamagak**

bimidasaa *na* thwart; *pl* **bimidasaag**; *also* **bimidasaagan**, **-an**
bimidaabaadan *vti* drag s.t. along; *1sg* **imbimidaabaadaan**; *prt* **bemidaabaadang**
bimidaabaazh /**bimidaabaaN-**/ *vta* drag s.o. along; *1sg* **imbimidaabaanaa**; *prt* **bemidaabaanaad**
bimidaabiiba'igo *vai* drive along quickly in a wagon or sleigh; *1sg* **imbimidaabiiba'ig**; *prt* **bemidaabiiba'igod**
bimidaabii'iwe *vai* drive along; *1sg* **imbimidaabii'iwe**; *prt* **bemidaabii'iwed**
bimide *ni* grease, oil; *loc* **bimideng**
bimijiwan *vii* flow along; *prt* **bemijiwang**
bimikawaan *ni* footprint, track; *pl* **bimikawaanan**
bimikawe *vai* leave tracks going along; *1sg* **imbimikawe**; *prt* **bemikawed**
biminaazhikaage *vai* send people along, chase people along; *1sg* **imbiminaazhikaage**; *prt* **beminaazhikaaged**
biminizha' /**biminizha'w-**/ *vta* chase s.o. along; *1sg* **imbiminizha'waa**; *prt* **beminizha'waad**
biminizha'an *vti* chase s.t. along; *1sg* **imbiminizha'aan**; *prt* **beminizha'ang**
biminizha'ige *vai* chase things along; *1sg* **imbiminizha'ige**; *prt* **beminizha'iged**
biminizhikaw *vta* send s.o. along; *1sg* **imbiminizhikawaa**; *prt* **beminizhikawaad**
biminizhimo *vai* run along in flight; *1sg* **imbiminizhim**; *prt* **beminizhimod**
bimipon /**bimipo-**/ *vii* snow goes along; *prt* **bemipog**
bimise *vai* fly along; *1sg* **imbimise**; *prt* **bemised**
bimise *vii* fly along; *prt* **bemiseg**; *aug* **bimisemagad**; *prt aug* **bemisemagak**
bimishimo *vai* dance along; *1sg* **imbimishim**; *prt* **bemishimod**
bimishkaa *vai* paddle along, go along by boat; *1sg* **imbimishkaa**; *prt* **bemishkaad**
bimitigweyaa *vii* flow along (as a river); *prt* **bemitigweyaag**; *aug* **bimitigweyaamagad**; *prt aug* **bemitigweyaamagak**
bimiwanaan *ni* pack, backpack; *pl* **bimiwanaanan**; *loc* **bimiwanaaning**; *dim* **bimiwanaanens**
bimiwane *vai* carry a pack along; *1sg* **imbimiwane**; *prt* **bemiwaned**
bimiwidoon *vti2* carry s.t. along, take s.t. along; *1sg* **imbimiwidoon**; *prt* **bemiwidood**
bimiwijige *vai* carry things along, be pregnant; *1sg* **imbimiwijige**; *prt* **bemiwijiged**
bimiwizh /**bimiwiN-**/ *vta* carry s.o. along, take s.o. along; *1sg* **imbimiwinaa**; *prt* **bemiwinaad**
bimiwizhiwe *vai* take people along, drive people along (as in a bus); *1sg* **imbimiwizhiwe**; *prt* **bemiwizhiwed**
bimiwizhiwewidaabaan *na* taxi; *pl* **bimiwizhiwewidaabaanag**; *loc* **bimiwizhiwewidaabaaning**; *dim* **bimiwizhiwewidaabaanens**
bimiwizhiwewinini *na* taxi driver, chauffeur; *pl* **bimiwizhiwewininiwag**
bimo /**bimw-**/ *vta* shoot s.o. with an arrow or other missile; *1sg* **imbimwaa**; *prt* **bemwaad**
bimodan *vti* shoot s.t. with an arrow or other missile; *1sg* **imbimodaan**; *prt* **bemodang**

bimojigan *ni* slingshot; *pl* **bimojiganan**; *dim* **bimojigaans**

bimojige *vai* shoot things with an arrow or other missile; *1sg* **imbimojige**; *prt* **bemojiged**

bimose *vai* walk along; *1sg* **imbimose**; *prt* **bemosed**

bimoode *vai* crawl along; *1sg* **imbimoode**; *prt* **bemooded**

bimoom *vta* carry s.o. along on one's back; *1sg* **imbimoomaa**; *prt* **bemoomaad**

bimoomaawaso *vai* carry a baby along on one's back; *1sg* **imbimoomaawas**; *prt* **bemoomaawasod**

bimoomigo *vai* ride along on horseback; *1sg* **imbimoomig**; *prt* **bemoomigod**

bimoomigoo-apabiwin *ni* saddle; *pl* **bimoomigoo-apabiwinan**; *loc* **bimoomigoo-apabiwining**; *dim* **bimoomigoo-apabiwinens**

bimoondan *vti* carry s.t. along on one's back; *1sg* **imbimoondaan**; *prt* **bemoondang**

bimoonjigan *ni* dance bustle, pack frame; *pl* **bimoonjiganan**; *loc* **bimoonjiganing**; *dim* **bimoonjigaans**

bimwewebide *vii* be heard speeding along, be heard driving along; *prt* **bemwewebideg**; *aug* **bimwewebidemagad**; *prt aug* **bemwewebidemagak**

bimwewebizo *vai* be heard speeding along, be heard driving along; *1sg* **imbimwewebiz**; *prt* **bemwewebizod**

bimweweshin *vai* be heard walking along, be heard going along and falling; *1sg* **imbimweweshin**; *prt* **bemweweshing**

bina' /**bina'w-**/ *vta* take s.o. down; *1sg* **imbina'waa**; *prt* **bena'waad**

bina'an *vti* take s.t. down; *1sg* **imbina'aan**; *prt* **bena'ang**

bi-naagozi *vai* appear, come into view; *1sg* **imbi-naagoz**; *prt* **ba-naagozid**

bi-naagwad *vii* appear, come into view; *prt* **ba-naagwak**

binaakwaan *ni* comb; *pl* **binaakwaanan**; *loc* **binaakwaaning**; *dim* **binaakwaanens**

binaakwe' /**binaakwe'w-**/ *vta* comb s.o.; *1sg* **imbinaakwe'waa**; *prt* **benaakwe'waad**

binaakwe'igan *ni* rake; *pl* **binaakwe'iganan**; *loc* **binaakwe'iganing**; *dim* **binaakwe'igaans**

binaakwe'ige *vai* rake things; *1sg* **imbinaakwe'ige**; *prt* **benaakwe'iged**

binaakwe'o *vai* comb one's hair; *1sg* **imbinaakwe'**; *prt* **benaakwe'od**

binaakwii *vai* fall (as a leaf); *1sg* **imbinaakwii**; *prt* **benaakwiid**

binaakwii-giizis *na* October; *also* **binaakwe-giizis**

bine *na* partridge; *pl* **binewag**; *dim* **binens**

bineshiinh *na* bird; *pl* **bineshiinyag**; *dim* **bineshiins**

bineshiinhwayaan *na* bird skin; *pl* **bineshiinhwayaanag**; *loc* **bineshiinhwayaaning**; *dim* **bineshiinhwayaanens**

binesi *na* bird (of large species, e.g., hawk or eagle), thunderbird; *pl* **binesiwag**

bingoshens *na* gnat; *pl* **bingoshensag**

bingwi *ni* sand, ashes; *loc* **bingwiing**; *dim* **bingwiins**

bingwiikaa *vii* be much sand; *prt* **bengwiikaag**; *aug* **bingwiikaamagad**; *prt aug* **bengwiikaamagak**

bingwii-miikana *ni* gravel road; *pl* **bingwii-miikanan**; *loc* **bingwii-miikanaang**; *dim* **bingwii-miikanaans**

biniweba' /**biniweba'w-**/ *vta* knock s.o. down using something; *1sg* **imbiniweba'waa**; *prt* **beniweba'waad**

biniweba'an *vti* knock s.t. down using something; *1sg* **imbiniweba'aan**; *prt* **beniweba'ang**

binzini *vai* have something in one's eye; *1sg* **imbinzin**; *prt* **benzinid**

bipakoombens *ni* cucumber; *pl* **bipakoombensan**

bishagaakwa'ige *vai* peel timber using something; *1sg* **imbishagaakwa'ige**; *prt* **beshagaakwa'iged**

bishagaaso *vai* peel from sunburn; *1sg* **imbishagaas**; *prt* **beshagaasod**

bishagibidoon *vti2* peel s.t. with hands; *1sg* **imbishagibidoon**; *prt* **beshagibidood**

bishagibijige *vai* peel things with hands; *1sg* **imbishagibijige**; *prt* **beshagibijiged**

bishagibizh /**bishagibiN-**/ *vta* peel s.o. with hands; *1sg* **imbishagibinaa**; *prt* **beshagibinaad**

bishagigidigweshin *vai* skin one's knee; *1sg* **imbishagigidigweshin**; *prt* **beshagigidigweshing**

bishagikodan *vti* peel s.t. with a knife; *1sg* **imbishagikodaan**; *prt* **beshagikodang**

bishagikozh /**bishagikoN-**/ *vta* peel s.o. with a knife; *1sg* **imbishagikonaa**; *prt* **beshagikozhwaad**

bishagishkaa *vai* peel off; *prt* **beshagishkaad**

bishagishkaa *vii* peel off; *prt* **beshagishkaag**; *aug* **bishagishkaamagad**; *prt aug* **beshagishkaamagak**

bishagiishkate *vii* be dark indoors; *prt* **beshagiishkateg**; *aug* **bishagiishkatemagad**; *prt aug* **beshagiishkatemagak**

bishagiishkaa *vii* be dark; *prt* **beshagiishkaag**; *aug* **bishagiishkaamagad**; *prt aug* **beshagiishkaamagak**

bishagiishkaande *vii* be dark colored; *prt* **beshagiishkaandeg**; *aug* **bishagiishkaandemagad**; *prt aug* **beshagiishkaandemagak**

bishagiishkaanzo *vai* be dark colored; *prt* **beshagiishkaanzod**

bisha'igobii *vai* peel wigob (inner bark of basswood); *1sg* **imbisha'igobii**; *prt* **besha'igobiid**

bishkonan *vti* shoot at s.t. and miss; *1sg* **imbishkonaan**; *prt* **beshkonang**

bishkonaw *vta* shoot at s.o. and miss; *1sg* **imbishkonawaa**; *prt* **beshkonawaad**

bishkonaage *vai* shoot and miss; *1sg* **imbishkonaage**; *prt* **beshkonaaged**

bishkongwashi *vai* doze; *1sg* **imbishkongwash**; *prt* **beshkongwashid**

bisigadanaaboo *ni* dumpling soup; *loc* **bisigadanaaboong**

biskane *vii* catch fire, ignite; *prt* **beskaneg**; *aug* **biskanemagad**; *prt aug* **beskanemagak**

biskanebidoon *vti2* switch s.t. on; *1sg*
imbiskanebidoon; *prt* beskanebidood
biskanesidoon *vti2* light s.t. by striking; *1sg*
imbiskanesidoon; *prt* beskanesidood
biskaa *vii* be bent over, be folded; *prt* beskaag; *aug*
biskaamagad; *prt aug* beskaamagak
biskaabii *vai* make a round trip in one day; *1sg*
imbiskaabii; *prt* beskaabiid
biskaakonebijigan *ni* switch; *pl*
biskaakonebijiganan; *loc*
biskaakonebijiganing; *dim*
biskaakonebijigaans
biskibidoon *vti2* bend s.t. over with hands, fold s.t.
with hands; *1sg* imbiskibidoon; *prt*
beskibidood
biskibizh /biskibiN-/ *vta* bend s.o. over with hands,
fold s.o. with hands; *1sg* imbiskibinaa; *prt*
beskibinaad
biskin *vta* bend s.o. over, fold s.o.; *1sg* imbiskinaa;
prt beskinaad
biskinan *vti* bend s.t. over, fold s.t.; *1sg*
imbiskinaan; *prt* beskinang
biskinigaade *vii* be bent over, be folded; *prt*
beskinigaadeg; *aug* biskinigaademagad; *prt*
aug beskinigaademagak
biskitenaagan *ni* sap bucket of folded birch bark;
pl biskitenaaganan; *loc* biskitenaaganing; *dim*
biskitenaagaans
biskiigin *vta* fold s.o. (as something sheet-like); *1sg*
imbiskiiginaa; *prt* beskiiginaad
biskiiginan *vti* fold s.t. (as something sheet-like);
1sg imbiskiiginaan; *prt* beskiiginang
bitaganaam *vta* accidentally hit s.o.; *1sg*
imbitaganaamaa; *prt* betaganaamaad
bitaganaandan *vti* accidentally hit s.t.; *1sg*
imbitaganaandaan; *prt* betaganaandang
bitaakondibeshin *vai* bump one's head; *1sg*
imbitaakondibeshin; *prt* betaakondibeshing
bitaakoshin *vai* bump something, hit against
something accidentally (as something stick- or
wood-like); *1sg* imbitaakoshin; *prt*
betaakoshing
bitaakoshkan *vti* bump into s.t.; *1sg*
imbitaakoshkaan; *prt* betaakoshkang
bitaakoshkaw *vta* bump into s.o.; *1sg*
imbitaakoshkawaa; *prt* betaakoshkawaad
bitaakoshkodaadiwag /bitaakoshkodaadi-/ *vai*
they have a collision; *1pl*
imbitaakoshkodaadimin; *prt*
betaakoshkodaadijig
bitaakosin *vii* bump something, hit against
something accidentally (as something stick- or
wood-like); *prt* betaakosing
bitizh /bitizhw-/ *vta* cut s.o. accidentally; *1sg*
imbitizhwaa; *prt* betizhwaad
bitizhan *vti* cut s.t. accidentally; *1sg* imbitizhaan;
prt betizhang
bizaan *pc* quiet, still
bizaan-ayaa *vai* be quiet; *1sg* imbizaan-ayaa; *prt*
bezaan-ayaad; *also* bizaani-ayaa
bizaanaakwadabi *vai* sit still; *1sg*
imbizaanaakwadab; *prt* bezaanaakwadabid
bizaanigaabawi *vai* stand quietly; *1sg*
imbizaanigaabaw; *prt* bezaanigaabawid

bizaanishin *vai* lie still; *1sg* imbizaanishin; *prt*
bezaanishing
bizhiki *na* cow, bison, buffalo; *pl* bizhikiwag; *dim*
bizhikiins
bizhikiwayaan *na* cowhide; *pl* bizhikiwayaanag;
dim bizhikiwayaanens
bizhiki-wiiyaas *ni* beef; *also* bizhikiwi-wiiyaas
bizhikiins *na* calf; *pl* bizhikiinsag
bizhikiinsiwayaan *na* calfhide; *pl*
bizhikiinsiwayaanag
bizhishigozi *vai* be empty; *prt* bezhishigozid
bizhishigwaa *vii* be empty; *prt* bezhishigwaag; *aug*
bizhishigwaamagad; *prt aug*
bezhishigwaamagak
bizhiw *na* lynx; *pl* bizhiwag; *dim* bizhiwens
bizhiwayaan *na* lynx hide; *pl* bizhiwayaanag; *loc*
bizhiwayaaning; *dim* bizhiwayaanens
bizindam *vai2* listen; *1sg* imbizindam; *prt*
bezindang
bizindamowin *ni* radio; *pl* bizindamowinan
bizindamoo-makak *ni* radio; *pl* bizindamoo-
makakoon; *loc* bizindamoo-makakong; *dim*
bizindamoo-makakoons
bizindan *vti* listen to s.t.; *1sg* imbizindaan; *prt*
bezindang
bizindaw *vta* listen to s.o.; *1sg* imbizindawaa; *prt*
bezindawaad
bizogeshin *vai* stumble; *1sg* imbizogeshin; *prt*
bezogeshing
bizokan *vti* stumble on s.t.; *1sg* imbizokaan; *prt*
bezokang
bizokaw *vta* stumble on s.o.; *1sg* imbizokawaa; *prt*
bezokawaad
bizozideshin *vai* stub one's toe, trip; *1sg*
imbizozideshin; *prt* bezozideshing
biibaagi *vai* call out, shout; *1sg* imbiibaag; *prt*
baabaagid
biibaagim *vta* call out to s.o., shout at s.o.; *1sg*
imbiibaagimaa; *prt* baabaagimaad
biibaagindan *vti* call out to s.t., shout at s.t.; *1sg*
imbiibaagindaan; *prt* baabaagindang
biibii *na* baby; *pl* biibiiyag; *dim* biibiiyens
biichibabagiwayaan *vai* put on one's shirt; *1sg*
imbiichibabagiwayaane; *prt*
baachibabagiwayaaned
biichibabiinzikawaagane *vai* put on one's coat;
1sg imbiichibabiinzikawaagane; *prt*
baachibabiinzikawaaganed
biichigiboodiyegwaazone *vai* put on one's pants;
1sg imbiichigiboodiyegwaazone; *prt*
baachigiboodiyegwaazoned
biichiminjikaawane *vai* put on one's mittens; *1sg*
imbiichiminjikaawane; *prt*
baachiminjikaawaned
biichiwakwaane *vai* put on one's hat; *1sg*
imbiichiwakwaane; *prt* baachiwakwaaned
biida'adoo *vai* follow a trail here; *1sg*
imbiida'adoo; *prt* baada'adood
biida'adoon *vti2* follow s.t. as a trail here; *1sg*
imbiida'adoon; *prt* baada'adood
biida'azh /biida'aN-/ *vta* follow s.o.'s trail here; *1sg*
imbiida'anaa; *prt* baada'anaad
biida'oodoon *vti2* bring here in a boat; *1sg*
imbiida'oodoon; *prt* baada'oodood

biida'oozh /biida'ooN-/ *vta* bring s.o. here in a boat; *1sg* imbiida'oonaa; *prt* baada'oonaad
biidakwazhiwe *vai* paddle here, swim here (as a fish); *1sg* imbiidakwazhiwe; *prt* baadakwazhiwed
biidaw *vta* bring (s.t.) for s.o.; *1sg* imbiidawaa; *prt* baadawaad; *also* biidamaw
biidaaban *vii* dawn comes, be daybreak; *prt* baadaabang
biidaadagaa *vai* swim here; *1sg* imbiidaadagaa; *prt* baadaadagaad
biidaadagaazii *vai* wade here; *1sg* imbiidaadagaazii; *prt* baadaadagaaziid
biidaada'e *vai* skate here; *1sg* imbiidaada'e; *prt* baadaada'ed
biidaajimo *vai* come telling news; *1sg* imbiidaajim; *prt* baadaajimod
biidaanakwad *vii* clouds approach; *prt* baadaanakwak
biidaandawe *vai* climb here; *1sg* imbiidaandawe; *prt* baadaandawed
biidaanimizi *vai* come in fear; *1sg* imbiidaanimiz; *prt* baadaanimizid
biidaapi *vai* come laughing; *1sg* imbiidaap; *prt* baadaapid
biidaasamabi *vai* sit facing this way; *1sg* imbiidaasamab; *prt* baadaasamabid
biidaasamishkaa *vai* paddle here, come in a boat; *1sg* imbiidaasamishkaa; *prt* baadaasamishkaad
biidaasamose *vai* walk here; *1sg* imbiidaasamose; *prt* baadaasamosed
biidaashi *vai* be blown here, sail here; *1sg* imbiidaash; *prt* baadaashid
biidaashkaa *vii* waves come in to shore; *prt* baadaashkaag; *aug* biidaashkaamagad; *prt aug* baadaashkaamagak
biidaasin *vii* be blown here, sail here; *prt* baadaasing
biidaazakonebizo *vai* drive here with a light; *1sg* imbiidaazakonebiz; *prt* baadaazakonebizod
biidaazakwanenjige *vai* come with a light; *1sg* imbiidaazakwanenjige; *prt* baadaazakwanenjiged
biidin *vta* hand s.o. over (here); *1sg* imbiidinaa; *prt* baadinaad
biidinamaw *vta* hand (s.t.) over (here) to s.o.; *1sg* imbiidinamawaa; *prt* baadinamawaad
biidinan *vti* hand s.t. over (here); *1sg* imbiidinaan; *prt* baadinang
biidoode *vai* crawl here; *1sg* imbiidoode; *prt* baadooded
biidoomigo *vai* ride here on horseback; *1sg* imbiidoomig; *prt* baadoomigod
biidoon *vti2* bring s.t.; *1sg* imbiidoon; *prt* baadood
biidwewebatoo *vai* be heard running here; *1sg* imbiidwewebatoo; *prt* baadwewebatood
biidwewebide *vii* be heard speeding here, be heard driving here; *prt* baadwewebideg; *aug* biidwewebidemagad; *prt aug* baadwewebidemagak
biidwewebizo *vai* be heard speeding here, be heard driving here; *1sg* imbiidwewebiz; *prt* baadwewebizod

biidwewekamigibatoo *vai* be heard running here on the ground; *1sg* imbiidwewekamigibatoo; *prt* baadwewekamigibatood
biidweweshin *vai* be heard walking here; *1sg* imbiidweweshin; *prt* baadweweshing
biidweweyaadagaa *vai* be heard swimming here; *1sg* imbiidweweyaadagaa; *prt* baadweweyaadagaad
biidwewidam *vai2* come making noise (e.g., thunder), come speaking; *1sg* imbiidwewidam; *prt* baadwewidang
biig *na* spade suite card; *pl* biigwag
biigobidoon *vti2* tear s.t., rip s.t.; *1sg* imbiigobidoon; *prt* baagobidood
biigobijigaade *vii* be torn, be ripped; *prt* baagobijigaadeg; *aug* biigobijigaademagad; *prt aug* baagobijigaademagak
biigobijigaazo *vai* be torn, be ripped; *prt* baagobijigaazod
biigobijige *vai* tear things, rip things; *1sg* imbiigobijige; *prt* baagobijiged
biigobizh /biigobiN-/ *vta* tear s.o., rip s.o.; *1sg* imbiigobinaa; *prt* baagobinaad
biigodaabaane *vai* have a broken-down car; *1sg* imbiigodaabaane; *prt* baagodaabaaned
biigode *vii* break by heat; *prt* baagodeg; *aug* biigodemagad; *prt aug* baagodemagak
biigojiishkaa *vai* burst open; *prt* baagojiishkaad
biigojiishkaa *vii* burst open; *prt* baagojiishkaag; *aug* biigojiishkaamagad; *prt aug* baagojiishkaamagak
biigon *vta* break s.o. by hand, dismantle s.o.; *1sg* imbiigonaa; *prt* baagonaad
biigonan *vti* break s.t. by hand, dismantle s.t.; *1sg* imbiigonaan; *prt* baagonang
biigoshim *vta* break s.o. by dropping, smash s.o.; *1sg* imbiigoshimaa; *prt* baagoshimaad
biigoshin *vai* break on impact; *1sg* imbiigoshin; *prt* baagoshing
biigoshkaa *vai* break, be broken, be broke (out of money); *prt* baagoshkaad
biigoshkaa *vii* break, be broken; *prt* baagoshkaag; *aug* biigoshkaamagad; *prt aug* baagoshkaamagak
biigosidoon *vti2* break s.t. by dropping, smash s.t.; *1sg* imbiigosidoon; *prt* baagosidood
biigosin *vii* break on impact; *prt* baagosing
biigozo *vai* break by heat; *prt* baagozod
biigwa' /biigwa'w-/ *vta* break s.o. using something; *1sg* imbiigwa'waa; *prt* baagwa'waad
biigwa'an *vti* break s.t. using something; *1sg* imbiigwa'aan; *prt* baagwa'ang
biigwakamigibidoon *vti2* break s.t. up (as ground), plow s.t.; *1sg* imbiigwakamigibidoon; *prt* baagwakamigibidood
biigwakamigibijigan *na* plow; *pl* biigwakamigibijiganag; *loc* biigwakamigibijiganing; *dim* biigwakamigibijigaans
biigwakamigibijige *vai* plow; *1sg* imbiigwakamigibijige; *prt* baagwakamigibijiged
biigwawe *vai* be bushy; *1sg* imbiigwawe; *prt* baagwawed

biigwaashi *vai* be blown apart; *prt* **baagwaashid**
biigwaasin *vii* be blown apart; *prt* **baagwaasing**
bii' *vta* wait for s.o.; *1sg* **imbii'aa**; *prt* **baa'aad**
bii'o *vai* wait; *1sg* **imbii'**; *prt* **baa'od**
biijiba'idiwag /biijiba'idi-/ *vai* they run here together; *1pl* **imbiijiba'idimin**; *prt* **baajiba'idijig**
biijibatoo *vai* run here; *1sg* **imbiijibatoo**; *prt* **baajibatood**
biijibide *vii* speed here, drive here, fly here; *prt* **baajibideg**; *aug* **biijibidemagad**; *prt aug* **baajibidemagak**
biijibizo *vai* speed here, drive here, fly here; *1sg* **imbiijibiz**; *prt* **baajibizod**
biijibii'amaw- *vta* write (s.t.) here to s.o. *in inverse forms: 1sg* **imbiijibii'amaag**; *prt* **baajibii'amaagod**
biijibii'ige *vai* write here, send a letter here; *prt* **baajibii'iged**
biijibiisaa *vii* rain comes; *prt* **baajibiisaag**; *aug* **biijibiisaamagad**; *prt aug* **baajibiisaamagak**
biijidaabaadan *vti* drag s.t. here; *1sg* **imbiijidaabaadaan**; *prt* **baajidaabaadang**
biijidaabaazh /biijidaabaaN-/ *vta* drag s.o. here; *1sg* **imbiijidaabaanaa**; *prt* **baajidaabaanaad**
biijidaabii *vai* drag here; *1sg* **imbiijidaabii**; *prt* **baajidaabiid**
biijidaabii'iwe *vai* drive here; *1sg* **imbiijidaabii'iwe**; *prt* **baajidaabii'iwed**
biijigaade *vii* be brought; *prt* **baajigaadeg**; *aug* **biijigaademagad**; *prt aug* **baajigaademagak**
biijigaazo *vai* be brought; *prt* **baajigaazod**
biijigidaazo *vai* come in anger; *1sg* **imbiijigidaaz**; *prt* **baajigidaazod**
biijigozi *vai* move one's residence here; *1sg* **imbiijigoz**; *prt* **baajigozid**
biijikawe *vai* come leaving tracks; *1sg* **imbiijikawe**; *prt* **baajikawed**
biijimaagozi *vai* give off a smell; *1sg* **imbiijimaagoz**; *prt* **baajimaagozid**
biijimaagwad *vii* give off a smell; *prt* **baajimaagwak**
biijimaam *vta* smell s.o.; *1sg* **imbiijimaamaa**; *prt* **baajimaamaad**
biijimaandan *vti* smell s.t.; *1sg* **imbiijimaandaan**; *prt* **baajimaandang**
biijimaaso *vai* give off a smell in cooking or burning; *prt* **baajimaasod**
biijimaate *vii* give off a smell in cooking or burning; *prt* **baajimaateg**; *aug* **biijimaatemagad**; *prt aug* **baajimaatemagak**
biijise *vai* fly here; *1sg* **imbiijise**; *prt* **baajised**
biijise *vii* fly here; *prt* **baajiseg**; *aug* **biijisemagad**; *prt aug* **baajisemagak**
biijwebin *vta* throw s.o. here; *1sg* **imbiijwebinaa**; *prt* **baajwebinaad**
biijwebinamaw *vta* throw (s.t.) here to s.o.; *1sg* **imbiijwebinamawaa**; *prt* **baajwebinamawaad**
biijwebinan *vti* throw s.t. here; *1sg* **imbiijwebinaan**; *prt* **baajwebinang**
biimashkwemaginigan *ni* bark torch; *pl* **biimashkwemaginiganan**; *loc* **biimashkwemaginiganing**; *dim* **biimashkwemaginigaans**

biimaakwad *ni* vine; *pl* **biimaakwadoon**; *loc* **biimaakwadong**; *dim* **biimaakwadoons**
biimidoon *vai* have a twisted mouth (as from a stroke); *1sg* **imbiimidoon**; *prt* **baamidoong**
biiminakwaan *ni* rope; *pl* **biiminakwaanan**; *loc* **biiminakwaaning**; *dim* **biiminakwaanens**
biiminakwaanens *ni* string; *pl* **biiminakwaanensan**; *loc* **biiminakwaanensing**
biiminakwe *vai* make rope, make string; *1sg* **imbiiminakwe**; *prt* **baaminakwed**
biiminigan *ni* brace and bit; *pl* **biiminiganan**
biimiskodisii *na* snail; *pl* **biimiskodisiig**
biimiskon *vta* turn s.o., twist s.o.; *1sg* **imbiimiskonaa**; *prt* **baamiskonaad**
biimiskonan *vti* turn s.t., twist s.t.; *1sg* **imbiimiskonaan**; *prt* **baamiskonang**
biimiskonigan *ni* screw; *pl* **biimiskoniganan**; *dim* **biimiskonigaans**
biimiskonikeshin *vai* fall and twist one's arm; *1sg* **imbiimiskonikeshin**; *prt* **baamiskonikeshing**
biimiskwa'an *vti* screw s.t.; *1sg* **imbiimiskwa'aan**; *prt* **baamiskwa'ang**
biimiskwa'igan *ni* screwdriver, wrench; *pl* **biimiskwa'iganan**; *loc* **biimiskwa'iganing**; *dim* **biimiskwa'igaans**
biimiskwa'igaans *ni* screw; *pl* **biimiskwa'igaansan**; *loc* **biimiskwa'igaansing**
biinad *vii* be clean; *prt* **baanak**
biina' /biina'w-/ *vta* put s.o. in; *1sg* **imbiina'waa**; *prt* **baana'waad**
biina'an *vti* put s.t. in; *1sg* **imbiina'aan**; *prt* **baana'ang**
biina'igaade *vii* be put in; *prt* **baana'igaadeg**; *aug* **biina'igaademagad**; *prt aug* **baana'igaademagak**
biina'igaazo *vai* be put in; *prt* **baana'igaazod**
biinaagamin /biinaagami-/ *vii* be clean (as a liquid); *prt* **baanaagamig**
biinda'am *vai2* be caught in a net; *1sg* **imbiinda'am**; *prt* **baanda'ang**
biindashkwaadan *vti* stuff s.t.; *1sg* **imbiindashkwaadaan**; *prt* **baandashkwaadang**
biindashkwaazh /biindashkwaaN-/ *vta* stuff s.o.; *1sg* **imbiindashkwaanaa**; *prt* **baandashkwaanaad**
biindaabikibijigan *ni* gearshift; *pl* **biindaabikibijiganan**
biindaabikibijige *vai* shift gears; *1sg* **imbiindaabikibijige**; *prt* **baandaabikibijiged**
biindaabikibizh /biindaabikibiN-/ *vta* shift s.o. (e.g., a car); *1sg* **imbiindaabikibinaa**; *prt* **baandaabikibinaad**
biindaakoojige *vai* make an offering of tobacco; *1sg* **imbiindaakoojige**; *prt* **baandaakoojiged**
biindaakoozh /biindaakooN-/ *vta* make an offering of tobacco to s.o.; *1sg* **imbiindaakoonaa**; *prt* **baandaakoonaad**
biindaakwaan *na* snuff; *loc* **biindaakwaaning**
biindaakwe *vai* chew snuff or tobacco; *1sg* **imbiindaakwe**; *prt* **baandaakwed**
biinde *vii* be in; *prt* **baandeg**; *aug* **biindemagad**; *prt aug* **baandemagak**
biindig *pc* inside

biindigadoon *vti2* bring s.t. inside, take s.t. inside; *1sg* **imbiindigadoon**; *prt* **baandigadood**

biindigaw *vta* enter into where s.o. is, come into where s.o. is; *1sg* **imbiindigawaa**; *prt* **baandigawaad**

biindigazh /**biindigaN-**/ *vta* bring s.o. inside, take s.o. inside; *1sg* **imbiindiganaa**; *prt* **baandiganaad**

biindige *vai* enter, go inside, come inside; *1sg* **imbiindige**; *prt* **baandiged**

biindigeba'idiwag /**biindigeba'idi-**/ *vai* they run inside together; *1pl* **imbiindigeba'idimin**; *prt* **baandigeba'idijig**

biindigeba'iwe *vai* run inside from people; *1sg* **imbiindigeba'iwe**; *prt* **baandigeba'iwed**

biindigebatoo *vai* run inside; *1sg* **imbiindigebatoo**; *prt* **baandigebatood**

biindigebatwaadan *vti* run inside with s.t.; *1sg* **imbiindigebatwaadaan**; *prt* **baandigebatwaadang**

biindigebatwaazh /**biindigebatwaaN-**/ *vta* run inside with s.o.; *1sg* **imbiindigebatwaanaa**; *prt* **baandigebatwaanaad**

biindigebide *vii* speed inside, drive inside, fly inside; *prt* **baandigebideg**; *aug* **biindigebidemagad**; *prt aug* **baandigebidemagak**

biindigebizo *vai* speed inside, drive inside, fly inside; *1sg* **imbiindigebiz**; *prt* **baandigebizod**

biindigenaazha' /**biindigenaazha'w-**/ *vta* tell s.o. to go inside; *1sg* **imbiindigenaazha'waa**; *prt* **baandigenaazha'waad**

biindigenaazhikaw *vta* chase s.o. inside; *1sg* **imbiindigenaazhikawaa**; *prt* **baandigenaazhikawaad**

biindigenise *vai* bring firewood inside; *1sg* **imbiindigenise**; *prt* **baandigenised**

biindigenizhikaw *vta* chase s.o. inside; *1sg* **imbiindigenizhikawaa**; *prt* **baandigenizhikawaad**

biindigeshimo *vai* dance inside (as in a Grand Entry); *1sg* **imbiindigeshim**; *prt* **baandigeshimod**

biindigewebin *vta* throw s.o. inside; *1sg* **imbiindigewebinaa**; *prt* **baandigewebinaad**

biindigewebinan *vti* throw s.t. inside; *1sg* **imbiindigewebinaan**; *prt* **baandigewebinang**

biindigewebinige *vai* throw things inside; *1sg* **imbiindigewebinige**; *prt* **baandigewebiniged**

biindigeyaashi *vai* be blown inside; *prt* **baandigeyaashid**

biindigeyaasin *vii* be blown inside; *prt* **baandigeyaasing**

biindoode *vii* crawl in; *prt* **baandooded**

biingeji *vai* feel cold; *1sg* **imbiingeji**; *prt* **baangejid**

biingeyendam *vai2* have something on one's mind, worry; *1sg* **imbiingeyendam**; *prt* **baangeyendang**

biinichigaade *vii* be cleaned; *prt* **baanichigaadeg**; *aug* **biinichigaademagad**; *prt aug* **baanichigaademagak**

biinichigaazo *vai* be cleaned; *prt* **baanichigaazod**

biinichige *vai* clean things; *1sg* **imbiinichige**; *prt* **baanichiged**

biinichigewikwe *na* cleaner (female), janitor (female); *pl* **biinichigewikweg**

biinichigewinini *na* cleaner, janitor; *pl* **biinichigewininiwag**

biini' *vta* clean s.o.; *1sg* **imbiini'aa**; *prt* **baani'aad**

biinininjii *vai* have a clean hand; *1sg* **imbiinininjii**; *prt* **baanininjiid**

biinish *pc* until, up to

biinitaw *vta* clean (s.t.) for s.o.; *1sg* **imbiinitawaa**; *prt* **baanitawaad**

biinitoon *vti2* clean s.t.; *1sg* **imbiinitoon**; *prt* **baanitood**

biinizi *vai* be clean; *1sg* **imbiiniz**; *prt* **baanizid**

biinizikaa *pc* spontaneously, for no purpose at all

biinjayi'ii *pc* inside it

biinjibide *vii* speed in, drive in, fly in, fall in; *prt* **baanjibideg**; *aug* **biinjibidemagad**; *prt aug* **baanjibidemagak**

biinjibizo *vai* speed in, drive in, fly in, fall in; *1sg* **imbiinjibiz**; *prt* **baanjibizod**

biinjiboonaagan *na* fish trap; *pl* **biinjiboonaaganag**; *loc* **biinjiboonaaganing**; *dim* **biinjiboonaagaans**

biinjidawaa *vii* be an outlet; *prt* **baanjidawaag**

biinjidoon *pc* inside the mouth

biinjijaanzh *pc* inside the nose

biinjijiwan *vii* flow in; *prt* **baanjijiwang**

biinjikomaan *ni* knife sheath; *pl* **biinjikomaanan**; *loc* **biinjikomaaning**; *dim* **biinjikomaanens**

biinjina *pc* inside the body

biinjise *vai* fly in, fall in; *1sg* **imbiinjise**; *prt* **baanjised**

biinjise *vii* fly in, fall in; *prt* **baanjiseg**; *aug* **biinjisemagad**; *prt aug* **baanjisemagak**

biinjitawag *pc* inside an ear

biinjwebin *vta* throw s.o. in; *1sg* **imbiinjwebinaa**; *prt* **baanjwebinaad**

biinjwebinan *vti* throw s.t. in; *1sg* **imbiinjwebinaan**; *prt* **baanjwebinang**

biinjwebinige *vai* throw things in, vote; *1sg* **imbiinjwebinige**; *prt* **baanjwebiniged**

biinjwebinigetamaw *vta* vote for s.o.; *1sg* **imbiinjwebinigetamawaa**; *prt* **baanjwebinigetamawaad**

biinjwebinigewi-giizhigad *vii* be election day; *prt* **baanjwebinigewi-giizhigak**

biinzibii *vai* burp grease; *1sg* **imbiinzibii**; *prt* **baanzibiid**

biinzo *vai* be in; *1sg* **imbiinz**; *prt* **baanzod**

biipiinjigana'onag *na* dew-claw game *plural*

biisa' /**biisa'w-**/ *vta* chop s.o. fine; *1sg* **imbiisa'waa**; *prt* **baasa'waad**

biisa'an *vti* chop s.t. fine; *1sg* **imbiisa'aan**; *prt* **baasa'ang**

biisaa *vii* be fine, be in particles; *prt* **baasaag**; *aug* **biisaamagad**; *prt aug* **baasaamagak**

biisibidoon *vti2* crumble s.t., pull s.t. into particles; *1sg* **imbiisibidoon**; *prt* **baasibidood**

biisibizh /**biisibiN-**/ *vta* crumble s.o., pull s.o. into particles; *1sg* **imbiisibinaa**; *prt* **baasibinaad**

biisiboodoon *vti2* grind s.t. up; *1sg* **imbiisiboodoon**; *prt* **baasiboodood**

biisiboojigan *na* cornmeal; *loc* **biisiboojiganing**

biisiboojigan *ni* grinder, mill; *pl* **biisiboojiganan**; *loc* **biisiboojiganing**; *dim* **biisiboojigaans**

biisiboozh /biisibooN-/ *vta* grind s.o. up; *1sg*
imbiisiboonaa; *prt* baasiboonaad
biisiga'isaan *ni* kindling wood; *pl* biisiga'isaanan;
loc biisiga'isaaning; *dim* biisiga'isaanens
biisiga'ise *vai* make kindling; *1sg* imbiisiga'ise; *prt*
baasiga'ised
biisitaagan *ni* bubble; *pl* biisitaaganan; *loc*
biisitaaganing; *dim* biisitaagaans
biisizi *vai* be fine, be in particles; *prt* baasizid
biitagoode *vai* put on one's dress; *1sg*
imbiitagoode; *prt* baatagoodeg
biitawagoodaan *ni* slip; *pl* biitawagoodaanan; *loc*
biitawagoodaaning; *dim* biitawagoodaanens
biitazhigane *vai* put on one's socks; *1sg*
imbiitazhigane; *prt* baatazhiganed
biite *ni* foam
biitewan *vii* be foamy; *prt* baatewang
biitewaaboo *ni* beer; *loc* biitewaaboong
biitoo- *pv4* as a layer
biitoo-babagiwayaan *ni* undershirt; *pl* biitoo-
babagiwayaanan; *loc* biitoo-
babagiwayaaning; *dim* biitoo-
babagiwayaanens
biitoo-giboodiyegwaazon *na* underpants; *pl*
biitoo-giboodiyegwaazonag; *loc* biitoo-
giboodiyegwaazoning; *dim* biitoo-
giboodiyegwaazonens
biitookizinaan *ni* overshoe; *pl* biitookizinaanan;
loc biitookizinaaning; *dim* biitookizinaanens;
also biitookizin
biitookizine *vai* wear overshoes; *1sg*
imbiitookizine; *prt* baatookizined
biitookonaye *vai* wear layers (as underwear); *1sg*
imbiitookonaye; *prt* baatookonayed
biitoon *vti2* wait for s.t.; *1sg* imbiitoon; *prt*
baatood
biitooshin *vai* lie in a layer; *prt* baatooshing
biitooshkigan *ni* men's underwear; *pl*
biitooshkiganan; *loc* biitooshkiganing; *dim*
biitooshkigaans
biitoosijigan *na* pie; *pl* biitoosijiganag; *loc*
biitoosijiganing; *dim* biitoosijigaans
biitoosijigani-bakwezhigan *na* pie; *pl*
biitoosijigani-bakwezhiganag; *loc*
biitoosijigani-bakwezhiganing; *dim*
biitoosijigani-bakwezhigaans
biitoosin *vii* lie in a layer; *prt* baatoosing
biiwan *vii* be a blizzard; *prt* baawang
biiwaabik *ni* (piece of) metal, iron; *pl*
biiwaabikoon; *loc* biiwaabikong; *dim*
biiwaabikoons
biiwaabiko-adaawewigamig *ni* hardware store; *pl*
biiwaabiko-adaawewigamigoon; *loc*
biiwaabiko-adaawewigamigong; *also*
biiwaabikwadaawewigamig
biiwaabiko-jiimaan *ni* aluminum canoe; *pl*
biiwaabiko-jiimaanan; *loc* biiwaabiko-
jiimaaning; *dim* biiwaabiko-jiimaanens
biiwaabikokaan *ni* mine; *pl* biiwaabikokaanan; *loc*
biiwaabikokaaning; *dim* biiwaabikokaanens
biiwaabikokewinini *na* miner; *pl*
biiwaabikokewininiwag
biiwaabikoons *ni* can, wire; *pl* biiwaabikoonsan;
loc biiwaabikoonsing

biiwaanag *na* flint; *pl* biiwaanagoog; *loc*
biiwaanagong; *dim* biiwaanagoons
biiwega'igan *ni* chip; *pl* biiwega'iganan; *loc*
biiwega'iganing; *dim* biiwega'igaans
biiwide *na* stranger, visitor; *pl* biiwideg
biiwise *vai* scatter, disperse; *prt* baawised
biiwise *vii* scatter, disperse; *prt* baawiseg; *aug*
biiwisemagad; *prt aug* baawisemagak
biiwiwebin *vta* scatter s.o.; *1sg* imbiiwiwebinaa;
prt baawiwebinaad
biiwiwebinan *vti* scatter s.t.; *1sg*
imbiiwiwebinaan; *prt* baawiwebinang
biizh /biiN-/ *vta* bring s.o.; *1sg* imbiinaa; *prt*
baanaad
biizikan *vti* wear s.t., have s.t. on (e.g., clothes),
put s.t. on (e.g., clothes); *1sg* imbiizikaan; *prt*
baazikang
biizikaw *vta* wear s.o., have s.o. on (e.g., clothes),
put s.o. on (e.g., clothes); *1sg* imbiizikawaa;
prt baazikawaad
biizikiigan *ni* item of clothing; *pl* biizikiiganan; *loc*
biizikiiganing; *dim* biizikiigaans
biizikonaye *vai* dress, be dressed, put on one's
clothes; *1sg* imbiizikonaye; *prt* baazikonayed
biizikonaye' *vta* dress s.o.; *1sg* imbiizikonaye'aa;
prt baazikonaye'aad
booch *pc* it is necessary, it is certain
boodawaade *vii* there is a fire made in a fireplace;
prt bwaadawaadeg; *aug* boodawaademagad;
prt aug bwaadawaademagak
boodawaan *ni* fireplace; *pl* boodawaanan; *loc*
boodawaaning; *dim* boodawaanens
boodawe *vai* build a fire; *1sg* imboodawe; *prt*
bwaadawed
boodawewinini *na* maintenance engineer, school
custodian; *pl* boodawewininiwag; *dim*
boodawewininiins
boodaadan *vti* blow on s.t.; *1sg* imboodaadaan;
prt bwaadaadang
boodaajige *vai* blow on things; *1sg* imboodaajige;
prt bwaadaajiged
boodaajii' /boodaajii'w-/ *vta* inflate s.o.; *1sg*
imboodaajii'waa; *prt* bwaadaajii'waad
boodaajii'an *vti* inflate s.t.; *1sg* imboodaajii'aan;
prt bwaadaajii'ang
boodaajii'igan *ni* tire pump, air pump; *pl*
boodaajii'iganan; *loc* boodaajii'iganing; *dim*
boodaajii'igaans
boodaajii'ige *vai* inflate things; *1sg*
imboodaajii'ige; *prt* bwaadaajii'iged
boodaakwe *vai+o* put (s.t.) in the kettle; *1sg*
imboodaakwe, imboodaakwen; *prt*
bwaadaakwed
boodaazh /boodaaN-/ *vta* blow on s.o.; *1sg*
imboodaanaa; *prt* bwaadaanaad
boodewaadamii *na* Potawatomi; *pl*
boodewaadamiig; *dim* boodewaadamiins
boodoonh *na* tadpole; *pl* boodoonyag
boogidi *vai* fart; *1sg* imboogid; *prt* bwaagidid
bookadiniganan *na* doughnut; *pl* bookadiniganag;
loc bookadiniganing; *dim* bookadinigaans;
also bwaakadinigaazod
bookobidoon *vti2* pull s.t. in two, break s.t. in two
with hands; *1sg* imboookobidoon; *prt*
bwaakobidood

bookobizh /bookobiN-/ *vta* pull s.o. in two, break
   s.o. in two with hands; *1sg* **imbookobinaa**; *prt*
   bwaakobinaad
bookoganaam *vta* break s.o. in two by hitting; *1sg*
   imbookoganaamaa; *prt* **bwaakoganaamaad**
bookoganaandan *vti* break s.t. in two by hitting;
   1sg **imbookoganaandaan**; *prt*
   bwaakoganaandang
bookogaade *vai* break one's leg, have a broken
   leg; *1sg* **imbookogaade**; *prt* **bwaakogaaded**
bookogaadeshin *vai* fall and break one's leg; *1sg*
   imbookogaadeshin; *prt* **bwaakogaadeshing**
bookogwebizh /bookogwebiN-/ *vta* wring s.o.'s
   neck; *1sg* **imbookogwebinaa**; *prt*
   bwaakogwebinaad
bookojaane *vai* have a broken nose; *1sg*
   imbookojaane; *prt* **bwaakojaaned**
bookonike *vai* break one's arm, have a broken
   arm; *1sg* **imbookonike**; *prt* **bwaakoniked**
bookonikeshin *vai* fall and break one's arm; *1sg*
   imbookonikeshin; *prt* **bwaakonikeshing**
bookoshkan *vti* break s.t. in two by foot or body;
   1sg **imbookoshkaan**; *prt* **bwaakoshkang**
bookoshkaw *vta* break s.o. in two by foot or body;
   1sg **imbookoshkawaa**; *prt* **bwaakoshkawaad**
bookoshkaa *vai* break in two, be broken in two;
   1sg **imbookoshkaa**; *prt* **bwaakoshkaad**
bookoshkaa *vii* break in two, be broken in two; *prt*
   bwaakoshkaag; *aug* **bookoshkaamagad**; *prt*
   aug **bwaakoshkaamagak**
bookwaabik *ni* piece of metal; *pl* **bookwaabikoon**;
   loc **bookwaabikong**; *dim* **bookwaabikoons**
bookwaawiganeshin *vai* fall and break one's back;
   1sg **imbookwaawiganeshin**; *prt*
   bwaakwaawiganeshing
boonakadoon *vti2* anchor s.t.; *1sg*
   imboonakadoon; *prt* **bwaanakadood**
boonakajigan *ni* anchor; *pl* **boonakajiganan**; *loc*
   boonakajiganing; *dim* **boonakajigaans**
boonam *vai2* lay an egg; *prt* **bwaanang**
boonaanimad *vii* wind lets up, wind dies down; *prt*
   bwaanaanimak
boonendam *vai2* give up, not think about, ignore;
   1sg **imboonendam**; *prt* **bwaanendang**
boonendan *vti* forget s.t., ignore s.t.; *1sg*
   imboonendaan; *prt* **bwaanendang**
boonenim *vta* forget s.o., ignore s.o.; *1sg*
   imboonenimaa; *prt* **bwaanenimaad**
boonichigaade *vii* be left alone; *prt*
   bwaanichigaadeg; *aug* **boonichigaademagad**;
   prt aug **bwaanichigaademagak**
boonichigaazo *vai* be left alone; *prt*
   bwaanichigaazod
booni' *vta* leave s.o. alone, quit s.o.; *1sg*
   imbooni'aa; *prt* **bwaani'aad**
boonim *vta* stop talking to s.o., avoid talking to
   s.o.; *1sg* **imboonimaa**; *prt* **bwaanimaad**
boonitoon *vti2* leave s.t. alone, quit s.t.; *1sg*
   imboonitoon; *prt* **bwaanitood**
boonii *vai* alight, land (from flight); *1sg* **imboonii**;
   prt **bwaaniid**
boopoogid= < boogid=
booshke *pc* it's up to you, it's your decision; *also*
   booshke giniin

bootaagan *na* mortar for wild rice; *pl*
   bootaaganag; *loc* **bootaaganing**; *dim*
   bootaagaans
bootaaganaak *ni* pestle; *pl* **bootaaganaakoon**; *loc*
   bootaaganaakong; *dim* **bootaaganaakoons**
bootaagaadan *vti* stamp s.t. in a mortar; *1sg*
   imbootaagaadaan; *prt* **bwaataagaadang**
bootaage *vai* stamp things in a mortar (e.g., wild
   rice); *1sg* **imbootaage**; *prt* **bwaataaged**
boozhoo *pc* hello!, greetings!
boozi *vai* get in a vehicle or boat, board, embark,
   get aboard; *1sg* **imbooz**; *prt* **bwaazid**
boozigwaashkwani *vai* jump in a vehicle or boat,
   jump aboard; *1sg* **imboozigwaashkwan**; *prt*
   bwaazigwaashkwanid
boozi' *vta* give a ride to s.o.; *1sg* **imboozi'aa**; *prt*
   bwaazi'aad
boozikinaagan *ni* bowl; *pl* **boozikinaaganan**; *loc*
   boozikinaaganing; *dim* **boozikinaagaans**
boozinaazha' /boozinaazha'w-/ *vta* tell s.o. to get
   in (a vehicle or boat), tell s.o. to go aboard; *1sg*
   imboozinaazha'waa; *prt* **bwaazinaazha'waad**
boozinodaw *vta* catch a ride with s.o.; *1sg*
   imboozinodawaa; *prt* **bwaazinodawaad**
boozitaw *vta* load (s.t.) with cargo for s.o.; *1sg*
   imboozitawaa; *prt* **bwaazitawaad**
boozitaaso *vai* load cargo; *1sg* **imboozitaas**; *prt*
   bwaazitaasod
boozitoon *vti2* load s.t. as cargo; *1sg*
   imboozitoon; *prt* **bwaazitood**
bwaa- *pv1* not able to, not before
bwaakadinigaazod *na-pt* doughnut; *pl*
   bwaakadinigaazojig; *also* **bookadinigan**
bwaan *na* Dakota (Sioux); *pl* **bwaanag**; *dim*
   bwaanens
bwaanawichige *vai* be unable (to do something);
   1sg **imbwaanawichige**; *prt* **bwayaanawichiged**
bwaanawi' *vta* be unable to do something to s.o.,
   be unable to manage s.o.; *1sg* **imbwaanawi'aa**;
   prt **bwayaanawi'aad**
bwaanawi'o *vai* be unable to do something, be
   stuck; *1sg* **imbwaanawi'**; *prt* **bwayaanawi'od**
bwaanawitoon *vti2* be unable to do s.t., be unable
   to manage s.t.; *1sg* **imbwaanawitoon**; *prt*
   bwayaanawitood
bwaanikwe *na* Dakota woman; *pl* **bwaanikweg**;
   dim **bwaanikwens**
bwaanimo *vai* speak Dakota; *1sg* **imbwaanim**; *prt*
   bwayaanimod
bwaanimotaw *vta* speak Dakota to s.o.; *1sg*
   imbwaanimotawaa; *prt* **bwayaanimotawaad**
bwaanzhii-nagamo *vai* sing war songs; *1sg*
   imbwaanzhii-nagam; *prt* **bwayaanzhii-**
   nagamod
bwaanzhii-niimi *vai* dance a war dance; *1sg*
   imbwaanzhii-niim; *prt* **bwayaanzhii-niimid**
bwaanzhii-niimi'idiwag /bwaanzhii-niimi'idi-/ *vai*
   they dance a war dance; *1pl* **imbwaanzhii-**
   niimi'idimin; *prt* **bwayaanzhii-niimi'idijig**
bwaanzhii-niimi'idiwin *ni* war dance; *pl*
   bwaanzhii-niimi'idiwinan
bwaanzhiiwi'o *vai* wear a dance outfit; *1sg*
   imbwaanzhiiwi'; *prt* **bwayaanzhiiwi'od**

bwaanzhiiwi'on *ni* dance outfit; *pl*
  bwaanzhiiwi'onan; *loc* bwaanzhiiwi'oning;
  dim bwaanzhiiwi'onens
bwaawane *vai* hardly be able to carry a pack; *1sg*
  imbwaawane; *prt* bwayaawaned

D

da- *pv1 future verb prefix in independent verbs with no
  personal prefix*
dabasagoode *vii* hang low; *prt* debasagoodeg; *aug*
  dabasagoodemagad; *prt aug*
  debasagoodemagak
dabasagoodoon *vti2* hang s.t. low; *1sg*
  indabasagoodoon; *prt* debasagoodood
dabasagoojin *vai* hang low; *prt* debasagoojing
dabasagoozh /dabasagooN-/ *vta* hang s.o. low;
  1sg indabasagoonaa; *prt* debasagoonaad
dabasakamigaa *vii* be low ground; *prt*
  debasakamigaag; *aug* dabasakamigaamagad;
  prt aug debasakamigaamagak
dabasaa *vii* be low; *prt* debasaag; *aug*
  dabasaamagad; *prt aug* debasaamagak
dabasendan *vti* hold s.t. in low regard; *1sg*
  indabasendaan; *prt* debasendang
dabasendaagozi *vai* be held in low regard; *1sg*
  indabasendaagoz; *prt* debasendaagozid
dabasendaagwad *vii* be held in low regard; *prt*
  debasendaagwak
dabasenim *vta* hold s.o. in low regard; *1sg*
  indabasenimaa; *prt* debasenimaad
dabazhish *pc* low
dabazi *vai* dodge; *1sg* indabaz; *prt* debazid; *also*
  dabazii*
dabinoo'igan *ni* shelter; *pl* dabinoo'iganan; *loc*
  dabinoo'iganing; *dim* dabinoo'igaans
dadaabas= < dabas=
dadaakw= < dakw=
dadaakwanagweyaa *vii* have short sleeves; *prt*
  dedaakwanagweyaag; *aug*
  dadaakwanagweyaamagad; *prt aug*
  dedaakwanagweyaamagak
dadaakwaanikwe *vai* have short hair; *1sg*
  indadaakwaanikwe; *prt* dedaakwaanikwed
dadaatabanaamo *vai* have fast respiration; *1sg*
  indadaatabanaam; *prt* dedaatabanaamod
dadaatabaanagidoon *vai* talk quickly; *1sg*
  indadaatabaanagidoon; *prt*
  dedaatabaanagidoong
dadaatabii *vai* be quick; *1sg* indadaatabii; *prt*
  dedaatabiid
dadibaajimo *vai* tell stories, report, narrate; *1sg*
  indadibaajim; *prt* dedibaajimod
dadibaajimotaw *vta* tell stories to s.o., narrate to
  s.o.; *1sg* indadibaajimotawaa; *prt*
  dedibaajimotawaad
dadibaajimoowinini *na* storyteller; *pl*
  dadibaajimoowininiwag

daga *pc* please!, come on!
dago- *pv4* in a place with
dagode *vii* be cooked with something else; *prt*
  degodeg; *aug* dagodemagad; *prt aug*
  degodemagak
dagon /dago-/ *vii* be in a certain place, be situated
  in a certain place; *prt* endagog
dagon *vta* add s.o. in, mix s.o. in; *1sg* indagonaa;
  prt degonaad
dagonan *vti* add s.t. in, mix s.t. in; *1sg*
  indagonaan; *prt* degonang
dagonigaade *vii* be added in, be mixed in; *prt*
  degonigaadeg; *aug* dagonigaademagad; *prt*
  aug degonigaademagak
dagonigaazo *vai* be added in, be mixed in; *prt*
  degonigaazod
dagonige *vai* mix things in; *1sg* indagonige; *prt*
  degoniged
dagoshim *vta* arrive with s.o., get s.o. to
  destination; *1sg* indagoshimaa; *prt*
  degoshimaad
dagoshin *vai* arrive; *1sg* indagoshin; *prt* degoshing
dagoshinoomagad *vii* arrive; *prt*
  degoshinoomagak
dagoz /dagozw-/ *vta* cook s.o. with something else;
  1sg indagozwaa; *prt* degozwaad
dagozan *vti* cook s.t. with something else; *1sg*
  indagozaan; *prt* degozang
dagozo *vai* be cooked with something else; *1sg*
  indagoz; *prt* degozod
dagwagim *vta* count s.o. in; *1sg* indagwagimaa;
  prt degwagimaad
dagwagindan *vti* count s.t. in; *1sg*
  indagwagindaan; *prt* degwagindang
dagwaginde *vii* be included, be counted in; *prt*
  degwagindeg; *aug* dagwagindemagad; *prt aug*
  degwagindemagak
dagwaginzo *vai* be included, be counted in; *1sg*
  indagwaginz; *prt* degwaginzod
dagwaagin /dagwaagi-/ *vii* be fall, be autumn; *prt*
  degwaagig
dagwaagishi *vai* spend the fall somewhere; *1sg*
  indagwaagish; *prt* degwaagishid
dagwaagong *pc* last fall, last autumn
dakaji *vai* get a chill, have a cold; *1sg* indakaj; *prt*
  dekajid
dakamanji'o *vai* be chilled, feel cold; *1sg*
  indakamanji'; *prt* dekamanji'od
dakate *vii* be cold (as a house or room); *prt*
  dekateg; *aug* dakatemagad; *prt aug*
  dekatemagak
dakaa *vii* be cool (of a thing); *prt* dekaag; *aug*
  dakaamagad; *prt aug* dekaamagak
dakaagamin /dakaagami-/ *vii* be cold (as a liquid);
  prt dekaagamig
dakaagamisin *vii* cool off (as a liquid); *prt*
  dekaagamising
dakaanimad *vii* be a cold wind; *prt* dekaanimak
dakaashi *vai* be cooled by the wind; *prt* dekaashid
dakaasin *vii* be cooled by the wind; *prt* dekaasing
dakaayaa *vii* be cool (weather); *prt* dekaayaag;
  aug dakaayaamagad; *prt aug*
  dekaayaamagak; *also* daki-ayaa
dakib *ni* cold water

dakibiisaa *vii* be cold rain; *prt* **dekibiisaag**; *aug* **dakibiisaamagad**; *prt aug* **dekibiisaamagak**
dakininjii *vai* have a cold hand; *1sg* **indakininjii**; *prt* **dekininjiid**
dakise *vai* cool; *prt* **dekised**
dakise *vii* cool; *prt* **dekiseg**; *aug* **dakisemagad**; *prt aug* **dekisemagak**
dakishim *vta* set s.o. to cool; *1sg* **indakishimaa**; *prt* **dekishimaad**
dakishin *vai* cool off; *prt* **dekishing**
dakisidoon *vti2* set s.t. to cool; *1sg* **indakisidoon**; *prt* **dekisidood**
dakisijigan *ni* refrigerator, freezer; *pl* **dakisijiganan**; *loc* **dakisijiganing**; *dim* **dakisijigaans**
dakisin *vii* cool off; *prt* **dekising**
dakizi *vai* be cool (of a thing); *prt* **dekizid**
dakobide *vii* be tied, be bound; *prt* **dekobideg**; *aug* **dakobidemagad**; *prt aug* **dekobidemagak**
dakobidoo *vai* tie wild rice; *1sg* **indakobidoo**; *prt* **dekobidood**
dakobidoon *vti2* tie s.t., bind s.t.; *1sg* **indakobidoon**; *prt* **dekobidood**
dakobijigan *ni* tied wild rice
dakobijige *vai* tie things, bind things; *1sg* **indakobijige**; *prt* **dekobijiged**
dakobinaawaso *vai* have a baby in a cradle board; *1sg* **indakobinaawaso**; *prt* **dekobinaawasod**
dakobinaawaswaan *na* baby in a cradle board; *pl* **dakobinaawaswaanag**; *dim* **dakobinaawaswaanens**
dakobizh /**dakobiN-**/ *vta* tie s.o., bind s.o.; *1sg* **indakobinaa**; *prt* **dekobinaad**
dakobizo *vai* be tied, be bound, be in a cradle board; *1sg* **indakobiz**; *prt* **dekobizod**
dakokaadan *vti* step on s.t.; *1sg* **indakokaadaan**; *prt* **dekokaadang**
dakokaazh /**dakokaaN-**/ *vta* step on s.o.; *1sg* **indakokaanaa**; *prt* **dekokaanaad**
dakokii *vai* step; *1sg* **indakokii**; *prt* **dekokiid**
dakon *vta* hold s.o., take hold of s.o., arrest s.o.; *1sg* **indakonaa**; *prt* **dekonaad**
dakonamaw *vta* hold (s.t.) for s.o.; *1sg* **indakonamawaa**; *prt* **dekonamawaad**
dakonan *vti* hold s.t., take hold of s.t.; *1sg* **indakonaan**; *prt* **dekonang**
dakoniwe *vai* arrest people; *1sg* **indakoniwe**; *prt* **dekoniwed**
dakoniwewidaabaan *na* police car; *pl* **dakoniwewidaabaanag**; *loc* **dakoniwewidaabaaning**; *dim* **dakoniwewidaabaanens**
dakoniwewigamig *ni* police station; *pl* **dakoniwewigamigoon**; *loc* **dakoniwewigamigong**
dakoniwewinini *na* sheriff, policeman; *pl* **dakoniwewininiwag**
dakoonagad *vii* be short (as a boat); *prt* **dekoonagak**
dakoozi *vai* be short; *1sg* **indakooz**; *prt* **dekoozid**
dakwam *vta* bite s.o.; *1sg* **indakwamaa**; *prt* **dekwamaad**
dakwandan *vti* bite s.t.; *1sg* **indakwandaan**; *prt* **dekwandang**
dakwange *vai* bite people; *1sg* **indakwange**; *prt* **dekwanged**

dakwanjigan *ni* pliers; *pl* **dakwanjiganan**; *loc* **dakwanjiganing**; *dim* **dakwanjigaans**
dakwanjige *vai* bite things; *1sg* **indakwanjige**; *prt* **dekwanjiged**
dakwaa *vii* be short; *prt* **dekwaag**; *aug* **dakwaamagad**; *prt aug* **dekwaamagak**
dakwaabikad *vii* be short (as something mineral); *prt* **dekwaabikak**
dakwaabikizi *vai* be short (as something mineral); *prt* **dekwaabikizid**
dakwaabiigad *vii* be short (as something string-like); *prt* **dekwaabiigak**
dakwaabiigizh /**dakwaabiigizhw-**/ *vta* cut s.o. short (as something string-like); *1sg* **indakwaabiigizhwaa**; *prt* **dekwaabiigizhwaad**
dakwaabiigizhan *vti* cut s.t. short (as something string-like); *1sg* **indakwaabiigizhaan**; *prt* **dekwaabiigizhang**
dakwaabiigizi *vai* be short (as something string-like); *prt* **dekwaabiigizid**
dakwaakozi *vai* be short (as something stick- or wood-like); *prt* **dekwaakozid**
dakwaakwad *vii* be short (as something stick- or wood-like); *prt* **dekwaakwak**
dakwegad *vii* be short (as something sheet-like); *prt* **dekwegak**
dakwegizi *vai* be short (as something sheet-like); *prt* **dekwegizid**
danakamigad *vii* take place in a certain place, happen in a certain place; *prt* **endanakamigak**
danakamigizi *vai* have an event in a certain place, play in a certain place; *1sg* **indanakamigiz**; *prt* **endanakamigizid**
danakii *vai* live in a certain place; *1sg* **indanakii**; *prt* **endanakiid**
dananjige *vai* eat in a certain place; *1sg* **indananjige**; *prt* **endananjiged**
dananokii *vai* work in a certain place; *1sg* **indananokii**; *prt* **endanokiid**
danaadodan *vti* tell of s.t. in a certain place; *1sg* **indanaadodaan**; *prt* **endanaadodang**
danaajim *vta* tell of s.o. in a certain place; *1sg* **indanaajimaa**; *prt* **endanaajimaad**
danendan *vti* think s.t. to be in a certain place, expect s.t. to be in a certain place; *1sg* **indanendaan**; *prt* **endanendang**
danenim *vta* think s.o. to be in a certain place, expect s.o. to be in a certain place; *1sg* **indanenimaa**; *prt* **endanenimaad**
danens *na* club suite card; *pl* **danensag**
dangishkan *vti* kick s.t.; *1sg* **indangishkaan**; *prt* **dengishkang**
dangishkaw *vta* kick s.o.; *1sg* **indangishkawaa**; *prt* **dengishkawaad**
dangishkaage *vai* kick people; *1sg* **indangishkaage**; *prt* **dengishkaaged**
dangishkige *vai* kick things; *1sg* **indangishkige**; *prt* **dengishkiged**
dani *vai* be rich; *1sg* **indan**; *prt* **denid**
danitan *vti* hear s.t. in a certain place; *1sg* **indanitaan**; *prt* **endanitang**
danitaw *vta* hear s.o. in a certain place; *1sg* **indanitawaa**; *prt* **endanitawaad**
danitaagozi *vai* be heard in a certain place; *1sg* **indanitaagoz**; *prt* **endanitaagozid**

danitaagwad *vii* be heard in a certain place; *prt* **endanitaagwak**

daniwin *ni* wealth, riches, property, belongings; *pl* **daniwinan**; *loc* **daniwining**; *dim* **daniwinens**

danwewe *vii* there is noise in a certain place; *prt* **endanweweg**; *aug* **danwewemagad**; *prt aug* **endanwewemagak**

danwewidam *vai2* be heard speaking in a certain place; *1sg* **indanwewidam**; *prt* **endanwewidang**

dapaabam *vta* peek through an opening at s.o., look through a window at s.o.; *1sg* **indapaabamaa**; *prt* **depaabamaad**

dapaabandan *vti* peek through an opening at s.t., look through a window at s.t.; *1sg* **indapaabandaan**; *prt* **depaabandang**

dapaabi *vai* peek through an opening, look through a window; *1sg* **indapaab**; *prt* **depaabid**

dapine *vai* suffer in a certain place, die in a certain place; *1sg* **indapine**; *prt* **endapined**

dash *pc* and; *also* **idash, -sh**

dashiwag /dashi-/ *vai* they are a certain number, they are so many; *1pl* **indashimin**; *prt* **endashijig**

dasing *pc* a certain number of times, so many times

dasinoon /dasin-/ *vii* they are a certain number, they are so many; *prt* **endasingin**

daso- *pv3* a certain number, so many, every

daso-anama'e-giizhik *pc* a certain number of weeks, so many weeks

daso-anama'e-giizhikwagad *vii* be a certain number of weeks, be so many weeks; *prt* **endaso-anama'e-giizhikwagad**; *also* **daswanama'e-giizhikwagad**

daso-biboon *pc* a certain number of years, so many years

daso-biboonagad *vii* be a certain number of years, be so many years; *prt* **endaso-biboonagak**

daso-biboonagizi *vai* be a certain number of years old; *1sg* **indaso-biboonagiz**; *prt* **endaso-biboonagizid**

daso-diba'igan *pc* a certain number of hours, so many hours, a certain number of miles, so many miles

daso-diba'iganed *vii* be a certain hour, be a certain time in hours; *prt* **endaso-diba'iganek**

daso-diba'igaans *pc* a certain number of minutes, a certain number of acres, so many minutes, so many acres

daso-diba'iminaan *pc* a certain number of bushels, so many bushels

daso-dibaabiishkoojigan *pc* a certain number of pounds, so many pounds

daso-dibik *pc* a certain number of nights, so many nights

daso-gikinoonowin *pc* a certain number of years, so many years

daso-giizhigad *vii* be a certain date; *prt* **endaso-giizhigak**

daso-giizhik *pc* a certain number of days, so many days

daso-giizis *pc* a certain number of months, so many months

dasogon *pc* a certain number of days, so many days

dasogonagad *vii* be a certain number of days, be so many days; *prt* **endasogonagak**

dasogonagizi *vai* be a certain day of the month, be a certain number of days old; *prt* **endasogonagizid**

dasogonendi *vai* be gone a certain number of days, be absent a certain number of days; *1sg* **indasogonend**; *prt* **endasogonendid**

dasonaagaans *pc* a certain number of cupfuls, so many cupfuls

dasoninj *pc* a certain number of inches, so many inches

dasosagoons *nm* a certain number of thousands, so many thousand

dasozid *pc* a certain number of feet, so many feet

dasoonaagan *ni* trap; *pl* **dasoonaaganan**; *loc* **dasoonaaganing**; *dim* **dasoonaagaans**

dasooshkin *pc* certain number of bags, so many bags

dasoozh /dasooN-/ *vta* trap s.o.; *1sg* **indasoonaa**; *prt* **desoonaad**

dasoozo *vai* be trapped, be pinned down; *1sg* **indasooz**; *prt* **desoozod**

daswaabik *pc* a certain number of dollars, so many dollars

daswewaan *pc* a certain number of sets, so many sets, a certain number of pairs, so many pairs

daswi *nm* a certain number, so many

datak= < **dak=**

datakw= < **dakw=**

datang= < **dang=**

datap= < **dap=**

dawaa *vii* be space, be room; *prt* **dewaamagak**; *aug* **dawaamagad**; *prt aug* **dewaamagak**

dawibidoon *vti2* pull s.t. apart to form a gap; *1sg* **indawibidoon**; *prt* **dewibidood**

dawibijige *vai* pull things apart to form a gap; *1sg* **indawibijige**; *prt* **dewibijiged**

dawibizh /dawibiN-/ *vta* pull s.o. apart to form a gap; *1sg* **indawibinaa**; *prt* **dewibinaad**

dazhi- *pv3* in a certain place, of a certain place, there

dazhim *vta* talk about s.o., gossip about s.o.; *1sg* **indazhimaa**; *prt* **endazhimaad**

dazhindan *vti* talk about s.t., gossip about s.t.; *1sg* **indazhindaan**; *prt* **endazhindang**

dazhinge *vai* talk about people, gossip; *1sg* **indazhinge**; *prt* **endazhinged**

dazhishimo *vai* dance in a certain place; *1sg* **indazhishim**; *prt* **endazhishimod**

dazhishin *vai* lie in a certain place, be buried in a certain place; *1sg* **indazhishin**; *prt* **endazhishing**

dazhisin *vii* lie in a certain place; *prt* **endazhising**

dazhitaa *vai* spend time in a certain place, play in a certain place; *1sg* **indazhitaa**; *prt* **endazhitaad**

dazhiikan *vti* work on s.t., be involved with s.t.; *1sg* **indazhiikaan**; *prt* **endazhiikang**

dazhiikaw *vta* work on s.o., be involved with s.o.; *1sg* **indazhiikawaa**; *prt* **endazhiikawaad**

dazhiike *vai* stay in a certain place, spend time in a certain place; *1sg* **indazhiike**; *prt* **endazhiiked**

dazhiikigaade *vii* be worked on; *prt* **endazhiikigaadeg;** *aug* **dazhiikigaademagad;** *prt aug* **endazhiikigaademagak**
daa *vai* live in a certain place; *1sg* **indaa;** *prt* **endaad**
daa- *pv1* would *modal,* could *modal,* should *modal,* can *modal,* might *modal*
daadwaa= < **dwaa=**
daangam *vta* taste a sample of s.o.; *1sg* **indaangamaa;** *prt* **dayaangamaad**
daangandan *vti* taste a sample of s.t.; *1sg* **indaangandaan;** *prt* **dayaangandang**
daangigwanenan *vti* sign s.t.; *1sg* **indaangigwanenaan;** *prt* **dayaangigwanenang**
daangigwanenige *vai* sign things; *1sg* **indaangigwanenige;** *prt* **dayaangigwaneniged**
daangin *vta* touch s.o. with hand; *1sg* **indaanginaa;** *prt* **dayaanginaad**
daanginan *vti* touch s.t. with hand; *1sg* **indaanginaan;** *prt* **dayaanginang**
daangishim *vta* put s.o. touching; *1sg* **indaangishimaa;** *prt* **dayaangishimaad**
daangishin *vai* lie touching; *1sg* **indaangishin;** *prt* **dayaangishing**
daangisidoon *vti2* put s.t. touching; *1sg* **indaangisidoon;** *prt* **dayaangisidood**
daangisin *vii* lie touching; *prt* **dayaangising**
daashkaa *vii* be split, be torn apart; *prt* **dayaashkaag;** *aug* **daashkaamagad;** *prt aug* **dayaashkaamagak**
daashkibidoon *vti2* split s.t. lengthwise with hands, tear s.t. apart; *1sg* **indaashkibidoon;** *prt* **dayaashkibidood**
daashkibizh /**daashkibiN-**/ *vta* split s.o. lengthwise with hands, tear s.o. apart; *1sg* **indaashkibinaa;** *prt* **dayaashkibinaad**
daashkiboodoon *vti2* saw s.t. apart lengthwise; *1sg* **indaashkiboodoon;** *prt* **dayaashkiboodood**
daashkiboojigan *na* saw mill, ripsaw; *pl* **daashkiboojiganag;** *loc* **daashkiboojiganing;** *dim* **daashkiboojigaans**
daashkiboojige *vai* saw things apart lengthwise; *1sg* **indaashkiboojige;** *prt* **dayaashkiboojiged**
daashkiboozh /**daashkibooN-**/ *vta* saw s.o. apart lengthwise; *1sg* **indaashkiboonaa;** *prt* **dayaashkiboonaad**
daashkiga' /**daashkiga'w-**/ *vta* split s.o. by chopping (as something of wood); *1sg* **indaashkiga'waa;** *prt* **dayaashkiga'waad**
daashkiga'an *vti* split s.t. by chopping (as something of wood); *1sg* **indaashkiga'aan;** *prt* **dayaashkiga'ang**
daashkiga'ige *vai* split wood; *1sg* **indaashkiga'ige;** *prt* **dayaashkiga'iged**
daashkiga'ise *vai* split firewood; *1sg* **indaashkiga'ise;** *prt* **dayaashkiga'ised**
daashkigishkaa *vai* split (as something of wood); *prt* **dayaashkigishkaad**
daashkigishkaa *vii* split (as something of wood); *prt* **dayaashkigishkaag;** *aug* **daashkigishkaamagad;** *prt aug* **dayaashkigishkaamagak**
daashkikaa *vii* split apart, crack apart; *prt* **dayaashkikaag;** *aug* **daashkikaamagad;** *prt aug* **dayaashkikaamagak**

daashkikwadin *vii* there is a crack in the ice; *prt* **dayaashkikwading**
daashkizh /**daashkizhw-**/ *vta* split s.o. by cutting; *1sg* **indaashkizhwaa;** *prt* **dayaashkizhwaad**
daashkizhan *vti* split s.t. by cutting; *1sg* **indaashkizhaan;** *prt* **dayaashkizhang**
daataagwa'igan *ni* rolled oats, oatmeal; *pl* **daataagwa'iganan;** *loc* **daataagwa'iganing;** *dim* **daataagwa'igaans**
daataang= < **daang=**
daataaw= < **daaw=**
daawani *vai* open one's mouth; *1sg* **indaawan;** *prt* **dayaawanid**
de- *pv4* sufficient, suitable, enough
deba'ookii *vai* have enough to give away; *1sg* **indeba'ookii;** *prt* **dayeba'ookiid**
deba'oozh /**deba'ooN-**/ *vta* have enough to give to or feed s.o.; *1sg* **indeba'oonaa;** *prt* **dayeba'oonaad**
debakii'ige *vai* determine the depth; *1sg* **indebakii'ige;** *prt* **dayebakii'iged**
debashkine *vai* fit, adequately hold; *prt* **dayebashkined**
debashkine *vii* fit, adequately hold; *prt* **dayebashkineg;** *aug* **debashkinemagad;** *prt aug* **dayebashkinemagak**
debaabam *vta* have s.o. in sight, see s.o. at a distance; *1sg* **indebaabamaa;** *prt* **dayebaabamaad**
debaabaminaagozi *vai* be in sight, be visible at a distance; *1sg* **indebaabaminaagoz;** *prt* **dayebaabaminaagozid**
debaabaminaagwad *vii* be in sight, be visible at a distance; *prt* **dayebaabaminaagwak**
debaabandan *vti* have s.t. in sight, see s.t. at a distance; *1sg* **indebaabandaan;** *prt* **dayebaabandang**
debibidaw *vta* grab (s.t.) for s.o., catch (s.t.) for s.o., get hold of (s.t.) for s.o.; *1sg* **indebibidawaa;** *prt* **dayebibidawaad**
debibidoon *vti2* grab s.t., catch s.t., get hold of s.t.; *1sg* **indebibidoon;** *prt* **dayebibidood**
debibizh /**debibiN-**/ *vta* grab s.o., catch s.o., get hold of s.o.; *1sg* **indebibinaa;** *prt* **dayebibinaad**
debibii *vii* fit (as something liquid), adequately hold (something liquid); *prt* **dayebibiig;** *aug* **debibiimagad;** *prt aug* **dayebibiimagak**
debi' *vta* satisfy s.o., benefit s.o., give s.o. something appropriate; *1sg* **indebi'aa;** *prt* **dayebi'aad**
debinaak *pc* badly, carelessly, any old way
debisachige *vai* have enough of things; *1sg* **indebisachige;** *prt* **dayebisachiged**
debisa' *vta* have enough of s.o.; *1sg* **indebisa'aa;** *prt* **dayebisa'aad**
debisatoon *vti2* have enough of s.t.; *1sg* **indebisatoon;** *prt* **dayebisatood**
debise *vai* be enough, be sufficient; *prt* **dayebised**
debise *vii* be enough, be sufficient; *prt* **dayebiseg;** *aug* **debisemagad;** *prt aug* **dayebisemagak**
debisewendam *vai2* feel satisfied, think there is enough; *1sg* **indebisewendam;** *prt* **dayebisewendang**
debishkan *vti* fit s.t. with foot or body; *1sg* **indebishkaan;** *prt* **dayebishkang**

debishkaw *vta* fit s.o. with foot or body; *1sg* indebishkawaa; *prt* dayebishkawaad

debisinii *vai* eat enough, be full (after eating); *1sg* indebisinii; *prt* dayebisiniid

debizi *vai* be satisfied, be lucky, have enough; *1sg* indebiz; *prt* dayebizid

debwe *vai* tell the truth; *1sg* indebwe; *prt* dayebwed

debwetam *vai2* believe, agree; *1sg* indebwetam; *prt* dayebwetang

debwetan *vti* believe s.t.; *1sg* indebwetaan; *prt* dayebwetang

debwetaw *vta* believe s.o., agree with s.o., obey s.o.; *1sg* indebwetawaa; *prt* dayebwetawaad

debwetaagozi *vai* be believable, be believed; *1sg* indebwetaagoz; *prt* dayebwetaagozid

debwetaagwad *vii* be believable, be believed; *prt* dayebwetaagwak

debwewidam *vai2* be heard speaking at a distance; *1sg* indebwewidam; *prt* dayebwewidang

debweyendam *vai2* believe; *1sg* indebweyendam; *prt* dayebweyendang

debweyendan *vti* believe in s.t.; *1sg* indebweyendaan; *prt* dayebweyendang

debweyenim *vta* believe in s.o.; *1sg* indebweyenimaa; *prt* dayebweyenimaad

dekaag *ni-pt* ice cream

de-miijin *vti3* eat enough of s.t.; *1sg* inde-miijin; *prt* daye-miijid

desabi *vai* sit astride; *1sg* indesab; *prt* dayesabid

desa'an *vti* prop s.t. up to be a level surface; *1sg* indesa'aan; *prt* dayesa'ang

desa'on *ni* platform, bench, bed (in wigwam); *pl* desa'onan; *loc* desa'oning; *dim* desa'onens

desaa *vii* be a level surface; *prt* dayesaag; *aug* desaamagad; *prt aug* dayesaamagak

desaabaan *ni* shelf; *pl* desaabaanan; *loc* desaabaaning; *dim* desaabaanens

desinaagan *ni* dinner plate; *pl* desinaaganan; *loc* desinaaganing; *dim* desinaagaans

desinaagaans *ni* saucer; *pl* desinaagaansan; *loc* desinaagaansing

deteba'agonjichigan *ni* bobber, float; *pl* deteba'agonjichiganan; *loc* deteba'agonjichiganing; *dim* deteba'agonjichigaans

detibised *na-pt* wheel; *pl* detibisejig

detiwe *pc* man's exclamation at making a small mistake

dewaabide *vai* have a toothache; *1sg* indewaabide; *prt* dayewaabided

dewaawigan *vai* have a backache; *1sg* indewaawigan; *prt* dayewaawigang

dewe'igan *na* drum; *pl* dewe'iganag; *loc* dewe'iganing; *dim* dewe'igaans

dewe'iganaak *na* drumstick; *pl* dewe'iganaakoon; *loc* dewe'iganaakong; *dim* dewe'iganaakoons; *also* dewe'iganaatig

dewigaade *vai* have an ache in one's leg; *1sg* indewigaade; *prt* dayewigaaded

dewikwe *vai* have a headache; *1sg* indewikwe; *prt* dayewikwed

dewikwe-mashkikiins *ni* aspirin; *pl* dewikwe-mashkikiinsan; *loc* dewikwe-mashkikiinsing

dewikwese *vai* get a sudden headache; *1sg* indewikwese; *prt* dayewikwesed

dewinike *vai* have an ache in one's arm; *1sg* indewinike; *prt* dayewiniked

dewininjii *vai* have an ache in one's hand; *1sg* indewininjii; *prt* dayewininjiid

dewipikwan *vai* have a backache; *1sg* indewipikwan; *prt* dayewipikwang

dewizi *vai* ache; *1sg* indewiz; *prt* dayewizid

dewizide *vai* have an ache in one's foot; *1sg* indewizide; *prt* dayewizided

di- *vai* be in a certain condition, have a certain thing the matter *used primarily in the conjunct*; *prt* endid

diba' /diba'w-/ *vta* pay for s.o., bail s.o. out; *1sg* indiba'waa; *prt* deba'waad

diba'akii *vai* survey land; *1sg* indiba'akii; *prt* deba'akiid

diba'akiiwinini *na* surveyor; *pl* diba'akiiwininiwag

diba'amaw *vta* pay s.o. for (s.t.), pay (s.t.) to s.o.; *1sg* indiba'amawaa; *prt* deba'amawaad

diba'amaadiwag /diba'amaadi-/ *vai* they pay each other for (s.t.); *1pl* indiba'amaadimin; *prt* deba'amaadijig

diba'amaage *vai* pay people for (s.t.); *1sg* indiba'amaage; *prt* deba'amaaged

diba'an *vti* pay for s.t.; *1sg* indiba'aan; *prt* deba'ang

diba'aatigwaan *ni* yardstick, measuring stick for timber; *pl* diba'aatigwaanan

diba'aatigwe *vai* scale timber; *1sg* indiba'aatigwe; *prt* deba'aatigwed

diba'ige *vai* pay things, measure things; *1sg* indiba'ige; *prt* deba'iged

diba'igese *vii* pay off, pay for itself; *prt* deba'igeseg; *aug* diba'igesemagad; *prt aug* deba'igesemagak

diba'igiiziswaan *na* clock; *pl* diba'igiiziswaanag; *loc* diba'igiiziswaaning; *dim* diba'igiiziswaanens

diba'igiiziswaanens *na* watch; *pl* diba'igiiziswaanensag; *loc* diba'igiiziswaanensing

dewe'igan (drum), dewe'iganaak (drumstick)

dibaabam *vta* inspect s.o., look s.o. over, check up on s.o.; *1sg* **indibaabamaa**; *prt* **debaabamaad**
dibaabandan *vti* inspect s.t., look s.t. over; *1sg* **indibaabandaan**; *prt* **debaabandang**
dibaabiigin *vta* measure s.o. (as with something string-like); *1sg* **indibaabiiginaa**; *prt* **debaabiiginaad**
dibaabiiginan *vti* measure s.t. (as with something string-like); *1sg* **indibaabiiginaan**; *prt* **debaabiiginang**
dibaabiishkoodoon *vti2* weigh s.t.; *1sg* **indibaabiishkoodoon**; *prt* **debaabiishkoodood**
dibaabiishkoojigan *ni* scale; *pl* **dibaabiishkoojiganan**; *loc* **dibaabiishkoojiganing**; *dim* **dibaabiishkoojigaans**
dibaabiishkoojige *vai* weigh things; *1sg* **indibaabiishkoojige**; *prt* **debaabiishkoojiged**
dibaabiishkoozh /**dibaabiishkooN-**/ *vta* weigh s.o.; *1sg* **indibaabiishkoonaa**; *prt* **debaabiishkoonaad**
dibaadodan *vti* tell of s.t.; *1sg* **indibaadodaan**; *prt* **debaadodang**
dibaajim *vta* tell of s.o.; *1sg* **indibaajimaa**; *prt* **debaajimaad**
dibaajimo *vai* tell, narrate; *1sg* **indibaajim**; *prt* **debaajimod**
dibaajimotaw *vta* tell (s.t.) to s.o., narrate (s.t.) to s.o.; *1sg* **indibaajimotawaa**; *prt* **debaajimotawaad**
dibaajimowin *ni* story, narrative; *pl* **dibaajimowinan**; *dim* **dibaajimowinens**
dibaakon *vta* judge s.o.; *1sg* **indibaakonaa**; *prt* **debaakonaad**
dibaakonan *vti* judge s.t.; *1sg* **indibaakonaan**; *prt* **debaakonang**
dibaakonigaade *vai* be a court matter; *1sg* **indibaakonigaade**; *prt* **debaakonigaaded**
dibaakonigaazo *vai* be judged, be sentenced; *prt* **debaakonigaazod**
dibaakonige *vai* judge things, be in politics; *1sg* **indibaakonige**; *prt* **debaakoniged**
dibaakonigewigamig *ni* courthouse; *pl* **dibaakonigewigamigoon**; *loc* **dibaakonigewigamigong**
dibaakonigewinini *na* judge, lawyer; *pl* **dibaakonigewininiwag**
dibendan *vti* control s.t., be the master of s.t., own s.t., earn s.t.; *1sg* **indibendaan**; *prt* **debendang**
dibendaagozi *vai* be controlled, be owned, belong, be a member; *1sg* **indibendaagoz**; *prt* **debendaagozid**
dibendaagwad *vii* be controlled, be owned, belong; *prt* **debendaagwak**
dibendaaso *vai* own for oneself; *1sg* **indibendaas**; *prt* **debendaasod**
dibenim *vta* control s.o., own s.o., be the master of s.o.; *1sg* **indibenimaa**; *prt* **debenimaad**
dibenindizo *vai* be independent, be one's own master; *1sg* **indibenindiz**; *prt* **debenindizod**
dibenjigaade *vii* be owned; *prt* **debenjigaadeg**; *aug* **dibenjigaademagad**; *prt aug* **debenjigaademagak**

dibenjigaazo *vai* be owned, be an initiated member; *prt* **debenjigaazod**
dibi *pc* I don't know where, I wonder where *dubitative*
dibi go *pc* wherever, anywhere *dubitative*
dibi' *vta* keep up even with s.o.; *1sg* **indibi'aa**; *prt* **debi'aad**
dibikad *vii* be night; *prt* **debikak**
dibikate *vii* be dark (as in a room or house); *prt* **debikateg**; *aug* **dibikatemagad**; *prt aug* **debikatemagak**
dibikaabaminaagwad *vii* be twilight; *prt* **debikaabaminaagwak**
dibik-giizis *na* moon; *pl* **dibik-giizisoog**; *also* **dibiki-giizis**
dibiki-ayaa *vai* be dark; *prt* **debiki-ayaad**
dibikong *pc* last night
dibinawe *pc* by oneself, inherently
dibishkaa *vai* have a birthday; *1sg* **indibishkaa**; *prt* **debishkaad**
dibishkoo *pc* just like, even, equal, direct
dibishkookamig *pc* right across, opposite
dibibide *vii* roll; *prt* **dedibibideg**; *aug* **didibibidemagad**; *prt aug* **dedibibidemagak**
dibibizo *vai* roll; *1sg* **indidibibiz**; *prt* **dedibibizod**
dibibin *vta* roll s.o.; *1sg* **indidibinaa**; *prt* **dedibinaad**
dibibinan *vti* roll s.t.; *1sg* **indidibinaan**; *prt* **dedibinang**
didibininjiibizon *na* ring; *pl* **didibininjiibizonag**; *loc* **didibininjiibizong**; *dim* **didibininjiibizonens**
didibise-apabiwin *ni* rocking chair; *pl* **didibise-apabiwinan**; *loc* **didibise-apabiwining**; *dim* **didibise-apabiwinens**
digow *na* wave; *pl* **digowag**; *also* **digo**
dikinaagan *ni* cradle board; *pl* **dikinaaganan**; *loc* **dikinaaganing**; *dim* **dikinaagaans**
dikineyaab *ni* cradle board wrapper; *pl* **dikineyaabiin**; *loc* **dikineyaabiing**; *dim* **dikineyaabiins**
dimii *vii* be deep (of a body of water); *prt* **demiig**; *aug* **dimiimagad**; *prt aug* **demiimagak**
dino *pc* sort inanimate, kind inanimate; *also* **dinowa**
dino *pc* sort animate, kind animate; *also* **dinowa**
ditibide *vii* roll along; *prt* **detibibideg**; *aug* **ditibibidemagad**; *prt aug* **detibibidemagak**
ditibidaaban *na* wagon, truck; *pl* **ditibidaabaanag**; *loc* **ditibidaabaaning**; *dim* **ditibidaabaanens**
ditibise *vai* roll, go around (e.g., a wheel); *prt* **detibised**
ditibise *vii* roll, go around; *prt* **detibiseg**; *aug* **ditibisemagad**; *prt aug* **detibisemagak**
ditibiwebishkigan *na* bicycle; *pl* **ditibiwebishkiganag**; *loc* **ditibiwebishkiganing**; *dim* **ditibiwebishkiganens**
ditibiwebishkige *vai* pedal, roll things along by kicking; *1sg* **inditibiwebishkige**; *prt* **detibiwebishkiged**
diindiisi *na* blue jay; *pl* **diindiisiwag**; *dim* **diindiisiins**
diitiba'an *vti* knock s.t. down off using something; *1sg* **indiitiba'aan**; *prt* **daatiba'ang**

diitiba' /diitiba'w-/ *vta* knock s.o. down off using something; *1sg* **indiitiba'waa;** *prt* **daatiba'waad**

diitibibidoon *vti2* knock s.t. down off something with hands; *1sg* **indiitibibidoon;** *prt* **daatibibidood**

diitibibizh /diitibibiN-/ *vta* knock s.o. down off something with hands; *1sg* **indiitibibinaa;** *prt* **daatibibinaad**

diitibishkan *vti* bump s.t. down off, knock s.t. down off something with foot or body; *1sg* **indiitibishkaan;** *prt* **daatibishkang**

diitibishkaw *vta* bump s.o. down off, knock s.o. down off something with foot or body; *1sg* **indiitibishkawaa;** *prt* **daatibishkawaad**

doodam *vai2* do something; *1sg* **indoodam;** *prt* **endoodang**

doodan *vti* do something to s.t.; *1sg* **indoodaan;** *prt* **endoodang**

doodaw *vta* do something to s.o.; *1sg* **indoodawaa;** *prt* **endoodawaad**

doodaadiwag /doodaadi-/ *vai* they do something to each other; *1pl* **indoodaadimin;** *prt* **endoodaadijig**

doodaadizo *vai* do something to oneself; *1sg* **indoodaadiz;** *prt* **endoodaadizod**

doodaazo *vai* do something to oneself; *1sg* **indoodaaz;** *prt* **endoodaazod**

doodooshaaboo *ni* milk; *loc* **doodooshaaboong**

doodooshaaboo-bimide *ni* butter; *loc* **doodooshaaboo-bimideng**

doonoo *na* bull; *pl* **doonoog**

dooskaabi *vai* open one's eyes; *1sg* **indooskaab;** *prt* **dwaaskaabid**

dootooban *vii* be springy ground; *prt* **dwaatoobang**

dwaa'ibaan *ni* hole made in the ice for water; *pl* **dwaa'ibaanan;** *loc* **dwaa'ibaaning;** *also* **dwaa'igan**

dwaa'ibii *vai* make a water hole in the ice; *1sg* **indwaa'ibii;** *prt* **dwayaa'ibiid;** *also* **dwaa'ige**

dwaa'ige *vai* make a hole in the ice; *1sg* **indwaa'ige;** *prt* **dwayaa'iged**

dwaashin *vai* fall through the ice; *1sg* **indwaashin;** *prt* **dwayaashing**

emikwaan *ni* spoon, ladle; *pl* **emikwaanan;** *dim* **emikwaanens**

emikwaanens *ni* spoon, teaspoon; *pl* **emikwaanensan;** *loc* **emikwaanensing**

enange *pc* sure! you bet!

enda- *pv4* just, real, very *nonitially:* **wenda-**

endaso- *pv3* so many, every: *changed form of:* **daso-**
endaso-dibik *pc* every night
endaso-gigizheb *pc* every morning
endaso-giizhik *pc* every day
endaso-giizis *pc* every month

endazhi- *pv3* in a certain place: *changed form of* **dazhi-**
endazhi-ataading *ni-pt* casino
endazhi-booniimagak *ni-pt* airport; *pl* **endazhi-booniimagakin**

endaad *vai* his/her home: *changed form of:* **daa**

endogwen *pc* I don't know, I am not sure

en' *pc* yes

eni- *pv2* going away from the speaker, coming up to in time *changed form of* **ani-**

enigok *pc* with effort, harder

enigoons *na* ant; *pl* **enigoonsag;** *also* **enig**

eniwek *pc* somewhat, a little bit, just so, middling

enyan' *pc* yes; *also* **en', eya'**

es *na* clam, shell; *pl* **esag**

eshkam *pc* gradually, more and more, less and less

eshkan *na* horn (of an animal); *pl* **eshkanag**

eshkan *ni* ice chisel; *pl* **eshkanan**

eshkandaming *ni-pt* watermelon; *pl* **eshkandamingin**

eshkwaa *pc* while

eshpabid *na-pt* leader, chairman; *pl* **eshpabijig**

esiban *na* raccoon; *pl* **esibanag;** *dim* **esibanens**

eta *pc* only

eya' *pc* yes

eyiishwaaswi *nm* eight each; *also* **nenishwaaswi***

eyiidawayi'ii *pc* on both sides of it

eyiidawininj *pc* at both hands

eyiizh *pc* both

ezhi- *pv3* in a certain way, to a certain place, thus, so, there *changed form of* **izhi-**

ezhininjiishin *vai* leave a handprint; *1sg* **indezhininjiishin;** *prt* **ayezhininjiishing**

ezhishin *vai* leave a mark; *1sg* **indezhishin;** *prt* **ayezhishing**

ezhisin *vii* leave a mark; *prt* **ezhising**

ezigaa *na* wood tick; *pl* **ezigaag;** *dim* **ezigaans**

E

edawayi'ii *pc* on both sides of it

edawi-zaka'o *vai* use crutches; *1sg* **indedawi-zaka';** *prt* **ayedawi-zaka'od**

edawi-zaka'on *ni* crutch; *pl* **edawi-zaka'onan;** *dim* **edawi-zaka'onens**

eko- *pv3* since, a certain length, as long as (in time): *changed form of* **ako-**

eko-nising *pc* the third

eko-niizhing *pc* the second

G

ga- *pv1* *future tense prefix after a personal prefix; also* **gad-**

gabaa *vai* get off a vehicle or boat, disembark; *1sg* **ingabaa;** *prt* **gebaad**

gabaa' *vta* get s.o. off a vehicle or boat, disembark s.o.; *1sg* **ingabaa'aa;** *prt* **gebaa'aad**

gabaanaazha' /gabaanaazha'w-/ *vta* tell s.o. to get off, tell s.o. to disembark; *1sg* ingabaanaazha'waa; *prt* gebaanaazha'waad
gabaashim *vta* cook s.o. by boiling; *1sg* ingabaashimaa; *prt* gebaashimaad
gabaatoon *vti2* cook s.t. by boiling; *1sg* ingabaatoon; *prt* gebaatood
gabe- *pv4* whole extent of, throughout
gabe-ayi'ii *pc* throughout it, a long time; *also* gabeyi'ii
gabe-dibik *pc* all night
gabe-dibikwe *vai* spend the whole night; *1sg* ingabe-dibikwe; *prt* gebe-dibikwed
gabe-gikendaasoowigamig *ni* college, university; *pl* gabe-gikendaasoowigamigoon; *loc* gabe-gikendaasoowigamigong
gabe-giizhik *pc* all day
gabekana *pc* at the end of the road or trail
gabenaw *vta* win from s.o. in a game, beat s.o. in a game; *1sg* ingabenawaa; *prt* gebenawaad
gabenaage *vai* score in a game, win; *1sg* ingabenaage; *prt* gebenaaged
gabe-onaagosh *pc* all evening
gabeshi *vai* camp, set up camp; *1sg* ingabesh; *prt* gebeshid
gabeshiwin *ni* campsite; *pl* gabeshiwinan; *loc* gabeshiwining; *dim* gabeshiwinens
gabeshkan *vti* go to the end of s.t.; *1sg* ingabeshkaan; *prt* gebeshkang
gabeshkaa *vai* go to the end; *1sg* ingabeshkaa; *prt* gebeshkaad
gabikan *vti* pass s.t. by; *1sg* ingabikaan; *prt* gebikang
gabikaw *vta* pass s.o. by; *1sg* ingabikawaa; *prt* gebikawaad
gad- *pv1 future tense prefix after a personal prefix, optional form before vowels*
gaganoonidiwag /gaganoonidi-/ *vai* they talk to each other, they converse with each other; *1pl* ingaganoonidimin; *prt* geganoonidijig
gaganoozh /gaganooN-/ *vta* talk to s.o., converse with s.o.; *1sg* ingaganoonaa; *prt* geganoonaad
gagaanonagweyaa *vii* have long sleeves; *prt* gegaanonagweyaag; *aug* gagaanonagweyaamagad; *prt aug* gegaanonagweyaamagak
gagaanw= < ginw=
gagaanwaanikwe *vai* have long hair; *1sg* ingagaanwaanikwe; *prt* gegaanwaanikwed
gagaanwaawan /gagaanwaa-/ *vii* be long *plural*; *prt* gegaanwaagin; *aug* gagaanwaamagadoon; *prt aug* gegaanwaamagakin
gagaanzitaw *vta* act contrary to s.o.'s instructions; *1sg* ingagaanzitawaa; *prt* gegaanzitawaad
gagaanzom *vta* persuade s.o., urge s.o., convince s.o.; *1sg* ingagaanzomaa; *prt* gegaanzomaad
gagaapag= < gipag=
gagiib= < gib=
gagiibanagaskwe *vai* stutter; *1sg* ingagiibanagaskwe; *prt* gegiibanagaskwed
gagiibaadad *vii* be foolish; *prt* gegiibaadak
gagiibaadaatese *vii* be a comedy, be a funny movie; *prt* gegiibaadaateseg; *aug* gagiibaadaatesemagad; *prt aug* gegiibaadaatesemagak

gagiibaadizi *vai* be foolish; *1sg* ingagiibaadiz; *prt* gegiibaadizid
gagiibaajichige *vai* do foolish things; *1sg* ingagiibaajichige; *prt* gegiibaajichiged
gagiibijaane *vai* have a stuffed-up nose; *1sg* ingagiibijaane; *prt* gegiibijaaned
gagiibishe *vai* be deaf; *1sg* ingagiibishe; *prt* gegiibished
gagiibiingwe *vai* be blind; *1sg* ingagiibiingwe; *prt* gegiibiingwed
gagiibw= < gibw=
gagiichii *vai* take off one's shoes, take off one's moccasins; *1sg* ingagiichii; *prt* gegiichiid
gagiidag= < gidag=
gagiidisk= < gidisk=
gagiigin *vta* select from s.o., pick from s.o.; *1sg* ingagiinaa; *prt* gegiiginaad
gagiiginan *vti* select from s.t., pick from s.t.; *1sg* ingagiiginan; *prt* gegiiginang
gagiij= < gij=
gagiik= < gik=
gagiikim *vta* preach to s.o.; *1sg* ingagiikimaa; *prt* gegiikimaad
gagiikimaawasowin *ni* education by preaching and exhortation
gagiikwe *vai* preach; *1sg* ingagiikwe; *prt* gegiikwed
gagiikwe-mazina'igan *ni* bible; *pl* gagiikwe-mazina'iganan; *loc* gagiikwe-mazina'iganing; *dim* gagiikwe-mazina'igaans
gagiikwewinini *na* preacher, minister; *pl* gagiikwewininiwag
gagiimood= < gimood=
gagiinawishki *vai* be a habitual liar; *1sg* ingagiinawishk; *prt* gegiinawishkid
gagiipidoon *vai* have chapped lips; *1sg* ingagiipidoon; *prt* gegiipidoong
gagiipizi *vai* be chapped; *1sg* ingagiipiz; *prt* gegiipizid
gagiipiingwe *vai* have a chapped face; *1sg* ingagiipiingwe; *prt* gegiipiingwed
gagiizh= < gizh=
gagiizhibaa= < gizhibaa=
gagiizhiib= < gizhiib=
gagwaadagitoo *vai* suffer; *1sg* ingagwaadagitoo; *prt* gegwaadagitood
gagwaanisagad *vii* be terrible; *prt* gegwaanisagak
gagwaanisagakamig *pc* terrible, awful
gagwaanisagendam *vai2* consider things to be terrible, suffer in one's mind; *1sg* ingagwaanisagendam; *prt* gegwaanisagendang
gagwaanisagendan *vti* consider s.t. terrible, consider s.t. disgusting; *1sg* ingagwaanisagendaan; *prt* gegwaanisagendang
gagwaanisagendaagozi *vai* be considered terrible, be considered disgusting; *1sg* ingagwaanisagendaagoz; *prt* gegwaanisagendaagozid
gagwaanisagendaagwad *vii* be considered terrible, be considered disgusting; *prt* gegwaanisagendaagwak
gagwaanisagenim *vta* consider s.o. to be terrible, consider s.o. disgusting; *1sg*

ingagwaanisagenimaa; *prt*
gegwaanisagenimaad
gagwaanisagizi *vai* be mean, be terrible; *1sg*
ingagwaanisagiz; *prt* gegwaanisagizid
gagwaayakw= < gwayakw=
gagwaazigw= < gozigw=
gagwe- *pv4* try
gagwedaganaam *vta* box s.o.; *1sg*
ingagwedaganaamaa; *prt*
gegwedaganaamaad
gagwedaganaandiwag /gagwedaganaandi-/ *vai*
they box each other; *1pl*
ingagwedaganaandimin; *prt*
gegwedaganaandijig
gagwedaganewinini *na* boxer; *pl*
gagwedaganewininiwag
gagweda'aakwe *vai* practice shooting; *1sg*
ingagweda'aakwe; *prt* gegweda'aakwed
gagwedin *vta* test s.o. by touch; *1sg*
ingagwedinaa; *prt* gegwedinaad
gagwedinan *vti* test s.t. by touch; *1sg*
ingagwedinaan; *prt* gegwedinang
gagwedoomigo *vai* practice riding on horseback;
1sg ingagwedoomig; *prt* gegwedoomigod
gagwedwe *vai* ask questions, inquire; *1sg*
ingagwedwe; *prt* gegwedwed
gagwejichige *vai* try things; *1sg* ingagwejichige;
prt gegwejichiged
gagweji' *vta* try to get s.o. to...; *1sg* ingagweji'aa;
prt gegweji'aad
gagwejikada' /gagwejikada'w-/ *vta* race s.o. in
boats; *1sg* ingagwejikada'waa; *prt*
gegwejikada'waad
gagwejikada'odiwag /gagwejikada'odi-/ *vai* they
race each other in boats; *1pl*
ingagwejikada'odimin; *prt* gegwejikada'odijig
gagwejikanidiwag /gagwejikanidi-/ *vai* they race
each other; *1pl* ingagwejikanidimin; *prt*
gegwejikanidijig
gagwejikazh /gagwejikaN-/ *vta* race s.o.; *1sg*
ingagwejikanaa; *prt* gegwejikanaad
gagwejikazhiwe *vai* race people; *1sg*
ingagwejikazhiwe; *prt* gegwejikazhiwed
gagwejikazhiwewidaabaan *na* race car; *pl*
gagwejikazhiwewidaabaanag
gagwejim *vta* ask s.o. questions; *1sg*
ingagwejimaa; *prt* gegwejimaad
gagwejindiwag /gagwejindi-/ *vai* they ask each
other questions; *1pl* ingagwejindimin; *prt*
gegwejindijig
gagwejitoon *vti2* try s.t., test s.t.; *1sg*
ingagwejitoon; *prt* gegwejitood
gagwejii *vai* test one's strength; *1sg* ingagwejii; *prt*
gegwejiid
gagwejiiwaanidiwag /gagwejiiwaanidi-/ *vai* they
wrestle each other; *1pl* ingagwejiiwaanidimin;
prt gegwejiiwaanidijig
gagwejiiwaazh /gagwejiiwaaN-/ *vta* wrestle s.o.;
1sg ingagwejiiwaanaa; *prt* gegwejiiwaanaad
gagwejiiwaazoowinini *na* wrestler; *pl*
gagwejiiwaazoowininiwag
gagwezikan *vti* test s.t. with foot or body; *1sg*
ingagwezikaan; *prt* gegwezikang
gagwezikaw *vta* test s.o. with foot or body; *1sg*
ingagwezikawaa; *prt* gegwezikawaad

gakakaa *vii* be square; *prt* gekakaag; *aug*
gakakaamagad; *prt* *aug* gekakaamagak
gakakaabikad *vii* be square (as something
mineral); *prt* gekakaabikak
gakakaabikizi *vai* be square (as something
mineral); *prt* gekakaabikizid
gakakaakozi *vai* be square (as something stick- or
wood-like); *prt* gekakaakozid
gakakaakwad *vii* be square (as something stick- or
wood-like); *prt* gekakaakwak
gakaki' *vta* make s.o. square; *1sg* ingakaki'aa; *prt*
gekaki'aad
gakakishin *vai* have a square pattern; *prt*
gekakishing
gakakisin *vii* have a square pattern; *prt* gekakising
gakakitoon *vti2* make s.t. square; *1sg*
ingakakitoon; *prt* gekakitood
gakakizi *vai* be square; *prt* gekakizid
gakakiigad *vii* be square (as something sheet-like);
prt gekakiigak
gakakiigizi *vai* be square (as something sheet-like);
prt gekakiigizid
Gakaabikaang *place* Minneapolis
gakaaga'ogaan *ni* house-like lodge; *pl*
gakaaga'ogaanan; *loc* gakaaga'ogaaning; *dim*
gakaaga'ogaanens
gakaamikijiwan *vii* be a waterfall; *prt*
gekaamikijiwang
gakeyaa *pc* in the direction of; *also* akeyaa, keyaa,
nakakeyaa*
gakijiwan *vii* be a waterfall; *prt* gekijiwang
gakina *pc* all; *also* akina, kina
gakina awiya *pr* everybody; *also* akina awiya, kina
awiya
gakina gegoo *pr* everything; *also* akina gegoo,
kina gegoo
gakiiwe *vai* go over a point, portage; *1sg*
ingakiiwe; *prt* gekiiwed
gakiiwenige *vai* carry things over a portage; *1sg*
ingakiiwenige; *prt* gekiiweniged
ganabaj *pc* perhaps, maybe
ganage *pc* in the least, by any means
ganakin *vta* take a handful of s.o.; *1sg*
inganakinaa; *prt* genakinaad
ganakinan *vti* take a handful of s.t.; *1sg*
inganakinaan; *prt* genakinang
ganawaabam *vta* look at s.o., watch s.o.; *1sg*
inganawaabamaa; *prt* genawaabamaad
ganawaabandan *vti* look at s.t., watch s.t.; *1sg*
inganawaabandaan; *prt* genawaabandang
ganawaabandiwag /ganawaabandi-/ *vai* they look
at each other, they watch each other; *1pl*
inganawaabandimin; *prt* genawaabandijig
ganawaabanjigaade *vii* be looked at, be watched;
prt genawaabanjigaadeg; *aug*
ganawaabanjigaademagad; *prt* *aug*
genawaabanjigaademagak
ganawaabanjigaazo *vai* be looked at, be watched,
be on parole; *prt* genawaabanjigaazod
ganawaabanjige *vai* look at things, watch things;
1sg inganawaabanjige; *prt* genawaabanjiged
ganawaabi *vai* look, watch; *1sg* inganawaab; *prt*
genawaabid
ganawendamaw *vta* take care of (s.t.) for s.o.; *1sg*
inganawendamawaa; *prt* genawendamawaad

ganawendan *vti* take care of s.t.; *1sg*
inganawendaan; *prt* **genawendang**
ganawendaagwad *vii* be taken care of; *prt*
genawendaagwak
ganawendaawaso *vai* take care of a child; *1sg*
inganawendaawas; *prt* **genawendaawasod**
ganawenim *vta* take care of s.o.; *1sg*
inganawenimaa; *prt* **genawenimaad**
ganawenindiwag /**ganawenindi-**/ *vai* they take
care of each other; *1pl* **inganawenindimin**; *prt*
genawenindijig
ganawenjigaade *vii* be taken care of; *prt*
genawenjigaadeg; *aug*
ganawenjigaademagad; *prt aug*
genawenjigaademagak
ganawenjigaazo *vai* be taken care of, be on parole;
prt **genawenjigaazod**
ganawenjige *vai* take care of things; *1sg*
inganawenjige; *prt* **genawenjiged**
ganoodan *vti* speak to s.t.; *1sg* **inganoodaan**; *prt*
genoodang
ganoonidiwag /**ganoonidi-**/ *vai* they speak to each
other; *1pl* **inganoonidimin**; *prt* **genoonidijig**
ganoozh /**ganooN-**/ *vta* address s.o., speak to s.o.,
call s.o. on the phone; *1sg* **inganoonaa**; *prt*
genoonaad
gashkadin *vii* freeze over, be frozen over; *prt*
geshkading
gashkadino-giizis *na* November
gashka'oode *vii* be knotted, be tangled; *prt*
geshka'oodeg; *aug* **gashka'oodemagad**; *prt*
aug **geshka'oodemagak**
gashka'oodoon *vti2* tie s.t. with a knot; *1sg*
ingashka'oodoon; *prt* **geshka'oodood**
gashka'oojigan *ni* knot; *pl* **gashka'oojiganan**; *dim*
gashka'oojigaans
gashka'oozh /**gashka'ooN-**/ *vta* tie s.o. with a
knot; *1sg* **ingashka'oonaa**; *prt* **geshka'oonaad**
gashka'oozo *vai* be knotted, be tangled; *prt*
geshka'oozod
gashkanokii *vai* be able to work; *1sg*
ingashkanokii; *prt* **geshkanokiid**
gashkapidoon *vti2* tie s.t. shut, tie s.t. in a bundle;
1sg **ingashkapidoon**; *prt* **geshkapidood**
gashkapizh /**gashkapiN-**/ *vta* tie s.o. shut, tie s.o.
in a bundle; *1sg* **ingashkapinaa**; *prt*
geshkapinaad
gashkawan *vii* be a dense fog; *prt* **geshkawang**
gashkaabika' /**gashkaabika'w-**/ *vta* lock s.o.; *1sg*
ingashkaabika'waa; *prt* **geshkaabika'waad**
gashkaabika'an *vti* lock s.t.; *1sg*
ingashkaabika'aan; *prt* **geshkaabika'ang**
gashkaabika'igan *ni* lock; *pl* **gashkaabika'iganan**;
loc **gashkaabika'iganing**; *dim*
gashkaabika'igaans
gashkaabika'igaade *vii* be locked; *prt*
geshkaabika'igaadeg; *aug*
gashkaabika'igaademagad; *prt aug*
geshkaabika'igaademagak
gashkaabika'igaazo *vai* be locked; *prt*
geshkaabika'igaazod
gashkaabika'ige *vai* lock things; *1sg*
ingashkaabika'ige; *prt* **geshkaabika'iged**
gashkaakonan *vti* bar s.t. (as something stick- or
wood-like), lock s.t. (as or as with something

stick- or wood-like); *1sg* **ingashkaakonaan**; *prt*
geshkaakonang
gashkaakwa'amaw *vta* lock (s.t.) for s.o. (as or as
with something stick- or wood-like); *1sg*
ingashkaakwa'amawaa; *prt*
geshkaakwa'amawaad
gashkaaso *vai* be sunburned; *1sg* **ingashkaas**; *prt*
geshkaasod
gashkendam *vai2* be lonely, be sad; *1sg*
ingashkendam; *prt* **geshkendang**
gashkibidaagan *na* a bag with closeable top, tobacco
bag, pipe bag, bandolier bag; *pl*
gashkibidaaganag; *loc* **gashkibidaaganing**;
dim **gashkibidaagaans**

**gashkibidaagan (bandolier bag;); see also
aazhooningwa'igan**

gashkibide *vii* be wrapped and tied in a bundle; *prt*
geshkibideg; *aug* **gashkibidemagad**; *prt aug*
geshkibidemagak
gashkibidoon *vti2* wrap and tie s.t. in a bundle; *1sg*
ingashkibidoon; *prt* **geshkibidood**
gashkibijigan *ni* bundle, package, packet; *pl*
gashkibijiganan; *loc* **gashkibijiganing**; *dim*
gashkibijigaans
gashkibijigaade *vii* be wrapped and tied in a
bundle; *prt* **geshkibijigaadeg**; *aug*
gashkibijigaademagad; *prt aug*
geshkibijigaademagak
gashkibijigaazo *vai* be wrapped and tied in a
bundle; *prt* **geshkibijigaazod**
gashkibijige *vai* wrap and tie things in a bundle;
1sg **ingashkibijige**; *prt* **geshkibijiged**
gashkibizh /**gashkibiN-**/ *vta* wrap and tie s.o. in a
bundle; *1sg* **ingashkibinaa**; *prt* **geshkibinaad**
gashkichige *vai* acquire, earn, be able (to do
something); *1sg* **ingashkichige**; *prt*
geshkichiged
gashkidaasebizo *vai* wear leg garters; *1sg*
ingashkidaasebiz; *prt* **geshkidaasebizod**
gashkidaasebizon *ni* leg garter; *pl*
gashkidaasebizonan; *loc*

gashkidaasebizoning; *dim*
gashkidaasebizonens
gashkigwaadan *vti* sew s.t.; *1sg*
ingashkigwaadaan; *prt* geshkigwaadang
gashkigwaade *vii* be sewn; *prt* geshkigwaadeg;
aug gashkigwaademagad; *prt aug*
geshkigwaademagak
gashkigwaaso *vai* sew; *1sg* ingashkigwaas; *prt*
geshkigwaasod
gashkigwaason *na* sewing machine; *pl*
gashkigwaasonag; *loc* gashkigwaasoning; *dim*
gashkigwaasonens
gashkigwaasoneyaab *ni* sewing thread; *pl*
gashkigwaasoneyaabiin; *loc*
gashkigwaasoneyaabiing; *dim*
gashkigwaasoneyaabiins
gashkigwaazh /gashkigwaaN-/ *vta* sew s.o. (e.g., a
pair of pants); *1sg* ingashkigwaanaa; *prt*
geshkigwaanaad
gashkigwaazo *vai* be sewn; *prt* geshkigwaazod
gashki' *vta* prevail over s.o., manage s.o., earn s.o.
(e.g., money); *1sg* ingashki'aa; *prt* geshki'aad
gashki'ewizi *vai* accomplish, succeed, have power;
1sg ingashki'ewiz; *prt* geshki'ewizid
gashki'o *vai* be able, get free; *1sg* ingashki'; *prt*
geshki'od
gashkitaw *vta* be able to get (s.t.) for s.o., be able
to manage (s.t.) for s.o.; *1sg* ingashkitawaa; *prt*
geshkitawaad
gashkitoon *vti2* be able to do s.t., succeed at s.t.,
manage s.t.; *1sg* ingashkitoon; *prt* geshkitood
gashkiwidoon *vti2* be able to take s.t., be able to
carry s.t.; *1sg* ingashkiwidoon; *prt*
geshkiwidood
gashkiwizh /gashkiwiN-/ *vta* be able to take s.o.,
be able to carry s.o.; *1sg* ingashkiwinaa; *prt*
geshkiwinaad
gashkii-dibikad *vii* be very dark at night; *prt*
geshkii-dibikak
gashkii-dibik-ayaa *vii* be dark as night; *prt* geshkii-
dibik-ayaag; *aug* gashkii-dibik-ayaamagad;
prt aug geshkii-dibik-ayaamagak
gawa' /gawa'w-/ *vta* fell s.o., chop s.o. down; *1sg*
ingawa'waa; *prt* gewa'waad
gawa'an *vti* fell s.t., chop s.t. down; *1sg*
ingawa'aan; *prt* gewa'ang
gawa'igaade *vii* be chopped down; *prt*
gewa'igaadeg; *aug* gawa'igaademagad; *prt*
aug gewa'igaademagak
gawa'igaazo *vai* be chopped down; *prt*
gewa'igaazod
gawaji *vai* freeze to death; *1sg* ingawaj; *prt* gewajid
gawanaandam *vai2* starve; *1sg* ingawanaandam;
prt gewanaandang
gawanokii *vai* collapse from overwork; *1sg*
ingawanokii; *prt* gewanokiid
gawaabaagwe *vai* suffer from thirst; *1sg*
ingawaabaagwe; *prt* gewaabaagwed
gawaakose *vai* fall over (as something stick- or
wood-like); *prt* gewaakosed
gawaakose *vii* fall over (as something stick- or
wood-like); *prt* gewaakoseg; *aug*
gawaakosemagad; *prt aug* gewaakosemagak

gawaashi *vai* be blown over; *prt* gewaashid
gawaasin *vii* be blown over; *prt* gewaasing
gawin *vta* upset s.o. by hand, tip s.o. over by hand;
1sg ingawinaa; *prt* gewinaad
gawinan *vti* upset s.t. by hand, tip s.t. over by
hand; *1sg* ingawinaan; *prt* gewinang
gawingwashi *vai* fall asleep; *1sg* ingawingwash; *prt*
gewingwashid
gawise *vai* fall over; *prt* gewised
gawise *vii* fall over; *prt* gewiseg; *aug*
gawisemagad; *prt aug* gewisemagak
gawishimo *vai* lie down, go to bed; *1sg*
ingawishim; *prt* gewishimod
gawiwebin *vta* throw s.o. down, knock s.o. down,
pull s.o. down with hands; *1sg* ingawiwebinaa;
prt gewiwebinaad
gawiwebinan *vti* throw s.t. down, knock s.t. down,
pull s.t. down with hands; *1sg*
ingawiwebinaan; *prt* gewiwebinang
gayat *pc* formerly, previously, some time ago
gayaashk *na* seagull; *pl* gayaashkwag; *dim*
gayaashkoons
gaye *pc* as for, also, too, and; *also* ge
gaa- *pv1* past tense prefix under initial change
gaadaw *vta* hide (s.t.) from s.o.; *1sg* ingaadawaa;
prt gayaadawaad
gaadoon *vti2* hide s.t.; *1sg* ingaadoon; *prt*
gayaadood
gaag *na* porcupine; *pl* gaagwag; *dim* gaagoons
gaagaagiw *na* raven; *pl* gaagaagiwag; *dim*
gaagaagiins; *also* gaagaagi*
gaagige- *pv4* forever
gaagiidaawigan *vai* have a sore back; *1sg*
ingaagiidaawigan; *prt* gayaagiidaawigang
gaagiidizi *vai* be sore; *1sg* ingaagiidiz; *prt*
gayaagiidizid
gaagiigido *vai* talk, speak; *1sg* ingaagiigid; *prt*
gayaagiigidod
gaagiigidoo-bineshiinh *na* parrot; *pl* gaagiigidoo-
bineshiinyag
gaagiigidoo-makakoons *ni* telephone,
phonograph, record player; *pl* gaagiigidoo-
makakoonsan; *loc* gaagiigidoo-
makakoonsing
gaagiigidoowinini *na* councillor; *pl*
gaagiigidoowininiwag
gaagiijidooskwan *vai* have a sore elbow; *1sg*
ingaagiijidooskwan; *prt* gayaagiijidooskwang
gaagiijigaade *vai* have a sore leg; *1sg*
ingaagiijigaade; *prt* gayaagiijigaaded
gaagiijinike *vai* have a sore arm; *1sg* ingaagiijinike;
prt gayaagiijiniked
gaagiijininjii *vai* have a sore hand, have a sore
finger; *1sg* ingaagiijininjii; *prt* gayaagiijininjiid
gaagiijizide *vai* have a sore foot; *1sg* ingaagiijizide;
prt gayaagiijizided
gaagiizom *vta* appease s.o., apologize to s.o.; *1sg*
ingaagiizomaa; *prt* gayaagiizomaad
gaajigaade *vii* be hidden; *prt* gayaajigaadeg; *aug*
gaajigaademagad; *prt aug*
gayaajigaademagak
gaajigaazo *vai* be hidden; *prt* gayaajigaazod

gaajige *vai* hide things; *1sg* **ingaajige**; *prt*
gayaajiged
gaakaabishiinh *na* screech owl; *pl*
gaakaabishiinyag
gaakaand= < gaand=
gaakaanj= < gaanj=
gaakaanz= < gaanz=
gaakaasii= < gaasii=
gaakaask= < gaask=
gaa mashi *pc* not yet; *also* **gaawiin mashi**
Gaa-miskwaawaakokaag *place* Cass Lake
gaanda'igwaason *ni* thimble; *pl*
gaanda'igwaasonan; *loc* **gaanda'igwaasoning**;
dim **gaanda'igwaasonens**
gaandakii'an *vti* pole s.t.; *1sg* **ingaandakii'aan**; *prt*
gayaandakii'ang
gaandakii'iganaak *ni* push pole; *pl*
gaandakii'iganaakoon; *loc*
gaandakii'iganaakong; *dim*
gaandakii'iganaakoons; *also*
gaandakii'iganaatig
gaandakii'ige *vai* pole a boat; *1sg* **ingaandakii'ige**;
prt **gayaandakii'iged**
gaandakii'o *vai* pole a boat; *1sg* **ingaandakii'**; *prt*
gayaandakii'od
gaandin *vta* push s.o.; *1sg* **ingaandinaa**; *prt*
gayaandinaad
gaandinamaw *vta* push (s.t.) for s.o.; *1sg*
ingaandinamawaa; *prt* **gayaandinamawaad**
gaandinan *vti* push s.t.; *1sg* **ingaandinaan**; *prt*
gayaandinang
gaandinige *vai* push things; *1sg* **ingaandinige**; *prt*
gayaandiniged
gaanjida' /gaanjida'w-/ *vta* push s.o. with a stick;
1sg **ingaanjida'waa**; *prt* **gayaanjida'waad**
gaanjida'an *vti* push s.t. with a stick; *1sg*
ingaanjida'aan; *prt* **gayaanjida'ang**
gaanjida'ige *vai* push things with a stick; *1sg*
ingaanjida'ige; *prt* **gayaanjida'iged**
gaanjweba' /gaanjweba'w-/ *vta* shove s.o. using
something; *1sg* **ingaanjweba'waa**; *prt*
gayaanjweba'waad
gaanjweba'an *vti* shove s.t. using something; *1sg*
ingaanjweba'aan; *prt* **gayaanjweba'ang**
gaanjweba'ige *vai* shove things using something,
pole logs; *1sg* **ingaanjweba'ige**; *prt*
gayaanjweba'iged
gaanjwebin *vta* shove s.o.; *1sg* **ingaanjwebinaa**; *prt*
gayaanjwebinaad
gaanjwebinan *vti* shove s.t.; *1sg* **ingaanjwebinaan**;
prt **gayaanjwebinang**
gaanjwebishkan *vti* shove s.t. with foot or body;
1sg **ingaanjwebishkaan**; *prt*
gayaanjwebishkang
gaanjwebishkaw *vta* shove s.o. with foot or body;
1sg **ingaanjwebishkawaa**; *prt*
gayaanjwebishkawaad
gaanoo *na* diamond suite card; *pl* **gaanoog**
gaanzikan *vti* push s.t. with foot or body; *1sg*
ingaanzikaan; *prt* **gayaanzikang**
gaanzikaw *vta* push s.o. with foot or body; *1sg*
ingaanzikawaa; *prt* **gayaanzikawaad**

gaapam *vta* crunch s.o. in mouth; *1sg*
ingaapamaa; *prt* **gayaapamaad**
gaapan *vii* be brittle; *prt* **gayaapang**; *also* **gaapaa**
gaapandan *vti* crunch s.t. in mouth; *1sg*
ingaapandaan; *prt* **gayaapandang**
gaapanjige *vai* crunch things in mouth; *1sg*
ingaapanjige; *prt* **gayaapanjiged**
gaapizan *vti* parch s.t.; *1sg* **ingaapizaan**; *prt*
gayaapizang
gaapizi *vai* be brittle; *prt* **gayaapizid**
gaapizigan *ni* popped wild rice; *pl* **gaapiziganan**;
loc **gaapiziganing**; *dim* **gaapizigaans**
gaapizige *vai* parch things; *1sg* **ingaapizige**; *prt*
gayaapiziged
gaapii *ni* coffee
gaashkakokwe'igan *ni* paddle for stirring boiling
maple sap; *pl* **gaashkakokwe'iganan**; *dim*
gaashkakokwe'igaans
gaashkibaajigan *ni* razor; *pl* **gaashkibaajiganan**;
loc **gaashkibaajiganing**; *dim*
gaashkibaajigaans
gaashkibaazh /gaashkibaaN-/ *vta* shave s.o.; *1sg*
ingaashkibaanaa; *prt* **gayaashkibaanaad**
gaashkibaazo *vai* shave; *1sg* **ingaashkibaaz**; *prt*
gayaashkibaazod
gaasiibii'an *vti* erase s.t.; *1sg* **ingaasiibii'aan**; *prt*
gayaasiibii'ang
gaasiibii'igan *na* eraser; *pl* **gaasiibii'iganag**; *loc*
gaasiibii'iganing; *dim* **gaasiibii'igaans**
gaasiibii'ige *vai* erase things; *1sg* **ingaasiibii'ige**; *prt*
gayaasiibii'iged
gaasiidoone'o *vai* wipe one's mouth; *1sg*
ingaasiidoone'; *prt* **gayaasiidoone'od**
gaasii' /gaasii'w-/ *vta* wipe s.o. using something;
1sg **ingaasii'waa**; *prt* **gayaasii'waad**
gaasii'an *vti* wipe s.t. using something; *1sg*
ingaasii'aan; *prt* **gayaasii'ang**
gaasii'ige *vai* wipe things using something; *1sg*
ingaasii'ige; *prt* **gayaasii'iged**
gaasiinaagane *vai* wipe dishes; *1sg*
ingaasiinaagane; *prt* **gayaasiinaaganed**
gaasiininjii *vai* wipe one's hands; *1sg* **ingaasiininjii**;
prt **gayaasiininjiid**
gaaskanazo *vai* whisper; *1sg* **ingaaskanaz**; *prt*
gayaaskanazod
gaaskanazootaw *vta* whisper to s.o.; *1sg*
ingaaskanazootawaa; *prt*
gayaaskanazootawaad
gaaskanaamo *vai* wheeze; *1sg* **ingaaskanaam**; *prt*
gayaaskanaamod
gaaskaaska' /gaaskaaska'w-/ *vta* scrape s.o. using
something; *1sg* **ingaaskaaska'waa**; *prt*
gayaaskaaska'waad
gaaskaaska'an *vti* scrape s.t. using something; *1sg*
ingaaskaaska'aan; *prt* **gayaaskaaska'ang**
gaaskide *vii* be dried out, be shrivelled; *prt*
gayaaskideg; *aug* **gaaskidemagad**; *prt aug*
gayaaskidemagak
gaaskiz /gaaskizw-/ *vta* dry s.o. by smoking; *1sg*
ingaaskizwaa; *prt* **gayaaskizwaad**
gaaskizan *vti* dry s.t. by smoking; *1sg*
ingaaskizaan; *prt* **gayaaskizang**

gaaskizo *vai* be dried out, be shrivelled; *1sg* ingaaskiz; *prt* gayaaskizod
gaawam *vta* be jealous of s.o.; *1sg* ingaawamaa; *prt* gayaawamaad
gaawaa *vii* be rough; *prt* gayaawaag; *aug* gaawaamagad; *prt aug* gayaawaamagak
Gaa-waabaabiganikaag *place* White Earth Reservation
gaawaabikad *vii* be rough (as something mineral); *prt* gayaawaabikak
gaawaabikizi *vai* be rough (as something mineral); *prt* gayaawaabikizid
gaawaandag *na* white spruce; *pl* gaawaandagoog; *loc* gaawaandagong; *dim* gaawaandagoons
gaawe *vai* be jealous; *1sg* ingaawe; *prt* gayaawed
gaawegad *vii* be rough (as something sheet-like); *prt* gayaawegak
gaawegizi *vai* be rough (as something sheet-like); *prt* gayaawegizid
gaawendam *vai2* be jealous; *1sg* ingaawendam; *prt* gayaawendang
gaawesa *pc* can't do it!, no way!, not at all
gaawizi *vai* be rough; *prt* gayaawizid
gaa wiikaa *pc* never; *also* gaawiin wiikaa
gaawiin *pc* no, not *negative*
gaawiin awiya *pr* nobody; *also* gaawiin awiiya
gaawiin ganage *pc* not in the least
gaawiin gegoo *pr* nothing
gaawiin geyaabi *pc* no more, no longer
gaawiin mashi *pc* not yet; *also* gaa mashi
gaawiin memwech *pc* it's not necessary, you don't have to
gaawiin wiikaa *pc* never; *also* gaa wiikaa
gaa-wiisagang *ni-pt* pepper
Gaa-zagaskwaajimekaag *place* Leech Lake Reservation
gaazh /gaaN-/ *vta* hide s.o.; *1sg* ingaanaa; *prt* gayaanaad
gaazhagens *na* cat; *pl* gaazhagensag
gaazo *vai* hide self; *1sg* ingaaz; *prt* gayaazod
gaazootaw *vta* hide from s.o.; *1sg* ingaazootawaa; *prt* gayaazootawaad
ge *pc* as for, also, too; *also* gaye
ge- *pv1 future tense prefix under initial change*
gebaakwa'ond *na-pt* prisoner; *pl* gebaakwa'onjig
gegapii *pc* after a while, eventually, finally
gegaa *pc* nearly, almost
geget *pc* sure, indeed, certainly, really
gego *pc* don't
gego bina *pc* just don't
gego ganage *pc* don't in any way
gego wiikaa *pc* don't ever
gegoo *pr* something *inanimate definite*, anything *inanimate indefinite*
gekek *na* hawk; *pl* gekekwag; *dim* gekekoons
gekinoo'amawind *na-pt* student; *pl* gekinoo'amawinjig
gekinoo'amaaged *na-pt* teacher; *pl* gekinoo'amaagejig
gemaa *pc* or, or maybe; *also* gemaa gaye
genwaabiigigwed *na-pt* giraffe; *pl* genwaabiigigwejig
genwaakwak apabiwin *ni* couch; *pl* genwaakwakin apabiwinan; *loc* genwaakwak apabiwining; *dim* genwaakwak apabiwinens

geshawishim *vta* put s.o. loosely; *1sg* ingeshawishimaa; *prt* gayeshawishimaad
geshawishkan *vti* fit s.t. loosely; *1sg* ingeshawishkaan; *prt* gayeshawishkang
geshawishkaw *vta* fit s.o. loosely; *1sg* ingeshawishkawaa; *prt* gayeshawishkawaad
geshawisidoon *vti2* put s.t. loosely; *1sg* ingeshawisidoon; *prt* gayeshawisidood
gete- *pv4* old, old-time
gete-aya'aa *na* someone old; *pl* gete-aya'aag
gete-ayi'ii *ni* something old; *pl* gete-ayi'iin
geyaabi *pc* still, yet
gezika *pc* suddenly
gezikwendam *vai2* vaguely remember; *1sg* ingezikwendam; *prt* gayezikwendang
gezikwendan *vti* vaguely remember s.t.; *1sg* ingezikwendaan; *prt* gayezikwendang
gezikwenim *vta* vaguely remember s.o.; *1sg* ingezikwenimaa; *prt* gayezikwenimaad
gi= *pre second person prefix before consonants in nouns and verbs*
gibadoonh *na* button; *pl* gibadoonyag; *loc* gibadoons; *also* gibodoonh
gibagoojigan *ni* cloth partition; *pl* gibagoojiganan; *loc* gibagoojiganing; *dim* gibagoojigaans
giba' /giba'w-/ *vta* stop s.o. up, plug s.o.; *1sg* ingiba'waa; *prt* geba'waad
giba'an *vti* stop s.t. up, plug s.t.; *1sg* ingiba'aan; *prt* geba'ang
giba'igaade *vii* be stopped up, be plugged; *prt* geba'igaadeg; *aug* giba'igaademagad; *prt aug* geba'igaademagak
giba'igaazo *vai* be stopped up, be plugged; *prt* geba'igaazod
giba'ige *vai* stop things up, plug things; *1sg* ingiba'ige; *prt* geba'iged
gibaabowe /gibaabowe'w-/ *vta* put a lid on s.o.; *1sg* ingibaabowe'waa; *prt* gebaabowe'waad
gibaabowe'an *vti* put a lid on s.t.; *1sg* ingibaabowe'aan; *prt* gebaabowe'ang
gibaabowe'igan *ni* pot lid; *pl* gibaabowe'iganan; *loc* gibaabowe'iganing; *dim* gibaabowe'igaans
gibaabowe'ige *vai* put a lid on things; *1sg* ingibaabowe'ige; *prt* gebaabowe'iged
gibaakobidoon *vti2* can s.t., pull s.t. shut (as something stick- or wood-like); *1sg* ingibaakobidoon; *prt* gebaakobidood
gibaakobijigan *ni* canned goods; *pl* gibaakobijiganan
gibaakowebinan *vti* slam s.t. shut (as something stick- or wood-like, e.g., a door); *1sg* ingibaakowebinaan; *prt* gebaakowebinang
gibaakwadin *vii* be frozen shut; *prt* gebaakwading
gibaakwa' /gibaakwa'w-/ *vta* shut s.o. (as or as with something stick- or wood-like), dam s.o., obstruct s.o., jail s.o.; *1sg* ingibaakwa'waa; *prt* gebaakwa'waad
gibaakwa'an *vti* shut s.t. (as or as with something stick- or wood-like), dam s.t., obstruct s.t.; *1sg* ingibaakwa'aan; *prt* gebaakwa'ang
gibaakwa'igan *ni* dam, stopper, plug; *pl* gibaakwa'iganan; *loc* gibaakwa'iganing; *dim* gibaakwa'igaans
gibaakwa'igaade *vii* be shut (as or as with something stick- or wood-like); *prt*

gebaakwa'igaadeg; *aug*
gibaakwa'igaademagad; *prt aug*
gebaakwa'igaademagak
gibaakwa'igaazo *vai* be imprisoned; *prt*
gebaakwa'igaazod
gibaakwa'ige *vai* dam things, plug things; *1sg*
ingibaakwa'ige; *prt* gebaakwa'iged
gibaakwa'odiiwigamig *ni* jail, prison; *pl*
gibaakwa'odiiwigamigoon; *loc*
gibaakwa'odiiwigamigong; *dim*
gibaakwa'odiiwigamigoons
gibaakwaji *vai* be frozen shut; *prt* gebaakwajid
gibichiitaa *vai* take a break; *1sg* ingibichiitaa; *prt*
gebichiitaad
gibide'ebizon *ni* vest; *pl* gibide'ebizonan; *loc*
gibide'ebizoning; *dim* gibide'ebizonens

gibide'ebizon (vest)

gibijaane *vai* have a stuffed-up nose; *1sg*
ingibijaane; *prt* gebijaaned; *also* gagiibijaane
gibinewen *vta* choke s.o.; *1sg* ingibinewenaa; *prt*
gebinewenaad
gibishaganzhii *vai* be constipated; *1sg*
ingibishaganzhii; *prt* gebishaganzhiid
gibishe *vai* be deaf (in one ear); *1sg* ingibishe; *prt*
gebished
gibishkan *vti* block s.t. with foot or body; *1sg*
ingibishkaan; *prt* gebishkang
gibishkaw *vta* block s.o. with foot or body; *1sg*
ingibishkawaa; *prt* gebishkawaad
gibishkwaande'on *ni* lodge door cover; *pl*
gibishkwaande'on
gibiskwe *vai* be hoarse; *1sg* ingibiskwe; *prt*
gebiskwed
gibitan *vai* have a nosebleed; *1sg* ingibitan; *prt*
gebitang; *also* gibitane*
gibitaneganaan *vta* bloody s.o.'s nose; *1sg*
ingibitaneganaamaa; *prt*
gebitaneganaamaad
gibitaneshin *vai* bloody one's nose falling; *1sg*
ingibitaneshin; *prt* gebitaneshing
gibiiga'igan *ni* curtain, drapes; *pl* gibiiga'iganan;
loc gibiiga'iganing; *dim* gibiiga'igaans
gibiiga'iganiigin *ni* window shade; *pl*
gibiiga'iganiiginoon; *loc* gibiiga'iganiiginong;
dim gibiiga'iganiiginoons

gibiiga'igaade *vii* be curtained; *prt*
gebiiga'igaadeg; *aug* gibiiga'igaademagad; *prt*
aug gebiiga'igaademagak
gibokiwas /gibokiwasw-/ *vta* glue s.o. shut; *1sg*
ingibokiwaswaa; *prt* gebokiwaswaad
gibokiwasan *vti* glue s.t. shut; *1sg* ingibokiwasaan;
prt gebokiwasang
gibokiwasigaade *vii* be glued shut; *prt*
gebokiwasigaadeg; *aug*
gibokiwasigaademagad; *prt aug*
gebokiwasigaademagak
gibokiwasigaazo *vai* be glued shut; *prt*
gebokiwasigaazod
giboz /gibozw-/ *vta* bake s.o., roast s.o. in the
oven; *1sg* ingibozwaa; *prt* gebozwaad
gibozan *vti* bake s.t., roast s.t. in the oven; *1sg*
ingibozaan; *prt* gebozang
giboziganaabik *ni* roasting pan; *pl*
giboziganaabikoon; *loc* giboziganaabikong;
dim giboziganaabikoons
gibozige *vai* roast things in the oven, bake things;
1sg ingibozige; *prt* geboziged
giboobijiganeyaab *ni* drawstring; *pl*
giboobijiganeyaabiin; *loc*
giboobijiganeyaabiing; *dim*
giboobijiganeyaabiins
giboobinidizo *vai* zip oneself up; *1sg*
ingiboobinidiz; *prt* geboobinidizod
giboodiyegwaazon *na* pants; *pl*
giboodiyegwaazonag; *loc*
giboodiyegwaazoning; *dim*
giboodiyegwaazonens
giboodiyegwaazoniigin *ni* denim; *pl*
giboodiyegwaazoniiginoon
giboogwaadan *vti* sew s.t. shut; *1sg*
ingiboogwaadaan; *prt* geboogwaadang
giboogwaazh /giboogwaaN-/ *vta* sew s.o. shut; *1sg*
ingiboogwaanaa; *prt* geboogwaanaad
gibwanaabaawe *vai* drown; *1sg*
ingibwanaabaawe; *prt* gebwanaabaawed
gibwanaamode *vii* be full of smoke; *prt*
gebwanaamodeg; *aug*
gibwanaamodemagad; *prt aug*
gebwanaamodemagak
gibwanaamoz /gibwanaamozw-/ *vta* smoke s.o.
out; *1sg* ingibwanaamozwaa; *prt*
gebwanaamozwaad
gibwanaamozo *vai* suffocate from smoke; *1sg*
ingibwanaamoz; *prt* gebwanaamozod
gichi- *pv4* big, great, very; *also* chi-
gichi-aniibiish *ni* cabbage; *pl* gichi-aniibiishan; *loc*
gichi-aniibiishing; *dim* gichi-aniibiishens
gichi-aya'aa *na* adult, elder; *pl* gichi-aya'aag
gichi-aya'aawi *vai* be an adult, be an elder; *1sg*
ingichi-aya'aaw; *prt* gechi-aya'aawid
gichi-aya'aawinaagozi *vai* look old; *1sg* ingichi-
aya'aawinaagoz; *prt* gechi-aya'aawinaagozid
gichi-dibaakonigewinini *na* judge; *pl* gichi-
dibaakonigewininiwag
gichigami *ni* sea, one of the Great Lakes, Lake
Superior; *pl* gichigamiin; *loc* gichigamiing; *dim*
gichigamiins
gichigamiiwashk *ni* reed; *pl* gichigamiiwashkoon;
loc gichigamiiwashkong; *dim*
gichigamiiwashkoons

gichi-gigizheb *pc* early in the morning
gichi-gizhizo *vai* have pneumonia; *1sg* **ingichi-gizhiz**; *prt* **gechi-gizhizod**
gichi-izhiwebad *vii* be stormy; *prt* **gechi-izhiwebak**
gichi-manidoo *na* Great Spirit, God; *pl* **gichi-manidoog**
gichi-manidoo-giizis *na* January; *also* **manidoo-giizis**
gichi-miikana *ni* highway; *pl* **gichi-miikanan**; *loc* **gichi-miikanaang**
gichi-mookomaan *na* white person, American; *pl* **gichi-mookomaanag**; *dim* **gichi-mookomaanens**
gichi-mookomaan *ni* large knife, butcher knife; *pl* **gichi-mookomaanan**; *loc* **gichi-mookomaaning**; *dim* **gichi-mookomaanens**
Gichi-mookomaan-aki *ni* United States; *loc* **Gichi-mookomaan-akiing**
gichi-mookomaanikwe *na* white woman; *pl* **gichi-mookomaanikweg**; *dim* **gichi-mookomaanikwens**
gichi-mookomaanimo *vai* speak English; *1sg* **ingichi-mookomaanim**; *prt* **gechi-mookomaanimod**
gichinik *ni* right hand *usually possessed*; *loc* **gichinikaang**
gichi-noodin *vii* be very windy, be a storm; *prt* **gechi-nooding**
gichi-ogimaa *na* highest leader, king; *pl* **gichi-ogimaag**; *dim* **gichi-ogimaans**
gichi-ogimaawi *vai* be the highest leader, be a king; *1sg* **ingichi-ogimaaw**; *prt* **gechi-ogimaawid**
gichi-ogin *na* tomato; *pl* **gichi-oginiig**; *loc* **gichi-oginiing**; *dim* **gichi-oginiins**
gichi-onaagan *ni* large pan, dish pan; *loc* **gichi-onaaganing**
Gichi-onigamiing *place* Grand Portage Reservation
gichi-oodena *ni* city; *pl* **gichi-oodenawan**; *loc* **gichi-oodenaang**
gichi-ziibi *ni* big river, Mississippi River; *pl* **gichi-ziibiwan**; *loc* **gichi-ziibiing**
gid= *pre second person prefix before vowels in verbs and non-dependent nouns*
gidagagwadaashi *na* crappie; *pl* **gidagagwadaashiwag**; *dim* **gidagagwadaashiins**
gidagaa *vii* be variegated, be spotted; *prt* **gedagaag**; *aug* **gidagaamagad**; *prt aug* **gedagaamagak**
gidagaa-bizhiw *na* bobcat; *pl* **gidagaa-bizhiwag**; *dim* **gidagaa-bizhiwens**
gidagaakoons *na* fawn; *pl* **gidagaakoonsag**
gidagizi *vai* be variegated, be spotted; *prt* **gedagizid**
gidagiigad *vii* be variegated (as something sheet-like), be spotted (as something sheet-like); *prt* **gedagiigak**
gidagiigin *na* calico, cotton cloth; *pl* **gidagiiginoon**
gidagiigizi *vai* be variegated (as something sheet-like), be spotted (as something sheet-like); *prt* **gedagiigizid**
gida' /gida'w-/ *vta* remove s.o. using something; *1sg* **ingida'waa**; *prt* **geda'waad**

gida'an *vti* remove s.t. using something; *1sg* **ingida'aan**; *prt* **geda'ang**
gidamo /gidamw-/ *vta* eat up s.o.; *1sg* **ingidamwaa**; *prt* **gedamwaad**
gidasan *vti* parch s.t. (e.g., wild rice); *1sg* **ingidasaan**; *prt* **gedasang**
gidasige *vai* parch things (e.g., wild rice); *1sg* **ingidasige**; *prt* **gedasiged**
gidaan *vti3* eat up of s.t.; *1sg* **ingidaan**; *prt* **gedaang**
gidaanawe *vai* eat everything up; *1sg* **ingidaanawe**; *prt* **gedaanawed**
gidimaagenim *vta* pity s.o.; *1sg* **ingidimaagenimaa**; *prt* **gedimaagenimaad**
gidimaaginaagozi *vai* look poor; *1sg* **ingidimaaginaagoz**; *prt* **gedimaaginaagozid**
gidimaaginaagwad *vii* look poor; *prt* **gedimaaginaagwak**
gidimaagizi *vai* be poor; *1sg* **ingidimaagiz**; *prt* **gedimaagizid**
gidiskaabiigishkaa *vii* come unconnected (as something string-like), come loose (as something string-like); *prt* **gediskaabiigishkaag**; *aug* **gidiskaabiigishkaamagad**; *prt aug* **gediskaabiigishkaamagak**
gidiskibidoon *vti2* pull s.t. free, disconnect s.t. with hands; *1sg* **ingidiskibidoon**; *prt* **gediskibidood**
gidiskibizh /gidiskibiN-/ *vta* pull s.o. free, disconnect s.o. with hands; *1sg* **ingidiskibinaa**; *prt* **gediskibinaad**
gidiskin *vta* free s.o., take s.o. off, disconnect s.o.; *1sg* **ingidiskinaa**; *prt* **gediskinaad**
gidiskinan *vti* free s.t., take s.t. off, disconnect s.t.; *1sg* **ingidiskinaan**; *prt* **gediskinang**
gidiskise *vai* come apart, come off; *prt* **gediskised**
gidiskise *vii* come apart, come off; *prt* **gediskiseg**; *aug* **gidiskisemagad**; *prt aug* **gediskisemagak**
gidoonagise *vai* fall out of a boat; *1sg* **ingidoonagise**; *prt* **gedoonagised**
gigazhigane *vai* wear socks; *1sg* **ingigazhigane**; *prt* **gegazhiganed**
gigaatigwaan *ni* sliver (in one's body); *pl* **gigaatigwaanan**; *loc* **gigaatigwaaning**; *dim* **gigaatigwaanens**
gigaatigwe *vai* have a sliver; *1sg* **ingigaatigwe**; *prt* **gegaatigwed**
gigibabagiwayaane *vai* wear a shirt; *1sg* **ingigibabagiwayaane**; *prt* **gegibabagiwayaaned**
gigibabiinzikawaagane *vai* wear a coat; *1sg* **ingigibabiinzikawaagane**; *prt* **gegibabiinzikawaaganed**
gigigiboodiyegwaazone *vai* wear pants; *1sg* **ingigigiboodiyegwaazone**; *prt* **gegigiboodiyegwaazoned**
gigiminjikaawane *vai* wear mittens; *1sg* **ingigiminjikaawane**; *prt* **gegiminjikaawaned**
gigishkan *vti* bear s.t. on one's body, have s.t. on one's body; *1sg* **ingigishkaan**; *prt* **gegishkang**
gigishkaw *vta* bear s.o. on one's body, be pregnant with s.o.; *1sg* **ingigishkawaa**; *prt* **gegishkawaad**
gigishkawaawaso *vai* be pregnant; *1sg* **ingigishkawaawas**; *prt* **gegishkawaawasod**

gigishkaajige *vai* be pregnant; *1sg* **ingigishkaajige;**
　prt **gegishkaajiged**
gigizheb *pc* in the morning
gigizhebaa-miijin *vti3* eat s.t. for breakfast; *1sg*
　ingigizhebaa-miijin; *prt* **gegizhebaa-miijid**
gigizhebaawagad *vii* be morning; *prt*
　gegizhebaawagak
gigizhebaa-wiisini *vai* eat breakfast; *1sg*
　ingigizhebaa-wiisin; *prt* **gegizhebaa-wiisinid**
gigizhebaa-wiisiniwin *ni* breakfast
gijibidoon *vti* remove s.t. with hands, pull s.t. off;
　1sg **ingijibidoon;** *prt* **gejibidood**
gijibizh /gijibiN-/ *vta* remove s.o. with hands, pull
　s.o. off; *1sg* **ingijibinaa;** *prt* **gejibinaad**
gijigijigaaneshiinh *na* chickadee; *pl*
　gijigijigaaneshiinyag
gijigwaadan *vti* remove s.t. with something sharp;
　1sg **ingijigwaadaan;** *prt* **gejigwaadang**
gijigwaazh /gijigwaaN-/ *vta* remove s.o. with
　something sharp; *1sg* **ingijigwaanaa;** *prt*
　gejigwaanaad
gijikonayezigan *na* hominy; *pl* **gijikonayeziganag**
gijinagizhiin *vta* disembowel s.o., gut s.o.; *1sg*
　ingijinagizhiinaa; *prt* **gejinagizhiinaad**
gijipizon *ni* belt; *pl* **gijipizonan;** *loc* **gijipizoning;**
　dim **gijipizonens**
gijipizonaabik *ni* belt buckle; *pl*
　gijipizonaabikoon; *loc* **gijipizonaabikong;** *dim*
　gijipizonaabikoons
gijipizonens *ni* fan belt; *loc* **gijipizonensing**
gikaa *vai* be elderly; *1sg* **ingikaa;** *prt* **gekaad**
gikendan *vti* know s.t.; *1sg* **ingikendaan;** *prt*
　gekendang
gikendaagozi *vai* be known; *1sg* **ingikendaagoz;**
　prt **gekendaagozid**
gikendaagwad *vii* be known; *prt* **gekendaagwak**
gikendaaso *vai* be smart, be educated; *1sg*
　ingikendaas; *prt* **gekendaasod**
gikenim *vta* know s.o.; *1sg* **ingikenimaa;** *prt*
　gekenimaad
gikenjige *vai* know things; *1sg* **ingikenjige;** *prt*
　gekenjiged
gikinawaabam *vta* learn by observation of s.o.; *1sg*
　ingikinawaabamaa; *prt* **gekinawaabamaad**
gikinawaabi *vai* learn by observation; *1sg*
　ingikinawaab; *prt* **gekinawaabid**
gikinawaajichige *vai* mark things; *1sg*
　ingikinawaajichige; *prt* **gekinawaajichiged**
gikinawaaji' *vta* mark s.o.; *1sg* **ingikinawaaji'aa;**
　prt **gekinawaaji'aad**
gikinawaajitoon *vti2* mark s.t.; *1sg*
　ingikinawaajitoon; *prt* **gekinawaajitood**
gikinjigwen *vta* embrace s.o., hug s.o.; *1sg*
　ingikinjigwenaa; *prt* **gekinjigwenaad**
gikinjigwenidiwag /gikinjigwenidi-/ *vai* they hug
　each other; *1pl* **ingikinjigwenidimin;** *prt*
　gekinjigwenidijig
gikinoo'amaw *vta* teach (s.t.) to s.o.; *1sg*
　ingikinoo'amawaa; *prt* **gekinoo'amawaad**
gikinoo'amaadizo *vai* teach oneself; *1sg*
　ingikinoo'amaadiz; *prt* **gekinoo'amaadizod**
gikinoo'amaadii-mazina'igan *ni* schoolbook; *loc*
　gikinoo'amaadii-mazina'iganing; *dim*
　gikinoo'amaadii-mazina'igaans

gikinoo'amaadiiwigamig *ni* school; *pl*
　gikinoo'amaadiiwigamigoon; *loc*
　gikinoo'amaadiiwigamigong; *dim*
　gikinoo'amaadiiwigamigoons
gikinoo'amaagan *na* student; *pl*
　gikinoo'amaaganag; *dim* **gikinoo'amaagaans**
gikinoo'amaage *vai* teach; *1sg* **ingikinoo'amaage;**
　prt **gekinoo'amaaged**
gikinoo'amaagewikwe *na* teacher (female); *pl*
　gikinoo'amaagewikweg
gikinoo'amaagewinini *na* teacher; *pl*
　gikinoo'amaagewininiwag
gikinoo'amaagozi *vai* be taught, go to school; *1sg*
　ingikinoo'amaagoz; *prt* **gekinoo'amaagozid**
gikinoonowagad *vii* a year passes; *prt*
　gekinoonowagak
gikinoonowin *ni* year
gikinootaw *vta* say something after s.o., follow
　s.o.'s instructions; *1sg* **ingikinootawaa;** *prt*
　gekinootawaad
gikiwe'on *ni* flag; *pl* **gikiwe'onan;** *loc*
　gikiwe'oning; *dim* **gikiwe'onens**
gimiwan *vii* rain; *prt* **gemiwang**
gimiwanoowayaan *ni* raincoat; *pl*
　gimiwanoowayaanan; *loc*
　gimiwanoowayaaning; *dim*
　gimiwanoowayaanens
gimoodi *vai+o* steal (s.t.); *1sg* **ingimood,**
　ingimoodin; *prt* **gemoodid**
gimoodim *vta* steal from s.o.; *1sg* **ingimoodimaa;**
　prt **gemoodimaad**
gimoodindiwag /gimoodindi-/ *vai* they steal from
　each other; *1pl* **ingimoodindimin;** *prt*
　gemoodindijig
gimoodishki *vai* be a thief; *1sg* **ingimoodishk;**
　prt **gemoodishkid**
gimoodishkiiwinini *na* thief, robber; *pl*
　gimoodishkiiwininiwag; *dim*
　gimoodishkiiwininiins
ginagaapi *vai* laugh, giggle; *1sg* **inginagaap;** *prt*
　genagaapid
ginagijiin *vta* tickle s.o. (at the mid-section); *1sg*
　inginagijiinaa; *prt* **genagijiinaad**
gina'amaw *vta* forbid s.o. to, warn s.o. against
　(s.t.); *1sg* **ingina'amawaa;** *prt* **gena'amawaad**
gina'amaadim /gina'amaadi-/ *vai* there is a
　prohibition, it is forbidden; *prt* **gena'amaading**
ginebig *na* snake; *pl* **ginebigoog;** *dim* **ginebigoons**
ginebigwayaan *na* snakeskin; *pl*
　ginebigwayaanag; *loc* **ginebigwayaaning;** *dim*
　ginebigwayaanens
ginigawin *vta* mix s.o.; *1sg* **inginigawinaa;** *prt*
　genigawinaad
ginigawinan *vti* mix s.t.; *1sg* **inginigawinaan;** *prt*
　genigawinang
ginigawinigaade *vii* be mixed; *prt*
　genigawinigaadeg; *aug*
　ginigawinigaademagad; *prt aug*
　genigawinigaademagak
ginigawinigaazo *vai* be mixed; *prt*
　genigawinigaazod
ginigawinige *vai* mix things; *1sg* **inginigawinige;**
　prt **genigawiniged**
ginigawisin *vii* be mixed; *prt* **genigawising**

ginigawiwebin *vta* mix s.o. by shaking; *1sg* **inginigawiwebinaa**; *prt* **genigawiwebinaad**
ginigawiwebinan *vti* mix s.t. by shaking; *1sg* **inginigawiwebinaan**; *prt* **genigawiwebinang**
giniw *na* golden eagle; *pl* **giniwag**; *dim* **giniwens**
ginjiba' *vta* flee from s.o., run away from s.o.; *1sg* **inginjiba'aa**; *prt* **genjiba'aad**
ginjiba'iwe *vai* flee from people, run away from people; *1sg* **inginjiba'iwe**; *prt* **genjiba'iwed**
ginjida' /**ginjida'w-**/ *vta* tap s.o. in, pound s.o. in; *1sg* **inginjida'waa**; *prt* **genjida'waad**
ginjida'an *vti* tap s.t. in, pound s.t. in; *1sg* **inginjida'aan**; *prt* **genjida'ang**
ginoodaawangaa *vii* be a long stretch of sand beach; *prt* **genoodaawangaag**; *aug* **ginoodaawangaamagad**; *prt aug* **genoodaawangaamagak**
ginoo' *vta* make s.o. long; *1sg* **inginoo'aa**; *prt* **genoo'aad**
ginoonagad *vii* be a long boat; *prt* **genoonagak**
ginoondawaan *ni* long lodge; *pl* **ginoondawaanan**; *loc* **ginoondawaaning**; *dim* **ginoondawaanens**
ginoozhe *na* northern pike; *pl* **ginoozheg**; *dim* **ginoozhens**
ginoozi *vai* be tall, be long; *1sg* **inginooz**; *prt* **genoozid**
ginwaa *vii* be long; *prt* **genwaag**; *aug* **ginwaamagad**; *prt aug* **genwaamagak**
ginwaabikad *vii* be long (as something mineral); *prt* **genwaabikak**
ginwaabikizi *vai* be long (as something mineral); *prt* **genwaabikizid**
ginwaabiigad *vii* be long (as something string-like); *prt* **genwaabiigak**
ginwaabiigizh /**ginwaabiigizhw-**/ *vta* cut s.o. long (as something string-like); *1sg* **inginwaabiigizhwaa**; *prt* **genwaabiigizhwaad**
ginwaabiigizhan *vti* cut s.t. long (as something string-like); *1sg* **inginwaabiigizhaan**; *prt* **genwaabiigizhang**
ginwaabiigizi *vai* be long (as something string-like); *prt* **genwaabiigizid**
ginwaako-apabiwin *ni* couch; *pl* **ginwaako-apabiwinan**; *loc* **ginwaako-apabiwining**; *dim* **ginwaako-apabiwinens**
ginwaakozi *vai* be tall (of a person), be long (as something wood or stick-like); *1sg* **inginwaakoz**; *prt* **genwaakozid**
ginwaakwad *vii* be long (as something stick- or wood-like); *prt* **genwaakwak**
ginwaatoon *vti2* make s.t. long; *1sg* **inginwaatoon**; *prt* **genwaatood**
ginwegad *vii* be long (as something sheet-like); *prt* **genwegak**
ginwegi' *vta* make s.o. long (as something sheet-like); *1sg* **inginwegi'aa**; *prt* **genwegi'aad**
ginwegitoon *vti2* make s.t. long (as something sheet-like); *1sg* **inginwegitoon**; *prt* **genwegitood**
ginwegizi *vai* be long (as something sheet-like); *prt* **genwegizid**
ginwenzh *pc* for a long time
ginzhizhawizi *vai* be a hard worker; *1sg* **inginzhizhawiz**; *prt* **genzhizhawizid**
gipagawe *vai* have thick fur; *prt* **gepagawed**

gipagaa *vii* be thick; *prt* **gepagaag**; *aug* **gipagaamagad**; *prt aug* **gepagaamagak**
gipagaabikad *vii* be thick (as something mineral); *prt* **gepagaabikak**
gipagaabikizi *vai* be thick (as something mineral); *prt* **gepagaabikizid**
gipagaabiigad *vii* be thick (as something string-like); *prt* **gepagaabiigak**
gipagaabiigizi *vai* be thick (as something string-like); *prt* **gepagaabiigizid**
gipagaakwadin *vii* be frozen thick; *prt* **gepagaakwading**
gipagaakwaji *vai* be frozen thick; *prt* **gepagaakwajid**
gipagikodan *vti* slice s.t. thick; *1sg* **ingipagikodaan**; *prt* **gepagikodang**
gipagikozh /**gipagikoN-**/ *vta* slice s.o. thick; *1sg* **ingipagikonaa**; *prt* **gepagikonaad**
gipagishin *vai* lie in a thick layer; *prt* **gepagishing**
gipagisin *vii* lie in a thick layer; *prt* **gepagising**
gipagizi *vai* be thick; *prt* **gepagizid**
gipagiigad *vii* be thick (as something sheet-like); *prt* **gepagiigak**
gipagiigizi *vai* be thick (as something sheet-like); *prt* **gepagiigizid**
gishkishenh *na* female dog; *pl* **gishkishenyag**
gisinaa *vii* be cold (weather); *prt* **gesinaag**; *aug* **gisinaamagad**; *prt aug* **gesinaamagak**
gitigaadan *vti* plant s.t.; *1sg* **ingitigaadaan**; *prt* **getigaadang**
gitigaade *vii* be planted; *prt* **getigaadeg**; *aug* **gitigaademagad**; *prt aug* **getigaademagak**
gitigaan *ni* garden, field, farm; *pl* **gitigaanan**; *loc* **gitigaaning**; *dim* **gitigaanens**
gitigaanens *ni* vegetable; *pl* **gitigaanensan**
gitigaazh /**gitigaaN-**/ *vta* plant s.o.; *1sg* **ingitigaanaa**; *prt* **getigaanaad**
gitigaazo *vai* be planted; *prt* **getigaazod**
gitige *vai* garden, farm, plant; *1sg* **ingitige**; *prt* **getiged**
gitigewinini *na* farmer; *pl* **gitigewininiwag**
gitimi *vai* be lazy; *1sg* **ingitim**; *prt* **getimid**
gitimishki *vai* be habitually lazy, be a lazybones; *1sg* **ingitimishk**; *prt* **getimishkid**
gitizi *vai* be older; *prt* **getizid**
gizhaabikiz /**gizhaabikizw-**/ *vta* heat s.o. (as something mineral); *1sg* **ingizhaabikizwaa**; *prt* **gezhaabikizwaad**
gizhaabikizan *vti* heat s.t. (as something mineral); *1sg* **ingizhaabikizaan**; *prt* **gezhaabikizang**
gizhaabikizigan *ni* stove; *pl* **gizhaabikiziganan**; *loc* **gizhaabikiziganing**; *dim* **gizhaabikizigaans**
gizhaabikizige *vai* heat things (as something mineral); *1sg* **ingizhaabikizige**; *prt* **gezhaabikiziged**
gizhaadan *vti* guard s.t., watch over s.t.; *1sg* **ingizhaadaan**; *prt* **gezhaadang**
gizhaadige *vai* guard things, watch over things; *1sg* **ingizhaadige**; *prt* **gezhaadiged**
gizhaadigewinini *na* game warden; *pl* **gizhaadigewininiwag**
gizhaagamide *vii* be hot (as a liquid); *prt* **gezhaagamideg**; *aug* **gizhaagamidemagad**; *prt aug* **gezhaagamidemagak**

gizhaagamizan *vti* heat s.t. (as a liquid); *1sg*
  ingizhaagamizaan; *prt* gezhaagamizang
gizhaagamizige *vai* heat things (as a liquid); *1sg*
  ingizhaagamizige; *prt* gezhaagamiziged
gizhaanimad *vii* be a hot wind; *prt* gezhaanimak
gizhaate *vii* be hot (weather); *prt* gezhaateg; *aug*
  gizhaatemagad; *prt aug* gezhaatemagak
gizhaawaso *vai* protect one's young; *1sg*
  ingizhaawas; *prt* gezhaawasod
gizhaawenim *vta* be jealous of s.o.; *1sg*
  ingizhaawenimaa; *prt* gezhaawenimaad
gizhaawenjige *vai* be jealous of things; *1sg*
  ingizhaawenjige; *prt* gezhaawenjiged
gizhaazh /gizhaaN-/ *vta* guard s.o., watch over
  s.o.; *1sg* ingizhaanaa; *prt* gezhaanaad
gizhe-manidoo *na* God (especially in Christian
  usage)
gizhewaadizi *vai* be kind, be generous; *1sg*
  ingizhewaadiz; *prt* gezhewaadizid
gizhibaabide *vii* spin, whirl, revolve; *prt*
  gezhibaabideg; *aug* gizhibaabidemagad; *prt*
  aug gezhibaabidemagak
gizhibaabise *vai* spin, whirl, revolve; *prt*
  gezhibaabised
gizhibaabise *vii* spin, whirl, revolve; *prt*
  gezhibaabiseg; *aug* gizhibaabisemagad; *prt*
  aug gezhibaabisemagak
gizhibaabizo *vai* spin, whirl, revolve; *prt*
  gezhibaabizod
gizhibaayaanimad *vii* be a whirlwind; *prt*
  gezhibaayaanimak
gizhibaayaasijigan *ni* rotary fan; *pl*
  gizhibaayaasijiganan; *loc*
  gizhibaayaasijiganing; *dim*
  gizhibaayaasijigaans
gizhide *vii* be hot; *prt* gezhideg; *aug*
  gizhidemagad; *prt aug* gezhidemagak
gizhizo *vai* be hot, have a fever; *1sg* ingizhiz; *prt*
  gezhizod
gizhiibatoo *vai* run fast; *1sg* ingizhiibatoo; *prt*
  gezhiibatood
gizhiibazhe *vai* have itchy skin; *1sg* ingizhiibazhe;
  prt gezhiibazhed
gizhiibide *vii* move fast, speed fast, fly fast; *prt*
  gezhiibideg; *aug* gizhiibidemagad; *prt aug*
  gezhiibidemagak
gizhiibizi *vai* itch; *1sg* ingizhiibiz; *prt* gezhiibizid
gizhiibizo *vai* move fast, speed fast, drive fast, fly
  fast; *1sg* ingizhiibiz; *prt* gezhiibizod
gizhiidaabii'iwe *vai* drive fast; *1sg*
  ingizhiidaabii'iwe; *prt* gezhiidaabii'iwed
gizhiigaa *vii* drip fast, leak fast; *prt* gezhiigaag; *aug*
  gizhiigaamagad; *prt aug* gezhiigaamagak
gizhiigi *vai* grow fast; *1sg* ingizhiig; *prt* gezhiigid
gizhiigin *vii* grow fast; *prt* gezhiiging
gizhiijiwan *vii* flow fast; *prt* gezhiijiwang
gizhiikaa *vai* go fast; *1sg* ingizhiikaa; *prt*
  gezhiikaad
gizhiikaabatoo *vai* run fast; *1sg* ingizhiikaabatoo;
  prt gezhiikaabatood
gizhiikaakwazhiwe *vai* paddle fast; *1sg*
  ingizhiikaakwazhiwe; *prt*
  gezhiikaakwazhiwed
gizhiise *vai* fly fast; *1sg* ingizhiise; *prt* gezhiised

gizhiise *vii* fly fast; *prt* gezhiiseg; *aug*
  gizhiisemagad; *prt aug* gezhiisemagak
gizhiiwe *vai* speak loud; *1sg* ingizhiiwe; *prt*
  gezhiiwed
gizhiiyaanimad *vii* wind blows fast; *prt*
  gezhiiyaanimak
gizizan *vti* heat s.t.; *1sg* ingizizaan; *prt* gezizang
giziibiiga' /giziibiiga'w-/ *vta* wash s.o. using
  something; *1sg* ingiziibiiga'waa; *prt*
  geziibiiga'waad
giziibiiga'an *vti* wash s.t. (clothes); *1sg*
  ingiziibiiga'aan; *prt* geziibiiga'ang
giziibiiga'igan *ni* soap; *pl* giziibiiga'iganan; *loc*
  giziibiiga'iganing; *dim* giziibiiga'igaans
giziibiiga'ige *vai* wash things, wash clothes; *1sg*
  ingiziibiiga'ige; *prt* geziibiiga'iged
giziibiiga'ige-makak *ni* washtub, washing
  machine; *pl* giziibiiga'ige-makakoon; *loc*
  giziibiiga'ige-makakong; *dim* giziibiiga'ige-
  makakoons
giziibiiga'igewigamig *ni* laundromat; *pl*
  giziibiiga'igewigamigoon; *loc*
  giziibiiga'igewigamigong; *dim*
  giziibiiga'igewigamigoons
giziibiigazhe *vai* take a bath, wash up; *1sg*
  ingiziibiigazhe; *prt* geziibiigazhed
giziibiigazhewaaboo *ni* rubbing alcohol
giziibiigin *vta* wash s.o. by hand; *1sg*
  ingiziibiiginaa; *prt* geziibiiginaad
giziibiiginakokwe *vai* wash pail, wash kettle; *1sg*
  ingiziibiiginakokwe; *prt* geziibiiginakokwed
giziibiiginan *vti* wash s.t. by hand; *1sg*
  ingiziibiiginaan; *prt* geziibiiginang
giziibiiginaage *vai* wash dishes; *1sg*
  ingiziibiiginaagane; *prt* geziibiiginaaganed
giziibiiginaaganewaaboo *ni* liquid detergent
giziibiigindibe *vai* wash one's hair; *1sg*
  ingiziibiigindibe; *prt* geziibiigindibed
giziibiigindiben *vta* wash s.o.'s hair; *1sg*
  ingiziibiigindibenaa; *prt* geziibiigindibenaad
giziibiiginigaade *vii* be washed; *prt*
  geziibiiginigaadeg; *aug*
  giziibiiginigaademagad; *prt aug*
  geziibiiginigaademagak
giziibiigininjii *vai* wash one's hands; *1sg*
  ingiziibiigininjii; *prt* geziibiigininjiid
giziibiigisaginige *vai* wash floors; *1sg*
  ingiziibiigisaginige; *prt* geziibiigisaginiged
giziibiigisaginige-giizhigad *vii* be Saturday; *prt*
  geziibiigisaginige-giizhigak
giziibiigii *vai* wash; *1sg* ingiziibiigii; *prt* geziibiigiid
giziibiigiingwe *vai* wash one's face; *1sg*
  ingiziibiigiingwe; *prt* geziibiigiingwed
giziibiigiingwewinaagan *ni* wash basin; *loc*
  giziibiigiingwewinaaganing; *dim*
  giziibiigiingwewinaagaans
giziibwewe *vai* squeak, creak; *prt* geziibwewed
giziibwewe *vii* squeak, creak; *prt* geziibweweg;
  aug giziibwewemagad; *prt aug*
  geziibwewemagak
giziibweweshkaa *vai* squeak in motion, creak; *prt*
  geziibweweshkaad
giziibweweshkaa *vii* squeak in motion, creak; *prt*
  geziibweweshkaag; *aug*

giziibweweshkaamagad; *prt aug*
geziibweweshkaamagak
giziibweweyaashi *vai* creak in the wind; *prt*
geziibweweyaashid
giziibweweyaasin *vii* creak in the wind; *prt*
geziibweweyaasing
giziidoone'on *ni* napkin; *pl* giziidoone'onan; *loc*
giziidoone'oning; *dim* giziidoone'onens
giziin *vta* wipe s.o. by hand; *1sg* ingiziinaa; *prt*
geziinaad
giziinan *vti* wipe s.t. by hand; *1sg* ingiziinaan; *prt*
geziinang
giziindime'o *vai* wipe oneself after defecating; *1sg*
ingiziindime'; *prt* geziindime'od
giziindime'on *ni* toilet tissue; *pl* giziindime'onan;
loc giziindime'oning; *dim* giziindime'onens
giziingwe'o *vai* wipe one's face with something;
1sg ingiziingwe'; *prt* geziingwe'od
giziingwe'on *ni* towel; *pl* giziingwe'onan; *loc*
giziingwe'oning; *dim* giziingwe'onens
giziininjii'on *ni* napkin; *pl* giziininjii'onan; *loc*
giziininjii'oning; *dim* giziininjii'onens
giziiyaabide'o *vai* brush one's teeth; *1sg*
ingiziiyaabide'; *prt* geziiyaabide'od
giziiyaabide'odizo *vai* brush one's teeth; *1sg*
ingiziiyaabide'odiz; *prt* geziiyaabide'odizod
giziiyaabide'on *ni* toothbrush; *pl*
giziiyaabide'onan; *loc* giziiyaabide'oning; *dim*
giziiyaabide'onens
giziiyaabika'igan *ni* dish towel; *pl*
giziiyaabika'iganan; *loc* giziiyaabika'iganing; *dim* giziiyaabika'igaans
gii- *pv1 past verb prefix*
giichibabagiwayaane *vai* take off one's shirt; *1sg*
ingiichibabagiwayaane; *prt*
gaachibabagiwayaaned
giichibabiinzikawaagane *vai* take off one's coat;
1sg ingiichibabiinzikawaagane; *prt*
gaachibabiinzikawaaganed
giichigiboodiyegwaazone *vai* take off one's pants;
1sg ingiichigiboodiyegwaazone; *prt*
gaachigiboodiyegwaazoned
giichigobidoon *vti2* pull s.t. off; *1sg*
ingiichigobidoon; *prt* gaachigobidood
giichigobizh /giichigobiN-/ *vta* pull s.t. off; *1sg*
ingiichigobinaa; *prt* gaachigobinaad
giichigon *vta* take s.o. off, extricate s.o.; *1sg*
ingiichigonaa; *prt* gaachigonaad
giichigonan *vti* take s.t. off, extricate s.t.; *1sg*
ingiichigonaan; *prt* gaachigonang
giichigwam *vta* pull s.o. off with teeth; *1sg*
ingiichigwamaa; *prt* gaachigwamaad
giichigwandan *vti* pull s.t. off with teeth; *1sg*
ingiichigwandaan; *prt* gaachigwandang
giichiminjikaawane *vai* take off one's mittens; *1sg*
ingiichiminjikaawane; *prt*
gaachiminjikaawaned
giichiwakwaane *vai* take off one's hat; *1sg*
ingiichiwakwaane; *prt* gaachiwakwaaned
giige *vai* heal up; *1sg* ingiige; *prt* gaaged
giigido *vai* speak; *1sg* ingiigid; *prt* gaagidod
giigidowin *ni* speech, telephone; *pl* giigidowinan;
loc giigidowining; *dim* giigidowinens

giigidoo-biiwaabikoons *ni* telephone, telephone
wire; *pl* giigidoo-biiwaabikoonsan; *loc*
giigidoo-biiwaabikoonsing
giigidoowinini *na* councillor, representative; *pl*
giigidoowininiwag
giigoonh *na* fish; *pl* giigoonyag
giigoonhwaaboo *ni* fish soup; *loc*
giigoonhwaaboong
giigoonyike *vai* fish; *1sg* ingiigoonyike; *prt*
gaagoonyiked
giigoonyikewinini *na* fisherman; *pl*
giigoonyikewininiwag
giigoozens *na* minnow; *pl* giigoozensag
gii' *vta* get away from s.o., escape from s.o.; *1sg*
ingii'aa; *prt* gaa'aad
gii'igoshimo *vai* fast for a vision; *1sg* ingii'igoshim;
prt gaa'igoshimod
gii'iwe *vai* escape from people; *1sg* ingii'iwe; *prt*
gaa'iwed
giikaji *vai* feel cold; *1sg* ingiikaj; *prt* gaakajid
giikanaamode *vii* be smoky inside; *prt*
gaakanaamodeg; *aug* giikanaamodemagad;
prt aug gaakanaamodemagak
giikanaamozigan *na* bacon
giikaam *vta* argue with s.o., quarrel with s.o.; *1sg*
ingiikaamaa; *prt* gaakaamaad
giikaandiwag /giikaandi-/ *vai* they argue with each
other, they quarrel with each other; *1pl*
ingiikaandimin; *prt* gaakaandijig
giikimanizi *vai* feel numb, tingle; *1sg* ingiikimaniz;
prt gaakimanizid
giikiibingwashi *vai* be sleepy; *1sg* ingiikiibingwash;
prt gaakiibingwashid
giimaabam *vta* peek at s.o., spy on s.o.; *1sg*
ingiimaabamaa; *prt* gaamaabamaad
giimaabi *vai* peek, spy; *1sg* ingiimaab; *prt*
gaamaabid
giimaadoode *vai* creep away; *1sg* ingiimaadoode;
prt gaamaadooded
giimitaw *vta* eavesdrop on s.o.; *1sg* ingiimitawaa;
prt gaamitawaad
giimii *vai* flee, escape; *1sg* ingiimii; *prt* gaamiid
giimoodad *vii* be secret; *prt* gaamoodak
giimoodanjige *vai* eat things secretly; *1sg*
ingiimoodanjige; *prt* gaamoodanjiged
giimoodaapi *vai* laugh secretly; *1sg* ingiimoodaap;
prt gaamoodaapid
giimooj *pc* secretly
giimoozaabi *vai* peek; *1sg* ingiimoozaab; *prt*
gaamoozaabid
giimoozikaw *vta* sneak up on s.o.; *1sg*
ingiimoozikawaa; *prt* gaamoozikawaad
giin *pr* you *second person singular personal pronoun*
giinawaa *pr* you *second person plural personal
pronoun*
giinawind *pr* we *first person inclusive personal
pronoun*, us *first person inclusive personal pronoun*
giinaa *vii* be sharp; *prt* gaanaag; *aug* giinaamagad;
prt aug gaanaamagak
giineta *pr* only you *second person singular personal
pronoun*
giinetawaa *pr* only you *second person plural
personal pronoun*
giinetawind *pr* only us *first person inclusive personal
pronoun*

giiniboodoon *vti2* file s.t. sharp; *1sg*
ingiiniboodoon; *prt* gaaniboodood
giiniboozh /giinibooN-/ *vta* file s.o. sharp; *1sg*
ingiiniboonaa; *prt* gaaniboonaad
giinitam *pr* your turn *second person singular personal
pronoun*
giinitamawaa *pr* your turn *second person plural
personal pronoun*
giinitamawind *pr* our turn *first person inclusive
personal pronoun*
giinizi *vai* be sharp; *prt* gaanizid
giishkada'igan *ni* cleaver, chopping tool; *pl*
giishkada'iganan; *loc* giishkada'iganing; *dim*
giishkada'igaans
giishkadinaa *vii* be a cliff, be a steep bank; *prt*
gaashkadinaag; *aug* giishkadinaamagad; *prt*
aug gaashkadinaamagak
giishka' /giishka'w-/ *vta* chop s.o. off; *1sg*
ingiishka'waa; *prt* gaashka'waad
giishka'an *vti* chop s.t. off; *1sg* ingiishka'aan; *prt*
gaashka'ang
giishka'aakwe *vai* cut timber; *1sg*
ingiishka'aakwe; *prt* gaashka'aakwed
giishka'aakwewigamig *ni* lumber camp; *pl*
giishka'aakwewigamigoon; *loc*
giishka'aakwewigamigong; *dim*
giishka'aakwewigamigoons
giishka'aakwewinini *na* lumberjack, logger; *pl*
giishka'aakwewininiwag
giishkam *vta* bite through s.o.; *1sg*
ingiishkamaa; *prt* gaashkamaad
giishkanakad *ni* stump; *pl* giishkanakadoon; *loc*
giishkanakadong; *dim* giishkanakadoons
giishkandan *vti* bite through s.t. cleanly; *1sg*
ingiishkandaan; *prt* gaashkandang
giishkashkimod *ni* cedar bark bag; *pl*
giishkashkimodan; *loc* giishkashkimodaang;
dim giishkashkimodens
giishkaabaagwe *vai* be thirsty; *1sg*
ingiishkaabaagwe; *prt* gaashkaabaagwed
giishkaabikaa *vii* be a steep rock face; *prt*
gaashkaabikaag; *aug* giishkaabikaamagad; *prt*
aug gaashkaabikaamagak
giishkaamikaa *vii* there is a drop-off; *prt*
gaashkaamikaag; *aug* giishkaamikaamagad;
prt aug gaashkaamikaamagak
giishkaazhibikaa *vii* there is a rock cliff; *prt*
gaashkaazhibikaag; *aug*
giishkaazhibikaamagad; *prt aug*
gaashkaazhibikaamagak
giishkibidoon *vti2* tear s.t. off; *1sg*
ingiishkibidoon; *prt* gaashkibidood
giishkibijigaade *vii* be torn off; *prt*
gaashkibijigaadeg; *aug*
giishkibijigaademagad; *prt aug*
gaashkibijigaademagak
giishkibijigaazo *vai* be torn off; *prt*
gaashkibijigaazod
giishkibijige *vai* tear things off; *1sg* ingiishkibijige;
prt gaashkibijiged
giishkibizh /giishkibiN-/ *vta* tear s.o. off; *1sg*
ingiishkibinaa; *prt* gaashkibinaad
giishkiboodoon *vti2* saw s.t. off; *1sg*
ingiishkiboodoon; *prt* gaashkiboodood

giishkiboojigan *ni* crosscut saw; *pl*
giishkiboojiganan; *loc* giishkiboojiganing; *dim*
giishkiboojigaans
giishkiboojige *vai* saw things off; *1sg*
ingiishkiboojige; *prt* gaashkiboojiged
giishkiboozh /giishkibooN-/ *vta* saw s.o. off; *1sg*
ingiishkiboonaa; *prt* gaashkiboonaad
giishkiga' /giishkiga'w-/ *vta* chop s.o. off; *1sg*
ingiishkiga'waa; *prt* gaashkiga'waad
giishkiga'an *vti* chop s.t. off; *1sg* ingiishkiga'aan;
prt gaashkiga'ang
giishkiganzhiikonidizo *vai* cut one's own nails; *1sg*
ingiishkiganzhiikonidiz; *prt*
gaashkiganzhiikonidizod
giishkijiin *vta* hug s.o., embrace s.o.; *1sg*
ingiishkijiinaa; *prt* gaashkijiinaad
giishkijiinidiwag /giishkijiinidi-/ *vai* they hug each
other, they embrace each other; *1pl*
ingiishkijiinidim; *prt* gaashkijiinidijig
giishkijiiwagooday *ni* skirt; *pl*
giishkijiiwagoodayan; *dim*
giishkijiiwagoodayens
giishkikaa *vai* tear, rip; *pl* gaashkikaad
giishkikaa *vii* tear, rip; *prt* gaashkikaag; *aug*
giishkikaamagad; *prt aug* gaashkikaamagak
giishkikozhiwe *vai* cut hair; *1sg* ingiishkikozhiwe;
prt gaashkikozhiwed
giishkikozhiwewikwe *na* barber (female); *pl*
giishkikozhiwewikweg
giishkikozhiwewinini *na* barber; *pl*
giishkikozhiwewininiwag
giishkishin *vai* get cut falling; *1sg* ingiishkishin; *prt*
gaashkishing
giishkizh /giishkizhw-/ *vta* cut s.o. off, cut through
s.o.; *1sg* ingiishkizhwaa; *prt* gaashkizhwaad
giishkizhan *vti* cut s.t. off, cut through s.o.; *1sg*
ingiishkizhaan; *prt* gaashkizhang
giishkizhigan *ni* scythe; *pl* giishkizhiganan; *loc*
giishkizhiganing; *dim* giishkizhiganans
giishkizhige *vai* cut things off, cut things; *1sg*
ingiishkizhige; *prt* gaashkizhiged
giishkizhodizo *vai* cut oneself; *1sg*
ingiishkizhodiz; *prt* gaashkizhodizod
giishkowe *vai* stop crying, stop making vocal
noise; *1sg* ingiishkowe; *prt* gaashkowed
giishpin *pc* if
giitagoode *vai* take off one's dress; *1sg*
ingiitagoode; *prt* gaatagooded
giitazhigane *vai* take off one's socks; *1sg*
ingiitazhigane; *prt* gaatazhiganed
giiwanaadingwaam *vai* have a bad dream, have a
nightmare; *1sg* ingiiwanaadingwaam; *prt*
gaawanaadingwaang
giiwanaadizi *vai* be crazy, be insane; *1sg*
ingiiwanaadiz; *prt* gaawanaadizid
giiwanaadiziiwigamig *ni* mental hospital; *pl*
giiwanaadiziiwigamigoon; *loc*
giiwanaadiziiwigamigong
giiwanim *vta* lie to s.o., deceive s.o. in speech; *1sg*
ingiiwanimaa; *prt* gaawanimaad
giiwanimo *vai* lie, be deceptive in speech; *1sg*
ingiiwanim; *prt* gaawanimod
giiwashkwe *vai* be dizzy; *1sg* ingiiwashkwe; *prt*
gaawashkwed

giiwashkwebazh /giiwashkwebaN-/ *vta* make s.o.
drunk; *1sg* ingiiwashkwebanaa; *prt*
gaawashkwebanaad
giiwashkwebii *vai* be drunk; *1sg* ingiiwashkwebii;
prt gaawashkwebiid
giiwashkweganaam *vta* knock s.o.
senseless; *1sg*
ingiiwashkweganaamaa; *prt*
gaawashkweganaamaad
giiwashkwe'ogo *vai* be seasick; *1sg*
ingiiwashkwe'og; *prt* gaawashkwe'ogod
giiwashkweshin *vai* be knocked senseless in
impact; *1sg* ingiiwashkweshin; *prt*
gaawashkweshing
giiwashkweshkaw- *vta* make s.o.
dizzy (especially
of a substance) *in inverse forms: 1sg*
ingiiwashkweshkaagon; *prt*
gaawashkweshkaagod
giiwashkweyaabandam *vai2* be dizzy, feel
unsteady; *1sg* ingiiwashkweyaabandam; *prt*
gaawashkweyaabandang
giiwashkweyendam *vai2* be confused; *1sg*
ingiiwashkweyendam; *prt*
gaawashkweyendang
giiwe *vai* go home, return; *1sg* ingiiwe; *prt* gaawed
giiwebatoo *vai* run back, run home; *1sg*
ingiiwebatoo; *prt* gaawebatood
giiwe-biboon *vii* be after mid-winter, be late
winter; *prt* gaawe-biboong
giiwedaabii'iwe *vai* drive home; *1sg*
ingiiwedaabii'iwe; *prt* gaawedaabii'iwed
giiwedin *ni* north wind, north; *loc* giiwedinong
giiwegidaazo *vai* go home mad; *1sg*
ingiiwegidaaz; *prt* gaawegidaazod
giiwe'o *vai* go home by boat; *1sg* ingiiwe'; *prt*
gaawe'od
giiwekii *vai* return to one's own country; *1sg*
ingiiwekii; *prt* gaawekiid
giiwenamaw *vta* give presents to s.o. in exchange;
1sg ingiiwenamawaa; *prt* gaawenamawaad
giiwenaazha' /giiwenaazha'w-/ *vta* tell s.o. to go
home; *1sg* ingiiwenaazha'waa; *prt*
gaawenaazha'waad
giiwenh *pc* so the story goes, so it is said
giiwenige *vai* give presents to relatives of someone
deceased in completion of mourning on anniversary of the death; *1sg* ingiiwenige; *prt*
gaaweniged
giiwe-niibin *vii* be after mid-summer, late summer;
prt gaawe-niibing
giiwewidaw *vta* take (s.t.) home for s.o., carry
(s.t.) home for s.o.; *1sg* ingiiwewidawaa; *prt*
gaawewidawaad
giiwewidoon *vti2* take s.t. home, carry s.t. home;
1sg ingiiwewidoon; *prt* gaawewidood
giiwewizh /giiwewiN-/ *vta* take s.o. home, carry
s.o. home; *1sg* ingiiwewinaa; *prt* gaawewinaad
giiweyendam *vai2* think about returning, think
about going home again; *1sg* ingiiweyendam;
prt gaaweyendang
giiwitaa-ayi'ii *pc* all around it; *also* giiwitaayi'ii
giiwitaabatoo *vai* run around something; *1sg*
ingiiwitaabatoo; *prt* gaawitaabatood
giiwitaabatwaadan *vti* run around s.t.; *1sg*
ingiiwitaabatwaadaan; *prt*
gaawitaabatwaadang

giiwitaashim *vta* lay s.o. down around; *1sg*
ingiiwitaashimaa; *prt* gaawitaashimaad
giiwitaashkan *vti* walk around s.t.; *1sg*
ingiiwitaashkaan; *prt* gaawitaashkang
giiwitaashkaw *vta* walk around s.o.; *1sg*
ingiiwitaashkawaa; *prt* gaawitaashkawaad
giiwitaashkaa *vai* go around, encircle; *1sg*
ingiiwitaashkaa; *prt* gaawitaashkaad
giiwitaashkode *pc* around the fire
giiwitaasidoon *vti2* lay s.t. down around; *1sg*
ingiiwitaasidoon; *prt* gaawitaasidood
giiwitaawose *vai* walk around something; *1sg*
ingiiwitaawose; *prt* gaawitaawosed; *also*
giiwitaa'ose
giiwitaayaazhagaame *vai* walk around the edge,
walk around a lake; *1sg*
ingiiwitaayaazhagaame; *prt*
gaawitaayaazhagaamed
giiwizi *vai* be orphaned; *1sg* ingiiwiz; *prt* gaawizid
giiwose *vai* hunt; *1sg* ingiiwose; *prt* gaawosed;
also giiyose
giiwosewasim *na* hunting dog; *pl*
giiwosewasimoog; *also* giiyosewasim
giiwosewinini *na* hunter; *pl* giiwosewininiwag;
also giiyosewinini
giiwoon *na* heart suite card; *pl* giiwoonag; *also*
giiyoon
giizhakidoon *vti2* finish setting s.t. up; *1sg*
ingiizhakidoon; *prt* gaazhakidood
giizhakizh /giizhakiN-/ *vta* finish setting s.o. up;
1sg ingiizhakinaa; *prt* gezhakinaad
giizhaa *pc* beforehand, in advance
giizhaajimo *vai* tell all; *1sg* ingiizhaajim; *prt*
gaazhaajimod
giizhaande *vii* be fully ripe; *prt* gaazhaandeg; *aug*
giizhaandemagad; *prt aug* gaazhaandemagak
giizhaanzo *vai* be fully ripe; *prt* gaazhaanzod
giizhendam *vai2* have one's mind made up;
resolve; *1sg* ingiizhendam; *prt* gaazhendang
giizhi- *pv4* finish, complete
giizhichigaade *vii* be finished; *prt*
gaazhichigaadeg; *aug* giizhichigaademagad;
prt aug gaazhichigaademagak
giizhichigaazo *vai* be finished; *prt*
gaazhichigaazod
giizhide *vii* be done cooking; *prt* gaazhideg; *aug*
giizhidemagad; *prt aug* gaazhidemagak
giizhig *na* sky, heaven, day; *loc* giizhigong
giizhigad *vii* be day; *prt* gaazhigak
giizhigamide *vii* finish boiling; *prt*
gaazhigamideg; *aug* giizhigamidemagad; *prt*
aug gaazhigamidemagak
giizhigamizige *vai* finish boiling things; *1sg*
ingiizhigamizige; *prt* gaazhigamiziged
giizhigaate *vii* there is moonlight; *prt*
gaazhigaateg; *aug* giizhigaatemagad; *prt aug*
gaazhigaatemagak
giizhige *vai* finish building a dwelling; *1sg*
ingiizhige; *prt* gaazhiged
giizhigi *vai* be ripe, be full grown; *1sg* ingiizhig; *prt*
gaazhigid
giizhigin *vii* be ripe, be full grown; *prt* gaazhiging
giizhi' *vta* finish s.o., finish making s.o.; *1sg*
ingiizhi'aa; *prt* gaazhi'aad

giizhik *na* white cedar; *pl* **giizhikag**; *loc* **giizhiking**; *dim* **giizhikens**
giizhikaandag *na* cedar bough; *pl* **giizhikaandagoog**; *loc* **giizhikaandagong**; *dim* **giizhikaandagoons**
giizhitoon *vti2* finish s.t., finish making s.t.; *1sg* **ingiizhitoon**; *prt* **gaazhitood**
giizhiikan *vti* finish with s.t.; *1sg* **ingiizhiikaan**; *prt* **gaazhiikang**
giizhiikaw *vta* finish with s.o.; *1sg* **ingiizhiikawaa**; *prt* **gaazhiikawaad**
giizhiitaa *vai* finish a task, finish work; *1sg* **ingiizhiitaa**; *prt* **gaazhiitaad**
giizhoo'o *vai* dress warmly; *1sg* **ingiizhoo'**; *prt* **gaazhoo'od**
giizhoopizo *vai* be wrapped up warm; *1sg* **ingiizhoopiz**; *prt* **gaazhoopizod**
giizhoopizon *na* scarf; *pl* **giizhoopizonag**; *loc* **giizhoopizoning**; *dim* **giizhoopizonens**
giizhooshin *vai* lie in warmth; *1sg* **ingiizhooshin**; *prt* **gaazhooshing**
giizhootawage'o *vai* wear earmuffs; *1sg* **ingiizhootawage'**; *prt* **gaazhootawage'od**
giizhootawage'on *na* earmuff; *pl* **giizhootawage'onag**; *dim* **giizhootawage'onens**
giizhoote *vii* be hot inside; *prt* **gaazhooteg**; *aug* **giizhootemagad**; *prt aug* **gaazhootemagak**
giizikan *vti* take s.t. off the body (e.g., clothes); *1sg* **ingiizikaan**; *prt* **gaazikang**
giizikaw *vta* take s.o. off the body (e.g., clothes); *1sg* **ingiizikawaa**; *prt* **gaazikawaad**
giizikonaye *vai* undress, take off one's clothes; *1sg* **ingiizikonaye**; *prt* **gaazikonayed**
giizikonaye' *vta* undress s.o.; *1sg* **ingiizikonaye'aa**; *prt* **gaazikonaye'aad**
giizis *na* sun, moon, month; *pl* **giizisoog**; *loc* **giizisong**; *dim* **giizisoons**
giizisoo-mazina'igan *ni* calendar; *pl* **giizisoo-mazina'iganan**; *loc* **giizisoo-mazina'iganing**; *dim* **giizisoo-mazina'igaans**
giiziz /giizizw-/ *vta* finish cooking s.o.; *1sg* **ingiizizwaa**; *prt* **gaazizwaad**
giizizamaw *vta* cook (s.t.) for s.o.; *1sg* **ingiizizamawaa**; *prt* **gaazizamawaad**
giizizan *vti* finish cooking s.t.; *1sg* **ingiizizaan**; *prt* **gaazizang**
giizizekwe *vai* cook; *1sg* **ingiizizekwe**; *prt* **gaazizekwed**
giizizo *vai* be done cooking; *prt* **gaazizod**; *also* **giizhizo**
go *pc emphatic word*; *also* **igo**
goda *pc emphatic word*
godam *vta* take a taste of s.t.; *1sg* **ingodamaa**; *prt* **gwedamaad**
godandan *vti* take a taste of s.o.; *1sg* **ingodandaan**; *prt* **gwedandang**
godigoshin *vai* fall and be injured; *1sg* **ingodigoshin**; *prt* **gwedigoshing**
godin *vta* test s.o. with hand; *1sg* **ingodinaa**; *prt* **gwedinaad**
godinan *vti* test s.t. with hand; *1sg* **ingodinaan**; *prt* **gwedinang**
godotaagan *ni* bell; *pl* **godotaaganan**; *loc* **gototaaganing**; *dim* **gototaagaans**

goji- *pv4* try, attempt
gojichige *vai* try things; *1sg* **ingojichige**; *prt* **gwejichiged**
goji'ewizi *vai* try, make an effort; *1sg* **ingoji'ewiz**; *prt* **gweji'ewizid**
gojimaam *vta* take a smell of s.o.; *1sg* **ingojimaamaa**; *prt* **gwejimaamaad**
gojimaandan *vti* take a smell of s.t.; *1sg* **ingojimaandaan**; *prt* **gwejimaandang**
goji-nagamo *vai* practice singing; *1sg* **ingoji-nagam**; *prt* **gweji-nagamod**
gojipidan *vti* take a taste of s.t., check s.t. by tasting; *1sg* **ingojipidaan**; *prt* **gwejipidang**
gojipijige *vai* taste things; *1sg* **ingojipijige**; *prt* **gwejipijiged**
gojipozh /gojipw-/ *vta* take a taste of s.o., check s.o. by tasting; *1sg* **ingojipwaa**; *prt* **gwejipwaad**
gomaa *pc* some amount, to a middling degree
gomaapii *pc* for some time, some distance
gondan *vti* swallow s.t.; *1sg* **ingondaan**; *prt* **gwendang**
gondaabiigin *vta* put s.o. in water, dip s.o.; *1sg* **ingondaabiiginaa**; *prt* **gwendaabiiginaad**
gondaabiiginan *vti* put s.t. in water, dip s.t.; *1sg* **ingondaabiiginaan**; *prt* **gwendaabiiginang**
gonzaabii *vii* sink in water; *prt* **gwenzaabiig**; *aug* **gonzaabiimagad**; *prt aug* **gwenzaabiimagak**
gonzaabiishkoojigan *ni* sinker (fishing tackle); *pl* **gonzaabiishkoojiganan**; *loc* **gonzaabiishkoojiganing**; *dim* **gonzaabiishkoojigaans**
gonzhi /gonN-/ *vta* swallow s.o.; *1sg* **ingonaa**; *prt* **gwenaad**
gopibatoo *vai* run inland; *1sg* **ingopibatoo**; *prt* **gwepibatood**
gopimine *vai* take wild rice inland; *1sg* **ingopimine**; *prt* **gwepimined**
gopiwidoon *vti2* take s.t. inland, carry s.t. inland; *1sg* **ingopiwidoon**; *prt* **gwepiwidood**
gopiwizh /gopiwiN-/ *vta* take s.o. inland, carry s.o. inland; *1sg* **ingopiwinaa**; *prt* **gwepiwinaad**
gopii *vai* go away from the water, go inland; *1sg* **ingopii**; *prt* **gwepiid**
gosha *pc emphatic particle*
goshi /goS-/ *vta* fear s.o.; *1sg* **ingosaa**; *prt* **gwesaad**
goshko' *vta* surprise s.o.; *1sg* **ingoshko'aa**; *prt* **gweshko'aad**
goshkokaa *vai* be surprised, be startled; *1sg* **ingoshkokaa**; *prt* **gweshkokaad**
goshkom *vta* surprise s.o. verbally; *1sg* **ingoshkomaa**; *prt* **gweshkomaad**
goshkozi *vai* wake up, be awake; *1sg* **ingoshkoz**; *prt* **gweshkozid**
goshkwaawaadabi *vai* sit quietly, remain tranquilly in place; *1sg* **ingoshkwaawaadab**; *prt* **gweshkwaawaadabid**
goshkwaawaadizi *vai* be still, be quiet; *1sg* **ingoshkwaawaadiz**; *prt* **gweshkwaawaadizid**
gotan *vti* be afraid of s.t., fear s.t.; *1sg* **ingotaan**; *prt* **gwetang**
gotaaji *vai* be afraid, have fear; *1sg* **ingotaaj**; *prt* **gwetaajid**
gotaajishki *vai* be timid; *1sg* **ingotaajishk**; *prt* **gwetaajishkid**

gotaamigozi *vai* be a good worker, be a good provider; *1sg* ingotaamigoz; *prt* gwetaamigozid

gotigobide *vii* roll over, go out of place; *prt* gwetigobideg; *aug* gotigobidemagad; *prt aug* gwetigobidemagak

gotigobidoon *vti2* roll s.t. over, tip s.t.; *1sg* ingotigobidoon; *prt* gwetigobidood

gotigobizh /gotigobiN-/ *vta* roll s.o. over, tip s.o.; *1sg* ingotigobinaa; *prt* gwetigobinaad

gotigobizo *vai* roll over, go out of place; *1sg* ingotigobiz; *prt* gwetigobizod

gozi *vai* move one's residence; *1sg* ingoz; *prt* gwezid

gozigwan *vii* be heavy; *prt* gwezigwang

gozigwani *vai* be heavy; *1sg* ingozigwan; *prt* gwezigwanid

gozigwaakomin *na* Juneberry; *pl* gozigwaakominag

gozigwaakominagaawanzh *na* Juneberry bush; *pl* gozigwaakominagaawanzhiig; *loc* gozigwaakominagaawanzhiing; *dim* gozigwaakominagaawanzhiins

gozikan *vti* test s.t. with foot or body, try on s.t. (e.g., clothes); *1sg* ingozikaan; *prt* gwezikang

gozikaw *vta* test s.o. with foot or body, try on s.o. (e.g., clothes); *1sg* ingozikawaa; *prt* gwezikawaad

googa'am *vai2* jump out of the water as a fish; *prt* gwaaga'ang

googii *vai* dive; *1sg* ingoogii; *prt* gwaagiid

gookooko'oo *na* owl; *pl* gookooko'oog; *dim* gookooko'oons

gookoosh *na* pig, pork; *pl* gookooshag; *dim* gookooshens

gookooshi-bimide *ni* lard

gookooshi-wiiyaas *ni* pork; *loc* gookooshi-wiiyaasing

goon *na* snow; *loc* gooning; *dim* goonens

goonikaa *vii* be much snow; *prt* gwaanikaag; *aug* goonikaamagad; *prt aug* gwaanikaamagak

goopadendan *vti* consider s.t. worthless; *1sg* ingoopadendaan; *prt* gwaapadendang

goopadenim *vta* consider s.o. worthless; *1sg* ingoopadenimaa; *prt* gwaapadenimaad

goopadizi *vai* be worthless, be useless; *1sg* ingoopadiz; *prt* gwaapadizid

goopaji' *vta* mistreat s.o., ruin s.o.; *1sg* ingoopaji'aa; *prt* gwaapaji'aad

goopajitoon *vti2* mistreat s.t., ruin s.t.; *1sg* ingoopajitoon; *prt* gwaapajitood

gwanabishkan *vti* tip s.t. with foot or body; *1sg* ingwanabishkaan; *prt* gwenabishkang

gwanabishkaa *vai* capsize, tip; *1sg* ingwanabishkaa; *prt* gwenabishkaad

gwayak *pc* straight, right, correct

gwayakobidoon *vti2* pull s.t. straight, tear s.t. straight; *1sg* ingwayakobidoon; *prt* gweyakobidood

gwayako-bimaadizi *vai* live a proper life; *1sg* ingwayako-bimaadiz; *prt* gweyako-bimaadizid

gwayakobizh /gwayakobiN-/ *vta* pull s.o. straight, tear s.o. straight; *1sg* ingwayakobinaa; *prt* gweyakobidood

gwayakobii'an *vti* write s.t. correctly; *1sg* ingwayakobii'aan; *prt* gweyakobii'ang

gwayakobii'ige *vai* write correctly; *1sg* ingwayakobii'ige; *prt* gweyakobii'iged

gwayakoboodoon *vti2* saw s.t. straight; *1sg* ingwayakoboodoon; *prt* gweyakoboodood

gwayakoboozh /gwayakobooN-/ *vta* saw s.o. straight; *1sg* ingwayakoboonaa; *prt* gweyakoboonaad

gwayakochige *vai* make things right, do things right; *1sg* ingwayakochige; *prt* gweyakochiged

gwayakogaabawi *vai* stand straight, have good posture; *1sg* ingwayakogaabaw; *prt* gweyakogaabawid

gwayakogi *vai* grow straight; *1sg* ingwayakog; *prt* gweyakogid

gwayakogin *vii* grow straight; *prt* gweyakoging

gwayakokweni *vai* hold one's head straight; *1sg* ingwayakokwen; *prt* gweyakokwenid

gwayakoshim *vta* lay s.o. straight; *1sg* ingwayakoshimaa; *prt* gweyakoshimaad

gwayakoshin *vai* lie straight, lie correctly; *1sg* ingwayakoshin; *prt* gweyakoshing

gwayakoshkaa *vai* go straight, go the right way; *1sg* ingwayakoshkaa; *prt* gweyakoshkaad

gwayakosidoon *vti2* lay s.t. straight; *1sg* ingwayakosidoon; *prt* gweyakosidood

gwayakosin *vii* lie straight, lie correctly; *prt* gweyakosing

gwayakotam *vai2* hear the right thing, find out the truth; *1sg* ingwayakotam; *prt* gweyakotang

gwayakowe *vai* speak correctly; *1sg* ingwayakowe; *prt* gweyakowed

gwayakozh /gwayakozhw-/ *vta* cut s.o. straight; *1sg* ingwayakozhwaa; *prt* gweyakozhwaad

gwayakozhan *vti* cut s.t. straight; *1sg* ingwayakozhaan; *prt* gweyakozhang

gwayako-zhooniyaa *na* cash, ready money

gwayakozi *vai* be straight; *prt* gweyakozid

gwayakwakamigaa *vii* be level ground; *prt* gweyakwakamigaag; *aug* gwayakwakamigaamagad; *prt aug* gwayakwakamigaamagak

gwayakwaa *vii* be straight, be the correct; *prt* gweyakwaag; *aug* gwayakwaamagad; *prt aug* gweyakwaamagak

gwayakwaabidoo'an *vti* thread s.t. correctly, bead s.t. correctly (on a loom); *1sg* ingwayakwaabidoo'aan; *prt* gweyakwaabidoo'ang

gwayakwaabidoo'ige *vai* bead things correctly (on a loom); *1sg* ingwayakwaabidoo'ige; *prt* gweyakwaabidoo'iged

gwayakwaabikad *vii* be straight (as something mineral); *prt* gweyakwaabikak

gwayakwaabikizi *vai* be straight (as something mineral); *prt* gweyakwaabikizid

gwayakwaabiigad *vii* be straight (as something string-like); *prt* gweyakwaabiigak

gwayakwaabiigizi *vai* be straight (as something string-like); *prt* gweyakwaabiigizid

gwayakwaakozi *vai* be straight (as something stick- or wood-like); *prt* gweyakwaakozid

gwayakwaakwad *vii* be straight (as something stick- or wood-like); *prt* gweyakwaakwak

gwayakwendam *vai2* think correctly, be certain; *1sg* **ingwayakwendam**; *prt* **gweyakwendang**
gwayakwendan *vti* consider s.t. right; *1sg* **ingwayakwendaan**; *prt* **gweyakwendang**
gwayakwendaagozi *vai* be considered right; *1sg* **ingwayakwendaagoz**; *prt* **gweyakwendaagozid**
gwayakwendaagwad *vii* be considered right; *prt* **gweyakwendaagwak**
gwaaba' *vta* scoop s.o. up; *1sg* **ingwaaba'aa**; *prt* **gwayaaba'aad**
gwaaba'amaw *vta* scoop (s.t.) up for s.o., get water for s.o.; *1sg* **ingwaaba'amawaa**; *prt* **gwayaaba'amawaad**
gwaaba'an *vti* scoop s.t. up; *1sg* **ingwaaba'aan**; *prt* **gwayaaba'ang**
gwaaba'ibii *vai* draw water, scoop up water; *1sg* **ingwaaba'ibii**; *prt* **gwayaaba'ibiid**
gwaaba'igan *ni* dipper; *pl* **gwaaba'iganan**; *loc* **gwaaba'iganing**; *dim* **gwaaba'igaans**
gwaaba'ige *vai* scoop up things, dip up things; *1sg* **ingwaaba'ige**; *prt* **gwayaaba'iged**
gwaaba'waawangwaan *ni* shovel (for dirt); *pl* **gwaaba'waawangwaanan**; *loc* **gwaaba'waawangwaaning**; *dim* **gwaaba'waawangwaanens**
gwaashkwani *vai* jump; *1sg* **ingwaashkwan**; *prt* **gwayaashkwanid**
gwaashkwaashkw= < gwaashkw=
gwaashkwesin *vii* bounce; *prt* **gwayaashkwesing**
gwaashkwezi *vai* be eager, be ambitious, be energetic; *1sg* **ingwaashkwez**; *prt* **gwayaashkwezid**
gwech *pc* enough, sufficient
gwekabi *vai* turn around while sitting; *1sg* **ingwekab**; *prt* **gwayekabid**
gwekaanimad *vii* wind shifts; *prt* **gwayekaanimak**
gwekendam *vai* change one's mind; *1sg* **ingwekendam**; *prt* **gwayekendang**
gwekibagizo *vai* turn quickly, right self; *1sg* **ingwekibagiz**; *prt* **gwayekibagizod**
gwekibatoo *vai* turn running; *1sg* **ingwekibatoo**; *prt* **gwayekibatood**
gwekibidoon *vti2* turn s.t. with hands; *1sg* **ingwekibidoon**; *prt* **gwayekibidood**
gwekibizh /gwekibiN-/ *vta* turn s.o. with hands; *1sg* **ingwekibinaa**; *prt* **gwayekibinaad**
gwekibizo *vai* turn driving; *1sg* **ingwekibiz**; *prt* **gwayekibizod**
gwekigaabawi *vai* turn while standing; *1sg* **ingwekigaabaw**; *prt* **gwayekigaabawid**
gwekikweni *vai* turn one's head around; *1sg* **ingwekikwen**; *prt* **gwayekikwenid**
gwekin *vta* turn s.o. by hand; *1sg* **ingwekinaa**; *prt* **gwayekinaad**
gwekinan *vti* turn s.t. by hand; *1sg* **ingwekinaan**; *prt* **gwekinang**
gwekinige *vai* turn things by hand; *1sg* **ingwekinige**; *prt* **gwayekiniged**
gwekishim *vta* put s.o. turned; *1sg* **ingwekishimaa**; *prt* **gwayekishimaad**
gwekishin *vai* turn lying in place; *1sg* **ingwekishin**; *prt* **gwayekishing**
gwekisidoon *vti2* put s.t. turned; *1sg* **ingwekisidoon**; *prt* **gwayekisidood**

gwekisin *vii* turn lying in place; *prt* **gwayekising**
gwekitaa *vai* turn (one's body); *1sg* **ingwekitaa**; *prt* **gwayekitaad**
gwekiwebinigan *na* pancake; *pl* **gwekiwebiniganag**; *loc* **gwekiwebiniganing**; *dim* **gwekiwebinigaans**
gwekiigin *vta* turn s.o. over (as something sheet-like); *1sg* **ingwekiiginaa**; *prt* **gwayekiiginaad**
gwekiiginan *vti* turn s.t. over (as something sheet-like); *1sg* **ingwekiiginaan**; *prt* **gwekiiginang**
gwekwek= < gwek=
gwendaaseg *ni-pt* liniment; *pl* **gwendaasegin**
gwiikwiin= < gwiin=
gwiinawaabam *vta* fail to see s.o.; *1sg* **ingwiinawaabamaa**; *prt* **gwaanawaabamaad**
gwiinawaabandan *vti* fail to see s.t.; *1sg* **ingwiinawaabandaan**; *prt* **gwaanawaabandang**
gwiinawendan *vti* miss s.t. absent; *1sg* **ingwiinawendaan**; *prt* **gwaanawendang**
gwiinawenim *vta* miss s.o. absent; *1sg* **ingwiinawenimaa**; *prt* **gwaanawenimaad**
gwiinawi- *pv4* not knowing, not able
gwiinawi-doodam *vai2* not know what to do; *1sg* **ingwiinawi-doodam**; *prt* **gwaanawi-doodang**
gwiinawi-inendam *vai2* not know what to think; *1sg* **ingwiinawi-inendam**; *prt* **gwaanawi-inendang**
gwiingwa'aage *na* wolverine; *pl* **gwiingwa'aageg**; *dim* **gwiingwa'aagens**
gwiinobii *vai* be unable to find a drink; *1sg* **ingwiinobii**; *prt* **gwaanobiid**
gwiishkoshi *vai* whistle; *1sg* **ingwiishkosh**; *prt* **gwaashkoshid**
gwiishkoshim *vta* whistle to s.o.; *1sg* **ingwiishkoshimaa**; *prt* **gwaashkoshimaad**
gwiishkoshwewegamide *vii* whistle from boiling; *prt* **gwaashkoshwewegamideg**; *aug* **gwiishkoshwewegamidemagad**; *prt aug* **gwaashkoshwewegamidemagak**
gwiishkoshwewegamizo *vai* whistle from boiling; *prt* **gwaashkoshwewegamizod**
gwiiwizens *na* boy; *pl* **gwiiwizensag**
gwiiwizensiwi *vai* be a boy; *1sg* **ingwiiwizensiw**; *prt* **gwaawizensiwid**

H

hay' *pc* expression of displeasure at accident or mistake

I

idan *vti* say so to s.t., speak to s.t.; *1sg* **indidaan**; *prt* **edang**

idash *pc* and, but; *also* **dash, -sh**

idiwag /**idi-**/ *vai* they say to each other, they speak to each other in a certain way; *1pl* **indidimin**; *prt* **edijig**

igaye *pc* and, as for; *also* **gaye, ge**

igiw* *pr* those *animate plural demonstrative*; *also* **ingiw, ingi, agiw***

igiwedig* *pr* those over there *animate plural demonstrative*; *also* **ingiwedig**

igo *pc* *emphatic word*; *also* **go**

i'imaa *pc* there; *also* **imaa**

i'iw *pr* that *inanimate singular demonstrative*; *also* **iw, 'iw, i'i, 'i**

i'iwedi *pr* that over there *inanimate singular demonstrative*; *also* **iwedi, 'iwedi**

ikido *vai* say, speak so; *1sg* **indikid**; *prt* **ekidod**

ikidowin *ni* word; *pl* **ikidowinan**; *dim* **ikidowinens**

iko *pc* used to, formerly, it was the custom to...; *also* **ko**

ikogaabawi *vai* stand out of the way; *1sg* **indikogaabaw**; *prt* **ekogaabawid**

ikon *vta* set s.o. out of the way; *1sg* **indikonaa**; *prt* **ekonaad**

ikonan *vti* set s.t. out of the way; *1sg* **indikonaan**; *prt* **ekonang**

ikonaazhikaw *vta* chase s.o. out of the way; *1sg* **indikonaazhikawaa**; *prt* **ekonaazhikawaad**

ikonigaade *vii* be set out of the way; *prt* **ekonigaadeg**; *aug* **ikonigaademagad**; *prt aug* **ekonigaademagak**

ikonigaazo *vai* be set out of the way, be evicted; *prt* **ekonigaazod**

ikoshim *vta* put s.o. out of the way; *1sg* **indikoshimaa**; *prt* **ekoshimaad**

ikoshin *vai* lie out of the way; *1sg* **indikoshin**; *prt* **ekoshing**

ikosidoon *vti2* put s.t. out of the way; *1sg* **indikosidoon**; *prt* **ekosidood**

ikosin *vii* lie out of the way; *prt* **ekosing**

ikoweba' /**ikoweba'w-**/ *vta* shove s.o. out of the way with something; *1sg* **indikoweba'waa**; *prt* **ekoweba'waad**

ikoweba'an *vti* shove s.t. out of the way with something; *1sg* **indikoweba'aan**; *prt* **ekoweba'ang**

ikowebin *vta* toss s.o. aside, shove aside s.o.; *1sg* **indikowebinaa**; *prt* **ekowebinaad**

ikowebinan *vti* toss s.t. aside, shove aside s.t.; *1sg* **indikowebinaan**; *prt* **ekowebinang**

ikowebishkan *vti* kick s.t. out of the way; *1sg* **indikowebishkaan**; *prt* **ekowebishkang**

ikowebishkaw *vta* kick s.o. out of the way; *1sg* **indikowebishkawaa**; *prt* **ekowebishkawaad**

ikwa *na* louse; *pl* **ikwag**

ikwabi *vai* sit aside, move out of the way sitting; *1sg* **indikwab**; *prt* **ekwabid**

ikwanagweni *vai* roll up one's sleeve; *1sg* **indikwanagwen**; *prt* **ekwanagwenid**

ikwanaamo *vai* draw breath in; *1sg* **indikwanaam**; *prt* **ekwanaamod**

ikwe *na* woman, queen (card); *pl* **ikwewag**; *dim* **ikwens**

ikwe-biizikiigan *ni* item of women's clothing; *loc* **ikwe-biizikiiganing**; *dim* **ikwe-biizikiigaans**

ikwe-niimi *vai* dance the women's dance; *1sg* **indikwe-niim**; *prt* **ekwe-niimid**

ikwe-niimi'idiwag /**ikwe-niimi'idi-**/ *vai* they dance the women's dance; *1pl* **indikwe-niimi'idimin**; *prt* **ekwe-niimi'idijig**

ikwe-niimi'idiwin *ni* women's dance; *pl* **ikwe-niimi'idiwinan**

ikwewi *vai* be a woman; *1sg* **indikwew**; *prt* **ekwewid**

ikwezens *na* girl; *pl* **ikwezensag**

ikwezensiwi *vai* be a girl; *1sg* **indikwezensiw**; *prt* **ekwezensiwid**

im= *pre first person prefix before b-*; *also* **nim=, m=**

imaa *pc* there; *also* **maa, i'imaa**

imbaabaa /**-baabaay-**/ *nad* my father; *pl* **imbaabaayag**

imbaabaayinaan *nad* our father = grandfather; *also* **imbaabaanaan, baabaanaan**

imbwaam /**-bwaam-**/ *nid* my thigh (back of thigh), my hindquarter; *pl* **imbwaaman**; *loc* **imbwaaming**; *dim* **imbwaamens**

in= *pre first person prefix before d-, j-, g-, z, zh-*; *also* **nin=, n=**

ina *pc* *yes-no question word*; *also* **na**

inabi *vai* sit a certain way; *1sg* **indinab**; *prt* **enabid**

inademo *vai* cry a certain way, go to a certain place crying; *1sg* **indinadem**; *prt* **enademod**

inagim *vta* set a certain price on s.o.; *1sg* **indinagimaa**; *prt* **enagimaad**

inagindamaw *vta* set a certain price on (s.t.) for s.o.; *1sg* **indinagindamawaa**; *prt* **enagindamawaad**

inagindan *vti* set a certain price on s.t.; *1sg* **indinagindaan**; *prt* **enagindang**

inaginde *vii* have a certain cost, have a certain price; *prt* **enagindeg**; *aug* **inagindemagad**; *prt aug* **enagindemagak**

inaginzo *vai* have a certain cost, have a certain price, be a certain date of the month; *prt* **enaginzod**

inagoode *vii* hang a certain way; *prt* **enagoodeg**; *aug* **inagoodemagad**; *prt aug* **enagoodemagak**

inagoodoon *vti2* hang s.t. a certain way; *1sg* **indinagoodoon**; *prt* **enagoodood**

inagoojin *vai* hang a certain way; *1sg* **indinagoojin**; *prt* **enagoojing**

inagoozh /**inagooN-**/ *vta* hang s.o. a certain way; *1sg* **indinagoonaa**; *prt* **enagoonaad**

ina'adoon *vti2* follow s.t. as a trail to a certain place; *1sg* **indina'adoon**; *prt* **ena'adood**

ina'am *vai2* sing a certain way; *1sg* **indina'am**; *prt* **ena'ang**

ina'azh /**ina'aN-**/ *vta* follow s.o.'s trail to a certain place; *1sg* **indina'anaa**; *prt* **ena'anaad**

ina'e *vai* shoot in a certain way or place; *1sg* **indina'e**; *prt* **ena'ed**

ina'o *vai* paddle to a certain place; *1sg* **indina'**; *prt* **ena'od**

ina'oodoo *vai* pole a boat to a certain place; *1sg* **indina'oodoo**; *prt* **ena'oodood**

ina'oodoon *vti2* take s.t. to a certain place by boat; *1sg* **indina'oodoon**; *prt* **ena'oodood**

ina'oozh /**ina'ooN-**/ *vta* take s.o. to a certain place by boat; *1sg* **indina'oonaa**; *prt* **ena'oonaad**

inakamigad *vii* be a certain event, happen a certain way; *prt* **enakamigak**

inakamigizi *vai* do a certain thing, have certain things happen to one; *1sg* **indinakamigiz**; *prt* **enakamigizid**

inakwazhiwe *vai* paddle a certain way, paddle to a certain place, swim to a certain place (as a fish); *1sg* **indinakwazhiwe**; *prt* **enakwazhiwed**

inamanji'o *vai* feel a certain way; *1sg* **indinamanji'**; *prt* **enamanji'od**

inamon /**inamo-**/ *vii* lead to a certain place (as a road or trail); *prt* **enamog**

inanjige *vai* eat a certain way, have a certain diet; *1sg* **indinanjige**; *prt* **enanjiged**

inanokii *vai* work a certain way, have a certain job; *1sg* **indinanokii**; *prt* **enanokiid**

inanokiitaw *vta* do a certain job for s.o.; *1sg* **indinanokiitawaa**; *prt* **enanokiitawaad**

inanoozh /**inanooN-**/ *vta* hire s.o. to do a certain job, hire s.o. to go to a certain place; *1sg* **indinanoonaa**; *prt* **enanoonaad**

inapizowin *ni* kitchen apron; *pl* **inapizowinan**; *loc* **inapizowining**; *dim* **inapizowinens**

inashke *pc* look!, behold!; *also* **nashke**

inawem *vta* be related to s.o.; *1sg* **indinawemaa**; *prt* **enawemaad**

inawendiwag /**inawendi-**/ *vai* they are related to each other; *1pl* **indinawendimin**; *prt* **enawendijig**

inaa *pc* emphatic particle; *also* **naa**

inaabadad *vii* be useful in a certain way, be employed in a certain way; *prt* **enaabadak**

inaabadizi *vai* be useful in a certain way, be employed in a certain way; *1sg* **indinaabadiz**; *prt* **enaabadizid**

inaabajichige *vai* use things a certain way; *1sg* **indinaabajichige**; *prt* **enaabajichiged**

inaabaji' *vta* use s.o. a certain way; *1sg* **indinaabaji'aa**; *prt* **enaabaji'aad**

inaabajitoon *vti2* use s.t. a certain way; *1sg* **indinaabajitoon**; *prt* **enaabajitood**

inaabam *vta* see s.o. a certain way as in a dream; *1sg* **indinaabamaa**; *prt* **enaabamaad**

inaabaminaagozi *vai* appear a certain way (especially as in a dream); *prt* **enaabaminaagozid**

inaabaminaagwad *vii* appear a certain way (especially as in a dream); *prt* **enaabaminaagwak**

inaabandam *vai2* dream a certain way; *1sg* **indinaabandam**; *prt* **enaabandang**

inaabandan *vti* see s.t. a certain way as in a dream; *1sg* **indinaabandaan**; *prt* **enaabandang**

inaabasige *vai* send smoke to a certain place; *1sg* **indinaabasige**; *prt* **enaabasiged**

inaabate *vii* go a certain direction (as smoke); *prt* **enaabateg**; *aug* **inaabatemagad**; *prt aug* **enaabatemagak**

inaabi *vai* peek, look to a certain place; *1sg* **indinaab**; *prt* **enaabid**

inaabikad *vii* be a certain way (as something mineral); *prt* **enaabikak**

inaabikizi *vai* be a certain way (as something mineral); *prt* **enaabikizid**

inaabiwin *ni* lightning

inaabiigad *vii* be a certain way (as something string-like); *prt* **enaabiigak**

inaabiigin *vta* string s.o. a certain way; *1sg* **inaabiiginaa**; *prt* **enaabiiginaad**

inaabiiginan *vti* string s.t. a certain way; *1sg* **indinaabiiginaan**; *prt* **enaabiiginang**

inaabiigizi *vai* be a certain way (as something string-like); *prt* **enaabiigizid**

inaadagaa *vai* swim to a certain place; *1sg* **indinaadagaa**; *prt* **enaadagaad**

inaadagaako *vai* go to a certain place on the ice; *1sg* **indinaadagaak**; *prt* **enaadagaakod**

inaadagaazii *vai* wade to a certain place; *1sg* **indinaadagaazii**; *prt* **enaadagaaziid**

inaada'e *vai* skate to a certain place; *1sg* **indinaada'e**; *prt* **enaada'ed**

inaadizi *vai* have a certain character, have a certain way of life; *1sg* **indinaadiz**; *prt* **enaadizid**

inaadiziwin *ni* way of life; *pl* **inaadiziwinan**

inaadodan *vti* tell a certain way about s.t., narrate a certain way about s.t.; *1sg* **indinaadodaan**; *prt* **enaadodang**

inaagamin /**inaagami-**/ *vii* be a certain way (as a liquid); *prt* **enaagamig**

inaagin *vta* bend s.o. a certain way; *1sg* **indinaaginaa**; *prt* **enaaginaad**

inaaginan *vti* bend s.t. a certain way; *1sg* **indinaaginaan**; *prt* **enaaginang**

inaaginigaade *vii* be bent a certain way; *prt* **enaaginigaadeg**; *aug* **inaaginigaademagad**; *prt aug* **enaaginigaademagak**

inaaginigaazo *vai* be bent a certain way; *prt* **enaaginigaazod**

inaajim *vta* tell of s.o. a certain way, narrate of s.o. a certain way; *1sg* **indinaajimaa**; *prt* **enaajimaad**

inaajimo *vai* tell a certain way, narrate a certain way; *1sg* **indinaajim**; *prt* **enaajimod**

inaajimotaw *vta* tell s.o. of (s.t.) a certain way, narrate (s.t.) to s.o. a certain way; *1sg* **indinaajimotawaa**; *prt* **enaajimotawaad**

inaakide *vii* burn a certain way; *prt* **enaakideg**; *aug* **inaakidemagad**; *prt aug* **enaakidemagak**

inaakiz /**inaakizw-**/ *vta* burn s.o. a certain way; *1sg* **indinaakizwaa**; *prt* **enaakizwaad**

inaakizan *vti* burn s.t. a certain way; *1sg* **indinaakizaan**; *prt* **enaakizang**

inaakizo *vai* burn a certain way; *prt* **enaakizod**

inaakon *vta* decide about s.o. a certain way, judge s.o. a certain way, sentence s.o. a certain way; *1sg* **indinaakonaa**; *prt* **enaakonaad**

inaakonan *vti* decide a certain way about s.t., judge s.t. a certain way; *1sg* **indinaakonaan**; *prt* **enaakonang**

inaakonigaade *vii* be decided in a certain way, be decreed a certain way; *prt* **enaakonigaadeg**; *aug* **inaakonigaademagad**

inaakonigaazo *vai* be judged a certain way, be sentenced a certain way; *prt* **enaakonigaazod**

inaakonige *vai* make a certain judgement, decide things a certain way, agree on something; *1sg* **indinaakonige**; *prt* **enaakoniged**

inaakonigewin *ni* law; *pl* **inaakonigewinan**

inaakozi *vai* be a certain way (as something stick- or wood-like); *prt* **enaakozid**

inaakwad *vii* be a certain way (as something stick- or wood-like); *prt* **enaakwak**

inaandawe *vai* climb to a certain place; *1sg* **indinaandawe**; *prt* **enaandawed**

inaande *vii* be colored a certain way; *prt* **enaandeg**; *aug* **inaandemagad**; *prt aug* **enaandemagak**

inaanzo *vai* be colored a certain way; *prt* **enaanzod**

inaapine *vai* be sick in a certain way; *1sg* **indinaapine**; *prt* **enaapined**

inaasamabi *vai* sit facing in a certain way; *1sg* **indinaasamab**; *prt* **enaasamabid**

inaasamigaabawi *vai* stand facing a certain way; *1sg* **indinaasamigaabaw**; *prt* **enaasamigaabawid**

inaasamishin *vai* lie facing a certain way; *1sg* **indinaasamishin**; *prt* **enaasamishing**

inaashi *vai* be blown a certain way, sail to a certain place; *1sg* **indinaash**; *prt* **enaashid**

inaasin *vii* be blown a certain way, sail to a certain place; *prt* **enaasing**

inaatese *vii* be a certain kind of movie; *prt* **enaateseg**; *aug* **inaatesemagad**; *prt aug* **enaatesemagak**

inaawadaaso *vai* haul something to a certain place; *1sg* **indinaawadaas**; *prt* **enaawadaasod**

inaawadoon *vti2* haul s.t. to a certain place; *1sg* **indinaawadoon**; *prt* **enaawadood**

inaawanidiwag /**inaawanidi-**/ *vai* they travel in a group to a certain place; *1pl* **indinaawanidimin**; *prt* **enaawanidijig**

inaawazh /**inaawaN-**/ *vta* haul s.o. to a certain place; *1sg* **indinaawanaa**; *prt* **enaawanaad**

inaazakonenjige *vai* go to a certain place with light; *1sg* **indinaazakonenjige**; *prt* **enaazakonenjiged**

inaazhagaame *vai* walk along shore to a certain place; *1sg* **indinaazhagaame**; *prt* **enaazhagaamed**

ind= *pre* first person prefix before vowels in verbs and non-dependent nouns; *also* **nind=, nd=**

indawaaj *pc* therefore, consequently, rather, preferably

indawemaa /**-dawemaaw-**/ *nad* my sibling of the opposite sex (brother or sister), my parallel cousin of the opposite sex; *pl* **indawemaag**

inday /**-day-**/ *nad* my dog, my horse; *pl* **indayag**; *dim* **indayens**

indaamikan /**-daamikan-**/ *nid* my chin, my jaw; *loc* **indaamikanaang**

indaan /**-daan-**/ *nad* my daughter; *pl* **indaanag**; *also* **indaanis**

indaangoshenh /**-daangosheny-**/ *nad* my (fe- male's) female cross-cousin (mother's brother's daughter or father's sister's daughter); *pl* **indaangoshenyag**

indaangwe /**-daangwew-**/ *nad* my (female's) sister- in-law, my (female's) female friend; *pl* **indaangweg**

indaanis /**-daanis-**/ *nad* my daughter; *pl* **indaanisag**; *loc* **indaanisens**; *also* **indaan**

indede /**-dedey-**/ *nad* my father; *pl* **indedeyag**

indedeyinaan *nad* our father = grandfather

inde' /**-de'-**/ *nid* my heart; *pl* **inde'an**; *loc* **inde'ing**

indenaniw /**-denaniw-**/ *nid* my tongue; *pl* **indenaniwan**; *loc* **indenaniwaang**

indengway /**-dengway-**/ *nid* my face; *pl* **indengwayan**; *loc* **indengwaang**

indenigom /**-denigom-**/ *nad* my nostril; *pl* **indenigomag**; *loc* **indenigomaang**

indigo *pc* just like, as if; *also* **nindigo***

indindawaa /**-dindawaa-**/ *nad* my fellow parent-in- law; *pl* **indindawaag**

indinimaangan /**-dinimaangan-**/ *nid* my shoulder; *pl* **indinimaanganan**; *loc* **indinimaanganaang**

indiniigan /**-diniigan-**/ *nid* my shoulder blade; *pl* **indiniiganag**; *loc* **indiniiganaang**

indis /**-disy-**/ *nid* my navel, my umbilical cord; *loc* **indis**; *dim* **indisiing**

indiskweyaab *nid* my vein; *pl* **indiskweyaabiin**

indiy /**-diy-**/ *nid* my rump, my rear end; *loc* **indiyaang**; *also* **indiyaash**

indoodem /**-doodem-**/ *nad* my totem, my clan; *pl* **indoodemag**

indoodikosiw /**-doodikosiw-**/ *na* my kidney; *pl* **indoodikosiwag**

indoodooshim /**-doodooshim-**/ *nad* my breast; *pl* **indoodooshimag**; *loc* **indoodooshimaang**

indoon /**-doon-**/ *nid* my mouth; *pl* **indoonan**; *loc* **indooning**

indoondan /**-doondan-**/ *nid* my heel; *pl* **indoondanan**; *loc* **indoondanaang**

indooskwan /**-dooskwan-**/ *nid* my elbow; *pl* **indooskwanan**; *loc* **indooskwanaang**

indoozhim /**-doozhim-**/ *nad* my parallel nephew (male's brother's son or female's sister's son); *pl* **indoozhimag**

indoozhimikwem /**-doozhimikwem-**/ *nad* my stepdaughter; *pl* **indoozhimikwemag**

indoozhimis /**-doozhimis-**/ *nad* my parallel niece (male's brother's daughter or female's sister's daughter); *pl* **indoozhimisag**

ine *pc* exclamation of denial

inendam *vai2* think a certain way, feel a certain way, decide, be of a certain mind, agree; *1sg* **indinendam**; *prt* **enendang**

inendan *vti* think a certain way of s.t.; *1sg* **indinendaan**; *prt* **enendang**

inendaagozi *vai* be thought of a certain way, seem to be a certain way, have a certain destiny; *1sg* **indinendaagoz**; *prt* **enendaagozid**

inendaagwad *vii* be thought of a certain way, seem to be a certain way; *prt* **enendaagwak**

inendi *vai* be gone a certain length of time, be absent a certain length of time; *1sg* **indinend**; *prt* **enendid**

inenim *vta* think of s.o. a certain way; *1sg* **indinenimaa**; *prt* **enenimaad**

inga *nad* my mother *archaic*; *obviative* **ogiin**

inge *pc* woman's expression of mild displeasure or disdain

ingidig /-gidigw-/ *nad* my knee; *pl* **ingidigwag**; *loc*
  ingidigwaang
ingitiziim /-gitiziim-/ *nad* my parent; *pl*
  ingitiziimag
ingiw *pr* those *animate plural demonstrative*; *also*
  ingi, igiw*, igi*, agiw*
ingiwedig *pr* those over there *animate plural
  demonstrative*; *also* **igiwedig***
ingo- /ningo-/ *pv4* one; *also* **ningo-***
ingo-anama'e-giizhik *pc* one week; *also* **ningo-
  anama'e-giizhik***
ingo-biboon *pc* one year; *also* **ningo-biboon***
ingo-biboonagad /ningo-biboonagad-/ *vii* be one
  year; *prt* **nengo-biboonagak**; *also* **ningo-
  biboonagad***
ingo-biboonagizi /ningo-biboonagizi-/ *vai* be one
  year old; *1sg* **niningo-biboonagiz**; *prt* **nengo-
  biboonagizid**; *also* **ningo-biboonagizi***
ingo-diba'igan *pc* one hour, one mile; *also* **ningo-
  diba'igan***
ingo-diba'iganed /ningo-diba'iganed-/ *vii* be one
  o'clock; *prt* **nengo-diba'iganek**; *also* **ningo-
  diba'iganed***
ingo-diba'igaans *pc* one minute, one acre; *also*
  ningo-diba'igaans*
ingo-dibik *pc* one night; *also* **ningo-dibik***
ingoding *pc* sometime, at one time; *also*
  ningoding*
ingodobaneninj *pc* one handful; *also*
  ningodobaneninj*
ingodoninj *pc* one inch; *also* **ningodoninj***
ingodosagoons *nm* one thousand; *also*
  ningodosagoons*
ingodozid *pc* one foot; *also* **ningodozid***
ingodooshkin *pc* one bag; *also* **ningodooshkin***
ingodwaaching *pc* six times; *also*
  ningodwaaching*
ingodwaachinoon /ningodwaachin-/ *vii* they are
  six; *prt* **nengodwaaching**; *also*
  ningodwaachinoon*
ingodwaachiwag /ningodwaachi-/ *vai* they are six;
  1pl **niningodwaachimin**; *prt* **nengodwaachijig**;
  also **ningodwaachiwag***
ingodwaak *nm* one hundred; *also* **ningodwaak***
ingodwaasimidana *nm* sixty; *also*
  ningodwaasimidana*
ingodwaaso- /ningodwaaso-/ *pv4* six; *also*
  ningodwaaso*
ingodwaaso-anama'e-giizhigad /ningodwaaso-
  anama'e-giizhigad-/ *vii* be six weeks; *prt*
  nengodwaaso-anama'e-giizhigak; *also*
  ningodwaaso-anama'e-giizhigad*
ingodwaaso-anama'e-giizhik *pc* six weeks; *also*
  ningodwaaso-anama'e-giizhik*
ingodwaaso-biboon *pc* six years; *also*
  ningodwaaso-biboon*
ingodwaaso-biboonagad /ningodwaaso-
  biboonagad-/ *vii* be six years; *prt*
  nengodwaaso-biboonagak; *also*
  ningodwaaso-biboonagad*
ingodwaaso-biboonagizi /ningodwaaso-
  biboonagizi-/ *vai* be six years old; *1sg*
  niningodwaaso-biboonagiz; *prt*
  nengodwaaso-biboonagizid; *also*
  ningodwaaso-biboonagaizi*

ingodwaaso-diba'igan *pc* six hours, six miles; *also*
  ningodwaaso-diba'igan*
ingodwaaso-diba'iganed /ningodwaaso-
  diba'iganed-/ *vii* be six o'clock; *prt*
  nengodwaaso-diba'iganek; *also*
  ningodwaaso-diba'iganed*
ingodwaaso-diba'igaans *pc* six minutes, six acres;
  also **ningodwaaso-diba'igaans***
ingodwaaso-dibik *pc* six nights; *also* **ningodwaaso-
  dibik***
ingodwaaso-giizhik *pc* six days; *also* **ningodwaaso-
  giizhik***
ingodwaaso-giizis *pc* six months; *also*
  ningodwaaso-giizis*
ingodwaasogon *pc* six days; *also*
  ningodwaasogon*
ingodwaasogonagad /ningodwaasogonagad-/ *vii*
  be six days; *prt* **nengodwaasogonagak**; *also*
  ningodwaasogonagad*
ingodwaasogonagizi /ningodwaasogonagizi-/ *vai*
  be the sixth day of the month, be six days old;
  prt **nengodwaasogonagizid**; *also*
  ningodwaasogonagizi*
ingodwaasoninj *pc* six inches; *also*
  ningodwaasoninj*
ingodwaasosagoons /ningodwaasosagoons-/ *nm*
  six thousand; *also* **ningodwaasosagoons***
ingodwaasoobii'igan *na* six (card); *pl*
  ingodwaasoobii'iganag; *also*
  ningodwaasoobii'igan*
ingodwaasooshkin *pc* six bags; *also*
  ningodwaasooshkin*
ingodwaaswaabik *pc* six dollars; *also*
  ningodwaaswaabik*
ingodwaaswaak *nm* six hundred; *also*
  ningodwaaswaak*
ingodwaaswi *nm* six; *also* **ningodwaaswi***
ingodwaaswewaan *pc* six sets, six pairs; *also*
  ningodwaaswewaan*
ingo-giizhik *pc* one day; *also* **ningo-giizhik***
ingo-giizis *pc* one month; *also* **ningo-giizis***
ingoji *pc* somewhere, approximately, nearly; *also*
  ningoji*
ingondashkway /-gondashkway-/ *nid* my throat; *pl*
  ingondashkway; *loc* **ingondashkwaang**
ingos /-gos-/ *nad* my son; *pl* **ingosag**; *also* **ingwis***
ingozis /-gozis-/ *nad* my son; *pl* **ingozisag**; *also*
  ingwizis*
ingoodaas /-goodaas-/ *nid* my dress; *pl*
  ingoodaasan
ingwana *pc* it was just so, it turns out that, so it
  was that; *also* **nangwana, ngwana**
inigaa' *vta* be mean to s.o., injure s.o.; *1sg*
  indinigaa'aa; *prt* **enigaa'aad**
inigaazi *vai* be poor, be pitiable, mourn; *1sg*
  indinigaaz; *prt* **enigaazid**
inigini *vai* be a certain size, be so big; *1sg* **indinigin**;
  prt **eniginid**
inigokwadeyaa *vii* be a certain width, be so wide;
  prt **enigokwadeyaag**; *aug*
  inigokwadeyaamagad; *prt aug*
  enigokwadeyaamagak
inigokwadeyaabikad *vii* be a certain width (as
  something mineral), be so wide (as something
  mineral); *prt* **enigokwadeyaabikak**

inigokwadeyaabikizi *vai* be a certain width (as something mineral), be so wide (as something mineral); *prt* **enigokwadeyaabikizid**

inigokwadeyaabiigad *vii* be a certain width (as something string-like), be so wide (as something string-like); *prt* **enigokwadeyaabiigak**

inigokwadeyaabiigizi *vai* be a certain width (as something string-like), be so wide (as something string-like); *prt* **enigokwadeyaabiigizid**

inigokwadeyaakozi *vai* be a certain width (as something stick- or wood-like), be so wide (as something stick- or wood-like); *prt* **enigokwadeyaakozid**

inigokwadeyaakwad *vii* be a certain width (as something stick- or wood-like), be so wide (as something stick- or wood-like); *prt* **enigokwadeyaakwak**

inigokwadeyiigad *vii* be a certain width (as something sheet-like), be so wide (as something sheet-like); *prt* **enigokwadeyiigak**

inigokwadeyiigizi *vai* be a certain width (as something sheet-like), be so wide (as something sheet-like); *prt* **enigokwadeyiigizid**

inigokwadezi *vai* be a certain width, be so wide; *prt* **enigokwadezid**

inigokwaa *vii* be a certain size, be so big; *prt* **enigokwaag**; *aug* **inigokwaamagad**; *prt aug* **enigokwaamagak**

inigokwaabikad *vii* be a certain size (as something mineral), be so big (as something mineral); *prt* **enigokwaabikak**

inigokwaabikizi *vai* be a certain size (as something mineral), be so big (as something mineral); *prt* **enigokwaabikizid**

inigokwaabiigad *vii* be a certain size (as something string-like), be so big (as something string-like); *prt* **enigokwaabiigak**

inigokwaabiigizi *vai* be a certain size (as something string-like), be so big (as something string-like); *prt* **enigokwaabiigizid**

inigokwaakozi *vai* be a certain size (as something stick- or wood-like), be so big (as something stick- or wood-like); *prt* **enigokwaakozid**

inigokwaakwad *vii* be a certain size (as something stick- or wood-like), be so big (as something stick- or wood-like); *prt* **enigokwaakwak**

inigokwegad *vii* be a certain size (as something sheet-like), be so big (as something sheet-like); *prt* **enigokwegak**

inigokwegizi *vai* be a certain size (as something sheet-like), be so big (as something sheet-like); *prt* **enigokwegizid**

inikodan *vti* slice s.t. a certain way; *1sg* **indinikodaan**; *prt* **enikodang**

inikonaye *vai* dress a certain way; *1sg* **indinikonaye**; *prt* **enikonayed**

inikozh /inikoN-/ *vta* slice s.o. a certain way; *1sg* **indinikonaa**; *prt* **enikonaad**

inikwe' /inikwe'w-/ *vta* steer s.o. a certain way; *1sg* **indinikwe'waa**; *prt* **enikwe'waad**

inikwe'an *vti* steer s.t. a certain way; *1sg* **indinikwe'aan**; *prt* **enikwe'ang**

inikweni *vai* put one's head a certain way; *1sg* **indinikwen**; *prt* **enikwenid**

inikweshin *vai* lie with one's head a certain way; *1sg* **indinikweshin**; *prt* **enikweshing**

inikwetaw *vta* nod one's head to s.o. a certain way; *1sg* **indinikwetawaa**; *prt* **enikwetawaad**

inin *vta* hold s.o. a certain way, handle s.o. a certain way; *1sg* **indininaa**; *prt* **eninaad**

ininamaw *vta* hand (s.t.) to s.o. a certain way; *1sg* **indininamawaa**; *prt* **eninamawaad**

ininan *vti* hold s.t. a certain way, handle s.t. a certain way; *1sg* **indininaan**; *prt* **eninang**

ininaatig *na* maple; *pl* **ininaatigoog**; *loc* **ininaatigong**; *also* **aninaatig**

inini *na* man; *pl* **ininiwag**; *dim* **ininiins**

ininaade *vii* be held a certain way, be handled a certain way; *prt* **eninigaadeg**; *aug* **ininigaademagad**; *prt aug* **eninigaademagak**

ininigaazo *vai* be held a certain way, be handled a certain way; *prt* **eninigaazod**

ininishib *na* mallard; *pl* **ininishibag**; *dim* **ininishibens**

ininii-biizikiigan *ni* item of men's clothing; *pl* **ininii-biizikiiganan**; *loc* **ininii-biizikiiganing**; *dim* **ininii-biizikiigaans**

ininiiwi *vai* be a man; *1sg* **indininiiw**; *prt* **eniniiwid**

initam *vai2* hear a certain noise, understand a certain way; *1sg* **indinitam**; *prt* **enitang**

initan *vti* hear s.t. a certain way, understand s.t. a certain way; *1sg* **indinitaan**; *prt* **enitang**

initaw *vta* hear s.o. a certain way, understand s.o. a certain way; *1sg* **indinitawaa**; *prt* **enitawaad**

initaagozi *vai* be heard a certain way, be understood a certain way; *prt* **enitaagozid**

initaagwad *vii* be heard a certain way, be understood a certain way; *prt* **enitaagwak**

iniw *pr* those *inanimate plural demonstrative*, that *obviative*, those *obviative*; *also* **niw, ini, ni, aniw***

iniwedin *pr* those over there *inanimate plural*, that over there *obiative*, those over there *obviative*; *also* **niwedin**

iniz /inizw-/ *vta* cook s.o. a certain way; *1sg* **indinizwaa**; *prt* **enizwaad**

inizan *vti* cook s.t. a certain way; *1sg* **indinizaan**; *prt* **enizang**

inizekwe *vai* cook (something) a certain way; *1sg* **indinizekwe**; *prt* **enizekwed**

inizh /inizhw-/ *vta* cut s.o. a certain way; *1sg* **indinizhwaa**; *prt* **enizhwaad**

inizhan *vti* cut s.t. a certain way; *1sg* **indinizhaan**; *prt* **enizhang**

injaanzh /-jaanzh-/ *nid* my nose; *pl* **injaanzhan**; *loc* **injaanzhing**

injichaag /-jichaagw-/ *nad* my soul, my spirit; *pl* **injichaagwag**; *loc* **injichaagong**

injiid /-jiidy-/ *nid* my rectum; *pl* **injiidiin**; *loc* **injiidiing**; *also* **injiidiish**

injiingwan /-jiingwan-/ *nad* my lap, my thigh (front of thigh); *pl* **injiingwanag**; *loc* **injiingwanaang**

injiitad /-jiitad-/ *nid* my sinew; *pl* **injiitadan**; *loc* **injiitadaang**

inose *vai* walk to a certain place, walk a certain way; *1sg* **indinose**; *prt* **enosed**

inoode *vai* crawl to a certain place, crawl a certain way; *1sg* **indinoode**; *prt* **enooded**

inoom *vta* carry s.o. to a certain place on one's back; *1sg* **indinoomaa;** *prt* **enoomaad**

inoomaawaso *vai* carry a baby to a certain place on one's back; *1sg* **indinoomaawas;** *prt* **enoomaawasod**

inoomigo *vai* ride to a certain place on horseback; *1sg* **indinoomig;** *prt* **enoomigod**

inoondan *vti* carry s.o. to a certain place on one's back; *1sg* **indinoondaan;** *prt* **enoondang**

inootaw *vta* quote s.o. a certain way; *1sg* **indinootawaa;** *prt* **enootawaad**

inootaage *vai* report what people say, quote people; *1sg* **indinootaage;** *prt* **enootaaged**

inwe *vai* make a characteristic call (neigh, etc.), speak a certain language; *1sg* **indinwe;** *prt* **enwed**

inwewe *vii* make a certain noise; *prt* **enweweg;** *aug* **inwewemagad;** *prt aug* **enwewemagak**

inwewidam *vai* be heard speaking going to a certain place; *1sg* **indinwewidam;** *prt* **enwewidang**

inwewin *ni* language; *pl* **inwewinan**

inzhaga'ay /**-zhaga'ay-**/ *nid* my skin; *loc* **inzhaga'aang**

inzhigwan /**zhigwan-**/ *nid* my tail (of a fish)

inzhishenh /**-zhisheny-**/ *nad* my cross-uncle (mother's brother); *pl* **inzhishenyag**

inzhiigan /**-zhiigan-**/ *nid* the small of my back; *loc* **inzhiiganaang**

inzid /**-zid-**/ *nid* my foot; *pl* **inzidan;** *loc* **inzidaang;** *dim* **inzidens**

inzigos /**-zigos-**/ *nad* my cross-aunt (father's sister); *pl* **inzigosag**

inzigozis /**-zigozis-**/ *nad* my mother-in-law; *pl* **inzigozisag**

inzinis /**-zinis-**/ *nad* my father-in-law; *pl* **inzinisag**

inzow /**-zow-**/ *nid* my tail (of an animal); *pl* **inzowan;** *loc* **inzowaang**

ipide *vii* speed to a certain place, drive to a certain place, fly to a certain place; *prt* **epideg;** *aug* **ipidemagad;** *prt aug* **epidemagak**

ipizo *vai* drive to a certain place, speed to a certain place, fly to a certain place; *1sg* **indipiz;** *prt* **epizod**

ipizoni' *vta* drive s.o. to a certain place; *1sg* **indipizoni'aa;** *prt* **epizoni'aad**

ipizonitoon *vti2* drive s.t. to a certain place; *1sg* **indipizonitoon;** *prt* **epizonitood**

ipogozi *vai* have a certain taste; *prt* **epogozid**

ipogwad *vii* have a certain taste; *prt* **epogwak**

isa *pc* emphatic word; *also* **sa**

ise *pc* for shame!

ishkendam *vai2* be disturbed, be upset; *1sg* **indishkendam;** *prt* **eshkendang**

ishkode *ni* fire; *pl* **ishkoden;** *loc* **ishkodeng;** *dim* **ishkodens**

ishkode-bingwi *ni* ashes

ishkode-jiimaan *ni* steamboat, ship; *pl* **ishkode-jiimaanan;** *loc* **ishkode-jiimaaning;** *dim* **ishkode-jiimaanens**

ishkodekaan *ni* lighter; *pl* **ishkodekaanan;** *loc* **ishkodekaaning;** *dim* **ishkodekaanens**

ishkodeke *vai* make a fire; *1sg* **indishkodeke;** *prt* **eshkodeked**

ishkode-makakoons *ni* battery; *pl* **ishkode-makakoonsan;** *loc* **ishkode-makakoonsing**

ishkodens *ni* match; *pl* **ishkodensan;** *loc* **ishkodensing**

ishkodewan *vii* be on fire; *prt* **eshkodewang**

ishkodewaaboo *ni* liquor; *loc* **ishkodewaaboong**

ishkodewidaabaan *na* train; *pl* **ishkodewidaabaanag;** *loc* **ishkodewidaabaaning;** *dim* **ishkodewidaabaanens;** *also* **mashkodewidaabaan***

ishkodewidaabaanikana *ni* train track; *pl* **ishkodewidaabaanikanan;** *loc* **ishkodewidaabaanikanaang**

ishkon *vta* reserve s.o., save s.o. back; *1sg* **indishkonaa;** *prt* **eshkonaad**

ishkonamaw *vta* reserve (s.t.) for s.o., save (s.t.) back for s.o.; *1sg* **indishkonamawaa;** *prt* **eshkonamawaad**

ishkonan *vti* reserve s.t., save s.t. back; *1sg* **indishkonaan;** *prt* **eshkonang**

ishkonigan *ni* reservation; *pl* **ishkoniganan;** *loc* **ishkoniganing;** *dim* **ishkonigaans**

ishkonigaade *vii* be reserved, be saved back; *prt* **eshkonigaadeg;** *aug* **ishkonigaademagad;** *prt aug* **eshkonigaademagak**

ishkonigaazo *vai* be reserved, be saved back; *prt* **eshkonigaazod**

ishkwam *vta* leave s.o. behind uneaten; *1sg* **indishkwamaa;** *prt* **eshkwamaad**

ishkwandan *vti* leave s.t. behind uneaten; *1sg* **indishkwandaan;** *prt* **eshkwandang**

ishkwanjigan *ni* leftover food; *pl* **ishkwanjiganan;** *loc* **ishkwanjiganing;** *dim* **ishkwanjigaans**

ishkwanjige *vai* leave leftovers; *1sg* **indishkwanjige;** *prt* **eshkwanjiged**

ishkwaa- *pv4* after

ishkwaa-anama'e-giizhigad *vii* be Monday; *prt* **eshkwaa-anama'e-giizhigak;** *also* **ishkwaa-aname-giizhigad**

ishkwaabiisaa *vii* stop raining; *prt* **eshkwaabiisaag;** *aug* **ishkwaabiisaamagad;** *prt aug* **eshkwaabiisaamagak**

ishkwaagamizige *vai* finish boiling sap; *1sg* **indishkwaagamizige;** *prt* **eshkwaagamiziged**

ishkwaagaa *vii* be the last run of sap; *prt* **eshkwaagaag;** *aug* **ishkwaagaamagad;** *prt aug* **eshkwaagaamagak**

ishkwaaj *pc* last, finally

ishkwaakajanokii-giizhigad *vii* be Saturday; *prt* **eshkwaajanokii-giizhigak**

ishkwaakamigad *vii* be over (of an event); *prt* **eshkwaakamigak**

ishkwaanaamo *vai* stop breathing; *1sg* **indishkwaanaam;** *prt* **eshkwaanaamod**

ishkwaa-naawakwe *vii* be afternoon; *prt* **eshkwaa-naawakweg;** *aug* **ishkwaa-naawakwemagad;** *prt aug* **eshkwaa-naawakwemagak**

ishkwaandem *ni* door; *pl* **ishkwaandeman;** *loc* **ishkwaandeming;** *dim* **ishkwaandemens**

ishkwaapon /**ishkwaapo-**/ *vii* stop snowing; *prt* **eshkwaapog**

ishkwaase *vii* come to an end; *prt* **eshkwaaseg;** *aug* **ishkwaasemagad;** *prt aug* **eshkwaasemagak**

ishkwaataa *vai* be at the end of an activity, stop an activity; *1sg* **indishkwaataa**; *prt* **eshkwaataad**
ishkwaayaanimad *vii* wind dies down; *prt* **eskwaayaanimak**
ishkwe-ayi'ii *pc* at the end of it; *also* **iskweya'ii**
ishkwebi *vai* sit at the end; *1sg* **indishkweb**; *prt* **eshkwebid**
ishkwegaabawi *vai* stand at the end; *1sg* **indishkwegaabaw**; *prt* **eshkwegaabawid**
ishkwege *vai* live at the end of town, live in the last house; *1sg* **indishkwege**; *prt* **eshkweged**
ishkwegoode *vii* hang at the end; *prt* **eshkwegoodeg**; *aug* **ishkwegoodemagad**; *prt aug* **eshkwegoodemagak**
ishkwegoodoon *vti2* hang s.t. at the end; *1sg* **indishkwegoodoon**; *prt* **eshkwegoodood**
ishkwegoojin *vai* hang at the end; *prt* **eshkwegoojing**
ishkwegoozh /ishkwegooN-/ *vta* hang s.o. at the end; *1sg* **indishkwegoonaa**; *prt* **eshkwegoonaad**
ishkwejaagan *na* last born child, youngest child; *pl* **ishkwejaaganag**
ishkwenikaazo *vai* have a last name; *1sg* **indishkwenikaaz**; *prt* **eshkwenikaazod**
ishkwenikaazowin *ni* last name; *pl* **ishkwenikaazowinan**
ishkweninj *ni* little finger; *pl* **ishkweninjiin**
ishkwesa'igan *na* toy top; *pl* **ishkwesa'iganag**; *loc* **ishkwesa'iganing**; *dim* **ishkwesa'igaans**
ishkweshin *vai* lie at the end; *1sg* **indishkweshin**; *prt* **eshkweshing**
ishkwesin *vii* lie at the end; *prt* **eshkwesing**
ishkweyaang *pc* behind, in the back, back (in time)
ishkwii *vai* stay behind; *1sg* **indishkwii**; *prt* **eshkwiid**
ishpadinaa *vii* be a hill, be a high place; *prt* **eshpadinaag**; *aug* **ishpadinaamagad**; *prt aug* **eshpadinaamagak**
ishpagindan *vti* charge a high price for s.t.; *1sg* **indishpagindaan**; *prt* **eshpagindang**
ishpagindaaso *vai* charge a high price; *1sg* **indishpagindaas**; *prt* **eshpagindaasod**
ishpaginde *vii* be high-priced; *prt* **eshpagindeg**; *aug* **ishpagindemagad**; *prt aug* **eshpagindemagak**
ishpaginzo *vai* be high-priced, be high in status or office; *1sg* **indishpaginz**; *prt* **eshpaginzod**
ishpagoode *vii* hang up high; *prt* **eshpagoodeg**; *aug* **ishpagoodemagad**; *prt aug* **eshpagoodemagak**
ishpagoodoon *vti2* hang s.t. up high; *1sg* **indishpagoodoon**; *prt* **eshpagoodood**
ishpagoojin *vai* hang up high, be high (e.g., the sun); *1sg* **indishpagoojin**; *prt* **eshpagoojing**
ishpagoozh /ishpagooN-/ *vta* hang s.o. up high; *1sg* **indishpagoonaa**; *prt* **eshpagoonaad**
ishpayi'ii *pc* above it, over it
ishpaa *vii* be high up; *prt* **eshpaag**; *aug* **ishpaamagad**; *prt aug* **eshpaamagak**
ishpaagonagaa *vii* be deep snow; *prt* **eshpaagonagaag**; *aug* **ishpaagonagaamagad**; *prt aug* **eshpaagonagaamagak**
ishpaatoon *vti2* make s.t. high; *1sg* **indishpaatoon**; *prt* **eshpaatood**

ishpenim *vta* think highly of s.o.; *1sg* **indishpenimaa**; *prt* **eshpenimaad**
ishpenimo *vai* be proud, have high aspirations; *1sg* **indishpenim**; *prt* **eshpenimod**
ishpi- *pv4* high, advanced into a time
ishpi-dibik *pc* late at night
ishpi-dibikad *vii* be late at night; *prt* **eshpi-dibikak**
ishpi-giizhigad *vii* be late morning or early afternoon; *prt* **eshpi-giizhigak**
ishpiming *pc* in the sky, above, in heaven
ishpimisag *ni* the floor above; *pl* **ishpimisagoon**; *loc* **ishpimisagong**
ishpimisagokaade *vii* have an upper story; *prt* **eshpimisagokaadeg**; *aug* **ishpimisagokaademagad**; *prt aug* **eshpimisagokaademagak**
ishpishin *vai* lie high up; *1sg* **indishpishin**; *prt* **eshpishing**
ishpisin *vii* lie high up; *prt* **eshpising**
ishwaaching *pc* eight times; *also* **nishwaaching***
ishwaachinoon /ishwaachin-/ *vii* they are eight; *prt* **eshwaachingin**; *also* **nishwaachinoon***
ishwaachiwag /ishwaachi-/ *vai* they are eight; *1pl* **indishwaachimin**; *prt* **eshwaachijig**; *also* **nishwaachiwag***
ishwaasimidana *nm* eighty; *also* **nishwaasimidana***
ishwaaso- *pv4* eight; *also* **nishwaaso-***
ishwaaso-anama'e-giizhigad *vii* be eight weeks; *also* **nishwaaso-anama'e-giizhigad***
ishwaaso-anama'e-giizhik *pc* eight weeks; *also* **nishwaaso-anama'e-giizhik***
ishwaaso-biboon *pc* eight years; *also* **nishwaaso-biboon***
ishwaaso-biboonagad *vii* be eight years; *prt* **eshwaaso-biboonagak**; *also* **nishwaaso-biboonagad***
ishwaaso-biboonagizi *vai* be eight years old; *1sg* **indishwaaso-biboonagiz**; *prt* **eshwaaso-biboonagizid**; *also* **nishwaaso-biboonagizi***
ishwaaso-diba'igan *pc* eight miles, eight hours; *also* **nishwaaso-diba'igan***
ishwaaso-diba'iganed *vii* be eight o'clock; *prt* **eshwaaso-diba'iganek**; *also* **nishwaaso-diba'iganed***
ishwaaso-diba'igaans *pc* eight minutes, eight acres; *also* **nishwaaso-diba'igaans***
ishwaaso-dibik *pc* eight nights; *also* **nishwaaso-dibik***
ishwaaso-giizhik *pc* eight days; *also* **nishwaaso-giizhik***
ishwaaso-giizis *pc* eight months; *also* **nishwaaso-giizis***
ishwaasogon *pc* eight days; *also* **nishwaasogon***
ishwaasogonagad *vii* be eight days; *prt* **eshwaasogonagak**; *also* **nishwaasogonagad***
ishwaasogonagizi *vai* be the eighth day of the month, be eight days old; *prt* **eshwaasogonagizid**; *also* **nishwaasogonagizi***
ishwaasoninj *pc* eight inches; *also* **nishwaasoninj***
ishwaasosagoons *nm* eight thousand; *also* **nishwaasosagoons***
ishwaasozid *pc* eight feet; *also* **nishwaasozid***

ishwaasoobii'igan *na* eight (card); *pl*
ishwaasoobii'iganag; *also*
nishwaasoobii'igan*
ishwaasooshkin *pc* eight bags; *also*
nishwaasooshkin*
ishwaaswaabik *pc* eight dollars; *also*
nishwaaswaabik*
ishwaaswaak *nm* eight hundred; *also*
nishwaaswaak*
ishwaaswewaan *pc* eight sets, eight pairs; *also*
nishwaaswewaan*
ishwaaswi *nm* eight; *also* **nishwaaswi***
iska'ibii *vai* bail; *1sg* **indiska'ibii;** *prt* **eska'ibiid**
iskandan *vti* drain s.t. dry; *1sg* **indiskandaan;** *prt*
eskandang
iskate *vii* go down (of a body of water), dry up (of
a body of water); *prt* **eskateg;** *aug*
iskatemagad; *prt aug* **eskatemagak**
iskaakizige *vai* run out of fuel; *1sg* **indiskaakizige;**
prt **eskaakiziged**
iskigamizan *vti* boil s.t. down; *1sg*
indiskigamizaan; *prt* **eskigamizang**
iskigamizide *vii* boil down; *prt* **eskigamizideg;** *aug*
iskigamizidemagad; *prt aug*
eskigamizidemagak
iskigamizigan *ni* sugar camp, sugar bush; *pl*
iskigamiziganan; *loc* **iskigamiziganing;** *dim*
iskigamizigaans
iskigamiziganaak *ni* frame for holding sap-boiling
kettles; *pl* **iskigamiziganaakoon;** *loc*
iskigamiziganaakong; *dim*
iskigamiziganaakoons
iskigamiziganaatig *ni* sap-boiling pole; *pl*
iskigamiziganaatigoon; *loc*
iskigamiziganaatigong; *dim*
iskigamiziganaatigoons
iskigamizige *vai* boil things down (e.g., maple
sap); *1sg* **indiskigamizige;** *prt* **eskigamiziged**
iskigamizige-giizis *na* April
iskigamizigewigamig *ni* sap-boiling lodge; *pl*
iskigamizigewigamigoon; *loc*
iskigamizigewigamigong; *dim*
iskigamizigewigamigoons
iskigamizo *vai* boil down; *prt* **eskigamizod**
iw *pr* that *inanimate singular demonstrative*; *also* **i'iw,**
i'i, 'i
iw apii *pr* at that time; *also* **i'iw apii**
iwedi *pr* that over there *inanimate singular
demonstrative*; *also* **i'iwedi**
iwidi *pc* over there
izhaa *vai* go to a certain place; *1sg* **indizhaa;** *prt*
ezhaad
izhaamagad *vii* go to a certain place; *prt*
ezhaamagak
izhi /iN-/ *vta* say to s.o., speak so to s.o.; *1sg*
indinaa; *prt* **enaad**
izhi- *pv3* in a certain way, to a certain place, thus,
so, there
izhi-ayaa *vai* be a certain way; *1sg* **indizhi-ayaa;** *prt*
ezhi-ayaad
izhibii'an *vti* write s.t. a certain way; *1sg*
indizhibii'aan; *prt* **ezhibii'ang**
izhibii'igaade *vii* be written a certain way; *prt*
ezhibii'igaadeg; *aug* **izhibii'igaademagad;** *prt*
aug **ezhibii'igaademagak**

izhibii'ige *vai* write things a certain way; *1sg*
indizhibii'ige; *prt* **ezhibii'iged**
izhichigaade *vii* be made a certain way; *prt*
ezhichigaadeg; *aug* **izhichigaademagad;** *prt*
aug **ezhichigaademagak**
izhichigaazo *vai* be made a certain way; *prt*
ezhichigaazod
izhichige *vai* do things a certain way; *1sg*
indizhichige; *prt* **ezhichiged**
izhichigewin *ni* way of doing, deed; *pl*
izhichigewinan; *dim* **izhichigewinens**
izhidaabaadan *vti* drag s.t. to a certain place; *1sg*
indizhidaabaadaan; *prt* **ezhidaabaadang**
izhidaabaazh /izhidaabaaN-/ *vta* drag s.o. to a
certain place; *1sg* **indizhidaabaanaa;** *prt*
ezhidaabaanaad
izhidaabii'iwe *vai* drive to a certain place; *1sg*
indizhidaabii'iwe; *prt* **ezhidaabii'iwed**
izhidoonem *vta* point s.o. out with lips; *1sg*
indizhidoonemaa; *prt* **ezhidoonemaad**
izhidooneni *vai* point a certain way with lips; *1sg*
indizhidoonen; *prt* **ezhidoonenid**
izhidoonetaw *vta* point (s.t.) out to s.o. with lips;
1sg **indizhidoonetawaa;** *prt* **ezhidoonetawaad**
izhi-giizhigad *vii* be a certain day of the week; *prt*
ezhi-giizhigak
izhigiizhwe *vai* talk a certain way; *1sg*
indizhigiizhwe; *prt* **ezhigiizhwed**
izhi' *vta* cause s.o. to do something, make s.o. do
something; *1sg* **indizhi'aa;** *prt* **ezhi'aad**
izhi'o *vai* dress a certain way; *1sg* **indizhi';** *prt*
ezhi'od
izhijiwan *vii* flow a certain way, flow to a certain
place; *prt* **ezhijiwang**
izhikawe *vai* leave tracks going to a certain place;
1sg **indizhikawe;** *prt* **ezhikawed**
izhimaagozi *vai* smell a certain way; *1sg*
indizhimaagoz; *prt* **ezhimaagozid**
izhimaagwad *vii* smell a certain way; *prt*
ezhimaagwak
izhimaam *vta* have s.o. smell a certain way to one;
1sg **indizhimaamaa;** *prt* **ezhimaamaad**
izhimaandan *vti* have s.t. smell a certain way to
one; *1sg* **indizhimaandaan;** *prt* **ezhimaandang**
izhimaaso *vai* smell a certain way cooking or
burning; *prt* **ezhimaasod**
izhimaate *vii* smell a certain way cooking or
burning; *prt* **ezhimaateg;** *aug*
izhimaatemagad; *prt aug* **ezhimaatemagak**
izhinan *vti* see s.t. a certain way, perceive s.t. a
certain way; *1sg* **indizhinaan;** *prt* **ezhinang**
izhinaw *vta* see s.o. a certain way, perceive s.o. a
certain way; *1sg* **indizhinawaa;** *prt* **ezhinawaad**
izhinaago' *vta* make s.o. look a certain way; *1sg*
indizhinaago'aa; *prt* **ezhinaago'aad**
izhinaago'idizo *vai* transform oneself in
appearance; *1sg* **indizhinaago'idiz;** *prt*
ezhinaago'idizod
izhinaagotoon *vti2* make s.t. look a certain way;
1sg **indizhinaagotoon;** *prt* **ezhinaagotood**
izhinaagozi *vai* have a certain appearance, have a
certain look; *1sg* **indizhinaagoz;** *prt*
ezhinaagozid
izhinaagwad *vii* have a certain appearance, have a
certain look; *prt* **ezhinaagwak**

izhinaazhikaw *vta* send s.o. to a certain place, chase s.o. to a certain place; *1sg* **indizhinaazhikawaa;** *prt* **ezhinaazhikawaad**

izhinikaadan *vti* name s.t. a certain way; *1sg* **indizihinikaadaan;** *prt* **ezhinikaadang**

izhinikaade *vii* be named a certain way; *prt* **ezhinikaadeg;** *aug* **izhinikaademagad;** *prt aug* **ezhinikaademagak**

izhinikaazh /izhinikaaN-/ *vta* name s.o. a certain way; *1sg* **indizhinikaanaa;** *prt* **ezhinikaanaad**

izhinikaazo *vai* be named a certain way; *1sg* **indizhinikaaz;** *prt* **ezhinikaazod**

izhinikeni *vai* move one's arm a certain way; *1sg* **indizhiniken;** *prt* **ezhinikenid**

izhininjiini *vai* move one's hand a certain way; *1sg* **indizhininjiin;** *prt* **ezhininjiinid**

izhinizha' /izhinizha'w-/ *vta* send s.o. to a certain place; *1sg* **indizhinizha'waa;** *prt* **ezhinizha'waad**

izhinizha'amaw *vta* send (s.t.) to s.o. to a certain place; *1sg* **indizhinizha'amawaa;** *prt* **ezhinizha'amawaad**

izhinizha'an *vti* send s.t. to a certain place; *1sg* **indizhinizha'aan;** *prt* **ezhinizha'ang**

izhinizha'igaade *vii* be sent to a certain place; *prt* **ezhinizha'igaadeg;** *aug* **izhinizha'igaademagad;** *prt aug* **ezhinizha'igaademagak**

izhinizha'igaazo *vai* be sent to a certain place; *prt* **ezhinizha'igaazod**

izhinizhikaw *vta* chase s.o. to a certain place; *1sg* **indizhinizhikawaa;** *prt* **ezhinizhikawaad**

izhinizhimo *vai* run to a certain place in flight; *1sg* **indizhinizhim;** *prt* **ezhinizhimod**

izhinoo' *vta* point to s.o. a certain way; *1sg* **indizhinoo'aa;** *prt* **ezhinoo'aad**

izhinoo'amaw *vta* point to (s.t.) for s.o.; *1sg* **indizhinoo'amawaa;** *prt* **ezhinoo'amawaad**

izhinoo'an *vti* point to s.t. a certain way; *1sg* **indizhinoo'aan;** *prt* **ezhinoo'ang**

izhinoo'iganinj *ni* index finger; *pl* **izhinoo'iganinjiin**

izhise *vai* fly to a certain place; *1sg* **indizhise;** *prt* **ezhised**

izhise *vii* fly to a certain place, pass (as time); *prt* **ezhiseg;** *aug* **izhisemagad;** *prt aug* **ezhisemagak**

izhishim *vta* lay s.o. a certain way, put s.o. a certain way; *1sg* **indizhishimaa;** *prt* **ezhishimaad**

izhishin *vai* lie a certain way; *1sg* **indizhishin;** *prt* **ezhishing**

izhisidoon *vti2* lay s.t. a certain way, set s.t. a certain way; *1sg* **indizhisidoon;** *prt* **ezhisidood**

izhisin *vii* lie a certain way, be written a certain way, be printed a certain way; *prt* **ezhising**

izhitigweyaa *vii* flow to a certain place (as a river); *prt* **ezhitigweyaag;** *aug* **izhitigweyaamagad;** *prt aug* **ezhitigweyaamagak**

izhitoon *vti2* cause s.t. to, make s.t. a certain way; *1sg* **indizhitoon;** *prt* **ezhitood**

izhitwaa *vai* have a certain custom, practice a certain religion; *1sg* **indizhitwaa;** *prt* **ezhitwaad**

izhiwebad *vii* happen a certain way, be a certain event, be a certain weather condition; *prt* **ezhiwebak**

izhiwebizi *vai* behave a certain way, have certain things happen to one, fare a certain way; *1sg* **indizhiwebiz;** *prt* **ezhiwebizid**

izhiwidaw *vta* take (s.t.) to s.o. at a certain place; *1sg* **indizhiwidawaa;** *prt* **ezhiwidawaad**

izhiwidoon *vti2* take s.t. to a certain place, carry s.t. to a certain place; *1sg* **indizhiwidoon;** *prt* **ezhiwidood**

izhiwijigaade *vii* be carried to a certain place, be taken to a certain place; *prt* **ezhiwijigaadeg;** *aug* **izhiwijigaademagad;** *prt aug* **ezhiwijigaademagak**

izhiwijigaazo *vai* be carried to a certain place, be taken to a certain place; *prt* **ezhiwijigaazod**

izhiwizh /izhiwiN-/ *vta* take s.o. to a certain place, carry s.o. to a certain place; *1sg* **indizhiwinaa;** *prt* **ezhiwinaad**

izhi-wiindan *vti* call s.t. a certain way, name s.t. a certain way; *1sg* **indizhi-wiindaan;** *prt* **ezhi-wiindang**

izhi-wiinde *vii* be called a certain way, be named a certain way; *prt* **ezhi-wiindeg;** *aug* **izhi-wiindemagad;** *prt aug* **ezhi-wiindemagak**

izhi-wiinzh /izhi-wiinN-/ *vta* call s.o. a certain way, name s.o. a certain way; *1sg* **indizhi-wiinaa;** *prt* **ezhi-wiinaad**

izhi-wiinzo *vai* be called a certain way, be named a certain way; *1sg* **indizhi-wiinz;** *prt* **ezhi-wiinzod**

izhizideni *vai* move one's foot a certain way; *1sg* **indizhiziden;** *prt* **ezhizidenid**

izhiigad *vii* be a certain way (as something sheetlike); *prt* **ezhiigak**

izhiigizi *vai* be a certain way (as something sheetlike); *prt* **ezhiigizid**

iidog *pc* maybe, must be

J

jachakan= < **jakan=**

jakanaamo *vai* have chest pains while breathing; *1sg* **injakanaam;** *prt* **jekanaamod**

jakiiwii *vai* strain self in lifting; *1sg* **injakiiwii;** *prt* **jekiiwiid**

jaachaag= < **jaag=**

jaachaamo *vai* sneeze; *1sg* **injaachaam;** *prt* **jayaachaamod**

jaagadaawaage *vai+o* sell out (of s.t.); *1sg* **injaagadaawaage, injaagadaawaagen;** *prt* **jayaagadaawaaged**

jaaga'e *vai* use up all of the ammunition; *1sg* **injaaga'e;** *prt* **jayaaga'ed**

jaagaabaji' *vta* use s.o. up; *1sg* **injaagaabaji'aa;** *prt* **jayaagaabaji'aad**

jaagaabajitoon *vti2* use s.t. up; *1sg* **injaagaabajitoon;** *prt* **jayaagaabajitood**

jaagaakide *vii* burn up; *prt* **jayaagaakideg;** *aug* **jaagaakidemagad;** *prt aug* **jayaagaakidemagak**

jaagaakiz /jaagaakizw-/ vta burn s.o. up; 1sg
  injaagaakizwaa; prt jayaagaakizwaad
jaagaakizan vti burn s.t. up; 1sg injaagaakizaan;
  prt jayaagaakizang
jaagaakizo vai burn up; prt jayaagaakizod
jaagide vii burn up; prt jayaagideg; aug
  jaagidemagad; prt aug jayaagidemagak
jaagin vta be out of s.o.; 1sg injaaginaa; prt
  jayaaginaad
jaaginan vti be out of s.t.; 1sg injaaginaan; prt
  jayaaginang
jaaginazh /jaaginaN-/ vta kill s.o. off; 1sg
  injaaginanaa; prt jayaaginanaad
jaaginigaade vii be used up; prt jayaaginigaadeg;
  aug jaaginigaademagad; prt aug
  jayaaginigaademagak
jaaginige vai use things up, take everything, spend
  everything; 1sg injaaginige; prt jayaaginiged
jaagise vai+o run out, become exhausted; 1sg
  injaagise, injaagisen; prt jayaagised
jaagise vii run out; prt jayaagiseg; aug
  jaagisemagad; prt aug jayaagisemagak
jaagiz /jaagizw-/ vta burn s.o. up; 1sg injaagizwaa;
  prt jayaagizwaad
jaagizan vti burn s.t. up; 1sg injaagizaan; prt
  jayaagizang
jaagizhooniyaaweshin vai use up all of the money;
  1sg injaagizhooniyaaweshin; prt
  jayaagizhooniyaaweshing
jaagizige vai use up all of the ammunition; 1sg
  injaagizige; prt jayaagiziged
jaagizo vai burn up; 1sg injaagiz; prt jayaagizod
jaagizodizo vai burn oneself; 1sg injaagizodiz; prt
  jayaagizodizod
jaangate vii be a corner of a room; prt
  jayaangateg; aug jaangatemagad; prt aug
  jayaangatemagak
jaangidiyeshin vai lie with one's rear end sticking
  out; 1sg injaangidiyeshin; prt
  jayaangidiyeshing
jejiibajikii na elephant; pl jejiibajikiig; dim
  jejiibajikiins
jekaagaminan vti dip s.t. in; 1sg
  injekaagaminaan; prt jayekaagaminang
jekaakwa'am vai2 go into the woods; 1sg
  injekaakwa'am; prt jayekaakwa'ang
jeko-mazina'igan ni check; pl jeko-
  mazina'iganan; loc jeko-mazina'iganing; dim
  jeko-mazina'igaans
ji- pv1 that, so that, in order to; future and modal
  prefix in unchanged conjunct
jibwaa- pv1 before; also ji-bwaa-
jiibadabi vai sit stiffly; 1sg injiibadab; prt
  jaabadabid
jiibadaakogaabawi vai stand stiffly; 1sg
  injiibadaakogaabaw; prt
  jaabadaakogaabawid
jiibadaakogaade vai have a stiff leg; 1sg
  injiibadaakogaade; prt jaabadaakogaaded
jiibadaakonike vai have a stiff arm; 1sg
  injiibadaakonike; prt jaabadaakoniked
jiibajigaade vai have a stiff leg; 1sg injiibajigaade;
  prt jaabajigaaded
jiibajigwayawe vai have a stiff neck; 1sg
  injiibajigwayawe; prt jaabajigwayawed

jiibajinike vai have a stiff arm; 1sg injiibajinike; prt
  jaabajiniked
jiibay na ghost, spirit; pl jiibayag
jiibayag niimi'idiwag /niimi'idi-/ vai they are the
  northern lights; prt jiibayag naami'idijig
jiibayaki ni graveyard, cemetery; pl jiibayakiin; loc
  jiibayakiing; dim jiibayakiins
jiibayaatig na grave marker; pl jiibayaatigoog; loc
  jiibayaatigong; dim jiibayaatigoons
jiibaakwaadan vti cook s.t.; 1sg injiibaakwaadaan;
  prt jaabaakwaadang
jiibaakwaazh /jiibaakwaaN-/ vta cook s.o.; 1sg
  injiibaakwaanaa; prt jaabaakwaanaad
jiibaakwe vai cook; 1sg injiibaakwe; prt
  jaabaakwed
jiibaakwe-gizhaabikizigan ni cook stove; pl
  jiibaakwe-gizhaabikiziganan; loc jiibaakwe-
  gizhaabikiziganing; dim jiibaakwe-
  gizhaabikizigaans
jiibaakwewakik na cooking pot, pan; pl
  jiibaakwewakikoog; loc jiibaakwewakikong;
  dim jiibaakwewakikoons
jiibaakwewigamig ni kitchen, cook shack; pl
  jiibaakwewigamigoon; loc
  jiibaakwewigamigong; dim
  jiibaakwewigamigoons
jiibaakwewikwe na cook (female); pl
  jiibaakwewikweg
jiibaakwewinini na cook (male); pl
  jiibaakwewininiwag
jiibegamig ni grave house, casket; pl
  jiibegamigoon; loc jiibegamigong; dim
  jiibegamigoons
jiibenaake vai have a feast honoring the dead; 1sg
  injiibenaake; prt jaabenaaked
jiibiingweni vai wink; 1sg injiibiingwen; prt
  jaabiingwenid
jiibiingwetaw vta wink at s.o.; 1sg
  injiibiingwetawaa; prt jaabiingwetawaad
jiichiibishkaa vai quiver; 1sg injiichiibishkaa; prt
  jaachiibishkaad
jiichiibizideni vai tap one's foot; 1sg
  injiichiibiziden; prt jaachiibizidenid
jiichiibiingwetaw vta wink at s.o.; 1sg
  injiichiibiingwetawaa; prt
  jaachiibiingwetawaad
jiichiigawiganebizh /jiichiigawiganebiN-/ vta
  scratch s.o.'s back; 1sg injiichiigawiganebinaa;
  prt jaachiigawiganebinaad
jiichiigibidoon vti2 scratch s.t. (leaving a visible
  mark); 1sg injiichiigibidoon; prt
  jaachiigibidood
jiichiigibizh /jiichiigibiN-/ vta scratch s.o. (leaving
  a visible mark); 1sg injiichiigibinaa; prt
  jaachiigibinaad
jiichiigii vai scratch (leaving a visible mark); 1sg
  injiichiigii; prt jaachiigiid
jiichiigom na wart; pl jiichiigomag
jiichiigwam vta chew on s.o.; 1sg injiichiigwamaa;
  prt jaachiigwamaad
jiichiigwandan vti chew on s.t.; 1sg
  injiichiigwandaan; prt jaachiigwandang
jiichiigwanjige vai chew on things; 1sg
  injiichiigwanjige; prt jaachiigwanjiged
jiichiishkinzhe'igan ni fire poker; pl
  jiichiishkinzhe'iganan; loc

jiichiishkinzhe'iganing; *dim*
jiichiishkinzhe'igaans
jiichiishkinzhe'ige *vai* stir the fire; *1sg*
   injiichiishkinzhe'ige; *prt* **jaachiishkinzhe'iged**
jiigada'igan *ni* broom; *pl* **jiigada'iganan**; *loc*
   jiigada'iganing; *dim* **jiigada'igaans**
jiiga'azh /**jiiga'aN-**/ *vta* scale s.o.; *1sg* **injiiga'anaa**;
   prt **jaaga'anaad**
jiiga'e *vai* scale fish; *1sg* **injiiga'e**; *prt* **jaaga'ed**
jiigashkosiw *pc* by a meadow
jiigayi'ii *pc* by it, along it
jiigaakwaa *pc* near the woods
jiigaatig *pc* by a tree, by a wall
jiigew *pc* along the shore
jiigewe *vai* go along the shore, go along the edge;
   1sg **injiigewe**; *prt* **jaagewed**
jiigewebatoo *vai* run along the shore; *1sg*
   injiigewebatoo; *prt* **jaagewebatood**
jiigewebizo *vai* drive along the shore, speed along
   the shore; *1sg* **injiigewebiz**; *prt* **jaagewebizod**
jiigewedaabii'iwe *vai* drive along the shore; *1sg*
   injiigewedaabii'iwe; *prt* **jaagewedaabii'iwed**
jiigewe'am *vai2* paddle along the shore; *1sg*
   injiigewe'am; *prt* **jaagewe'ang**
jiigewe'o *vai* paddle along the shore; *1sg*
   injiigewe'; *prt* **jaagewe'od**
jiigewekwazhiwe *vai* paddle along the shore; *1sg*
   injiigewekwazhiwe; *prt* **jaagewekwazhiwed**
jiigeweyaazhagaame *vai* walk along the shore; *1sg*
   injiigeweyaazhagaame; *prt*
   jaageweyaazhagaamed
jiigeweyaazhagaamebatoo *vai* run along the
   shore; *1sg* **injiigeweyaazhagaamebatoo**; *prt*
   jaageweyaazhagaamebatood
jiigi- *pn* near, by
jiigibiig *pc* along the shore, by the water
jiigigamig *pc* by a house
jiigikana *pc* by a road or trail
jiigishkode *pc* by a fire
jiigishkwaand *pc* by a door
jiimaan *ni* canoe, boat; *pl* **jiimaanan**; *loc*
   jiimaaning; *dim* **jiimaanens**
jiimaanike *vai* make a canoe, make a boat; *1sg*
   injiimaanike; *prt* **jaamaaniked**
jiime *vai* go by canoe, paddle; *1sg* **injiime**; *prt*
   jaamed
jiingwe *vii* rumble; *prt* **jaangweg**; *aug*
   jiingwemagad; *prt aug* **jaangwemagak**
jiis *ni* rutabaga; *pl* **jiisan**; *loc* **jiising**; *dim* **jiisens**
jiisakaan *ni* shaking tent; *pl* **jiisakaanan**; *loc*
   jiisakaaning; *dim* **jiisakaanens**
jiisakii *vai* practice divination in a shaking tent; *1sg*
   injiisakii; *prt* **jaasakiid**
jiisakiiwinini *na* seer who uses a shaking tent; *pl*
   jiisakiiwininiwag
jiishada'igan *ni* broom; *pl* **jiishada'iganan**; *loc*
   jiishada'iganing; *dim* **jiishada'igaans**
jiishada'ige *vai* sweep; *1sg* **injiishada'ige**; *prt*
   jaashada'iged
jiishakamiga'igan *ni* rake; *pl* **jiishakamiga'iganan**;
   loc **jiishakamiga'iganing**; *dim*
   jiishakamiga'igaans
jiishaakwa' /**jiishaakwa'w-**/ *vta* scrape s.o. to
   remove hair (e.g., a hide); *1sg*
   injiishaakwa'waa; *prt* **jaashaakwa'aad**

jiishaakwa'igan *ni* hide scraper; *pl*
   jiishaakwa'iganan
jiishaakwa'ige *vai* scrape hides; *1sg*
   injiishaakwa'ige; *prt* **jaashaakwa'iged**
jiisibizh /**jiisibiN-**/ *vta* pinch s.o.; *1sg* **injiisibinaa**;
   prt **jaasibinaad**
jiiskinikebizo *vai* wear a bracelet, wear arm
   garters; *1sg* **injiiskinikebiz**; *prt* **jaaskinikebizod**
jiiskinikebizon *ni* arm garter, bracelet; *pl*
   jiiskinikebizonan; *loc* **jiiskinikebizoning**; *dim*
   jiiskinikebizonens

M

madaabii *vai* go to the shore; *1sg* **nimadaabii**; *prt*
   medaabiid
madaabiibatoo *vai* run to the shore; *1sg*
   nimadaabiibatoo; *prt* **medaabiibatood**
madaabiiwidoon *vti2* take s.t. to the shore, carry
   s.t. to the shore; *1sg* **nimadaabiiwidoon**; *prt*
   medaabiiwidood
madaabiiwizh /**madaabiiwiN-**/ *vta* take s.o. to the
   shore, carry s.o. to the shore; *1sg*
   nimadaabiiwinaa; *prt* **medaabiiwinaad**
madaagamin /**madaagami-**/ *vii* be turbulent
   water; *prt* **medaagamig**
madoodiswan *ni* sweat lodge; *pl* **madoodiswanan**;
   loc **madoodiswaning**
madoodoo *vai* take a sweat bath; *1sg*
   nimadoodoo; *prt* **medoodood**
madoodoowasin *na* rock for sweat lodge; *pl*
   madoodoowasiniig; *loc* **madoodoowasiniing**
madoodoowinini *na* Finn; *pl*
   madoodoowininiwag
madwe- *pv4* being heard, making noise
madwebiisaa *vii* rain is heard; *prt* **medwebiisaag**;
   aug **madwebiisaamagad**; *prt aug*
   medwebiisaamagak
madwegamide *vii* make noise boiling; *prt*
   medwegamideg; *aug* **madwegamidemagad**;
   prt aug **medwegamidemagak**
madwegamijii *vai* one's stomach growls; *1sg*
   nimadwegamijii; *prt* **medwegamijiid**
madwegamizo *vai* make noise boiling; *prt*
   medwegamizod
madwe' /**madwe'w-**/ *vta* drum on s.o.; *1sg*
   nimadwe'; *prt* **medwe'waad**
madwe'an *vti* drum on s.t.; *1sg* **nimadwe'aan**; *prt*
   medwe'ang
madwejiwan *vii* be heard flowing (e.g., a rapids);
   prt **medwejiwang**
madwekwadin *vii* be heard cracking (as ice); *prt*
   medwekwading
madwengwaam *vai* make noise in one's sleep,
   snore; *1sg* **nimadwengwaam**; *prt*
   medwengwaang
madwenjige *vai* be heard eating; *1sg*
   nimadwenjige; *prt* **medwenjiged**

madwesagishin *vai* be heard falling on the floor, be heard walking on the floor; *1sg* **nimadwesagishin;** *prt* **medwesagishing**
madweshin *vai* ring, make noise hitting; *1sg* **nimadweshin;** *prt* **medweshing**
madwesidoon *vti2* ring s.t.; *1sg* **nimadwesidoon;** *prt* **medwesidood**
madwesijige *vai* ring things, make noise hitting things; *1sg* **nimadwesijige;** *prt* **medwesijiged**
madwesin *vii* ring, make noise hitting; *prt* **medwesing**
madwetaa *vai* be heard in an activity; *1sg* **nimadwetaa;** *prt* **medwetaad**
madwewe *vii* make noise; *prt* **medweweg;** *aug* **madwewemagad;** *prt aug* **medwewemagak**
madwewechigan *ni* musical instrument, piano, organ; *pl* **madwewechiganan;** *loc* **madwewechiganing;** *dim* **madwewechigaans**
madwewechige *vai* make sounds on things, play music; *1sg* **nimadwewechige;** *prt* **medwewechiged**
madwewetaw *vta* play music for s.o.; *1sg* **nimadwewetawaa;** *prt* **medwewetawaad;** *also* **madwewetamaw**
madwewetoon *vti2* make sounds on s.t., make noise on s.t.; *1sg* **nimadwewetoon;** *prt* **medwewetood**
madweyaabiigibijigan *ni* guitar; *pl* **madweyaabiigibijiganan;** *loc* **madweyaabiigibijiganing;** *dim* **madweyaabiigibijigaans**
madweyaabiigibijige *vai* play a guitar; *1sg* **nimadweyaabiigibijige;** *prt* **medweyaabiigibijiged**
madwezige *vai* be heard shooting; *1sg* **nimadwezige;** *prt* **medweziged**
ma'iingan *na* wolf; *pl* **ma'iinganag;** *dim* **ma'iingaans**
ma'iinganasim *na* German shepherd; *pl* **ma'iinganasimoog;** *dim* **ma'iinganasimoons**
ma'iinganiwayaan *na* wolf hide; *pl* **ma'iinganiwayaanag;** *loc* **ma'iinganiwayaaning;** *dim* **ma'iinganiwayaanens**
maji- *pv4* bad
majigiizhwe *vai* swear; *1sg* **nimajigiizhwe;** *prt* **mejigiizhwed**
majigoode *ni* dress; *pl* **majigoodeyan**
maji-izhiwebizi *vai* misbehave, lead an evil life; *1sg* **nimaji-izhiwebiz;** *prt* **meji-izhiwebizid**
maji-manidoo *na* evil manitou, devil; *pl* **maji-manidoog;** *dim* **maji-manidoons**
maji-manidoowaadizi *vai* be evil, be possessed by an evil spirit; *1sg* **nimaji-manidoowaadiz;** *prt* **meji-manidoowaadizid**
maji-mashkiki *ni* poison; *pl* **maji-mashkikiwan;** *loc* **maji-mashkikiing;** *dim* **maji-mashkikiins**
makade *ni* black gunpowder; *loc* **makadeng**
makade- *pv4* black
makade-aniibiish *ni* black tea; *loc* **makade-aniibiishing**
makade-bigiw *na* tar, asphalt
makadeke *vai* undergo puberty fast; *1sg* **nimakadeke;** *prt* **mekadeked**
makade-mashkikiwaaboo *ni* coffee; *loc* **makade-mashkikiwaaboong**

makadeshib *na* black duck; *pl* **makadeshibag;** *dim* **makadeshibens**
makadewaa *vii* be black, be dark; *prt* **mekadewaag;** *aug* **makadewaamagad;** *prt aug* **mekadewaamagak**
makadewaabikad *vii* be black (as something mineral); *prt* **mekadewaabikak**
makadewaabikizi *vai* be black (as something mineral), be in eclipse; *prt* **mekadewaabikizid**
makadewaabiigad *vii* be black (as something string-like); *prt* **mekadewaabiigak**
makadewaabiigizi *vai* be black (as something string-like); *prt* **mekadewaabiigizid**
makadewaagamin /**makadewaagami-**/ *vii* be black (as a liquid), be dark (as a liquid); *prt* **mekadewaagamig**
makade-waagosh *na* fox (in black phase); *pl* **makade-waagoshag;** *dim* **makade-waagoshens**
makadewaakozi *vai* be black (as something stick- or wood-like); *prt* **mekadewaakozid**
makadewaakwad *vii* be black (as something stick- or wood-like); *prt* **mekadewaakwak**
makadewaande *vii* be colored black; *prt* **mekadewaandeg;** *aug* **makadewaandemagad;** *prt aug* **mekadewaandemagak**
makadewaanzo *vai* be colored black; *prt* **mekadewaanzod**
makadewegad *vii* be black (as something sheet-like); *prt* **mekadewegak**
makadewegizi *vai* be black (as something sheet-like); *prt* **mekadewegizid**
makadewi'o *vai* wear black; *1sg* **nimakadewi';** *prt* **mekadewi'od**
makadewindibe *vai* have black hair; *1sg* **nimakadewindibe;** *prt* **mekadewindibed**
makadewizi *vai* be black, be dark; *prt* **mekadewizid**
makade-wiiyaas *na* Black person, person of African descent; *pl* **makade-wiiyaasag**
makade-wiiyaasikwe *na* Black woman, woman of African descent; *pl* **makade-wiiyaasikweg**
makadeyaanakwad *vii* there are dark clouds; *prt* **mekadeyaanakwak**
makak *ni* box, birch bark basket; *pl* **makakoon;** *loc* **makakong;** *dim* **makakoons**

makak (birch bark basket)

makakoke *vai* make a box, make a birch bark basket; *1sg* **nimakakoke**; *prt* **mekakoked**
makakosag *ni* tub, barrel; *pl* **makakosagoon**; *loc* **makakosagong**; *dim* **makakosagoons**
makam *vta* take (s.t.) from s.o. forcibly, rob s.o. of (s.t.); *1sg* **nimakamaa**; *prt* **mekamaad**
makandwe *vai* rob people, take captives; *1sg* **nimakandwe**; *prt* **mekandwed**
makizin *ni* moccasin, shoe; *pl* **makizinan**; *loc* **makizining**; *dim* **makizinens**

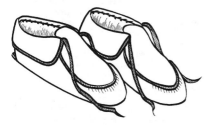

makizinan (moccasins); see also
bashweginwakizinan, bashkwegino-makizinan

makizinataadiwag /**makizinataadi-**/ *vai* they play the moccasin game with each other; *1pl* **nimakizinataadimin**; *prt* **mekizinataadijig**
makizinataage *vai* play the moccasin game; *1sg* **nimakizinataage**; *prt* **mekizinataaged**
makizinataage-nagamon *ni* moccasin game song; *pl* **makizinataage-nagamonan**
makizinataagewin *ni* moccasin game
makizineyaab *ni* shoelace; *pl* **makizineyaabiin**; *loc* **makizineyaabiing**; *dim* **makizineyaabiins**
makizinike *vai* make moccasins, make shoes; *1sg* **nimakizinike**; *prt* **mekiziniked**
makominagaawanzh *na* mountain ash; *pl* **makominagaawanzhiig**; *loc* **makominagaawanzhiing**; *dim* **makominagaawanzhiins**
makoons *na* bear cub; *pl* **makoonsag**
makwa *na* bear; *pl* **makwag**; *dim* **makoons**
makwasaagim *na* bear paw snowshoe; *pl* **makwasaagimag**; *loc* **makwasaagiming**; *dim* **makwasaagimens**
mamadweyaashkaa *vii* roar (as waves); *prt* **memadweyaashkaag**; *aug* **mamadweyaashkaamagad**; *prt aug* **memadweyaashkaamagak**
mamagoniishkwe *vai* have the mumps; *1sg* **nimamagoniishkwe**; *prt* **memagoniishkwed**
mamakiziwin *ni* smallpox
mamakii' *vta* allot s.o. land; *1sg* **nimamakii'aa**; *prt* **memakii'aad**
mamakii'idim /**mamakii'idi-**/ *vai* there is an allotment of land; *prt* **memakii'iding**
mamaw *vta* take (s.t.) from s.o., pick (s.t.) up from s.o.; *1sg* **nimamawaa**; *prt* **memawaad**
mamaach= < **mich=**
mamaachaawan /**mamaachaa-**/ *vii* they are big; *prt* **memaachaagin**; *aug*

mamaachaamagadoon; *prt aug* **memaachaamagakin**
mamaadwe *vai* groan; *1sg* **nimamaadwe**; *prt* **memaadwed**
mamaajide'eshkaa *vai* have a heart attack; *1sg* **nimamaajide'eshkaa**; *prt* **memaajide'eshkaad**
mamaajise *vai* move; *1sg* **nimamaajise**; *prt* **memaajised**
mamaajise *vii* move; *prt* **memaajiseg**; *aug* **mamaajisemagad**; *prt aug* **memaajisemagak**
mamaajii *vai* move, be in motion; *1sg* **nimamaajii**; *prt* **memaajiid**
mamaakadew= < **makadew=**
mamaandaagochige *vai* perform tricks; *1sg* **nimamaandaagochige**; *prt* **memaandaagochiged**
mamaandaagochigewin *ni* circus, carnival; *pl* **mamaandaagochigewinan**
mamaandid= < **mindid=**
mamaandidowag /**mamaandido-**/ *vai* they are big; *prt* **memaandidojig**
mamaang= < **mang=**
mamaangade= < **mangade=**
mamaangadepon /**mamaangadepo-**/ *vii* snow in large flakes; *prt* **memaangadepog**
mamaangaashkaa *vii* be big waves; *prt* **memaangaashkaag**; *aug* **mamaangaashkaamagad**; *prt aug* **memaangaashkaamagak**
mamaashkaw= < **mashkaw=**
mamaayag= < **mayag=**
mamaazhi' *vta* prevail over s.o., conquer s.o.; *1sg* **nimamaazhi'aa**; *prt* **memaazhi'aad**
mamaazhitoon *vti2* prevail over s.t., conquer s.t.; *1sg* **nimamaazhitoon**; *prt* **memaazhitood**
mamaazhii *vai* make things badly, do a poor job; *1sg* **nimamaazhii**; *prt* **memaazhiid**
mamaazikaa *vai* move, agitate; *1sg* **nimamaazikaa**; *prt* **memaazikaad**
mami /**mam-**/ *vta* take s.o., pick s.o. up; *1sg* **nimamaa**; *prt* **memaad**
mamigaade *vii* be taken, be picked up; *prt* **memigaadeg**; *aug* **mamigaademagad**; *prt aug* **memigaademagak**
mamigaazo *vai* be taken, be picked up; *prt* **memigaazod**
mamige *vai* take things, pick up things; *1sg* **nimamige**; *prt* **memiged**
maminaadendam *vai2* have proud thoughts, have an arrogant attitude; *1sg* **nimaminaadendam**; *prt* **meminaadendang**
maminaadizi *vai* be arrogant; *1sg* **nimaminaadiz**; *prt* **meminaadizid**
mamizh /**mamizhw-**/ *vta* cut s.o. out; *1sg* **nimamizhwaa**; *prt* **memizhwaad**
mamizhan *vti* cut s.t. out; *1sg* **nimamizhaan**; *prt* **memizhang**
mamiidaawendam *vai2* be disturbed in one's mind, be troubled in one's mind; *1sg* **nimamiidaawendam**; *prt* **memiidaawendang**
mamiikw= < **mikw=**
mamiisaw= < **misaw=**
mamiiziwe= < **miziwe=**

mamoon *vti2* take s.t., pick s.t. up; *1sg*
  nimamoon; *prt* **memood**
manashkikiiwe *vai* gather medicine; *1sg*
  nimanashkikiiwe; *prt* **menashkikiiwed**
manaaji' *vta* spare s.o., go easy on s.o.; *1sg*
  nimanaaji'aa; *prt* **menaaji'aad**
manaajitoon *vti2* spare s.t., go easy on s.t.; *1sg*
  nimanaajitoon; *prt* **menaajitood**
mandaamin *na* corn, kernel of corn; *pl*
  mandaaminag; *loc* **mandaamining**; *dim*
  mandaaminens
mandaaminashk *ni* cornstalk; *pl*
  mandaaminashkoon; *loc*
  mandaaminashkong; *dim*
  mandaaminashkoons
mandaaminaaboo *ni* corn soup; *loc*
  mandaaminaaboong
mandaaminaak *ni* ear of corn; *pl*
  mandaaminaakoon; *loc* **mandaaminaakong**;
  dim **mandaaminaakoons**
mandaamini-gitigaan *ni* cornfield; *pl*
  mandaamini-gitigaanan; *loc* **mandaamini-**
  gitigaaning; *dim* **mandaamini-gitigaanens**
mandaaminiwazh *ni* gunnysack; *pl*
  mandaaminiwazhan; *loc*
  mandaaminiwazhing; *dim*
  mandaaminiwazhens
manepwaa *vai* be short of tobacco, need to smoke;
  1sg **nimanepwaa**; *prt* **menepwaad**
manezi *vai-o* be in need of (s.t.), be short of (s.t.);
  1sg **nimanez, nimanezin**; *prt* **menezid**
mangade' *vta* make s.o. wide, widen s.o.; *1sg*
  nimangade'aa; *prt* **mengade'aad**
mangademon /**mangademo-**/ *vii* be wide (as a
  road or trail); *prt* **mengademog**; *also*
  mangadademon
mangadengwe *vai* have a broad face; *1sg*
  nimangadengwe; *prt* **mengadengwed**
mangadetoon *vti2* make s.t. wide, widen s.t.; *1sg*
  nimangadetoon; *prt* **mengadetood**
mangadeyaa *vii* be wide; *prt* **mengadeyaag**; *aug*
  mangadeyaamagad; *prt aug*
  mengadeyaamagak
mangadeyoonagad *vii* be wide (as a boat); *prt*
  mengadeyoonagak
mangadezi *vai* be wide; *prt* **mengadezid**
mangadinaa *vii* there is a big hill; *prt*
  mengadinaag; *aug* **mangadinaamagad**; *prt*
  aug **mengadinaamagak**
mangate *vii* be roomy; *prt* **mengateg**; *aug*
  mangatemagad; *prt aug* **mengatemagak**
mangaanibaadan *vti* shovel s.t.; *1sg*
  nimangaanibaadaan; *prt* **mengaanibaadang**
mangaanibaajigan *ni* shovel; *pl*
  mangaanibaajiganan; *loc*
  mangaanibaajiganing; *dim*
  mangaanibaajigaans
mangaanibaajige *vai* shovel things (e.g., snow);
  1sg **nimangaanibaajige**; *prt*
  mengaanibaajiged
mangaanibaazh /**mangaanibaaN-**/ *vta* shovel s.o.
  (e.g., snow); *1sg* **nimangaanibaanaa**; *prt*
  mengaanibaanaad
mangaanibii *vai* shovel; *1sg* **nimangaanibii**; *prt*
  mengaanibiid

mangide'e *vai* be courageous; *1sg* **nimangide'e**;
  prt **mengide'ed**
mangi' *vta* make s.o. big; *1sg* **nimangi'aa**; *prt*
  mengi'aad
mangindibe *vai* have a big head; *1sg*
  nimangindibe; *prt* **mengindibed**
mangininjii *vai* have a big hand; *1sg* **nimangininjii**;
  prt **mengininjiid**
mangishkiinzhigwe *vai* have a big eye; *1sg*
  nimangishkiinzhigwe; *prt*
  mengishkiinzhigwed
mangitigweyaa *vii* be wide (as a river); *prt*
  mengitigweyaag; *aug* **mangitigweyaamagad**;
  prt aug **mengitigweyaamagak**
mangiwane *vai* carry a big pack; *1sg*
  nimangiwane; *prt* **mengiwaned**
mangizide *vai* have a big foot; *1sg* **nimangizide**;
  prt **mengizided**
manidoo *na* god, spirit, manitou; *pl* **manidoog**;
  dim **manidoons**
manidoo-biiwaabik *ni* steel, magnet; *loc* **manidoo-**
  biiwaabikong; *dim* **manidoo-biiwaabikoons**
manidoo-giizis *na* January; *also* **gichi-manidoo-**
  giizis
manidoo-giizisoons *na* December
manidookaazo *vai* take on spiritual power by
  one's own authority; *1sg* **nimanidookaaz**; *prt*
  menidookaazod
manidooke *vai* have spiritual power, conduct a
  ceremony; *1sg* **nimanidooke**; *prt* **menidooked**
manidoominens *na* bead; *pl* **manidoominensag**;
  loc **manidoominensing**
manidoominensikaan *na* item of bead work; *pl*
  manidoominensikaanag; *loc*
  manidoominensikaaning; *dim*
  manidoominensikaanens
manidoo-nagamon *ni* spiritual song; *pl* **manidoo-**
  nagamonan; *loc* **manidoo-nagamoning**; *dim*
  manidoo-nagamonens
manidoons *na* bug, insect; *pl* **manidoonsag**
manidoonsikaa *vii* there are many bugs; *prt*
  menidoonsikaag; *aug* **manidoonsikaamagad**;
  prt aug **menidoonsikaamagak**
manidoo-waabooz *na* cottontail rabbit; *pl*
  manidoo-waaboozoog; *dim* **manidoo-**
  waaboozoons
manidoowaadizi *vai* have a spiritual nature; *1sg*
  nimanidoowaadiz; *prt* **menidoowaadizid**
manidoowi *vai* be a spirit, be a manitou; *1sg*
  nimanidoow; *prt* **menidoowid**
manisaw *vta* cut (s.t.) as firewood for s.o.; *1sg*
  nimanisawaa; *prt* **menisawaad**
manisaadan *vti* cut s.t. as firewood; *1sg*
  nimanisaadaan; *prt* **menisaadang**
manise *vai* cut firewood; *1sg* **nimanise**; *prt*
  menised
maniwiigwaase *vai* gather birch bark; *1sg*
  nimaniwiigwaase; *prt* **meniwiigwaased**
manoomin *ni* wild rice; *loc* **manoomining**; *dim*
  manoominens; *also* **anishinaabe-manoomin**
manoominaganzh *ni* wild rice stalk; *pl*
  manoominaganzhiin
manoominaaboo *ni* wild rice broth; *loc*
  manoominaaboong

manoominikaa *vii* there is much wild rice; *prt* **menoominikaag**; *aug* **manoominikaamagad**; *prt aug* **menoominikaamagak**
manoominike *vai* harvest wild rice, make rice; *1sg* **nimanoominike**; *prt* **menoominiked**
manoominike-giizis *na* the month of ricing: September, August
manoominike-mazina'igaans *ni* ricing license; *pl* **manoominike-mazina'igaansan**
manoominikeshiinh *na* rice bird; *pl* **manoominikeshiinyag**
manoomini-mashkimod *ni* rice bag; *pl* **manoomini-mashkimodan**; *loc* **manoominimashkimodaang**
manoominiwazh *ni* rice bag; *pl* **manoominiwazhan**; *loc* **manoominiwazhing**
mashkawadin *vii* freeze, be frozen; *prt* **meshkawading**
mashkawaji *vai* freeze, be frozen, be frostbitten; *1sg* **nimashkawaj**; *prt* **meshkawajid**
mashkawaji-bimide *ni* tallow; *loc* **mashkawajibimideng**
mashkawajininjiiwaji *vai* have a hand stiff from cold; *1sg* **nimashkawajininjiiwaj**; *prt* **meshkawajininjiiwajid**
mashkawapide *vii* be tied tight; *prt* **meshkawapideg**; *aug* **mashkawapidemagad**; *prt aug* **meshkawapidemagak**
mashkawapidoon *vti2* tie s.t. tight; *1sg* **nimashkawapidoon**; *prt* **meshkawapidood**
mashkawapizh /**mashkawapiN-**/ *vta* tie s.o. tight; *1sg* **nimashkawapinaa**; *prt* **meshkawapinaad**
mashkawapizo *vai* be tied tight; *1sg* **nimashkawapiz**; *prt* **meshkawapizod**
mashkawaa *vii* be strong, be hard, be dense; *prt* **meshkawaag**; *aug* **mashkawaamagad**; *prt aug* **meshkawaamagak**
mashkawaagamin /**mashkawaagami-**/ *vii* be strong (as a liquid); *prt* **meshkawaagamig**
mashkawaakwadin *vii* be frozen stiff; *prt* **meshkawaakwading**
mashkawaakwaji *vai* be frozen stiff, be frostbitten; *1sg* **nimashkawaakwaj**; *prt* **meshkawaakwajid**
mashkawaakwajidoon *vti2* freeze s.t. stiff; *1sg* **nimashkawaakwajidoon**; *prt* **meshkawaakwajidood**
mashkawaakwajim *vta* freeze s.o. stiff; *1sg* **nimashkawaakwajimaa**; *prt* **meshkawaakwajimaad**
mashkawaakwajininjiiwaji *vai* have a frozen hand; *1sg* **nimashkawaakwajininjiiwaj**; *prt* **meshkawaakwajininjiiwajid**
mashkawimaaso *vai* smell strong burning or cooking; *prt* **meshkawimaasod**
mashkawimaate *vii* smell strong burning or cooking; *prt* **meshkawimaateg**; *aug* **mashkawimaatemagad**; *prt aug* **meshkawimaatemagak**
mashkawizi *vai* be strong, be dense, be hard; *prt* **meshkawizid**
mashkawizii *vai* be strong (of a person), have inner strength; *1sg* **nimashkawizii**; *prt* **meshkawiziid**

mashkawiziiwin *ni* power; muscle; *pl* **mashkawiziiwinan**; *loc* **mashkawiziiwining**; *dim* **mashkawiziiwinens**
mashkiki *ni* medicine; *pl* **mashkikiwan**; *loc* **mashkikiing**; *dim* **mashkikiins**
mashkikiwaaboo *ni* liquid medicine; *pl* **mashkikiwaaboon**; *loc* **mashkikiwaaboong**
mashkikii-adaawewigamig *ni* pharmacy, drugstore; *pl* **mashkikii-adaawewigamigoon**; *loc* **mashkikii-adaawewigamigong**; *dim* **mashkikii-adaawewigamigoons**; *also* **mashkikiiwi-adaawewigamig**
mashkikii-adaawewinini *na* pharmacist, druggist; *pl* **mashkikii-adaawewininiwag**; *also* **mashkikiiwi-adaawewinini**
mashkikiikaazh /**mashkikiikaaN-**/ *vta* doctor s.o.; *1sg* **nimashkikiikaanaa**; *prt* **meshkikiikaanaad**
mashkikiike *vai* make medicine; *1sg* **nimashkikiike**; *prt* **meshkikiiked**
mashkikiins *ni* pill; *pl* **mashkikiinsan**
mashkikiiwikwe *na* nurse (female); *pl* **mashkikiiwikweg**; *dim* **mashkikiiwikwens**
mashkikiiwinini *na* doctor; *pl* **mashkikiiwininiwag**; *dim* **mashkikiiwininiins**
mashkikiiwininiikwe *na* doctor (female); *pl* **mashkikiiwininiikweg**
mashkimod *ni* bag, sack; *pl* **mashkimodan**; *loc* **mashkimodaang**; *dim* **mashkimodens**, **mashkimodaans**
mashkimodegwaajigan *ni* pocket; *pl* **mashkimodegwaajiganan**; *loc* **mashkimodegwaajiganing**; *dim* **mashkimodegwaajigaans**
mashkimodens *ni* envelope; *pl* **mashkimodensan**; *loc* **mashkimodensing**
mashkiigimin *na* lowbush cranberry; *pl* **mashkiigiminag**; *loc* **mashkiigimining**; *dim* **mashkiigiminens**
mashkiigiminagaawanzh *ni* lowbush cranberry bush; *pl* **mashkiigiminagaawanzhiin**; *loc* **mashkiigiminagaawanzhiing**; *dim* **mashkiigiminagaawanzhiins**
mashkiigwaatig *na* tamarack; *pl* **mashkiigwaatigoog**; *loc* **mashkiigwaatigong**; *dim* **mashkiigwaatigoons**
mashkode *ni* prairie, plain; *pl* **mashkoden**; *loc* **mashkodeng**; *dim* **mashkodens**
mashkode-bizhiki *na* bison, buffalo; *pl* **mashkode-bizhikiwag**; *dim* **mashkodebizhikiins**
mashkodesimin *na* bean; *pl* **mashkodesiminag**; *loc* **mashkodesimining**; *dim* **mashkodesiminens**; *also* **mashkodiisimin**
mashkodesiminaaboo *ni* bean soup; *loc* **mashkodesiminaaboong**
mashkosiw *ni* grass, hay; *pl* **mashkosiwan**; *loc* **mashkosiing**; *dim* **mashkosiins**
mashkosiigaan *ni* lodge of grass; *pl* **mashkosiigaanan**; *loc* **mashkosiigaaning**; *dim* **mashkosiigaanens**
mawadish /**mawadiS-**/ *vta* visit s.o.; *1sg* **nimawadisaa**; *prt* **mewadisaad**
mawadishiwe *vai* visit people; *1sg* **nimawadishiwe**; *prt* **mewadishiwed**

mawadisidiwag /mawadisidi-/ *vai* they visit each
other; *1pl* nimawadisidimin; *prt* mewadisidijig
mawi *vai* cry, weep; *1sg* nimaw; *prt* mewid
mawim *vta* cry for s.o.; *1sg* nimawimaa; *prt*
mewimaad
mawinazh /mawinaN-/ *vta* run at s.o., attack s.o.;
1sg nimawinanaa; *prt* mewinanaad
mawindan *vti* cry for s.t.; *1sg* nimawindaan; *prt*
mewindang
mawinzo *vai* pick berries; *1sg* nimawinz; *prt*
mewinzod
mawishki *vai* be a crybaby; *1sg* nimawishk; *prt*
mewishkid
mawiikaazo *vai* pretend to cry; *1sg* nimawiikaaz;
prt mewiikaazod
mawiinsiwi *vai* cry a little; *1sg* nimawiinsiw; *prt*
mewiinsiwid
mayagendam *vai2* feel strange; *1sg*
nimayagendam; *prt* meyagendang
mayagendaagwad *vii* be considered strange; *prt*
meyagendaagwak
mayagenim *vta* consider s.o. strange; *1sg*
nimayagenimaa; *prt* meyagenimaad
mayagi- *pv4* strange, foreign, exotic
mayagi-anishinaabe *na* non-local Indian; *pl*
mayagi-anishinaabeg; *dim* mayagi-
anishinaabens
mayagi-bine *na* pheasant; *pl* mayagi-binewag; *dim*
mayagi-binens
mayaginaagozi *vai* look strange, look foreign; *1sg*
nimayaginaagoz; *prt* meyaginaagozid
mayaginaagwad *vii* look strange, look foreign; *prt*
meyaginaagwak
mayagitaagozi *vai* sound strange, sound foreign;
prt meyagitaagozid
mayagitaagwad *vii* sound strange, sound foreign;
prt meyagitaagwak
mayagizi *vai* be strange, be foreign; *1sg*
nimayagiz; *prt* meyagizid
mayagwe *vai* speak a strange language; *1sg*
nimayagwe; *prt* meyagwed
mayagwewinini *na* foreigner, speaker of a strange
language; *pl* mayagwewininiwag
mayaajiibizod *na-pt* engine; *pl* maayaajiibizojig
mazaanag /mazaan-/ *na* chaff from wild rice
plural; *loc* mazaaning; *dim* mazaanens
mazaanaatig *na* thistle; *pl* mazaanaatigoog; *loc*
mazaanaatigong; *dim* mazaanaatigoons
mazhi /maN-/ *vta* have sexual intercourse with
s.o.; *1sg* nimanaa; *prt* menaad
mazhiwe *vai* have sexual intercourse; *1sg*
nimazhiwe; *prt* mezhiwed
mazhii'igan *ni* cut-over clearing; *pl* mazhii'iganan;
loc mazhii'iganing; *dim* mazhii'igaans
mazhii'ige *vai* clear land; *1sg* nimazhii'ige; *prt*
mezhii'iged
mazina'amaw *vta* owe (s.t.) to s.o., get credit
from s.o.; *1sg* nimazina'amawaa; *prt*
mezina'amawaad
mazina'igan *ni* book, paper, letter, document; *pl*
mazina'iganan; *loc* mazina'iganing; *dim*
mazina'igaans
mazina'igani-makak *ni* cardboard box; *pl*
mazina'igani-makakoon; *loc* mazina'igani-
makakong; *dim* mazina'igani-makakoons

mazina'igani-mashkimodens *ni* paper bag; *pl*
mazina'igani-mashkimodensan; *loc*
mazina'igani-mashkimodensing
mazina'iganiiwidaabaan *na* mail truck; *pl*
mazina'iganiiwidaabaanag; *loc*
mazina'iganiiwidaabaaning; *dim*
mazina'iganiiwidaabaanens
mazina'iganiiwigamig *ni* post office; *pl*
mazina'iganiiwigamigoon; *loc*
mazina'iganiiwigamigong; *dim*
mazina'iganiiwigamigoons
mazina'iganiiwinini *na* postman; *pl*
mazina'iganiiwininiwag
mazina'igaans *ni* ticket, license; *pl*
mazina'igaansan; *loc* mazina'igaansing
mazina'ige *vai* owe, go into debt, get credit; *1sg*
nimazina'ige; *prt* mezina'iged
mazinashkibijigan *na* doll of hay or grass; *pl*
mazinashkibijiganag; *loc*
mazinashkibijiganing; *dim*
mazinashkibijigaans
mazinaabidoo'an *vti* bead s.t. on a loom; *1sg*
nimazinaabidoo'aan; *prt* mezinaabidoo'ang
mazinaabidoo'iganaatig *ni* bead loom; *pl*
mazinaabidoo'iganaatigoon; *loc*
mazinaabidoo'iganaatigong; *dim*
mazinaabidoo'iganaatigoons
mazinaabidoo'ige *vai* bead things on a loom; *1sg*
nimazinaabidoo'ige; *prt* mezinaabidoo'iged
mazinaabikiwebinigan *ni* typewriter, computer; *pl*
mazinaabikiwebiniganan; *loc*
mazinaabikiwebiniganing; *dim*
mazinaabikiwebinigaans
mazinaabikiwebinige *vai* type; *1sg*
nimazinaabikiwebinige; *prt*
mezinaabikiwebiniged
mazinaadin *vta* make an image of s.o.; *1sg*
nimazinaadinaa; *prt* mezinaadinaad
mazinaakide *vii* be pictured, be photographed; *prt*
mezinaakideg; *aug* mazinaakidemagad; *prt*
aug mezinaakidemagak
mazinaakiz /mazinaakizw-/ *vta* take pictures of
s.o., photograph s.o.; *1sg* nimazinaakizwaa;
prt mezinaakizwaad
mazinaakizan *vti* take pictures of s.t., photograph
s.t.; *1sg* nimazinaakizaan; *prt* mezinaakizang
mazinaakizigan *ni* camera; *pl* mazinaakiziganan;
loc mazinaakiziganing; *dim* mazinaakizigaans
mazinaakizige *vai* take pictures, photograph
things; *1sg* nimazinaakizige; *prt*
mezinaakiziged
mazinaakizo *vai* be pictured, be photographed;
1sg nimazinaakiz; *prt* mezinaakizod
mazinaakizon *ni* picture, photograph; *pl*
mazinaakizonan; *loc* mazinaakizoning; *dim*
mazinaakizonens
mazinaatese *vii* be a movie; *prt* mezinaateseg;
aug mazinaatesemagad; *prt aug*
mezinaatesemagak
mazinaatesewigamig *ni* movie theater; *pl*
mazinaatesewigamigoon; *loc*
mazinaatesewigamigong; *dim*
mazinaatesewigamigoons; *also*
mazinaatesijigewigamig

mazinaatesijigan *ni* television set; *pl* **mazinaatesijiganan;** *loc* **mazinaatesijiganing;** *dim* **mazinaatesijigaans**

mazinaatewebinigan *ni* movie projector; *pl* **mazinaatewebiniganan;** *loc* **mazinaatewebiniganing;** *dim* **mazinaatewebinigaans**

mazinibaganjigan *ni* dental pictograph on birch bark; *pl* **mazinibaganjiganan;** *loc* **mazinibaganjiganing;** *dim* **mazinibaganjigaans**

mazinibaganjige *vai* make a dental pictograph on birch bark; *1sg* **nimazinibaganijge;** *prt* **mezinibaganjiged**

mazinibii' /mazinibii'w-/ *vta* draw s.o.; *1sg* **nimazinibii'waa;** *prt* **mezinibii'waad**

mazinibii'an *vti* draw s.t.; *1sg* **nimazinibii'aan;** *prt* **mezinibii'ang**

mazinibii'igan *ni* drawing, design; *pl* **mazinibii'iganan;** *loc* **mazinibii'iganing;** *dim* **mazinibii'igaans**

mazinibii'ige *vai* draw things; *1sg* **nimazinibii'ige;** *prt* **mezinibii'iged**

mazinibii'igewinini *na* artist; *pl* **mazinibii'igewininiwag**

mazinichigan *na* doll, image, statue; *pl* **mazinichiganag;** *loc* **mazinichiganing;** *dim* **mazinichigaans**

mazinigwaadan *vti* embroider s.t., bead s.t.; *1sg* **nimazinigwaadaan;** *prt* **mezinigwaadang**

mazinigwaaso *vai* embroider, bead; *1sg* **nimazinigwaas;** *prt* **mezinigwaasod**

mazinigwaazh /mazinigwaaN-/ *vta* embroider s.o., bead on s.o.; *1sg* **nimazinigwaanaa;** *prt* **mezinigwaanaad**

mazinishin *vai* be imprinted, have a design; *prt* **mezinishing**

mazinisin *vii* be imprinted, have a design; *prt* **mezinising**

maadaginzo *vai* start a month, be the first day (of a month); *prt* **mayaadaginzod**

maada'adoo *vai* go off following a trail; *1sg* **nimaada'adoo;** *prt* **mayaada'adood**

maada'azh /maada'aN-/ *vta* go off following s.o.'s trail; *1sg* **nimaada'anaa;** *prt* **mayaada'anaad**

maada'ookii *vai* share, distribute; *1sg* **nimaada'ookii;** *prt* **mayaada'ookiid**

maada'oonidiwag /maada'oonidi-/ *vai* they distribute (s.t.) to each other, they share (s.t.); *1pl* **nimaada'oonidimin;** *prt* **mayaada'oonidijig**

maada'oozh /maada'ooN-/ *vta* distribute (s.t.) to s.o., share (s.t.) out to s.o.; *1sg* **nimaada'oonaa;** *prt* **mayaada'oonaad**

maadakamigad *vii* start (as an event); *prt* **mayaadakamigak**

maadakamigizi *vai* start (in some event); *1sg* **nimaadakamigiz;** *prt* **mayaadakamigizid**

maadanjige *vai* start eating; *1sg* **nimaadanjige;** *prt* **mayaadanjiged**

maadanokaadan *vti* start to work on s.t.; *1sg* **nimaadanokaadaan;** *prt* **mayaadanokaadang**

maadanokaazh /maadanokaaN-/ *vta* start to work on s.o.; *1sg* **nimaadanokaanaa;** *prt* **mayaadanokaanaad**

maadanoki *vai* start to work; *1sg* **nimaadanokii;** *prt* **mayaadanokiid**

maadaaboode *vii* drift off on the current; *prt* **mayaadaaboodeg;** *aug* **maadaaboodemagad;** *prt aug* **mayaadaaboodemagak**

maadaaboono *vai* drift off on the current; *prt* **mayaadaaboonod**

maadaadizi *vai* start a journey; *1sg* **nimaadaadiz;** *prt* **mayaadaadizid**

maadaa'an *vii* drift off on the waves; *prt* **mayaadaa'ang**

maadaa'ogo *vai* drift off on the waves; *prt* **mayaadaa'ogod**

maadaajim *vta* start to tell of s.o.; *1sg* **nimaadaajimaa;** *prt* **mayaadaajimaad**

maadaajimo *vai* start to tell; *1sg* **nimaadaajim;** *prt* **mayaadaajimod**

maadaajimotaw *vta* start to tell (s.t.) to s.o.; *1sg* **nimaadaajimotawaa;** *prt* **mayaadaajimotawaad**

maadaanimad *vii* wind picks up; *prt* **mayaadaanimak**

maadaawanidiwag /maadaawanidi-/ *vai* they start off in a group; *1pl* **nimaadaawanidimin;** *prt* **mayaadaawanidijig**

maadodan *vti* start to tell of s.t.; *1sg* **nimaadodaan;** *prt* **mayaadodang**

maadoode *vai* crawl off; *1sg* **nimaadoode;** *prt* **mayaadooded**

maadoom *vta* carry s.o. off on one's back; *1sg* **nimaadoomaa;** *prt* **mayaadoomaad**

maadoondan *vti* carry s.t. off on one's back; *1sg* **nimaadoondaan;** *prt* **mayaadoondang**

maadwewebizoni' *vta* start s.o. (e.g., a car); *1sg* **nimaadwewebizoni'aa;** *prt* **mayaadwewebizoni'aad**

maagizhaa *pc* maybe, perhaps; *also* **maazhaa**

maagobidoon *vti2* squeeze s.t.; *1sg* **nimaagobidoon;** *prt* **mayaagobidood**

maagobizh /maagobiN-/ *vta* squeeze s.o.; *1sg* **nimaagobinaa;** *prt* **mayaagobinaad**

maagon *vta* press on s.o.; *1sg* **nimaaagonaa;** *prt* **mayaagonaad**

maagonan *vti* press on s.t.; *1sg* **nimaagonaan;** *prt* **mayaagonang**

maa'ishkam *vai2* shop; *1sg* **nimaa'ishkam;** *prt* **mayaa'ishkang**

maajaa *vai* leave, depart, start off; *1sg* **nimaajaa;** *prt* **mayaajaad;** *also* **ani-maajaa**

maajaa' *vta* hold a funeral for s.o.; *1sg* **nimaajaa'aa;** *prt* **mayaajaa'aad**

maajaa'iwe *vai* hold a funeral, speak at a funeral; *1sg* **nimaajaa'iwe;** *prt* **mayaajaa'iwed**

maajiibiisaa *vii* start to rain; *prt* **mayaajiibiisaag;** *aug* **maajiibiisaamagad;** *prt aug* **mayaajiibiisaamagak**

maajiidaabiiba'igo *vai* drive off in a wagon; *1sg* **nimaajidaabiiba'ig;** *prt* **mayaajidaabiiba'igod**

maajidaabii'iwe *vai* drive off; *1sg* **nimaajidaabii'iwe;** *prt* **mayaajidaabii'iwed**

maajigaa *vii* start to leak, start to drip, start to run with sap; *prt* **mayaajigaag;** *aug* **maajigaamagad;** *prt aug* **mayaajigaamagak**

maaji' *vta* start to make s.o.; *1sg* **nimaaji'aa;** *prt* **mayaaji'aad**

maajijiwan *vii* start to flow, be a whirlpool; *prt*
mayaajijiwang

maajinaazha' /**maajinaazha'w-**/ *vta* send s.o. off;
1sg **nimaajinaazha'waa**; *prt*
mayaajinaazha'waad

maajinizha' /**maajinizha'w-**/ *vta* send s.o. off; *1sg*
nimaajinizha'waa; *prt* **mayaajinizha'waad**
maajinizha'amaw *vta* send (s.t.) off to s.o.; *1sg*
nimaajinizha'amawaa; *prt*
mayaajinizha'amawaad

maajinizha'an *vti* send s.t. off; *1sg*
nimaajinizha'aan; *prt* **mayaajinizha'ang**

maajinizhikaw *vta* chase s.o. off; *1sg*
nimaajinizhikawaa; *prt* **maayaajinizhikawaad**

maajipon /**maajipo-**/ *vii* start to snow; *prt*
mayaajipog

maajise *vai* begin, start, move off; *1sg* **nimaajise**;
prt **mayaajised**

maajise *vii* begin, start, move off; *prt* **mayaajiseg**;
aug **maajisemagad**; *prt aug* **mayaajisemagak**

maajitaa *vai* start an activity; *1sg* **nimaajitaa**; *prt*
mayaajitaad

maajitoon *vti2* start to make s.t.; *1sg* **nimaajitoon**;
prt **mayaajitood**

maajii- *pv4* start, begin, start off

maajiiba'idiwag /**maajiiba'idi-**/ *vai* they run off
together; *1pl* **nimaajiiba'idimin**; *prt*
mayaajiiba'idijig

maajiiba'igo *vai* drive off drawn by horses; *1sg*
nimaajiiba'ig; *prt* **mayaajiiba'igod**

maajiiba'iwe *vai* start to flee; *1sg* **nimaajiiba'iwe**;
prt **mayaajiiba'iwed**

maajiibatoo *vai* start to run, run off; *1sg*
nimaajiibatoo; *prt* **mayaajiibatood**

maajiibide *vii* drive off, speed off, start to run (as a
machine); *prt* **mayaajiibideg**; *aug*
maajiibidemagad; *prt aug*
mayaajiibidemagak

maajiibizo *vai* drive off, speed off, start to run (as
a machine); *1sg* **nimaajiibiz**; *prt* **mayaajiibizod**

maajiibii'amaw *vta* write a letter to s.o.; *1sg*
nimaajiibii'amawaa; *prt*
mayaajiibii'amawaad

maajiibii'igan *ni* letter; *pl* **maajiibii'iganan**; *loc*
maajiibii'iganing; *dim* **maajiibii'igaans**

maajiibii'ige *vai* write a letter; *1sg* **nimaajiibii'ige**;
prt **mayaajiibii'iged**

maajiibii'ige-mashkimodens *ni* envelope; *pl*
maajiibii'ige-mashkimodensan; *loc*
maajiibii'ige-mashkimodensing

maajiidaw *vta* take (s.t.) along for s.o.; *1sg*
nimaajiidawaa; *prt* **mayaajiidawaad**

maajiidoon *vti2* take s.t. away, take s.t. along; *1sg*
nimaajiidoon; *prt* **mayaajiidood**

maajiigi *vai* grow up, start to grow; *1sg* **nimaajiig**;
prt **mayaajiigid**

maajiigidaazo *vai* go off mad; *1sg* **nimaajiigidaaz**;
prt **mayaajiigidaazod**

maajiigin *vii* grow up, start to grow; *prt*
mayaajiiging

maajii'am *vai2* start to sing; *1sg* **nimaajii'am**; *prt*
mayaajii'ang

maajiijigaade *vii* be taken along; *prt*
mayaajiijigaadeg; *aug* **maajiijigaademagad**;
prt aug **mayaajiijigaademagak**

maajiijigaazo *vai* be taken along; *prt*
mayaajiijigaazod

maajiikan *vti* start to work on s.t.; *1sg*
nimaajiikaan; *prt* **mayaajiikang**

maajiikaw *vta* start to work on s.o.; *1sg*
nimaajiikawaa; *prt* **mayaajiikawaad**

maajiikwazhiwe *vai* paddle off, swim off (as a
fish); *1sg* **nimaajiikwazhiwe**; *prt*
mayaajiikwazhiwed

maajiishkaa *vii* start to move; *prt* **mayaajiishkaag**;
aug **maajiishkaamagad**; *prt aug*
mayaajiishkaamagak

maajiishkaa' *vta* start s.o. (e.g., a car, a clock); *1sg*
nimaajiishkaa'aa; *prt* **mayaajiishkaa'aad**

maajiiyaadagaako *vai* start off on the ice; *1sg*
nimaajiiyaadagaak; *prt* **mayaajiiyaadagaakod**

maajiizh /**maajiiN-**/ *vta* take s.o. away, take s.o.
along; *1sg* **nimaajiinaa**; *prt* **mayaajiinaad**

maajiizhiwe *vai* take people away; *1sg*
nimaajiizhiwe; *prt* **mayaajiizhiwed**

maakigaade *vai* have a lame leg; *1sg*
nimaakigaade; *prt* **mayaakigaaded**

maakinaw *vta* shoot and wound s.o.; *1sg*
nimaakinawaa; *prt* **mayaakinawaad**

maakizi *vai* be lame; *1sg* **nimaakiz**; *prt*
mayaakizid

maamakaadakamig *pc* amazing!, astonishing!

maamakaadendam *vai2* be amazed, be
astonished; *1sg* **nimaamakaadendam**; *prt*
mayaamakaadendang

maamakaadendan *vti* be amazed at s.t., be
astonished at s.t., wonder at s.t.; *1sg*
nimaamakaadendaan; *prt*
mayaamakaadendang

maamakaadendaagwad *vii* be considered
amazing, be considered astonishing; *prt*
mayaamakaadendaagwak

maamakaadenim *vta* be amazed at s.o., be
astonished at s.o., wonder at s.o.; *1sg*
nimaamakaadenimaa; *prt*
mayaamakaadenimaad

maamakaadizi *vai* be amazing, astonish; *1sg*
nimaamakaadiz; *prt* **mayaamakaadizid**

maamakaaj *pc* amazing, astonishing

maamakaajichige *vai* do amazing things; *1sg*
nimaamakaajichige; *prt*
mayaamakaajichiged

maamakaazitaw *vta* be amazed at what s.o. says;
1sg **nimaamakaazitawaa**; *prt*
mayaamakaazitawaad

maamawi *pc* together

maamawoo- *pv4* together

maamigin *vta* pick s.o. up, gather s.o.; *1sg*
nimaamiginaa; *prt* **mayaamiginaad**

maamiginan *vti* pick s.t. up, gather s.t.; *1sg*
nimaamiginaan; *prt* **mayaamiginang**

maaminonendam *vai2* think, consider, ponder;
1sg **nimaaminonendam**; *prt*
mayaaminonendang

maaminonendan *vti* think on s.t., consider s.t.,
realize of s.t.; *1sg* **nimaaminonendaan**; *prt*
mayaaminonendang

maaminonenim *vta* think on s.o., consider s.o.,
realize s.o. that; *1sg* **nimaaminonenimaa**;
prt **mayaaminonenimaad**

maanabi *vai* sit uncomfortably; *1sg* nimaanab; *prt* mayaanabid
maanadamon /maanadamo-/ *vii* be bad (as a road or trail); *prt* mayaanadamog
maanadikoshens *na* goat; *pl* maanadikoshensag
maana'e *vai* take a shot; *1sg* nimaana'e; *prt* mayaana'ed
maanamanji'o *vai* feel bad, be in poor health; *1sg* nimaanamanji'; *prt* mayaanamanji'od
maanameg *na* catfish; *pl* maanamegwag; *dim* maanamegoons
maananoons *na* hop hornbeam, ironwood; *pl* maananoonsag; *loc* maananoonsing
maanashigan *na* sheepshead (fish); *pl* maanashiganag; *dim* maanashigaans
maanazaadi *na* balsam poplar, Balm of Gilead tree; *pl* maanazaadiwag; *loc* maanazaadiing; *dim* maanazaadiins
maanaadad *vii* be ugly; *prt* mayaanaadak
maanaadizi *vai* be ugly, be homely; *1sg* nimaanaadiz; *prt* mayaanaadizid
maanaagamin /maanaagami-/ *vii* taste bad (as a liquid); *prt* mayaanaagamig
maanaaji' *vta* make s.o. wrong, make s.o. odd; *1sg* nimaanaaji'aa; *prt* mayaanaaji'aad
maanaajitoon *vti2* make s.t. wrong, make s.t. odd; *1sg* nimaanaajitoon; *prt* mayaanaajitood
maanendam *vai2* feel bad, feel depressed; *1sg* nimaanendam; *prt* mayaanendang; *also* maazhendam
maanendan *vti* feel bad about s.t., consider s.t. disagreeable; *1sg* nimaanendaan; *prt* mayaanendang
maanendaagozi *vai* be considered bad-off, be considered disagreeable; *1sg* nimaanendaagoz; *prt* mayaanendaagozid
maanendaagwad *vii* be considered bad, be considered disagreeable; *prt* mayaanendaagwak
maanenim *vta* consider s.o. bad-off, consider s.o. disagreeable; *1sg* nimaanenimaa; *prt* mayaanenimaad
maang *na* loon; *pl* maangwag; *dim* maangoons
maanikaw- *vta* disagree with s.o. (of something consumed) *in inverse forms: 1sg* nimaanikaagon; *prt* mayaanikaagod
maanishtaanish *na* sheep; *pl* maanishtaanishag; *dim* maanishtaanishens; *also* maanitaanish
maanishtaanishiwayaan *ni* sheepskin
maanitan *vti* hear s.t. sounding bad; *1sg* nimaanitaan; *prt* mayaanitang
maanitaw *vta* hear s.o. sounding bad; *1sg* nimaanitawaa; *prt* mayaanitawaad
maanose *vai* walk with discomfort; *1sg* nimaanose; *prt* mayaanosed
maanowe *vai* be hoarse, have a bad voice; *1sg* nimaanowe; *prt* mayaanowed
maanoo *pc* never mind, let it be, don't bother, don't care
maashkinoozhe *na* muskellunge; *pl* maashkinoozheg; *dim* maashkinoozhens
maawandoobiwag /maawandoobi-/ *vai* they sit together; *1pl* nimaawandoobimin; *prt* mayaawandoobijig

maawandoogindan *vti* total up s.t. (as an account); *1sg* nimaawandoogindaan; *prt* mayaawandoogindang
maawandoogindaaso *vai* total up (as an account); *1sg* nimaawandoogindaas; *prt* mayaawandoogindaasod
maawandoogwaadan *vti* sew s.t. together (e.g., pieces for a quilt); *1sg* nimaawandoogwaadaan; *prt* mayaawandoogwaadang
maawandoogwaaso *vai* sew together; *1sg* nimaawandoogwaas; *prt* mayaawandoogwaasod
maawandoogwaason *ni* quilt; *pl* maawandoogwaasonan; *loc* maawandoogwaasoning; *dim* maawandoogwaasonens
maawandoogwaazh /maawandoogwaaN-/ *vta* sew s.o. together; *1sg* nimaawandoogwaanaa; *prt* mayaawandoogwaanaad
maawandoonan *vti* bring s.t. together; *1sg* nimaawandoonaan; *prt* mayaawandoonang
maawanji' *vta* collect s.o.; *1sg* nimaawanji'aa; *prt* mayaawanji'aad
maawanji'idiwag /maawanji'idi-/ *vai* they come together, they meet with each other, they have a meeting; *1pl* nimaawanji'idimin; *prt* mayaawanji'idijig
maawanjitoon *vti2* collect s.t.; *1sg* nimaawanjitoon; *prt* mayaawanjitood
maazhaa *pc* maybe, perhaps; *also* maagizhaa
maazhendam *vai2* feel out of sorts; *1sg* nimaazhendam; *prt* mayaazhendang
maazhi- *pv4* bad, ill-formed
maazhi-ayaa *vai* be bad-off, be in poor health; *1sg* nimaazhi-ayaa; *prt* mayaazhi-ayaad
maazhibide *vii* run poorly (e.g., a machine), operate poorly; *prt* mayaazhibideg; *aug* maazhibidemagad; *prt aug* mayaazhibidemagak
maazhi-bimaadizi *vai* behave badly, lead a bad life; *1sg* nimaazhi-bimaadiz; *prt* mayaazhi-bimaadizid
maazhibizo *vai* run poorly (e.g., a car), operate poorly; *prt* mayaazhibizod
maazhide'e *vai* have heartburn; *1sg* nimaazhide'e; *prt* mayaazhide'ed
maazhi-giizhigad *vii* be a bad day; *prt* mayaazhi-giizhigak
maazhigiizhwe *vai* have difficulty speaking, have abnormal speech; *1sg* nimaazhigiizhwe; *prt* mayaazhigiizhwed
maazhigondaagan *vai* have difficulty with one's voice; *1sg* nimaazhigondaagan; *prt* mayaazhigondaagang
maazhi-izhiwebizi *vai* behave badly; *1sg* nimaazhi-izhiwebiz; *prt* mayaazhi-izhiwebizid
maazhimaagozi *vai* smell bad; *1sg* nimaazhimaagoz; *prt* mayaazhimaagozid
maazhimaagwad *vii* smell bad; *prt* mayaazhimaagwak
maazhimaagwanaamo *vai* have bad breath; *1sg* nimaazhimaagwanaam; *prt* mayaazhimaagwanaamod

maazhimaaso *vai* smell bad burning or cooking;
prt **mayaazhimaasod**
maazhimaate *vii* smell bad burning or cooking;
prt **mayaazhimaateg**
maazhingwaam *vai* sleep uncomfortably; *1sg*
nimaazhingwaam; *prt* **mayaazhingwaang**
maazhinikaade *vii* have an ugly name; *prt*
mayaazhinikaadeg; *aug*
maazhinikaademagad; *prt aug*
mayaazhinikaademagak
maazhinikaazo *vai* have an ugly name; *1sg*
nimaazhinikaaz; *prt* **mayaazhinikaazod**
maazhipogozi *vai* taste bad; *prt*
mayaazhipogozid
maazhipogwad *vii* taste bad; *prt*
mayaazhipogwak
maazhise *vai* have things go wrong, have bad luck;
1sg **nimaazhise**; *prt* **mayaazhised**
maazhishin *vai* lie uncomfortably; *1sg*
nimaazhishin; *prt* **mayaazhishing**
megade *vai* burp; *1sg* **nimegade**; *prt* **mayegaded**
megwaa *pc* while, during
megwe- *pn* among, in the midst of
megwe-aya'ii *pc* in among it; *also* **megweya'ii**
megwejiishkiwag *pc* in the mud
megwekob *pc* in the brush
megwaayaak *pc* in the woods
mekadewikonayed *na-pt* priest; *pl*
mekadewikonayejig
mekadewikonayewikwe *na* nun; *pl*
mekadewikonayewikweg; *dim*
mekadewikonayewikwens; *also*
mekadewikonayekwe
mekadewikonayewinini *na* priest; *pl*
mekadewikonayewininiwag
memaangishens *na* mule; *pl* **memaangishensag**
meme *na* red-headed woodpecker; *pl* **memeg**; *dim*
memens
memegwesi *na* hairy-faced bank-dwelling dwarf
spirit; *pl* **memegwesiwag**; *dim* **memegwesiins**
memengwaa *na* butterfly; *pl* **memengwaag**; *dim*
memengwaans
memeshkwad *pc* in turns, alternately
memidaaswi *nm* ten each
memindage *pc* of course, especially, above all
memookiwidoo *na* pocket gopher; *pl*
memookiwidoog; *dim* **memookiwidoons**
memwech *pc* just that, exactly, it is so
menwaagamig *ni-pt* soft drink; *pl*
menwaagamigin
meshkwad *pc* in turn, in exchange
meshkwadoon *vta* trade s.o., exchange s.o.; *1sg*
nimeshkwadoonaa; *prt* **mayeshkwadoonaad**
meshkwadoonamaw *vta* trade (s.t.) with s.o.; *1sg*
nimeshkwadoonamawaa; *prt*
mayeshkwadoonamawaad
meshkwadoonamaage *vai* trade things with
people; *1sg* **nimeshkwadoonamaage**; *prt*
mayeshkwadoonamaaged
meshkwadoonan *vti* trade s.t., exchange s.t.; *1sg*
nimeshkwadoonaan; *prt*
mayeshkwadoonang
meshkwadoonige *vai* trade for things, exchange
things; *1sg* **nimeshkwadoonige**; *prt*
mayeshkwadooniged

meskwanagekozid *na-pt* cinnamon; *pl*
meskwanagekozijig
meskwaazhigwaneshi *na* redhorse (fish); *pl*
meskwaazhigwaneshiwag; *dim*
meskwaazhigwaneshiins
meta *pc* it is only that; *also* **mii eta**
mewinzha *pc* a long time ago, long ago
michayi'ii *pc* on a bare surface
michaa *vii* be big; *prt* **mechaag**; *aug*
michaamagad; *prt aug* **mechaamagak**
michaabaminaagwad *vii* appear big; *prt*
mechaabaminaagwak
michaabikad *vii* be big (as something mineral); *prt*
mechaabikak
michaabikizi *vai* be big (as something mineral), be
full (as something mineral, e.g., the moon); *prt*
mechaabikizid
michaakozi *vai* be big (as something stick- or
wood-like); *prt* **mechaakozid**
michaakwad *vii* be big (as something stick- or
wood-like); *prt* **mechaakwak**
michaatoon *vti2* make s.t. big; *1sg* **nimichaatoon**;
prt **mechaatood**
michi- *pv4* by hand, without anything special,
barely
michininjiikanjige *vai* eat with one's fingers; *1sg*
nimichininjiikanjige; *prt* **mechininjiikanjiged**
michisag *ni* floor; *pl* **michisagoon**; *loc*
michisagong
michishin *vai* lie uncovered; *prt* **mechishing**
michisin *vii* lie uncovered; *prt* **mechising**
michiigad *vii* be big (as something sheet-like); *prt*
mechiigak
michiigizi *vai* be big (as something sheet-like); *prt*
mechiigizid
midaaching *pc* ten times
midaachinoon /midaachin-/ *vii* they are ten; *prt*
medaaching
midaachiwag /midaachi-/ *vai* they are ten; *1pl*
nimidaachimin; *prt* **medaachijig**
midaaso- *pv4* ten
midaaso-anama'e-giizhigad *pc* ten weeks
midaaso-anama'e-giizhik *pc* ten weeks
midaaso-biboon *pc* ten years
midaaso-biboonagad *vii* be ten years; *prt*
medaaso-biboonagak
midaaso-biboonagizi *vai* be ten years old; *1sg*
nimidaaso-biboonagiz; *prt* **medaaso-
biboonagizid**
midaaso-diba'igan *pc* ten miles, ten hours
midaaso-diba'iganed *vii* be ten o'clock; *prt*
medaaso-diba'iganek
midaaso-diba'igaans *pc* ten minutes
midaaso-dibik *pc* ten nights
midaaso-giizhik *pc* ten days
midaaso-giizis *pc* ten months
midaasogon *pc* ten days
midaasogonagad *vii* be ten days; *prt*
medaasogonagak
midaasogonagizi *vai* be the tenth day of the
month, be ten days old; *prt* **medaasogonagizid**
midaasoninj *pc* ten inches
midaasozid *pc* ten feet
midaasosagoons *nm* ten thousand

midaasoobii'igan *na* ten (card); *pl*
 midaasoobii'iganag
midaasooshkin *pc* ten bags
midaaswaabik *pc* ten dollars
midaaswaak *nm* thousand
midaaswewaan *pc* ten sets, ten pairs
midaaswi *nm* ten
midaaswi ashi-bezhig *nm* eleven
midaaswi ashi-ingodwaaswi *nm* sixteen; *also*
 midaaswi ashi-ningodwaaswi*
midaaswi ashi-ishwaaswi *nm* eighteen; *also*
 midaaswi ashi-nishwaaswi*
midaaswi ashi-naanan *nm* fifteen
midaaswi ashi-ningodwaaswi* *nm* sixteen; *also*
 midaaswi ashi-ingodwaaswi
midaaswi ashi-nishwaaswi* *nn* eighteen; *also*
 midaaswi ashi-ishwaaswi
midaaswi ashi-niswi *nm* thirteen
midaaswi ashi-niiwin *nm* fourteen
midaaswi ashi-niizh *nm* twelve
midaaswi ashi-niizhwaaswi *nm* seventeen
midaaswi ashi-zhaangaswi *nm* nineteen
midechininj *ni* thumb; *pl* **midechininjiin**
midechizid *ni* big toe; *pl* **midechizidan**
midewayaan *na* Mide medicine bag; *pl*
 midewayaanag; *loc* **midewayaaning**; *dim*
 midewayaanens
midewi *vai* join the Midewiwin, participate in the
 Midewiwin; *1sg* **nimidew**; *prt* **medewid**
midewigaan *ni* Mide lodge; *pl* **midewigaanan**; *loc*
 midewigaaning; *dim* **midewigaanens**
midewigaanaak *ni* Mide lodge frame; *pl*
 midewigaanaakoon; *loc* **midewigaamaakong**
midewiwin *ni* Midewiwin, Medicine Dance,
 Grand Medicine Society
migi *vai* bark; *1sg* **nimig**; *prt* **megid**
migidan *vti* bark at s.t.; *1sg* **nimigidaan**; *prt*
 megidang
migiskan *ni* fish hook; *pl* **migiskanan**; *loc*
 migiskaning; *dim* **migiskaans**
migiskanaak *ni* fishing pole; *pl* **migiskanaakoon**;
 loc **migiskanaakong**; *dim* **migiskanaakoons**;
 also **migiskanaatig**
migiskaneyaab *ni* hook and line; *pl*
 migiskaneyaabiin; *loc* **migiskaneyaabiing**; *dim*
 migiskaneyaabiins
migizh /**migiN-**/ *vta* bark at s.o.; *1sg* **nimiginaa**; *prt*
 meginaad
migizi *na* bald eagle; *pl* **migiziwag**; *dim* **migiziins**
migoshkaadendam *vai2* be annoyed; *1sg*
 nimigoshkaadendam; *prt*
 megoshkaadendang
migoshkaaji' *vta* annoy s.o., bother s.o.; *1sg*
 nimigoshkaaji'aa; *prt* **megoshkaaji'aad**
migoos *ni* awl; *pl* **migoosan**; *loc* **migoosing**; *dim*
 migoosens

migoos (awl)

mikamaw *vta* find (s.t.) for s.o., find (s.t.) of
 s.o.'s; *1sg* **nimikamawaa**; *prt* **mekamawaad**
mikan *vti* find s.t.; *1sg* **nimikaan**; *prt* **mekang**
mikaw *vta* find s.o.; *1sg* **nimikawaa**; *prt*
 mekawaad
mikawi *vai* come to, regain consciousness; *1sg*
 nimikaw; *prt* **mekawid**
mikaage *vai* find people; *1sg* **nimikaage**; *prt*
 mekaaged
mikigaade *vii* be found; *prt* **mekigaadeg**; *aug*
 mikigaademagad; *prt* *aug* **mekigaademagak**
mikigaazo *vai* be found; *prt* **mekigaazod**
mikige *vai* find things; *1sg* **nimikige**; *prt* **mekiged**
mikinaak *na* snapping turtle; *pl* **mikinaakwag**; *dim*
 mikinaakoons
mikobidaw *vta* find (s.t.) for s.o. with hands; *1sg*
 nimikobidawaa; *prt* **mekobidawaad**
mikobidoon *vti2* find s.t. with hands; *1sg*
 nimikobidoon; *prt* **mekobidood**
mikobijige *vai* find things with hands; *1sg*
 nimikobijige; *prt* **mekobijiged**
mikobizh /**mikobiN-**/ *vta* find s.o. with hands; *1sg*
 nimikobinaa; *prt* **mekobinaad**
mikom *vta* mention s.o. come to one's mind; *1sg*
 nimikomaa; *prt* **mekomaad**
mikond *na* binding stick; *pl* **mikondiig**; *loc*
 mikondiing; *dim* **mikondiins**; *also* **mikwand**
mikondan *vti* mention s.t. come to one's mind; *1sg*
 nimikondaan; *prt* **mekondang**
mikoojiin *vta* feel s.o., feel for s.o.; *1sg*
 nimikoojiinaa; *prt* **mekoojiinaad**
mikoojiinan *vti* feel s.t., feel for s.t.; *1sg*
 nimikoojiinaan; *prt* **mekoojiinang**
mikwam *na* ice; *pl* **mikwamiig**; *loc* **mikwamiing**;
 dim **mikwamiins**
mikwamiikaa *vii* there is much ice; *prt*
 mekwamiikaag; *aug* **mikwamiikaamagad**; *prt*
 aug **mekwamiikaamagak**
mikwamii-makak *ni* ice box, refrigerator; *pl*
 mikwamii-makakoon; *loc* **mikwamii-**
 makakong; *dim* **mikwamii-makakoons**
mikwamiiwadamon /**mikwamiiwadamo-**/ *vii* be
 icy (as a road or trail); *prt*
 mekwamiiwadamog
mikwamiiwinaagaans *ni* drinking glass; *pl*
 mikwamiiwinaagaansan; *loc*
 mikwamiiwinaagaansing
mikwendam *vai2* recollect, remember, have things
 come to one's mind; *1sg* **nimikwendam**; *prt*
 mekwendang
mikwendan *vti* recollect s.t., remember s.t., come
 to think of s.t.; *1sg* **nimikwendaan**; *prt*
 mekwendang
mikwendaagozi *vai* be remembered, be recollected, come to mind; *1sg* **nimikwendaagoz**;
 prt **mekwendaagozid**
mikwendaagwad *vii* be remembered, be recollected, come to mind; *prt* **mekwendaagwak**
mikwenim *vta* recollect s.o., remember s.o., come
 to think of s.o.; *1sg* **nimikwenimaa**; *prt*
 mekwenimaad
mimigosaga'igan *ni* scrub brush; *pl*
 mimigosaga'iganan; *loc* **mimigosaga'iganing**;
 dim **mimigosaga'igaans**

mimigoshkam *vai2* thresh something, jig something (e.g., wild rice); *1sg* **nimimigoshkam**; *prt* **memigoshkang**
mimigoshkamwaagan *ni* barrel or tub used in threshing wild rice; *pl* **mimigoshkamwaaganan**; *loc* **mimigoshkamwaaganing**
mimigoshkan *vti* thresh s.t. (e.g., wild rice), jig s.t. (e.g., wild rice); *1sg* **nimimigoshkaan**; *prt* **memigoshkang**
mimigwaabika'igan *ni* pot scrubber; *pl* **mimigwaabika'iganan**; *loc* **mimigwaabika'iganing**; *dim* **mimigwaabika'igaans**
mimigwaakosijigan *ni* washboard; *pl* **mimigwaakosijiganan**; *loc* **mimigwaakosijiganing**; *dim* **mimigwaakosijigaans**
mina' *vta* give s.o. a drink, give s.o. (s.t.) to drink; *1sg* **nimina'aa**; *prt* **mena'aad**
minawaanigozi *vai* be happy, be joyous, have a good time; *1sg* **niminawaanigoz**; *prt* **menawaanigozid**
minawaanigwad *vii* be happy, be exciting; *prt* **menawaanigwak**
mindawe *vai* be dissatisfied (with what has been given), pout; *1sg* **nimindawe**; *prt* **mendawed**
mindaweganzhii *vai* have white spots on fingernails; *1sg* **nimindaweganzhii**; *prt* **mendaweganzhiid**
mindido *vai* be big; *1sg* **nimindid**; *prt* **mendidod**
mindido' *vta* make s.o. big; *1sg* **nimindido'aa**; *prt* **mendido'aad**
mindimooyenh *na* old woman, old lady; *pl* **mindimooyenyag**; *dim* **mindimooyens**
mindimooyenyiwi *vai* be an old woman, be an old lady; *1sg* **nimindimooyenyiw**; *prt* **mendimooyenyiwid**
mindookad *vii* there is dew; *prt* **mendookak**
mini /miny-/ *ni* pus
minik *pc* a certain amount, a certain number, so much, so many
minikwaajigan *ni* drinking vessel; *pl* **minikwaajiganan**; *loc* **minikwaajiganing**; *dim* **minikwaajigaans**
minikwe *vai+o* drink (s.t.); *1sg* **niminikwe, niminikwen**; *prt* **menikwed**
minikwewigamig *ni* tavern, bar; *pl* **minikwewigamigoon**; *loc* **minikwewigamigong**; *dim* **minikwewigamigoons**
minis *ni* island; *pl* **minisan**; *loc* **minising**; *dim* **minisens**
minisaabik *ni* rocky island; *pl* **minisaabikoon**; *loc* **minisaabikong**; *dim* **minisaabikoons**
miniiwaabide *vai* have an abscessed tooth; *1sg* **niminiiwaabide**; *prt* **meniiwaabided**
miniiwitawage *vai* have an infected ear; *1sg* **niminiiwitawage**; *prt* **meniiwitawaged**
minjikanaakobijigan *ni* fence; *pl* **minjikanaakobijiganan**; *loc* **minjikanaakobijiganing**; *dim* **minjikanaakobijigaans**
minjikaawan *na* mitten; *pl* **minjikaawanag**; *loc* **minjikaawaning**

minjimaakwii *vai* cling (as to something stick- or wood-like), hold on (as to something stick- or wood-like); *1sg* **niminjimaakwii**; *prt* **menjimaakwiid**
minjimendan *vti* keep s.t. in one's mind, remember s.t.; *1sg* **niminjimendaan**; *prt* **menjimendang**
minjimenim *vta* keep s.o. in one's mind, remember s.o.; *1sg* **niminjimenimaa**; *prt* **menjimenimaad**
minjimin *vta* hold s.o. in place, steady s.o.; *1sg* **niminjiminaa**; *prt* **menjiminaad**
minjiminamaw *vta* hold (s.t.). in place for s.o., steady (s.t.) for s.o.; *1sg* **niminjiminamawaa**; *prt* **menjiminamawaad**
minjiminan *vti* hold s.t. in place, steady s.t.; *1sg* **niminjiminaan**; *prt* **menjiminang**
minjiminigan *ni* handle; *pl* **minjiminiganan**; *loc* **minjiminiganing**; *dim* **minjiminigaans**
minjimishkan *vti* hold s.t. in place with foot or body, steady s.t. with foot or body; *1sg* **niminjimishkaan**; *prt* **menjimishkang**
minjimishkaw *vta* hold s.o. in place with foot or body, steady s.o. with foot or body; *1sg* **niminjimishkawaa**; *prt* **menjimishkawaad**
minjimishkoode *vii* be held in place with weight; *prt* **menjimishkoodeg**; *aug* **minjimishkoodemagad**; *prt aug* **menjimishkoodemagak**
minjimishkoodoon *vti2* hold s.t. in place with weight; *1sg* **niminjimishkoodoon**; *prt* **menjimishkoodood**
minjimishkoozh /minjimishkooN-/ *vta* hold s.o. in place with weight; *1sg* **niminjimishkoonaa**; *prt* **menjimishkoonaad**
minjimishkoozo *vai* be held in place with weight; *1sg* **niminjimishkooz**; *prt* **menjimishkoozod**
minjimii *vai* cling, hold on; *1sg* **niminjimii**; *prt* **menjimiid**
minjinawezi *vai* have regrets, be disappointed; *1sg* **niminjinawez**; *prt* **menjinawezid**
mino- *pv4* good, nice, well
mino-ayaa *vai* be good, be fine, be well; *1sg* **nimino-ayaa**; *prt* **meno-ayaad**
minobide *vii* run well (e.g., a machine); *prt* **menobideg**; *aug* **minobidemagad**; *prt aug* **menobidemagak**
mino-bimaadizi *vai* live well, have good health, lead a good life; *1sg* **nimino-bimaadiz**; *prt* **meno-bimaadizid**
minobizo *vai* run well (e.g., a car); *prt* **menobizod**
minobii *vai* drink and be merry; *1sg* **niminobii**; *prt* **menobiid**
minochige *vai* do things well, do good things; *1sg* **niminochige**; *prt* **menochiged**
minode *vii* be well cooked; *prt* **menodeg**; *aug* **minodemagad**; *prt aug* **menodemagak**
minode'e *vai* be kind; *1sg* **niminode'e**; *prt* **menode'ed**
mino-doodaw *vta* treat s.o. well; *1sg* **nimino-doodawaa**; *prt* **meno-doodawaad**
minogi *vai* grow well; *1sg* **niminog**; *prt* **menogid**
minogin *vii* grow well; *prt* **menoging**
mino-giizhigad *vii* be a nice day; *prt* **meno-giizhigak**

mino-giizhiganishi *vai* have good travelling weather; *1sg* nimino-giizhiganish; *prt* meno-giizhiganishid

minogondaagan *vai* have a good voice; *1sg* niminogondaagan; *prt* menogondaagang

mino'o *vai* dress well; *1sg* nimino'; *prt* meno'od

mino-izhiwebizi *vai* behave well, lead a good life; *1sg* nimino-izhiwebiz; *prt* meno-izhiwebizid

minokan *vti* fit s.t. well; *1sg* niminokaan; *prt* menokang

minokaw *vta* fit s.o. well (e.g., pants), agree with s.o. (especially of something consumed); *in inverse forms: 1sg* niminokaagon; *prt* menokaagod

minomaagochigan *ni* perfume; *pl* minomaagochiganan; *loc* minomaagochiganing; *dim* minomaagochigaans

minomaagochige *vai* use perfume; *1sg* niminomaagochige; *prt* menomaagochiged

minomaagozi *vai* have a good smell; *1sg* niminomaagoz; *prt* menomaagozid

minomaagwad *vii* have a good smell; *prt* menomaagwak

minomaam *vta* like the smell of s.o.; *1sg* niminomaamaa; *prt* menomaamaad

minomaandan *vti* like the smell of s.t.; *1sg* niminomaandaan; *prt* menomaandang

minomaaso *vai* smell good burning or cooking; *prt* menomaasod

minomaate *vii* smell good burning or cooking; *prt* menomaateg; *aug* minomaatemagad; *prt aug* menomaatemagak

minopidan *vti* find a good taste in s.t.; *1sg* niminopidaan; *prt* menopidang

minopijige *vai* like the taste of things; *1sg* niminopijige; *prt* menopijiged

minopogozi *vai* taste good; *prt* menopogozid

minopogwad *vii* taste good; *prt* menopogwak

minopozh /**minopw-**/ *vta* find a good taste in s.o.; *1sg* niminopwaa; *prt* menopwaad

minose *vai* have things go well for one, get along well, have good luck; *1sg* niminose; *prt* menosed

minose *vii* go well; *prt* menoseg; *aug* minosemagad; *prt aug* menosemagak

minoshim *vta* put s.o. in the right position; *1sg* niminoshimaa; *prt* menoshimaad

minoshin *vai* lie comfortably, lie in a good position; *1sg* niminoshin; *prt* menoshing

minosidoon *vti2* put s.t. in the right position; *1sg* niminosidoon; *prt* menosidood

minosin *vii* lie in a good position, lie well in place; *prt* menosing

minotam *vai2* like hearing something, like the sound; *1sg* niminotam; *prt* menotang

minotan *vti* like hearing s.t., hear s.t. sounding good; *1sg* niminotaan; *prt* menotang

minotaw *vta* like hearing s.o., hear s.o. sounding good; *1sg* niminotawaa; *prt* menotawaad

minotaagozi *vai* sound good; *1sg* niminotaagoz; *prt* menotaagozid

minotaagwad *vii* sound good; *prt* menotaagwak

minowe *vai* have a good voice, speak well; *1sg* niminowe; *prt* menowed

minoz /**minozw-**/ *vta* cook s.o. well; *1sg* niminozwaa; *prt* menozwaad

minozan *vti* cook s.t. well; *1sg* niminozaan; *prt* menozang

minozekwe *vai* cook well; *1sg* niminozekwe; *prt* menozekwed

minozo *vai* be well cooked; *prt* menozod

minwabi *vai* sit comfortably; *1sg* niminwab; *prt* menwabid

minwamanji'o *vai* feel good, be in good health; *1sg* niminwamanji'; *prt* menwamanji'od

minwanjige *vai* eat well; *1sg* niminwanjige; *prt* menwanjiged

minwashkine *vai* fit well, be well filled; *prt* menwashkined

minwashkine *vii* fit well, be well filled; *prt* menwashkineg; *aug* minwashkinemagad; *prt aug* menwashkinemagak

minwaabadad *vii* be very useful, be of good use; *prt* menwaabadak

minwaabadizi *vai* be very useful, be of good use; *1sg* niminwaabadiz; *prt* menwaabadizid

minwaabaji' *vta* get good use of s.o.; *1sg* niminwaabaji'aa; *prt* menwaabaji'aad

minwaabajitoon *vti2* get good use of s.t.; *1sg* niminwaabajitoon; *prt* menwaabajitood

minwaabam *vta* like the look of s.o.; *1sg* niminwaabamaa; *prt* menwaabamaad

minwaabamewizi *vai* be admired, be respected; *1sg* niminwaabamewiz; *prt* menwaabamewizid

minwaabaminaagozi *vai* look good; *1sg* niminwaabaminaagoz; *prt* menwaabaminaagozid

minwaabaminaagwad *vii* look good; *prt* menwaabaminaagwak

minwaabandan *vti* like the look of s.t.; *1sg* niminwaabandaan; *prt* menwaabandang

minwaabewizi *vai* have a good body; *1sg* niminwaabewiz; *prt* menwaabewizid

minwaabi *vai* have good eyesight, see well; *1sg* niminwaab; *prt* menwaabid

minwaabikad *vii* be good (as something mineral); *prt* menwaabikak

minwaabikizi *vai* be good (as something mineral); *prt* menwaabikizid

minwaadizi *vai* lead a good life; *1sg* niminwaadiz; *prt* menwaadizid

minwaadodan *vti* tell good news of s.t.; *1sg* niminwaadodaan; *prt* menwaadodang

minwaagamin /**minwaagami-**/ *vii* taste good (as a liquid); *prt* menwaagamig

minwaajim *vta* tell good news of s.o.; *1sg* niminwaajimaa; *prt* menwaajimaad

minwaajimo *vai* tell good news, tell a good story; *1sg* niminwaajim; *prt* menwaajimod

minwaakozi *vai* be good (as something stick- or wood-like); *prt* menwaakozid

minwaakwad *vii* be good (as something stick- or wood-like); *prt* menwaakwak

minwaande *vii* be a good color; *prt* menwaandeg; *aug* minwaandemagad; *prt aug* menwaandemagak

minwaanimad *vii* there is a good breeze, there is a favorable wind; *prt* menwaanimak

minwaanzo *vai* be a good color; *1sg* **niminwaanz;** *prt* **menwaanzod**

minwaatese *vii* be a good movie; *prt* **menwaateseg;** *aug* **minwaatesemagad;** *prt* *aug* **menwaatesemagak**

minwegad *vii* be good (as something sheet-like); *prt* **menwegak**

minwegizi *vai* be good (as something sheet-like); *prt* **menwegizid**

minwendam *vai2* be happy, be glad; *1sg* **niminwendam;** *prt* **menwendang**

minwendan *vti* like s.t.; *1sg* **niminwendaan;** *prt* **menwendang**

minwendaagozi *vai* be likeable, be agreeable, be fun; *prt* **menwendaagozid**

minwendaagwad *vii* be likeable, be fun; *prt* **menwendaagwak**

minwenim *vta* like s.o.; *1sg* **niminwenimaa;** *prt* **menwenimaad**

misajidamoo *na* grey squirrel; *pl* **misajidamoog;** *dim* **misajidamoons**

misakakojiish *na* badger; *pl* **misakakojiishag;** *dim* **misakakojiishens**

misan /miS-/ *ni* firewood *plural of:* **mishi;** *loc* **mising**

misawendam *vai2* desire, want; *1sg* **nimisawendam;** *prt* **mesawendang**

misawendan *vti* desire s.t., want s.t.; *1sg* **nimisawendaan;** *prt* **mesawendang**

misawenim *vta* desire s.o., want s.o.; *1sg* **nimisawenimaa;** *prt* **mesawenimaad**

misawenjige *vai* desire things, want things; *1sg* **nimisawenjige;** *prt* **mesawenjiged**

misaabe *na* giant; *pl* **misaabeg;** *dim* **misaabens**

misaabooz *na* jack rabbit; *pl* **misaaboozoog;** *dim* **misaaboozoons**

mishi /miS-/ *ni* piece of firewood; *pl* **misan;** *loc* **mising**

mishibizhii *na* lion, panther, underwater panther; *pl* **mishibizhiig;** *dim* **mishibizhiins**

mishiikenh *na* snapping turtle; *pl* **mishiikenyag**

mishiimin *na* apple; *pl* **mishiiminag;** *loc* **mishiimining;** *dim* **mishiiminens**

mishiiminaaboo *ni* apple juice; *loc* **mishiiminaaboong**

mishiiminaatig *na* apple tree; *pl* **mishiiminaatigoog;** *loc* **mishiiminaatigong;** *dim* **mishiiminaatigoons**

mishiiwaatig *ni* dry wood; *pl* **mishiiwaatigoon;** *loc* **mishiiwaatigong;** *dim* **mishiiwaatigoons**

Misi-zaaga'iganiing *place* Mille Lacs Reservation

misko- *pv4* red

miskobagaa *vii* there are red leaves on the trees; *prt* **meskobagag;** *aug* **miskobagaamagad;** *prt* *aug* **meskobagaamagak**

miskobagizi *vai* have red leaves; *prt* **meskobagizid**

misko-bineshiinh *na* cardinal; *pl* **misko-bineshiinyag;** *dim* **misko-bineshiins**

miskodoonechigan *ni* lipstick; *pl* **miskodoonechiganan;** *loc* **miskodoonechiganing;** *dim* **miskodoonechigaans**

miskogaadeyaab *ni* yarn; *pl* **miskogaadeyaabiin**

misko'o *vai* wear red; *1sg* **nimisko';** *prt* **mesko'od**

miskojaane *vai* have a red nose; *1sg* **nimiskojaane;** *prt* **meskojaaned**

misko-jiis *ni* beet; *pl* **misko-jiisan;** *loc* **misko-jiising;** *dim* **misko-jiisens**

miskomin *na* raspberry; *pl* **miskominag;** *loc* **miskomining;** *dim* **miskominens**

miskondibe *vai* be red-headed; *1sg* **nimiskondibe;** *prt* **meskondibed**

miskozi *vai* be red; *prt* **meskozid**

miskwakone *vii* blaze up; *prt* **meskwakoneg;** *aug* **miskwakonemagad;** *prt* *aug* **meskwakonemagak**

miskwanowe *vai* have a red cheek; *1sg* **nimiskwanowe;** *prt* **meskwanowed**

miskwanowechigan *ni* rouge; *pl* **miskwanowechiganan;** *loc* **miskwanowechiganing;** *dim* **miskwanowechigaans**

miskwanowechige *vai* use rouge; *1sg* **nimiskwanowechige;** *prt* **meskwanowechiged**

miskwazhe *vai* have measles; *1sg* **nimiskwazhe;** *prt* **meskwazhed**

miskwaa *vii* be red; *prt* **meskwaag;** *aug* **miskwaamagad;** *prt* *aug* **meskwaamagak**

miskwaabik *ni* (piece of) copper; *loc* **miskwaabikong;** *dim* **miskwaabikoons**

miskwaabikad *vii* be red (as something mineral); *prt* **meskwaabikak**

miskwaabikide *vii* be red-hot (as something mineral); *prt* **meskwaabikideg;** *aug* **miskwaabikidemagad;** *prt* *aug* **meskwaabikidemagak**

miskwaabikizi *vai* be red (as something mineral); *prt* **meskwaabikizid**

miskwaabikizo *vai* be red-hot (as something mineral); *prt* **meskwaabikizod**

miskwaabikoons *na* cent, penny; *pl* **miskwaabikoonsag;** *loc* **miskwaabikoonsing**

miskwaabiigad *vii* be red (as something string-like); *prt* **meskwaabiigak**

miskwaabiigizi *vai* be red (as something string-like); *prt* **meskwaabiigizid**

miskwaabiimizh *na* red osier (locally known as dogwood); *pl* **miskwaabiimizhiig;** *loc* **miskwaabiimizhiing;** *dim* **miskwaabiimizhiins**

miskwaadesi *na* painted turtle; *pl* **miskwaadesiwag;** *dim* **miskwaadesiins**

Miskwaagamiiwi-zaaga'iganiing *place* Red Lake Reservation

miskwaakonaye *vai* dress in red; *1sg* **nimiskwaakonaye;** *prt* **meskwaakonayed**

miskwaakozi *vai* be red (as something stick- or wood-like); *prt* **meskwaakozid**

miskwaakwad *vii* be red (as something stick- or wood-like); *prt* **meskwaakwak**

miskwaanakwad *vii* be red clouds; *prt* **meskwaanakwak**

miskwaande *vai* be colored red; *prt* **meskwaandeg;** *aug* **miskwaandemagad;** *prt* *aug* **meskwaandemagak**

miskwaanzigan *ni* roach headdress; *pl* **miskwaanziganan;** *loc* **miskwaanziganing;** *dim* **miskwaanzigaans**

miskwaanzo *vai* be colored red; *prt* **meskwaanzod**

miskwaawaak *na* red cedar; *pl* **miskwaawaakoog;** *loc* **miskwaawaakong;** *dim* **miskwaawaakoons**

miskwegad *vii* be red (as something sheet-like); *prt* **meskwegak**

miskwegizi *vai* be red (as something sheet-like); *prt* **meskwegizid**

miskwi *ni* blood; *loc* **miskwiing**

miskwiingwese *vai* blush; *1sg* **nimiskwiingwese;** *prt* **meskwiingwesed**

miskwiiwi *vai* bleed, be bloody; *1sg* **nimiskwiiw;** *prt* **meskwiiwid**

miskwiiwijaane *vai* have a bloody nose; *1sg* **nimiskwiiwijaane;** *prt* **meskwiiwijaaned**

mitabi *vai* sit on the bare ground; *1sg* **nimitab;** *prt* **metabid**

mitagwazhe *vai* be naked; *1sg* **nimitagwazhe;** *prt* **metagwazhed**

mitakamig *pc* on bare ground

mitaakondibe *vai* be bare-headed; *1sg* **nimitaakondibe;** *prt* **metaakondibed**

mitaawangaa *vii* be a sandy beach; *prt* **metaawangaag;** *aug* **mitaawangaamagad;** *prt aug* **metaawangaamagak**

mitig *na* tree; *pl* **mitigoog;** *loc* **mitigong;** *dim* **mitigoons**

mitig *ni* stick, piece of wood; *pl* **mitigoon;** *loc* **mitigong;** *dim* **mitigoons**

mitigo-jiimaan *ni* wooden boat, wooden canoe; *pl* **mitigo-jiimaanan;** *loc* **mitigo-jiimaaning;** *dim* **mitigo-jiimaanens**

mitigokaa *vii* there are many trees; *prt* **metigokaag;** *aug* **mitigokaamagad;** *prt aug* **metigokaamagak**

mitigo-makak *ni* wooden box, crate; *pl* **mitigo-makakoon;** *loc* **mitigo-makakong;** *dim* **mitigo-makakoons**

mitigomin *ni* acorn; *pl* **mitigominan;** *loc* **mitigomining;** *dim* **mitigominens**

mitigomizh *na* oak; *pl* **mitigomizhiig;** *loc* **mitigomizhiing;** *dim* **mitigomizhiins**

mitigonaagan *ni* wooden dish; *pl* **mitigonaaganan;** *loc* **mitigonaaganing;** *dim* **mitigonaagaans**

mitigo-waakaa'igan *ni* log cabin; *pl* **mitigo-waakaa'iganan;** *loc* **mitigo-waakaa'iganing;** *dim* **mitigo-waakaa'igaans**

mitigoons *ni* stick; *pl* **mitigoonsan;** *loc* **mitigoonsing**

mitigwakik *na* Mide drum; *pl* **mitigwakikoog;** *loc* **mitigwakikong;** *dim* **mitigwakikoons**

mitigwaab *na* bow; *pl* **mitigwaabiig;** *loc* **mitigwaabiing;** *dim* **mitigwaabiins**

mitigwaabaak *na* hickory; *pl* **mitigwaabaakoog;** *loc* **mitigwaabaakong;** *dim* **mitigwaabaakoons**

mitigwemikwaan *ni* wooden spoon, wooden ladle; *pl* **mitigwemikwaanan;** *dim* **mitigwemikwaanens**

mitose *vai* go on foot; *1sg* **nimitose;** *prt* **metosed**

mizay *na* ling, eelpout, burbot, mariah, lawyer (fish); *pl* **mizayag**

mizhagaa *vai* come ashore in canoe; *1sg* **nimizhagaa;** *prt* **mezhagaad**

mizhakiise *vai* hit the bottom; *1sg* **nimizhakiise;** *prt* **mezhakiised**

mizhakiise *vii* hit the bottom; *prt* **mezhakiiseg;** *aug* **mizhakiisemagad;** *prt aug* **mezhakiisemagak**

mizhakwad *vii* be clear sky, be good weather; *prt* **mezhakwak**

mizhaakigwe *vai* get a cold; *1sg* **nimizhaakigwe;** *prt* **mezhaakigwed**

mizhisha *pc* in plain view

mizho /**mizhw-**/ *vta* hit s.o. (in shooting); *1sg* **nimizhwaa;** *prt* **mezhwaad**

mizhodam *vai2* win, hit the target; *1sg* **nimizhodam;** *prt* **mezhodang**

mizhodan *vti* hit s.t. (in shooting); *1sg* **nimizhodaan;** *prt* **mezhodang**

mizise *na* turkey; *pl* **miziseg;** *dim* **mizisens**

miziwe *pc* all over, everywhere

miziwebii'an *vti* write s.t. all over; *1sg* **nimiziwebii'aan;** *prt* **meziwebii'ang**

miziwebii'igaade *vii* be written on all over; *prt* **meziwebii'igaadeg;** *aug* **miziwebii'igaademagad;** *prt aug* **meziwebii'igaademagak**

miziwebii'ige *vai* write all over; *1sg* **nimiziwebii'ige;** *prt* **meziwebii'iged**

miziwe' *vta* make s.o. of a whole piece; *1sg* **nimiziwe'aa;** *prt* **meziwe'aad**

miziwekamig *pc* all over the world

miziweshkaa *vii* be everywhere, go everywhere, spread all over; *prt* **meziweshkaag;** *aug* **miziweshkaamagad;** *prt aug* **meziweshkaamagak**

miziwetoon *vti2* make s.t. of a whole piece; *1sg* **nimiziwetoon;** *prt* **meziwetood**

miziweyaa *vii* be whole, be intact; *prt* **meziweyaag;** *aug* **miziweyaamagad;** *prt aug* **meziweyaamagak**

miziweyaabikizi *vai* be full (as something mineral, e.g., the moon); *prt* **meziweyaabikizid**

miziwezi *vai* be whole, be intact; *1sg* **nimiziwez;** *prt* **meziwezid**

mizizaak *na* horsefly; *pl* **mizizaakwag;** *dim* **mizizaakoons**

mitigwemikwaan
(wooden spoon, wooden ladle)

mizizi *vai* start to get sick, catch a disease; *1sg*
   nimiziz; *prt* **mezizid**
mii *pc* it is thus that, it is that *existential particle*
mii dash *pc* and then; *also* **miish**
miigaadiwag /**miigaadi-**/ *vai* they fight each other;
   1pl **nimiigaadimin**; *prt* **maagaadijig**
miigaadiwin *ni* battle, war; *pl* **miigaadiwinan**
miigaazh /**miigaaN-**/ *vta* fight s.o.; *1sg*
   nimiigaanaa; *prt* **maagaanaad**
miigaazo *vai* fight; *1sg* **nimiigaaz**; *prt* **maagaazod**
miigis *na* Mide shell, pearl; *pl* **miigisag**; *loc*
   miigising; *dim* **miigisens**
miigiwe *vai+o* give away (s.t.); *1sg* **nimiigiwe**,
   nimiigiwen; *prt* **maagiwed**
miigwan *na* feather; *pl* **miigwanag**; *loc*
   miigwaning; *dim* **miigwaans**
miigwani-wiiwakwaan *ni* feather headdress,
   feather bonnet; *pl* **miigwani-wiiwakwaanan**;
   loc **miigwani-wiiwakwaaning**; *dim* **miigwani-**
   wiiwakwaanens
miigwech *pc* thanks!
miigwechiwendam *vai2* be thankful; *1sg*
   nimiigwechiwendam; *prt*
   maagwechiwendang
miigwechiwendan *vti* be thankful for s.t.; *1sg*
   nimiigwechiwendaan; *prt*
   maagwechiwendang
miigwechiwenim *vta* be thankful for s.o.; *1sg*
   nimiigwechiwenimaa; *prt*
   maagwechiwenimaad
miigwechiwi-giizhigad *vii* be Thanksgiving Day;
   prt **maagwechiwi-giizhigak**
miigwechiwi' *vta* thank s.o.; *1sg*
   nimiigwechiwi'aa; *prt* **maagwechiwi'aad**
miijim *ni* food; *pl* **miijiman**
miijimadaawe *vai* buy food; *1sg* **nimiijimadaawe**;
   prt **maajimadaawed**
miijimikanjigan *ni* bait; *pl* **miijimikanjiganan**; *loc*
   miijimikanjiganing; *dim* **miijimikanjigaans**
miijimikanjige *vai* bait things; *1sg*
   nimiijimikanjige; *prt* **maajimikanjiged**
miijin *vti3* eat s.t.; *1sg* **nimiijin**; *prt* **maajid**
miikana *ni* road, trail; *pl* **miikanan**; *loc*
   miikanaang; *dim* **miikanens, miikaans**
miikanaake *vai* make a road or trail; *1sg*
   nimiikanaake; *prt* **maakanaaked**
miikanaakewinini *na* road worker; *pl*
   miikanaakewininiwag
miikanaawan *vii* be a road, be a trail; *prt*
   maakanaawang
miikawaadad *vii* be handsome, be beautiful; *prt*
   maakawaadak
miikawaadizi *vai* be handsome, be beautiful; *1sg*
   nimiikawaadiz; *prt* **mekawaadizid**
miikindizi *vai* tease; *1sg* **nimiikindiz**; *prt*
   maakindizid
miikinji' *vta* tease s.o., harass s.o.; *1sg*
   nimiikinji'aa; *prt* **maakinji'aad**
miikonan *vti* shoot and hit s.t.; *1sg* **nimiikonaan**;
   prt **maakonang**
miikonaw *vta* shoot and hit s.o.; *1sg*
   nimiikonawaa; *prt* **maakonawaad**
miikwa' /**miikwa'w-**/ *vta* hit s.o. dead center with
   something; *1sg* **nimiikwa'waa**; *prt*
   maakwa'waad

miikwa'an *vti* hit s.t. dead center with something;
   1sg **nimiikwa'aan**; *prt* **maakwa'ang**
miinagaawanzh *na* blueberry plant; *pl*
   miinagaawanzhiig; *loc* **miinagaawanzhiing**;
   dim **miinagaawanzhiins**
miinan /**miin-**/ *ni* blueberries *plural*; *loc* **miining**;
   dim **miinensan**
mii nange *pc* yes, for sure, certainly
miinawaa *pc* and, also, again
miinens *na* hawthorn fruit; *pl* **miinensag**
miinensagaawanzh *na* hawthorn tree; *pl*
   miinensagaawanzhiig; *loc*
   miinensagaawanzhiing; *dim*
   miinensagaawanzhiins
miini-baashkiminasigan *ni* blueberry sauce
miinidiwag /**miinidi-**/ *vai* they give (s.t.) to each
   other, they have a give-away; *1pl* **nimiinidimin**;
   prt **maanidijig**
miini-giizis *na* August, July; *also* **miinike-giizis**
miinikaan *ni* seed; *pl* **miinikaanan**; *loc*
   miinikaaning; *dim* **miinikaanens**
miish *pc* it is thus that, and then
miishaabiwinaan *ni* eyelash; *pl*
   miishaabiwinaanan
miishidaamikan *vai* have a beard; *1sg*
   nimiishidaamikan; *prt* **maashidaamikang**
miishidoon *vai* have a moustache; *1sg*
   nimiishidoon; *prt* **maashidoong**
miishiigin *ni* velvet; *pl* **miishiiginoon**; *loc*
   miishiiginong; *dim* **miishiiginoons**
miishiijiimin *na* peach; *pl* **miishiijiiminag**; *loc*
   miishiijiimining; *dim* **miishiijiiminens**
miizh /**miiN-**/ *vta* give (s.t.) to s.o.; *1sg* **nimiinaa**;
   prt **maanaad**
miizii *vai* defecate; *1sg* **nimiizii**; *prt* **maaziid**
miiziiwigamig *ni* toilet, bathroom; *pl*
   miiziiwigamigoon; *loc* **miiziiwigamigong**; *dim*
   miiziiwigamigoons
moshwe *na* shawl; *pl* **moshweg**; *loc* **moshweng**;
   dim **moshwens**
moshwens *ni* handkerchief; *pl* **moshwensan**; *loc*
   moshwensing
moo *ni* feces, excrement; *pl* **moowan**
moo' *vta* make s.o. cry; *1sg* **nimoo'aa**; *prt*
   mwaa'aad
mooka'am *vai2* be sunrise, rise (as the sun); *1sg*
   nimooka'am; *prt* **mwaaka'ang**
mookawaakii *vai* cry to go along; *1sg*
   nimookawaakii; *prt* **mwaakawaakiid**
mookibii *vai* emerge from the water; *prt*
   mwaakibiid
mookijiwanibiig *ni* spring (water source); *loc*
   mookijiwanibiigong; *dim*
   mookijiwanibiigoons
mookii *vai* emerge from surface; *1sg* **nimookii**; *prt*
   mwaakiid
mookiitaw *vta* attack s.o. from hiding; *1sg*
   nimookiitawaa; *prt* **mwaakiitawaad**
mookodaaso *vai* carve, whittle; *1sg* **nimookodaas**;
   prt **mwaakodaasod**
mookodaasowinini *na* carpenter, carver; *pl*
   mookodaasowininiwag
mookojigan *ni* drawknife, plane (tool); *pl*
   mookojiganan; *loc* **mookojiganing**; *dim*
   mookojigaans

mookomaan *ni* knife; *pl* **mookomaanan**; *loc* **mookomaaning**; *dim* **mookomaanens**

moona' /**moona'w-**/ *vta* dig up s.o.; *1sg* **nimoona'waa**; *prt* **mwaana'waad**

moona'an *vti* dig up s.t.; *1sg* **nimoona'aan**; *prt* **mwaana'ang**

moona'ige *vai* dig up things; *1sg* **nimoona'ige**; *prt* **mwaana'iged**

moonenim *vta* suspect s.o.; *1sg* **nimoonenimaa**; *prt* **mwaanenimaad**

moonikaan *ni* cellar; *pl* **moonikaanan**; *loc* **moonikaaning**; *dim* **moonikaanens**

mooningwane *na* yellow-shafted flicker; *pl* **mooningwaneg**; *dim* **mooningwanens**

moose *na* worm; *pl* **mooseg**; *dim* **moosens**

moosewiingwe *vai* have acne on one's face; *1sg* **nimoosewiingwe**; *prt* **mwaasewiingwed**

mooshka'an *vii* be flooded, there is a flood; *prt* **mwaashka'ang**

mooshka'osi *na* American bittern (locally called shypoke); *pl* **mooshka'osiwag**; *dim* **mooshka'osiins**

mooshkamo *vai* come up to the surface of the water; *1sg* **nimooshkam**; *prt* **mwaashkamod**

mooshkinadoon *vti2* fill s.t. (with solids); *1sg* **nimooshkinadoon**; *prt* **mwaashkinadood**

mooshkina' *vta* fill s.o. (with solids); *1sg* **nimooshkina'aa**; *prt* **mwaashkina'aad**

mooshkine *vai* be full (of solids); *1sg* **nimooshkine**; *prt* **mwaashkined**

mooshkine *vii* be full (of solids); *prt* **mwaashkineg**; *aug* **mooshkinemagad**; *prt aug* **mwaashkinemagak**

mooshkinebadoon *vti2* fill s.t. (with a liquid); *1sg* **nimooshkinebadoon**; *prt* **mwaashkinebadood**

mooshkinebazh /**mooshkinebaN-**/ *vta* fill s.o. (with a liquid); *1sg* **nimooshkinebanaa**; *prt* **mwaashkinebanaad**

mooshkinebii *vii* be full (of a liquid); *prt* **mwaashkinebiig**; *aug* **mooshkinebiimagad**; *prt aug* **mwaashkinebiimagak**

mooshkinebii'ige *vai* fill out a form; *1sg* **nimooshkinebii'ige**; *prt* **mwaashkinebii'iged**

mooshkineyaabate *vii* be filled with smoke; *prt* **mwaashkineyaabateg**; *aug* **mooshkineyaabatemagad**; *prt aug* **mwaashkineyaabatemagak**

mooz *na* moose; *pl* **moozoog**; *dim* **moozoons**

moozhag *pc* always, often, all the time

moozhaabe *na* unmarried man; *pl* **moozhaabeg**

moozhi' *vta* feel s.o. in or on one's body; *1sg* **nimoozhi'aa**; *prt* **mwaazhi'aad**

moozhikwe *na* unmarried woman; *pl* **moozhikweg**

moozhitoon *vti2* feel s.t. in or on one's body; *1sg* **nimoozhitoon**; *prt* **mwaazhitood**

moozhwaagan *ni* scissors; *pl* **moozhwaaganan**; *loc* **moozhwaaganing**; *dim* **moozhwaagaans**

N

n= *pre first person prefix before long vowels in dependent noun stems*

na *pc* yes-no question word

nabagaa *vii* be flat; *prt* **nebagaag**; *aug* **nabagaamagad**; *prt aug* **nebagaamagak**

nabagidaabaan *na* toboggan; *pl* **nabagidaabaanag**; *loc* **nabagidaabaaning**; *dim* **nabagidaabaanens**

nabagijaane *vai* have a flat nose; *1sg* **ninabagijaane**; *prt* **nebagijaaned**

nabagijiishin *vai* have a flat tire; *prt* **nebagijiishing**

nabagisag *na* board; *pl* **nabagisagoog**; *loc* **nabagisagong**; *dim* **nabagisagoons**

nabagizi *vai* be flat; *prt* **nebagizid**

nabon *vta* fold s.o. over; *1sg* **ninabonaa**; *prt* **nebonaad**

nabonan *vti* fold s.t. over; *1sg* **ninabonaan**; *prt* **nebonang**

naboob *ni* soup; *pl* **naboobiin**; *loc* **naboobiing**; *dim* **naboobiins**

naboobiike *vai* make soup; *1sg* **ninaboobiike**; *prt* **neboobiiked**

nagadamaw *vta* leave (s.t.) behind for s.o.; *1sg* **ninagadamawaa**; *prt* **negadamawaad**

nagadan *vti* abandon s.t., leave s.t. behind; *1sg* **ninagadaan**; *prt* **negadang**

nagadendan *vti* be used to s.t., be familiar with s.t.; *1sg* **ninagadendaan**; *prt* **negadendang**

nagadenim *vta* be used to s.o., be familiar with s.o., be acquainted with s.o.; *1sg* **ninagadenimaa**; *prt* **negadenimaad**

nagadenindiwag /**nagadenindi-**/ *vai* they are acquainted with each other, they are friends with each other; *1pl* **ninagadenindimin**; *prt* **negadenindijig**

nagaji *vta* be used to making s.o., know how to handle s.o.; *1sg* **ninagaji'aa**; *prt* **negaji'aad**

nagajitoon *vti2* be used to making s.t., know how to handle s.t.; *1sg* **ninagajitoon**; *prt* **negajitood**

nagamo *vai* sing; *1sg* **ninagam**; *prt* **negamod**

nagamon *ni* song; *pl* **nagamonan**; *dim* **nagamonens**

nagamotaw *vta* sing for s.o.; *1sg* **ninagamotawaa**; *prt* **negamotawaad**

nagamowin *ni* singing, song

nagamoo-makak *ni* phonograph, record player; *pl* **nagamoo-makakoon**; *loc* **nagamoo-makakong**; *dim* **nagamoo-makakoons**

nagazh /**nagaN-**/ *vta* abandon s.o., leave s.o. behind; *1sg* **ninaganaa**; *prt* **neganaad**

nagazhiwe *vai* abandon people; *1sg* **ninagazhiwe**; *prt* **negazhiwed**

Nagaajiwanaang *place* Fond du Lac Reservation

nagaashkaa *vai* halt, stop moving; *1sg* **ninagaashkaa**; *prt* **negaashkaad**

nagaashkaa *vii* halt, stop moving; *prt* **negaashkaag**; *aug* **nagaashkaamagad**; *prt aug* **negaashkaamagak**

nagaashkaa' *vta* make s.o. stop (e.g., a car); *1sg*
  ninagaashkaa'aa; *prt* **negaashkaa'aad**
nagaashkaatoon *vti2* make s.t. stop; *1sg*
  ninagaashkaatoon; *prt* **negaashkaatood**
nagaawebishkigan *ni* brakes; *pl*
  nagaawebishkiganan; *loc*
  nagaawebishkiganing
nagaawebishkige *vai* apply the brakes; *1sg*
  ninagaawebishkige; *prt* **negaawebishkiged**
nagishkan *vti* meet s.t. (while going somewhere);
  1sg **ninagishkaan**; *prt* **negishkang**
nagishkaw *vta* meet s.o. (while going somewhere);
  1sg **ninagishkawaa**; *prt* **negishkawaad**
nagishkodaadiwag /**nagishkodaadi-**/ *vai* they meet
  each other; *1pl* **ninagishkodaadimin**; *prt*
  negishkodaadijig
nagwaagan *ni* snare; *pl* **nagwaaganan**; *loc*
  nagwaaganing; *dim* **nagwaagaans**
nagwaaganeyaab *ni* snare wire; *pl*
  nagwaaganeyaabiin; *loc*
  nagwaaganeyaabiing; *dim*
  nagwaaganeyaabiins
nagwaazh /**nagwaaN-**/ *vta* snare s.o.; *1sg*
  ninagwaanaa; *prt* **negwaanaad**
nagweyaab *ni* rainbow; *pl* **nagweyaabiin**; *loc*
  nagweyaabiing; *dim* **nagweyaabiins**
na'aanganikwe *na* daughter-in-law; *pl*
  na'aanganikweg
na'aangish *na* son-in-law; *pl* **na'aangishiig**
na'egaaj *pc* not too hard!, go easy!
na'enimo *vai* store things away; *1sg* **nina'enim**; *prt*
  ne'enimod
na'idaa *pc* right at the time, just then
na'isijige *vai* put things in order; *1sg* **nina'isijige**;
  prt **ne'isijiged**
nakodan *vti* answer s.t.; *1sg* **ninakodaan**; *prt*
  nekodang
nakom *vta* answer s.o., reply to s.o.; *1sg*
  ninakomaa; *prt* **nekomaad**
nakondiwag /**nakondi-**/ *vai* they answer each
  other, they reply to each other; *1pl*
  ninakondimin; *prt* **nekondijig**
nakwebidoon *vti2* catch s.t. with hands; *1sg*
  ninakwebidoon; *prt* **nekwebidood**
nakwebijige *vai* catch things with hands; *1sg*
  ninakwebijige; *prt* **nekwebijiged**
nakwebijigewinini *na* catcher (in baseball); *pl*
  nakwebijigewininiwag; *dim*
  nakwebijigewininiins
nakwebizh /**nakwebiN-**/ *vta* catch s.o. with hands;
  1sg **ninakwebinaa**; *prt* **nekwebinaad**
nakwebii'amaw *vta* write (s.t.) back to s.o.; *1sg*
  ninakwebii'amawaa; *prt* **nekwebii'amawaad**
nakwebii'amaadiwag /**nakwebii'amaadi-**/ *vai*
  they write back to each other; *1pl*
  ninakwebii'amaadimin; *prt*
  nekwebii'amaadijig
nakweshkaw *vta* meet s.o.; *1sg* **ninakweshkawaa**;
  prt **nekweshkawaad**
nakweshkodaadiwag /**nakweshkodaadi-**/ *vai* they
  meet each other; *1pl* **ninakweshkodaadimin**;
  prt **nekweshkodaadijig**

nakwetam *vai2* answer; *1sg* **ninakwetam**; *prt*
  nekwetang
nakwetan *vti* answer s.t.; *1sg* **ninakwetaan**; *prt*
  nekwetang
nakwetaw *vta* answer s.o.; *1sg* **ninakwetawaa**; *prt*
  nekwetawaad
namadabi *vai* sit, sit down; *1sg* **ninamadab**; *prt*
  nemadabid
namanjinik *ni* left hand *usually possessed*; *pl*
  namanjinikan; *loc* **namanjinikaang**
namanjii *vai* be left-handed; *1sg* **ninamanjii**; *prt*
  nemanjiid
name *na* sturgeon; *pl* **namewag**; *dim* **namens**
namebin *na* sucker (fish); *pl* **namebinag**; *dim*
  namebinens
namebini-giizis *na* February
name' *vta* find signs of s.o.'s presence; *1sg*
  niname'aa; *prt* **neme'aad**
nameshin *vai* leave signs of one's presence; *1sg*
  ninameshin; *prt* **nemeshing**
namesin *vii* leave signs of its presence; *prt*
  nemesing
nametoo *vai* leave signs of one's presence; *1sg*
  ninametoo; *prt* **nemetood**
nanagin *vta* hold s.o. back, prevent s.o. (from
  doing something); *1sg* **ninanaginaa**; *prt*
  nenaginaad
nanaabag= < **nabag=**
nanaa'ichige *vai* fix things, repair things; *1sg*
  ninanaa'ichige; *prt* **nenaa'ichiged**
nanaa'idaabaane *vai* repair a car; *1sg*
  ninanaa'idaabaane; *prt* **nenaa'idaabaaned**
nanaa'idaabaanewinini *na* automobile mechanic;
  pl **nanaa'idaabaanewininiwag**
nanaa'idaabaanikewinini *na* automobile mechanic; *pl* **nanaa'idaabaanikewininiwag**
nanaa'in *vta* put s.o. in order, put s.o. away, fix
  s.o.; *1sg* **ninanaa'inaa**; *prt* **nenaa'inaad**
nanaa'inan *vti* put s.t. in order, put s.t. away, fix
  s.t.; *1sg* **ninanaa'inaan**; *prt* **nenaa'inang**
nanaa'itaw *vta* fix (s.t.) for s.o., repair (s.t.) for
  s.o.; *1sg* **ninanaa'itawaa**; *prt* **nenaa'itawaad**;
  also **nanaa'itamaw**
nanaa'itoon *vti2* fix s.t., repair s.t.; *1sg*
  ninanaa'itoon; *prt* **nenaa'itood**
nanaa'ii *vai* be dressed up; *1sg* **ninanaa'ii**; *prt*
  nenaa'iid
nanaamad= < **namad=**
nanaandaw= < **nandaw=**
nanaandawi' *vta* heal s.o., doctor s.o.; *1sg*
  ninanaandawi'aa; *prt* **nenaandawi'aad**
nanaandawi'iwe *vai* heal people, doctor people;
  1sg **ninanaandawi'iwe**; *prt* **nenaandawi'iwed**
nanaando= < **nando=**
nanaawad= < **nawad=**
nanda- *pv4* seek, look for
nanda-anokii *vai* look for work; *1sg* **ninanda-
  anokii**; *prt* **nenda-anokiid**
nanda-gikendan *vti* seek to know s.t., seek to learn
  s.t.; *1sg* **ninanda-gikendaan**; *prt* **nenda-
  gikendang**
nanda-gikenim *vta* seek to know s.o.; *1sg* **ninanda-
  gikenimaa**; *prt* **nenda-gikenimaad**

nanda-mikwendan *vti* try to think of s.t., try to
remember s.t.; *1sg* ninanda-mikwendaan; *prt*
nenda-mikwendang
nanda-mikwenim *vta* try to think of s.o., try to remember s.o.; *1sg* ninanda-mikwenimaa; *prt*
nenda-mikwenimaad
nandawaabam *vta* look for s.o., search for s.o.; *1sg*
ninandawaabamaa; *prt* nendawaabamaad
nandawaabandan *vti* look for s.t., search for s.t.;
1sg ninandawaabandaan; *prt*
nendawaabandang
nandawaabanjige *vai* look for things, search for
things; *1sg* ninandawaabanjige; *prt*
nendawaabanjiged
nandawaaboozwe *vai* hunt for rabbits; *1sg*
ninandawaaboozwe; *prt* nendawaaboozwed
nandawaatoo *vai* scout; *1sg* ninandawaatoo; *prt*
nendawaatood
nandawendam *vai2* want, desire; *1sg*
ninandawendam; *prt* nendawendang
nandawendan *vti* want s.t., desire s.t.; *1sg*
ninandawendaan; *prt* nendawendang
nandawendaagozi *vai* be suitable, be desirable; *prt*
nendawendaagozid
nandawendaagwad *vii* be suitable, be desirable;
prt nendawendaagwak
nandawenim *vta* want s.o. (to do...), desire s.o.;
1sg ninandawenimaa; *prt* nendawenimaad
nandawenjige *vai* get food by hunting or fishing;
1sg ninandawenjige; *prt* nendawenjiged
nandawishibe *vai* hunt ducks; *1sg*
ninandawishibe; *prt* nendawishibed
nandawisimwe *vai* look for horses; *1sg*
ninandawisimwe; *prt* nendawisimwed
nandobani *vai* go to war *archaic*; *1sg* ninandoban;
prt nendobanid
nandodamaw *vta* ask s.o. for (s.t.), beg s.o. for
(s.t.); *1sg* ninandodamawaa; *prt*
nendodamawaad
nandodamaage *vai* ask people for (s.t.), beg
people for (s.t.); *1sg* ninandodamaage; *prt*
nendodamaaged
nandodan *vti* ask for s.t.; *1sg* ninandodaan; *prt*
nendodang
nandokawechige *vai* look for tracks; *1sg*
ninandokawechige; *prt* nendokawechiged
nandokawe' *vta* look for s.o.'s tracks, be on s.o.'s
trail; *1sg* ninandokawe'aa; *prt* nendokawe'aad
nandom *vta* call s.o., summon s.o.; *1sg*
ninandomaa; *prt* nendomaad
nandomaam *vta* smell for s.o., sniff s.o.; *1sg*
ninandomaamaa; *prt* nendomaamaad
nandomaandan *vti* smell for s.t., sniff s.t.; *1sg*
ninandomaandaan; *prt* nendomaandang
nandone' /nandone'w-/ *vta* look for s.o.; *1sg*
ninandone'waa; *prt* nendone'waad
nandone'an *vti* look for s.t.; *1sg* ninandone'aan;
prt nendone'ang
nandone'igaade *vii* be looked for; *prt*
nendone'igaadeg; *aug*
nandone'igaademagad; *prt aug*
nendone'igaademagak
nandone'igaazo *vai* be looked for; *prt*
nendone'igaazod

nandone'ige *vai* look for things; *1sg*
ninandone'iged; *prt* nendone'iged
nandotam *vai2* listen for something; *1sg*
ninandotam; *prt* nendotang
nandotan *vti* listen for s.t.; *1sg* ninandotaan; *prt*
nendotang
nandotaw *vta* listen for s.o.; *1sg* ninandotawaa;
prt nendotawaad
nandoobii *vai* look for a drink; *1sg* ninandoobii;
prt nendoobiid
nandoojiin *vta* feel for s.o., grope for s.o.; *1sg*
ninandoojiinaa; *prt* nendoojiinaad
nandoojiinan *vti* feel for s.t., grope for s.t.; *1sg*
ninandoojiinaan; *prt* nendoojiinang
nandoojiinige *vai* feel for things, grope for things;
1sg ninandoojiinige; *prt* nendoojiiniged
nandookome *vai* look for lice; *1sg*
ninandookome; *prt* nendookomed
nandookomeshiinh *na* monkey; *pl*
nandookomeshiinyag
nandwaanikaadan *vti* dig for s.t.; *1sg*
ninandwaanikaadaan; *prt* nendwaanikaadang
nandwaanikaazh /nandwaanikaaN-/ *vta* dig for
s.o.; *1sg* ninandwaanikaanaa; *prt*
nendwaanikaanaad
nandwewem *vta* go and ask for s.o.; *1sg*
ninandwewemaa; *prt* nendwewemaad
nandwewendamaw *vta* go and ask s.o. (for s.t.);
1sg ninandwewendamawaa; *prt*
nendwewendamawaad
nandwewendan *vti* go and ask for s.t.; *1sg*
ninandwewendaan; *prt* nendwewendang
nandwewezige *vai* signal by shooting; *1sg*
ninandwewezige; *prt* nendweweziged
nangwana *pc* it turns out that, it happens to be;
also ngwana, ingwana
naniibikim *vta* scold s.o.; *1sg* ninaniibikimaa; *prt*
neniibikimaad
naniisido= < nisido=
naniizaanad *vii* be dangerous; *prt* neniizaanak
naniizaanendan *vti* consider s.t. dangerous; *1sg*
ninaniizaanendaan; *prt* neniizaanendang
naniizaanendaagwad *vii* be considered dangerous;
prt neniizaanendaagwak
naniizaanenim *vta* consider s.o. dangerous, think
s.o. to be in danger; *1sg* ninaniizaanenimaa;
prt neniizaanenimaad
naniizaanizi *vai* be dangerous; *1sg* ninaniizaaniz;
prt neniizaanizid
napaazikan *vti* wear s.t. the wrong way; *1sg*
ninapaazikaan; *prt* nepaazikang
napaazikaw *vta* wear s.o. the wrong way; *1sg*
ninapaazikawaa; *prt* nepaazikawaad
napodin *na* dumpling; *pl* napodinag; *loc*
napodining; *dim* napodinens
napodinike *vai* make dumplings; *1sg*
ninapodinike; *prt* nepodiniked
nasanaamo *vai* exhale, recover one's breath; *1sg*
ninasanaam; *prt* nesanaamod
nase'an *vti* stir s.t. to form sugar; *1sg* ninase'aan;
prt nese'ang
nase'igan *ni* granulated maple sugar
nase'ige *vai* stir to form sugar; *1sg* ninase'ige; *prt*
nese'iged

naseyaawangwaan *ni* sugaring trough; *pl*
  naseyaawangwaanan; *loc*
  naseyaawangwaaning; *dim*
  naseyaawangwaanens

naseyaawangwaan (sugaring trough)

naseyaawangwe *vai* granulate sugar; *1sg*
  ninaseyaawangwe; *prt* **neseyaawangwed**
nashke *pc* look!, behold!; *also* **inashke**
nawadam *vta* take hold of s.o. in mouth, take a
  bite of s.o.; *1sg* **ninawadamaa;** *prt*
  newadamaad
nawadandan *vti* take hold of s.t. in mouth, take
  a bite of s.t.; *1sg* **ninawadandaan;** *prt*
  newadandang
nawadanjige *vai* take hold of things in mouth, take
  a bite of things; *1sg* **ninawadanjige;** *prt*
  newadanjiged
nawadide *vii* catch fire; *prt* **newadideg;** *aug*
  nawadidemagad; *prt aug* **newadidemagak**
nawadin *vta* grab s.o., seize s.o.; *1sg* **ninawadinaa;**
  prt **newadinaad**
nawadinamaw *vta* grab (s.t.) of s.o.'s, seize (s.t.)
  of s.o.'s; *1sg* **ninawadinamawaa;** *prt*
  newadinamawaad
nawadinan *vti* grab s.t., seize s.t.; *1sg*
  ninawadinaan; *prt* **newadinang**
nawadiniwe *vai* grab people, seize people, take
  captives; *1sg* **ninawadiniwe;** *prt* **newadiniwed**
nawadizo *vai* catch fire; *prt* **newadizod**
nawaj *pc* more
nawajii *vai* take a lunch break; *1sg* **ninawajii;** *prt*
  newajiid
nawapo *vai* take a lunch along; *1sg* **ninawap;** *prt*
  newapod
nawapwaan *ni* lunch taken along; *pl*
  nawapwaanan; *dim* **nawapwaanens**
nawapwaanike *vai* make a lunch to take along; *1sg*
  ninawapwaanike; *prt* **newapwaaniked**
nayaag *pc* ahead of time
nayenzh *pc* both
nazhikewaakwadabi *vai* sit alone; *1sg*
  ninazhikewaakwadab; *prt*
  nezhikewaakwadabid
nazhikewige *vai* live alone; *1sg* **ninazhikewige;** *prt*
  nezhikewiged
nazhikewizi *vai* be alone; *1sg* **ninazhikewiz;** *prt*
  nezhikewizid

nazikwe' /**nazikwe'w-**/ *vta* comb s.o.'s hair; *1sg*
  ninazikwe'waa; *prt* **nezikwe'waad**
nazikwe'o *vai* comb one's hair; *1sg* **ninazikwe';** *prt*
  nezikwe'od
naa *pc emphatic particle*
naaba'anidizo *vai* step in the same tracks; *1sg*
  ninaaba'anidizo; *prt* **nayaaba'anidizod**
naabe- *pv4* male
naabese *na* male bird, rooster; *pl* **naabeseg;** *dim*
  naabesens
naabesim *na* male dog, stallion; *pl* **naabesimoog;**
  dim **naabesimoons**
naabidoo' /**naabidoo'w-**/ *vta* thread s.o., string s.o.
  (e.g., beads); *1sg* **ninaabidoo'waa;** *prt*
  nayaabidoo'waad
naabidoo'an *vti* thread s.t., string s.t.; *1sg*
  ninaabidoo'aan; *prt* **nayaabidoo'ang**
naabidoo'igan *ni* beading needle; *pl*
  naabidoo'iganan; *loc* **naabidoo'iganing;** *dim*
  naabidoo'igaans
naabidoo'ige *vai* thread things, string things; *1sg*
  ninaabidoo'ige; *prt* **nayaabidoo'iged**
naabikan *vti* wear s.t. around one's neck; *1sg*
  ninaabikaan; *prt* **nayaabikang**
naabikaw *vta* wear s.o. around one's neck; *1sg*
  ninaabikawaa; *prt* **nayaabikawaad**
naabikawaagan *na* necktie, necklace; *pl*
  naabikawaaganag; *loc* **naabikawaaganing;**
  dim **naabikawaagaans**
naabikwaan *ni* ship, vessel; *pl* **naabikwaanan;** *loc*
  naabikwaaning; *dim* **naabikwaanens**
naabinootaw *vta* repeat what s.o. says, mock s.o.;
  1sg **ninaabinootawaa;** *prt* **nayaabinootawaad**
naabinootaage *vai* repeat what people say, mock
  people; *1sg* **ninaabinootaage;** *prt*
  nayaabinootaaged
naabinootaage-makak *ni* tape recorder; *pl*
  naabinootaage-makakoon; *loc*
  naabinootaage-makakong; *dim*
  naabinootaage-makakoons
naabishebizon *ni* earring; *pl* **naabishebizonan;** *loc*
  naabishebizoning; *dim* **naabishebizonens**
naabishkaw *vta* take s.o.'s place; *1sg*
  ninaabishkawaa; *prt* **nayaabishkawaad**
naabishkaage *vai* take someone's place; *1sg*
  ninaabishkaage; *prt* **nayaabishkaaged**
naabizhigan *ni* pattern (in sewing); *pl*
  naabizhiganan; *loc* **naabizhiganing;** *dim*
  naabizhigaans
naada'oodoon *vti2* go to get s.t. by boat; *1sg*
  ninaada'oodoon; *prt* **nayaada'oodood**
naadagoodoo *vai* check one's snares; *1sg*
  ninaadagoodoo; *prt* **nayaadagoodood**
naada' /**naada'w-**/ *vta* go get s.o. by boat; *1sg*
  ninaada'waa; *prt* **nayaada'waad**
naada'an *vti* go get s.t. by boat; *1sg* **ninaada'aan;**
  prt **nayaada'ang**
naada'oozh /**naada'ooN-**/ *vta* go to get s.o. by
  boat; *1sg* **ninaada'oonaa;** *prt* **nayaada'oonaad**
naadamaw *vta* help s.o.; *1sg* **ninaadamawaa;** *prt*
  nayaadamawaad
naadamaadiwag /**naadamaadi-**/ *vai* they help
  each other; *1pl* **ninaadamaadimin;** *prt*
  nayaadamaadijig

naadamaage *vai* help people; *1sg* **ninaadamaage**; *prt* **nayaadamaaged**
naadasabii *vai* go get a net, pick up a net; *1sg* **ninaadasabii**; *prt* **nayaadasabiid**
naadashkosiwe *vai* go after hay; *1sg* **ninaadashkosiwe**; *prt* **nayaadashkosiwed**
naadasoonaagane *vai* check one's traps, go get one's traps; *1sg* **ninaadasoonaagane**; *prt* **nayaadasoonaaganed**
naadaw *vta* go get (s.t.) for s.o., fetch (s.t.) for s.o.; *1sg* **ninaadawaa**; *prt* **nayaadawaad**
naadazina'igane *vai* go get mail; *1sg* **ninaadazina'igane**; *prt* **nayaadazina'iganed**
naadazina'ige *vai* go collect a debt; *1sg* **ninaadazina'ige**; *prt* **nayaadazina'iged**
naadin *vti3* go get s.t., fetch s.t., go after s.t.; *1sg* **ninaadin**; *prt* **nayaadid**
naadinise *vai* go get firewood; *1sg* **ninaadinise**; *prt* **nayaadinised**; *also* **naajinise**
naadoobii *vai* go get water or other liquid, gather sap; *1sg* **ninaadoobii**; *prt* **nayaadoobiid**
naagadawaabam *vta* observe s.o.; *1sg* **ninaagadawaabamaa**; *prt* **nayaagadawaabamaad**
naagadawaabandan *vti* observe s.t.; *1sg* **ninaagadawaabandaan**; *prt* **nayaagadawaabandang**
naagadawendam *vai2* think; *1sg* **ninaagadawendam**; *prt* **nayaagadawendang**
naagadawendan *vti* think about s.t.; *1sg* **ninaagadawendaan**; *prt* **nayaagadawendang**
naagadawenim *vta* think about s.o.; *1sg* **ninaagadawenimaa**; *prt* **nayaagadawenimaad**
naagaj *pc* later, after a while
naago' *vta* make s.o. show, reveal s.o.; *1sg* **ninaago'aa**; *prt* **nayaago'aad**
naagotoon *vti2* make s.t. show, reveal s.t.; *1sg* **ninaagotoon**; *prt* **nayaagotood**
naagozi *vai* be visible; *1sg* **ninaagoz**; *prt* **nayaagozid**
naagwad *vii* be visible; *prt* **nayaagwak**
naajibatwaadan *vti* run to get s.t.; *1sg* **ninaajibatwaadaan**; *prt* **nayaajibatwaadang**
naajibatwaazh /naajibatwaaN-/ *vta* run to get s.o.; *1sg* **ninaajibatwaanaa**; *prt* **nayaajibatwaanaad**
naajigaade *vii* be fetched, be picked up; *prt* **nayaajigaadeg**; *aug* **naajigaademagad**; *prt aug* **nayaajigaademagak**
naajigaazo *vai* be fetched, be picked up; *prt* **nayaajigaazod**
naajimiijime *vai* go get food; *1sg* **ninaajimiijime**; *prt* **nayaajimiijimed**
naajinizha'an *vti* go after s.t., send for s.t.; *1sg* **ninaajinizha'aan**; *prt* **nayaajinizha'ang**
naajinizha' /naajinizha'w-/ *vta* go after s.o., send for s.o.; *1sg* **ninaajinizha'waa**; *prt* **nayaajinizha'waad**
naajinizha'amaw *vta* order (s.t.) for s.o.; *1sg* **ninaajinizha'amawaa**; *prt* **nayaajinizha'amawaad**
naajinizha'ige *vai* order things; *1sg* **ninaajinizha'ige**; *prt* **nayaajinizha'iged**
naajiwanii'ige *vai* go after traps; *1sg* **ninaajiwanii'ige**; *prt* **nayaajiwanii'iged**

naan *nad* grandma (vocative of **nimaamaanaan** grandmother)
naanabem *pc* too late, it should have been done
naanan *nm* five
naananinoon /naananin-/ *vii* they are five; *prt* **nayaananingin**
naananiwag /naanani-/ *vai* they are five; *1pl* **ninaananimin**; *prt* **nayaananijig**
naanaabishebizo *vai* wear earrings; *1sg* **ninaanaabishebiz**; *prt* **nayaanaabishebizod**
naanaagadawaabam *vta* watch s.o. carefully, observe s.o.; *1sg* **ninaanaagadawaabamaa**; *prt* **nayaanaagadawaabamaad**
naanaagadawaabandan *vti* watch s.t. carefully, observe s.t.; *1sg* **ninaanaagadawaabandaan**; *prt* **nayaanaagadawaabandang**
naanaagadawendam *vai2* consider, think; *1sg* **ninaanaagadawendam**; *prt* **nayaanaagadawendang**
naanaagadawendan *vti* consider s.t., think about s.t.; *1sg* **ninaanaagadawendaan**; *prt* **nayaanaagadawendang**
naanaagadawenim *vta* consider s.o., think about s.o.; *1sg* **ninaanaagadawenimaa**; *prt* **nayaanaagadawenimaad**
naangan *vii* be light in weight; *prt* **nayaangang**
naangendan *vti* consider s.t. light in weight; *1sg* **ninaangendaan**; *prt* **nayaangendang**
naangenim *vta* consider s.o. light in weight; *1sg* **ninaangenimaa**; *prt* **nayaangenimaad**
naangide'e *vai* be carefree; *1sg* **ninaangide'e**; *prt* **nayaangide'ed**
naangiwane *vai* carry a light pack; *1sg* **ninaangiwane**; *prt* **nayaangiwaned**
naangizi *vai* be light in weight; *1sg* **ninaangiz**; *prt* **nayaangizid**
naanibaayawe *vai* yawn; *1sg* **ninaanibaayawe**; *prt* **nayaanibaayawed**
naanimidana *nm* fifty
naaning *pc* five times
naaningim *pc* often
naaningodinong* *pc* now and then, every once in a while, sometimes; *also* **naangodinong***
naano- *pv4* five
naano-anama'e-giizhigad *vii* be five weeks; *prt* **nayaano-anama'e-giizhigak**
naano-anama'e-giizhik *pc* five weeks
naano-biboon *pc* five years
naano-biboonagad *vii* be five years; *prt* **nayaano-biboonagak**
naano-biboonagizi *vai* be five years old; *1sg* **ninaano-biboonagiz**; *prt* **nayaano-biboonagizid**
naano-diba'igan *pc* five miles, five hours
naano-diba'iganed *vii* be five o'clock; *prt* **nayaano-diba'iganek**
naano-diba'igaans *pc* five minutes, five acres
naano-dibik *pc* five nights
naano-giizhigad *vii* be Friday; *prt* **nayaano-giizhigak**
naano-giizhik *pc* five days
naano-giizis *pc* five months
naanogon *pc* five days
naanogonagad *vii* be five days; *prt* **nayaanogonagak**

naanogonagizi *vai* be the fifth day of the month, be five days old; *prt* **nayaanogonagizid**
naanoninj *pc* five inches
naanosagoons *nm* five thousand
naanozid *pc* five feet
naanoobii'igan *na* five (card); *pl* **naanoobii'iganag**
naanoomaya *pc* a little while ago
naanooshkin *pc* five bags
naanwaabik *pc* five dollars
naanwaak *nm* five hundred
naanwewaan *pc* five sets, five pairs
naasanaa *pc* look out!, come on!
naasaab *pc* like, the same
naasaabibii'an *vti* copy s.t. in writing; *1sg* **ninaasaabibii'aan**; *prt* **nayaasaabibii'ang**
naasaabibii'ige *vai* copy things in writing; *1sg* **ninaasaabibii'ige**; *prt* **nayaasaabibii'iged**
naawagaam *pc* in the middle of the lake
naawakwe *vii* be noon; *prt* **nayaawakweg**; *aug* **naawakwemagad**; *prt aug* **nayaawakwemagak**
naawakwe-miijin *vti3* eat s.t. for dinner (noon meal), eat s.t. for lunch (noon meal); *1sg* **ninaawakwe-miijin**; *prt* **nayaawakwe-miijid**
naawakwe-wiisini *vai* eat dinner (noon meal), eat lunch (noon meal); *1sg* **ninaawakwe-wiisin**; *prt* **nayaawakwe-wiisinid**
naawashkosiw *pc* in the middle of a meadow
naawayi'ii *pc* in the middle of it
naawaakigan *pc* in the middle of the chest
naawaakwaa *pc* in the middle of the woods
naawaawigan *pc* in the middle of the back
naawi- *pn* in the middle of
naawigatig *pc* in the middle of the forehead
naawij *pc* out in the lake
naawikana *pc* in the middle of the road or trail
naawinaagozi *vai* be barely visible, be a distant sight; *1sg* **ninaawinaagoz**; *prt* **nayaawinaagozid**
naawinaagwad *vii* be barely visible, be a distant sight; *prt* **nayaawinaagwak**
naawininj *ni* middle finger; *pl* **naawininjiin**
naawisag *pc* in the middle of the floor
naawoonag *pc* in the middle of a boat
naayanh *pc* correct?, right?
naazh /naaN-/ *vta* go get s.o., fetch s.o., go after s.o.; *1sg* **ninaanaa**; *prt* **nayaanaad**
naazhaabii'igan *ni* violin, fiddle; *pl* **naazhaabii'iganan**; *loc* **naazhaabii'iganing**; *dim* **naazhaabii'igaans**
naazhiiga'igan *ni* hide stretcher; *pl* **naazhiiga'iganan**; *loc* **naazhiiga'iganing**; *dim* **naazhiiga'igaans**
naazhiiga'ige *vai* stretch a hide; *1sg* **ninaazhiiga'ige**; *prt* **nayaazhiiga'iged**
naazikan *vti* go to s.t., approach s.t.; *1sg* **ninaazikaan**; *prt* **nayaazikang**
naazikaw *vta* go to s.o., approach s.o.; *1sg* **ninaazikawaa**; *prt* **nayaazikawaad**
naazikaage *vai* go to people, approach people; *1sg* **ninaazikaage**; *prt* **nayaazikaaged**
negwaabam *vta* look malevolently out of corner of one's eye at s.o.; *1sg* **ninegwaabamaa**; *prt* **nayegwaabamaad**

negwaakwaan *ni* tap, spile (for sugaring); *pl* **negwaakwaanan**; *loc* **negwaakwaaning**; *dim* **negwaakwaanens**
nemaab *ni* marble, pool ball; *pl* **nemaabiin**
nemaabii *vai* play pool; *1sg* **ninemaabii**; *prt* **nayemaabiid**
nemaabiiwigamig *ni* pool hall; *pl* **nemaabiiwigamigoon**; *loc* **nemaabiiwigamigong**; *dim* **nemaabiiwigamigoons**
nenaandawi'iwed *na-pt* traditional healer; *pl* **nenaandawi'iwejig**
nenaapaajinikesi *na* mole; *pl* **nenaapaajinikesiwag**; *dim* **nenaapaajinikesiins**
nendodamaageshkid *na-pt* beggar; *pl* **nendodamaageshkijig**
neningo= < ingo=
neningodwaaso= < ingodwaaso=
neningodwaaswi *nm* six each
neniswi *nm* three each
neniibowa *pc* a whole lot
neniiwin *nm* four each
neniizh *nm* two each
neniizhwaaswi *nm* seven each
nenookaasi *na* hummingbird; *pl* **nenookaasiwag**; *dim* **nenookaasiins**
nesezo *vai* pant; *1sg* **ninesez**; *prt* **nayesezod**
neshangaa *vii* be limber, be slack; *prt* **nayeshangaag**; *aug* **neshangaamagad**; *prt aug* **nayeshangaamagak**
neshangaabiigad *vii* be slack (as something stringlike); *prt* **nayeshangaabiigak**
neshangaabiigizi *vai* be slack (as something stringlike); *prt* **nayeshangaabiigizid**
neshangishin *vai* be relaxed, lie limp; *1sg* **nineshangishin**; *prt* **nayeshangishing**
neshangisin *vii* lie limp, lie slack; *prt* **nayeshangising**
neshangizi *vai* be limber, be slack; *1sg* **nineshangiz**; *prt* **nayeshangizid**
newe *na* bull snake; *pl* **neweg**; *dim* **newens**
neyaab *pc* back to previous place or condition, as before
neyaashi *ni* point of land, peninsula; *pl* **neyaashiwan**; *loc* **neyaashiing**; *dim* **neyaashiins**
neyaashiiwan *vii* there is a peninsula, there is a point of land; *prt* **nayeyaashiiwang**
ni= *pre* first person prefix; *also* **ni=, in=, im=, n=, nin=*, nim=***
ni- *pv2* going away, coming up to in time; *also* **ani-**
nibaa *vai* sleep; *1sg* **ninibaa**; *prt* **nebaad**
nibaagan *ni* bed; *pl* **nibaaganan**; *loc* **nibaaganing**; *dim* **nibaagaans**
nibaaganaatig *ni* bed frame; *pl* **nibaaganaatigoon**; *loc* **nibaaganaatigong**; *dim* **nibaaganaatigoons**
nibe' *vta* make s.o. sleep, put s.o. to bed; *1sg* **ninibe'aa**; *prt* **nebe'aad**
nibekaazo *vai* pretend to sleep; *1sg* **ninibekaaz**; *prt* **nebekaazod**
nibendaw *vta* stay overnight with s.o.; *1sg* **ninibendawaa**; *prt* **nebendawaad**
nibendaage *vai* stay overnight with people; *1sg* **ninibendaage**; *prt* **nebendaaged**

nibeshkaw- *vta* make s.o. sleep *in inverse forms: 1sg*
  ninibeshkaagon; *prt* nebeshkaagod
nibewigamig *ni* bedroom; *pl* nibewigamigoon; *loc*
  nibewigamigong; *dim* nibewigamigoons
nibi *ni* water; *loc* nibiing
nibinaadi *vai* get water; *1sg* ninibinaad; *prt*
  nebinaadid
nibiikaa *vii* be much water; *prt* nebiikaag; *aug*
  nibiikaamagad; *prt aug* nebiikaamagak
nibiiwadamon /nibiiwadamo-/ *vii* be wet (as a
  road or trail); *prt* nebiiwadamog
nibiiwakamigaa *vii* be wet ground; *prt*
  nebiiwakamigaag; *aug*
  nibiiwakamigaamagad; *prt aug*
  nebiiwakamigaamagak
nibiiwakik *na* water pail; *pl* nibiiwakikoog; *loc*
  nibiiwakikong; *dim* nibiiwakikoons
nibiiwan *vii* be wet, be watery; *prt* nebiiwang
nibiiwi *vai* be wet; *1sg* ninibiiw; *prt* nebiiwid
nibo *vai* die, be dead; *1sg* ninib; *prt* nebod
nibooke *vai* have a death in one's family; *1sg*
  ninibooke; *prt* nebooked
niboowi *vai* be paralyzed; *1sg* niniboow; *prt*
  neboowid
niboowidaabaan *na* hearse; *pl*
  niboowidaabaanag; *loc* niboowidaabaaning;
  dim niboowidaabaanens
niboowigamig *ni* mortuary; *pl* niboowigamigoon;
  loc niboowigamigong
niboowigaade *vai* have a numb leg; *1sg*
  niniboowigaade; *prt* neboowigaaded
niboowinike *vai* have a numb arm; *1sg*
  niniboowinike; *prt* neboowiniked
niboowininjii *vai* have a numb hand; *1sg*
  niniboowininjii; *prt* neboowininjiid
niboowise *vai* have a stroke, become paralyzed,
  fall ill from bad medicine; *1sg* niniboowise; *prt*
  neboowised
niboowizide *vai* have a numb foot; *1sg*
  niniboowizide; *prt* neboowizided
nibwaakaa *vai* be wise, be intelligent; *1sg*
  ninibwaakaa; *prt* nebwaakaad
nichiiwad *vii* there is a severe storm, there is a catastrophe; *prt* nechiiwad
nigig *na* otter; *pl* nigigwag; *dim* nigigoons
nigigwayaan *na* otter hide; *pl* nigigwayaanag
nika *na* Canada goose; *pl* nikag; *dim* nikens
nikakwan /-kakwan-/ *nid* my shin; *pl* nikakwanan;
  loc nikakwanaang
nikan /-kan-/ *nid* my bone; *pl* nikanan; *loc* nikaning
nikanendi *vai* be gone overnight; *1sg* ninikanend;
  prt nekanendid
nikatig /-katigw-/ *nid* my forehead; *pl* nikatigoon;
  loc nikatigwaang
nikaad /-kaad-/ *nid* my leg; *pl* nikaadan; *loc*
  nikaading
nikaakigan /-kaakigan-/ *nid* my chest; *pl*
  nikaakiganan; *loc* nikaakiganaang
nikibii *vai* be flooded; *prt* nekibiid
nikibii *vii* be flooded; *prt* nekibiig; *aug*
  nikibiimagad; *prt aug* nekibiimagak
nikidin /-kidin-/ *nad* my vulva
nikon /-kon-/ *nid* my liver; *pl* nikonan; *loc* nikoning
nikonaas /-konaas-/ *nid* my blanket; *pl* nikonaasan

nikoonzh /-koonzh-/ *nid* my bill, my beak; *loc*
  nikoonzhing
nikwegan /-kwegan-/ *nid* the back of my neck; *pl*
  nikweganan; *loc* nikweganaang
nimaamaa /-maamaay-/ *nad* my mother; *pl*
  nimaamaayag
nimaamaa /-maamaay-/ *nad* my eyebrow hair; *pl*
  nimaamaayag
niminaawe'o *vai* paddle out from shore; *1sg*
  niniminaawe'; *prt* neminaawe'od
niminaaweyaadagaako *vai* go out from shore on
  the ice; *1sg* niniminaaweyaadagaak; *prt*
  neminaaweyaadagaakod
niminaaweyaandawaagan *ni* dock; *pl*
  niminaaweyaandawaaganan; *loc*
  niminaaweyaandawaaganing; *dim*
  niminaaweyaandawaagaans
nimisad /-misad-/ *nid* my stomach; *pl* nimisadan;
  loc nimisadaang
nimisenh /-miseny-/ *nad* my older sister, my older
  female parallel cousin; *pl* nimisenyag
nimishoo *nad* grandpa *vocative of* nimishoomis
nimishoome /-mishoomey-/ *nad* my parallel uncle
  (father's brother); *pl* nimishoomeyag
nimishoomis /-mishoomis-/ *nad* my grandfather;
  pl nimishoomisag
nimiishigwaan /-miishigwaan-/ *nid* my pubic hair;
  pl nimiishigwaanan
ninaga'ayag /-naga'ay-/ *nad* my scales *plural*
ninagaskway /-nagaskway-/ *nid* my palate; *loc*
  ninagaskwaang
ninagaakininj /-nagaakininjy-/ *nid* my palm; *pl*
  ninagaakininjiin; *loc* ninagaakininjiing
ninagaakizid /-nagaakizid-/ *nid* my sole; *pl*
  ninagaakizidan; *loc* ninagaakizidaang
ninagizh /-nagizhy-/ *nid* my intestine; *pl*
  ninagizhiin; *loc* ninagizhiing
ninagway /-nagway-/ *nid* my sleeve; *pl*
  ninagwayan; *loc* ninagwayag; *dim* ninagwens
ninashkid /-nashkidy-/ *nid* my tail (of a bird); *pl*
  ninashkidiin; *loc* ninashkidiing
ninasid /-nasid-/ *nid* my hoof; *loc* ninasidaang
ninaabem /-naabem-/ *nad* my husband; *pl*
  ninaabemag
ninaan /-naan-/ *nad* my calf; *pl* ninaanag; *loc*
  ninaaning
nindigo *pc* as if, just like; *also* indigo
ningaabii'an *ni* west; *loc* ningaabii'anong
ningaasimoo-jiimaan *ni* sailboat; *pl* ningaasimoo-
  jiimaanan; *loc* ningaasimoo-jiimaaning; *dim*
  ningaasimoo-jiimaanens
ningaasimoono *vai* sail (in a boat); *1sg*
  niningaasimoon; *prt* nengaasimoonod
ningaasimoonowin *ni* sail; *loc*
  ningaasimoonowining; *dim*
  ningaasimoonowinens
ningaasimoowinini *na* sailor; *pl*
  ningaasimoowininiwag
ningide *vii* melt, thaw; *prt* nengideg; *aug*
  ningidemagad; *prt aug* nengidemagak
ningiz /ningizw-/ *vta* melt s.o.; *1sg* niningizwaa;
  prt nengizwaad
ningizan *vti* melt s.t.; *1sg* niningizaan; *prt*
  nengizang
ningizo *vai* melt, thaw; *prt* nengizod

ningiigwadin *vii* be frosted; *prt* **nengiigwading**
ningiigwaji *vai* be frosted; *prt* **nengiigwajid**
ningo-* *pv4* one; *also* **ingo-**
ningo-anama'e-giizhik* *pc* one week; *also* **ingo-anama'e-giizhik**
ningo-biboon* *pc* one year; *also* **ingo-biboon**
ningo-biboonagad* *vii* be one year; *prt* **nengo-biboonagak**; *also* **ingo-biboonagad**
ningo-diba'igan* *pc* one hour, one mile; *also* **ingo-diba'igan**
ningo-diba'iganed* *vii* be one o'clock; *prt* **nengo-diba'iganek**; *also* **ingo-diba'iganed**
ningo-diba'igaans* *pc* one minute, one acre; *also* **ingo-diba'igaans**
ningo-dibik* *pc* one night; *also* **ingo-dibik**
ningoding* *pc* sometime, at one time; *also* **ingoding**
ningodoninj* *pc* one inch; *also* **ingodoninj**
ningodozid* *pc* one foot; *also* **ingodozid**
ningodooshkin* *pc* one bag; *also* **ingodooshkin**
ningodwaaching* *pc* six times; *also* **ingodwaaching**
ningodwaachinoon* /**ningodwaachin-**/ *vii* they are six; *prt* **nengodwaachingin**; *also* **ingodwaachinoon**
ningodwaachiwag* /**ningodwaachi-**/ *vai* they are six; *1pl* **niningodwaachimin**; *prt* **nengodwaachijig**; *also* **ingodwaachiwag**
ningodwaak* *nm* one hundred; *also* **ingodwaak**
ningodwaasimidana* *nm* sixty; *also* **ingodwaasimidana**
ningodwaaso-* *pv4* six; *also* **ingodwaaso-**
ningodwaaso-anama'e-giizhik* *pc* six weeks; *also* **ingodwaaso-anama'e-giizhik**
ningodwaasosagoons* *nm* six thousand; *also* **ingodwaasosagoons**
ningodwaasoobii'igan* *na* six (card); *pl* **ningodwaasoobii'iganag**
ningodwaasooshkin* *pc* six bags; *also* **ingodwaasooshkin**
ningodwaaswaabik* *pc* six dollars; *also* **ingodwaaswaabik**
ningodwaaswaak* *nm* six hundred; *also* **ingodwaaswaak**
ningodwaaswewaan* *pc* six sets, six pairs; *also* **ingodwaaswewaan**
ningodwaaswi* *nm* six; *also* **ingodwaaswi**
ningodwewaan* *pc* one pair, one set; *also* **ingodwewaan**
ningo-giizhik* *pc* one day; *also* **ingo-giizhik**
ningo-giizis* *pc* one month; *also* **ingo-giizis**
ningoji* *pc* somewhere; *also* **ingoji**
ningwa' /**ningwa'w-**/ *vta* bury s.o.; *1sg* **niningwa'waa**; *prt* **nengwa'waad**
ningwa'abwaan *na* bread baked under the ashes; *pl* **ningwa`abwaanag**
ningwa'abwe *vai+o* cook (s.t.) under the ashes; *1sg* **niningwa'abwe, niningwa'abwen**; *prt* **nengwa'abwed**
ningwa'an *vti* bury s.t.; *1sg* **niningwa'aan**; *prt* **nengwa'ang**
ningwa'igaazo *vai* be buried; *prt* **nengwa'igaazod**
ningwaja' /**ningwaja'w-**/ *vta* hoe s.o.; *1sg* **niningwaja'waa**; *prt* **nengwaja'waad**

ningwaja'an *vti* hoe s.t.; *1sg* **niningwaja'aan**; *prt* **nengwaja'ang**
ningwaja'ige *vai* hoe; *1sg* **niningwaja'ige**; *prt* **nengwaja'iged**
ningwakamigin *vta* put s.o. under the ground; *1sg* **niningwakamiginaa**; *prt* **nengwakamiginaad**
ningwaanakwad *vii* be cloudy; *prt* **nengwaanakwak**
ninik /**-nik-**/ *nid* my arm; *pl* **ninikan**; *loc* **ninikaang**
nining /**-ningwy-**/ *nid* my armpit; *pl* **niningwiin**; *loc* **niningwiing**
niningwan *nad* my son-in-law; *pl* **niningwanag**
niningwanis /**-ningwanis-**/ *nad* my cross-nephew (male's sister's son or female's brother's son); *pl* **niningwanisag**
niningwiigan /**-ningwiigan-**/ *nid* my wing; *pl* **niningwiiganan**; *loc* **niningwiiganaang**
nininj /**-ninjy-**/ *nid* my hand, my finger; *pl* **nininjiin**; *loc* **nininjiing**; *dim* **nininjiins**
nininjiins /**-ninjiins-**/ *nid* my finger; *pl* **nininjiinsan**; *loc* **nininjiinsing**
ninishiwag /**-nishiw-**/ *nad* my testicles *plural*; *loc* **ninishiwaang**
niniigi'igoog /**-niigi'igw-**/ *nad* my parents *plural*
niniijaanis /**-niijaanis-**/ *nad* my child; *pl* **niniijaanisag**; *dim* **niniijaanisens**
niniishk /**-niishkw-**/ *nad* my gland (lymph node); *pl* **niniishkwag**
ninoshenh /**-nosheny-**/ *nad* my parallel aunt (mother's sister); *pl* **ninoshenyag**
ninow /**-now-**/ *nid* my cheek; *pl* **ninowan**; *loc* **ninowaang**
ninoogan /**-noogan-**/ *nid* my hip; *pl* **ninooganan**; *loc* **ninooganaang**
nipan /**-pan-**/ *nid* my lung; *pl* **nipanan**; *loc* **nipaning**
nipigemag /**-pigemagw-**/ *nid* my rib; *pl* **nipigemagoon**; *loc* **nipigemagong**
nipikwan /**-pikwan-**/ *nid* my back; *pl* **nipikwanan**; *loc* **nipikwanaang**
nisawa'ogaan *ni* lodge with peaked roof; *pl* **nisawa'ogaanan**; *loc* **nisawa'ogaaning**; *dim* **nisawa'ogaanens**
nisawayi'ii *pc* in between it
nisayenh /**-sayeny-**/ *nad* my older brother, my older male parallel cousin; *pl* **nisayenyag**
nisaabaawe *vai* get wet; *1sg* **ninisaabaawe**; *prt* **nesaabaawed**
nisaabaawe *vii* get wet; *prt* **nesaabaaweg**; *aug* **nisaabaawemagad**; *prt aug* **nesaabaawemagak**
nishi /**niS-**/ *vta* kill s.o.; *1sg* **ninisaa**; *prt* **nesaad**
nishimis /**-shimis-**/ *nad* my cross-niece (female's brother's daughter or male's sister's daughter); *pl* **nishimisag**
nishiwe *vai* kill people; *1sg* **ninishiwe**; *prt* **neshiwed**
nishiime /**-shiimey-**/ *nad* my younger sibling, my younger brother, my younger sister, my younger parallel cousin; *pl* **nishiimeyag**
nishkanzh /**-shkanzhy-**/ *nad* my nail (fingernail, toenail), my claw; *pl* **nishkanzhiig**; *loc* **nishkanzhiing**
nishkatay /**-shkatay-**/ *nid* my skin
nishkaadizi *vai* be angry, be mad; *1sg* **ninishkaadiz**; *prt* **neshkaadizid**

nishkaajitaa *vai* behave angrily, act up in anger; *1sg* **ninishkaajitaa**; *prt* **neshkaajitaad**

nishkendam *vai2* feel angry, feel mad; *1sg* **ninishkendam**; *prt* **neshkendang**

nishkenim *vta* be angry at s.o., be mad at s.o.; *1sg* **ninishkenimaa**; *prt* **neshkenimaad**

nishki' *vta* anger s.o., make s.o. mad; *1sg* **ninishki'aa**; *prt* **neshki'aad**

nishki'idiwag /nishki'idi-/ *vai* they anger each other, they make each other mad; *1pl* **ninishki'idimin**; *prt* **neshki'idijig**

nishkim *vta* anger s.o. by speech, speak and make s.o. mad; *1sg* **ninishkimaa**; *prt* **neshkimaad**

nishkitaa *vai* anger people, make people mad; *1sg* **ninishkitaa**; *prt* **neshkitaad**

nishkiinzhig /-shkiinzhigw-/ *nid* my eye; *pl* **nishkiinzhigoon**; *loc* **nishkiinzhigong**

nishkoonzh *nid* my snout

nishtigwaan /-shtigwaan-/ *nid* my head; *pl* **nishtigwaanan**; *loc* **nishtigwaaning**

nishtigwaanigegan /-shtigwaanigegan-/ *nid* my skull; *pl* **nishtigwaanigeganan**

nishwanaajichige *vai* waste things, spoil things, destroy things; *1sg* **ninishwanaajichige**; *prt* **neshwanaajichiged**

nishwanaaji' *vta* waste s.o., spoil s.o., destroy s.o.; *1sg* **ninishwanaaji'aa**; *prt* **neshwanaaji'aad**

nishwanaajitoon *vti2* waste s.t., spoil s.t., destroy s.t.; *1sg* **ninishwanaajitoon**; *prt* **neshwanaajitood**

nishwaaching* *pc* eight times; *also* **ishwaaching**

nishwaachinoon* /nishwaachin-/ *vii* they are eight; *prt* **neshwaachingin**; *also* **ishwaachinoon**

nishwaachiwag* /nishwaachi-/ *vai* they are eight; *1pl* **ninishwaachimin**; *prt* **neshwaachijig**; *also* **ishwaachiwag**

nishwaasimidana* *nm* eighty; *also* **ishwaasimidana**

nishwaaso-* *pv4* eight; *also* **ishwaaso-**

nishwaaso-anama'e-giizhik* *pc* eight weeks; *also* **ishwaaso-anama'e-giizhik**

nishwaaso-biboon* *pc* eight years; *also* **ishwaaso-biboon**

nishwaaso-biboonagad* *vii* be eight years; *prt* **neshwaaso-biboonagak**; *also* **ishwaaso-biboonagad**

nishwaaso-biboonagizi* *vai* be eight years old; *1sg* **ninishwaaso-biboonagiz**; *prt* **neshwaaso-biboonagizid**; *also* **ishwaaso-biboonagizi**

nishwaaso-diba'igan* *pc* eight miles, eight hours; *also* **ishwaaso-diba'igan**

nishwaaso-diba'iganed* *vii* be eight o'clock; *prt* **neshwaaso-diba'iganek**; *also* **ishwaaso-diba'iganed**

nishwaaso-diba'igaans* *pc* eight minutes, eight acres; *also* **ishwaaso-diba'igaans**

nishwaaso-dibik* *pc* eight nights; *also* **ishwaaso-dibik**

nishwaaso-giizhik* *pc* eight days; *also* **ishwaaso-giizhik**

nishwaaso-giizis* *pc* eight months; *also* **ishwaaso-giizis**

nishwaasogon* *pc* eight days; *also* **ishwaasogon**

nishwaasogonagad* *vii* be eight days; *prt* **neshwaasogonagak**; *also* **ishwaasogonagad**

nishwaasogonagizi* *vai* be the eighth day of the month, be eight days old; *prt* **neshwaasogonagizid**; *also* **ishwaasogonagizi**

nishwaasoninj* *pc* eight inches; *also* **ishwaasoninj**

nishwaasosagoons* *nm* eight thousand; *also* **ishwaasosagoons**

nishwaasozid* *pc* eight feet; *also* **ishwaasozid**

nishwaasoobii'igan* *na* eight (card); *pl* **nishwaasoobii'iganag**; *also* **ishwaasoobii'igan**

nishwaasooshkin *pc* eight bags; *also* **ishwaasooshkin**

nishwaaswaabik* *pc* eight dollars; *also* **ishwaaswaabik**

nishwaaswaak* *nm* eight hundred; *also* **ishwaaswaak**

nishwaaswewaan* *pc* eight sets, eight pairs; *also* **ishwaaswewaan**

nishwaaswi* *nm* eight; *also* **ishwaaswi**

nisidawinan *vti* recognize s.t. by sight; *1sg* **ninisidawinaan**; *prt* **nesidawinang**

nisidawinaw *vta* recognize s.o. by sight; *1sg* **ninisidawinawaa**; *prt* **nesidawinawaad**

nisidawinaadiwag /nisidawinaadi-/ *vai* they recognize each other; *1pl* **ninisidawinaadimin**; *prt* **nesidawinaadijig**

nisidiwag /nisidi-/ *vai* they kill each other; *1pl* **ninisidimin**; *prt* **nesidijig**

nisidizo *vai* kill oneself, commit suicide; *1sg* **ninisidiz**; *prt* **nesidizod**

nisidomaam *vta* recognize s.o. by smell; *1sg* **ninisidomaamaa**; *prt* **nesidomaamaad**

nisidomaandan *vti* recognize s.t. by smell; *1sg* **ninisidomaandaan**; *prt* **nesidomaandang**

nisidotam *vai2* understand; *1sg* **ninisidotam**; *prt* **nesidotang**

nisidotan *vti* understand s.t., recognize s.t. by sound; *1sg* **ninisidotaan**; *prt* **nesidotang**

nisidotaw *vta* understand s.o., recognize s.o. by sound; *1sg* **ninisidotawaa**; *prt* **nesidotawaad**

nisidotaadiwag /nisidotaadi-/ *vai* they understand each other; *1pl* **ninisidotaadimin**; *prt* **nesidotaadijig**

nisidotaagozi *vai* be understood; *prt* **nesidotaagozid**

nisidotaagwad *vii* be understood; *prt* **nesidotaagwak**

nisimidana *nm* thirty

nisinoon /nisin-/ *vii* they are three; *prt* **nesingin**

nising *pc* three times, thrice

nisiwag /nisi-/ *vai* they are three; *1pl* **ninisimin**; *prt* **nesijig**

niso- *pv4* three

niso-anama'e-giizhigad *vii* be three weeks; *prt* **neso-anama'e-giizhigak**

niso-anama'e-giizhik *pc* three weeks

niso-biboon *pc* three years

niso-biboonagad *vii* be three years; *prt* **neso-biboonagak**

niso-biboonagizi *vai* be three years old; *1sg* **niniso-biboonagiz**; *prt* **neso-biboonagizid**

niso-diba'igan *pc* three hours, three miles

niso-diba'iganed *vii* be three o'clock; *prt* **neso-diba'iganek**

niso-diba'igaans *pc* three minutes, three acres
niso-dibik *pc* three nights
niso-giizhik *pc* three days
niso-giizis *pc* three months
nisogon *pc* three days
nisogonagad *vii* be three days; *prt* **nesogonagak**
nisogonagizi *vai* be the third day of the month, be three days old; *prt* **nesogonagizid**
nisoninj *pc* three inches
nisosagoons *nm* three thousand
nisozid *pc* three feet
nisoobii'igan *na* three (card), trey; *pl* **nisoobii'iganag**
nisooshkin *pc* three bags
niswaabik *pc* three dollars
niswaak *nm* three hundred
niswaakodaabaan *ni* travois; *pl* **niswaakodaabaanan**
niswewaan *pc* three sets, three pairs
niswi *nm* three
nitam *pc* first
nitamaw *vta* kill (s.t.) for s.o.; *1sg* **ninitamawaa**; *prt* **netamawaad**
nitamaage *vai* kill (s.t.) for people; *1sg* **ninitamaage**; *prt* **netamaaged**
nitamaazo *vai* kill (s.t.) for oneself; *1sg* **ninitamaaz**; *prt* **netamaazod**
nitamige *vai* live in the first house; *1sg* **ninitamige**; *prt* **netamiged**
nitamoozhaan *na* eldest child, first-born; *pl* **nitamoozhaanag**; *dim* **nitamoozhaanens**
nitawag /-tawag-/ *nid* my ear; *pl* **nitawagan**; *loc* **nitawagaang**
nitaa- *pv4* know how to do something, being good at, being skilled at, frequently do
nitaage *vai* kill game, mourn; *1sg* **ninitaage**; *prt* **netaaged**
nitaawe *vai* be skilled in speaking or singing; *1sg* **ninitaawe**; *prt* **netaawed**
nitaawichige *vai* be skilled at things, know how to make things; *1sg* **ninitaawichige**; *prt* **netaawichiged**
nitaawigi *vai* grow up; *1sg* **ninitaawig**; *prt* **netaawigid**
nitaawigi' *vta* grow s.o., raise s.o. (e.g., a child); *1sg* **ninitaawigi'aa**; *prt* **netaawigi'aad**
nitaawigin *vii* grow up; *prt* **netaawiging**
nitaawigitoon *vti2* grow s.t., raise s.t. (e.g., a crop); *1sg* **ninitaawigitoon**; *prt* **netaawigitood**
nitaawi' *vta* know how to make s.o.; *1sg* **ninitaawi'aa**; *prt* **netaawi'aad**
nitaawitoon *vti2* know how to make s.t.; *1sg* **ninitaawitoon**; *prt* **netaawitood**
nitoon *vti2* kill s.t.; *1sg* **ninitoon**; *prt* **netood**
niwiidigemaagan /-wiidigemaagan-/ *na* my spouse, my wife, my husband, my companion; *pl* **niwiidigemaaganag**
niwiiw /-wiiw-/ *nad* my wife; *pl* **niwiiwag**
niibawi *vai* stand; *1sg* **niniibaw**; *prt* **naabawid**
niibawi' *vta* make s.o. stand up; *1sg* **niniibawi'aa**; *prt* **naabawi'aad**
niibawitoon *vti2* make s.t. stand up; *1sg* **niniibawitoon**; *prt* **naabawitood**
niibaa- *pv4* at night

niibaa-anama'e-giizhigad *vii* be Christmas; *prt* **naabaa-anama'e-giizhigak**
niibaabizo *vai* drive at night; *1sg* **niniibaabiz**; *prt* **naabaabizod**
niibaa-dibik *pc* late at night
niibaashkaa *vai* travel at night; *1sg* **niniibaashkaa**; *prt* **naabaashkaad**
niibid /-iibid-/ *nid* my tooth; *pl* **niibidan**; *loc* **niibidaang**
niibidebiwag /niibidebi-/ *vai* they sit side by side in a row; *1pl* **niniibidebimin**; *prt* **naabidebijig**
niibideshinoog /niibideshin-/ *vai* they lie side-by-side in a row; *1pl* **niniibideshinimin**; *prt* **naabideshingig**
niibidesinoon /niibidesin-/ *vii* they lie side by side in a row; *prt* **naabidesingin**
niibidoon *vti2* weave s.t.; *1sg* **niniibidoon**; *prt* **naabidood**
niibin *vii* be summer; *prt* **naabing**
niibinaakwaanininj *ni* finger; *pl* **niibinaakwaanininjiin**; *loc* **niibinakwaanininjiing**; *dim* **niibinaakwaanininjiins**
niibinaakwaanizidaan *ni* toe; *pl* **niibinaakwaanizidaanan**; *loc* **niibinaakwaanizidaaning**; *dim* **niibinaakwaanizidaanens**
niibinishi *vai* spend the summer somewhere; *1sg* **niniibinish**; *prt* **naabinishid**
niibinishiiwigamig *ni* cottage, resort; *pl* **niibinishiiwigamigoon**; *loc* **niibinishiiwigamigong**; *dim* **niibinishiiwigamigoons**
niibinong *pc* last summer
niibowa *pc* many, much; *also* **niibiwa***
niibowagadoon /niibowagad-/ *vii* they are many, there is much of it; *prt* **naabowagakin**
niibowagiziwag /niibowagizi-/ *vai* they are many, there is much of it; *prt* **naabowagizijig**
niigaan *pc* ahead, leading, at the front
niigaanabi *vai* sit in front; *1sg* **niniigaanab**; *prt* **naagaanabid**
niigaanagoode *vii* hang in front; *prt* **naagaanagoodeg**; *aug* **niigaanagoodemagad**; *prt aug* **naagaanagoodemagak**
niigaanagoozh /niigaanagooN-/ *vta* hang s.o. in front; *1sg* **niniigaanagoonaa**; *prt* **naagaanagoonaad**
niigaanagoodoon *vti2* hang s.t. in front; *1sg* **niniigaanagoodoon**; *prt* **naagaanagoodood**
niigaanagoojin *vai* hang in front; *prt* **naagaanagoojing**
niigaanigaabawi *vai* stand in front; *1sg* **niniigaanigaabaw**; *prt* **naagaanigaabawid**
niigaaniwizh /nigaaniwiN-/ *vta* lead s.o.; *1sg* **niniigaaniwinaa**; *prt* **naagaaniwinaad**
niigaanii *vai* go ahead, lead; *1sg* **niniigaanii**; *prt* **naagaaniid**
niigi *vai* be born, increase in number; *1sg* **niniig**; *prt* **naagid**
niigi' *vta* bear s.o., make s.o. grow, make s.o. increase in number; *1sg* **niniigi'aa**; *prt* **naagi'aad**
niigitoon *vti2* make s.t. grow, make s.t. increase in number; *1sg* **niniigitoon**; *prt* **naagitood**

niigode *vii* break by heat; *prt* naagodeg; *aug*
niigodemagad; *prt aug* naagodemagak
niigoshin *vai* break on impact; *prt* naagoshing
niigoshkan *vti* break s.t. with foot or body; *1sg*
niniigoshkaan; *prt* naagoshkang
niigoshkaa *vii* be broken; *prt* naagoshkaag; *aug*
niigoshkaamagad; *prt aug* naagoshkaamagak
niigosidoon *vti2* break s.t. by dropping; *1sg*
niniigosidoon; *prt* naagosidood
niigosin *vii* break on impact; *prt* naagosing
niigozo *vai* break by heat; *prt* naagozod
niiji- *pn* my fellow
niijikiwenh /-iijikiweny-/ *nad* my (male's) brother,
my (male's) male friend; *pl* niijikiwenyag
niijikwe /-iijikwew-/ *nad* my (female's) female
friend; *pl* niijikweg
niijii *nad* my friend *vocative form, usually male to
male*
niijiinini *nad* my fellow man
niikaan /-iikaan-/ *nad* my (male's) male friend
ritual use, my (male's) brother *ritual use*; *pl*
niikaanag
niikaanis /-iikaanis-/ *nad* my (male's) brother *ritual
use*, my (male's) male friend *ritual use*; *pl*
niikaanisag
niikimo *vai* growl (of a dog); *1sg* niniikim; *prt*
naakimod
niima' /niima'w-/ *vta* pick s.o. up using something,
carry s.o. using something; *1sg* niniima'waa;
prt naama'waad
niima'an *vti* pick s.t. up using something, carry s.t.
using something; *1sg* niniima'aan; *prt*
naama'ang
niimam *vta* pick s.o. up in mouth, carry s.o. in
mouth; *1sg* niniimamaa; *prt* naamamaad
niimandan *vti* pick s.t. up in mouth, carry s.t. in
mouth; *1sg* niniimandaan; *prt* naamandang
niimaakwa' /niimaakwa'w-/ *vta* pick s.o. up (as or
as with something stick- or wood-like); *1sg*
niniimaakwa'waa; *prt* naamaakwa'waad
niimaakwa'an *vti* pick s.t. up (as or as with
something stick- or wood-like); *1sg*
niniimaakwa'aan; *prt* naamaakwa'ang
niimi *vai* dance; *1sg* niniim; *prt* naamid
niimibaashkizigane *vai* take along a gun; *1sg*
niniimibaashkizigane; *prt*
naamibaashkiziganed
niimidana *nm* forty
niimi'idii-nagamon *ni* dance song; *pl* niimi'idii-
nagamonan
niimi' *vta* make s.o. dance; *1sg* niniimi'aa; *prt*
naami'aad
niimi'idiwag /niimi'idi-/ *vai* they dance; *1pl*
niniimi'idimin; *prt* naami'idijig
niimi'idiiwigamig *ni* dance hall; *pl*
niimi'idiiwigamigoon; *loc*
niimi'idiiwigamigong; *dim*
niimi'idiiwigamigoons
niimi'iwe *vai* give a dance; *1sg* niniimi'iwe; *prt*
naami'iwed
niimikaw *vta* dance for s.o.; *1sg* niniimikawaa; *prt*
naamikawaad
niimikaage *vai* dance for people (for a purpose);
1sg niniimikaage; *prt* naamikaaged
niin *pr* I, me *first person singular personal pronoun*

niinag /-iinag-/ *nid* my penis; *loc* niinagaang
niinamad *vii* be weak; *prt* naanamak
niinaminaagozi *vai* look weak; *1sg*
niniinaminaagoz; *prt* naanaminaagozid
niinaminaagwad *vii* look weak; *prt*
naanaminaagwak
niinamizi *vai* be weak, be frail; *1sg* niniinamiz; *prt*
naanamizid
niinawind *pr* we *first person exclusive plural pronoun*,
us *first person exclusive plural pronoun*
niindaa' *vta* send (s.t.) to s.o.; *1sg* niniindaa'aa; *prt*
naandaa'aad
niindaa'iwe *vai* send (s.t.) to people; *1sg*
niniindaa'iwe; *prt* naandaa'iwed
niineta *pr* only me *first person singular personal
pronoun*
niinetawind *pr* only us *first person exclusive plural
personal pronoun*
niingidawadamon /niingidawadamo-/ *vii* fork (as
a road or trail); *prt* naangidawadamog
niingidawitigweyaa *vii* fork (as a river); *prt*
naangidawitigweyaag; *aug*
niingidawitigweyaamagad; *prt aug*
naangidawitigweyaamagak
niinim /-iinimw-/ *nad* my sibling-in-law of the opposite sex, my (female's) brother-in-law, my
(male's) sister-in-law; *pl* niinimoog
niinimoshenh /-iinimosheny-/ *nad* my sweetheart,
my cross-cousin of the opposite sex; *pl*
niinimoshenyag
niinindib /-iinindib-/ *nid* my brain; *loc*
niinindibaang
niinitam *pr* my turn *first person singular personal
pronoun*
niinitamawind *pr* our turn *first person exclusive
plural personal pronoun*
niinizis /-iinisiz-/ *nid* my (strand of) hair; *pl*
niinizisan; *loc* niinizising
niinzob /-iinzoby-/ *nid* my gallbladder; *pl*
niinzobiin; *loc* niinzobiing
niisayi'ii *pc* down from it
niisaajiwan *pc* downstream
niisaakiiwe *vai* go downhill; *1sg* niniisaakiiwe; *prt*
naasaakiiwed
niisaakiiwebatoo *vai* run downhill; *1sg*
niniisaakiiwebatoo; *prt* naasaakiiwebatood
niisaandawe *vai* climb down, go downstairs; *1sg*
niniisaandawe; *prt* naasaandawed
niisaandawebatoo *vai* run down; *1sg*
niniisaandawebatoo; *prt*
naasaandawebatood
niisaandawebizo *vai* climb down fast; *1sg*
niniisaandawebiz; *prt* naasaandawebizod
niisaanendam *vai* feel depressed; *1sg*
niniisaanendam; *prt* naasaanendang
niishtana *nm* twenty
niishtana-ashi-niizh *ni* twenty-two (gun)
niisibidoon *vti2* pull s.t. down, tear s.t. down; *1sg*
niniisibidoon; *prt* naasibidood
niisibizh /niisibiN-/ *vta* pull s.o. down, tear s.o.
down; *1sg* niniisibinaa; *prt* naasibinaad
niisiiwe-minjikaawan *na* glove; *pl* niisiiwe-
minjikaawanag
niisiiwezh /niisiiwezhw-/ *vta* cut fringe in s.o.; *1sg*
niniisiiwezhwaa; *prt* naasiiwezhwaad

niisiiwezhan *vti* cut fringe in s.t.; *1sg*
  niniisiiwezhaan; *prt* **naasiiwezhang**
niisiiwezhigan *ni* fringe; *pl* **niisiiwezhiganan;** *loc*
  niisiiwezhiganing; *dim* **niisiiwezhigaans**
niisiiwezhigaade *vii* be fringed; *prt*
  naasiiwezhigaadeg; *aug*
  niisiiwezhigaademagad; *prt aug*
  naasiiwezhigaademagak
niisiiwezhigaazo *vai* be fringed; *prt*
  naasiiwezhigaazod
niiskaadad *vii* be bad weather; *prt* **naaskaadak**
niiskindibe *vai* have messy hair; *1sg* **niniiskindibe;**
  prt **naaskindibed**
niitaa /-**iitaaw-**/ *nad* my (male's) brother-in-law; *pl*
  niitaag
niitaawis /-**iitaawis-**/ *nad* my (male's) male cross-
  cousin (male's father's sister's son or male's
  mother's brother's son); *pl* **niitaawisag**
niiwana' /niiwana'w-/ *vta* slaughter s.o., beat s.o.
  to death; *1sg* **niniiwana'waa;** *prt*
  naawana'waad
niiwanishin *vai* die in an accident; *1sg*
  niniiwanishin; *prt* **naawanishing**
niiwaabik *pc* four dollars
niiwaak *nm* four hundred
niiwewaan *pc* four sets, four pairs
niiwezh /niiweN-/ *vta* defeat s.o. in a contest or
  game, beat s.o.; *1sg* **niniiwenaa;** *prt*
  naawenaad
niiwezhiwe *vai* defeat people in a contest or game;
  1sg **niniiwezhiwe;** *prt* **naawezhiwed**
niiwin *nm* four
niiwing *pc* four times
niiwinoon /niiwin-/ *vii* they are four; *prt* **naawingin**
niiwiwag /niiwi-/ *vai* they are four; *1pl* **niniiwimin;**
  prt **naawijig**
niiwo- *pv4* four; *also* **niiyo-**
niiwo-anama'e-giizhigad *vii* be four weeks; *prt*
  naawo-anama'e-giizhigak; *also* **niiyo-
  anama'e-giizhigad**
niiwo-anama'e-giizhik *pc* four weeks; *also* **niiyo-
  anama'e-giizhik**
niiwo-biboon *pc* four years; *also* **niiyo-biboon**
niiwo-biboonagad *vii* be four years; *prt* **naawo-
  biboonagak;** *also* **niiyo-biboonagad**
niiwo-biboonagizi *vai* be four years old; *1sg*
  niniiwo-biboonagiz; *prt* **naawo-biboonagizid;**
  also **niiyo-biboonagizi**
niiwo-diba'igan *pc* four hours, four miles; *also*
  niiyo-diba'igan
niiwo-diba'igaans *pc* four minutes, four acres; *also*
  niiyo-diba'igaans
niiwo-dibik *pc* four nights; *also* **niiyo-dibik**
niiwo-giizhigad *vii* be Thursday; *prt* **naawo-
  giizhigak;** *also* **niiyo-giizhigad**
niiwo-giizhik *pc* four days; *also* **niiyo-giizhik**
niiwo-giizis *pc* four months; *also* **niiyo-giizis**
niiwogon *pc* four days; *also* **niiyogon**
niiwogonagad *vii* be four days; *prt*
  naawogonagak; *also* **niiyogonagad**
niiwogonagizi *vai* be the fourth day of the month,
  be four days old; *prt* **naawogonagizid;** *also*
  niiyogonagizi
niiwoninj *pc* four inches; *also* **niiyoninj**

niiwosagoons *nm* four thousand; *also*
  niiyosagoons
niiwozid *pc* four feet; *also* **niiyozid**
niiwoobii'igan *na* four (card); *pl* **niiwoobii'iganag;**
  also **niiyoobii'igan**
niiwooshkin *pc* four bags; *also* **niiyooshkin**
niiyaw /-iiyaw-/ *nid* my body; *pl* **niiyawan;** *loc*
  niiyawing
niiyawen'enh /-iiyawen'eny-/ *nad* my namesake
  (reciprocal relationship between name-giving
  sponsor and child); *pl* **niiyawen'enyag**
niiyaas /-iiyaas-/ *nid* my flesh, my meat (of the
  body); *loc* **niiyaasing**
niiyo- *pv4* four; *also* **niiwo-**
niiyo-anama'e-giizhigad *vii* be four weeks; *prt*
  naayo-anama'e-giizhigak; *also* **niiwo-
  anama'e-giizhigad**
niiyo-anama'e-giizhik *pc* four weeks; *also* **niiwo-
  anama'e-giizhik**
niiyo-biboon *pc* four years; *also* **niiwo-biboon**
niiyo-biboonagad *vii* be four years; *prt* **naayo-
  biboonagak;** *also* **niiwo-biboonagad**
niiyo-biboonagizi *vai* be four years old; *1sg*
  niniiyo-biboonagiz; *prt* **naayo-biboonagizid;**
  also **niiwo-biboonagizi**
niiyo-diba'igan *pc* four hours, four miles; *also*
  niiwo-diba'igan
niiyo-diba'iganed *vii* be four o'clock; *prt* **naayo-
  diba'iganek;** *also* **niiwo-diba'iganed**
niiyo-diba'igaans *pc* four minutes, four acres; *also*
  niiwo-diba'igaans
niiyo-dibik *pc* four nights; *also* **niiwo-dibik**
niiyo-giizhigad *vii* be Thursday; *prt* **naayo-
  giizhigak;** *also* **niiwo-giizhigad**
niiyo-giizhik *pc* four days; *also* **niiwo-giizhik**
niiyo-giizis *pc* four months; *also* **niiwo-giizis**
niiyogon *pc* four days; *also* **niiwogon**
niiyogonagad *vii* be four days; *prt* **naayogonagak;**
  also **niiwogonagad**
niiyogonagizi *vai* be the fourth day of the month,
  be four days old; *prt* **naayogonagizid;** *also*
  niiwogonagizi
niiyoninj *pc* four inches; *also* **niiwoninj**
niiyosagoons *nm* four thousand; *also*
  niiwosagoons
niiyoobii'igan *na* four (card); *pl* **niiyoobii'iganag;**
  also **niiwoobii'igan**
niizh *nm* two
niizhing *pc* two times, twice
niizhinoon /niizhin-/ *vii* they are two; *prt*
  naazhingin
niizhiwag /niizhi-/ *vai* they are two; *1pl*
  niniizhimin; *prt* **naazhijig**
niizho- *pv4* two
niizho-anama'e-giizhigad *pc* be two weeks
niizho-anama'e-giizhik *pc* two weeks
niizho-biboon *pc* two years
niizho-biboonagad *vii* be two years; *prt* **naazho-
  biboonagak**
niizho-biboonagizi *vai* be two years old; *1sg*
  niniizho-biboonagiz; *prt* **naazho-
  biboonagizid**
niizho-diba'igan *pc* two hours, two miles
niizho-diba'iganed *vii* be two o'clock; *prt* **naazho-
  diba'iganek**

niizho-diba'igaans *pc* two minutes, two acres
niizho-dibik *pc* two nights
niizho-giizhigad *vii* be Tuesday; *prt* naazho-giizhigak
niizho-giizhik *pc* two days
niizho-giizis *pc* two months
niizhogon *pc* two days
niizhogonagad *vii* be two days; *prt* naazhogonagak
niizhogonagizi *vai* be the second day of the month, be two days old; *prt* naazhogonagizid
niizhoninj *pc* two inches
niizhosagoons *nm* two thousand
niizhozid *pc* two feet
niizhoobii'igan *na* deuce, two (card); *pl* niizhoobii'iganag
niizhoodenh *na* twin; *pl* niizhoodenyag
niizhooshkin *pc* two bags
niizhwaabik *pc* two dollars
niizhwaaching *pc* seven times
niizhwaachinoon /niizhwaachin-/ *vii* they are seven; *prt* naazhwaachingin
niizhwaachiwag /niizhwaachi-/ *vai* they are seven; *1pl* niniizhwaachimin; *prt* naazhwaachijig
niizhwaak *nm* two hundred
niizhwaasimidana *nm* seventy
niizhwaaso- *pv4* seven
niizhwaaso-anama'e-giizhigad *pc* be seven weeks
niizhwaaso-anama'e-giizhik *pc* seven weeks
niizhwaaso-biboon *pc* seven years
niizhwaaso-biboonagad *vii* be seven years; *prt* naazhwaaso-biboonagak
niizhwaaso-biboonagizi *vai* be seven years old; *1sg* niniizhwaaso-biboonagiz; *prt* naazhwaaso-biboonagizid
niizhwaaso-diba'igan *pc* seven hours, seven miles
niizhwaaso-diba'iganed *vii* be seven o'clock; *prt* naazhwaaso-diba'iganek
niizhwaaso-diba'igaans *pc* seven minutes, seven acres
niizhwaaso-dibik *pc* seven nights
niizhwaaso-giizhik *pc* seven days
niizhwaaso-giizis *pc* seven months
niizhwaasogon *pc* seven days
niizhwaasogonagad *vii* be seven days; *prt* naazhwaasogonagak
niizhwaasogonagizi *vai* be the seventh day of the month, be seven days old; *prt* naazhwaasogonagizid
niizhwaasoninj *pc* seven inches
niizhwaasosagoons *nm* seven thousand
niizhwaasozid *pc* seven feet
niizhwaasoobii'igan *na* seven (card); *pl* niizhwaasoobii'iganag
niizhwaasooshkin *pc* seven bags
niizhwaaswaabik *pc* seven dollars
niizhwaaswaak *nm* seven hundred
niizhwaaswewaan *pc* seven sets, seven pairs
niizhwaaswi *nm* seven
niizhwewaan *pc* two sets, two pairs
noodamikwe *vai* hunt beaver, trap beaver; *1sg* ninoodamikwe; *prt* nwaadamikwed
noodendam *vai2* flirt; *1sg* ninoodendam; *prt* nwaadendang
noodin *vii* be windy, there is a wind; *prt* nwaading

noogibatoo *vai* stop running; *1sg* ninoogibatoo; *prt* nwaagibatood
noogibide *vii* stop speeding, stop driving; *prt* nwaagibideg; *aug* noogibidemagad; *prt aug* nwaagibidemagak
noogibizo *vai* stop speeding, stop driving; *1sg* ninoogibiz; *prt* nwaagibizod
noogigaabawi *vai* stop and stand in place; *1sg* ninoogigaabaw; *prt* nwaagigaabawid
noogin *vta* stop s.o. by hand; *1sg* ninooginaa; *prt* nwaaginaad
nooginan *vti* stop s.t. by hand; *1sg* ninooginaan; *prt* nwaaginang
noogise *vai* come to a stop; *1sg* ninoogise; *prt* nwaagised
noogishkaa *vai* stop (moving); *1sg* ninoogishkaa; *prt* nwaagishkaad
noogishkaa *vii* stop (moving); *prt* nwaagishkaag; *aug* noogishkaamagad; *prt aug* nwaagishkaamagak
noogishkaawigamig *ni* hotel; *pl* noogishkaawigamigoon; *loc* noogishkaawigamigong; *dim* noogishkaawigamigoons
noojigiigoonyiwe *vai* go fishing; *1sg* ninoojigiigoonyiwe; *prt* nwaajigiigoonyiwed
nooji' *vta* seek s.o., go after s.o., hunt for s.o.; *1sg* ninooji'aa; *prt* nwaaji'aad
nooji'iwe *vai* seek people, hunt for people; *1sg* ninooji'iwe; *prt* nwaaji'iwed
noojimo *vai* recover from an illness; *1sg* ninoojim; *prt* nwaajimod
noojitoon *vti2* seek s.t., go after s.t., hunt for s.t.; *1sg* ninoojitoon; *prt* nwaajitood
noojiikwewe *vai* actively seek the company of women; *1sg* ninoojiikwewe; *prt* nwaajiikwewed
nookaa *vii* be soft, be tender; *prt* nwaakaag; *aug* nookaamagad; *prt aug* nwaakaamagak
nookaabaawe *vai* be softened in water; *prt* nwaakaabaawed
nookaabaawe *vii* be softened in water; *prt* nwaakaabaaweg; *aug* nookaabaawemagad; *prt aug* nwaakaabaawemagak
nookaadad *vii* be mild; *prt* nwaakaadak
nookaadizi *vai* be meek, be mild; *1sg* ninookaadiz; *prt* nwaakaadizid
nookide *vii* be cooked tender; *prt* nwaakideg; *aug* nookidemagad; *prt aug* nwaakidemagak
nookiz /nookizw-/ *vta* cook s.o. tender; *1sg* ninookizwaa; *prt* nwaakizwaad
nookizan *vti* cook s.t. tender; *1sg* ninookizaan; *prt* nwaakizang
nookizi *vai* be soft, be tender; *prt* nwaakizid
nookizo *vai* be cooked tender; *prt* nwaakizod
nookiigad *vii* be soft (as something sheet-like); *prt* nwaakiigak
nookiigizi *vai* be soft (as something sheet-like); *prt* nwaakiigizid
nookomis /-ookomis-/ *nad* my grandmother; *pl* nookomisag
nookoo *nad* grandma *vocative form of* nookomis my grandmother
nookwezan *vti* burn s.t. as medicine; *1sg* ninookwezaan; *prt* nwaakwezang

nookwezigan *ni* medicine for burning; *pl*
    nookweziganan
nookwezige *vai* burn things as medicine; *1sg*
    ninookwezige; *prt* **nwaakweziged**
noomag *pc* for a spell, a short while
noomaya *pc* recently
noomininjii *vai* put lotion on one's hand; *1sg*
    ninoomininjii; *prt* **nwaamininjiid**
noomininjiiwin *ni* hand lotion; *pl*
    noomininjiiwinan
noonaawaso *vai* nurse a child; *1sg* **ninoonaawas**;
    prt **nwaanaawasod**
noondam *vai2* hear; *1sg* **ninoondam**; *prt*
    nwaandang
noondan *vti* hear s.t.; *1sg* **ninoondaan**; *prt*
    nwaandang
noondaw *vta* hear s.o.; *1sg* **ninoondawaa**; *prt*
    nwaandawaad
noondaagochigan *ni* musical instrument (espe-
    cially a wind instrument), whistle, horn,
    harmonica; *pl* **noondaagochiganan**; *loc*
    noondaagochiganing; *dim*
    noondaagochigaans

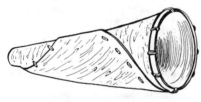

noondaagochigan (horn)

noondaagochige *vai* play a wind instrument; *1sg*
    ninoondaagochige; *prt* **nwaandaagochiged**
noondaagotoon *vti2* play s.t. as a wind instru-
    ment; *1sg* **ninoondaagotoon**; *prt*
    nwaandaagotood
noondaagozi *vai* can be heard, make noise, make
    a characteristic call (e.g., neigh, moo); *1sg*
    ninoondaagoz; *prt* **nwaandaagozid**
noondaagwad *vii* be heard, make noise; *prt*
    nwaandaagwak
noonde- *pv4* need to, before the usual time
noondesachige *vai* run short of things; *1sg*
    ninoondesachige; *prt* **nwaandesachiged**
noondesa' *vta* run short of s.o.; *1sg*
    ninoondesa'aa; *prt* **nwaandesa'aad**
noondesatoon *vti2* run short of s.t.; *1sg*
    ninoondesatoon; *prt* **nwaandesatood**
noondese *vai* run short; *1sg* **ninoondese**; *prt*
    nwaandesed
noondeshin *vai* be fatigued, be exhausted; *1sg*
    ninoondeshin; *prt* **nwaandeshing**
noongom *pc* now, today, nowadays
nooni *vai* suckle (of child or offspring); *1sg*
    ninoon; *prt* **nwaanid**
nooni' *vta* breast feed s.o.; *1sg* **ninooni'aa**; *prt*
    nwaani'aad
noopiming *pc* inland, in the woods, in the bush

noopinadoon *vti2* go after s.t., follow s.t.; *1sg*
    ninoopinadoon; *prt* **nwaapinadood**
noopinazh /**noopinaN-**/ *vta* go after s.o., follow
    s.o.; *1sg* **ninoopinanaa**; *prt* **nwaapinanaad**
noos /**-oos-**/ *nad* my father *old-fashioned*; *pl* **noosag**
nooshkaachigaade *vii* be winnowed; *prt*
    nwaashkaachigaadeg; *aug*
    nooshkaachigaademagad; *prt aug*
    nwaashkaachigaademagak
nooshkaachige *vai* winnow things (e.g., wild rice);
    1sg **ninooshkaachige**; *prt* **nwaashkaachiged**
nooshkaachinaagan *ni* winnowing tray; *pl*
    nooshkaachinaaganan; *loc*
    nooshkaachinaaganing; *dim*
    nooshkaachinaagaans

nooshkaachinaagan (winnowing tray)

nooshkaatoon *vti2* winnow s.t. (e.g., wild rice);
    1sg **ninooshkaatoon**; *prt* **nwaashkaatood**
nooskwaada' /**nooskwaada'w-**/ *vta* lick s.o.; *1sg*
    ninooskwaada'waa; *prt* **nwaaskwaada'waad**
nooskwaada'an *vti* lick s.t.; *1sg*
    ninooskwaada'aan; *prt* **nwaaskwaada'ang**
noozh /**nooN-**/ *vta* nurse s.o. (e.g., a baby); *1sg*
    ninoonaa; *prt* **nwaanaad**
noozhishenh /**-oozhisheny-**/ *nad* my grandchild; *pl*
    noozhishenyag
noozis *nad* grandchild *vocative form of*
    noozhishenh my grandchild

o= *pre third person prefix before consonants in verbs
    and nouns*
o- *pv2* go over to; *also* **a'o-, awi-**
obikwaaj *nid* bulb; *pl* **obikwaajiin**; *loc*
    obikwaajiing; *dim* **obikwaajiins**
obiigomakakii *na* toad; *pl* **obiigomakakiig**; *dim*
    obiigomakakiins
obiimiskodisii *na* snail; *pl* **obiimiskodisiig**; *dim*
    obiimiskodisiins
oboodashkwaanishiinh *na* dragonfly; *pl*
    oboodashkwaanishiinyag

od= *pre third person prefix before vowels in verbs and non-dependent nouns*

odakiimi *vai* have land; *1sg* **indoodakiim**; *prt* **wedakiimid**

odamino *vai* play; *1pl* **indoodamin**; *prt* **wedaminod**

odaminoowigamig *ni* recreation building; *pl* **odaminoowigamigoon**; *loc* **odaminoowigamigong**; *dim* **odaminoowigamigoons**

odaminwaagan *na* doll; *pl* **odaminwaaganag**; *loc* **odaminwaaganing**; *dim* **odaminwaagaans**

odaminwaagan (doll)

odaminwaagan *ni* toy, plaything; *pl* **odaminwaaganan**; *loc* **odaminwaaganing**; *dim* **odaminwaagaans**

odaminwaage *vai+o* use (s.t.) as a toy; *1sg* **indoodaminwaage, indoodaminwaagen**; *prt* **wedaminwaaged**

odasiniinsimi *vai* have gallstones; *1sg* **indoodasiniinsimi**; *prt* **wedasiniinsimid**

odatagaagomin *na* blackberry; *pl* **odatagaagominag**; *dim* **odatagaagominens**

odatagaagominagaawanzh *na* blackberry bush; *pl* **odatagaagominagaawanzhiig**; *loc* **odatagaagominagaawanzhiing**; *dim* **odatagaagominagaawanzhiins**

odayi *vai* have a dog, have a horse; *1sg* **indooday**; *prt* **wedayid**

odaabaadan *vti* drag s.t.; *1sg* **indoodaabaadaan**; *prt* **wedaabaadang**

odaabaan *na* car, wagon, sled, sleigh; *pl* **odaabaanag**; *loc* **odaabaaning**; *dim* **odaabaanens**

odaabaanikewigamig *ni* repair garage; *pl* **odaabaanikewigamigoon**; *loc* **odaabaanikewigamigong**; *dim* **odaabaanikewigamigoons**

odaabaanikewinini *na* mechanic; *pl* **odaabaanikewininiwag**

odaabaazh /odaabaaN-/ *vta* drag s.o.; *1sg* **indoodaabaanaa**; *prt* **wedaabaanaad**

odaabii *vai* drag (something); *1sg* **indoodaabii**; *prt* **wedaabiid**

odaabii' *vta* drive s.o. (e.g., a draft animal or a car); *1sg* **indoodaabii'aa**; *prt* **wedaabii'aad**

odaabii'aagan *na* draft animal; *pl* **odaabii'aaganag**; *dim* **odaabii'aagaans**

odaabii'iwe *vai* drive; *1sg* **indoodaabii'iwe**; *prt* **wedaabii'iwed**

odaabii'iwe-mazina'igaans *ni* driver's license; *pl* **odaabii'iwe-mazina'igaansan**

odaabii'iwewinini *na* driver; *pl* **odaabii'iwewininiwag**; *dim* **odaabii'iwewininiins**

odaake *vai* steer, direct affairs; *1sg* **indoodaake**; *prt* **wedaaked**

odaakewigimaa *na* director, governor; *pl* **odaakewigimaag**; *dim* **odaakewigimaans**; *also* **odaake-ogimaa**

odaani *vai* have a daughter; *1sg* **indoodaan**; *prt* **wedaanid**

odaanisi *vai* have a daughter; *1sg* **indoodaanis**; *prt* **wedaanisid**

odaapin *vta* accept s.o., take s.o. offered, pick s.o. up; *1sg* **indoodaapinaa**; *prt* **wedaapinaad**

odaapinamaw *vta* accept (s.t.) from s.o., take (s.t.) offered by s.o., pick (s.t.) up from s.o.; *1sg* **indoodaapinamawaa**; *prt* **wedaapinamawaad**

odaapinan *vti* accept s.t., take s.t. offered, pick s.t. up; *1sg* **indoodaapinaan**; *prt* **wedaapinang**

odaapinigaade *vii* be taken, be accepted; *prt* **wedaapinigaadeg**; *aug* **odaapinigaademagad**; *prt aug* **wedaapinigaademagak**

odaapinigaazo *vai* be taken, be accepted; *prt* **wedaapinigaazod**

odaapinige *vai* accept things, take things offered, pick up things; *1sg* **indoodaapinige**; *prt* **wedaapiniged**

odaapishkaa *vii* shrink; *prt* **wedaapishkaag**; *aug* **odaapishkaamagad**; *prt aug* **wedaapishkaamagak**

odaapishkaa *vai* shrink; *prt* **wedaapishkaad**

odaawaa *na* Odawa (Ottawa); *pl* **odaawaag**; *dim* **odaawaans**

odaawaamo *vai* speak Odawa (Ottawa); *1sg* **indoodaawaam**; *prt* **wedaawaamod**

ode'imin *ni* strawberry; *pl* **ode'iminan**; *dim* **ode'iminens**

ode'imini-giizis *na* June

odish /odiS-/ *vta* come up to s.o., visit s.o., reach s.o.; *1sg* **indoodisaa**; *prt* **wedisaad**

odishiwe *vai* visit people; *1sg* **indoodishiwe**; *prt* **wedishiwed**

oditan *vti* come up to s.t., reach s.t.; *1sg* **indooditaan**; *prt* **weditang**

odoodemi *vai* have a totem (clan); *1sg* **indoodoodem**; *prt* **wedoodemid**

odoodemindiwag /odoodemindi-/ *vai* they have a mutual totem (clan); *1pl* **indoodoodemindimin**; *prt* **wedoodemindijig**

odoondanegwaajigan *ni* tab at heel of moccasin; *pl* **odoondanegwaajiganan**; *dim* **odoondanegwaajigaans**

odoonibii *na* tullibee; *pl* **odoonibiig**; *dim* **odoonibiins**; *also* **odoonibiins, -ag**

ogaa *na* pickerel, walleye; *pl* **ogaawag**; *dim* **ogaans**
ogichidaa *na* warrior, ceremonial headman; *pl* **ogichidaag**
ogichidaakwe *na* ceremonial headwoman, wife of ceremonial headman; *pl* **ogichidaakweg**
ogidajiw* *pc* on top of a mountain; *also* **agidajiw, wagidajiw**
ogidakamig* *pc* on top of the ground; *also* **agidakamig, wagidakamig**
ogidasin* *pc* on top of a rock; *also* **agidasin, wagidasin**
ogidaabik* *pc* on something mineral (e.g., metal, glass, rock); *also* **agidaabik, wagidaabik**
ogidaajiwan* *pc* upstream; *also* **agidaajiwan, wagidaajiwan**
ogidaaki* *pc* on top of a hill; *also* **agidaaki, wagidaaki**
ogidibiig* *pc* on top of the water; *also* **agidibiig, wagidibiig**
ogidigamig* *pc* on top of the house; *also* **agidigamig, wagidigamig**
ogidiskwam* *pc* on top of the ice; *also* **agidiskwam, wagidiskwam**
ogijayi'ii* *pc* on top of it; *also* **agijayi'ii, wagijayi'ii**
ogiji-* *pn* on top of; *also* **agiji-, wagiji-**
ogimaa *na* chief, boss, leader; *pl* **ogimaag**; *dim* **ogimaans**
ogimaa *na* king (card); *pl* **ogimaag**
ogimaakandan *vti* rule s.t., govern s.t.; *1sg* **indoogimaakandaan**; *prt* **wegimaakandang**
ogimaakandaw *vta* rule s.o., govern s.o.; *1sg* **indoogimaakandawaa**; *prt* **wegimaakandawaad**
ogimaakaw *vta* make s.o. chief, make s.o. leader; *1sg* **indoogimaakawaa**; *prt* **wegimaakawaad**
ogimaakwe *na* wife of chief or leader, woman leader, queen; *pl* **ogimaakweg**; *dim* **ogimaakwens**
ogimaakwens *na* princess; *pl* **ogimaakwensag**
ogimaawi *vai* be a leader, be a chief; *1sg* **indoogimaaw**; *prt* **wegimaawid**
ogimaawigamig *ni* head office, administration office; *pl* **ogimaawigamigoon**; *loc* **ogimaawigamigong**; *dim* **ogimaawigamigoons**
ogimaawiwin *ni* government, authority, leadership; *pl* **ogimaawiwinan**
ogin *na* rose hip, tomato; *pl* **oginiig**; *loc* **oginiing**; *dim* **oginiins**
oginii-dagonigan *ni* catsup
oginii-waabigwan *ni* rose; *pl* **oginii-waabigwaniin**; *loc* **oginii-waabigwaniing**; *dim* **oginii-waabigwaniins**
ogiishkimanisii *na* kingfisher; *pl* **ogiishkimanisiig**; *dim* **ogiishkimanisiins**
ogow* *pr* these *animate plural demonstrative; also* **ogo*, ongow, ongo**
ogowedig* *pr* these over here *animate plural demonstrative; also* **ongowedig**
o'o *pr* this *inanimate singular demonstrative; also* **o'ow, 'ow, 'o, o'o**
o'omaa *pc* here; *also* **omaa**
o'owedi *pr* this over here *inanimate singular demonstrative; also* **owedi**

ojaanimendam *vai2* be anxious, be impatient; *1sg* **indoojaanimendam**; *prt* **wejaanimendang**
ojaanimi- *pv4* busy, noisy
ojaanimi' *vta* make s.o. hurry, rush s.o.; *1sg* **indoojaanimi'aa**; *prt* **wejaanimi'aad**
ojaanimim *vta* hurry s.o. by speech; *1sg* **indoojaanimimaa**; *prt* **wejaanimimaad**
ojaanimitaa *vai* be busy (in some work or activity); *1sg* **indoojaanimitaa**; *prt* **wejaanimitaad**
ojaanimitoon *vti2* be eager to do s.t.; *1sg* **indoojaanimitoon**; *prt* **wejaanimitood**
ojaanimizekwe *vai* cook in a hurry; *1sg* **indoojaanimizekwe**; *prt* **wejaanimizekwed**
ojaanimizi *vai* be busy; *1sg* **indoojaanimiz**; *prt* **wejaanimizid**
ojibwe *na* Ojibwe; *pl* **ojibweg**; *dim* **ojibwens**
ojibwekwe *na* Ojibwe woman; *pl* **ojibwekweg**; *dim* **ojibwekwens**
ojibwemo *vai* speak Ojibwe; *1sg* **indoojibwem**; *prt* **wejibwemod**
ojibwemotaw *vta* speak Ojibwe to s.o.; *1sg* **indoojibwemotawaa**; *prt* **wejibwemotawaad**
ojibwemowin *ni* Ojibwe language; *pl* **ojibwemowinan**
ojibwewanishinaabe *na* Ojibwe; *pl* **ojibwewanishinaabeg**; *dim* **ojibwewanishinaabens**; *also* **ojibwe-anishinaabe**
ojibwewi *vai* be Ojibwe; *1sg* **indoojibwew**; *prt* **wejibwewid**
ojibwewibii'an *vti* write s.t. in Ojibwe; *1sg* **indoojibwewibii'aan**; *prt* **wejibwewibii'ang**
ojibwewibii'igaade *vii* be written in Ojibwe; *prt* **wejibwewibii'igaadeg**; *aug* **ojibwewibii'igaademagad**; *prt aug* **wejibwewibii'igaademagak**
ojibwewibii'ige *vai* write things in Ojibwe; *1sg* **indoojibwewibii'ige**; *prt* **wejibwewibii'iged**
ojibwewisidoon *vti2* put s.t. into Ojibwe; *1sg* **indoojibwewisidoon**; *prt* **wejibwewisidood**
ojibwewisin *vii* be written in Ojibwe (e.g., a book); *prt* **wejibwewising**
ojichaagobiishin *vii* reflect in water; *prt* **wejichaagobiishing**
ojichaagobiisin *vii* reflect in water; *prt* **wejichaagobiising**
ojijise *vii* come (as time), pass (as time); *prt* **wejijiseg**; *aug* **ojijisemagad**; *prt aug* **wejijisemagak**
ojijiingwanabi *vai* kneel; *1sg* **indoojijiingwanab**; *prt* **wejijiingwanabid**
ojiibik *ni* root; *pl* **ojiibikan**; *loc* **ojiibikaang**; *dim* **ojiibikens**
ojiibikaawan *vii* have roots; *prt* **wejiibikaawang**
ojiibikaawi *vai* have roots; *prt* **wejiibikaawid**
ojiig *na* fisher; *pl* **ojiigag**; *dim* **ojiigens**
ojiigwayaan *na* fisher hide; *pl* **ojiigwayaanag**; *loc* **ojiigwayaaning**; *dim* **ojiigwayaanens**
ojiim *vta* kiss s.o.; *1sg* **indoojiimaa**; *prt* **wejiimaad**
ojiindiwag /**ojiindi-**/ *vai* they kiss each other; *1pl* **indoojiindimin**; *prt* **wejiindijig**
ojiishigi *vai* have a scar; *1sg* **indoojiishig**; *prt* **wejiishigid**
ojiishinike *vai* have scar on one's arm; *1sg* **indoojiishinike**; *prt* **wejiishineked**

ojiishininjii *vai* have scar on one's hand; *1sg*
indoojiishininjii; *prt* wejiishininjiid
ojiishiingwe *vai* have scar on one's face; *1sg*
indoojiishiingwe; *prt* wejiishiingwed
okanakosimaan *ni* squash; *pl* okanakosimaanan;
loc okanakosimaaning; *dim*
okanakosimaanens
okanaapine *vai* have arthritis, have rheumatism;
1sg indookanaapine; *prt* wekanaapined
okawi' *vta* find s.o.'s tracks; *1sg* indookawi'aa; *prt*
wekawi'aad
okawitoon *vti2* find the tracks of s.t.; *1sg*
indookawitoon; *prt* wekawitood
okaadakik *na* legged kettle, treaty kettle; *pl*
okaadakikoog; *loc* okaadakikong; *dim*
okaadakikoons
okaadaak *ni* carrot; *pl* okaadaakoon; *loc*
okaadaakong; *dim* okaadaakoons
okaaden *vta* braid s.o., braid s.o.'s hair; *1sg*
indookaadenaa; *prt* wekaadenaad
okaadenan *vti* braid s.t.; *1sg* indookaadenaan; *prt*
wekaadenang
okaadenigan *ni* braided rug, braid; *pl*
okaadeniganan; *loc* okaadeniganing; *dim*
okaadenigaans
okaadenigaade *vii* be braided; *prt*
wekaadenigaadeg; *aug*
okaadenigaademagad; *prt aug*
wekaadenigaademagak
okaadenige *vai* braid things, have braids; *1sg*
indookaadenige; *prt* wekaadeniged
okeyaw *na* fish decoy; *pl* okeyawag
okij *ni* pipestem; *pl* okijiin; *loc* okijiing; *dim* okijiins
okijaabik *ni* stovepipe, tailpipe; *pl* okijaabikoon;
loc okijaabikong; *dim* okijaabikoons
okikaandag *na* jack pine; *pl* okikaandagoog; *loc*
okikaandagong; *dim* okikaandagoons; *also*
wakikaandag
okoshim *vta* pile s.o.; *1sg*
indookoshimaa; *prt* wekoshimaad
okoshin *vai* lie in a pile; *prt* wekoshing
okosidoon *vti2* pile s.t., stack s.t.; *1sg*
indookosidoon; *prt* wekosidood
okosimaan *ni* pumpkin, squash; *pl* okosimaanan;
loc okosimaaning; *dim* okosimaanens
okosin *vii* lie in a pile; *prt* wekosing
okwapide *vii* be tied in a bunch; *prt* wekwapideg;
aug okwapidemagad; *prt aug*
wekwapidemagak
okwapidoon *vti2* tie s.t. in a bunch; *1sg*
indookwapidoon; *prt* wekwapidood
okwapizh /okwapiN-/ *vta* tie s.o. in a bunch; *1sg*
indookwapinaa; *prt* wekwapinaad
okwapizo *vai* be tied in a bunch; *prt* wekwapizod
okwaakoshim *vta* stack s.o. (as something stick-
or wood-like); *1sg* indookwaakoshimaa; *prt*
wekwaakoshimaad
okwaakosidoon *vti2* stack s.t. (as something stick-
or wood-like); *1sg* indookwaakosidoon; *prt*
wekwaakosidood
omakakii *na* frog; *pl* omakakiig; *dim* omakakiins
omakakiiwinini *na* Finn; *pl* omakakiiwininiwag
omanoominii *na* Menominee; *pl* omanoominiig
omashkiigoo *na* Cree; *pl* omashkiigoog

omashkiigoomo *vai* speak Cree; *1sg*
indoomashkiigoom; *prt* wemashkiigoomod
omashkooz *na* elk; *pl* omashkoozoog; *dim*
omashkoozoons
omaa *pc* here; *also* o'omaa
omaamaayi *vai* have a mother; *1sg*
indoomaamaay; *prt* wemaamaayid
ombaabate *vii* go upwards as smoke; *prt*
wembaabateg
ombaabiigin *vta* hoist s.o., lift s.o. (as with something string-like); *1sg* indoombaabiiginaa; *prt*
wembaabiiginaad
ombaabiiginan *vti* hoist s.t., lift s.t. (as with something string-like); *1sg* indoombaabiiginaan; *prt*
wembaabiiginang
ombaakwa' /ombaakwa'w-/ *vta* raise s.o. (as or as
with something stick- or wood-like); *1sg*
indoombaakwa'waa; *prt* wembaakwa'waad
ombaakwa'an *vti* raise s.t. (as or as with something stick- or wood-like); *1sg*
indoombaakwa'aan; *prt* wembaakwa'ang
ombaashi *vai* be blown upwards; *1sg*
indoombaash; *prt* wembaashid
ombaasin *vii* be blown upwards; *prt* wembaasing
ombendam *vai2* be excited, be hopeful; *1sg*
indoombendam; *prt* wembendang
ombibide *vii* fly upwards, speed upwards; *prt*
wembibideg; *aug* ombibidemagad; *prt aug*
wembibidemagak
ombibizo *vai* fly upwards, speed upwards; *1sg*
indoombibiz; *prt* wembibizod
ombigamizan *vti* boil s.t. to sugar; *1sg*
indoombigamizaan; *prt* wembigamizang
ombigamizigan *ni* boiling sugar; *pl*
ombigamiziganan; *loc* ombigamiziganing
ombigamizige *vai* boil to sugar, sugar off; *1sg*
indoombigamizige; *prt* wembigamiziged
ombigwaashkwani *vai* jump upwards; *1sg*
indoombigwaashkwan; *prt*
wembigwaashkwanid
ombi' *vta* excite s.o., stir s.o. up; *1sg* indoombi'aa;
prt wembi'aad
ombijiishkaa *vai* have a swollen stomach; *1sg*
indoombijiishkaa; *prt* wembijiishkaad
ombin *vta* lift s.o.; *1sg* indoombinaa; *prt*
wembinaad
ombinamaw *vta* lift (s.t.) for s.o.; *1sg*
indoombinamawaa; *prt* wembinamawaad
ombinan *vti* lift s.t.; *1sg* indoombinaan; *prt*
wembinang
ombinikeni *vai* lift one's arm; *1sg* indoombiniken;
prt wembinikenid
ombishkaa *vai* go upwards; *1sg* indoombishkaa;
prt wembishkaad
ombishkaa *vii* go upwards; *prt* wembishkaag; *aug*
ombishkaamagad; *prt aug*
wembishkaamagak
ombisijigaans *ni* baking powder; *pl*
ombisijigaansan; *loc* ombisijigaansing
ombiwane *vai* lift a pack to one's back; *1sg*
indoombiwane; *prt* wembiwaned
ombiwebin *vta* throw s.o. upwards; *1sg*
indoombiwebinaa; *prt* wembiwebinaad
ombiwebinan *vti* throw s.t. upwards; *1sg*
indoombiwebinaan; *prt* wembiwebinang

ombiwidoon *vti2* lift and carry s.t.; *1sg*
indoombiwidoon; *prt* wembiwidood
ombiwizh /ombiwiN-/ *vta* lift and carry s.o.; *1sg*
indoombiwinaa; *prt* wembiwinaad
ombizigan *ni* baking soda; *loc* ombiziganing
ombiigizi *vai* be loud, be noisy; *1sg* indoombiigiz;
prt wembiigizid
ombiigwewe *vai* be loud (in operation); *prt*
wembiigwewed
ombiigwewe *vii* be loud (in operation); *prt*
wembiigweweg; *aug* ombiigwewemagad; *prt*
aug wembiigwewemagak
omboom *vta* lift s.o. on one's back; *prt*
wemboomaad
omboondan *vti* lift s.t. on one's back; *1sg*
indoomboondaan; *prt* wemboondang
ombwewebinige *vai* throw things around, make a
mess; *1sg* indoombwewebinige; *prt*
wembwewebiniged
omigii *vai* have sores, have scabs; *1sg* indoomigii;
prt wemigiid
omigiingwe *vai* have scabs on one's face; *1sg*
indoomigiingwe; *prt* wemigiingwed
omiimii *na* dove, pigeon; *pl* omiimiig; *dim*
omiimiins
omiimiisi *na* mayfly; *pl* omiimiisiwag
omooday *ni* bottle; *pl* omoodayan; *loc*
omoodaang
omoodayaabik *ni* (piece of) glass, broken glass (as
from a bottle); *pl* omoodayaabikoon; *loc*
omoodayaabikong; *dim* omoodayaabikoons
onabi *vai* take a seat; *1sg* indoonab; *prt* wenabid
onabi' *vta* seat s.o.; *1sg* indoonabi'aa; *prt*
wenabi'aad
onabi'iwe *vai* seat people; *1sg* indoonabi'iwe; *prt*
wenabi'iwed
onadin *vta* mold s.o., knead s.o., sculpt s.o.; *1sg*
indoonadinaa; *prt* wenadinaad
onadinan *vti* mold s.t., knead s.t., sculpt s.t.; *1sg*
indoonadinaan; *prt* wenadinang
onadinige *vai* knead things, mold things; *1sg*
indoonadinige; *prt* wenadiniged
onagim *vta* decide on s.o., appoint s.o., set a price
on s.o.; *1sg* indoonagimaa; *prt* wenagimaad
onagindan *vti* set a price on s.t.; *1sg*
indoonagindaan; *prt* wenagindang
onagindaaso *vai* set a price; *1sg* indoonagindaas;
prt wenagindaasod
onagizh *ni* sausage; *pl* onagizhiin; *loc* onagizhiing;
dim onagizhiins; *also* onagizhiins
onagizhiinsan /onagizhiins-/ *ni* macaroni *plural*
onagoode *vii* hang in place; *prt* wenagoodeg; *aug*
onagoodemagad; *prt aug* wenagoodemagak
onagoodoon *vti2* hang s.t. in place; *1sg*
indoonagoodoon; *prt* wenagoodood
onagoojin *vai* hang in place; *prt* wenagoojing
onagoozh /onagooN-/ *vta* hang s.o. in place; *1sg*
indoonagoonaa; *prt* wenagoonaad
onakidoon *vti2* set s.t. up; *1sg* indoonakidoon; *prt*
wenakidood
onakizh /onakiN-/ *vta* set s.o. up; *1sg*
indoonakinaa; *prt* wenakinaad
onapide *vii* be tied in place; *prt* wenapideg; *aug*
onapidemagad; *prt aug* wenapidemagak

onapidoon *vti2* tie s.t. in place; *1sg*
indoonapidoon; *prt* wenapidood
onapijige *vai* harness up; *1sg* indoonapijige; *prt*
wenapijiged
onapizh /onapiN-/ *vta* tie s.o. in place, harness
s.o.; *1sg* indoonapinaa; *prt* wenapinaad
onapizo *vai* be harnessed; *prt* wenapizod
onashkinade *vii* be loaded; *prt* wenashkinadeg;
aug onashkinademagad; *prt aug*
wenashkinademagak
onashkinadoon *vti2* load s.t. (e.g., a gun); *1sg*
indoonashkinadoon; *prt* wenashkinadood
onashkina' *vta* load s.o. (e.g., a pipe); *1sg*
indoonashkina'aa; *prt* wenashkina'aad
onwaawe *vai* hiccough; *1sg* indoonwaawe; *prt*
wenwaawed
onaabam *vta* choose s.o., pick s.o.; *1sg*
indoonaabamaa; *prt* wenaabamaad
onaabanad *vii* there is a crust on the snow; *prt*
wenaabanak
onaabandan *vti* choose s.t., pick s.t.; *1sg*
indoonaabandaan; *prt* wenaabandang
onaabani-giizis *na* March
onaabanjigaade *vii* be chosen, be picked; *prt*
wenaabanjigaadeg; *aug*
onaabanjigaademagad; *prt aug*
wenaabanjigaademagak
onaabanjigaazo *vai* be chosen, be picked; *prt*
wenaabanjigaazod
onaabanjige *vai* choose things, pick things; *1sg*
indoonaabanjige; *prt* wenaabanjiged
onaabemi *vai* have a husband; *1sg* indoonaabem;
prt wenaabemid
onaagan *ni* dish, plate; *pl* onaaganan; *loc*
onaaganing; *dim* onaagaans

onaagan (dish) or boozikinaagan (bowl)

onaagaans *ni* cup, small plate; *pl* onaagaansan; *loc*
onaagaansing
onaagin *vta* bend s.o. into form; *1sg*
indoonaaginaa; *prt* wenaaginaad
onaaginan *vti* bend s.t. into form; *1sg*
indoonaaginaan; *prt* wenaaginang
onaagoshi-miijin *vti3* eat s.t. for supper; *1sg*
indoonaagoshi-miijin; *prt* wenaagoshi-miijid
onaagoshin /onaagoshi-/ *vii* be evening; *prt*
wenaagoshig

onaagoshi-wiisini *vai* eat supper; *1sg*
 indoonaagoshi-wiisin; *prt* **wenaagoshi-
 wiisinid**
onaakon *vta* decide on s.o., judge s.o.; *1sg*
 indoonaakonaa; *prt* **wenaakonaad**
onaakonan *vti* decide on s.t., plan s.t.; *1sg*
 indoonaakonaan; *prt* **wenaakonang**
onaakonige *vai* plan things, decide things, judge
 things, be in court; *1sg* **indoonaakonige;** *prt*
 wenaakoniged
onaakosidoon *vti2* set s.t. up as a frame; *1sg*
 indoonaakosidoon; *prt* **wenaakosidood**
ondadamon /ondadamo-/ *vii* lead from a certain
 place (as a road or trail); *prt* **wendadamog**
ondademo *vai* cry for a certain reason, come from
 a certain place crying; *1sg* **indoondadem;** *prt*
 wendademod
onda'ibaan *ni* water well, water source; *pl*
 onda'ibaanan; *loc* **onda'ibaaning;** *dim*
 onda'ibaanens
onda'ibii *vai* get water from a certain place; *1sg*
 indoonda'ibii; *prt* **wenda'ibiid**
ondakwazhiwe *vai* paddle from a certain place,
 swim from a certain place (as a fish); *1sg*
 indoondakwazhiwe; *prt* **wendakwazhiwed**
ondamanokii *vai* be kept busy in work; *1sg*
 indoondamanokii; *prt* **wendamanokiid**
ondamendam *vai2* be preoccupied, be worried;
 1sg **indoondamendam;** *prt* **wendamendang**
ondamendan *vti* worry about s.t., be preoccupied
 with s.t.; *1sg* **indoondamendaan;** *prt*
 wendamendang
ondamenim *vta* worry about s.o., be preoccupied
 with s.o.; *1sg* **indoondamenimaa;** *prt*
 wendamenimaad
ondami' *vta* hinder s.o., get in s.o.'s way; *1sg*
 indoondami'aa; *prt* **wendami'aad**
ondamitaa *vai* be kept busy in an activity; *1sg*
 indoondamitaa; *prt* **wendamitaad**
ondamizi *vai* be busy; *1sg* **indoondamiz;** *prt*
 wendamizid
ondaabate *vii* come from a certain place (as
 smoke); *prt* **wendaabateg;** *aug*
 ondaabatemagad; *prt aug* **wendaabatemagak**
ondaadad *vii* come from a certain place, originate
 in a certain place; *prt* **wendaadak**
ondaadagaa *vai* swim from a certain place; *1sg*
 indoondaadagaa; *prt* **wendaadagaad**
ondaadagaazii *vai* wade from a certain place; *1sg*
 indoondaadagaazii; *prt* **wendaadagaaziid**
ondaada'e *vai* skate from a certain place; *1sg*
 indoondaada'e; *prt* **wendaada'ed**
ondaadizi *vai* be born, come from a certain place;
 1sg **indoondaadiz;** *prt* **wendaadizid**
ondaadiziike *vai* give birth; *1sg* **indoondaadiziike;**
 prt **wendaadiziiked**
ondaanimad *vii* come as wind from a certain
 direction; *prt* **wendaanimak**
ondaas *pc* on this side, come here!
ondaasagaam *pc* on this side of the water
ondaasayi'ii *pc* on this side of it
ondaashaan *pc* come here! (especially said to
 children)

ondaashi *vai* be blown from a certain place, sail
 from a certain place; *1sg* **indoondaash;** *prt*
 wendaashid
ondaasikana *pc* on this side of the road, on this
 side of the trail
ondaasin *vii* be blown from a certain place, sail
 from a certain place; *prt* **wendaasing**
ondaasishkode *pc* on this side of the fire
onde *vii* boil; *prt* **wendeg;** *aug* **ondemagad;** *prt*
 aug **wendemagak**
ondendam *vai2* strongly desire; *1sg*
 indoondendam; *prt* **wendendang**
ondendi *vai* be gone from a certain place, be
 absent from a certain place; *1sg* **indoondend;**
 prt **wendendid**
ondenim *vta* envy s.o.; *1sg* **indoondenimaa;** *prt*
 wendenimaad
ondin *vii* wind comes from a certain direction; *prt*
 wending
ondin *vta* get s.o. from a certain place, obtain s.o.
 from a certain place; *1sg* **indoondinaa;** *prt*
 wendinaad
ondinamaw *vta* get (s.t.) for s.o. from a certain
 place, obtain (s.t.) for s.o. from a certain place;
 1sg **indoondinamawaa;** *prt* **wendinamawaad**
ondinamaazo *vai* get (s.t.) for oneself from a
 certain place; *1sg* **indoondinamaaz;** *prt*
 wendinamaazod
ondinan *vti* get s.t. from a certain place, obtain s.t.
 from a certain place; *1sg* **indoondinaan;** *prt*
 wendinang
ondinigaade *vii* be obtained from a certain place;
 prt **wendinigaadeg;** *aug* **ondinigaademagad;**
 prt aug **wendinigaademagak**
ondinigaazo *vai* be obtained from a certain place;
 prt **wendinigaazod**
ondinige *vai* get things from a certain place, obtain
 things from a certain place; *1sg* **indoondinige;**
 prt **wendiniged**
ondizi *vai* make a living a certain way, earn from a
 certain place, inherit from a certain source; *1sg*
 indoondiz; *prt* **wendizid**
ondose *vai* walk from a certain place; *1sg*
 indoondose; *prt* **wendosed**
ondoode *vai* crawl from a certain place; *1sg*
 indoondoode; *prt* **wendooded**
ondoom *vta* carry s.o. on back from a certain
 place; *1sg* **indoondoomaa;** *prt* **wendoomaad**
ondoomigo *vai* ride from a certain place on
 horseback; *1sg* **indoondoomig;** *prt*
 wendoomigod
ondoondan *vti* carry s.t. on back from a certain
 place; *1sg* **indoondoondaan;** *prt*
 wendoondang
onendam *vai2* decide what to do, figure something
 out; *1sg* **indoonendam;** *prt* **wenendang**
ongow *pr* these *animate plural demonstrative; also*
 ongo, ogow*, ogo*
ongowedig *pr* these over here *animate plural
 demonstrative; also* **ogowedig***
Onigamiinsing *place* Duluth
onikodan *vti* cut s.t. to shape; *1sg* **indoonikodaan;**
 prt **wenikodang**
onikozh /onikoN-/ *vta* cut s.o. to shape; *1sg*
 indoonikonaa; *prt* **wenikonaad**

onin *vta* put s.o. in order, assemble s.o., deal s.o.
(e.g., cards); *1sg* **indooninaa**; *prt* **weninaad**
oninan *vti* put s.t. in order, assemble s.t.; *1sg*
indooninan; *prt* **weninang**
oninasabii *vai* prepare a net for setting; *1sg*
indooninasabii; *prt* **weninasabiid**
oninige *vai* put things in order, assemble things,
deal cards; *1sg* **indooninige**; *prt* **weniniged**
oninjii-baashkizigan *ni* handgun; *pl* **oninjii-
baashkiziganan**; *loc* **oninjii-baashkiziganing**;
dim **oninjii-baashkizigaans**
onishkaa *vai* get up (from a prone position); *1sg*
indoonishkaa; *prt* **wenishkaad**
onizhishi *vai* be nice, be pretty; *1sg* **indoonizhish**;
prt **wenizhishid**
onizhishi' *vta* make s.o. nice, make s.o. well; *1sg*
indoonizhishi'aa; *prt* **wenizhishi'aad**
onizhishin *vii* be nice, be pretty; *prt* **wenizhishing**
onizhishitoon *vti2* make s.t. nice, make s.t. well;
1sg **indoonizhishitoon**; *prt* **wenizhishitood**
oniijaanisensi *vai* have a small child; *1sg*
indooniijaanisens; *prt* **weniijaanisensid**
oniijaanisi *vai* have a child; *1sg* **indooniijaanis**; *prt*
weniijaanisid
oniijaaniw *na* doe; *pl* **oniijaaniwag**; *dim*
oniijaaniins
onji- *pv3* from a certain place, for a certain reason,
because
onjibatoo *vai* run from a certain place; *1sg*
indoonjibatoo; *prt* **wenjibatood**
onjibaa *vai* come from a certain place; *1sg*
indoonjibaa; *prt* **wenjibaad**
onjibide *vii* speed from a certain place, drive from
a certain place, fall from a certain place; *prt*
wenjibideg; *aug* **onjibidemagad**; *prt aug*
wenjibidemagak
onjibizo *vai* speed from a certain place, drive from
a certain place, fall from a certain place; *1sg*
indoonjibiz; *prt* **wenjibizod**
onjida *pc* on purpose
onjidaabii'iwe *vai* drive from a certain place; *1sg*
indoonjidaabii'iwe; *prt* **wenjidaabii'iwed**
onjigaa *vii* leak, drip, run with sap; *prt* **wenjigaag**;
aug **onjigaamagad**; *prt aug* **wenjigaamagak**
onjijiwan *vii* flow from a certain place; *prt*
wenjijiwang
onjinawe' *vta* anger s.o. for a certain reason, make
s.o. mad for a certain reason; *1sg*
indoonjinawe'aa; *prt* **wenjinawe'aad**
onjinazh /**onjinaN-**/ *vta* kill s.o. for a certain
reason; *1sg* **indoonjinanaa**; *prt* **wenjinanaad**
onjinizhimo *vai* run from a certain place in flight;
1sg **indoonjinizhim**; *prt* **wenjinizhimod**
onjise *vai* fly from a certain place; *1sg* **indoonjise**;
prt **wenjised**
onjise *vii* fly from a certain place; *prt* **wenjiseg**; *aug*
onjisemagad; *prt aug* **wenjisemagak**
onjishkawa'o *vai* paddle against the wind; *1sg*
indoonjishkawa'; *prt* **wenjishkawa'od**; *also*
onjishkawa'am
onjishkawishkaa *vai* go against the wind; *1sg*
indoonjishkawishkaa; *prt* **wenjishkawishkaad**
onjiwidoon *vti2* take s.t. from a certain place, carry
s.t. from a certain place; *1sg* **indoonjiwidoon**;
prt **wenjiwidood**

onjiwizh /**onjiwiN-**/ *vta* take s.o. from a certain
place, carry s.o. from a certain place; *1sg*
indoonjiwinaa; *prt* **wenjiwinaad**
onjii *vai* come from a certain place; *1sg* **indoonjii**;
prt **wenjiid**
onow *pr* these *inanimate plural demonstrative*, this,
these *animate obviative demonstrative*; *also* **ono**
onowedin *pr* these over here *inanimate plural
demonstrative*, this/these over here *obviative
demonstrative*
onwaachige *vai* foretell the future; *1sg*
indoonwaachige; *prt* **wenwaachiged**
onzan *vti* boil s.t.; *1sg* **indoonzaan**; *prt* **wenzang**
onzaabi *vai* look out from a certain place; *1sg*
indoonzaab; *prt* **wenzaabid**
onzaam *pc* too much, excessively, extremely
onzaamashkinadoon *vti2* overfill s.t. with solids;
1sg **indoonzaamashkinadoon**; *prt*
wenzaamashkinadood
onzaamashkina' *vta* overfill s.o. with solids; *1sg*
indoonzaamashkina'aa; *prt*
wenzaamashkina'aad
onzaamaakide *vii* be burnt crisp; *prt*
wenzaamaakideg; *aug* **onzaamaakidemagad**;
prt aug **wenzaamaakidemagak**
onzaamaakizo *vai* be burnt crisp; *prt*
wenzaamaakizod
onzaamendam *vai2* give too much consideration;
1sg **indoonzaamendam**; *prt* **wenzaamendang**
onzaamenimo *vai* be elated, be overexcited; *1sg*
indoonzaamenim; *prt* **wenzaamenimod**
onzaamibadoon *vti2* overfill s.t. (with a liquid);
1sg **indoonzaamibadoon**; *prt*
wenzaamibadood
onzaamibazh /**onzaamibaN-**/ *vta* give s.o. too
much to drink; *1sg* **indoonzaamibanaa**; *prt*
wenzaamibanaad
onzaamibii *vai* drink too much; *1sg*
indoonzaamibii; *prt* **wenzaamibiid**
onzaamichige *vai* overdo things; *1sg*
indoonzaamichige; *prt* **wenzaamichiged**
onzaamide *vii* be overcooked; *prt* **wenzaamideg**;
aug **onzaamidemagad**; *prt aug*
wenzaamidemagak
onzaamidoon *vai* talk too much; *1sg*
indoonzaamidoon; *prt* **wenzaamidoong**
onzaamine *vai* be very sick; *1sg* **indoonzaamine**;
prt **wenzaamined**
onzaamingwaam *vai* oversleep; *1sg*
indoonzaamingwaam; *prt*
wenzaamingwaang
onzaamiwane *vai* pack too much of a load; *1sg*
indoonzaamiwane; *prt* **wenzaamiwaned**
onzaamiz /**onzaamizw-**/ *vta* overcook s.o.,
overheat s.o.; *1sg* **indoonzaamizwaa**; *prt*
wenzaamizwaad
onzaamizan *vti* overcook s.t., overheat s.t.; *1sg*
indoonzaamizaan; *prt* **wenzaamizang**
onzaamizo *vai* be overcooked; *prt* **wenzaamizod**
onzaamiinad *vii* be too much, be too many; *prt*
wenzaamiinak
onzaamiino *vai* be too much, be too many; *prt*
wenzaamiinod
onzo *vai* boil; *prt* **wenzod**

onzo /onzw-/ *vta* boil s.o.; *1sg* indoonzwaa; *prt* wenzwaad
opichi *na* robin; *pl* opichiwag; *dim* opichiins
opime-ayi'ii *pc* on the side of it; *also* opimeya'ii
opimekana *pc* along the side of the road, along the side of the trail
opimese *vai* fall on the side; *prt* wepimesed
opimeshim *vai* lay s.o. on side; *1sg* indoopimeshimaa; *prt* wepimeshimaad
opimeshin *vai* lie on one's side; *1sg* indoopimeshin; *prt* wepimeshing
opimesidoon *vti2* lay s.t. on side; *1sg* indoopimesidoon; *prt* wepimesidood
opimesin *vii* lie on side; *prt* wepimesing
opin *na* potato; *pl* opiniig; *dim* opiniins
opwaagan *na* pipe (for smoking); *pl* opwaaganag; *loc* opwaaganing; *dim* opwaagaans

opwaagan (pipe), okij (pipe stem)

opwaaganasin *na* pipestone; *pl* opwaaganasiniig
opwaagaans *na* cigarette; *pl* opwaagaansag; *loc* opwaagaansing
oshaakaw *vta* scare s.o. away (e.g., game); *1sg* indooshaakawaa; *prt* weshaakawaad
oshedinaa *vii* there is a ridge; *prt* weshedinaag; *aug* oshedinaamagad; *prt aug* weshedinaamagak
oshkagoojin *vai* be new (of a moon); *prt* weshkagoojing; *also* oshki-agoojin
oshkanzhiikaajigan *ni* horseshoe; *pl* oshkanzhiikaajiganan; *loc* oshkanzhiikaajiganing; *dim* oshkanzhiikaajigaans
oshkaya'aawi *vai* be young; *1sg* indooshkaya'aaw; *prt* wedooshkaya'aawid; *also* oshki-aya'aawi
oshkaya'aa *na* someone new, someone young; *pl* oshkaya'aag; *dim* oshkaya'aans; *also* oshki-aya'aa
oshkayi'ii *ni* something new, something young; *pl* oshkayi'iin; *dim* oshkayi'iins; *also* oshki-ayi'ii
oshkayi'iiwan *vii* be young, be new; *prt* weshkayi'iiwang
oshkaabewis *na* ceremonial attendant, ceremonial messenger; *pl* oshkaabewisag; *dim* oshkaabewisens
oshki- *pv4* new, young, for the first time
oshki-bimaadizi *vai* be young; *1sg* indooshki-bimaadiz; *prt* weshki-bimaadizid
oshki-dibikad *vii* be early in the night; *prt* weshki-dibikak
oshki'o *vai* wear new clothes; *1sg* indooshki'; *prt* weshki'od
oshki-inini *na* young man; *pl* oshki-ininiwag
oshkikonaye *vai* dress in a new outfit; *1sg* indooshkikonaye; *prt* weshkikonayed

oshkinawe *na* young man, adolescent boy; *pl* oshkinaweg; *dim* oshkinawens
oshkinawewi *vai* be a young man, be an adolescent boy; *1sg* indooshkinawew; *prt* weshkinawewid
oshkiniigi *vai* be young, be an adolescent; *1sg* indooshkiniig; *prt* weshkiniigid
oshkiniigikwe *na* young woman, adolescent girl; *pl* oshkiniigikweg; *dim* oshkiniigikwens
oshkiniigikwewi *vai* be a young woman, be an adolescent girl; *1sg* indooshkiniigikwew; *prt* weshkiniigikwewid
oshkiinaagozi *vai* look young, look new; *1sg* indooshkiinaagoz; *prt* weshkiinaagozid
oshkiinaagwad *vii* look new; *prt* weshkiinaagwak
oshkiinzhigokaajiganan *ni* eyeglasses *plural*; *loc* oshkiinzhigokaajiganing; *dim* oshkiinzhigokaajigaansan; *also* oshkiinzhigokaajigaan; *also* oshkiinzhikokaanan
oshkiinzhigokewinini *na* optometrist; *pl* oshkiinzhigokewininiwag
oshtigwaanens *ni* postage stamp; *pl* oshtigwaanensan; *loc* oshtigwaanensing
oshtigwaanzhaabonigan *ni* common pin; *pl* oshtigwaanzhaaboniganan
osidaawendam *vai2* be sad, be dejected, be sorrowful; *1sg* indoosidaawendam; *prt* wesidaawendang
owa *pc* exclamation of agreeable surprise
owedi *pr* this over here *inanimate singular demonstrative; also* o'owedi
owidi *pc* over here; *also* o'owidi
owiiyawen'enyi *vai* be a namesake; *1sg* indoowiiyawen'enh; *prt* wewiiyawen'enyid
ozagaskwaajime *na* leech, bloodsucker; *pl* ozagaskwaajimeg; *dim* ozagaskwaajimens; *also* zagaskwaajime
ozaawaa *vii* be brown, be yellow; *prt* wezaawaag; *aug* ozaawaamagad; *prt aug* wezaawaamagak
ozaawaabik *ni* (piece of) brass; *pl* ozaawaabikoon; *loc* ozaawaabikong
ozaawaabikad *vii* be brown (as something mineral), be yellow (as something mineral), be brass; *prt* wezaawaabikak
ozaawaabikizi *vai* be brown (as something mineral), be yellow (as something mineral), be brass; *prt* wezaawaabikizid
ozaawaabikoons *na* cent, penny; *pl* ozaawaabikoonsag; *loc* ozaawaabikoonsing
ozaawaabiigad *vii* be brown (as something string-like), be yellow (as something string-like); *prt* wezaawaabiigak
ozaawaabiigizi *vai* be brown (as something string-like), be yellow (as something string-like); *prt* wezaawaabiigizid
ozaawaakizan *vti* brown s.t. by fire, toast s.t. brown; *1sg* indoozaawaakizaan; *prt* wezaawaakizang
ozaawaakozi *vai* be brown (as something stick- or wood-like), be yellow (as something stick- or wood-like); *prt* wezaawaakozid
ozaawaakwad *vii* be brown (as something stick- or wood-like), be yellow (as something stick- or wood-like); *prt* wezaawaakwak

ozaawaande *vii* be colored brown, be colored yellow; *prt* **wezaawaandeg**; *aug* **ozaawaandemagad**; *prt aug* **wezaawaandemagak**
ozaawaanzo *vai* be colored brown, be colored yellow; *prt* **wezaawaanzod**
ozaawaa-zhooniyaa *ni* gold; *loc* **ozaawaazhooniyaang**; *dim* **ozaawaa-zhooniyaans**; *also* **ozhaawaa-zhooniyaa**
ozaawaa-zhooniyaawaande *vii* be colored gold; *prt* **wezaawaa-zhooniyaawaandeg**; *aug* **ozaawaa-zhooniyaawaandemagad**; *prt aug* **wezaawaa-zhooniyaawaandemagak**; *also* **ozhaawaa-zhooniyaawaande**
ozaawaa-zhooniyaawaanzo *vai* be colored gold; *prt* **wezaawaa-zhooniyaawaanzod**; *also* **ozhaawaa-zhooniyaanzo**
ozaawegad *vii* be brown (as something sheet-like), be yellow (as something sheet-like); *prt* **wezaawegak**
ozaawegizi *vai* be brown (as something sheet-like), be yellow (as something sheet-like); *prt* **wezaawegizid**
ozaawi- *pv4* brown, yellow
ozaawi-bimide *ni* butter; *loc* **ozaawi-bimideng**
ozaawi'o *vai* wear brown, wear yellow; *1sg* **indoozaawi'**; *prt* **wezaawi'od**
ozaawikaadaak *ni* carrot; *pl* **ozaawikaadaakoon**; *loc* **ozaawikaadaakong**; *dim* **ozaawikaadaakoons**
ozaawikosimaan *ni* pumpkin; *pl* **ozaawikosimaanan**; *loc* **ozaawikosimaaning**; *dim* **ozaawikosimaanens**
ozaawindibe *vai* be blond, have brown hair; *1sg* **indoozaawindibe**; *prt* **wezaawindibed**
ozaawizi *vai* be brown, be yellow; *prt* **wezaawizid**
ozhaashadamon /ozhaashadamo-/ *vii* be slippery (as a road or trail); *prt* **wezhaashadamog**
ozhaashaa *vii* be slippery, be slick; *prt* **wezhaashaag**; *aug* **ozhaashaamagad**; *prt aug* **wezhaashaamagak**
ozhaashaabikad *vii* be slippery (as something mineral); *prt* **wezhaashaabikak**
ozhaashaabikizi *vai* be slippery (as something mineral); *prt* **wezhaashaabikizid**
ozhaashaakozi *vai* be slippery (as something stick- or wood-like); *prt* **wezhaashaakozid**
ozhaashaakwad *vii* be slippery (as something stick- or wood-like); *prt* **wezhaashaakwak**
ozhaashigob *na* slippery elm; *pl* **ozhaashigobiig**; *loc* **ozhaashigobiing**; *dim* **ozhaashigobiins**
ozhaashikoshin *vai* slip and fall on the ice; *1sg* **indoozhaashikoshin**; *prt* **wezhaashikoshing**
ozhaashikwadamon /ozhaashikwadamo-/ *vii* be slippery with ice (as a road or trail); *prt* **wezhaashikwadamog**
ozhaashikwaa *vii* there is slippery ice; *prt* **wezhaashikwaag**; *aug* **ozhaashikwaamagad**; *prt aug* **wezhaashikwaamagak**
ozhaashishin *vai* slip and fall; *1sg* **indoozhaashishin**; *prt* **wezhaashishing**
ozhaashizi *vai* be slippery, be slick; *prt* **wezhaashizid**
ozhaawashko- *pv4* blue, green

ozhaawashko-aniibiish *ni* green tea; *loc* **ozhaawashko-aniibiishing**
ozhaawashko-bineshiinh *na* bluebird; *pl* **ozhaawashko-bineshiinyag**
ozhaawashko'o *vai* wear blue, wear green; *1sg* **indoozhaawashko'**; *prt* **wezhaawashko'od**
ozhaawashko-manoomin *ni* green wild rice; *loc* **ozhaawashko-manoomining**
ozhaawashkozi *vai* be blue, be green; *prt* **wezhaawashkozid**
ozhaawashkwaa *vii* be blue, be green; *prt* **wezhaawashkwaag**; *aug* **ozhaawashkwaamagad**; *prt aug* **wezhaawashkwaamagak**
ozhaawashkwaabi *vai* have a black eye; *1sg* **indoozhaawashkwaab**; *prt* **wezhaawashkwaabid**
ozhaawashkwaabikad *vii* be blue (as something mineral), be green (as something mineral); *prt* **wezhaawashkwaabikak**
ozhaawashkwaabikizi *vai* be blue (as something mineral), be green (as something mineral); *prt* **wezhaawashkwaabikizid**
ozhaawashkwaabiigad *vii* be blue (as something string-like), be green (as something string-like); *prt* **wezhaawashkwaabiigak**
ozhaawashkwaabiigizi *vai* be blue (as something string-like), be green (as something string-like); *prt* **wezhaawashkwaabiigizid**
ozhaawashkwaakozi *vai* be blue (as something stick- or wood-like), be green (as something stick- or wood-like); *prt* **wezhaawashkwaakozid**
ozhaawashkwaakwad *vii* be blue (as something stick- or wood-like), be green (as something stick- or wood-like); *prt* **wezhaawashkwaakwak**
ozhaawashkwaanagiingwe *vai* have a bruised face; *1sg* **indoozhaawashkwaanagiingwe**; *prt* **wezhaawashkwaanagiingwed**
ozhaawashkwegad *vii* be blue (as something sheet-like), be green (as something sheet-like); *prt* **wezhaawashkwegak**
ozhaawashkwegizi *vai* be blue (as something sheet-like), be green (as something sheet-like); *prt* **wezhaawashkwegizid**
ozhibii' */ozhibii'w-/* *vta* write s.o. down; *1sg* **indoozhibii'waa**; *prt* **wezhibii'waad**
ozhibii'amaw *vta* write (s.t.) for s.o.; *1sg* **indoozhibii'amawaa**; *prt* **wezhibii'amawaad**
ozhibii'an *vti* write s.t., write s.t. down; *1sg* **indoozhibii'aan**; *prt* **wezhibii'ang**
ozhibii'igan *ni* letter of the alphabet, something written; *pl* **ozhibii'iganan**; *loc* **ozhibii'iganing**; *dim* **ozhibii'igaans**
ozhibii'iganaaboo *ni* ink; *loc* **ozhibii'iganaaboong**
ozhibii'iganaak *ni* pen, pencil; *pl* **ozhibii'iganaakoon**; *loc* **ozhibii'iganaakong**; *dim* **ozhibii'iganaakoons**
ozhibii'igaade *vii* be written; *prt* **wezhibii'igaadeg**; *aug* **ozhibii'igaademagad**; *prt aug* **wezhibii'igaademagak**
ozhibii'ige *vai* write; *1sg* **indoozhibii'ige**; *prt* **wezhibii'iged**

ozhibii'ige-adoopowin *ni* desk; *pl* ozhibii'ige-adoopowinan; *loc* ozhibii'ige-adoopowining; *dim* ozhibii'ige-adoopowinens
ozhibii'igewigamig *ni* office; *pl* ozhibii'igewigamigoon; *loc* ozhibii'igewigamigong; *dim* ozhibii'igewigamigoons
ozhibii'igewikwe *na* secretary (female), clerk (female); *pl* ozhibii'igewikweg
ozhibii'igewinini *na* secretary (male), clerk (male); *pl* ozhibii'igewininiwag
ozhichigaade *vii* be made, be built; *prt* wezhichigaadeg; *aug* ozhichigaademagad; *prt aug* wezhichigaademagak
ozhichigaazo *vai* be made, be built; *prt* wezhichigaazod
ozhichige *vai* make things; *1sg* indoozhichige; *prt* wezhichiged
ozhiga'ige *vai* tap trees; *1sg* indoozhiga'ige; *prt* wezhiga'iged
ozhigaw *vta* build a house for s.o.; *1sg* indoozhigawaa; *prt* wezhigawaad
ozhige *vai* build a lodge; *1sg* indoozhige; *prt* wezhiged
ozhi' *vta* make s.o., build s.o., form s.o.; *1sg* indoozhi'aa; *prt* wezhi'aad
ozhim *vta* escape from s.o.; *1sg* indoozhimaa; *prt* wezhimaad
ozhimo *vai* flee; *1sg* indoozhim; *prt* wezhimod
ozhitamaw *vta* make (s.t.) for s.o., build (s.t.) for s.o.; *1sg* indoozhitamawaa; *prt* wezhitamawaad
ozhitaw *vta* make (s.t.) for s.o., build (s.t.) for s.o.; *1sg* indoozhitawaa; *prt* wezhitawaad
ozhitoon *vti2* make s.t., build s.t., form s.t.; *1sg* indoozhitoon; *prt* wezhitood
ozhiwanikaadan *vti* make a pack of s.t.; *1sg* indoozhiwanikaadaan; *prt* wezhiwanikaadang
ozhiwanike *vai* pack up; *1sg* indoozhiwanike; *prt* wezhiwaniked
ozhiitaa *vai* get ready, prepare; *1sg* indoozhiitaa; *prt* wezhiitaad
ozhooniyaami *vai* have money; *1sg* indoozhooniyaam; *prt* wezhooniyaamid
ozide-miikana *ni* footpath; *pl* ozide-miikanan; *loc* ozide-miikanaang; *dim* ozide-miikanens, ozide-miikanaans
ozisijige *vai* make a bed; *1sg* indoozisijige; *prt* wezisijiged; *also* ozhisijige
ozisinaagane *vai* set the table; *1sg* indoozisinaagane; *prt* wezisinaaganed
oziigaa *vii* be wrinkled; *prt* weziigaag; *aug* oziigaamagad; *prt aug* weziigaamagak
oziigishkaa *vai* wrinkle up; *prt* weziigishkaad
oziigishkaa *vii* wrinkle up; *prt* weziigishkaag; *aug* oziigishkaamagad; *prt aug* weziigishkaamagak
oziigizi *vai* be wrinkled; *1sg* indooziigiz; *prt* weziigizid
oziigiingwe *vai* have a wrinkled face; *1sg* indooziigiingwe; *prt* weziigiingwed
oziisigobimizh *na* willow; *pl* oziisigobimizhiig; *loc* oziisigobimizhiing; *dim* oziisigobimizhiins

oziisigobimizhii-makak *ni* willow basket; *pl* oziisigobimizhii-makakoon; *loc* oziisigobimizhii-makakong; *dim* oziisigobimizhii-makakoons
ozosodam *vai2* cough; *1sg* indoozosodam; *prt* wezosodang
ozosodamoo-mashkiki *ni* cough medicine
ozosodamwaapine *vai* have a respiratory illness, have tuberculosis; *1sg* indoozosodamwaapine; *prt* wezosodamwaapined
ozosodamwaapinewin *ni* tuberculosis
oo *pc* oh!
oodena *ni* town; *pl* oodenawan; *loc* oodenaang; *dim* oodenawens, oodenaans
oojii *na* fly (insect); *pl* oojiig; *dim* oojiins; *also* oojiins
ookwe *na* maggot; *pl* ookweg; *dim* ookwens
ookwemin *ni* black cherry; *pl* ookweminan; *dim* ookweminens
ookweminagaawanzh *na* black cherry bush; *pl* ookweminagaawanzhiig; *loc* ookweminagaawanzhiing; *dim* ookweminagaawanzhiins
oonh *pc* oh!, so...

P

pane *pc* always, continuously; *also* apane

S

sa *pc* emphatic; *also* isa
-sh *pc* and, and then; *also* dash, idash
shi *pc* plus *used in counting; also* ashi

T

taayaa *pc* man's expression of mild displeasure or disdain; *also* aatayaa

w= *pre third person prefix before an initial ii of a dependent noun stem*

wabaashiiwan *vii* there is a narrows; *prt* **webaashiiwang**

wabigamaa *vii* there is a channel between lakes, there is a narrows; *prt* **webigamaag**; *aug* **wabigamaamagad**; *prt aug* **webigamaamagak**

wadab *na* spruce root; *pl* **wadabiig**; *loc* **wadabiing**; *dim* **wadabiins**

wadabii-makak *ni* basket of spruce root; *pl* **wadabii-makakoon**; *loc* **wadabii-makakong**; *dim* **wadabii-makakoons**

wadikwan *ni* branch; *pl* **wadikwanan**; *loc* **wadikwaning**; *dim* **wadikwaans**

wadiswan *ni* bird nest; *pl* **wadiswanan**; *loc* **wadiswaning**; *dim* **wadiswaans**

wado *na* blood clot; *pl* **wadowag**

wadoop *ni* alder; *pl* **wadoopiin**; *loc* **wadoopiing**; *dim* **wadoopiins**

wagidajiw *pc* on top of a mountain; *also* **ogidajiw***, **agidajiw**

wagidakamig *pc* on top of the ground; *also* **ogidakamig***, **agidakamig**

wagidasin *pc* on top of a rock; *also* **ogidasin***, **agidasin**

wagidaabik *pc* on something mineral (e.g., metal, glass, rock); *also* **ogidaabik***, **agidaabik**

wagidaajiwan *pc* upstream; *also* **ogidaajiwan***, **agidaajiwan**

wagidaaki *pc* on top of a hill; *also* **ogidaaki***, **agidaaki**

wagidibiig *pc* on top of the water; *also* **ogidibiig***, **agidibiig**

wagidigamig *pc* on top of the house; *also* **ogidigamig***, **agidigamig**

wagidiskwam *pc* on top of the ice; *also* **ogidiskwam***, **agidiskwam**

wagijayi'ii *pc* on top of it; *also* **ogijayi'ii***, **agijayi'ii**

wagiji- *pn* on top of; *also* **ogiji-***, **agiji-**

wa'aw *pr* this *animate singular demonstrative*

wa'awedi *pr* this over here *animate singular demonstrative*

wajepii *vai* be fast; *1sg* **niwajepii**; *prt* **wejepiid**

wajiw *ni* mountain; *pl* **wajiwan**; *loc* **wajiwing**; *dim* **wajiwens**

wakewaji *vai* can't take the cold, get chilled easily; *1sg* **niwakewaj**; *prt* **wekewajid**

wanagek *na* bark (of a tree); *pl* **wanagekwag**; *loc* **wanagekong**; *dim* **wanagekoons**

wanagekogamig *ni* bark lodge; *pl* **wanagekogamigoon**; *loc* **wanagekogamigong**; *dim* **wanagekogamigoons**

wanagim *vta* miscount s.o.; *1sg* **niwanagimaa**; *prt* **wenagimaad**

wanagindan *vti* miscount s.t., misread s.t.; *1sg* **niwanagindaan**; *prt* **wenagindang**

wanagindaaso *vai* miscount, misread; *1sg* **niwanagindaas**; *prt* **wenagindaasod**

wanakong *pc* on the tip, on the treetop

wanaabidoo'an *vti* make a mistake beading s.t. on a loom; *1sg* **niwanaabidoo'aan**; *prt* **wenaabidoo'ang**

wanaabidoo'ige *vai* make a mistake beading things on a loom; *1sg* **niwanaabidoo'ige**; *prt* **wenaabidoo'iged**

wanaanimizi *vai* have stage fright, be confused; *1sg* **niwanaanimiz**; *prt* **wenaanimizid**

wanendam *vai2* forget; *1sg* **niwanendam**; *prt* **wenendang**

wanendamaa *vai* faint; *1sg* **niwanendamaa**; *prt* **wenendamaad**

wanendan *vti* forget s.t.; *1sg* **niwanendaan**; *prt* **wenendang**

wanenim *vta* forget s.o.; *1sg* **niwanenimaa**; *prt* **wenenimaad**

wani- *pv4* in error, by mistake

wanibatoo *vai* run the wrong way; *1sg* **niwanibatoo**; *prt* **wenibatood**

wanibizo *vai* get lost driving; *1sg* **niwanibiz**; *prt* **wenibizod**

wanibii'an *vti* make a mistake writing s.t.; *1sg* **niwanibii'aan**; *prt* **wenibii'ang**

wanibii'ige *vai* make a mistake writing; *1sg* **niwanibii'ige**; *prt* **wenibii'iged**

wanichige *vai* make a mistake; *1sg* **niwanichige**; *prt* **wenichiged**

wanigiizhwe *vai* make a mistake speaking, mispronounce; *1sg* **niwanigiizhwe**; *prt* **wenigiizhwed**

wanigwaadan *vti* make a mistake sewing on s.t.; *1sg* **niwanigwaadaan**; *prt* **wenigwaadang**

wanigwaaso *vai* make a mistake sewing; *1sg* **niwanigwaas**; *prt* **wenigwaasod**

wanigwaazh /wanigwaaN-/ *vta* make a mistake sewing on s.o.; *1sg* **niwanigwaanaa**; *prt* **wenigwaanaad**

wani' *vta* lose s.o.; *1sg* **niwani'aa**; *prt* **weni'aad**

wanim *vta* mislead s.o. by speech, confuse s.o. by speech; *1sg* **niwanimaa**; *prt* **wenimaad**

wanin *vta* take s.o. who/that is the wrong one, touch s.o. who/that is the wrong one; *1sg* **niwaninaa**; *prt* **weninaad**

waninan *vti* take s.t. that is the wrong one, touch s.t. that is the wrong one; *1sg* **niwaninaan**; *prt* **weninang**

waninawe'an *vti* stir s.t.; *1sg* **niwaninawe'aan**; *prt* **weninawe'ang**

waninawe'igan *ni* eggbeater, mixer; *pl* **waninawe'iganan**; *loc* **waninawe'iganing**; *dim* **waninawe'igaans**

wanishim *vta* misplace s.o.; *1sg* **niwanishimaa**; *prt* **wenishimaad**

wanishin *vai* be lost, get lost; *1sg* **niwanishin**; *prt* **wenishing**

wanishkwe' *vta* distract s.o., interrupt s.o.; *1sg* **niwanishkwe'aa**; *prt* **wenishkwe'aad**

wanishkwem *vta* disturb s.o. by speech, interrupt s.o. by speech; *1sg* **niwanishkwemaa**; *prt* **wenishkwemaad**

wanishkweyendam *vai* be distracted; *1sg* **niwanishkweyendam**; *prt* **wenishkweyendang**

wanisidoon *vti2* misplace s.t.; *1sg* **niwanisidoon**; *prt* **wenisidood**

wanisin *vii* be lost, get lost; *prt* **wenising**

wanitam *vai2* misunderstand something heard; *1sg* **niwanitam;** *prt* **wenitang**

wanitaw *vta* misunderstand (what) s.o. (says); *1sg* **niwanitawaa;** *prt* **wenitawaad**

wanitoon *vti2* lose s.t.; *1sg* **niwanitoon;** *prt* **wenitood**

wanii'amaw *vta* trap for s.o.; *1sg* **niwanii'amawaa;** *prt* **wenii'amawaad**

wanii'igan *ni* trap; *pl* **wanii'iganan;** *loc* **wanii'iganing;** *dim* **wanii'igaans**

wanii'ige *vai* trap; *1sg* **niwanii'ige;** *prt* **wenii'iged**

wanii'igewinini *na* trapper; *pl* **wanii'igewininiwag**

waniike *vai+o* forget (s.t.); *1sg* **niwaniike,** **niwaniiken;** *prt* **weniiked**

wapaa' *vta* disturb s.o.'s sleep; *1sg* **niwapaa'aa;** *prt* **wepaa'aad**

washkibagizo *vai* turn in place; *1sg* **niwashkibagiz;** *prt* **weshkibagizod**

washkigaabawi *vai* turn while standing; *1sg* **niwashkigaabaw;** *prt* **weshkigaabawid**

washki-giiwe *vai* turn and go back; *1sg* **niwashki-giiwe;** *prt* **weshki-giiwed**

washkitigweyaa *vii* flow around a bend (as a river); *prt* **weshkitigweyaag;** *aug* **washkitigweyaamagad;** *prt aug* **weshkitigweyaamagak**

wawaase= < waase

wawaasese *vii* there is lightning; *prt* **wewaaseseg;** *aug* **wawaasesemagad;** *prt aug* **wewaasesemagak**

wawenabi *vai* sit down, be seated; *1sg* **niwawenab;** *prt* **wewenabid**

wawezhichigaade *vii* be decorated, be made pretty; *prt* **wewezhichigaadeg;** *aug* **wawezhichigaademagad;** *prt aug* **wewezhichigaademagak**

wawezhichigaazo *vai* be decorated; *prt* **wewezhichigaazod**

wawezhichige *vai* decorate things; *1sg* **niwawezhichige;** *prt* **wewezhichiged**

wawezhi' *vta* decorate s.o., dress s.o. up, make s.o. up; *1sg* **niwawezhi'aa;** *prt* **wewezhi'aad**

wawezhi'o *vai* dress up, make up oneself; *1sg* **niwawezhi';** *prt* **wewezhi'od**

wawezhitoon *vti2* decorate s.t.; *1sg* **niwawezhitoon;** *prt* **wewezhitood**

wawiyadendaagozi *vai* be considered cute, be considered funny (comical); *1sg* **niwawiyadendaagoz;** *prt* **wewiyadendaagozid**

wawiyadendaagwad *vii* be cute; *prt* **wewiyadendaagwak**

wawiyadenim *vta* think s.o. cute, think s.o. comical; *1sg* **niwawiyadenimaa;** *prt* **wewiyadenimaad**

wawiyazh *pc* funny, comical

wawiyazhinaagozi *vai* look cute, look funny (comical); *1sg* **niwawiyazhinaagoz;** *prt* **wewiyazhinaagozid**

wawiyazhinaagwad *vii* look cute, look funny (comical); *prt* **wewiyazhinaagwak**

wawiyazhitaagozi *vai* sound cute, sound funny (comical); *1sg* **niwawiyazhitaagoz;** *prt* **wewiyazhitaagozid**

wawiyazhitaagwad *vii* sound cute, sound funny (comical); *prt* **wewiyazhitaagwak**

wawiinge *pc* well, properly, carefully, completely

wawiingechige *vai* do exactly, do skilfully; *1sg* **niwawiingechige;** *prt* **wewiingechiged**

wawiinge' *vta* make s.o. skilfully; *1sg* **niwawiinge'aa;** *prt* **wewiinge'aad**

wawiingetoon *vti2* make s.t. skilfully; *1sg* **niwawiingetoon;** *prt* **wewiingetood**

wawiingezi *vai* be skilful; *1sg* **niwawiingez;** *prt* **wewiingezid**

way *pc* exclamation

wayaabishkiiwed *na-pt* white person; *pl* **wayaabishkiiwejig**

wayekwaase *vii* come to an end; *prt* **weyekwaaseg;** *aug* **wayekwaasemagad;** *prt aug* **weyekwaasemagak**

wayeshkad *pc* at first, in the beginning

wayezhim *vta* cheat s.o., deceive s.o.; *1sg* **niwayezhimaa;** *prt* **weyezhimaad**

wayezhinge *vai* cheat people, deceive people; *1sg* **niwayezhinge;** *prt* **weyezhinged**

wayiiba *pc* soon, early, in a little while; *also* **wiiba***

wazhashk *na* muskrat; *pl* **wazhashkwag;** *dim* **wazhashkoons**

wazhashkwayaan *na* muskrat hide; *pl* **wazhashkwayaanag;** *loc* **wazhashkwayaaning;** *dim* **wazhashkwayaanens**

wazhashkwedo *na* fungus; *pl* **wazhashkwedowag;** *dim* **wazhashkwedoons**

wazhashkwedoons *na* mushroom; *pl* **wazhashkwedoonsag**

wazhashkwiish *ni* muskrat lodge; *pl* **wazhashkwiishan;** *loc* **wazhashkwiishing**

waa *pc* exclamation

waa- *pv1* will, want to *changed form of future/desiderative verb prefix*

waabam *vta* see s.o.; *1sg* **niwaabamaa;** *prt* **wayaabamaad**

waabamoojichaagwaan *ni* mirror; *pl* **waabamoojichaagwaanan;** *loc* **waabamoojichaagwaaning;** *dim* **waabamoojichaagwaanens**

waaban *vii* be dawn, be tomorrow; *prt* **wayaabang**

waabananokii *vai* work until dawn; *1sg* **niwaabananokii;** *prt* **wayaabananokiid**

waabanda' *vta* show (s.t.) to s.o.; *1sg* **niwaabanda'aa;** *prt* **wayaabanda'aad**

waabanda'iwe *vai* show (s.t.) to people; *1sg* **niwaabanda'iwe;** *prt* **wayaabanda'iwed**

waabanda'iwewin *ni* show, exhibition; *pl* **waabanda'iwewinan;** *loc* **waabanda'iwewining**

waabandan *vti* see s.t.; *1sg* **niwaabandaan;** *prt* **wayaabandang**

waabandiwag /waabandi-/ *vai* they see each other; *1pl* **niwaabandimin;** *prt* **wayaabandijig**

waabandizo *vai* see oneself; *1sg* **niwaabandiz;** *prt* **wayaabandizod**

waabandizowin *ni* mirror; *pl* **waabandizowinan;** *loc* **waabandizowining;** *dim* **waabandizowinens**

waabang *vii* tomorrow *conjunct form of verb* **waaban**

waabange *vai* observe people, be a spectator, be a witness; *1sg* **niwaabange**; *prt* **wayaabanged**

waabani-noodin *ni* east wind

waabanjigaade *vii* be seen; *prt* **wayaabanjigaadeg**; *aug* **waabanjigaademagad**; *prt aug* **wayaabanjigaademagak**

waabanjigaazo *vai* be seen; *prt* **wayaabanjigaazod**

waabanong *pc* in the east, to the east

waabashkiki *ni* swamp; *pl* **waabashkikiin**; *loc* **waabashkikiing**; *dim* **waabashkikiins**

waabashkikiiwan *vii* be swampy; *prt* **wayaabashkikiiwang**

waabaabigan *na* white clay

waabaaso *vai* fade from light; *prt* **wayaabaasod**

waabaate *vii* fade from light; *prt* **wayaabaateg**; *aug* **waabaatemagad**; *prt aug* **wayaabaatemagak**

waabi *vai* have vision, see; *1sg* **niwaab**; *prt* **wayaabid**

waabide *vii* be faded, be bleached; *prt* **wayaabideg**; *aug* **waabidemagad**; *prt aug* **wayaabidemagak**

waabigan *na* clay; *loc* **waabiganing**

waabiganikaade *vii* be made of clay, be made of concrete; *prt* **wayaabiganikaadeg**; *aug* **waabiganikaademagad**; *prt aug* **wayaabiganikaademagak**

waabigwan *ni* flower; *pl* **waabigwaniin**; *loc* **waabigwaniing**; *dim* **waabigwaniins**

waabigwanii-giizis *na* May

waabijiiyaa *vii* be grey; *prt* **wayaabijiiyaag**; *aug* **waabijiiyaamagad**; *prt aug* **wayaabijiiyaamagak**

waabijiizi *vai* be grey; *prt* **wayaabijiizid**

waabikwe *vai* have grey hair; *1sg* **niwaabikwe**; *prt* **wayaabikwed**

waabi-makade *ni* smokeless gunpowder

waabi-manoomin *ni* white rice; *loc* **waabimanoomining**

waabishkawedoon *vai* have white whiskers; *1sg* **niwaabishkawedoon**; *prt* **wayaabishkawedoong**

waabishkaa *vii* be white; *prt* **wayaabishkaag**; *aug* **waabishkaamagad**; *prt aug* **wayaabishkaamagak**

waabishkaabikad *vii* be white (as something mineral); *prt* **wayaabishkaabikak**

waabishkaabikizi *vai* be white (as something mineral); *prt* **wayaabishkaabikizid**

waabishkaabiigad *vii* be white (as something string-like); *prt* **wayaabishkaabiigak**

waabishkaabiigizi *vai* be white (as something string-like); *prt* **wayaabishkaabiigizid**

waabishkaakozi *vai* be white (as something stick- or wood-like); *prt* **wayaabishkaakozid**

waabishkaakwad *vii* be white (as something stick- or wood-like); *prt* **wayaabishkaakwak**

waabishkaanakwad *vii* there are white clouds; *prt* **wayaabishkaanakwak**

waabishkaande *vii* be colored white; *prt* **wayaabishkaandeg**; *aug*

waabishkaandemagad; *prt aug* **wayaabishkaandemagak**

waabishkaanzo *vai* be colored white; *prt* **wayaabishkaanzod**

waabishki- *pv4* white

waabishki'o *vai* wear white; *1sg* **niwaabishki'**; *prt* **wayaabishki'od**

waabishkindibe *vai* have white hair; *1sg* **niwaabishkindibe**; *prt* **wayaabishkindibed**

waabishkizi *vai* be white; *prt* **wayaabishkizid**

waabishkiigad *vii* be white (as something sheet-like); *prt* **wayaabishkiigak**

waabishkiigin *ni* sheet, white cloth; *pl* **waabishkiiginoon**; *loc* **waabishkiiginong**; *dim* **waabishkiiginoons**

waabishkiigizi *vai* be white (as something sheet-like); *prt* **wayaabishkiigizid**

waabishkiingwechigan *ni* face powder; *loc* **waabishkiingwechiganing**; *dim* **waabishkiingwechigaans**

waabishkiingwechige *vai* use face powder; *1sg* **niwaabishkiingwechige**; *prt* **wayaabishkiingwechiged**

waabishkiiwe *vai* be a white person; *1sg* **niwaabishkiiwe**; *prt* **wayaabishkiiwed**

waabizhagindibe *vai* be bald; *1sg* **niwaabizhagindibe**; *prt* **wayaabizhagindibed**

waabizheshi *na* marten; *pl* **waabizheshiwag**; *dim* **waabizheshiins**

waabizheshiwayaan *na* marten hide; *pl* **waabizheshiwayaanag**; *loc* **waabizheshiwayaaning**; *dim* **waabizheshiwayaanens**

waabizii *na* swan; *pl* **waabiziig**; *dim* **waabiziins**

waabizo *vai* be faded, be bleached; *prt* **wayaabizod**

waabiingwe *vai* be pale faced; *1sg* **niwaabiingwe**; *prt* **wayaabiingwed**

waaboozwayaan *na* rabbit skin; *pl* **waaboozwayaanag**; *dim* **waaboozwayaanens**

waabooyaan *ni* blanket; *pl* **waabooyaanan**; *loc* **waabooyaaning**; *dim* **waabooyaanens**; *also* **waabowayaan**

waabooz *na* snowshoe hare, rabbit; *pl* **waaboozoog**; *dim* **waaboozoons**

waaboozwaaboo *ni* rabbit soup; *loc* **waaboozwaaboong**

waagaa *vii* be bent; *prt* **wayaagaag**; *aug* **waagaamagad**; *prt aug* **wayaagaamagak**

waagaabikad *vii* be bent (as something mineral); *prt* **wayaagaabikak**

waagaabikizi *vai* be bent (as something mineral); *prt* **wayaagaabikizid**

waagaakozi *vai* be bent (as something stick- or wood-like); *prt* **wayaagaakozid**

waagaakwad *ni* ax; *pl* **waagaakwadoon**; *loc* **waagaakwadong**; *dim* **waagaakwadoons**

waagaakwad *vii* be bent (as something stick- or wood-like); *prt* **wayaagaakwak**

waagaakwadoons *ni* hatchet; *pl* **waagaakwadoonsan**; *loc* **waagaakwadoonsing**

waagaakwadwaatig *ni* ax handle; *pl*
  waagaakwadwaatigoon; *loc*
  waagaakwadwaatigong; *dim*
  waagaakwadwaatigoons
waagibidoon *vti2* bend s.t. with hands; *1sg*
  niwaagibidoon; *prt* wayaagibidood
waagibizh /waagibiN-/ *vta* bend s.o. with hands;
  1sg niwaagibinaa; *prt* wayaagibinaad
waagikomaan *ni* crooked knife; *pl*
  waagikomaanan; *dim* waagikomaanens

waagikomaan (crooked knife)

waagin *vta* bend s.o. with hand; *1sg* niwaaginaa;
  prt wayaaginaad
waaginan *vti* bend s.t. with hand; *1sg*
  niwaaginaan; *prt* wayaaginang
waaginaa *na* canoe rib; *pl* waaginaag; *loc*
  waaginaang; *dim* waaginaans
waaginogaan *ni* domed lodge, wigwam; *pl*
  waaginogaanan; *loc* waaginogaaning; *dim*
  waaginogaanens

waaginogaan (domed lodge, wigwam)

waagizi *vai* be bent; *prt* wayaagizid
waagosh *na* fox; *pl* waagoshag; *dim* waagoshens
waagoshiwayaan *na* fox hide; *pl*
  waagoshiwayaanag; *dim* waagoshiwayaanens
waak *ni* fish egg; *pl* waakwan
waakaa'igan *ni* house, building; *pl* waakaa'iganan;
  loc waakaa'iganing; *dim* waakaa'igaans
waakaa'ige *vai* build a house; *1sg* niwaakaa'ige;
  prt wayaakaa'iged
waakaa'igewinini *na* carpenter; *pl*
  waakaa'igewininiwag

waangawi' *vta* tame s.o.; *1sg* niwaangawi'aa; *prt*
  wayaangawi'aad
waangawizi *vai* be tame; *1sg* niwaangawiz; *prt*
  wayaangawizid
waangoom *vta* adopt s.o.; *1sg* niwaangoomaa; *prt*
  wayaangoomaad
waanikaan *ni* excavated hole; *pl* waanikaanan; *loc*
  waanikaaning; *dim* waanikaanens
waanike *vai* dig a hole; *1sg* niwaanike; *prt*
  wayaaniked
waanzh *ni* den, cave, burrow; *pl* waanzhan; *loc*
  waanzhing; *dim* waanzhens
waanzhibiiyaa *vii* be a pond, be a pothole of
  water, be a puddle; *prt* wayaanzhibiiyaag; *aug*
  waanzhibiiyaamagad; *prt aug*
  wayaanzhibiiyaamagak
waasa *pc* far, distant
waasamowin *ni* lightning, electricity
waasamoo- *pv4* powered, electric
waasamoo-anokiiwinini *na* electrician; *pl*
  waasamoo-anokiiwininiwag
waasamoo-bimide *ni* gasoline; *loc* waasamoo-
  bimideng
waasamoo-jiimaan *ni* motor launch; *pl*
  waasamoo-jiimaanan; *loc* waasamoo-
  jiimaaning; *dim* waasamoo-jiimaanens
waasamoo-waazakonenjigan *ni* electric lamp; *pl*
  waasamoo-waazakonenjiganan; *loc*
  waasamoo-waazakonenjiganing; *dim*
  waasamoo-waazakonenjigaans
waasamoowidaabaan *na* car; *pl*
  waasamoowidaabaanag; *loc*
  waasamoowidaabaaning; *dim*
  waasamoowidaabaanens
waasawad *vii* be far; *prt* wayaasawak
waasaabikide *vii* shine (as something mineral),
  reflect (as something mineral); *prt*
  wayaasaabikideg; *aug* waasaabikidemagad;
  prt aug wayaasaabikidemagak
waasaabikizo *vai* shine (as something mineral),
  reflect (as something mineral); *prt*
  wayaasaabikizod
waasechigan *ni* window; *pl* waasechiganan; *loc*
  waasechiganing; *dim* waasechigaans
waasechiganaabik *ni* window glass, window pane;
  pl waasechiganaabikoon; *loc*
  waasechiganaabikong; *dim*
  waasechiganaabikoons
waasese *vii* there is a flash of lightning; *prt*
  wayaaseseg; *aug* waasesemagad; *prt aug*
  wayaasesemagak
waasete *vii* be bright inside; *prt* wayaaseteg; *aug*
  waasetemagad; *prt aug* wayaasetemagak
waaseyaa *vii* be bright, be sunny; *prt*
  wayaaseyaag; *aug* waaseyaamagad; *prt aug*
  wayaaseyaamagak
waaseyaaban *vii* be light at dawn; *prt*
  wayaaseyaabang
waaseyaanakwad *vii* clouds can be seen through;
  prt wayaaseyaanakwak
waaseyiigad *vii* be bright (as something sheet-
  like), be shiny (as something sheet-like); *prt*
  wayaaseyiigak

waaseyiigizi *vai* be bright (as something sheet-like), be shiny (as something sheet-like); *prt* **wayaaseyiigizid**
waashkobaagamig *ni-pt* soft drink; *pl* **waashkobaagamigin**
waashkobizid bakwezhigan *na-pt* sweet roll, pastry, cake; *pl* **waashkobizijig bakwezhiganag**
Waashtanong *place* Washington, D.C.
waasiko' *vta* make s.o. shiny; *1sg* **niwaasiko'aa**; *prt* **wayaasiko'aad**
waasikotoon *vti2* make s.t. shiny; *1sg* **niwaasikotoon**; *prt* **wayaasikotood**
waasikwa' *vta* polish s.o., shine s.o.; *1sg* **niwaasikwa'waa**; *prt* **wayaasikwa'waad**
waasikwa'an *vti* polish s.t., shine s.t.; *1sg* **niwaasikwa'aan**; *prt* **wayaasikwa'ang**
waaswaa *vai* shine for game or fish, jacklight; *1sg* **niwaaswaa**; *prt* **wayaaswaad**
waaswaagan *ni* torch; *pl* **waaswaaganan**; *loc* **waaswaaganing**; *dim* **waaswaagaans**
waatebagaa *vii* there are bright leaves; *prt* **wayaatebagaag**; *aug* **waatebagaamagad**; *prt* *aug* **wayaatebagaamagak**
waatebagaa-giizis *na* October, September; *also* **waatebago-giizis**
waawan *ni* egg; *pl* **waawanoon**; *loc* **waawanong**; *dim* **waawanoons**
waawaabiganoojiinh *na* mouse; *pl* **waawaabiganoojiinyag**; *dim* **waawaabiganoojiins**
waawaashkeshi *na* deer; *pl* **waawaashkeshiwag**; *dim* **waawaashkeshiins**
waawaashkeshiwayaan *na* deer hide; *pl* **waawaashkeshiwayaanag**; *loc* **waawaashkeshiwayaaning**; *dim* **waawaashkeshiwayaanens**
waawaashkeshiwi-wiiyaas *ni* deer meat
waawaatesi *na* firefly; *pl* **waawaatesiwag**; *dim* **waawaatesiins**; *also* **wewaatesi**
waawiyebii'igan *ni* compass (drawing instrument); *pl* **waawiyebii'iganan**; *loc* **waawiyebii'iganing**; *dim* **waawiyebii'igaans**
waawiyebii'ige *vai* draw a circle; *1sg* **niwaawiyebii'ige**; *prt* **wayaawiyebii'iged**
waawiye' *vta* make s.o. round; *1sg* **niwaawiye'aa**; *prt* **wayaawiye'aad**
waawiyeminagad *vii* be round (as something ball-like); *prt* **wayaawiyeminagak**
waawiyeminagizi *vai* be round (as something ball-like); *prt* **wayaawiyeminagizid**
waawiyetoon *vti2* make s.t. round; *1sg* **niwaawiyetoon**; *prt* **wayaawiyetood**
waawiyeyaa *vii* be round, be circular; *prt* **wayaawiyeyaag**; *aug* **waawiyeyaamagad**; *prt* *aug* **wayaawiyeyaamagak**
waawiyeyaabikad *vii* be round (as something mineral); *prt* **wayaawiyeyaabikak**
waawiyeyaabikizi *vai* be round (as something mineral); *prt* **wayaawiyeyaabikizid**
waawiyeyaakozi *vai* be round (as something stick- or wood-like); *prt* **wayaawiyeyaakozid**
waawiyeyaakwad *vii* be round (as something stick- or wood-like); *prt* **wayaawiyeyaakwak**

waawiyezi *vai* be round, be circular; *1sg* **niwaawiyez**; *prt* **wayaawiyezid**
waawiindamaw *vta* explain (s.t.) to s.o., tell about (s.t.) to s.o., promise (s.t.) to s.o.; *1sg* **niwaawiindamawaa**; *prt* **wayaawiindamawaad**
waawiindamaage *vai* explain (s.t.) to people, promise (s.t.) to people; *1sg* **niwaawiindamaage**; *prt* **wayaawiindamaaged**
waawiinjigaade *vii* be explained, be talked about all the time; *prt* **wayaawiinjigaadeg**; *aug* **waawiinjigaademagad**; *prt* *aug* **wayaawiinjigaademagak**
waawiinjigaazo *vai* be talked about all the time; *prt* **wayaawiinjigaazod**
waawiinzh /waawiinN-/ *vta* mention s.o., name s.o.; *1sg* **ninwaawiinaa**; *prt* **wayaawiinaad**
waawoono *vai* howl (e.g., a dog); *prt* **wayaawoonod**
waazakone *vii* glow, give off light; *prt* **wayaazakoneg**; *aug* **waazakonemagad**; *prt* *aug* **wayaazakonemagak**
waazakonebidoon *vti2* turn s.t. on for a light; *1sg* **niwaazakonebidoon**; *prt* **wayaazakonebidood**
waazakonenjigan *ni* lamp; *pl* **waazakonenjiganan**; *loc* **waazakonenjiganing**; *dim* **waazakonenjigaans**
waazakonenjiganaaboo *ni* kerosene; *loc* **waazakonenjiganaaboong**
waazakonenjiganaaboowadaawewigamig *ni* gas station; *also* **waazakonenjiganaaboo-adaawewigamig**
waazakonenjiganaaboowakik *na* gas tank, gas can; *pl* **waazakonenjiganaaboowakikoog**; *loc* **waazakonenjiganaaboowakikong**; *dim* **waazakonenjiganaaboowakikoons**
waazakonenjiganaatig *ni* light pole; *pl* **waazakonenjiganaatigoon**; *loc* **wazakonenjiganaatigong**; *dim* **waazakonenjiganaatigoons**
weba' /weba'w-/ *vta* shove s.o. away using something; *1sg* **niweba'waa**; *prt* **wayeba'waad**
weba'an *vti* shove s.t. away using something; *1sg* **niweba'aan**; *prt* **wayeba'ang**
webaashi *vai* be blown away; *1sg* **niwebaash**; *prt* **wayebaashid**
webaasin *vii* be blown away; *prt* **wayebaasing**
webin *vta* throw s.o. away; *1sg* **niwebinaa**; *prt* **wayebinaad**
webinan *vti* throw s.t. away; *1sg* **niwebinaan**; *prt* **wayebinang**
webinidiwag /webinidi-/ *vai* they separate from each other, they divorce each other; *1pl* **niwebinidimin**; *prt* **wayebinidijig**
webinigan *na* someone abandoned; *pl* **webiniganag**; *dim* **webinigaans**
webinigaade *vii* be thrown away; *prt* **wayebinigaadeg**; *aug* **webinigaademagad**; *prt* *aug* **wayebinigaademagak**
webinigaazo *vai* be thrown away; *prt* **wayebinigaazod**
webinige *vai* throw things away; *1sg* **niwebinige**; *prt* **wayebiniged**

wegimaawabid *na-pt* councillor, government official; *pl* **wegimaawabijig**

wegodogwen *pr* I don't know what *inanimate dubitative*, I wonder what *inanimate dubitative; plural* **wegodogwenan**

wegodogwen *igo pr* whatever it might be *inanimate dubitative*

wegonen *pr* what *inanimate interrogative; plural* **wegonenan**; *also* **awegonen**

wegonesh *pr* what, and what *inanimate interrogative*

wegwaagi *pc* behold!

wemitigoozhi *na* Frenchman; *pl* **wemitigoozhiwag**; *dim* **wemitigoozhiins**

wemitigoozhiimo *vai* speak French; *1sg* **niwemitigoozhiim**; *prt* **wayemitigoozhiimod**

Wenabozho *na* name of **aadizookaan** character viewed as culture hero and trickster; *also* **Nenabozho***

wenda- *pv4* really, completely, just so

wendad *vii* be easy, be cheap; *prt* **wayendak**

wendaginde *vii* be cheap; *prt* **wayendagindeg**; *aug* **wendagindemagad**; *prt aug* **wayendagindemagak**

wendaginzo *vai* be cheap; *prt* **wayendaginzod**

wendaabang *vii* east, where the dawn comes from *conjunct of:* **ondaaban**

wendizi *vai* be easy, be cheap; *prt* **wayendizid**

weniban *pc* disappeared!, gone!

wenipanad *vii* be easy, be cheap; *prt* **wayenipanak**

wenipanendan *vti* consider s.t. easy; *1sg* **niwenipanendaan**; *prt* **wayenipanendang**

wenipanizi *vai* be easy; *prt* **wayenipanizid**

wenipazh *pc* at hand, easily

wenipazhi' *vta* get s.o. easily; *1sg* **niwenipazhi'aa**; *prt* **wayenipazhi'aad**

wenipazhitoon *vti2* get s.t. easily; *1sg* **niwenipazhitoon**; *prt* **wayenipazhitood**

wenji- *pv3* from a certain place, for a certain reason, because *changed from of* **onji-**

wese'an *vii* be a tornado; *prt* **wayese'ang**

wetotwaag *ni-pt* jello

wewayiiba *pc* every little while; *also* **wewiiba***

wewaagijiizid *ni-pt* banana; *pl* **wewaagijiizijig**

wewebanaabii *vai* fish with a hook and line; *1sg* **niwewebanaabii**; *prt* **wayewebanaabiid**

wewebaanoweni *vai* wag one's tail; *prt* **wayewebaanowenid**

wewebikweni *vai* nod one's head; *1sg* **niwewebikwen**; *prt* **wayewebikwenid**

wewebikwetaw *vta* shake one's head at s.o.; *1sg* **niwewebikwetawaa**; *prt* **wayewebikwetawaad**

wewebizo *vai* swing; *1sg* **niwewebiz**; *prt* **wayewebizod**

wewebizon *ni* swing; *pl* **wewebizonan**; *loc* **wewebizoning**; *dim* **wewebizonens**

wewebizoo-apabiwin *ni* rocking chair; *pl* **wewebizoo-apabiwinan**; *loc* **wewebizoo-apabiwining**; *dim* **wewebizoo-apabiwinens**

weweni *pc* properly, correctly, carefully

wewese' /**wewese'w-**/ *vta* fan s.o.; *1sg* **niwewese'waa**; *prt* **wayewese'waad**

wewese'idizo *vai* fan oneself; *1sg* **niwewese'idiz**; *prt* **wayewese'idizod**

wewese'igan *ni* hand fan; *pl* **wewese'iganan**; *loc* **wewese'iganing**; *dim* **wewese'igaans**

wewese'ige *vai* fan things; *1sg* **niwewese'ige**; *prt* **wayewese'iged**

wewiib *pc* in a hurry, quickly, hurry

wewiibendam *vai* be eager, want to hurry; *1sg* **niwewiibendam**; *prt* **wayewiibendang**

wewiibi' *vta* hurry s.o., hurry making s.o.; *1sg* **niwewiibi'aa**; *prt* **wayewiibi'aad**

wewiibim *vta* tell s.o. to hurry; *1sg* **niwewiibimaa**; *prt* **wayewiibimaad**

wewiibingwaange *na* teal; *pl* **wewiibingwaangeg**; *dim* **wewiibingwaangens**

wewiibishkaa *vai* hurry; *1sg* **niwewiibishkaa**; *prt* **wayewiibishkaad**

wewiibitaa *vai* hurry (in some work or activity); *1sg* **niwewiibitaa**; *prt* **wayewiibitaad**

wewiibitoon *vti* hurry s.t., hurry making s.t.; *1sg* **niwewiibitoon**; *prt* **wayewiibitood**

wewiibizi *vai* be in a hurry; *1sg* **niwewiibiz**; *prt* **wayewiibizid**

wezaawiminagazid *na-pt* orange (fruit); *pl* **wezaawiminagizijig**

wii- *pv1* want to, will *future/desiderative verb prefix*

wiibidaakaajiganan *ni* false teeth *plural; also* **wiibidaakaanan**

wiibidaa-mashkikiiwinini *na* dentist; *pl* **wiibidaa-mashkikiiwininiwag**

wiibwaa *vii* become narrow, constrict; *prt* **waabwaag**; *aug* **wiibwaamagad**; *prt aug* **waabwaamagak**

wiidabim *vta* sit with s.o.; *1sg* **niwiidabimaa**; *prt* **waadabimaad**

wiidagwazhem *vta* share a cover with s.o.; *1sg* **niwiidagwazhemaa**; *prt* **waadagwazhemaad**

wiidanokiim *vta* work with s.o.; *1sg* **niwiidanokiimaa**; *prt* **waadanokiimaad**

wiidige *vai* marry, be married; *1sg* **niwiidige**; *prt* **waadiged**

wiidigem *vta* marry s.o., be married to s.o.; *1sg* **niwiidigemaa**; *prt* **waadigemaad**

wiidigendiwag /**wiidigendi-**/ *vai* they marry each other, they are married to each other; *1pl* **niwiidigendimin**; *prt* **waadigendijig**

wiidosem *vta* walk with s.o.; *1sg* **niwiidosemaa**; *prt* **waadosemaad**

wiidookaw *vta* help s.o.; *1sg* **niwiidookawaa**; *prt* **waadookawaad**

wiidookaage *vai* help people; *1sg* **niwiidookaage**; *prt* **waadookaaged**

wiidookaazo *vai* help; *1sg* **niwiidookaaz**; *prt* **waadookaazod**

wiidookodaadiwag /**wiidookodaadi-**/ *vai* they help each other; *1pl* **niwiidookodaadimin**; *prt* **waadookodaadijig**

wiidoopam *vta* eat with s.o.; *1sg* **niwiidoopamaa**; *prt* **waadoopamaad**

wiidoopange *vai* eat with people; *1sg* **niwiidoopange**; *prt* **waadoopanged**

wiigiwaam *ni* wigwam, lodge; *pl* **wiigiwaaman**; *loc* **wiigiwaaming**; *dim* **wiigiwaamens**

wiigiwaamaak *ni* wigwam frame; *pl* **wiigiwaamaakoon**; *loc* **wiigiwaamaakong**; *dim* **wiigiwaamaakoons**

wiigiwaamaatig *ni* wigwam pole; *pl*
  wiigiwaamaatigoon; *loc* **wiigiwaamaatigong;**
  dim **wiigiwaamaatigoons**
wiigiwaamige *vai* live in a wigwam; *1sg*
  niwiigiwaamige; *prt* **waagiwaamiged**
wiigiwaamike *vai* make a wigwam; *1sg*
  niwiigiwaamike; *prt* **waagiwaamiked**
wiigob *na* basswood tree; *pl* **wiigobiig**
wiigob *ni* inner bark of basswood; *pl* **wiigobiin;** *loc*
  wiigobiing; *dim* **wiigobiins**
wiigobaatig *na* basswood tree; *pl* **wiigobaatigoog;**
  loc **wiigobaatigong;** *dim* **wiigobaatigoons**
wiigobimizh *na* basswood tree; *pl* **wiigobimizhiig;**
  dim **wiigobimizhiins**
wiigwaas *na* birch tree; *pl* **wiigwaasag;** *loc*
  wiigwaasing; *dim* **wiigwaasens**
wiigwaas *ni* birch bark; *pl* **wiigwaasan;** *loc*
  wiigwaasing; *dim* **wiigwaasens**
wiigwaasabakway *ni* birch bark covering, roll of
  birch bark roofing; *pl* **wiigwaasabakwayan**
wiigwaasabakwaan *na* birch bark roof; *pl*
  wiigwaasabakwaanag; *loc*
  wiigwaasabakwaaning
wiigwaasigamig *ni* birch bark lodge; *pl*
  wiigwaasigamigoon; *loc* **wiigwaasigamigong;**
  dim **wiigwaasigamigoons**
wiigwaasi-jiimaan *ni* birch bark canoe; *pl*
  wiigwaasi-jiimaanan; *loc* **wiigwaasi-**
  jiimaaning; *dim* **wiigwaasi-jiimanens**
wiigwaasikaa *vii* there are many birches; *prt*
  waagwaasikaag; *aug* **wiigwaasikaamagad;** *prt*
  aug **waagwaasikaamagak**
wiigwaasike *vai* remove birch bark from the tree;
  1sg **niwiigwaasike;** *prt* **waagwaasiked**
wiigwaasi-makak *ni* birch bark box, birch bark
  basket; *pl* **wiigwaasi-makakoon;** *loc* **wiigwaasi-**
  makakong; *dim* **wiigwaasi-makakoons**
wiigwaasi-mitig *na* birch (tree); *pl* **wiigwaasi-**
  mitigoog; *loc* **wiigwaasi-mitigong;** *dim*
  wiigwaasi-mitigoons; *also* **wiigwaasaatig**
wiigwaasinaagan *ni* birch bark dish; *pl*
  wiigwaasinaaganan; *loc* **wiigwaasinaaganing;**
  dim **wiigwaasinaagaans**
wiij'anokiim *vta* work with s.o.; *1sg*
  niwiij'anokiimaa; *prt* **waaj'anokiimaad;** *also*
  wiiji-anokiim
wiij'ayaaw *vta* be with s.o., stay with s.o.; *1sg*
  niwiij'ayaawaa; *prt* **waaj'ayaawaad;** *also* **wiiji-**
  ayaaw
wiiji- *pv4* with, in company with
wiijigamigishkaw *vta* be a neighbor to s.o.; *1sg*
  niwiijigamigishkawaa; *prt*
  waajigamigishkawaad
wiijigim *vta* be the same age as s.o.; *1sg*
  niwiijigimaa; *prt* **waajigimaad**
wiijigindiwag /**wiijigindi-**/ *vai* they are the same
  age; *1pl* **niwiijigindimin;** *prt* **waajigindijig**
wiiji' *vta* play with s.o.; *1sg* **niwiiji'aa;** *prt* **waaji'aad**
wiijishimotaw *vta* dance with s.o.; *1sg*
  niwiijishimotawaa; *prt* **waajishimotawaad**
wiijii'iwe *vai* go with people, accompany people;
  1sg **niwiijii'iwe;** *prt* **waajii'iwed**
wiijiindiwag /**wiijiindi-**/ *vai* they go with each
  other, they accompany each other; *1pl*
  niwiijiindimin; *prt* **waajiindijig**

wiijiiw *vta* go with s.o., accompany s.o.; *1sg*
  niwiijiiwaa; *prt* **waajiiwaad**
wiijiiwaagan *na* companion, partner; *pl*
  wiijiiwaaganag
wiikaa *pc* late, seldom, ever
wiikenh *na* sweet flag; *pl* **wiikenyag**
wiikobidaw *vta* pull (s.t.) for s.o.; *1sg*
  niwiikobidawaa; *prt* **waakobidawaad**
wiikobidoon *vti2* pull s.t.; *1sg* **niwiikobidoon;** *prt*
  waakobidood
wiikobijigan *ni* dresser, chest of drawers; *pl*
  wiikobijiganan; *loc* **wiikobijiganing;** *dim*
  wiikobijigaans
wiikobijigaade *vii* be pulled; *prt* **waakobijigaadeg;**
  aug **wiikobijigaademagad;** *prt* *aug*
  waakobijigaademagak
wiikobijigaazo *vai* be pulled; *prt* **waakobijigaazod**
wiikobijige *vai* pull things; *1sg* **niwiikobijige;** *prt*
  waakobijiged
wiikobizh /**wiikobiN-**/ *vta* pull s.o.; *1sg*
  niwiikobinaa; *prt* **waakobinaad**
wiikom *vta* invite s.o. to a feast (especially as part
  of a religious ceremony); *1sg* **niwiikomaa;** *prt*
  waakomaad
wiikondiwag /**wiikondi-**/ *vai* they have a feast; *1pl*
  niwiikondimin; *prt* **waakondijig**
wiikonge *vai* give a feast, invite people to a feast
  (especially as part of a religious ceremony); *1sg*
  niwiikonge; *prt* **waakonged**
wiikwa'ibaan *ni* pump; *pl* **wiikwa'ibaanan;** *loc*
  wiikwa'ibaaning; *dim* **wiikwa'ibaanens**
wiikwa'ibii *vai* pump water; *1sg* **niwiikwa'ibii;** *prt*
  waakwa'ibiid
wiikwaji'o *vai* try to get free; *1sg* **niwiikwaji';** *prt*
  waakwaji'od
wiikwajitoon *vti2* try to do s.t., try to get free of
  s.t.; *1sg* **niwiikwajitoon;** *prt* **waakwajitood**
wiikwam *vta* suck on s.o., draw on s.o. with
  mouth (e.g., a pipe); *1sg* **niwiikwamaa;** *prt*
  waakwamaad
wiikwamo *vai* suck; *1sg* **niwiikwam;** *prt*
  waakwamod
wiikwandan *vti* suck on s.t., draw on s.t. with
  mouth; *1sg* **niwiikwandaan;** *prt* **waakwandang**
wiikwanjige *vai* suck on things, draw on things
  with mouth; *1sg* **niwiikwanjige;** *prt*
  waakwanjiged
wiikwaabiigin *vta* pull s.o. (as with something
  string-like); *1sg* **niwiikwaabiiginaa;** *prt*
  waakwaabiiginaad
wiikwaabiiginan *vti* pull s.t. (as with something
  string-like); *1sg* **niwiikwaabiiginaan;** *prt*
  waakwaabiiginang
wiikwegamaa *vii* be a bay; *prt* **waakwegamaag;**
  aug **wiikwegamaamagad;** *prt* *aug*
  waakwegamaamagak
wiimaashkaa *vai* detour; *1sg* **niwiimaashkaa;** *prt*
  waamaashkaad
wiimbaa *vii* be hollow; *prt* **waambaag;** *aug*
  wiimbaamagad; *prt* *aug* **waambaamagak**
wiimbizi *vai* be hollow; *1sg* **niwiimbiz;** *prt*
  waambizid
wiimbwewe *vii* give a hollow sound; *prt*
  waambweweg; *aug* **wiimbwewemagad;** *prt*
  aug **waambwewemagak**

wiin *pc* contrastive particle
wiin *pr* *third person singular personal pronoun*, she *third person singular personal pronoun*
wiinad *vii* be dirty; *prt* **waanak**
wiinawaa *pr* they *third person plural personal pronoun*
wiinaagamin /wiinaagami-/ *vii* be dirty (as a liquid); *prt* **waanaagamig**
wiinaajimo *vai* tell a dirty story; *1sg* **niwiinaajim**; *prt* **waanaajimod**
wiindamaw *vta* tell s.o. about (s.t.); *1sg* **niwiindamawaa**; *prt* **waandamawaad**
wiindamaage *vai* tell about (s.t.) to people, announce (s.t.) to people; *1sg* **niwiindamaage**; *prt* **waandamaaged**
wiindan *vti* name s.t., mention the name of s.t.; *1sg* **niwiindaan**; *prt* **waandang**
wiinde *vii* have a name; *prt* **waandeg**; *aug* **wiindemagad**; *prt aug* **waandemagak**
wiindigoo *na* windigo: winter cannibal monster; *pl* **wiindigoog**; *dim* **wiindigoons**
wiindigoo-bineshiinh *na* kingbird; *pl* **wiindigoo-bineshiinyag**
wiindigoowi *vai* be a windigo; *1sg* **niwiindigoow**; *prt* **waandigoowid**
wiineta *pr* only him *third person singular personal pronoun*, only her *third person singular personal pronoun*
wiinetawaa *pr* only them *third person plural personal pronoun*
wiingashk *ni* sweet grass; *pl* **wiingashkoon**; *loc* **wiingashkong**; *dim* **wiingashkoons**
wiinibiigoo *na* Winnebago; *pl* **wiinibiigoog**; *dim* **wiinibiigoons**
wiinichige *vai* dirty things; *1sg* **niwiinichige**; *prt* **waanichiged**
wiinigiizhwe *vai* speak nastily; *1sg* **niwiinigiizhwe**; *prt* **waanigiizhwed**
wiini' *vta* make s.o. dirty; *1sg* **niwiini'aa**; *prt* **waani'aad**
wiinijiishkiwagaa *vii* there is a muddy patch; *prt* **waanijiishkiwagaag**; *aug* **wiinijiishkiwagaamagad**; *prt aug* **waanijiishkiwagaamagak**
wiinin *ni* fat; *loc* **wiininong**
wiinininjii *vai* have a dirty hand; *1sg* **niwiininjii**; *prt* **waanininjiid**
wiinino *vai* be fat; *1sg* **niwiinin**; *prt* **waaninod**
wiinishagaandibaan *ni* dandruff
wiinishagaandibe *vai* have a dirty scalp; *1sg* **niwiinishagaandibe**; *prt* **waanishagaandibed**
wiinitam *pr* his turn *third person singular personal pronoun*, her turn *third person singular personal pronoun*
wiinitamawaa *pr* their turn *third person plural personal pronoun*
wiinitoon *vti2* dirty s.t.; *1sg* **niwiinitoon**; *prt* **waanitood**
wiinizi *vai* be dirty; *1sg* **niwiiniz**; *prt* **waanizid**
wiinizik *na* yellow birch; *pl* **wiinizikoog**; *dim* **wiinizikoons**
wiinizisimaani-zagaakwa'igan *ni* hairpin; *pl* **wiinizisimaani-zagaakwa'iganan**; *dim* **wiinizisimaani-zagaakwa'igaans**

wiinzh /wiinN-/ *vta* name s.o., mention the name of s.o., give s.o. a name; *1sg* **niwiinaa**; *prt* **waanaad**
wiinzo *vai* have a name; *1sg* **niwiinz**; *prt* **waanzod**
wiipem *vta* sleep with s.o.; *1sg* **niwiipemaa**; *prt* **waapemaad**
wiipendan *vti* sleep with s.t.; *1sg* **niwiipendaan**; *prt* **waapendang**
wiipemaawaso *vai* sleep with children protectively; *1sg* **niwiipemaawas**; *prt* **waapemaawasod**
wiipendiwag /wiipendi-/ *vai* they sleep with each other; *1pl* **niwiipendimin**; *prt* **waapendijig**
wiisagan *vii* be bitter; *prt* **waasagang**; *also* **wiisagaa**
wiisagaagamin /wiisagaagami-/ *vii* be bitter (as a liquid); *prt* **waasagaagamig**
wiisagendam *vai* suffer pain; *1sg* **niwiisagendam**; *prt* **waasagendang**
wiisagigonewe *vai* have a sore throat; *1sg* **niwiisagigonewe**; *prt* **waasagigonewed**
wiisagi-jiisens *ni* radish; *pl* **wiisagi-jiisensan**; *loc* **wiisagi-jiisensing**
wiisagine *vai* be in pain; *1sg* **niwiisagine**; *prt* **waasagined**
wiisagipogozi *vai* taste bitter; *prt* **waasagipogozid**
wiisagipogwad *vii* taste bitter; *prt* **waasagipogwak**
wiisagishin *vai* get hurt; *1sg* **niwiisagishin**; *prt* **waasagishing**
wiisagishkaw *vta* hurt s.o. with foot or body; *1sg* **niwiisagishkawaa**; *prt* **waasagishkawaad**
wiisagizi *vai* be bitter; *prt* **waasagizid**
wiisaakodewikwe *na* woman of mixed ancestry, Metis woman; *pl* **wiisaakodewikweg**
wiisaakodewinini *na* person of mixed ancestry, Metis; *pl* **wiisaakodewininiwag**
wiishkoban *vii* be sweet; *prt* **waashkobang**
wiishkobaaboo *ni* maple sap; *loc* **wiishkobaaboong**
wiishkobaagamin /wiishkobaagami-/ *vii* be sweet (as a liquid); *prt* **waashkobaagamig**
wiishkobi- *pv4* sweet
wiishkobi-bakwezhigan *na* sweet roll, pastry, cake; *pl* **wiishkobi-bakwezhiganag**; *loc* **wiishkobi-bakwezhiganing**; *dim* **wiishkobi-bakwezhigaans**
wiishkobi-jiis *ni* sugar beet; *pl* **wiishkobi-jiisan**
wiishkobipogozi *vai* taste sweet; *prt* **waashkobipogozid**
wiishkobipogwad *vii* taste sweet; *prt* **waashkobipogwak**
wiishkobizi *vai* be sweet; *prt* **waashkobizid**
wiisini *vai* eat; *1sg* **niwiisin**; *prt* **waasinid**
wiisiniwin *ni* food; *pl* **wiisiniwinan**; *loc* **wiisiniwining**
wiisinii-adaawewigamig *ni* grocery store; *pl* **wiisinii-adaawewigamigoon**; *loc* **wiisinii-adaawewigamigong**; *dim* **wiisinii-adaawewigamigoons**
wiisiniiwigamig *ni* restaurant, cafe; *pl* **wiisiniiwigamigoon**; *loc* **wiisiniiwigamigong**; *dim* **wiisiniiwigamigoons**
wiisookaw *vta* associate with s.o.; *1sg* **niwiisookawaa**; *prt* **waasookawaad**

wiiwakwaan *ni* hat; *pl* **wiiwakwaanan**; *loc*
   wiiwakwaaning; *dim* **wiiwakwaanens**
wiiwegin *vta* wrap s.o. (as or as with something
   sheet-like); *1sg* **niwiiweginaa**; *prt*
   waaweginaad
wiiweginan *vti* wrap s.t. (as or as with something
   sheet-like); *1sg* **niwiiweginaan**; *prt*
   waaweginang
wiiweginigan *ni* wrapped package; *pl*
   wiiweginiganan; *loc* **wiiweginiganing**; *dim*
   wiiweginigaans
wiiyagasenh *ni* dust, dirt; *pl* **wiiyagasenyan**
wiiyaas *ni* meat; *loc* **wiiyaasing**; *dim* **wiiyaasens**
wiiyaas-adaawewigamig *ni* meat market; *pl*
   wiiyaas-adaawewigamigoon; *loc* **wiiyaas-
   adaawewigamigong**
wiiyaasaaboo *ni* broth; *loc* **wiiyaasaaboong**
wiiyaasi-dakoniwewinini *na* game warden,
   conservation officer; *pl* **wiiyaasi-
   dakoniwewininiwag**
wiiyaasi-naboob *ni* stew; *loc* **wiiyaasi-naboobiing**
wiizhaam *vta* ask s.o. along, urge s.o. to come; *1sg*
   niwiizhaamaa; *prt* **waazhaamaad**

Z

zaga' /**zaga'w-**/ *vta* fasten s.o. together; *1sg*
   inzaga'waa; *prt* **zega'waad**
zaga'an *vti* fasten s.t. together; *1sg* **inzaga'aan**; *prt*
   zega'ang
zaga'igan *ni* nail; *pl* **zaga'iganan**; *loc* **zaga'iganing**;
   dim **zaga'igaans**
zagakim *vta* tell s.o. to settle down; *1sg*
   inzagakimaa; *prt* **zegakimaad**
zagakin *vta* put s.o. away, tidy s.o.; *1sg*
   inzagakinaa; *prt* **zegakinaad**
zagakinan *vti* put s.t. away, tidy s.t.; *1sg*
   inzagakinaan; *prt* **zegakinang**
zagakinigaade *vii* be put away, be tidied; *prt*
   zegakinigaadeg; *aug* **zagakinigaademagad**;
   prt aug **zegakinigaademagak**
zagakinigaazo *vai* be put away, be tidied; *prt*
   zegakinigaazod
zagakinige *vai* put things away, tidy things; *1sg*
   inzagakinige; *prt* **zegakiniged**
zagakishim *vta* put s.o. in order; *1sg*
   inzagakishimaa; *prt* **zegakishimaad**
zagakisidoon *vti2* put s.t. in order; *1sg*
   inzagakisidoon; *prt* **zegakisidood**
zagakisijige *vti* put things in order; *1sg*
   inzagakisijige; *prt* **zegakisijiged**
zagapide *vii* be tied on, be towed; *prt* **zegapideg**;
   aug **zagapidemagad**; *prt aug* **zegapidemagak**
zagapidoon *vti2* tie s.t. on, tow s.t.; *1sg*
   inzagapidoon; *prt* **zegapidood**
zagapijigan *ni* trailer; *pl* **zagapijiganan**; *loc*
   zagapijiganing; *dim* **zagapijigaans**

zagapizh /**zagapiN-**/ *vta* tie s.o. on, tow s.o.; *1sg*
   inzagapinaa; *prt* **zegapinaad**
zagapizo *vai* be tied on, be towed; *1sg* **inzagapiz**;
   prt **zegapizod**
zagaswaa *vai* smoke (tobacco); *1sg* **inzagaswaa**;
   prt **zegaswaad**
zagaswaadan *vti* smoke s.t. (e.g., kinnickinnick);
   1sg **inzagaswaadaan**; *prt* **zegaswaadang**
zagaswaazh /**zagaswaaN-**/ *vta* smoke s.o. (e.g.,
   tobacco); *1sg* **inzagaswaanaa**; *prt*
   zegaswaanaad
zagaswe' *vta* give a smoke to s.o., share a smoke
   with s.o. (especially a pipe in a ceremony); *1sg*
   inzagaswe'aa; *prt* **zegaswe'aad**
zagaswe'idiwag /**zagaswe'idi-**/ *vai* they have a
   council meeting; *1pl* **inzagaswe'idimin**; *prt*
   zegaswe'idijig
zagaswe'idiiwinini *na* councillor; *pl*
   zagaswe'idiiwininiwag
zagaswe'iwe *vai* give a ceremony, convene a council; *1sg* **inzagaswe'iwe**; *prt* **zegaswe'iwed**
zagataagan *na* tinder, punk; *pl* **zagataaganag**; *loc*
   zagataaganing
zagaakwa' /**zagaakwa'w-**/ *vta* fasten s.o., pin s.o.,
   button s.o. up; *1sg* **inzagaakwa'waa**; *prt*
   zegaakwa'waad
zagaakwa'an *vti* fasten s.t., pin s.t.; *1sg*
   inzagaakwa'aan; *prt* **zegaakwa'ang**
zagaakwa'igan *ni* pin, safety pin; *pl*
   zagaakwa'iganan; *loc* **zagaakwa'iganing**; *dim*
   zagaakwa'igaans
zagaakwa'igaade *vii* be fastened, be pinned; *prt*
   zegaakwa'igaadeg; *aug*
   zagaakwa'igaademagad; *prt aug*
   zegaakwa'igaademagak
zagaakwa'igaazo *vai* be fastened, be pinned; *prt*
   zegaakwa'igaazod
zagaakwa'ige *vai* fasten things, pin things; *1sg*
   inzagaakwa'ige; *prt* **zegaakwa'iged**
zagaakwa'odizo *vai* button up oneself; *1sg*
   inzagaakwa'odiz; *prt* **zegaakwa'odizod**
zagaakwa'on *na* brooch, pin; *pl* **zagaakwa'onag**;
   loc **zagaakwa'oning**; *dim* **zagaakwa'onens**
zagaakwajin *vai* get snagged on a limb; *1sg*
   inzagaakwajin; *prt* **zegaakwajing**
zagaakwaa *vii* be dense woods; *prt* **zegaakwaag**;
   aug **zagaakwaamagad**; *prt aug*
   zegaakwaamagak
zagidoonebijigan *ni* bridle, bit; *pl*
   zagidoonebijiganan; *loc* **zagidoonebijiganing**;
   dim **zagidoonebijigaans**
zagime *na* mosquito; *pl* **zagimeg**; *dim* **zagimens**
zagimekaa *vii* there are many mosquitoes; *prt*
   zegimekaag; *aug* **zagimekaamagad**; *prt aug*
   zegimekaamagak
zagimewayaan *na* mosquito net; *pl*
   zagimewayaanag; *loc* **zagimewayaaning**; *dim*
   zagimewayaanens
zagininjiin *vta* shake hands with s.o.; *1sg*
   inzagininjiinaa; *prt* **zegininjiinaad**
zagininjiinidiwag /**zagininjiinidi-**/ *vai* they shake
   hands with each other; *1pl* **inzagininjiinidimin**;
   prt **zegininjiinidijig**
zaka' /**zaka'w-**/ *vta* set s.o. on fire, light s.o. (e.g., a
   pipe); *1sg* **inzaka'waa**; *prt* **zeka'waad**

zaka'amaw *vta* set (s.t.) on fire for s.o., light (s.t.) for s.o.; *1sg* inzaka'amawaa; *prt* zeka'amawaad

zaka'an *vti* set s.t. on fire, light s.t.; *1sg* inzaka'aan; *prt* zeka'ang

zaka'igan *ni* lighter; *pl* zaka'iganan; *loc* zaka'iganing; *dim* zaka'igaans

zaka'ipwaagane *vai* light a pipe; *1sg* inzaka'ipwaagane; *prt* zeka'ipwaaganed

zaka'o *vai* use a cane; *1sg* inzaka'; *prt* zeka'od

zaka'on *ni* cane; *pl* zaka'onan; *loc* zaka'oning; *dim* zaka'onens

zakaasigan *ni* flashlight; *pl* zakaasiganan; *loc* zakaasiganing; *dim* zakaasigaans

zakide *vii* burn; *prt* zekideg; *aug* zakidemagad; *prt aug* zekidemagak

zakiz /zakizw-/ *vta* burn s.o., light s.o.; *1sg* inzakizwaa; *prt* zekizwaad

zakizan *vti* burn s.t., light s.t.; *1sg* inzakizaan; *prt* zekizang

zakizige *vai* burn things, light things; *1sg* inzakizige; *prt* zekiziged

zakizo *vai* burn, have a fire at one's place; *1sg* inzakiz; *prt* zekizod

zanagad *vii* be difficult, be hard (to manage); *prt* zenagak

zanagendam *vai2* consider things hard, consider things difficult; *1sg* inzanagendam; *prt* zenagendang

zanagendan *vti* consider s.t. hard, consider s.t. difficult; *1sg* inzanagendaan; *prt* zenagendang

zanagenim *vta* consider s.o. hard, consider s.o. difficult; *1sg* inzanagenimaa; *prt* zenagenimaad

zanagi' *vta* make it difficult for s.o.; *1sg* inzanagi'aa; *prt* zenagi'aad

zanagizi *vai* be difficult; *1sg* inzanagiz; *prt* zenagizid

zasag= < zag=

zasak= < zak=

zasakwaa *vii* there is a heavy frost; *prt* zesakwaag

zasaswe < zaswe=

zasiko= < ziko=

zasiiko= < ziiko=

zaswebidoon *vti2* scatter s.t. with hands; *1sg* inzaswebidoon; *prt* zeswebidood

zaswebizh /zaswebiN-/ *vta* scatter s.o. with hands; *1sg* inzaswebinaa; *prt* zeswebinaad

zaswebiiga'andaw *vta* splash s.o.; *1sg* inzaswebiiga'andawaa; *prt* zeswebiiga'andawaad

zaswe'an *vti* scatter s.t. using something; *1sg* inzaswe'aan; *prt* zeswe'ang

zasweshkan *vti* scatter s.t. with foot or body; *1sg* inzasweshkaan; *prt* zesweshkang

zasweshkaw *vta* scatter s.o. with foot or body; *1sg* inzasweshkawaa; *prt* zesweshkawaad

zazagaa *vii* there is dense underbrush; *prt* zezagaag; *aug* zazagaamagad; *prt aug* zezagaamagak

zazaagizi *vai* be stingy; *1sg* inzazaagiz; *prt* zezaagizid

zazaanag= < zanag=

zazegaa *pc* dressed up, decorated

zazegaa'o *vai* dress up; *1sg* inzazegaa'; *prt* zezegaa'od

zazegaa-ikwe *na* dressed-up woman; *pl* zazegaa-ikwewag; *dim* zazegaa-ikwens

zazegaa-inini *na* dressed-up man; *pl* zazegaa-ininiwag; *dim* zazegaa-ininiins

zaziikizi *vai* be the eldest (of siblings); *1sg* inzaziikiz; *prt* zeziikizid

zaaga'am *vai2* go out, exit, go to the toilet; *1sg* inzaaga'am; *prt* zayaaga'ang

zaaga'amoowigamig *ni* toilet, outhouse, privy; *pl* zaaga'amoowigamigoon; *loc* zaaga'amoowigamigong; *dim* zaaga'amoowigamigoons

zaaga'igan *ni* lake; *pl* zaaga'iganiin; *loc* zaaga'iganiing; *dim* zaaga'igaans

zaagajiwe *vai* come out over a hill; *1sg* inzaagajiwe; *prt* zayaagajiwed

zaagakii *vai* sprout; *prt* zayaagakiid

zaagakii *vii* sprout; *prt* zayaagakiig; *aug* zaagakiimagad; *prt aug* zayaagakiimagak

zaagaakoshin *vai* lie sticking out (as something stick- or wood-like); *1sg* inzaagaakoshin; *prt* zayaagaakoshing

zaagaakosin *vii* lie sticking out (as something stick- or wood-like); *prt* zayaagaakosing

zaagewe *vai* come suddenly into view as from around a corner; *1sg* inzaagewe; *prt* zayaagewed

zaagewebatoo *vai* run suddenly into view; *1sg* inzaagewebatoo; *prt* zayaagewebatood

zaagewebide *vii* speed suddenly into view, drive suddenly into view; *prt* zayaagewebideg; *aug* zaagewebidemagad; *prt aug* zayaagewebidemagak

zaagewebizo *vai* speed suddenly into view, drive suddenly into view; *1sg* inzaagewebiz; *prt* zayaagewebizod

zaagewe *vai* paddle suddenly into view; *1sg* inzaagewe'; *prt* zayaagewe'od

zaagewekwazhiwe *vai* paddle suddenly into view, swim as a fish suddenly into view; *1sg* inzaagewekwazhiwe; *prt* zayaagewekwazhiwed

zaagibagaa *vii* leaves bud; *prt* zayaagibagaag; *aug* zaagibagaamagad; *prt aug* zayaagibagaamagak

zaagibagaa-giizis *na* May

zaagichigaade *vii* be loved, be treasured, be held stingily; *prt* zayaagichigaadeg; *aug* zaagichigaademagad; *prt aug* zayaagichigaademagak

zaagichigaazo *vai* be loved, be treasured, be held stingily; *prt* zayaagichigaazod

zaagidawaa *vii* flow into a lake, be an inlet; *prt* zayaagidawaag; *aug* zaagidawaamagad; *prt aug* zayaagidawaamagak

zaagidaawanidiwag /zaagidaawanidi-/ *vai* they go out in a group; *1pl* inzaagidaawanidimin; *prt* zayaagidaawanidijig

zaagidenaniweni *vai* stick out one's tongue; *1sg* inzaagidenaniwen; *prt* zayaagidenaniwenid

zaagidenaniwetaw *vta* stick out one's tongue at s.o.; *1sg* inzaagidenaniwetawaa; *prt* zayaagidenaniwetawaad

zaagidin *vta* put s.o. out, evict s.o.; *1sg*
inzaagidinaa; *prt* **zayaagidinaad**
zaagidinan *vti* put s.t. out; *1sg* **inzaagidinaan**; *prt*
zayaagidinang
zaagidinidiwag /**zaagidinidi-**/ *vai* they are let out
together (as from school or a meeting); *prt*
zayaagidinidijig
zaagidoode *vai* crawl out; *1sg* **inzaagidoode**; *prt*
zayaagidooded
zaagigi *vai* sprout, grow out; *prt* **zayaagigid**
zaagigin *vii* sprout, grow out; *prt* **zayaagiging**
zaagi' *vta* love s.o., treasure s.o.; *1sg* **inzaagi'aa**; *prt*
zayaagi'aad
zaagi'idiwag /**zaagi'idi-**/ *vai* they love each other;
1pl **inzaagi'idimin**; *prt* **zayaagi'idijig**
zaagijinaazha' /**zaagijinaazha'w-**/ *vta* tell s.o. to
go outside; *1sg* **inzaagijinaazha'waa**; *prt*
zayaagijinaazha'waad
zaagijinizhikaw *vta* chase s.o. outside; *1sg*
inzaagijinizhikawaa; *prt*
zayaagijinizhikawaad
zaagijiwan *vii* flow out; *prt* **zayaagijiwang**
zaagijiwebin *vta* throw s.o. outside; *1sg*
inzaagijiwebinaa; *prt* **zayaagijiwebinaad**
zaagijiwebinan *vti* throw s.t. outside; *1sg*
inzaagijiwebinaan; *prt* **zayaagijiwebinang**
zaagijiwebinigaade *vii* be thrown outside; *prt*
zayaagijiwebinigaadeg; *aug*
zaagijiwebinigaademagad; *prt aug*
zayaagijiwebinigaademagak
zaagijiwebinige *vai* throw things outside; *1sg*
inzaagijiwebinige; *prt* **zayaagijiwebiniged**
zaagikweni *vai* stick out one's head; *1sg*
inzaagikwen; *prt* **zayaagikwenid**
zaagitoon *vti2* love s.t., treasure s.t.; *1sg*
inzaagitoon; *prt* **zayaagitood**
zaagiziba' *vta* run out with s.o.; *1sg*
inzaagiziba'aa; *prt* **zayaagiziba'aad**
zaagiziba'idiwag /**zaagiziba'idi-**/ *vai* they run out
together; *1pl* **inzaagiziba'idimin**; *prt*
zayaagiziba'idijig
zaagizibatoo *vai* run out; *1sg* **inzaagizibatoo**; *prt*
zayaagizibatood
zaagizibatwaadan *vti* run out with s.t.; *1sg*
inzaagizibatwaadaan; *prt*
zayaagizibatwaadang
zaagizibatwaazh /**zaagizibatwaaN-**/ *vta* run out
with s.o.; *1sg* **inzaagizibatwaanaa**; *prt*
zayaagizibatwaanaad
zaagizi' *vta* take s.o. out, make s.o. go out; *1sg*
inzaagizi'aa; *prt* **zayaagizi'aad**
zaagizitaw *vta* take (s.t.) out for s.o.; *1sg*
inzaagizitawaa; *prt* **zayaagizitawaad**
zaagizitoon *vti2* take s.t. out; *1sg* **inzaagizitoon**;
prt **zayaagizitood**
zaagiing *pc* at the inlet
zaasakokwaadan *vti* fry s.t.; *1sg*
inzaasakokwaadaan; *prt* **zayaasakokwaadang**
zaasakokwaade *vii* be fried; *prt*
zayaasakokwaadeg; *aug*
zaasakokwaademagad; *prt aug*
zayaasakokwaademagak
zaasakokwaan *na* fry bread; *pl* **zaasakokwaanag**;
loc **zaasakokwaaning**; *dim* **zaasakokwaanens**

zaasakokwaazh /**zaasakokwaaN-**/ *vta* fry s.o.; *1sg*
inzaasakokwaanaa; *prt* **zayaasakokwaanaad**
zaasakokwaazo *vai* be fried; *prt*
zayaasakokwaazod
zaasakokwe *vai* fry; *1sg* **inzaasakokwe**; *prt*
zayaasakokwed
zaasaag= < zaag=
zaasaakwe *vai* give war whoops, whoop; *1sg*
inzaasaakwe; *prt* **zayaasaakwed**
zaasigan *na* cracklings; *pl* **zaasiganag**
zaasijiwan *vii* flow with a ripple; *prt* **zayaasijiwang**
zaasoong= < zoong=
zaatemaagozi *vai* smell rancid; *prt*
zayaatemaagozid
zaatemaagwad *vii* smell rancid; *prt*
zayaatemaagwak
zaatepogozi *vai* taste rancid; *prt* **zayaatepogozid**
zaatepogwad *vii* taste rancid; *prt* **zayaatepogwak**
zaateshin *vai* turn rancid; *prt* **zayaateshing**
zaatesin *vii* turn rancid; *prt* **zayaatesing**
zegaabandam *vai2* have a scary dream; *1sg*
inzegaabandam; *prt* **zayegaabandang**
zegaanakwad *vii* there are storm clouds; *prt*
zayegaanakwak
zegaatese *vii* be a scary movie; *prt* **zayegaateseg**;
aug **zegaatesemagad**; *prt aug*
zayegaatesemagak
zegendam *vai2* be nervous, be fearful; *1sg*
inzegendam; *prt* **zayegendang**
zegendaagozi *vai* be considered scary, be considered dangerous; *1sg* **inzegendaagoz**; *prt*
zayegendaagozid
zegendaagwad *vii* be considered scary, be considered dangerous; *prt* **zayegendaagwak**
zegibanwaanishiinh *na* cedar waxwing; *pl*
zegibanwaanishiinyag
zegigaadeshin *vai* sprain one's leg; *1sg*
inzegigaadeshin; *prt* **zayegigaadeshing**
zegi' *vta* scare s.o., frighten s.o.; *1sg* **inzegi'aa**; *prt*
zayegi'aad
zegim *vta* intimidate s.o. by speech; *1sg*
inzegimaa; *prt* **zayegimaad**
zeginaagozi *vai* look scary; *1sg* **inzeginaagoz**; *prt*
zayeginaagozid
zeginaagwad *vii* look scary; *prt* **zayeginaagwak**
zegingwashi *vai* have a nightmare; *1sg*
inzegingwash; *prt* **zayegingwashid**
zeginikeshin *vai* sprain one's arm; *1sg*
inzeginikeshin; *prt* **zayeginikeshing**
zegizi *vai* be scared, be afraid; *1sg* **inzegiz**; *prt*
zayegizid
zegizideshin *vai* sprain one's foot; *1sg*
inzegizideshin; *prt* **zayegizideshing**
zegwewe *vii* rumble; *prt* **zayegweweg**; *aug*
zegwewemagad; *prt aug* **zayegwewemagak**
zenibaanh *na* ribbon, silk; *pl* **zenibaanyag**; *loc*
zenibaanying; *dim* **zenibaans**
zenibaawegin *ni* silk, satin; *pl* **zenibaaweginoon**;
loc **zenibaaweginong**; *dim* **zenibaaweginoons**
zesab *na* nettle; *pl* **zesabiig**; *loc* **zesabiing**
zeseg= < zeg=
zesegwaabide'o *vai* pick one's teeth; *1sg*
inzesegwaabide'; *prt* **zayesegwaabide'od**

zesegwaabide'on *ni* toothpick; *pl*
zesegwaabide'onan; *loc* zesegwaabide'oning;
dim **zesegwaabide'onens**
zhagashkaandawe *na* flying squirrel; *pl*
zhagashkaandaweg; *dim*
zhagashkaandawens
zhagashkitaa *vai* bend down; *1sg* inzhagashkitaa;
prt **zhegashkitaad**
zhakamo *vai* put (something) in one's mouth; *1sg*
inzhakam; *prt* **zhekamod**
zhakamodaw *vta* spoon feed s.o.; *1sg*
inzhakamodawaa; *prt* **zhekamodawaad**
zhakaa *vii* be damp; *prt* **zhekaag**; *aug*
zhakaamagad; *prt aug* **zhekaamagak**
zhakaagonagaa *vii* there is soft snow; *prt*
zhekaagonagaag; *aug* zhakaagonagaamagad;
prt aug **zhekaagonagaamagak**
zhakipon /**zhakipo-**/ *vii* there is heavy wet snow
falling; *prt* **zhekipog**
zhakizi *vai* be damp; *prt* **zhekizid**
zhakiigad *vii* be damp (as something sheet-like);
prt **zhekiigak**
zhakiigizi *vai* be damp (as something sheet-like);
prt **zhekiigizid**
zhashagi *na* blue heron; *pl* **zhashagiwag**; *dim*
zhashagiins
zhashingade= < **zhingade=**
zhawendaagozi *vai* be blessed, be pitied, be fortunate; *1sg* inzhawendaagoz; *prt*
zhewendaagozid
zhawenim *vta* bless s.o., pity s.o.; *1sg*
inzhawenimaa; *prt* **zhewenimaad**
zhawenjige *vai* be merciful, be kind-hearted, have
pity; *1sg* inzhawenjige; *prt* **zhewenjiged**
zhawimin *ni* grape; *pl* **zhawiminan**; *also* **zhoomin**
zhayiigwa *pc* now, already *old-fashioned*
zhazhiibitam *vai2* be stubborn, be disobedient;
1sg inzhazhiibitam; *prt* **zhezhiibitang**
zhaabobatoo *vai* run through; *1sg*
inzhaabobatoo; *prt* **zhayaabobatood**
zhaabobii *vii* be saturated; *prt* **zhayaabobiig**; *aug*
zhaabobiimagad; *prt aug* **zhayaabobiimagak**
zhaabobiiginan *vti* strain s.t.; *1sg*
inzhaabobiiginaan; *prt* **zhayaabobiiginang**
zhaabobiiginigan *ni* strainer; *pl*
zhaabobiiginiganan; *loc* zhaabobiiginiganing;
dim **zhaabobiiginigaans**
zhaabokaawizi *vai* have diarrhea; *1sg*
inzhaabokaawiz; *prt* **zhayaabokaawizid**
zhaabon *vta* put s.o. through; *1sg* inzhaabonaa;
prt **zhayaabonaad**
zhaabonan *vti* put s.t. through; *1sg* inzhaabonaan;
prt **zhayaabonang**
zhaabonigan *ni* needle; *pl* **zhaaboniganan**; *loc*
zhaaboniganing; *dim* **zhaabonigaans**
zhaabose *vii* go through, pass through; *prt*
zhayaaboseg; *aug* zhaabosemagad; *prt aug*
zhayaabosemagak
zhaaboshkaachigan *ni* sifter; *pl*
zhaaboshkaachiganan; *loc*
zhaaboshkaachiganing; *dim*
zhaaboshkaachigaans
zhaaboshkaachige *vai* sift things; *1sg*
inzhaaboshkaachige; *prt*
zhayaaboshkaachiged

zhaaboshkaas /**zhaaboshkaasw-**/ *vta* sift s.o.; *1sg*
inzhaaboshkaaswaa; *prt*
zhayaaboshkaaswaad
zhaaboshkaatoon *vti2* sift s.t.; *1sg*
inzhaaboshkaatoon; *prt* **zhayaaboshkaatood**
zhaabowe *vai* sing an accompaniment (of
women); *1sg* inzhaabowe; *prt* **zhayaabowed**
zhaabozigan *ni* laxative; *pl* **zhaaboziganan**; *loc*
zhaaboziganing
zhaaboomin *na* gooseberry; *pl* **zhaaboominag**;
dim **zhaaboominens**
zhaaboominagaawanzh *na* gooseberry bush; *pl*
zhaaboominagaawanzhiig; *loc*
zhaaboominagaawanzhiing; *dim*
zhaaboominagaawanzhiins
zhaaboondawaan *ni* long lodge with doors at both
ends; *pl* **zhaaboondawaanan**; *loc*
zhaaboondawaaning; *dim*
zhaaboondawaanens
zhaabwayi'ii *pc* through it
zhaabwaabam *vta* see through s.o.; *1sg*
inzhaabwaabamaa; *prt* **zhayaabwaabamaad**
zhaabwaabandan *vti* see through s.t.; *1sg*
inzhaabwaabandaan; *prt*
zhayaabwaabandang
zhaabwaakizigan *ni* x-ray plate; *pl*
zhaabwaakiziganan
zhaabwaakizo *vai* get an x-ray; *1sg*
inzhaabwaakiz; *prt* **zhayaabwaakizod**
zhaabwii *vai* go through, pass through, survive; *1sg*
inzhaabwii; *prt* **zhayaabwiid**
zhaaganaash *na* Englishman; *pl* **zhaaganaashag**;
also **zhaaganaashii**
zhaaganaashiimo *vai* speak English; *1sg*
inzhaaganaashiim; *prt* **zhayaaganaashiimod**
zhaaganaashiimotaw *vta* speak English to s.o.; *1sg*
inzhaaganaashiimotawaa; *prt*
zhayaaganaashiimotawaad
Zhaaganaashiiwaki *ni* Canada; *loc*
Zhaaganaashiiwakiing
zhaaganaashiiwibii'amaw *vta* write in English to
s.o.; *1sg* inzhaaganaashiiwibii'amawaa; *prt*
zhayaaganaashiiwibii'amawaad
zhaaganaashiiwibii'an *vti* write s.t. in English; *1sg*
inzhaaganaashiiwibii'aan; *prt*
zhayaaganaashiiwibii'ang
zhaaganaashiiwibii'ige *vai* write in English; *1sg*
inzhaaganaashiiwibii'ige; *prt*
zhayaaganaashiiwibii'iged
zhaagode'e *vai* be cowardly; *1sg* inzhaagode'e; *prt*
zhayaagode'ed
zhaagoodenim *vta* think s.o. is inadequate; *1sg*
inzhaagoodenimaa; *prt* **zhayaagoodenimaad**
zhaagooji' *vta* defeat s.o., overcome s.o.; *1sg*
inzhaagooji'aa; *prt* **zhayaagooji'aad**
zhaagooji'iwe *vai* defeat people, overcome people;
1sg inzhaagooji'iwe; *prt* **zhayaagooji'iwed**
zhaagoojitoon *vti2* defeat s.t., overcome s.t.; *1sg*
inzhaagoojitoon; *prt* **zhayaagoojitood**
zhaagoozom *vta* defeat s.o. in speech, overcome
s.o. with speech; *1sg* inzhaagoozomaa; *prt*
zhayaagoozomaad
zhaagwaadad *vii* be weak in power, be ineffective;
prt **zhayaagwaadak**

zhaagwaadizi *vai* be weak in power, be ineffective; *1sg* **inzhaagwaadiz**; *prt* **zhayaagwaadizid**
zhaagwaagamin /**zhaagwaagami-**/ *vii* be weak (as a liquid); *prt* **zhayaagwaagamig**
zhaagwendan *vti* consider s.t. weak; *1sg* **inzhaagwendaan**; *prt* **zhayaagwendang**
zhaagwenim *vta* consider s.o. weak, have doubts about s.o.; *1sg* **inzhaagwenimaa**; *prt* **zhayaagwenimaad**
zhaagwenimo *vai* lack self-confidence, be introverted; *1sg* **inzhaagwenim**; *prt* **zhayaagwenimod**
zhaagwiiwii *vai* be weak in muscular strength; *1sg* **inzhaagwiiwii**; *prt* **zhayaagwiiwiid**
zhaangaching *pc* nine times
zhaangachinoon /**zhaangachin-**/ *vii* they are nine; *prt* **zhayaangachingin**
zhaangachiwag /**zhaangachi-**/ *vai* they are nine; *1pl* **inzhaangachimin**; *prt* **zhayaangachijig**
zhaangasimidana *nm* ninety
zhaangaso- *pv4* nine
zhaangaso-anama'e-giizhik *pc* nine weeks
zhaangaso-biboon *pc* nine years
zhaangaso-biboonagad *vii* be nine years; *prt* **zhayaangaso-biboonagak**
zhaangaso-biboonagizi *vai* be nine years old; *1sg* **inzhaangaso-biboonagiz**; *prt* **zhayaangaso-biboonagizid**
zhaangaso-diba'igan *pc* nine hours, nine miles
zhaangaso-diba'iganed *vii* be nine o'clock; *prt* **zhayaangaso-diba'iganek**
zhaangaso-diba'igaans *pc* nine minutes, nine acres
zhaangaso-giizhik *pc* nine days
zhaangaso-giizis *pc* nine months
zhaangasogon *pc* nine days
zhaangasogonagad *vii* be nine days; *prt* **zhayaangasogonagak**
zhaangasogonagizi *vai* be the ninth day of the month, be nine days old; *prt* **zhayaangasogonagizid**
zhaangasoninj *pc* nine inches
zhaangasosagoons *nm* nine thousand
zhaangasozid *pc* nine feet
zhaangasoobii'igan *na* nine (card); *pl* **zhaangasoobii'iganag**
zhaangasooshkin *pc* nine bags
zhaangaswaabik *pc* nine dollars
zhaangaswaak *nm* nine hundred
zhaangaswewaan *pc* nine sets, nine pairs
zhaangaswi *nm* nine
zhaangweshi *na* mink; *pl* **zhaangweshiwag**; *dim* **zhaangweshiins**
zhaangweshiwayaan *na* mink hide; *pl* **zhaangweshiwayaanag**; *dim* **zhaangweshiwayaanens**
zhaashaabw= < **zhaabw=**
zhaashaaginizide *vai* be barefoot; *1sg* **inzhaashaaginizide**; *prt* **zhayaashaaginizided**
zhaashaagw= < **zhaagw=**
zhaashaagwam *vta* chew s.o.; *1sg* **inzhaashaagwamaa**; *prt* **zhayaashaagwamaad**
zhaashaagwamikiwe *vai* chew gum; *1sg* **inzhaashaagwamikiwe**; *prt* **zhayaashaagwamikiwed**

zhaashaagwandan *vti* chew s.t.; *1sg* **inzhaashaagwandaan**; *prt* **zhayaashaagwandang**
zhaashaagwanjige *vai* chew things; *1sg* **inzhaashaagwanjige**; *prt* **zhayaashaagwanjiged**
zhaashaawanibiisens *na* purple martin; *pl* **zhaashaawanibiisensag**
zhaashiing= < **zhiing=**
zhaawan *pc* south
zhaawani-noodin *na* south wind
zhaawanong *pc* in the south, to the south
zhaawaabookaadeg bipakoombens *ni* pickle; *pl* **zhaawaabookaadegin bipakoombensan**
zhebaa *pc* this morning (just past)
zhede *na* pelican; *pl* **zhedeg**; *dim* **zhedens**
zhegon *vta* stick s.o. in a tight place; *1sg* **inzhegonaa**; *prt* **zhayegonaad**
zhegonan *vti* stick s.t. in a tight place; *1sg* **inzhegonaan**; *prt* **zhayegonang**
zhegoshim *vta* put s.o. in a tight place; *1sg* **inzhegoshimaa**; *prt* **zhayegoshimaad**
zhegoshin *vai* lie in a tight place; *1sg* **inzhegoshin**; *prt* **zhayegoshing**
zhegosidoon *vti2* put s.t. in a tight place; *1sg* **inzhegosidoon**; *prt* **zhayegosidood**
zhegosin *vii* lie in a tight place; *prt* **zhayegosing**
zhegoode *vai* crawl in a tight place; *1sg* **inzhegoode**; *prt* **zhayegoodeg**
zhezhaangaswi *nm* nine each
zhigagowe *vai* vomit; *1sg* **inzhigagowe**; *prt* **zhegagowed**
zhigajibii' *vta* be tired of waiting for s.o.; *1sg* **inzhigajibii'aa**; *prt* **zhegajibii'aad**
zhigajibii'o *vai* be tired of waiting; *1sg* **inzhigajibii'**; *prt* **zhegajibii'od**
zhigajibiitoon *vti2* be tired of waiting for s.t.; *1sg* **inzhigajibiitoon**; *prt* **zhegajibiitood**
zhigajii *vai* be tired, be impatient; *1sg* **inzhigajii**; *prt* **zhegajiid**
zhigaag *na* skunk; *pl* **zhigaagwag**; *dim* **zhigaagoons**
zhigaagawanzh *na* onion; *pl* **zhigaagawanzhiig**; *loc* **zhigaagawanzhiing**; *dim* **zhigaagawanzhiins**
zhigidan *vti* urinate on s.t.; *1sg* **inzhigidaan**; *prt* **zhegidang**
zhigingwaam *vai* wet the bed; *1sg* **inzhigingwaam**; *prt* **zhegingwaang**
zhiginidizo *vai* urinate on oneself; *1sg* **inzhiginidiz**; *prt* **zheginidizod**
zhigizh /**zhigiN-**/ *vta* urinate on s.o.; *1sg* **inzhiginaa**; *prt* **zheginaad**
zhigwa *pc* now, at this time; *also* **azhigwa, zhigo**
zhigwameg *na* dogfish; *pl* **zhigwamegwag**; *dim* **zhigwamegoons**
zhigwaajiganaak *ni* tool for extracting marrow from bones; *pl* **zhigwaajiganaakoon**
zhigwaajige *vai* extract marrow from bones; *1sg* **inzhigwaajige**; *prt* **zhegwaajiged**
zhigweyaabam *vta* aim at s.o.; *1sg* **inzhigweyaabamaa**; *prt* **zhegweyaabamaad**
zhigweyaabandan *vti* aim at s.t.; *1sg* **inzhigweyaabandaan**; *prt* **zhegweyaabandang**

zhigweyaabi *vai* aim sights; *1sg* **inzhigweyaab**; *prt* **zhegweyaabid**
zhimaagan *ni* spear, lance; *pl* **zhimaaganan**; *loc* **zhimaaganing**; *dim* **zhimaagaans**
zhimaaganish *na* soldier, jack (card); *pl* **zhimaaganishag**; *dim* **zhimaaganishens**
zhimaaganishii-aakoziiwigamig *ni* veteran's hospital; *pl* **zhimaaganishii-aakoziiwigamigoon**; *loc* **zhimaaganishii-aakoziiwigamigong**; *dim* **zhimaaganishii-aakoziiwigamigoons**
zhimaaganishii-ogimaa *na* military officer; *pl* **zhimaaganishii-ogimaag**
zhimaaganishiiwigamig *ni* veteran's home; *pl* **zhimaaganishiiwigamigoon**; *loc* **zhimaaganishiiwigamigong**
zhinawa'oojigan *ni* small round bell, sleigh bell, dance bell; *pl* **zhinawa'oojiganan**; *loc* **zhinawa'oojiganing**; *dim* **zhinawa'oojigaans**
zhingaden *vta* spread s.o. out; *1sg* **inzhingadenaa**; *prt* **zhengadenaad**
zhingadenan *vti* spread s.t. out; *1sg* **inzhingadenaan**; *prt* **zhengadenang**
zhingadeshim *vta* lay s.o. spread out; *1sg* **inzhingadeshimaa**; *prt* **zhengadeshimaad**
zhingadeshin *vai* lie spread out; *1sg* **inzhingadeshin**; *prt* **zhengadeshing**
zhingadesidoon *vti2* lay s.t. spread out; *1sg* **inzhingadesidoon**; *prt* **zhengadesidood**
zhingadesin *vii* lie spread out; *prt* **zhengadesing**
zhingibis *na* grebe *locally called* hell diver; boil, carbuncle; *pl* **zhingibisag**; *dim* **zhingibisens**
zhingishin *vai* lie down; *1sg* **inzhingishin**; *prt* **zhengishing**
zhingob *na* balsam fir; *pl* **zhingobiig**; *loc* **zhingobiing**; *dim* **zhingobiins**
zhingobaaboo *ni* beer; *loc* **zhingobaaboong**
zhingobaandag *na* fir bough; *pl* **zhingobaandagoog**; *loc* **zhingobaandagong**; *dim* **zhingobaandagoons**
zhingos *na* weasel; *pl* **zhingosag**; *dim* **zhingosens**
zhingosiwayaan *na* weasel skin; *pl* **zhingosiwayaanag**; *loc* **zhingosiwayaaning**; *dim* **zhingosiwayaanens**
zhingwaak *na* white pine; *pl* **zhingwaakwag**; *loc* **zhingwaakong**; *dim* **zhingwaakoons**
zhingwaakwaandag *na* pine bough; *pl* **zhingwaakwaandagoog**; *loc* **zhingwaakwaandagong**; *dim* **zhingwaakwaandagoons**
zhinoodaagan *ni* net cord; *pl* **zhinoodaaganan**; *dim* **zhinoodaagaans**
zhishigagowe *vai* keep vomiting; *1sg* **inzhishigagowe**; *prt* **zheshigagowed**
zhishigobidoon *vti2* crush s.t. with hands; *1sg* **inzhishigobidoon**; *prt* **zheshigobidood**
zhishigobizh /zhishigobiN-/ *vta* crush s.o. with hands; *1sg* **inzhishigobinaa**; *prt* **zheshigobinaad**
zhishigoshkan *vti* crush s.t. by foot or body; *1sg* **inzhishigoshkaan**; *prt* **zheshigoshkang**
zhishigoshkaw *vta* crush s.o. by foot or body; *1sg* **inzhishigoshkawaa**; *prt* **zheshigoshkawaad**
zhishigwam *vta* gnaw s.o., chew s.o. to bits; *1sg* **inzhishigwamaa**; *prt* **zheshigwamaad**

zhishigwandan *vti* gnaw s.t., chew s.t. to bits; *1sg* **inzhishigwandaan**; *prt* **zheshigwandang**
zhishwajayi'ii *pc* alongside it
zhishwajigamig *pc* alongside the house
zhishwajikana *pc* alongside the road
zhizhoobii' /zhizhoobii'w-/ *vta* paint s.o.; *1sg* **inzhizhoobii'waa**; *prt* **zhezhoobii'waad**
zhizhoobii'amaw *vta* paint (s.t.) for s.o.; *1sg* **inzhizhoobii'amawaa**; *prt* **zhezhoobii'amawaad**
zhizhoobii'an *vti* paint s.t.; *1sg* **inzhizhoobii'aan**; *prt* **zhezhoobii'ang**
zhizhoobii'igan *ni* paint; *pl* **zhizhoobii'iganan**; *loc* **zhizhoobii'iganing**
zhizhoobii'iganaatig *ni* paint brush; *pl* **zhizhoobii'iganaatigoon**; *loc* **zhizhoobii'iganaatigong**; *dim* **zhizhoobii'iganaatigoons**
zhizhoobii'ige *vai* paint things; *1sg* **inzhizhoobii'ige**; *prt* **zhezhoobii'iged**
zhizhoobii'igewinini *na* painter; *pl* **zhizhoobii'igewininiwag**
zhizhoo' /zhizhoo'w-/ *vta* spread s.o. using something; *1sg* **inzhizhoo'waa**; *prt* **zhezhoo'waad**
zhizhoo'an *vti* spread s.t. using something; *1sg* **inzhizhoo'aan**; *prt* **zhezhoo'ang**
zhizhoo'ige *vai* spread things using something; *1sg* **inzhizhoo'ige**; *prt* **zhezhoo'iged**
zhiibawaaseyaa *vii* be transparent; *prt* **zhaabawaaseyaag**; *aug* **zhiibawaaseyaamagad**; *prt aug* **zhaabawaaseyaamagak**
zhiibawaasezi *vai* be transparent; *1sg* **inzhiibawaasez**; *prt* **zhaabawaasezid**
zhiibaakwa' /zhiibaakwa'w-/ *vta* stretch s.o. on a hide stretcher; *1sg* **inzhiibaakwa'waa**; *prt* **zhaabaakwa'waad**
zhiibaakwa'ataan *ni* flat hide stretcher (especially for muskrats); *pl* **zhiibaakwa'ataanan**; *loc* **zhiibaakwa'ataaning**; *dim* **zhiibaakwa'ataanens**
zhiibaangwashi *vai* take a quick nap; *1sg* **inzhiibaangwash**; *prt* **zhaabaangwashid**
zhiibaayaabanjigan *ni* telescope, binoculars; *pl* **zhiibaayaabanjiganan**; *loc* **zhiibaayaabanjiganing**; *dim* **zhiibaayaabanjigaans**
zhiibaayaakizo *vai* get x-rayed; *1sg* **inzhiibaayaakiz**; *prt* **zhaabaayaakizod**
zhiibii *vai* stretch one's body; *1sg* **inzhiibii**; *prt* **zhaabiid**
zhiibiiga' /zhiibiiga'w-/ *vta* stretch s.o. using something (as something sheet-like); *1sg* **inzhiibiiga'waa**; *prt* **zhaabiiga'waad**
zhiibiiga'an *vti* stretch s.t. using something (as something sheet-like); *1sg* **inzhiibiiga'aan**; *prt* **zhaabiiga'ang**
zhiibiigibidoon *vti2* stretch s.t. by pulling (as something sheet-like); *1sg* **inzhiibiigibidoon**; *prt* **zhaabiigibidood**
zhiibiigibizh /zhiibiigibiN-/ *vta* stretch s.o. by pulling (as something sheet-like); *1sg* **inzhiibiigibinaa**; *prt* **zhaabiigibinaad**
zhiibiigishkaa *vii* stretch (as something sheet-like); *prt* **zhaabiigishkaag**; *aug*

zhiibiigishkaamagad; *prt aug*
zhaabiigishkaamagak
zhiigaa *na* widow, widower; *pl* **zhiigaag**
zhiigaawi *vai* be a widow, be a widower; *1sg*
inzhiigaaw; *prt* **zhaagaawid**
zhiigon *vta* empty s.o.; *1sg* **inzhiigonaa**; *prt*
zhaagonaad
zhiigonan *vti* empty s.t.; *1sg* **inzhiigonaan**; *prt*
zhaagonang
zhiigonigaade *vii* be emptied; *prt*
zhaagonigaadeg; *aug* **zhiigonigaademagad**;
prt aug **zhaagonigaademagak**
zhiigonigaazo *vai* be emptied; *prt*
zhaagonigaazod
zhiigonige *vai* empty things; *1sg* **inzhiigonige**; *prt*
zhaagoniged
zhiigoshkigani-adaawewigamig *ni* secondhand
clothing store; *pl* **zhiigoshkigani-
adaawewigamigoon**; *loc* **zhiigoshkigani-
adaawewigamigong**
zhiigozhigan *ni* carcass; *pl* **zhiigozhiganan**; *loc*
zhiigozhiganing; *dim* **zhiigozhigaans**
zhiigoojiinan *vti* deflate s.t.; *1sg* **inzhiigoojiinaan**;
prt **zhaagoojiinang**
zhiigwanaabik *na* grindstone; *pl*
zhiigwanaabikoog; *loc* **zhiigwanaabikong**; *dim*
zhiigwanaabikoons
zhiingendan *vti* dislike s.t., disapprove of s.t., hate
s.t.; *1sg* **inzhiingendaan**; *prt* **zhaangendang**
zhiingendaagozi *vai* be disliked, be disapproved
of, be hated; *1sg* **inzhiingendaagoz**; *prt*
zhaangendaagozid
zhiingendaagwad *vii* be disliked, be disapproved
of, be hated; *prt* **zhaangendaagwak**
zhiingenim *vta* dislike s.o., disapprove of s.o., hate
s.o.; *1sg* **inzhiingenimaa**; *prt* **zhaangenimaad**
zhiingenindiwag /**zhiingenindi-**/ *vai* they dislike
each other, they disapprove of each other, they
hate each other; *1pl* **inzhiingenindimin**; *prt*
zhaangeninindijig
zhiishiib= < **zhiib=**
zhiishiib *na* duck; *pl* **zhiishiibag**; *dim* **zhiishiibens**
zhiishiibanwii-baashkizigan *ni* shotgun; *pl*
zhiishiibanwii-baashkiziganan; *loc*
zhiishiibanwii-baashkiziganing; *dim*
zhiishiibanwii-baashkizigaans
zhiishiibikojigan *na* duck decoy; *pl*
zhiishiibikojigan; *loc* **zhiishiibikojiganing**; *dim*
zhiishiibikojigaans
zhiishiig= < **zhig=**
zhiishiigi *vai* urinate; *1sg* **inzhiishiig**; *prt*
zhaashiigid
zhiishiigwan *na* rattle; *pl* **zhiishiigwanag**; *loc*
zhiishiigwaning; *dim* **zhiishiigwaans**
zhiishiigwaans *na* sugar cone; *pl*
zhiishiigwaansag; *loc* **zhiishiigwaansing**
zhiishiigwe *na* rattlesnake; *pl* **zhiishiigweg**; *dim*
zhiishiigwens
zhiiwan *vii* be sour; *prt* **zhaawang**
zhiiwaaboo *ni* vinegar; *loc* **zhiiwaaboong**
zhiiwaabookaade *vii* be pickled; *prt*
zhaawaabookaadeg; *aug*
zhiiwaabookaademagad; *prt aug*
zhaawaabookaademagak

zhiiwaagamide *vii* thicken into syrup; *prt*
zhaawaagamideg; *aug*
zhiiwaagamidemagad; *prt aug*
zhaawaagamidemagak
zhiiwaagamin /**zhiiwaagami-**/ *vii* be sour (as a
liquid); *prt* **zhaawaagamig**
zhiiwaagamizigan *ni* syrup; *loc*
zhiiwaagamiziganing
zhiiwaagamiziganike *vai* make syrup; *1sg*
inzhiiwaagamiziganike; *prt*
zhaawaagamiziganiked
zhiiwaagamizige *vai* make syrup; *1sg*
inzhiiwaagamizige; *prt* **zhaawaagamiziged**
zhiiwibag *ni* rhubarb; *pl* **zhiiwibagoon**; *loc*
zhiiwibagong; *dim* **zhiiwibagoons**
zhiiwi-bipakoombens *ni* pickle; *pl* **zhiiwi-
bipakoombensan**
zhiiwisijigan *na* sourdough; *pl* **zhiiwisijiganag**; *loc*
zhiiwisijiganing
zhiiwitaagan *ni* salt; *loc* **zhiiwitaaganing**
zhiiwitaagana' /**zhiiwitaagana'w-**/ *vta* salt s.o.; *1sg*
inzhiiwitaagana'waa; *prt*
zhaawitaagana'waad
zhiiwitaagana'an *vti* salt s.t.; *1sg*
inzhiiwitaagana'aan; *prt* **zhaawitaagana'ang**
zhiiwitaagana'ige *vai* salt things; *1sg*
inzhiiwitaagana'ige; *prt* **zhaawitaagana'iged**
zhiiwitaaganaagamin /**zhiiwitaaganaagami-**/ *vii*
be salty (as a liquid); *prt*
zhaawitaaganaagamig
zhiiwitaaganipogozi *vai* taste salty; *1sg*
zhaawitaaganipogozid
zhiiwitaaganipogwad *vii* taste salty; *prt*
zhaawitaaganipogwak
zhiiwitaagani-gookoosh *na* salt pork
zhiiwizi *vai* be sour; *prt* **zhaawizid**
zhoobi' *vta* attract s.o., please s.o.; *1sg*
inzhoobi'aa; *prt* **zhwaabi'aad**
zhoobizi *vai* be tempted; *1sg* **inzhoobiz**; *prt*
zhwaabizid
zhoominaaboo *ni* wine; *loc* **zhoominaaboong**;
also **zhawiminaaboo**
zhoominens *ni* raisin; *pl* **zhoominensan**

zhiishiigwan (rattle)

zhoomiingweni *vai* smile; *1sg* inzhoomiingwen; *prt* zhwaamiingwenid

zhoomiingwetaw *vta* smile at s.o.; *1sg* inzhoomiingwetawaa; *prt* zhwaamiingwetawaad

zhooniyaa *na* money; *loc* zhooniyaang; *dim* zhooniyaans

zhooniyaake *vai* make money, earn money; *1sg* inzhooniyaake; *prt* zhwaaniyaaked

zhooniyaa-mashkimod *ni* purse, handbag; *pl* zhooniyaa-mashkimodan; *loc* zhooniyaa-mashkimodaang; *dim* zhooniyaa-mashkimodens; *also* zhooniyaa-mashkimodens

zhooniyaans *na* coin, dime; *pl* zhooniyaansag; *loc* zhooniyaansing

zhooniyaawaabik *na* coin; *pl* zhooniyaawaabikoog; *loc* zhooniyaawaabikong; *dim* zhooniyaawaabikoons

zhooniyaawaabik *ni* silver; *pl* zhooniyaawaabikoon; *dim* zhooniyaawaabikoons

zhooniyaawigamig *ni* bank; *pl* zhooniyaawigamigoon; *loc* zhooniyaawigamigong

zhooshkodaabaan *na* toboggan; *pl* zhooshkodaabaanag; *loc* zhooshkodaabaaning; *dim* zhooshkodaanaanens

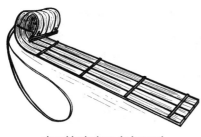

zhooshkodaabaan (toboggan)

zhooshkon *vta* slide s.o. with hand; *1sg* inzhooshkonaa; *prt* zhwaashkonaad

zhooshkonan *vti* slide s.t. with hand; *1sg* inzhooshkonaan; *prt* zhwaashkonang

zhooshkonige *vai* slide things, play checkers; *1sg* inzhooshkonige; *prt* zhwaashkoniged

zhooshkoshimaan *na* ski; *pl* zhooshkoshimaanag; *also* zhooshkoshime-aagim

zhooshkozi *vai* be smooth, be slick; *prt* zhwaashkozid

zhooshkwabi *vai* slide over sitting; *1sg* inzhooshkwab; *prt* zhwaashkwabid

zhooshkwadamon /zhooshkwadamo-/ *vii* be slippery (as a road or trail); *prt* zhwaashkwadamog

zhooshkwajiwe *vai* go sliding; *1sg* inzhooshkwajiwe; *prt* zhwaashkwajiwed

zhooshkwaa *vii* be smooth, be slick; *prt* zhwaashkwaag; *aug* zhooshkwaamagad; *prt* *aug* zhwaashkwaamagak

zhooshkwaabikad *vii* be smooth (as something mineral), be rustless; *prt* zhwaashkwaabikak

zhooshkwaabikizi *vai* be smooth (as something mineral), be rustless; *prt* zhwaashkwaabikizid

zhooshkwaada'aagan *ni* skate; *pl* zhooshkwaada'aaganan; *loc* zhooshkwaada'aaganing; *dim* zhooshkwaada'aagaans

zhooshkwaada'e *vai* skate; *1sg* inzhooshkwaada'e; *prt* zhwaashkwaada'ed

zhooshkwaada'ewigamig *ni* arena, rink; *pl* zhooshkwaada'ewigamigoon; *loc* zhooshkwaada'ewigamigong; *dim* zhooshkwaada'ewigamigoons

zhooshkwaagim *na* ski; *pl* zhooshkwaagimag; *loc* zhooshkwaagiming; *dim* zhooshkwaagimens

zhooshkwaagime *vai* ski; *1sg* inzhooshkwaagime; *prt* zhwaashkwaagimed

zhooshkwaakozi *vai* be smooth (as something stick- or wood-like); *prt* zhwaashkwaakozid

zhooshkwaakwad *vii* be smooth (as something stick- or wood-like); *prt* zhwaashkwaakwak

zhooshkwegad *vii* be smooth (as something sheet-like); *prt* zhwaashkwegak

zhooshkwega' /zhooshkwega'w-/ *vta* iron s.o. (e.g., pants); *1sg* inzhooshkwega'waa; *prt* zhwaashkwega'waad

zhooshkwega'an *vti* iron s.t.; *1sg* inzhooshkwega'aan; *prt* zhwaashkwega'ang

zhooshkwega'igan *ni* clothes iron; *pl* zhooshkwega'iganan; *loc* zhooshkwega'iganing; *dim* zhooshkwega'igaans

zhooshkwega'ige *vai* iron clothes; *1sg* inzhooshkwega'ige; *prt* zhwaashkwega'iged

zhooshkwegizi *vai* be smooth (as something sheet-like); *prt* zhwaashkwegizid

ziko *vai* spit; *1sg* inzik; *prt* zekod

zikowin *ni* saliva, spit

zikwaadan *vti* spit on s.t.; *1sg* inzikwaadaan; *prt* zekwaadaan

zikwaajige *vai* spit on things; *1sg* inzikwaajige; *prt* zekwaajiged

zikwaazh /zikwaaN-/ *vta* spit on s.o.; *1sg* inzikwaanaa; *prt* zekwaanaad

zinigobidoon *vti2* massage s.t. with something; *1sg* inzinigobidoon; *prt* zenigobidood

zinigobizh /zinigobiN-/ *vta* massage s.o. with something; *1sg* inzinigobinaa; *prt* zenigobinaad

zinigon *vta* rub s.o. with something; *1sg* inzinigonaa; *prt* zenigonaad

zinigonan *vti* rub s.t. with something; *1sg* inzinigonaan; *prt* zenigonang

zisiboodoon *vti2* file s.t., grind s.t. down; *1sg* inzisiboodoon; *prt* zesiboodood

zisiboojigan *ni* file, rasp; *pl* zisiboojiganan; *loc* zisiboojiganing; *dim* zisiboojigaans

zisiboojige *vai* file things; *1sg* inzisiboojige; *prt* zesiboojiged

zisiboozh /zisibooN-/ *vta* file s.o., grind s.o. down; *1sg* inzisiboonaa; *prt* zesiboonaad

ziibaaska'igan *ni* jingle (on dress); *pl*
    ziibaaska'iganan; *loc* **ziibaaska'iganing**; *dim*
    ziibaaska'igaans
ziibaaska'iganagooday *ni* jingle dress; *pl*
    ziibaaska'iganagoodayan

ziibaaska'iganagooday (jingle dress)

ziibaaskobijige *vai* set a net under the ice; *1sg*
    inziibaaskobijige; *prt* **zaabaaskobijiged**
ziibi *ni* river; *pl* **ziibiwan**; *loc* **ziibiing**; *dim* **ziibiins**
ziibiins *ni* creek; *pl* **ziibiinsan**; *loc* **ziibiinsing**
ziiga'andan *vti* water s.t., pour liquid on s.t.; *1sg*
    inziiga'andaan; *prt* **zaaga'andang**
ziiga'andaw *vta* pour liquid on s.o., baptize s.o.;
    1sg **inziiga'andawaa**; *prt* **zaaga'andawaad**
ziiga'igan *ni* sugar cake, sugar cone; *pl*
    ziiga'iganan; *loc* **ziiga'iganing**; *dim*
    ziiga'igaans
ziiga'iganike *vai* make a sugar cone; *1sg*
    inziiga'iganike; *prt* **zaaga'iganiked**
ziiga'ige *vai* cast sugar cones; *1sg* **inziiga'ige**; *prt*
    zaaga'iged
ziigana' /**ziigana'w-**/ *vta* spoon feed s.o. a liquid;
    1sg **inziigana'waa**; *prt* **zaagana'waad**
ziigashkinadoon *vti2* fill s.t. to overflowing with
    solids; *1sg* **inziigashkinadoon**; *prt*
    zaagashkinadood
ziigashkina' *vta* fill s.o. to overflowing with solids;
    1sg **inziigashkina'aa**; *prt* **zaagashkina'aad**
ziigibadoon *vti2* fill s.t. to overflowing with a
    liquid; *1sg* **inziigibadoon**; *prt* **zaagibadood**
ziigigamide *vii* boil over; *prt* **zaagigamideg**; *aug*
    ziigigamidemagad; *prt aug*
    zaagigamidemagak
ziigigamizo *vai* boil over; *prt* **zaagigamizod**
ziiginan *vti* pour s.t., spill s.t.; *1sg* **inziiginaan**; *prt*
    zaaginang
ziiginige *vai* pour things, spill things; *1sg*
    inziiginige; *prt* **zaaginiged**
ziiginigewigamig *ni* tavern, bar; *pl*
    ziiginigewigamigon; *loc*
    ziiginigewigamigong; *dim*
    ziiginigewigamigoons
ziiginigewikwe *na* barmaid; *pl* **ziiginigewikweg**

ziiginigewinini *na* bartender; *pl*
    ziiginigewininiwag
ziiginishaan *ni* ear drops
ziiginiingwaan *ni* eye drops
ziigise *vii* pour out, spill out; *prt* **zaagiseg**; *aug*
    ziigisemagad; *prt aug* **zaagisemagak**
ziigwan *vii* be spring; *prt* **zaagwang**
ziigwanishi *vai* spend the spring somewhere; *1sg*
    inziigwanish; *prt* **zaagwanishid**
ziigwanong *pc* last spring
ziigwebinan *vti* spill s.t.; *1sg* **inziigwebinaan**; *prt*
    zaagwebinang
ziigwebinigan *ni* dump, trash; *pl* **ziigwebiniganan**;
    loc **ziigwebiniganing**; *dim* **ziigwebinigaans**
ziigwebinigewakik *na* slop pail; *pl*
    ziigwebinigewakikoog; *loc*
    ziigwebinigewakikong; *dim*
    ziigwebinigewakikoons
ziikaa *na* car *old fashioned*; *pl* **ziikaag**; *loc* **ziikaang**;
    dim **ziikaans**
ziikaapidan *vti* drink s.t. quickly; *1sg*
    inziikaapidaan; *prt* **zaakaapidang**
ziikoobiiginan *vti* strain s.t.; *1sg*
    inziikoobiiginaan; *prt* **zaakoobiiginang**
ziinaakwa'igan *ni* clothes wringer, clothespin; *pl*
    ziinaakwa'iganan; *loc* **ziinaakwa'iganing**; *dim*
    ziinaakwa'igaans
ziindaakoshin *vai* be wedged in tightly (as some-
    thing stick- or wood-like); *1sg* **inziindaakoshin**;
    prt **zaandaakoshing**
ziindaakosin *vii* be wedged in tightly (as some-
    thing stick- or wood-like); *prt* **zaandaakosing**
ziinibidoon *vti2* squeeze s.t., wring s.t.; *1sg*
    inziinibidoon; *prt* **zaanibidood**
ziinibizh /**ziinibiN-**/ *vta* squeeze s.o., wring s.o.;
    1sg **inziinibinaa**; *prt* **zaanibinaad**
ziinikiigomaan *na* snot
ziinikiigome *vai* blow one's nose; *1sg*
    inziinikiigome; *prt* **zaanikiigomed**
ziinin *vta* milk s.o.; *1sg* **inziininaa**; *prt* **zaaninaad**
ziininiwe *vai* milk cows; *1sg* **inziininiwe**; *prt*
    zaaniniwed
ziinzibaakwad *ni* maple sugar, sugar; *loc*
    ziinzibaakwadong; *dim* **ziinzibaakwadoons**
ziinzibaakwado-makak *ni* birch bark basket for
    maple sugar; *pl* **ziinzibaakwado-makakoon**
ziinzibaakwad-onaagaans *ni* sugar bowl; *pl*
    ziinzibaakwad-onaagaansan; *loc*
    ziinzibaakwad-onaagaansing
ziinzibaakwadowaapine *vai* have diabetes; *1sg*
    inziinzibaakwadowaapine; *prt*
    zaanzibaakwadowaapined; *also*
    ziinzibaakwadwaapine
ziinzibaakwadoons *ni* candy; *pl*
    ziinzibaakwadoonsan; *loc*
    ziinzibaakwadoonsing
ziinzibaakwadwaaboo *ni* maple sap; *loc*
    ziinzibaakwadwaaboong
ziinzoopizon *ni* bandage; *pl* **ziinzoopizonan**; *loc*
    ziinzoopizoning; *dim* **ziinzoopizonens**
zoobam *vta* suck out of s.o.; *1sg* **inzoobamaa**; *prt*
    zwaabamaad
zoobandan *vti* suck out of s.t.; *1sg* **inzoobandaan**;
    prt **zwaabandang**
zoogipon /**zoogipo-**/ *vii* snow; *prt* **zwaagipog**

zoongan *vii* be solid, be strong; *prt* **zwaangang**
zoongide'e *vai* be brave; *1sg* **inzoongide'e**; *prt*
zwaangide'ed
zoongigane *vai* have strong bones; *1sg*
inzoongigane; *prt* **zwaangiganed**
zoongi' *vta* make s.o. strong, make s.o. solid; *1sg*
inzoongi'aa; *prt* **zwaangi'aad**
zoongingwashi *vai* sleep deeply
zoonginike *vai* have a strong arm; *1sg*
inzoonginike; *prt* **zwaanginiked**

zoongininjii *vai* have a strong hand; *1sg*
inzoongininjii; *prt* **zwaangininjiid**
zoongishin *vai* lie firmly fixed in place; *1sg*
inzoongishin; *prt* **zwaangishing**
zoongisin *vii* lie firmly fixed in place; *prt*
zwaangising
zoongitoon *vti2* make s.t. strong, make s.t. solid;
1sg **inzoongitoon**; *prt* **zwaangitood**
zoongizi *vai* be solid, be strong; *1sg* **inzoongiz**; *prt*
zwaangizid

Part II

English–Ojibwe Index

A

ABANDON

ABANDON: abandon s.o. **nagazh** /**nagaN-**/ *vta;* abandon s.t. **nagadan** *vti;* abandon people **nagazhiwe** *vai*

ABLE

ABLE: be able **gashki'o** *vai;* be able (to do something) **gashkichige** *vai*

ABLE TO CARRY: be able to carry s.o. **gashkiwizh** /**gashkiwiN-**/ *vta;* be able to carry s.t. **gashkiwidoon** *vti2*

ABLE TO DO: be able to do s.t. **gashkitoon** *vti2*

ABLE TO GET: be able to get (s.t.) for s.o. **gashkitaw** *vta*

ABLE TO MANAGE: be able to manage (s.t.) for s.o. **gashkitaw** *vta*

ABLE TO TAKE: be able to take s.o. **gashkiwizh** /**gashkiwiN-**/ *vta;* be able to take s.t. **gashkiwidoon** *vti2*

ABLE TO WORK: be able to work **gashkanokii** *vai*

NOT ABLE: not able to **bwaa-** *pv1*

ABOARD

GET ABOARD: **boozi** *vai*

JUMP ABOARD: **boozigwaashkwani** *vai*

TELL TO GO ABOARD: tell s.o. to go aboard **boozinaazha'** /**boozinaazha'w-**/ *vta*

ABOUT

ABOUT: going about **babaa-** *pv2*

BLOWN ABOUT: be blown about **babaamaashi** *vai;* **babaamaasin** *vii*

CARRY ABOUT: carry s.o. about **babaamiwizh** /**babaamiwiN-**/ *vta;* carry s.t. about **babaamiwidoon** *vti2*

CHASE ABOUT: chase s.o. about **babaaminizha'** /**babaaminizha'w-**/ *vta;* chase s.t. about **babaaminizha'an** *vti;* chase things about **babaaminizha'ige** *vai*

CLOUDS MOVE ABOUT: **babaamaanakwad** *vii*

CRAWL ABOUT: **babaamoode** *vai*

DANCE ABOUT: **babaamishimo** *vai*

DRIVE ABOUT: **babaamibide**, **babaamibidemagad** *vii;* **babaamibizo** *vai;* **babaamidaabii'iwe** *vai*

FLY ABOUT: **babaamibide**, **babaamibidemagad** *vii;* **babaamibizo** *vai;* **babaamise** *vai;* **babaamise**, **babaamisemagad** *vii*

GO ABOUT CRYING: **babaamademo** *vai*

GO ABOUT IN A BOAT: **babaamishkaa** *vai*

GO ABOUT ON BUSINESS: go about on one's business **babaamizi** *vai*

GO ABOUT ON THE ICE: **babaamaadagaako** *vai*

GO ABOUT TRADING: **babaamadaawe** *vai*

GOING ABOUT: **babaa-** *pv2*

GUIDE ABOUT: guide s.o. about **babaamiwizh** /**babaamiwiN-**/ *vta*

LIVE ABOUT: **babaamaadizi** *vai*

MOVE RESIDENCE ABOUT: move one's residence about **babaamigozi** *vai*

PADDLE ABOUT: **babaamishkaa** *vai*

RIDE ABOUT ON HORSEBACK: **babaamoomigo** *vai*

RUN ABOUT: **babaamibatoo** *vai;* they run about together **babaamiba'idiwag** /**babaamiba'idi-**/ *vai*

SAIL ABOUT: **babaamaashi** *vai;* **babaamaasin** *vii*

SKATE ABOUT: **babaamaada'e** *vai*

SPEED ABOUT: **babaamibide**, **babaamibidemagad** *vii;* **babaamibizo** *vai*

SPREAD THE NEWS ABOUT: **babaamaajimo** *vai*

SWIM ABOUT: **babaamaadagaa** *vai*

TAKE ABOUT: take s.o. about **babaamiwizh** /**babaamiwiN-**/ *vta;* take s.t. about **babaamiwidoon** *vti2*

TRAVEL ABOUT: **babaamaadizi** *vai*

WADE ABOUT: **babaamaadagaazii** *vai*

WALK ABOUT: **babaamose** *vai;* **babimose** *vai*

WANDER ABOUT: **babaa-ayaa** *vai*

ABOVE

ABOVE: **ishpiming** *pc;* above it **ishpayi'ii** *pc*

ABOVE ALL

ABOVE ALL: **memindage** *pc*

ABSCESSED

ABSCESSED TOOTH: have an abscessed tooth **miniiwaabide** *vai*

ABSENT

ABSENT A CERTAIN LENGTH OF TIME: be absent a certain length of time **apiitendi** *vai;* **inendi** *vai*

ABSENT A CERTAIN NUMBER OF DAYS: be absent a certain number of days **dasogonendi** *vai*

ABSENT FROM A CERTAIN PLACE: be absent from a certain place **ondendi** *vai*

ABUSE

ABUSE: abuse s.o. **aanimi'** *vta;* abuse s.t. **aanimitoon** *vti2*

ACCEPT

ACCEPT: accept s.o. **odaapin** *vta;* accept s.t. **odaapinan** *vti;* accept (s.t.) from s.o. **odaapinamaw** *vta;* accept things **odaapinige** *vai*

ACCEPTED

ACCEPTED: be accepted **odaapinigaade**, **odaapinigaademagad** *vii;* **odaapinigaazo** *vai*

ACCIDENT

DIE IN AN ACCIDENT: **niiwanishin** *vai*

ACCIDENTALLY

ACCIDENTALLY: **bichi-** *pv4*

ACCIDENTALLY HIT: accidentally hit s.o. **bitaganaam** *vta;* accidentally hit s.t. **bitaganaandan** *vti*

CUT ACCIDENTALLY: cut s.o. accidentally **bitizh** /**bitizhw-**/ *vta;* cut s.t. accidentally **bitizhan** *vti*

HIT AGAINST ACCIDENTALLY: hit against something accidentally (as something stick- or wood-like) **bitaakoshin** *vai;* **bitaakosin** *vii*
SHOOT ACCIDENTALLY: shoot s.o. accidentally **bichinaw** *vta;* shoot s.t. accidentally **bichinan** *vti;* shoot things accidentally **bichinaage** *vai;* shoot oneself accidentally **bichinaadizo** *vai*

ACCOMPANY
ACCOMPANY: accompany s.o. **wiijiiw** *vta;* accompany people **wiijii'iwe** *vai;* they accompany each other **wiijiindiwag** /**wiijiindi-**/ *vai*

ACCOMPLISH
ACCOMPLISH: **gashki'ewizi** *vai*

ACCUSE
ACCUSE: accuse s.o. **anaamim** *vta*

ACE
ACE: ace (card) **bezhigoobii'igan, -ag** *na*

ACHE
ACHE: **dewizi** *vai*
ACHE IN ARM: have an ache in one's arm **dewinike** *vai*
ACHE IN BACK: have a backache **dewaawigan** *vai;* **dewipikwan** *vai*
ACHE IN FOOT: have an ache in one's foot **dewizide** *vai*
ACHE IN HAND: have an ache in one's hand **dewininjii** *vai*
ACHE IN LEG: have an ache in one's leg **dewigaade** *vai*
TOOTHACHE: have a toothache **dewaabide** *vai*

ACNE
ACNE ON FACE: have acne on one's face **moosewiingwe** *vai*

ACORN
ACORN: **mitigomin, -an** *ni*

ACQUAINTED
ACQUAINTED: be acquainted with s.o. **nagadenim** *vta;* they are acquainted with each other **nagadenindiwag** /**nagadenindi-**/ *vai*

ACQUIRE
ACQUIRE: **gashkichige** *vai*

ACRE
CERTAIN NUMBER OF ACRES: a certain number of acres **daso-diba'igaans** *pc*

ACROSS
ACROSS: **agaami-** *pn;* across it **agaamayi'ii** *pc*
ACROSS THE LAKE: **agaaming** *pc*
ACROSS THE ROAD: across the road or trail **agaamikana** *pc*
CARRY ACROSS: carry s.o. across **aazhogewizh** /**aazhogewiN-**/ *vta;* carry s.t. across **aazhogewidoon** *vti2*
CLIMB ACROSS: **aazhawaandawe** *vai*
DRIVE ACROSS: **aazhogebizo** *vai;* **aazhogedaabii'iwe** *vai;* **aazhoodaabii'iwe** *vai*

FERRY ACROSS: ferry s.o. across **aazhawa'oozh** /**aazhawa'ooN-**/ *vta;* ferry s.t. across **aazhawa'oodoon** *vti2*
GO ACROSS: **aazhooshkaa** *vai*
GO ACROSS BY BOAT: **aazhawa'am** *vai2,* also **aazhawa'o**
GO ACROSS WATER: **aazhoge** *vai*
JUMP ACROSS: **aazhawigwaashkwani** *vai*
LAY ACROSS: lay s.o. across (as something stick- or wood-like) **aazhawaakoshim** *vta;* lay s.t. across (as something stick- or wood-like) **aazhawaakosidoon** *vti2*
LIE ACROSS: lie across (as something stick- or wood-like) **aazhawaakoshin** *vai;* **aazhawaakosin** *vii*
OVER ACROSS: **awasi-** *pn;* over across it **awasayi'ii** *pc*
OVER ACROSS THE FIRE: **awasishkode** *pc*
OVER ACROSS THE MOUNTAIN: **awasajiw** *pc*
OVER ACROSS THE WATER: **awasagaam** *pc*
OVER ACROSS THE WOODS: **awasaakwaa** *pc*
RIGHT ACROSS: **dibishkookamig** *pc*
ROAD GOES ACROSS: go across (as a road or trail) **aazhoodamon** /**aazhoodamo-**/ *vii*
RUN ACROSS: **aazhoobatoo** *vai,* also **aazhawibatoo;** they run across together **aazhogeba'idiwag** /**aazhogeba'idi-**/ *vai;* **aazhooba'idiwag** /**aazhooba'idi-**/ *vai*
RUN ACROSS WADING: **aazhawagaaziibatoo** *vai*
SWIM ACROSS: **aazhawaadagaa** *vai*
TAKE ACROSS: take s.o. across **aazhogewizh** /**aazhogewiN-**/ *vta;* take s.t. across **aazhogewidoon** *vti2*
TAKE ACROSS BY BOAT: take s.o. across by boat **aazhawa'oozh** /**aazhawa'ooN-**/ *vta;* take s.t. across by boat **aazhawa'oodoon** *vti2*
TRAIL GOES ACROSS: go across (as a road or trail) **aazhoodamon** /**aazhoodamo-**/ *vii*
WADE ACROSS: **aazhawagaazii** *vai*

ADD
ADD IN: add s.o. in **dagon** *vta;* add s.t. in **dagonan** *vti*
ADD TOGETHER: **asigagindaaso** *vai;* add s.o. together (e.g., money) **asigagim** *vta;* add s.t. together **asigagindan** *vti*

ADDED
ADDED IN: be added in **dagonigaade, dagonigaademagad** *vii;* **dagonigaazo** *vai*

ADDRESS
ADDRESS: address s.o. **ganoozh** /**ganooN-**/ *vta*

ADHERE
ADHERE: **agoke** *vai;* **agoke, agokemagad** *vii;* **bazagoke;** **bazagoke, bazagokemagad** *vii*

ADMIRED
ADMIRED: be admired **minwaabamewizi** *vai*

ADOLESCENT
ADOLESCENT: be an adolescent **oshkiniigi** *vai*
ADOLESCENT BOY: **oshkinawe, -g** *na;* be an adolescent boy **oshkinawewi** *vai*
ADOLESCENT GIRL: **oshkiniigikwe, -g** *na;* be an adolescent girl **oshkiniigikwewi** *vai*

ADOPT
ADOPT: adopt s.o. **bami'** *vta;* **waangoom** *vta*

ADOPTED
ADOPTED ONE: **bami'aagan, -ag** *na*

ADULT
ADULT: **gichi-aya'aa, -g** *na;* be an adult **gichi-aya'aawi** *vai*

ADVANCE
IN ADVANCE: **giizhaa** *pc*

ADVANCED
ADVANCED INTO A TIME: **ishpi-** *pv4*

AFRAID
AFRAID: be afraid **gotaaji** *vai;* **zegizi** *vai;* be afraid of s.t. **gotan** *vti*

AFRICAN
AFRICAN: person of African descent **makade-wiiyaas, -ag** *na*
AFRICAN WOMAN: woman of African descent **makade-wiiyaasikwe, -g** *na*

AFTER
AFTER: **ishkwaa-** *pv4*

AFTER A WHILE
AFTER A WHILE: **baanimaa** *pc, also* **baamaa; baanimaa apii** *pc, also* **baanimaapii, baamaapii; bijiinag** *pc;* **gegapii** *pc;* **naagaj** *pc*

AFTERNOON
AFTERNOON: be afternoon **ishkwaa-naawakwe, ishkwaa-naawakwemagad** *vii*
LATE MORNING OR EARLY AFTERNOON: be late morning or early afternoon **ishpi-giizhigad** *vii*

AGAIN
AGAIN: **miinawaa** *pc*

AGAINST THE WIND
GO AGAINST THE WIND: **onjishkawishkaa** *vai*
PADDLE AGAINST THE WIND: **onjishkawa'o** *vai, also* **onjishkawa'am**

AGE
CERTAIN AGE: be a certain age **apiitizi** *vai*
SAME AGE: they are the same age **wiijigindiwag** /**wiijigindi-**/ *vai;* be the same age as s.o. **wiijigim** *vta*

AGITATE
AGITATE: **mamaazikaa** *vai*

AGO
A LITTLE WHILE AGO: **naanoomaya** *pc*
LONG AGO: **mewinzha** *pc*

AGREE
AGREE: **debwetam** *vai2;* **inendam** *vai2;* agree on something **inaakonige** *vai;* agree with s.o. **debwetaw** *vta;* agree with s.o. *especially of something consumed; inverse forms of:* **minokaw-** *vta*

AGREEABLE
AGREEABLE: be agreeable **minwendaagozi** *vai*

AHEAD
AHEAD: **niigaan** *pc*
GO AHEAD: **niigaanii** *vai*

AHEAD OF TIME
AHEAD OF TIME: **nayaag** *pc*

AIM
AIM: aim at s.o. **zhigweyaabam** *vta;* aim at s.t. **zhigweyaabandan** *vti*
AIM SIGHTS: **zhigweyaabi** *vai*

AIR PUMP
AIR PUMP: **boodaajii'igan, -an** *ni*

AIRPLANE
AIRPLANE: **bemisemagak, -in** *ni-pt*

AIRPORT
AIRPORT: **endazhi-booniimagak, -in** *ni-pt*

ALARMED
ALARMED: be alarmed **amaniso** *vai;* be alarmed by s.o. **amanisodaw** *vta*

ALCOHOL
RUBBING ALCOHOL: **giziibiigazhewaaboo** *ni*

ALDER
ALDER: **wadoop, -iin** *ni*

ALGAE
ALGAE: **ataagib** *ni*

ALIGHT
ALIGHT: **boonii** *vai*

ALIVE
ALIVE: be alive **bimaadizi** *vai*
COME ALIVE: **aabijiibaa** *vai*

ALL
ALL: **akina** *pc, also* **kina, gakina**
ALL DAY: **gabe-giizhik** *pc*
ALL EVENING: **gabe-onaagosh** *pc*
ALL KINDS: **anooj** *pc*
ALL NIGHT: **gabe-dibik** *pc*
ALL OVER: **miziwe** *pc*
ALL THE TIME: **apane** *pc*

ALLOT
ALLOT LAND: allot s.o. land **mamakii'** *vta*

ALLOTMENT
ALLOTMENT OF LAND: there is an allotment of land **mamakii'idim** /**mamakii'idi-**/ *vai*

ALLOW
ALLOW: allow s.o. **bagidin** *vta;* allow s.t. **bagidinan** *vti;* allow (s.t.) to s.o. **bagidinamaw** *vta;* allow things **bagidinige** *vai*

ALLOWED
ALLOWED: be allowed **bagidinigaade, bagidinigaademagad** *vii;* **bagidinigaazo** *vai*

ALMOST
ALMOST: **gegaa** *pc*

ALONE
ALONE: be alone **bezhigo** *vai;* **nazhikewizi** *vai*
LIVE ALONE: **nazhikewige** *vai*

SIT ALONE: **nazhikewaakwadabi** *vai*
ALONG
ALONG: **bimi-** *pv2;* along it **jiigayi'ii** *pc*
ALONG THE SHORE: **jiigew** *pc;* **jiigibiig** *pc*
BLOWN ALONG: be blown along **bimaashi**
vai; **bimaasin** *vii*
CARRY A BABY ALONG ON BACK: carry a
baby along on one's back **bimoomaawaso**
vai
CARRY A PACK ALONG: **bimiwane** *vai*
CARRY ALONG: carry s.o. along **bimiwizh**
/bimiwiN-/ *vta;* carry s.t. along
bimiwidoon *vti2;* carry things along
bimiwijige *vai*
CARRY ALONG ON BACK: carry s.o. along
on one's back **bimoom** *vta;* carry s.t. along
on one's back **bimoondan** *vti*
CHASE ALONG: chase s.o. along **biminizha'**
/biminizha'w-/ *vta;* **biminizhikaw** *vta;*
chase s.t. along **biminizha'an** *vti;* chase
things along **biminizha'ige** *vai;* chase
people along **biminaazhikaage** *vai*
CLIMB ALONG: **bimaandawe** *vai*
CLOUDS GO ALONG: **bimaanakwad** *vii*
CRAWL ALONG: **bimoode** *vai*
CRY WALKING ALONG: **bimademo** *vai*
DANCE ALONG: **bimishimo** *vai*
DRAG ALONG: drag s.o. along
bimidaabaazh /bimidaabaaN-/ *vta;* drag
s.t. along **bimidaabaadan** *vti*
DRIFT ALONG ON CURRENT:
bimaaboode, bimaaboodemagad *vii;*
bimaaboono *vai*
DRIVE ALONG: **bimibide, bimibidemagad**
vii; **bimibizo** *vai;* **bimidaabii'iwe** *vai;*
drive s.o. along **bimibizoni'** *vta;* drive s.t.
along **bimibizonitoon** *vti2;* drive people
along (as in a bus) **bimiwizhiwe** *vai*
DRIVE ALONG IN A WAGON OR
SLEIGH: drive along quickly in a wagon
or sleigh **bimidaabiiba'igo** *vai*
FLOW ALONG: **bimijiwan** *vii*
FLY ALONG: **bimibide, bimibidemagad** *vii;*
bimibizo *vai;* **bimise** *vai;* **bimise,**
bimisemagad *vii*
FOLLOW A TRAIL ALONG: **bima'adoo**
vai; follow s.o.'s trail along **bima'azh**
/bima'aN-/ *vta;* follow s.t. along as a trail
bima'adoon *vti2*
GO ALONG: **bimi-ayaa** *vai*
GO ALONG BY BOAT: **bimishkaa** *vai*
GO ALONG SINGING: **bima'amaazo** *vai*
GO ALONG THE EDGE: **bimaazhagaame** *vai*
GO ALONG THE SHORE: **bimaazhagaame**
vai
GO ALONG WITH A LIGHT:
bimaazakonenjige *vai*
GOING ALONG: **ani-** *pv2,* also **ni-;** **bimi-** *pv2*
HEARD DRIVING ALONG: be heard driving
along **bimwewebide,**
bimwewebidemagad *vii;* **bimwewebizo**
vai
HEARD SPEEDING ALONG: be heard
speeding along **bimwewebide,**

bimwewebidemagad *vii;* **bimwewebizo**
vai
HEARD WALKING ALONG: be heard
walking along **bimweweshin** *vai*
LEAD ALONG: lead along (as something
string-like) **bimaabiigamon**
/bimaabiigamo-/ *vii*
LEAVE TRACKS GOING ALONG:
bimikawe *vai*
LIE ALONG: lie along (as something stick- or
wood-like) **bimaakoshin** *vai;* **bimaakosin**
vii
PADDLE ALONG: **bimakwazhiwe** *vai;*
bimishkaa *vai*
POLE A BOAT ALONG: **bima'oodoo** *vai;*
bima'ookii *vai*
PUT ALONG: put s.o. along (as something
stick- or wood-like) **bimaakoshim** *vta;* put
s.t. along (as something stick- or wood-
like) **bimaakosidoon** *vti2*
RAIN GOES ALONG: **bimibiisaa,**
bimibiisaamagad *vii*
RIDE ALONG DRAWN BY HORSES:
bimiba'igo *vai*
RIDE ALONG ON HORSEBACK:
bimoomigo *vai*
RIVER FLOWS ALONG: flow along (as a
river) **bimitigweyaa, bimitigweyaamagad**
vii
ROAD LEADS ALONG: lead along (as a road
or trail) **bimamon /bimamo-/,**
bimamoomagad *vii*
RUN ALONG: **bimibatoo** *vai;* they run along
together **bimiba'idiwag /bimiba'idi-/** *vai*
RUN ALONG IN FLIGHT: **biminizhimo**
vai; run along in flight from someone
bimiba'iwe *vai*
SAIL ALONG: **bimaashi** *vai;* **bimaasin** *vii*
SEND ALONG: send s.o. along **biminizhikaw**
vta; send people along **biminaazhikaage**
vai
SKATE ALONG: **bimaada'e** *vai*
SNOW GOES ALONG: **bimipon /bimipo-/**
vii
SPEED ALONG: **bimibide, bimibidemagad**
vii; **bimibizo** *vai*
STRING ALONG: string s.o. along
bimaabiigin *vta;* string s.t. along
bimaabiiginan *vti*
SWIM ALONG: **bimaadagaa** *vai;* swim along
(as a fish) **bimakwazhiwe** *vai*
TAKE ALONG: take s.o. along **bimiwizh**
/bimiwiN-/ *vta;* take s.t. along **bimiwidoon**
vti2; take people along **bimiwizhiwe** *vai*
TAKE ALONG FOR A RIDE: take s.o. along
for a ride **bimibizoni'** *vta*
TAKE ALONG IN A BOAT: take s.o. along
in a boat **bima'oozh /bima'ooN-/** *vta;* take
s.t. along in a boat **bima'oodoon** *vti2*
TRAIL LEADS ALONG: lead along (as a
road or trail) **bimamon /bimamo-/,**
bimamoomagad *vii*
TRAVEL ALONG: **bimi-ayaa** *vai;* travel
along in a group (as a school of fish)
bimaawadaaso *vai*

WADE ALONG: **bimaadagaazii** *vai*
WALK ALONG: **bimose** *vai*
WALK ALONG ON THE ICE:
  bimaadagaako *vai*
ALONGSIDE
  ALONGSIDE: alongside it **zhishwajayi'ii** *pc*
  ALONGSIDE THE HOUSE:
    zhishwajigamig *pc*
  ALONGSIDE THE ROAD: **zhishwajikana** *pc*
ALPHABET
  LETTER OF THE ALPHABET:
    ozhibii'igan, -an *ni*
ALREADY
  ALREADY: **azhigwa** *pc, also* **zhigwa, zhigo;**
    already *old-fashioned* **zhayiigwa** *pc*
ALSO
  ALSO: **gaye** *pc, also* **ge; miinawaa** *pc*
ALTERNATELY
  ALTERNATELY: **memeshkwad** *pc*
ALTHOUGH
  ALTHOUGH: **aanawi** *pc*
ALWAYS
  ALWAYS: **apane** *pc;* **moozhag** *pc*
AMAZED
  AMAZED: be amazed **maamakaadendam**
    vai2; be amazed at s.o. **maamakaadenim**
    vta; be amazed at s.t. **maamakaadendan**
    vti; be amazed at what s.o. says
    maamakaazitaw *vta*
AMAZING
  AMAZING: **maamakaaj** *pc;* amazing!
    maamakaadakamig *pc;* be amazing
    maamakaadizi *vai*
  CONSIDERED AMAZING: be considered
    amazing **maamakaadendaagwad** *vii*
  DO AMAZING THINGS: **maamakaajichige**
    vai
AMBITIOUS
  AMBITIOUS: be ambitious **gwaashkwezi** *vai*
AMBULANCE
  AMBULANCE: **aakoziiwidaabaan, -ag** *na*
AMERICAN
  AMERICAN: **gichi-mookomaan, -ag** *na*
AMERICAN BITTERN
  AMERICAN BITTERN: American bittern
    (locally called shypoke) **mooshka'osi,**
    -wag *na*
AMMUNITION
  USE UP AMMUNITION: use up all of the
    ammunition **jaaga'e** *vai;* **jaagizige** *vai*
AMONG
  AMONG: **megwe-** *pn*
  IN AMONG: in among it **megwe-aya'ii** *pc,*
    also **megweya'ii**
AMOUNT
  CERTAIN AMOUNT: a certain amount
    minik *pc*
  SOME AMOUNT: **gomaa** *pc*
ANCESTOR
  ANCESTOR: **aanikoobijigan, -ag** *na*
ANCHOR
  ANCHOR: **boonakajigan, -an** *ni;* anchor s.t.
    boonakadoon *vti2*

AND
  AND: **dash** *pc, also* **idash, -sh; gaye** *pc, also* **ge;**
    miinawaa *pc*
  AND THEN: **mii dash** *pc, also* **miish**
ANGER
  ANGER: anger s.o. **nishki'** *vta;* anger people
    nishkitaa *vai;* they anger each other
    nishki'idiwag /nishki'idi-/ *vai*
  ACT UP IN ANGER: **nishkaajitaa** *vai*
  ANGER FOR A CERTAIN REASON: anger
    s.o. for a certain reason **onjinawe'** *vta*
  COME IN ANGER: **biijigidaazo** *vai*
ANGRILY
  BEHAVE ANGRILY: **nishkaajitaa** *vai*
ANGRY
  ANGRY: be angry **nishkaadizi** *vai;* be angry at
    s.o. **nishkenim** *vta*
  ANGRY TO A CERTAIN EXTENT: be
    angry to a certain extent **apiichigidaazo**
    vai
  FEEL ANGRY: **nishkendam** *vai2*
ANIMAL
  DOMESTIC ANIMAL: **awakaan, -ag** *na*
  DRAFT ANIMAL: **odaabii'aagan, -ag** *na*
  WILD ANIMAL: **awesiinh, -yag** *na*
ANKLE JOINT
  ANKLE JOINT: **bikwaakoganaan, -an** *ni*
ANNOUNCE
  ANNOUNCE: announce (s.t.) to people
    wiindamaage *vai*
ANNOY
  ANNOY: annoy s.o. **migoshkaaji'** *vta*
ANNOYED
  ANNOYED: be annoyed **migoshkaadendam**
    vai2
ANSWER
  ANSWER: **nakwetam** *vai2;* answer s.o.
    nakom *vta;* **nakwetaw** *vta;* answer s.t.
    nakodan *vti;* **nakwetan** *vti;* they answer
    each other **nakondiwag** /nakondi-/ *vai*
  ANSWER BACK: answer back to s.o.
    aazhidem *vta*
ANT
  ANT: **enigoons, -ag** *na, also* **enig**
ANXIOUS
  ANXIOUS: be anxious **ojaanimendam** *vai2*
ANYBODY
  ANYBODY: anybody *animate indefinite* **awiya,**
    -g *pr, also* **awiiya**
ANYHOW
  ANYHOW: **aanawi** *pc;* **bagwana** *pc*
ANYTHING
  ANYTHING: anything *inanimate indefinite*
    gegoo *pr*
ANYTIME
  ANYTIME: anytime *dubitative* **amanj igo apii**
    pc
ANYWHERE
  ANYWHERE: anywhere *dubitative* **dibi go** *pc*
APART
  COME APART: **gidiskise** *vai;* **gidiskise,**
    gidiskisemagad *vii*

APOLOGIZE
APOLOGIZE: apologize to s.o. gaagiizom *vta*
APPEAR
APPEAR: bi-naagozi *vai;* bi-naagwad *vii*
APPEAR A CERTAIN WAY: appear a certain way (especially as in a dream) inaabaminaagozi *vai;* inaabaminaagwad *vii*
APPEARANCE
CHANGE APPEARANCE: change s.o.'s appearance aanzinaago' *vta;* change s.t.'s appearance aanzinaagotoon *vti2;* change one's own appearance aanzinaago'idizo *vai*
HAVE A CERTAIN APPEARANCE: izhinaagozi *vai;* izhinaagwad *vii*
APPEASE
APPEASE: appease s.o. gaagiizom *vta*
APPLE
APPLE: mishiimin, -ag *na*
APPLE JUICE
APPLE JUICE: mishiiminaaboo *ni*
APPLE TREE
APPLE TREE: mishiiminaatig, -oog *na*
APPLIQUE
APPLIQUE: appliqué piece agogwaajigan, -an *ni*
APPOINT
APPOINT: appoint s.o. onagim *vta*
APPROACH
APPROACH: approach s.o. naazikaw *vta;* approach s.t. naazikan *vti;* approach people naazikaage *vai*
APPROXIMATELY
APPROXIMATELY: ingoji *pc, also* ningoji*
APRIL
APRIL: iskigamizige-giizis *na*
APRON
KITCHEN APRON: inapizowin, -an *ni*
MAN'S APRON: man's apron (traditional dress) aanziyaan, -an *ni*
ARENA
ARENA: zhooshkwaada'ewigamig, -oon *ni*
ARGUE
ARGUE: argue with s.o. giikaam *vta;* they argue with each other giikaandiwag /giikaandi-/ *vai*
ARM
ARM: my arm ninik, -an /-nik-/ *nid*
ACHE IN ARM: have an ache in one's arm dewinike *vai*
BREAK ARM: break one's arm bookonike *vai*
BROKEN ARM: have a broken arm bookonike *vai*
FALL AND BREAK ARM: fall and break one's arm bookonikeshin *vai*
FALL AND TWIST ARM: fall and twist one's arm biimiskonikeshin *vai*
HAVE SCAR ON ARM: have scar on one's arm ojiishinike *vai*
LIFT ARM: lift one's arm ombinikeni *vai*
MOVE ARM A CERTAIN WAY: move one's arm a certain way izhinikeni *vai*

NUMB ARM: have a numb arm niboowinike *vai*
SORE ARM: have a sore arm gaagiijinike *vai*
SPRAIN ARM: sprain one's arm zeginikeshin *vai*
STIFF ARM: have a stiff arm jiibadaakonike *vai;* jiibajinike *vai*
STRONG ARM: have a strong arm zoonginike *vai*
ARM GARTER
ARM GARTER: jiiskinikebizon, -an *ni*
WEAR ARM GARTERS: jiiskinikebizo *vai*
ARMPIT
ARMPIT: my armpit nining, -wiin /-ningwy-/ *nid*
AROUND
ALL AROUND: all around it giiwitaa-ayi'ii *pc, also* giiwitaayi'ii
AROUND THE FIRE: giiwitaashkode *pc*
GO AROUND: giiwitaashkaa *vai*
LAY DOWN AROUND: lay s.o. down around giiwitaashim *vta;* lay s.t. down around giiwitaasidoon *vti2*
RUN AROUND: run around s.t. giiwitaabatwaadan *vti;* run around something giiwitaabatoo *vai*
WALK AROUND: walk around s.o. giiwitaashkaw *vta;* walk around s.t. giiwitaashkan *vti;* walk around something giiwitaawose *vai, also* giiwitaa'ose
WALK AROUND THE EDGE: giiwitaayaazhagaame *vai*
ARREST
ARREST: arrest s.o. dakon *vta;* arrest people dakoniwe *vai*
ARRIVE
ARRIVE: dagoshin *vai;* dagoshinoomagad *vii;* bagami-ayaa *vai;* bagami-ayaa, bagami-ayaamagad *vii;* arrive with s.o. dagoshim *vta;* arriving bagami- *pv4*
ARRIVE BY BOAT: bagamishkaa *vai*
ARRIVE CARRYING: arrive carrying s.o. bagamiwizh /bagamiwiN-/ *vta;* arrive carrying s.t. bagamiwidoon *vti2*
ARRIVE CRAWLING: bagamoode *vai*
ARRIVE DRIVING: bagamibide, bagamibidemagad *vii;* bagamibizo *vai;* bagamidaabii'iwe *vai*
ARRIVE FLEEING: arrive fleeing from people bagamiba'iwe *vai*
ARRIVE FLYING: bagamibide, bagamibidemagad *vii;* bagamibizo *vai;* bagamise *vai;* bagamise, bagamisemagad *vii*
ARRIVE LAUGHING: bagamaapi *vai*
ARRIVE MAD: bagamigidaazo *vai*
ARRIVE ON HORSEBACK: bagamoomigo *vai*
ARRIVE ON THE RUN: bagamibatoo *vai;* they arrive on the run together bagamiba'idiwag /bagamiba'idi-/ *vai*
ARRIVE PADDLING: bagamishkaa *vai*
ARRIVE SPEEDING: bagamibide, bagamibidemagad *vii;* bagamibizo *vai*

ARRIVE SWIMMING: **bagamaadagaa** *vai*
ARRIVE WALKING: **bagamose** *vai*
ARRIVE WITH NEWS: **bagamaajimo** *vai*
ARROGANT
   ARROGANT: be arrogant **maminaadizi** *vai*
   ARROGANT ATTITUDE: have an arrogant
   attitude **maminaadendam** *vai2*
ARROW
   ARROW: **bikwak, -oon** *ni*
   SHOOT WITH AN ARROW: shoot s.o. with
   an arrow or other missile **bimo /bimw-/**
   vta; shoot s.t. with an arrow or other
   missile **bimodan** *vti;* shoot things with an
   arrow or other missile **bimojige** *vai*
ARTHRITIS
   ARTHRITIS: have arthritis **okanaapine** *vai*
ARTIST
   ARTIST: **mazinibii'igewinini, -wag** *na*
AS FOR
   AS FOR: **gaye** *pc, also* **ge**
AS IF
   AS IF: **indigo** *pc, also* **nindigo***
ASH
   BLACK ASH: black ash (tree) **aagimaak,**
   -wag *na*
   WHITE ASH: white ash (tree)
   baapaagimaak, -wag *na*
ASHAMED
   ASHAMED: be ashamed **agadendam** *vai2;*
   agadendaagozi *vai;* be ashamed before
   s.o. **agajiitaw** *vta;* be ashamed of s.o.
   agadenim *vta;* be ashamed of s.t.
   agadendan *vti*
   MAKE ASHAMED: make s.o. ashamed **agaji'**
   vta
ASHES
   ASHES: **bingwi** *ni;* **ishkode-bingwi** *ni*
   HOT ASHES: be hot ashes **akakanzhekaa,**
   akakanzhekaamagad *vii*
ASHORE
   BLOWN ASHORE: be blown ashore
   agwaayaashi *vai;* **agwaayaasin** *vii*
   COME ASHORE: **agwaataa** *vai;* come ashore
   in a boat **agwaa'o** *vai, also* **agwaa'am;**
   come ashore in canoe **mizhagaa** *vai*
   DRAG ASHORE: drag s.o. ashore
   agwaadaabaazh /agwaadaabaaN-/ *vta;*
   drag s.t. ashore **agwaadaabaadan** *vti;* drag
   something ashore **agwaadaabii** *vai*
   GO ASHORE: **agwaataa** *vai*
   PULL ASHORE: pull s.o. ashore **agwaabizh**
   /agwaabiN-/ *vta;* pull s.t. ashore
   agwaabidoon *vti2*
   RUN ASHORE: **agwaabatoo** *vai*
   SAIL ASHORE: **agwaayaashi** *vai*
   SWIM ASHORE: **agwaayaadagaa** *vai*
   TAKE ASHORE BY BOAT: take s.t. ashore
   by boat **agwaa'oodoon** *vti2*
   TAKEN ASHORE: be taken ashore
   agwaasijigaade, agwaasijigaademagad
   vii; **agwaasijigaazo** *vai*

ASK
   ASK: ask for s.t. **nandodan** *vti;* ask s.o. for
   (s.t.) **nandodamaw** *vta;* ask people for
   (s.t.) **nandodamaage** *vai*
   ASK ALONG: ask s.o. along **wiizhaam** *vta*
   ASK QUESTIONS: **gagwedwe** *vai;* ask s.o.
   questions **gagwejim** *vta;* they ask each
   other questions **gagwejindiwag**
   /gagwejindi-/ *vai*
   GO AND ASK: go and ask for s.o.
   nandwewem *vta;* go and ask for s.t.
   nandwewendan *vti;* go and ask s.o. (for
   s.t.) **nandwewendamaw** *vta*
ASLEEP
   FALL ASLEEP: **gawingwashi** *vai*
ASPHALT
   ASPHALT: **makade-bigiw** *na*
ASPHALT ROAD
   ASPHALT ROAD: **bigii-miikana, -n** *ni*
ASPIRIN
   ASPIRIN: **dewikwe-mashkikiins, -an** *ni*
ASSEMBLE
   ASSEMBLE: assemble s.o. **onin** *vta;* assemble
   s.t. **oninan** *vti;* assemble things **oninige** *vai*
ASSINIBOIN
   ASSINIBOIN: **asinii-bwaan, -ag** *na*
ASSOCIATE
   ASSOCIATE: associate with s.o. **wiisookaw**
   vta
ASTONISH
   ASTONISH: **maamakaadizi** *vai*
ASTONISHED
   ASTONISHED: be astonished
   maamakaadendam *vai2;* be astonished at
   s.o. **maamakaadenim** *vta;* be astonished
   at s.t. **maamakaadendan** *vti*
ASTONISHING
   ASTONISHING: **maamakaaj** *pc;* astonishing!
   maamakaadakamig *pc*
   CONSIDERED ASTONISHING: be consid-
   ered astonishing **maamakaadendaagwad**
   vii
ASTRIDE
   SIT ASTRIDE: **desabi** *vai*
AT HAND
   AT HAND: **wenipazh** *pc*
AT RANDOM
   AT RANDOM: **bagwana** *pc*
ATTACK
   ATTACK: attack s.o. **mawinazh /mawinaN-/**
   vta; attack s.o. from hiding **mookiitaw** *vta*
ATTEMPT
   ATTEMPT: **goji-** *pv4*
ATTENDANT
   CEREMONIAL ATTENDANT:
   oshkaabewis, -ag *na*
ATTENTION
   ATTENTION: attention! **ambe** *pc*
ATTRACT
   ATTRACT: attract s.o. **zhoobi'** *vta*

AUGUST

AUGUST: manoominike-giizis *na;* miini-
giizis *na, also* miinike-giizis

AUNT

AUNT: my cross aunt (father's sister) inzigos,
-ag */*-zigos-/ *nad;* my parallel aunt
(mother's sister) ninoshenh, -yag
/-nosheny-/ *nad*

AUTHORITY

AUTHORITY: ogimaawiwin, -an *ni*

AUTOMOBILE MECHANIC

AUTOMOBILE MECHANIC:
nanaa'idaabaanewinini, -wag *na;*
nanaa'idaabaanikewinini, -wag *na*

AUTUMN

AUTUMN: be autumn dagwaagin
*/*dagwaagi-/ *vii*
LAST AUTUMN: dagwaagong *pc*

AVOID

AVOID TALKING: avoid talking to s.o.
boonim *vta*

AWAKE

AWAKE: be awake goshkozi *vai*
COME AWAKE: amajise *vai*
SHAKE AWAKE: shake s.o. awake
amajwebin *vta*

AWAY

BLOWN AWAY: be blown away animaashi
vai; animaasin *vii*
CARRY AWAY: carry s.o. away animiwizh
*/*animiwiN-/ *vta;* carry s.t. away
animiwidoon *vti2*
CARRY AWAY ON BACK: carry s.o. away
on one's back animoom *vta;* carry s.t.
away on one's back animoondan *vti*
CLOUDS GO AWAY: animaanakwad *vii*
CRAWL AWAY: animoode *vai*
DANCE AWAY: animishimo *vai*
DRAG AWAY: animidaabii *vai*
DRIFT AWAY: animaabogo *vai;*
animaaboode, animaaboodemagad *vii*
DRIFT AWAY ON THE WAVES: animaa'an
vii; animaa'ogo *vai*
DRIVE AWAY: animibide, animibidemagad
vii; animibizo *vai;* animidaabii'iwe *vai;*
drive away with horses animiba'igo *vai;*
drive away with s.o. (e.g., a car)
animibizoni' *vta;* drive away with s.t.
animibizonitoon *vti2*
DRIVE AWAY MAKING NOISE:
animwewebide, animwewebidemagad
vii; animwewebizo *vai*
DRIVE AWAY WITH A LIGHT:
animaazakonenjigebizo *vai*
FLOAT AWAY: animaabogo *vai;*
animaaboode, animaaboodemagad *vii*
FLOW AWAY: animijiwan *vii*
FLY AWAY: animibide, animibidemagad *vii;*
animibizo *vai;* animise *vai;* animise,
animisemagad *vii*
FLY AWAY MAKING NOISE:
animwewebide, animwewebidemagad
vii; animwewebizo *vai*

FOLLOW A TRAIL AWAY: anima'adoo *vai;*
follow s.o.'s trail away anima'azh
*/*anima'aN-/ *vta;* follow s.t. away as a trail
anima'adoon *vti2*
GO AWAY: go away! awas *pc*
GO AWAY IN A CANOE: animishkaa *vai*
GO AWAY LAUGHING: animaapi *vai*
GO AWAY MAD: animigidaazo *vai*
GO AWAY ON THE ICE: animaadagaako
vai
GO AWAY SINGING: anima'amaazo *vai*
GO AWAY SPEAKING: animwewidam *vai2*
GO AWAY WITH A LIGHT:
animaazakonenjige *vai*
GOING AWAY: ani- *pv2, also* ni-
LEAVE TRACKS GOING AWAY:
animikawe *vai*
PADDLE AWAY: animishkaa *vai*
RAIN GOES AWAY: animibiisaa,
animibiisaamagad *vii*
RIDE AWAY ON HORSEBACK:
animoomigo *vai*
RUN AWAY: animibatoo *vai;* run away (in
the other direction) with s.o.
animibatwaazh */*animibatwaaN-/ *vta;* run
away (in the other direction) with s.t.
animibatwaadan *vti;* they run away (in the
other direction) together animiba'idiwag
*/*animiba'idi-/ *vai*
RUN AWAY MAKING NOISE:
animwewebatoo *vai*
RUN AWAY SCARED: animinizhimo *vai*
SAIL AWAY: animaashi *vai;* animaasin *vii*
SKATE AWAY: animaada'e *vai*
SPEED AWAY: animibide, animibidemagad
vii; animibizo *vai*
SPEED AWAY MAKING NOISE:
animwewebide, animwewebidemagad
vii; animwewebizo *vai*
SWIM AWAY: animaadagaa *vai*
TAKE AWAY: take s.o. away animiwizh
*/*animiwiN-/ *vta;* take s.t. away
animiwidoon *vti2*
TAKE AWAY BY BOAT: take s.o. away by
boat anima'oozh */*anima'ooN-/ *vta;* take
s.t. away by boat anima'oodoon *vti2*
WADE AWAY: animaadagaazii *vai*
WALK AWAY: animose *vai*
WALK AWAY MAKING NOISE:
animwewetoo *vai*

AWFUL

AWFUL: gagwaanisagakamig *pc*

AWL

AWL: migoos, -an *ni*

AX

AX: waagaakwad, -oon *ni*

AX HANDLE

AX HANDLE: waagaakwadwaatig, -oon *ni*

B

BABY
BABY: **abinoojiiyens**, **-ag** *na*, also **abinoojiins**;
biibii, **-yag** *na*
BABY IN A CRADLE BOARD:
dakobinaawaswaan, **-ag** *na*
CARRY A BABY ALONG ON BACK: carry a
baby along on one's back **bimoomaawaso**
vai
CARRY A BABY TO A CERTAIN PLACE
ON BACK: carry a baby to a certain place
on one's back **inoomaawaso** *vai*
HAVE A BABY IN A CRADLE BOARD:
dakobinaawaso *vai*
BABY-SIT
BABY-SIT: **bamoozhe** *vai*
BACK
BACK: my back **nipikwan**, **-an** /**-pikwan-**/ *nid*
FALL AND BREAK BACK: fall and break
one's back **bookwaawiganeshin** *vai*
MIDDLE OF THE BACK: in the middle of
the back **naawaawigan** *pc*
SCRATCH BACK: scratch s.o.'s back
jiichiigawiganebizh /**jiichiigawiganebiN-**/
vta
SMALL OF BACK: the small of my back
inzhiigan /**-zhiigan-**/ *nid*
SORE BACK: have a sore back
gaagiidaawigan *vai*
WARM BACK: warm one's back
abaawiganezo *vai*
BACK
BACK: back (in time) **ishkweyaang** *pc*; back
to previous place or condition **neyaab** *pc*
BACK UP: **azhetaa** *vai*
GO BACK: **azhe-** *pv4*; **azhegiiwe** *vai*
HAND BACK: hand s.o. back **azhen** *vta*;
hand s.t. back **azhenan** *vti*
IN THE BACK: **ishkweyaang** *pc*
PULL BACK: pull s.o. back **azhebizh**
/**azhebiN-**/ *vta*; pull s.t. back **azhebidoon**
vti2
TAKE BACK: take s.o. back **azhen** *vta*; take
s.t. back **azhenan** *vti*; take (s.t.) back to
s.o. **azhenamaw** *vta*
TURN AND LOOK BACK: **aabanaabi** *vai*;
turn and look back at s.o. **aabanaabam**
vta; turn and look back at s.t.
aabanaabandan *vti*
BACK UP
BACK UP A VEHICLE: **azhebizo** *vai*
BACKACHE
BACKACHE: have a backache **dewaawigan**
vai; **dewipikwan** *vai*
BACKPACK
BACKPACK: **bimiwanaan**, **-an** *ni*
BACKWARDS
FALL OVER BACKWARDS: **aazhigijishin**
vai; **aazhigijisin** *vii*

GO BACKWARDS: **azheshkaa** *vai*; **azhetaa**
vai
LAY OVER BACKWARDS: lay s.o. over
backwards **aazhigijishim** *vta*; lay s.t. over
backwards **aazhigijisidoon** *vti2*
PADDLE BACKWARDS: **azhe'o** *vai*
SIT FACING BACKWARDS: **animikwabi**
vai
THROW OVER BACKWARDS: throw s.o.
over backwards **aazhigidwebin** *vta*; throw
s.t. over backwards **aazhigidwebinan** *vti*
TURN OVER BACKWARDS: **aazhigijise**
vai; **aazhigijise**, **aazhigijisemagad** *vii*
TURN TO FACE BACKWARDS: turn s.o. to
face backwards **animikon** *vta*; turn s.t. to
face backwards **animikonan** *vti*
TURNED TO FACE BACKWARDS: be
turned to face backwards **animikonigaade**,
animikonigaademagad *vii*;
animikonigaazo *vai*
BACON
BACON: **giikanaamozigan** *na*
BAD
BAD: **maji-** *pv4*; **maazhi-** *pv4*
BAD BREATH: have bad breath
maazhimaagwanaamo *vai*
BAD DAY: be a bad day **maazhi-giizhigad** *vii*
BAD DREAM: have a bad dream
giiwanaadingwaam *vai*
BAD LUCK: have bad luck **maazhise** *vai*
BAD ROAD: be bad (as a road or trail)
maanadamon /**maanadamo-**/ *vii*
BAD TRAIL: be bad (as a road or trail)
maanadamon /**maanadamo-**/ *vii*
BAD VOICE: have a bad voice **maanowe** *vai*
BAD WEATHER: be bad weather **niiskaadad**
vii
CONSIDERED BAD: be considered bad
maanendaagwad *vii*
FEEL BAD: **maanamanji'o** *vai*; **maanendam**
vai2, also **maazhendam**; feel bad about s.t.
maanendan *vti*
HAVE A BAD FALL: **aapijishin** *vai*
LEAD A BAD LIFE: **maazhi-bimaadizi** *vai*
SMELL BAD: **maazhimaagozi** *vai*;
maazhimaagwad *vii*
SMELL BAD BURNING OR COOKING:
maazhimaaso *vai*; **maazhimaate** *vii*
SOUND BAD: hear s.o. sounding bad
maanitaw *vta*; hear s.t. sounding bad
maanitan *vti*
TASTE BAD: **maazhipogozi** *vai*;
maazhipogwad *vii*; taste bad (as a liquid)
maanaagamin /**maanaagami-**/ *vii*
BAD OFF
BAD OFF: be bad off **maazhi-ayaa** *vai*
CONSIDER BAD OFF: consider s.o. bad off
maanenim *vta*
CONSIDERED BAD OFF: be considered bad
off **maanendaagozi** *vai*
BADGER
BADGER: **misakakojiish**, **-ag** *na*
BADLY
BADLY: **debinaak** *pc*

BEHAVE BADLY: **maazhi-bimaadizi** *vai;* **maazhi-izhiwebizi** *vai*
BAG
BAG: **mashkimod, -an** *ni*
BAG WITH CLOSEABLE TOP: **gashkibidaagan, -ag** *na*
CEDAR BARK BAG: **giishkashkimod, -an** *ni*
CERTAIN NUMBER OF BAGS: **dasooshkin** *pc*
CLOTH BAG: **bagiwayaaneshkimod, -an** *ni*
HALF A BAG: **aabitooshkin** *pc*
MEDICINE BAG: Mide medicine bag **midewayaan, -ag** *na*
PAPER BAG: **mazina'igani-mashkimodens, -an** *ni*
RICE BAG: **manoomini-mashkimod, -an** *ni;* **manoominiwazh, -an** *ni*
BAIL
BAIL: **iska'ibii** *vai*
BAIL OUT: bail s.o. out **diba' /diba'w-/** *vta*
BAIT
BAIT: **miijimikanjigan, -an** *ni;* bait things **miijimikanjige** *vai*
BAKE
BAKE: bake s.o. **giboz /gibozw-/** *vta;* bake s.t. **gibozan** *vti;* bake things **gibozige** *vai*
BAKER
BAKER: **bakwezhiganikewinini, -wag** *na;* baker (female) **bakwezhiganikewikwe, -g** *na*
BAKERY
BAKERY: **bakwezhiganikewigamig, -oon** *ni*
BAKING POWDER
BAKING POWDER: **ombisijigaans, -an** *ni*
BAKING SODA
BAKING SODA: **ombizigan** *ni*
BALD
BALD: be bald **waabizhagindibe** *vai*
BALD EAGLE
BALD EAGLE: **migizi, -wag** *na*
BALL
BALL: **bikwaakwad, -oon** *ni*
BALL OF TWINE OR YARN: **bikoojaan, -an** *ni*
POOL BALL: **nemaab, -iin** *ni*
BALM OF GILEAD
BALM OF GILEAD TREE: **maanazaadi, -wag** *na*
BALSAM FIR
BALSAM FIR: **zhingob, -iig** *na*
BALSAM POPLAR
BALSAM POPLAR: **maanazaadi, -wag** *na*
BANANA
BANANA: **wewaagijiizid** *ni-pt*
BANDAGE
BANDAGE: **ziinzoopizon, -an** *ni*
BANDOLIER BAG
BANDOLIER BAG: **gashkibidaagan, -ag** *na,* also **aazhoningwa'igan**
BANK
BANK: **zhooniyaawigamig, -oon** *ni*

BANK
STEEP BANK: be a steep bank **giishkadinaa, giishkadinaamagad** *vii*
BAPTIZE
BAPTIZE: baptize s.o. **ziiga'andaw** *vta*
BAR
BAR: **minikwewigamig, -oon** *ni;* **ziiginigewigamig, -oon** *ni*
BAR
BAR: bar s.t. (as something stick- or wood-like) **gashkaakonan** *vti*
BARBER
BARBER: **baapaagokozhiwewinini, -wag** *na;* **giishkikozhiwewinini, -wag** *na*
BARBER SHOP
BARBER SHOP: **baapaagokozhiwewigamig, -oon** *ni*
BARE
ON A BARE SURFACE: **michayi'ii** *pc*
BARE GROUND
ON BARE GROUND: **mitakamig** *pc*
SIT ON THE BARE GROUND: **mitabi** *vai*
BARE-HEADED
BARE-HEADED: be bare-headed **mitaakondibe** *vai*
BAREFOOT
BAREFOOT: be barefoot **zhaashaaginizide** *vai*
BARELY
BARELY: **agaawaa** *pc;* **michi-** *pv4*
BARK
BARK: **migi** *vai;* bark at s.o. **migizh /migiN-/** *vta;* bark at s.t. **migidan** *vti*
BARK
BARK: bark (of a tree) **wanagek, -wag** *na*
INNER BARK OF BASSWOOD: **wiigob, -iin** *ni*
BARK LODGE
BARK LODGE: **wanagekogamig, -oon** *ni*
BARK TORCH
BARK TORCH: **biimashkwemaginigan, -an** *ni*
BARMAID
BARMAID: **ziiginigewikwe, -g** *na*
BARN
BARN: **awakaanigamig, -oon** *ni*
BARREL
BARREL: **makakosag, -oon** *ni*
BARTENDER
BARTENDER: **ziiginigewinini, -wag** *na*
BASEBALL
PLAY BASEBALL: **bakitejii'ige** *vai*
BASEBALL BAT
BASEBALL BAT: **bakitejii'iganaak, -oon** *ni*
BASEBALL PLAYER
BASEBALL PLAYER: **bakitejii'igewinini, -wag** *na*
BASEMENT
IN THE BASEMENT: **anaamisag** *pc*
BASHFUL
BASHFUL: be bashful **agaji** *vai*

BASK
BASK: bask in the sun **abaasandeke** *vai*
BASKET
BASKET OF SPRUCE ROOT: **wadabii-makak, -oon** *ni*
BIRCH BARK BASKET: **makak, -oon** *ni;* **wiigwasi-makak, -oon** *ni;* birch bark basket for maple sugar **ziinzibaakwado-makak, -oon** *ni*
WILLOW BASKET: **oziisigobimizhii-makak, -oon** *ni*
BASS
LARGEMOUTH BASS: **ashigan, -ag** *na*
BASSWOOD
BASSWOOD: basswood tree **wiigob, -iig** *na;* **wiigobaatig, -oog** *na;* **wiigobimizh, -iig** *na*
INNER BARK OF BASSWOOD: **wiigob, -iin** *ni*
BASSWOOD BARK FIBER
BASSWOOD BARK FIBER: processed basswood bark fiber **asigobaan** *ni*
BAT
BASEBALL BAT: **bakitejii'iganaak, -oon** *ni*
BAT
BAT: **bapakwaanaajiinh, -yag** *na, also* **apakwaanaajiinh**
BATH
TAKE A BATH: **giziibiigazhe** *vai*
BATHE
BATHE: **bagizo** *vai*
BATHROOM
BATHROOM: **miiziiwigamig, -oon** *ni*
BATHTUB
BATHTUB: **bagizowin, -an** *ni*
BATTERY
BATTERY: **ishkode-makakoons, -an** *ni*
BATTLE
BATTLE: **miigaadiwin, -an** *ni*
BAY
BAY: be a bay **wiikwegamaa, wiikwegamaamagad** *vii*
BE
BE: be (in a certain place) **ayaa** *vai;* **ayaa, ayaamagad** *vii;* be a certain thing **aawan** *vii;* be a certain thing or being **aaw** *vai*
BE A CERTAIN WAY: **izhi-ayaa** *vai;* be a certain way (as a liquid) **inaagamin /inaagami-/** *vii;* be a certain way (as something mineral) **inaabikad** *vii;* **inaabikizi** *vai;* be a certain way (as something sheet-like) **izhiigad** *vii;* **izhiigizi** *vai;* be a certain way (as something stick- or wood-like) **inaakozi** *vai;* **inaakwad** *vii;* be a certain way (as something string-like) **inaabiigad** *vii;* **inaabiigizi** *vai*
BE IN: **biinde, biindemagad** *vii;* **biinzo** *vai*
BE IN A CERTAIN PLACE: **abi** *vai;* **ate, atemagad** *vii;* **dagon /dago-/** *vii;* be (in a certain place) **ayaa** *vai;* **ayaa, ayaamagad** *vii*
BE IN A CERTAIN STATE: *with a pv4* be in a certain state **ayaa, ayaamagad** *vii;* **ayaa** *vai*

BE IN THE SKY: be in the sky (e.g., a star, the sun, or the moon) **agoojin** *vai*
BE WITH: be with s.o. **wiij'ayaaw** *vta, also* **wiiji-ayaaw**
COME TO BE: **bagami-ayaa, bagami-ayaamagad** *vii*
SEEM TO BE A CERTAIN WAY: **inendaagwad** *vii*
THINK TO BE IN A CERTAIN PLACE: think s.o. to be in a certain place **danenim** *vta;* think s.t. to be in a certain place **danendan** *vti*
BEACH
LONG STRETCH OF SAND BEACH: be a long stretch of sand beach **ginoodaawangaa, ginoodaawangaamagad** *vii*
SANDY BEACH: be a sandy beach **mitaawangaa, mitaawangaamagad** *vii*
BEAD
BEAD: **manidoominens, -ag** *na;* **mazinigwaaso** *vai;* bead on s.o. **mazinigwaazh /mazinigwaaN-/** *vta;* bead s.t. **mazinigwaadan** *vti*
BEAD CORRECTLY: bead s.t. correctly (on a loom) **gwayakwaabidoo'an** *vti;* bead things correctly (on a loom) **gwayakwaabidoo'ige** *vai*
BEAD ON A LOOM: bead s.t. on a loom **mazinaabidoo'an** *vti;* bead things on a loom **mazinaabidoo'ige** *vai*
MAKE A MISTAKE BEADING: make a mistake beading s.t. on a loom **wanaabidoo'an** *vti;* make a mistake beading things on a loom **wanaabidoo'ige** *vai*
BEAD LOOM
BEAD LOOM: **mazinaabidoo'iganaatig, -oon** *ni*
BEAD WORK
BEAD WORK: item of bead work **manidoominensikaan, -ag** *na*
BEADING NEEDLE
BEADING NEEDLE: **naabidoo'igan, -an** *ni*
BEAK
BEAK: my beak **nikoonzh /-koonzh-/** *nid*
BEAN
BEAN: **mashkodesimin, -ag** *na, also* **mashkodiisimin**
BEAN SOUP
BEAN SOUP: **mashkodesiminaaboo** *ni*
BEAR
BEAR: bear s.o. (e.g., a child) **niigi'** *vta*
BEAR ON BODY: bear s.o. on one's body **gigishkaw** *vta;* bear s.t. on one's body **gigishkan** *vti*
BEAR
BEAR: **makwa, -g** *na*
BEAR CUB: **makoons, -ag** *na*
BEAR PAW SNOWSHOE
BEAR PAW SNOWSHOE: **makwasaagim, -ag** *na*

BEARD
BEARD: have a beard **miishidaamikan** *vai*
BEAT
BEAT: beat s.o. **niiwezh /niiweN-/** *vta*
BEAT IN A CONTEST: beat s.o. in a contest **bakinaw** *vta;* beat people in a contest **bakinaage** *vai*
BEAT IN A GAME: beat s.o. in a game **gabenaw** *vta*
BEAT TO DEATH: beat s.o. to death **niiwana' /niiwana'w-/** *vta*
BEAUTIFUL
BEAUTIFUL: be beautiful **miikawaadad** *vii;* **miikawaadizi** *vai*
BEAVER
BEAVER: **amik, -wag** *na*
HUNT BEAVER: **noodamikwe** *vai*
BEAVER HIDE
BEAVER HIDE: **amikwayaan, -ag** *na*
BEAVER LODGE
BEAVER LODGE: **amikwiish, -an** *ni*
BECAUSE
BECAUSE: **onji-** *pv3*
BED
BED: **nibaagan, -an** *ni;* bed (in wigwam) **desa'on, -an** *ni;* bed (made on the floor or ground) **apishimon, -an** *ni*
GO TO BED: **gawishimo** *vai*
MAKE A BED: **ozisijige** *vai, also* **ozhisijige;** make a bed (as in camp) **apishimonike** *vai*
PUT TO BED: put s.o. to bed **nibe'** *vta*
WET THE BED: **zhigingwaam** *vai*
BED FRAME
BED FRAME: **nibaaganaatig, -oon** *ni*
BEDROOM
BEDROOM: **nibewigamig, -oon** *ni*
BEE
BEE: **aamoo, -g** *na*
BEEHIVE
BEEHIVE: **aamoo-wadiswan, -an** *ni*
BEEF
BEEF: **bizhiki-wiiyaas** *ni, also* **bizhikiwi- wiiyaas**
BEER
BEER: **biitewaaboo** *ni;* **zhingobaaboo** *ni*
BEET
BEET: **misko-jiis, -an** *ni*
SUGAR BEET: **wiishkobi-jiis, -an** *ni*
BEFORE
BEFORE: **jibwaa-** *pv1, also* **ji-bwaa-**
AS BEFORE: **neyaab** *pc*
BEFORE THE USUAL TIME: **noonde-** *pv4*
BEFOREHAND
BEFOREHAND: **giizhaa** *pc*
BEG
BEG: beg s.o. for (s.t.) **nandodamaw** *vta;* beg people for (s.t.) **nandodamaage** *vai*
BEGGAR
BEGGAR: **nendodamaageshkid** *na-pt*
BEGIN
BEGIN: **maajii-** *pv4;* **maajise** *vai;* **maajise, maajisemagad** *vii*

BEGINNING
IN THE BEGINNING: **wayeshkad** *pc*
BEHAVE
BEHAVE A CERTAIN WAY: **izhiwebizi** *vai*
BEHAVE ANGRILY: **nishkaajitaa** *vai*
BEHAVE BADLY: **maazhi-bimaadizi** *vai;* **maazhi-izhiwebizi** *vai*
BEHAVE WELL: **mino-izhiwebizi** *vai*
BEHIND
BEHIND: **ishkweyaang** *pc*
BEHOLD
BEHOLD: behold! **inashke** *pc, also* **nashke;** **wegwaagi** *pc*
BEING
BEING: a being **aya'aa, -g** *pr*
BELIEVABLE
BELIEVABLE: be believable **debwetaagozi** *vai;* **debwetaagwad** *vii*
BELIEVE
BELIEVE: **debwetam** *vai2;* **debweyendam** *vai2;* believe s.o. **debwetaw** *vta;* believe s.t. **debwetan** *vti*
BELIEVE IN: believe in s.o. **debweyenim** *vta;* believe in s.t. **debweyendan** *vti*
NOT BELIEVE: not believe s.t. said **aagonwetan** *vti;* not believe what s.o. says **aagonwetaw** *vta*
BELIEVED
BELIEVED: be believed **debwetaagozi** *vai;* **debwetaagwad** *vii*
BELL
BELL: **godotaagan, -an** *ni*
SMALL ROUND BELL: **zhinawa'oojigan, -an** *ni*
BELONG
BELONG: **dibendaagozi** *vai;* **dibendaagwad** *vii*
BELONG TO A GROUP: **aginzo** *vai*
BELONGING
BELONGINGS: **daniwin, -an** *ni*
BELT
BELT: **gijipizon, -an** *ni*
BELT BUCKLE
BELT BUCKLE: **gijipizonaabik, -oon** *ni*
BENCH
BENCH: **desa'on, -an** *ni*
BEND
BEND A CERTAIN WAY: bend s.o. a certain way **inaagin** *vta;* bend s.t. a certain way **inaaginan** *vti*
BEND DOWN: **zhagashkitaa** *vai*
BEND INTO FORM: bend s.o. into form **onaagin** *vta;* bend s.t. into form **onaaginan** *vti*
BEND OVER: bend s.o. over **biskin** *vta;* bend s.t. over **biskinan** *vti*
BEND OVER WITH HANDS: bend s.o. over with hands **biskibizh /biskibiN-/** *vta;* bend s.t. over with hands **biskibidoon** *vti2*
BEND WITH HAND: bend s.o. with hand **waagin** *vta;* bend s.t. with hand **waaginan** *vti*

BEND WITH HANDS: bend s.o. with hands
waagibizh /waagibiN-/ vta; bend s.t. with
hands waagibidoon vti2
BENEFIT
BENEFIT: benefit s.o. debi' vta
BENT
BENT: be bent waagaa, waagaamagad vii;
waagizi vai; be bent (as something min-
eral) waagaabikad vii; waagaabikizi vai;
be bent (as something stick- or wood-like)
waagaakozi vai; waagaakwad vii
BENT A CERTAIN WAY: be bent a certain
way inaaginigaade, inaaginigaademagad
vii; inaaginigaazo vai
BENT OVER: be bent over biskaa,
biskaamagad vii; biskinigaade,
biskinigaademagad vii
BERRY
PICK BERRIES: mawinzo vai
BET
BET: ataage vai; they bet with each other
ataadiwag /ataadi-/ vai
PLACE A BET: achige vai
BETWEEN
IN BETWEEN: in between it nisawayi'ii pc
BEWARE
BEWARE: beware! (a warning based on a
premonition) baapiniziwaagan pc
BEYOND
BEYOND: awasi- pn; beyond it awasayi'ii pc
BEYOND THE FIRE: awasishkode pc
BEYOND THE MOUNTAIN: awasajiw pc
BEYOND THE WOODS: awasaakwaa pc
BIBLE
BIBLE: gagiikwe-mazina'igan, -an ni
BICYCLE
BICYCLE: ditibiwebishkigan, -ag na
BIG
BIG: gichi- pv4, also chi-; be big michaa,
michaamagad vii; mindido vai; they are
big mamaachaawan /mamaachaa-/,
mamaachaamagadoon vii;
mamaandidowag /mamaandido-/ vai; be
big (as something mineral) michaabikad
vii; michaabikizi vai; be big (as something
sheet-like) michiigad vii; michiigizi vai; be
big (as something stick- or wood-like)
michaakozi vai; michaakwad vii
APPEAR BIG: michaabaminaagwad vii
BIG EYE: have a big eye mangishkiinzhigwe
vai
BIG FOOT: have a big foot mangizide vai
BIG HAND: have a big hand mangininjii vai
BIG HEAD: have a big head mangindibe vai
BIG HILL: there is a big hill mangadinaa,
mangadinaamagad vii
MAKE BIG: make s.o. big mangi' vta;
mindido' vta; make s.t. big michaatoon
vti2
SO BIG: be so big inigini vai; inigokwaa,
inigokwaamagad vii; be so big (as something mineral) inigokwaabikad vii;
inigokwaabikizi vai; be so big (as
something sheet-like) inigokwegad vii;

inigokwegizi vai; be so big (as something
stick- or wood-like) inigokwaakozi vai;
inigokwaakwad vii; be so big (as some-
thing string-like) inigokwaabiigad vii;
inigokwaabiigizi vai
BILL
BILL: my bill nikoonzh /-koonzh-/ nid
BIND
BIND: bind s.o. dakobizh /dakobiN-/ vta;
bind s.t. dakobidoon vti2; bind things
dakobijige vai
BINDING
BINDING STICK: mikond, -ag na, also
mikwand
BINOCULARS
BINOCULARS: zhiibaayaabanjigan, -an ni
BIRCH
BIRCH: birch (tree) wiigwaasi-mitig, -oog
na, also wiigwaasaatig; wiigwaas, -ag na
MANY BIRCHES: there are many birches
wiigwaasikaa, wiigwaasikaamagad vii
YELLOW BIRCH: wiinizik, -oog na
BIRCH BARK
BIRCH BARK: wiigwaas, -an ni
GATHER BIRCH BARK: maniwiigwaase
vai
REMOVE BIRCH BARK: remove birch bark
from the tree wiigwaasike vai
BIRCH BARK BASKET
BIRCH BARK BASKET: makak, -oon ni;
wiigwaasi-makak, -oon ni; birch bark
basket for maple sugar ziinzibaakwado-
makak, -oon ni
MAKE A BIRCH BARK BASKET:
makakoke vai
BIRCH BARK BOX
BIRCH BARK BOX: wiigwaasi-makak, -oon
ni
BIRCH BARK CANOE
BIRCH BARK CANOE: wiigwaasi-jiimaan,
-an ni
BIRCH BARK COVERING
BIRCH BARK COVERING:
wiigwaasabakway, -an ni
BIRCH BARK DISH
BIRCH BARK DISH: wiigwaasinaagan, -an
ni
BIRCH BARK LODGE
BIRCH BARK LODGE: wiigwaasigamig,
-oon ni
BIRCH BARK ROOF
BIRCH BARK ROOF: wiigwaasabakwaan,
-ag na
BIRCH BARK ROOFING
ROLL OF BIRCH BARK ROOFING:
wiigwaasabakway, -an ni
BIRD
BIRD: bineshiinh, -yag na; bird (of large
species, e.g., hawk or eagle) binesi, -wag
na
BABY BIRD: banajaanh, -yag na
MALE BIRD: naabese, -g na

BIRD SKIN
BIRD SKIN: **bineshiinhwayaan, -ag** *na*
BIRTH
GIVE BIRTH: **ondaadiziike** *vai*
BIRTHDAY
HAVE A BIRTHDAY: **dibishkaa** *vai*
BISON
BISON: **bizhiki, -wag** *na;* **mashkode-bizhiki, -wag** *na*
BIT
BIT: **zagidoonebijigan, -an** *ni*
BITE
BITE: bite s.o. **dakwam** *vta;* bite s.t. **dakwandan** *vti;* bite things **dakwanjige** *vai;* bite people **dakwange** *vai*
BITE A PIECE OFF: bite a piece off s.o. **bakwem** *vta;* bite a piece off s.t. **bakwendan** *vti*
BITE THROUGH: bite s.o. through (e.g., something string-like) **bakam** *vta;* bite s.t. through (e.g., something string-like) **bakandan** *vti;* bite through s.o. cleanly **giishkam** *vta;* bite through s.t. cleanly **giishkandan** *vti*
TAKE A BITE: take a bite of s.o. **nawadam** *vta;* take a bite of s.t. **nawadandan** *vti;* take a bite of things **nawadanjige** *vai*
BITTER
BITTER: be bitter **wiisagan** *vii, also* **wiisagaa;** **wiisagizi** *vai;* be bitter (as a liquid) **wiisagaagamin** /wiisagaagami-/ *vii*
TASTE BITTER: **wiisagipogozi** *vai;* **wiisagipogwad** *vii*
BITTERN
AMERICAN BITTERN: **mooshka'osi, -wag** *na*
BLACK
BLACK: **makade-** *pv4;* be black **makadewaa, makadewaamagad** *vii;* **makadewizi** *vai;* be black (as a liquid) **makadewaagamin** /makadewaagami-/ *vii;* be black (as something mineral) **makadewaabikad** *vii;* **makadewaabikizi** *vai;* be black (as something sheet-like) **makadewegad** *vii;* **makadewegizi** *vai;* be black (as something stick- or wood-like) **makadewaakozi** *vai;* **makadewaakwad** *vii;* be black (as something string-like) **makadewaabiigad** *vii;* **makadewaabiigizi** *vai*
BLACK HAIR: have black hair **makadewindibe** *vai*
COLORED BLACK: be colored black **makadewaande, makadewaandemagad** *vii;* **makadewaanzo** *vai*
HAVE A BLACK EYE: **ozhaawashkwaabi** *vai*
WEAR BLACK: **makadewi'o** *vai*
BLACK ASH
BLACK ASH: black ash (tree) **aagimaak, -wag** *na*
BLACK CHERRY
BLACK CHERRY: **ookwemin, -an** *ni*

BLACK CHERRY BUSH
BLACK CHERRY BUSH: **ookweminagaawanzh, -iig** *na*
BLACK DUCK
BLACK DUCK: **makadeshib, -ag** *na*
BLACK
BLACK PERSON: **makade-wiiyaas, -ag** *na*
BLACK WOMAN: **makade-wiiyaasikwe, -g** *na*
BLACKBERRY
BLACKBERRY: **odatagaagomin, -ag** *na*
BLACKBERRY BUSH
BLACKBERRY BUSH: **odatagaagominagaawanzh, -iig** *na*
BLACKBIRD
BLACKBIRD: **asiginaak, -wag** *na*
BLACKSMITH
BLACKSMITH: **awashtoyaa, -g** *na, also* **awishtoyaa**
BLAME
BLAME: blame s.o. (in speech) **anaamim** *vta;* blame people **anaaminge** *vai;* they blame each other **anaamindiwag** /anaamindi-/ *vai;* blame oneself **anaamindizo** *vai*
BLANKET
BLANKET: **waabooyaan, -an** *ni, also* **waabowayaan; agwazhe'on, -an** *ni;* my blanket **nikonaas, -an** /-konaas-/ *nid*
COVER WITH BLANKETS: cover s.o. with blankets **agwazhe'** *vta*
COVERED WITH BLANKETS: be covered with blankets **agwazhe** *vai*
BLAST
BLAST: blast s.o. **baasaabikiz** /baasaabikizw-/ *vta;* blast s.t. **baasaabikizan** *vti;* blast things **baasaabikizige** *vai*
BLAZE
BLAZE UP: **miskwakone, miskwakonemagad** *vii*
BLEACHED
BLEACHED: be bleached **waabide, waabidemagad** *vii;* **waabizo** *vai*
BLEED
BLEED: **miskwiiwi** *vai*
BLESS
BLESS: bless s.o. **zhawenim** *vta*
BLESSED
BLESSED: be blessed **zhawendaagozi** *vai*
BLIND
HUNTING BLIND: **akandoowin, -an** *ni*
USE A BLIND: **akandoo** *vai*
BLIND
BLIND: be blind **gagiibiingwe** *vai*
BLINDFOLD
BLINDFOLD: **basangwaabapijigan, -an** *ni;* blindfold s.o. **basangwaabapizh** /basangwaabapiN-/ *vta*
BLINDFOLDED
BLINDFOLDED: be blindfolded **basangwaabapizo** *vai*

BLISTER
BLISTER: have a blister **abashkwebiigizi** *vai*
BLISTER ON FOOT: get a blister on one's
foot **abashkwebiigizideshin** *vai*
BLISTER ON HAND: get a blister on one's
hand **abashkwebiigininjiishin** *vai*
BLIZZARD
BLIZZARD: be a blizzard **biiwan** *vii*
BLOATED
BLOATED: be bloated **baasinigo** *vai*
BLOCK
BLOCK WITH FOOT OR BODY: block s.o.
with foot or body **gibishkaw** *vta;* block s.t.
with foot or body **gibishkan** *vti*
BLOND
BLOND: be blond **ozaawindibe** *vai*
BLOOD
BLOOD: **miskwi** *ni*
BLOOD CLOT
BLOOD CLOT: **wado, -wag** *na*
BLOODSUCKER
BLOODSUCKER: **ozagaskwaajime, -g** *na,*
also **zagaskwaajime**
BLOODY
BLOODY: be bloody **miskwiiwi** *vai*
BLOODY NOSE: bloody s.o.'s nose
gibitaneganaam *vta;* have a bloody nose
miskwiiwijaane *vai*
BLOODY NOSE FALLING: bloody one's
nose falling **gibitaneshin** *vai*
BLOOM
BLOOM: **baashkaabigwanii,**
baashkaabigwaniimagad *vii*
BLOSSOM
BLOSSOM: **baashkaabigwanii,**
baashkaabigwaniimagad *vii*
BLOW
BLOW: blow on s.o. **boodaazh /boodaaN-/**
vta; blow on s.t. **boodaadan** *vti;* blow on
things **boodaajige** *vai*
BLOW NOSE: blow one's nose **ziinikiigome**
vai
BLOW UP: **baashkide, baashkidemagad** *vii;*
baashkizo *vai*
BLOWN
BLOWN A CERTAIN WAY: be blown a
certain way **inaashi** *vai;* **inaasin** *vii*
BLOWN ABOUT: be blown about
babaamaashi *vai;* **babaamaasin** *vii*
BLOWN ALONG: be blown along **bimaashi**
vai; **bimaasin** *vii*
BLOWN APART: be blown apart **biigwaashi**
vai; **biigwaasin** *vii*
BLOWN ASHORE: be blown ashore
agwaayaashi *vai;* **agwaayaasin** *vii*
BLOWN AWAY: be blown away **animaashi**
vai; **animaasin** *vii;* **webaashi** *vai;*
webaasin *vii*
BLOWN FROM A CERTAIN PLACE: be
blown from a certain place **ondaashi** *vai;*
be blown from a certain place **ondaasin** *vii*
BLOWN HERE: be blown here **biidaashi** *vai;*
biidaasin *vii*

BLOWN IN: be blown in **bagamaashi** *vai;*
bagamaasin *vii*
BLOWN INSIDE: be blown inside
biindigeyaashi *vai;* **biindigeyaasin** *vii*
BLOWN INTO THE WATER: be blown into
the water **bakobiiyaashi** *vai;*
bakobiiyaasin *vii*
BLOWN OVER: be blown over **gawaashi** *vai;*
gawaasin *vii*
BLOWN UPWARDS: be blown upwards
ombaashi *vai;* **ombaasin** *vii*
BLOWOUT
BLOWOUT: have a blowout **baashkijiisijige**
vai
BLUE
BLUE: **ozhaawashko-** *pv4;* be blue
ozhaawashkozi *vai;* **ozhaawashkwaa,**
ozhaawashkwaamagad *vii;* be blue (as
something mineral) **ozhaawashkwaabikad**
vii; **ozhaawashkwaabikizi** *vai;* be blue (as
something sheet-like) **ozhaawashkwegad**
vii; **ozhaawashkwegizi** *vai;* be blue (as
something stick- or wood-like)
ozhaawashkwaakozi *vai;*
ozhaawashkwaakwad *vii;* be blue (as
something string-like)
ozhaawashkwaabiigad *vii;*
ozhaawashkwaabiigizi *vai*
WEAR BLUE: **ozhaawashko'o** *vai*
BLUE HERON
BLUE HERON: **zhashagi, -wag** *na*
BLUE JAY
BLUE JAY: **diindiisi, -wag** *na*
BLUEBERRY
BLUEBERRY: blueberries *plural* **miinan**
/miin-/ *ni*
BLUEBERRY PLANT
BLUEBERRY PLANT: **miinagaawanzh, -iig**
na
BLUEBERRY SAUCE
BLUEBERRY SAUCE: **miini-**
baashkiminasigan *ni*
BLUEBIRD
BLUEBIRD: **ozhaawashko-bineshiinh, -yag**
na
BLUSH
BLUSH: **miskwiingwese** *vai*
BOARD
BOARD: **nabagisag, -oog** *na*
BOARD
BOARD: **boozi** *vai*
BOAT
BOAT: **jiimaan, -an** *ni*
ARRIVE BY BOAT: **bagamishkaa** *vai*
COME IN A BOAT: **biidaasamishkaa** *vai*
GO ABOUT IN A BOAT: **babaamishkaa** *vai*
GO HOME BY BOAT: **giiwe'o** *vai*
LONG BOAT: be a long boat **ginoonagad** *vii*
MAKE A BOAT: **jiimaanike** *vai*
MIDDLE OF A BOAT: in the middle of a
boat **naawoonag** *vii*
NARROW BOAT: be narrow (as a boat)
agaasadeyoonagad *vii*

POLE A BOAT: **gaandakii'ige** *vai;*
gaandakii'o *vai*
POLE A BOAT ALONG: **bima'ookii** *vai*
SHORT BOAT: be short (as a boat)
dakoonagad *vii*
UNDER A BOAT: **anaamoonag** *pc*
WIDE BOAT: be wide (as a boat)
mangadeyoonagad *vii*
WOODEN BOAT: **mitigo-jiimaan, -an** *ni*
BOBBER
BOBBER: **deteba'agonjichigan, -an** *ni*
BOBCAT
BOBCAT: **gidagaa-bizhiw, -ag** *na*
BODY
BODY: my body **niiyaw, -an /-iiyaw-/** *nid*
GOOD BODY: have a good body
minwaabewizi *vai*
INSIDE BODY: inside the body **biinjina** *pc*
BOIL
BOIL: **onde, ondemagad** *vii;* **onzo** *vai;* boil
s.o. **onzo /onzw-/** *vta;* boil s.t. **onzan** *vti*
BOIL DOWN: **iskigamizide,**
iskigamizidemagad *vii;* **iskigamizo** *vai;*
boil s.t. down **iskigamizan** *vti;* boil things
down (e.g., maple sap) **iskigamizige** *vai*
BOIL OVER: **ziigigamide,**
ziigigamidemagad *vii;* **ziigigamizo** *vai*
BOIL TO SUGAR: **ombigamizige** *vai;* boil
s.t. to sugar **ombigamizan** *vti*
COOK BY BOILING: cook s.o. by boiling
gabaashim *vta;* cook s.t. by boiling
gabaatoon *vti2*
FINISH BOILING: **giizhigamide,**
giizhigamidemagad *vii;* finish boiling
things **giizhigamizige** *vai*
FINISH BOILING SAP: **ishkwaagamizige**
vai
MAKE NOISE BOILING: **madwegamide,**
madwegamidemagad *vii;* **madwegamizo**
vai
WHISTLE FROM BOILING:
gwiishkoshwewegamide,
gwiishkoshwewegamidemagad *vii;*
gwiishkoshwewegamizo *vai*
BONE
BONE: my bone **nikan, -an /-kan-/** *nid*
STRONG BONES: have strong bones
zoongigane *vai*
BOOK
BOOK: **mazina'igan, -an** *ni*
PRAYER BOOK: **anama'e-mazina'igan, -an**
ni
SCHOOLBOOK: **gikinoo'amaadii-**
mazina'igan *ni*
BORN
BORN: be born **niigi** *vai;* **ondaadizi** *vai*
BORROW
BORROW: borrow (s.t.) from people
adaawange *vai+o;* borrow (s.t.) from s.o.
adaawam *vta*
BOSS
BOSS: **ogimaa, -g** *na*
BOTH
BOTH: **eyiizh** *pc;* **nayenzh** *pc*

AT BOTH HANDS: **eyiidawininj** *pc*
ON BOTH SIDES: on both sides of it
edawayi'ii *pc*
BOTHER
BOTHER: bother s.o. **babaamenim** *vta;*
migoshkaaji' *vta;* bother s.t.
babaamendan *vti*
BOTTLE
BOTTLE: **omooday, -an** *ni*
BOUGH
CEDAR BOUGH: **giizhikaandag, -oog** *na*
FIR BOUGH: **zhingobaandag, -oog** *na*
PINE BOUGH: **zhingwaakwaandag, -oog** *na*
BOUNCE
BOUNCE: **gwaashkwesin** *vii*
BOUND
BOUND: be bound **dakobide,**
dakobidemagad *vii;* **dakobizo** *vai*
BOW
BOW: **mitigwaab, -iig** *na*
BOWL
BOWL: **boozikinaagan, -an** *ni*
BOWSTRING
BOWSTRING: **achaab, -iin** *ni*
BOX
BOX: **makak, -oon** *ni*
BIRCH BARK BOX: **wiigwaasi-makak, -oon**
ni
CARDBOARD BOX: **mazina'igani-makak,**
-oon *ni*
MAKE A BOX: **makakoke** *vai*
WOODEN BOX: **mitigo-makak, -oon** *ni*
BOX
BOX: box s.o. **gagwedaganaam** *vta;* they box
each other **gagwedaganaandiwag**
/gagwedaganaandi-/ *vai*
BOXER
BOXER: **gagwedaganewinini, -wag** *na*
BOY
BOY: **gwiiwizens, -ag** *na;* be a boy
gwiiwizensiwi *vai*
ADOLESCENT BOY: **oshkinawe, -g** *na;* be
an adolescent boy **oshkinawewi** *vai*
BRACE AND BIT
BRACE AND BIT: **biiminigan, -an** *ni*
BRACELET
BRACELET: **jiiskinikebizon, -an** *ni*
WEAR A BRACELET: **jiiskinikebizo** *vai*
BRAID
BRAID: **okaadenigan, -an** *ni;* braid s.o.'s hair
okaaden *vta;* braid s.t. **okaadenan** *vti;*
braid things **okaadenige** *vai*
HAVE BRAIDS: **okaadenige** *vai*
BRAIDED
BRAIDED: be braided **okaadenigaade,**
okaadenigaademagad *vii*
BRAIDED RUG
BRAIDED RUG: **okaadenigan, -an** *ni*
BRAIN
BRAIN: my brain **niinindib /-iinindib-/** *nid*
BRAKES
BRAKES: **nagaawebishkigan, -an** *ni*

APPLY THE BRAKES: **nagaawebishkige** *vai*
BRANCH
    BRANCH: **wadikwan, -an** *ni*
    RIVER BRANCHES: branch (as a river)
        baketigweyaa, baketigweyaamagad *vii*
BRASS
    BRASS: (piece of) brass **ozaawaabik, -oon** *ni;*
        be brass **ozaawaabikad** *vii;* **ozaawaabikizi**
        vai
BRASSIERE
    BRASSIERE: **aasodoodooshimebizon, -an** *ni*
BRAVE
    BRAVE: be brave **zoongide'e** *vai*
BREAD
    BREAD: **bakwezhigan, -ag** *na;* bread cooked
        over an open fire **abwaajigan, -ag** *na*
    BREAD BAKED UNDER THE ASHES:
        ningwa'abwaan, -ag *na*
    FRY BREAD: **zaasakokwaan, -ag** *na*
    MAKE BREAD: **bakwezhiganike** *vai*
BREAD BOX
    BREAD BOX: **bakwezhigani-makak, -oon** *ni*
BREAK
    BREAK: **biigoshkaa** *vai;* **biigoshkaa,**
        biigoshkaamagad *vii*
    BREAK APART: break apart (e.g., something
        string-like) **bakise** *vai;* **bakise,**
        bakisemagad *vii*
    BREAK APART FROM RUBBING: break
        apart from rubbing (e.g., something string-
        like) **bakiboode, bakiboodemagad** *vii;*
        bakiboozo *vai*
    BREAK ARM: break one's arm **bookonike** *vai*
    BREAK BY DROPPING: break s.o. by drop-
        ping **biigoshim** *vta;* break s.t. by dropping
        biigosidoon *vti2;* **niigosidoon** *vti2*
    BREAK BY HAND: break s.o. by hand **biigon**
        vta; break s.t. by hand **biigonan** *vti*
    BREAK BY HEAT: **biigode, biigodemagad**
        vii; **biigozo** *vai;* **niigode, niigodemagad**
        vii; **niigozo** *vai*
    BREAK IN TWO: **bookoshkaa** *vai;*
        bookoshkaa, bookoshkaamagad *vii*
    BREAK IN TWO BY FOOT OR BODY:
        break s.o. in two by foot or body
        bookoshkaw *vta;* break s.t. in two by foot
        or body **bookoshkan** *vti*
    BREAK IN TWO BY HITTING: break s.o. in
        two by hitting **bookoganaam** *vta;* break
        s.t. in two by hitting **bookoganaandan** *vti*
    BREAK IN TWO WITH HANDS: break s.o.
        in two with hands **bookobizh** /**bookobiN-**/
        vta; break s.t. in two with hands
        bookobidoon *vti2*
    BREAK LEG: break one's leg **bookogaade** *vai*
    BREAK OFF: break s.o. off (e.g., something
        string-like) **bakibizh** /**bakibiN-**/ *vta;* break
        s.t. off (e.g., something string-like)
        bakibidoon *vti2*
    BREAK ON IMPACT: **biigoshin** *vai;* **biigosin**
        vii; **niigoshin** *vai;* **niigosin** *vii*
    BREAK UP: break s.t. up (as ground)
        biigwakamigibidoon *vti2*

BREAK USING SOMETHING: break s.o.
    using something **biigwa'** /**biigwa'w-**/ *vta;*
    break s.t. using something **biigwa'an** *vti*
FALL AND BREAK ARM: fall and break
    one's arm **bookonikeshin** *vai*
FALL AND BREAK BACK: fall and break
    one's back **bookwaawiganeshin** *vai*
FALL AND BREAK LEG: fall and break
    one's leg **bookogaadeshin** *vai*
BREAK
    TAKE A BREAK: **gibichiitaa** *vai*
BREAKFAST
    BREAKFAST: **gigizhebaa-wiisiniwin** *ni*
    EAT BREAKFAST: **gigizhebaa-wiisini** *vai;*
        eat s.t. for breakfast **gigizhebaa-miijin** *vti3*
BREAST
    BREAST: my breast **indoodooshim, -ag**
        /**-doodooshim-**/ *nad*
BREAST FEED
    BREAST FEED: breast feed s.o. **nooni'** *vta*
BREATH
    BAD BREATH: have bad breath
        maazhimaagwanaamo *vai*
    DRAW BREATH IN: **ikwanaamo** *vai*
    RECOVER ONE'S BREATH: **nasanaamo**
        vai
    SHORT OF BREATH: be short of breath
        akwanaamo *vai*
    TAKE SHORT BREATHS: **akwanaamo** *vai*
BREATHE
    BREATHE: **bagidanaamo** *vai*
    STOP BREATHING: **ishkwaanaamo** *vai*
BREECH CLOUT
    BREECH CLOUT: **aanziyaan, -an** *ni*
BREEZE
    GOOD BREEZE: there is a good breeze
        minwaanimad *vii*
BRIDGE
    BRIDGE: **aazhogan, -an** *ni;* foot bridge
        aazhawaandawaagan, -an *ni*
BRIDLE
    BRIDLE: **zagidoonebijigan, -an** *ni*
BRIGHT
    BRIGHT: be bright **waaseyaa,**
        waaseyaamagad *vii;* be bright (as
        something sheet-like) **waaseyiigad** *vii;*
        waaseyiigizi *vai*
    BRIGHT INSIDE: be bright inside **waasete,**
        waasetemagad *vii*
    BRIGHT LEAVES: there are bright leaves
        waatebagaa, waatebagaamagad *vii*
BRING
    BRING: bring s.o. **biizh** /**biiN-**/ *vta;* bring s.t.
        biidoon *vti2;* bring (s.t.) for s.o. **biidaw**
        vta, also **biidamaw**
    BRING FIREWOOD INSIDE: **biindigenise**
        vai
    BRING HERE IN A BOAT: **biida'oodoon**
        vti2; bring s.o. here in a boat **biida'oozh**
        /**biida'ooN-**/ *vta*
    BRING INSIDE: bring s.o. inside **biindigazh**
        /**biindigaN-**/ *vta;* bring s.t. inside
        biindigadoon *vti2*

BRING TOGETHER: bring s.t. together
maawandoonan *vti*
BRITTLE
BRITTLE: be brittle **gaapan** *vii, also* **gaapaa;**
gaapizi *vai*
BROKE
BROKE: be broke (out of money) **biigoshkaa**
vai
BROKEN
BROKEN: be broken **biigoshkaa** *vai;*
biigoshkaa, biigoshkaamagad *vii;*
niigoshkaa, niigoshkaamagad *vii*
BROKEN ARM: have a broken arm
bookonike *vai*
BROKEN IN TWO: be broken in two
bookoshkaa *vai;* **bookoshkaa,**
bookoshkaamagad *vii*
BROKEN LEG: have a broken leg
bookogaade *vai*
HAVE A BROKEN NOSE: **bookojaane** *vai*
BROKEN GLASS
BROKEN GLASS: broken glass (as from a
bottle) **omoodayaabik, -oon** *ni*
BROOCH
BROOCH: **zagaakwa'on, -ag** *na*
BROOM
BROOM: **jiigada'igan, -an** *ni;* **jiishada'igan,**
-an *ni*
BROTH
BROTH: **wiiyaasaaboo** *ni*
WILD RICE BROTH: **manoominaaboo** *ni*
BROTHER
BROTHER: my (male's) brother **niijikiwenh,**
-yag /**-iijikiweny-**/ *nad;* my (male's) brother
ritual use **niikaan, -ag** /**-iikaan-**/ *nad;*
niikaanis, -ag /**-iikaanis-**/ *nad;* my sibling
of the opposite sex (brother or sister)
indawemaa, -g /**-dawemaaw-**/ *nad*
OLDER BROTHER: my older brother
nisayenh, -yag /**-sayeny-**/ *nad*
YOUNGER BROTHER: my younger brother
nishiime, -yag /**-shiimey-**/ *nad*
BROTHER-IN-LAW
BROTHER-IN-LAW: my (female's) brother-
in-law **niinim, -oog** /**-iinimw-**/ *nad;* my
(male's) brother-in-law **niitaa, -g** /**-iitaaw-**/
nad
BROUGHT
BROUGHT: be brought **biijigaade,**
biijigaademagad *vii;* **biijigaazo** *vai*
BROWN
BROWN: **ozaawi-** *pv4;* be brown **ozaawaa,**
ozaawaamagad *vii;* **ozaawizi** *vai;* be
brown (as something mineral)
ozaawaabikad *vii;* **ozaawaabikizi** *vai;* be
brown (as something sheet-like)
ozaawegad *vii;* **ozaawegizi** *vai;* be brown
(as something stick- or wood-like)
ozaawaakozi *vai;* **ozaawaakwad** *vii;* be
brown (as something string-like)
ozaawaabiigad *vii;* **ozaawaabiigizi** *vai*
BROWN BY FIRE: brown s.t. by fire
ozaawaakizan *vti*

COLORED BROWN: be colored brown
ozaawaande, ozaawaandemagad *vii;*
ozaawaanzo *vai*
HAVE BROWN HAIR: **ozaawindibe** *vai*
TOAST BROWN: toast s.t. brown
ozaawaakizan *vti*
WEAR BROWN: **ozaawi'o** *vai*
BRUISED
BRUISED FACE: have a bruised face
ozhaawashkwaanagiingwe *vai*
BRUSH
BRUSH: brush s.o. using something (as something sheet-like) **bawega'** /**bawega'w-**/ *vta;*
brush s.t. using something (as something
sheet-like) **bawega'an** *vti*
BRUSH SNOW: brush snow off s.o. by hand
bawaagonen *vta;* brush snow off s.o. using
something **bawaagone'** /**bawaagone'w-**/
vta; brush snow off s.t. by hand
bawaagonenan *vti;* brush snow off s.t.
using something **bawaagone'an** *vti*
BRUSH TEETH: brush one's teeth
giziiyaabide'o *vai;* **giziiyaabide'odizo** *vai*
PAINT BRUSH: **zhizhoobii'iganaatig, -oon**
ni
SCRUB BRUSH: **mimigosaga'igan, -an** *ni*
BRUSH
IN THE BRUSH: **megwekob** *pc*
BUBBLE
BUBBLE: **biisitaagan, -an** *ni*
BUCK
BUCK: **ayaabe, -g** *na*
BUCKLE
BELT BUCKLE: **gijipizonaabik, -oon** *ni*
BUCKSKIN DRESS
BUCKSKIN DRESS: **bashkweginagooday,**
-an *ni*
BUD
LEAVES BUD: **zaagibagaa,**
zaagibagaamagad *vii*
BUFFALO
BUFFALO: **bizhiki, -wag** *na;* **mashkode-**
bizhiki, -wag *na*
BUG
BUG: **manidoons, -ag** *na*
MANY BUGS: there are many bugs
manidoonsikaa, manidoonsikaamagad
vii
BUILD
BUILD: build s.o. **ozhi'** *vta;* build s.t.
ozhitoon *vti2;* build (s.t.) for s.o.
ozhitaw *vta;* **ozhitaw** *vta*
BUILD A HOUSE: **waakaa'ige** *vai;* build a
house for s.o. **ozhigaw** *vta*
BUILD A LODGE: **ozhige** *vai*
FINISH BUILDING A DWELLING:
giizhige *vai*
BUILDING
BUILDING: **waakaa'igan, -an** *ni*
BUILT
BUILT: be built **ozhichigaade,**
ozhichigaademagad *vii;* **ozhichigaazo** *vai*

BULB
BULB: obikwaaj, -iin *nid*
BULL
BULL: doonoo, -g *na*
BULL SNAKE
BULL SNAKE: newe, -g *na*
BULLET
BULLET: anwi, -in *ni*
TWENTY-TWO BULLET: anwiins, -an *ni*
BULLHEAD
BULLHEAD: awaazisii, -g *na, also* owaazisii,
wawaazisii
BUMP
BUMP: bump into s.o. bitaakoshkaw *vta;*
bump into s.t. bitaakoshkan *vti;* bump
something bitaakoshin *vai;* bitaakosin *vii*
BUMP DOWN OFF: bump s.o. down off
diitibishkaw *vta;* bump s.t. down off
diitibishkan *vti*
BUMP HEAD: bump one's head
bitaakondibeshin *vai*
BUNCH
TIE IN A BUNCH: tie s.o. in a bunch
okwapizh /okwapiN-/ *vta;* tie s.t. in a
bunch okwapidoon *vti2*
TIED IN A BUNCH: be tied in a bunch
okwapide, okwapidemagad *vii;*
okwapizo *vai*
BUNDLE
BUNDLE: gashkibijigan, -an *ni*
TIE IN A BUNDLE: tie s.o. in a bundle
gashkapizh /gashkapiN-/ *vta;* tie s.t. in a
bundle gashkapidoon *vti2*
WRAP AND TIE IN A BUNDLE: wrap and
tie s.o. in a bundle gashkibizh /gashkibiN-
/ *vta;* wrap and tie s.t. in a bundle
gashkibidoon *vti2;* wrap and tie things in
bundle gashkibijige *vai*
WRAPPED AND TIED IN A BUNDLE: be
wrapped and tied in a bundle gashkibide,
gashkibidemagad *vii;* gashkibijigaade,
gashkibijigaademagad *vii;*
gashkibijigaazo *vai*
BURBOT
BURBOT: mizay, -ag *na*
BURIED
BURIED: be buried (of a person)
bagidenjigaazo *vai;* ningwa'igaazo *vai*
BURIED IN A CERTAIN PLACE: be buried
in a certain place dazhishin *vai*
BURN
BURN: zakide, zakidemagad *vii;* zakizo *vai;*
burn s.o. zakiz /zakizw-/ *vta;* burn s.t.
zakizan *vti;* burn things zakizige *vai;* burn
oneself jaagizodizo *vai*
BURN A CERTAIN WAY: inaakide,
inaakidemagad *vii;* inaakizo *vai;* burn s.o.
a certain way inaakiz /inaakizw-/ *vta;* burn
s.t. a certain way inaakizan *vti*
BURN A HOLE: burn a hole in s.o.
bagwaakiz /bagwaakizw-/ *vta;* burn a hole
in s.t. bagwaakizan *vti*

BURN AS MEDICINE: burn s.t. as medicine
nookwezan *vti;* burn things as medicine
nookwezige *vai*
BURN TO THE PAN: agwaabikide,
agwaabikidemagad *vii;* agwaabikizo *vai;*
burn s.o. to the pan agwaabikiz
/agwaabikizw-/ *vta;* burn s.t. to the pan
agwaabikizan *vti*
BURN UP: jaagaakide, jaagaakidemagad *vii;*
jaagaakizo *vai;* jaagide, jaagidemagad
vii; jaagizo *vai;* burn s.o. up jaagaakiz
/jaagaakizw-/ *vta;* jaagiz /jaagizw-/ *vta;*
burn s.t. up jaagaakizan *vti;* jaagizan *vti*
BURNED
HAVE A HOLE BURNED IN: bagwaakide,
bagwaakidemagad *vii;* bagwaakizo *vai*
BURP
BURP: aagade *vai;* megade *vai*
BURP GREASE: biinzibii *vai*
BURROW
BURROW: waanzh, -an *ni*
BURST
BURST: burst s.o. using something baashka'
/baashka'w-/ *vta;* burst s.t. using some-
thing baashka'an *vti*
BURST ON IMPACT: burst s.o. on impact
baashkishim *vta;* burst s.t. on impact
baashkisidoon *vti2*
BURST OPEN: biigojiishkaa *vai;*
biigojiishkaa, biigojiishkaamagad *vii*
BURST OPEN USING SOMETHING: burst
s.o. open using something baashkijii'
/baashkijii'w-/ *vta;* burst s.t. open using
something baashkijii'an *vti*
BURST OUT LAUGHING: baashkaapi *vai*
BURY
BURY: bury s.o. (e.g., a person) bagidenim
vta; bury s.o. ningwa' /ningwa'w-/ *vta;*
bury s.t. ningwa'an *vti*
BUSH
IN THE BUSH: noopiming *pc*
BUSHEL
CERTAIN NUMBER OF BUSHELS: a
certain number of bushels daso-
diba'iminaan *pc*
BUSHY
BUSHY: be bushy biigwawe *vai*
BUSINESS
DO BUSINESS: babaamizi *vai*
GO ABOUT ON BUSINESS: go about on
one's business babaamizi *vai*
BUSTLE
DANCE BUSTLE: bimoonjigan, -an *ni*
BUSY
BUSY: ojaanimi- *pv4;* be busy ojaanimizi *vai;*
ondamizi *vai;* be busy (in some work or
activity) ojaanimitaa *vai*
KEPT BUSY IN AN ACTIVITY: be kept
busy in an activity ondamitaa *vai*
KEPT BUSY IN WORK: be kept busy in
work ondamanokii *vai*
BUT
BUT: aanawi *pc*

BUTTER
BUTTER: **doodooshaaboo-bimide** *ni;*
ozaawi-bimide *ni*
BUTTERFLY
BUTTERFLY: **memengwaa, -g** *na*
BUTTON
BUTTON: **gibadoonh, -yag** *na, also*
gibodoonh
BUTTON UP: button s.o. up **zagaakwa'**
/zagaakwa'w-/ *vta;* button up oneself
zagaakwa'odizo *vai*
BUY
BUY: buy (s.t.) **adaawe** *vai+o;* buy (s.t.) for
oneself **adaawetamaazo** *vai;* buy (s.t.) for
s.o. **adaawetamaw** *vta;* buy (s.t.) from s.o.
adaam *vta*
BUY FOOD: **miijimadaawe** *vai*
BY
BY: **jiigi-** *pn;* by it **jiigayi'ii** *pc*
BY A DOOR: **jiigishkwaand** *pc*
BY A FIRE: **jiigishkode** *pc*
BY A HOUSE: **jiigigamig** *pc*
BY A MEADOW: **jiigashkosiw** *pc*
BY A ROAD: by a road or trail **jiigikana** *pc*
BY A TRAIL: by a road or trail **jiigikana** *pc*
BY A TREE: **jiigaatig** *pc*
BY A WALL: **jiigaatig** *pc*
GOING BY: **bimi-** *pv2*
BY ONESELF
BY ONESELF: **dibinawe** *pc*
BYPASS
BYPASS: bypass s.o. **bakekazh /bakekaN-/**
vta; bypass people **bakekazhiwe** *vai*

C

CABBAGE
CABBAGE: **gichi-aniibiish, -an** *ni*
CABIN
LOG CABIN: **mitigo-waakaa'igan, -an** *ni*
CACHE
CACHE: **asanjigoowin, -an** *ni;* cache (s.t.)
asanjigo *vai+o*
CAFE
CAFE: **wiisiniiwigamig, -oon** *ni*
CAKE
CAKE: **waashkobizid bakwezhigan, -ag** *na-*
pt; **wiishkobi-bakwezhigan, -ag** *na*
CALENDAR
CALENDAR: **giizisoo-mazina'igan, -an** *ni*
CALF
CALF: **bizhikiins, -ag** *na*
CALF
CALF: my calf **ninaan, -ag /-naan-/** *nad*
CALFHIDE
CALFHIDE: **bizhikiinsiwayaan, -ag** *na*

CALICO
CALICO: **gidagiigin, -oon** *ni*
CALL
CALL: call s.o. **nandom** *vta*
CALL A CERTAIN WAY: call s.o. a certain
way **izhi-wiinzh /izhi-wiinN-/** *vta;* call s.t. a
certain way **izhi-wiindan** *vti*
CALL IN INDIAN: call s.o. in Indian
(Ojibwe) **anishinaabewinikaazh**
/anishinaabewinikaaN-/ *vta;* call s.t. in
Indian (Ojibwe) **anishinaabewinikaadan**
vti
CALL IN OJIBWE: call s.o. in Indian
(Ojibwe) **anishinaabewinikaazh**
/anishinaabewinikaaN-/ *vta;* call s.t. in
Indian (Ojibwe) **anishinaabewinikaadan**
vti
CALL ON THE PHONE: call s.o. on the
phone **ganoozh /ganooN-/** *vta*
CALL OUT: **biibaagi** *vai;* call out to s.o.
biibaagim *vta;* call out to s.t. **biibaagindan**
vti
MAKE A CHARACTERISTIC CALL: make
a characteristic call (e.g., neigh, moo)
noondaagozi *vai;* make a characteristic
call (neigh, etc.) **inwe** *vai*
CALLED
CALLED A CERTAIN WAY: be called a
certain way **izhi-wiinde, izhi-**
wiindemagad *vii;* **izhi-wiinzo** *vai*
CALLED IN INDIAN: be called in Indian
(Ojibwe) **anishinaabewinikaade,**
anishinaabewinikaademagad *vii;*
anishinaabewinikaazo *vai*
CALLED IN OJIBWE: be called in Indian
(Ojibwe) **anishinaabewinikaade,**
anishinaabewinikaademagad *vii;*
anishinaabewinikaazo *vai*
CALM
CALM: be calm **awibaa, awibaamagad** *vii*
CALM WEATHER: be calm weather
anwaatin *vii*
CAMEL
CAMEL: **bekwaawigang** *na-pt*
CAMERA
CAMERA: **mazinaakizigan, -an** *ni*
CAMP
CAMP: **gabeshi** *vai*
CAMPSITE
CAMPSITE: **gabeshiwin, -an** *ni*
CAN
CAN: *modal* **daa-** *pv1*
CAN
CAN: **biiwaabikoons, -an** *ni;* can s.t.
gibaakobidoon *vti2*
CAN OPENER
CAN OPENER: **baakaakozhigan, -an** *ni*
CAN'T DO IT
CAN'T DO IT: can't do it! **gaawesa** *pc*
CANADA
CANADA: **Zhaaganaashiiwaki** *ni*
CANADA GOOSE
CANADA GOOSE: **nika, -g** *na*

CANDY
CANDY: **ziinzibaakwadoons, -an** *ni*
CANE
CANE: **zaka'on, -an** *ni*
USE A CANE: **zaka'o** *vai*
CANNED GOODS
CANNED GOODS: **gibaakobijigan, -an** *ni*
CANNIBAL
WINTER CANNIBAL MONSTER: windigo:
winter cannibal monster **wiindigoo, -g** *na*
CANOE
CANOE: **jiimaan, -an** *ni*
ALUMINUM CANOE: **biiwaabiko-jiimaan,**
-an *ni*
BIRCH BARK CANOE: **wiigwaasi-jiimaan,**
-an *ni*
GO BY CANOE: **jiime** *vai*
MAKE A CANOE: **atoono** *vai;* **jiimaanike**
vai
WOODEN CANOE: **mitigo-jiimaan, -an** *ni*
CANOE RIB
CANOE RIB: **waaginaa, -g** *na*
CANOPY
CANOPY: **agwanogaan, -an** *ni*
CANVAS
CANVAS: **babagiwayaanegamigwegin, -oon**
ni
CANVAS SHOE
CANVAS SHOE: **babagiwayaanekizin, -an**
ni, also **bagiwayaanekizin**
CAPSIZE
CAPSIZE: **gwanabishkaa** *vai*
CAPTIVE
TAKE CAPTIVES: **makandwe** *vai;*
nawadiniwe *vai*
CAR
CAR: **odaabaan, -ag** *na;*
waasamoowidaabaan, -ag *na;* car *old*
fashioned **ziikaa, -g** *na*
HAVE A BROKEN-DOWN CAR:
biigodaabaane *vai*
POLICE CAR: **dakoniwewidaabaan, -ag** *na*
RACE CAR: **gagwejikazhiwewidaabaan, -ag**
na
REPAIR A CAR: **nanaa'idaabaane** *vai*
CARCASS
CARCASS: **zhiigozhigan, -an** *ni*
CARD
CARD: playing card **ataadiwin, -ag** *na*
CLUB SUITE CARD: **danens, -ag** *na*
CUT CARDS: **bakwenige** *vai*
DIAMOND SUITE CARD: **gaanoo, -g** *na*
HEART SUITE CARD: **giiwoon, -ag** *na, also*
giiyoon
SPADE SUITE CARD: **biig, -wag** *na*
CARDBOARD BOX
CARDBOARD BOX: **mazina'igani-makak,**
-oon *ni*
CARDINAL
CARDINAL: **misko-bineshiinh, -yag** *na*
CARE
CARE: care for s.o. **bamenim** *vta;* care for s.t.
bamendan *vti*

CAREFREE
CAREFREE: be carefree **naangide'e** *vai*
CAREFUL
CAREFUL: be careful **ayaangwaamizi** *vai*
CAREFULLY
CAREFULLY: **wawiinge** *pc;* **weweni** *pc*
CARELESSLY
CARELESSLY: **debinaak** *pc* *
CARGO
LOAD CARGO: **boozitaaso** *vai;* load s.t. as
cargo **boozitoon** *vti2;* load (s.t.) with cargo
for s.o. **boozitaw** *vta*
CARIBOU
CARIBOU: **adik, -wag** *na*
CARNIVAL
CARNIVAL: **mamaandaagochigewin, -an** *ni*
CARPENTER
CARPENTER: **mookodaasowinini, -wag** *na;*
waakaa'igewinini, -wag *na*
CARRIED
CARRIED TO A CERTAIN PLACE: be
carried to a certain place **izhiwijigaade,**
izhiwijigaademagad *vii;* **izhiwijigaazo** *vai*
CARROT
CARROT: **okaadaak, -oon** *ni;*
ozaawikaadaak, -oon *ni*
CARRY
ABLE TO CARRY: be able to carry s.o.
gashkiwizh /**gashkiwiN-**/ *vta;* be able to
carry s.t. **gashkiwidoon** *vti2*
ARRIVE CARRYING: arrive carrying s.o.
bagamiwizh /**bagamiwiN-**/ *vta;* arrive
carrying s.t. **bagamiwidoon** *vti2*
CARRY A BABY ALONG ON BACK: carry a
baby along on one's back **bimoomaawaso**
vai
CARRY A BABY TO A CERTAIN PLACE
ON BACK: carry a baby to a certain place
on one's back **inoomaawaso** *vai*
CARRY A BIG PACK: **mangiwane** *vai*
CARRY A PACK ALONG: **bimiwane** *vai*
CARRY ABOUT: carry s.o. about
babaamiwizh /**babaamiwiN-**/ *vta;* carry
s.t. about **babaamiwidoon** *vti2*
CARRY ACROSS: carry s.o. across
aazhogewizh /**aazhogewiN-**/ *vta;* carry s.t.
across **aazhogewidoon** *vti2*
CARRY ALONG: carry s.o. along **bimiwizh**
/**bimiwiN-**/ *vta;* carry s.t. along
bimiwidoon *vti2;* carry things along
bimiwijige *vai*
CARRY ALONG ON BACK: carry s.o. along
on one's back **bimoom** *vta;* carry s.t. along
on one's back **bimoondan** *vti*
CARRY AWAY: carry s.o. away **animiwizh**
/**animiwiN-**/ *vta;* carry s.t. away
animiwidoon *vti2*
CARRY AWAY ON BACK: carry s.o. away
on one's back **animoom** *vta;* carry s.t.
away on one's back **animoondan** *vti*
CARRY FROM A CERTAIN PLACE: carry
s.o. from a certain place **onjiwizh**

/onjiwiN-/ *vta;* carry s.t. from a certain
place **onjiwidoon** *vti2*
CARRY HOME: carry s.o. home **giiwewizh**
/giiwewiN-/ *vta;* carry s.t. home
giiwewidoon *vti2;* carry (s.t.) home for s.o.
giiwewidaw *vta*
CARRY IN MOUTH: carry s.o. in mouth
niimam *vta;* carry s.t. in mouth
niimandan *vti*
CARRY INLAND: carry s.o. inland **gopiwizh**
/gopiwiN-/ *vta;* carry s.t. inland
gopiwidoon *vti2*
CARRY OFF ON BACK: carry s.o. off on
one's back **maadoom** *vta;* carry s.t. off on
one's back **maadoondan** *vti*
CARRY ON BACK FROM A CERTAIN
PLACE: carry s.o. on back from a certain
place **ondoom** *vta;* carry s.t. on back from
a certain place **ondoondan** *vti*
CARRY OVER A PORTAGE: carry things
over a portage **gakiiwenige** *vai*
CARRY TO A CERTAIN PLACE: carry s.o.
to a certain place **izhiwizh** /izhiwiN-/ *vta;*
carry s.t. to a certain place **izhiwidoon** *vti2*
CARRY TO A CERTAIN PLACE ON
BACK: carry s.o. to a certain place on
one's back **inoom** *vta;* carry s.t. to a certain place on one's back **inoondan** *vti*
CARRY TO THE SHORE: carry s.o. to the
shore **madaabiiwizh** /madaabiiwiN-/ *vta;*
carry s.t. to the shore **madaabiiwidoon**
vti2
CARRY USING SOMETHING: carry s.o.
using something **niima'** /niima'w-/ *vta;*
carry s.t. using something **niima'an** *vti*
HARDLY BE ABLE TO CARRY THE
PACK: hardly be able to carry a pack
bwaawane *vai*
LIFT AND CARRY: lift and carry s.o.
ombiwizh /ombiwiN-/ *vta;* lift and carry
s.t. **ombiwidoon** *vti2*
CARVE
CARVE: **mookodaaso** *vai*
CARVER
CARVER: **mookodaasowinini, -wag** *na*
CASH
CASH: **gwayako-zhooniyaa** *na*
CASINO
CASINO: **endazhi-ataading** *ni-pt*
CASKET
CASKET: **jiibegamig, -oon** *ni*
CASS LAKE
CASS LAKE: **Gaa-miskwaawaakokaag** *place*
CAST
CAST SUGAR CONES: **ziiga'ige** *vai*
CAT
CAT: **gaazhagens, -ag** *na*
CATASTROPHE
CATASTROPHE: there is a catastrophe
nichiiwad *vii*
CATCH
CATCH: catch s.o. **debibizh** /debibiN-/ *vta;*
catch s.t. **debibidoon** *vti2;* catch (s.t.) for
s.o. **debibidaw** *vta*

CATCH A DISEASE: **mizizi** *vai*
CATCH A RIDE: catch a ride with s.o.
boozinodaw *vta*
CATCH WITH HANDS: catch s.o. with
hands **nakwebizh** /nakwebiN-/ *vta;* catch
s.t. with hands **nakwebidoon** *vti2;* catch
things with hands **nakwebijige** *vai*
CATCH FIRE
CATCH FIRE: **biskane, biskanemagad** *vii;*
nawadide, nawadidemagad *vii;* **nawadizo**
vai
CATCH UP
CATCH UP: catch up to s.o. **adim** *vta;* catch
up to s.t. **adindan** *vti*
CATCH UP IN A BOAT: catch up to s.o. in a
boat **adima'** /adima'w-/ *vta*
CATCHER
CATCHER: catcher (in baseball)
nakwebijigewinini, -wag *na*
CATFISH
CATFISH: **maanameg, -wag** *na*
CATSUP
CATSUP: **oginii-dagonigan** *ni*
CATTAIL
CATTAIL: **apakweshkway, -ag** *na*
CATTAIL MAT: **apakweshkway, -ag** *na*
CAUGHT
CAUGHT IN A NET: be caught in a net
biinda'am *vai2*
CAUSE
CAUSE: cause s.o. to do something **izhi'** *vta;*
cause s.t. to **izhitoon** *vti2*
CAUTION
CAUTION: caution s.o. **ayaangwaamim** *vta*
CAUTIOUS
CAUTIOUS: be cautious **ayaangwaamizi** *vai*
CAVE
CAVE: **waanzh, -an** *ni*
CEDAR
RED CEDAR: **miskwaawaak, -oog** *na*
WHITE CEDAR: **giizhik, -ag** *na*
CEDAR BARK BAG
CEDAR BARK BAG: **giishkashkimod, -an** *ni*
CEDAR BOUGH
CEDAR BOUGH: **giizhikaandag, -oog** *na*
CEDAR WAXWING
CEDAR WAXWING: **zegibanwaanishiinh,
-yag** *na*
CELLAR
CELLAR: **moonikaan, -an** *ni*
CEMETERY
CEMETERY: **jiibayaki, -in** *ni*
CENSE
CENSE: cense s.o. **abaabas** /abaabasw-/ *vta;*
cense s.t. **abaabasan** *vti;* cense oneself
abaabaso *vai;*
CENT
CENT: **miskwaabikoons, -ag** *na;*
ozaawaabikoons, -ag *na*
CEREMONY
CONDUCT A CEREMONY: **manidooke** *vai*
GIVE A CEREMONY: **zagaswe'iwe** *vai*

CERTAIN
CERTAIN: be certain **gwayakwendam** *vai2;*
it is certain **booch** *pc*
CERTAIN EVENT: be a certain event
inakamigad *vii*
CERTAINLY
CERTAINLY: **geget** *pc;* **mii nange** *pc*
CHAFF
CHAFF: chaff from wild rice *plural* **mazaanag**
/**mazaan-**/ *na*
CHAIN
CHAIN OF LAKES: be a chain of lakes
aanikegamaa, aanikegamaamagad *vii*
CHAIR
CHAIR: **apabiwin, -an** *ni*
ROCKING CHAIR: **didibise-apabiwin, -an**
ni; **wewebizoo-apabiwin, -an** *ni*
CHAIRMAN
CHAIRMAN: **eshpabid** *na-pt*
CHANGE
CHANGE: **aanji-** *pv4;* change s.o. **aanji'** *vta;*
change s.o. with foot or body (e.g., clothes)
aanzikaw *vta;* change s.t. **aanjitoon** *vti2;*
change s.t. with foot or body (e.g., clothes)
aanzikan *vti*
CHANGE APPEARANCE: change one's own
appearance **aanzinaago'idizo** *vai;* change
s.o.'s appearance **aanzinaago'** *vta;* change
s.t.'s appearance **aanzinaagotoon** *vti2*
CHANGE CLOTHES: change one's clothes
aanzikonaye *vai;* change s.o. with foot or
body (e.g., clothes) **aanzikaw** *vta;* change
s.o.'s clothes **aanzikonaye'** *vta;* change s.t.
with foot or body (e.g., clothes) **aanzikan**
vti
CHANGE COUNTRIES: **aandakii** *vai*
CHANGE DRESS: change one's dress
aandagoode *vai*
CHANGE LAWS: **aandaakonige** *vai*
CHANGE LIFE: change one's life **aanji-
bimaadizi** *vai*
CHANGE MIND: change one's mind
aanizhiitam *vai2;* **gwekendam** *vai*
CHANGE PLANS: **aandaakonige** *vai*
CHANGE SEAT: **aandabi** *vai*
CHANGE
LOOSE CHANGE: **bigishki-zhooniyaans,
-ag** *na*
CHANGED
LOOK CHANGED: **aanzinaagozi** *vai;*
aanzinaagwad *vii*
CHANNEL
CHANNEL: there is a channel between lakes
wabigamaa, wabigamaamagad *vii*
CHAPPED
CHAPPED: be chapped **gagiipizi** *vai*
CHAPPED FACE: have a chapped face
gagiipiingwe *vai*
CHAPPED LIPS: have chapped lips
gagiipidoon *vai*
CHARACTER
CERTAIN CHARACTER: have a certain
character **inaadizi** *vai*

CHARCOAL
CHARCOAL: **akakanzhe** *ni*
CHARGE
CHARGE A HIGH PRICE: **ishpagindaaso**
vai; charge a high price for s.t.
ishpagindan *vti*
CHASE
CHASE ABOUT: chase s.o. about
babaaminizha' /**babaaminizha'w-**/ *vta;*
chase s.t. about **babaaminizha'an** *vti;*
chase things about **babaaminizha'ige** *vai*
CHASE ALONG: chase s.o. along **biminizha'**
/**biminizha'w-**/ *vta;* **biminizhikaw** *vta;*
chase s.t. along **biminizha'an** *vti;* chase
things along **biminizha'ige** *vai;* chase
people along **biminaazhikaage** *vai*
CHASE INSIDE: chase s.o. inside
biindigenaazhikaw *vta;* **biindigenizhikaw**
vta
CHASE OFF: chase s.o. off **maajinizhikaw**
vta
CHASE OUT OF THE WAY: chase s.o. out
of the way **ikonaazhikaw** *vta*
CHASE OUTSIDE: chase s.o. outside
zaagijinizhikaw *vta*
CHASE TO A CERTAIN PLACE: chase s.o.
to a certain place **izhinaazhikaw** *vta;*
izhinizhikaw *vta*
CHAUFFEUR
CHAUFFEUR: **bimiwizhiwewinini, -wag** *na*
CHEAP
CHEAP: be cheap **wendad** *vii;* **wendaginde,
wendagindemagad** *vii;* **wendaginzo** *vai;*
wendizi *vai;* **wenipanad** *vii*
CHEAT
CHEAT: cheat s.o. **wayezhim** *vta;* cheat
people **wayezhinge** *vai*
CHECK
CHECK BY TASTING: check s.o. by tasting
gojipozh /**gojipw-**/ *vta;* check s.t. by tasting
gojipidan *vti*
CHECK SNARES: check one's snares
naadagoodoo *vai*
CHECK TRAPS: check one's traps
naadasoonaagane *vai*
CHECK UP: check up on s.o. **dibaabam** *vta*
CHECK
CHECK: **jeko-mazina'igan, -an** *ni*
CHECKERS
PLAY CHECKERS: **zhooshkonige** *vai*
CHEEK
CHEEK: my cheek **ninow, -an** /**-now-**/ *nid*
RED CHEEK: have a red cheek **miskwanowe**
vai
CHERRY
BLACK CHERRY: **ookwemin, -an** *ni*
CHEST
CHEST: my chest **nikaakigan, -an**
/**-kaakigan-**/ *nid*
CHEST PAINS: have chest pains while
breathing **jakanaamo** *vai*
MIDDLE OF THE CHEST: in the middle of
the chest **naawaakigan** *pc*

CHEST OF DRAWERS
  CHEST OF DRAWERS: **wiikobijigan, -an** *ni*
CHEW
  CHEW: chew s.o. **zhaashaagwam** *vta;* chew
    s.t. **zhaashaagwandan** *vti;* chew things
    zhaashaagwanjige *vai*
  CHEW GUM: **zhaashaagwamikiwe** *vai*
  CHEW ON: chew on s.o. **jiichiigwam** *vta;*
    chew on s.t. **jiichiigwandan** *vti;* chew on
    things **jiichiigwanjige** *vai*
  CHEW SNUFF OR TOBACCO: **biindaakwe**
    vai
  CHEW TO BITS: chew s.o. to bits
    zhishigwam *vta;* chew s.t. to bits
    zhishigwandan *vti*
  CHEW TOBACCO: **agwanenjige** *vai*
CHEWING GUM
  CHEWING GUM: **bigiins, -ag** *na*
CHICKADEE
  CHICKADEE: **gijigijigaaneshiinh, -yag** *na*
CHICKEN
  CHICKEN: **baaka'aakwenh, -yag** *na*
CHICKEN COOP
  CHICKEN COOP: **baaka'aakwenhwigamig,
    -oon** *ni*
CHICKEN SOUP
  CHICKEN SOUP: **baaka'aakwenhwaaboo**
    ni
CHIEF
  CHIEF: **ogimaa, -g** *na;* be a chief **ogimaawi**
    vai
  MAKE CHIEF: make s.o. chief **ogimaakaw**
    vta
  WIFE OF CHIEF OR LEADER:
    ogimaakwe, -g *na*
CHILD
  CHILD: **abinoojiinh, -yag** *na;* be a child
    abinoojiinyiwi *vai;* my child **niniijaanis,
    -ag** /**-niijaanis-**/ *nad*
  ELDEST CHILD: **nitamoozhaan, -ag** *na*
  HAVE A CHILD: **oniijaanisi** *vai;* have a small
    child **oniijaanisensi** *vai*
  PRETEND TO BE A CHILD:
    abinoojiinyikaazo *vai*
  TAKE CARE OF A CHILD: **bamoozhe** *vai;*
    ganawendaawaso *vai*
  YOUNGEST CHILD: **ishkwejaagan, -ag** *na*
CHILL
  GET A CHILL: **dakaji** *vai*
CHILLED
  CHILLED: be chilled **dakamanji'o** *vai*
  GET CHILLED EASILY: **wakewaji** *vai*
CHIN
  CHIN: my chin **indaamikan, -an** /**-daamikan-**
    / *nid*
CHINESE
  CHINESE: **aniibiishaabookewinini, -wag** *na;*
    be Chinese **aniibiishaabookewininiiwi** *vai*
CHIP
  CHIP: **biiwega'igan, -an** *ni*
CHIPMUNK
  CHIPMUNK: **agongos, -ag** *na*

CHISEL
  ICE CHISEL: **eshkan, -an** *ni*
CHOKE
  CHOKE: choke on food **bakwenishkaago** *vai;*
    choke on something stuck in one's throat
    ana'o *vai;* choke s.o. **gibinewen** *vta*
  CHOKE WHILE DRINKING: **bakwenibii**
    vai
CHOKECHERRY
  CHOKECHERRY: **asasawemin, -an** *ni*
CHOKECHERRY BUSH
  CHOKECHERRY BUSH:
    asasaweminagaawanzh, -iig *na*
CHOOSE
  CHOOSE: choose s.o. **onaabam** *vta;* choose
    s.t. **onaabandan** *vti;* choose things
    onaabanjige *vai*
CHOP
  CHOP A PIECE OFF: chop a piece off s.o. (as
    something of wood) **bakwega'**
    /**bakwega'w-**/ *vta;* chop a piece off s.t. (as
    something of wood) **bakwega'an** *vti*
  CHOP DOWN: chop s.o. down **gawa'**
    /**gawa'w-**/ *vta;* chop s.t. down **gawa'an** *vti*
  CHOP FINE: chop s.o. fine **biisa'** /**biisa'w-**/
    vta; chop s.t. fine **biisa'an** *vti*
  CHOP INTO SMALL PIECES: chop s.o. into
    small pieces (as something of wood)
    baasiga' /**baasiga'w-**/ *vta;* chop s.t. into
    small pieces (as something of wood)
    baasiga'an *vti*
  CHOP OFF: chop s.o. off **giishka'** /**giishka'w-**/
    vta; chop s.t. off **giishka'an** *vti*
  CHOP OFF WITH AX: chop s.o. off with ax
    giishkiga' /**giishkiga'w-**/ *vta;* chop s.t. off
    with ax **giishkiga'an** *vti*
  CHOP POINTED: chop s.o. pointed
    bajiishkiga' /**bajiishkiga'w-**/ *vta;* chop s.t.
    pointed **bajiishkiga'an** *vti*
CHOPPED
  CHOPPED DOWN: be chopped down
    gawa'igaade, gawa'igaademagad *vii;*
    gawa'igaazo *vai*
CHOSE
  CHOSE: be chosen **onaabanjigaade,
    onaabanjigaademagad** *vii*
CHOSEN
  CHOSEN: be chosen **onaabanjigaazo** *vai*
CHRISTIAN
  CHRISTIAN: **anama'e-** *pv4, also* **aname-**; be
    Christian **anami'aa** *vai*
CHRISTMAS
  CHRISTMAS: be Christmas **niibaa-anama'e-
    giizhigad** *vii*
CHURCH
  CHURCH: **anama'ewigamig, -oon** *ni, also*
    anamewigamig
CIGARETTE
  CIGARETTE: **asemaawipwaagaans, -ag** *na,
    also* **asemaa-opwaagaans; opwaagaans,
    -ag** *na*
CINNAMON
  CINNAMON: **meskwanagekozid** *na-pt*

CIRCLE
 DRAW A CIRCLE: **waawiyebii'ige** *vai*
CIRCULAR
 CIRCULAR: be circular **waawiyeyaa,
  waawiyeyaamagad** *vii;* **waawiyezi** *vai*
CIRCUS
 CIRCUS: **mamaandaagochigewin, -an** *ni*
CITY
 CITY: **gichi-oodena, -wan** *ni*
CLAM
 CLAM: **es, -ag** *na*
CLAN
 CLAN: my clan **indoodem, -ag /-doodem-/**
  nad
CLAP
 CLAP HANDS: clap one's hands
  bapasininjii'odizo *vai*
CLAW
 CLAW: my claw **nishkanzh, -iig /-shkanzhy-/**
  nad
CLAY
 CLAY: **waabigan** *na*
 MADE OF CLAY: be made of clay
  waabiganikaade, waabiganikaademagad
  vii
 WHITE CLAY: **waabaabigan** *na*
CLEAN
 CLEAN: be clean **biinad** *vii;* **biinizi** *vai;* be
  clean (as a liquid) **biinaagamin
  /biinaagami-/** *vii;* clean s.o. **biini'** *vta;*
  clean s.t. **biinitoon** *vti2;* clean (s.t.) for s.o.
  biinitaw *vta;* clean things **biinichige** *vai*
 CLEAN A FISH: **bakazhaawe** *vai*
 CLEAN HAND: have a clean hand **biinininjii**
  vai
CLEANED
 CLEANED: be cleaned **biinichigaade,
  biinichigaademagad** *vii;* **biinichigaazo** *vai*
CLEANER
 CLEANER: **biinichigewinini, -wag** *na;*
  cleaner (female) **biinichigewikwe, -g** *na*
CLEAR
 CLEAR LAND: **mazhii'ige** *vai*
 CLEAR OFF: clear off after a storm
  aabaakawad *vii;* ice clears off the lake
  baakibii'an *vii*
 CLEAR SKY: be clear sky **mizhakwad** *vii*
CLEARING
 CUT-OVER CLEARING: **mazhii'igan, -an** *ni*
 ON THE OTHER SIDE OF THE
  CLEARING: **agaamaakwaa** *pc*
CLEARLY
 SEE CLEARLY: **bagakaabi** *vai;* see s.o.
  clearly **bagakaabam** *vta;* see s.t. clearly
  bagakaabandan *vti*
CLEAVER
 CLEAVER: **giishkada'igan, -an** *ni*
CLERK
 CLERK: clerk (female) **ozhibii'igewikwe, -g**
  na; clerk (male) **ozhibii'igewinini, -wag** *na*
CLIFF
 CLIFF: be a cliff **giishkadinaa,
  giishkadinaamagad** *vii*

ROCK CLIFF: **aazhibik, -oon** *ni;* there is a
  rock cliff **giishkaazhibikaa,
  giishkaazhibikaamagad** *vii*
CLIMB
 CLIMB ACROSS: **aazhawaandawe** *vai*
 CLIMB ALONG: **bimaandawe** *vai*
 CLIMB DOWN: **niisaandawe** *vai;* climb
  down fast **niisaandawebizo** *vai*
 CLIMB HERE: **biidaandawe** *vai*
 CLIMB OVER: **baazhidaandawe** *vai*
 CLIMB TO CERTAIN PLACE: climb to a
  certain place **inaandawe** *vai*
 CLIMB UP: **akwaandawe** *vai*
 CLIMB UP FAST: **akwaandawebatoo** *vai;*
  climb up fast (e.g., in an elevator)
  akwaandawebizo *vai*
CLING
 CLING: **minjimii** *vai;* cling (as to something
  stick- or wood-like) **minjimaakwii** *vai*
CLOCK
 CLOCK: **diba'igiiziswaan, -ag** *na*
CLOSE
 CLOSE: **besho** *pc;* be close **beshowad** *vii*
 APPEAR TO BE CLOSE: **beshonaagozi** *vai;*
  beshonaagwad *vii*
 THINK TO BE CLOSE: think s.t. to be close
  beshwendan *vti*
CLOSET
 CLOSET: **ataasowin, -an** *ni*
CLOT
 BLOOD CLOT: **wado, -wag** *na*
CLOTH
 CLOTH: **babagiwayaaniigin, -oon** *ni, also*
  bagiwayaaniigin
 CLOTH BAG: **bagiwayaaneshkimod, -an** *ni*
 COTTON CLOTH: **gidagiigin, -oon** *ni*
 WHITE CLOTH: **waabishkiigin, -oon** *ni*
CLOTHES
 CLOTHES: item of clothing **biizikiigan, -an** *ni*
 CHANGE CLOTHES: change one's clothes
  aanzikonaye *vai;* change s.o. with foot or
  body (e.g., clothes) **aanzikaw** *vta;* change
  s.o.'s clothes **aanzikonaye'** *vta;* change s.t.
  with foot or body (e.g., clothes) **aanzikan**
  vti
 PUT ON CLOTHES: put on one's clothes
  biizikonaye *vai*
 TAKE OFF CLOTHES: take off one's clothes
  giizikonaye *vai;* take s.o. off the body
  (e.g., clothes) **giizikaw** *vta;* take s.t. off the
  body (e.g., clothes) **giizikan** *vti*
 WASH CLOTHES: **giziibiiga'ige** *vai*
 WEAR NEW CLOTHES: **oshki'o** *vai*
CLOTHES IRON
 CLOTHES IRON: **zhooshkwega'igan, -an** *ni*
CLOTHES WRINGER
 CLOTHES WRINGER: **ziinaakwa'igan, -an**
  ni
CLOTHESLINE
 CLOTHESLINE: **agoojiganeyaab, -iin** *ni*
 CLOTHESLINE POLE: **agoojiganaatig, -
  oon** *ni*

CLOTHESPIN
CLOTHESPIN: **ziinaakwa'igan, -an** *ni*

CLOTHING
CHILDREN'S CLOTHING: item of children's clothing **abinoojiinh-biizikaagan, -an** *ni*

ITEM OF CLOTHING: **biizikiigan, -an** *ni*

MEN'S CLOTHING: item of men's clothing **ininii-biizikiigan** *ni*

WOMEN'S CLOTHING: item of women's clothing **ikwe-biizikiigan** *ni*

CLOUD
CLOUD: **aanakwad, -oon** *ni*

CLOUDS APPROACH: **biidaanakwad** *vii*

CLOUDS GO ALONG: **bimaanakwad** *vii*

CLOUDS GO AWAY: **animaanakwad** *vii*

CLOUDS MOVE ABOUT: **babaamaanakwad** *vii*

CLOUDS SEEN THROUGH: clouds can be seen through **waaseyaanakwad** *vii*

DARK CLOUDS: there are dark clouds **makadeyaanakwad** *vii*

RED CLOUDS: be red clouds **miskwaanakwad** *vii*

STORM CLOUDS: there are storm clouds **zegaanakwad** *vii*

WHITE CLOUDS: there are white clouds **waabishkaanakwad** *vii*

CLOUDY
CLOUDY: be cloudy **ningwaanakwad** *vii*

CLUB
CLUB SUITE CARD: **danens, -ag** *na*

CLUB
BALL-HEADED CLUB: ball-headed club **bikwaakwado-bagamaagan, -an** *ni*

WAR CLUB: war club **bagamaagan, -an** *ni*

COAL
COAL: **akakanzhe** *ni*

COALS
COALS: **akakanzhe** *ni;* be coals **akakanzhekaa, akakanzhekaamagad** *vii*

COAT
COAT: **babiinzikawaagan, -an** *ni*

PUT ON COAT: put on one's coat **biichibabiinzikawaagane** *vai*

TAKE OFF COAT: take off one's coat **giichibabiinzikawaagane** *vai*

WEAR A COAT: **gigibabiinzikawaagane** *vai*

COFFEE
COFFEE: **makade-mashkikiwaaboo** *ni;* **gaapii** *ni*

COIN
COIN: **zhooniyaans, -ag** *na;* **zhooniyaawaabik, -oog** *na*

COLD
COLD: be cold (as a liquid) **dakaagamin /dakaagami-/** *vii*

CAN'T TAKE THE COLD: **wakewaji** *vai*

COLD HAND: have a cold hand **dakininjii** *vai*

COLD HOUSE: be cold (as a house or room) **dakate, dakatemagad** *vii*

COLD RAIN: be cold rain **dakibiisaa, dakibiisaamagad** *vii*

COLD ROOM: be cold (as a house or room) **dakate, dakatemagad** *vii*

COLD WATER: **dakib** *ni*

COLD WEATHER: be cold (weather) **gisinaa, gisinaamagad** *vii*

COLD WIND: be a cold wind **dakaanimad** *vii*

FEEL COLD: **biingeji** *vai;* **dakamanji'o** *vai;* **giikaji** *vai*

HAVE A COLD: **dakaji** *vai*

WAKE FROM BEING COLD: **amadaji** *vai*

COLD
GET A COLD: **mizhaakigwe** *vai*

HAVE A COLD: **agigokaa** *vai*

COLLAPSE
COLLAPSE FROM OVERWORK: **gawanokii** *vai*

COLLAR
COLLAR: **apigwayawegwaajigan, -an** *ni*

COLLECT
COLLECT: collect s.o. **asigin** *vta;* **maawanji' ** *vta;* collect s.t. **asiginan** *vti;* **maawanjitoon** *vti2*

COLLECT MONEY AS A DONATION: **asigizhooniyaawe** *vai*

COLLEGE
COLLEGE: **gabe-gikendaasoowigamig, -oon** *ni*

COLLISION
COLLISION: they have a collision **bitaakoshkodaadiwag /bitaakoshkodaadi-/** *vai*

COLOR
GOOD COLOR: be a good color **minwaande, minwaandemagad** *vii;* **minwaanzo** *vai*

COLORED
COLORED A CERTAIN WAY: be colored a certain way **inaande, inaandemagad** *vii;* **inaanzo** *vai*

COMB
COMB: **binaakwaan, -an** *ni;* comb one's hair **binaakwe'o** *vai;* **nazikwe'o** *vai;* comb s.o. **binaakwe' /binaakwe'w-/** *vta;* **nazikwe' /nazikwe'w-/** *vta*

COME
COME: **bi-izhaa** *vai;* come (as time) **ojijise, ojijisemagad** *vii*

COME AS WIND FROM A CERTAIN PLACE: come as wind from a certain direction **ondaanimad** *vii*

COME ASHORE: **agwaataa** *vai;* come ashore in a boat **agwaa'o** *vai, also* **agwaa'am**; come ashore in canoe **mizhagaa** *vai*

COME FROM A CERTAIN PLACE: **ondaadad** *vii;* **ondaadizi** *vai;* **onjibaa** *vai;* **onjii** *vai;* come from a certain place (as smoke) **ondaabate, ondaabatemagad** *vii*

COME FROM A CERTAIN PLACE CRYING: **ondademo** *vai*

COME HERE: come here! **ondaas** *pc;* **ondaashaan** *pc*

COME IN: come into where s.o. is **biindigaw** *vta*

COME IN A BOAT: **biidaasamishkaa** *vai*

COME IN ANGER: **biijigidaazo** *vai*

COME IN FEAR: **biidaanimizi** *vai*
COME INSIDE: **biindige** *vai*
COME INTO VIEW: **bi-naagozi** *vai;* **bi-naagwad** *vii*
COME LAUGHING: **biidaapi** *vai*
COME LEAVING TRACKS: **biijikawe** *vai*
COME MAKING NOISE: come making noise (e.g., thunder) **biidwewidam** *vai2*
COME OUT OF THE WOODS: **bapaakwa'am** *vai2*
COME OUT OVER A HILL: **zaagajiwe** *vai*
COME SPEAKING: **biidwewidam** *vai2*
COME SUDDENLY INTO VIEW: come suddenly into view as from around a corner **zaagewe** *vai*
COME TELLING NEWS: **biidaajimo** *vai*
COME TO AN END: **ishkwaase, ishkwaasemagad** *vii*
COME TO BE: **bagami-ayaa, bagami-ayaamagad** *vii*
COME TO PASS: **bagami-ayaa, bagami-ayaamagad** *vii*
COME UP: come up to the surface of the water **mooshkamo** *vai*
COME UP TO: come up to s.o. **odish /odiS-/** *vta;* come up to s.t. **oditan** *vti*
COME WITH A LIGHT: **biidaazakwanenjige** *vai*
RAIN COMES: **biijibiisaa, biijibiisaamagad** *vii*

COME ON
COME ON: come on! **ambe** *pc;* **daga** *pc;* **naasanaa** *pc*

COME TO
COME TO: **aabaakawizi** *vai;* **mikawi** *vai*

COMEDY
COMEDY: be a comedy **gagiibaadaatese, gagiibaadaatesemagad** *vii*

COMFORTABLY
LIE COMFORTABLY: **minoshin** *vai*
SIT COMFORTABLY: **minwabi** *vai*

COMICAL
COMICAL: **wawiyazh** *pc*
THINK COMICAL: think s.o. comical **wawiyadenim** *vta*

COMING UP TO
COMING UP TO IN TIME: **ani-** *pv2,* also **ni-**

COMMISSION
COMMISSION: **anookii** *vai;* commission s.o. **anoozh /anooN-/** *vta*

COMMODITY FOOD
COMMODITY FOOD: **ashandiwin, -an** *ni*

COMMODITY STORE
COMMODITY STORE: **ashangewigamig, -oon** *ni*

COMMON PIN
COMMON PIN: **oshtigwaanzhaabonigan, -an** *ni*

COMPANION
COMPANION: **wiijiiwaagan, -ag** *na;* my companion **niwiidigemaagan, -ag /-wiidigemaagan-/** *na*

COMPANY
IN COMPANY WITH: **wiiji-** *pv4*

COMPASS
COMPASS: compass (drawing instrument) **waawiyebii'igan, -an** *ni*

COMPLETE
COMPLETE: **giizhi-** *pv4*

COMPLETELY
COMPLETELY: **wawiinge** *pc;* **wenda-** *pv4*

COMPUTER
COMPUTER: **mazinaabikiwebinigan, -an** *ni*

CONCRETE
MADE OF CONCRETE: be made of concrete **waabiganikaade, waabiganikaademagad** *vii*

CONCRETE ROAD
CONCRETE ROAD: **asinii-miikana, -n** *ni*

CONFUSE
CONFUSE: confuse s.o. by speech **wanim** *vta*

CONFUSED
CONFUSED: be confused **giiwashkweyendam** *vai2;* **wanaanimizi** *vai*

CONQUER
CONQUER: conquer s.o. **mamaazhi'** *vta;* conquer s.t. **mamaazhitoon** *vti2*

CONSCIOUSNESS
REGAIN CONSCIOUSNESS: **mikawi** *vai*

CONSEQUENTLY
CONSEQUENTLY: **indawaaj** *pc*

CONSERVATION OFFICER
CONSERVATION OFFICER: **wiiyaasi-dakoniwewinini, -wag** *na*

CONSIDER
CONSIDER: **maaminonendam** *vai2;* **naanaagadawendam** *vai2;* consider s.o. **maaminonenim** *vta;* **naanaagadawenim** *vta;* consider s.t. **maaminonendan** *vti;* **naanaagadawendan** *vti*

CONSIDERATION
GIVE TOO MUCH CONSIDERATION: **onzaamendam** *vai2*

CONSTIPATED
CONSTIPATED: be constipated **gibishaganzhii** *vai*

CONSTRICT
CONSTRICT: **wiibwaa, wiibwaamagad** *vii*

CONTEST
BEAT IN A CONTEST: beat s.o. in a contest **bakinaw** *vta;* beat people in a contest **bakinaage** *vai*

CONTINUALLY
CONTINUALLY: **apane** *pc;* **aabiji-** *pv4*

CONTRADICT
CONTRADICT: **aagonwetam** *vai2;* contradict s.o. **aagonwetaw** *vta;* contradict s.t. **aagonwetan** *vti*

CONTRARY
ACT CONTRARY TO INSTRUCTIONS: act contrary to s.o.'s instructions **gagaanzitaw** *vta*

CONTROL
CONTROL: control s.o. **dibenim** *vta;* control s.t. **dibendan** *vti*

CONTROLLED
CONTROLLED: be controlled **dibendaagozi** *vai;* **dibendaagwad** *vii*

CONVENE
CONVENE A COUNCIL: **zagaswe'iwe** *vai*

CONVERSE
CONVERSE: converse with s.o. **gaganoozh** /**gaganooN-**/ *vta;* they converse with each other **gaganoonidiwag** /**gaganoonidi-**/ *vai*

CONVINCE
CONVINCE: convince s.o. **gagaanzom** *vta*

COOK
COOK: cook (female) **jiibaakwewikwe**, **-g** *na;* cook (male) **jiibaakwewinini**, **-wag** *na;* **giizizekwe** *vai;* **jiibaakwe** *vai;* cook s.o. **jiibaakwaazh** /**jiibaakwaaN-**/ *vta;* cook s.t. **jiibaakwaadan** *vti;* cook (s.t.) for s.o. **giizizamaw** *vta*
COOK A CERTAIN WAY: cook (something) a certain way **inizekwe** *vai;* cook s.o. a certain way **iniz** /**inizw-**/ *vta;* cook s.t. a certain way **inizan** *vti*
COOK BY BOILING: cook s.o. by boiling **gabaashim** *vta;* cook s.t. by boiling **gabaatoon** *vti2*
COOK IN A HURRY: **ojaanimizekwe** *vai*
COOK ON THE COALS: cook (s.t.) on the coals **akakanzhebwe** *vai+o*
COOK OVER A FIRE: cook (s.t.) over a fire **abwe** *vai+o;* cook s.o. over a fire **abwaazh** /**abwaaN-**/ *vta;* cook s.t. over a fire **abwaadan** *vti*
COOK TENDER: cook s.o. tender **nookiz** /**nookizw-**/ *vta;* cook s.t. tender **nookizan** *vti*
COOK UNDER THE ASHES: cook (s.t.) under the ashes **ningwa'abwe** *vai+o*
COOK WELL: **minozekwe** *vai;* cook s.o. well **minoz** /**minozw-**/ *vta;* cook s.t. well **minozan** *vti*
COOK WITH: cook s.o. with something else **dagoz** /**dagozw-**/ *vta;* cook s.t. with something else **dagozan** *vti*
DONE COOKING: be done cooking **giizhide**, **giizhidemagad** *vii;* **giizizo** *vai, also* **giizhizo**
FINISH COOKING: finish cooking s.o. **giiziz** /**giizizw-**/ *vta;* finish cooking s.t. **giizizan** *vti*

COOK SHACK
COOK SHACK: **jiibaakwewigamig**, **-oon** *ni*

COOKED
COOKED TENDER: be cooked tender **nookide, nookidemagad** *vii;* **nookizo** *vai*
COOKED WITH: be cooked with something else **dagode, dagodemagad** *vii;* **dagozo** *vai*
INCOMPLETELY COOKED: be incompletely cooked **ashkide, ashkidemagad** *vii;* **ashkizo** *vai*
WELL COOKED: be well cooked **minode, minodemagad** *vii;* **minozo** *vai*

COOKIE
COOKIE: **bakwezhigaans, -ag** *na*

COOKING POT
COOKING POT: **jiibaakwewakik, -oog** *na*

COOL
COOL: **dakise** *vai;* **dakise, dakisemagad** *vii;* be cool (of a thing) **dakaa, dakaamagad** *vii;* **dakizi** *vai*
COOL OFF: **dakishin** *vai;* **dakisin** *vii;* cool off (as a liquid) **dakaagamisin** *vii*
COOL WEATHER: be cool (weather) **dakaayaa, dakaayaamagad** *vii, also* **dakiayaa**
SET TO COOL: set s.o. to cool **dakishim** *vta;* set s.t. to cool **dakisidoon** *vti2*

COOLED
COOLED BY THE WIND: be cooled by the wind **dakaashi** *vai;* **dakaasin** *vii*

COOP
CHICKEN COOP: **baaka'aakwenhwigamig, -oon** *ni*

COOT
COOT: **aajigade, -g** *na*

COPPER
COPPER: (piece of) copper **miskwaabik** *ni*

COPY
COPY IN WRITING: copy s.t. in writing **naasaabibii'an** *vti;* copy things in writing **naasaabibii'ige** *vai*

CORN
CORN: **mandaamin, -ag** *na*
EAR OF CORN: **mandaaminaak, -oon** *ni*
KERNEL OF CORN: **mandaamin, -ag** *na*

CORNFIELD
CORNFIELD: **mandaamini-gitigaan, -an** *ni*

CORNMEAL
CORNMEAL: **biisiboojigan** *na*

CORN SOUP
CORN SOUP: **mandaaminaaboo** *ni*

CORNER
CORNER OF A ROOM: be a corner of a room **jaangate, jaangatemagad** *vii*

CORNSTALK
CORNSTALK: **mandaaminashk, -oon** *ni*

CORRECT
CORRECT: **gwayak** *pc;* correct? **naayanh** *pc*

CORRECTLY
CORRECTLY: **weweni** *pc*
BEAD CORRECTLY: bead s.t. correctly (on a loom) **gwayakwaabidoo'an** *vti;* bead things correctly (on a loom) **gwayakwaabidoo'ige** *vai*
LIE CORRECTLY: **gwayakoshin** *vai;* **gwayakosin** *vii*
SPEAK CORRECTLY: **gwayakowe** *vai*
THINK CORRECTLY: **gwayakwendam** *vai2*
THREAD CORRECTLY: thread s.t. correctly **gwayakwaabidoo'an** *vti*
WRITE CORRECTLY: **gwayakobii'ige** *vai;* write s.t. correctly **gwayakobii'an** *vti*

COST
HAVE A CERTAIN COST: **inaginde, inagindemagad** *vii;* **inaginzo** *vai*

COTTAGE
COTTAGE: **niibinishiiwigamig**, **-oon** *ni*

COTTON
COTTON CLOTH: **babagiwayaaniigin**, **-oon** *ni, also* **bagiwayaaniigin; gidagiigin**, **-oon** *ni*

COTTONTAIL RABBIT
COTTONTAIL RABBIT: **manidoo-waabooz**, **-oog** *na*

COUCH
COUCH: **genwaakwak apabiwin** *ni;* **ginwaako-apabiwin**, **-an** *ni*

COUGH
COUGH: **ozosodam** *vai2*

COUGH MEDICINE
COUGH MEDICINE: **ozosodamoo-mashkiki** *ni*

COULD
COULD: could *modal* **daa-** *pv1*

COUNCIL
CONVENE A COUNCIL: **zagaswe'iwe** *vai*
COUNCIL MEETING: they have a council meeting **zagaswe'idiwag** /**zagaswe'idi-**/ *vai*

COUNCILLOR
COUNCILLOR: **gaagiigidoowinini**, **-wag** *na;* **giigidoowinini**, **-wag** *na;* **wegimaawabid** *na-pt;* **zagaswe'idiiwinini**, **-wag** *na*

COUNT
COUNT: **agindaaso** *vai;* count s.o. **agim** *vta;* count s.t. **agindan** *vti;* count (s.t.) for s.o. **agindamaw** *vta;* count (s.t.) for people **agindamaage** *vai*
COUNT IN: count s.o. in **dagwagim** *vta;* count s.t. in **dagwagindan** *vti*
COUNT OVER: **aandaginzo** *vai;* count s.o. over **aandagim** *vta;* count s.t. over **aandagindan** *vti*

COUNTED
COUNTED: be counted **aginjigaade**, **aginjigaademagad** *vii;* **aginjigaazo** *vai;* **aginzo** *vai*
COUNTED IN: be counted in **dagwaginde**, **dagwagindemagad** *vii;* **dagwaginzo** *vai*

COUNTRY
COUNTRY: **aki**, **-in** *ni*
CHANGE COUNTRIES: **aandakii** *vai*
RETURN TO OWN COUNTRY: return to one's own country **giiwekii** *vai*

COURAGEOUS
COURAGEOUS: be courageous **mangide'e** *vai*

COURT
IN COURT: be in court **onaakonige** *vai*

COURT MATTER
COURT MATTER: be a court matter **dibaakonigaade** *vai*

COURTHOUSE
COURTHOUSE: **dibaakonigewigamig**, **-oon** *ni*

COUSIN
CROSS-COUSIN: my (female's) female cross-cousin (mother's brother's daughter or father's sister's daughter) **indaangoshenh**, **-yag** /**-daangosheny-**/ *nad;* my (male's) male cross-cousin (male's father's sister's son or male's mother's brother's son) **niitaawis**, **-ag** /**-iitaawis-**/ *nad;* my cross-cousin of the opposite sex **niinimoshenh**, **-yag** /**-iinimosheny-**/ *nad*
PARALLEL COUSIN: my older male parallel cousin **nisayenh**, **-yag** /**-sayeny-**/ *nad;* my older female parallel cousin **nimisenh**, **-yag** /**-miseny-**/ *nad;* my parallel cousin of the opposite sex **indawemaa**, **-g** /**-dawemaaw-**/ *nad;* my younger parallel cousin **nishiime**, **-yag** /**-shiimey-**/ *nad*

COVER
COVER: cover s.o. **badagwana'** /**badagwana'w-**/ *vta;* cover s.t. **badagwana'an** *vti;* cover things **badagwana'ige** *vai*
COVER WITH BLANKETS: cover s.o. with blankets **agwazhe'** *vta*
COVER WITH BODY: cover s.o. with body **badagoshkaw** *vta;* cover s.t. with body **badagoshkan** *vti*
SHARE COVER WITH: share a cover with s.o. **wiidagwazhem** *vta*

COVERED
COVERED: be covered **badagwana'igaade**, **badagwana'igaademagad** *vii;* **badagwana'igaazo** *vai*
COVERED WITH BLANKETS: be covered with blankets **agwazhe** *vai*
LIE WITH FACE COVERED: lie with one's face covered **badagwiingweshin** *vai*

COVERING
COVERING: **agwazhe'on**, **-an** *ni*

COW
COW: **bizhiki**, **-wag** *na*

COWARDLY
COWARDLY: be cowardly **zhaagode'e** *vai*

COWHIDE
COWHIDE: **bizhikiwayaan**, **-ag** *na*

CRAB
CRAB: **ashaageshiinh**, **-yag** *na*

CRACK
CRACK: crack (e.g., glass or china) **baasikaa**, **baasikaamagad** *vii;* crack on impact **baasishin** *vai;* **baasisin** *vii;* crack s.o. **baasishim** *vta;* crack s.t. **baasisidoon** *vti2*
CRACK APART: **daashkikaa**, **daashkikaamagad** *vii*
CRACK BY HEAT: crack s.o. by heat **baasiz** /**baasizw-**/ *vta;* crack s.t. by heat **baasizan** *vti*
CRACK FROM HEAT: **baaside**, **baasidemagad** *vii;* **baasizo** *vai*
CRACK IN THE ICE: there is a crack in the ice **daashkikwadin** *vii*
CRACK USING SOMETHING: crack s.o. using something **baasa'** /**baasa'w-**/ *vta;* crack s.t. using something **baasa'an** *vti;* crack things using something **baasa'ige** *vai*
FALL AND CRACK HEAD: fall and crack one's head **baasindibeshin** *vai*

HEARD CRACKING: be heard cracking (as ice) **madwekwadin** *vii*

CRACKER
CRACKER: **bakwezhigaans, -ag** *na*

CRACKLINGS
CRACKLINGS: **zaasigan, -ag** *na*

CRADLE BOARD
CRADLE BOARD: **dikinaagan, -an** *ni*
BABY IN A CRADLE BOARD: **dakobinaawaswaan, -ag** *na*
HAVE A BABY IN A CRADLE BOARD: **dakobinaawaso** *vai*
IN CRADLE BOARD: be in a cradle board **dakobizo** *vai*

CRADLE BOARD FOOTREST
CRADLE BOARD FOOTREST: **apizideyaakwa'igan, -an** *ni*

CRADLE BOARD WRAPPER
CRADLE BOARD WRAPPER: **dikineyaab, -iin** *ni*

CRAFT
CRAFT: **anokaajigan, -an** *ni*

CRANBERRY
HIGHBUSH CRANBERRY: **aniibiimin, -an** *ni*
LOWBUSH CRANBERRY: **mashkiigimin, -ag** *na*

CRANBERRY BUSH
HIGHBUSH CRANBERRY BUSH: **aniibiiminagaawanzh, -iig** *na*
LOWBUSH CRANBERRY BUSH: **mashkiigiminagaawanzh, -iin** *ni*

CRANE
SANDHILL CRANE: **ajijaak, -wag** *na*

CRAPPIE
CRAPPIE: **gidagagwadaashi, -wag** *na*

CRATE
CRATE: **mitigo-makak, -oon** *ni*

CRAWL
ARRIVE CRAWLING: **bagamoode** *vai*
CRAWL A CERTAIN WAY: **inoode** *vai*
CRAWL ABOUT: **babaamoode** *vai*
CRAWL ALONG: **bimoode** *vai*
CRAWL AWAY: **animoode** *vai*
CRAWL FROM A CERTAIN PLACE: **ondoode** *vai*
CRAWL HERE: **biidoode** *vai*
CRAWL IN: **biindoode** *vii*
CRAWL IN A TIGHT PLACE: **zhegoode** *vai*
CRAWL OFF: **maadoode** *vai*
CRAWL OUT: **zaagidoode** *vai*
CRAWL TO A CERTAIN PLACE: **inoode** *vai*

CRAYFISH
CRAYFISH: **ashaageshiinh, -yag** *na*

CRAZY
CRAZY: be crazy **giiwanaadizi** *vai*

CREAK
CREAK: **giziibwewe** *vai*; **giziibwewe, giziibwewemagad** *vii*; **giziibweweshkaa** *vai*; **giziibweweshkaa, giziibweweshkaamagad** *vii*

CREAK IN THE WIND: **giziibweweyaashi** *vai*; **giziibweweyaasin** *vii*

CREDIT
GET CREDIT: **mazina'ige** *vai*; get credit from s.o. **mazina'amaw** *vta*

CREE
CREE: **omashkiigoo, -g** *na*
SPEAK CREE: **omashkiigoomo** *vai*

CREEK
CREEK: **ziibiins, -an** *ni*

CREEP
CREEP AWAY: **giimaadoode** *vai*

CRISP
BURNT CRISP: be burnt crisp **onzaamaakide, onzaamaakidemagad** *vii*; **onzaamaakizo** *vai*

CROOKED KNIFE
CROOKED KNIFE: **waagikomaan, -an** *ni*

CROSS
CROSS: **aazhideyaatig, -oog** *na*

CROSSCUT SAW
CROSSCUT SAW: **giishkiboojigan, -an** *ni*

CROSSED
SIT WITH LEGS CROSSED: **aazhoogaadebi** *vai*

CROW
CROW: **aandeg, -wag** *na*

CRUMBLE
CRUMBLE: crumble s.o. **biisibizh /biisibiN-/** *vta*; crumble s.t. **biisibidoon** *vti2*

CRUNCH
CRUNCH IN MOUTH: crunch s.o. in mouth **gaapam** *vta*; crunch s.t. in mouth **gaapandan** *vti*; crunch things in mouth **gaapanjige** *vai*

CRUSH
CRUSH BY FOOT OR BODY: crush s.o. by foot or body **zhishigoshkaw** *vta*; crush s.t. by foot or body **zhishigoshkan** *vti*
CRUSH WITH HANDS: crush s.o. with hands **zhishigobizh /zhishigobiN-/** *vta*; crush s.t. with hands **zhishigobidoon** *vti2*

CRUST
CRUST ON THE SNOW: there is a crust on the snow **onaabanad** *vii*

CRUTCH
CRUTCH: **aajiningwa'on, -an** *ni*; **edawi-zaka'on, -an** *ni*
USE CRUTCHES: **edawi-zaka'o** *vai*

CRY
CRY: **mawi** *vai*; cry for s.o. **mawim** *vta*; cry for s.t. **mawindan** *vti*
COME FROM A CERTAIN PLACE CRYING: **ondademo** *vai*
CRY A CERTAIN WAY: **inademo** *vai*
CRY A LITTLE: **mawiinsiwi** *vai*
CRY FOR A CERTAIN REASON: **ondademo** *vai*
CRY TO GO ALONG: **mookawaakii** *vai*
CRY WALKING ALONG: **bimademo** *vai*
GO ABOUT CRYING: **babaamademo** *vai*
GO TO A CERTAIN PLACE CRYING: **inademo** *vai*

MAKE CRY: make s.o. cry **moo'** *vta*
PRETEND TO CRY: **mawiikaazo** *vai*
STOP CRYING: **giishkowe** *vai*
CRYBABY
CRYBABY: be a crybaby **mawishki** *vai*
CUB
BEAR CUB: **makoons, -ag** *na*
CUCUMBER
CUCUMBER: **bipakoombens, -an** *ni*
CUFF
MOCCASIN CUFF: **apiganegwaajigan, -an** *ni, also* **apigwanegwaason, -an**
CULTURE HERO
CULTURE HERO: name of **aadizookaan** character viewed as culture hero and trickster **Wenabozho** *na, also* **Nenabozho***
CUP
CUP: **onaagaans, -an** *ni*
CUPBOARD
CUPBOARD: **ataasowin, -an** *ni*
CUPFUL
CERTAIN NUMBER OF CUPFULS: a certain number of cupfuls **dasonaagaans** *pc*
CURE
CURE OVER A FIRE: cure s.o. over a fire **abwewas /abwewasw-/** *vta;* cure s.t. over a fire **abwewasan** *vti;* cure things over a fire **abwewasige** *vai*
CURL
CURL HAIR BY HEAT: curl s.o.'s hair by heat **babiizigaakiz /babiizigaakizw-/** *vta*
CURLY
CURLY HAIR: have curly hair **babiizigindibe** *vai*
CURRENT
DRIFT ALONG ON CURRENT: **bimaaboode, bimaaboodemagad** *vii;* **bimaaboono** *vai*
DRIFT OFF ON THE CURRENT: **maadaaboode, maadaaboodemagad** *vii;* **maadaaboono** *vai*
CURTAIN
CURTAIN: **gibiiga'igan, -an** *ni*
CURTAINED
CURTAINED: be curtained **gibiiga'igaade, gibiiga'igaademagad** *vii*
CUSHION
CUSHION: **apisijigan, -an** *ni*
CUSTOM
HAVE A CERTAIN CUSTOM: **izhitwaa** *vai*
IT WAS THE CUSTOM TO: it was the custom to... **iko** *pc, also* **ko**
CUT
CUT: cut things **giishkizhige** *vai;* cut oneself **giishkizhodizo** *vai*
CUT A CERTAIN WAY: cut s.o. a certain way **inizh /inizhw-/** *vta;* cut s.t. a certain way **inizhan** *vti*
CUT A PIECE OFF: cut a piece off s.o. **bakwezh /bakwezhw-/** *vta;* cut a piece off s.t. **bakwezhan** *vti*

CUT ACCIDENTALLY: cut s.o. accidentally **bitizh /bitizhw-/** *vta;* cut s.t. accidentally **bitizhan** *vti*
CUT CARDS: **bakwenige** *vai*
CUT FIREWOOD: **manise** *vai;* cut s.t. as firewood **manisaadan** *vti;* cut (s.t.) as firewood for s.o. **manisaw** *vta*
CUT FRINGE: cut fringe in s.o. **niisiiwezh /niisiiwezhw-/** *vta;* cut fringe in s.t. **niisiiwezhan** *vti*
CUT HAIR: **giishkikozhiwe** *vai*
CUT INTO STRIPS: cut s.t. into strips **baanizhan** *vti*
CUT LONG: cut s.t. long (as something string-like) **ginwaabiigizh /ginwaabiigizhw-/** *vta;* cut s.t. long (as something string-like) **ginwaabiigizhan** *vti*
CUT MEAT INTO STRIPS: cut meat into strips for preservation **baanizhaawe** *vai*
CUT NAILS: cut one's own nails **giishkiganzhiikonidizo** *vai*
CUT OFF: cut s.o. off **giishkizh /giishkizhw-/** *vta;* cut s.t. off **giishkizhan** *vti;* cut things off **giishkizhige** *vai*
CUT OUT: cut s.o. out **mamizh /mamizhw-/** *vta;* cut s.t. out **mamizhan** *vti*
CUT SHORT: cut s.o. short (as something string-like) **dakwaabiigizh /dakwaabiigizhw-/** *vta;* cut s.t. short (as something string-like) **dakwaabiigizhan** *vti*
CUT STRAIGHT: cut s.o. straight **gwayakozh /gwayakozhw-/** *vta;* cut s.t. straight **gwayakozhan** *vti*
CUT THROUGH: cut through s.o. **giishkizh /giishkizhw-/** *vta;* cut s.t. **giishkizhan** *vti*
CUT TIMBER: **giishka'aakwe** *vai*
CUT TO PIECES: cut s.o. to pieces **bigishkizh /bigishkizhw-/** *vta;* cut s.t. to pieces **bigishkizhan** *vti*
CUT TO SHAPE: cut s.o. to shape **onikozh /onikoN-/** *vta;* cut s.t. to shape **onikodan** *vti*
GET CUT FALLING: **giishkishin** *vai*
MAKE A CUT: make a cut on s.o. **beshizh /beshizhw-/** *vta;* make a cut on s.t. **beshizhan** *vti*
CUTE
CUTE: be cute **wawiyadendaagwad** *vii*
CONSIDERED CUTE: be considered cute **wawiyadendaagozi** *vai*
LOOK CUTE: **wawiyazhinaagozi** *vai;* **wawiyazhinaagwad** *vii*
SOUND CUTE: **wawiyazhitaagozi** *vai;* **wawiyazhitaagwad** *vii*
THINK CUTE: think s.o. cute **wawiyadenim** *vta*

D

DAKOTA
DAKOTA: Dakota (Sioux) **bwaan, -ag** *na*
DAKOTA WOMAN: **bwaanikwe, -g** *na*
SPEAK DAKOTA: **bwaanimo** *vai;* speak
Dakota to s.o. **bwaanimotaw** *vta*

DAM
DAM: **gibaakwa'igan, -an** *ni;* dam s.o.
gibaakwa' /gibaakwa'w-/ *vta;* dam s.t.
gibaakwa'an *vti;* dam things **gibaakwa'ige**
vai

DAMAGE
DAMAGE: damage s.o. **banaaji'** *vta;* damage
s.t. **banaajitoon** *vti2*
DAMAGE WITH HANDS: damage s.o. with
hands **banaajibizh /banaajibiN-/** *vta;*
damage s.t. with hands **banaajibidoon** *vti2*

DAMAGED
DAMAGED: be damaged **banaadad** *vii;*
banaadizi *vai*

DAMMED
DAMMED: be shut (as or as with something
stick- or wood-like) **gibaakwa'igaade,**
gibaakwa'igaademagad *vii*

DAMP
DAMP: be damp **zhakaa, zhakaamagad** *vii;*
zhakizi *vai;* be damp (as something sheet-
like) **zhakiigad** *vii;* **zhakiigizi** *vai*

DANCE
DANCE: **niimi** *vai;* dance a war dance
bwaanzhii-niimi *vai;* dance for s.o.
niimikaw *vta;* they dance **niimi'idiwag**
/niimi'idi-/ *vai;* they dance a war dance
bwaanzhii-niimi'idiwag /bwaanzhii-
niimi'idi-/ *vai;* war dance **bwaanzhii-**
niimi'idiwin, -an *ni;* dance for people (for a
purpose) **niimikaage** *vai*
DANCE ABOUT: **babaamishimo** *vai*
DANCE ALONG: **bimishimo** *vai*
DANCE AWAY: **animishimo** *vai*
DANCE IN A CERTAIN PLACE:
dazhishimo *vai*
DANCE INSIDE: dance inside (as in a Grand
Entry) **biindigeshimo** *vai*
DANCE THE WOMEN'S DANCE: **ikwe-**
niimi *vai;* they dance the women's dance
ikwe-niimi'idiwag /ikwe-niimi'idi-/ *vai*
DANCE WITH: dance with s.o.
wiijishimotaw *vta*
GIVE A DANCE: **niimi'iwe** *vai*
MAKE DANCE: make s.o. dance **niimi'** *vta*
WOMEN'S DANCE: **ikwe-niimi'idiwin, -an**
ni

DANCE BELL
DANCE BELL: **zhinawa'oojigan, -an** *ni*

DANCE BUSTLE
DANCE BUSTLE: **bimoonjigan, -an** *ni*

DANCE HALL
DANCE HALL: **niimi'idiiwigamig, -oon** *ni*

DANCE OUTFIT
DANCE OUTFIT: **bwaanzhiiwi'on, -an** *ni*
WEAR A DANCE OUTFIT: **bwaanzhiiwi'o**
vai

DANCE SONG
DANCE SONG: **niimi'idii-nagamon, -an** *ni*

DANDRUFF
DANDRUFF: **wiinishagaandibaan** *ni*

DANGER
DANGER: be danger **aanimad** *vii*
THINK TO BE IN DANGER: think s.o. to be
in danger **naniizaanenim** *vta*

DANGEROUS
DANGEROUS: be dangerous **naniizaanad**
vii; **naniizaanizi** *vai*
CONSIDER DANGEROUS: consider s.o.
dangerous **naniizaanenim** *vta;* consider
s.t. dangerous **naniizaanendan** *vti*
CONSIDERED DANGEROUS: be
considered dangerous
naniizaanendaagwad *vii;* **zegendaagozi**
vai; **zegendaagwad** *vii*

DARK
DARK: be dark **bishagiishkaa,**
bishagiishkaamagad *vii;* **dibiki-ayaa** *vai;*
makadewaa, makadewaamagad *vii;*
makadewizi *vai;* be dark (as a liquid)
makadewaagamin /makadewaagami-/ *vii*
DARK AS NIGHT: be dark as night **gashkii-**
dibik-ayaa, gashkii-dibik-ayaamagad *vii*
DARK AT NIGHT: be very dark at night
gashkii-dibikad *vii*
DARK COLORED: be dark colored
bishagiishkaande,
bishagiishkaandemagad *vii;*
bishagiishkaanzo *vai*
DARK HOUSE: be dark (as in a room or
house) **dibikate, dibikatemagad** *vii*
DARK INDOORS: be dark indoors
bishagiishkate, bishagiishkatemagad *vii*
DARK ROOM: be dark (as in a room or
house) **dibikate, dibikatemagad** *vii*

DARKENED
DARKENED: be darkened (e.g. the moon or
sun in an eclipse) **aateyaabikishin** *vai*

DATE
CERTAIN DATE: be a certain date **daso-**
giizhigad *vii*
CERTAIN DATE OF THE MONTH: be a
certain date of the month **inaginzo** *vai*

DAUGHTER
DAUGHTER: my daughter **indaanis, -ag**
/-daanis-/ *nad, also* **indaan**
HAVE A DAUGHTER: **odaani** *vai;* **odaanisi**
vai

DAUGHTER-IN-LAW
DAUGHTER-IN-LAW: **na'aanganikwe, -g**
na

DAWN
DAWN: be dawn **waaban** *vii*
DAWN COMES: **biidaaban** *vii*
LIGHT AT DAWN: be light at dawn
waaseyaaban *vii*

WORK UNTIL DAWN: **waabananokii** *vai*

DAY

DAY: **giizhig** *na;* be day **giizhigad** *vii*

ABSENT A CERTAIN NUMBER OF
DAYS: be absent a certain number of days
dasogonendi *vai*

ALL DAY: **gabe-giizhik** *pc*

BAD DAY: be a bad day **maazhi-giizhigad** *vii*

CERTAIN DAY OF THE MONTH: be a
certain day of the month **dasogonagizi** *vai*

CERTAIN DAY OF THE WEEK: be a
certain day of the week **izhi-giizhigad** *vii*

CERTAIN NUMBER OF DAYS: a certain
number of days **daso-giizhik** *pc;* **dasogon**
pc; be a certain number of days
dasogonagad *vii*

CERTAIN NUMBER OF DAYS OLD: be a
certain number of days old **dasogonagizi**
vai

DAY AFTER TOMORROW: **awas-waabang**
pc

DAY BEFORE YESTERDAY: **awasonaago**
pc

EVERY DAY: **endaso-giizhik** *pc*

GONE A CERTAIN NUMBER OF DAYS:
be gone a certain number of days
dasogonendi *vai*

NICE DAY: be a nice day **mino-giizhigad** *vii*

SO LATE IN THE DAY: be so late in the day
apiichi-giizhigad *vii*

THE FIRST DAY: be the first day (of a
month) **maadaginzo** *vai*

DAYBREAK

DAYBREAK: be daybreak **biidaaban** *vii*

DEAD

DEAD: be dead **nibo** *vai*

HAVE A FEAST HONORING THE DEAD:
jiibenaake *vai*

DEAF

DEAF: be deaf **gagiibishe** *vai;* be deaf (in one
ear) **gibishe** *vai*

DEAL

DEAL: deal cards **oninige** *vai;* deal s.o. (e.g.,
cards) **onin** *vta*

DEATH

BEAT TO DEATH: beat s.o. to death
niiwana' /**niiwana'w-**/ *vta*

HAVE A DEATH IN FAMILY: have a death
in one's family **nibooke** *vai*

DEBT

GO COLLECT A DEBT: **naadazina'ige** *vai*

GO INTO DEBT: **mazina'ige** *vai*

DECEIVE

DECEIVE: deceive s.o. **wayezhim** *vta;* deceive s.o. in speech **giiwanim** *vta;* deceive
people **wayezhinge** *vai*

DECEMBER

DECEMBER: **manidoo-giizisoons** *na*

DECEPTIVE

DECEPTIVE: be deceptive in speech
giiwanimo *vai*

DECIDE

DECIDE: **inendam** *vai2;* decide what to do
onendam *vai2*

DECIDE A CERTAIN WAY: decide a certain
way about s.t. **inaakonan** *vti;* decide about
s.o. a certain way **inaakon** *vta;* decide
things a certain way **inaakonige** *vai*

DECIDE AGAINST: **aanizhiitam** *vai2*

DECIDE ON: decide on s.o. **onagim** *vta;*
onaakon *vta;* decide on s.t. **onaakonan** *vti*

DECIDED

DECIDED IN A CERTAIN WAY: be
decided in a certain way **inaakonigaade,**
inaakonigaademagad *vii*

DECISION

IT'S YOUR DECISION: **booshke** *pc, also*
booshke giniin

DECORATE

DECORATE: decorate s.o. **wawezhi'** *vta;*
decorate s.t. **wawezhitoon** *vti2;* decorate
things **wawezhichige** *vai*

DECORATED

DECORATED: **zazegaa** *pc;* be decorated
wawezhichigaade,
wawezhichigaademagad *vii;*
wawezhichigaazo *vai*

DECOY

DUCK DECOY: **zhiishiibikojigan, -ag** *na*

FISH DECOY: **okeyaw, -ag** *na*

DECREED

DECREED A CERTAIN WAY: be decreed a
certain way **inaakonigaade,**
inaakonigaademagad *vii*

DEED

DEED: **izhichigewin, -an** *ni*

DEEP

DEEP: be deep (of a body of water) **dimii,**
dimiimagad *vii*

DEEP SNOW: be deep snow **ishpaagonagaa,**
ishpaagonagaamagad *vii*

DEEP TO A CERTAIN EXTENT: be deep
to a certain extent **akwiindimaa,**
akwiindimaamagad *vii*

DEER

DEER: **waawaashkeshi, -wag** *na*

DEER HIDE

DEER HIDE: **waawaashkeshiwayaan, -ag** *na*

DEER MEAT

DEER MEAT: **waawaashkeshiwi-wiiyaas** *ni*

DEFEAT

DEFEAT: defeat s.o. **zhaagooji'** *vta;* defeat
s.o. in speech **zhaagoozom** *vta;* defeat s.t.
zhaagoojitoon *vti2;* defeat people
zhaagooji'iwe *vai*

DEFEAT IN A CONTEST OR GAME:
defeat s.o. in a contest or game **niiwezh**
/**niiweN-**/ *vta;* defeat people in a contest or
game **niiwezhiwe** *vai*

DEFECATE

DEFECATE: **miizii** *vai*

DEFLATE

DEFLATE: deflate s.t. **zhiigoojiinan** *vti*

DEJECTED
    DEJECTED: be dejected **osidaawendam** *vai2*
DEN
    DEN: **waanzh, -an** *ni*
DENIAL
    DENIAL: exclamation of denial **ine** *pc*
DENIM
    DENIM: **giboodiyegwaazoniigin, -oon** *ni*
DENSE
    DENSE: be dense **mashkawaa,
    mashkawaamagad** *vii;* **mashkawizi** *vai*
DENTAL PICTOGRAPH
    DENTAL PICTOGRAPH: dental pictograph
    on birch bark **mazinibaganjigan, -an** *ni*
    MAKE A DENTAL PICTOGRAPH: make a
    dental pictograph on birch bark
    mazinibaganjige *vai*
DENTIST
    DENTIST: **wiibidaa-mashkikiiwinini, -wag**
    na
DENY
    DENY: **aagonwetam** *vai2;* deny s.t.
    aagonwetan *vti;* deny what s.o. says
    aagonwetaw *vta*
DEPART
    DEPART: **maajaa** *vai,* also **ani-maajaa**
DEPEND
    DEPEND ON: depend on (s.t.) **apenimo**
    vai+o; depend on s.o. **apenimonodaw** *vta,*
    also **apenimodaw;** depend on s.t.
    apenimonodan *vti*
DEPRESSED
    FEEL DEPRESSED: **maanendam** *vai2,* also
    maazhendam; niisaanendam *vai*
DEPTH
    DETERMINE THE DEPTH: **debakii'ige** *vai*
    LIE TO A CERTAIN DEPTH: **apiichishin**
    vai; **apiichisin** *vii*
DEPTHS
    IN THE DEPTHS OF A BODY OF
    WATER: **anaamiindim** *pc*
DESIGN
    DESIGN: **mazinibii'igan, -an** *ni*
    HAVE A DESIGN: **mazinishin** *vai;* **mazinisin**
    vii
DESIRABLE
    DESIRABLE: be desirable **nandawendaagozi**
    vai; **nandawendaagwad** *vii*
DESIRE
    DESIRE: **misawendam** *vai2;* **nandawendam**
    vai2; desire s.o. **agaawaazh /agaawaaN-/**
    vta; **misawenim** *vta;* **nandawenim** *vta;*
    desire s.t. **agaawaadan** *vti;* **misawendan**
    vti; **nandawendan** *vti;* desire things
    misawenjige *vai*
    STRONGLY DESIRE: **ondendam** *vai2*
DESIRES
    HAVE INTENSE FEELINGS OR DESIRES:
    aakwendam *vai2*
DESK
    DESK: **apibii'igan, -an** *ni;* **ozhibii'ige-
    adoopowin, -an** *ni*

DESPAIR
    DESPAIR: **banaadendam** *vai2;* despair of s.o.
    banaadenim *vta;* despair of s.t.
    banaadendan *vti*
DESPITE
    DESPITE: **aanawi** *pc*
DESTINY
    HAVE A CERTAIN DESTINY: **inendaagozi**
    vai
DESTROY
    DESTROY: destroy s.t. **nishwanaajitoon**
    vti2; destroy s.o. **nishwanaaji'** *vta;* destroy
    things **nishwanaajichige** *vai*
DETERGENT
    LIQUID DETERGENT:
    giziibiiginaaganewaaboo *ni*
DETOUR
    DETOUR: **wiimaashkaa** *vai*
DEUCE
    DEUCE: **niizhoobii'igan, -ag** *na*
DEVIL
    DEVIL: **maji-manidoo, -g** *na*
DEW
    DEW: there is dew **mindookad** *vii*
DEW-CLAW GAME
    DEW-CLAW GAME: dew-claw game *plural*
    biipiinjigana'onag *na*
DIABETES
    HAVE DIABETES: **ziinzibaakwadowaapine**
    vai, also **ziinzibaakwadwaapine**
DIAMOND
    DIAMOND SUITE CARD: **gaanoo, -g** *na*
DIAPER
    DIAPER: **aanziyaan, -an** *ni*
DIARRHEA
    HAVE DIARRHEA: **zhaabokaawizi** *vai*
DIE
    DIE: **nibo** *vai*
    DIE FROM A FALL: **aapijishin** *vai*
    DIE IN A CERTAIN PLACE: **dapine** *vai*
    DIE IN AN ACCIDENT: **niiwanishin** *vai*
DIFFERENT
    DIFFERENT: **bakaan** *pc;* be different
    bakaanad *vii;* **bakaanizi** *vai*
    ALL DIFFERENT: **bebakaan** *pc*
DIFFICULT
    DIFFICULT: be difficult **zanagad** *vii;*
    zanagizi *vai*
    CONSIDER DIFFICULT: consider s.o. dif-
    ficult **zanagenim** *vta;* consider s.t. difficult
    zanagendan *vti;* consider things difficult
    zanagendam *vai2*
    MAKE IT DIFFICULT: make it difficult for
    s.o. **zanagi'** *vta*
DIG
    DIG: dig for s.o. **nandwaanikaazh
    /nandwaanikaaN-/** *vta;* dig for s.t.
    nandwaanikaadan *vti*
    DIG A HOLE: **waanike** *vai*
    DIG UP: dig up s.o. **moona' /moona'w-/** *vta;*
    dig up s.t. **moona'an** *vti;* dig up things
    moona'ige *vai*

DIME
DIME: **bezhizhooniyaans, -ag** *na;*
   zhooniyaans, -ag *na*
DINNER
EAT DINNER: eat dinner (noon meal)
   naawakwe-wiisini *vai;* eat s.t. for dinner
   (noon meal) **naawakwe-miijin** *vti3*
DINNER PLATE
DINNER PLATE: **desinaagan, -an** *ni*
DIP
DIP: dip s.o. **gondaabiigin** *vta;* dip s.t
   gondaabiiginan *vti*
DIP IN: dip s.t. in **jekaagaminan** *vti*
DIP UP: dip up things **gwaaba'ige** *vai*
DIPPER
DIPPER: **gwaaba'igan, -an** *ni*
DIRECT
DIRECT: **dibishkoo** *pc*
DIRECTION
IN THE DIRECTION OF: **gakeyaa** *pc, also*
   akeyaa, keyaa, nakakeyaa*
DIRECTOR
DIRECTOR: **odaakewigimaa, -g** *na, also*
   odaake-ogimaa
DIRT
DIRT: **wiiyagasenh** *ni*
DIRTY
DIRTY: be dirty **wiinad** *vii;* **wiinizi** *vai;* be
   dirty (as a liquid) **wiinaagamin**
   /wiinaagami-/ *vii*
DIRTY HAND: have a dirty hand **wiinininjii**
   vai
DIRTY SCALP: have a dirty scalp
   wiinishagaandibe *vai*
MAKE DIRTY: make s.o. dirty **wiini'** *vta;*
   make s.t. dirty **wiinitoon** *vti2;* make things
   dirty **wiinichige** *vai*
TELL A DIRTY STORY: **wiinaajimo** *vai*
DISAGREE
DISAGREE: disagree with s.o. (of something
   consumed) *inverse forms of:* **maanikaw-** *vta*
DISAGREEABLE
CONSIDER DISAGREEABLE: consider s.o.
   disagreeable **maanenim** *vta;* consider s.t.
   disagreeable **maanendan** *vti*
CONSIDERED DISAGREEABLE: be considered disagreeable **maanendaagozi** *vai;*
   maanendaagwad *vii*
DISAPPEARED
DISAPPEARED: disappeared! **weniban** *pc*
DISAPPOINTED
DISAPPOINTED: be disappointed
   minjinawezi *vai*
DISAPPROVE
DISAPPROVE: disapprove of s.o. **zhiingenim**
   vta; disapprove of s.t. **zhiingendan** *vti;*
   they disapprove of each other
   zhiingenindiwag /zhiingenindi-/ *vai*
DISAPPROVED
DISAPPROVED OF: be disapproved of
   zhiingendaagozi *vai;* **zhiingendaagwad**
   vii

DISBELIEVE
DISBELIEVE: disbelieve s.o. **aagonweyenim**
   vta
DISCOMFORT
WALK WITH DISCOMFORT: **maanose** *vai*
DISCONNECT
DISCONNECT: disconnect s.o. **gidiskin** *vta;*
   disconnect s.t. **gidiskinan** *vti*
DISCONNECT WITH HANDS: disconnect
   s.o. with hands **gidiskibizh /gidiskibiN-/**
   vta; disconnect s.t. with hands
   gidiskibidoon *vti2*
DISCOURAGE
DISCOURAGE: discourage s.o. **aanishim** *vta*
DISEASE
DISEASE: **aakoziwin, -an** *ni*
CATCH A DISEASE: **mizizi** *vai*
DISEMBARK
DISEMBARK: **gabaa** *vai;* disembark s.o.
   gabaa' *vta*
TELL TO DISEMBARK: tell s.o. to
   disembark **gabaanaazha'**
   /gabaanaazha'w-/ *vta*
DISEMBOWEL
DISEMBOWEL: disembowel s.o.
   gijinagizhiin *vta*
DISGUSTING
CONSIDER DISGUSTING: consider s.o.
   disgusting **gagwaanisagenim** *vta;* consider
   s.t. disgusting **gagwaanisagendan** *vti*
CONSIDERED DISGUSTING: be consid-
   ered disgusting **gagwaanisagendaagozi**
   vai; **gagwaanisagendaagwad** *vii*
DISH
DISH: **onaagan, -an** *ni*
BIRCH BARK DISH: **wiigwaasinaagan, -an**
   ni
WASH DISHES: **giziibiiginaagane** *vai*
WIPE DISHES: **gaasiinaagane** *vai*
WOODEN DISH: **mitigonaagan, -an** *ni*
DISH GAME
PLAY THE DISH GAME: **bagese** *vai*
DISH PAN
DISH PAN: **gichi-onaagan** *ni*
DISH TOWEL
DISH TOWEL: **giziiyaabika'igan, -an** *ni*
DISLIKE
DISLIKE: dislike s.o. **aanawenim** *vta;*
   zhiingenim *vta;* dislike s.t. **aanawendan**
   vti; **zhiingendan** *vti;* they dislike each other
   zhiingenindiwag /zhiingenindi-/ *vai;* dis-
   like things **aanawenjige** *vai*
DISLIKED
DISLIKED: be disliked **aanawendaagozi** *vai;*
   aanawendaagwad *vii;* **zhiingendaagozi**
   vai; **zhiingendaagwad** *vii*
DISMANTLE
DISMANTLE: dismantle s.o. **biigon** *vta;*
   dismantle s.t. **biigonan** *vti*
DISOBEDIENT
DISOBEDIENT: be disobedient
   zhazhiibitam *vai2*

DISPERSE
DISPERSE: **biiwise** *vai;* **biiwise, biiwise꞉magad** *vii*

DISRESPECT
SHOW DISRESPECT: show disrespect for s.o. **baapinodaw** *vta*

DISSATISFIED
DISSATISFIED: be dissatisfied (with what has been given) **mindawe** *vai*

DISTANCE
CERTAIN DISTANCE: be a certain distance **apiichaa, apiichaamagad** *vii*
HEARD SPEAKING AT A DISTANCE: be heard speaking at a distance **debwewidam** *vai2*
SOME DISTANCE: **gomaapii** *pc*

DISTANT
DISTANT: **waasa** *pc*
DISTANT SIGHT: be a distant sight **naawinaagozi** *vai;* **naawinaagwad** *vii*

DISTRACT
DISTRACT: distract s.o. **wanishkwe'** *vta*

DISTRACTED
DISTRACTED: be distracted **wanishkweyendam** *vai*

DISTRESS
IN DISTRESS: be in distress **aanimizi** *vai*

DISTRIBUTE
DISTRIBUTE: **maada'ookii** *vai;* distribute (s.t.) to s.o. **maada'oozh /maada'ooN-/** *vta;* they distribute (s.t.) to each other **maada'oonidiwag /maada'oonidi-/** *vai*

DISTURB
DISTURB BY SPEECH: disturb s.o. by speech **wanishkwem** *vta*
DISTURB SLEEP: disturb s.o.'s sleep **wapaa'** *vta*

DISTURBANCE
DISTURBANCE: be a disturbance **aanimad** *vii*

DISTURBED
DISTURBED: be disturbed **ishkendam** *vai2;* be disturbed in one's mind **mamiidaawendam** *vai2*

DIVE
DIVE: **googii** *vai*

DIVIDE
RIVER DIVIDES: divide (as a river) **baketigweyaa, baketigweyaamagad** *vii*

DIVORCE
DIVORCE: they divorce each other **webinidiwag /webinidi-/** *vai*

DIZZY
DIZZY: be dizzy **giiwashkwe** *vai;* **giiwashkweyaabandam** *vai2*
MAKE DIZZY: make s.o. dizzy (especially of a substance) *inverse forms of:* **giiwashkweshkaw-** *vta*

DO
DO: do something **doodam** *vai2;* do something to s.o. **doodaw** *vta;* do something to s.t. **doodan** *vti;* they do something to each other **doodaadiwag /doodaadi-/** *vai;* do

something to oneself **doodaadizo** *vai;* **doodaazo** *vai*
DO A CERTAIN THING: **inakamigizi** *vai*
DO A CERTAIN WAY: do things a certain way **izhichige** *vai*
DO AMAZING THINGS: **maamakaajichige** *vai*
DO EXACTLY: **wawiingechige** *vai*
DO GOOD: do good things **minochige** *vai*
DO IN VAIN: **aanawewizi** *vai*
DO RIGHT: do things right **gwayakochige** *vai*
DO SKILFULLY: **wawiingechige** *vai*
DO WELL: do things well **minochige** *vai*
FREQUENTLY DO: **nitaa-** *pv4*
MAKE DO: make s.o. do something **izhi'** *vta*
NOT KNOW WHAT TO DO: **gwiinawi-doodam** *vai2*
TRY TO DO: try to do s.t. **wiikwajitoon** *vti2*
UNABLE TO DO: be unable to do something **bwaanawi'o** *vai;* be unable to do s.t. **bwaanawitoon** *vti2;* be unable to do something to s.o. **bwaanawi'** *vta*

DOCK
DOCK: **niminaaweyaandawaagan, -an** *ni*

DOCTOR
DOCTOR: **mashkikiiwinini, -wag** *na;* doctor (female) **mashkikiiwininiikwe, -g** *na;* doctor s.o. **mashkikiikaazh /mashkikiikaaN-/** *vta;* **nanaandawi'** *vta;* doctor people **nanaandawi'iwe** *vai*

DOCUMENT
DOCUMENT: **mazina'igan, -an** *ni*

DODGE
DODGE: **dabazi** *vai, also* **dabazii***

DOE
DOE: **oniijaaniw, -ag** *na*

DOG
DOG: **animosh, -ag** *na;* my dog **inday, -ag /-day-/** *nad*
FEMALE DOG: **gishkishenh, -yag** *na*
HAVE A DOG: **odayi** *vai*
HUNTING DOG: **giiwosewasim, -oog** *na, also* **giiyosewasim**
MALE DOG: **naabesim, -oog** *na*

DOGFISH
DOGFISH: **zhigwameg, -wag** *na*

DOGWOOD
DOGWOOD: red osier (locally known as dogwood) **miskwaabiimizh, -iig** *na*

DOING
WAY OF DOING: **izhichigewin, -an** *ni*

DOLL
DOLL: **mazinichigan, -ag** *na;* **odaminwaagan, -ag** *na*
DOLL OF HAY OR GRASS: **mazinashkibijigan, -ag** *na*
DOLL OF PROCESSED BASSWOOD BARK FIBER: **asigobaani-mazinichigan, -ag** *na*

DOLLAR
CERTAIN NUMBER OF DOLLARS: a certain number of dollars **daswaabik** *pc*

EIGHT DOLLARS: **ishwaaswaabik** *pc, also* **nishwaaswaabik***
FIVE DOLLARS: **naanwaabik** *pc*
FOUR DOLLARS: **niiwaabik** *pc*
NINE DOLLARS: **zhaangaswaabik** *pc*
ONE DOLLAR: **bezhigwaabik** *pc*
SEVEN DOLLARS: **niizhwaaswaabik** *pc*
SIX DOLLARS: **ingodwaaswaabik** *pc, also* **ningodwaaswaabik***
TEN DOLLARS: **midaaswaabik** *pc*
THREE DOLLARS: **niswaabik** *pc*
TWO DOLLARS: **niizhwaabik** *pc*

DOMESTIC ANIMAL
DOMESTIC ANIMAL: **awakaan, -ag** *na*

DON'T
DON'T: **gego** *pc*
DON'T BOTHER: **maanoo** *pc*
DON'T CARE: **maanoo** *pc*
DON'T EVER: **gego wiikaa** *pc*
DON'T IN ANY WAY: **gego ganage** *pc*
I DON'T KNOW WHAT: I don't know what *inanimate dubitative* **wegodogwen, -an** *pr*
JUST DON'T: **gego bina** *pc*
YOU DON'T HAVE TO: **gaawiin memwech** *pc*

DONATION
COLLECT MONEY AS A DONATION: **asigizhooniyaawe** *vai*

DOOR
DOOR: **ishkwaandem, -an** *ni*
BY A DOOR: **jiigishkwaand** *pc*
LODGE DOOR COVER: **gibishkwaande'on, -an** *ni*

DOUBTS
HAVE DOUBTS: have doubts about s.o. **zhaagwenim** *vta*

DOUGHNUT
DOUGHNUT: **bookadinigan, -ag** *na, also* **bwaakadinigaazod**

DOVE
DOVE: **omiimii, -g** *na*

DOWN
DOWN: down from it **niisayi'ii** *pc*
CLIMB DOWN: **niisaandawe** *vai;* climb down fast **niisaandawebizo** *vai*
KNOCK DOWN OFF WITH HANDS: knock s.o. down off something with hands **diitibibizh /diitibibiN-/** *vta;* knock s.t. down off something with hands **diitibibidoon** *vti2*
PULL DOWN: pull s.o. down **niisibizh /niisibiN-/** *vta;* pull s.t. down **niisibidoon** *vti2*
RUN DOWN: **niisaandawebatoo** *vai*
TEAR DOWN: tear s.o. down **niisibizh /niisibiN-/** *vta;* tear s.t. down **niisibidoon** *vti2*

DOWNHILL
GO DOWNHILL: **niisaakiiwe** *vai*
RUN DOWNHILL: **niisaakiiwebatoo** *vai*

DOWNSTAIRS
GO DOWNSTAIRS: **niisaandawe** *vai*

DOWNSTREAM
DOWNSTREAM: **niisaajiwan** *pc*

DOZE
DOZE: **bishkongwashi** *vai*

DRAFT ANIMAL
DRAFT ANIMAL: **odaabii'aagan, -ag** *na*

DRAG
DRAG: drag (something) **odaabii** *vai;* drag s.o. **odaabaazh /odaabaaN-/** *vta;* drag s.t. **odaabaadan** *vti*
DRAG ALONG: drag s.o. along **bimidaabaazh /bimidaabaaN-/** *vta;* drag s.t. along **bimidaabaadan** *vti*
DRAG ASHORE: drag s.o. ashore **agwaadaabaazh /agwaadaabaaN-/** *vta;* drag s.t. ashore **agwaadaabaadan** *vti;* drag something ashore **agwaadaabii** *vai*
DRAG AWAY: **animidaabii** *vai*
DRAG HERE: **biijidaabii** *vai;* drag s.o. here **biijidaabaazh /biijidaabaaN-/** *vta;* drag s.t. here **biijidaabaadan** *vti*
DRAG INTO THE WATER: drag s.o. into the water **bakobiidaabaazh /bakobiidaabaaN-/** *vta;* drag s.t. into the water **bakobiidaabaadan** *vti*
DRAG TO A CERTAIN PLACE: drag s.o. to a certain place **izhidaabaazh /izhidaabaaN-/** *vta;* drag s.t. to a certain place **izhidaabaadan** *vti*

DRAGONFLY
DRAGONFLY: **oboodashkwaanishiinh, -yag** *na*

DRAIN
DRAIN DRY: drain s.t. dry **iskandan** *vti*

DRAPES
DRAPES: **gibiiga'igan, -an** *ni*

DRAW
DRAW WITH MOUTH: draw on s.o. with mouth (e.g., a pipe) **wiikwam** *vta;* draw on s.t. with mouth **wiikwandan** *vti;* draw on things with mouth **wiikwanjige** *vai*

DRAW WATER
DRAW WATER: **gwaaba'ibii** *vai*

DRAW
DRAW: draw s.o. **mazinibii' /mazinibii'w-/** *vta;* draw s.t. **mazinibii'an** *vti;* draw things **mazinibii'ige** *vai*
DRAW A CIRCLE: **waawiyebii'ige** *vai*

DRAWING
DRAWING: **mazinibii'igan, -an** *ni*

DRAWKNIFE
DRAWKNIFE: **mookojigan, -an** *ni*

DRAWSTRING
DRAWSTRING: **giboobijiganeyaab, -iin** *ni*

DREAM
DREAM: dream of s.o. **bawaazh /bawaaN-/** *vta;* dream of s.t. **bawaadan** *vti;* have dreams **bawaajige** *vai*
BAD DREAM: have a bad dream **giiwanaadingwaam** *vai*
DREAM A CERTAIN WAY: **inaabandam** *vai2*

SCARY DREAM: have a scary dream
zegaabandam *vai2*
SEE A CERTAIN WAY AS IN A DREAM:
see s.o. a certain way as in a dream
inaabam *vta;* see s.t. a certain way as in a
dream **inaabandan** *vti*

DRESS
DRESS: **majigoode, -yan** *ni;* my dress
ingoodaas, -an /-goodaas-/ *nid*
BUCKSKIN DRESS: buckskin dress
bashkweginagooday, -an *ni*
CHANGE DRESS: change one's dress
aandagoode *vai*
JINGLE DRESS: **ziibaaska'iganagooday, -an**
ni
PUT ON DRESS: put on one's dress
biitagoode *vai*
TAKE OFF DRESS: take off one's dress
giitagoode *vai*

DRESS
DRESS: **biizikonaye** *vai;* dress s.o.
biizikonaye' *vta*
DRESS A CERTAIN WAY: **inikonaye** *vai;*
izhi'o *vai*
DRESS IN A NEW OUTFIT: **oshkikonaye**
vai
DRESS IN RED: **miskwaakonaye** *vai*
DRESS UP: **wawezhi'o** *vai;* **zazegaa'o** *vai;*
dress s.o. up **wawezhi'** *vta*
DRESS WARMLY: **giizhoo'o** *vai*
DRESS WELL: **mino'o** *vai*

DRESSED
DRESSED: be dressed **biizikonaye** *vai*
DRESSED UP: **zazegaa** *pc;* be dressed up
nanaa'ii *vai*

DRESSED-UP
DRESSED-UP MAN: **zazegaa-inini, -wag** *na*
DRESSED-UP WOMAN: **zazegaa-ikwe,**
-wag *na*

DRESSER
DRESSER: **wiikobijigan, -an** *ni*

DRIED
DRIED: **baate-** *pv4;* be dried **baasigaade,**
baasigaademagad *vii;* **baasigaazo** *vai*
DRIED OUT: be dried out **gaaskide,**
gaaskidemagad *vii;* **gaaskizo** *vai*

DRIFT
DRIFT ALONG ON CURRENT:
bimaaboode, bimaaboodemagad *vii;*
bimaaboono *vai*
DRIFT AWAY: **animaabogo** *vai;*
animaaboode, animaaboodemagad *vii*
DRIFT AWAY ON THE WAVES: **animaa'an**
vii; **animaa'ogo** *vai*
DRIFT OFF ON THE CURRENT:
maadaaboode, maadaaboodemagad *vii;*
maadaaboono *vai*
DRIFT OFF ON THE WAVES: **maadaa'an**
vii; **maadaa'ogo** *vai*

DRILL
DRILL: **bagone'igan, -an** *ni;* drill s.o. **bagone'**
/bagone'w-/ *vta;* drill s.t. **bagone'an** *vti*

DRINK
DRINK: drink (s.t.) **minikwe** *vai+o*

CHOKE WHILE DRINKING: **bakwenibii**
vai
DRINK AND BE MERRY: **minobii** *vai*
DRINK QUICKLY: drink s.t. quickly
ziikaapidan *vti*
DRINK TOO MUCH: **onzaamibii** *vai*
GIVE A DRINK: give s.o. a drink **mina'** *vta*
GIVE TOO MUCH TO DRINK: give s.o. too
much to drink **onzaamibazh**
/onzaamibaN-/ *vta*
LOOK FOR A DRINK: **nandoobii** *vai*
UNABLE TO FIND A DRINK: be unable to
find a drink **gwiinobii** *vai*

DRINKING GLASS
DRINKING GLASS: **mikwamiiwinaagaans,**
-an *ni*

DRINKING VESSEL
DRINKING VESSEL: **minikwaajigan, -an** *ni*

DRIP
DRIP: **onjigaa, onjigaamagad** *vii*
DRIP DOWN: **bangigaa, bangigaamagad** *vii*
DRIP FAST: **gizhiigaa, gizhiigaamagad** *vii*
START TO DRIP: **maajigaa,**
maajigaamagad *vii*

DRIVE
DRIVE: **odaabii'iwe** *vai;* drive s.o. (e.g., a
draft animal or a car) **odaabii'** *vta*
ARRIVE DRIVING: **bagamibide,**
bagamibidemagad *vii;* **bagamibizo** *vai;*
bagamidaabii'iwe *vai*
DRIVE ABOUT: **babaamibide,**
babaamibidemagad *vii;* **babaamibizo**
vai; **babaamidaabii'iwe** *vai*
DRIVE ACROSS: **aazhogebizo** *vai;*
aazhogedaabii'iwe *vai;* **aazhoodaabii'iwe**
vai
DRIVE ALONG: **bimibide, bimibidemagad**
vii; **bimibizo** *vai;* **bimidaabii'iwe** *vai;*
drive s.o. along **bimibizoni'** *vta;* drive s.t.
along **bimibizonitoon** *vti2;* drive people
along (as in a bus) **bimiwizhiwe** *vai*
DRIVE ALONG IN A WAGON OR
SLEIGH: drive along quickly in a wagon
or sleigh **bimidaabiiba'igo** *vai*
DRIVE ALONG THE SHORE: **jiigewebizo**
vai; **jiigewedaabii'iwe** *vai*
DRIVE AT A CERTAIN SPEED:
apiichibide, apiichibidemagad *vii;*
apiichibizo *vai*
DRIVE AT NIGHT: **niibaabizo** *vai*
DRIVE AWAY: **animibide, animibidemagad**
vii; **animibizo** *vai;* **animidaabii'iwe** *vai;*
drive away with horses **animiba'igo** *vai;*
drive away with s.o. (e.g., a car)
animibizoni' *vta;* drive away with s.t.
animibizonitoon *vti2*
DRIVE AWAY MAKING NOISE:
animwewebide, animwewebidemagad
vii; **animwewebizo** *vai*
DRIVE AWAY WITH A LIGHT:
animaazakonenjigebizo *vai*
DRIVE FAST: **gizhiibizo** *vai;* **gizhiidaabii'iwe**
vai

DRIVE FROM A CERTAIN PLACE:
  onjibide, onjibidemagad *vii;* onjibizo *vai;*
  onjidaabii'iwe *vai*
DRIVE HERE: biijibide, biijibidemagad *vii;*
  biijibizo *vai;* biijidaabii'iwe *vai*
DRIVE HERE WITH A LIGHT:
  biidaazakonebizo *vai*
DRIVE HOME: giiwedaabii'iwe *vai*
DRIVE IN: drive in biinjibide,
  biinjibidemagad *vii;* biinjibizo *vai*
DRIVE INSIDE: biindigebide,
  biindigebidemagad *vii;* biindigebizo *vai*
DRIVE OFF: maajidaabii'iwe *vai;*
  maajiibide, maajiibidemagad *vii;*
  maajiibizo *vai;* drive off in a wagon
  maajidaabiiba'igo *vai*
DRIVE OFF DRAWN BY HORSES:
  maajiiba'igo *vai*
DRIVE OFF TO THE SIDE: bakebide,
  bakebidemagad *vii;* bakebizo *vai*
DRIVE SLOWLY: bejibide, bejibidemagad
  vii; bejibizo *vai*
DRIVE SUDDENLY INTO VIEW:
  zaagewebide, zaagewebidemagad *vii;*
  zaagewebizo *vai*
DRIVE TO A CERTAIN PLACE: ipide,
  ipidemagad *vii;* ipizo *vai;* izhidaabii'iwe
  vai; drive s.o. to a certain place ipizoni'
  vta; drive s.t. to a certain place ipizonitoon
  vti2
GET LOST DRIVING: wanibizo *vai*
HEARD DRIVING ALONG: be heard driving
  along bimwewebide,
  bimwewebidemagad *vii;* bimwewebizo
  vai
HEARD DRIVING HERE: be heard driving
  here biidwewebide, biidwewebidemagad
  vii; biidwewebizo *vai*
STOP DRIVING: noogibide,
  noogibidemagad *vii;* noogibizo *vai*
TURN DRIVING: gwekibizo *vai*
DRIVE GAME
  DRIVE GAME: apagajinaazhikaage *vai;*
  drive game for s.o. apagajinaazhikamaw
  vta; drive game as s.o. apagajinaazhikaw
  vta
DRIVER
  DRIVER: odaabii'iwewinini, -wag *na*
  TAXI DRIVER: bimiwizhiwewinini, -wag *na*
DRIVER'S LICENSE
  DRIVER'S LICENSE: odaabii'iwe-
  mazina'igaans, -an *ni*
DROP
  DROP: drop s.o. bangishim *vta;* drop s.t.
  bangisidoon *vti2*
  LET DROP: let s.o. drop banin *vta;* let s.t.
  drop baninan *vti*
  LET DROP FROM MOUTH: let s.o. drop
  from one's mouth bagidam *vta;* let s.t.
  drop from one's mouth bagidandan *vti*
DROP-OFF
  DROP-OFF: there is a drop-off
  giishkaamikaa, giishkaamikaamagad *vii*

DROWN
  DROWN: gibwanaabaawe *vai*
DRUGGIST
  DRUGGIST: mashkikii-adaawewinini, -wag
  na, also mashkikiiwi-adaawewinini
DRUGSTORE
  DRUGSTORE: mashkikii-adaawewigamig,
  -oon *ni,* also mashkikiiwi-adaawewigamig
DRUM
  DRUM: dewe'igan, -ag *na;* drum on s.o.
  madwe' /madwe'w-/ *vta;* drum on s.t.
  madwe'an *vti*
  MIDE DRUM: mitigwakik, -oog *na*
  POUND ON DRUM: baaga'akokwe *vai*
DRUMSTICK
  DRUMSTICK: dewe'iganaak, -oon *na,* also
  dewe'iganaatig; drumstick for hand drum
  baaga'akokwaan, -an *ni*
DRUNK
  DRUNK: be drunk giiwashkwebii *vai*
  MAKE DRUNK: make s.o. drunk
  giiwashkwebazh /giiwashkwebaN-/ *vta*
DRY
  DRY: be dry baaso *vai;* baate, baatemagad
  vii; bengozi *vai;* bengwan *vii;* dry s.o.
  baas /baasw-/ *vta;* dry s.o. using something
  bengwa' /bengwa'w-/ *vta;* dry s.t. baasan
  vti; dry s.t. using something bengwa'an *vti*
  DRAIN DRY: drain s.t. dry iskandan *vti*
  DRY BY SMOKING: dry s.o. by smoking
  gaaskiz /gaaskizw-/ *vta;* dry s.t. by
  smoking gaaskizan *vti*
  DRY UP: dry up (of a body of water) iskate,
  iskatemagad *vii*
DRY WOOD
  DRY WOOD: mishiiwaatig, -oon *ni*
DRYING RACK
  DRYING RACK: drying rack for strips of
  meat over a fire abwaanaak, -oon *ni*
DUCK
  DUCK: zhiishiib, -ag *na*
  HUNT DUCKS: nandawishibe *vai*
DUCK DECOY
  DUCK DECOY: zhiishiibikojigan, -ag *na*
DULL
  DULL: be dull ashiwaa, ashiwaamagad *vii*
DULUTH
  DULUTH: Onigamiinsing *place*
DUMB
  DUMB: be dumb bagwanawizi *vai*
DUMP
  DUMP: ziigwebinigan, -an *ni*
DUMPLING
  DUMPLING: napodin, -ag *na*
  MAKE DUMPLINGS: napodinike *vai*
DUMPLING SOUP
  DUMPLING SOUP: bisigadanaaboo *ni*
DURING
  DURING: megwaa *pc*
DUST
  DUST: wiiyagasenh *ni*

DWARF
HAIRY-FACED BANK-DWELLING
DWARF SPIRIT: **memegwesi, -wag** *na*
DYE
DYE: **atisigan, -an** *ni, also* **adisigan**; dye s.o.
atis /atisw-/ *vta, also* **adis**; dye s.t. **atisan**
vti, also **adisan**; dye things **atisige** *vai, also*
adisige
DYNAMITE
DYNAMITE: **baasaabikizigan, -an** *ni*

E

EAGER
EAGER: be eager **gwaashkwezi** *vai;*
wewiibendam *vai;* be eager to do s.t.
ojaanimitoon *vti2*
EAGLE
BALD EAGLE: **migizi, -wag** *na*
GOLDEN EAGLE: **giniw, -ag** *na*
EAR
EAR: my ear **nitawag, -an /-tawag-/** *nid*
INFECTED EAR: have an infected ear
miniiwitawage *vai*
INSIDE EAR: inside an ear **biinjitawag** *pc*
EAR DROPS
EAR DROPS: **ziiginishaan, -an** *ni*
EAR OF CORN
EAR OF CORN: **mandaaminaak, -oon** *ni*
EARLY
EARLY: **wayiiba** *pc, also* **wiiba**
EARLY IN THE MORNING: **gichi-gigizheb**
pc
EARLY IN THE NIGHT: be early in the
night **oshki-dibikad** *vii*
EARMUFF
EARMUFF: **giizhootawage'on, -ag** *na*
WEAR EARMUFFS: **giizhootawage'o** *vai*
EARN
EARN: **gashkichige** *vai;* earn s.o. (e.g.,
money) **gashki'** *vta;* earn s.t. **dibendan** *vti*
EARN FROM A CERTAIN PLACE: **ondizi**
vai
EARN MONEY: **zhooniyaake** *vai*
EARRING
EARRING: **naabishebizon, -an** *ni*
WEAR EARRINGS: **naanaabishebizo** *vai*
EARTH
EARTH: **aki, -in** *ni;* be the earth **akiiwan** *vii*
EARTH LODGE
EARTH LODGE: **akiiwe-wiigiwaam, -an** *ni*
EASILY
EASILY: **wenipazh** *pc*
GET EASILY: get s.o. easily **wenipazhi'** *vta;*
get s.t. easily **wenipazhitoon** *vti2*

EAST
EAST: east: where the dawn comes from
conjunct of **ondaaban: wendaabang** *vii*
IN THE EAST: **waabanong** *pc*
TO THE EAST: **waabanong** *pc*
EAST WIND
EAST WIND: **waabani-noodin** *ni*
EASY
EASY: be easy **wendad** *vii;* **wendizi** *vai;*
wenipanad *vii;* **wenipanizi** *vai*
CONSIDER EASY: consider s.t. easy
wenipanendan *vti*
EASY GOING: be easygoing **bekaadizi** *vai*
GO EASY: go easy on s.o. **manaaji'** *vta;* go
easy on s.t. **manaajitoon** *vti2;* go easy!
na'egaaj *pc*
EAT
EAT: **wiisini** *vai;* eat s.o. **amo /amw-/** *vta;* eat
s.t. **miijin** *vti3*
EAT A CERTAIN WAY: **inanjige** *vai*
EAT BREAKFAST: **gigizhebaa-wiisini** *vai;*
eat s.t. for breakfast **gigizhebaa-miijin** *vti3*
EAT DINNER: eat dinner (noon meal)
naawakwe-wiisini *vai;* eat s.t. for dinner
(noon meal) **naawakwe-miijin** *vti3*
EAT ENOUGH: **debisinii** *vai;* eat enough of
s.t. **de-miijin** *vti3*
EAT IN A CERTAIN PLACE: **dananjige** *vai*
EAT LUNCH: eat lunch (noon meal)
naawakwe-wiisini *vai;* eat s.t. for lunch
(noon meal) **naawakwe-miijin** *vti3*
EAT SECRETLY: eat things secretly
giimoodanjige *vai*
EAT SUPPER: **onaagoshi-wiisini** *vai;* eat s.t.
for supper **onaagoshi-miijin** *vti3*
EAT UP: eat everything up **gidaanawe** *vai;* eat
up s.t. **gidaan** *vti3;* eat up s.o. **gidamo**
/gidamw-/ *vta*
EAT WELL: **minwanjige** *vai*
EAT WITH: eat with s.o. **wiidoopam** *vta;* eat
with people **wiidoopange** *vai*
EAT WITH FINGERS: eat with one's fingers
michininjiikanjige *vai*
EAT WITH SOMETHING ELSE: eat things
with something else (e.g., butter with
bread) **apanjige** *vai*
HEARD EATING: be heard eating
madwenjige *vai*
LEAVE BEHIND UNEATEN: leave s.o.
behind uneaten **ishkwam** *vta;* leave s.t.
behind uneaten **ishkwandan** *vti*
START EATING: **maadanjige** *vai*
EAVESDROP
EAVESDROP: eavesdrop on s.o. **giimitaw** *vta*
ECHO
ECHO: **baswewe** *vai;* **baswewe,**
baswewemagad *vii*
ECLIPSE
IN ECLIPSE: be in eclipse **makadewaabikizi**
vai
EDGE
WALK AROUND THE EDGE:
giiwitaayaazhagaame *vai*

EDUCATED
EDUCATED: be educated **gikendaaso** *vai*
EDUCATION
EDUCATION BY PREACHING AND
EXHORTATION: **gagiikimaawasowin** *ni*
EELPOUT
EELPOUT: **mizay, -ag** *na*
EFFORT
MAKE AN EFFORT: **goji'ewizi** *vai*
WITH EFFORT: **enigok** *pc*
EGG
EGG: **waawan, -oon** *ni*
FISH EGG: **waak, -wan** *ni*
LAY AN EGG: **boonam** *vai2*
EGGBEATER
EGGBEATER: **waninawe'igan, -an** *ni*
EIGHT
EIGHT: **ishwaaswi** *nm, also* **nishwaaswi***;
ishwaaso- *pv4, also* **nishwaaso-***; eight
(card) **ishwaasoobii'igan, -ag** *na, also*
nishwaasoobii'igan*; they are eight
ishwaachinoon /**ishwaachin-**/ *vii, also*
nishwaachinoon*; **ishwaachiwag**
/**ishwaachi-**/ *vai, also* **nishwaachiwag***
AND EIGHT: **ashi-ishwaaso-** *pv4, also* **ashi-
nishwaaso-***; **ashi-ishwaaswi** *nm, also*
ashi-nishwaaswi*
EIGHT ACRES: **ishwaaso-diba'igaans** *pc,
also* **nishwaaso-diba'igaans***
EIGHT DAYS: **ishwaaso-giizhik** *pc, also*
nishwaaso-giizhik*; **ishwaasogon** *pc, also*
nishwaasogon*; be eight days
ishwaasogonagad *vii, also*
nishwaasogonagad*
EIGHT DAYS OLD: be eight days old
ishwaasogonagizi *vai, also*
nishwaasogonagizi*
EIGHT DOLLARS: **ishwaaswaabik** *pc, also*
nishwaaswaabik*
EIGHT EACH: **eyishwaaswi** *nm, also*
nenishwaaswi*
EIGHT FEET: **ishwaasozid** *pc, also*
nishwaasozid*
EIGHT HOURS: **ishwaaso-diba'igan** *pc, also*
nishwaaso-diba'igan*
EIGHT HUNDRED: **ishwaaswaak** *nm, also*
nishwaaswaak*
EIGHT INCHES: **ishwaasoninj** *pc, also*
nishwaasoninj*
EIGHT MILES: **ishwaaso-diba'igan** *pc, also*
nishwaaso-diba'igan*
EIGHT MINUTES: **ishwaaso-diba'igaans** *pc,
also* **nishwaaso-diba'igaans***
EIGHT MONTHS: **ishwaaso-giizis** *pc, also*
nishwaaso-giizis*
EIGHT NIGHTS: **ishwaaso-dibik** *pc, also*
nishwaaso-dibik*
EIGHT O'CLOCK: be eight o'clock
ishwaaso-diba'iganed *vii, also* **nishwaaso-
diba'iganed***
EIGHT PAIRS: **íshwaaswewaan** *pc, also*
nishwaaswewaan*
EIGHT SETS: **ishwaaswewaan** *pc, also*
nishwaaswewaan*

EIGHT THOUSAND: **ishwaasosagoons** *nm,
also* **nishwaasosagoons***
EIGHT TIMES: **ishwaaching** *pc, also*
nishwaaching*
EIGHT WEEKS: **ishwaaso-anama'e-giizhik**
pc, also **nishwaaso-anama'e-giizhik***; be
eight weeks **ishwaaso-anama'e-giizhigad**
vii, also **nishwaaso-anama'e-giizhigad***
EIGHT YEARS: **ishwaaso-biboon** *pc, also*
nishwaaso-biboon*; be eight years
ishwaaso-biboonagad *vii, also* **nishwaaso-
biboonagad***
EIGHT YEARS OLD: be eight years old
ishwaaso-biboonagizi *vai, also* **nishwaaso-
biboonagizi***
EIGHTEEN
EIGHTEEN: **ashi-ishwaaswi** *nm, also* **ashi-
nishwaaswi***; **midaaswi ashi-ishwaaswi**
nm, also **midaaswi ashi-nishwaaswi***
EIGHTH
THE EIGHTH DAY OF THE MONTH: be
the eighth day of the month
ishwaasogonagizi *vai, also*
nishwaasogonagizi*
EIGHTY
EIGHTY: **ishwaasimidana** *nm, also*
nishwaasimidana*
EJACULATE
EJACULATE: **baashkizige** *vai*
ELATED
ELATED: be elated **onzaamenimo** *vai*
ELBOW
ELBOW: my elbow **indooskwan, -an**
/**-dooskwan-**/ *nid*
SORE ELBOW: have a sore elbow
gaagiijidooskwan *vai*
ELDER
ELDER: **gichi-aya'aa, -g** *na*
ELDERLY
ELDERLY: be elderly **gikaa** *vai*
ELDEST
ELDEST CHILD: **nitamoozhaan, -ag** *na*
THE ELDEST: be the eldest (of siblings)
zaziikizi *vai*
ELECTION DAY
ELECTION DAY: be election day
biinjwebinigewi-giizhigad *vii*
ELECTRIC
ELECTRIC: **waasamoo-** *pv4*
ELECTRIC LAMP
ELECTRIC LAMP: **waasamoo-
waazakonenjigan, -an** *ni*
ELECTRICIAN
ELECTRICIAN: **waasamoo-anokiiwinini,
-wag** *na*
ELECTRICITY
ELECTRICITY: **waasamowin** *ni*
ELEPHANT
ELEPHANT: **jejiibajikii, -g** *na*
ELEVATOR
ELEVATOR: **akwaandawaagan, -an** *ni;*
akwaandawebizon, -an *ni*

ELEVEN
    ELEVEN: **ashi-bezhig** *nm;* **midaaswi ashi-bezhig** *nm;* **ashi-bezhigo-** *pv4*
ELK
    ELK: **omashkooz, -oog** *na*
ELM
    ELM: **aniib, -iig** *na*
    SLIPPERY ELM: **ozhaashigob, -iig** *na*
EMBARK
    EMBARK: **boozi** *vai*
EMBARRASS
    EMBARRASS: embarrass s.o. **agaji'** *vta*
    EMBARRASS BY SPEECH: embarrass s.o. by speech **agazom** *vta*
EMBARRASSED
    EMBARRASSED: be embarrassed **agadendaagozi** *vai;* be embarrassed by s.o. **agadenim** *vta*
EMBARRASSING
    EMBARRASSING: be embarrassing **agadendaagwad** *vii*
EMBRACE
    EMBRACE: embrace s.o. **gikinjigwen** *vta;* **giishkijiin** *vta;* they embrace each other **giishkijiinidiwag** /**giishkijiinidi-**/ *vai*
EMBROIDER
    EMBROIDER: **mazinigwaaso** *vai;* embroider s.o. **mazinigwaazh** /**mazinigwaaN-**/ *vta;* embroider s.t. **mazinigwaadan** *vti*
EMERGE
    EMERGE FROM SURFACE: **mookii** *vai*
    EMERGE FROM THE WATER: **mookibii** *vai*
EMPLOYED
    EMPLOYED IN A CERTAIN WAY: be employed in a certain way **inaabadad** *vii;* **inaabadizi** *vai*
EMPTIED
    EMPTIED: be emptied **zhiigonigaade, zhiigonigaademagad** *vii;* **zhiigonigaazo** *vai*
EMPTY
    EMPTY: be empty **bizhishigozi** *vai;* **bizhishigwaa, bizhishigwaamagad** *vii;* empty s.o. **zhiigon** *vta;* empty s.t. **zhiigonan** *vti;* empty things **zhiigonige** *vai*
ENCIRCLE
    ENCIRCLE: **giiwitaashkaa** *vai*
END
    AT THE END: at the end of it **ishkwe-ayi'ii** *pc,* also **iskweya'ii**
    AT THE END OF AN ACTIVITY: be at the end of an activity **ishkwaataa** *vai*
    AT THE END OF THE ROAD: at the end of the road or trail **gabekana** *pc*
    AT THE END OF THE TRAIL: at the end of the road or trail **gabekana** *pc*
    COME TO AN END: **ishkwaase, ishkwaasemagad** *vii;* **wayekwaase, wayekwaasemagad** *vii*
    GO TO THE END: **gabeshkaa** *vai;* go to the end of s.t. **gabeshkan** *vti*

HANG AT THE END: ishkwegoode, ishkwegoodemagad *vii;* **ishkwegoojin** *vai;* hang s.o. at the end **ishkwegoozh** /**ishkwegooN-**/ *vta;* hang s.t. at the end **ishkwegoodoon** *vti2*
    LIE AT THE END: **ishkweshin** *vai;* **ishkwesin** *vii*
    LIVE ON THE END OF TOWN: live at the end of town **ishkwege** *vai*
    SIT AT THE END: **ishkwebi** *vai*
    STAND AT THE END: **ishkwegaabawi** *vai*
ENERGETIC
    ENERGETIC: be energetic **gwaashkwezi** *vai*
ENGAGED
    ENGAGED IN AN ACTIVITY TO A CERTAIN EXTENT: be engaged in an activity to a certain extent **apiichitaa** *vai*
ENGAGED
    ENGAGED: be engaged **asho-wiidige** *vai;* they are engaged to each other **asho-wiidigendiwag** /**asho-wiidigendi-**/ *vai*
ENGINE
    ENGINE: **mayaajiibizod** *na-pt*
ENGLISH
    SPEAK ENGLISH: **gichi-mookomaanimo** *vai;* **zhaaganaashiimo** *vai;* speak English to s.o. **zhaaganaashiimotaw** *vta*
    WRITE IN ENGLISH: **zhaaganaashiiwibii'ige** *vai;* write in English to s.o. **zhaaganaashiiwibii'amaw** *vta;* write s.t. in English **zhaaganaashiiwibii'an** *vti*
ENGLISHMAN
    ENGLISHMAN: **zhaaganaash, -ag** *na,* also **zhaaganaashi, -wag**
ENOUGH
    ENOUGH: **de-** *pv4;* **gwech** *pc;* be enough **debise** *vai;* **debise, debisemagad** *vii*
    EAT ENOUGH: **debisinii** *vai;* eat enough of s.t. **de-miijin** *vti3*
    HAVE ENOUGH: **debizi** *vai;* have enough of s.o. **debisa'** *vta;* have enough of s.t. **debisatoon** *vti2;* have enough of things **debisachige** *vai*
    HAVE ENOUGH TO GIVE: have enough to give away **deba'ookii** *vai;* have enough to give to or feed s.o. **deba'oozh** /**deba'ooN-**/ *vta*
    THINK THERE IS ENOUGH: **debisewendam** *vai2*
ENTER
    ENTER: **biindige** *vai;* enter into where s.o. is **biindigaw** *vta*
ENVELOPE
    ENVELOPE: **mashkimodens, -an** *ni;* **maajiibii'ige-mashkimodens, -an** *ni*
ENVY
    ENVY: envy s.o. **ondenim** *vta*
EQUAL
    EQUAL: **dibishkoo** *pc*
ERASE
    ERASE: erase s.t. **gaasiibii'an** *vti;* erase things **gaasiibii'ige** *vai*

ERASER
ERASER: **gaasiibii'igan, -ag** *na*
ERROR
IN ERROR: **wani-** *pv4*
ESCAPE
ESCAPE: **giimii** *vai;* escape from s.o. **gii'** *vta;*
ozhim *vta;* escape from people **gii'iwe** *vai*
ESPECIALLY
ESPECIALLY: **memindage** *pc*
EUROPE
IN EUROPE: **agaamakiing** *pc*
EVEN
EVEN: **dibishkoo** *pc*
KEEP UP EVEN: keep up even with s.o. **dibi'**
vta
EVEN THOUGH
EVEN THOUGH: **awanjish** *pc*
EVENING
EVENING: be evening **onaagoshin**
/onaagoshi-/ *vii*
ALL EVENING: **gabe-onaagosh** *pc*
EVENT
CERTAIN EVENT: be a certain event
inakamigad *vii;* **izhiwebad** *vii*
HAVE AN EVENT IN A CERTAIN PLACE:
danakamigizi *vai*
EVENTUALLY
EVENTUALLY: **gegapii** *pc*
EVER
EVER: **wiikaa** *pc*
DON'T EVER: **gego wiikaa** *pc*
EVERY
EVERY: **akina** *pc, also* **kina, gakina; daso-** *pv3*
EVERY DAY: **endaso-giizhik** *pc*
EVERY MONTH: **endaso-giizis** *pc*
EVERY MORNING: **endaso-gigizheb** *pc*
EVERY NIGHT: **endaso-dibik** *pc*
EVERY ONCE IN A WHILE: **aayaapii** *pc*
EVERYTHING
EVERYTHING: **akina gegoo** *pr, also* **kina**
gegoo, gakina gegoo
EVERYWHERE
EVERYWHERE: **miziwe** *pc;* be everywhere
miziweshkaa, miziweshkaamagad *vii*
GO EVERYWHERE: **miziweshkaa,**
miziweshkaamagad *vii*
EVICT
EVICT: evict s.o. **zaagidin** *vta*
EVICTED
EVICTED: be evicted **ikonigaazo** *vai*
EVIL
EVIL: be evil **maji-manidoowaadizi** *vai*
EVIL MANITOU: **maji-manidoo, -g** *na*
LEAD AN EVIL LIFE: **maji-izhiwebizi** *vai*
EXACTLY
EXACTLY: **memwech** *pc*
DO EXACTLY: **wawiingechige** *vai*
EXCESSIVELY
EXCESSIVELY: **onzaam** *pc*

EXCHANGE
EXCHANGE: exchange s.o. **meshkwadoon**
vta; exchange s.t. **meshkwadoonan** *vti;*
exchange things **meshkwadoonige** *vai*
IN EXCHANGE: **meshkwad** *pc*
EXCITE
EXCITE: excite s.o. **ombi'** *vta*
EXCITED
EXCITED: be excited **baapinakamigizi** *vai;*
ombendam *vai2*
EXCITING
EXCITING: be exciting **minawaanigwad** *vii*
EXCREMENT
EXCREMENT: **moo, -wan** *ni*
EXHALE
EXHALE: **bagidanaamo** *vai;* **nasanaamo** *vai*
EXHAUSTED
EXHAUSTED: be exhausted **noondeshin** *vai*
EXHIBITION
EXHIBITION: **waabanda'iwewin, -an** *ni*
EXHORTATION
EDUCATION BY PREACHING AND
EXHORTATION: **gagiikimaawasowin** *ni*
EXIT
EXIT: **zaaga'am** *vai2*
EXOTIC
EXOTIC: **mayagi-** *pv4*
EXPECT
EXPECT: **akawaabi** *vai;* expect s.o. to come
akawaabam *vta;* expect s.t. to come
akawaabandan *vti*
EXPECT TO BE IN A CERTAIN PLACE:
expect s.o. to be in a certain place
danenim *vta;* expect s.t. to be in a certain
place **danendan** *vti*
EXPLAIN
EXPLAIN: explain (s.t.) to s.o.
waawiindamaw *vta;* explain (s.t.) to
people **waawiindamaage** *vai*
EXPLAINED
EXPLAINED: be explained **waawiinjigaade,**
waawiinjigaademagad *vii*
EXPLODE
EXPLODE: **baashkide, baashkidemagad** *vii;*
baashkizo *vai*
EXTENT
CERTAIN EXTENT: a certain extent **apiichi-**
pv3
WHOLE EXTENT OF: **gabe-** *pv4*
EXTINGUISH
EXTINGUISH: extinguish s.t. **aate'an** *vti*
EXTINGUISHED
EXTINGUISHED: be extinguished **aate,**
aatemagad *vii*
APPEAR TO BE EXTINGUISHED: appear
to be extinguished (e.g., the moon or sun
in an eclipse) **aatenaagozi** *vai*
EXTREMELY
EXTREMELY: **onzaam** *pc*
EXTRICATE
EXTRICATE: extricate s.o. **giichigon** *vta;* ex-
tricate s.t. **giichigonan** *vti*

EYE

EYE: my eye **nishkiinzhig, -oon /-shkiinzhigw-/** *nid*

BIG EYE: have a big eye **mangishkiinzhigwe** *vai*

HAVE A BLACK EYE: **ozhaawashkwaabi** *vai*

HAVE SOMETHING IN EYE: have something in one's eye **binzini** *vai*

OPEN EYES: open one's eyes **dooskaabi** *vai*

SHUT EYES: shut one's eyes **basangwaabi** *vai*

SWOLLEN EYES: have swollen eyes **baagishkiinzhigwe** *vai*

EYE DROPS

EYE DROPS: **ziiginiingwaan** *ni*

EYEGLASSES

EYEGLASSES: eyeglasses *plural* **oshkiinzhigokaajiganan** *ni, also* **oshkiinzhikokaanan**

EYEBROW

EYEBROW HAIR: my eyebrow hair **nimaamaa, -yag /-maamaay-/** *nad*

EYELASH

EYELASH: **miishaabiwinaan, -an** *ni*

EYESIGHT

GOOD EYESIGHT: have good eyesight **minwaabi** *vai*

F

FACE

FACE: my face **indengway, -an /-dengway-/** *nid*

ACNE ON FACE: have acne on one's face **moosewiingwe** *vai*

BROAD FACE: have a broad face **mangadengwe** *vai*

BRUISED FACE: have a bruised face **ozhaawashkwaanagiingwe** *vai*

CHAPPED FACE: have a chapped face **gagiipiingwe** *vai*

FALL ON FACE: fall on one's face **ajijiingwese** *vai*

HAVE SCAR ON FACE: have scar on one's face **ojiishiingwe** *vai*

LIE WITH FACE COVERED: lie with one's face covered **badagwiingweshin** *vai*

NARROW FACE: have a narrow face **agaasadengwe** *vai*

SCABS ON FACE: have scabs on one's face **omigiingwe** *vai*

SLAP ON FACE: slap s.o. on the face **basiingwe' /basiingwe'w-/** *vta*

SWOLLEN FACE: have a swollen face **baagiingwe** *vai*

WASH FACE: wash one's face **giziibiigiingwe** *vai*

WIPE FACE: wipe one's face with something **giziingwe'o** *vai*

WRINKLED FACE: have a wrinkled face **oziigiingwe** *vai*

FACE POWDER

FACE POWDER: **waabishkiingwechigan** *ni*

USE FACE POWDER: **waabishkiingwechige** *vai*

FACE DOWN

FALL FACE DOWN: **animikose** *vai;* **animikose, animikosemagad** *vii*

LAY FACE DOWN: lay s.o. face down **animikoshim** *vta;* lay s.t. face down **animikosidoon** *vti2*

LIE FACE DOWN: **animikoshin** *vai;* **animikosin** *vii*

TURN FACE DOWN: turn s.o. face down **animikon** *vta;* turn s.t. face down **animikonan** *vti*

TURNED FACE DOWN: be turned face down **animikonigaade, animikonigaademagad** *vii;* **animikonigaazo** *vai*

FACE UP

LAY FACE UP: lay s.o. face up **aazhigijishim** *vta;* lay s.t. face up **aazhigijisidoon** *vti2*

LIE FACE UP: **aazhigijishin** *vai;* **aazhigijisin** *vii*

TURN FACE UP: **aazhigijise** *vai;* **aazhigijise, aazhigijisemagad** *vii*

FACTORY

FACTORY: **anokiiwigamig, -oon** *ni*

FADE

FADE: fade from light **waabaaso** *vai;* **waabaate, waabaatemagad** *vii*

FADED

FADED: be faded **waabide, waabidemagad** *vii;* **waabizo** *vai*

FAIL

FAIL TO SEE: fail to see s.o. **gwiinawaabam** *vta;* fail to see s.t. **gwiinawaabandan** *vti*

FAINT

FAINT: **wanendamaa** *vai*

FALL

FALL: **bangishin** *vai;* **bangisin** *vii;* fall (as a leaf) **binaakwii** *vai*

DIE FROM A FALL: **aapijishin** *vai*

FALL AND BREAK ARM: fall and break one's arm **bookonikeshin** *vai*

FALL AND BREAK BACK: fall and break one's back **bookwaawiganeshin** *vai*

FALL AND BREAK LEG: fall and break one's leg **bookogaadeshin** *vai*

FALL AND CRACK HEAD: fall and crack one's head **baasindibeshin** *vai*

FALL AND TWIST ARM: fall and twist one's arm **biimiskonikeshin** *vai*

FALL DOWN AGAINST: **apangishin** *vai;* **apangisin** *vii*

FALL DOWN HARD: **bakiteshin** *vai*

FALL FACE DOWN: **animikose** *vai;* **animikose, animikosemagad** *vii*

FALL FROM A CERTAIN PLACE:
  onjibide, onjibidemagad *vii;* onjibizo *vai*
FALL HEAD FIRST: ajijibizo *vai*
FALL IN: biinjibide, biinjibidemagad *vii;*
  biinjibizo *vai;* biinjise *vai;* biinjise,
  biinjisemagad *vii*
FALL INTO THE WATER: bakobiise *vai;*
  bakobiise, bakobiisemagad *vii*
FALL OFF A HORSE: banoomigo *vai*
FALL ON FACE: fall on one's face
  ajijiingwese *vai*
FALL ON THE SIDE: opimese *vai*
FALL OUT OF A BOAT: gidoonagise *vai*
FALL OVER: gawise *vai;* gawise,
  gawisemagad *vii;* fall over (as something
  stick- or wood-like) gawaakose *vai;*
  gawaakose, gawaakosemagad *vii*
FALL OVER BACKWARDS: aazhigijishin
  vai; aazhigijisin *vii*
FALL THROUGH THE ICE: dwaashin *vai*
HAVE A BAD FALL: aapijishin *vai*
HEARD FALLING: be heard falling on the
  floor madwesagishin *vai;* be heard going
  along and falling bimweweshin *vai*
SLIP AND FALL: ozhaashishin *vai*
SLIP AND FALL ON THE ICE:
  ozhaashikoshin *vai*
FALL
  FALL: be fall dagwaagin /dagwaagi-/ *vii*
  FALL BEFORE LAST: awas-dagwaagong *pc*
  LAST FALL: dagwaagong *pc*
  SPEND THE FALL: spend the fall
  somewhere dagwaagishi *vai*
FALSE TEETH
  FALSE TEETH: false teeth *plural*
  wiibidaakaajiganan *ni, also*
  wiibidaakaanan
FAMILIAR
  FAMILIAR: be familiar with s.o. nagadenim
  vta; be familiar with s.t. nagadendan *vti*
FAN
  FAN: fan s.o. wewese' /wewese'w-/ *vta;* fan
  things wewese'ige *vai;* fan oneself
  wewese'idizo *vai*
  HAND FAN: wewese'igan, -an *ni*
  ROTARY FAN: gizhibaayaasijigan, -an *ni*
FAN BELT
  FAN BELT: apikaans, -an *ni;* gijipizonens *ni*
FAR
  FAR: waasa *pc;* be far waasawad *vii*
  AS FAR AS: ako- *pv3*
  SO FAR ALONG IN AN ACTIVITY: be so
  far along in an activity apiichitaa *vai*
FARE
  FARE A CERTAIN WAY: izhiwebizi *vai*
FARM
  FARM: gitigaan, -an *ni;* gitige *vai*
FARMER
  FARMER: gitigewinini, -wag *na*
FART
  FART: boogidi *vai*
FAST
  FAST: be fast wajepii *vai*

CLIMB UP FAST: akwaandawebatoo *vai*
DRIP FAST: gizhiigaa, gizhiigaamagad *vii*
DRIVE FAST: gizhiibizo *vai;* gizhiidaabii'iwe
  vai
FLOW FAST: gizhiijiwan *vii*
FLY FAST: gizhiibide, gizhiibidemagad *vii;*
  gizhiibizo *vai;* gizhiise *vai;* gizhiise,
  gizhiisemagad *vii*
GO AS FAST AS POSSIBLE: apiizikaa *vai*
GO FAST: gizhiikaa *vai*
GROW FAST: gizhiigi *vai;* gizhiigin *vii*
LEAK FAST: gizhiigaa, gizhiigaamagad *vii*
MOVE FAST: gizhiibide, gizhiibidemagad
  vii; gizhiibizo *vai*
PADDLE FAST: gizhiikaakwazhiwe *vai*
RUN FAST: gizhiibatoo *vai;* gizhiikaabatoo
  vai
SPEED FAST: gizhiibide, gizhiibidemagad
  vii; gizhiibizo *vai*
WIND BLOWS FAST: gizhiiyaanimad *vii*
FAST
  FAST FOR A VISION: gii'igoshimo *vai*
  UNDERGO A PUBERTY FAST: makadeke
  vai
FASTEN
  FASTEN: fasten s.o. zagaakwa'
  /zagaakwa'w-/ *vta;* fasten s.t.
  zagaakwa'an *vti;* fasten things
  zagaakwa'ige *vai*
  FASTEN TOGETHER: fasten s.o. together
  zaga' /zaga'w-/ *vta;* fasten s.t. together
  zaga'an *vti*
FASTENED
  FASTENED: be fastened zagaakwa'igaade,
  zagaakwa'igaademagad *vii;*
  zagaakwa'igaazo *vai*
FAT
  FAT: wiinin *ni;* be fat wiinino *vai*
FATHER
  FATHER: my father imbaabaa, -yag
  /-baabaay-/ *nad;* indede, -yag /-dedey-/
  nad; my father *old-fashioned* noos, -ag
  /-oos-/ *nad*
FATHER-IN-LAW
  FATHER-IN-LAW: my father-in-law inzinis,
  -ag /-zinis-/ *nad*
FATIGUED
  FATIGUED: be fatigued noondeshin *vai*
FAWN
  FAWN: gidagaakoons, -ag *na*
FEAR
  FEAR: fear s.o. goshi /goS-/ *vta;* fear s.t.
  gotan *vti*
  COME IN FEAR: biidaanimizi *vai*
  HAVE FEAR: gotaaji *vai*
FEARFUL
  FEARFUL: be fearful zegendam *vai2*
FEAST
  GIVE A FEAST: wiikonge *vai*
  HAVE A FEAST: they have a feast
  wiikondiwag /wiikondi-/ *vai*
  HAVE A FEAST HONORING THE DEAD:
  jiibenaake *vai*

INVITE TO A FEAST: invite s.o. to a feast (especially as part of a religious ceremony) **wiikom** *vta;* invite people to a feast (especially as part of a religious ceremony) **wiikonge** *vai*

FEATHER
FEATHER: **miigwan, -ag** *na*
STICK IN A FEATHER: stick a feather in one's hair or hat **badakibine'o** *vai*

FEATHER HEADDRESS
FEATHER HEADDRESS: **miigwani-wiiwakwaan, -an** *ni*

FEBRUARY
FEBRUARY: **namebini-giizis** *na*

FECES
FECES: **moo, -wan** *ni*

FEED
FEED: feed (s.t.) to s.o. **asham** *vta;* feed people **ashange** *vai*

FEEL
FEEL: feel s.o. **mikoojiin** *vta;* feel s.o. in or on one's body **moozhi'** *vta;* feel s.t. **mikoojiinan** *vti;* feel s.t. in or on one's body **moozhitoon** *vti2*
FEEL A CERTAIN WAY: **inamanji'o** *vai;* **inendam** *vai2*
FEEL ABOUT TO A CERTAIN EXTENT: feel about s.o. to a certain extent **apiitenim** *vta*
FEEL BAD: **maanamanji'o** *vai;* **maanendam** *vai2, also* **maazhendam;** feel bad about s.t. **maanendan** *vti*
FEEL COLD: **biingeji** *vai;* **dakamanji'o** *vai;* **giikaji** *vai*
FEEL DEPRESSED: **maanendam** *vai2, also* **maazhendam**
FEEL FOR: feel for s.o. **mikoojiin** *vta;* **nandoojiin** *vta;* feel for s.t. **mikoojiinan** *vti;* **nandoojiinan** *vti;* feel for things **nandoojiinige** *vai*
FEEL GOOD: **minwamanji'o** *vai*
FEEL NUMB: **giikimanizi** *vai*
FEEL OUT OF SORTS: **maazhendam** *vai2*
FEEL SATISFIED: **debisewendam** *vai2*
FEEL STRANGE: **mayagendam** *vai2*
FEEL TIRED: **ayekwamanji'o** *vai*

FEELINGS
HAVE INTENSE FEELINGS OR DESIRES: **aakwendam** *vai2*

FELL
FELL: fell s.o. **gawa' /gawa'w-/** *vta;* fell s.t. **gawa'an** *vti*

FELLOW
FELLOW: my fellow **niiji-** *pn*
FELLOW MAN: my fellow man **niijiinini** *nad*

FENCE
FENCE: **minjikanaakobijigan, -an** *ni*

FERRY
FERRY ACROSS: ferry s.o. across **aazhawa'oozh /aazhawa'ooN-/** *vta;* ferry s.t. across **aazhawa'oodoon** *vti2*

FESTIVITIES
FESTIVITIES: there are festivities **baapinakamigad** *vii*

FETCH
FETCH: fetch s.o. **naazh /naaN-/** *vta;* fetch s.t. **naadin** *vti3;* fetch (s.t.) for s.o. **naadaw** *vta*

FETCHED
FETCHED: be fetched **naajigaade, naajigaademagad** *vii;* **naajigaazo** *vai*

FEVER
HAVE A FEVER: **gizhizo** *vai*

FEW
FEW: **bangii** *pc;* be few **bangiiwagad** *vii;* **bangiiwagizi** *vai*
VERY FEW: be very few **bangiishenhwagad** *vii;* **bangiishenhwagizi** *vai*

FIDDLE
FIDDLE: **naazhaabii'igan, -an** *ni*

FIELD
FIELD: **gitigaan, -an** *ni*
CORNFIELD: **mandaamini-gitigaan, -an** *ni*

FIERCE
FIERCE: be fierce **aakwaadizi** *vai*

FIFTEEN
FIFTEEN: **ashi-naanan** *nm;* **midaaswi ashi-naanan** *nm*

FIFTH
THE FIFTH DAY OF THE MONTH: be the fifth day of the month **naanogonagizi** *vai*

FIFTY
FIFTY: **naanimidana** *nm*

FIGHT
FIGHT: **miigaazo** *vai;* fight s.o. **miigaazh /miigaaN-/** *vta;* they fight each other **miigaadiwag /miigaadi-/** *vai*

FIGURE
FIGURE OUT: figure something out **onendam** *vai2*

FILE
FILE: **zisiboojigan, -an** *ni;* file s.o. **zisiboozh /zisibooN-/** *vta;* file s.t. **zisiboodoon** *vti2;* file things **zisiboojige** *vai*
FILE SHARP: file s.o. sharp **giiniboozh /giinibooN-/** *vta;* file s.t. sharp **giiniboodoon** *vti2*

FILL
FILL: fill s.o. (with a liquid) **mooshkinebazh /mooshkinebaN-/** *vta;* fill s.o. (with solids) **mooshkina'** *vta;* fill s.t. (with a liquid) **mooshkinebadoon** *vti2;* fill s.t. (with solids) **mooshkinadoon** *vti2*
FILL HALF FULL: fill s.o. half full (of liquid) **aabitoobazh /aabitoobaN-/** *vta;* fill s.o. half full (of solids) **aabitooshkina'** *vta;* fill s.t. half full **aabitooshkinadoon** *vti2;* fill s.t. half full (of liquid) **aabitoobadoon** *vti2*
FILL TO OVERFLOWING: fill s.o. to overflowing with solids **ziigashkina'** *vta;* fill s.t. to overflowing with a liquid **ziigibadoon** *vti2;* fill s.t. to overflowing with solids **ziigashkinadoon** *vti2*

FILL OUT
  FILL OUT A FORM: **mooshkinebii'ige** *vai*
FILLED
  FILLED WITH SMOKE: be filled with smoke
    mooshkineyaabate,
    mooshkineyaabatemagad *vii*
  WELL FILLED: be well filled **minwashkine**
    vai; **minwashkine, minwashkinemagad**
    vii
FINALLY
  FINALLY: **gegapii** *pc;* **ishkwaaj** *pc*
FIND
  FIND: find s.o. **mikaw** *vta;* find s.t. **mikan** *vti;*
    find (s.t.) for s.o. **mikamaw** *vta;* find
    things **mikige** *vai;* find people **mikaage** *vai*
  FIND TRACKS: find s.o.'s tracks **okawi'** *vta;*
    find the tracks of s.t. **okawitoon** *vti2*
  FIND WITH HANDS: find s.o. with hands
    mikobizh /mikobiN-/ *vta;* find s.t. with
    hands **mikobidoon** *vti2;* find (s.t.) for s.o.
    with hands **mikobidaw** *vta;* find things
    with hands **mikobijige** *vai*
FINE
  FINE: be fine **biisaa, biisaamagad** *vii;* **biisizi**
    vai; be fine (as something string-like)
    agaasaabiigad *vii;* **agaasaabiigizi** *vai*
  CHOP FINE: chop s.o. fine **biisa' /biisa'w-/**
    vta; chop s.t. fine **biisa'an** *vti*
FINE
  FINE: be fine **mino-ayaa** *vai*
FINGER
  FINGER: **niibinaakwaanininj, -iin** *ni;* my
    finger **nininj, -iin /-ninjy-/** *nid;* **nininjiins,**
    -an /-ninjiins-/ *nid*
  EAT WITH FINGERS: eat with one's fingers
    michininjiikanjige *vai*
  INDEX FINGER: **izhinoo'iganinj, -iin** *ni*
  LITTLE FINGER: **ishkweninj, -iin** *ni*
  MIDDLE FINGER: **naawininj, -iin** *ni*
  SORE FINGER: have a sore finger
    gaagiijininjii *vai*
FINGERNAIL
  FINGERNAIL: my nail (fingernail, toenail)
    nishkanzh, -iig /-shkanzhy-/ *nad*
  WHITE SPOTS ON FINGERNAILS: have
    white spots on fingernails **mindaweganzhii**
    vai
FINISH
  FINISH: **giizhi-** *pv4;* finish (in work or an
    activity) **anwaataa** *vai;* finish a task
    giizhiitaa *vai;* finish s.o. **giizhi'** *vta;* finish
    s.t. **giizhitoon** *vti2;* finish with s.o.
    giizhiikaw *vta;* finish with s.t. **giizhiikan**
    vti
  FINISH A TASK: **giizhiitaa** *vai*
  FINISH BOILING: **giizhigamide,**
    giizhigamidemagad *vii;* finish boiling
    things **giizhigamizige** *vai*
  FINISH BOILING SAP: **ishkwaagamizige**
    vai
  FINISH BUILDING A DWELLING:
    giizhige *vai*

FINISH COOKING: finish cooking s.o. **giiziz**
  /giizizw-/ *vta;* finish cooking s.t. **giizizan**
  vti
FINISH MAKING: finish making s.o. **giizhi'**
  vta; finish making s.t. **giizhitoon** *vti2*
FINISH WORK: **giizhiitaa** *vai*
FINISHED
  FINISHED: be finished **giizhichigaade,**
    giizhichigaademagad *vii;* **giizhichigaazo**
    vai
FINN
  FINN: **madoodoowinini, -wag** *na;*
    omakakiiwinini, -wag *na*
FIR
  BALSAM FIR: **zhingob, -iig** *na*
FIR BOUGH
  FIR BOUGH: **zhingobaandag, -oog** *na*
FIRE
  FIRE: **ishkode, -n** *ni;* there is a fire made in a
    fireplace **boodawaade,**
    boodawaademagad *vii*
  AROUND THE FIRE: **giiwitaashkode** *pc*
  BEYOND THE FIRE: **awasishkode** *pc*
  BUILD A FIRE: **boodawe** *vai*
  BY A FIRE: **jiigishkode** *pc*
  CATCH FIRE: **nawadide, nawadidemagad**
    vii; **nawadizo** *vai*
  HAVE A FIRE: have a fire at one's place
    zakizo *vai*
  MAKE A FIRE: **ishkodeke** *vai*
  ON FIRE: be on fire **ishkodewan** *vii*
  ON THE OTHER SIDE OF THE FIRE:
    agaamishkode *pc*
  ON THIS SIDE OF THE FIRE:
    ondaasishkode *pc*
  OVER ACROSS THE FIRE: **awasishkode** *pc*
  PUT WOOD ON THE FIRE: **bagidinise** *vai*
  SET ON FIRE: set s.o. on fire **zaka' /zaka'w-/**
    vta; set s.t. on fire **zaka'an** *vti;* set (s.t.) on
    fire for s.o. **zaka'amaw** *vta*
  STIR THE FIRE: **jiichiishkinzhe'ige** *vai*
  TAKEN OFF THE FIRE: be taken off the fire
    agwaasijigaade, agwaasijigaademagad
    vii; **agwaasijigaazo** *vai*
  WARM BY THE FIRE: warm oneself by the
    fire **awazo** *vai*
FIRE EXTINGUISHER
  FIRE EXTINGUISHER: **aate'igan, -an** *ni*
FIRE POKER
  FIRE POKER: **jiichiishkinzhe'igan, -an** *ni*
FIRE TRUCK
  FIRE TRUCK: **aate'ishkodawewidaabaan** *na*
FIREFLY
  FIREFLY: **waawaatesi, -wag** *na, also*
    wewaatesi
FIREMAN
  FIREMAN: **aate'ishkodawewinini, -wag** *na*
FIREPLACE
  FIREPLACE: **boodawaan, -an** *ni*
FIREWOOD
  FIREWOOD: piece of firewood **mishi /miS-/**
    ni

BRING FIREWOOD INSIDE: **biindigenise** *vai*

CUT FIREWOOD: **manise** *vai;* cut s.t. as firewood **manisaadan** *vti;* cut (s.t.) as firewood for s.o. **manisaw** *vta*

GO GET FIREWOOD: **naadinise** *vai, also* **naajinise**

SPLIT FIREWOOD: **daashkiga'ise** *vai*

FIRST
FIRST: **nitam** *pc;* first (in a time sequence) **akawe** *pc, also* **kawe**

AT FIRST: **wayeshkad** *pc*

FIRST OF ALL: **akawe** *pc, also* **kawe**

LIVE IN THE FIRST HOUSE: **nitamige** *vai*

THE FIRST DAY: be the first day (of a month) **maadaginzo** *vai*

FIRST PERSON
FIRST PERSON: *first person prefix* **ni=** *pre; also* **n=, in=, ind=, im=, nin=*, nim=*, nind=***

FIRST PERSON EXCLUSIVE PLURAL: we *first person exclusive plural personal pronoun* **niinawind** *pr;* only us *first person exclusive plural personal pronoun* **niinetawind** *pr;* our turn *first person exclusive plural personal pronoun* **niinitamawind** *pr*

FIRST PERSON INCLUSIVE PLURAL: we *first person inclusive personal pronoun* **giinawind** *pr;* only us *first person inclusive personal pronoun* **giinetawind** *pr;* our turn *first person inclusive personal pronoun* **giinitamawind** *pr*

FIRST PERSON SINGULAR: I *first person singular personal pronoun* **niin** *pr;* my turn *first person singular personal pronoun* **niinitam** *pr;* only me *first person singular personal pronoun* **niineta** *pr*

FIRST TIME
FOR THE FIRST TIME: **oshki-** *pv4*

FIRST-BORN
FIRST-BORN: **nitamoozhaan, -ag** *na*

FISH
FISH: **giigoonh, -yag** *na;* **giigoonyike** *vai*

CLEAN A FISH: **bakazhaawe** *vai*

FIRE-CURED MEAT OR FISH: **abwewasigan, -an** *ni*

FISH THROUGH THE ICE WITH SPEAR: **akwa'waa** *vai*

FISH WITH A HOOK AND LINE: **wewebanaabii** *vai*

FISH WITH A NET: **bagida'waa** *vai*

FISH WITH SET LINES: **bagidaabii** *vai*

GO FISHING: **noojigiigoonyiwe** *vai*

SCALE FISH: **jiiga'e** *vai*

FISH DECOY
FISH DECOY: **okeyaw, -ag** *na*

FISH EGG
FISH EGG: **waak, -wan** *ni*

FISH HOOK
FISH HOOK: **migiskan, -an** *ni*

FISH HOUSE
FISH HOUSE FOR SPEARING: **akwa'wewigamig, -oon** *ni*

FISH SOUP
FISH SOUP: **giigoonhwaaboo** *ni*

FISH SPEAR
FISH SPEAR: **anit, -iin** *ni*

FISH TRAP
FISH TRAP: **biinjiboonaagan, -ag** *na*

FISHER
FISHER: **ojiig, -ag** *na*

FISHER HIDE
FISHER HIDE: **ojiigiwayaan, -ag** *na*

FISHERMAN
FISHERMAN: **giigoonyikewinini, -wag** *na*

FISHING POLE
FISHING POLE: **migiskanaak, -oon** *ni, also* **migiskanaatig**

FIT
FIT: **debashkine** *vai;* **debashkine, debashkinemagad** *vii;* fit (as something liquid) **debibii, debibiimagad** *vii*

FIT LOOSELY: fit s.o. loosely **geshawishkaw** *vta;* fit s.t. loosely **geshawishkan** *vti*

FIT WELL: **minwashkine** *vai;* **minwashkine, minwashkinemagad** *vii;* fit s.o. well (e.g., pants) **minokaw** *vta;* fit s.t. well **minokan** *vti*

FIT WITH FOOT OR BODY: fit s.o. with foot or body **debishkaw** *vta;* fit s.t. with foot or body **debishkan** *vti*

FIVE
FIVE: **naanan** *nm;* **naano-** *pv4;* they are five **naananinoon /naananin-/** *vii;* **naananiwag /naanani-/** *vai;* five (card) **naanoobii'igan, -ag** *na*

AND FIVE: **ashi-naanan** *nm;* **ashi-naano-** *pv4*

FIVE ACRES: **naano-diba'igaans** *pc*

FIVE DAYS: **naano-giizhik** *pc;* **naanogon** *pc;* be five days **naanogonagad** *vii*

FIVE DAYS OLD: be five days old **naanogonagizi** *vai*

FIVE DOLLARS: **naanwaabik** *pc*

FIVE FEET: **naanozid** *pc*

FIVE HOURS: **naano-diba'igan** *pc*

FIVE HUNDRED: **naanwaak** *nm*

FIVE INCHES: **naanoninj** *pc*

FIVE MILES: **naano-diba'igan** *pc*

FIVE MINUTES: **naano-diba'igaans** *pc*

FIVE MONTHS: **naano-giizis** *pc*

FIVE NIGHTS: **naano-dibik** *pc*

FIVE O'CLOCK: be five o'clock **naano-diba'iganed** *vii*

FIVE PAIRS: **naanwewaan** *pc*

FIVE SETS: **naanwewaan** *pc*

FIVE THOUSAND: **naanosagoons** *nm*

FIVE TIMES: **naaning** *pc*

FIVE WEEKS: **naano-anama'e-giizhik** *pc;* be five weeks **naano-anama'e-giizhigad** *vii*

FIVE YEARS: **naano-biboon** *pc;* be five years **naano-biboonagad** *vii*

FIVE YEARS OLD: be five years old **naano-biboonagizi** *vai*

FIX
FIX: fix s.o. **nanaa'in** *vta;* fix s.t. **nanaa'inan** *vti;* **nanaa'itoon** *vti2;* fix (s.t.) for s.o. **nanaa'itaw** *vta, also* **nanaa'itamaw;** fix things **nanaa'ichige** *vai*

FLAG
   FLAG: **gikiwe'on, -an** *ni*
FLASHLIGHT
   FLASHLIGHT: **zakaasigan, -an** *ni*
FLAT
   FLAT: be flat **nabagaa, nabagaamagad** *vii;*
   nabagizi *vai*
   FLAT NOSE: have a flat nose **nabagijaane** *vai*
   FLAT TIRE: have a flat tire **nabagijiishin** *vai*
FLAVOR
   FLAVOR: flavor (s.t.) **apaabowe** *vai+o*
FLEA
   FLEA: **babig, -wag** *na*
FLEE
   FLEE: **giimii** *vai;* **ozhimo** *vai;* flee from s.o.
   ginjiba' *vta;* flee from people **ginjiba'iwe**
   vai
   ARRIVE FLEEING: arrive fleeing from people
   bagamiba'iwe *vai*
   FLEE FOR GOOD: **aapijinizhimo** *vai*
   START TO FLEE: **maajiiba'iwe** *vai*
FLESH
   FLESH: my flesh **niiyaas /-iiyaas-/** *nid*
FLIGHT
   RUN ALONG IN FLIGHT: **biminizhimo**
   vai; run along in flight from someone
   bimiba'iwe *vai*
   RUN FROM CERTAIN PLACE IN
   FLIGHT: run from a certain place in flight
   onjinizhimo *vai*
   RUN TO A CERTAIN PLACE IN FLIGHT:
   izhinizhimo *vai*
FLING
   FLING OPEN: fling s.t. open (as something
   stick- or wood-like, e.g., a door)
   baakaakowebinan *vti*
FLINT
   FLINT: **biiwaanag, -oog** *na*
FLIRT
   FLIRT: **noodendam** *vai2*
FLOAT
   FLOAT: **agomo** *vai;* **agonde** *vii*
   FLOAT AWAY: **animaabogo** *vai;*
   animaaboode, animaaboodemagad *vii*
FLOAT
   FLOAT: **deteba'agonjichigan, -an** *ni;* net
   float **agonjoonaagan, -an** *ni*
FLOOD
   FLOOD: there is a flood **mooshka'an** *vii*
FLOODED
   FLOODED: be flooded **mooshka'an** *vii;*
   nikibii *vai;* **nikibii, nikibiimagad** *vii*
FLOOR
   FLOOR: **michisag, -oon** *ni*
   FLOOR ABOVE: the floor above **ishpimisag,
   -oon** *ni*
   FLOOR PIECE OF CANOE: **apisidaagan,
   -ag** *na*
   IN THE MIDDLE OF THE FLOOR:
   naawisag *pc*
   UNDER THE FLOOR: **anaamisag** *pc*
   WASH FLOORS: **giziibiigisaginige** *vai*

FLOUR
   FLOUR: **bakwezhigan, -ag** *na;* **bebinezid
   bakwezhigan** *na;* **bibine-bakwezhigan** *na*
FLOUR BOX
   FLOUR BOX: **bakwezhigani-makak, -oon** *ni*
FLOW
   FLOW A CERTAIN WAY: **izhijiwan** *vii*
   FLOW ALONG: **bimijiwan** *vii*
   FLOW AWAY: **animijiwan** *vii*
   FLOW FAST: **gizhiijiwan** *vii*
   FLOW FROM A CERTAIN PLACE:
   onjijiwan *vii*
   FLOW IN: **biinjijiwan** *vii*
   FLOW INTO A LAKE: **zaagidawaa,
   zaagidawaamagad** *vii*
   FLOW OUT: **zaagijiwan** *vii*
   FLOW TO A CERTAIN PLACE: **izhijiwan**
   vii
   FLOW WITH A RIPPLE: **zaasijiwan** *vii*
   HEARD FLOWING: be heard flowing (e.g., a
   rapids) **madwejiwan** *vii*
   RIVER FLOWS ALONG: flow along (as a
   river) **bimitigweyaa, bimitigweyaamagad**
   vii
   RIVER FLOWS AROUND A BEND: flow
   around a bend (as a river)
   washkitigweyaa, washkitigweyaamagad
   vii
   RIVER FLOWS TO A CERTAIN PLACE:
   flow to a certain place (as a river)
   izhitigweyaa, izhitigweyaamagad *vii*
   START TO FLOW: **maajijiwan** *vii*
FLOWER
   FLOWER: **waabigwan, -iin** *ni*
FLUTE
   FLUTE: **bibigwan, -an** *ni*
   PLAY THE FLUTE: **bibigwe** *vai*
FLY
   ARRIVE FLYING: **bagamibide,
   bagamibidemagad** *vii;* **bagamibizo** *vai;*
   bagamise *vai;* **bagamise,
   bagamisemagad** *vii*
   FLY ABOUT: **babaamibide,
   babaamibidemagad** *vii;* **babaamibizo**
   vai; **babaamise** *vai;* **babaamise,
   babaamisemagad** *vii*
   FLY ALONG: **bimibide, bimibidemagad** *vii;*
   bimibizo *vai;* **bimise** *vai;* **bimise,
   bimisemagad** *vii*
   FLY AT A CERTAIN SPEED: **apiichibide,
   apiichibidemagad** *vii;* **apiichibizo** *vai*
   FLY AWAY: **animibide, animibidemagad** *vii;*
   animibizo *vai;* **animise** *vai;* **animise,
   animisemagad** *vii*
   FLY AWAY MAKING NOISE:
   animwewebide, animwewebidemagad
   vii; **animwewebizo** *vai*
   FLY FAST: **gizhiibide, gizhiibidemagad** *vii;*
   gizhiibizo *vai;* **gizhiise** *vai;* **gizhiise,
   gizhiisemagad** *vii*
   FLY FROM A CERTAIN PLACE: **onjise** *vai;*
   onjise, onjisemagad *vii*

FLY HERE: biijibide, biijibidemagad *vii;*
biijibizo *vai;* biijise *vai;* biijise,
biijisemagad *vii*
FLY IN: biinjibide, biinjibidemagad *vii;*
biinjibizo *vai;* biinjise *vai;* biinjise,
biinjisemagad *vii*
FLY INSIDE: biindigebide,
biindigebidemagad *vii;* biindigebizo *vai*
FLY OPEN: fly open (as something stick- or
wood-like, e.g., a door) baakaakose,
baakaakosemagad *vii*
FLY TO A CERTAIN PLACE: ipide,
ipidemagad *vii;* ipizo *vai;* izhise *vai;*
izhise, izhisemagad *vii*
FLY UPWARDS: ombibide,
ombibidemagad *vii;* ombibizo *vai*
FLY
FLY: fly (insect) oojii, -g *na,* also oojiins
FLYING SQUIRREL
FLYING SQUIRREL: zhagashkaandawe, -g
na
FOAM
FOAM: biite *ni*
FOAMY
FOAMY: be foamy biitewan *vii*
FOG
FOG: there is a fog awan *vii*
DENSE FOG: be a dense fog gashkawan *vii*
FOGGY
FOGGY: be foggy awan *vii*
FOLD
FOLD: fold s.o. biskin *vta;* fold s.o. (as some-
thing sheet-like) biskiigin *vta;* fold s.t.
biskinan *vti;* fold s.t. (as something sheet-
like) biskiiginan *vti*
FOLD OVER: fold s.o. over nabon *vta;* fold
s.t. over nabonan *vti*
FOLD WITH HANDS: fold s.o. with hands
biskibizh /biskibiN-/ *vta;* fold s.t. with
hands biskibidoon *vti2*
FOLDED
FOLDED: be folded biskaa, biskaamagad *vii;*
biskinigaade, biskinigaademagad *vii*
FOLLOW
FOLLOW: follow in s.o.'s steps aanikeshkaw
vta; follow s.o. noopinazh /noopinaN-/
vta; follow s.t. noopinadoon *vti2*
FOLLOW A TRAIL: go off following a trail
maada'adoo *vai;* go off following s.o.'s
trail maada'azh /maada'aN-/ *vta*
FOLLOW A TRAIL ALONG: bima'adoo
vai; follow s.o.'s trail along bima'azh
/bima'aN-/ *vta;* follow s.t. along as a trail
bima'adoon *vti2*
FOLLOW A TRAIL AWAY: anima'adoo *vai;*
follow s.o.'s trail away anima'azh
/anima'aN-/ *vta;* follow s.t. away as a trail
anima'adoon *vti2*
FOLLOW A TRAIL HERE: biida'adoo *vai;*
follow s.o.'s trail here biida'azh /biida'aN-/
vta; follow s.t. as a trail here biida'adoon
vti2
FOLLOW A TRAIL TO A CERTAIN
PLACE: follow s.o.'s trail to a certain place

ina'azh /ina'aN-/ *vta;* follow s.t. as a trail
to a certain place ina'adoon *vti2*
FOND DU LAC
FOND DU LAC: Fond du Lac Reservation
Nagaajiwanaang *place*
FOOD
FOOD: miijim, -an *ni;* wiisiniwin *ni*
BUY FOOD: miijimadaawe *vai*
GET FOOD: get food by hunting or fishing
nandawenjige *vai*
GO GET FOOD: naajimiijime *vai*
SERVE FOOD: serve food to people ashange
vai
FOOLISH
FOOLISH: be foolish gagiibaadad *vii;*
gagiibaadizi *vai*
DO FOOLISH THINGS: gagiibaajichige *vai*
FOOT
FOOT: my foot inzid, -an /-zid-/ *nid*
ACHE IN FOOT: have an ache in one's foot
dewizide *vai*
BIG FOOT: have a big foot mangizide *vai*
BLISTER ON FOOT: get a blister on one's
foot abashkwebiigizideshin *vai*
CERTAIN NUMBER OF FEET: a certain
number of feet dasozid *pc*
MOVE FOOT A CERTAIN WAY: move
one's foot a certain way izhizideni *vai*
MUDDY FEET: have muddy feet
azhashkiiwizide *vai*
NUMB FOOT: have a numb foot
niboowizide *vai*
SORE FOOT: have a sore foot gaagiijizide *vai*
SPRAIN FOOT: sprain one's foot
zegizideshin *vai*
SWEATY FOOT: have a sweaty foot
abwezide *vai*
SWOLLEN FOOT: have a swollen foot
baagizide *vai*
TAP FOOT: tap one's foot jiichiibizideni *vai*
WARM FEET: warm one's feet abizidezo *vai*
FOOTBRIDGE
FOOTBRIDGE: foot bridge
aazhawaandawaagan, -an *ni*
FOOTPATH
FOOTPATH: ozide-miikana, -n *ni*
FOOTPRINT
FOOTPRINT: bimikawaan, -an *ni*
FOOTREST
CRADLE BOARD FOOTREST:
apizideyaakwa'igan, -an *ni*
FOOTSTOOL
FOOTSTOOL: apizideshinowin, -an *ni*
FORBID
FORBID: forbid s.o. to gina'amaw *vta*
FORBIDDEN
FORBIDDEN: it is forbidden gina'amaadim
vai
FOREHEAD
FOREHEAD: my forehead nikatig, -oon
/-katigw-/ *nid*
MIDDLE OF THE FOREHEAD: in the
middle of the forehead naawigatig *pc*

FOREIGN
FOREIGN: **mayagi-** *pv4;* be foreign **mayagizi** *vai*
LOOK FOREIGN: **mayaginaagozi** *vai;* **mayaginaagwad** *vii*
SOUND FOREIGN: **mayagitaagozi** *vai;* **mayagitaagwad** *vii*

FOREIGNER
FOREIGNER: **mayagwewinini, -wag** *na*

FORETELL
FORETELL THE FUTURE: **onwaachige** *vai*

FOREVER
FOREVER: **gaagige-** *pv4*

FORGET
FORGET: **wanendam** *vai2;* forget (s.t.) **waniike** *vai+o;* forget s.o. **boonenim** *vta;* **wanenim** *vta;* forget s.t. **boonendan** *vti;* **wanendan** *vti*

FORK
FORK: **badaka'igan, -an** *ni*
USE A FORK ON: use a fork on s.o. **badaka' /badaka'w-/** *vta;* use a fork on s.t. **badaka'an** *vti*

FORK
RIVER FORKS: fork (as a river) **niingidawitigweyaa, niingidawitigweyaamagad** *vii*
ROAD FORKS: fork (as a road or trail) **niingidawadamon /niingidawadamo-/** *vii*
TRAIL FORKS: fork (as a road or trail) **niingidawadamon /niingidawadamo-/** *vii*

FORM
FORM: form s.o. **ozhi'** *vta;* form s.t. **ozhitoon** *vti2*

FORMERLY
FORMERLY: **gayat** *pc;* **iko** *pc,* also **ko**

FORTUNATE
FORTUNATE: be fortunate **zhawendaagozi** *vai*

FORTY
FORTY: **niimidana** *nm*

FOUND
FOUND: be found **mikigaade, mikigaademagad** *vii;* **mikigaazo** *vai*

FOUR
FOUR: **niiwin** *nm;* **niiwo-** *pv4,* also **niiyo-**; they are four **niiwinoon /niiwin-/** *vii;* **niiwiwag /niiwi-/** *vai;* four (card) **niiwoobii'igan, -ag** *na,* also **niiyoobii'igan**
AND FOUR: **ashi-niiwin** *nm;* **ashi-niiwo-** *pv4,* also **ashi-niiyo-**; **ashi-niiyo-** *pv4,* also **ashi-niiwo-**
FOUR ACRES: **niiwo-diba'igaans** *pc,* also **niiyo-diba'igaans**
FOUR DAYS: **niiwo-giizhik** *pc,* also **niiyo-giizhik**; **niiwogon** *pc,* also **niiyogon**; be four days **niiwogonagad** *vii,* also **niiyogonagad**
FOUR DAYS OLD: be four days old **niiwogonagizi** *vai,* also **niiyogonagizi**
FOUR DOLLARS: **niiwaabik** *pc*
FOUR EACH: **neniiwin** *nm*
FOUR FEET: **niiwozid** *pc,* also **niiyozid**

FOUR HOURS: **niiwo-diba'igan** *pc,* also **niiyo-diba'igan**
FOUR HUNDRED: **niiwaak** *nm*
FOUR INCHES: **niiwoninj** *pc,* also **niiyoninj**
FOUR MILES: **niiwo-diba'igan** *pc,* also **niiyo-diba'igan**
FOUR MINUTES: **niiwo-diba'igaans** *pc,* also **niiyo-diba'igaans**
FOUR MONTHS: **niiwo-giizis** *pc,* also **niiyo-giizis**
FOUR NIGHTS: **niiwo-dibik** *pc,* also **niiyo-dibik**
FOUR PAIRS: **niiwewaan** *pc*
FOUR SETS: **niiwewaan** *pc*
FOUR THOUSAND: **niiwosagoons** *nm,* also **niiyosagoons**
FOUR TIMES: **niiwing** *pc*
FOUR WEEKS: **niiwo-anama'e-giizhik** *pc,* also **niiyo-anama'e-giizhik**; **niiwo-anama'e-giizhik** *pc,* also **niiyo-anama'e-giizhik**; be four weeks **niiwo-anama'e-giizhigad** *vii,* also **niiyo-anama'e-giizhigad**
FOUR YEARS: **niiwo-biboon** *pc,* also **niiyo-biboon**; be four years **niiwo-biboonagad** *vii*
FOUR YEARS OLD: be four years old **niiwo-biboonagizi** *vai,* also **niiyo-biboonagizi**

FOURTEEN
FOURTEEN: **ashi-niiwin** *nm;* **midaaswi ashi-niiwin** *nm*

FOURTH
THE FOURTH DAY OF THE MONTH: be the fourth day of the month **niiwogonagizi** *vai,* also **niiyogonagizi**

FOURTH OF JULY
FOURTH OF JULY: be the Fourth of July **baapaashkizige-giizhigad** *vii*

FOX
FOX: **waagosh, -ag** *na*

FOX HIDE
FOX HIDE: **waagoshiwayaan, -ag** *na*

FRAIL
FRAIL: be frail **niinamizi** *vai*

FRAME
SAP-BOILING FRAME: frame for holding sap-boiling kettles **iskigamiziganaak, -oon** *ni*
SET UP AS A FRAME: set s.t. up as a frame **onaakosidoon** *vti2*

FREE
FREE: free s.o. **gidiskin** *vta;* free s.t. **gidiskinan** *vti*
GET FREE: **gashki'o** *vai*
PULL FREE: pull s.o. free **gidiskibizh /gidiskibiN-/** *vta;* pull s.t. free **gidiskibidoon** *vti2*
TRY TO GET FREE: **wiikwaji'o** *vai;* try to get free of s.t. **wiikwajitoon** *vti2*

FREEZE
FREEZE: **mashkawadin** *vii;* **mashkawaji** *vai*
FREEZE OVER: **gashkadin** *vii*
FREEZE STIFF: freeze s.o. stiff **mashkawaakwajim** *vta;* freeze s.t. stiff **mashkawaakwajidoon** *vti2*

FREEZE TO DEATH: **gawaji** *vai*
FREEZER
   FREEZER: **dakisijigan, -an** *ni*
FRENCH
   SPEAK FRENCH: **wemitigoozhiimo** *vai*
FRENCHMAN
   FRENCHMAN: **wemitigoozhi, -wag** *na*
FRIDAY
   FRIDAY: be Friday **naano-giizhigad** *vii*
FRIED
   FRIED: be fried **zaasakokwaade,
   zaasakokwaademagad** *vii;*
   zaasakokwaazo *vai*
FRIEND
   FRIEND: my (female's) female friend
   niijikwe, -g /-iijikwew-/ *nad;* my (female's)
   female friend **indaangwe, -g /-daangwew-/**
   nad; my (male's) male friend **niijikiwenh,
   -yag /-iijikiweny-/** *nad;* my (male's) male
   friend *ritual use* **niikaan, -ag /-iikaan-/** *nad;*
   niikaanis, -ag /-iikaanis-/ *nad;* my friend
   (vocative form, usually male to male) **niijii**
   nad
   CLOSE FRIENDS: be close friends with s.o.
   beshwaji' *vta*
   FRIENDS: they are friends with each other
   nagadenindiwag /nagadenindi-/ *vai*
FRIGHTEN
   FRIGHTEN: frighten s.o. **zegi'** *vta*
FRINGE
   FRINGE: **niisiiwezhigan, -an** *ni*
   CUT FRINGE: cut fringe in s.o. **niisiiwezh
   /niisiiwezhw-/** *vta;* cut fringe in s.t.
   niisiiwezhan *vti*
FRINGED
   FRINGED: be fringed **niisiiwezhigaade,
   niisiiwezhigaademagad** *vii;*
   niisiiwezhigaazo *vai*
FROG
   FROG: **omakakii, -g** *na*
FROM
   ABSENT FROM A CERTAIN PLACE: be
   absent from a certain place **ondendi** *vai*
   BLOWN FROM A CERTAIN PLACE: be
   blown from a certain place **ondaashi** *vai;*
   be blown from a certain place **ondaasin** *vii*
   CARRY FROM A CERTAIN PLACE: carry
   s.o. from a certain place **onjiwizh
   /onjiwiN-/** *vta;* carry s.t. from a certain
   place **onjiwidoon** *vti2*
   CARRY ON BACK FROM A CERTAIN
   PLACE: carry s.o. on back from a certain
   place **ondoom** *vta;* carry s.t. on back from
   a certain place **ondoondan** *vti*
   COME AS WIND FROM A CERTAIN
   PLACE: come as wind from a certain
   direction **ondaanimad** *vii*
   COME FROM A CERTAIN PLACE:
   ondaadad *vii;* **ondaadizi** *vai;* **onjibaa** *vai;*
   onjii *vai;* come from a certain place (as
   smoke) **ondaabate, ondaabatemagad** *vii*
   COME FROM A CERTAIN PLACE
   CRYING: **ondademo** *vai*

CRAWL FROM A CERTAIN PLACE:
   ondoode *vai*
DRIVE FROM A CERTAIN PLACE:
   onjibide, onjibidemagad *vii;* **onjibizo** *vai;*
   onjidaabii'iwe *vai*
EARN FROM A CERTAIN PLACE: **ondizi**
   vai
FALL FROM A CERTAIN PLACE:
   onjibide, onjibidemagad *vii;* **onjibizo** *vai*
FLOW FROM A CERTAIN PLACE:
   onjijiwan *vii*
FLY FROM A CERTAIN PLACE: **onjise** *vai;*
   onjise, onjisemagad *vii*
FROM A CERTAIN PLACE: **onji-** *pv3*
GET FROM A CERTAIN PLACE: get (s.t.)
   for oneself from a certain place
   ondinamaazo *vai;* get s.o. from a certain
   place **ondin** *vta;* get s.t. from a certain
   place **ondinan** *vti;* get (s.t.) for s.o. from a
   certain place **ondinamaw** *vta;* get things
   from a certain place **ondinige** *vai*
GET WATER FROM A CERTAIN PLACE:
   onda'ibii *vai*
GONE FROM A CERTAIN PLACE: be gone
   from a certain place **ondendi** *vai*
INHERIT FROM A CERTAIN SOURCE:
   ondizi *vai*
LOOK OUT FROM A CERTAIN PLACE:
   onzaabi *vai*
OBTAIN FROM A CERTAIN PLACE: ob-
   tain s.o. from a certain place **ondin** *vta;* obtain s.t. from a certain place **ondinan** *vti;*
   obtain (s.t.) for s.o. from a certain place
   ondinamaw *vta;* obtain things from a certain place **ondinige** *vai*
OBTAINED FROM A CERTAIN PLACE:
   be obtained from a certain place
   ondinigaade, ondinigaademagad *vii;*
   ondinigaazo *vai*
PADDLE FROM A CERTAIN PLACE:
   ondakwazhiwe *vai*
RIDE FROM A CERTAIN PLACE ON
   HORSEBACK: **ondoomigo** *vai*
ROAD LEADS FROM A CERTAIN PLACE:
   lead from a certain place (as a road or trail)
   ondadamon /ondadamo-/ *vii*
RUN FROM CERTAIN PLACE IN
   FLIGHT: run from a certain place in flight
   onjinizhimo *vai*
RUN FROM A CERTAIN PLACE:
   onjibatoo *vai*
SAIL FROM A CERTAIN PLACE: **ondaashi**
   vai; **ondaasin** *vii*
SKATE FROM A CERTAIN PLACE:
   ondaada'e *vai*
SPEED FROM A CERTAIN PLACE:
   onjibide, onjibidemagad *vii;* **onjibizo** *vai*
SWIM FROM A CERTAIN PLACE:
   ondaadagaa *vai;* swim from a certain place
   (as a fish) **ondakwazhiwe** *vai*
TAKE FROM A CERTAIN PLACE: take s.o.
   from a certain place **onjiwizh /onjiwiN-/**
   vta; take s.t. from a certain place
   onjiwidoon *vti2*

TRAIL LEADS FROM A CERTAIN
PLACE: lead from a certain place (as a
road or trail) **ondadamon** /**ondadamo-**/ *vii*
WADE FROM A CERTAIN PLACE:
ondaadagaazii *vai*
WALK FROM A CERTAIN PLACE: **ondose**
vai

FRONT
AT THE FRONT: **niigaan** *pc*
HANG IN FRONT: **niigaanagoode**,
niigaanagoodemagad *vii;* **niigaanagoojin**
vai; hang s.o. in front **niigaanagoozh**
/**niigaanagooN-**/ *vta;* hang s.t. in front
niigaanagoodoon *vti2*
SIT IN FRONT: **niigaanabi** *vai*
STAND IN FRONT: **niigaanigaabawi** *vai*

FROST
HEAVY FROST: there is a heavy frost
zasakwaa *vii*

FROSTBITTEN
FROSTBITTEN: be frostbitten **mashkawaji**
vai; **mashkawaakwaji** *vai*

FROSTED
FROSTED: be frosted **ningiigwadin** *vii;*
ningiigwaji *vai*

FROZEN
FROZEN: be frozen **mashkawadin** *vii;*
mashkawaji *vai*
FROZEN HAND: have a frozen hand
mashkawaakwajininjiiwaji *vai*
FROZEN OVER: be frozen over **gashkadin** *vii*
FROZEN SHUT: be frozen shut **gibaakwadin**
vii; **gibaakwaji** *vai*
FROZEN STIFF: be frozen stiff
mashkawaakwadin *vii;* **mashkawaakwaji**
vai
FROZEN THICK: be frozen thick
gipagaakwadin *vii;* **gipagaakwaji** *vai*
FROZEN THIN: be frozen thin
bibagaakwadin *vii;* **bibagaakwaji** *vai*

FRY
FRY: **zaasakokwe** *vai;* fry s.o.
zaasakokwaazh /**zaasakokwaaN-**/ *vta;* fry
s.t. **zaasakokwaadan** *vti*

FRY BREAD
FRY BREAD: **zaasakokwaan**, **-ag** *na*

FRYING PAN
FRYING PAN: **abwewin**, **-an** *ni*

FUEL
RUN OUT OF FUEL: **iskaakizige** *vai*

FULL
FULL: be full (after eating) **debisinii** *vai;* be
full (of a liquid) **mooshkinebii**,
mooshkinebiimagad *vii;* be full (of solids)
mooshkine, **mooshkine**,
mooshkinemagad *vii*
FULL MOON: be full (as something mineral,
e.g., the moon) **miziweyaabikizi** *vai*
FULL OF SMOKE: be full of smoke
gibwanaamode, **gibwanaamodemagad**
vii

FULLY
FULLY RIPE: be fully ripe **giizhaande**,
giizhaandemagad *vii;* **giizhaanzo** *vai*

FUN
FUN: be fun **minwendaagozi** *vai;*
minwendaagwad *vii*
JUST FOR FUN: **anishaa** *pc*

FUNERAL
HOLD A FUNERAL: **bagidenjige** *vai;*
maajaa'iwe *vai;* hold a funeral for s.o.
maajaa' *vta*
SPEAK AT A FUNERAL: **maajaa'iwe** *vai*

FUNGUS
FUNGUS: **wazhashkwedo**, **-wag** *na*

FUNNY
FUNNY: **wawiyazh** *pc*
CONSIDERED FUNNY: be considered
funny (comical) **wawiyadendaagozi** *vai*
FUNNY MOVIE: be a funny movie
gagiibaadaatese, **gagiibaadaatesemagad**
vii
LOOK FUNNY: look funny (comical)
wawiyazhinaagozi *vai;*
wawiyazhinaagwad *vii*
SOUND FUNNY: sound funny (comical)
wawiyazhitaagozi *vai;*
wawiyazhitaagwad *vii*

FUR
FUR FOR TRADE: **adaawaagan**, **-an** *ni*
THICK FUR: have thick fur **gipagawe** *vai*

FUTURE
FORETELL THE FUTURE: **onwaachige** *vai*

FUTURE TENSE
FUTURE TENSE: *future tense prefix after a
personal prefix* **ga-** *pv1; future tense prefix
optional form after a personal prefix and before
a vowel* **gad-**; *future tense prefix in independent order with no personal prefix* **da-** *pv1;
future tense prefix in unchanged conjunct order*
ji- *pv1*
FUTURE/DESIDERATIVE TENSE: want to
wii- *pv1*

G

GALLBLADDER
GALLBLADDER: my gall bladder **niinzob**,
-iin /**-iinzoby-**/ *nid*

GALLSTONE
HAVE GALLSTONES: **odasiniinsimi** *vai*

GAMBLE
GAMBLE: **ataage** *vai;* they gamble with each
other **ataadiwag** /**ataadi-**/ *vai*

GAME WARDEN
GAME WARDEN: **gizhaadigewinini**, **-wag**
na; **wiiyaasi-dakoniwewinini**, **-wag** *na*

GAP

PULL APART TO FORM A GAP: pull s.o. apart to form a gap **dawibizh** /**dawibiN-**/ *vta;* pull s.t. apart to form a gap **dawibidoon** *vti2;* pull things apart to form a gap **dawibijige** *vai*

GARDEN

GARDEN: **gitigaan, -an** *ni;* **gitige** *vai*

GARTER

ARM GARTER: **jiiskinikebizon, -an** *ni* LEG GARTER: **gashkidaasebizon, -an** *ni*

GAS CAN

GAS CAN: **waazakonenjiganaaboowakik, -oog** *na*

GAS STATION

GAS STATION: **waazakonenjiganaaboowadaawewigamig, -oon** *ni, also* **waazakonenjiganaabooadaawewigamig**

GAS TANK

GAS TANK: **waazakonenjiganaaboowakik, -oog** *na*

GASOLINE

GASOLINE: **waasamoo-bimide** *ni;* **waazakonenjiganaaboo** *ni*

GATHER

GATHER: gather s.o. **maamigin** *vta;* gather s.t. **maamiginan** *vti* GATHER SAP: **naadoobii** *vai* GATHER UP: gather s.o. up **asigin** *vta;* gather s.t. up **asiginan** *vti*

GATHERED

GATHERED UP: be gathered up **asiginigaade, asiginigaademagad** *vii;* **asiginigaazo** *vai*

GEAR

GEARSHIFT: **aandaabikinigan, -an** *ni* SHIFT GEARS: **aandaabikinige** *vai;* **biindaabikibijige** *vai*

GEARSHIFT

GEARSHIFT: **biindaabikibijigan, -an** *ni*

GENEROUS

GENEROUS: be generous **gizhewaadizi** *vai*

GERMAN SHEPHERD

GERMAN SHEPHERD: **ma'iinganasim, -oog** *na*

GET

GET EASILY: get s.o. easily **wenipazhi'** *vta;* get s.t. easily **wenipazhitoon** *vti2* GET FROM A CERTAIN PLACE: get s.o. from a certain place **ondin** *vta;* get s.t. from a certain place **ondinan** *vti;* get (s.t.) for s.o. from a certain place **ondinamaw** *vta;* get things from a certain place **ondinige** *vai;* get (s.t.) for oneself from a certain place **ondinamaazo** *vai* GET WATER: **nibinaadi** *vai;* get water for s.o. **gwaaba'amaw** *vta* GO GET: go get s.o. **naazh** /**naaN-**/ *vta;* go get s.t. **naadin** *vti3;* go get (s.t.) for s.o. **naadaw** *vta* GO GET A NET: **naadasabii** *vai*

GO GET BY BOAT: go get s.o. by boat **naada'** /**naada'w-**/ *vta;* go get s.t. by boat **naada'an** *vti* GO GET FIREWOOD: **naadinise** *vai, also* **naajinise** GO GET FOOD: **naajimiijime** *vai* GO GET MAIL: **naadazina'igane** *vai* GO GET TRAPS: go get one's traps **naadasoonaagane** *vai* GO GET WATER: go get water or other liquid **naadoobii** *vai* GO TO GET: go to get s.o. by boat **naada'oozh** /**naada'ooN-**/ *vta;* go to get s.t. by boat **naada'oodoon** *vti* RUN TO GET: run to get s.o. **naajibatwaazh** /**naajibatwaaN-**/ *vta;* run to get s.t. **naajibatwaadan** *vti*

GET AWAY

GET AWAY: get away from s.o. **gii'** *vta*

GET IN

GET IN: get in a vehicle or boat **boozi** *vai* TELL TO GET IN: tell s.o. to get in (a vehicle or boat) **boozinaazha'** /**boozinaazha'w-**/ *vta*

GET OFF

GET OFF: get off a vehicle or boat **gabaa** *vai;* get s.o. off a vehicle or boat **gabaa'** *vta* TELL TO GET OFF: tell s.o. to get off **gabaanaazha'** /**gabaanaazha'w-**/ *vta*

GET UP

GET UP: get up (from a prone position) **onishkaa** *vai*

GHOST

GHOST: **jiibay, -ag** *na*

GIANT

GIANT: **misaabe, -g** *na*

GIGGLE

GIGGLE: **ginagaapi** *vai*

GIRAFFE

GIRAFFE: **genwaabiigigwed** *na-pt*

GIRL

GIRL: **ikwezens, -ag** *na;* be a girl **ikwezensiwi** *vai* ADOLESCENT GIRL: **oshkiniigikwe, -g** *na;* be an adolescent girl **oshkiniigikwewi** *vai*

GIVE

GIVE: give (s.t.) to s.o. **miizh** /**miiN-**/ *vta;* they give (s.t.) to each other **miinidiwag** /**miinidi-**/ *vai* GIVE AWAY: give away (s.t.) **miigiwe** *vai+o* GIVE PRESENTS: give presents to relatives of someone deceased in completion of mourning on anniversary of the death **giiwenige** *vai* GIVE PRESENTS IN EXCHANGE: give presents to s.o. in exchange **giiwenamaw** *vta* GIVE SOMETHING APPROPRIATE: give s.o. something appropriate **debi'** *vta* HAVE ENOUGH TO GIVE: have enough to give away **deba'ookii** *vai;* have enough to give to or feed s.o. **deba'oozh** /**deba'ooN-**/ *vta*

GIVE UP
GIVE UP: **aanizhiitam** *vai2;* **boonendam**
vai2
GIVEAWAY
GIVEAWAY: they have a giveaway
miinidiwag /**miinidi-**/ *vai*
GLAD
GLAD: be glad **minwendam** *vai2*
GLAND
GLAND: my gland (lymph node) **niniishk,**
-wag /**-niishkw-**/ *nad*
SWOLLEN GLAND: have a swollen gland
(lymph node) **baaginiishkwe** *vai*
GLASS
GLASS: (piece of) glass **omoodayaabik, -oon**
ni
BROKEN GLASS: (piece of) glass
omoodayaabik, -oon *ni*
DRINKING GLASS: **mikwamiiwinaagaans,**
-an *ni*
WINDOW GLASS: **waasechiganaabik, -oon**
ni
GLASSES
EYEGLASSES: eyeglasses *plural*
oshkiinzhigokaajiganan *ni,* also
oshkiinzhikokaanan
GLOVE
GLOVE: **niisiiwe-minjikaawan, -ag** *na*
GLOW
GLOW: **waazakone, waazakonemagad** *vii*
GLUE
GLUE: **agokiwasigan, -an** *ni;* glue s.o.
agokiwas /**agokiwasw-**/ *vta;* **bazagokazh**
/**bazagokaN-**/ *vta;* glue s.t. **agokiwasan**
vti; **bazagokadoon** *vti2*
GLUE SHUT: glue s.o. shut **gibokiwas** *vta;*
glue s.t. shut **gibokiwasan** *vti*
GLUED
GLUED: be glued **agokiwaso** *vai;* **agokiwate,**
agokiwatemagad *vii*
GLUED SHUT: be glued shut
gibokiwasigaade, gibokiwasigaademagad
vii; **gibokiwasigaazo** *vai*
GNAT
GNAT: **bingoshens, -ag** *na*
GNAW
GNAW: gnaw s.o. **zhishigwam** *vta;* gnaw s.t.
zhishigwandan *vti*
GO
GO: go to a certain place **izhaa** *vai;*
izhaamagad *vii*
GO A CERTAIN DIRECTION: go a certain
direction (as smoke) **inaabate,**
inaabatemagad *vii*
GO A CERTAIN SPEED: **apiizikaa** *vai*
GO ACROSS: **aazhooshkaa** *vai*
GO ACROSS BY BOAT: **aazhawa'am** *vai2,*
also **aazhawa'o**
GO ACROSS WATER: **aazhoge** *vai*
GO AFTER: go after s.o. **naajinizha'**
/**naajinizha'w-**/ *vta;* **naazh** /**naaN-**/ *vta;*
nooji' *vta;* **noopinazh** /**noopinaN-**/ *vta;* go

after s.t. **naadin** *vti3;* **naajinizha'an** *vti;*
noojitoon *vti2;* **noopinadoon** *vti2*
GO AFTER HAY: **naadashkosiwe** *vai*
GO AFTER TRAPS: **naajiwanii'ige** *vai*
GO AGAINST THE WIND:
onjishkawishkaa *vai*
GO AHEAD: **niigaanii** *vai*
GO ALONG: **bimi-ayaa** *vai*
GO ALONG THE EDGE: **jiigewe** *vai*
GO ALONG THE SHORE: **bimaazhagaame**
vai; **jiigewe** *vai*
GO AND ASK: go and ask for s.o.
nandwewem *vta;* go and ask for s.t.
nandwewendan *vti;* go and ask s.o. (for
s.t.) **nandwewendamaw** *vta*
GO AND NOT RETURN: **aapidendi** *vai*
GO AROUND: **ditibise, ditibisemagad** *vii;*
giiwitaashkaa *vai;* go around (e.g., a
wheel) **ditibise** *vai*
GO AS FAST AS POSSIBLE: **apiizikaa** *vai*
GO ASHORE: **agwaataa** *vai*
GO AWAY: go away! **awas** *pc*
GO AWAY FROM THE WATER: **gopii** *vai*
GO AWAY IN A CANOE: **animishkaa** *vai*
GO BACK: **azhe-** *pv4;* **azhegiiwe** *vai*
GO BACKWARDS: **azheshkaa** *vai;* **azhetaa**
vai
GO BY CANOE: **jiime** *vai*
GO DOWN: go down (of a body of water)
iskate, iskatemagad *vii*
GO DOWN INTO THE WATER: **bakobii**
vai
GO DOWNHILL: **niisaakiiwe** *vai*
GO DOWNSTAIRS: **niisaandawe** *vai*
GO EASY: go easy on s.o. **manaaji'** *vta;* go
easy on s.t. **manaajitoon** *vti2*
GO EVERYWHERE: **miziweshkaa,**
miziweshkaamagad *vii*
GO FAST: **gizhiikaa** *vai*
GO GET: go get s.o. **naazh** /**naaN-**/ *vta;* go get
s.t. **naadin** *vti3;* go get (s.t.) for s.o.
naadaw *vta*
GO GET A NET: **naadasabii** *vai*
GO GET BY BOAT: go get s.o. by boat
naada' /**naada'w-**/ *vta;* go get s.t. by boat
naada'an *vti*
GO GET FIREWOOD: **naadinise** *vai,* also
naajinise
GO GET FOOD: **naajimiijime** *vai*
GO GET MAIL: **naadazina'igane** *vai*
GO GET TRAPS: go get one's traps
naadasoonaagane *vai*
GO GET WATER: go get water or other
liquid **naadoobii** *vai*
GO HOME: **giiwe** *vai*
GO HOME BY BOAT: **giiwe'o** *vai*
GO HOME MAD: **giiwegidaazo** *vai*
GO INLAND: **gopii** *vai*
GO INSIDE: **biindige** *vai*
GO INTO THE WOODS: **jekaakwa'am** *vai2*
GO OFF MAD: **maajiigidaazo** *vai*
GO OFF TO THE SIDE: **bake** *vai*
GO ON FOOT: **mitose** *vai*
GO OUT: **zaaga'am** *vai2*

GO OUT OF PLACE: **gotigobide,
gotigobidemagad** *vii;* **gotigobizo** *vai*
GO OUT OF SIGHT: **ani-naagozi** *vai;* **ani-naagwad** *vii;* go out of sight (as around a corner) **aagawe** *vai*
GO OVER A POINT: **gakiiwe** *vai*
GO OVER TO: go over to; *after a personal prefix:* **a'o- awi-** *pv2, also* **'o-**
GO STRAIGHT: **gwayakoshkaa** *vai*
GO THE RIGHT WAY: **gwayakoshkaa** *vai*
GO THROUGH: **zhaabose, zhaabosemagad** *vii;* **zhaabwii** *vai*
GO TO: go to s.o. **naazikaw** *vta;* go to s.t. **naazikan** *vti;* go to people **naazikaage** *vai*
GO TO A CERTAIN PLACE: **izhaa** *vai;* **izhaamagad** *vii*
GO TO BED: **gawishimo** *vai*
GO TO GET: go to get s.o. by boat **naada'oozh /naada'ooN-/** *vta;* go to get s.t. by boat **naada'oodoon** *vti2*
GO TO SCHOOL: **gikinoo'amaagozi** *vai*
GO TO THE END: **gabeshkaa** *vai;* go to the end of s.t. **gabeshkan** *vti*
GO TO THE SHORE: **madaabii** *vai*
GO TO THE TOILET: **zaaga'am** *vai2*
GO TO WAR: go to war *archaic* **nandobani** *vai*
GO UPHILL: **agidaakiiwe** *vai*
GO UPSTAIRS: **akwaandawe** *vai*
GO UPWARDS: **ombishkaa** *vai;* **ombishkaa, ombishkaamagad** *vii*
GO UPWARDS AS SMOKE: **ombaabate** *vii*
GO WELL: **minose, minosemagad** *vii;* have things go well for one **minose** *vai*
GO WITH: go with s.o. **wiijiiw** *vta;* go with people **wiijii'iwe** *vai;* they go with each other **wiijiindiwag /wiijiindi-/** *vai*
GO WITH IN A BOAT: go with s.o. in a boat **aadawa'am** *vta*
GO WRONG: have things go wrong **maazhise** *vai*

GOAT
GOAT: **maanadikoshens, -ag** *na*

GOD
GOD: **gichi-manidoo, -g** *na;* **manidoo, -g** *na;* God (especially in Christian usage) **gizhe-manidoo** *na*

GOLD
GOLD: **ozaawaa-zhooniyaa** *ni, also* **ozhaawaa-zhooniyaa**
COLORED GOLD: be colored gold **ozaawaa-zhooniyaawaande, ozaawaa-zhooniyaawaandemagad** *vii, also* **ozhaawaa-zhooniyaawaande; ozaawaa-zhooniyaawaanzo** *vai, also* **ozhaawaa-zhooniyaawaanzo**

GOLDEN EAGLE
GOLDEN EAGLE: **giniw, -ag** *na*

GONE
GONE: gone! **weniban** *pc*
GONE A CERTAIN LENGTH OF TIME: be gone a certain length of time **apiitendi** *vai;* **inendi** *vai*

GONE A CERTAIN NUMBER OF DAYS: be gone a certain number of days **dasogonendi** *vai*
GONE FOREVER: be gone forever **aapidendi** *vai*
GONE FROM A CERTAIN PLACE: be gone from a certain place **ondendi** *vai*
GONE OVERNIGHT: be gone overnight **nikanendi** *vai*

GOOD
GOOD: **mino-** *pv4;* be good **mino-ayaa** *vai;* be good (as something mineral) **minwaabikad** *vii;* **minwaabikizi** *vai;* be good (as something sheet-like) **minwegad** *vii;* **minwegizi** *vai;* be good (as something stick- or wood-like) **minwaakozi** *vai;* **minwaakwad** *vii*
DO GOOD: do good things **minochige** *vai*
FEEL GOOD: **minwamanji'o** *vai*
FIND A GOOD TASTE: find a good taste in s.o. **minopozh /minopw-/** *vta;* find a good taste in s.t. **minopidan** *vti*
GET GOOD USE: get good use of s.o. **minwaabaji'** *vta;* get good use of s.t. **minwaabajitoon** *vti2*
GOOD AT: being good at **nitaa-** *pv4*
GOOD BODY: have a good body **minwaabewizi** *vai*
GOOD BREEZE: there is a good breeze **minwaanimad** *vii*
GOOD COLOR: be a good color **minwaande, minwaandemagad** *vii;* **minwaanzo** *vai*
GOOD EYESIGHT: have good eyesight **minwaabi** *vai*
GOOD HEALTH: have good health **mino-bimaadizi** *vai*
GOOD LUCK: have good luck **minose** *vai*
GOOD MOVIE: be a good movie **minwaatese, minwaatesemagad** *vii*
GOOD PROVIDER: be a good provider **gotaamigozi** *vai*
GOOD SMELL: have a good smell **minomaagozi** *vai;* **minomaagwad** *vii*
GOOD USE: be of good use **minwaabadad** *vii;* **minwaabadizi** *vai*
GOOD VOICE: have a good voice **minogondaagan** *vai;* **minowe** *vai*
GOOD WEATHER: be good weather **mizhakwad** *vii*
GOOD WORKER: be a good worker **gotaamigozi** *vai*
HAVE A GOOD TIME: **minawaanigozi** *vai*
IN GOOD HEALTH: be in good health **minwamanji'o** *vai*
LEAD A GOOD LIFE: **mino-izhiwebizi** *vai;* **minwaadizi** *vai*
LIE IN A GOOD POSITION: **minosin** *vii*
LOOK GOOD: **minwaabaminaagozi** *vai;* **minwaabaminaagwad** *vii*
SMELL GOOD: have a good smell **minomaagozi** *vai;* **minomaagwad** *vii*
SMELL GOOD BURNING OR COOKING: **minomaaso** *vai;* **minomaate, minomaatemagad** *vii*

SOUND GOOD: **minotaagozi** *vai;*
minotaagwad *vii*
SOUNDING GOOD: hear s.o. sounding good
minotaw *vta;* hear s.t. sounding good
minotan *vti*
TASTE GOOD: **minopogozi** *vai;*
minopogwad *vii;* taste good (as a liquid)
minwaagamin /minwaagami-/ *vii*
TELL A GOOD STORY: **minwaajimo** *vai*
TELL GOOD NEWS: **minwaajimo** *vai;* tell
good news of s.o. **minwaajim** *vta;* tell good
news of s.t. **minwaadodan** *vti*
GOOSE
CANADA GOOSE: **nika, -g** *na*
GOOSEBERRY
GOOSEBERRY: **zhaaboomin, -ag** *na*
GOOSEBERRY BUSH
GOOSEBERRY BUSH:
zhaaboominagaawanzh, -iig *na*
GOPHER
POCKET GOPHER: **memookiwidoo, -g** *na*
GOSSIP
GOSSIP: **dazhinge** *vai;* gossip about s.o.
dazhim *vta;* gossip about s.t. **dazhindan**
vti
GOVERN
GOVERN: govern s.o. **ogimaakandaw** *vta;*
govern s.t. **ogimaakandan** *vti*
GOVERNMENT
GOVERNMENT: **ogimaawiwin, -an** *ni*
GOVERNOR
GOVERNOR: **odaakewigimaa, -g** *na, also*
odaake-ogimaa
GRAB
GRAB: grab s.o. **debibizh** /debibiN-/ *vta;*
nawadin *vta;* grab s.t. **debibidoon** *vti2;*
nawadinan *vti;* grab (s.t.) for s.o.
debibidaw *vta;* grab (s.t.) of s.o.'s
nawadinamaw *vta;* grab people
nawadiniwe *vai*
GRADUALLY
GRADUALLY: **eshkam** *pc*
GRAND MEDICINE SOCIETY
GRAND MEDICINE SOCIETY: **midewiwin**
ni
GRAND PORTAGE
GRAND PORTAGE: Grand Portage Reserva-
tion **gichi-onigamiing** *place*
GRANDCHILD
GRANDCHILD: grandchild *vocative form of*
noozhishenh my grandchild **noozis** *nad;*
my grandchild **noozhishenh, -yag**
/-oozhisheny-/ *nad*
GRANDFATHER
GRANDFATHER: my grandfather
nimishoomis, -ag /-mishoomis-/ *nad*
GRANDMA
GRANDMA: grandma! **naan** *nad (vocative);*
nookoo *nad (vocative)*
GRANDMOTHER
GRANDMOTHER: my grandmother
nookomis, -ag /-ookomis-/ *nad*

GRANDPA
GRANDPA: grandpa! **nimishoo** *nad (vocative)*
GRANULATE
GRANULATE SUGAR: **naseyaawangwe** *vai*
GRANULATED SUGAR
GRANULATED SUGAR: **bibine-**
ziinzibaakwad *ni*
GRAPE
GRAPE: **zhawimin, -an** *ni, also* **zhoomin**
GRASS
GRASS: **mashkosiw, -an** *ni*
GRASSHOPPER
GRASSHOPPER: **bapakine, -g** *na*
GRAVE HOUSE
GRAVE HOUSE: **jiibegamig, -oon** *ni*
GRAVE MARKER
GRAVE MARKER: **jiibayaatig, -oog** *na*
GRAVEL ROAD
GRAVEL ROAD: **bingwii-miikana, -n** *ni*
GRAVEYARD
GRAVEYARD: **jiibayaki, -in** *ni*
GRAVY
GRAVY: **bakwezhiganaaboo** *ni*
GREASE
GREASE: **bimide** *ni*
BURP GREASE: **biinzibii** *vai*
GREAT
GREAT: **gichi-** *pv4, also* **chi-**
GREAT SPIRIT
GREAT SPIRIT: **gichi-manidoo, -g** *na*
GREAT-GRANDCHILD
GREAT-GRANDCHILD: **aanikoobijigan,**
-ag *na*
GREAT-GRANDPARENT
GREAT-GRANDPARENT: **aanikoobijigan,**
-ag *na*
GREBE
GREBE: **zhingibis, -ag** *na*
GREEN
GREEN: **ozhaawashko-** *pv4;* be green
ozhaawashkozi *vai;* **ozhaawashkwaa,**
ozhaawashkwaamagad *vii;* be green (as
something mineral) **ozhaawashkwaabikad**
vii; **ozhaawashkwaabikizi** *vai;* be green
(as something sheet-like)
ozhaawashkwegad *vii;*
ozhaawashkwegizi *vai;* be green (as something stick- or wood-like)
ozhaawashkwaakozi *vai;*
ozhaawashkwaakwad *vii;* be green (as
something string-like)
ozhaawashkwaabiigad *vii;*
ozhaawashkwaabiigizi *vai;* be leaf-green
ashkibagong inaande, ashkibagong
inaandemagad *vii;* **ashkibagong inaanzo**
vai
GREEN LEAVES: there are green leaves
ashkibagaa, ashkibagaamagad *vii*
WEAR GREEN: **ozhaawashko'o** *vai*
GREEN TEA
GREEN TEA: **ozhaawashko-aniibiish** *ni*

GREET

GREET: greet s.o. **anamikaw** *vta;* greet people **anamikaage** *vai;* they greet each other **anamikaadiwag** /**anamikaadi-**/ *vai*

GREETINGS

GREETINGS: greetings! **aaniin** *pc;* **boozhoo** *pc*

GREY

GREY: be grey **waabijiiyaa, waabijiiyaamagad** *vii;* **waabijiizi** *vai*
GREY HAIR: have grey hair **waabikwe** *vai*

GREY SQUIRREL

GREY SQUIRREL: **misajidamoo, -g** *na*

GRILL

GRILL: grill (s.t.) **akakanzhebwe** *vai+o*

GRIND

GRIND DOWN: grind s.o. down **zisiboozh** /**zisibooN-**/ *vta;* grind s.t. down **zisiboodoon** *vti2*
GRIND UP: grind s.o. up **biisiboozh** /**biisibooN-**/ *vta;* grind s.t. up **biisiboodoon** *vti2*

GRINDER

GRINDER: **biisiboojigan, -an** *ni*

GRINDSTONE

GRINDSTONE: **zhiigwanaabik, -oog** *na*

GROAN

GROAN: **mamaadwe** *vai*

GROCERY STORE

GROCERY STORE: grocery store **wiisinii-adaawewigamig, -oon** *ni*

GROPE

GROPE: grope for s.o. **nandoojiin** *vta;* grope for s.t. **nandoojiinan** *vti;* grope for things **nandoojiinige** *vai*

GROUND

GROUND: **aki, -in** *ni*
LEVEL GROUND: be level ground **gwayakwakamigaa, gwayakwakamigaamagad** *vii*
LOW GROUND: be low ground **dabasakamigaa, dabasakamigaamagad** *vii*
ON TOP OF THE GROUND: **agidakamig** *pc,* also **ogidakamig*, wagidakamig**
PUT UNDER THE GROUND: put s.o. under the ground **ningwakamigin** *vta*
SPRINGY GROUND: be springy ground **dootooban** *vii*
UNDER THE GROUND: **anaamakamig** *pc*
WET GROUND: be wet ground **nibiiwakamigaa, nibiiwakamigaamagad** *vii*

GROW

GROW: grow s.o. **nitaawigi'** *vta;* grow s.t. **nitaawigitoon** *vti2;* make s.o. grow **niigi' ** *vta;* make s.t. grow **niigitoon** *vti2*
GROW AT A CERTAIN SPEED: **apiichigi** *vai;* **apiichigin** *vii*
GROW FAST: **gizhiigi** *vai;* **gizhiigin** *vii*
GROW OUT: **zaagigi** *vai;* **zaagigin** *vii*
GROW STRAIGHT: **gwayakogi** *vai;* **gwayakogin** *vii*

GROW UP: **maajiigi** *vai;* **maajiigin** *vii;* **nitaawigi** *vai;* **nitaawigin** *vii*
GROW UP A CERTAIN EXTENT: **apiichigi** *vai;* **apiichigin** *vii*
GROW WELL: **minogi** *vai;* **minogin** *vii*
START TO GROW: **maajiigi** *vai;* **maajiigin** *vii*

GROWL

GROWL: growl (of a dog) **niikimo** *vai*
STOMACH GROWLS: one's stomach growls **madwegamijii** *vai*

GUARD

GUARD: guard s.o. **gizhaazh** /**gizhaaN-**/ *vta;* guard s.t. **gizhaadan** *vti;* guard things **gizhaadige** *vai*

GUIDE

GUIDE ABOUT: guide s.o. about **babaamiwizh** /**babaamiwiN-**/ *vta*

GUITAR

GUITAR: **madweyaabiigibijigan, -an** *ni*
PLAY A GUITAR: **madweyaabiigibijige** *vai*

GUM

CHEW GUM: **zhaashaagwamikiwe** *vai*
CHEWING GUM: **bigiins, -ag** *na*

GUN

GUN: **baashkizigan, -an** *ni*
HANDGUN: **oninjii-baashkizigan, -an** *ni*
TAKE ALONG A GUN: **niimibaashkizigane** *vai*

GUNNYSACK

GUNNYSACK: **mandaaminiwazh, -an** *ni*

GUNPOWDER

BLACK GUNPOWDER: **makade** *ni*
SMOKELESS GUNPOWDER: **waabi-makade** *ni*

GUT

GUT: gut s.o. **bagojiin** *vta;* **gijinagizhiin** *vta*

H

HAIR

HAIR: my (strand of) hair **niinizis, -an** /**-iinisiz-**/ *nid*
BLACK HAIR: have black hair **makadewindibe** *vai*
CURL HAIR BY HEAT: curl s.o.'s hair by heat **babiizigaakiz** /**babiizigaakizw-**/ *vta*
CURLY HAIR: have curly hair **babiizigindibe** *vai*
CUT HAIR: **giishkikozhiwe** *vai*
GREY HAIR: have grey hair **waabikwe** *vai*
HAVE BROWN HAIR: **ozaawindibe** *vai*
LONG HAIR: have long hair **gagaanwaanikwe** *vai*
MESSY HAIR: have messy hair **niiskindibe** *vai*

PUBIC HAIR: my pubic hair **nimiishigwaan, -an /-miishigwaan-/** *nid*
SHORT HAIR: have short hair **dadaakwaanikwe** *vai*
WASH HAIR: wash one's hair **giziibiigindibe** *vai*
WHITE HAIR: have white hair **waabishkindibe** *vai*

HAIRPIN
HAIRPIN: **wiinizisimaani-zagaakwa'igan, -an** *ni*

HAIRCUT
GET A HAIRCUT: **baapaagokozo** *vai*
GIVE A HAIRCUT: give s.o. a haircut **baapaagokozh /baapaagokoN-/** *vta*

HAIRDRESSER
HAIRDRESSER: hairdresser (female) **baapaagokozhiwewikwe, -g** *na;* hairdresser (male) **baapaagokozhiwewinini, -wag** *na*

HAIRDRESSING SALON
HAIRDRESSING SALON: **baapaagokozhiwewigamig, -oon** *ni*

HALF
HALF: **aabita** *pc;* **aabita-** *pv4*
AND A HALF: **ashi-aabita** *nm*
HALF A BAG: **aabitooshkin** *pc*
HALF MOON: be half (as something mineral, e.g., the moon) **aabitawaabikizi** *vai*

HALF FULL
HALF FULL: be half full (of liquid) **aabitoobii** *vai;* **aabitoobii, aabitoobiimagad** *vii;* be half full (of solids) **aabitooshkine** *vai;* **aabitooshkine, aabitooshkinemagad** *vii*
FILL HALF FULL: fill s.o. half full (of liquid) **aabitoobazh /aabitoobaN-/** *vta;* fill s.o. half full (of solids) **aabitooshkina'** *vta;* fill s.t. half full **aabitooshkinadoon** *vti2;* fill s.t. half full (of liquid) **aabitoobadoon** *vti2*

HALF-DOLLAR
HALF-DOLLAR: **aabitawaabik** *na*

HALFWAY
HALFWAY: halfway along it **aabitawayi'ii** *pc*

HALT
HALT: **nagaashkaa** *vai;* **nagaashkaa, nagaashkaamagad** *vii*

HAMMER
HAMMER: **bakite'igan, -an** *ni,* also **bakite'igaans**
HAND HAMMER: **bakite'igaans, -an** *ni*

HAMMER HANDLE
HAMMER HANDLE: **bakite'iganaak, -oon** *ni*

HAND
HAND A CERTAIN WAY: hand (s.t.) to s.o. a certain way **ininamaw** *vta*
HAND BACK: hand s.o. back **azhen** *vta;* hand s.t. back **azhenan** *vti*
HAND OVER: hand s.o. over (here) **biidin** *vta;* hand s.t. over (here) **biidinan** *vti;* hand (s.t.) over (here) to s.o. **biidinamaw** *vta*

HAND
HAND: my hand **nininj, -iin /-ninj-/** *nid*
ACHE IN HAND: have an ache in one's hand **dewininjii** *vai*
AT BOTH HANDS: **eyiidawininj** *pc*
BIG HAND: have a big hand **mangininjii** *vai*
BLISTER ON HAND: get a blister on one's hand **abashkwebiigininjiishin** *vai*
BY HAND: **michi-** *pv4*
CLAP HANDS: clap one's hands **bapasininjii'odizo** *vai*
CLEAN HAND: have a clean hand **biinininjii** *vai*
COLD HAND: have a cold hand **dakininjii** *vai*
DIRTY HAND: have a dirty hand **wiinininjii** *vai*
FROZEN HAND: have a frozen hand **mashkawaakwajininjiiwaji** *vai*
HAVE SCAR ON HAND: have scar on one's hand **ojiishininjii** *vai*
LEFT HAND: left hand *usually possessed* **namanjinik, -an** *ni*
MOVE HAND A CERTAIN WAY: move one's hand a certain way **izhininjiini** *vai*
NUMB HAND: have a numb hand **niboowininjii** *vai*
PUT LOTION ON HAND: put lotion one's hand **noomininjii** *vai*
RIGHT HAND: right hand *usually possessed* **gichinik** *ni*
SHAKE HANDS: shake hands with s.o. **zagininjii** *vta;* they shake hands with each other **zagininjiinidiwag /zagininijiinidi-/** *vai*
SORE HAND: have a sore hand **gaagiijininjii** *vai*
STIFF HAND: have a hand stiff from cold **mashkawajininjiiwaji** *vai*
STRONG HAND: have a strong hand **zoongininjii** *vai*
SWEATY HAND: have a sweaty hand **abweninjii** *vai*
SWOLLEN HAND: have a swollen hand **baagininjii** *vai*
WARM HANDS: warm one's hands **abininjiizo** *vai*
WASH HANDS: wash one's hands **giziibiigininjii** *vai*
WIPE HANDS: wipe one's hands **gaasiininjii** *vai*

HAND LOTION
HAND LOTION: **noomininjiiwin, -an** *ni*

HANDBAG
HANDBAG: **zhooniyaa-mashkimod, -an** *ni,* also **zhooniyaa-mashkimodens**

HANDFUL
ONE HANDFUL: **ingodobaneninj** *pc,* also **ningodobaneninj***
TAKE A HANDFUL: take a handful of s.o. **ganakin** *vta;* take a handful of s.t. **ganakinan** *vti*

HANDGUN
HANDGUN: **oninjii-baashkizigan, -an** *ni*

HANDKERCHIEF
HANDKERCHIEF: **moshwens, -an** *ni*
HANDLE
HANDLE: **minjiminigan, -an** *ni*
HANDLE A CERTAIN WAY: handle s.o. a certain way **inin** *vta;* handle s.t. a certain way **ininan** *vti*
HANDLED
HANDLED A CERTAIN WAY: be handled a certain way **ininigaade, ininigaademagad** *vii;* **ininigaazo** *vai*
HANDPRINT
LEAVE HANDPRINT: leave a handprint **ezhininjiishin** *vai*
HANDSOME
HANDSOME: be handsome **miikawaadad** *vii;* **miikawaadizi** *vai*
HANG
HANG: **agoode, agoodemagad** *vii;* **agoojin** *vai;* hang s.o. **agoozh /agooN-/** *vta;* hang s.t. **agoodoon** *vti2;* hang (s.t.) for s.o. **agoodaw** *vta;* hang things **agoojige** *vai*
HANG A CERTAIN WAY: **inagoode, inagoodemagad** *vii;* **inagoojin** *vai;* hang s.o. a certain way **inagoozh /inagooN-/** *vta;* hang s.t. a certain way **inagoodoon** *vti2*
HANG AT THE END: **ishkwegoode, ishkwegoodemagad** *vii;* **ishkwegoojin** *vai;* hang s.o. at the end **ishkwegoozh /ishkwegooN-/** *vta;* hang s.t. at the end **ishkwegoodoon** *vti2*
HANG IN FRONT: **niigaanagoode, niigaanagoodemagad** *vii;* **niigaanagoojin** *vai;* hang s.o. in front **niigaanagoozh /niigaanagooN-/** *vta;* hang s.t. in front **niigaanagoodoon** *vti2*
HANG IN PLACE: **onagoode, onagoodemagad** *vii;* **onagoojin** *vai;* hang s.o. in place **onagoozh /onagooN-/** *vta;* hang s.t. in place **onagoodoon** *vti2*
HANG LOW: **dabasagoode, dabasagoodemagad** *vii;* **dabasagoojin** *vai;* hang s.o. low **dabasagoozh /dabasagooN-/** *vta;* hang s.t. low **dabasagoodoon** *vti2*
HANG UP A NET: **agoodasabii** *vai*
HANG UP HIGH: **ishpagoode, ishpagoodemagad** *vii;* **ishpagoojin** *vai;* hang s.o. up high **ishpagoozh /ishpagooN-/** *vta;* hang s.t. up high **ishpagoodoon** *vti2*
HANG UP LAUNDRY: **agoojige** *vai*
HANG UPSIDE DOWN: **ajidagoode, ajidagoodemagad** *vii;* **ajidagoojin** *vai;* hang s.o. upside down **ajidagoozh /ajidagooN-/** *vta;* hang s.t. upside down **ajidagoodoon** *vti2*
HANGER
KETTLE HANGER: **agoodakikwaan, -an** *ni*
HAPPEN
HAPPEN A CERTAIN WAY: **inakamigad** *vii;* **izhiwebad** *vii*

HAPPEN IN A CERTAIN PLACE: **danakamigad** *vii*
HAPPENS TO BE: it happens to be **nangwana** *pc, also* **ngwana, ingwana**
HAVE CERTAIN THINGS HAPPEN: have certain things happen to one **inakamigizi** *vai;* **izhiwebizi** *vai*
HAPPY
HAPPY: be happy **minawaanigozi** *vai;* **minawaanigwad** *vii;* **minwendam** *vai2*
HARASS
HARASS: harass s.o. **miikinji'** *vta*
HARD
CONSIDER HARD: consider s.o. hard **zanagenim** *vta;* consider s.t. hard **zanagendan** *vti;* consider things hard **zanagendam** *vai2*
HARD TO MANAGE: be hard (to manage) **zanagad** *vii*
HARD WORKER
HARD WORKER: be a hard worker **ginzhizhawizi** *vai*
HARD
HARD: be hard **mashkawaa, mashkawaamagad** *vii;* **mashkawizi** *vai*
HARDER
HARDER: **enigok** *pc*
HARDLY
HARDLY: **agaawaa** *pc*
HARDWARE STORE
HARDWARE STORE: **biiwaabiko-adaawewigamig, -oon** *ni, also* **biiwaabikwadaawewigamig**
HARE
SNOWSHOE HARE: snowshoe hare **waabooz, -oog** *na*
HARMONICA
HARMONICA: **noondaagochigan, -an** *ni*
HARNESS
HARNESS: **apikan, -an** *ni;* harness s.o. **onapizh /onapiN-/** *vta;* harness up **onapijige** *vai*
HARNESSED
HARNESSED: be harnessed **onapizo** *vai*
HARVEST
HARVEST WILD RICE: **bawa'am** *vai2;* **manoominike** *vai*
HAT
HAT: **wiiwakwaan, -an** *ni*
PUT ON HAT: put on one's hat **biichiwakwaane** *vai*
TAKE OFF HAT: take off one's hat **giichiwakwaane** *vai*
HATCH
HATCH: **baashkaawe'am** *vai2, also* **baashkaawe'o**
HATCHET
HATCHET: **waagaakwadoons, -an** *ni*
HATE
HATE: hate s.o. **zhiingenim** *vta;* hate s.t. **zhiingendan** *vti;* they hate each other **zhiingenindiwag /zhiingenindi-/** *vai*

HATED
HATED: be hated **zhiingendaagozi** *vai;*
zhiingendaagwad *vii*
HAUL
HAUL: haul s.o. **aawazh /aawaN-/** *vta;* haul
s.t. **aawadoon** *vti2;* haul something
aawadaaso *vai;* haul (s.t.) for s.o.
aawadaw *vta;* haul people **aawazhiwe** *vai*
HAUL ON SHOULDER: haul s.o. on one's
shoulder **aawajinigaazh /aawajinigaaN-/**
vta; haul s.t. on one's shoulder
aawajinigaadan *vti;* haul things on one's
shoulder **aawajinige** *vai*
HAUL TO A CERTAIN PLACE: haul s.o. to
a certain place **inaawazh /inaawaN-/** *vta;*
haul s.t. to a certain place **inaawadoon**
vti2; haul something to a certain place
inaawadaaso *vai*
HAUL WILD RICE: **aawajimine** *vai*
HAVE
HAVE: have s.o. **ayaaw** *vta;* have s.t. **ayaan**
vti3
HAVE ON
HAVE ON: have s.o. on (e.g., clothes)
biizikaw *vta;* have s.t. on (e.g., clothes)
biizikan *vti*
HAWK
HAWK: **gekek, -wag** *na*
HAWTHORN
HAWTHORN: hawthorn tree
miinensagaawanzh, -iig *na*
HAWTHORN FRUIT
HAWTHORN FRUIT: **miinens, -ag** *na*
HAY
HAY: **mashkosiw, -an** *ni*
GO AFTER HAY: **naadashkosiwe** *vai*
HAZELNUT
HAZELNUT: **bagaan, -ag** *na*
HAZELNUT BUSH
HAZELNUT BUSH: **bagaaniminzh, -iig** *na*
HE
HE: he *third person singular personal pronoun*
wiin *pr*
HEAD
HEAD: my head **nishtigwaan, -an**
/-shtigwaan-/ *nid*
BIG HEAD: have a big head **mangindibe** *vai*
BUMP HEAD: bump one's head
bitaakondibeshin *vai*
FALL AND CRACK HEAD: fall and crack
one's head **baasindibeshin** *vai*
HOLD HEAD STRAIGHT: hold one's head
straight **gwayakokweni** *vai*
LIE WITH HEAD A CERTAIN WAY: lie
with one's head a certain way **inikweshin**
vai
LIE WITH HEAD ON: lie with head on
something **apikweshimo** *vai*
NOD HEAD: nod one's head **wewebikweni**
vai
NOD HEAD A CERTAIN WAY: nod one's
head to s.o. a certain way **inikwetaw** *vta*

PUT HEAD A CERTAIN WAY: put one's
head a certain way **inikweni** *vai*
SHAKE HEAD: shake head at s.o.
wewebikwetaw *vta*
SLAP ON HEAD: slap s.o. on the head
basindibe' /basindibe'w-/ *vta*
STICK OUT HEAD: stick out one's head
zaagikweni *vai*
TURN HEAD AROUND: turn one's head
around **gwekikweni** *vai*
HEAD OFFICE
HEAD OFFICE: **ogimaawigamig, -oon** *ni*
HEADACHE
HEADACHE: have a headache **dewikwe** *vai*
GET A SUDDEN HEADACHE: **dewikwese**
vai
HEADBAND
HEADBAND: **basikwebizon, -an** *ni*
HEADDRESS
FEATHER HEADDRESS: feather bonnet
miigwani-wiiwakwaan, -an *ni*
HEADMAN
CEREMONIAL HEADMAN: **ogichidaa, -g**
na
HEADWOMAN
CEREMONIAL HEADWOMAN:
ogichidaakwe, -g *na*
HEAL
HEAL: heal s.o. **nanaandawi'** *vta;* heal people
nanaandawi'iwe *vai*
HEAL UP: **giige** *vai*
HEALER
TRADITIONAL HEALER:
nenaandawi'iwed *na-pt*
HEAR
HEAR: **noondam** *vai2;* hear s.o. **noondaw**
vta; hear s.t. **noondan** *vti*
HEAR A CERTAIN NOISE: **initam** *vai2*
HEAR A CERTAIN WAY: hear s.o. a certain
way **initaw** *vta;* hear s.t. a certain way
initan *vti*
HEAR IN A CERTAIN PLACE: hear s.o. in a
certain place **danitaw** *vta;* hear s.t. in a certain place **danitan** *vti*
HEAR RIGHT: hear the right thing
gwayakotam *vai2*
LIKE HEARING: like hearing s.o. **minotaw**
vta; like hearing s.t. **minotan** *vti;* like hearing something **minotam** *vai2*
HEARD
HEARD: be heard **noondaagwad** *vii;* can be
heard **noondaagozi** *vai*
BEING HEARD: **madwe-** *pv4*
HEARD A CERTAIN WAY: be heard a cer-
tain way **initaagozi** *vai;* **initaagwad** *vii*
HEARD DRIVING ALONG: be heard driving
along **bimwewebide,**
bimwewebidemagad *vii;* **bimwewebizo**
vai
HEARD DRIVING HERE: be heard driving
here **biidwewebide, biidwewebidemagad**
vii; **biidwewebizo** *vai*
HEARD FALLING: be heard going along and
falling **bimweweshin** *vai*

HEARD IN A CERTAIN PLACE: be heard
in a certain place **danitaagozi** *vai;*
danitaagwad *vii*
HEARD IN AN ACTIVITY: be heard in an
activity **madwetaa** *vai*
HEARD RUNNING HERE: be heard running
here **biidwewebatoo** *vai*
HEARD RUNNING HERE ON THE
GROUND: be heard running here on the
ground **biidwewekamigibatoo** *vai*
HEARD SPEEDING ALONG: be heard
speeding along **bimwewebide**,
bimwewebidemagad *vii;* **bimwewebizo**
vai
HEARD SPEEDING HERE: be heard
speeding here **biidwewebide**,
biidwewebidemagad *vii;* **biidwewebizo**
vai
HEARD SWIMMING HERE: be heard
swimming here **biidweweyaadagaa** *vai*
HEARD WALKING ALONG: be heard
walking along **bimweweshin** *vai*
HEARD WALKING HERE: be heard walking
here **biidweweshin** *vai*

HEARSE
HEARSE: **niboowidaabaan, -ag** *na*

HEART
HEART: my heart **inde', -an /-de'-/** *nid*

HEART ATTACK
HAVE A HEART ATTACK:
mamaajide'eshkaa *vai*

HEART
HEART SUITE CARD: **giiwoon, -ag** *na, also*
giiyoon

HEARTBURN
HAVE HEARTBURN: **maazhide'e** *vai*

HEAT
HEAT: heat s.o. (as something mineral)
gizhaabikiz /gizhaabikizw-/ *vta;* heat s.t.
gizizan *vti;* heat s.t. (as a liquid)
gizhaagamizan *vti;* heat s.t. (as something
mineral) **gizhaabikizan** *vti;* heat things (as
a liquid) **gizhaagamizige** *vai;* heat things
(as something mineral) **gizhaabikizige** *vai*

HEATER
HEATER: **awazowin, -an** *ni*

HEAVEN
HEAVEN: **giizhig** *na*
IN HEAVEN: **ishpiming** *pc*

HEAVY
HEAVY: be heavy **gozigwan** *vii;* **gozigwani**
vai
SO HEAVY: be so heavy **apiitinigozi** *vai;*
apiitinigwad *vii*

HEEL
HEEL: my heel **indoondan, -an /-doondan-/**
nid

HEIGHT
CERTAIN HEIGHT: be a certain height
akoozi *vai;* **akwaa, akwaamagad** *vii;*
akwaakozi *vai;* **akwaakwad** *vii;* **apiitaa,**
apiitaamagad *vii*

HELD
HELD A CERTAIN WAY: be held a certain
way **ininigaade, ininigaademagad** *vii;*
ininigaazo *vai*
HELD IN PLACE: be held in place with
weight **minjimishkoode**,
minjimishkoodemagad *vii;*
minjimishkoozo *vai*

HELL DIVER
HELL DIVER: **zhingibis, -ag** *na*

HELLO
HELLO: hello! **aaniin** *pc;* **boozhoo** *pc*

HELP
HELP: **wiidookaazo** *vai;* help s.o. **naadamaw**
vta; **wiidookaw** *vta;* help people
naadamaage *vai;* **wiidookaage** *vai;* they
help each other **naadamaadiwag**
/naadamaadi-/ *vai;* **wiidookodaadiwag**
/wiidookodaadi-/ *vai*

HERE
HERE: **bi-** *pv2;* **omaa** *pc,* also **o'omaa**
BLOWN HERE: be blown here **biidaashi** *vai;*
biidaasin *vii*
BRING HERE IN A BOAT: **biida'oodoon**
vti2; bring s.o. here in a boat **biida'oozh**
/biida'ooN-/ *vta*
CLIMB HERE: **biidaandawe** *vai*
CRAWL HERE: **biidoode** *vai*
DRAG HERE: **biijidaabii** *vai;* drag s.o. here
biijidaabaazh /biijidaabaaN-/ *vta;* drag s.t.
here **biijidaabaadan** *vti*
DRIVE HERE: **biijibide, biijibidemagad** *vii;*
biijibizo *vai;* **biijidaabii'iwe** *vai*
DRIVE HERE WITH A LIGHT:
biidaazakonebizo *vai*
FLY HERE: **biijibide, biijibidemagad** *vii;*
biijibizo *vai;* **biijise** *vai;* **biijise,**
biijisemagad *vii*
FOLLOW A TRAIL HERE: **biida'adoo** *vai;*
follow s.o.'s trail here **biida'azh /biida'aN-/**
vta; follow s.t. as a trail here **biida'adoon**
vti2
HEARD DRIVING HERE: be heard driving
here **biidwewebide, biidwewebidemagad**
vii; **biidwewebizo** *vai*
HEARD RUNNING HERE: be heard running
here **biidwewebatoo** *vai*
HEARD RUNNING HERE ON THE
GROUND: be heard running here on the
ground **biidwewekamigibatoo** *vai*
HEARD SPEEDING HERE: be heard
speeding here **biidwewebide**,
biidwewebidemagad *vii;* **biidwewebizo**
vai
HEARD SWIMMING HERE: be heard
swimming here **biidweweyaadagaa** *vai*
HEARD WALKING HERE: be heard walking
here **biidweweshin** *vai*
MOVE RESIDENCE HERE: move one's residence here **biijigozi** *vai*
OVER HERE: **owidi** *pc,* also **o'owidi**
PADDLE HERE: **biidakwazhiwe** *vai;*
biidaasamishkaa *vai*

RIDE HERE ON HORSEBACK: **biidoomigo**
vai
RUN HERE: **biijibatoo** *vai;* they run here
together **biijiba'idiwag** /**biijiba'idi-**/ *vai*
SAIL HERE: **biidaashi** *vai;* **biidaasin** *vii*
SEND A LETTER HERE: **biijibii'ige** *vai*
SKATE HERE: **biidaada'e** *vai*
SPEED HERE: **biijibide, biijibidemagad** *vii;*
biijibizo *vai*
SWIM HERE: **biidaadagaa** *vai;* swim here (as
a fish) **biidakwazhiwe** *vai*
THROW HERE: throw s.o. here **biijwebin**
vta; throw s.t. here **biijwebinan** *vti;* throw
(s.t.) here to s.o. **biijwebinamaw** *vta*
WADE HERE: **biidaadagaazii** *vai*
WALK HERE: **biidaasamose** *vai*
WRITE HERE: **biijibii'ige** *vai;* write (s.t.) here
to s.o. *inverse forms of:* **biijibii'amaw-** *vta*

HERON
BLUE HERON: **zhashagi, -wag** *na*

HICCOUGH
HICCOUGH: **onwaawe** *vai*

HICKORY
HICKORY: **mitigwaabaak, -oog** *na*

HIDDEN
HIDDEN: be hidden **gaajigaade,**
gaajigaademagad *vii;* **gaajigaazo** *vai*

HIDE
HIDE: hide from s.o. **gaazootaw** *vta;* hide s.o.
gaazh /**gaaN-**/ *vta;* hide s.t. **gaadoon** *vti2;*
hide self **gaazo** *vai;* hide (s.t.) from s.o.
gaadaw *vta;* hide things **gaajige** *vai*

HIDE
HIDE: **bashkwegin, -oon** *ni*
BEAVER HIDE: **amikwayaan, -ag** *na*
CALFHIDE: **bizhikiinsiwayaan, -ag** *na*
DEER HIDE: **waawaashkeshiwayaan, -ag** *na*
FISHER HIDE: **ojiigiwayaan, -ag** *na*
FOX HIDE: **waagoshiwayaan, -ag** *na*
LYNX HIDE: **bizhiwayaan, -ag** *na*
MARTEN HIDE: **waabizheshiwayaan, -ag**
na
MINK HIDE: **zhaangweshiwayaan, -ag** *na*
MUSKRAT HIDE: **wazhashkwayaan, -ag** *na*
OTTER HIDE: **nigigwayaan, -ag** *na*
STRETCH A HIDE: **naazhiiga'ige** *vai*
TANNED HIDE: **asekaan, -ag** *na*
WOLF HIDE: **ma'iinganiwayaan, -ag** *na*

HIDE SCRAPER
HIDE SCRAPER: **jiishaakwa'igan, -an** *ni*

HIDE STRETCHER
HIDE STRETCHER: **naazhiiga'igan, -an** *ni*
FLAT HIDE STRETCHER: flat hide stretcher (especially for muskrats)
zhiibaakwa'ataan, -an *ni*

HIGH
HIGH: **ishpi-** *pv4;* be high (e.g., the sun)
ishpagoojin *vai*
CHARGE A HIGH PRICE: **ishpagindaaso**
vai; charge a high price for s.t.
ishpagindan *vti*
HANG UP HIGH: **ishpagoode,**
ishpagoodemagad *vii;* **ishpagoojin** *vai;*
hang s.o. up high **ishpagoozh**

/**ishpagooN-**/ *vta;* hang s.t. up high
ishpagoodoon *vti2*
HIGH IN STATUS OR OFFICE: be high in
status or office **ishpaginzo** *vai*
HIGH PLACE: be a high place **ishpadinaa,**
ishpadinaamagad *vii*
HIGH UP: be high up **ishpaa, ishpaamagad**
vii
LIE HIGH UP: **ishpishin** *vai;* **ishpisin** *vii*
MAKE HIGH: make s.t. high **ishpaatoon** *vti2*

HIGH-PRICED
HIGH-PRICED: be high-priced **ishpaginde,**
ishpagindemagad *vii;* **ishpaginzo** *vai*

HIGHLY
THINK HIGHLY: think highly of s.o.
ishpenim *vta*

HIGHWAY
HIGHWAY: **gichi-miikana, -n** *ni*

HILL
HILL: be a hill **ishpadinaa, ishpadinaamagad**
vii
BIG HILL: there is a big hill **mangadinaa,**
mangadinaamagad *vii*
COME OUT OVER A HILL: **zaagajiwe** *vai*
ON TOP OF A HILL: **agidaaki** *pc, also*
ogidaaki*, wagidaaki
SMALL HILL: there is a small hill **bikwadinaa,**
bikwadinaamagad *vii;* there is a small hill
agaasadinaa, agaasadinaamagad *vii*

HINDER
HINDER: hinder s.o. **ondami'** *vta*

HINDQUARTER
HINDQUARTER: my hindquarter
imbwaam, -an /**-bwaam-**/ *nid*

HIP
HIP: my hip **ninoogan, -an** /**-noogan-**/ *nid*

HIRE
HIRE: **anookii** *vai;* hire s.o. **anoozh** /**anooN-**/
vta
HIRE TO DO A CERTAIN JOB: hire s.o. to
do a certain job **inanoozh** /**inanooN-**/ *vta*
HIRE TO GO TO A CERTAIN PLACE: hire
s.o. to go to a certain place **inanoozh**
/**inanooN-**/ *vta*

HIT
HIT: be hit **bakite'igaade,**
bakite'igaademagad *vii;* **bakite'igaazo**
vai; hit s.o. **bakite'** /**bakite'w-**/ *vta;* hit s.o.
(in shooting) **mizho** /**mizhw-**/ *vta;* hit s.t.
bakite'an *vti;* hit s.t. (in shooting)
mizhodan *vti;* hit things **bakite'ige** *vai;*
they hit each other **bakite'odiwag**
/**bakite'odi-**/ *vai*
ACCIDENTALLY HIT: accidentally hit s.o.
bitaganaam *vta;* accidentally hit s.t.
bitaganaandan *vti*
HIT AGAINST ACCIDENTALLY: hit
against something accidentally (as something stick- or wood-like) **bitaakoshin** *vai;*
bitaakosin *vii*
HIT DEAD CENTER: hit s.o. dead center
with something **miikwa'** /**miikwa'w-**/ *vta;*
hit s.t. dead center with something
miikwa'an *vti*

HIT THE BOTTOM: **mizhakiise** *vai;*
mizhakiise, mizhakiisemagad *vii*
HIT THE TARGET: **mizhodam** *vai2*
MAKE NOISE HITTING: **madweshin** *vai;*
madwesin *vii;* make noise hitting s.t.
madwesidoon *vti2;* make noise hitting
things **madwesijige** *vai*
SHOOT AND HIT: shoot and hit s.o.
miikonaw *vta;* shoot and hit s.t. **miikonan**
vti

HITCHED
HITCHED ON: be hitched on
agwapijigaade, agwapijigaademagad *vii;*
agwapijigaazo *vai*

HITHER
HITHER: **bi-** *pv2*

HIVE
BEEHIVE: **aamoo-wadiswan, -an** *ni*

HOARSE
HOARSE: be hoarse **gibiskwe** *vai;* **maanowe**
vai

HOE
HOE: **ningwaja'ige** *vai;* hoe s.o. **ningwaja'**
/**ningwaja'w-**/ *vta;* hoe s.t. **ningwaja'an** *vti*

HOIST
HOIST: hoist s.o. **ombaabiigin** *vta;* hoist s.t.
ombaabiiginan *vti*

HOLD
HOLD: hold s.o. **dakon** *vta;* hold s.t. **dakonan**
vti; hold (s.t.) for s.o. **dakonamaw** *vta*
ADEQUATELY HOLD: **debashkine** *vai;*
debashkine, debashkinemagad *vii;* adequately hold (something liquid) **debibii,**
debibiimagad *vii*
GET HOLD: get hold of s.o. **debibizh**
/**debibiN-**/ *vta;* get hold of s.t. **debibidoon**
vti2; get hold of (s.t.) for s.o. **debibidaw**
vta
HOLD A CERTAIN WAY: hold s.o. a certain
way **inin** *vta;* hold s.t. a certain way **ininan**
vti
HOLD AGAINST: hold s.o. against **ashidin**
vta; hold s.t. against **ashidinan** *vti*
HOLD BACK: hold s.o. back **nanagin** *vta*
HOLD IN MOUTH: hold s.o. in one's mouth
agwanem *vta;* hold s.t. in one's mouth
agwanendan *vti;* hold things in one's
mouth **agwanenjige** *vai*
HOLD IN PLACE: hold s.o. in place
minjimin *vta;* hold s.o. in place with foot
or body **minjimishkaw** *vta;* hold s.o. in
place with weight **minjimishkoozh**
/**minjimishkooN-**/ *vta;* hold s.t. in place
minjiminan *vti;* hold s.t. in place with foot
or body **minjimishkan** *vti;* hold s.t. in
place with weight **minjimishkoodoon** *vti2;*
hold (s.t.). in place for s.o. **minjiminamaw**
vta
HOLD ON: **minjimii** *vai;* hold on (as to something stick- or wood-like) **minjimaakwii**
vai
HOLD UP AGAINST: hold s.o. up against
agon *vta;* hold s.t. up against **agonan** *vti*

HOLD UPSIDE DOWN: hold s.o. upside
down **ajidin** *vta;* hold s.t. upside down
ajidinan *vti*
TAKE HOLD: take hold of s.o. **dakon** *vta;*
take hold of s.t. **dakonan** *vti*

HOLD ON
HOLD ON: hold on! **bekaa** *pc*

HOLE
BURN A HOLE: burn a hole in s.o.
bagwaakiz /**bagwaakizw-**/ *vta;* burn a hole
in s.t. **bagwaakizan** *vti*
DIG A HOLE: **waanike** *vai*
EXCAVATED HOLE: **waanikaan, -an** *ni*
GET A HOLE: **bagoshkaa** *vai;* **bagoshkaa,**
bagoshkaamagad *vii*
HAVE A HOLE: **bagoneyaa,**
bagoneyaamagad *vii;* **bagonezi** *vai*
HAVE A HOLE BURNED IN: **bagwaakide,**
bagwaakidemagad *vii;* **bagwaakizo** *vai*
HOLE MADE IN THE ICE FOR WATER:
dwaa'ibaan, -an *ni, also* **dwaa'igan**
MAKE A HOLE IN THE ICE: **dwaa'ige** *vai*
MAKE A HOLE USING SOMETHING:
make a hole in s.o. using something
bagone' /**bagone'w-**/ *vta;* make a hole in
s.t. using something **bagone'an** *vti*
MAKE A WATER HOLE IN THE ICE:
dwaa'ibii *vai, also* **dwaa'ige**

HOLLOW
HOLLOW: be hollow **wiimbaa,**
wiimbaamagad *vii;* **wiimbizi** *vai*
GIVE A HOLLOW SOUND: **wiimbwewe,**
wiimbwewemagad *vii*

HOME
HOME: his/her home: **endaad** *changed form of:*
daa *vai*
BE AT HOME: **abi** *vai*
CARRY HOME: carry s.o. home **giiwewizh**
/**giiwewiN-**/ *vta;* carry s.t. home
giiwewidoon *vti2;* carry (s.t.) home for s.o.
giiwewidaw *vta*
DRIVE HOME: **giiwedaabii'iwe** *vai*
GO HOME: **giiwe** *vai*
GO HOME BY BOAT: **giiwe'o** *vai*
GO HOME MAD: **giiwegidaazo** *vai*
RUN HOME: **giiwebatoo** *vai*
TAKE HOME: take s.o. home **giiwewizh**
/**giiwewiN-**/ *vta;* take s.t. home
giiwewidoon *vti2;* take (s.t.) home for s.o.
giiwewidaw *vta*
TELL TO GO HOME: tell s.o. to go home
giiwenaazha' /**giiwenaazha'w-**/ *vta*

HOMELY
HOMELY: be homely **maanaadizi** *vai*

HOMINY
HOMINY: **gijikonayezigan, -ag** *na*

HONEY
HONEY: **aamoo-ziinzibaakwad** *ni*

HOOF
HOOF: my hoof **ninasid** /**-nasid-**/ *nid*

HOOK
FISH HOOK: **migiskan, -an** *ni*
FISH WITH A HOOK AND LINE:
wewebanaabii *vai*

HOOK AND LINE: **migiskaneyaab, -iin** *ni*
HOP HORNBEAM
HOP HORNBEAM: **maananoons, -ag** *na*
HOPE
HOPE: **bagosendam** *vai2;* hope for s.o., have hope for s.o. **bagosenim** *vta;* hope for s.t. **bagosendan** *vti*
LOSE HOPE: lose hope in s.o. **banaadenim** *vta;* lose hope in s.t. **banaadendan** *vti*
HOPEFUL
HOPEFUL: be hopeful **ombendam** *vai2*
HORN
HORN: **noondaagochigan, -an** *ni*
HORN
HORN: horn (of an animal) **eshkan, -ag** *na*
HORSE
HORSE: **bebezhigooganzhii, -g** *na,* also **mishtadim*, mashtadim***; my horse **inday, -ag /-day-/** *nad*
FALL OFF A HORSE: **banoomigo** *vai*
HAVE A HORSE: **odayi** *vai*
LOOK FOR HORSES: **nandawisimwe** *vai*
RIDE TO A CERTAIN PLACE WITH HORSES: **apa'igo** *vai*
HORSEBACK
ARRIVE ON HORSEBACK: **bagamoomigo** *vai*
RIDE ABOUT ON HORSEBACK: **babaamoomigo** *vai*
RIDE ALONG ON HORSEBACK: **bimoomigo** *vai*
RIDE AWAY ON HORSEBACK: **animoomigo** *vai*
RIDE FROM A CERTAIN PLACE ON HORSEBACK: **ondoomigo** *vai*
RIDE HERE ON HORSEBACK: **biidoomigo** *vai*
RIDE TO A CERTAIN PLACE ON HORSEBACK: ride to a certain place on horseback **inoomigo** *vai*
HORSEFLY
HORSEFLY: **mizizaak, -wag** *na*
HORSESHOE
HORSESHOE: **oshkanzhiikaajigan, -an** *ni*
HOSPITAL
HOSPITAL: **aakoziiwigamig, -oon** *ni*
MENTAL HOSPITAL: **giiwanaadiziiwigamig, -oon** *ni*
VETERAN'S HOSPITAL: **zhimaaganishii-aakoziiwigamig, -oon** *ni*
HOT
HOT: be hot **gizhide, gizhidemagad** *vii;* **gizhizo** *vai;* be hot (as a liquid) **gizhaagamide, gizhaagamidemagad** *vii*
HOT INSIDE: be hot inside **giizhoote, giizhootemagad** *vii*
HOT WEATHER: be hot (weather) **gizhaate, gizhaatemagad** *vii*
HOT WIND: be a hot wind **gizhaanimad** *vii*
HOTEL
HOTEL: **noogishkaawigamig, -oon** *ni*

HOUR
CERTAIN HOUR: be a certain hour **daso-diba'iganed** *vii*
CERTAIN NUMBER OF HOURS: a certain number of hours **daso-diba'igan** *pc*
CERTAIN TIME IN HOURS: be a certain time in hours **daso-diba'iganed** *vii*
HOUSE
HOUSE: **waakaa'igan, -an** ni
ALONGSIDE THE HOUSE: **zhishwajigamig** *pc*
BUILD A HOUSE: **waakaa'ige** *vai;* build a house for s.o. **ozhigaw** *vta*
BY A HOUSE: **jiigigamig** *pc*
COLD HOUSE: be cold (as a house or room) **dakate, dakatemagad** *vii*
DARK HOUSE: be dark (as in a room or house) **dibikate, dibikatemagad** *vii*
ON TOP OF THE HOUSE: **agidigamig** *pc,* also **ogidigamig*, wagidigamig**
QUIET HOUSE: be a quiet house **bangate, bangatemagad** *vii*
SMALL HOUSE: be small (as a room or house) **agaasate, agaasatemagad** *vii*
HOW
HOW: how? **aaniin** *pc;* **aaniish** *pc*
HOW MANY: how many? **aaniin minik** *pc*
HOW MUCH: how much? *interrogative* **aaniin minik** *pc*
I DON'T KNOW HOW: **amanj** *dubitative pc,* also **amanj iidog, namanj*, namanj iidog***
I WONDER HOW: I wonder how *dubitative* **amanj** *pc,* also **amanj iidog, namanj*, namanj iidog***
HOWEVER
HOWEVER: however *dubitative* **amanj igo** *pc*
HOWL
HOWL: howl **waawoono** *vai*
HUG
HUG: hug s.o. **gikinjigwen** *vta;* **giishkijiin** *vta;* they hug each other **gikinjigwenidiwag /gikinjigwenidi-/** *vai;* **giishkijiinidiwag /giishkijiinidi-/** *vai*
HUMAN
HUMAN: human (in contrast to non-human beings) **anishinaabe, -g** *na;* be human (in contrast to non-human beings) **anishinaabewi** *vai*
HUMMINGBIRD
HUMMINGBIRD: **nenookaasi, -wag** *na*
HUNDRED
CERTAIN NUMBER OF HUNDREDS: **daswaak** *nm*
EIGHT HUNDRED: **ishwaaswaak** *nm,* also **nishwaaswaak***
FIVE HUNDRED: **naanwaak** *nm*
FOUR HUNDRED: **niiwaak** *nm*
NINE HUNDRED: **zhaangaswaak** *nm*
ONE HUNDRED: **ingodwaak** *nm,* also **ningodwaak***
SEVEN HUNDRED: **niizhwaaswaak** *nm*
SIX HUNDRED: **ingodwaaswaak** *nm,* also **ningodwaaswaak***
THREE HUNDRED: **niswaak** *nm*

TWO HUNDRED: niizhwaak *nm*

HUNGRY
HUNGRY: be hungry **bakade** *vai*
PRETEND TO BE HUNGRY: **bakadekaazo** *vai*

HUNT
HUNT: **giiwose** *vai*, also **giiyose**; get food by hunting or fishing **nandawenjige** *vai*; hunt for s.o. **nooji'** *vta*; hunt for s.t. **noojitoon** *vti2*; hunt for people **nooji'iwe** *vai*
HUNT BEAVER: **noodamikwe** *vai*
HUNT DUCKS: **nandawishibe** *vai*
HUNT FOR RABBITS: **nandawaaboozwe** *vai*

HUNTER
HUNTER: **giiwosewinini, -wag** *na*, also **giiyosewinini**

HUNTING BLIND
HUNTING BLIND: **akandoowin, -an** *ni*

HUNTING DOG
HUNTING DOG: **giiwosewasim, -oog** *na*, also **giiyosewasim**

HURRY
HURRY: **wewiib** *pc*; **wewiibishkaa** *vai*; hurry (in some work or activity) **wewiibitaa** *vai*; hurry s.o. **wewiibi'** *vta*; hurry s.t. **wewiibitoon** *vti*
COOK IN A HURRY: **ojaanimizekwe** *vai*
HURRY BY SPEECH: hurry s.o. by speech **ojaanimim** *vta*
HURRY MAKING: hurry making s.o. **wewiibi'** *vta*; hurry making s.t. **wewiibitoon** *vti*
IN A HURRY: **wewiib** *pc*; be in a hurry **wewiibizi** *vai*
MAKE HURRY: make s.o. hurry **ojaanimi'** *vta*
TELL TO HURRY: tell s.o. to hurry **wewiibim** *vta*
WANT TO HURRY: **wewiibendam** *vai*

HURT
GET HURT: **wiisagishin** *vai*
HURT WITH FOOT OR BODY: hurt s.o. with foot or body **wiisagishkaw** *vta*

HUSBAND
HUSBAND: my husband **ninaabem, -ag /-naabem-/** *nad*; **niwiidigemaagan, -ag /-wiidigemaagan-/** *na*
HAVE A HUSBAND: **onaabemi** *vai*

HYMN
HYMN: **anama'e-nagamon, -an** *ni*

I

I: I *first person singular personal pronoun* **niin** *pr*

I DON'T KNOW
I DON'T KNOW HOW: *dubitative* **amanj** *pc*, also **amanj iidog, namanj*, namanj iidog***
I DON'T KNOW WHEN: *dubitative* **amanj apii** *pc*
I DON'T KNOW WHERE: *dubitative* **dibi** *pc*
I DON'T KNOW WHO: I don't know who *animate dubitative* **awegwen, -ag** *pr*

I DON'T REMEMBER
I DON'T REMEMBER WHAT: **ayi'ii, -n** *pr*
I DON'T REMEMBER WHO: **aya'aa, -g** *pr*

ICE
ICE: **mikwam, -iig** *na*
CRACK IN THE ICE: there is a crack in the ice **daashkikwadin** *vii*
FALL THROUGH THE ICE: **dwaashin** *vai*
FISH THROUGH THE ICE WITH SPEAR: **akwa'waa** *vai*
GO ABOUT ON THE ICE: **babaamaadagaako** *vai*
GO AWAY ON THE ICE: **animaadagaako** *vai*
GO OUT FROM SHORE ON THE ICE: **niminaaweyaadagaako** *vai*
GO TO A CERTAIN PLACE ON THE ICE: **inaadagaako** *vai*
HOLE MADE IN THE ICE FOR WATER: **dwaa'ibaan, -an** *ni*, also **dwaa'igan**
MAKE A HOLE IN THE ICE: **dwaa'ige** *vai*
MAKE A WATER HOLE IN THE ICE: **dwaa'ibii** *vai*, also **dwaa'ige**
MUCH ICE: there is much ice **mikwamiikaa, mikwamiikaamagad** *vii*
ON TOP OF THE ICE: **agidiskwam** *pc*, also **ogidiskwam*, wagidiskwam**
SLIP AND FALL ON THE ICE: **ozhaashikoshin** *vai*
SLIPPERY ICE: there is slippery ice **ozhaashikwaa, ozhaashikwaamagad** *vii*
START OFF ON THE ICE: **maajiiyaadagaako** *vai*
UNDER THE ICE: **anaamiskwam** *pc*
WALK ALONG ON THE ICE: **bimaadagaako** *vai*

ICE BOX
ICE BOX: **mikwamii-makak, -oon** *ni*

ICE CHISEL
ICE CHISEL: **eshkan, -an** *ni*

ICE CREAM
ICE CREAM: **dekaag** *ni-pt*

ICY
ICY ROAD: be icy (as a road or trail) **mikwamiiwadamon /mikwamiiwadamo-/** *vii*
ICY TRAIL: be icy (as a road or trail) **mikwamiiwadamon /mikwamiiwadamo-/** *vii*

IDENTIFY
IDENTIFY: identify s.o. **aawenim** *vta*; identify s.t. **aawendan** *vti*
IDENTIFY BY SIGHT: identify s.o. by sight **aawenaw** *vta*; identify s.t. by sight **aawenan** *vti*

IDENTIFY BY SOUND: identify s.o. by
sound **aawetaw** *vta;* identify s.t. by sound
aawetan *vti*

IF
IF: **giishpin** *pc*

IGNITE
IGNITE: **biskane, biskanemagad** *vii*

IGNORANT
IGNORANT: be ignorant **bagwanawizi** *vai*

IGNORE
IGNORE: **boonendam** *vai2;* ignore s.o.
boonenim *vta;* ignore s.t. **boonendan** *vti*

ILL
ILL: be ill **aakozi** *vai+o*
FALL ILL FROM BAD MEDICINE:
niboowise *vai*
SERIOUSLY ILL: be seriously ill **aanimizi** *vai*

ILL-FORMED
ILL-FORMED: **maazhi-** *pv4*

ILLNESS
HAVE A RESPIRATORY ILLNESS:
ozosodamwaapine *vai*

IMAGE
IMAGE: **mazinichigan, -ag** *na*
MAKE AN IMAGE: make an image of s.o.
mazinaadin *vta*

IMPATIENT
IMPATIENT: be impatient **ojaanimendam**
vai2; **zhigajii** *vai*

IMPRINTED
IMPRINTED: be imprinted **mazinishin** *vai;*
mazinisin *vii*

IMPRISONED
IMPRISONED: be imprisoned
gibaakwa'igaazo *vai*

IN
IN: be in **biinde, biindemagad** *vii;* **biinzo** *vai*
CRAWL IN: **biindoode** *vii*
DRIVE IN: speed in **biinjibide,**
biinjibidemagad *vii;* **biinjibizo** *vai*
FALL IN: **biinjibide, biinjibidemagad** *vii;*
biinjibizo *vai;* **biinjise** *vai;* **biinjise,**
biinjisemagad *vii*
FLOW IN: **biinjijiwan** *vii*
FLY IN: **biinjibide, biinjibidemagad** *vii;*
biinjibizo *vai;* **biinjise** *vai;* **biinjise,**
biinjisemagad *vii*
IN A CERTAIN PLACE: **dazhi-** *pv3;* be in a
certain place **dagon /dago-/** *vii*
IN A PLACE WITH: **dago-** *pv4*
IN AMONG: in among it **megwe-aya'ii** *pc,*
also **megweya'ii**
IN THE BRUSH: **megwekob** *pc*
IN THE MIDST: in the midst of **megwe-** *pn*
IN THE MUD: **megwejiishkiwag** *pc*
IN THE WOODS: **megwaayaak** *pc*
SPEED IN: drive in **biinjibide,**
biinjibidemagad *vii;* **biinjibizo** *vai*
THROW IN: throw s.o. in **biinjwebin** *vta;*
throw s.t. in **biinjwebinan** *vti;* throw things
in **biinjwebinige** *vai*

IN ORDER TO
IN ORDER TO: **ji-** *pv1*

IN TURN
IN TURN: **meshkwad** *pc*

IN TURNS
IN TURNS: **memeshkwad** *pc*

IN VAIN
IN VAIN: **aano-** *pv1*
DO IN VAIN: **aanawewizi** *vai*

INADEQUATE
INADEQUATE: be inadequate **aanawewizi**
vai
THINK INADEQUATE: think s.o. is
inadequate **zhaagoodenim** *vta*

INCH
CERTAIN NUMBER OF INCHES: a certain
number of inches **dasoninj** *pc*

INCLUDED
INCLUDED: be included **dagwaginde,**
dagwagindemagad *vii;* **dagwaginzo** *vai*

INCOMPETENT
INCOMPETENT: be incompetent **bagandizi**
vai

INCREASE
INCREASE IN NUMBER: **niigi** *vai;* make
s.o. increase in number **niigi'** *vta;* make s.t.
increase in number **niigitoon** *vti2*

INDEED
INDEED: **geget** *pc*

INDEPENDENT
INDEPENDENT: be independent
dibenindizo *vai*

INDEX FINGER
INDEX FINGER: **izhinoo'iganinj, -iin** *ni*

INDIAN
INDIAN: Indian (in contrast to non-Indians)
anishinaabe, -g *na;* be Indian (in contrast
to non-Indians) **anishinaabewi** *vai*
CALL IN INDIAN: call s.o. in Indian
(Ojibwe) **anishinaabewinikaazh**
/anishinaabewinikaaN-/ *vta;* call s.t. in
Indian (Ojibwe) **anishinaabewinikaadan**
vti
CALLED IN INDIAN: be called in Indian
(Ojibwe) **anishinaabewinikaade,**
anishinaabewinikaademagad *vii;*
anishinaabewinikaazo *vai*
INDIAN WRITING: Indian (Ojibwe) writing
anishinaabewibii'igan, -an *ni*
MANY INDIANS: there are many Indians
anishinaabekaa *vii*
NON-LOCAL INDIAN: **mayagi-**
anishinaabe, -g *na*
SOMETHING WRITTEN IN INDIAN:
something written in Indian (Ojibwe)
anishinaabewibii'igan, -an *ni*
SPEAK IN AN INDIAN LANGUAGE: speak
in an Indian language (especially in
Ojibwe) **anishinaabe-gaagiigido** *vai*
WRITE IN INDIAN: write in Indian (Ojibwe)
anishinaabewibii'ige *vai;* write s.t. in
Indian (Ojibwe) **anishinaabewibii'an** *vti;*
write s.t. in Indian (Ojibwe) (e.g., a book)
anishinaabewisidoon *vti2;* write (s.t.) in

Indian (Ojibwe) to s.o.
anishinaabewibii'amaw *vta*
WRITTEN IN INDIAN: be written in Indian
(Ojibwe) **anishinaabewibii'igaade,
anishinaabewibii'igaademagad** *vii;* be
written in Indian (Ojibwe) (e.g., a book or
document) **anishinaabewisin** *vii*

INDIAN CENTER
INDIAN CENTER: **anishinaabe-
maawanjii'idiiwigamig, -oon** *ni*

INDIAN COUNTRY
INDIAN COUNTRY: **anishinaabewaki** *ni*

INDIAN LANGUAGE
INDIAN LANGUAGE: Indian language
(especially Ojibwe) **anishinaabemowin,
-an** *ni*
SPEAK AN INDIAN LANGUAGE: speak an
Indian language (especially Ojibwe) to s.o.
anishinaabemotaw *vta;* speak an Indian
language (especially Ojibwe)
anishinaabemo *vai*

INDIAN WOMAN
INDIAN WOMAN: **anishinaabekwe, -g** *na;*
be an Indian woman **anishinaabekwewi**
vai

INEFFECTIVE
INEFFECTIVE: be ineffective **aanawewizi**
vai; **zhaagwaadad** *vii;* **zhaagwaadizi** *vai*

INFECT
INFECT: infect s.o. with something
aazhookoodin *vta*

INFECTED
INFECTED EAR: have an infected ear
miniiwitawage *vai*

INFLATE
INFLATE: inflate s.o. **boodaajii'
/boodaajii'w-/** *vta;* inflate s.t. **boodaajii'an**
vti; inflate things **boodaajii'ige** *vai*

INHERENTLY
INHERENTLY: **dibinawe** *pc*

INHERIT
INHERIT FROM A CERTAIN SOURCE:
ondizi *vai*

INJURE
INJURE: injure s.o. **inigaa'** *vta*

INJURED
INJURED: fall and be injured **godigoshin** *vai*

INK
INK: **ozhibii'iganaaboo** *ni*

INLAND
INLAND: **noopiming** *pc*
CARRY INLAND: carry s.o. inland **gopiwizh
/gopiwiN-/** *vta;* carry s.t. inland
gopiwidoon *vti2*
GO INLAND: **gopii** *vai*
RUN INLAND: **gopibatoo** *vai*
TAKE INLAND: take s.o. inland **gopiwizh
/gopiwiN-/** *vta;* take s.t. inland
gopiwidoon *vti2*

INLET
INLET: at the inlet **zaagiing** *pc;* be an inlet
zaagidawaa, zaagidawaamagad *vii*

INQUIRE
INQUIRE: **gagwedwe** *vai*

INSANE
INSANE: be insane **giiwanaadizi** *vai*

INSECT
INSECT: **manidoons, -ag** *na*

INSIDE
INSIDE: **biindig** *pc;* inside it **biinjayi'ii** *pc*
BLOWN INSIDE: be blown inside
biindigeyaashi *vai;* **biindigeyaasin** *vii*
BRING FIREWOOD INSIDE: **biindigenise**
vai
BRING INSIDE: bring s.o. inside **biindigazh
/biindigaN-/** *vta;* bring s.t. inside
biindigadoon *vti2*
CHASE INSIDE: chase s.o. inside
biindigenaazhikaw *vta;* **biindigenizhikaw**
vta
COME INSIDE: **biindige** *vai*
DANCE INSIDE: dance inside (as in a Grand
Entry) **biindigeshimo** *vai*
DRIVE INSIDE: **biindigebide,
biindigebidemagad** *vii;* **biindigebizo** *vai*
FLY INSIDE: **biindigebide,
biindigebidemagad** *vii;* **biindigebizo** *vai*
GO INSIDE: **biindige** *vai*
INSIDE BODY: inside the body **biinjina** *pc*
INSIDE EAR: inside an ear **biinjitawag** *pc*
INSIDE MOUTH: inside the mouth
biinjidoon *pc*
INSIDE NOSE: inside the nose **biinjijaanzh** *pc*
RUN INSIDE: **biindigebatoo** *vai;* they run
inside together **biindigeba'idiwag
/biindigeba'idi-/** *vai;* run inside with s.o.
biindigebatwaazh /biindigebatwaaN-/
vta; run inside with s.t.
biindigebatwaadan *vti;* run inside from
people **biindigeba'iwe** *vai*
SPEED INSIDE: **biindigebide,
biindigebidemagad** *vii;* **biindigebizo** *vai*
TAKE INSIDE: take s.o. inside **biindigazh
/biindigaN-/** *vta;* take s.t. inside
biindigadoon *vti2*
TELL TO GO INSIDE: tell s.o. to go inside
biindigenaazha' /biindigenaazha'w-/ *vta*
THROW INSIDE: throw s.o. inside
biindigewebin *vta;* throw s.t. inside
biindigewebinan *vti;* throw things inside
biindigewebinige *vai*

INSIDE OUT
TURN INSIDE OUT: **aaboozikaa** *vai;*
aaboozikaa, aaboozikaamagad *vii;* turn
s.o. inside out **aaboodin** *vta;* turn s.t. inside out **aaboodinan** *vti*
WEAR INSIDE OUT: wear s.o. inside out
aaboozikaw *vta;* wear s.t. inside out
aaboozikan *vti*

INSIGNIFICANT
CONSIDER INSIGNIFICANT: consider s.o.
insignificant **agaasenim** *vta;* consider s.t.
insignificant **agaasendan** *vti*
CONSIDERED INSIGNIFICANT: be considered insignificant **agaasendaagozi** *vai;*
agaasendaagwad *vii*

INSPECT
INSPECT: inspect s.o. **dibaabam** *vta;* inspect
s.t. **dibaabandan** *vti*

INSTRUMENT
MUSICAL INSTRUMENT:
madwewechigan, -an *ni;* musical instrument (especially a wind instrument)
noondaagochigan, -an *ni*

INTACT
INTACT: be intact **miziweyaa,
miziweyaamagad** *vii;* **miziwezi** *vai*

INTELLIGENT
INTELLIGENT: be intelligent **nibwaakaa** *vai*

INTENSE
HAVE INTENSE FEELINGS OR DESIRES:
aakwendam *vai2*

INTERCOURSE
HAVE SEXUAL INTERCOURSE: **mazhiwe**
vai; have sexual intercourse with s.o.
mazhi /maN-/ *vta*

INTERPRET
INTERPRET: interpret s.o. **aanikanootaw**
vta; interpret s.t. **aanikanootan** *vti;*
interpret for people **aanikanootaage** *vai*

INTERPRETED
INTERPRETED: be interpreted
aanikanootaagozi *vai*

INTERPRETER
INTERPRETER: **aanikanootaagewinini,
-wag** *na*

INTERRUPT
INTERRUPT: interrupt s.o. **wanishkwe'** *vta*
INTERRUPT BY SPEECH: interrupt s.o. by
speech **wanishkwem** *vta*

INTESTINE
INTESTINE: my intestine **ninagizh, -iin
/-nagizhy-/** *nid*

INTIMIDATE
INTIMIDATE: intimidate s.o. by speech
zegim *vta*

INTROVERTED
INTROVERTED: be introverted
zhaagwenimo *vai*

INVITE
INVITE TO A FEAST: invite s.o. to a feast
(especially as part of a religious ceremony)
wiikom *vta;* invite people to a feast (especially as part of a religious ceremony)
wiikonge *vai*

INVOLVED
INVOLVED: be involved with s.o. **dazhiikaw**
vta; be involved with s.t. **dazhiikan** *vti*

IRON
IRON: **biiwaabik, -oon** *ni;* clothes iron
zhooshkwega'igan, -an *ni;* iron s.o. (e.g.,
pants) **zhooshkwega' /zhooshkwega'w-/**
vta; iron s.t. **zhooshkwega'an** *vti*
IRON CLOTHES: **zhooshkwega'ige** *vai*

IRONWOOD
IRONWOOD: **maananoons, -ag** *na*

ISLAND
ISLAND: **minis, -an** *ni*
ROCKY ISLAND: **minisaabik, -oon** *ni*

IT IS SO
IT IS SO: **memwech** *pc*

IT IS THUS THAT
IT IS THUS THAT: **miish** *pc;* **mii** *pc*

ITCH
ITCH: **gizhiibizi** *vai*

ITCHY
ITCHY SKIN: have itchy skin **gizhiibazhe** *vai*

J

JACK
JACK: jack (card) **zhimaaganish, -ag** *na*

JACK PINE
JACK PINE: **okikaandag, -oog** *na, also*
wakikaandag

JACK RABBIT
JACK RABBIT: **misaabooz, -oog** *na*

JACKET
JACKET: **babiinzikawaagan, -an** *ni*

JACKLIGHT
JACKLIGHT: **waaswaa** *vai*

JAIL
JAIL: **gibaakwa'odiiwigamig, -oon** *ni;* jail s.o.
gibaakwa' /gibaakwa'w-/ *vta*

JAM
JAM: **baashkiminasigan, -an** *ni*

JANITOR
JANITOR: **biinichigewinini, -wag** *na;* janitor
(female) **biinichigewikwe, -g** *na*

JANUARY
JANUARY: **gichi-manidoo-giizis** *na, also*
manidoo-giizis

JAW
JAW: my jaw **indaamikan, -an /-daamikan-/**
nid

JAY
BLUE JAY: **diindiisi, -wag** *na*

JEALOUS
JEALOUS: be jealous **gaawe** *vai;* **gaawendam**
vai2; be jealous of s.o. **gaawam** *vta;*
gizhaawenim *vta;* be jealous of things
gizhaawenjige *vai*

JELLO
JELLO: **wetotwaag** *ni-pt*

JIG
JIG: jig s.t. (e.g., wild rice) **mimigoshkan** *vti;*
jig something (e.g., wild rice)
mimigoshkam *vai2*

JINGLE
JINGLE: jingle (on dress) **ziibaaska'igan, -an**
ni

JINGLE DRESS
JINGLE DRESS: jingle dress
ziibaaska'iganagooday, -an *ni*

JOB

JOB: **anokiiwin, -an** *ni*
DO A CERTAIN JOB: do a certain job for s.o. **inanokiitaw** *vta*
HAVE A CERTAIN JOB: **inanokii** *vai*
HIRE TO DO A CERTAIN JOB: hire s.o. to do a certain job **inanoozh /inanooN-/** *vta*

JOINING

LAY JOINING: lay s.o. joining something else **aanikooshim** *vta;* lay s.t. joining something else **aanikoosidoon** *vti2*
LIE JOINING: lie joining something else **aanikooshin** *vai;* **aanikoosin** *vii*

JOURNEY

START A JOURNEY: **maadaadizi** *vai*

JOYOUS

JOYOUS: be joyous **minawaanigozi** *vai*

JUDGE

JUDGE: **dibaakonigewinini, -wag** *na;* **gichi-dibaakonigewinini, -wag** *na;* judge s.o. **dibaakon** *vta;* **onaakon** *vta;* judge s.t. **dibaakonan** *vti;* judge things **dibaakonige** *vai;* **onaakonige** *vai*
JUDGE A CERTAIN WAY: judge s.o. a certain way **inaakon** *vta;* judge s.t. a certain way **inaakonan** *vti*

JUDGED

JUDGED: be judged **dibaakonigaazo** *vai*
JUDGED A CERTAIN WAY: be judged a certain way **inaakonigaazo** *vai*

JUDGEMENT

MAKE A CERTAIN JUDGEMENT: **inaakonige** *vai*

JUICE

APPLE JUICE: **mishiiminaaboo** *ni*

JULY

JULY: **aabita-niibino-giizis** *na;* **baapaashkizige-giizis** *na;* **miini-giizis** *na,* also **miinike-giizis**

JUMP

JUMP: **gwaashkwani** *vai*
JUMP ABOARD: **boozigwaashkwani** *vai*
JUMP ACROSS: **aazhawigwaashkwani** *vai*
JUMP IN A VEHICLE OR BOAT: **boozigwaashkwani** *vai*
JUMP INTO THE WATER: **bakobiigwaashkwani** *vai*
JUMP OUT OF THE WATER: jump out of the water as a fish **googa'am** *vai2*
JUMP OVER: **baazhijigwaashkwani** *vai*
JUMP UPWARDS: **ombigwaashkwani** *vai*

JUNE

JUNE: **ode'imini-giizis** *na*

JUNEBERRY

JUNEBERRY: **gozigwaakomin, -ag** *na*

JUNEBERRY BUSH

JUNEBERRY BUSH: **gozigwaakominagaawanzh, -iig** *na*

JUST

JUST: **enda-** *pv4*
JUST DON'T: **gego bina** *pc*
JUST FOR FUN: **anishaa** *pc*
JUST FOR NOTHING: **anishaa** *pc*

JUST LIKE: **indigo** *pc,* also **nindigo***
JUST NOW: **bijiinag** *pc*
JUST SO: **eniwek** *pc;* **wenda-** *pv4*
JUST THAT: **memwech** *pc*
JUST THEN: **na'idaa** *pc*

K

KEROSENE

KEROSENE: **waazakonenjiganaaboo** *ni*

KETTLE

KETTLE: **akik, -oog** *na*
LEGGED KETTLE: **okaadakik, -oog** *na*
PUT IN THE KETTLE: put (s.t.) in the kettle **boodaakwe** *vai+o*
WASH KETTLE: **giziibiiginakokwe** *vai*

KETTLE HANGER

KETTLE HANGER: **agoodakikwaan, -an** *ni*

KEY

KEY: **aabaabika'igan, -an** *ni*

KICK

KICK: kick s.o. **basikawaazh /basikawaaN-/** *vta;* **dangishkaw** *vta;* kick s.t. **basikawaadan** *vti;* **dangishkan** *vti;* kick things **dangishkige** *vai;* kick people **dangishkaage** *vai*
KICK IN REAR: kick s.o. in the rear **basidiyeshkaw** *vta*
KICK OUT OF THE WAY: kick s.o. out of the way **ikowebishkaw** *vta;* kick s.t. out of the way **ikowebishkan** *vti*

KIDNEY

KIDNEY: my kidney **indoodikosiw, -ag /-doodikosiw-/** *na*

KILL

KILL: kill game **nitaage** *vai;* kill s.o. **nishi /niS-/** *vta;* kill s.t. **nitoon** *vti2;* kill oneself **nisidizo** *vai;* kill (s.t.) for s.o. **nitamaw** *vta;* kill (s.t.) of people or for people **nitamaage** *vai;* kill (s.t.) for oneself **nitamaazo** *vai;* kill people **nishiwe** *vai;* they kill each other **nisidiwag /nisidi-/** *vai*
FINALLY AND COMPLETELY KILL: finally and completely kill s.o. **aapijinazh /aapijinaN-/** *vta*
KILL FOR A CERTAIN REASON: kill s.o. for a certain reason **onjinazh /onjinaN-/** *vta*
KILL OFF: kill s.o. off **jaaginazh /jaaginaN-/** *vta*

KIND

KIND: be kind **gizhewaadizi** *vai;* **minode'e** *vai*

KIND

KIND: kind *animate* **dino, -wag** *pr,* also **dinowa;** kind *inanimate* **dino, -wan** *pr,* also **dinowa**

ALL KINDS: **anooj** *pc*
KIND-HEARTED
KIND-HEARTED: be kind-hearted
zhawenjige *vai*
KINDLING
KINDLING WOOD: **biisiga'isaan, -an** *ni*
MAKE KINDLING: **biisiga'ise** *vai*
KING
KING: **gichi-ogimaa, -g** *na;* be a king **gichi-ogimaawi** *vai;* king (card) **ogimaa, -g** *na*
KINGBIRD
KINGBIRD: **wiindigoo-bineshiinh, -yag** *na*
KINGFISHER
KINGFISHER: **ogiishkimanisii, -g** *na*
KINNIKINNICK
KINNIKINNICK: kinnikinnick (tobacco and bark smoking mixture) **apaakozigan** *ni*
MAKE KINNIKINNICK: **apaakozige** *vai*
KISS
KISS: kiss s.o. **ojiim** *vta;* they kiss each other **ojiindiwag** /ojiindi-/ *vai*
KITCHEN
KITCHEN: **jiibaakwewigamig, -oon** *ni*
KITCHEN APRON
KITCHEN APRON: **inapizowin, -an** *ni*
KNEAD
KNEAD: knead s.o. **onadin** *vta;* knead s.t. **onadinan** *vti;* knead things **onadinige** *vai*
KNEE
KNEE: my knee **ingidig, -wag** /-gidigw-/ *nad*
SKIN KNEE: skin one's knee **bishagigidigweshin** *vai*
KNEEL
KNEEL: **ojijiingwanabi** *vai*
KNIFE
KNIFE: **mookomaan, -an** *ni*
BUTCHER KNIFE: **gichi-mookomaan, -an** *ni*
CROOKED KNIFE: **waagikomaan, -an** *ni*
LARGE KNIFE: **gichi-mookomaan, -an** *ni*
KNIFE SHEATH
KNIFE SHEATH: **biinjikomaan, -an** *ni*
KNOCK
KNOCK: knock on s.o. (as something stick- or wood-like) **baapaagaakwa'** /baapaagaakwa'w-/ *vta;* knock on s.t. (as something stick- or wood-like, e.g., a door) **baapaagaakwa'an** *vti;* knock on things (as something stick- or wood-like, e.g., a door) **baapaagaakwa'ige** *vai*
KNOCK DOWN: knock s.o. down **gawiwebin** *vta;* knock s.t. down **gawiwebinan** *vti*
KNOCK DOWN OFF: knock s.o. down off something with foot or body **diitibishkaw** *vta;* knock s.t. down off something with foot or body **diitibishkan** *vti*
KNOCK DOWN OFF USING SOMETHING: knock s.o. down off using something **diitiba'** /diitiba'w-/ *vta;* knock s.t. down off using something **diitiba'an** *vti*
KNOCK DOWN OFF WITH HANDS: knock s.o. down off something with hands

diitibibizh /diitibibiN-/ *vta;* knock s.t. down off something with hands **diitibibidoon** *vti2*
KNOCK DOWN USING SOMETHING: knock s.o. down using something **biniweba'** /biniweba'w-/ *vta;* knock s.t. down using something **biniweba'an** *vti*
KNOCK SENSELESS: knock s.o. senseless **giiwashkweganaam** *vta*
KNOCK WILD RICE: **bawa'am** *vai2*
KNOCKER
RICE KNOCKER: rice knocker (stick for wild rice harvesting) **bawa'iganaak, -oog** *na*
KNOLL
KNOLL: be a knoll **bikwadinaa, bikwadinaamagad** *vii*
KNOT
KNOT: **gashka'oojigan, -an** *ni*
TIE WITH A KNOT: tie s.o. with a knot **gashka'oozh** /gashka'ooN-/ *vta;* tie s.t. with a knot **gashka'oodoon** *vti2*
KNOTTED
KNOTTED: be knotted **gashka'oode, gashka'oodemagad** *vii;* **gashka'oozo** *vai*
KNOW
KNOW: know s.o. **gikenim** *vta;* know s.t. **gikendan** *vti;* know things **gikenjige** *vai*
KNOW HOW: know how to do something **nitaa-** *pv4;* know how to handle s.o. **nagaji'** *vta;* know how to handle s.t. **nagajitoon** *vti2*
KNOW HOW TO MAKE: know how to make s.o. **nitaawi'** *vta;* know how to make s.t. **nitaawitoon** *vti2;* know how to make things **nitaawichige** *vai*
SEEK TO KNOW: seek to know s.o. **nanda-gikenim** *vta;* seek to know s.t. **nanda-gikendan** *vti*
KNOWN
KNOWN: be known **gikendaagozi** *vai;* **gikendaagwad** *vii*

L

LACROSSE
PLAY LACROSSE: **baaga'adowe** *vai*
LACROSSE STICK
LACROSSE STICK: **baaga'adowaan, -an** *ni*
LADDER
LADDER: **akwaandawaagan, -an** *ni*
LADLE
LADLE: spoon **emikwaan, -an** *ni*
WOODEN LADLE: **mitigwemikwaan, -an** *ni*
LAKE
LAKE: **zaaga'igan, -iin** *ni*
ACROSS THE LAKE: **agaaming** *pc*
AT THE LAKE: **agamiing** *pc*

CHAIN OF LAKES: be a chain of lakes
aanikegamaa, aanikegamaamagad *vii*
FLOW INTO A LAKE: **zaagidawaa,
zaagidawaamagad** *vii*
GREAT LAKE: one of the Great Lakes
gichigami, -in *ni*
IN THE MIDDLE OF THE LAKE:
naawagaam *pc*
LAKE GOES OFF FROM ANOTHER:
bakegamaa, bakegamaamagad *vii*
ON THE OTHER SIDE OF THE LAKE:
agaaming *pc*
OUT IN THE LAKE: **naawij** *pc*
WALK AROUND A LAKE:
giiwitaayaazhagaame *vai*

LAKE SUPERIOR
LAKE SUPERIOR: **gichigami** *ni usually in
locative* **gichigamiing**

LAME
LAME: be lame **maakizi** *vai*
LAME LEG: have a lame leg **maakigaade** *vai*

LAMP
LAMP: **waazakonenjigan, -an** *ni*
ELECTRIC LAMP: **waasamoo-
waazakonenjigan, -an** *ni*

LANCE
LANCE: **zhimaagan, -an** *ni*

LAND
LAND: **aki, -in** *ni*
ALLOT LAND: allot s.o. land **mamakii'** *vta*
ALLOTMENT OF LAND: there is an allot-
ment of land **mamakii'idim /mamakii'idi-/**
vai
CLEAR LAND: **mazhii'ige** *vai*
HAVE LAND: **odakiimi** *vai*
SURVEY LAND: **diba'akii** *vai*

LAND
LAND: **agwaa'o** *vai, also* **agwaa'am**; land
(from flight) **boonii** *vai*

LANGUAGE
LANGUAGE: **inwewin, -an** *ni*
OJIBWE LANGUAGE: **ojibwemowin** *ni;*
Indian language (especially Ojibwe)
anishinaabemowin, -an *ni*

LAP
LAP: my lap **injiingwan, -ag /-jiingwan-/** *nad*

LARD
LARD: **gookooshi-bimide** *ni*

LAST
LAST: **ishkwaaj** *pc*
LAST AUTUMN: **dagwaagong** *pc*
LAST BORN CHILD: **ishkwejaagan, -ag** *na*
LAST FALL: **dagwaagong** *pc*
LAST NIGHT: **dibikong** *pc*
LAST SPRING: **ziigwanong** *pc*
LAST SUMMER: **niibinong** *pc*
LAST WINTER: **biboonong** *pc*

LAST NAME
LAST NAME: **ishkwenikaazowin, -an** *ni*
HAVE A LAST NAME: **ishkwenikaazo** *vai*

LATE
LATE: **wiikaa** *pc*

LATE AT NIGHT: **ishpi-dibik** *pc;* **niibaa-
dibik** *pc;* be late at night **ishpi-dibikad** *vii*
LATE SUMMER: **giiwe-niibin** *vii*
LATE WINTER: be late winter **giiwe-biboon**
vii
SO LATE IN THE DAY: be so late in the day
apiichi-giizhigad *vii*
TOO LATE: **naanabem** *pc*

LATER
LATER: **baanimaa** *pc, also* **baamaa;**
baanimaa apii *pc, also* **baanimaapii,**
baamaapii; naagaj *pc*

LAUGH
LAUGH: **baapi** *vai;* **ginagaapi** *vai;* laugh at
s.o. **baapi'** *vta;* laugh at s.t. **baapitoon** *vti2*
ARRIVE LAUGHING: **bagamaapi** *vai*
BURST OUT LAUGHING: **baashkaapi** *vai*
COME LAUGHING: **biidaapi** *vai*
GO AWAY LAUGHING: **animaapi** *vai*
LAUGH SECRETLY: **giimoodaapi** *vai*

LAUNCH
MOTOR LAUNCH: **waasamoo-jiimaan, -an**
ni

LAUNDROMAT
LAUNDROMAT: **giziibiiga'igewigamig,
-oon** *ni*

LAUNDRY
HANG UP LAUNDRY: **agoojige** *vai*

LAW
LAW: **inaakonigewin, -an** *ni*
CHANGE LAWS: **aandaakonige** *vai*

LAWYER
LAWYER: **dibaakonigewinini, -wag** *na*

LAWYER
LAWYER: lawyer (fish) **mizay, -ag** *na*

LAXATIVE
LAXATIVE: **zhaabozigan, -an** *ni*

LAY
LAY A CERTAIN WAY: lay s.o. a certain way
izhishim *vta;* lay s.t. a certain way
izhisidoon *vti2*
LAY ACROSS: lay s.o. across (as something
stick- or wood-like) **aazhawaakoshim** *vta;*
lay s.t. across (as something stick- or wood-
like) **aazhawaakosidoon** *vti2*
LAY AN EGG: **boonam** *vai2*
LAY DOWN AROUND: lay s.o. down around
giiwitaashim *vta;* lay s.t. down around
giiwitaasidoon *vti2*
LAY FACE DOWN: lay s.o. face down
animikoshim *vta;* lay s.t. face down
animikosidoon *vti2*
LAY FACE UP: lay s.o. face up **aazhigijishim**
vta; lay s.t. face up **aazhigijisidoon** *vti2*
LAY JOINING: lay s.o. joining something else
aanikooshim *vta;* lay s.t. joining something else **aanikoosidoon** *vti2*
LAY ON SIDE: lay s.o. on side **opimeshim**
vai; lay s.t. on side **opimesidoon** *vti2*
LAY OVER BACKWARDS: lay s.o. over
backwards **aazhigijishim** *vta;* lay s.t. over
backwards **aazhigijisidoon** *vti2*

LAY SOMETHING FOR PROTECTION:
lay something on or under s.t. for
protection **apisidoon** *vti2*
LAY SPREAD OUT: lay s.o. spread out
zhingadeshim *vta;* lay s.t. spread out
zhingadesidoon *vti2*
LAY STRAIGHT: lay s.o. straight
gwayakoshim *vta;* lay s.t. straight
gwayakosidoon *vti2*

LAYER
AS A LAYER: **biitoo-** *pv4*
LIE IN A LAYER: **biitooshin** *vai;* **biitoosin**
vii
LIE IN A THICK LAYER: **gipagishin** *vai;*
gipagisin *vii*
LIE IN A THIN LAYER: **bibagishin** *vai;*
bibagisin *vii*
WEAR LAYERS: wear layers (as underwear)
biitookonaye *vai*

LAZY
LAZY: be habitually lazy **gitimishki** *vai;* be
lazy **bagandizi** *vai;* **gitimi** *vai*

LAZYBONES
LAZYBONES: be a lazybones **gitimishki** *vai*

LEAD
LEAD: **niigaanii** *vai;* lead s.o. **niigaaniwizh**
/nigaaniwiN-/ *vta*
LEAD ALONG: lead along (as something
string-like) **bimaabiigamon**
/bimaabiigamo-/ *vii*
ROAD LEADS ALONG: lead along (as a road
or trail) **bimamon /bimamo-/,**
bimamoomagad *vii*
ROAD LEADS FROM A CERTAIN PLACE:
lead from a certain place (as a road or trail)
ondadamon /ondadamo-/ *vii*
ROAD LEADS TO A CERTAIN PLACE:
lead to a certain place (as a road or trail)
inamon /inamo-/ *vii*
TRAIL LEADS ALONG: lead along (as a
road or trail) **bimamon /bimamo-/,**
bimamoomagad *vii*
TRAIL LEADS FROM A CERTAIN
PLACE: lead from a certain place (as a
road or trail) **ondadamon /ondadamo-/** *vii*
TRAIL LEADS TO A CERTAIN PLACE:
lead to a certain place (as a road or trail)
inamon /inamo-/ *vii*

LEAD
LEAD: lead (metal) **ashkikomaan** *ni*

LEADER
LEADER: **eshpabid** *na-pt;* **ogimaa, -g** *na;* be a
leader **ogimaawi** *vai*
HIGHEST LEADER: **gichi-ogimaa, -g** *na;* be
the highest leader **gichi-ogimaawi** *vai*
MAKE LEADER: make s.o. leader
ogimaakaw *vta*
WIFE OF CHIEF OR LEADER:
ogimaakwe, -g *na*
WOMAN LEADER: **ogimaakwe, -g** *na*

LEADERSHIP
LEADERSHIP: **ogimaawiwin, -an** *ni*

LEADING
LEADING: **niigaan** *pc*

LEAF
LEAF: **aniibiish, -an** *ni;* **aniibiishibag, -oon** *ni*
BRIGHT LEAVES: there are bright leaves
waatebagaa, waatebagaamagad *vii*
GREEN LEAVES: there are green leaves
ashkibagaa, ashkibagaamagad *vii*
LEAVES BUD: **zaagibagaa,**
zaagibagaamagad *vii*
MANY LEAVES: there are many leaves
aniibiishikaa, aniibiishikaamagad *vii*
RED LEAVES: have red leaves **miskobagizi**
vai; there are red leaves on the trees
miskobagaa, miskobagaamagad *vii*

LEAF-GREEN
LEAF-GREEN: be leaf-green **ashkibagong**
inaande, ashkibagong inaandemagad *vii;*
ashkibagong inaanzo *vai*

LEAK
LEAK: **onjigaa, onjigaamagad** *vii*
LEAK FAST: **gizhiigaa, gizhiigaamagad** *vii*
START TO LEAK: **maajigaa,**
maajigaamagad *vii*

LEAN
LEAN AGAINST: lean against (as something
stick- or wood-like) **aatwaakoshin** *vai;*
aatwaakosin *vii;* lean s.o. against (as
something stick- or wood-like)
aatwaakoshim *vta;* lean s.t. against (as
something stick- or wood-like)
aatwaakosidoon *vti2*
STAND LEANING AGAINST: stand leaning
against something **aatwaakogaabawi** *vai*

LEARN
LEARN BY OBSERVATION: **gikinawaabi**
vai; learn by observation of s.o.
gikinawaabam *vta*
SEEK TO LEARN: seek to learn s.t. **nanda-**
gikendan *vti*

LEAST
IN THE LEAST: **ganage** *pc*

LEATHER
LEATHER: **bashkwegin, -oon** *ni;*
bashkweginowayaan, -an *ni*

LEAVE
LEAVE: **maajaa** *vai, also* **ani-maajaa**
LEAVE ALONE: leave s.o. alone **booni'** *vta;*
leave s.t. alone **boonitoon** *vti2*
LEAVE BEHIND: leave s.o. behind **nagazh**
/nagaN-/ *vta;* leave s.t. behind **nagadan**
vti; leave (s.t.) behind for s.o. **nagadamaw**
vta; abandon people **nagazhiwe** *vai*
LEAVE BEHIND UNEATEN: leave s.o.
behind uneaten **ishkwam** *vta;* leave s.t.
behind uneaten **ishkwandan** *vti*

LEECH
LEECH: **ozagaskwaajime, -g** *na, also*
zagaskwaajime

LEECH LAKE
LEECH LAKE: Leech Lake Reservation **Gaa-**
zagaskwaajimekaag *place*

LEFT
LEFT HAND: left hand *usually possessed*
namanjinik, -an *ni*

LEFT ALONE
LEFT ALONE: be left alone **boonichigaade, boonichigaademagad** *vii;* **boonichigaazo** *vai*

LEFT-HANDED
LEFT-HANDED: be left-handed **namanjii** *vai*

LEFTOVERS
LEFTOVERS: leftover food **ishkwanjigan, -an** *ni*
LEAVE LEFTOVERS: **ishkwanjige** *vai*

LEG
LEG: my leg **nikaad, -an** */-kaad-/* *nid*
ACHE IN LEG: have an ache in one's leg **dewigaade** *vai*
BREAK LEG: break one's leg **bookogaade** *vai*
BROKEN LEG: have a broken leg **bookogaade** *vai*
FALL AND BREAK LEG: fall and break one's leg **bookogaadeshin** *vai*
LAME LEG: have a lame leg **maakigaade** *vai*
NUMB LEG: have a numb leg **niboowigaade** *vai*
SIT WITH LEGS CROSSED: **aazhoogaadebi** *vai*
SORE LEG: have a sore leg **gaagiijigaade** *vai*
SPRAIN LEG: sprain one's leg **zegigaadeshin** *vai*
STIFF LEG: have a stiff leg **jiibadaakogaade** *vai;* **jiibajigaade** *vai*

LEG GARTER
LEG GARTER: **gashkidaasebizon, -an** *ni*
WEAR LEG GARTERS: **gashkidaasebizo** *vai*

LEGEND
LEGEND: **aadizookaan, -ag** *na*
CHARACTER OF A LEGEND OR MYTH: **aadizookaan, -ag** *na*
TELL A LEGEND: **aadizooke** *vai;* tell a legend to s.o. **aadizookaw** *vta*

LEGGING
LEGGING: **aas, -an** *ni*

LEND
LEND: lend (s.t.) to s.o. **awi'** *vta;* lend (s.t.) to people **awi'iwe** *vai*

LENGTH
CERTAIN LENGTH: **ako-** *pv3;* be a certain length **akoozi** *vai;* **akwaa, akwaamagad** *vii;* be a certain length (as something mineral) **akwaabikad** *vii;* **akwaabikizi** *vai;* be a certain length (as something sheet-like) **akwegad** *vii;* **akwegizi** *vai;* be a certain length (as something stick- or wood-like) **akwaakozi** *vai;* **akwaakwad** *vii;* be a certain length (as something string-like) **akwaabiigad** *vii;* **akwaabiigizi** *vai*
MAKE A CERTAIN LENGTH: make s.o. a certain length **akoo'** *vta;* make s.t. a certain length **akootoon** *vti2*

LESS AND LESS
LESS AND LESS: **eshkam** *pc*

LET GO
LET GO: be let go **bagidinigaade, bagidinigaademagad** *vii;* **bagidinigaazo**

vai; let s.o. go **bagidin** *vta;* let s.t. go **bagidinan** *vti;* let things go **bagidinige** *vai*

LET IT BE
LET IT BE: **maanoo** *pc*

LET OUT
LET OUT: they are let out together (as from school or a meeting) **zaagidinidiwag** */zaagidinidi-/* *vai*

LET'S GO
LET'S GO: let's go! **ambe** *pc*

LETTER
LETTER: **mazina'igan, -an** *ni;* **maajiibii'igan, -an** *ni*
LETTER OF THE ALPHABET: **ozhibii'igan, -an** *ni*
SEND A LETTER HERE: **biijibii'ige** *vai*
WRITE A LETTER: **maajiibii'ige** *vai;* write a letter to s.o. **maajiibii'amaw** *vta*

LEVEL
LEVEL GROUND: be level ground **gwayakwakamigaa, gwayakwakamigaamagad** *vii*
LEVEL SURFACE: be a level surface **desaa, desaamagad** *vii*

LIAR
LIAR: be a habitual liar **gagiinawishki** *vai*

LIBRARY
LIBRARY: **agindaasoowigamig, -oon** *ni*

LICE
LOOK FOR LICE: **nandookome** *vai*

LICENSE
LICENSE: **mazina'igaans, -an** *ni*
DRIVER'S LICENSE: **odaabii'iwe- mazina'igaans, -an** *ni*
MARRIAGE LICENSE: **aapiji-wiidige- mazina'igan, -an** *ni*
RICING LICENSE: **manoominike- mazina'igaans, -an** *ni*

LICK
LICK: lick s.o. **nooskwaada'** */nooskwaada'w-/* *vta;* lick s.t. **nooskwaada'an** *vti*

LID
POT LID: **gibaabowe'igan, -an** *ni*
PUT A LID ON: put a lid on s.o. **gibaabowe'** */gibaabowe'w-/* *vta;* put a lid on s.t. **gibaabowe'an** *vti;* put a lid on things **gibaabowe'ige** *vai*

LIE
LIE A CERTAIN WAY: **izhishin** *vai;* **izhisin** *vii*
LIE ACROSS: lie across (as something stick- or wood-like) **aazhawaakoshin** *vai;* **aazhawaakosin** *vii*
LIE ALONG: lie along (as something stick- or wood-like) **bimaakoshin** *vai;* **bimaakosin** *vii*
LIE AS PADDING: **apishin** *vai;* **apisin** *vii*
LIE AT THE END: **ishkweshin** *vai;* **ishkwesin** *vii*
LIE COMFORTABLY: **minoshin** *vai*
LIE CORRECTLY: **gwayakoshin** *vai;* **gwayakosin** *vii*

LIE DOWN: **gawishimo** *vai;* **zhingishin** *vai*
LIE FACE DOWN: animikoshin *vai;*
  animikosin *vii*
LIE FACE UP: **aazhigijishin** *vai;* **aazhigijisin**
  vii
LIE FACING A CERTAIN WAY:
  inaasamishin *vai*
LIE FIRMLY FIXED: lie firmly fixed in place
  zoongishin *vai;* **zoongisin** *vii*
LIE HIGH UP: **ishpishin** *vai;* **ishpisin** *vii*
LIE IN A CERTAIN PLACE: **dazhishin** *vai;*
  dazhisin *vii*
LIE IN A GOOD POSITION: **minoshin** *vai;*
  minosin *vii*
LIE IN A LAYER: **biitooshin** *vai;* **biitoosin**
  vii
LIE IN A PILE: **okoshin** *vai;* **okosin** *vii*
LIE IN A THICK LAYER: **gipagishin** *vai;*
  gipagisin *vii*
LIE IN A THIN LAYER: **bibagishin** *vai;*
  bibagisin *vii*
LIE IN A TIGHT PLACE: **zhegoshin** *vai;*
  zhegosin *vii*
LIE IN WAIT: lie in wait for game **akandoo**
  vai; lie in wait for s.o. **akamaw** *vta*
LIE IN WARMTH: **giizhooshin** *vai*
LIE JOINING: lie joining something else
  aanikooshin *vai;* **aanikoosin** *vii*
LIE LIMP: **neshangishin** *vai;* **neshangisin** *vii*
LIE ON: lie on something **apishimo** *vai*
LIE ON SIDE: **opimesin** *vii;* lie on one's side
  opimeshin *vai*
LIE OUT OF THE WAY: **ikoshin** *vai;* **ikosin**
  vii
LIE PROTECTIVELY ON: lie protectively on
  s.o. **badagoshkaw** *vta;* lie protectively on
  s.t. **badagoshkan** *vti*
LIE SIDE BY SIDE IN A ROW: they lie side
  by side in a row **niibidesinoon** /**niibidesin-**/
  vii; they lie side by side in a row
  niibideshinoog /**niibideshin-**/ *vai*
LIE SLACK: **neshangisin** *vii*
LIE SPREAD OUT: **zhingadeshin** *vai;*
  zhingadesin *vii*
LIE STICKING OUT: lie sticking out (as
  something stick- or wood-like)
  zaagaakoshin *vai;* **zaagaakosin** *vii*
LIE STILL: **bizaanishin** *vai*
LIE STRAIGHT: **gwayakoshin** *vai;*
  gwayakosin *vii*
LIE TO A CERTAIN DEPTH: **apiichishin**
  vai; **apiichisin** *vii*
LIE TOUCHING: **daangishin** *vai;* **daangisin**
  vii
LIE UNCOMFORTABLY: **maazhishin** *vai*
LIE UNCOVERED: **baakishin** *vai;* **baakisin**
  vii; **michishin** *vai;* **michisin** *vii*
LIE WELL IN PLACE: **minosin** *vii*
LIE WITH FACE COVERED: lie with one's
  face covered **badagwiingweshin** *vai*
LIE WITH HEAD A CERTAIN WAY: lie
  with one's head a certain way **inikweshin**
  vai
LIE WITH HEAD ON: lie with head on
  something **apikweshimo** *vai*

LIE WITH REAR END STICKING OUT: lie
  with one's rear end sticking out
  jaangidiyeshin *vai*
TURN LYING IN PLACE: **gwekishin** *vai;*
  gwekisin *vii*

LIE
  LIE: **giiwanimo** *vai;* lie to s.o. **giiwanim** *vta*

LIFE
  CHANGE LIFE: change one's life **aanji-**
    bimaadizi *vai*
  LEAD A BAD LIFE: **maazhi-bimaadizi** *vai*
  LEAD A GOOD LIFE: **mino-bimaadizi** *vai;*
    mino-izhiwebizi *vai;* **minwaadizi** *vai*
  LEAD AN EVIL LIFE: **maji-izhiwebizi** *vai*
  LIVE A PROPER LIFE: **gwayako-bimaadizi**
    vai
  SAVE LIFE: save the life of s.o. **bimaaji'** *vta*

LIFT
  LIFT: lift s.o. **ombin** *vta;* lift s.o. (as with
    something string-like) **ombaabiigin** *vta;* lift
    s.t. **ombinan** *vti;* lift s.t. (as with something
    string-like) **ombaabiiginan** *vti;* lift (s.t.) for
    s.o. **ombinamaw** *vta*
  LIFT A PACK: lift a pack to one's back
    ombiwane *vai*
  LIFT AND CARRY: lift and carry s.o.
    ombiwizh /**ombiwiN-**/ *vta;* lift and carry
    s.t. **ombiwidoon** *vti2*
  LIFT ARM: lift one's arm **ombinikeni** *vai*
  LIFT ON BACK: lift s.o. on one's back
    omboom *vta;* lift s.t. on one's back
    omboondan *vti*
  STRAIN IN LIFTING: strain self in lifting
    jakiiwii *vai*

LIGHT
  LIGHT: light s.o. **zakiz** /**zakizw-**/ *vta;* light
    s.o. (e.g., a pipe) **zaka'** /**zaka'w-**/ *vta;* light
    s.t. **zaka'an** *vti;* **zakizan** *vti;* light (s.t.) for
    s.o. **zaka'amaw** *vta;* light things **zakizige**
    vai
  COME WITH A LIGHT:
    biidaazakwanenjige *vai*
  DRIVE AWAY WITH A LIGHT:
    animaazakonenjigebizo *vai*
  DRIVE HERE WITH A LIGHT:
    biidaazakonebizo *vai*
  GIVE OFF LIGHT: **waazakone,**
    waazakonemagad *vii*
  GO ALONG WITH A LIGHT:
    bimaazakonenjige *vai*
  GO AWAY WITH A LIGHT:
    animaazakonenjige *vai*
  GO TO A CERTAIN PLACE WITH
    LIGHT: **inaazakonenjige** *vai*
  LIGHT A PIPE: **zaka'ipwaagane** *vai*
  LIGHT AT DAWN: be light at dawn
    waaseyaaban *vii*
  LIGHT BY STRIKING: light s.t. by striking
    biskanesidoon *vti2*
  TURN ON A LIGHT: turn s.t. on for a light
    waazakonebidoon *vti2*

LIGHT
  LIGHT: be light in weight **naangan** *vii;*
    naangizi *vai*

CARRY A LIGHT PACK: **naangiwane** *vai*
CONSIDER LIGHT: consider s.o. light in
weight **naangenim** *vta;* consider s.t. light
in weight **naangendan** *vti*

LIGHT POLE
LIGHT POLE: **waazakonenjiganaatig, -oon**
ni

LIGHTER
LIGHTER: **ishkodekaan, -an** *ni;* **zaka'igan,
-an** *ni*

LIGHTNING
LIGHTNING: **inaabiwin** *ni;* **waasamowin** *ni;*
there is a flash of lightning **waasese,
waasesemagad** *vii;* there is lightning
wawaasese, wawaasesemagad *vii*
STRUCK BY LIGHTNING: be struck by
lightning **baagijigaade,
baagijigaademagad** *vii;* **baagijigaazo** *vai*

LIKE
LIKE: like s.o. **minwenim** *vta;* like s.t.
minwendan *vti*

LIKE
LIKE: **naasaab** *pc*
JUST LIKE: **dibishkoo** *pc;* **indigo** *pc, also*
nindigo*

LIKEABLE
LIKEABLE: be likeable **minwendaagozi** *vai;*
minwendaagwad *vii*

LIMBER
LIMBER: be limber **neshangaa,
neshangaamagad** *vii;* **neshangizi** *vai*

LIMP
LIE LIMP: **neshangishin** *vai;* **neshangisin** *vii*

LINE
FISH WITH A HOOK AND LINE:
wewebanaabii *vai*
HAVE A LINE: **beshaa, beshaamagad** *vii;*
beshizi *vai*
HOOK AND LINE: **migiskaneyaab, -iin** *ni*

LING
LING: **mizay, -ag** *na*

LINIMENT
LINIMENT: **gwendaaseg** *ni-pt*

LION
LION: **mishibizhii, -g** *na*

LIP
CHAPPED LIPS: have chapped lips
gagiipidoon *vai*

LIPSTICK
LIPSTICK: **miskodoonechigan, -an** *ni*

LIQUOR
LIQUOR: **ishkodewaaboo** *ni*

LISTEN
LISTEN: **bizindam** *vai2;* listen to s.o.
bizindaw *vta;* listen to s.t. **bizindan** *vti;* listen for
something **nandotam** *vai2*
LISTEN FOR: listen for s.o. **nandotaw** *vta;*
listen for s.t. **nandotan** *vti;* listen for

LITTLE
A LITTLE: **bangii** *pc*
JUST A LITTLE: **bangiishenh** *pc*

THINK LITTLE OF: think little of s.o.
agaasenim *vta;* think little of s.t.
agaasendan *vti*

LITTLE BIT
LITTLE BIT: be a little bit **bangiiwagad** *vii;*
bangiiwagizi *vai*
A LITTLE BIT: **bangii** *pc;* **eniwek** *pc*
A LITTLE BIT EACH: **bebangii** *pc*
A VERY LITTLE BIT: **bangiishenh** *pc*
VERY LITTLE BIT: be a very little bit
bangiishenhwagad *vii;* **bangiishenhwagizi**
vai

LITTLE FINGER
LITTLE FINGER: **ishkweninj, -iin** *ni*

LITTLE WHILE
A LITTLE WHILE: **ajina** *pc*
A LITTLE WHILE AGO: **naanoomaya** *pc*
IN A LITTLE WHILE: **wayiiba** *pc*

LIVE
LIVE: **bimaadizi** *vai*
LIVE A PROPER LIFE: **gwayako-bimaadizi**
vai
LIVE ABOUT: **babaamaadizi** *vai*
LIVE ALONE: **nazhikewige** *vai*
LIVE IN: live in s.t. **abiitan** *vti*
LIVE IN A CERTAIN PLACE: **danakii** *vai;*
daa *vai*
LIVE IN A WIGWAM: **wiigiwaamige** *vai*
LIVE IN THE FIRST HOUSE: **nitamige** *vai*
LIVE IN THE LAST HOUSE: **ishkwege** *vai*
LIVE ON THE END OF TOWN: live at the
end of town **ishkwege** *vai*
LIVE SOMEWHERE ELSE: **aandakii** *vai*
LIVE THE INDIAN WAY: **anishinaabe-
bimaadizi** *vai*
LIVE WELL: **mino-bimaadizi** *vai*

LIVER
LIVER: my liver **nikon, -an** */-kon-/* *nid*

LIVING
MAKE A LIVING A CERTAIN WAY: **ondizi**
vai

LIVING ROOM
LIVING ROOM: **abiwin, -an** *ni;* **abiiwigamig,
-oon** *ni*

LOAD
LOAD: load s.o. (e.g., a pipe) **onashkina'** *vta;*
load s.t. (e.g., a gun) **onashkinadoon** *vti2*
LOAD CARGO: **boozitaaso** *vai;* load s.t. as
cargo **boozitoon** *vti2;* load (s.t.) with cargo
for s.o. **boozitaw** *vta*
PACK TOO MUCH OF A LOAD:
onzaamiwane *vai*

LOADED
LOADED: be loaded **onashkinade,
onashkinademagad** *vii*

LOCK
LOCK: **gashkaabika'igan, -an** *ni;* lock s.o.
gashkaabika' */gashkaabika'w-/* *vta;* lock
s.t. **gashkaabika'an** *vti;* lock s.t. (as or as
with something stick- or wood-like
gashkaakonan *vti;* lock (s.t.) for s.o. (as or
as with something stick- or wood-like)
gashkaakwa'amaw *vta;* lock things
gashkaabika'ige *vai*

LOCKED
LOCKED: be locked **gashkaabika'igaade, gashkaabika'igaademagad** *vii;* **gashkaabika'igaazo** *vai*

LODGE
LODGE: **wiigiwaam, -an** *ni*
BARK LODGE: **wanagekogamig, -oon** *ni*
BEAVER LODGE: **amikwiish, -an** *ni*
BIRCH BARK LODGE: **wiigwaasigamig, -oon** *ni*
BUILD A LODGE: **ozhige** *vai*
DOMED LODGE: **waaginogaan, -an** *ni*
EARTH LODGE: **akiiwe-wiigiwaam, -an** *ni*
HOUSE-LIKE LODGE: **gakaaga'ogaan, -an** *ni*
LODGE OF GRASS: **mashkosiigaan, -an** *ni*
LODGE WITH PEAKED ROOF: **nisawa'ogaan, -an** *ni*
LODGE WITH POINTED TOP: **bajiishka'ogaan, -an** *ni*
LONG LODGE: **ginoondawaan, -an** *ni;* long lodge with doors at both ends **zhaaboondawaan, -an** *ni*
MIDE LODGE: **midewigaan, -an** *ni*
OTHER SIDE OF THE LODGE: **agaamindesi** *pc;* on the other side of the lodge **agaamindesing** *pc*
SAP-BOILING LODGE: **iskigamizigewigamig, -oon** *ni*
STORAGE LODGE: **asanjigoowigamig, -oon** *ni*
SWEAT LODGE: **madoodiswan, -an** *ni*

LODGE POLE
LODGE POLE: **abanzh, -iin** *ni*

LOG CABIN
LOG CABIN: **mitigo-waakaa'igan, -an** *ni*

LOGGER
LOGGER: **giishka'aakwewinini, -wag** *na*

LONELY
LONELY: be lonely **gashkendam** *vai2*

LONG
LONG: be long **ginoozi** *vai;* **ginwaa, ginwaamagad** *vii;* they are long *plural* **gagaanwawan** /**gagaanwaa-**/, **gagaanwaamagadoon** *vii;* be long (as something mineral) **ginwaabikad** *vii;* **ginwaabikizi** *vai;* be long (as something sheet-like) **ginwegad** *vii;* **ginwegizi** *vai;* be long (as something stick- or wood-like) **ginwaakozi** *vai;* **ginwaakwad** *vii;* be long (as something string-like) **ginwaabiigad** *vii;* **ginwaabiigizi** *vai*
AS LONG AS: **ako-** *pv3*
CUT LONG: cut s.o. long (as something string-like) **ginwaabiigizh** /**ginwaabiigizhw-**/ *vta;* cut s.t. long (as something string-like) **ginwaabiigizhan** *vti*
HAVE LONG SLEEVES: **gagaanonagweyaa, gagaanonagweyaamagad** *vii*
LONG BOAT: be a long boat **ginoonagad** *vii*
LONG HAIR: have long hair **gagaanwaanikwe** *vai*
MAKE LONG: make s.o. long **ginoo'** *vta;* make s.t. long **ginwaatoon** *vti2;* make s.o.

long (as something sheet-like) **ginwegi' ** *vta;* make s.t. so long (as something sheet-like) **ginwegitoon** *vti2*
MAKE SO LONG: make s.o. so long **akoo'** *vta;* make s.t. so long **akootoon** *vti2*
SO LONG: be so long **akoozi** *vai;* **akwaa, akwaamagad** *vii;* be so long (as something mineral) **akwaabikad** *vii;* **akwaabikizi** *vai;* be so long (as something sheet-like) **akwegad** *vii;* **akwegizi** *vai;* be so long (as something string-like) **akwaabiigad** *vii;* **akwaabiigizi** *vai*

LONG TIME
A LONG TIME: **gabe-ayi'ii** *pc, also* **gabeyi'ii**
A LONG TIME AGO: **mewinzha** *pc*
FOR A LONG TIME: **ginwenzh** *pc*

LOOK
HAVE A CERTAIN LOOK: **izhinaagozi** *vai;* **izhinaagwad** *vii*
LOOK GOOD: **minwaabaminaagozi** *vai;* **minwaabaminaagwad** *vii*
LOOK NEW: **oshkiinaagozi** *vai;* **oshkiinaagwad** *vii*
LOOK OLD: **gichi-aya'aawinaagozi** *vai*
LOOK POOR: **gidimaaginaagozi** *vai;* **gidimaaginaagwad** *vii*
LOOK SICK: **aakoziiwinaagozi** *vai*
LOOK WEAK: **niinaminaagozi** *vai;* **niinaminaagwad** *vii*
LOOK YOUNG: **oshkiinaagozi** *vai*
MAKE LOOK A CERTAIN WAY: make s.o. look a certain way **izhinaago'** *vta;* make s.t. look a certain way **izhinaagotoon** *vti2*

LOOK
LOOK: **ganawaabi** *vai;* look! **inashke** *pc, also* **nashke**
LIKE THE LOOK: like the look of s.o. **minwaabam** *vta;* like the look of s.t. **minwaabandan** *vti*
LOOK AT: look at s.o. **ganawaabam** *vta;* look at s.t. **ganawaabandan** *vti;* look at things **ganawaabanjige** *vai;* they look at each other **ganawaabandiwag** /**ganawaabandi-**/ *vai*
LOOK MALEVOLENTLY: look malevolently out of corner of one's eye at s.o. **negwaabam** *vta*
LOOK OUT FROM A CERTAIN PLACE: **onzaabi** *vai*
LOOK OVER: look s.o. over **dibaabam** *vta;* look s.t. over **dibaabandan** *vti*
LOOK THROUGH A WINDOW: **dapaabi** *vai;* look through a window at s.o. **dapaabam** *vta;* look through a window at s.t. **dapaabandan** *vti*
LOOK TO A CERTAIN PLACE: **inaabi** *vai*
TURN AND LOOK BACK: **aabanaabi** *vai;* turn and look back at s.o. **aabanaabam** *vta;* turn and look back at s.t. **aabanaabandan** *vti*

LOOK FOR
LOOK FOR: **nanda-** *pv4;* look for s.o. **nandawaabam** *vta;* **nandone' ** /**nandone'w-**/ *vta;* look for s.t.

nandawaabandan *vti;* nandone'an *vti;*
look for things nandawaabanjige *vai;*
nandone'ige *vai*
LOOK FOR A DRINK: nandoobii *vai*
LOOK FOR HORSES: nandawisimwe *vai*
LOOK FOR LICE: nandookome *vai*
LOOK FOR TRACKS: nandokawechige *vai;*
look for s.o.'s tracks nandokawe' *vta*
LOOK FOR WORK: nanda-anokii *vai*

LOOK OUT
LOOK OUT: look out! naasanaa *pc*

LOOKED
LOOKED AT: be looked at
ganawaabanjigaade,
ganawaabanjigaademagad *vii;*
ganawaabanjigaazo *vai*

LOOKED FOR
LOOKED FOR: be looked for
nandone'igaade, nandone'igaademagad
vii; nandone'igaazo *vai*

LOOM
BEAD LOOM: mazinaabidoo'iganaatig,
-oon *ni*
BEAD ON A LOOM: bead s.t. on a loom
mazinaabidoo'an *vti;* bead things on a
loom mazinaabidoo'ige *vai*

LOON
LOON: maang, -wag *na*

LOOSE
COME LOOSE: come loose (as something
string-like) gidiskaabiigishkaa,
gidiskaabiigishkaamagad *vii*

LOOSELY
FIT LOOSELY: fit s.o. loosely geshawishkaw
vta; fit s.t. loosely geshawishkan *vti*
PUT LOOSELY: put s.o. loosely
geshawishim *vta;* put s.t. loosely
geshawisidoon *vti2*

LOSE
LOSE: lose s.o. wani' *vta;* lose s.t. wanitoon
vti2
LOSE HOPE: lose hope in s.o. banaadenim
vta; lose hope in s.t. banaadendan *vti*

LOST
LOST: be lost wanishin *vai;* wanisin *vii*
GET LOST: wanishin *vai;* wanisin *vii*
GET LOST DRIVING: wanibizo *vai*

LOTION
HAND LOTION: noomininjiiwin, -an *ni*
PUT LOTION ON HAND: put lotion on
one's hand noomininjii *vai*

LOUD
LOUD: be loud ombiigizi *vai;* be loud (in operation) ombiigwewe *vai;* ombiigwewe,
ombiigwewemagad *vii*
SPEAK LOUD: gizhiiwe *vai*

LOUSE
LOUSE: ikwa, -g *na*

LOVE
LOVE: love s.o. zaagi' *vta;* love s.t. zaagitoon
vti2; they love each other zaagi'idiwag
/zaagi'idi-/ *vai*

LOVED
LOVED: be loved zaagichigaade,
zaagichigaademagad *vii;* zaagichigaazo
vai

LOW
LOW: dabazhish *pc;* be low dabasaa,
dabasaamagad *vii*
HANG LOW: dabasagoode,
dabasagoodemagad *vii;* dabasagoojin
vai; hang s.o. low dabasagoozh
/dabasagooN-/ *vta;* hang s.t. low
dabasagoodoon *vti2*
LOW GROUND: be low ground
dabasakamigaa, dabasakamigaamagad
vii

LOW REGARD
HELD IN LOW REGARD: be held in low
regard dabasendaagozi *vai;*
dabasendaagwad *vii*
HOLD IN LOW REGARD: hold s.o. in low
regard dabasenim *vta;* hold s.t. in low
regard dabasendan *vti*

LUCKY
LUCKY: be lucky debizi *vai*

LUMBER CAMP
LUMBER CAMP: giishka'aakwewigamig,
-oon *ni*

LUMBERJACK
LUMBERJACK: giishka'aakwewinini, -wag
na

LUNCH
EAT LUNCH: eat lunch (noon meal)
naawakwe-wiisini *vai;* eat s.t. for lunch
(noon meal) naawakwe-miijin *vti3*
LUNCH TAKEN ALONG: nawapwaan, -an
ni
MAKE A LUNCH TO TAKE ALONG:
nawapwaanike *vai*
TAKE A LUNCH ALONG: nawapo *vai*
TAKE A LUNCH BREAK: nawajii *vai*

LUNG
LUNG: my lung nipan, -an /-pan-/ *nid*

LYMPH NODE
LYMPH NODE: my gland (lymph node)
niniishk, -wag /-niishkw-/ *nad*

LYNX
LYNX: bizhiw, -ag *na*

LYNX HIDE
LYNX HIDE: bizhiwayaan, -ag *na*

MACARONI
MACARONI: macaroni *plural* onagizhiinsan
/onagizhiins-/ *ni*

MAD

MAD: be mad **nishkaadizi** *vai;* be mad at s.o.
nishkenim *vta*
ARRIVE MAD: **bagamigidaazo** *vai*
FEEL MAD: **nishkendam** *vai2*
GO AWAY MAD: **animigidaazo** *vai*
GO HOME MAD: **giiwegidaazo** *vai*
GO OFF MAD: **maajiigidaazo** *vai*
MAKE MAD: make s.o. mad **nishki'** *vta;*
speak and make s.o. mad **nishkim** *vta;*
make people mad **nishkitaa** *vai;* they make
each other mad **nishki'idiwag** /**nishki'idi-**/
vai
MAKE MAD FOR A CERTAIN REASON:
make s.o. mad for a certain reason
onjinawe' *vta*

MADE

MADE: be made **ozhichigaade,**
ozhichigaademagad *vii;* **ozhichigaazo** *vai*
MADE A CERTAIN WAY: be made a certain
way **izhichigaade, izhichigaademagad** *vii;*
izhichigaazo *vai*

MAGGOT

MAGGOT: **ookwe, -g** *na*

MAGNET

MAGNET: **manidoo-biiwaabik** *ni*

MAIL

GO GET MAIL: **naadazina'igane** *vai*

MAIL TRUCK

MAIL TRUCK: **mazina'iganiiwidaabaan, -ag**
na

MAINTENANCE ENGINEER

MAINTENANCE ENGINEER:
boodawewinini, -wag *na*

MAKE

MAKE: make s.o. **ozhi'** *vta;* make s.t.
ozhitoon *vti2;* make (s.t.) for s.o.
ozhitamaw *vta;* **ozhitaw** *vta;* make things
ozhichige *vai*
FINISH MAKING: finish making s.t.
giizhitoon *vti2*
HURRY MAKING: hurry making s.o.
wewiibi' *vta;* hurry making s.t.
wewiibitoon *vti*
KNOW HOW TO MAKE: know how to make
s.o. **nitaawi'** *vta;* know how to make s.t.
nitaawitoon *vti2;* know how to make
things **nitaawichige** *vai*
MAKE A BED: **ozisijige** *vai, also* **ozhisijige**
MAKE A CERTAIN WAY: make s.t. a certain
way **izhitoon** *vti2*
MAKE BADLY: make things badly
mamaazhii *vai*
MAKE DO: make s.o. do something **izhi'** *vta*
MAKE NICE: make s.o. nice **onizhishi'** *vta;*
make s.t. nice **onizhishitoon** *vti2*
MAKE OVER: make s.o. over **aanji'** *vta;* make
s.t. over **aanjitoon** *vti2*
MAKE SKILFULLY: make s.o. skilfully
wawiinge' *vta;* make s.t. skilfully
wawiingetoon *vti2*
MAKE WELL: make s.o. well **onizhishi'** *vta;*
make s.t. well **onizhishitoon** *vti2*

START TO MAKE: start to make s.o. **maaji'**
vta; start to make s.t. **maajitoon** *vti2*

MAKE UP

MAKE UP: make s.o. up **wawezhi'** *vta;* make
up oneself **wawezhi'o** *vai*

MALE

MALE: **naabe-** *pv4*

MALLARD

MALLARD: **ininishib, -ag** *na*

MAN

MAN: **inini, -wag** *na;* be a man **ininiiwi** *vai*
DRESSED-UP MAN: **zazegaa-inini, -wag** *na*
FELLOW MAN: my fellow man **niijiinini** *nad*
OLD MAN: **akiwenzii, -yag** *na*
UNMARRIED MAN: **moozhaabe, -g** *na*
YOUNG MAN: **oshki-inini, -wag** *na;*
oshkinawe, -g *na;* be a young man
oshkinawewi *vai*

MANAGE

MANAGE: manage s.o. **gashki'** *vta;* manage
s.t. **gashkitoon** *vti2*
UNABLE TO MANAGE: be unable to
manage s.o. **bwaanawi'** *vta;* be unable to
manage s.t. **bwaanawitoon** *vti2*

MANITOU

MANITOU: **manidoo, -g** *na;* be a manitou
manidoowi *vai*

MANUFACTURE

MANUFACTURE: **anokaajigan, -an** *ni*

MANY

MANY: **niibowa** *pc, also* **niibiwa*;** they are
many **baatayiinadoon** /**baatayiinad-**/ *vii;*
baatayiinowag /**baatayiino-**/ *vai, also*
/**baatayiini-**/; **niibowagadoon**
/**niibowagad-**/ *vii;* **niibowagiziwag**
/**niibowagizi-**/ *vai*
HAVE MANY: have many of s.o. **baatayiino'**
vta; have many of s.t. **baatayiinatoon** *vti2*
HOW MANY: how many? **aaniin minik** *pc*
SO MANY: **minik** *pc*

MAP

MAP: **akii-mazina'igan, -an** *ni*

MAPLE

MAPLE: **aninaatig, -oog** *na, also* **ininaatig**

MAPLE SAP

MAPLE SAP: **wiishkobaaboo** *ni;*
ziinzibaakwadwaaboo *ni*

MAPLE SUGAR

MAPLE SUGAR: **ziinzibaakwad** *ni;*
anishinaabe-ziinzibaakwad *ni*
GRANULATED MAPLE SUGAR: **nase'igan**
ni

MAPLE TAFFY

MAPLE TAFFY: **bigiwizigan** *ni*

MARBLE

MARBLE: **nemaab, -iin** *ni*

MARCH

MARCH: **onaabani-giizis** *na*

MARIAH

MARIAH: **mizay, -ag** *na*

MARK

MARK: mark s.o. **gikinawaaji'** *vta;* mark s.t.
gikinawaajitoon *vti2;* mark things
gikinawaajichige *vai*

LEAVE A MARK: **ezhishin** *vai;* **ezhisin** *vii*

MARK WITH A STRIPE: mark s.o. with a
stripe **beshibii'** /**beshibii'w-**/ *vta;* mark s.t.
with a stripe **beshibii'an** *vti;* mark things
with a stripe **beshibii'ige** *vai*

MARRIAGE LICENSE

MARRIAGE LICENSE: **aapiji-wiidige-
mazina'igan, -an** *ni*

MARRIED

MARRIED: be legally married **aapiji-wiidige**
vai; be married **wiidige** *vai;* be married to
s.o. **wiidigem** *vta;* they are married to each
other **wiidigendiwag** /**wiidigendi-**/ *vai*

MARROW

EXTRACT MARROW: extract marrow from
bones **zhigwaajige** *vai*

TOOL FOR EXTRACTING MARROW: tool
for extracting marrow from bones
zhigwaajiganaak, -oon *ni*

MARRY

MARRY: **wiidige** *vai;* marry s.o. **wiidigem**
vta; they marry each other **wiidigendiwag**
/**wiidigendi-**/ *vai*

MARTEN

MARTEN: **waabizheshi, -wag** *na*

MARTEN HIDE

MARTEN HIDE: **waabizheshiwayaan, -ag**
na

MARTIN

MARTIN: **zhaashaawanibiisens, -ag** *na*

MASSAGE

MASSAGE: massage s.o. with something
zinigobizh /**zinigobiN-**/ *vta;* massage s.t.
with something **zinigobidoon** *vti2*

MASTER

MASTER: be the master of s.t. **dibendan** *vti;*
be the master to s.o. **dibenim** *vta;* be one's
own master **dibenindizo** *vai*

MAT

CATTAIL MAT: **apakweshkway, -ag** *na*

MAT ON BOTTOM OF A CANOE: mat on
bottom of canoe **apishkaamon, -an** *ni*

PROTECTIVE MAT: **apisijigan, -an** *ni*

WOVEN MAT: **anaakan, -an** *ni*

MATCH

MATCH: **ishkodens, -an** *ni*

MATTRESS

MATTRESS: **apishimon, -an** *ni*

MAY

MAY: **waabigwanii-giizis** *na;* **zaagibagaa-
giizis** *na*

MAYBE

MAYBE: **ganabaj** *pc;* **iidog** *pc;* **maagizhaa** *pc,*
also **maazhaa**

OR MAYBE: **gemaa** *pc, also* **gemaa gaye**

MAYFLY

MAYFLY: **omiimiisi, -wag** *na*

ME

ME: **niin** *pr first person singular person pronoun*

MEADOW

BY A MEADOW: **jiigashkosiw** *pc*

MIDDLE OF A MEADOW: in the middle of
a meadow **naawashkosiw** *pc*

ON THE OTHER SIDE OF THE
MEADOW: **agaamashkosiw** *pc*

MEAN

MEAN: be mean **gagwaanisagizi** *vai;* be mean
to s.o. **inigaa'** *vta*

MEANS

BY ANY MEANS: **ganage** *pc*

MEASLES

HAVE MEASLES: **miskwazhe** *vai*

MEASURE

MEASURE: measure s.o. (as with something
string-like) **dibaabiigin** *vta;* measure s.t.
(as with something string-like)
dibaabiiginan *vti;* measure things **diba'ige**
vai

MEASURING STICK

MEASURING STICK FOR TIMBER:
diba'aatigwaan, -an *ni*

MEAT

MEAT: **wiiyaas** *ni;* my meat (of the body)
niiyaas /**-iiyaas-**/ *nid*

CUT MEAT INTO STRIPS: cut meat into
strips for preservation **baanizhaawe** *vai*

DEER MEAT: **waawaashkeshiwi-wiiyaas** *ni*

FIRE-CURED MEAT OR FISH:
abwewasigan, -an *ni*

RAW MEAT: be raw (as meat) **ashkin** *vii;*
ashkini *vai*

MEAT MARKET

MEAT MARKET: **wiiyaas-adaawewigamig,
-oon** *ni*

MECHANIC

MECHANIC: **odaabaanikewinini, -wag** *na*

MEDICINE

MEDICINE: **mashkiki, -wan** *ni;* medicine for
burning **nookwezigan, -an** *ni*

BURN AS MEDICINE: burn s.t. as medicine
nookwezan *vti;* burn things as medicine
nookwezige *vai*

GATHER MEDICINE: **manashkikiiwe** *vai*

LIQUID MEDICINE: **mashkikiwaaboo, -n**
ni

MAKE MEDICINE: **mashkikiike** *vai*

MEDICINE DANCE

MEDICINE DANCE: **midewiwin** *ni*

MEEK

MEEK: be meek **nookaadizi** *vai*

MEET

MEET: meet s.o. **nakweshkaw** *vta;* meet s.o.
(while going somewhere) **nagishkaw** *vta;*
meet s.t. (while going somewhere)
nagishkan *vti;* they meet each other
nagishkodaadiwag /**nagishkodaadi-**/ *vai;*
nakweshkodaadiwag /**nakweshkodaadi-**/
vai

MEETING

COUNCIL MEETING: they have a council
meeting **zagaswe'idiwag** /**zagaswe'idi-**/
vai

HAVE A MEETING: they have a meeting
maawanji'idiwag /maawanji'idi-/ *vai*

MELT
MELT: **ningide, ningidemagad** *vii;* **ningizo**
vai; melt s.o. **ningiz /ningizw-/** *vta;* melt
s.t. **ningizan** *vti*

MEMBER
MEMBER: be a member **dibendaagozi** *vai*
INITIATED MEMBER: be an initiated
member **dibenjigaazo** *vai*

MENOMINEE
MENOMINEE: **omanoominii, -g** *na*

MENSES
SECLUDED AT FIRST MENSES: be
secluded at first menses **bakaanige** *vai*

MENTAL HOSPITAL
MENTAL HOSPITAL:
giiwanaadiziiwigamig, -oon *ni*

MENTION
MENTION: mention s.o. **waawiinzh**
/waawiinN-/ *vta;* mention s.o. come to
one's mind **mikom** *vta;* mention s.t. come
to one's mind **mikondan** *vti;* mention the
name of s.o. **wiinzh /wiinN-/** *vta;* mention
the name of s.t. **wiindan** *vti*

MERCIFUL
MERCIFUL: be merciful **zhawenjige** *vai*

MERRY
DRINK AND BE MERRY: **minobii** *vai*

MESS
MAKE A MESS: **ombwewebinige** *vai*

MESSENGER
CEREMONIAL MESSENGER:
oshkaabewis, -ag *na*

MESSY
MESSY HAIR: have messy hair **niiskindibe**
vai

METAL
METAL: metal **biiwaabik, -oon** *ni*
ON METAL: on something mineral (e.g.,
metal, glass, rock) **agidaabik** *pc, also*
ogidaabik*, wagidaabik
PIECE OF METAL: **bookwaabik, -oon** *ni*

METIS
METIS: Metis **wiisaakodewinini, -wag** *na*

METIS WOMAN
METIS WOMAN: **wiisaakodewikwe, -g** *na*

MID-SUMMER
AFTER MID-SUMMER: be after mid-
summer **giiwe-niibin** *vii*

MID-WINTER
AFTER MID-WINTER: be after mid-winter
giiwe-biboon *vii*

MIDDLE
IN THE MIDDLE: in the middle of **naawi-**
pn; in the middle of it **naawayi'ii** *pc*
IN THE MIDDLE OF THE FLOOR:
naawisag *pc*
IN THE MIDDLE OF THE LAKE:
naawagaam *pc*
IN THE MIDDLE OF THE ROAD: in the
middle of the road or trail **naawikana** *pc*

IN THE MIDDLE OF THE TRAIL: in the
middle of the road or trail **naawikana** *pc*
MIDDLE OF A BOAT: in the middle of a
boat **naawoonag** *pc*
MIDDLE OF A MEADOW: in the middle of
a meadow **naawashkosiw** *pc*
MIDDLE OF THE BACK: in the middle of
the back **naawaawigan** *pc*
MIDDLE OF THE CHEST: in the middle of
the chest **naawaakigan** *pc*
MIDDLE OF THE FOREHEAD: in the
middle of the forehead **naawigatig** *pc*
MIDDLE OF THE WOODS: in the middle of
the woods **naawaakwaa** *pc*

MIDDLE FINGER
MIDDLE FINGER: **naawininj, -iin** *ni*

MIDDLING
MIDDLING: **eniwek** *pc*
MIDDLING DEGREE: to a middling degree
gomaa *pc*

MIDE DRUM
MIDE DRUM: **mitigwakik, -oog** *na*

MIDE LODGE
MIDE LODGE: **midewigaan, -an** *ni*

MIDE LODGE FRAME
MIDE LODGE FRAME: **midewigaanaak,**
-oon *ni*

MIDE SHELL
MIDE SHELL: **miigis, -ag** *na*

MIDEWIWIN
MIDEWIWIN: **midewiwin** *ni*
JOIN THE MIDEWIWIN: **midewi** *vai*

MIDNIGHT
MIDNIGHT: be midnight **aabitaa-dibikad** *vii*

MIGHT
MIGHT: might *modal* **daa-** *pv1*

MILD
MILD: be mild **nookaadad** *vii;* **nookaadizi**
vai
MILD WEATHER: be mild weather
aabawaa, aabawaamagad *vii*

MILE
CERTAIN NUMBER OF MILES: a certain
number of miles **daso-diba'igan** *pc*

MILK
MILK: **doodooshaaboo** *ni;* milk cows
ziininiwe *vai;* milk s.o. **ziinin** *vta*

MILL
MILL: **biisiboojigan, -an** *ni*
SAW MILL: **daashkiboojigan, -ag** *na*

MILLE LACS
MILLE LACS: Mille Lacs Reservation **Misi-**
zaaga'iganiing *place*

MIND
CHANGE MIND: change one's mind
aanizhiitam *vai2*
COME TO MIND: **mikwendaagozi** *vai;*
mikwendaagwad *vii;* have things come to
one's mind **mikwendam** *vai2*
HAVE MIND MADE UP: have one's mind
made up **giizhendam** *vai2*
HAVE ON MIND: have something on one's
mind **biingeyendam** *vai2*

KEEP IN MIND: keep s.o. in one's mind
minjimenim *vta;* keep s.t. in one's mind
minjimendan *vti*
OF A CERTAIN MIND: be of a certain mind
inendam *vai2*
RELEASE FROM MIND: release s.o. from
one's mind **bagidenim** *vta;* release s.t.
from one's mind **bagidendan** *vti;* release
things from one's mind **bagidenjige** *vai*

MINE
MINE: **biiwaabikokaan, -an** *ni*

MINER
MINER: **biiwaabikokewinini, -wag** *na*

MINISTER
MINISTER: **gagiikwewinini, -wag** *na*

MINK
MINK: **zhaangweshi, -wag** *na*

MINK HIDE
MINK HIDE: **zhaangweshiwayaan, -ag** *na*

MINNEAPOLIS
MINNEAPOLIS: **Gakaabikaang** *place*

MINNOW
MINNOW: **giigoozens, -ag** *na*

MINUTE
CERTAIN NUMBER OF MINUTES: a certain number of minutes **daso-diba'igaans**
pc

MIRROR
MIRROR: **waabamoojichaagwaan, -an** *ni;*
waabandizowin, -an *ni*

MISBEHAVE
MISBEHAVE: **maji-izhiwebizi** *vai*

MISCOUNT
MISCOUNT: **wanagindaaso** *vai;* miscount
s.o. **wanagim** *vta;* miscount s.t.
wanagindan *vti*

MISHEAR
MISHEAR: mishear s.o. **banitaw** *vta;* mishear
s.t. **banitan** *vti*

MISLEAD
MISLEAD: mislead s.o. by speech **wanim** *vta*

MISPLACE
MISPLACE: misplace s.o. **wanishim** *vta;*
misplace s.t. **wanisidoon** *vti2*

MISPRONOUNCE
MISPRONOUNCE: **wanigiizhwe** *vai*

MISREAD
MISREAD: **wanagindaaso** *vai;* misread s.t.
wanagindan *vti*

MISS
MISS: miss s.o. absent **gwiinawenim** *vta;* miss
s.t. absent **gwiinawendan** *vti*
MISS OUT: **banizi** *vai*
MISS USING SOMETHING: miss s.o. using
something **bana' /bana'w-/** *vta;* miss s.t.
using something **bana'an** *vti*
SHOOT AND MISS: **bishkonaage** *vai;* shoot
at s.o. and miss **bishkonaw** *vta;* shoot at
s.t. and miss **bishkonan** *vti*

MISSED
MISSED: missed it! **hay'** *pc*

MISSISSIPPI RIVER
MISSISSIPPI RIVER: **Gichi-ziibi, -wan** *ni*

MISTAKE
BY MISTAKE: **bichi-** *pv4;* **wani-** *pv4*
MAKE A MISTAKE: **wanichige** *vai*
MAKE A MISTAKE BEADING: make a
mistake beading s.t. on a loom
wanaabidoo'an *vti;* make a mistake
beading things on a loom **wanaabidoo'ige**
vai
MAKE A MISTAKE SEWING: **wanigwaaso**
vai; make a mistake sewing on s.o.
wanigwaazh /wanigwaaN-/ *vta;* make a
mistake sewing on s.t. **wanigwaadan** *vti*
MAKE A MISTAKE SPEAKING:
wanigiizhwe *vai*
MAKE A MISTAKE WRITING: **wanibii'ige**
vai; make a mistake writing s.t. **wanibii'an**
vti

MISTREAT
MISTREAT: mistreat s.o. **goopaji'** *vta;*
mistreat s.t. **goopajitoon** *vti2*

MISTY
MISTY: be misty **awanibiisaa,**
awanibiisaamagad *vii*

MISUNDERSTAND
MISUNDERSTAND: misunderstand (what)
s.o. (says) **wanitaw** *vta;* misunderstand
something heard **wanitam** *vai2*

MITTEN
MITTEN: **minjikaawan, -ag** *na*
PUT ON MITTENS: put on one's mittens
biichiminjikaawane *vai*
TAKE OFF MITTENS: take off one's mittens
giichiminjikaawane *vai*
WEAR MITTENS: **gigiminjikaawane** *vai*

MIX
MIX: mix s.o. **ginigawin** *vta;* mix s.t.
ginigawinan *vti;* mix things **ginigawinige**
vai
MIX BY SHAKING: mix s.o. by shaking
ginigawiwebin *vta;* mix s.t. by shaking
ginigawiwebinan *vti*
MIX IN: mix s.o. in **dagon** *vta;* mix s.t. in
dagonan *vti;* mix things in **dagonige** *vai*

MIXED
MIXED: be mixed **ginigawinigaade,**
ginigawinigaademagad *vii;*
ginigawinigaazo *vai;* **ginigawisin** *vii*
MIXED IN: be mixed in **dagonigaade,**
dagonigaademagad *vii;* **dagonigaazo** *vai*

MIXED ANCESTRY
PERSON OF MIXED ANCESTRY:
wiisaakodewinini, -wag *na*
WOMAN OF MIXED ANCESTRY:
wiisaakodewikwe, -g *na*

MIXER
MIXER: **waninawe'igan, -an** *ni*

MOCCASIN
MOCCASIN: **makizin, -an** *ni*
HIDE MOCCASIN: **bashkweginwakizin, -an**
ni, also **bashkwegino-makizin**
MAKE MOCCASINS: **makizinike** *vai*

PUT ON MOCCASINS: put on one's
moccasins **babiichii** *vai*
TAKE OFF MOCCASINS: take off one's
moccasins **gagiichii** *vai*
MOCCASIN CUFF
MOCCASIN CUFF: **apiganegwaajigan, -an**
ni, also **apigwanegwaason, -an**
MOCCASIN GAME
MOCCASIN GAME: **makizinataagewin** *ni*
PLAY THE MOCCASIN GAME:
makizinataage *vai;* they play the moccasin
game with each other **makizinataadiwag**
/makizinataadi-/ *vai*
MOCCASIN GAME SONG
MOCCASIN GAME SONG: **makizinataage-**
nagamon, -an *ni*
MOCCASIN VAMP
MOCCASIN VAMP: **apiingwe'igan, -an** *ni*
MOCK
MOCK: mock s.o. **naabinootaw** *vta;* mock
people **naabinootaage** *vai*
MOCK DISRESPECTFULLY: mock s.o.
disrespectfully **baapinodaw** *vta*
MOLD
MOLD: mold s.o. **onadin** *vta;* mold s.t.
onadinan *vti;* mold things **onadinige** *vai*
MOLDY
MOLDY: be moldy **agwaagoshi** *vai;*
agwaagosin *vii*
MOLE
MOLE: **nenaapaajinikesi, -wag** *na*
MONDAY
MONDAY: be Monday **ishkwaa-anama'e-**
giizhigad *vii, also* **ishkwaa-aname-**
giizhigad
MONEY
MONEY: **zhooniyaa** *na*
COLLECT MONEY AS A DONATION:
asigizhooniyaawe *vai*
EARN MONEY: **zhooniyaake** *vai*
HAVE MONEY: **ozhooniyaami** *vai*
MAKE MONEY: **zhooniyaake** *vai*
USE UP MONEY: use up all of the money
jaagizhooniyaaweshin *vai*
MONKEY
MONKEY: **nandookomeshiinh, -yag** *na*
MONSTER
WINTER CANNIBAL MONSTER: windigo:
winter cannibal monster **wiindigoo, -g** *na*
MONTH
MONTH: **giizis, -oog** *na*
CERTAIN DATE OF THE MONTH: be a
certain date of the month **inaginzo** *vai*
CERTAIN NUMBER OF MONTHS: a
certain number of months **daso-giizis** *pc*
EVERY MONTH: **endaso-giizis** *pc*
START A MONTH: **maadaginzo** *vai*
MOON
MOON: **dibik-giizis, -oog** *na, also* **dibiki-**
giizis; giizis, -oog *na*
FULL MOON: be full (as something mineral,
e.g., the moon) **michaabikizi** *vai;*
miziweyaabikizi *vai*

HALF MOON: be half (as something mineral,
e.g., the moon) **aabitawaabikizi** *vai*
NEW MOON: be new (of a moon)
oshkagoojin *vai, also* **oshki-agoojin**
MOONLIGHT
MOONLIGHT: there is moonlight
giizhigaate, giizhigaatemagad *vii*
MOOSE
MOOSE: **mooz, -oog** *na*
MORE
MORE: **nawaj** *pc*
MUCH MORE: **awashime** *pc*
MORE AND MORE
MORE AND MORE: **eshkam** *pc*
MORNING
MORNING: be morning **gigizhebaawagad** *vii*
EARLY IN THE MORNING: **gichi-gigizheb**
pc
EVERY MORNING: **endaso-gigizheb** *pc*
IN THE MORNING: **gigizheb** *pc*
LATE MORNING OR EARLY
AFTERNOON: be late morning or early
afternoon **ishpi-giizhigad** *vii*
THIS MORNING: this morning (just past)
zhebaa *pc*
MORTAR
MORTAR: mortar for wild rice **bootaagan,**
-ag *na*
STAMP IN A MORTAR: stamp s.t. in a mor-
tar **bootaagaadan** *vti;* stamp things in a
mortar (e.g., wild rice) **bootaage** *vai*
MORTUARY
MORTUARY: **niboowigamig, -oon** *ni*
MOSQUITO
MOSQUITO: **zagime, -g** *na*
MANY MOSQUITOES: there are many
mosquitoes **zagimekaa,**
zagimekaamagad *vii*
MOSQUITO NET
MOSQUITO NET: **zagimewayaan, -ag** *na*
MOSS
MOSS: **aasaakamig, -oon** *ni*
MOTHER
MOTHER: my mother **nimaamaa, -yag**
/-maamaay-/ *nad;* my mother old-fashioned
inga *nad*
HAVE A MOTHER: **omaamaayi** *vai*
MOTHER-IN-LAW
MOTHER-IN-LAW: my mother-in-law
inzigozis, -ag /-zigozis-/ *nad*
MOTION
IN MOTION: be in motion **mamaajii** *vai*
MOTOR
OUTBOARD MOTOR: **akikoons, -ag** *na*
MOTOR LAUNCH
MOTOR LAUNCH: **waasamoo-jiimaan, -an**
ni
MOUNTAIN
MOUNTAIN: **wajiw, -an** *ni*
BEYOND THE MOUNTAIN: **awasajiw** *pc*
ON TOP OF A MOUNTAIN: **agidajiw** *pc,*
also **ogidajiw*, wagidajiw**

OVER ACROSS THE MOUNTAIN:
awasajiw *pc*
MOUNTAIN ASH
  MOUNTAIN ASH: **makominagaawanzh,
-iig** *na*
MOURN
  MOURN: **inigaazi** *vai;* **nitaage** *vai*
  COMPLETE MOURNING: complete
  mourning for s.o. **bagidenim** *vta*
MOUSE
  MOUSE: **waawaabiganoojiinh, -yag** *na*
MOUSTACHE
  MOUSTACHE: have a moustache
  miishidoon *vai*
MOUTH
  MOUTH: my mouth **indoon, -an /-doon-/** *nid*
  INSIDE MOUTH: inside the mouth
  biinjidoon *pc*
  OPEN MOUTH: open one's mouth **daawani**
  vai
  PUT IN MOUTH: put (something) in one's
  mouth **zhakamo** *vai*
  TWISTED MOUTH: have a twisted mouth
  (as from a stroke) **biimidoon** *vai*
  WIPE MOUTH: wipe one's mouth
  gaasiidoone'o *vai*
MOVE
  MOVE: **mamaajise** *vai;* **mamaajise,
  mamaajisemagad** *vii;* **mamaajii** *vai;*
  mamaazikaa *vai*
  MOVE A CERTAIN WAY: *with a pv4* move a
  certain way **ayaa** *vai;* **ayaa,
  ayaamagad** *vii*
  MOVE ARM A CERTAIN WAY: move one's
  arm a certain way **izhinikeni** *vai*
  MOVE FAST: **gizhiibide, gizhiibidemagad**
  vii; **gizhiibizo** *vai*
  MOVE FOOT A CERTAIN WAY: move
  one's foot a certain way **izhizideni** *vai*
  MOVE HAND A CERTAIN WAY: move
  one's hand a certain way **izhininjiini** *vai*
  MOVE OFF: **maajise** *vai;* **maajise,
  maajisemagad** *vii*
  MOVE RESIDENCE: move one's residence
  gozi *vai*
  MOVE RESIDENCE ABOUT: move one's
  residence about **babaamigozi** *vai*
  MOVE RESIDENCE HERE: move one's
  residence here **biijigozi** *vai*
  MOVE SLOWLY: **bejibide, bejibidemagad**
  vii; **bejibizo** *vai;* **bezikaa** *vai*
  MOVE TO A NEW RESIDENCE: **aanjigozi**
  vai
  START TO MOVE: **maajiishkaa,
  maajiishkaamagad** *vii*
MOVIE
  MOVIE: be a movie **mazinaatese,
  mazinaatesemagad** *vii*
  CERTAIN KIND OF MOVIE: be a certain
  kind of movie **inaatese, inaatesemagad**
  vii
  FUNNY MOVIE: be a funny movie
  gagiibaadaatese, gagiibaadaatesemagad
  vii

GOOD MOVIE: be a good movie
  minwaatese, minwaatesemagad *vii*
  SCARY MOVIE: be a scary movie **zegaatese,
  zegaatesemagad** *vii*
MOVIE PROJECTOR
  MOVIE PROJECTOR: **mazinaatewebinigan,
  -an** *ni*
MOVIE THEATER
  MOVIE THEATER: **mazinaatesewigamig,
  -oon** *ni, also* **mazinaatesijigewigamig**
MUCH
  MUCH: **niibowa** *pc, also* **niibiwa*;** be much
  baatayiinad *vii;* **baatayiino** *vai, also*
  baatayiini; there is much of it **niibowagad**
  vii; **niibowagizi** *vai*
  HAVE MUCH: have much of s.o. **baatayiino'**
  vta; have much of s.t. **baatayiinatoon** *vti2*
  HOW MUCH: how much? *interrogative* **aaniin
  minik** *pc*
  SO MUCH: **minik** *pc*
  TOO MUCH: **onzaam** *pc*
MUD
  MUD: **azhashki** *ni*
  IN THE MUD: **megwejiishkiwag** *pc*
  MUCH MUD: there is much mud
  azhashkiikaa, azhashkiikaamagad *vii*
MUD HEN
  MUD HEN: **aajigade, -g** *na*
MUDDY
  MUDDY: be muddy **azhashkiiwan** *vii;* there
  is a muddy patch **wiinijiishkiwagaa,
  wiinijiishkiwagaamagad** *vii*
  MUDDY FEET: have muddy feet
  azhashkiiwizide *vai*
MULE
  MULE: **memaangishens, -ag** *na*
MUMPS
  HAVE THE MUMPS: **mamagoniishkwe** *vai*
MUSCLE
  MUSCLE: **mashkawiziiwin, -an** *ni*
MUSHROOM
  MUSHROOM: **wazhashkwedoons, -ag** *na*
MUSIC
  PLAY MUSIC: **madwewechige** *vai;* play
  music for s.o. **madwewetaw** *vta, also*
  madwewetamaw
MUSICAL INSTRUMENT
  MUSICAL INSTRUMENT:
  madwewechigan, -an *ni;* musical instru-
  ment (especially a wind instrument)
  noondaagochigan, -an *ni*
MUSKELLUNGE
  MUSKELLUNGE: **maashkinoozhe, -g** *na*
MUSKRAT
  MUSKRAT: **wazhashk, -wag** *na*
MUSKRAT HIDE
  MUSKRAT HIDE: **wazhashkwayaan, -ag** *na*
MUSKRAT LODGE
  MUSKRAT LODGE: **wazhashkwiish, -an** *ni*
MUST BE
  MUST BE: **iidog** *pc*
MYTH
  MYTH: **aadizookaan, -ag** *na*

CHARACTER OF A LEGEND OR MYTH:
aadizookaan, -ag *na*
TELL A MYTH: **aadizooke** *vai;* tell a myth to
s.o. **aadizookaw** *vta*

N

NAIL
NAIL: **zaga'igan, -an** *ni*
NAIL UP AGAINST THE WALL: nail s.t. up
against the wall **agwaakwa'an** *vti*
NAIL
NAIL: my nail (fingernail, toenail) **nishkanzh,
-iig** */-shkanzhy-/* *nad*
CUT NAILS: cut one's own nails
giishkiganzhiikonidizo *vai*
NAKED
NAKED: be naked **mitagwazhe** *vai*
NAME
NAME: name s.o. **waawiinzh** */waawiinN-/*
vta; **wiinzh** */wiinN-/* *vta;* name s.t. **wiindan**
vti
GIVE A NAME: give s.o. a name **wiinzh**
/wiinN-/ *vta*
HAVE A NAME: **wiinde, wiindemagad** *vii;*
wiinzo *vai*
HAVE AN UGLY NAME: **maazhinikaade,
maazhinikaademagad** *vii;*
maazhinikaazo *vai*
NAME A CERTAIN WAY: name s.o. a
certain way **izhinikaazh** */izhinikaaN-/* *vta;*
izhi-wiinzh */izhi-wiinN-/* *vta;* name s.t. a
certain way **izhinikaadan** *vti;* **izhi-wiindan**
vti
NAMED
NAMED A CERTAIN WAY: be named a
certain way **izhinikaade,
izhinikaademagad** *vii;* **izhinikaazo** *vai;*
izhi-wiinde, izhi-wiindemagad *vii;* **izhi-
wiinzo** *vai*
NAMESAKE
NAMESAKE: be a namesake **owiiyawen'enyi**
vai; my namesake (reciprocal relationship
between name-giving sponsor and child)
niiyawen'enh, -ag */-iiyawen'eny-/* *nad*
NAP
TAKE A QUICK NAP: **zhiibaangwashi** *vai*
NAPKIN
NAPKIN: **giziidoone'on, -an** *ni;* **giziininjii'on,
-an** *ni*
NARRATE
NARRATE: **dibaajimo** *vai;* narrate (s.t.) to
s.o. **dibaajimotaw** *vta*
NARRATE A CERTAIN WAY: **inaajimo** *vai;*
narrate a certain way about s.t. **inaadodan**
vti; narrate of s.o. a certain way **inaajim**

vta; narrate (s.t.) to s.o. a certain way
inaajimotaw *vta*
NARRATIVE
NARRATIVE: **dibaajimowin, -an** *ni*
NARROW
NARROW: be narrow **agaasadeyaa,
agaasadeyaamagad** *vii;* **agaasadezi** *vai;*
be narrow (as something mineral)
agaasadeyaabikad *vii;* **agaasadeyaabikizi**
vai; be narrow (as something sheet-like)
agaasadeyiigad *vii;* **agaasadeyiigizi** *vai;*
be narrow (as something string-like)
agaasadeyaabiigad *vii;*
agaasadeyaabiigizi *vai*
BECOME NARROW: **wiibwaa,
wiibwaamagad** *vii*
MAKE NARROW: make s.o. narrow
agaasade' *vta;* make s.t. narrow
agaasadetoon *vti2*
NARROW BOAT: be narrow (as a boat)
agaasadeyoonagad *vii*
NARROW FACE: have a narrow face
agaasadengwe *vai*
NARROW RIVER: be narrow (as a river)
**agaasadetigweyaa,
agaasadetigweyaamagad** *vii*
NARROW ROAD: be narrow (as a road or
trail) **agaasademon** */agaasademo-/* *vii*
NARROW TRAIL: be narrow (as a road or
trail) **agaasademon** */agaasademo-/* *vii*
NARROWS
NARROWS: there is a narrows **wabaashiiwan**
vii; **wabigamaa, wabigamaamagad** *vii*
NAVEL
NAVEL: my navel **indis** */-disy-/* *nid*
NEAR
NEAR: **besho** *pc;* **jiigi-** *pn;* be near **beshowad**
vii
NEAR WOODS: near the woods **jiigaakwaa**
pc
THOUGHT NEAR: be thought near
beshwendaagozi *vai;* **beshwendaagwad**
vii
NEARLY
NEARLY: **gegaa** *pc;* **ingoji** *pc, also* **ningoji***
NECESSARY
NECESSARY: it is necessary **booch** *pc*
NECK
BACK OF NECK: the back of my neck
nikwegan, -an */-kwegan-/* *nid*
STIFF NECK: have a stiff neck
jiibajigwayawe *vai*
WEAR AROUND NECK: wear s.o. around
one's neck **naabikaw** *vta;* wear s.t. around
one's neck **naabikan** *vti*
WRING NECK: wring s.o.'s neck
bookogwebizh */bookogwebiN-/* *vta*
NECKLACE
NECKLACE: **naabikawaagan, -ag** *na*
NECKTIE
NECKTIE: **naabikawaagan, -ag** *na*
NEED
IN NEED: be in need of (s.t.) **manezi** *vai-o*

NEED TO: **noonde-** *pv4*
NEEDLE
  NEEDLE: **zhaabonigan, -an** *ni*
  BEADING NEEDLE: **naabidoo'igan, -an** *ni*
NEIGHBOR
  NEIGHBOR: be a neighbor to s.o.
  wiijigamigishkaw *vta*
NEPHEW
  NEPHEW: my cross-nephew (male's sister's
  son or female's brother's son) **niningwanis,
  -ag /-ningwanis-/** *nad;* my parallel nephew
  (male's brother's son or female's sister's
  son) **indoozhim, -ag /-doozhim-/** *nad*
NERVOUS
  NERVOUS: be nervous **zegendam** *vai2*
NEST
  BIRD NEST: **wadiswan, -an** *ni*
NESTLING
  NESTLING: **banajaanh, -yag** *na*
NET
  NET: **asab, -iig** *na*
  CAUGHT IN A NET: be caught in a net
  biinda'am *vai2*
  FISH WITH A NET: **bagida'waa** *vai*
  GO GET A NET: **naadasabii** *vai*
  HANG UP A NET: **agoodasabii** *vai*
  MAKE NETS: **asabike** *vai*
  MOSQUITO NET: **zagimewayaan, -ag** *na*
  PICK UP A NET: **naadasabii** *vai*
  PREPARE A NET: prepare a net for setting
  oninasabii *vai*
  SET A NET: **bagida'waa** *vai*
NET CORD
  NET CORD: **zhinoodaagan, -an** *ni*
NET FLOAT
  NET FLOAT: **agonjoonaagan, -an** *ni*
NET SINKER
  NET SINKER: **asinaab, -iig** *na*
NETT LAKE
  NETT LAKE: Nett Lake Reservation
  Asabikone-zaaga'iganiing *place, also*
  Asabikonaye-zaaga'iganiing
NETTLE
  NETTLE: **zesab, -iig** *na*
NEVER
  NEVER: **gaa wiikaa** *pc, also* **gaawiin wiikaa**
  NEVER MIND: **maanoo** *pc*
NEW
  NEW: **oshki-** *pv4;* be new **oshkayi'iiwan** *vii*
  LOOK NEW: **oshkiinaagozi** *vai;*
  oshkiinaagwad *vii*
  SOMEONE NEW: **oshkaya'aa, -g** *na, also*
  oshki-aya'aa
  SOMETHING NEW: **oshkayi'ii, -n** *ni, also*
  oshki-ayi'ii
  WEAR NEW CLOTHES: **oshki'o** *vai*
NEW MOON
  NEW MOON: be new (of a moon)
  oshkagoojin *vai, also* **oshki-agoojin**
NEWS
  ARRIVE WITH NEWS: **bagamaajimo** *vai*
  COME TELLING NEWS: **biidaajimo** *vai*

  SPREAD THE NEWS ABOUT:
  babaamaajimo *vai*
  TELL GOOD NEWS: **minwaajimo** *vai;* tell
  good news of s.o. **minwaajim** *vta;* tell good
  news of s.t. **minwaadodan** *vti*
NEWSPAPER
  NEWSPAPER: **babaamaajimoo-
  mazina'igan, -an** *ni*
NEXT
  NEXT: they are next to each other
  aanikeshkodaadiwag /aanikeshkodaadi-/
  vai
  NEXT ROOM: in the next room **aajisag** *pc*
  NEXT TO: be next to s.o. **aanikeshkaw** *vta*
  SOMEONE NEXT IN SUCCESSION TO
  THE LEADER: someone next in
  succession to the leader (e.g., a vice
  president) **aanike-ogimaa, -g** *na*
NICE
  NICE: **mino-** *pv4;* be nice **onizhishi** *vai;*
  onizhishin *vii*
  MAKE NICE: make s.o. nice **onizhishi'** *vta;*
  make s.t. nice **onizhishitoon** *vti2*
  NICE DAY: be a nice day **mino-giizhigad** *vii*
NICKEL
  NICKEL: nickel (coin) **aabita-zhooniyaans,
  -ag** *na*
NIECE
  NIECE: my cross-niece (female's brother's
  daughter or male's sister's daughter)
  nishimis, -ag /-shimis-/ *nad;* my parallel
  niece (male's brother's daughter or
  female's sister's daughter) **indoozhimis,
  -ag /-doozhimis-/** *nad*
NIGHT
  NIGHT: be night **dibikad** *vii*
  ALL NIGHT: **gabe-dibik** *pc*
  AT NIGHT: **niibaa-** *pv4*
  CERTAIN NUMBER OF NIGHTS: a certain
  number of nights **daso-dibik** *pc*
  DARK AS NIGHT: be dark as night **gashkii-
  dibik-ayaa, gashkii-dibik-ayaamagad** *vii*
  DARK AT NIGHT: be very dark at night
  gashkii-dibikad *vii*
  DRIVE AT NIGHT: **niibaabizo** *vai*
  EARLY IN THE NIGHT: be early in the
  night **oshki-dibikad** *vii*
  EVERY NIGHT: **endaso-dibik** *pc*
  LAST NIGHT: **dibikong** *pc*
  LATE AT NIGHT: **ishpi-dibik** *pc;* **niibaa-
  dibik** *pc;* be late at night **ishpi-dibikad** *vii*
  SPEND THE WHOLE NIGHT: **gabe-
  dibikwe** *vai*
  TRAVEL AT NIGHT: **niibaashkaa** *vai*
NIGHTMARE
  NIGHTMARE: have a nightmare
  giiwanaadingwaam *vai;* **zegingwashi** *vai*
NINE
  NINE: **zhaangaswi** *nm;* **zhaangaso-** *pv4;* nine
  (card) **zhaangasoobii'igan, -ag** *na;* they
  are nine **zhaangachinoon /zhaangachin-/**
  vii; **zhaangachiwag /zhaangachi-/** *vai*
  AND NINE: **ashi-zhaangaswi** *nm,* **ashi-
  zhaangaso-** *pv4*

NINE ACRES: **zhaangaso-diba'igaans** *pc*
NINE DAYS: **zhaangaso-giizhik** *pc;*
  zhaangasogon *pc;* be nine days
  zhaangasogonagad *vii*
NINE DAYS OLD: be nine days old
  zhaangasogonagizi *vai*
NINE DOLLARS: **zhaangaswaabik** *pc*
NINE EACH: **zhezhaangaswi** *nm*
NINE FEET: **zhaangasozid** *pc*
NINE HOURS: **zhaangaso-diba'igan** *pc*
NINE HUNDRED: **zhaangaswaak** *nm*
NINE INCHES: **zhaangasoninj** *pc*
NINE MILES: **zhaangaso-diba'igan** *pc*
NINE MINUTES: **zhaangaso-diba'igaans** *pc*
NINE MONTHS: **zhaangaso-giizis** *pc*
NINE O'CLOCK: be nine o'clock **zhaangaso-diba'iganed** *vii*
NINE PAIRS: **zhaangaswewaan** *pc*
NINE SETS: **zhaangaswewaan** *pc*
NINE THOUSAND: **zhaangasosagoons** *nm*
NINE TIMES: **zhaangaching** *pc*
NINE WEEKS: **zhaangaso-anama'e-giizhik** *pc;* be nine weeks **zhaangaso-anama'e-giizhigad** *vii*
NINE YEARS: **zhaangaso-biboon** *pc;* be nine years **zhaangaso-biboonagad** *vii;* be nine years old **zhaangaso-biboonagizi** *vai*

NINETEEN
NINETEEN: **ashi-zhaangaswi** *nm;* **midaaswi ashi-zhaangaswi** *nm*
NINETY
NINETY: **zhaangasimidana** *nm*
NINTH
NINTH DAY OF THE MONTH: be the ninth day of the month **zhaangasogonagizi** *vai*
NO
NO: **gaawiin** *pc*
NO LONGER: **gaawiin geyaabi** *pc*
NO MORE: **gaawiin geyaabi** *pc*
NO PURPOSE AT ALL: for no purpose at all **biinizikaa** *pc*
NO WAY: no way! **gaawesa** *pc*
NOBODY
NOBODY: **gaawiin awiya** *pr, also* **gaawiin awiiya**
NOD
NOD HEAD: nod one's head **wewebikweni** *vai*
NOD HEAD A CERTAIN WAY: nod one's head to s.o. a certain way **inikwetaw** *vta*
NOISE
DRIVE AWAY MAKING NOISE: **animwewebide, animwewebidemagad** *vii*
HEAR A CERTAIN NOISE: **initam** *vai2*
MAKE A CERTAIN NOISE: **inwewe, inwewemagad** *vii*
MAKE NOISE: **madwewe, madwewemagad** *vii;* **noondaagozi** *vai;* **noondaagwad** *vii;* make noise on s.t. **madwewetoon** *vti2*
MAKE NOISE BOILING: **madwegamide, madwegamidemagad** *vii;* **madwegamizo** *vai*

MAKE NOISE HITTING: **madweshin** *vai;* **madwesin** *vii;* make noise hitting s.t. **madwesidoon** *vti2;* make noise hitting things **madwesijige** *vai*
MAKING NOISE: **madwe-** *pv4*
NOISE IN A CERTAIN PLACE: there is noise in a certain place **danwewe, danwewemagad** *vii*
STOP MAKING VOCAL NOISE: **giishkowe** *vai*
WAKE BY VOCAL NOISE: wake s.o. by vocal noise **amajim** *vta*
WALK AWAY MAKING NOISE: **animwewetoo** *vai*
NOISY
NOISY: **ojaanimi-** *pv4;* be noisy **ombiigizi** *vai*
NOON
NOON: be noon **naawakwe, naawakwemagad** *vii*
NORTH
NORTH: **giiwedin** *ni*
NORTH WIND: **giiwedin** *ni*
NORTHERN LIGHTS
NORTHERN LIGHTS: they are the northern lights **jiibayag niimi'idiwag /niimi'idi-/** *vai*
NORTHERN PIKE
NORTHERN PIKE: **ginoozhe, -g** *na*
NOSE
NOSE: my nose **injaanzh, -an /-jaanzh-/** *nid*
BLOODY NOSE: bloody s.o.'s nose **gibitaneganaam** *vta;* have a bloody nose **miskwiiwijaane** *vai*
BLOODY NOSE FALLING: bloody one's nose falling **gibitaneshin** *vai*
BLOW NOSE: blow one's nose **ziinikiigome** *vai*
FLAT NOSE: have a flat nose **nabagijaane** *vai*
HAVE A BROKEN NOSE: **bookojaane** *vai*
HAVE A STUFFED-UP NOSE: **gibijaane** *vai, also* **gagiibijaane**
INSIDE NOSE: inside the nose **biinjijaanzh** *pc*
RED NOSE: have a red nose **miskojaane** *vai*
SWOLLEN NOSE: have a swollen nose **baagijaane** *vai*
NOSEBLEED
NOSEBLEED: have a nosebleed **gibitan** *vai, also* **gibitane***
NOSTRIL
NOSTRIL: my nostril **indenigom, -ag /-denigom-/** *nad*
NOT
NOT: not *negative* **gaawiin** *pc*
NOT ABLE: **gwiinawi-** *pv4*
NOT AT ALL: **gaawesa** *pc*
NOT BEFORE: **bwaa-** *pv1*
NOT IN THE LEAST: **gaawiin ganage** *pc*
NOT KNOW WHAT TO DO: **gwiinawi-doodam** *vai2*
NOT KNOW WHAT TO THINK: **gwiinawi-inendam** *vai2*
NOT KNOWING: **gwiinawi-** *pv4*
NOT NECESSARY: it's not necessary **gaawiin memwech** *pc*
NOT REALLY: **anishaa** *pc*

NOT TOO HARD: not too hard! **na'egaaj** *pc*
NOT YET: **gaa mashi** *pc, also* **gaawiin mashi**

NOTCHED
NOTCHED: be notched **aajikode, aajikodemagad** *vii*

NOTHING
NOTHING: **gaawiin gegoo** *pr*

NOTICE
NOTICE: **agwaakwa'igan, -an** *ni*

NOVEMBER
NOVEMBER: **gashkadino-giizis** *na*

NOW
NOW: **azhigwa** *pc, also* **zhigwa, zhigo**; **noongom** *pc;* **zhayiigwa** *pc*
JUST NOW: **bijiinag** *pc*

NOWADAYS
NOWADAYS: **noongom** *pc*

NUMB
FEEL NUMB: **giikimanizi** *vai*
NUMB ARM: have a numb arm **niboowinike** *vai*
NUMB FOOT: have a numb foot **niboowizide** *vai*
NUMB HAND: have a numb hand **niboowininjii** *vai*
NUMB LEG: have a numb leg **niboowigaade** *vai*

NUMBER
NUMBER: **asigibii'igan, -an** *ni*
CERTAIN NUMBER: a certain number **daso-** *pv3;* **daswi** *nm;* **minik** *pc;* they are a certain number **dashiwag /dashi-/** *vai;* **dasinoon /dasin-/** *vii*
CERTAIN NUMBER OF TIMES: a certain number of times **dasing** *pc*
WRITE NUMBERS: **asigibii'ige** *vai*

NUN
NUN: **anama'ewikwe, -g** *na;* **mekadewikonayewikwe, -g** *na, also* **mekadewikonayekwe**

NURSE
NURSE: nurse s.o. (e.g., a baby) **noozh /nooN-/** *vta*
NURSE A CHILD: **noonaawaso** *vai*

NURSE
NURSE: nurse (female) **mashkikiiwikwe, -g** *na*

NUT
NUT: **bagaan, -ag** *na*

OAK
OAK: **mitigomizh, -iig** *na*

OAR
OAR: **azheboyaanaak, -oon** *ni*

OATMEAL
OATMEAL: **daataagwa'igan, -an** *ni*

OBSERVATION
LEARN BY OBSERVATION: **gikinawaabi** *vai;* learn by observation of s.o. **gikinawaabam** *vta*

OBSERVE
OBSERVE: observe s.o. **naagadawaabam** *vta;* **naanaagadawaabam** *vta;* observe s.t. **naagadawaabandan** *vti;* **naanaagadawaabandan** *vti;* observe people **waabange** *vai*

OBSTRUCT
OBSTRUCT: obstruct s.o. **gibaakwa' /gibaakwa'w-/** *vta;* obstruct s.t. **gibaakwa'an** *vti*

OBTAIN
OBTAIN FROM A CERTAIN PLACE: obtain s.o. from a certain place **ondin** *vta;* obtain s.t. from a certain place **ondinan** *vti;* obtain (s.t.) for s.o. from a certain place **ondinamaw** *vta;* obtain things from a certain place **ondinige** *vai*

OBTAINED
OBTAINED FROM A CERTAIN PLACE: be obtained from a certain place **ondinigaade, ondinigaademagad** *vii;* **ondinigaazo** *vai*

OCCASIONALLY
OCCASIONALLY: **ayaangodinong** *pc, also* **aangodinong**

OCCUPIED
OCCUPIED: be occupied **abiichigaade, abiichigaademagad** *vii*

OCCUPY
OCCUPY: occupy s.t. **abiitan** *vti*

OCTOBER
OCTOBER: **binaakwii-giizis** *na, also* **binaakwe-giizis; waatebagaa-giizis** *na, also* **waatebago-giizis**

ODAWA
ODAWA: Odawa (Ottawa) **odaawaa, -g** *na*
SPEAK ODAWA: speak Odawa (Ottawa) **odaawaamo** *vai*

ODD
MAKE ODD: make s.o. odd **maanaaji'** *vta;* make s.t. odd **maanaajitoon** *vti2*

OF COURSE
OF COURSE: **memindage** *pc*

OFF
COME OFF: **gidiskise** *vai;* **gidiskise, gidiskisemagad** *vii*

OFFER
OFFER: offer s.o. **bagidin** *vta;* offer s.t. **bagidinan** *vti;* offer (s.t.) to s.o. **bagidinamaw** *vta;* offer things **bagidinige** *vai*

OFFERED
OFFERED: be offered **bagidinigaade, bagidinigaademagad** *vii;* **bagidinigaazo** *vai*

OFFERING
OFFERING: **bagijigan, -an** *ni*

MAKE AN OFFERING: **bagijige** *vai*
MAKE AN OFFERING OF TOBACCO:
biindaakoojige *vai;* make an offering of tobacco to s.o. **biindaakoozh**
/**biindaakooN-**/ *vta*

OFFICE
OFFICE: **ozhibii'igewigamig, -oon** *ni*
ADMINISTRATION OFFICE:
ogimaawigamig, -oon *ni*

OFFICER
MILITARY OFFICER: **zhimaaganishii-
ogimaa, -g** *na*

OFFICIAL
GOVERNMENT OFFICIAL:
wegimaawabid *na-pt*

OFTEN
OFTEN: **moozhag** *pc;* **naaningim** *pc*

OH
OH: oh! **oo** *pc;* **oonh** *pc*

OIL
OIL: **bimide** *ni*

OJIBWE
OJIBWE: **anishinaabe, -g** *na;* **ojibwe, -g** *na;*
ojibwewanishinaabe, -g *na,* also **ojibwe-
anishinaabe;** be Ojibwe **anishinaabewi**
vai; **ojibwewi** *vai*
CALL IN OJIBWE: call s.o. in Indian
(Ojibwe) **anishinaabewinikaazh**
/**anishinaabewinikaaN-**/ *vta;* call s.t. in
Indian (Ojibwe) **anishinaabewinikaadan**
vti
CALLED IN OJIBWE: be called in Indian
(Ojibwe) **anishinaabewinikaade,
anishinaabewinikaademagad** *vii;*
anishinaabewinikaazo *vai*
OJIBWE WRITING: Indian (Ojibwe) writing
anishinaabewibii'igan, -an *ni*
PUT INTO OJIBWE: put s.t. into Ojibwe
ojibwewisidoon *vti2*
SPEAK OJIBWE: **ojibwemo** *vai;* speak
Ojibwe to s.o. **ojibwemotaw** *vta;* speak an
Indian language (especially Ojibwe) to s.o.
anishinaabemotaw *vta;* speak an Indian
language (especially Ojibwe)
anishinaabemo *vai*
WRITE IN OJIBWE: write in Indian (Ojibwe)
anishinaabewibii'ige *vai;* write s.t. in
Indian (Ojibwe) **anishinaabewibii'an** *vti;*
write s.t. in Indian (Ojibwe) (e.g., a book)
anishinaabewisidoon *vti2;* write s.t. in
Ojibwe **ojibwewibii'an** *vti;* write (s.t.) in
Indian (Ojibwe) to s.o.
anishinaabewibii'amaw *vta;* write things
in Ojibwe **ojibwewibii'ige** *vai*
WRITTEN IN OJIBWE: be written in Indian
(Ojibwe) **anishinaabewibii'igaade,
anishinaabewibii'igaademagad** *vii;* be
written in Indian (Ojibwe) (e.g., a book or
document) **anishinaabewisin** *vii;* be written in Ojibwe **ojibwewibii'igaade,
ojibwewibii'igaademagad** *vii;* be written
in Ojibwe (e.g., a book) **ojibwewisin** *vii*

OJIBWE LANGUAGE
OJIBWE LANGUAGE: **ojibwemowin** *ni;* Indian language (especially Ojibwe)
anishinaabemowin, -an *ni*

OJIBWE WOMAN
OJIBWE WOMAN: **ojibwekwe, -g** *na*

OLD
OLD: **gete-** *pv4*
CERTAIN NUMBER OF DAYS OLD: be a
certain number of days old **dasogonagizi**
vai
CERTAIN NUMBER OF YEARS OLD: be a
certain number of years old **daso-
biboonagizi** *vai*
LOOK OLD: **gichi-aya'aawinaagozi** *vai*
SO MANY YEARS OLD: be so many years
old **daso-biboonagizi** *vai*
SOMEONE OLD: **gete-aya'aa, -g** *na*
SOMETHING OLD: **gete-ayi'ii, -n** *ni*

OLD LADY
OLD LADY: **mindimooyenh, -yag** *na;* be an
old lady **mindimooyenyiwi** *vai*

OLD MAN
OLD MAN: **akiwenzii, -yag** *na;* be an old
man **akiwenziiyiwi** *vai*

OLD WOMAN
OLD WOMAN: **mindimooyenh, -yag** *na;* be
an old woman **mindimooyenyiwi** *vai*

OLD-TIME
OLD-TIME: **gete-** *pv4*

OLDER
OLDER: be older **gitizi** *vai*

ON
ON METAL: on something mineral (e.g.,
metal, glass, rock) **agidaabik** *pc,* also
ogidaabik*, wagidaabik
ON ROCK: on something mineral (e.g., metal,
glass, rock) **agidaabik** *pc,* also **ogidaabik*,
wagidaabik**
ON THE SHORE: **agamiing** *pc*
ON TOP: on top of **agiji-** *pn,* also **ogiji-*,
wagiji-;** on top of it **agijayi'ii** *pc,* also
ogijayi'ii*, wagijayi'ii
ON TOP OF A HILL: **agidaaki** *pc,* also
ogidaaki*, wagidaaki
ON TOP OF A MOUNTAIN: **agidajiw** *pc,*
also **ogidajiw*, wagidajiw**
ON TOP OF A ROCK: **agidasin** *pc,* also
ogidasin*, wagidasin
ON TOP OF THE GROUND: **agidakamig**
pc, also **ogidakamig*, wagidakamig**
ON TOP OF THE HOUSE: **agidigamig** *pc,*
also **ogidigamig*, wagidigamig**
ON TOP OF THE ICE: **agidiskwam** *pc,* also
ogidiskwam*, wagidiskwam
ON TOP OF THE WATER: **agidibiig** *pc,* also
ogidibiig*, wagidibiig

ON PURPOSE
ON PURPOSE: **onjida** *pc*

ONCE
ONCE: **aabiding** *pc*

ONE

ONE: **bezhig** *nm;* **bezhigo-** *pv4;* **ingo-** /**ningo-**/
pv4, also **ningo-***; be one **bezhigwan** *vii*
AND ONE: **ashi-bezhig** *nm;* **ashi-bezhigo-**
pv4
AT ONE TIME: **aabiding** *pc;* **ingoding** *pc, also*
ningoding*
GONE A CERTAIN LENGTH OF TIME:
be gone a certain length of time **apiitendi**
vai
IN ONE PLACE: **bezhigwanong** *pc*
ONE ACRE: **ingo-diba'igaans** *pc, also* **ningo-**
diba'igaans*
ONE DAY: **ingo-giizhik** *pc, also* **ningo-**
giizhik*
ONE DOLLAR: **bezhigwaabik** *na*
ONE FOOT: **ingodozid** *pc, also* **ningodozid***
ONE HOUR: **ingo-diba'igan** *pc, also* **ningo-**
diba'igan*
ONE HUNDRED: **ingodwaak** *nm, also*
ningodwaak*
ONE INCH: **ingodoninj** *pc, also* **ningodoninj***
ONE MILE: **ingo-diba'igan** *pc, also* **ningo-**
diba'igan*
ONE MINUTE: **ingo-diba'igaans** *pc, also*
ningo-diba'igaans*
ONE MONTH: **ingo-giizis** *pc, also* **ningo-**
giizis*
ONE NIGHT: **ingo-dibik** *pc, also* **ningo-dibik***
ONE O'CLOCK: be one o'clock **ingo-**
diba'iganed /**ningo-diba'iganed-**/ *vii, also*
ningo-diba'iganed*
ONE PLACE: **bezhigwanong** *pc*
ONE THOUSAND: **ingodosagoons** *nm, also*
ningodosagoons*
ONE WEEK: **ingo-anama'e-giizhik** *pc, also*
ningo-anama'e-giizhik*
ONE YEAR: **ingo-biboon** *pc, also* **ningo-**
biboon*; be one year **ingo-biboonagad**
/**ningo-biboonagad-**/ *vii, also* **ningo-**
biboonagad*
ONE YEAR OLD: be one year old **ingo-**
biboonagizi /**ningo-biboonagizi-**/ *vai, also*
ningo-biboonagizi*

ONE-BY-ONE

ONE-BY-ONE: **bebezhig** *nm*

ONION

ONION: **zhigaagawanzh, -iig** *na*

ONLY

ONLY: **eta** *pc*
ONLY HER: only her *third person singular*
personal pronoun **wiineta** *pr*
ONLY HIM: only him *third person singular*
personal pronoun **wiineta** *pr*
ONLY ME: only me *first person singular*
personal pronoun **niineta** *pr*
ONLY THEM: only them *third person plural*
personal pronoun **wiinetawaa** *pr*
ONLY US: only us *first person exclusive plural*
personal pronoun **niinetawind** *pr;* only us
first person inclusive personal pronoun
giinetawind *pr*
ONLY YOU: only you *second person singular*
personal pronoun **giineta** *pr;* only you *second*

personal plural personal pronoun **giinetawaa**
pr
THE ONLY ONE: be the only one **bezhigo**
vai; **bezhigwan** *vii*

OPEN

OPEN: be open **baakishin** *vai;* **baakisin** *vii;* be
open (as something stick- or wood-like,
e.g., a door) **baakaakosin** *vii;* open s.t. (as
something stick- or wood-like, e.g., a door)
baakaakonan *vti;* open (s.t.) for s.o. (as
something stick- or wood-like, e.g., a door)
baakaakonamaw *vta*
COME OPEN: **baakise, baakisemagad** *vii*
FLING OPEN: fling s.t. open (as something
stick- or wood-like, e.g., a door)
baakaakowebinan *vti*
FLY OPEN: **baakise, baakisemagad** *vii;* fly
open (as something stick- or wood-like,
e.g., a door) **baakaakose,**
baakaakosemagad *vii*
OPEN EYES: open one's eyes **dooskaabi** *vai*
OPEN MOUTH: open one's mouth **daawani**
vai
OPEN UP: open s.o. up **baakin** *vta;* open s.t.
up **baakinan** *vti;* open things up **baakinige**
vai
RIP OPEN: rip s.o.open **aabibizh** /**aabibiN-**/
vta; rip s.t. open **aabibidoon** *vti2*

OPENED

OPENED: be opened (as something stick- or
wood-like, e.g., a door) **baakaakonigaade,**
baakaakonigaademagad *vii*

OPENER

CAN OPENER: **baakaakozhigan, -an** *ni*

OPERATE

OPERATE POORLY: **maazhibide,**
maazhibidemagad *vii;* **maazhibizo** *vai*

OPPOSITE

OPPOSITE: **dibishkookamig** *pc*

OPTOMETRIST

OPTOMETRIST: **oshkiinzhigokewinini,**
-wag *na*

OR

OR: **gemaa** *pc, also* **gemaa gaye**

ORANGE

ORANGE: orange (fruit) **wezaawiminagazid**
na-pt

ORDER

ORDER: order (s.t.) for s.o. **naajinizha'amaw**
vta; order things **naajinizha'ige** *vai*
GIVE AN ORDER: **anookii** *vai;* give an order
to s.o. **anoozh** /**anooN-**/ *vta*
PUT IN ORDER: put s.o. in order **onin** *vta;*
put s.t. in order **oninan** *vti;* put things in
order **oninige** *vai*

ORGAN

ORGAN: **madwewechigan, -an** *ni*

ORIENTAL

ORIENTAL: **aniibiishaabookewinini, -wag**
na; be Oriental **aniibiishaabookewininiiwi**
vai

ORIGINATE
ORIGINATE IN A CERTAIN PLACE:
ondaadad *vii*

ORPHANED
ORPHANED: be orphaned **giiwizi** *vai*

OSIER
RED OSIER: **miskwaabiimizh, -iig** *na*

OTHER SIDE
ON THE OTHER SIDE: on the other side of
it **agaamayi'ii** *pc;* **aazhawayi'ii** *pc*
ON THE OTHER SIDE OF: **agaami-** *pn*
ON THE OTHER SIDE OF THE
CLEARING: **agaamaakwaa** *pc*
ON THE OTHER SIDE OF THE FIRE:
agaamishkode *pc*
ON THE OTHER SIDE OF THE LAKE:
agaaming *pc*
ON THE OTHER SIDE OF THE
MEADOW: **agaamashkosiw** *pc*
ON THE OTHER SIDE OF THE ROAD: on
the other side of the road or trail
agaamikana *pc*
ON THE OTHER SIDE OF THE TRAIL: on
the other side of the road or trail
agaamikana *pc*
OTHER SIDE OF THE LODGE:
agaamindesi *pc;* on the other side of the
lodge **agaamindesing** *pc*

OTTER
OTTER: **nigig, -wag** *na*

OTTER HIDE
OTTER HIDE: **nigigwayaan, -ag** *na*

OUT
CRAWL OUT: **zaagidoode** *vai*
FLOW OUT: **zaagijiwan** *vii*
GO OUT IN A GROUP: they go out in a
group **zaagidaawanidiwag**
/zaagidaawanidi-/ *vai*
GROW OUT: **zaagigi** *vai;* **zaagigin** *vii*
MAKE GO OUT: make s.o. go out **zaagizi'**
vta
PUT OUT: put s.o. out **zaagidin** *vta;* put s.t.
out **zaagidinan** *vti*
RUN OUT: **zaagizibatoo** *vai;* run out with
s.o. **zaagiziba'** *vta;* **zaagizibatwaazh**
/zaagizibatwaaN-/ *vta;* run out with s.t.
zaagizibatwaadan *vti;* they run out
together **zaagiziba'idiwag /zaagiziba'idi-/**
vai
STICK OUT HEAD: stick out one's head
zaagikweni *vai*
TAKE OUT: take s.o. out **zaagizi'** *vta;* take
s.t. out **zaagizitoon** *vti2;* take (s.t.) out for
s.o. **zaagizitaw** *vta*

OUT FROM SHORE
GO OUT FROM SHORE ON THE ICE:
niminaaweyaadagaako *vai*
PADDLE OUT FROM SHORE:
niminaawe'o *vai*

OUT OF
OUT OF: be out of s.o. **jaagin** *vta;* be out of
s.t. **jaaginan** *vti*

OUT OF SIGHT
GO OUT OF SIGHT: **ani-naagozi** *vai;* **ani-
naagwad** *vii;* go out of sight (as around a
corner) **aagawe** *vai*

OUT OF SORTS
FEEL OUT OF SORTS: **maazhendam** *vai2*

OUT OF THE WAY
STAND OUT OF THE WAY: **ikogaabawi**
vai

OUTBOARD MOTOR
OUTBOARD MOTOR: **akikoons, -ag** *na*

OUTDOORS
OUTDOORS: **agwajiing** *pc*

OUTHOUSE
OUTHOUSE: **zaaga'amoowigamig, -oon** *ni*

OUTLET
OUTLET: be an outlet **biinjidawaa** *vii*

OUTSIDE
OUTSIDE: **agwajiing** *pc*
CHASE OUTSIDE: chase s.o. outside
zaagijinizhikaw *vta*
TELL TO GO OUTSIDE: tell s.o. to go
outside **zaagijinaazha' /zaagijinaazha'w-/**
vta
THROW OUTSIDE: throw s.o. outside
zaagijiwebin *vta;* throw s.t. outside
zaagijiwebinan *vti;* throw things outside
zaagijiwebinige *vai*
THROWN OUTSIDE: be thrown outside
zaagijiwebinigaade,
zaagijiwebinigaademagad *vii*

OVEN
ROAST IN THE OVEN: roast s.o. in the oven
giboz /gibozw-/ *vta;* roast s.t. in the oven
gibozan *vti;* roast things in the oven
gibozige *vai*

OVER
OVER: be over (of an event) **ishkwaakamigad**
vii; over it **ishpayi'ii** *pc*
CLIMB OVER: **baazhidaandawe** *vai*
JUMP OVER: **baazhijigwaashkwani** *vai*
STEP OVER: step over s.o. **baazhida'**
/baazhida'w-/ *vta;* step over s.t.
baazhida'an *vti*
THROW OVER: throw s.o. over
baazhijiwebin *vta;* throw s.t. over
baazhijiwebinan *vti*

OVERCOME
OVERCOME: overcome s.o. **zhaagooji'** *vta;*
overcome s.o. with speech **zhaagoozom**
vta; overcome s.t. **zhaagoojitoon** *vti2;*
overcome people **zhaagooji'iwe** *vai*

OVERCOOK
OVERCOOK: overcook s.o. **onzaamiz**
/onzaamizw-/ *vta;* overcook s.t.
onzaamizan *vti*

OVERCOOKED
OVERCOOKED: be overcooked **onzaamide,**
onzaamidemagad *vii;* **onzaamizo** *vai*

OVERDO
OVERDO: overdo things **onzaamichige** *vai*

OVEREXCITED
OVEREXCITED: be overexcited
onzaamenimo *vai*

OVERFILL
OVERFILL: overfill s.o. with solids
onzaamashkina' *vta;* overfill s.t. (with a
liquid) **onzaamibadoon** *vti2;* overfill s.t.
with solids **onzaamashkinadoon** *vti2*

OVERFLOW
OVERFLOW: overflow (as a liquid)
bazhidebii, bazhidebiimagad *vii*
FILL TO OVERFLOWING: fill s.o. to
overflowing with solids **ziigashkina'** *vta;* fill
s.t. to overflowing with a liquid
ziigibadoon *vti2;* fill s.t. to overflowing
with solids **ziigashkinadoon** *vti2*

OVERHEAT
OVERHEAT: overheat s.o. **onzaamiz**
/onzaamizw-/ *vta;* overheat s.t.
onzaamizan *vti*

OVERNIGHT
GONE OVERNIGHT: be gone overnight
nikanendi *vai*
STAY OVERNIGHT: stay overnight with s.o.
nibendaw *vta;* stay overnight with people
nibendaage *vai*

OVERSEAS
OVERSEAS: **agaamakiing** *pc*

OVERSHOE
OVERSHOE: **biitookizinaan, -an** *ni, also*
biitookizin
WEAR OVERSHOES: **biitookizine** *vai*

OVERSLEEP
OVERSLEEP: **onzaamingwaam** *vai*

OVERTAKE
OVERTAKE: overtake s.o. **adim** *vta;* overtake
s.t. **adindan** *vti*
OVERTAKE IN A BOAT: overtake s.o. in a
boat **adima'** **/adima'w-/** *vta*

OVERWORK
COLLAPSE FROM OVERWORK:
gawanokii *vai*

OWE
OWE: **mazina'ige** *vai;* owe (s.t.) to s.o.
mazina'amaw *vta*

OWL
OWL: **gookooko'oo, -g** *na*
SCREECH OWL: **gaakaabishiinh, -yag** *na*

OWN
OWN: own s.o. **ayaaw** *vta;* **dibenim** *vta;* own
s.t. **ayaan** *vti3;* **dibendan** *vti;* own for
oneself **dibendaaso** *vai*

OWNED
OWNED: be owned **dibendaagozi** *vai;*
dibendaagwad *vii;* **dibenjigaade,**
dibenjigaademagad *vii;* **dibenjigaazo** *vai*

P

PACK
PACK: **bimiwanaan, -an** *ni*
CARRY A BIG PACK: **mangiwane** *vai*
CARRY A LIGHT PACK: **naangiwane** *vai*
CARRY A PACK ALONG: **bimiwane** *vai*
HARDLY BE ABLE TO CARRY THE
PACK: hardly be able to carry a pack
bwaawane *vai*
LIFT A PACK: lift a pack to one's back
ombiwane *vai*
MAKE A PACK: make a pack of s.t.
ozhiwanikaadan *vti*
PACK TOO MUCH OF A LOAD:
onzaamiwane *vai*
PACK UP: **ozhiwanike** *vai*
SET DOWN PACK: set down one's pack
bagijiwane *vai*

PACK FRAME
PACK FRAME: **bimoonjigan, -an** *ni*

PACKAGE
PACKAGE: **gashkibijigan, -an** *ni*
WRAPPED PACKAGE: **wiiweginigan, -an** *ni*

PACKET
PACKET: **gashkibijigan, -an** *ni*

PADDING
LIE AS PADDING: **apishin** *vai;* **apisin** *vii*

PADDLE
PADDLE: **abwi, -in** *ni;* **jiime** *vai*
ARRIVE PADDLING: **bagamishkaa** *vai*
PADDLE A CERTAIN WAY: **inakwazhiwe**
vai
PADDLE ABOUT: **babaamishkaa** *vai*
PADDLE AGAINST THE WIND:
onjishkawa'o *vai, also* **onjishkawa'am**
PADDLE ALONG: **bimakwazhiwe** *vai;*
bimishkaa *vai*
PADDLE ALONG THE SHORE:
jiigewe'am *vai2;* **jiigewe'o** *vai;*
jiigewekwazhiwe *vai*
PADDLE AWAY: **animishkaa** *vai*
PADDLE BACKWARDS: **azhe'o** *vai*
PADDLE FAST: **gizhiikaakwazhiwe** *vai*
PADDLE FOR STIRRING BOILING
MAPLE SAP: **gaashkakokwe'igan, -an** *ni*
PADDLE FROM A CERTAIN PLACE:
ondakwazhiwe *vai*
PADDLE HERE: **biidakwazhiwe** *vai;*
biidaasamishkaa *vai*
PADDLE OFF: **maajiikwazhiwe** *vai*
PADDLE OUT FROM SHORE:
niminaawe'o *vai*
PADDLE SUDDENLY INTO VIEW:
zaagewe'o *vai;* **zaagewekwazhiwe** *vai*
PADDLE TO A CERTAIN PLACE: **ina'o**
vai; **inakwazhiwe** *vai*

PAIL
PAIL: **akik, -oog** *na*
WASH PAIL: **giziibiiginakokwe** *vai*
WATER PAIL: **nibiiwakik, -oog** *na*

PAIN
PAIN: be in pain **wiisagine** *vai*
CHEST PAINS: have chest pains while
breathing **jakanaamo** *vai*
SUFFER PAIN: **wiisagendam** *vai*
WAKE FROM PAIN: **amajine** *vai*

PAINT
PAINT: **zhizhoobii'igan, -an** *ni;* paint s.o.
zhizhoobii' /**zhizhoobii'w-**/ *vta;* paint s.t.
zhizhoobii'an *vti;* paint (s.t.) for s.o.
zhizhoobii'amaw *vta;* paint things
zhizhoobii'ige *vai*

PAINT BRUSH
PAINT BRUSH: **zhizhoobii'iganaatig, -oon**
ni

PAINTED TURTLE
PAINTED TURTLE: **miskwaadesi, -wag** *na*

PAINTER
PAINTER: **zhizhoobii'igewinini, -wag** *na*

PAIR
CERTAIN NUMBER OF PAIRS: a certain
number of pairs **daswewaan** *pc*

PALATE
PALATE: my palate **ninagaskway**
/**-nagaskway-**/ *nid*

PALE
PALE FACED: be pale faced **waabiingwe** *vai*

PALM
PALM: my palm **ninagaakininj, -iin**
/**-nagaakininjy-**/ *nid*

PAN
PAN: **akik, -oog** *na;* **jiibaakwewakik, -oog** *na*
FRYING PAN: **abwewin, -an** *ni*
LARGE PAN: **gichi-onaagan** *ni*
ROASTING PAN: **giboziganaabik, -oon** *ni*

PANCAKE
PANCAKE: **gwekiwebinigan, -ag** *na*

PANT
PANT: **nesezo** *vai*

PANTHER
PANTHER: **mishibizhii, -g** *na*

PANTS
PANTS: **giboodiyegwaazon, -ag** *na*
PUT ON PANTS: put on one's pants
biichigiboodiyegwaazone *vai*
TAKE OFF PANTS: take off one's pants
giichigiboodiyegwaazone *vai*
WEAR PANTS: **gigigiboodiyegwaazone** *vai*

PAPER
PAPER: **mazina'igan, -an** *ni*

PAPER BAG
PAPER BAG: **mazina'igani-mashkimodens,
-an** *ni*

PARALYZED
PARALYZED: be paralyzed **niboowi** *vai*
BECOME PARALYZED: **niboowise** *vai*

PARCH
PARCH: parch s.t. **gaapizan** *vti;* parch s.t.
(e.g., wild rice) **gidasan** *vti;* parch things
gaapizige *vai;* parch things (e.g., wild rice)
gidasige *vai*

PARENT
PARENT: my parent **ingitiziim, -ag**
/**-gitiziim-**/ *nad*
PARENTS: my parents *plural* **niniigi'igoog**
/**-niigi'igw-**/ *nad*

PARENT-IN-LAW
PARENT-IN-LAW: my fellow parent-in-law
indindawaa, -g /**-dindawaa-**/ *nad*

PAROLE
ON PAROLE: be on parole
ganawaabanjigaazo *vai;* **ganawenjigaazo**
vai

PARROT
PARROT: **gaagiigidoo-bineshiinh, -yag** *na*

PART
PART: **bakise** *vai;* **bakise, bakisemagad** *vii*

PARTICLES
IN PARTICLES: be in particles **biisaa,
biisaamagad** *vii;* **biisizi** *vai*
PULL INTO PARTICLES: pull s.o. into par-
ticles **biisibizh** /**biisibiN-**/ *vta;* pull s.t. into
particles **biisibidoon** *vti2*

PARTITION
CLOTH PARTITION: **gibagoojigan, -an** *ni*

PARTNER
PARTNER: **wiijiiwaagan, -ag** *na*

PARTRIDGE
PARTRIDGE: **bine, -wag** *na*

PASS
PASS: pass (as time) **izhise, izhisemagad** *vii;*
ojiise, ojiisemagad *vii*
COME TO PASS: **bagami-ayaa, bagami-
ayaamagad** *vii*
PASS BY: pass s.o. by **gabikaw** *vta;* pass s.t.
by **gabikan** *vti*
PASS THROUGH: **zhaabose,
zhaabosemagad** *vii;* **zhaabwii** *vai*

PAST
GOING PAST: **bimi-** *pv2*

PAST TENSE
PAST TENSE: *past verb prefix* **gii-** *pv1*

PASTE
PASTE: **agokiwasigan, -an** *ni;* paste something on s.o. **agokiwas** /**agokiwasw-**/ *vta;*
paste something on s.t. **agokiwasan** *vti*

PASTED
PASTED: be pasted on **agokiwaso** *vai;*
agokiwate, agokiwatemagad *vii*

PASTRY
PASTRY: **waashkobizid bakwezhigan** *na-pt;*
wiishkobi-bakwezhigan, -ag *na*

PATCH
PATCH: **bagwa'igan, -an** *ni;* patch s.o.
bagwa' /**bagwa'w-**/ *vta;* patch s.t.
bagwa'an *vti;* patch (s.t.) for s.o.
bagwa'amaw *vta;* patch things **bagwa'ige**
vai
WEAR PATCHES: **bagwa'igaazo** *vai*

PATCHED
PATCHED: be patched **bagwa'igaade,
bagwa'igaademagad** *vii;* **bagwa'igaazo**
vai

PATTERN
  PATTERN: pattern (in sewing) **naabizhigan, -an** *ni*
  HAVE A SQUARE PATTERN: **gakakishin** *vai;* **gakakisin** *vii*
PAY
  PAY: pay for s.o. **diba' /diba'w-/** *vta;* pay for s.t. **diba'an** *vti;* pay (s.t.) to s.o. **diba'amaw** *vta;* pay s.o. for (s.t.) **diba'amaw** *vta;* pay things **diba'ige** *vai;* pay people for (s.t.) **diba'amaage** *vai;* they pay each other for (s.t.) **diba'amaadiwag /diba'amaadi-/** *vai*
  PAY OFF: **diba'igese, diba'igesemagad** *vii*
PAY ATTENTION
  PAY ATTENTION: **babaamendam** *vai2;* pay attention to s.o. **babaamenim** *vta;* pay attention to s.t. **babaamendan** *vti*
PEA
  PEAS: peas *plural* **anijiiminan /anijiimin-/** *ni*
PEA SOUP
  PEA SOUP: **anijiiminaaboo** *ni*
PEACEFUL
  PEACEFUL: be peaceful **bangan** *vii*
PEACH
  PEACH: **miishiijiimin, -ag** *na*
PEANUT
  PEANUT: **bagaan, -ag** *na*
PEANUT BUTTER
  PEANUT BUTTER: **bagaani-bimide** *ni, also* **bagaanensi-bimide**
PEARL
  PEARL: **miigis, -ag** *na*
PEDAL
  PEDAL: **ditibiwebishkige** *vai*
PEDDLER
  PEDDLER: **babaamadaawewinini, -wag** *na, also* **babaamadaawaagewinini;** be a peddlar **babaamadaawe** *vai*
PEEK
  PEEK: **giimaabi** *vai;* **giimoozaabi** *vai;* **inaabi** *vai;* peek at s.o. **giimaabam** *vta*
  PEEK THROUGH AN OPENING: **dapaabi** *vai;* peek through an opening at s.o. **dapaabam** *vta;* peek through an opening at s.t. **dapaabandan** *vti*
PEEL
  PEEL FROM SUNBURN: **bishagaaso** *vai*
  PEEL OFF: **bishagishkaa** *vai;* **bishagishkaa, bishagishkaamagad** *vii*
  PEEL TIMBER USING SOMETHING: **bishagaakwa'ige** *vai*
  PEEL WIGOB: peel wigob (inner bark of basswood) **bisha'igobii** *vai*
  PEEL WITH A KNIFE: peel s.o. with a knife **bishagikozh /bishagikoN-/** *vta;* peel s.t. with a knife **bishagikodan** *vti*
  PEEL WITH HANDS: peel s.o. with hands **bishagibizh /bishagibiN-/** *vta;* peel s.t. with hands **bishagibidoon** *vti2;* peel things with hands **bishagibijige** *vai*
PELICAN
  PELICAN: **zhede, -g** *na*

PEN
  PEN: **ozhibii'iganaak, -oon** *ni*
PENCIL
  PENCIL: **ozhibii'iganaak, -oon** *ni*
PENINSULA
  PENINSULA: **neyaashi, -wan** *ni;* there is a peninsula **neyaashiiwan** *vii*
PENIS
  PENIS: my penis **niinag /-iinag-/** *nid*
PENNY
  PENNY: **miskwaabikoons, -ag** *na;* **ozaawaabikoons, -ag** *na*
PEOPLE
  MANY PEOPLE: there are many people **anishinaabekaa** *vii*
PEPPER
  PEPPER: **gaa-wiisagang** *ni-pt*
PERCEIVE
  PERCEIVE A CERTAIN WAY: perceive s.o. a certain way **izhinaw** *vta;* perceive s.t. a certain way **izhinan** *vti*
PERCH
  PERCH: **asaawe, -g** *na*
PERCHED
  PERCHED UP: be perched up on something **agoozi** *vai*
PERFORM
  PERFORM TRICKS: **mamaandaagochige** *vai*
PERFUME
  PERFUME: **minomaagochigan, -an** *ni*
  USE PERFUME: **minomaagochige** *vai*
PERHAPS
  PERHAPS: **ganabaj** *pc;* **maagizhaa** *pc, also* **maazhaa**
PERSISTENTLY
  PERSISTENTLY: **awanjish** *pc*
PERSON
  PERSON: **anishinaabe, -g** *na;* **bemaadizid** *na-pt*
PERSUADE
  PERSUADE: persuade s.o. **gagaanzom** *vta*
PESTLE
  PESTLE: **bootaaganaak, -oon** *ni*
PET
  PET: **bami'aagaans, -ag** *na*
PHARMACIST
  PHARMACIST: **mashkikii-adaawewinini, -wag** *na, also* **mashkikiiwi-adaawewinini**
PHARMACY
  PHARMACY: **mashkikii-adaawewigamig, -oon** *ni, also* **mashkikiiwi-adaawewigamig**
PHEASANT
  PHEASANT: **mayagi-bine, -wag** *na*
PHLEGM
  PHLEGM: **agig** *na*
PHONE
  CALL ON THE PHONE: call s.o. on the phone **ganoozh /ganooN-/** *vta*
PHONOGRAPH
  PHONOGRAPH: **gaagiigidoo-makakoons, -an** *ni;* **nagamoo-makak, -oon** *ni*

PHOTOGRAPH
PHOTOGRAPH: **mazinaakizon, -an** *ni;* photograph s.o. **mazinaakiz** /**mazinaakizw-**/ *vta;* photograph s.t. **mazinaakizan** *vti;* photograph things **mazinaakizige** *vai*

PHOTOGRAPHED
PHOTOGRAPHED: be photographed **mazinaakide, mazinaakidemagad** *vii;* **mazinaakizo** *vai*

PIANO
PIANO: **madwewechigan, -an** *ni*

PICK
PICK: pick s.o. **onaabam** *vta;* pick s.t. **onaabandan** *vti;* pick things **onaabanjige** *vai*
PICK BERRIES: **mawinzo** *vai*
PICK FROM: pick from s.o. **gagiigin** *vta;* pick from s.t. **gagiiginan** *vti*
PICK TEETH: pick one's teeth **zesegwaabide'o** *vai*

PICK UP
PICK UP: pick s.o. up **mami** /**mam-**/ *vta;* **maamigin** *vta;* **odaapin** *vta;* pick s.t. up **mamoon** *vti2;* **maamiginan** *vti;* **odaapinan** *vti;* pick (s.t.) up from s.o. **mamaw** *vta;* **odaapinamaw** *vta;* pick up things **mamige** *vai;* **odaapinige** *vai*
PICK UP A NET: **naadasabii** *vai*
PICK UP IN MOUTH: pick s.o. up in mouth **niimam** *vta;* pick s.t. up in mouth **niimandan** *vti*
PICK UP USING SOMETHING: pick s.o. up (as or as with something stick- or wood-like) **niimaakwa'** /**niimaakwa'w-**/ *vta;* pick s.o. up using something **niima'** /**niima'w-**/ *vta;* pick s.t. up (as or as with something stick- or wood-like) **niimaakwa'an** *vti;* pick s.t. up using something **niima'an** *vti*

PICKED
PICKED: be picked **onaabanjigaade, onaabanjigaademagad** *vii;* **onaabanjigaazo** *vai*

PICKED UP
PICKED UP: be picked up **mamigaade, mamigaademagad** *vii;* **mamigaazo** *vai;* **naajigaade, naajigaademagad** *vii;* **naajigaazo** *vai*

PICKEREL
PICKEREL: **ogaa, -wag** *na*

PICKLE
PICKLE: **zhaawaabookaadeg bipakoombens** *ni;* **zhiiwi-bipakoombens, -an** *ni*

PICKLED
PICKLED: be pickled **zhiiwaabookaade, zhiiwaabookaademagad** *vii*

PICTURE
PICTURE: **mazinaakizon, -an** *ni*
TAKE PICTURES: **mazinaakizige** *vai;* take pictures of s.o. **mazinaakiz** /**mazinaakizw-**/ *vta;* take pictures of s.t. **mazinaakizan** *vti*

PICTURED
PICTURED: be pictured **mazinaakide, mazinaakidemagad** *vii;* **mazinaakizo** *vai*

PIE
PIE: **biitoosijigan, -ag** *na;* **biitoosijiganibakwezhigan, -ag** *na*

PIECE
BITE A PIECE OFF: bite a piece off s.o. **bakwem** *vta;* bite a piece off s.t. **bakwendan**
CHOP A PIECE OFF: chop a piece off s.o. (as something of wood) **bakwega'** /**bakwega'w-**/ *vta;* chop a piece off s.t. (as something of wood) **bakwega'an** *vti*
CUT A PIECE OFF: cut a piece off s.o. **bakwezh** /**bakwezhw-**/ *vta;* cut a piece off s.t. **bakwezhan** *vti*
TAKE A PIECE OFF BY HAND: take a piece off s.o. by hand **bakwen** *vta;* take a piece off s.t. by hand **bakwenan** *vti*
TAKE A PIECE OFF USING SOMETHING: take a piece off s.o. using something **bakwe'** *vta;* take a piece off s.t. using something **bakwe'an** *vti*
TEAR A PIECE OFF: tear a piece off of s.o. **bakwebizh** /**bakwebiN-**/ *vta;* tear a piece off of s.t. **bakwebidoon** *vti2*

PIECES
CUT TO PIECES: cut s.o. to pieces **bigishkizh** /**bigishkizhw-**/ *vta;* cut s.t. to pieces **bigishkizhan** *vti*
FALL TO PIECES: **bigishkanad** *vii;* **bigishkanani** *vai*
GO TO PIECES: **bigishkise** *vai;* **bigishkise, bigishkisemagad** *vii*
TEAR TO PIECES: tear s.o. to pieces **bigishkibizh** /**bigishkibiN-**/ *vta;* tear s.t. to pieces **bigishkibidoon** *vti2*

PIG
PIG: **gookoosh, -ag** *na*

PIGEON
PIGEON: **omiimii, -g** *na*

PIKE
NORTHERN PIKE: **ginoozhe, -g** *na*

PILE
PILE: pile s.o. **okoshim** *vta;* pile s.t. **okosidoon** *vti2*
LIE IN A PILE: **okoshin** *vai;* **okosin** *vii*

PILL
PILL: **bebiikominagak** *ni-pt;* **mashkikiins, -an** *ni*

PILLOW
PILLOW: **apikweshimon, -an** *ni*

PILLOWCASE
PILLOWCASE: **apikweshimoniigin, -oon** *ni*

PIN
PIN: **zagaakwa'igan, -an** *ni;* **zagaakwa'on, -ag** *na;* pin s.o. **zagaakwa'** /**zagaakwa'w-**/ *vta;* pin s.t. **zagaakwa'an** *vti;* pin things **zagaakwa'ige** *vai*
COMMON PIN: **oshtigwaanzhaabonigan, -an** *ni*

HAIRPIN: **wiinizisimaani-zagaakwa'igan, -an** *ni*

PINCH
PINCH: pinch s.o. **jiisibizh /jiisibiN-/** *vta*

PINCHERRY
PINCHERRY: **bawa'iminaan, -an** *ni*

PINCHERRY BUSH
PINCHERRY BUSH: **bawa'iminagaawanzh, -iig** *na*

PINE
JACK PINE: **okikaandag, -oog** *na, also* **wakikaandag**
WHITE PINE: **zhingwaak, -wag** *na*

PINE BOUGH
PINE BOUGH: **zhingwaakwaandag, -oog** *na*

PINNED
PINNED: be pinned **zagaakwa'igaade, zagaakwa'igaademagad** *vii;* **zagaakwa'igaazo** *vai*
PINNED DOWN: be pinned down **dasoozo** *vai*

PIPE
PIPE: pipe (for smoking) **opwaagan, -ag** *na*
LIGHT A PIPE: **zaka'ipwaagane** *vai*
STONE PIPE: **asinii-opwaagan** *na*

PIPE BAG
PIPE BAG: **gashkibidaagan, -ag** *na*

PIPE STEM
PIPE STEM: **okij, -iin** *ni*

PIPESTONE
PIPESTONE: **opwaaganasin, -iig** *na*

PITCH
PITCH: **bigiw** *ni*
APPLY PITCH: **bigiike** *vai;* apply pitch to s.t. (e.g., a canoe) **bigiikaadan** *vti*

PITCHER
PITCHER: pitcher (in baseball) **apagijigewinini, -wag** *na*

PITIABLE
PITIABLE: be pitiable **inigaazi** *vai*

PITIED
PITIED: be pitied **zhawendaagozi** *vai*

PITY
PITY: pity s.o. **gidimaagenim** *vta;* **zhawenim** *vta*
HAVE PITY: **zhawenjige** *vai*

PLACE
PLACE A BET: **achige** *vai*

PLAIN
PLAIN: **mashkode, -n** *ni*

PLAIN VIEW
IN PLAIN VIEW: **mizhisha** *pc*

PLAN
PLAN: plan s.t. **onaakonan** *vti*
CHANGE PLANS: **aandaakonige** *vai*

PLANE
PLANE: airplane **bemisemagak, -in** *ni-pt*

PLANE
PLANE: plane (tool) **mookojigan, -an** *ni*

PLANT
PLANT: **gitige** *vai;* plant s.o. **gitigaazh /gitigaaN-/** *vta;* plant s.t. **gitigaadan** *vti*

PLANT IN: plant s.o. in **badakizh /badakiN-/** *vta;* plant s.t. **badakidoon** *vti2;* plant things in **bagidinige** *vai*

PLANTED
PLANTED: be planted **gitigaade, gitigaademagad** *vii;* **gitigaazo** *vai*
PLANTED IN: be planted in **badakide, badakidemagad** *vii;* **badakizo** *vai*

PLATE
PLATE: **onaagan, -an** *ni*
DINNER PLATE: **desinaagan, -an** *ni*
SMALL PLATE: **onaagaans, -an** *ni*

PLATFORM
PLATFORM: **desa'on, -an** *ni*

PLAY
PLAY: **odamino** *vai*
PLAY A GUITAR: **madweyaabiigibijige** *vai*
PLAY A WIND INSTRUMENT: **noondaagochige** *vai;* play s.t. as a wind instrument **noondaagotoon** *vti2*
PLAY BASEBALL: **bakitejii'ige** *vai*
PLAY IN A CERTAIN PLACE: **danakamigizi** *vai;* **dazhitaa** *vai*
PLAY LACROSSE: **baaga'adowe** *vai*
PLAY MUSIC: **madwewechige** *vai;* play music for s.o. **madwewetaw** *vta, also* **madwewetamaw**
PLAY POOL: **nemaabii** *vai*
PLAY SHINNY: **bapasikawe** *vai*
PLAY THE DISH GAME: **bagese** *vai*
PLAY THE FLUTE: **bibigwe** *vai*
PLAY THE MOCCASIN GAME: **makizinataage** *vai;* they play the moccasin game with each other **makizinataadiwag /makizinataadi-/** *vai*
PLAY WITH: play with s.o. **wiiji'** *vta*

PLAYING CARD
PLAYING CARD: **ataadiwin, -ag** *na*

PLAYTHING
PLAYTHING: **odaminwaagan, -an** *ni*

PLEASE
PLEASE: please s.o. **zhoobi'** *vta;* please! **daga** *pc*

PLIERS
PLIERS: **dakwanjigan, -an** *ni*

PLOW
PLOW: **biigwakamigibijigan, -ag** *na;* **biigwakamigibijige** *vai;* plow s.t. **biigwakamigibidoon** *vti2*

PLUCK
PLUCK: pluck s.o. (e.g., a bird) **bashkobizh /bashkobiN-/** *vta;* pluck s.t. **bakwajibidoon** *vti2;* pluck s.t. (as a plant) **bashkwashkibidoon** *vti2*

PLUG
PLUG: **gibaakwa'igan, -an** *ni;* plug s.o. **giba' /giba'w-/** *vta;* plug s.t. **giba'an** *vti;* plug things **giba'ige** *vai;* **gibaakwa'ige** *vai*

PLUGGED
PLUGGED: be plugged **giba'igaade, giba'igaademagad** *vii;* **giba'igaazo** *vai*

PLUM
PLUM: **bagesaan, -ag** *na*

PLUM BUSH
PLUM BUSH: **bagesaaniminagaawanzh, -iig**
na
PLUM TREE
PLUM TREE: **bagesaanaatig, -oog** *na*
PNEUMONIA
HAVE PNEUMONIA: **gichi-gizhizo** *vai*
POCKET
POCKET: **mashkimodegwaajigan, -an** *ni*
POINT
POINT A CERTAIN WAY: point to s.o. a
certain way **izhinoo'** *vta;* point to s.t. a cer-
tain way **izhinoo'an** *vti;* point to (s.t.) for
s.o. **izhinoo'amaw** *vta*
POINT WITH LIPS: point a certain way with
lips **izhidooneni** *vai;* point s.o. out with
lips **izhidoonem** *vta;* point (s.t.) out to s.o.
with lips **izhidoonetaw** *vta*
POINT
POINT: point of land **neyaashi, -wan** *ni;* there
is a point of land **neyaashiiwan** *vii*
GO OVER A POINT: **gakiiwe** *vai*
POINTED
POINTED: be pointed **bajiishkaa,
bajiishkaamagad** *vii;* **bajiishkizi** *vai*
CHOP POINTED: chop s.o. pointed
bajiishkiga' /bajiishkiga'w-/ *vta;* chop s.t.
pointed **bajiishkiga'an** *vti*
POISON
POISON: **maji-mashkiki, -wan** *ni*
POKER
POKER: fire poker **jiichiishkinzhe'igan, -an** *ni*
POLE
POLE: pole s.t. **gaandakii'an** *vti*
LIGHT POLE: **waazakonenjiganaatig, -oon**
ni
POLE A BOAT: **gaandakii'ige** *vai;*
gaandakii'o *vai*
POLE A BOAT ALONG: **bima'oodoo** *vai;*
bima'ookii *vai*
POLE A BOAT TO A CERTAIN PLACE:
ina'oodoo *vai*
POLE IN A BOAT: pole s.t. along in a boat
bima'oodoon *vti2;* pole s.o. along in a
boat **bima'oozh** /bima'ooN-/ *vta*
POLE LOGS: **gaanjweba'ige** *vai*
POLICE CAR
POLICE CAR: **dakoniwewidaabaan, -ag** *na*
POLICE STATION
POLICE STATION: **dakoniwewigamig,
-oon** *ni*
POLICEMAN
POLICEMAN: **dakoniwewinini, -wag** *na*
POLISH
POLISH: polish s.o. **waasikwa'** *vta;* polish s.t.
waasikwa'an *vti*
POLITICS
IN POLITICS: be in politics **dibaakonige** *vai*
POND
POND: be a pond **waanzhibiiyaa,
waanzhibiiyaamagad** *vii*
PONDER
PONDER: **maaminonendam** *vai2*

POOL
PLAY POOL: **nemaabii** *vai*
POOL HALL
POOL HALL: **nemaabiiwigamig, -oon** *ni*
POOR
POOR: be poor **gidimaagizi** *vai;* **inigaazi** *vai*
LOOK POOR: **gidimaaginaagozi** *vai;*
gidimaaginaagwad *vii*
POOR HEALTH
IN POOR HEALTH: be in poor health
maanamanji'o *vai;* **maazhi-ayaa** *vai*
POOR JOB
POOR JOB: do a poor job **mamaazhii** *vai*
POORLY
RUN POORLY: run poorly (e.g., a car)
maazhibizo *vai;* run poorly (e.g., a ma-
chine) **maazhibide, maazhibidemagad** *vii*
POPLAR
POPLAR: **azaadi, -wag** *na*
BALSAM POPLAR: **maanazaadi, -wag** *na*
PORCUPINE
PORCUPINE: **gaag, -wag** *na*
PORK
PORK: **gookoosh, -ag** *na;* **gookooshi-wiiyaas**
ni
SALT PORK: **zhiiwitaagani-gookoosh** *na*
PORTAGE
PORTAGE: **gakiiwe** *vai*
CARRY OVER A PORTAGE: carry things
over a portage **gakiiwenige** *vai*
POSSESSED
POSSESSED: be possessed by an evil spirit
maji-manidoowaadizi *vai*
POST
POST: post s.t. up **agwaakwa'an** *vti*
POST OFFICE
POST OFFICE: **mazina'iganiiwigamig, -oon**
ni
POSTAGE STAMP
POSTAGE STAMP: **oshtigwaanens, -an** *ni*
POSTER
POSTER: **agwaakwa'igan, -an** *ni*
POSTMAN
POSTMAN: **mazina'iganiiwinini, -wag** *na*
POSTURE
HAVE GOOD POSTURE: **gwayakogaabawi**
vai
POT
POT: **akik, -oog** *na*
COOKING POT: **jiibaakwewakik, -oog** *na*
POT LID
POT LID: **gibaabowe'igan, -an** *ni*
POT SCRUBBER
POT SCRUBBER: **mimigwaabika'igan, -an**
ni
POTATO
POTATO: **opin, -iig** *na*
WILD POTATO: **bagwajipin, -iig** *na, also*
bagwaji-opin
POTAWATOMI
POTAWATOMI: **boodewaadamii, -g** *na*

POTBELLY
POTBELLY: have a potbelly **bikonagizhii** *vai*
POTHOLDER
POTHOLDER: **apaabikinigan, -an** *ni*
POTHOLE
POTHOLE: be a pothole of water
waanzhibiiyaa, waanzhibiiyaamagad *vii*
POUND
POUND IN: pound s.o. in **ginjida' /ginjida'w-/**
vta; pound s.t. in **ginjida'an** *vti*
POUND ON DRUM: **baaga'akokwe** *vai*
POUND
CERTAIN NUMBER OF POUNDS: a
certain number of pounds **daso-
dibaabiishkoojigan** *pc*
POUR
POUR: pour s.t. **ziiginan** *vti;* pour things
ziiginige *vai*
POUR ON: pour liquid on s.o. **ziiga'andaw**
vta; pour liquid on s.t. **ziiga'andan** *vti*
POUR OUT: **ziigise, ziigisemagad** *vii*
POUT
POUT: **mindawe** *vai*
POWDER
FACE POWDER: **waabishkiingwechigan** *ni*
POWER
HAVE POWER: **gashki'ewizi** *vai*
POWERED
POWERED: **waasamoo-** *pv4*
PRACTICE
PRACTICE RIDING: practice riding on
horseback **gagwedoomigo** *vai*
PRACTICE SHOOTING: **gagweda'aakwe**
vai
PRACTICE SINGING: **goji-nagamo** *vai*
PRAIRIE
PRAIRIE: **mashkode, -n** *ni*
PRAIRIE CHICKEN
PRAIRIE CHICKEN: **aagask, -wag** *na*
PRAY
PRAY: **anami'aa** *vai;* pray for s.o.
anama'etaw *vta*
PRAYER BOOK
PRAYER BOOK: **anama'e-mazina'igan, -an**
ni
PREACH
PREACH: **gagiikwe** *vai;* preach to s.o.
gagiikim *vta*
PREACHER
PREACHER: **gagiikwewinini, -wag** *na*
PREACHING
EDUCATION BY PREACHING AND EX-
HORTATION: **gagiikimaawasowin** *ni*
PREGNANT
PREGNANT: be pregnant **anjiko** *vai;*
bimiwijige *vai;* **gigishkawaawaso** *vai;*
gigishkaajige *vai;* be pregnant with s.o.
gigishkaw *vta*
PREOCCUPIED
PREOCCUPIED: be preoccupied
ondamendam *vai2;* be preoccupied with

s.o. **ondamenim** *vta;* be preoccupied with
s.t. **ondamendan** *vti*
PREPARE
PREPARE: **ozhiitaa** *vai*
PRESERVES
PRESERVES: **baashkiminasigan, -an** *ni*
PRESS
PRESS: press on s.o. **maagon** *vta;* press on s.t.
maagonan *vti*
PRETTY
PRETTY: be pretty **onizhishi** *vai;* **onizhishin**
vii
MADE PRETTY: be made pretty
wawezhichigaade,
wawezhichigaademagad *vii*
PREVAIL
PREVAIL: prevail over s.o. **gashki'** *vta;*
mamaazhi' *vta;* prevail over s.t.
mamaazhitoon *vti2*
PREVENT
PREVENT: prevent s.o. (from doing some-
thing) **nanagin** *vta*
PREVIOUSLY
PREVIOUSLY: **gayat** *pc*
PRICE
CHARGE A HIGH PRICE: **ishpagindaaso**
vai; charge a high price for s.t.
ishpagindan *vti*
HAVE A CERTAIN PRICE: **inaginde,**
inagindemagad *vii;* **inaginzo** *vai*
HAVE A PRICE OF A CERTAIN HEIGHT:
apiitaginde, apiitagindemagad *vii;*
apiitaginzo *vai*
SET A CERTAIN PRICE: set a certain price
on s.o. **inagim** *vta;* set a certain price on
s.t. **inagindan** *vti;* set a certain price on
(s.t.) for s.o. **inagindamaw** *vta*
SET A PRICE: **onagindaaso** *vai;* set a price
on s.o. **onagim** *vta;* set a price on s.t.
onagindan *vti*
SET A PRICE OF A CERTAIN HEIGHT:
set a price of a certain height on s.o.
apiitagim *vta;* set a price of a certain
height on s.t. **apiitagindan** *vti*
PRICK
PRICK: prick s.o. **badaka' /badaka'w-/** *vta;*
prick s.t. **badaka'an** *vti;* prick things
badaka'ige *vai*
PRICKED
GET PRICKED: **badakijin** *vai*
PRIEST
PRIEST: **mekadewikonayed** *na-pt;*
mekadewikonayewinini, -wag *na*
PRINCESS
PRINCESS: **ogimaakwens, -ag** *na*
PRINTED
PRINTED A CERTAIN WAY: be printed a
certain way **izhisin** *vii*
PRISON
PRISON: **gibaakwa'odiiwigamig, -oon** *ni*
PRISONER
PRISONER: **gebaakwa'ond** *na-pt*

PRIVY
PRIVY: **zaaga'amoowigamig, -oon** *ni*
PROGRESS
IN PROGRESS: **ani-** *pv2, also* **ni-**
PROHIBITION
PROHIBITION: there is a prohibition
gina'amaadim *vii*
PROJECT
PROJECT: **anokaajigan, -an** *ni*
PROJECTOR
MOVIE PROJECTOR: **mazinaatewebinigan,
-an** *ni*
PROMISE
PROMISE: promise (s.t.) to s.o.
waawiindamaw *vta;* promise (s.t.) to
people **waawiindamaage** *vai*
PROP
PROP UP TO BE A LEVEL SURFACE: prop
s.t. up to be a level surface **desa'an** *vti*
PROPER
LIVE A PROPER LIFE: **gwayako-bimaadizi**
vai
PROPERLY
PROPERLY: **wawiinge** *pc;* **weweni** *pc*
PROPERTY
PROPERTY: **daniwin, -an** *ni*
PROTECT
PROTECT YOUNG: protect one's young
gizhaawaso *vai*
PROTECTION
LAY SOMETHING FOR PROTECTION:
lay something on or under s.t. for protec-
tion **apisidoon** *vti2*
PROUD
PROUD: be proud **ishpenimo** *vai;* be proud
of oneself **apiitenimo** *vai*
PROUD THOUGHTS: have proud thoughts
maminaadendam *vai2*
PROUD TO A CERTAIN EXTENT: be
proud of s.o. to a certain extent **apiitenim**
vta; be proud of s.t. to a certain extent
apiitendan *vti*
PUBIC HAIR
PUBIC HAIR: my pubic hair **nimiishigwaan,
-an** */-miishigwaan-/ nid*
PUDDLE
PUDDLE: be a puddle **waanzhibiiyaa,
waanzhibiiyaamagad** *vii*
PULL
PULL: pull s.o. **wiikobizh** */wiikobiN-/ vta;*
pull s.o. (as with something string-like)
wiikwaabiigin *vta;* pull s.t. **wiikobidoon**
vti2; pull s.t. (as with something string-
like) **wiikwaabiiginan** *vti;* pull (s.t.) for s.o.
wiikobidaw *vta;* pull things **wiikobijige** *vai*
PULL APART TO FORM A GAP: pull s.o.
apart to form a gap **dawibizh** */dawibiN-/
vta;* pull s.t. apart to form a gap
dawibidoon *vti2;* pull things apart to form
a gap **dawibijige** *vai*
PULL ASHORE: pull s.o. ashore **agwaabizh**
/agwaabiN-/ vta; pull s.t. ashore
agwaabidoon *vti2*

PULL BACK: pull s.o. back **azhebizh**
/azhebiN-/ vta; pull s.t. back **azhebidoon**
vti2
PULL DOWN: pull s.o. down **niisibizh**
/niisibiN-/ vta; pull s.t. down **niisibidoon**
vti2
PULL DOWN WITH HANDS: pull s.o.
down with hands **gawiwebin** *vta;* pull s.t.
down with hands **gawiwebinan** *vti*
PULL FREE: pull s.o. free **gidiskibizh**
/gidiskibiN-/ vta; pull s.t. free
gidiskibidoon *vti2*
PULL FROM THE WATER: pull s.o. from
the water **agwaabizh** */agwaabiN-/ vta;* pull
s.t. from the water **agwaabidoon** *vti2*
PULL IN TWO: pull s.o. in two **bookobizh**
/bookobiN-/ vta; pull s.t. in two
bookobidoon *vti2*
PULL INTO PARTICLES: pull s.o. into particles **biisibizh** */biisibiN-/ vta;* pull s.t. into
particles **biisibidoon** *vti2*
PULL OFF: pull s.o. off **gijibizh** */gijibiN-/ vta;*
pull s.t. off **gijibidoon** *vti;* **giichigobidoon**
vti2; **giichigobizh** */giichigobiN-/ vta*
PULL OFF WITH TEETH: pull s.o. off with
teeth **giichigwam** *vta;* pull s.t. off with
teeth **giichigwandan** *vti*
PULL SHUT: pull s.t. shut (as something
stick- or wood-like) **gibaakobidoon** *vti2*
PULL STRAIGHT: pull s.o. straight
gwayakobizh */gwayakobiN-/ vta;* pull s.t.
straight **gwayakobidoon** *vti2*
PULL UP: pull s.t. up **bakwajibidoon** *vti2*
PULLED
PULLED: be pulled **wiikobijigaade,
wiikobijigaademagad** *vii;* **wiikobijigaazo**
vai
PUMP
PUMP: **wiikwa'ibaan, -an** *ni*
PUMP WATER: **wiikwa'ibii** *vai*
TIRE PUMP: **boodaajii'igan, -an** *ni*
PUMPKIN
PUMPKIN: **okosimaan, -an** *ni;*
ozaawikosimaan, -an *ni*
PUNK
PUNK: **zagataagan, -ag** *na*
PUPPY
PUPPY: **animoons, -ag** *na*
PURSE
PURSE: **zhooniyaa-mashkimod, -an** *ni, also*
zhooniyaa-mashkimodens
PUS
PUS: **mini** */miny-/ ni*
PUSH
PUSH: push s.o. **gaandin** *vta;* push s.t.
gaandinan *vti;* push (s.t.) for s.o.
gaandinamaw *vta;* push things **gaandinige**
vai
PUSH WITH A STICK: push s.o. with a stick
gaanjida' */gaanjida'w-/ vta;* push s.t. with
a stick **gaanjida'an** *vti;* push things with a
stick **gaanjida'ige** *vai*

PUSH WITH FOOT OR BODY: push s.o.
with foot or body **gaanzikaw** *vta;* push s.t.
with foot or body **gaanzikan** *vti*
PUSH POLE
PUSH POLE: **gaandakii'iganaak, -oon** *ni,*
also **gaandakii'iganaatig**
PUT
PUT ALONG: put s.o. along (as something
stick- or wood-like) **bimaakoshim** *vta;* put
s.t. along (as something stick- or wood-
like) **bimaakosidoon** *vti2*
PUT AWAY: be put away **zagakinigaade,
zagakinigaademagad** *vii;* **zagakinigaazo**
vai; put s.o. away **nanaa'in** *vta;* **zagakin**
vta; put s.t. away **nanaa'inan** *vti;*
zagakinan *vti;* put things away **zagakinige**
vai
PUT HEAD A CERTAIN WAY: put one's
head a certain way **inikweni** *vai*
PUT IN: be put in **biina'igaade,
biina'igaademagad** *vii;* **biina'igaazo** *vai;*
put s.o. in **biina' /biina'w-/** *vta;* put s.t. in
biina'an *vti*
PUT IN A CERTAIN PLACE: be put in a
certain place **achigaade, achigaademagad**
vii; **achigaazo** *vai;* put s.o. in a certain
place **ashi /aS-/** *vta;* put s.t. in a certain
place **atoon** *vti2;* put (s.t.) in a certain
place for s.o. **ataw** *vta;* put things in a
certain place **achige** *vai*
PUT IN A TIGHT PLACE: put s.o. in a tight
place **zhegoshim** *vta;* put s.t. in a tight
place **zhegosidoon** *vti2*
PUT IN MOUTH: put (something) in one's
mouth **zhakamo** *vai;* put s.o. in one's
mouth **agwanem** *vta;* put s.t. in one's
mouth **agwanendan** *vti;* put things in
one's mouth **agwanenjige** *vai*
PUT IN ORDER: put s.o. in order **nanaa'in**
vta; **onin** *vta;* **zagakishim** *vta;* put s.t. in
order **nanaa'inan** *vti;* **oninan** *vti;*
zagakisidoon *vti2;* put things in order
zagakisijige *vti;* **na'isijige** *vai;* **oninige** *vai*
PUT IN THE KETTLE: put (s.t.) in the
kettle **boodaakwe** *vai+o*
PUT IN THE RIGHT POSITION: put s.o. in
the right position **minoshim** *vta;* put s.t. in
the right position **minosidoon** *vti2*
PUT IN TO SOAK: be put in to soak
agonjijigaade, agonjijigaademagad *vii;*
agonjijigaazo *vai;* put s.o. in to soak
agonjim *vta;* put s.t. in to soak **agonjidoon**
vti2
PUT IN WATER: put s.o. in water
gondaabiigin *vta;* put s.t. in water
gondaabiiginan *vti*
PUT LOOSELY: put s.o. loosely
geshawishim *vta;* put s.t. loosely
geshawisidoon *vti2*
PUT ON A ROOF: **apakwe** *vai*
PUT OUT: put s.o. out **zaagidin** *vta;* put s.t.
out **zaagidinan** *vti*
PUT OUT OF THE WAY: put s.o. out of the
way **ikoshim** *vta;* put s.t. out of the way
ikosidoon *vti2*

PUT THROUGH: put s.o. through **zhaabon**
vta; put s.t. through **zhaabonan** *vti*
PUT TOUCHING: put s.o. touching
daangishim *vta;* put s.t. touching
daangisidoon *vti2*
PUT TURNED: put s.o. turned **gwekishim**
vta; put s.t. turned **gwekisidoon** *vti2*
PUT UNDER THE GROUND: put s.o.
under the ground **ningwakamigin** *vta*
PUT WOOD ON THE FIRE: **bagidinise** *vai*
PUT ON
PUT ON: put s.t. on (e.g., clothes) **biizikan**
vti; put s.o. on (e.g., clothes) **biizikaw** *vta*
PUT ON CLOTHES: put on one's clothes
biizikonaye *vai*
PUT ON COAT: put on one's coat
biichibabiinzikawaagane *vai*
PUT ON DRESS: put on one's dress
biitagoode *vai*
PUT ON HAT: put on one's hat
biichiwakwaane *vai*
PUT ON MITTENS: put on one's mittens
biichiminjikaawane *vai*
PUT ON MOCCASINS: put on one's
moccasins **babiichii** *vai*
PUT ON PANTS: put on one's pants
biichigiboodiyegwaazone *vai*
PUT ON SHIRT: put on one's shirt
biichibabagiwayaane *vai*
PUT ON SHOES: put on one's shoes
babiichii *vai*
PUT ON SOCKS: put on one's socks
biitazhigane *vai*
PUT OUT
PUT OUT: put s.t. out (e.g., fire or light)
aate'an *vti*
PUT OUT A FIRE: put out a fire on s.o. with
hands **aatebizh /aatebiN-/** *vta*
PUT OUT QUICKLY: put s.t. out quickly
(e.g., fire or light) **aatewebinan** *vti*
PUTTY
PUTTY: **bigiike** *vai;* putty s.t. **bigiikaadan** *vti*

Q

QUARREL
QUARREL: quarrel with s.o. **giikaam** *vta;*
they quarrel with each other **giikaandiwag**
/giikaandi-/ *vai*
QUEEN
QUEEN: **ogimaakwe, -g** *na;* queen (card)
ikwe, -wag *na*
QUESTION
YES-NO QUESTION: *yes-no question word* **ina**
pc, also **na**
QUICK
QUICK: be quick **dadaatabii** *vai*

QUICKLY
    QUICKLY: **wewiib** *pc*
QUIET
    QUIET: **bizaan** *pc;* be quiet **bangan** *vii;*
    bekaadizi *vai;* **bizaan-ayaa** *vai, also*
    bizaani-ayaa; goshkwaawaadizi *vai*
    QUIET HOUSE: be a quiet house **bangate,**
    bangatemagad *vii*
QUIETLY
    SIT QUIETLY: **goshkwaawaadabi** *vai*
    STAND QUIETLY: **bizaanigaabawi** *vai*
QUILT
    QUILT: **maawandoogwaason, -an** *ni*
QUIT
    QUIT: quit s.o. **booni'** *vta;* quit s.t. **boonitoon**
    vti2
    QUIT WORKING: **aanizhiitam** *vai2*
QUITE
    QUITE: **aapiji** *pc*
QUIVER
    QUIVER: **jiichiibishkaa** *vai*
QUOTE
    QUOTE: quote s.o. a certain way **inootaw**
    vta; quote people **inootaage** *vai*

R

RABBIT
    RABBIT: **waabooz, -oog** *na*
    COTTONTAIL RABBIT: **manidoo-**
    waabooz, -oog *na*
    HUNT FOR RABBITS: **nandawaaboozwe**
    vai
    JACK RABBIT: **misaabooz, -oog** *na*
RABBIT SKIN
    RABBIT SKIN: **waaboozwayaan, -ag** *na*
RABBIT SOUP
    RABBIT SOUP: **waaboozwaaboo** *ni*
RACCOON
    RACCOON: **esiban, -ag** *na*
RACE
    RACE: race s.o. **gagwejikazh /gagwejikaN-/**
    vta; race people **gagwejikazhiwe** *vai;* they
    race each other **gagwejikanidiwag**
    /gagwejikanidi-/ *vai*
    RACE IN BOATS: race s.o. in boats
    gagwejikada' /gagwejikada'w-/ *vta;* they
    race each other in boats
    gagwejikada'odiwag /gagwejikada'odi-/
    vai
RACE CAR
    RACE CAR: **gagwejikazhiwewidaabaan, -ag**
    na
RACK
    HANGING RACK FOR FOOD DRYING:
    agoojiwanaanaak, -oon *ni*

RADIO
    RADIO: **bizindamowin, -an** *ni;* **bizindamoo-**
    makak, -oon *ni*
RADISH
    RADISH: **wiisagi-jiisens, -an** *ni*
RAFTER
    RAFTER: **abanzh, -iin** *ni*
RAIN
    RAIN: **gimiwan** *vii*
    COLD RAIN: be cold rain **dakibiisaa,**
    dakibiisaamagad *vii*
    RAIN COMES: **biijibiisaa, biijibiisaamagad**
    vii
    RAIN GOES ALONG: **bimibiisaa,**
    bimibiisaamagad *vii*
    RAIN GOES AWAY: **animibiisaa,**
    animibiisaamagad *vii*
    RAIN IS HEARD: **madwebiisaa,**
    madwebiisaamagad *vii*
    RAIN IS ON THE WAY: **bagamibiisaa,**
    bagamibiisaamagad *vii*
    SPRINKLING RAIN: be sprinkling rain
    awanibiisaa, awanibiisaamagad *vii*
    START TO RAIN: **maajibiisaa,**
    maajibiisaamagad *vii*
    STOP RAINING: **ishkwaabiisaa,**
    ishkwaabiisaamagad *vii*
RAINBOW
    RAINBOW: **nagweyaab, -iin** *ni*
RAINCOAT
    RAINCOAT: **gimiwanoowayaan, -an** *ni*
RAISE
    RAISE: raise s.o. (e.g., a child) **nitaawigi'** *vta;*
    raise s.t. **nitaawigitoon** (e.g., a crop) *vti2*
    RAISE USING SOMETHING: raise s.o. (as
    or as with something stick- or wood-like)
    ombaakwa' /ombaakwa'w-/ *vta;* raise s.t.
    (as or as with something stick- or wood-
    like) **ombaakwa'an** *vti*
RAISIN
    RAISIN: **zhoominens, -an** *ni*
RAKE
    RAKE: **binaakwe'igan, -an** *ni;*
    jiishakamiga'igan, -an *ni;* rake things
    binaakwe'ige *vai*
RANCID
    SMELL RANCID: **zaatemaagozi** *vai;*
    zaatemaagwad *vii*
    TASTE RANCID: **zaatepogozi** *vai;*
    zaatepogwad *vii*
    TURN RANCID: **zaateshin** *vai;* **zaatesin** *vii*
RANK
    AT A CERTAIN RANK: be at a certain rank
    apiitendaagozi *vai;* **apiitendaagwad** *vii*
RASP
    RASP: **zisiboojigan, -an** *ni*
RASPBERRY
    RASPBERRY: **miskomin, -ag** *na*
RATHER
    RATHER: **indawaaj** *pc*
RATIONS
    RATIONS: **ashandiwin, -an** *ni*

RATTLE
    RATTLE: **zhiishiigwan, -ag** *na*

RATTLESNAKE
    RATTLESNAKE: **zhiishiigwe, -g** *na*

RAVEN
    RAVEN: **gaagaagiw, -ag** *na, also* **gaagaagi***

RAW
    RAW: **ashki-** *pv4*
    RAW MEAT: be raw (as meat) **ashkin** *vii;* **ashkini** *vai*

RAZOR
    RAZOR: **gaashkibaajigan, -an** *ni*

REACH
    REACH: reach s.o. **odish /odiS-/** *vta;* reach s.t. **oditan** *vti*

READ
    READ: **agindaaso** *vai;* be read **aginjigaade, aginjigaademagad** *vii;* read s.t. **agindan** *vti;* read (s.t.) for s.o. **agindamaw** *vta;* read (s.t.) for people **agindamaage** *vai*

READY
    GET READY: **ozhiitaa** *vai*

REAL
    REAL: **enda-** *pv4*

REALIZE
    REALIZE: realize of s.o. that **maaminonenim** *vta;* realize of s.t. that **maaminonendan** *vti*

REALLY
    REALLY: **geget** *pc;* **enda-** *pv4*

REAR END
    REAR END: my rear end **indiy /-diy-/** *nid, also* **indiyaash**
    LIE WITH REAR END STICKING OUT: lie with one's rear end sticking out **jaangidiyeshin** *vai*

REASON
    FOR A CERTAIN REASON: **onji-** *pv3*

RECENTLY
    RECENTLY: **bijiinag** *pc;* **noomaya** *pc*

RECOGNIZE
    RECOGNIZE: recognize s.o. **aawekaazh /aawekaaN-/** *vta;* **aawenim** *vta;* recognize s.t. **aawendan** *vti;* they recognize each other **nisidawinaadiwag /nisidawinaadi-/** *vai*
    RECOGNIZE BY SIGHT: recognize s.o. by sight **aawenaw** *vta;* **nisidawinaw** *vta;* recognize s.t. by sight **aawenan** *vti;* **nisidawinan** *vti*
    RECOGNIZE BY SMELL: recognize s.o. by smell **nisidomaam** *vta;* recognize s.t. by smell **nisidomaandan** *vti*
    RECOGNIZE BY SOUND: recognize s.o. by sound **aawetaw** *vta;* **nisidotaw** *vta;* recognize s.t. by sound **aawetan** *vti;* **nisidotan** *vti*

RECOLLECT
    RECOLLECT: **mikwendam** *vai2;* recollect s.o. **mikwenim** *vta;* recollect s.t. **mikwendan** *vti*

RECOLLECTED
    RECOLLECTED: be recollected **mikwendaagozi** *vai;* **mikwendaagwad** *vii*

RECORD PLAYER
    RECORD PLAYER: **gaagiigidoo-makakoons, -an** *ni;* **nagamoo-makak, -oon** *ni*

RECOVER
    RECOVER FROM AN ILLNESS: **noojimo** *vai*

RECREATION BUILDING
    RECREATION BUILDING: **odaminoowigamig, -oon** *ni*

RECTUM
    RECTUM: my rectum **injiid, -iin /-jiidy-/** *nid, also* **injiidiish**

RED
    RED: **misko-** *pv4;* be red **miskozi** *vai;* **miskwaa, miskwaamagad** *vii;* be red (as something mineral) **miskwaabikad** *vii;* **miskwaabikizi** *vai;* be red (as something sheet-like) **miskwegad** *vii;* **miskwegizi** *vai;* be red (as something stick- or wood-like) **miskwaakozi** *vai;* **miskwaakwad** *vii;* be red (as something string-like) **miskwaabiigad** *vii;* **miskwaabiigizi** *vai*
    COLORED RED: be colored red **miskwaande, miskwaandemagad** *vii;* **miskwaanzo** *vai*
    DRESS IN RED: **miskwaakonaye** *vai*
    RED CHEEK: have a red cheek **miskwanowe** *vai*
    RED CLOUDS: be red clouds **miskwaanakwad** *vii*
    RED LEAVES: have red leaves **miskobagizi** *vai;* there are red leaves on the trees **miskobagaa, miskobagaamagad** *vii*
    RED NOSE: have a red nose **miskojaane** *vai*
    WEAR RED: **misko'o** *vai*

RED CEDAR
    RED CEDAR: **miskwaawaak, -oog** *na*

RED LAKE
    RED LAKE: Red Lake Reservation **Miskwaagamiiwi-zaaga'iganiing** *place*

RED OSIER
    RED OSIER: red osier (locally known as dogwood) **miskwaabiimizh, -iig** *na*

RED SQUIRREL
    RED SQUIRREL: **ajidamoo, -g** *na*

RED-HEADED
    RED-HEADED: be red-headed **miskondibe** *vai*

RED-HEADED WOODPECKER
    RED-HEADED WOODPECKER: **meme, -g** *na*

RED-HOT
    RED-HOT: be red-hot (as something mineral) **miskwaabikide, miskwaabikidemagad** *vii;* **miskwaabikizo** *vai*

REDHORSE
    REDHORSE: redhorse (fish) **meskwaazhigwaneshi, -wag** *na*

REDUCE
    REDUCE TO NOTHING: reduce s.o. to nothing **ango'** *vta;* reduce s.t. to nothing **angotoon** *vti2*

REED
REED: anaakanashk, -oon *ni;*
gichigamiiwashk, -oon *ni*
REFLECT
REFLECT: reflect (as something mineral)
waasaabikide, waasaabikidemagad *vii;*
waasaabikizo *vai*
REFLECT IN WATER: ojichaagobiishin *vii;*
ojichaagobiisin *vii*
REFRIGERATOR
REFRIGERATOR: dakisijigan, -an *ni;*
mikwamii-makak, -oon *ni*
REGARD
REGARD TO A CERTAIN DEGREE: regard
s.t. to a certain degree **apiitendan** *vti*
REGRETS
REGRETS: have regrets **minjinawezi** *vai*
REINDEER
REINDEER: adik, -wag *na*
REJECT
REJECT: reject s.o. **aanawenim** *vta;* reject s.t.
aanawendan *vti;* reject things
aanawenjige *vai*
REJECTED
REJECTED: be rejected **aanawendaagozi** *vai;*
aanawendaagwad *vii*
RELATED
RELATED: be related to s.o. **inawem** *vta;*
they are related to each other **inawendiwag**
/inawendi-/ *vai*
RELAXED
RELAXED: be relaxed **neshangishin** *vai*
RELEASE
RELEASE: release s.o. **bagidin** *vta;* release s.t.
bagidinan *vti;* release (s.t.) to s.o.
bagidinamaw *vta;* release things
bagidinige *vai*
RELEASE FROM MIND: release s.o. from
one's mind **bagidenim** *vta;* release s.t.
from one's mind **bagidendan** *vti;* release
things from one's mind **bagidenjige** *vai*
RELEASE QUICKLY: release s.o. quickly
bagijwebin *vta;* release s.t. quickly
bagijwebinan *vti*
RELEASED
RELEASED: be released **bagidinigaade,**
bagidinigaademagad *vii;* **bagidinigaazo**
vai
RELIGION
PRACTICE A CERTAIN RELIGION:
izhitwaa *vai*
RELY
RELY ON: rely on (s.t.) **apenimo** *vai+o*
REMAIN
REMAIN TRANQUILLY IN PLACE:
goshkwaawaadabi *vai*
REMEMBER
REMEMBER: mikwendam *vai2;* remember
s.o. **mikwenim** *vta;* **minjimenim** *vta;* remember s.t. **mikwendan** *vti;*
minjimendan *vti*

TRY TO REMEMBER: try to remember s.o.
nanda-mikwenim *vta;* try to remember s.t.
nanda-mikwendan *vti*
VAGUELY REMEMBER: gezikwendam
vai2; vaguely remember s.o. **gezikwenim**
vta; vaguely remember s.t. **gezikwendan**
vti
REMEMBERED
REMEMBERED: be remembered
mikwendaagozi *vai;* **mikwendaagwad** *vii*
REMOVE
REMOVE USING SOMETHING: remove
s.o. using something **gida' /gida'w-/** *vta;*
remove s.t. using something **gida'an** *vti*
REMOVE WITH HANDS: remove s.o. with
hands **gijibizh /gijibiN-/** *vta;* remove s.t.
with hands **gijibidoon** *vti*
REMOVE WITH SOMETHING SHARP:
remove s.o. with something sharp
gijigwaazh /gijigwaaN-/ *vta;* remove s.t.
with something sharp **gijigwaadan** *vti*
RENT
RENT: rent (s.t.) from people **adaawange**
vai+o; rent (s.t.) from s.o. **adaawam** *vta;*
rent (s.t.) to people **awi'iwe** *vai*
REPAIR
REPAIR: repair s.t. **nanaa'itoon** *vti2;* repair
(s.t.) for s.o. **nanaa'itaw** *vta, also*
nanaa'itamaw; repair things **nanaa'ichige**
vai
REPAIR A CAR: nanaa'idaabaane *vai*
REPAIR GARAGE
REPAIR GARAGE: odaabaanikewigamig,
-oon *ni*
REPEAT
REPEAT: repeat what s.o. says **naabinootaw**
vta; repeat what people say **naabinootaage**
vai
REPLY
REPLY: reply to s.o. **nakom** *vta;* they reply to
each other **nakondiwag /nakondi-/** *vai*
REPORT
REPORT: dadibaajimo *vai;* report what
people say **inootaage** *vai*
REPRESENTATIVE
REPRESENTATIVE: giigidoowinini, -wag
na
REPRIMAND
REPRIMAND: reprimand s.o. **aanimim** *vta*
RESERVATION
RESERVATION: ishkonigan, -an *ni*
RESERVE
RESERVE: reserve s.o. **ishkon** *vta;* reserve s.t.
ishkonan *vti;* reserve (s.t.) for s.o.
ishkonamaw *vta*
RESERVED
RESERVED: be reserved **ishkonigaade,**
ishkonigaademagad *vii;* **ishkonigaazo** *vai*
RESIDENCE
MOVE RESIDENCE: move one's residence
gozi *vai*
MOVE RESIDENCE ABOUT: move one's
residence about **babaamigozi** *vai*

MOVE TO A NEW RESIDENCE: **aanji-gozi** *vai*

RESORT
RESORT: **niibinishiiwigamig, -oon** *ni*

RESOUND
RESOUND: **baswewe** *vai;* **baswewe, baswewemagad** *vii*

RESPECTED
RESPECTED: be respected **minwaabamewizi** *vai*

RESPIRATION
HAVE FAST RESPIRATION: **dadaatabanaamo** *vai*

RESPIRATORY
HAVE A RESPIRATORY ILLNESS: **ozosodamwaapine** *vai*

REST
REST: **anwebi** *vai*
REST LYING DOWN: **anweshin** *vai*

RESTAURANT
RESTAURANT: **wiisiniiwigamig, -oon** *ni*

RETURN
RETURN: **azhegiiwe** *vai;* **giiwe** *vai;* return s.o. **azhen** *vta;* return s.t. **azhenan** *vti;* return (s.t.) to s.o. **azhenamaw** *vta;* return (s.t.) to people **azhenamaage** *vai*
RETURN TO OWN COUNTRY: return to one's own country **giiwekii** *vai*
THINK ABOUT RETURNING: **giiweyendam** *vai2*

REVEAL
REVEAL: reveal s.o. **naago'** *vta;* reveal s.t. **naagotoon** *vti2*

REVIVE
REVIVE: **aabaakawad** *vii;* **aabaakawizi** *vai;* **aabijiibaa** *vai;* revive s.o. **aabaakawi'** *vta*

REVOLVE
REVOLVE: **gizhibaabide, gizhibaabidemagad** *vii;* **gizhibaabise** *vai;* **gizhibaabise, gizhibaabisemagad** *vii;* **gizhibaabizo** *vai*

RHEUMATISM
RHEUMATISM: have rheumatism **okanaapine** *vai*

RHUBARB
RHUBARB: **zhiiwibag, -oon** *ni*

RIB
RIB: my rib **nipigemag, -oon** */-pigemagw-/ nid*
CANOE RIB: **waaginaa, -g** *na*

RIBBON
RIBBON: **zenibaanh, -yag** *na*

RICE
MAKE RICE: **manoominike** *vai*
WHITE RICE: **waabi-manoomin** *ni*
WILD RICE: **manoomin** *ni, also* **anishinaabe-manoomin**

RICE BAG
RICE BAG: **manoomini-mashkimod, -an** *ni;* **manoominiwazh, -an** *ni*

RICE BIRD
RICE BIRD: **manoominikeshiinh, -yag** *na*

RICE KNOCKER
RICE KNOCKER: rice knocker (stick for wild rice harvesting) **bawa'iganaak, -oog** *na*

RICH
RICH: be rich **dani** *vai*

RICHES
RICHES: **daniwin, -an** *ni*

RICING LICENSE
RICING LICENSE: **manoominike-mazina'igaans, -an** *ni*

RIDE
CATCH A RIDE: catch a ride with s.o. **boozinodaw** *vta*
GIVE A RIDE: give a ride to s.o. **boozi'** *vta*
PRACTICE RIDING: practice riding on horseback **gagwedoomigo** *vai*
RIDE ABOUT ON HORSEBACK: **babaamoomigo** *vai*
RIDE ALONG DRAWN BY HORSES: **bimiba'igo** *vai*
RIDE ALONG ON HORSEBACK: **bimoomigo** *vai*
RIDE AWAY ON HORSEBACK: **animoomigo** *vai*
RIDE FROM A CERTAIN PLACE ON HORSEBACK: **ondoomigo** *vai*
RIDE HERE ON HORSEBACK: **biidoomigo** *vai*
RIDE TO A CERTAIN PLACE ON HORSE-BACK: ride to a certain place on horseback **inoomigo** *vai*
RIDE TO A CERTAIN PLACE WITH HORSES: **apa'igo** *vai*

RIDGE
RIDGE: there is a ridge **oshedinaa, oshedinaamagad** *vii*

RIGHT
RIGHT: **gwayak** *pc;* right? **naayanh** *pc*
CONSIDER RIGHT: consider s.t. right **gwayakwendan** *vti*
CONSIDERED RIGHT: be considered right **gwayakwendaagozi** *vai;* **gwayakwendaagwad** *vii*
DO RIGHT: do things right **gwayakochige** *vai*
HEAR RIGHT: hear the right thing **gwayakotam** *vai2*
MAKE RIGHT: make things right **gwayakochige** *vai*

RIGHT ACROSS
RIGHT ACROSS: **dibishkookamig** *pc*

RIGHT AT THE TIME
RIGHT AT THE TIME: **na'idaa** *pc*

RIGHT
RIGHT HAND: right hand *usually possessed* **gichinik** *ni*

RING
RING: **madweshin** *vai;* **madwesin** *vii;* ring s.t. **madwesidoon** *vti2*

RING
RING: **didibininjiibizon, -ag** *na*

RINK
RINK: **zhooshkwaada'ewigamig, -oon** *ni*

RIP
RIP: **giishkikaa** *vai;* **giishkikaa, giishkikaamagad** *vii;* rip s.o. **biigobizh /biigobiN-/** *vta;* rip s.t. **biigobidoon** *vti2;* rip things **biigobijige** *vai*

RIP OPEN: rip s.o. **aabibizh /aabibiN-/** *vta;* rip s.t. open **aabibidoon** *vti2*

RIPE
RIPE: be ripe **atiso** *vai, also* **adiso; atite, atitemagad** *vii, also* **adite; giizhigi** *vai;* **giizhigin** *vii*

FULLY RIPE: be fully ripe **giizhaande, giizhaandemagad** *vii;* **giizhaanzo** *vai*

RIPPED
RIPPED: be ripped **biigobijigaade, biigobijigaademagad** *vii;* **biigobijigaazo** *vai*

RIPPLE
FLOW WITH A RIPPLE: **zaasijiwan** *vii*

RIPSAW
RIPSAW: **daashkiboojigan, -ag** *na*

RISE
RISE: rise (as the sun) **mooka'am** *vai2*

RIVER
RIVER: **ziibi, -wan** *ni*

BIG RIVER: **gichi-ziibi, -wan** *ni*

NARROW RIVER: be narrow (as a river) **agaasadetigweyaa, agaasadetigweyaamagad** *vii*

RIVER BRANCHES: branch (as a river) **baketigweyaa, baketigweyaamagad** *vii*

RIVER DIVIDES: divide (as a river) **baketigweyaa, baketigweyaamagad** *vii*

RIVER FLOWS ALONG: flow along (as a river) **bimitigweyaa, bimitigweyaamagad** *vii*

RIVER FLOWS AROUND A BEND: flow around a bend (as a river) **washkitigweyaa, washkitigweyaamagad** *vii*

RIVER FLOWS TO A CERTAIN PLACE: flow to a certain place (as a river) **izhitigweyaa, izhitigweyaamagad** *vii*

RIVER FORKS: fork (as a river) **niingidawitigweyaa, niingidawitigweyaamagad** *vii*

WIDE RIVER: be wide (as a river) **mangitigweyaa, mangitigweyaamagad** *vii*

ROACH HEADDRESS
ROACH HEADDRESS: **miskwaanzigan, -an** *ni*

ROAD
ROAD: **miikana, -n** *ni;* be a road **miikanaawan** *vii*

ACROSS THE ROAD: across the road or trail **agaamikana** *pc*

ALONG THE SIDE OF THE ROAD: **opimekana** *pc*

ALONGSIDE THE ROAD: **zhishwajikana** *pc*

ASPHALT ROAD: **bigii-miikana, -n** *ni*

AT THE END OF THE ROAD: at the end of the road or trail **gabekana** *pc*

BAD ROAD: be bad (as a road or trail) **maanadamon /maanadamo-/** *vii*

BY A ROAD: by a road or trail **jiigikana** *pc*

CONCRETE ROAD: **asinii-miikana, -n** *ni*

GRAVEL ROAD: **bingwii-miikana, -n** *ni*

ICY ROAD: be icy (as a road or trail) **mikwamiiwadamon /mikwamiiwadamo-/** *vii*

IN THE MIDDLE OF THE ROAD: in the middle of the road or trail **naawikana** *pc*

MAKE A ROAD: make a road or trail **miikanaake** *vai*

NARROW ROAD: be narrow (as a road or trail) **agaasademon /agaasademo-/** *vii*

ON THE OTHER SIDE OF THE ROAD: on the other side of the road or trail **agaamikana** *pc*

ON THIS SIDE OF THE ROAD: **ondaasikana** *pc*

ROAD FORKS: fork (as a road or trail) **niingidawadamon /niingidawadamo-/** *vii*

ROAD GOES ACROSS: go across (as a road or trail) **aazhoodamon /aazhoodamo-/** *vii*

ROAD GOES OFF TO THE SIDE: go off to the side (as a road or trail) **bakemon /bakemo-/** *vii*

ROAD LEADS ALONG: lead along (as a road or trail) **bimamon /bimamo-/, bimamoomagad** *vii*

ROAD LEADS FROM A CERTAIN PLACE: lead from a certain place (as a road or trail) **ondadamon /ondadamo-/** *vii*

ROAD LEADS TO A CERTAIN PLACE: lead to a certain place (as a road or trail) **inamon /inamo-/** *vii*

SLIPPERY ROAD: be slippery (as a road or trail) **ozhaashadamon /ozhaashadamo-/** *vii;* **zhooshkwadamon /zhooshkwadamo-/** *vii;* be slippery with ice (as a road or trail) **ozhaashikwadamon /ozhaashikwadamo-/** *vii*

WET ROAD: be wet (as a road or trail) **nibiiwadamon /nibiiwadamo-/** *vii*

WIDE ROAD: be wide (as a road or trail) **mangademon /mangademo-/** *vii, also* **mangadademon**

ROAD WORKER
ROAD WORKER: **miikanaakewinini, -wag** *na*

ROAR
ROAR: roar (as waves) **mamadweyaashkaa, mamadweyaashkaamagad** *vii*

ROAST
ROAST: roast (s.t.) **abwe** *vai+o;* roast s.o. **abwaazh /abwaaN-/** *vta;* roast s.t. **abwaadan** *vti;* roast things **abwaajige** *vai*

ROAST IN THE OVEN: roast s.o. in the oven **giboz /gibozw-/** *vta;* roast s.t. in the oven **gibozan** *vti;* roast things in the oven **gibozige** *vai*

ROASTED FISH
ROASTED FISH: **abwaajigan, -an** *ni*

ROASTED MEAT
ROASTED MEAT: **abwaajigan, -an** *ni*

ROASTING PAN
  ROASTING PAN: **giboziganaabik, -oon** *ni*
ROB
  ROB: rob s.o. of (s.t.) **makam** *vta;* rob people
    makandwe *vai*
ROBBER
  ROBBER: **gimoodishkiiwinini, -wag** *na*
ROBIN
  ROBIN: **opichi, -wag** *na*
ROCK
  ROCK: **asin, -iig** *na;* be of rock **asiniiwan** *vii*
  MANY ROCKS: there are many rocks
    asiniikaa, asiniikaamagad *vii*
  ON ROCK: on something mineral (e.g., metal,
    glass, rock) **agidaabik** *pc, also* **ogidaabik*,
    wagidaabik**
  ON TOP OF A ROCK: **agidasin** *pc, also*
    ogidasin*, wagidasin
  ROCK CLIFF: **aazhibik, -oon** *ni;* there is a
    rock cliff **giishkaazhibikaa,
    giishkaazhibikaamagad** *vii*
  ROCK FOR SWEAT LODGE:
    madoodoowasin, -iig *na*
  STEEP ROCK FACE: be a steep rock face
    giishkaabikaa, giishkaabikaamagad *vii*
ROCKING CHAIR
  ROCKING CHAIR: **didibise-apabiwin, -an**
    ni; **wewebizoo-apabiwin, -an** *ni*
ROLL
  ROLL: **didibibide, didibibidemagad** *vii;*
    didibibizo *vai;* **ditibise** *vai;* **ditibise,
    ditibisemagad** *vii;* roll s.o. **didibin** *vta;* roll
    s.t. **didibinan** *vti*
  ROLL ALONG: **ditibibide, ditibibidemagad**
    vii
  ROLL ALONG KICKING: roll things along
    by kicking **ditibiwebishkige** *vai*
  ROLL OVER: **gotigobide, gotigobidemagad**
    vii; **gotigobizo** *vai;* roll s.o. over
    gotigobizh /gotigobiN-/ *vta;* roll s.t. over
    gotigobidoon *vti2*
  ROLL UP SLEEVE: roll up one's sleeve
    ikwanagweni *vai*
ROLL
  ROLL: **bakwezhigaans, -ag** *na*
ROLLED OATS
  ROLLED OATS: **daataagwa'igan, -an** *ni*
ROOF
  PUT ON A ROOF: **apakwe** *vai*
ROOFING
  ROOFING: **apakwaan, -an** *ni*
ROOM
  ROOM: **abiwin, -an** *ni;* be room **dawaa,
    dawaamagad** *vii*
  COLD ROOM: be cold (as a house or room)
    dakate, dakatemagad *vii*
  DARK ROOM: be dark (as in a room or
    house) **dibikate, dibikatemagad** *vii*
  NEXT ROOM: in the next room **aajisag** *pc*
  SMALL ROOM: be small (as a room or
    house) **agaasate, agaasatemagad** *vii*

ROOMY
  ROOMY: be roomy **mangate,
    mangatemagad** *vii*
ROOSTER
  ROOSTER: **naabese, -g** *na*
ROOT
  ROOT: **ojiibik, -an** *ni*
  HAVE ROOTS: **ojiibikaawan** *vii;* **ojiibikaawi**
    vai
ROOT HOUSE
  ROOT HOUSE: **akiiwigamig, -oon** *ni*
ROPE
  ROPE: **biiminakwaan, -an** *ni*
  MAKE ROPE: **biiminakwe** *vai*
ROSARY
  ROSARY: rosary *plural* **anama'eminensag** *na*
ROSE
  ROSE: **oginii-waabigwan, -iin** *ni*
ROSE HIP
  ROSE HIP: **ogin, -iig** *na*
ROTARY FAN
  ROTARY FAN: **gizhibaayaasijigan, -an** *ni*
ROTTEN
  ROTTEN: be rotten **bigishkanad** *vii;*
    bigishkanani *vai*
ROUGE
  ROUGE: **miskwanowechigan, -an** *ni*
  USE ROUGE: **miskwanowechige** *vai*
ROUGH
  ROUGH: be rough **gaawaa, gaawaamagad**
    vii; **gaawizi** *vai;* be rough (as something
    mineral) **gaawaabikad** *vii;* **gaawaabikizi**
    vai; be rough (as something sheet-like)
    gaawegad *vii;* **gaawegizi** *vai*
ROUND
  ROUND: be round **waawiyeyaa,
    waawiyeyaamagad** *vii;* **waawiyezi** *vai;* be
    round (as something ball-like)
    waawiyeminagad *vii;* **waawiyeminagizi**
    vai; be round (as something mineral)
    waawiyeyaabikad *vii;* **waawiyeyaabikizi**
    vai; be round (as something stick- or
    wood-like) **waawiyeyaakozi** *vai;*
    waawiyeyaakwad *vii*
  MAKE ROUND: make s.o. round **waawiye'**
    vta; make s.t. round **waawiyetoon** *vti2*
ROUND TRIP
  MAKE A ROUND TRIP: make a round trip
    in one day **biskaabii** *vai*
ROW
  LIE SIDE BY SIDE IN A ROW: they lie side
    by side in a row **niibidesinoon /niibidesin-/**
    vii; they lie side by side in a row
    niibideshinoog /niibideshin-/ *vai*
  SIT SIDE BY SIDE IN A ROW: they sit side
    by side in a row **niibidebiwag /niibidebi-/**
    vai
ROW
  ROW: row (a boat) **azheboye** *vai*
RUB
  RUB: rub s.o. with something **zinigon** *vta;* rub
    s.t. with something **zinigonan** *vti*

RUBBING ALCOHOL
RUBBING ALCOHOL: **giziibiigazhewaaboo** *ni*
RUG
RUG: **anaakan, -an** *ni*
BRAIDED RUG: **okaadenigan, -an** *ni*
RUIN
RUIN: ruin s.o. **goopaaji'** *vta;* ruin s.t.
gopajitoon *vti2*
RULE
RULE: rule s.o. **dibenim** *vta;* **ogimaakandaw**
vta; rule s.t. **ogimaakandan** *vti*
RUMBLE
RUMBLE: **jiingwe, jiingwemagad** *vii;*
zegwewe, zegwewemagad *vii*
RUMP
RUMP: my rump **indiy** */-diy-/ nid, also*
indiyaash
RUN
ARRIVE ON THE RUN: **bagamibatoo** *vai;*
they arrive on the run together
bagamiba'idiwag */bagamiba'idi-/ vai*
HEARD RUNNING HERE: be heard running
here **biidwewebatoo** *vai*
HEARD RUNNING HERE ON THE
GROUND: be heard running here on the
ground **biidwewekamigibatoo** *vai*
RUN ABOUT: **babaamibatoo** *vai;* they run
about together **babaamiba'idiwag**
/babaamiba'idi-/ vai
RUN ACROSS: **aazhoobatoo** *vai, also*
aazhawibatoo; they run across together
aazhogeba'idiwag */aazhogeba'idi-/ vai;*
aazhooba'idiwag */aazhooba'idi-/ vai*
RUN ACROSS WADING:
aazhawagaaziibatoo *vai*
RUN ALONG: **bimibatoo** *vai;* they run along
together **bimiba'idiwag** */bimiba'idi-/ vai*
RUN ALONG IN FLIGHT: **biminizhimo**
vai; run along in flight from someone
bimiba'iwe *vai*
RUN ALONG THE SHORE: **jiigewebatoo**
vai; **jiigeweyaazhagaamebatoo** *vai*
RUN AROUND: run around s.t.
giiwitaabatwaadan *vti;* run around something **giiwitaabatoo** *vai*
RUN ASHORE: **agwaabatoo** *vai*
RUN AT: run at s.o. **mawinazh** */mawinaN-/*
vta
RUN AT A CERTAIN SPEED: **apiichibatoo**
vai; run at a certain speed (e.g., a machine)
apiichibide, apiichibidemagad *vii;*
apiichibizo *vai*
RUN AWAY: **animibatoo** *vai;* run away (in
the other direction) with s.o.
animibatwaazh */animibatwaaN-/ vta;* run
away (in the other direction) with s.t.
animibatwaadan *vti;* they run away (in the
other direction) together **animiba'idiwag**
/animiba'idi-/ vai
RUN AWAY FOR GOOD: **aapijibatoo** *vai*
RUN AWAY MAKING NOISE:
animwewebatoo *vai*
RUN AWAY SCARED: **animinizhimo** *vai*

RUN BACK: **giiwebatoo** *vai*
RUN DOWN: **niisaandawebatoo** *vai*
RUN DOWNHILL: **niisaakiiwebatoo** *vai*
RUN FAST: **gizhiibatoo** *vai;* **gizhiikaabatoo**
vai
RUN FROM CERTAIN PLACE IN
FLIGHT: run from a certain place in flight
onjinizhimo *vai*
RUN FROM A CERTAIN PLACE:
onjibatoo *vai*
RUN HERE: **biijibatoo** *vai;* they run here
together **biijiba'idiwag** */biijiba'idi-/ vai*
RUN HOME: **giiwebatoo** *vai*
RUN IN A CERTAIN WAY: **apatoo** *vai*
RUN INLAND: **gopibatoo** *vai*
RUN INSIDE: **biindigebatoo** *vai;* they run
inside together **biindigeba'idiwag**
/biindigeba'idi-/ vai; run inside with s.o.
biindigebatwaazh */biindigebatwaaN-/*
vta; run inside with s.t.
biindigebatwaadan *vti;* run inside from
people **biindigeba'iwe** *vai*
RUN INTO THE WATER: **bakobiibatoo** *vai*
RUN OFF: **maajiibatoo** *vai;* they run off
together **maajiiba'idiwag** */maajiiba'idi-/*
vai
RUN OFF TO THE SIDE: **bakebatoo** *vai*
RUN OUT: **zaagizibatoo** *vai;* run out with
s.o. **zaagiziba'** *vta;* **zaagizibatwaazh**
/zaagizibatwaaN-/ vta; run out with s.t.
zaagizibatwaadan *vti;* they run out together **zaagiziba'idiwag** */zaagiziba'idi-/*
vai
RUN POORLY: run poorly (e.g., a car)
maazhibizo *vai;* run poorly (e.g., a
machine) **maazhibide, maazhibidemagad**
vii
RUN SLOWLY: **bejibatoo** *vai;* **bezikaabatoo**
vai
RUN SUDDENLY INTO VIEW:
zaagewebatoo *vai*
RUN THE WRONG WAY: **wanibatoo** *vai*
RUN THROUGH: **zhaabobatoo** *vai*
RUN TO A CERTAIN PLACE: **apatoo** *vai;*
run with s.o. to a certain place **apa'** *vta*
RUN TO A CERTAIN PLACE IN FLIGHT:
izhinizhimo *vai*
RUN TO A CERTAIN PLACE TOGETH-
ER: they run to a certain place together
apa'idiwag */apa'idi-/ vai*
RUN TO GET: run to get s.o. **naajibatwaazh**
/naajibatwaaN-/ vta; run to get s.t.
naajibatwaadan *vti*
RUN TO THE SHORE: **madaabiibatoo** *vai*
RUN UPHILL: **agidaakiiwebatoo** *vai*
RUN WELL: run well (e.g., a machine)
minobide, minobidemagad *vii;* **minobizo**
vai
RUN WITH SAP: **onjigaa, onjigaamagad** *vii*
START TO RUN: **maajiibatoo** *vai;* start to
run (e.g., a machine) **maajiibide,**
maajiibidemagad *vii;* **maajiibizo** *vai*
START TO RUN WITH SAP: **maajigaa,**
maajigaamagad *vii*
STOP RUNNING: **noogibatoo** *vai*

TURN RUNNING: **gwekibatoo** *vai*

RUN AWAY

RUN AWAY: run away from s.o. **ginjiba'** *vta;*
run away from people **ginjiba'iwe** *vai*
RUN AWAY TO A CERTAIN PLACE: run
away from people to a certain place
apa'iwe *vai*

RUN OUT

RUN OUT: **jaagise** *vai+o;* **jaagise,
jaagisemagad** *vii*
RUN OUT OF FUEL: **iskaakizige** *vai*

RUN SHORT

RUN SHORT: **noondese** *vai;* run short of s.o.
noondesa' *vta;* run short of s.t.
noondesatoon *vti2;* run short of things
noondesachige *vai*

RUSH

RUSH: rush s.o. **ojaanimi'** *vta*

RUSH

RUSH: **anaakanashk, -oon** *ni*

RUSTLESS

RUSTLESS: be rustless **zhooshkwaabikad**
vii; **zhooshkwaabikizi** *vai*

RUSTY

RUSTY: be rusty **agwaagwaabikad** *vii;*
agwaagwaabikizi *vai*
TURN RUSTY: **agwaagwaabikishin** *vai;*
agwaagwaabikisin *vii*

RUTABAGA

RUTABAGA: **jiis, -an** *ni*

S

SACK

SACK: **mashkimod, -an** *ni*
GUNNYSACK: **mandaaminiwazh, -an** *ni*

SAD

SAD: be sad **gashkendam** *vai2;*
osidaawendam *vai2*

SADDLE

SADDLE: **bimoomigoo-apabiwin, -an** *ni*

SAFETY PIN

SAFETY PIN: **zagaakwa'igan, -an** *ni*

SAIL

SAIL: **ningaasimoonowin** *ni;* sail (in a boat)
ningaasimoono *vai*
SAIL ABOUT: **babaamaashi** *vai;*
babaamaasin *vii*
SAIL ALONG: **bimaashi** *vai;* **bimaasin** *vii*
SAIL ASHORE: **agwaayaashi** *vai*
SAIL AWAY: **animaashi** *vai;* **animaasin** *vii*
SAIL FROM A CERTAIN PLACE: **ondaashi**
vai; **ondaasin** *vii*
SAIL HERE: **biidaashi** *vai;* **biidaasin** *vii*
SAIL IN: **bagamaashi** *vai;* **bagamaasin** *vii*

SAIL TO A CERTAIN PLACE: **inaashi** *vai;*
inaasin *vii*

SAILBOAT

SAILBOAT: **ningaasimoo-jiimaan, -an** *ni*

SAILOR

SAILOR: **ningaasimoowinini, -wag** *na*

SALIVA

SALIVA: **zikowin** *ni*

SALT

SALT: **zhiiwitaagan** *ni;* salt s.o.
zhiiwitaagana' /zhiiwitaagana'w-/ *vta;* salt
s.t. **zhiiwitaagana'an** *vti;* salt things
zhiiwitaagana'ige *vai*

SALT PORK

SALT PORK: **zhiiwitaagani-gookoosh** *na*

SALTY

SALTY: be salty (as a liquid)
**zhiiwitaaganaagamin
/zhiiwitaaganaagami-/** *vii*
TASTE SALTY: **zhiiwitaaganipogozi** *vai;*
zhiiwitaaganipogwad *vii*

SAME

SAME: be the same **bezhigwan** *vii;* the same
naasaab *pc*
AT THE SAME TIME: **bekish** *pc*
SAME AGE: they are the same age
wiijigindiwag /wiijigindi-/ *vai*
STEP IN THE SAME TRACKS:
naaba'anidizo *vai*
THE SAME AGE: be the same age as s.o.
wiijigim *vta*

SAND

SAND: **bingwi** *ni*
MUCH SAND: be much sand **bingwiikaa,
bingwiikaamagad** *vii*

SANDHILL CRANE

SANDHILL CRANE: **ajijaak, -wag** *na*

SANDY

SANDY BEACH: be a sandy beach
mitaawangaa, mitaawangaamagad *vii*

SAP

FINISH BOILING SAP: **ishkwaagamizige**
vai
GATHER SAP: **naadoobii** *vai*
MAPLE SAP: **wiishkobaaboo** *ni;*
ziinzibaakwadwaaboo *ni*
START TO RUN WITH SAP: **maajigaa,
maajigaamagad** *vii*
THE LAST RUN OF SAP: be the last run of
sap **ishkwaagaa, ishkwaagaamagad** *vii*

SAP BUCKET

SAP BUCKET OF FOLDED BIRCH BARK:
biskitenaagan, -an *ni*

SAP-BOILING FRAME

SAP-BOILING FRAME: frame for holding
sap-boiling kettles **iskigamiziganaak, -oon**
ni

SAP-BOILING LODGE

SAP-BOILING LODGE:
iskigamizigewigamig, -oon *ni*

SAP-BOILING POLE

SAP-BOILING POLE: **iskigamiziganaatig,
-oon** *ni*

SATIN
SATIN: **zenibaawegin, -oon** *ni*
SATISFIED
SATISFIED: be satisfied **debizi** *vai*
FEEL SATISFIED: **debisewendam** *vai2*
SATISFY
SATISFY: satisfy s.o. **debi'** *vta*
SATURATED
SATURATED: be saturated **zhaabobii,
zhaabobiimagad** *vii*
SATURDAY
SATURDAY: be Saturday **giziibiigisaginige-
giizhigad** *vii;* **ishwaajanokii-giizhigad** *vii*
SAUCER
SAUCER: **desinaagaans, -an** *ni*
SAUSAGE
SAUSAGE: **onagizh, -iin** *ni, also* **onagizhiins**
SAVE
SAVE BACK: save s.o. back **ishkon** *vta;* save
s.t. back **ishkonan** *vti;* save (s.t.) back for
s.o. **ishkonamaw** *vta*
SAVE LIFE: save the life of s.o. **bimaaji'** *vta*
SAVED
SAVED BACK: be saved back **ishkonigaade,
ishkonigaademagad** *vii;* **ishkonigaazo** *vai*
SAW
CROSSCUT SAW: **giishkiboojigan, -an** *ni*
SAW APART LENGTHWISE: saw s.o. apart
lengthwise **daashkiboozh /daashkibooN-/**
vta; saw s.t. apart lengthwise
daashkiboodoon *vti2;* saw things apart
lengthwise **daashkiboojige** *vai*
SAW OFF: saw s.o. off **giishkiboozh
/giishkibooN-/** *vta;* saw s.t. off
giishkiboodoon *vti2;* saw things off
giishkiboojige *vai*
SAW STRAIGHT: saw s.o. straight
gwayakoboozh /gwayakobooN-/ *vta;* saw
s.t. straight **gwayakoboodoon** *vti2*
SAW MILL
SAW MILL: **daashkiboojigan, -ag** *na*
SAY
SAY: **ikido** *vai;* say so to s.t. **idan** *vti;* say to
s.o. **izhi /iN-/** *vta;* they say to each other
idiwag /idi-/ *vai*
SAY AFTER: say something after s.o.
gikinootaw *vta*
SCAB
SCABS: have scabs **omigii** *vai*
SCABS ON FACE: have scabs on one's face
omigiingwe *vai*
SCALE
SCALE: scale s.o. **jiiga'azh /jiiga'aN-/** *vta*
SCALE FISH: **jiiga'e** *vai*
SCALES: my scales *plural* **ninaga'ayag
/-naga'ay-/** *nad*
SCALE
SCALE: **dibaabiishkoojigan, -an** *ni*
SCALE TIMBER
SCALE TIMBER: **diba'aatigwe** *vai*
SCALP
DIRTY SCALP: have a dirty scalp
wiinishagaandibe *vai*

SCANDINAVIAN
SCANDINAVIAN: **agongos, -ag** *na*
SCANDINAVIAN LANGUAGE
SPEAK A SCANDINAVIAN LANGUAGE:
agongosimo *vai*
SCAR
HAVE A SCAR: **ojiishigi** *vai*
HAVE SCAR ON ARM: have scar on one's
arm **ojiishinike** *vai*
HAVE SCAR ON FACE: have scar on one's
face **ojiishiingwe** *vai*
HAVE SCAR ON HAND: have scar on one's
hand **ojiishininjii** *vai*
SCARE
SCARE: scare s.o. **zegi'** *vta*
SCARE AWAY: scare s.o. away (e.g., game)
oshaakaw *vta*
SCARED
SCARED: be scared **zegizi** *vai*
RUN AWAY SCARED: **animinizhimo** *vai*
SCARF
SCARF: **giizhoopizon, -ag** *na*
SCARY
CONSIDERED SCARY: be considered scary
zegendaagozi *vai;* **zegendaagwad** *vii*
LOOK SCARY: **zeginaagozi** *vai;*
zeginaagwad *vii*
SCARY DREAM: have a scary dream
zegaabandam *vai2*
SCARY MOVIE: be a scary movie **zegaatese,
zegaatesemagad** *vii*
SCATTER
SCATTER: **biiwise** *vai;* **biiwise,
biiwisemagad** *vii;* scatter s.o. **biiwiwebin**
vta; scatter s.t. **biiwiwebinan** *vti*
SCATTER USING SOMETHING: scatter
s.t. using something **zaswe'an** *vti*
SCATTER WITH FOOT OR BODY: scatter
s.o. with foot or body **zasweshkaw** *vta;*
scatter s.t. with foot or body **zasweshkan**
vti
SCATTER WITH HANDS: scatter s.o. with
hands **zaswebizh /zaswebiN-/** *vta;* scatter
s.t. with hands **zaswebidoon** *vti2*
SCHOOL
SCHOOL: **gikinoo'amaadiiwigamig, -oon** *ni*
GO TO SCHOOL: **gikinoo'amaagozi** *vai*
SCHOOL CUSTODIAN
SCHOOL CUSTODIAN: **boodawewinini,
-wag** *na*
SCHOOLBOOK
SCHOOLBOOK: **gikinoo'amaadii-
mazina'igan** *ni*
SCISSORS
SCISSORS: **moozhwaagan, -an** *ni*
SCOLD
SCOLD: scold s.o. **naniibikim** *vta*
SCOOP
SCOOP UP: scoop s.o. up **gwaaba'** *vta;* scoop
s.t. up **gwaaba'an** *vti;* scoop (s.t.) up for
s.o. **gwaaba'amaw** *vta;* scoop up things
gwaaba'ige *vai*
SCOOP UP WATER: **gwaaba'ibii** *vai*

SCORE
SCORE IN A GAME: **gabenaage** *vai*
SCOUT
SCOUT: **nandawaatoo** *vai*
SCRAPE
SCRAPE HIDES: **jiishaakwa'ige** *vai;* scrape s.o. to remove hair (e.g., a hide) **jiishaakwa'** /**jiishaakwa'w-**/ *vta*

SCRAPE USING SOMETHING: scrape s.o. using something **gaaskaaska'** /**gaaskaaska'w-**/ *vta;* scrape s.t. using something **gaaskaaska'an** *vti*
SCRAPER
HIDE SCRAPER: **jiishaakwa'igan, -an** *ni*
SCRATCH
SCRATCH: scratch (leaving a visible mark) **jiichiigii** *vai;* scratch s.o. **baazagobizh** /**baazagobiN-**/ *vta;* scratch s.o. (leaving a visible mark) **jiichiigibizh** /**jiichiigibiN-**/ *vta;* scratch s.t. (leaving a visible mark) **jiichiigibidoon** *vti2*

SCRATCH BACK: scratch s.o.'s back **jiichiigawiganebizh** /**jiichiigawiganebiN-**/ *vta*
SCREAM
SCREAM: **aazhikwe** *vai*
SCREECH OWL
SCREECH OWL: **gaakaabishiinh, -yag** *na*
SCREW
SCREW: **biimiskonigan, -an** *ni;* **biimiskwa'igaans, -an** *ni;* screw s.t. **biimiskwa'an** *vti*
SCREWDRIVER
SCREWDRIVER: **biimiskwa'igan, -an** *ni*
SCRUB BRUSH
SCRUB BRUSH: **mimigosaga'igan, -an** *ni*
SCULPT
SCULPT: sculpt s.o. **onadin** *vta;* sculpt s.t. **onadinan** *vti*
SCYTHE
SCYTHE: **giishkizhigan, -an** *ni*
SEA
SEA: **gichigami, -in** *ni*
SEAGULL
SEAGULL: **gayaashk, -wag** *na*
SEARCH
SEARCH: search for s.o. **nandawaabam** *vta;* search for s.t. **nandawaabandan** *vti;* search for things **nandawaabanjige** *vai*
SEASICK
SEASICK: be seasick **giiwashkwe'ogo** *vai*
SEASON
SEASON: season (s.t.) **apaabowe** *vai+o*
SEAT
SEAT: seat s.o. **onabi'** *vta;* seat people **onabi'iwe** *vai*

CHANGE SEAT: **aandabi** *vai*

TAKE A SEAT: **onabi** *vai*
SEATED
SEATED: be seated **wawenabi** *vai*
SECOND
SECOND: the second **eko-niizhing** *pc*

THE SECOND DAY OF THE MONTH: be the second day of the month **niizhogonagizi** *vai*
SECOND PERSON
SECOND PERSON: *second person prefix before consonants in nouns and verbs* **gi=** *pre;second person prefix before vowels in verbs and non-dependent nouns* **gid=** *pre; second person prefix before vowels in dependent nouns* **g=** *pre*

SECOND PERSON PLURAL: you *second person plural personal pronoun* **giinawaa** *pr;* only you *second personal plural personal pronoun* **giinetawaa** *pr;* your turn *second person plural personal pronoun* **giinitamawaa** *pr*

SECOND PERSON SINGULAR: you *second person singular personal pronoun* **giin** *pr;* only you *second person singular personal pronoun* **giineta** *pr;* your turn *second person singular personal pronoun* **giinitam** *pr*
SECONDHAND CLOTHING STORE
SECONDHAND CLOTHING STORE: **zhiigoshkigani-adaawewigamig, -oon** *ni*
SECRET
SECRET: be secret **giimoodad** *vii*
SECRETARY
SECRETARY: secretary (female) **ozhibii'igewikwe, -g** *na*
SECRETLY
SECRETLY: **giimooj** *pc*

EAT SECRETLY: eat things secretly **giimoodanjige** *vai*

LAUGH SECRETLY: **giimoodaapi** *vai*
SEE
SEE: **waabi** *vai;* see s.o. **waabam** *vta;* see s.t. **waabandan** *vti;* see oneself **waabandizo** *vai;* they see each other **waabandiwag** /**waabandi-**/ *vai*

FAIL TO SEE: fail to see s.o. **gwiinawaabam** *vta;* fail to see s.t. **gwiinawaabandan** *vti*

SEE A CERTAIN WAY: see s.o. a certain way **izhinaw** *vta;* see s.t. a certain way **izhinan** *vti*

SEE A CERTAIN WAY AS IN A DREAM: see s.o. a certain way as in a dream **inaabam** *vta;* see s.t. a certain way as in a dream **inaabandan** *vti*

SEE AT A DISTANCE: see s.o. at a distance **debaabam** *vta;* see s.t. at a distance **debaabandan** *vti*

SEE CLEARLY: **bagakaabi** *vai;* see s.o. clearly **bagakaabam** *vta;* see s.t. clearly **bagakaabandan** *vti*

SEE THROUGH: see through s.o. **zhaabwaabam** *vta;* see through s.t. **zhaabwaabandan** *vti*

SEE WELL: **minwaabi** *vai*
SEED
SEED: **miinikaan, -an** *ni*
SEEK
SEEK: **nanda-** *pv4;* seek s.o. **nooji'** *vta;* seek s.t. **noojitoon** *vti2;* seek people **nooji'iwe** *vai*

SEEK TO KNOW: seek to know s.o. **nandagikenim** *vta;* seek to know s.t. **nandagikendan** *vti*

SEEK TO LEARN: seek to learn s.t. **nandagikendan** *vti*

SEEM
SEEM TO BE A CERTAIN WAY: **inendaagozi** *vai;* **inendaagwad** *vii*

SEEN
SEEN: be seen **waabanjigaade, waabanjigaademagad** *vii;* **waabanjigaazo** *vai*

SEIZE
SEIZE: seize s.o. **nawadin** *vta;* seize s.t. **nawadinan** *vti;* seize (s.t.) of s.o.'s **nawadinamaw** *vta;* seize people **nawadiniwe** *vai*

SELDOM
SELDOM: **wiikaa** *pc*

SELECT
SELECT FROM: select from s.o. **gagiigin** *vta;* select from s.t. **gagiiginan** *vti*

SELF-CONFIDENCE
LACK SELF-CONFIDENCE: **zhaagwenimo** *vai*

SELL
SELL: sell (s.t.) **adaawaage** *vai+o*
SELL OUT: sell out (of s.t.) **jaagadaawaage** *vai+o*

SEND
SEND: send for s.o. **naajinizha' /naajinizha'w-/** *vta;* send for s.t. **naajinizha'an** *vti;* send (s.t.) to s.o. **niindaa'** *vta;* send (s.t.) to people **niindaa'iwe** *vai*
SEND A LETTER HERE: **biijibii'ige** *vai*
SEND ALONG: send s.o. along **biminizhikaw** *vta;* send people along **biminaazhikaage** *vai*
SEND OFF: send s.o. off **maajinaazha' /maajinaazha'w-/** *vta;* **maajinizha' /maajinizha'w-/** *vta;* send s.t. off **maajinizha'an** *vti;* send (s.t.) off to s.o. **maajinizha'amaw** *vta*
SEND TO A CERTAIN PLACE: send s.o. to a certain place **izhinaazhikaw** *vta;* **izhinizha' /izhinizha'w-/** *vta;* send s.t. to a certain place **izhinizha'an** *vti;* send (s.t.) to s.o. to a certain place **izhinizha'amaw** *vta*

SENSELESS
KNOCK SENSELESS: knock s.o. senseless **giiwashkweganaam** *vta*
KNOCKED SENSELESS IN IMPACT: be knocked senseless in impact **giiwashkweshin** *vai*

SENT
SENT TO A CERTAIN PLACE: be sent to a certain place **izhinizha'igaade, izhinizha'igaademagad** *vii;* **izhinizha'igaazo** *vai*

SENTENCE
SENTENCE A CERTAIN WAY: sentence s.o. a certain way **inaakon** *vta*

SENTENCED
SENTENCED: be sentenced **dibaakonigaazo** *vai*
SENTENCED A CERTAIN WAY: be sentenced a certain way **inaakonigaazo** *vai*

SEPARATE
SEPARATE: they separate from each other **webinidiwag /webinidi-/** *vai*

SEPTEMBER
SEPTEMBER: **waatebagaa-giizis** *na, also* **waatebago-giizis; manoominike-giizis** *na*

SERVE
SERVE FOOD: serve food to people **ashange** *vai*

SET
SET A CERTAIN PRICE: set a certain price on s.o. **inagim** *vta;* set a certain price on s.t. **inagindan** *vti;* set a certain price on (s.t.) for s.o. **inagindamaw** *vta*
SET A CERTAIN WAY: set s.o. a certain way **izhishim** *vta;* set s.t. a certain way **izhisidoon** *vti2*
SET A NET: **bagida'waa** *vai;* set a net under the ice **ziibaaskobijige** *vai*
SET A PRICE: **onagindaaso** *vai;* set a price on s.o. **onagim** *vta;* set a price on s.t. **onagindan** *vti*
SET A PRICE OF A CERTAIN HEIGHT: set a price of a certain height on s.o. **apiitagim** *vta;* set a price of a certain height on s.t. **apiitagindan** *vti*
SET A SNARE: **agoodoo** *vai;* set a snare for s.o. **agoodaw** *vta*
SET DOWN: be set down **bagidinigaade, bagidinigaademagad** *vii;* **bagidinigaazo** *vai;* set s.o. down **bagidin** *vta;* set s.t. down **bagidinan** *vti;* set (s.t.) down for s.o. **bagidinamaw** *vta;* set things down **bagidinige** *vai*
SET DOWN OFF BACK: set s.o. down off one's back **bagidoom** *vta;* set s.t. down off one's back **bagidoondan** *vti*
SET DOWN PACK: set down one's pack **bagijiwane** *vai*
SET IN THE GROUND: set s.o. in the ground **badakishim** *vta;* set s.t. in the ground **badakisidoon** *vti2;* set things in the ground **badakisijige** *vai*
SET OUT OF THE WAY: be set out of the way **ikonigaade, ikonigaademagad** *vii;* **ikonigaazo** *vai;* set s.o. out of the way **ikon** *vta;* set s.t. out of the way **ikonan** *vti*
SET THE TABLE: **ozisinaagane** *vai*
SET TO COOL: set s.o. to cool **dakishim** *vta;* set s.t. to cool **dakisidoon** *vti2*
SUN SETS: set as the sun; *conjunct* **bangishimog** in the west **bangishimon /bangishimo-/** *vii*

SET
CERTAIN NUMBER OF SETS: a certain number of sets **daswewaan** *pc*

SET LINE
FISH WITH SET LINES: **bagidaabii** *vai*

SET UP

SET UP: set s.t. up **onakidoon** *vti2;* set s.o. up
onakizh /**onakiN-**/ *vta*

FINISH SETTING UP: finish setting s.o. up
giizhakizh /**giizhakiN-**/ *vta;* finish setting
s.t. up **giizhakidoon** *vti2*

SET UP AS A FRAME: set s.t. up as a frame
onaakosidoon *vti2*

SET UP CAMP: **gabeshi** *vai*

SETTLE DOWN

TELL TO SETTLE DOWN: tell s.o. to settle
down **zagakim** *vta*

SEVEN

SEVEN: **niizhwaaswi** *nm;* **niizhwaaso-** *pv4;*
seven (card) **niizhwaasoobii'igan, -ag** *na;*
they are seven **niizhwaachinoon**
/**niizhwaachin-**/ *vii;* **niizhwaachiwag**
/**niizhwaachi-**/ *vai*

AND SEVEN: **ashi-niizhwaaswi** *nm;* **ashi-
niizhwaaso-** *pv4*

SEVEN ACRES: **niizhwaaso-diba'igaans** *pc*

SEVEN DAYS: **niizhwaaso-giizhik** *pc;*
niizhwaasogon *pc;* be seven days
niizhwaasogonagad *vii*

SEVEN DAYS OLD: be seven days old
niizhwaasogonagizi *vai*

SEVEN DOLLARS: **niizhwaaswaabik** *pc*

SEVEN EACH: **neniizhwaaswi** *nm*

SEVEN FEET: **niizhwaasozid** *pc*

SEVEN HOURS: **niizhwaaso-diba'igan** *pc*

SEVEN HUNDRED: **niizhwaaswaak** *nm*

SEVEN INCHES: **niizhwaasoninj** *pc*

SEVEN MILES: **niizhwaaso-diba'igan** *pc*

SEVEN MINUTES: **niizhwaaso-diba'igaans**
pc

SEVEN MONTHS: **niizhwaaso-giizis** *pc*

SEVEN NIGHTS: **niizhwaaso-dibik** *pc*

SEVEN O'CLOCK: be seven o'clock
niizhwaaso-diba'iganed *vii*

SEVEN PAIRS: **niizhwaaswewaan** *pc*

SEVEN SETS: **niizhwaaswewaan** *pc*

SEVEN THOUSAND: **niizhwaasosagoons**
nm

SEVEN TIMES: **niizhwaaching** *pc*

SEVEN WEEKS: **niizhwaaso-anama'e-
giizhik** *pc;* be seven weeks **niizhwaaso-
anama'e-giizhigad** *pc*

SEVEN YEARS: **niizhwaaso-biboon** *pc;* be
seven years **niizhwaaso-biboonagad** *vii*

SEVEN YEARS OLD: be seven years old
niizhwaaso-biboonagizi *vai*

SEVENTEEN

SEVENTEEN: **ashi-niizhwaaswi** *nm;*
midaaswi ashi-niizhwaaswi *nm*

SEVENTH

THE SEVENTH DAY OF THE MONTH:
be the seventh day of the month
niizhwaasogonagizi *vai*

SEVENTY

SEVENTY: **niizhwaasimidana** *nm*

SEW

SEW: **gashkigwaaso** *vai;* sew s.o. (e.g., a pair
of pants) **gashkigwaazh** /**gashkigwaaN-**/
vta; sew s.t. **gashkigwaadan** *vti*

MAKE A MISTAKE SEWING: **wanigwaaso**
vai; make a mistake sewing on s.o.
wanigwaazh /**wanigwaaN-**/ *vta;* make a
mistake sewing on s.t. **wanigwaadan** *vti*

SEW ON: sew s.o. on **agogwaazh**
/**agogwaaN-**/ *vta;* sew s.t. on **agogwaadan**
vti; sew something on **agogwaaso** *vai*

SEW SHUT: sew s.o. shut **giboogwaazh**
/**giboogwaaN-**/ *vta;* sew s.t. shut
giboogwaadan *vti*

SEW TOGETHER: **maawandoogwaaso** *vai;*
sew s.o. together **maawandoogwaazh**
/**maawandoogwaaN-**/ *vta;* sew s.t. together (e.g., pieces for a quilt)
maawandoogwaadan *vti*

SEWING MACHINE

SEWING MACHINE: **gashkigwaason, -ag** *na*

SEWING THREAD

SEWING THREAD: **gashkigwaasoneyaab,
-iin** *ni*

SEWN

SEWN: be sewn **gashkigwaade,
gashkigwaademagad** *vii;* **gashkigwaazo**
vai

SHADE

SHADE: shade s.o. **agawaateshkaw** *vta;*
shade s.t. **agawaateshkan** *vti;* there is
shade **agawaateyaa, agawaateyaamagad**
vii

IN SHADE: be in shade **agawaateshin** *vai;*
agawaatesin *vii*

WINDOW SHADE: **gibiiga'iganiigin, -oon** *ni*

SHADOW

SHADOW: there is shadow **agawaateyaa,
agawaateyaamagad** *vii*

CAST A SHADOW: cast a shadow on s.o.
agawaateshkaw *vta;* cast a shadow on s.t.
agawaateshkan *vti*

CAST A SHADOW FLYING: **agawaatese**
vai; **agawaatese, agawaatesemagad** *vii*

IN SHADOW: be in shadow **agawaateshin**
vai; **agawaatesin** *vii*

SHAKE

SHAKE: **baapagishkaa** *vai;* **baapagishkaa,
baapagishkaamagad** *vii;* shake s.o. **bawin**
vta; shake s.t. **bawinan** *vti*

SHAKE AWAKE: shake s.o. awake
amajwebin *vta*

SHAKE HANDS: shake hands with s.o.
zagininjiin *vta;* they shake hands with each
other **zagininjiinidiwag** /**zagininjiinidi-**/
vai

SHAKE HEAD: shake one's head at s.o.
wewebikwetaw *vta*

SHAKE OUT: hold and shake s.o. out
baapaawin *vta;* hold and shake s.t. out
baapaawinan *vti;* shake s.o. out (as something sheet-like) **bawegin** *vta;* shake s.t.
out (as something sheet-like) **baweginan**
vti

SHAKE WINGS: shake one's wings
bapawaangeni *vai*

SHAKING TENT

SHAKING TENT: **jiisakaan, -an** *ni*

PRACTICE DIVINATION IN A SHAKING
TENT: **jiisakii** *vai*
SEER WHO USES A SHAKING TENT:
jiisakiiwinini, -wag *na*

SHALLOW
SHALLOW: be shallow **baagwaa,
baagwaamagad** *vii*

SHAME
FOR SHAME: for shame! **ise** *pc*

SHAMEFUL
SHAMEFUL: be shameful **agadendaagwad**
vii

SHARE
SHARE: **maada'ookii** *vai;* share (s.t.) out to
s.o. **maada'oozh /maada'ooN-/** *vta;* they
share (s.t.) **maada'oonidiwag
/maada'oonidi-/** *vai*

SHARP
SHARP: be sharp **giinaa, giinaamagad** *vii;*
giinizi *vai*
FILE SHARP: file s.o. sharp **giiniboozh
/giinibooN-/** *vta;* file s.t. sharp
giiniboodoon *vti2*

SHATTER
SHATTER: shatter (e.g., glass or china)
baasikaa, baasikaamagad *vii;* shatter on
impact **baasishin** *vai;* **baasisin** *vii;* shatter
s.o. **baasishim** *vta;* shatter s.t. **baasisidoon**
vti2
SHATTER BY HEAT: shatter s.o. by heat
baasiz /baasizw-/ *vta;* shatter s.t. by heat
baasizan *vti*
SHATTER FROM HEAT: **baaside,
baasidemagad** *vii;* **baasizo** *vai*
SHATTER USING SOMETHING: shatter
s.o. using something **baasa' /baasa'w-/** *vta;*
shatter s.t. using something **baasa'an** *vti;*
shatter things using something **baasa'ige**
vai
SHATTER WITH FOOT OR BODY: shatter
s.o. with foot or body **baasikaw** *vta;* shatter
s.t. with foot or body **baasikan** *vti*

SHAVE
SHAVE: **gaashkibaazo** *vai;* shave s.o.
gaashkibaazh /gaashkibaaN-/ *vta*

SHAWL
SHAWL: **moshwe, -g** *na*

SHE
SHE: she *third person singular personal pronoun*
wiin *pr*

SHEATH
KNIFE SHEATH: **biinjikomaan, -an** *ni*

SHED
SHED: **ataasoowigamig, -oon** *ni*

SHEEP
SHEEP: **maanishtaanish, -ag** *na, also*
maanitaanish

SHEEPSHEAD
SHEEPSHEAD: sheepshead (fish)
maanashigan, -ag *na*

SHEEPSKIN
SHEEPSKIN: **maanishtaanishiwayaan** *ni*

SHEET
SHEET: **apishimoniigin, -oon** *ni;*
waabishkiigin, -oon *ni*

SHELF
SHELF: **desaabaan, -an** *ni*

SHELL
SHELL: **es, -ag** *na*
MIDE SHELL: **miigis, -ag** *na*

SHELTER
SHELTER: **dabinoo'igan, -an** *ni*

SHERIFF
SHERIFF: **dakoniwewinini, -wag** *na*

SHIFT
SHIFT: shift s.o. (e.g., a car) **biindaabikibizh
/biindaabikibiN-/** *vta*
GEAR SHIFT: **aandaabikinigan, -an** *ni*
SHIFT GEARS: **aandaabikinige** *vai;*
biindaabikibijige *vai*

SHIFTLESS
SHIFTLESS: be shiftless **bagandizi** *vai*

SHIN
SHIN: my shin **nikakwan, -an /-kakwan-/** *nid*

SHINE
SHINE: shine (as something mineral)
waasaabikide, waasaabikidemagad *vii;*
waasaabikizo *vai;* shine s.o. **waasikwa'**
vta; shine s.t. **waasikwa'an** *vti*
SHINE FOR GAME OR FISH: **waaswaa** *vai*

SHINNY
PLAY SHINNY: **bapasikawe** *vai*

SHINY
SHINY: be shiny (as something sheet-like)
waaseyiigad *vii;* **waaseyiigizi** *vai*
MAKE SHINY: make s.o. shiny **waasiko'** *vta;*
make s.t. shiny **waasikotoon** *vti2*

SHIP
SHIP: **ishkode-jiimaan, -an** *ni;* **naabikwaan,
-an** *ni*

SHIRT
SHIRT: **babagiwayaan, -an** *ni, also*
bagiwayaan
PUT ON SHIRT: put on one's shirt
biichibabagiwayaane *vai*
TAKE OFF SHIRT: take off one's shirt
giichibabagiwayaane *vai*
WEAR A SHIRT: **gigibabagiwayaane** *vai*

SHOE
SHOE: **makizin, -an** *ni*
MAKE SHOES: **makizinike** *vai*
PUT ON SHOES: put on one's shoes
babiichii *vai*
TAKE OFF SHOES: take off one's shoes
gagiichii *vai*
TENNIS SHOE: **babagiwayaanekizin, -an** *ni,*
also **bagiwayaanekizin**

SHOELACE
SHOELACE: **makizineyaab, -iin** *ni*

SHOOT
SHOOT: shoot s.o. **baashkiz /baashkizw-/**
vta; shoot s.t. **baashkizan** *vti;* shoot oneself
baashkizodizo *vai;* shoot things
baashkizige *vai*

HEARD SHOOTING: be heard shooting
madwezige *vai*
PRACTICE SHOOTING: **gagweda'aakwe**
vai
SHOOT ACCIDENTALLY: shoot s.o. accidentally **bichinaw** *vta;* shoot s.t. accidentally **bichinan** *vti;* shoot oneself accidentally **bichinaadizo** *vai;* shoot things accidentally **bichinaage** *vai*
SHOOT AND HIT: shoot and hit s.o.
miikonaw *vta;* shoot and hit s.t. **miikonan**
vti
SHOOT AND MISS: **bishkonaage** *vai;* shoot
at s.o. and miss **bishkonaw** *vta;* shoot at
s.t. and miss **bishkonan** *vti*
SHOOT AND WOUND: shoot and wound
s.o. **maakinaw** *vta*
SHOOT IN A CERTAIN WAY OR PLACE:
ina'e *vai*
SHOOT WITH AN ARROW: shoot s.o. with
an arrow or other missile **bimo** /bimw-/
vta; shoot s.t. with an arrow or other
missile **bimodan** *vti;* shoot things with an
arrow or other missile **bimojige** *vai*
SIGNAL BY SHOOTING: **nandwewezige**
vai

SHOP
SHOP: **maa'ishkam** *vai2*

SHORE
ALONG THE SHORE: **jiigew** *pc;* **jiigibiig** *pc*
CARRY TO THE SHORE: carry s.o. to the
shore **madaabiiwizh** /madaabiiwiN-/ *vta;*
carry s.t. to the shore **madaabiiwidoon**
vti2
DRIVE ALONG THE SHORE: **jiigewebizo**
vai; **jiigewedaabii'iwe** *vai*
GO ALONG THE SHORE: **bimaazhagaame**
vai; **jiigewe** *vai*
GO TO THE SHORE: **madaabii** *vai*
ON THE SHORE: **agamiing** *pc*
PADDLE ALONG THE SHORE:
jiigewe'am *vai2;* **jiigewe'o** *vai;*
jiigewekwazhiwe *vai*
RUN ALONG THE SHORE: **jiigewebatoo**
vai; **jiigeweyaazhagaamebatoo** *vai*
RUN TO THE SHORE: **madaabiibatoo** *vai*
SPEED ALONG THE SHORE: **jiigewebizo**
vai
TAKE TO THE SHORE: take s.o. to the
shore **madaabiiwizh** /madaabiiwiN-/ *vta;*
take s.t. to the shore **madaabiiwidoon** *vti2*
WALK ALONG SHORE TO A CERTAIN
PLACE: **inaazhagaame** *vai*
WALK ALONG THE SHORE:
jiigeweyaazhagaame *vai*

SHORT
SHORT: be short **dakoozi** *vai;* **dakwaa**,
dakwaamagad *vii;* be short (as something
mineral) **dakwaabikad** *vii;* **dakwaabikizi**
vai; be short (as something sheet-like)
dakwegad *vii;* **dakwegizi** *vai;* be short (as
something stick- or wood-like)
dakwaakozi *vai;* **dakwaakwad** *vii;* be

short (as something string-like)
dakwaabiigad *vii;* **dakwaabiigizi** *vai*
CUT SHORT: cut s.o. short (as something
string-like) **dakwaabiigizh**
/dakwaabiigizhw-/ *vta;* cut s.t. short (as
something string-like) **dakwaabiigizhan** *vti*
SHORT BOAT: be short (as a boat)
dakoonagad *vii*
SHORT HAIR: have short hair
dadaakwaanikwe *vai*
SHORT SLEEVES: have short sleeves
dadaakwanagweyaa,
dadaakwanagweyaamagad *vii*

SHORT
SHORT: be short of (s.t.) **manezi** *vai-o*
RUN SHORT: run short **noondese** *vai;* run
short of s.o. **noondesa'** *vta;* run short of
s.t. **noondesatoon** *vti2;* run short of things
noondesachige *vai*
SHORT OF BREATH: be short of breath
akwanaamo *vai*
SHORT OF TOBACCO: be short of tobacco
manepwaa *vai*

SHORT WHILE
A SHORT WHILE: **noomag** *pc*

SHOT
TAKE A BAD SHOT: **maana'e** *vai*

SHOTGUN
SHOTGUN: **zhiishiibanwii-baashkizigan**, -an
ni

SHOTGUN SHELL
SHOTGUN SHELL: **anwi**, -in *ni*

SHOULD
SHOULD: should *modal* **daa-** *pv1;* it should
have been done **naanabem** *pc*

SHOULDER
SHOULDER: my shoulder **indinimaangan**,
-an /-dinimaangan-/ *nid*
HAUL ON SHOULDER: haul s.o. on one's
shoulder **aawajinigaazh** /aawajinigaaN-/
vta; haul s.t. on one's shoulder
aawajinigaadan *vti;* haul things on one's
shoulder **aawajinige** *vai*
WEAR ACROSS THE SHOULDER: wear
s.t. across the shoulder **aazhooningwa'an**
vti

SHOULDER BLADE
SHOULDER BLADE: my shoulder blade
indiniigan, -ag /-diniigan-/ *nad*

SHOUT
SHOUT: **biibaagi** *vai;* shout at s.o. **biibaagim**
vta; shout at s.t. **biibaagindan** *vti*

SHOVE
SHOVE: shove s.o. **gaanjwebin** *vta;* shove s.t.
gaanjwebinan *vti*
SHOVE ASIDE: shove aside s.o. **ikowebin**
vta; shove aside s.t. **ikowebinan** *vti*
SHOVE AWAY USING SOMETHING:
shove s.o. away using something **weba'**
/weba'w-/ *vta;* shove s.t. away using
something **weba'an** *vti*
SHOVE OUT OF THE WAY WITH
SOMETHING: shove s.o. out of the way
with something **ikoweba'** /ikoweba'w-/

vta; shove s.t. out of the way with
something **ikoweba'an** *vti*
SHOVE USING SOMETHING: shove s.o.
using something **gaanjweba'**
/gaanjweba'w-/ *vta;* shove s.t. using
something **gaanjweba'an** *vti;* shove things
using something **gaanjweba'ige** *vai*
SHOVE WITH FOOT OR BODY: shove s.o.
with foot or body **gaanjwebishkaw** *vta;*
shove s.t. with foot or body
gaanjwebishkan *vti*

SHOVEL
SHOVEL: **mangaanibaajigan, -an** *ni;*
mangaanibii *vai;* shovel (for dirt)
gwaaba'waawangwaan, -an *ni;* shovel s.o.
(e.g., snow) **mangaanibaazh**
/mangaanibaaN-/ *vta;* shovel s.t.
mangaanibaadan *vti;* shovel things
mangaanibaajige *vai*

SHOW
SHOW: **waabanda'iwewin, -an** *ni;* show (s.t.)
to s.o. **waabanda'** *vta;* show (s.t.) to
people **waabanda'iwe** *vai*
MAKE SHOW: make s.o. show **naago'** *vta;*
make s.t. show **naagotoon** *vti2*

SHRINK
SHRINK: **odaapishkaa, odaapishkaamagad**
vii; **odaapishkaa** *vai*

SHRIVELLED
SHRIVELLED: be shrivelled **gaaskide,**
gaaskidemagad *vii;* **gaaskizo** *vai*

SHUT
SHUT: be shut (as or as with something stick-
or wood-like) **gibaakwa'igaade,**
gibaakwa'igaademagad *vii;* shut s.o. (as
or as with something stick- or wood-like)
gibaakwa' /gibaakwa'w-/ *vta;* shut s.t. (as
or as with something stick- or wood-like)
gibaakwa'an *vti*
FROZEN SHUT: be frozen shut **gibaakwadin**
vii; **gibaakwaji** *vai*
GLUE SHUT: glue s.o. shut **gibokiwas** *vta;*
glue s.t. shut **gibokiwasan** *vti*
GLUED SHUT: be glued shut
gibokiwasigaade, gibokiwasigaademagad
vii; **gibokiwasigaazo** *vai*
PULL SHUT: pull s.t. shut (as something
stick- or wood-like) **gibaakobidoon** *vti2*
SEW SHUT: sew s.o. shut **giboogwaazh**
/giboogwaaN-/ *vta;* sew s.t. shut
giboogwaadan *vti*
SHUT EYES: shut one's eyes **basangwaabi**
vai
SLAM SHUT: slam s.t. shut (as something
stick- or wood-like, e.g., a door)
gibaakowebinan *vti*
TIE SHUT: tie s.o. shut **gashkapizh**
/gashkapiN-/ *vta;* tie s.t. shut
gashkapidoon *vti2*

SHY
SHY: be a shy person **agajishki** *vai;* be shy
agaji *vai;* be shy in front of s.o. **agajiitaw**
vta
FEEL SHY: **agadendam** *vai2*

SHYPOKE
SHYPOKE: American bittern (locally called
shypoke) **mooshka'osi, -wag** *na*

SIBLING
SIBLING: my sibling of the opposite sex
(brother or sister) **indawemaa, -g**
/-dawemaaw-/ *nad*
YOUNGER SIBLING: my younger sibling
(brother or sister) **nishiime, -yag**
/-shiimey-/ *nad*

SIBLING-IN-LAW
SIBLING-IN-LAW: my sibling-in-law of the
opposite sex **niinim, -oog /-iinimw-/** *nad*

SICK
SICK: be sick **aakozi** *vai+o*
LOOK SICK: **aakoziiwinaagozi** *vai*
MAKE SICK: make s.o. sick (especially of a
substance consumed); *inverse forms of:*
aakoziishkaw- *vta*
PRETEND TO SICK: pretend to be sick
aakoziikaazo *vai*
SICK IN A BODY PART: be sick (in s.t.)
aakozi *vai+o*
SICK IN A CERTAIN WAY: be sick in a
certain way **inaapine** *vai*
START TO GET SICK: **mizizi** *vai*
VERY SICK: be very sick **aanimizi** *vai;*
onzaamine *vai*

SICKLY
CONSIDERED SICKLY: be considered
sickly **aakoziiwendaagozi** *vai*

SICKNESS
SICKNESS: **aakoziwin, -an** *ni*
MUCH SICKNESS: there is much sickness
aakoziwinikaa, aakoziwinikaamagad *vii*

SIDE
ALONG THE SIDE OF THE ROAD:
opimekana *pc*
ALONG THE SIDE OF THE TRAIL:
opimekana *pc*
DRIVE OFF TO THE SIDE: **bakebide,**
bakebidemagad *vii;* **bakebizo** *vai*
FALL ON THE SIDE: **opimese** *vai*
GO OFF TO THE SIDE: **bake** *vai*
LAY ON SIDE: lay s.o. on side **opimeshim**
vai; lay s.t. on side **opimesidoon** *vti2*
LIE ON SIDE: **opimesin** *vii;* lie on one's side
opimeshin *vai*
ON THE SIDE: on the side of it **opime-ayi'ii**
pc, also **opimeya'ii**
ON THIS SIDE: **ondaas** *pc;* on this side of it
ondaasayi'ii *pc*
ON THIS SIDE OF THE FIRE:
ondaasishkode *pc*
ON THIS SIDE OF THE ROAD:
ondaasikana *pc*
ON THIS SIDE OF THE TRAIL:
ondaasikana *pc*
ON THIS SIDE OF THE WATER:
ondaasagaam *pc*
ROAD GOES OFF TO THE SIDE: go off to
the side (as a road or trail) **bakemon**
/bakemo-/ *vii*
RUN OFF TO THE SIDE: **bakebatoo** *vai*

SPEED OFF TO THE SIDE: **bakebide,
bakebidemagad** *vii;* **bakebizo** *vai*
TRAIL GOES OFF TO THE SIDE: go off to
the side (as a road or trail) **bakemon
/bakemo-/** *vii*

SIFT
SIFT: sift s.o. **zhaaboshkaas
/zhaaboshkaasw-/** *vta;* sift s.t.
zhaaboshkaatoon *vti2;* sift things
zhaaboshkaachige *vai*
SIFTER
SIFTER: **zhaaboshkaachigan, -an** *ni*
SIGHT
DISTANT SIGHT: be a distant sight
naawinaagozi *vai;* **naawinaagwad** *vii*
HAVE IN SIGHT: have s.o. in sight
debaabam *vta;* have s.t. in sight
debaabandan *vti*
IN SIGHT: be in sight **debaabaminaagozi**
vai; **debaabaminaagwad** *vii*
SIGN
SIGN: sign s.t. **daangigwanenan** *vti;* sign
things **daangigwanenige** *vai*
SIGN
SIGN: **agwaakwa'igan, -an** *ni*
SIGNAL
SIGNAL BY SHOOTING: **nandwewezige**
vai
SIGNS
FIND SIGNS: find signs of s.o.'s presence
name' *vta*
LEAVE SIGNS: leave signs of its presence
namesin *vii;* leave signs of one's presence
nameshin *vai;* **nametoo** *vai*
SILK
SILK: **zenibaanh, -yag** *na;* **zenibaawegin,
-oon** *ni*
SILVER
SILVER: **zhooniyaawaabik, -oon** *ni*
SINCE
SINCE: **ako-** *pv3*
SINEW
SINEW: my sinew **injiitad, -an /-jiitad-/** *nid*
SING
SING: **nagamo** *vai;* sing for s.o. **nagamotaw**
vta
GO ALONG SINGING: **bima'amaazo** *vai*
GO AWAY SINGING: **anima'amaazo** *vai*
PRACTICE SINGING: **goji-nagamo** *vai*
SING A CERTAIN WAY: **ina'am** *vai2*
SING AN ACCOMPANIMENT: sing an ac-
companiment (of women) **zhaabowe** *vai*
SING WAR SONGS: **bwaanzhii-nagamo** *vai*
START TO SING: **maajii'am** *vai2*
SINGE
SINGE: singe s.o. **banzo /banzw-/** *vta;* singe
s.t. **banzan** *vti*
SINGED
SINGED: be singed **bande, bandemagad** *vii;*
banzo *vai*
SINGING
SINGING: **nagamowin** *ni*

SINK
SINK: sink in water **gonzaabii,
gonzaabiimagad** *vii*
SINKER
SINKER: net sinker **asinaab, -iig** *na;* sinker
(fishing tackle) **gonzaabiishkoojigan, -an**
ni
SISTER
OLDER SISTER: my older sister **nimisenh,
-yag /-miseny-/** *nad*
YOUNGER SISTER: my younger sister
nishiime, -yag /-shiimey-/ *nad*
SISTER-IN-LAW
SISTER-IN-LAW: my (female's) sister-in-law
indaangwe, -g /-daangwew-/ *nad;* my
(male's) sister-in-law **niinim, -oog
/-iinimw-/** *nad*
SIT
SIT: **namadabi** *vai*
SIT A CERTAIN WAY: **inabi** *vai*
SIT ALONE: **nazhikewaakwadabi** *vai*
SIT ASIDE: **ikwabi** *vai*
SIT ASTRIDE: **desabi** *vai*
SIT AT THE END: **ishkwebi** *vai*
SIT COMFORTABLY: **minwabi** *vai*
SIT DOWN: **namadabi** *vai;* **wawenabi** *vai*
SIT FACING BACKWARDS: **animikwabi**
vai
SIT FACING IN A CERTAIN WAY:
inaasamabi *vai*
SIT FACING THIS WAY: **biidaasamabi** *vai*
SIT IN A CERTAIN PLACE: **abi** *vai*
SIT IN FRONT: **niigaanabi** *vai*
SIT ON THE BARE GROUND: **mitabi** *vai*
SIT OUT OF THE WAY: move out of the
way sitting **ikwabi** *vai*
SIT QUIETLY: **goshkwaawaadabi** *vai*
SIT SIDE BY SIDE IN A ROW: they sit side
by side in a row **niibidebiwag /niibidebi-/**
vai
SIT STIFFLY: **jiibadabi** *vai*
SIT STILL: **bizaanaakwadabi** *vai*
SIT TOGETHER: they sit together
maawandoobiwag /maawandoobi-/ *vai*
SIT UNCOMFORTABLY: **maanabi** *vai*
SIT UP WITH AT A WAKE: sit up with s.o.
(e.g., the deceased at a wake) **abiitaw** *vta*
SIT WITH: sit with s.o. **wiidabim** *vta*
SIT WITH BACK TO: sit with back to s.o.
animikwabiitaw *vta*
SIT WITH LEGS CROSSED:
aazhoogaadebi *vai*
TURN AROUND WHILE SITTING:
gwekabi *vai*
SITUATED
SITUATED IN A CERTAIN PLACE: be
situated in a certain place **dagon /dago-/** *vii*
SIX
SIX: **ingodwaaswi** *nm,* also **ningodwaaswi***;
ingodwaaso- /ningodwaaso-/ *pv4,* also
ningodwaaso*; six (card)
ingodwaasoobii'igan, -ag *na,* also
ningodwaasoobii'igan*;
ningodwaasoobii'igan*, -ag *na;* they are

six **ingodwaachinoon** /ningodwaachin-/ *vii, also* **ningodwaachinoon***; **ingodwaachiwag** /ningodwaachi-/ *vai, also* **ningodwaachiwag***
AND SIX: **ashi-ingodwaaso-** *pv4, also* **ashi-ningodwaaso-***; **ashi-ingodwaaswi** *nm, also* **ashi-ningodwaaswi***
SIX ACRES: **ingodwaaso-diba'igaans** *pc, also* **ningodwaaso-diba'igaans***
SIX DAYS: **ingodwaaso-giizhik** *pc, also* **ningodwaaso-giizhik***; **ingodwaasogon** *pc, also* **ningodwaasogon***; be six days **ingodwaasogonagad** /ningodwaasogonagad-/ *vii, also* **ningodwaasogonagad***
SIX DAYS OLD: be six days old **ingodwaasogonagizi** /ningodwaasogonagizi-/ *vai, also* **ningodwaasogonagizi***
SIX DOLLARS: **ingodwaaswaabik** *pc, also* **ningodwaaswaabik***
SIX EACH: **neningodwaaswi** *nm*
SIX HOURS: **ingodwaaso-diba'igan** *pc, also* **ningodwaaso-diba'igan***
SIX HUNDRED: **ingodwaaswaak** *nm, also* **ningodwaaswaak***
SIX INCHES: **ingodwaasoninj** *pc, also* **ningodwaasoninj***
SIX MILES: **ingodwaaso-diba'igan** *pc, also* **ningodwaaso-diba'igan***
SIX MINUTES: **ingodwaaso-diba'igaans** *pc, also* **ningodwaaso-diba'igaans***
SIX MONTHS: **ingodwaaso-giizis** *pc, also* **ningodwaaso-giizis***
SIX NIGHTS: **ingodwaaso-dibik** *pc, also* **ningodwaaso-dibik***
SIX O'CLOCK: be six o'clock **ingodwaaso-diba'iganed** /ningodwaaso-diba'iganed-/ *vii, also* **ningodwaaso-diba'iganed***
SIX PAIRS: **ingodwaaswewaan** *pc, also* **ningodwaaswewaan***
SIX SETS: **ingodwaaswewaan** *pc, also* **ningodwaaswewaan***
SIX THOUSAND: **ingodwaasosagoons** /ningodwaasosagoons-/ *pc, also* **ningodwaasosagoons***
SIX TIMES: **ingodwaaching** *pc, also* **ningodwaaching***
SIX WEEKS: **ingodwaaso-anama'e-giizhik** *pc, also* **ningodwaaso-anama'e-giizhik***; be six weeks **ingodwaaso-anama'e-giizhigad** /ningodwaaso-anama'e-giizhigad-/ *vii, also* **ningodwaaso-anama'e-giizhigad***
SIX YEARS: **ingodwaaso-biboon** *pc, also* **ningodwaaso-biboon***; be six years **ingodwaaso-biboonagad** /ningodwaaso-biboonagad-/ *vii, also* **ningodwaaso-biboonagad***
SIX YEARS OLD: be six years old **ingodwaaso-biboonagizi** /ningodwaaso-biboonagizi-/ *vai, also* **ningodwaaso-biboonagaizi***

SIXTEEN
SIXTEEN: **ashi-ingodwaaswi** *nm, also* **ashi-ningodwaaswi***; **midaaswi ashi-ingodwaaswi** *nm, also* **midaaswi ashi-ningodwaaswi***
SIXTH
THE SIXTH DAY OF THE MONTH: be the sixth day of the month **ingodwaasogonagizi** /ningodwaasogonagizi-/ *vai, also* **ningodwaasogonagizi***
SIXTY
SIXTY: **ingodwaasimidana** *nm, also* **ningodwaasimidana***
SIZE
CERTAIN SIZE: be a certain size **inigini** *vai;* **inigokwaa, inigokwaamagad** *vii;* be a certain size (as something mineral) **inigokwaabikad** *vii;* **inigokwaabikizi** *vai;* be a certain size (as something sheet-like) **inigokwegad** *vii;* **inigokwegizi** *vai;* be a certain size (as something stick- or wood-like) **inigokwaakozi** *vai;* **inigokwaakwad** *vii;* be a certain size (as something string-like) **inigokwaabiigad** *vii;* **inigokwaabiigizi** *vai*
SKATE
SKATE: **zhooshkwaada'aagan, -an** *ni;* **zhooshkwaada'e** *vai*
SKATE ABOUT: **babaamaada'e** *vai*
SKATE ALONG: **bimaada'e** *vai*
SKATE AWAY: **animaada'e** *vai*
SKATE FROM A CERTAIN PLACE: **ondaada'e** *vai*
SKATE HERE: **biidaada'e** *vai*
SKATE TO A CERTAIN PLACE: **inaada'e** *vai*
SKI
SKI: **zhooshkoshimaan, -ag** *na;* **zhooshkwaagim, -ag** *na;* **zhooshkwaagime** *vai*
SKILFUL
SKILFUL: be skilful **wawiingezi** *vai*
SKILFULLY
DO SKILFULLY: **wawiingechige** *vai*
MAKE SKILFULLY: make s.o. skilfully **wawiinge'** *vta;* make s.t. skilfully **wawiingetoon** *vti2*
SKILLED
SKILLED: being skilled at **nitaa-** *pv4;* be skilled at things **nitaawichige** *vai*
SKILLED IN SPEAKING OR SINGING: be skilled in speaking or singing **nitaawe** *vai*
SKIM
SKIM: skim s.t. **bima'an** *vti;* skim things **bima'ige** *vai*
SKIN
SKIN: my skin **inzhaga'ay** /-zhaga'ay-/ *nid;* **nishkatay** /-shkatay-/ *nid*
ITCHY SKIN: have itchy skin **gizhiibazhe** *vai*
SKIN
SKIN: skin s.o. **bakon** *vta;* skin things **bakonige** *vai*

SKIN KNEE: skin one's knee
  bishagigidigweshin *vai*
SKINNY
  SKINNY: be skinny **bakaakadozo** *vai*
SKIRT
  SKIRT: **giishkijiiwagooday, -an** *ni*
SKULL
  SKULL: my skull **nishtigwaanigegan, -an**
  /-shtigwaanigegan-/ *nid*
SKUNK
  SKUNK: **zhigaag, -wag** *na*
SKY
  SKY: **giizhig** *na*
  CLEAR SKY: be clear sky **mizhakwad** *vii*
  IN THE SKY: **ishpiming** *pc;* be in the sky
    (e.g., a star, the sun, or the moon) **agoojin**
    vai
SLACK
  SLACK: be slack **neshangaa,**
    neshangaamagad *vii;* **neshangizi** *vai;* be
    slack (as something string-like)
    neshangaabiigad *vii;* **neshangaabiigizi** *vai*
  LIE SLACK: **neshangisin** *vii*
SLAM
  SLAM SHUT: slam s.t. shut (as something
    stick- or wood-like, e.g., a door)
    gibaakowebinan *vti*
SLAP
  SLAP ON FACE: slap s.o. on the face
    basiingwe' /basiingwe'w-/ *vta*
  SLAP ON HEAD: slap s.o. on the head
    basindibe' /basindibe'w-/ *vta*
  SLAP ON REAR: slap s.o. on the rear
    basidiye' /basidiye'w-/ *vta*
SLAUGHTER
  SLAUGHTER: slaughter s.o. **niiwana'**
    /niiwana'w-/ *vta*
SLAVE
  SLAVE: **awakaan, -ag** *na*
SLED
  SLED: **biboonodaabaanens, -ag** *na;*
    odaabaan, -ag *na*
SLEEP
  SLEEP: **nibaa** *vai*
  DISTURB SLEEP: disturb s.o.'s sleep **wapaa'**
    vta
  MAKE NOISE IN SLEEP: make noise in
    one's sleep **madwengwaam** *vai*
  MAKE SLEEP: make s.o. sleep **nibe'** *vta;*
    make s.o. sleep *inverse forms of:* **nibeshkaw-**
    vta
  PRETEND TO SLEEP: **nibekaazo** *vai*
  SLEEP DEEPLY: **zoongingwashi** *vai*
  SLEEP UNCOMFORTABLY:
    maazhingwaam *vai*
  SLEEP WITH: sleep with s.o. **wiipem** *vta;*
    sleep with s.t. **wiipendan** *vti;* they sleep
    with each other **wiipendiwag /wiipendi-/**
    vai
  SLEEP WITH CHILDREN
    PROTECTIVELY: **wiipemaawaso** *vai*
SLEEPY
  SLEEPY: be sleepy **giikiibingwashi** *vai*

SLEEVE
  SLEEVE: my sleeve **ninagway, -an /-nagway-/**
    nid
  HAVE LONG SLEEVES: **gagaanonagweyaa,**
    gagaanonagweyaamagad *vii*
  ROLL UP SLEEVE: roll up one's sleeve
    ikwanagweni *vai*
  SHORT SLEEVES: have short sleeves
    dadaakwanagweyaa,
    dadaakwanagweyaamagad *vii*
SLEIGH
  SLEIGH: **biboonodaabaan, -ag** *na;*
    odaabaan, -ag *na*
  DRIVE ALONG IN A WAGON OR
    SLEIGH: drive along quickly in a wagon
    or sleigh **bimidaabiiba'igo** *vai*
SLEIGH BELL
  SLEIGH BELL: **zhinawa'oojigan, -an** *ni*
SLICE
  SLICE A CERTAIN WAY: slice s.o. a certain
    way **inikozh /inikoN-/** *vta;* slice s.t. a
    certain way **inikodan** *vti*
  SLICE THICK: slice s.o. thick **gipagikozh**
    /gipagikoN-/ *vta;* slice s.t. thick
    gipagikodan *vti*
  SLICE THIN: slice s.o. thin **bibagikozh**
    /bibagikoN-/ *vta;* slice s.t. thin
    bibagikodan *vti*
SLICK
  SLICK: be slick **ozhaashaa,**
    ozhaashaamagad *vii;* **ozhaashizi** *vai;*
    zhooshkozi *vai;* **zhooshkwaa,**
    zhooshkwaamagad *vii*
SLIDE
  SLIDE: slide s.o. with hand **zhooshkon** *vta;*
    slide s.t. with hand **zhooshkonan** *vti;* slide
    things **zhooshkonige** *vai*
  GO SLIDING: **zhooshkwajiwe** *vai*
  SLIDE OVER SITTING: **zhooshkwabi** *vai*
  SLIDE WITH HAND: slide s.o. with hand
    zhooshkon *vta;* slide s.t. with hand
    zhooshkonan *vti*
SLINGSHOT
  SLINGSHOT: **bimojigan, -an** *ni*
SLIP
  SLIP AND FALL: **ozhaashishin** *vai*
  SLIP AND FALL ON THE ICE:
    ozhaashikoshin *vai*
SLIP
  SLIP: **biitawagoodaan, -an** *ni*
SLIPPERY
  SLIPPERY: be slippery **ozhaashaa,**
    ozhaashaamagad *vii;* **ozhaashizi** *vai;* be
    slippery (as something mineral)
    ozhaashaabikad *vii;* **ozhaashaabikizi** *vai;*
    be slippery (as something stick- or wood-
    like) **ozhaashaakozi** *vai;* **ozhaashaakwad**
    vii
  SLIPPERY ICE: there is slippery ice
    ozhaashikwaa, ozhaashikwaamagad *vii*
  SLIPPERY ROAD: be slippery (as a road or
    trail) **ozhaashadamon /ozhaashadamo-/**
    vii; **zhooshkwadamon**
    /zhooshkwadamo-/ *vii;* be slippery with

ice (as a road or trail) **ozhaashikwadamon** **/ozhaashikwadamo-/** *vii*
SLIPPERY TRAIL: be slippery (as a road or trail) **ozhaashadamon /ozhaashadamo-/** *vii;* **zhooshkwadamon** **/zhooshkwadamo-/** *vii;* be slippery with ice (as a road or trail) **ozhaashikwadamon** **/ozhaashikwadamo-/** *vii*

SLIPPERY ELM
SLIPPERY ELM: **ozhaashigob, -iig** *na*

SLIVER
SLIVER: sliver (in one's body) **gigaatigwaan, -an** *ni*
HAVE A SLIVER: **gigaatigwe** *vai*

SLOP PAIL
SLOP PAIL: **ziigwebinigewakik, -oog** *na*

SLOW
SLOW DOWN: slow down! **bekaa** *pc*

SLOWLY
DRIVE SLOWLY: **bejibide, bejibidemagad** *vii;* **bejibizo** *vai*
MOVE SLOWLY: **bejibide, bejibidemagad** *vii;* **bejibizo** *vai;* **bezikaa** *vai*
RUN SLOWLY: **bejibatoo** *vai;* **bezikaabatoo** *vai*
WALK SLOWLY: **bedose** *vai*

SMALL
SMALL: be small **agaasaa, agaasaamagad** *vii;* **agaashiinyi** *vai;* be small (as something ball-like) **agaasiminagad** *vii;* **agaasiminagizi** *vai;* be small (as something mineral) **agaasaabikad** *vii;* **agaasaabikizi** *vai;* be small (as something sheet-like) **agaasiigad** *vii;* **agaasiigizi** *vai;* be small (as something stick- or wood-like) **agaasaakozi** *vai;* **agaasaakwad** *vii;* be small (as something string-like) **agaasaabiigad** *vii;* **agaasaabiigizi** *vai*
APPEAR SMALL: **agaasaabaminaagozi** *vai;* **agaasaabaminaagwad** *vii*
LOOK SMALL: **agaasaabaminaagozi** *vai;* **agaasaabaminaagwad** *vii*
MAKE SMALL: make s.o. small **agaasi'** *vta;* make s.t. small **agaasaatoon** *vti2*
SMALL HILL: there is a small hill **agaasadinaa, agaasadinaamagad** *vii*
SMALL HOUSE: be small (as a room or house) **agaasate, agaasatemagad** *vii*
SMALL ROOM: be small (as a room or house) **agaasate, agaasatemagad** *vii*

SMALL OF BACK
SMALL OF BACK: the small of my back **inzhiigan /-zhiigan-/** *nid*

SMALLPOX
SMALLPOX: **mamakiziwin** *ni*

SMART
SMART: be smart **gikendaaso** *vai*

SMASH
SMASH: smash s.o. **biigoshim** *vta;* smash s.t. **biigosidoon** *vti2*

SMELL
SMELL: smell s.o. **biijimaam** *vta;* smell s.t. **biijimaandan** *vti*

GIVE OFF A SMELL: **biijimaagozi** *vai;* **biijimaagwad** *vii*
GIVE OFF A SMELL IN COOKING OR BURNING: **biijimaaso** *vai;* **biijimaate, biijimaatemagad** *vii*
GOOD SMELL: have a good smell **minomaagozi** *vai;* **minomaagwad** *vii*
HAVE SMELL A CERTAIN WAY: have s.o. smell a certain way to one **izhimaam** *vta;* have s.t. smell a certain way to one **izhimaandan** *vti*
LIKE THE SMELL: like the smell of s.o. **minomaam** *vta;* like the smell of s.t. **minomaandan** *vti*
RECOGNIZE BY SMELL: recognize s.o. by smell **nisidomaam** *vta;* recognize s.t. by smell **nisidomaandan** *vti*
SMELL A CERTAIN WAY: **izhimaagozi** *vai;* **izhimaagwad** *vii*
SMELL A CERTAIN WAY COOKING OR BURNING: **izhimaaso** *vai;* **izhimaate, izhimaatemagad** *vii*
SMELL BAD: **maazhimaagozi** *vai;* **maazhimaagwad** *vii*
SMELL BAD BURNING OR COOKING: **maazhimaaso** *vai;* **maazhimaate** *vii*
SMELL FOR: smell for s.o. **nandomaam** *vta;* smell for s.t. **nandomaandan** *vti*
SMELL GOOD: have a good smell **minomaagozi** *vai;* **minomaagwad** *vii*
SMELL GOOD BURNING OR COOKING: **minomaaso** *vai;* **minomaate, minomaatemagad** *vii*
SMELL RANCID: **zaatemaagozi** *vai;* **zaatemaagwad** *vii*
SMELL STRONG BURNING OR COOKING: **mashkawimaaso** *vai;* **mashkawimaate, mashkawimaatemagad** *vii*
TAKE A SMELL: take a smell of s.o. **gojimaam** *vta;* take a smell of s.t. **gojimaandan** *vti*

SMILE
SMILE: **zhoomiingweni** *vai;* smile at s.o. **zhoomiingwetaw** *vta*

SMOKE
SMOKE: **bakwene, bakwenemagad** *vii*
FILLED WITH SMOKE: be filled with smoke **mooshkineyaabate, mooshkineyaabatemagad** *vii*
FULL OF SMOKE: be full of smoke **gibwanaamode, gibwanaamodemagad** *vii*
GO UPWARDS AS SMOKE: **ombaabate** *vii*
SEND SMOKE TO A CERTAIN PLACE: **inaabasige** *vai*
SMOKE OUT: smoke s.o. out **gibwanaamoz /gibwanaamozw-/** *vta*
SUFFOCATE FROM SMOKE: **gibwanaamozo** *vai*

SMOKE
SMOKE: smoke (tobacco) **zagaswaa** *vai;* smoke s.o. (e.g., tobacco) **zagaswaazh**

/zagaswaaN-/ *vta;* smoke s.t. (e.g., kinnickinnick) **zagaswaadan** *vti*
GIVE A SMOKE: give a smoke to s.o.
zagaswe' *vta*
NEED TO SMOKE: **manepwaa** *vai*
SHARE A SMOKE: share a smoke with s.o.
(especially a pipe in a ceremony) **zagaswe'**
vta

SMOKY
SMOKY: be smoky **bakwene,
bakwenemagad** *vii*
SMOKY INSIDE: be smoky inside
giikanaamode, giikanaamodemagad *vii*

SMOOTH
SMOOTH: be smooth **zhooshkozi** *vai;*
zhooshkwaa, zhooshkwaamagad *vii;* be
smooth (as something mineral)
zhooshkwaabikad *vii;* **zhooshkwaabikizi**
vai; be smooth (as something sheet-like)
zhooshkwegad *vii;* **zhooshkwegizi** *vai;* be
smooth (as something stick- or wood-like)
zhooshkwaakozi *vai;* **zhooshkwaakwad**
vii

SNAGGED
SNAGGED: get snagged on a limb
zagaakwajin *vai*

SNAIL
SNAIL: **biimiskodisii, -g** *na;* **obiimiskodisii,
-g** *na*

SNAKE
SNAKE: **ginebig, -oog** *na*

SNAKESKIN
SNAKESKIN: **ginebigwayaan, -ag** *na*

SNAP
SNAP OFF: snap s.o. off (e.g., something
string-like) **bakibizh /bakibiN-/** *vta;* snap
s.t. off (e.g., something string-like)
bakibidoon *vti2*
SNAP OFF WITH FOOT OR BODY: snap
s.o. off with foot or body (e.g., something
string-like) **bakishkaw** *vta;* snap s.t. off
with foot or body (e.g., something string-
like) **bakishkan** *vti*

SNAPPING TURTLE
SNAPPING TURTLE: **mikinaak, -wag** *na;*
mishiikenh, -yag *na*

SNARE
SNARE: **agoodwaagan, -an** *ni;* **nagwaagan,
-an** *ni;* snare s.o. **nagwaazh /nagwaaN-/**
vta
CHECK SNARES: check one's snares
naadagoodoo *vai*
SET A SNARE: **agoodoo** *vai;* set a snare for
s.o. **agoodaw** *vta*

SNARE WIRE
SNARE WIRE: **agoodwaaganeyaab, -iin** *ni;*
nagwaaganeyaab, -iin *ni*

SNEAK
SNEAK UP: sneak up on s.o. **giimoozikaw**
vta

SNEEZE
SNEEZE: **jaachaamo** *vai*

SNIFF
SNIFF: sniff s.o. **nandomaam** *vta;* sniff s.t.
nandomaandan *vti*

SNIP
SNIP OFF: snip s.o. off (e.g., something
string-like) **bakizh /bakizhw-/** *vta;* snip s.t.
off (e.g., something string-like) **bakizhan**
vti

SNOT
SNOT: **ziinikiigomaan** *na*

SNOUT
SNOUT: my snout **nishkoonzh** *nid*

SNOW
SNOW: **goon** *na;* **zoogipon /zoogipo-/** *vii*
BRUSH SNOW: brush snow off s.o. by hand
bawaagonen *vta;* brush snow off s.o. using
something **bawaagone' /bawaagone'w-/**
vta; brush snow off s.t. by hand
bawaagonenan *vti;* brush snow off s.t.
using something **bawaagone'an** *vta*
CRUST ON THE SNOW: there is a crust on
the snow **onaabanad** *vii*
DEEP SNOW: be deep snow **ishpaagonagaa,
ishpaagonagaamagad** *vii*
HEAVY WET SNOW: there is heavy wet
snow falling **zhakipon /zhakipo-/** *vii*
MUCH SNOW: be much snow **goonikaa,
goonikaamagad** *vii*
SNOW GOES ALONG: **bimipon /bimipo-/**
vii
SNOW IN LARGE FLAKES:
mamaangadepon /mamaangadepo-/ *vii*
SOFT SNOW: there is soft snow
zhakaagonagaa, zhakaagonagaamagad
vii
START TO SNOW: **maajipon /maajipo-/** *vii*
STOP SNOWING: **ishkwaapon /ishkwaapo-/**
vii
UNDER THE SNOW: **anaamaagon** *pc, also*
anaamaagonag

SNOWSHOE
SNOWSHOE: **aagim, -ag** *na;* **aagimose** *vai*
BEAR PAW SNOWSHOE: **makwasaagim,
-ag** *na*

SNOWSHOE HARE
SNOWSHOE HARE: **waabooz, -oog** *na*

SNUFF
SNUFF: **biindaakwaan** *na*
CHEW SNUFF OR TOBACCO: **biindaakwe**
vai

SO
SO: **izhi-** *pv3;* so... **oonh** *pc*
JUST SO: **eniwek** *pc*
SO IT IS SAID: **giiwenh** *pc*
SO THAT: **ji-** *pv1*
SO THE STORY GOES: **giiwenh** *pc*

SO MANY
SO MANY: **daso-** *pv3;* **daswi** *nm;* they are so
many **dashiwag /dashi-/** *vai;* **dasinoon
/dasin-/** *vii*
SO MANY ACRES: **daso-diba'igaans** *pc*
SO MANY BAGS: **dasooshkin** *pc*
SO MANY BUSHELS: so many bushels **daso-
diba'iminaan** *pc*

SO MANY CUPFULS: **dasonaagaans** *pc*
SO MANY DAYS: **daso-giizhik** *pc;* **dasogon**
  pc; be so many days **dasogonagad** *vii*
SO MANY DOLLARS: **daswaabik** *pc*
SO MANY FEET: **dasozid** *pc*
SO MANY HOURS: **daso-diba'igan** *pc*
SO MANY INCHES: **dasoninj** *pc*
SO MANY MILES: **daso-diba'igan** *pc*
SO MANY MINUTES: **daso-diba'igaans** *pc*
SO MANY MONTHS: **daso-giizis** *pc*
SO MANY NIGHTS: **daso-dibik** *pc*
SO MANY PAIRS: **daswewaan** *pc*
SO MANY POUNDS: **daso-
  dibaabiishkoojigan** *pc*
SO MANY SETS: so many sets **daswewaan** *pc*
SO MANY THOUSAND: **dasosagoons** *nm*
SO MANY TIMES: **dasing** *pc*
SO MANY WEEKS: **daso-anama'e-giizhik**
  pc; be so many weeks **daso-anama'e-
  giizhikwagad** *vii, also* **daswanama'e-
  giizhikwagad**
SO MANY YEARS: **daso-biboon** *pc;* **daso-
  gikinoonowin** *pc;* be so many years **daso-
  biboonagad** *vii*
SO MANY YEARS OLD: be so many years
  old **daso-biboonagizi** *vai*
SOAK
  SOAK: soak s.o. **agonjim** *vta;* soak s.t.
    agonjidoon *vti2*
  PUT IN TO SOAK: be put in to soak
    agonjijigaade, agonjijigaademagad *vii;*
    agonjijigaazo *vai;* put s.o. in to soak
    agonjim *vta;* put s.t. in to soak **agonjidoon**
    vti2
SOAP
  SOAP: **giziibiiga'igan, -an** *ni*
SOBER
  SOBER UP: **aatebii** *vai*
SOCIAL WORKER
  SOCIAL WORKER: **ashangewinini, -wag** *na;*
    social worker (female) **ashangewikwe, -g**
    na
SOCK
  SOCK: **azhigan, -an** *ni*
  PUT ON SOCKS: put on one's socks
    biitazhigane *vai*
  TAKE OFF SOCKS: take off one's socks
    giitazhigane *vai*
  WEAR SOCKS: **gigazhigane** *vai*
SOD HOUSE
  SOD HOUSE: **akiiwigamig, -oon** *ni*
SODA
  BAKING SODA: **ombizigan** *ni*
SOFT
  SOFT: be soft **nookaa, nookaamagad** *vii;*
    nookizi *vai;* be soft (as something sheet-
    like) **nookiigad** *vii;* **nookiigizi** *vai*
  HAVE A SOFT VOICE: **bedowe** *vai*
  SOFT SNOW: there is soft snow
    zhakaagonagaa, zhakaagonagaamagad
    vii
SOFT DRINK
  SOFT DRINK: **menwaagamig, -in** *ni-pt;*
    waashkobaagamig, -in *ni-pt*

SOFTENED
  SOFTENED: be softened in water
    nookaabaawe *vai;* **nookaabaawe,
    nookaabaawemagad** *vii*
SOLDIER
  SOLDIER: **zhimaaganish, -ag** *na*
SOLE
  SOLE: my sole **ninagaakizid, -an
    /-nagaakizid-/** *nid*
SOLID
  SOLID: be solid **zoongan** *vii;* **zoongizi** *vai*
  MAKE SOLID: make s.o. solid **zoongi'** *vta;*
    make s.t. solid **zoongitoon** *vti2*
SOME
  SOME: **aanind** *pc*
  FOR SOME TIME: **gomaapii** *pc*
  SOME AMOUNT: **gomaa** *pc*
  SOME DISTANCE: **gomaapii** *pc*
SOMEBODY
  SOMEBODY: somebody *animate indefinite*
    awiya, -g *pr, also* **awiiya**
SOMEONE
  SOMEONE: **aya'aa, -g** *pr*
SOMETHING
  SOMETHING: **ayi'ii, -n** *pr;* something
    inanimate indefinite **gegoo** *pr*
SOMETIME
  SOMETIME: **ingoding** *pc, also* **ningoding***
SOMETIMES
  SOMETIMES: **ayaangodinong** *pc, also*
    aangodinong
SOMEWHAT
  SOMEWHAT: **eniwek** *pc*
SOMEWHERE
  SOMEWHERE: **ingoji** *pc, also* **ningoji***
SON
  SON: my son **ingozis, -ag /-gozis-/** *nad, also*
    ingos, ingwizis*
SON-IN-LAW
  SON-IN-LAW: **na'aangish, -iig** *na;* my son-in-
    law **niningwan, -ag** *nad*
SONG
  SONG: **nagamon, -an** *ni;* **nagamowin** *ni*
  DANCE SONG: **niimi'idii-nagamon, -an** *ni*
  MOCCASIN GAME SONG: **makizinataage-
    nagamon, -an** *ni*
  SPIRITUAL SONG: **manidoo-nagamon, -an**
    ni
SOON
  SOON: **wayiiba** *pc; also* **wiiba***
SORE
  SORE: be sore **gaagiidizi** *vai*
  SORE ARM: have a sore arm **gaagiijinike** *vai*
  SORE BACK: have a sore back
    gaagiidaawigan *vai*
  SORE ELBOW: have a sore elbow
    gaagiijidooskwan *vai*
  SORE FINGER: have a sore finger
    gaagiijininjii *vai*
  SORE FOOT: have a sore foot **gaagiijizide** *vai*
  SORE HAND: have a sore hand **gaagiijininjii**
    vai
  SORE LEG: have a sore leg **gaagiijigaade** *vai*

SORE THROAT: have a sore throat
wiisagigonewe *vai*
SORES
SORES: have sores **omigii** *vai*
SORROWFUL
SORROWFUL: be sorrowful **osidaawendam**
vai2
SORT
SORT: sort *animate* **dino, -wag** *pr, also*
dinowa; sort *inanimate* **dino, -wan** *pr, also*
dinowa
SOUL
SOUL: my soul **injichaag, -wag /-jichaagw-/**
nad
SOUND
LIKE THE SOUND: **minotam** *vai2*
MAKE SOUNDS: make sounds on s.t.
madwewetoon *vti2;* make sounds on
things **madwewechige** *vai*
SOUND FOREIGN: **mayagitaagozi** *vai*
SOUND GOOD: **minotaagozi** *vai;*
minotaagwad *vii*
SOUND STRANGE: **mayagitaagozi** *vai*
SOUNDING GOOD: hear s.o. sounding good
minotaw *vta;* hear s.t. sounding good
minotan *vti*
SOUP
SOUP: **naboob, -iin** *ni*
BEAN SOUP: **mashkodesiminaaboo** *ni*
CHICKEN SOUP: **baaka'aakwenhwaaboo**
ni
CORN SOUP: **mandaaminaaboo** *ni*
DUMPLING SOUP: **bisigadanaaboo** *ni*
FISH SOUP: **giigoonhwaaboo** *ni*
MAKE SOUP: **naboobiike** *vai*
PEA SOUP: **anijiiminaaboo** *ni*
RABBIT SOUP: **waaboozwaaboo** *ni*
SOUR
SOUR: be sour **zhiiwan** *vii;* **zhiiwizi** *vai;* be
sour (as a liquid) **zhiiwaagamin**
/zhiiwaagami-/ *vii*
SOURDOUGH
SOURDOUGH: **zhiiwisijigan, -ag** *na*
SOUTH
SOUTH: **zhaawan** *pc*
IN THE SOUTH: **zhaawanong** *pc*
SOUTH WIND: **zhaawani-noodin** *na*
TO THE SOUTH: **zhaawanong** *pc*
SPACE
SPACE: be space **dawaa, dawaamagad** *vii*
SPADE
SPADE SUITE CARD: **biig, -wag** *na*
SPANK
SPANK: spank s.o. **bapasidiye'**
/bapasidiye'w-/ *vta*
SPARE
SPARE: spare s.o. **manaaji'** *vta;* spare s.t.
manaajitoon *vti2*
SPAWN
SPAWN: they spawn **aamiwag /aami-/** *vai*
SPEAK
SPEAK: **gaagiigido** *vai;* **giigido** *vai;* speak to
s.o. **ganoozh /ganooN-/** *vta;* speak to s.t.

ganoodan *vti;* idan *vti;* they speak to each
other **ganoonidiwag /ganoonidi-/** *vai*
COME SPEAKING: **biidwewidam** *vai2*
GO AWAY SPEAKING: **animwewidam** *vai2*
HAVE DIFFICULTY SPEAKING:
maazhigiizhwe *vai*
HEARD SPEAKING AT A DISTANCE: be
heard speaking at a distance **debwewidam**
vai2
HEARD SPEAKING GOING TO A CER-
TAIN PLACE: be heard speaking going to
a certain place **inwewidam** *vai*
HEARD SPEAKING IN A CERTAIN
PLACE: be heard speaking in a certain
place **danwewidam** *vai2*
MAKE A MISTAKE SPEAKING:
wanigiizhwe *vai*
SPEAK A CERTAIN LANGUAGE: **inwe** *vai*
SPEAK A SCANDINAVIAN LANGUAGE:
agongosimo *vai*
SPEAK A STRANGE LANGUAGE:
mayagwe *vai*
SPEAK AN INDIAN LANGUAGE: speak an
Indian language (especially Ojibwe) to s.o.
anishinaabemotaw *vta;* speak an Indian
language (especially Ojibwe)
anishinaabemo *vai*
SPEAK CORRECTLY: **gwayakowe** *vai*
SPEAK CREE: **omashkiigoomo** *vai*
SPEAK DAKOTA: **bwaanimo** *vai;* speak Da-
kota to s.o. **bwaanimotaw** *vta*
SPEAK ENGLISH: **zhaaganaashiimo** *vai;*
speak English to s.o. **zhaaganaashiimotaw**
vta
SPEAK FRENCH: **wemitigoozhiimo** *vai*
SPEAK IN A CERTAIN WAY: they speak to
each other in a certain way **idiwag /idi-/** *vai*
SPEAK IN AN INDIAN LANGUAGE: speak
in an Indian language (especially in
Ojibwe) **anishinaabe-gaagiigido** *vai*
SPEAK LOUD: **gizhiiwe** *vai*
SPEAK NASTILY: **wiinigiizhwe** *vai*
SPEAK ODAWA: speak Odawa (Ottawa)
odaawaamo *vai*
SPEAK OJIBWE: **ojibwemo** *vai;* speak Ojib-
we to s.o. **ojibwemotaw** *vta;* speak an In-
dian language (especially Ojibwe) to s.o.
anishinaabemotaw *vta;* speak an Indian
language (especially Ojibwe)
anishinaabemo *vai*
SPEAK SO: **ikido** *vai;* speak so to s.o. **izhi**
/iN-/ *vta*
SPEAK WELL: **minowe** *vai*
SPEAKER
SPEAKER: speaker (for others)
aanikanootaagewinini, -wag *na*
SPEAR
SPEAR: **zhimaagan, -an** *ni;* spear s.t.
badaka'an *vti;* spear things **badaka'ige** *vai*
FISH SPEAR: **anit, -iin** *ni*
FISH THROUGH THE ICE WITH SPEAR:
akwa'waa *vai*
SPECTATOR
SPECTATOR: be a spectator **waabange** *vai*

SPEECH
SPEECH: **giigidowin, -an** *ni*
HAVE ABNORMAL SPEECH:
maazhigiizhwe *vai*
SPEED
ARRIVE SPEEDING: **bagamibide,
bagamibidemagad** *vii;* **bagamibizo** *vai*
DRIVE AT A CERTAIN SPEED:
apiichibide, apiichibidemagad *vii;*
apiichibizo *vai*
FLY AT A CERTAIN SPEED: **apiichibide,
apiichibidemagad** *vii;* **apiichibizo** *vai*
GO A CERTAIN SPEED: **apiizikaa** *vai*
GROW AT A CERTAIN SPEED: **apiichigi**
vai; **apiichigin** *vii*
HEARD SPEEDING ALONG: be heard
speeding along **bimwewebide,
bimwewebidemagad** *vii;* **bimwewebizo**
vai
HEARD SPEEDING HERE: be heard
speeding here **biidwewebide,
biidwewebidemagad** *vii;* **biidwewebizo**
vai
RUN AT A CERTAIN SPEED: **apiichibatoo**
vai; run at a certain speed (e.g., a machine)
apiichibide, apiichibidemagad *vii;*
apiichibizo *vai*
SPEED ABOUT: **babaamibide,
babaamibidemagad** *vii;* **babaamibizo** *vai*
SPEED ALONG: **bimibide, bimibidemagad**
vii; **bimibizo** *vai*
SPEED ALONG THE SHORE: **jiigewebizo**
vai
SPEED AWAY: **animibide, animibidemagad**
vii; **animibizo** *vai*
SPEED AWAY MAKING NOISE:
animwewebide, animwewebidemagad
vii; **animwewebizo** *vai*
SPEED FAST: **gizhiibide, gizhiibidemagad**
vii; **gizhiibizo** *vai*
SPEED FROM A CERTAIN PLACE:
onjibide, onjibidemagad *vii;* **onjibizo** *vai*
SPEED HERE: **biijibide, biijibidemagad** *vii;*
biijibizo *vai*
SPEED IN: drive in **biinjibide,
biinjibidemagad** *vii;* **biinjibizo** *vai*
SPEED INSIDE: **biindigebide,
biindigebidemagad** *vii;* **biindigebizo** *vai*
SPEED OFF: **maajiibide, maajiibidemagad**
vii; **maajiibizo** *vai*
SPEED OFF TO THE SIDE: **bakebide,
bakebidemagad** *vii;* **bakebizo** *vai*
SPEED SUDDENLY INTO VIEW:
zaagewebide, zaagewebidemagad *vii;*
zaagewebizo *vai*
SPEED TO A CERTAIN PLACE: **ipide,
ipidemagad** *vii;* **ipizo** *vai*
SPEED UPWARDS: **ombibide,
ombibidemagad** *vii;* **ombibizo** *vai*
STOP SPEEDING: **noogibide,
noogibidemagad** *vii;* **noogibizo** *vai*
WIND HAS A CERTAIN SPEED: the wind
has a certain speed **apiitaanimad** *vii*

SPEND
SPEND EVERYTHING: **jaaginige** *vai*
SPEND TIME
SPEND TIME IN A CERTAIN PLACE:
dazhitaa *vai;* **dazhiike** *vai*
SPIDER
SPIDER: **asabikeshiinh, -yag** *na*
SPILE
SPILE: spile (for sugaring) **negwaakwaan, -an**
ni
SPILL
SPILL: spill s.t. **ziiginan** *vti;* **ziigwebinan** *vti;*
spill things **ziiginige** *vai*
SPILL OUT: **ziigise, ziigisemagad** *vii*
SPIN
SPIN: **gizhibaabide, gizhibaabidemagad** *vii;*
gizhibaabise *vai;* **gizhibaabise,
gizhibaabisemagad** *vii;* **gizhibaabizo** *vai*
SPIRIT
SPIRIT: **jiibay, -ag** *na;* **manidoo, -g** *na;* be a
spirit **manidoowi** *vai;* my spirit **injichaag,
-wag** */-jichaagw-/* *nad*
GREAT SPIRIT: **gichi-manidoo, -g** *na*
SPIRITUAL
SPIRITUAL NATURE: have a spiritual
nature **manidoowaadizi** *vai*
SPIRITUAL POWER
SPIRITUAL POWER: have spiritual power
manidooke *vai;* take on spiritual power by
one's own authority **manidookaazo** *vai*
SPIRITUAL SONG
SPIRITUAL SONG: **manidoo-nagamon, -an**
ni
SPIT
SPIT: **ziko** *vai;* **zikowin** *ni;* spit on s.o.
zikwaazh */zikwaaN-/* *vta;* spit on s.t.
zikwaadan *vti;* spit on things **zikwaajige**
vai
SPLASH
SPLASH: splash s.o. **zaswebiiga'andaw** *vta*
SPLIT
SPLIT: be split **daashkaa, daashkaamagad**
vii; split (as something of wood)
daashkigishkaa *vai;* **daashkigishkaa,
daashkigishkaamagad** *vii*
SPLIT APART: **daashkikaa,
daashkikaamagad** *vii*
SPLIT BY CHOPPING: split s.o. by chopping
(as something of wood) **daashkiga'**
/daashkiga'w-/ *vta;* split s.t. by chopping
(as something of wood) **daashkiga'an** *vti*
SPLIT BY CUTTING: split s.o. by cutting
daashkizh */daashkizhw-/* *vta;* split s.t. by
cutting **daashkizhan** *vti*
SPLIT FIREWOOD: **daashkiga'ise** *vai*
SPLIT LENGTHWISE WITH HANDS: split
s.o. lengthwise with hands **daashkibizh**
/daashkibiN-/ *vta;* split s.t. lengthwise with
hands **daashkibidoon** *vti2*
SPLIT WOOD: **daashkiga'ige** *vai*
SPOIL
SPOIL: **banaajishin** *vai;* **banaajisin** *vii;* spoil
s.o. **banaaji'** *vta;* **nishwanaaji'** *vta;* spoil

s.t. banaajitoon *vti2;* nishwanaajitoon
vti2; spoil things nishwanaajichige *vai*
SPOILED
    SPOILED: be spoiled banaadad *vii;* banaadizi
    vai
SPONTANEOUSLY
    SPONTANEOUSLY: biinizikaa *pc*
SPOOL
    SPOOL: spool (for thread) asabaabiiwaatig,
    -oon *ni*
SPOON
    SPOON: emikwaanens, -an *ni;* ladle
    emikwaan, -an *ni*
    WOODEN SPOON: mitigwemikwaan, -an *ni*
SPOON FEED
    SPOON FEED: spoon feed s.o. zhakamodaw
    vta
    SPOON FEED A LIQUID: spoon feed s.o. a
    liquid ziigana' /ziigana'w-/ *vta*
SPOTTED
    SPOTTED: be spotted gidagaa,
    gidagaamagad *vii;* gidagizi *vai;* be spotted
    (as something sheet-like) gidagiigad *vii;*
    gidagiigizi *vai*
SPOUSE
    SPOUSE: my spouse niwiidigemaagan, -ag
    /-wiidigemaagan-/ *na*
SPRAIN
    SPRAIN ARM: sprain one's arm zeginikeshin
    vai
    SPRAIN FOOT: sprain one's foot
    zegizideshin *vai*
    SPRAIN LEG: sprain one's leg zegigaadeshin
    vai
SPREAD
    SPREAD ALL OVER: miziweshkaa,
    miziweshkaamagad *vii*
    SPREAD THE NEWS ABOUT:
    babaamaajimo *vai*
    SPREAD USING SOMETHING: spread s.o.
    using something zhizhoo' /zhizhoo'w-/
    vta; spread s.t. using something
    zhizhoo'an *vti;* spread things using some-
    thing zhizhoo'ige *vai*
SPREAD OUT
    SPREAD OUT: spread s.o. out zhingaden
    vta; spread s.t. out zhingadenan *vti*
    LAY SPREAD OUT: lay s.o. spread out
    zhingadeshim *vta;* lay s.t. spread out
    zhingadesidoon *vti2*
    LIE SPREAD OUT: zhingadeshin *vai;*
    zhingadesin *vii*
SPRING
    SPRING: be spring ziigwan *vii*
    LAST SPRING: ziigwanong *pc*
    SPEND THE SPRING: spend the spring
    somewhere ziigwanishi *vai*
    SPRING BEFORE LAST: awas-ziigwanong
    pc
SPRING
    SPRING: spring (water source)
    mookijiwanibiig *ni*

SPRINGY
    SPRINGY GROUND: be springy ground
    dootooban *vii*
SPRINKLING
    SPRINKLING RAIN: be sprinkling rain
    awanibiisaa, awanibiisaamagad *vii*
SPROUT
    SPROUT: zaagakii *vai;* zaagakii,
    zaagakiimagad *vii;* zaagigi *vai;* zaagigin
    vii
SPRUCE
    WHITE SPRUCE: gaawaandag, -oog *na*
SPRUCE ROOT
    SPRUCE ROOT: wadab, -iig *na*
    BASKET OF SPRUCE ROOT: wadabii-
    makak, -oon *ni*
SPY
    SPY: giimaabi *vai;* spy on s.o. giimaabam *vta*
SQUARE
    SQUARE: be square gakakaa, gakakaamagad
    vii; gakakizi *vai;* be square (as something
    mineral) gakakaabikad *vii;* gakakaabikizi
    vai; be square (as something sheet-like)
    gakakiigad *vii;* gakakiigizi *vai;* be square
    (as something stick- or wood-like)
    gakakaakozi *vai;* gakakaakwad *vii*
    HAVE A SQUARE PATTERN: gakakishin
    vai; gakakisin *vii*
    MAKE SQUARE: make s.o. square gakaki'
    vta; make s.t. square gakakitoon *vti2*
SQUASH
    SQUASH: okanakosimaan, -an *ni;*
    okosimaan, -an *ni*
SQUEAK
    SQUEAK: giziibwewe *vai;* giziibwewe,
    giziibwewemagad *vii;* squeak in motion
    giziibweweshkaa *vai;* giziibweweshkaa,
    giziibweweshkaamagad *vii*
SQUEEZE
    SQUEEZE: squeeze s.o. maagobizh
    /maagobiN-/ *vta;* ziinibizh /ziinibiN-/ *vta;*
    squeeze s.t. maagobidoon *vti2;*
    ziinibidoon *vti2*
SQUIRREL
    SQUIRREL: red squirrel ajidamoo, -g *na*
    FLYING SQUIRREL: zhagashkaandawe, -g
    na
    GREY SQUIRREL: misajidamoo, -g *na*
STAB
    STAB: stab s.o. bazhiba' /bazhiba'w-/ *vta;*
    stab s.t. bazhiba'an *vti*
STACK
    STACK: stack s.o. okoshim *vta;* stack s.o. (as
    something stick- or wood-like)
    okwaakoshim *vta;* stack s.t. okosidoon
    vti2
STAGE FRIGHT
    STAGE FRIGHT: have stage fright
    wanaanimizi *vai*
STAIRWAY
    STAIRWAY: akwaandawaagan, -an *ni*
STALLION
    STALLION: naabesim, -oog *na*

STAMP
POSTAGE STAMP: **oshtigwaanens, -an** *ni*
STAND
STAND: **niibawi** *vai*
STAND AT THE END: **ishkwegaabawi** *vai*
STAND BACK: **azhegaabawi** *vai*
STAND FACING A CERTAIN WAY:
inaasamigaabawi *vai*
STAND IN FRONT: **niigaanigaabawi** *vai*
STAND IN PLACE OF: stand in place of s.o.
aanikeshkaw *vta*
STAND LEANING AGAINST: stand leaning
against something **aatwaakogaabawi** *vai*
STAND OUT OF THE WAY: **ikogaabawi**
vai
STAND QUIETLY: **bizaanigaabawi** *vai*
STAND STIFFLY: **jiibadaakogaabawi** *vai*
STAND STRAIGHT: **gwayakogaabawi** *vai*
STAND UP: **bazigwii** *vai;* make s.o. stand up
niibawi' *vta;* make s.t. stand up
niibawitoon *vti2*
STAND UP FROM A SURFACE: **badakide,**
badakidemagad *vii;* **badakizo** *vai*
STAND UP SUDDENLY: **bazigonjise** *vai*
STAND WITH THE BACK OUT:
animikogaabawi *vai*
STOP AND STAND IN PLACE: stop and
stand in place **noogigaabawi** *vai*
TURN STANDING: turn while standing
gwekigaabawi *vai;* **washkigaabawi** *vai*
STAR
STAR: **anang, -oog** *na*
START
START: **maajise** *vai;* **maajise,**
maajisemagad *vii;* **maajii-** *pv4;* start (as
an event) **maadakamigad** *vii;* start (in
some event) **maadakamigizi** *vai;* start s.o.
(e.g., a car) **maadwewebizoni'** *vta;* start
s.o. (e.g., a car, a clock) **maajiishkaa'** *vta*
START A JOURNEY: **maadaadizi** *vai*
START A MONTH: **maadaginzo** *vai*
START AN ACTIVITY: **maajitaa** *vai*
START EATING: **maadanjige** *vai*
START OFF: **maajaa** *vai,* also **ani-maajaa;**
maajii- *pv4;* they start off in a group
maadaawanidiwag /**maadaawanidi-**/ *vai*
START OFF ON THE ICE:
maajiiyaadagaako *vai*
START TO DRIP: **maajigaa,**
maajigaamagad *vii*
START TO FLEE: **maajiiba'iwe** *vai*
START TO FLOW: **maajijiwan** *vii*
START TO GET SICK: **mizizi** *vai*
START TO GROW: **maajiigi** *vai;* **maajiigin**
vii
START TO LEAK: **maajigaa,**
maajigaamagad *vii*
START TO MAKE: start to make s.o. **maaji'**
vta; start to make s.t. **maajitoon** *vti2*
START TO MOVE: **maajiishkaa,**
maajiishkaamagad *vii*
START TO RAIN: **maajibiisaa,**
maajibiisaamagad *vii*

START TO RUN: **maajiibatoo** *vai;* start to
run (as a machine) **maajiibide,**
maajiibidemagad *vii;* **maajiibizo** *vai*
START TO SING: **maajii'am** *vai2*
START TO SNOW: **maajipon** /**maajipo-**/ *vii*
START TO TELL: **maadaajim** *vai;* start to
tell of s.o. **maadaajim** *vta;* start to tell of
s.t. **maadodan** *vti;* start to tell (s.t.) to s.o.
maadaajimotaw *vta*
START TO WORK: **maadanoki** *vai;* start to
work on s.o. **maadanokaazh**
/**maadanokaaN-**/ *vta;* **maajiikaw** *vta;* start
to work on s.t. **maadanokaadan** *vti;*
maajiikan *vti*
STARTLED
STARTLED: be startled **goshkokaa** *vai*
STARVE
STARVE: **gawanaandam** *vai2*
STATUE
STATUE: **mazinichigan, -ag** *na*
STAY
STAY BEHIND: **ishkwii** *vai*
STAY IN A CERTAIN PLACE: **dazhiike** *vai*
STAY OVERNIGHT: stay overnight with s.o.
nibendaw *vta;* stay overnight with people
nibendaage *vai*
STAY WITH: stay with s.o. **wiij'ayaaw** *vta,*
also **wiiji-ayaaw**
STEADY
STEADY: steady s.o. **minjimin** *vta;* steady s.o.
with foot or body **minjimishkaw** *vta;*
steady s.t. **minjiminan** *vti;* steady s.t. with
foot or body **minjimishkan** *vti;* steady (s.t.)
for s.o. **minjiminamaw** *vta*
STEAL
STEAL: steal (s.t.) **gimoodi** *vai+o;* steal from
s.o. **gimoodim** *vta;* they steal from each
other **gimoodindiwag** /**gimoodindi-**/ *vai*
STEAM
STEAM: **baashkinede, baashkinedemagad**
vii; **baashkinezo** *vai*
STEAMBOAT
STEAMBOAT: **ishkode-jiimaan, -an** *ni*
STEEL
STEEL: **manidoo-biiwaabik** *ni*
STEEP
STEEP BANK: be a steep bank **giishkadinaa,**
giishkadinaamagad *vii*
STEER
STEER: **odaake** *vai*
STEER A CERTAIN WAY: steer s.o. a
certain way **inkwe'** /**inkwe'w-**/ *vta;* steer
s.t. a certain way **inkwe'an** *vti*
STEM
PIPE STEM: **okij, -iin** *ni*
STEP
STEP: **dakokii** *vai;* step on s.o. **dakokaazh**
/**dakokaaN-**/ *vta;* step on s.t. **dakokaadan**
vti
STEP IN THE SAME TRACKS:
naaba'anidizo *vai*

STEP OVER: step over s.o. **baazhida'**
/**baazhida'w-**/ *vta;* step over s.t.
baazhida'an *vti*
STEPDAUGHTER
STEPDAUGHTER: my stepdaughter
indoozhimikwem, -ag /**-doozhimikwem-**/
nad
STEW
STEW: **wiiyaasi-naboob** *ni*
STICK
STICK IN: stick s.o. in **badakishim** *vta;*
badakizh /**badakiN-**/ *vta;* stick s.t. in
badakidoon *vti2;* **badakisidoon** *vti2;* stick
something in s.o. **badaka'** /**badaka'w-**/ *vta;*
stick something in s.t. **badaka'an** *vti;* stick
something in things **badaka'ige** *vai;* stick
things in **badakisijige** *vai*
STICK IN A FEATHER: stick a feather in
one's hair or hat **badakibine'o** *vai*
STICK IN A SURFACE: **badakise** *vai;*
badakise, badakisemagad *vii*
STICK IN A TIGHT PLACE: stick s.o. in a
tight place **zhegon** *vta;* stick s.t. in a
tight place **zhegonan** *vti*
STICK OUT HEAD: stick out one's head
zaagikweni *vai*
STICK OUT TONGUE: stick out one's
tongue **zaagidenaniweni** *vai;* stick out
one's tongue at s.o. **zaagidenaniwetaw** *vta*
STICK
STICK: **mitig, -oon** *ni;* **mitigoons, -an** *ni*
STICK
STICK: **bazagoke** *vai;* **bazagoke,**
bazagokemagad *vii;* stick on **agoke** *vai;*
agoke, agokemagad *vii;* stick s.o. on
agokazh /**agokaN-**/ *vta;* stick s.t. on
agokadoon *vti2*
STICKY
STICKY: be sticky **bazagozi** *vai;* **bazagwaa,**
bazagwaamagad *vii*
STIFF
FREEZE STIFF: freeze s.o. stiff
mashkawaakwajim *vta;* freeze s.t. stiff
mashkawaakwajidoon *vti2*
FROZEN STIFF: be frozen stiff
mashkawaakwadin *vii;* **mashkawaakwaji**
vai
STIFF ARM: have a stiff arm **jiibadaakonike**
vai; **jiibajinike** *vai*
STIFF HAND: have a hand stiff from cold
mashkawajininjiiwaji *vai*
STIFF LEG: have a stiff leg **jiibadaakogaade**
vai; **jiibajigaade** *vai*
STIFF NECK: have a stiff neck
jiibajigwayawe *vai*
STIFFLY
SIT STIFFLY: **jiibadabi** *vai*
STAND STIFFLY: **jiibadaakogaabawi** *vai*
STILL
STILL: **bizaan** *pc;* be still **goshkwaawaadizi**
vai
LIE STILL: **bizaanishin** *vai*
SIT STILL: **bizaanaakwadabi** *vai*

STILL
STILL: **geyaabi** *pc*
STINGILY
HELD STINGILY: be held stingily
zaagichigaade, zaagichigaademagad *vii;*
zaagichigaazo *vai*
STINGY
STINGY: be stingy **zazaagizi** *vai*
STIR
STIR: stir s.t. **waninawe'an** *vti*
STIR THE FIRE: **jiichiishkinzhe'ige** *vai*
STIR TO FORM SUGAR: **nase'ige** *vai;* stir
s.t. to form sugar **nase'an** *vti*
STIR UP: stir s.o. up **ombi'** *vta*
STOMACH
STOMACH: my stomach **nimisad, -an**
/**-misad-**/ *nid*
SWOLLEN STOMACH: have a swollen
stomach **ombijiishkaa** *vai*
STOMACHACHE
GIVE A STOMACHACHE: give s.o. a
stomachache; *inverse forms of:*
aakoshkadekaw- *vta*
HAVE A STOMACHACHE: **aakoshkade** *vai*
STONE
STONE: **asin, -iig** *na;* be of stone **asiniiwan** *vii*
MANY STONES: there are many stones
asiniikaa, asiniikaamagad *vii*
STOP
STOP: stop (moving) **noogishkaa** *vai;*
noogishkaa, noogishkaamagad *vii*
COME TO A STOP: **noogise** *vai*
MAKE STOP: make s.o. stop (e.g., a car)
nagaashkaa' *vta;* make s.t. stop
nagaashkaatoon *vti2*
STOP AN ACTIVITY: **ishkwaataa** *vai*
STOP AND STAND IN PLACE: stop and
stand in places **noogigaabawi** *vai*
STOP BREATHING: **ishkwaanaamo** *vai*
STOP BY HAND: stop s.o. by hand **noogin**
vta; stop s.t. by hand **nooginan** *vti*
STOP CRYING: **giishkowe** *vai*
STOP DRIVING: **noogibide,**
noogibidemagad *vii;* **noogibizo** *vai*
STOP MAKING VOCAL NOISE: **giishkowe**
vai
STOP MOVING: **nagaashkaa** *vai;*
nagaashkaa, nagaashkaamagad *vii*
STOP RAINING: **ishkwaabiisaa,**
ishkwaabiisaamagad *vii*
STOP RUNNING: **noogibatoo** *vai*
STOP SNOWING: **ishkwaapon** /**ishkwaapo-**/
vii
STOP SPEEDING: **noogibide,**
noogibidemagad *vii;* **noogibizo** *vai*
STOP TALKING: stop talking to s.o. **boonim**
vta
STOP UP: stop s.o. up **giba'** /**giba'w-**/ *vta;*
stop s.t. up **giba'an** *vti;* stop things up
giba'ige *vai*
STOPPED
STOPPED UP: be stopped up **giba'igaade,**
giba'igaademagad *vii;* **giba'igaazo** *vai*

STOPPER
STOPPER: **gibaakwa'igan, -an** *ni*
STORAGE LODGE
STORAGE LODGE: **asanjigoowigamig,
-oon** *ni;* **ataasoowigamig, -oon** *ni*
STORE
STORE: store something, store (s.t.) **ataaso**
vai+o
STORE AWAY: store things away **na'enimo**
vai
STORE
STORE: **adaawewigamig, -oon** *ni*
GROCERY STORE: **wiisinii-
adaawewigamig, -oon** *ni*
SECOND-HAND CLOTHING STORE:
second-hand clothing store
zhiigoshkigani-adaawewigamig, -oon *ni*
STORE CLERK
STORE CLERK: **adaawewinini, -wag** *na;*
store clerk (female) **adaawewininiikwe** *na*
STORM
STORM: be a storm **gichi-noodin** *vii;* there is
a severe storm **nichiiwad** *vii*
STORM CLOUD
STORM CLOUDS: there are storm clouds
zegaanakwad *vii*
STORMY
STORMY: be stormy **gichi-izhiwebad** *vii*
STORY
STORY: **dibaajimowin, -an** *ni*
TELL A GOOD STORY: **minwaajimo** *vai*
TELL A STORY: tell a story of s.o. **aajim** *vta;*
tell a story of s.t. **aadodan** *vti*
TELL A TRADITIONAL STORY:
aadizooke *vai*
TELL STORIES: **dadibaajimo** *vai;* tell stories
to s.o. **dadibaajimotaw** *vta*
TRADITIONAL STORY: **aadizookaan, -ag**
na
STORYTELLER
STORYTELLER: **aadizookewinini, -wag** *na;*
dadibaajimoowinini, -wag *na*
STOVE
STOVE: **gizhaabikizigan, -an** *ni*
COOK STOVE: **jiibaakwe-gizhaabikizigan,
-an** *ni*
STOVEPIPE
STOVEPIPE: **okijaabik, -oon** *ni*
STRAIGHT
STRAIGHT: **gwayak** *pc;* be straight
gwayakozi *vai;* **gwayakwaa,
gwayakwaamagad** *vii;* be straight (as
something mineral) **gwayakwaabikad** *vii;*
gwayakwaabikizi *vai;* be straight (as
something stick- or wood-like)
gwayakwaakozi *vai;* **gwayakwaakwad** *vii;*
be straight (as something string-like)
gwayakwaabiigad *vii;* **gwayakwaabiigizi**
vai
CUT STRAIGHT: cut s.o. straight
gwayakozh /gwayakozhw-/ *vta;* cut s.t.
straight **gwayakozhan** *vti*
GO STRAIGHT: **gwayakoshkaa** *vai*

GROW STRAIGHT: **gwayakogi** *vai;*
gwayakogin *vii*
HOLD HEAD STRAIGHT: hold one's head
straight **gwayakokweni** *vai*
LAY STRAIGHT: lay s.o. straight
gwayakoshim *vta;* lay s.t. straight
gwayakosidoon *vti2*
LIE STRAIGHT: **gwayakoshin** *vai;*
gwayakosin *vii*
PULL STRAIGHT: pull s.o. straight
gwayakobizh /gwayakobiN-/ *vta;* pull s.t.
straight **gwayakobidoon** *vti2*
SAW STRAIGHT: saw s.o. straight
gwayakoboozh /gwayakobooN-/ *vta;* saw
s.t. straight **gwayakoboodoon** *vti2*
STAND STRAIGHT: **gwayakogaabawi** *vai*
TEAR STRAIGHT: tear s.o. straight
gwayakobizh /gwayakobiN-/ *vta;* tear s.t.
straight **gwayakobidoon** *vti2*
STRAIN
STRAIN: strain s.t. **zhaabobiiginan** *vti;*
ziikoobiiginan *vti*
STRAIN
STRAIN IN LIFTING: strain self in lifting
jakiiwii *vai*
STRAINER
STRAINER: **zhaabobiiginigan, -an** *ni*
STRANGE
STRANGE: **mayagi-** *pv4;* be strange **mayagizi**
vai
CONSIDER STRANGE: consider s.o. strange
mayagenim *vta*
CONSIDERED STRANGE: be considered
strange **mayagendaagwad** *vii*
FEEL STRANGE: **mayagendam** *vai2*
LOOK STRANGE: **mayaginaagozi** *vai;*
mayaginaagwad *vii*
SOUND STRANGE: **mayagitaagozi** *vai;*
mayagitaagwad *vii*
SPEAK A STRANGE LANGUAGE:
mayagwe *vai*
SPEAKER OF A STRANGE LANGUAGE:
mayagwewinini, -wag *na*
STRANGER
STRANGER: **biiwide, -g** *na*
STRAP
STRAP: **apikan, -an** *ni*
STRAWBERRY
STRAWBERRY: **ode'imin, -an** *ni*
STRENGTH
TEST STRENGTH: test one's strength
gagwejii *vai*
STRETCH
STRETCH: stretch (as something sheet-like)
zhiibiigishkaa, zhiibiigishkaamagad *vii;*
stretch s.o. on a hide stretcher **zhiibaakwa'
/zhiibaakwa'w-/** *vta*
STRETCH A HIDE: **naazhiiga'ige** *vai*
STRETCH BODY: stretch one's body **zhiibii**
vai
STRETCH BY PULLING: stretch s.o. by
pulling (as something sheet-like)
zhiibiigibizh /zhiibiigibiN-/ *vta;* stretch s.t.

by pulling (as something sheet-like)
zhiibiigibidoon *vti2*
STRETCH USING SOMETHING: stretch
s.o. using something (as something sheet-
like) **zhiibiiga'** /**zhiibiiga'w-**/ *vta;* stretch
s.t. using something (as something sheet-
like) **zhiibiiga'an** *vti*

STRETCHER
HIDE STRETCHER: flat hide stretcher
(especially for muskrats)
zhiibaakwa'ataan, -an *ni*

STRIKE
STRIKE: strike s.o. **bakite'** /**bakite'w-**/ *vta;*
strike s.t. **bakite'an** *vti;* strike things
bakite'ige *vai;* they strike each other
bakite'odiwag /**bakite'odi-**/ *vai*

STRING
STRING: string s.o. (e.g., beads) **naabidoo'**
/**naabidoo'w-**/ *vta;* string s.t. **naabidoo'an**
vti; string things **naabidoo'ige** *vai*
STRING A CERTAIN WAY: string s.o. a certain way **inaabiigin** *vta;* string s.t. a certain
way **inaabiiginan** *vti*
STRING ALONG: string s.o. along
bimaabiigin *vta;* string s.t. along
bimaabiiginan *vti*

STRING
STRING: **biiminakwaanens, -an** *ni*
MAKE STRING: **biiminakwe** *vai*

STRIPE
HAVE A STRIPE: **beshaa, beshaamagad** *vii;*
beshizi *vai*
MARK WITH A STRIPE: mark s.o. with a
stripe **beshibii'** /**beshibii'w-**/ *vta;* mark s.t.
with a stripe **beshibii'an** *vti;* mark things
with a stripe **beshibii'ige** *vai*

STRIPS
CUT INTO STRIPS: cut s.t. into strips
baanizhan *vti*

STROKE
HAVE A STROKE: **niboowise** *vai*

STROLL
TAKE A STROLL: **babimose** *vai*

STRONG
STRONG: be strong **mashkawaa,
mashkawaamagad** *vii;* **mashkawizi** *vai;*
zoongan *vii;* **zoongizi** *vai;* be strong (as a
liquid) **mashkawaagamin**
/**mashkawaagami-**/ *vii;* be strong (of a
person) **mashkawizii** *vai*
MAKE STRONG: make s.o. strong **zoongi'**
vta; make s.t. strong **zoongitoon** *vti2*
SMELL STRONG BURNING OR
COOKING: **mashkawimaaso** *vai;*
**mashkawimaate,
mashkawimaatemagad** *vii*
STRONG ARM: have a strong arm
zoonginike *vai*
STRONG BONES: have strong bones
zoongigane *vai*
STRONG HAND: have a strong hand
zoongininjii *vai*

STRUCK
STRUCK: be struck **bakite'igaade,
bakite'igaademagad** *vii;* **bakite'igaazo**
vai
STRUCK BY LIGHTNING: be struck by
lightning **baagijigaade,
baagijigaademagad** *vii;* **baagijigaazo** *vai*

STUB
STUB TOE: stub one's toe **bizozideshin** *vai*

STUBBORN
STUBBORN: be stubborn **zhazhiibitam** *vai2*

STUBBORNLY
STUBBORNLY: **awanjish** *pc*

STUCK
STUCK: be stuck **baataashin** *vai;* **baataasin**
vii; **bwaanawi'o** *vai*
GET STUCK: **baataase** *vai;* **baataase,
baataasemagad** *vii*

STUDENT
STUDENT: **gekinoo'amawind** *na-pt;*
gikinoo'amaagan, -ag *na*

STUFF
STUFF: stuff s.o. **biindashkwaazh**
/**biindashkwaaN-**/ *vta;* stuff s.t.
biindashkwaadan *vti*

STUFFED-UP
HAVE A STUFFED-UP NOSE: **gibijaane**
vai, also **gagiibijaane**

STUMBLE
STUMBLE: **bizogeshin** *vai;* stumble on s.o.
bizokaw *vta;* stumble on s.t. **bizokan** *vti*

STUMP
STUMP: **giishkanakad, -oon** *ni*

STURGEON
STURGEON: **name, -wag** *na*

STUTTER
STUTTER: **gagiibanagaskwe** *vai*

SUCCEED
SUCCEED: **gashki'ewizi** *vai;* succeed at s.t.
gashkitoon *vti2*

SUCCESSION
SOMEONE NEXT IN SUCCESSION TO
THE LEADER: someone next in succession to the leader (e.g., a vice president)
aanike-ogimaa, -g *na*

SUCK
SUCK: **wiikwamo** *vai;* suck on s.o. **wiikwam**
vta; suck on s.t. **wiikwandan** *vti;* suck on
things **wiikwanjige** *vai*
SUCK OUT: suck out of s.o. **zoobam** *vta;*
suck out of s.t. **zoobandan** *vti*

SUCKER
SUCKER: sucker (fish) **namebin, -ag** *na*

SUCKLE
SUCKLE: suckle (of child or offspring) **nooni**
vai

SUDDENLY
SUDDENLY: **gezika** *pc*

SUFFER
SUFFER: **aanimizi** *vai;* **gagwaadagitoo** *vai*
MAKE SUFFER: make s.o. suffer **aanimi'** *vta*
SUFFER EMOTIONALLY: **aanimendam**
vai2

SUFFER IN A CERTAIN PLACE: suffer in a certain place **dapine** *vai*
SUFFER IN MIND: suffer in one's mind **gagwaanisagendam** *vai2*
SUFFER MENTALLY: **aanimendam** *vai2*
SUFFER PAIN: **wiisagendam** *vai*
SUFFICIENT
　SUFFICIENT: **de-** *pv4;* **gwech** *pc;* be sufficient **debise** *vai;* **debise, debisemagad** *vii*
SUFFOCATE
　SUFFOCATE FROM SMOKE: **gibwanaamozo** *vai*
SUGAR
　SUGAR: **ziinzibaakwad** *ni*
　BOIL TO SUGAR: **ombigamizige** *vai;* boil s.t. to sugar **ombigamizan** *vti*
　BOILING SUGAR: **ombigamizigan, -an** *ni*
　GRANULATE SUGAR: **naseyaawangwe** *vai*
　GRANULATED SUGAR: **bibine-ziinzibaakwad** *ni*
　MAPLE SUGAR: **anishinaabe-ziinzibaakwad** *ni;* **ziinzibaakwad** *ni*
　STIR TO FORM SUGAR: stir s.t. to form sugar **nase'an** *vti*
　SUGAR OFF: **ombigamizige** *vai*
SUGAR BEET
　SUGAR BEET: **wiishkobi-jiis, -an** *ni*
SUGAR BOWL
　SUGAR BOWL: **ziinzibaakwad-onaagaans, -an** *ni*
SUGAR BUSH
　SUGAR BUSH: **iskigamizigan, -an** *ni*
SUGAR CAKE
　SUGAR CAKE: **ziiga'igan, -an** *ni*
SUGAR CAMP
　SUGAR CAMP: **iskigamizigan, -an** *ni*
SUGAR CONE
　SUGAR CONE: **zhiishiigwaans, -ag** *na;* **ziiga'igan, -an** *ni*
　CAST SUGAR CONES: **ziiga'ige** *vai*
　MAKE A SUGAR CONE: **ziiga'iganike** *vai*
SUICIDE
　COMMIT SUICIDE: **nisidizo** *vai*
SUITABLE
　SUITABLE: **de-** *pv4;* be suitable **nandawendaagozi** *vai;* **nandawendaagwad** *vii*
SUITCASE
　SUITCASE: **babaamaadizii-makak, -oon** *ni*
SUMMER
　SUMMER: be summer **niibin** *vii*
　LAST SUMMER: **niibinong** *pc*
　LATE SUMMER: **giiwe-niibin** *vii*
　SPEND THE SUMMER: spend the summer somewhere **niibinishi** *vai*
　SUMMER BEFORE LAST: **awas-niibinong** *pc*
SUMMON
　SUMMON: summon s.o. **nandom** *vta*
SUN
　SUN: **giizis, -oog** *na*

SUN SETS: set as the sun **bangishimon /bangishimo-/** *vii*
SUNBURN
　PEEL FROM SUNBURN: **bishagaaso** *vai*
SUNBURNED
　SUNBURNED: be sunburned **gashkaaso** *vai*
SUNDAY
　SUNDAY: be Sunday **anama'e-giizhigad** *vii,* also **aname-giizhigad**
SUNFISH
　SUNFISH: **agwadaashi, -wag** *na*
SUNNY
　SUNNY: be sunny **waaseyaa, waaseyaamagad** *vii*
SUNRISE
　SUNRISE: be sunrise **mooka'am** *vai2*
SUPPER
　EAT SUPPER: **onaagoshi-wiisini** *vai;* eat s.t. for supper **onaagoshi-miijin** *vti3*
SUPPORT
　SUPPORT: support s.o. **bami'** *vta*
SUPPORTED
　SUPPORTED ONE: **bami'aagan, -ag** *na*
SURE
　SURE: **geget** *pc;* sure! **enange** *pc*
　FOR SURE: **mii nange** *pc*
SURPRISE
　SURPRISE: surprise s.o. **goshko'** *vta*
　SURPRISE VERBALLY: surprise s.o. verbally **goshkom** *vta*
SURPRISED
　SURPRISED: be surprised **goshkokaa** *vai*
SURVEY
　SURVEY LAND: **diba'akii** *vai*
SURVEYOR
　SURVEYOR: **diba'akiiwinini, -wag** *na*
SURVIVE
　SURVIVE: **zhaabwii** *vai*
SUSPECT
　SUSPECT: suspect s.o. **anaamenim** *vta;* **moonenim** *vta;* suspect s.t. **anaamendan** *vti*
SUSPENDED
　SUSPENDED IN WATER: be suspended in water **agomo** *vai;* **agonde** *vii*
SUSPENDERS
　SUSPENDERS: suspenders *plural* **anikamaanan /anikamaan-/** *ni*
SWALLOW
　SWALLOW: swallow s.o. **gonzhi /gonN-/** *vta;* swallow s.t. **gondan** *vti*
SWAMP
　SWAMP: **waabashkiki, -in** *ni*
SWAMPY
　SWAMPY: be swampy **waabashkikiiwan** *vii*
SWAN
　SWAN: **waabizii, -g** *na*
SWEAR
　SWEAR: **majigiizhwe** *vai*
SWEAT
　SWEAT: **abwezo** *vai*

SWEAT BATH
TAKE A SWEAT BATH: **madoodoo** *vai*

SWEAT LODGE
SWEAT LODGE: **madoodiswan, -an** *ni*
ROCK FOR SWEAT LODGE:
madoodoowasin, -iig *na*

SWEATY
SWEATY FOOT: have a sweaty foot
abwezide *vai*
SWEATY HAND: have a sweaty hand
abweninjii *vai*

SWEEP
SWEEP: **jiishada'ige** *vai*

SWEET
SWEET: **wiishkobi-** *pv4;* be sweet **wiishkoban**
vii; **wiishkobizi** *vai;* be sweet (as a liquid)
wiishkobaagamin /wiishkobaagami-/ *vii*
TASTE SWEET: **wiishkobipogozi** *vai;*
wiishkobipogwad *vii*

SWEET FLAG
SWEET FLAG: **wiikenh, -yag** *na*

SWEET GRASS
SWEET GRASS: **wiingashk, -oon** *ni*

SWEET ROLL
SWEET ROLL: **waashkobizid bakwezhigan,**
-ag *na-pt;* **wiishkobi-bakwezhigan, -ag** *na*

SWEETHEART
SWEETHEART: my sweetheart
niinimoshenh, -yag /-iinimosheny-/ *nad*

SWIM
ARRIVE SWIMMING: **bagamaadagaa** *vai*
GO SWIMMING: **bagizo** *vai*
HEARD SWIMMING HERE: be heard
swimming here **biidweweyaadagaa** *vai*
SWIM ABOUT: **babaamaadagaa** *vai*
SWIM ACROSS: **aazhawaadagaa** *vai*
SWIM ALONG: **bimaadagaa** *vai;* swim along
(as a fish) **bimakwazhiwe** *vai*
SWIM ASHORE: **agwaayaadagaa** *vai*
SWIM AWAY: **animaadagaa** *vai*
SWIM FROM A CERTAIN PLACE:
ondaadagaa *vai;* swim from a certain place
(as a fish) **ondakwazhiwe** *vai*
SWIM HERE: **biidaadagaa** *vai;* swim here (as
a fish) **biidakwazhiwe** *vai*
SWIM OFF: swim off (as a fish)
maajiikwazhiwe *vai*
SWIM SUDDENLY INTO VIEW: swim as a
fish suddenly into view **zaagewekwazhiwe**
vai
SWIM TO A CERTAIN PLACE: **inaadagaa**
vai; swim to a certain place (as a fish)
inakwazhiwe *vai*

SWING
SWING: **wewebizo** *vai;* **wewebizon, -an** *ni*

SWITCH
SWITCH: **biskaakonebijigan, -an** *ni*
SWITCH ON: switch s.t. on **biskanebidoon**
vti2

SWOLLEN
SWOLLEN: be swollen **baagishi** *vai;* **baagisin**
vii
SWOLLEN EYES: have swollen eyes
baagishkiinzhigwe *vai*
SWOLLEN FACE: have a swollen face
baagiingwe *vai*
SWOLLEN FOOT: have a swollen foot
baagizide *vai*
SWOLLEN GLAND: have a swollen gland
(lymph node) **baaginiishkwe** *vai*
SWOLLEN HAND: have a swollen hand
baagininjii *vai*
SWOLLEN NOSE: have a swollen nose
baagijaane *vai*
SWOLLEN STOMACH: have a swollen
stomach **ombijiishkaa** *vai*

SWORD
SWORD: **ashaweshk, -oon** *ni*

SYRUP
SYRUP: **zhiiwaagamizigan** *ni*
MAKE SYRUP: **zhiiwaagamiziganike** *vai;*
zhiiwaagamizige *vai*
THICKEN INTO SYRUP: **zhiiwaagamide,**
zhiiwaagamidemagad *vii*

T

TAB
TAB AT HEEL OF MOCCASIN:
odoondanegwaajigan, -an *ni*

TABLE
TABLE: **adoopowin, -an** *ni*
SET THE TABLE: **ozisinaagane** *vai*

TABLE CLOTH
TABLE CLOTH: **adoopowiniigin, -oon** *ni*

TADPOLE
TADPOLE: **boodoonh, -yag** *na*

TAFFY
MAKE TAFFY: **bigiwizige** *vai*
MAPLE TAFFY: **bigiwizigan** *ni*

TAIL
ANIMAL TAIL: my tail (of an animal) **inzow,**
-an /-zow-/ *nid*
BIRD TAIL: my tail (of a bird) **ninashkid, -iin**
/-nashkidy-/ *nid*
FISH TAIL: my tail (of a fish) **inzhigwan**
/-zhigwan-/ *nid*
WAG TAIL: wag one's tail **wewebaanoweni**
vai

TAILPIPE
TAILPIPE: **okijaabik, -oon** *ni*

TAKE
TAKE: take s.o. **mami /mam-/** *vta;* take s.o.
offered **odaapin** *vta;* take s.t. **mamoon**
vti2; take s.t. offered **odaapinan** *vti;* take
(s.t.) from s.o. **mamaw** *vta;* take (s.t.)
offered by s.o. **odaapinamaw** *vta;* take
things **mamige** *vai;* take things offered
odaapinige *vai*

ABLE TO TAKE: be able to take s.o.
gashkiwizh /gashkiwiN-/ *vta;* be able to
take s.t. **gashkiwidoon** *vti2*
TAKE A HANDFUL: take a handful of s.o.
ganakin *vta;* take a handful of s.t.
ganakinan *vti*
TAKE A PIECE OFF BY HAND: take a piece
off s.o. by hand **bakwen** *vta;* take a piece
off s.t. by hand **bakwenan** *vti*
TAKE A PIECE OFF USING
SOMETHING: take a piece off s.o. using
something **bakwe'** *vta;* take a piece off s.t.
using something **bakwe'an** *vti*
TAKE A TASTE: take a taste of s.o.
godandan *vti;* take a taste of s.t. **godam**
vta; **gojipidan** *vti*
TAKE ABOUT: take s.o. about **babaamiwizh**
/babaamiwiN-/ *vta;* take s.t. about
babaamiwidoon *vti2*
TAKE ACROSS: take s.o. across
aazhogewizh /aazhogewiN-/ *vta;* take s.t.
across **aazhogewidoon** *vti2*
TAKE ACROSS BY BOAT: take s.o. across
by boat **aazhawa'oozh /aazhawa'ooN-/**
vta; take s.t. across by boat
aazhawa'oodoon *vti2*
TAKE ALONG: take s.o. along **bimiwizh**
/bimiwiN-/ *vta;* **maajiizh /maajiiN-/** *vta;*
take s.t. along **bimiwidoon** *vti2;*
maajiidoon *vti2;* take (s.t.) along for s.o.
maajiidaw *vta;* take people along
bimiwizhiwe *vai*
TAKE ALONG A GUN: **niimibaashkizigane**
vai
TAKE ALONG FOR A RIDE: take s.o. along
for a ride **bimibizoni'** *vta*
TAKE ALONG IN A BOAT: take s.o. along
in a boat **bima'oozh /bima'ooN-/** *vta;* take
s.t. along in a boat **bima'oodoon** *vti2*
TAKE ASHORE: take s.o. ashore **agwaashim**
vta; take s.t. ashore **agwaasidoon** *vti2*
TAKE ASHORE BY BOAT: take s.t. ashore
by boat **agwaa'oodoon** *vti2*
TAKE AWAY: take s.o. away **animiwizh**
/animiwiN-/ *vta;* **maajiizh /maajiiN-/** *vta;*
take s.t. away **animiwidoon** *vti2;*
maajiidoon *vti2;* take people away
maajiizhiwe *vai*
TAKE AWAY BY BOAT: take s.o. away by
boat **anima'oozh /anima'ooN-/** *vta;* take
s.t. away by boat **anima'oodoon** *vti2*
TAKE BACK: take s.o. back **azhen** *vta;* take
s.t. back **azhenan** *vti;* take (s.t.) back to
s.o. **azhenamaw** *vta*
TAKE DOWN: take s.o. down **bina' /bina'w-/**
vta; take s.t. down **bina'an** *vti*
TAKE EVERYTHING: **jaaginige** *vai*
TAKE FORCIBLY: take (s.t.) from s.o.
forcibly **makam** *vta*
TAKE FROM A CERTAIN PLACE: take s.o.
from a certain place **onjiwizh /onjiwiN-/**
vta; take s.t. from a certain place
onjiwidoon *vti2*
TAKE HOME: take s.o. home **giiwewizh**
/giiwewiN-/ *vta;* take s.t. home

giiwewidoon *vti2;* take (s.t.) home for s.o.
giiwewidaw *vta*
TAKE INLAND: take s.o. inland **gopiwizh**
/gopiwiN-/ *vta;* take s.t. inland
gopiwidoon *vti2*
TAKE INSIDE: take s.o. inside **biindigazh**
/biindigaN-/ *vta;* take s.t. inside
biindigadoon *vti2*
TAKE OFF INTO THE AIR: **bazikwa'o** *vai*
TAKE OFF THE FIRE: take s.o. off the fire
agwaabiigin *vta;* **agwaashim** *vta;* take s.t.
off the fire **agwaabiiginan** *vti;*
agwaasidoon *vti2*
TAKE OFF THE WATER: take s.o. off the
water **agwaabiigin** *vta;* take s.t. off the
water **agwaabiiginan** *vti*
TAKE OFF THE WATER USING
SOMETHING: take s.o. off the water
using something **agwaabiiga'**
/agwaabiiga'w-/ *vta;* take s.t. off the water
using something **agwaabiiga'an** *vti*
TAKE OUT: take s.o. out **zaagizi'** *vta;* take
s.t. out **zaagizitoon** *vti2;* take (s.t.) out for
s.o. **zaagizitaw** *vta*
TAKE PICTURES: **mazinaakizige** *vai;* take
pictures of s.o. **mazinaakiz**
/mazinaakizw-/ *vta;* take pictures of s.t.
mazinaakizan *vti*
TAKE PLACE: take s.o.'s place **naabishkaw**
vta; take someone's place **naabishkaage**
vai
TAKE TO A CERTAIN PLACE: take s.o. to
a certain place **izhiwizh /izhiwiN-/** *vta;*
take s.t. to a certain place **izhiwidoon** *vti2;*
take (s.t.) to s.o. at a certain place
izhiwidaw *vta*
TAKE TO A CERTAIN PLACE BY BOAT:
take s.o. to a certain place by boat
ina'oozh /ina'ooN-/ *vta;* take s.t. to a
certain place by boat **ina'oodoon** *vti2*
TAKE TO THE SHORE: take s.o. to the
shore **madaabiiwizh /madaabiiwiN-/** *vta;*
take s.t. to the shore **madaabiiwidoon** *vti2*
TAKE WILD RICE INLAND: **gopimine** *vai*
TAKE WRONG ONE: take s.o. who/that is
the wrong one **wanin** *vta;* take s.t. that is
the wrong one **waninan** *vti*

TAKE CARE

TAKE CARE: take care of s.o. **ganawenim**
vta; take care of s.t. **ganawendan** *vti;* take
care of (s.t.) for s.o. **ganawendamaw** *vta;*
take care of things **ganawenjige** *vai;* they
take care of each other **ganawenindiwag**
/ganawenindi-/ *vai*
TAKE CARE OF A CHILD: **bamoozhe** *vai;*
ganawendaawaso *vai*

TAKE OFF

TAKE OFF: take s.o. off **gidiskin** *vta;*
giichigon *vta;* take s.t. off **gidiskinan** *vti;*
giichigonan *vti*
TAKE OFF CLOTHES: take off one's clothes
giizikonaye *vai;* take s.o. off the body
(e.g., clothes) **giizikaw** *vta;* take s.t. off the
body (e.g., clothes) **giizikan** *vti*

TAKE OFF COAT: take off one's coat
giichibabiinzikawaagane *vai*
TAKE OFF DRESS: take off one's dress
giitagoode *vai*
TAKE OFF HAT: take off one's hat
giichiwakwaane *vai*
TAKE OFF MITTENS: take off one's mittens
giichiminjikaawane *vai*
TAKE OFF MOCCASINS: take off one's
moccasins **gagiichii** *vai*
TAKE OFF PANTS: take off one's pants
giichigiboodiyegwaazone *vai*
TAKE OFF SHIRT: take off one's shirt
giichibabagiwayaane *vai*
TAKE OFF SHOES: take off one's shoes
gagiichii *vai*
TAKE OFF SOCKS: take off one's socks
giitazhigane *vai*
TAKE PLACE
TAKE PLACE IN A CERTAIN PLACE:
danakamigad *vii*
TAKEN
TAKEN: be taken **mamigaade,**
mamigaademagad *vii;* **mamigaazo** *vai;*
odaapinigaade, odaapinigaademagad *vii;*
odaapinigaazo *vai*
TAKEN ALONG: be taken along
maajiijigaade, maajiijigaademagad *vii;*
maajiijigaazo *vai*
TAKEN ASHORE: be taken ashore
agwaasijigaade, agwaasijigaademagad
vii; **agwaasijigaazo** *vai*
TAKEN OFF THE FIRE: be taken off the fire
agwaasijigaade, agwaasijigaademagad
vii; **agwaasijigaazo** *vai*
TAKEN TO A CERTAIN PLACE: be taken
to a certain place **izhiwijigaade,**
izhiwijigaademagad *vii;* **izhiwijigaazo** *vai*
TAKEN CARE
TAKEN CARE: be taken care of
ganawendaagwad *vii;* **ganawenjigaade,**
ganawenjigaademagad *vii;*
ganawenjigaazo *vai*
TALK
TALK: **gaagiigido** *vai;* talk to s.o. **gaganoozh**
/gaganooN-/ *vta;* they talk to each other
gaganoonidiwag /gaganoonidi-/ *vai*
AVOID TALKING: avoid talking to s.o.
boonim *vta*
STOP TALKING: stop talking to s.o. **boonim**
vta
TALK A CERTAIN WAY: **izhigiizhwe** *vai*
TALK ABOUT: talk about s.o. **dazhim** *vta;*
talk about s.t. **dazhindan** *vti;* talk about
people **dazhinge** *vai*
TALK BACK: talk back to s.o. **aazhidem** *vta*
TALK QUICKLY: **dadaatabaanagidoon** *vai*
TALK TOO MUCH: **onzaamidoon** *vai*
TALK WITHOUT STOPPING:
aabidaanagidoon *vai;* **aapidaanagidoon**
vai
TALKED
TALKED ABOUT: be talked about all the
time **waawiinjigaade,**

waawiinjigaademagad *vii;*
waawiinjigaazo *vai*
TALL
TALL: be tall **ginoozi** *vai;* be tall (of a person)
ginwaakozi *vai*
SO TALL: be so tall **akoozi** *vai;* **akwaa,**
akwaamagad *vii*
TALLOW
TALLOW: **mashkawaji-bimide** *ni*
TAMARACK
TAMARACK: **mashkiigwaatig, -oog** *na*
TAME
TAME: be tame **waangawizi** *vai;* tame s.o.
waangawi' *vta*
TAN
TAN: tan hides **aseke** *vai;* tan s.o. (e.g., a
hide) **asekaazh /asekaaN-/** *vta*
TANGLED
TANGLED: be tangled **gashka'oode,**
gashka'oodemagad *vii;* **gashka'oozo** *vai*
TANK
TANK: **atoobaan, -an** *ni*
TANNED HIDE
TANNED HIDE: **asekaan, -ag** *na*
TANNING
TANNING: **asekewin** *ni*
TAP
TAP: **negwaakwaan, -an** *ni*
TAP FOOT: tap one's foot **jiichiibizideni** *vai*
TAP IN: tap s.o. in **ginjida' /ginjida'w-/** *vta;*
tap s.t. in **ginjida'an** *vti*
TAP TREES: **ozhiga'ige** *vai*
TAPE RECORDER
TAPE RECORDER: **naabinootaage-makak,**
-oon *ni*
TAR
TAR: **bigiw** *ni;* **bigiike** *vai;* **makade-bigiw** *na;*
tar s.t. **bigiikaadan** *vti*
TARGET
HIT THE TARGET: **mizhodam** *vai2*
TASTE
TASTE: taste things **gojipijige** *vai*
FIND A GOOD TASTE: find a good taste in
s.o. **minopozh /minopw-/** *vta;* find a good
taste in s.t. **minopidan** *vti*
HAVE A CERTAIN TASTE: **ipogozi** *vai;*
ipogwad *vii*
LIKE THE TASTE: like the taste of things
minopijige *vai*
TAKE A TASTE: take a taste of s.o.
godandan *vti;* **gojipozh /gojipw-/** *vta;* take
a taste of s.t. **godam** *vta;* **gojipidan** *vti*
TASTE A SAMPLE: taste a sample of s.o.
daangam *vta;* taste a sample of s.t.
daangandan *vti*
TASTE BAD: **maazhipogozi** *vai;*
maazhipogwad *vii;* taste bad (as a liquid)
maanaagamin /maanaagami-/ *vii*
TASTE BITTER: **wiisagipogozi** *vai;*
wiisagipogwad *vii*
TASTE GOOD: **minopogozi** *vai;*
minopogwad *vii;* taste good (as a liquid)
minwaagamin /minwaagami-/ *vii*

TASTE RANCID: **zaatepogozi** *vai;*
zaatepogwad *vii*
TASTE SALTY: **zhiiwitaaganipogozi** *vai;*
zhiiwitaaganipogwad *vii*
TASTE SWEET: **wiishkobipogozi** *vai;*
wiishkobipogwad *vii*

TAUGHT
TAUGHT: be taught **gikinoo'amaagozi** *vai*

TAVERN
TAVERN: **minikwewigamig, -oon** *ni;*
ziiginigewigamig, -oon *ni*

TAXI
TAXI: **bimiwizhiwewidaabaan, -ag** *na*

TAXI DRIVER
TAXI DRIVER: **bimiwizhiwewinini, -wag** *na*

TEA
TEA: **aniibiish, -an** *ni;* **aniibiishaaboo** *ni*
BLACK TEA: **makade-aniibiish** *ni*
GREEN TEA: **ozhaawashko-aniibiish** *ni*
MAKE TEA: **aniibiishaabooke** *vai;*
aniibiishike *vai*

TEACH
TEACH: **gikinoo'amaage** *vai;* teach (s.t.) to
s.o. **gikinoo'amaw** *vta;* teach oneself
gikinoo'amaadizo *vai*

TEACHER
TEACHER: **gekinoo'amaaged** *na-pt;*
gikinoo'amaagewinini, -wag *na;* teacher
(female) **gikinoo'amaagewikwe, -g** *na*

TEAKETTLE
TEAKETTLE: **aniibiishakik, -oog** *na*

TEAL
TEAL: **wewiibingwaange, -g** *na*

TEAR
TEAR: **giishkikaa** *vai;* **giishkikaa,
giishkikaamagad** *vii;* tear s.o. **biigobizh
/biigobiN-/** *vta;* tear s.t. **biigobidoon** *vti2;*
tear things **biigobijige** *vai*
TEAR A PIECE OFF: tear a piece off of s.o.
bakwebizh /bakwebiN-/ *vta;* tear a piece
off of s.t. **bakwebidoon** *vti2*
TEAR APART: tear s.o. apart **daashkibizh
/daashkibiN-/** *vta;* tear s.t. apart
daashkibidoon *vti2*
TEAR DOWN: tear s.o. down **niisibizh
/niisibiN-/** *vta;* tear s.t. down **niisibidoon**
vti2
TEAR OFF: tear s.o. off **giishkibizh
/giishkibiN-/** *vta;* tear s.t. off **giishkibidoon**
vti2; tear things off **giishkibijige** *vai*
TEAR STRAIGHT: tear s.o. straight
gwayakobizh /gwayakobiN-/ *vta;* tear s.t.
straight **gwayakobidoon** *vti2*
TEAR TO PIECES: tear s.o. to pieces
bigishkibizh /bigishkibiN-/ *vta;* tear s.t. to
pieces **bigishkibidoon** *vti2*

TEASE
TEASE: **miikindizi** *vai;* tease s.o. **miikinji'** *vta*

TEASPOON
TEASPOON: **emikwaanens, -an** *ni*

TELEPHONE
TELEPHONE: **gaagiigidoo-makakoons, -an**
ni; **giigidowin, -an** *ni;* **giigidoo-
biiwaabikoons, -an** *ni*

TELEPHONE WIRE
TELEPHONE WIRE: **giigidoo-
biiwaabikoons, -an** *ni*

TELESCOPE
TELESCOPE: **zhiibaayaabanjigan, -an** *ni*

TELEVISION
TELEVISION SET: **mazinaatesijigan, -an** *ni*

TELL
TELL: **dibaajimo** *vai;* tell of s.o. **dibaajim** *vta;*
tell of s.t. **dibaadodan** *vti;* tell (s.t.) to s.o.
dibaajimotaw *vta*
COME TELLING NEWS: **biidaajimo** *vai*
START TO TELL: **maadaajimo** *vai;* start to
tell of s.o. **maadaajim** *vta;* start to tell of
s.t. **maadodan** *vti;* start to tell (s.t.) to s.o.
maadaajimotaw *vta*
TELL A CERTAIN WAY: **inaajimo** *vai;* tell a
certain way about s.t. **inaadodan** *vti;* tell of
s.o. a certain way **inaajim** *vta;* tell s.o. of
(s.t.) a certain way **inaajimotaw** *vta*
TELL A LEGEND: **aadizooke** *vai;* tell a
legend to s.o. **aadizookaw** *vta*
TELL A MYTH: **aadizooke** *vai;* tell a myth to
s.o. **aadizookaw** *vta*
TELL A STORY: tell a story of s.o. **aajim** *vta;*
tell a story of s.t. **aadodan** *vti*
TELL A TRADITIONAL STORY:
aadizooke *vai*
TELL ABOUT: tell s.o. about (s.t.)
wiindamaw *vta;* tell about (s.t.) to people
wiindamaage *vai*
TELL ALL: **giizhaajimo** *vai*
TELL GOOD NEWS: **minwaajimo** *vai;* tell
good news of s.o. **minwaajim** *vta;* tell good
news of s.t. **minwaadodan** *vti*
TELL IN A CERTAIN PLACE: tell of s.o. in
a certain place **danaajim** *vta;* tell of s.t. in a
certain place **danaadodan** *vti*
TELL ON: tell on s.o. **baataam** *vta*
TELL STORIES: **dadibaajimo** *vai;* tell stories
to s.o. **dadibaajimotaw** *vta*
TELL THE TRUTH: **debwe** *vai*
TELL TO GET IN: tell s.o. to get in (a vehicle
or boat) **boozinaazha' /boozinaazha'w-/**
vta
TELL TO GO ABOARD: tell s.o. to go
aboard **boozinaazha' /boozinaazha'w-/**
vta
TELL TO HURRY: tell s.o. to hurry
wewiibim *vta*
TELL TO SETTLE DOWN: tell s.o. to settle
down **zagakim** *vta*

TEMPTED
TEMPTED: be tempted **zhoobizi** *vai*

TEN
TEN: **midaaswi** *nm;* **midaaso-** *pv4;* they are
ten **midaachinoon /midaachin-/** *vii;*
midaachiwag /midaachi-/ *vai;* ten (card)
midaasoobii'igan, -ag *na*

TEN DAYS: **midaaso-giizhik** *pc;* **midaasogon**
pc; be ten days **midaasogonagad** *vii*
TEN DAYS OLD: be ten days old
midaasogonagizi *vai*
TEN DOLLARS: **midaaswaabik** *pc*
TEN EACH: **memidaaswi** *nm*
TEN HOURS: **midaaso-diba'igan** *pc*
TEN INCHES: **midaasoninj** *pc*
TEN MILES: **midaaso-diba'igan** *pc*
TEN MINUTES: **midaaso-diba'igaans** *pc*
TEN MONTHS: **midaaso-giizis** *pc*
TEN NIGHTS: **midaaso-dibik** *pc*
TEN O'CLOCK: be ten o'clock **midaaso-
diba'iganed** *vii*
TEN PAIRS: **midaaswewaan** *pc*
TEN SETS: **midaaswewaan** *pc*
TEN THOUSAND: **midaasosagoons** *nm*
TEN TIMES: **midaaching** *pc*
TEN WEEKS: **midaaso-anama'e-giizhik** *pc;*
midaaso-anama'e-giizhigad *pc*
TEN YEARS: **midaaso-biboon** *pc;* be ten
years **midaaso-biboonagad** *vii*
TEN YEARS OLD: be ten years old **midaaso-
biboonagizi** *vai*
TENDER
TENDER: be tender **nookaa, nookaamagad**
vii; **nookizi** *vai*
COOK TENDER: cook s.o. tender **nookiz**
/nookizw-/ *vta;* cook s.t. tender **nookizan**
vti
COOKED TENDER: be cooked tender
nookide, nookidemagad *vii;* **nookizo** *vai*
TENNIS SHOE
TENNIS SHOE: **babagiwayaanekizin, -an** *ni,*
also **bagiwayaanekizin**
TENT
TENT: **babagiwayaanegamig, -oon** *ni, also*
bagiwayaanegamig
TENTH
THE TENTH DAY OF THE MONTH: be
the tenth day of the month
midaasogonagizi *vai*
TERRIBLE
TERRIBLE: **gagwaanisagakamig** *pc;* be terrible **gagwaanisagad** *vii;* **gagwaanisagizi** *vai*
CONSIDER TERRIBLE: consider s.o. to be
terrible **gagwaanisagenim** *vta;* consider
s.t. terrible **gagwaanisagendan** *vti;*
consider things to be terrible
gagwaanisagendam *vai2*
CONSIDERED TERRIBLE: be considered
terrible **gagwaanisagendaagozi** *vai;*
gagwaanisagendaagwad *vii*
TEST
TEST: test s.t. **gagwejitoon** *vti2*
TEST BY TOUCH: test s.o. by touch
gagwedin *vta;* test s.t. by touch
gagwedinan *vti*
TEST STRENGTH: test one's strength
gagwejii *vai*
TEST WITH FOOT OR BODY: test s.o. with
foot or body **gagwezikaw** *vta;* **gozikaw**
vta; test s.t. with foot or body **gagwezikan**
vti; **gozikan** *vti*

TEST WITH HAND: test s.o. with hand
godin *vta;* test s.t. with hand **godinan** *vti*
TESTICLE
TESTICLES: my testicles *plural* **ninishiwag**
/-nishiw-/ *nad*
TESTIFY
TESTIFY AGAINST: testify against s.o.
baataam *vta*
THANK
THANK: thank s.o. **miigwechiwi'** *vta*
THANKS: thanks! **miigwech** *pc*
THANKFUL
THANKFUL: be thankful
miigwechiwendam *vai2;* be thankful for
s.o. **miigwechiwenim** *vta;* be thankful for
s.t. **miigwechiwendan** *vti*
THANKSGIVING DAY
THANKSGIVING DAY: be Thanksgiving
Day **miigwechiwi-giizhigad** *vii*
THAT
THAT: that *animate singular demonstrative*
a'aw *pr, also* **aw, 'aw, 'a;** that *inanimate
singular demonstrative* **i'iw** *pr, also* **iw, 'iw,
i'i, 'i;** that *obviative demonstrative* **iniw** *pr,
also* **niw, ini, ni, aniw***
THAT OVER THERE: that over there *animate singular demonstrative* **a'awedi** *pr, also*
awedi; that over there *inanimate singular
demonstrative* **iwedi** *pr, also* **i'iwedi;** that/
those over there *obviative demonstrative*
iniwedin *pr, also* **niwedin**
THAT
THAT: **ji-** *pv1*
THAW
THAW: **ningide, ningidemagad** *vii;* **ningizo**
vai
THEATER
MOVIE THEATER: **mazinaatesewigamig,
-oon** *ni, also* **mazinaatesijigewigamig**
THEN
THEN: **apii** *pc;* **azhigwa** *pc, also* **zhigwa,
zhigo**
AND THEN: **mii dash** *pc, also* **miish**
JUST THEN: **na'idaa** *pc*
THERE
THERE: **imaa** *pc, also* **maa, i'imaa; izhi-** pv3;
dazhi- *pv3*
OVER THERE: **iwidi** *pc*
THEREFORE
THEREFORE: **indawaaj** *pc*
THESE
THESE: these *animate plural demonstrative*
ongow *pr, also* **ongo, ogow*, ogo*;** these
inanimate plural demonstrative, **onow** *pr;*
also **ono;** this/these *obviative demonstrative*
onow *pr, also* **ono**
THESE OVER HERE: these over here *animate
plural demonstrative* **ongowedig** *pr, also*
ogowedig*; these over here *inanimate plural demonstrative* **onowedin** *pr;* this/these
over here *obviative demonstrative* **onowedin**
pr

THEY

THEY: they *third person plural personal pronoun* **wiinawaa** *pr*

THICK

THICK: be thick **gipagaa, gipagaamagad** *vii;* **gipagizi** *vai;* be thick (as something mineral) **gipagaabikad** *vii;* **gipagaabikizi** *vai;* be thick (as something sheet-like) **gipagiigad** *vii;* **gipagiigizi** *vai;* be thick (as something string-like) **gipagaabiigad** *vii;* **gipagaabiigizi** *vai*

FROZEN THICK: be frozen thick **gipagaakwadin** *vii;* **gipagaakwaji** *vai*

LIE IN A THICK LAYER: **gipagishin** *vai;* **gipagisin** *vii*

SLICE THICK: slice s.o. thick **gipagikozh** /**gipagikoN-**/ *vta;* slice s.t. thick **gipagikodan** *vti*

THICK FUR: have thick fur **gipagawe** *vai*

THICKEN

THICKEN INTO SYRUP: **zhiiwaagamide, zhiiwaagamidemagad** *vii*

THICKNESS

CERTAIN THICKNESS: be a certain thickness **apiitaa, apiitaamagad** *vii*

HAVE A CERTAIN THICKNESS: **apiitizi** *vai*

THIEF

THIEF: **gimoodishkiiwinini, -wag** *na;* be a thief **gimoodishki** *vai*

THIGH

THIGH: my thigh (back of thigh) **imbwaam, -an** /**-bwaam-**/ *nid;* my thigh (front of thigh) **injiingwan, -ag** /**-jiingwan-**/ *nad*

THIMBLE

THIMBLE: **gaanda'igwaason, -an** *ni*

THIN

THIN: be thin **bibagaa, bibagaamagad** *vii;* **bibagizi** *vai;* be thin (as something mineral) **bibagaabikaad** *vii;* **bibagaabikizi** *vai;* be thin (as something sheet-like) **bibagiigad** *vii;* **bibagiigizi** *vai;* be thin (of a person) **bakaakadozo** *vai*

FROZEN THIN: be frozen thin **bibagaakwadin** *vii;* **bibagaakwaji** *vai*

LIE IN A THIN LAYER: **bibagishin** *vai;* **bibagisin** *vii*

SLICE THIN: slice s.o. thin **bibagikozh** /**bibagikoN-**/ *vta;* slice s.t. thin **bibagikodan** *vti*

THING

THING: **ayi'ii, -n** *pr*

VARIETY OF THINGS: a variety of things **anooj gegoo** *pr,* also **anooji-gegoo**

THINK

THINK: **maaminonendam** *vai2;* **naagadawendam** *vai2;* **naanaagadawendam** *vai2;* think on s.o. **maaminonenim** *vta;* think on s.t. **maaminonendan** *vti*

COME TO THINK OF: come to think of s.o. **mikwenim** *vta;* come to think of s.t. **mikwendan** *vti*

NOT KNOW WHAT TO THINK: **gwiinawi-inendam** *vai2*

THINK A CERTAIN WAY: **inendam** *vai2;* think a certain way of s.t. **inendan** *vti;* think of s.o. a certain way **inenim** *vta*

THINK ABOUT: think about s.o. **naagadawenim** *vta;* **naanaagadawenim** *vta;* think about s.t. **naagadawendan** *vti;* **naanaagadawendan** *vti*

THINK ABOUT GOING HOME: think about going home again **giiweyendam** *vai2*

THINK ABOUT RETURNING: **giiweyendam** *vai2*

THINK CORRECTLY: **gwayakwendam** *vai2*

TRY TO THINK: try to think of s.o. **nanda-mikwenim** *vta;* try to think of s.t. **nanda-mikwendan** *vti*

THIRD

THIRD: the third **eko-nising** *pc*

THE THIRD DAY OF THE MONTH: be the third day of the month **nisogonagizi** *vai*

THIRD PERSON

THIRD PERSON: *third person prefix before consonants in verbs and nouns* **o=** *pre; third person prefix before vowels in verbs and non-dependent nouns* **od=** *pre; third person prefix before initial* **ii** *dependent noun stems* **w=** *pre*

THIRD PERSON PLURAL: they *third person plural personal pronoun* **wiinawaa** *pr;* their turn *third person plural personal pronoun* **wiinitamawaa** *pr;* only them *third person plural personal pronoun* **wiinetawaa** *pr*

THIRD PERSON SINGULAR: she/he *third person singular personal pronoun* **wiin** *pr;* his/her turn *third person singular personal pronoun* **wiinitam** *pr;* only her/him *third person singular pronoun* **wiineta** *pr*

THIRST

SUFFER FROM THIRST: **gawaabaagwe** *vai*

THIRSTY

THIRSTY: be thirsty **giishkaabaagwe** *vai*

THIRTEEN

THIRTEEN: **ashi-niswi** *nm;* **midaaswi ashi-niswi** *nm*

THIRTY

THIRTY: **nisimidana** *nm*

THIS

THIS: this *animate singular demonstrative* **wa'aw** *pr;* this *inanimate singular demonstrative* **o'o** *pr,* also **o'ow, 'ow, 'o, o'o**; this/these *obviative demonstrative* **onow,** also **ono** *pr*

THIS OVER HERE: this over here *animate singular demonstrative* **wa'awedi** *pr;* this over here *inanimate singular demonstrative* **o'owedi,** also **owedi** *pr;* this/these over here *obviative demonstrative* **onowedin** *pr*

THISTLE

THISTLE: **mazaanaatig, -oog** *na*

THOSE

THOSE: those *animate plural demonstrative*
ingiw *pr, also* ingi, igiw*, igi*, agiw*; those
inanimate plural demonstrative iniw *pr, also*
niw, ini, ni, aniw*; those *obviative* iniw *pr,
also* niw, ini, ni, aniw*

THOSE OVER THERE: those over there
animate plural demonstrative ingiwedig *pr,
also* igiwedig*; those over there *inanimate
plural* iniwedin *pr, also* niwedin; those over
there *obviative demonstrative* iniwedin *pr,
also* niwedin

THOUGHT

THOUGHT OF A CERTAIN WAY: be
thought of a certain way inendaagozi *vai;*
inendaagwad *vii*

THOUSAND

THOUSAND: midaaswaak *nm*

CERTAIN NUMBER OF THOUSANDS: a
certain number of thousands dasosagoons
nm

EIGHT THOUSAND: ishwaasosagoons *nm,
also* nishwaasosagoons*

FIVE THOUSAND: naanosagoons *nm*

FOUR THOUSAND: niiwosagoons *nm, also*
niiyosagoons

NINE THOUSAND: zhaangasosagoons *nm*

ONE THOUSAND: ingodosagoons *nm, also*
ningodosagoons*

SEVEN THOUSAND: niizhwaasosagoons
nm

SIX THOUSAND: ingodwaasosagoons
/ningodwaasosagoons-/ *nm, also*
ningodwaasosagoons*

TEN THOUSAND: midaasosagoons *nm*

THREE THOUSAND: nisosagoons *nm*

TWO THOUSAND: niizhosagoons *nm*

THREAD

THREAD: asabaab, -iin *ni;* thread s.o.
naabidoo' /naabidoo'w-/ *vta;* thread s.t.
naabidoo'an *vti;* thread things
naabidoo'ige *vai*

SEWING THREAD: gashkigwaasoneyaab,
-iin *ni*

THREAD CORRECTLY: thread s.t. correctly
gwayakwaabidoo'an *vti*

THREE

THREE: niswi *nm;* niso- *pv4;* they are three
nisinoon /nisin-/ *vii;* nisiwag /nisi-/ *vai;*
three (card) nisoobii'igan, -ag *na*

AND THREE: ashi-niso- *pv4;* ashi-niswi *nm*

THREE ACRES: niso-diba'igaans *pc*

THREE DAYS: niso-giizhik *pc;* nisogon *pc;*
be three days nisogonagad *vii*

THREE DAYS OLD: be three days old
nisogonagizi *vai*

THREE DOLLARS: niswaabik *pc*

THREE EACH: neniswi *nm*

THREE FEET: nisozid *pc*

THREE HOURS: niso-diba'igan *pc*

THREE HUNDRED: niswaak *nm*

THREE INCHES: nisoninj *pc*

THREE MILES: niso-diba'igan *pc*

THREE MINUTES: niso-diba'igaans *pc*

THREE MONTHS: niso-giizis *pc*

THREE NIGHTS: niso-dibik *pc*

THREE O'CLOCK: be three o'clock niso-
diba'iganed *vii*

THREE PAIRS: niswewaan *pc*

THREE SETS: niswewaan *pc*

THREE THOUSAND: nisosagoons *nm*

THREE TIMES: nising *pc*

THREE WEEKS: niso-anama'e-giizhik *pc;* be
three weeks niso-anama'e-giizhigad *vii*

THREE YEARS: niso-biboon *pc;* be three
years niso-biboonagad *vii*

THREE YEARS OLD: be three years old
niso-biboonagizi *vai*

THRESH

THRESH: thresh field crops bakiteshka'ige
vai; thresh s.t. (e.g., wild rice)
mimigoshkan *vti*

BARREL OR TUB USED IN THRESHING
WILD RICE: mimigoshkamwaagan, -an
ni

THRESH WILD RICE: thresh something
mimigoshkam *vai2*

THRICE

THRICE: nising *pc*

THROAT

THROAT: my throat ingondashkway
/-gondashkway-/ *nid*

SORE THROAT: have a sore throat
wiisagigonewe *vai*

THROUGH

THROUGH: through it zhaabwayi'ii *pc*

BITE THROUGH: bite s.o. through (e.g.,
something string-like) bakam *vta;* bite s.t.
through (e.g., something string-like)
bakandan *vti*

GO THROUGH: zhaabose, zhaabosemagad
vii; zhaabwii *vai*

PASS THROUGH: zhaabose,
zhaabosemagad *vii;* zhaabwii *vai*

PUT THROUGH: put s.o. through zhaabon
vta; put s.t. through zhaabonan *vti*

RUN THROUGH: zhaabobatoo *vai*

SEE THROUGH: see through s.o.
zhaabwaabam *vta;* see through s.t.
zhaabwaabandan *vti*

THROUGHOUT

THROUGHOUT: gabe- *pv4;* throughout it
gabe-ayi'ii *pc, also* gabeyi'ii

THROW

THROW: throw s.o. apagizh /apagiN-/ *vta;*
throw s.t. apagidan *vti, also* apagidoon;
throw (s.t.) at s.o. apagidaw *vta;* throw
things apagijige *vai;* they throw (s.t.) at
each other apagidaadiwag /apagidaadi-/
vai

THROW AROUND: throw things around
ombwewebinige *vai*

THROW AWAY: throw s.o. away webin *vta;*
throw s.t. away webinan *vti;* throw things
away webinige *vai*

THROW DOWN: throw s.o. down
gawiwebin *vta;* throw s.t. down
gawiwebinan *vti*

THROW DOWN QUICKLY: throw s.o.
down quickly **bagijwebin** *vta;* throw s.t.
down quickly **bagijwebinan** *vti*
THROW HERE: throw s.o. here **biijwebin**
vta; throw s.t. here **biijwebinan** *vti;* throw
(s.t.) here to s.o. **biijwebinamaw** *vta*
THROW IN: throw s.o. in **biinjwebin** *vta;*
throw s.t. in **biinjwebinan** *vti;* throw things
in **biinjwebinige** *vai*
THROW INSIDE: throw s.o. inside
biindigewebin *vta;* throw s.t. inside
biindigewebinan *vti;* throw things inside
biindigewebinige *vai*
THROW INTO THE WATER: throw s.o.
into the water **bakobiiwebin** *vta;* throw s.t.
into the water **bakobiiwebinan** *vti*
THROW OUT OF THE WATER: throw s.o.
out of the water **agwaawebin** *vta;* throw
s.t. out of the water **agwaawebinan** *vti;*
throw (s.t.) out of the water for s.o.
agwaawebinamaw *vta*
THROW OUTSIDE: throw s.o. outside
zaagijiwebin *vta;* throw s.t. outside
zaagijiwebinan *vti;* throw things outside
zaagijiwebinige *vai*
THROW OVER: throw s.o. over
baazhijiwebin *vta;* throw s.t. over
baazhijiwebinan *vti*
THROW OVER BACKWARDS: throw s.o.
over backwards **aazhigidwebin** *vta;* throw
s.t. over backwards **aazhigidwebinan** *vti*
THROW SELF DOWN AGAINST
SOMETHING: **apagizo** *vai*
THROW UP AGAINST: throw s.o. up against
(as something stick- or wood-like)
aatwaakowebin *vta;* throw s.t. up against
(as something stick- or wood-like)
aatwaakowebinan *vti*
THROW UPWARDS: throw s.o. upwards
ombiwebin *vta;* throw s.t. upwards
ombiwebinan *vti*

THROWN
THROWN AWAY: be thrown away
webinigaade, webinigaademagad *vii;*
webinigaazo *vai*
THROWN OUTSIDE: be thrown outside
zaagijiwebinigaade,
zaagijiwebinigaademagad *vii*

THUMB
THUMB: **midechininj, -iin** *ni*

THUNDER
THUNDER: come making noise (e.g.,
thunder) **biidwewidam** *vai2;* there is
thunder **animikiikaa, animikiikaamagad**
vii

THUNDERBIRD
THUNDERBIRD: **animikii, -g** *na;* **binesi,**
-wag *na*

THUNDERCLAP
MAKE A THUNDERCLAP: make a thunderclap (of the thunderers) **baashkakwa'am**
vai2

THUNDERER
THUNDERER: **animikii, -g** *na*

THURSDAY
THURSDAY: be Thursday **niiwo-giizhigad**
vii, also **niiyo-giizhigad**

THUS
THUS: **izhi-** *pv3*

THWART
THWART: **bimidasaa, -g** *na, also*
bimidasaagan, -an

TICK
WOOD TICK: **ezigaa, -g** *na*

TICKET
TICKET: **mazina'igaans, -an** *ni*

TICKLE
TICKLE: tickle s.o. (at the mid-section)
ginagijiin *vta*

TIDIED
TIDIED: be tidied **zagakinigaade,**
zagakinigaademagad *vii;* **zagakinigaazo**
vai

TIDY
TIDY: tidy s.o. **zagakin** *vta;* tidy s.t.
zagakinan *vti;* tidy things **zagakinige** *vai*

TIE
TIE: tie s.o. **dakobizh** /**dakobiN-**/ *vta;* tie s.t.
dakobidoon *vti2;* tie things **dakobijige** *vai*
TIE IN A BUNCH: tie s.o. in a bunch
okwapizh /**okwapiN-**/ *vta;* tie s.t. in a
bunch **okwapidoon** *vti2*
TIE IN A BUNDLE: tie s.o. in a bundle
gashkapizh /**gashkapiN-**/ *vta;* tie s.t. in a
bundle **gashkapidoon** *vti2*
TIE IN PLACE: tie s.o. in place **onapizh**
/**onapiN-**/ *vta;* tie s.t. in place **onapidoon**
vti2
TIE ON: tie s.o. on **zagapizh** /**zagapiN-**/ *vta;*
tie s.o. on something **agwapizh** /**agwapiN-**/
vta; tie s.t. on **zagapidoon** *vti2;* tie s.t. on
something **agwapidoon** *vti2*
TIE SHUT: tie s.o. shut **gashkapizh**
/**gashkapiN-**/ *vta;* tie s.t. shut
gashkapidoon *vti2*
TIE TIGHT: tie s.o. tight **mashkawapizh**
/**mashkawapiN-**/ *vta;* tie s.t. tight
mashkawapidoon *vti2*
TIE WILD RICE: **dakobidoo** *vai*
TIE WITH A KNOT: tie s.o. with a knot
gashka'oozh /**gashka'ooN-**/ *vta;* tie s.t.
with a knot **gashka'oodoon** *vti2*

TIED
TIED: be tied **dakobide, dakobidemagad** *vii;*
dakobizo *vai*
TIED IN A BUNCH: be tied in a bunch
okwapide, okwapidemagad *vii;*
okwapizo *vai*
TIED IN PLACE: be tied in place **onapide,**
onapidemagad *vii*
TIED ON: be tied on **agwapijigaade,**
agwapijigaademagad *vii;* **agwapijigaazo**
vai; **zagapide, zagapidemagad** *vii;*
zagapizo *vai*
TIED TIGHT: be tied tight **mashkawapide,**
mashkawapidemagad *vii;* **mashkawapizo**
vai
TIED WILD RICE: **dakobijigan, -an** *ni*

TIGHT PLACE

CRAWL IN A TIGHT PLACE: **zhegoode** *vai*

LIE IN A TIGHT PLACE: **zhegoshin** *vai;* **zhegosin** *vii*

PUT IN A TIGHT PLACE: put s.o. in a tight place **zhegoshim** *vta;* put s.t. in a tight place **zhegosidoon** *vti2*

STICK IN A TIGHT PLACE: stick s.o. in a tight place **zhegon** *vta;* stick s.t. in a tight place **zhegonan** *vti*

TIMBER

CUT TIMBER: **giishka'aakwe** *vai*

PEEL TIMBER USING SOMETHING: **bishagaakwa'ige** *vai*

TIME

AT ONE TIME: **aabiding** *pc;* **ingoding** *pc, also* **ningoding***

AT THAT TIME: **iw apii** *pr, also* **i'iw apii**

AT THE TIME: **apii** *pc*

AT THIS TIME: **azhigwa** *pc, also* **zhigwa, zhigo**

CERTAIN TIME IN HOURS: be a certain time in hours **daso-diba'iganed** *vii*

COMING UP TO IN TIME: **ani-** *pv2, also* **ni-**

FOR SOME TIME: **gomaapii** *pc*

TIMES

CERTAIN NUMBER OF TIMES: a certain number of times **dasing** *pc*

SO MANY TIMES: **dasing** *pc*

TIMID

TIMID: be timid **gotaajishki** *vai*

TINDER

TINDER: **zagataagan, -ag** *na*

TINGLE

TINGLE: **giikimanizi** *vai*

TINY

TINY: they are tiny **babiiwaawan /babiiwaa-/** *vii;* **babiiwizhiinyiwag /babiiwizhiinyi-/** *vai;* they are tiny (as something ball-like) **babiiwiminagadoon /babiiwiminagad-/** *vii;* **babiiwiminagiziwag /babiiwiminagizi-/** *vai*

TIP

TIP: **gwanabishkaa** *vai;* tip s.o. **gotigobizh /gotigobiN-/** *vta;* tip s.t. **gotigobidoon** *vti2*

TIP OVER BY HAND: tip s.o. over by hand **gawin** *vta;* tip s.t. over by hand **gawinan** *vti*

TIP WITH FOOT OR BODY: tip s.t. with foot or body **gwanabishkan** *vti*

TIP

ON THE TIP: **wanakong** *pc*

TIPI

TIPI: **bajiishka'ogaan, -an** *ni*

TIRE

FLAT TIRE: have a flat tire **nabagijiishin** *vai*

TIRE PUMP

TIRE PUMP: **boodaajii'igan, -an** *ni*

TIRED

TIRED: be tired **ayekozi** *vai;* **zhigajii** *vai*

FEEL TIRED: **ayekwamanji'o** *vai*

MAKE TIRED: make s.o. tired **ayeko'** *vta*

TIRED OF WAITING: be tired of waiting **zhigajibii'o** *vai;* be tired of waiting for s.o. **zhigajibii'** *vta;* be tired of waiting for s.t. **zhigajibiitoon** *vti2*

TO

TO: to a certain place **izhi-** *pv3*

CARRIED TO A CERTAIN PLACE: be carried to a certain place **izhiwijigaade, izhiwijigaademagad** *vii;* **izhiwijigaazo** *vai*

CARRY A BABY TO A CERTAIN PLACE ON BACK: carry a baby to a certain place on one's back **inoomaawaso** *vai*

CARRY TO A CERTAIN PLACE: carry s.o. to a certain place **izhiwizh /izhiwiN-/** *vta;* carry s.t. to a certain place **izhiwidoon** *vti2*

CARRY TO A CERTAIN PLACE ON BACK: carry s.o. to a certain place on one's back **inoom** *vta;* carry s.t. to a certain place on one's back **inoondan** *vti*

CHASE TO A CERTAIN PLACE: chase s.o. to a certain place **izhinaazhikaw** *vta;* **izhinizhikaw** *vta*

CLIMB TO CERTAIN PLACE: climb to a certain place **inaandawe** *vai*

CRAWL TO A CERTAIN PLACE: **inoode** *vai*

DRAG TO A CERTAIN PLACE: drag s.o. to a certain place **izhidaabaazh /izhidaabaaN-/** *vta;* drag s.t. to a certain place **izhidaabaadan** *vti*

DRIVE TO A CERTAIN PLACE: **ipide, ipidemagad** *vii;* **ipizo** *vai;* **izhidaabii'iwe** *vai;* drive s.o. to a certain place **ipizoni'** *vta;* drive s.t. to a certain place **ipizonitoon** *vti2*

FLOW TO A CERTAIN PLACE: **izhijiwan** *vii*

FLY TO A CERTAIN PLACE: **ipide, ipidemagad** *vii;* **ipizo** *vai;* **izhise** *vai;* **izhise, izhisemagad** *vii*

FOLLOW A TRAIL TO A CERTAIN PLACE: follow s.o.'s trail to a certain place **ina'azh /ina'aN-/** *vta;* follow s.t. as a trail to a certain place **ina'adoon** *vti2*

GO TO A CERTAIN PLACE: **izhaa** *vai;* **izhaamagad** *vii*

GO TO A CERTAIN PLACE CRYING: **inademo** *vai*

GO TO A CERTAIN PLACE ON THE ICE: **inaadagaako** *vai*

GO TO A CERTAIN PLACE WITH LIGHT: **inaazakonenjige** *vai*

HAUL TO A CERTAIN PLACE: haul s.o. to a certain place **inaawazh /inaawaN-/** *vta;* haul s.t. to a certain place **inaawadoon** *vti2;* haul something to a certain place **inaawadaaso** *vai*

LEAVE TRACKS GOING TO A CERTAIN PLACE: **izhikawe** *vai*

LOOK TO A CERTAIN PLACE: **inaabi** *vai*

PADDLE TO A CERTAIN PLACE: **ina'o** *vai;* **inakwazhiwe** *vai*

POLE A BOAT TO A CERTAIN PLACE: **ina'oodoo** *vai*

RIDE TO A CERTAIN PLACE ON
HORSEBACK: ride to a certain place on
horseback **inoomigo** *vai*
RIDE TO A CERTAIN PLACE WITH
HORSES: **apa'igo** *vai*
RIVER FLOWS TO A CERTAIN PLACE:
flow to a certain place (as a river)
izhitigweyaa, izhitigweyaamagad *vii*
ROAD LEADS TO A CERTAIN PLACE:
lead to a certain place (as a road or trail)
inamon /inamo-/ *vii*
RUN AWAY TO A CERTAIN PLACE: run
away from people to a certain place
apa'iwe *vai*
RUN TO A CERTAIN PLACE: **apatoo** *vai;*
run with s.o. to a certain place **apa'** *vta*
RUN TO A CERTAIN PLACE IN FLIGHT:
izhinizhimo *vai*
RUN TO A CERTAIN PLACE
TOGETHER: they run to a certain place
together **apa'idiwag /apa'idi-/** *vai*
SAIL TO A CERTAIN PLACE: **inaashi** *vai;*
inaasin *vii*
SEND SMOKE TO A CERTAIN PLACE:
inaabasige *vai*
SEND TO A CERTAIN PLACE: send s.o. to
a certain place **izhinaazhikaw** *vta;*
izhinizha' /izhinizha'w-/ *vta;* send s.t. to a
certain place **izhinizha'an** *vti;* send (s.t.) to
s.o. to a certain place **izhinizha'amaw** *vta*
SENT TO A CERTAIN PLACE: be sent to a
certain place **izhinizha'igaade,**
izhinizha'igaademagad *vii;*
izhinizha'igaazo *vai*
SKATE TO A CERTAIN PLACE: **inaada'e**
vai
SPEED TO A CERTAIN PLACE: **ipide,**
ipidemagad *vii;* **ipizo** *vai*
SWIM TO A CERTAIN PLACE: **inaadagaa**
vai; swim to a certain place (as a fish)
inakwazhiwe *vai*
TAKE TO A CERTAIN PLACE: take s.o. to
a certain place **izhiwizh /izhiwiN-/** *vta;*
take s.t. to a certain place **izhiwidoon** *vti2;*
take (s.t.) to s.o. at a certain place
izhiwidaw *vta*
TAKE TO A CERTAIN PLACE BY BOAT:
take s.o. to a certain place by boat
ina'oozh /ina'ooN-/ *vta;* take s.t. to a
certain place by boat **ina'oodoon** *vti2*
TAKEN TO A CERTAIN PLACE: be taken
to a certain place **izhiwijigaade,**
izhiwijigaademagad *vii;* **izhiwijigaazo** *vai*
TO A CERTAIN PLACE: **izhi-** *pv3*
TRAIL LEADS TO A CERTAIN PLACE:
lead to a certain place (as a road or trail)
inamon /inamo-/ *vii*
TRAVEL TO A CERTAIN PLACE: travel in
a group to a certain place **inaawanidiwag**
/inaawanidi-/ *vai*
WADE TO A CERTAIN PLACE:
inaadagaazii *vai*
WALK ALONG SHORE TO A CERTAIN
PLACE: **inaazhagaame** *vai*

WALK TO CERTAIN PLACE: walk to a
certain place **inose** *vai*
TOAD
    TOAD: **babiigomakakii, -g** *na;*
    obiigomakakii, -g *na*
TOAST
    TOAST BROWN: toast s.t. brown
    ozaawaakizan *vti*
TOBACCO
    TOBACCO: **asemaa** *na*
    CHEW SNUFF OR TOBACCO: **biindaakwe**
    vai
    CHEW TOBACCO: **agwanenjige** *vai*
    MAKE AN OFFERING OF TOBACCO:
    biindaakoojige *vai;* make an offering of
    tobacco to s.o. **biindaakoozh**
    /biindaakooN-/ *vta*
    SHORT OF TOBACCO: be short of tobacco
    manepwaa *vai*
TOBACCO BAG
    TOBACCO BAG: **gashkibidaagan, -ag** *na*
TOBOGGAN
    TOBOGGAN: **nabagidaabaan, -ag** *na;*
    zhooshkodaabaan, -ag *na*
TODAY
    TODAY: **noongom** *pc*
TOE
    TOE: **niibinaakwaanizidaan, -an** *ni*
    BIG TOE: **midechizid, -an** *ni*
TOGETHER
    TOGETHER: **maamawi** *pc;* **maamawoo-** *pv4*
    ADD TOGETHER: **asigagindaaso** *vai;* add
    s.o. together (e.g., money) **asigagim** *vta;*
    add s.t. together **asigagindan** *vti*
    BRING TOGETHER: bring s.t. together
    maawandoonan *vti*
    COME TOGETHER: they come together
    maawanji'idiwag /maawanji'idi-/ *vai*
    SEW TOGETHER: **maawandoogwaaso** *vai;*
    sew s.o. together **maawandoogwaazh**
    /maawandoogwaaN-/ *vta;* sew s.t. to-
    gether (e.g., pieces for a quilt)
    maawandoogwaadan *vti*
    SIT TOGETHER: they sit together
    maawandoobiwag /maawandoobi-/ *vai*
TOILET
    TOILET: **miiziiwigamig, -oon** *ni;*
    zaaga'amoowigamig, -oon *ni*
    GO TO THE TOILET: **zaaga'am** *vai2*
TOILET TISSUE
    TOILET TISSUE: **giziindime'on, -an** *ni*
TOMATO
    TOMATO: **gichi-ogin, -iig** *na;* **ogin, -iig** *na*
TOMORROW
    TOMORROW: be tomorrow **waaban** *vii*
    DAY AFTER TOMORROW: **awas-waabang**
    pc
TONGUE
    TONGUE: my tongue **indenaniw, -an**
    /-denaniw-/ *nid*
    STICK OUT TONGUE: stick out one's
    tongue **zaagidenaniweni** *vai;* stick out
    one's tongue at s.o. **zaagidenaniwetaw** *vta*

TOO
TOO: gaye *pc, also* ge
DRINK TOO MUCH: onzaamibii *vai*
GIVE TOO MUCH TO DRINK: give s.o. too much to drink onzaamibazh /onzaamibaN-/ *vta*
PACK TOO MUCH OF A LOAD: onzaamiwane *vai*
TALK TOO MUCH: onzaamidoon *vai*
TOO LATE: naanabem *pc*
TOO MANY: be too many onzaamiinad *vii;* onzaamiino *vai*
TOO MUCH: onzaam *pc;* be too much onzaamiinad *vii;* onzaamiino *vai*

TOOL
TOOL: aabajichigan, -an *ni*

TOOTH
TOOTH: my tooth niibid, -an /-iibid-/ *nid*
ABSCESSED TOOTH: have an abscessed tooth miniiwaabide *vai*
BRUSH TEETH: brush one's teeth giziiyaabide'o *vai;* giziiyaabide'odizo *vai*
FALSE TEETH: false teeth *plural* wiibidaakaajiganan *ni, also* wiibidaakaanan
PICK TEETH: pick one's teeth zesegwaabide'o *vai*

TOOTHACHE
TOOTHACHE: have a toothache dewaabide *vai*

TOOTHBRUSH
TOOTHBRUSH: giziiyaabide'on, -an *ni*

TOOTHLESS
TOOTHLESS: be toothless bashkwanige *vai*

TOOTHPICK
TOOTHPICK: zesegwaabide'on, -an *ni*

TOP
ON TOP: on top of agiji- *pn, also* ogiji-*, wagiji-; on top of it agijayi'ii *pc, also* ogijayi'ii*, wagijayi'ii
ON TOP OF A HILL: agidaaki *pc, also* ogidaaki*, wagidaaki
ON TOP OF A MOUNTAIN: agidajiw *pc, also* ogidajiw*, wagidajiw
ON TOP OF A ROCK: agidasin *pc, also* ogidasin*, wagidasin
ON TOP OF THE GROUND: agidakamig *pc, also* ogidakamig*, wagidakamig
ON TOP OF THE HOUSE: agidigamig *pc, also* ogidigamig*, wagidigamig
ON TOP OF THE ICE: agidiskwam *pc, also* ogidiskwam*, wagidiskwam
ON TOP OF THE WATER: agidibiig *pc, also* ogidibiig*, wagidibiig

TOP
TOY TOP: ishkwesa'igan, -ag *na*

TORCH
TORCH: waaswaagan, -an *ni*
BARK TORCH: biimashkwemaginigan, -an *ni*

TORN
TORN: be torn biigobijigaade, biigobijigaademagad *vii;* biigobijigaazo *vai*

TORN APART
TORN APART: be torn apart daashkaa, daashkaamagad *vii*
TORN OFF: be torn off giishkibijigaade, giishkibijigaademagad *vii;* giishkibijigaazo *vai*

TORNADO
TORNADO: be a tornado wese'an *vii*

TOSS
TOSS ASIDE: toss s.o. aside ikowebin *vta;* toss s.t. aside ikowebinan *vti*

TOTAL
TOTAL UP: asigagindaaso *vai;* total up (as an account) maawandoogindaaso *vai;* total up s.t. (as an account) maawandoogindan *vti*

TOTEM
TOTEM: my totem indoodem, -ag /-doodem-/ *nad*
HAVE A TOTEM: have a totem (clan) odoodemi *vai;* they have a mutual totem (clan) odoodemindiwag /odoodemindi-/ *vai*

TOUCH
TOUCH: touch s.o. with hand daangin *vta;* touch s.t. with hand daanginan *vti*
LIE TOUCHING: daangishin *vai;* daangisin *vii*
PUT TOUCHING: put s.o. touching daangishim *vta;* put s.t. touching daangisidoon *vti2*
TEST BY TOUCH: test s.o. by touch gagwedin *vta;* test s.t. by touch gagwedinan *vti*
TOUCH WRONG ONE: touch s.o. who/that is the wrong one wanin *vta;* touch s.t. that is the wrong one waninan *vti*

TOURIST
TOURIST: bebaamaadizid *na-pt*

TOW
TOW: tow s.o. zagapizh /zagapiN-/ *vta;* tow s.t. zagapidoon *vti2*

TOWARD
TOWARD THE SPEAKER: bi- *pv2*

TOWED
TOWED: be towed zagapide, zagapidemagad *vii;* zagapizo *vai*

TOWEL
TOWEL: giziingwe'on, -an *ni*
DISH TOWEL: giziiyaabika'igan, -an *ni*

TOWN
TOWN: oodena, -wan *ni*
LIVE ON THE END OF TOWN: live at the end of town ishkwege *vai*

TOY
TOY: odaminwaagan, -an *ni*
USE AS A TOY: use (s.t.) as a toy odaminwaage *vai+o*

TRACK
TRACK: bimikawaan, -an *ni*
COME LEAVING TRACKS: biijikawe *vai*
FIND TRACKS: find s.o.'s tracks okawi' *vta;* find the tracks of s.t. okawitoon *vti2*

LEAVE TRACKS GOING ALONG:
bimikawe *vai*
LEAVE TRACKS GOING AWAY:
animikawe *vai*
LEAVE TRACKS GOING TO A CERTAIN
PLACE: **izhikawe** *vai*
LOOK FOR TRACKS: **nandokawechige** *vai;*
look for s.o.'s tracks **nandokawe'** *vta*

TRADE
TRADE: trade s.o. **meshkwadoon** *vta;* trade
s.t. **meshkwadoonan** *vti;* trade (s.t.) with
s.o. **meshkwadoonamaw** *vta;* trade for
things **meshkwadoonige** *vai;* trade things
with people **meshkwadoonamaage** *vai*
GO ABOUT TRADING: **babaamadaawe** *vai*

TRADER
TRADER: **adaawewinini, -wag** *na;* trader
(female) **adaawewininiikwe** *na*

TRAIL
TRAIL: **miikana, -n** *ni;* be a trail
miikanaawan *vii*
ALONG THE SIDE OF THE TRAIL:
opimekana *pc*
AT THE END OF THE TRAIL: at the end of
the road or trail **gabekana** *pc*
BAD TRAIL: be bad (as a road or trail)
maanadamon /maanadamo-/ *vii*
BY A TRAIL: by a road or trail **jiigikana** *pc*
FOLLOW A TRAIL: go off following a trail
maada'adoo *vai;* go off following s.o.'s
trail **maada'azh** /maada'aN-/ *vta*
FOLLOW A TRAIL ALONG: **bima'adoo**
vai; follow s.o.'s trail along **bima'azh**
/bima'aN-/ *vta;* follow s.t. along as a trail
bima'adoon *vti2*
FOLLOW A TRAIL AWAY: **anima'adoo** *vai;*
follow s.o.'s trail away **anima'azh**
/anima'aN-/ *vta;* follow s.t. away as a trail
anima'adoon *vti2*
FOLLOW A TRAIL HERE: **biida'adoo** *vai;*
follow s.o.'s trail here **biida'azh** /biida'aN-/
vta; follow s.t. as a trail here **biida'adoon**
vti2
FOLLOW A TRAIL TO A CERTAIN
PLACE: follow s.o.'s trail to a certain place
ina'azh /ina'aN-/ *vta;* follow s.t. as a trail
to a certain place **ina'adoon** *vti2*
ICY TRAIL: be icy (as a road or trail)
mikwamiiwadamon
/mikwamiiwadamo-/ *vii*
IN THE MIDDLE OF THE TRAIL: in the
middle of the road or trail **naawikana** *pc*
MAKE A TRAIL: make a road or trail
miikanaake *vai*
NARROW TRAIL: be narrow (as a road or
trail) **agaasademon** /agaasademo-/ *vii*
ON THE OTHER SIDE OF THE TRAIL: on
the other side of the road or trail
agaamikana *pc*
ON THIS SIDE OF THE TRAIL:
ondaasikana *pc*
SLIPPERY TRAIL: be slippery (as a road or
trail) **ozhaashadamon** /ozhaashadamo-/
vii; **zhooshkwadamon**

/zhooshkwadamo-/ *vii;* be slippery with
ice (as a road or trail) **ozhaashikwadamon**
/ozhaashikwadamo-/ *vii*
TRAIL FORKS: fork (as a road or trail)
niingidawadamon /niingidawadamo-/ *vii*
TRAIL GOES ACROSS: go across (as a road
or trail) **aazhoodamon** /aazhoodamo-/ *vii*
TRAIL GOES OFF TO THE SIDE: go off to
the side (as a road or trail) **bakemon**
/bakemo-/ *vii*
TRAIL LEADS ALONG: lead along (as a
road or trail) **bimamon** /bimamo-/,
bimamoomagad *vii*
TRAIL LEADS FROM A CERTAIN
PLACE: lead from a certain place (as a
road or trail) **ondadamon** /ondadamo-/ *vii*
TRAIL LEADS TO A CERTAIN PLACE:
lead to a certain place (as a road or trail)
inamon /inamo-/ *vii*
WET TRAIL: be wet (as a road or trail)
nibiiwadamon /nibiiwadamo-/ *vii*
WIDE TRAIL: be wide (as a road or trail)
mangademon /mangademo-/ *vii,* also
mangadademon

TRAILER
TRAILER: **zagapijigan, -an** *ni*

TRAIN
TRAIN: **ishkodewidaabaan, -ag** *na,* also
mashkodewidaabaan*

TRAIN TRACK
TRAIN TRACK: **ishkodewidaabaanikana, -n**
ni

TRANQUILLY
REMAIN TRANQUILLY IN PLACE:
goshkwaawaadabi *vai*

TRANSFORM
TRANSFORM: transform oneself in appearance **izhinaago'idizo** *vai;* transform s.o.
aanzinaago' *vta;* transform s.t.
aanzinaagotoon *vti2;* transform oneself
aanzinaago'idizo *vai*

TRANSLATE
TRANSLATE: translate s.o. **aanikanootaw**
vta; translate s.t. **aanikanootan** *vti;* translate for people **aanikanootaage** *vai*

TRANSLATOR
TRANSLATOR: **aanikanootaagewinini,**
-wag *na*

TRANSPARENT
TRANSPARENT: be transparent
zhiibawaaseyaa, zhiibawaaseyaamagad
vii; **zhiibawaasezi** *vai*

TRAP
TRAP: **dasoonaagan, -an** *ni;* **wanii'igan, -an**
ni; **wanii'ige** *vai;* trap for s.o. **wanii'amaw**
vta; trap s.o. **dasoozh** /dasooN-/ *vta*
CHECK TRAPS: check one's traps
naadasoonaagane *vai*
GO AFTER TRAPS: **naajiwanii'ige** *vai*
GO GET TRAPS: go get one's traps
naadasoonaagane *vai*
TRAP BEAVER: **noodamikwe** *vai*

TRAPPED
TRAPPED: be trapped **dasoozo** *vai*

TRAPPER
    TRAPPER: wanii'igewinini, -wag *na*
TRASH
    TRASH: ziigwebinigan, -an *ni*
TRAVEL
    TRAVEL ABOUT: babaamaadizi *vai*
    TRAVEL ALONG: bimi-ayaa *vai;* travel
        along in a group (as a school of fish)
        bimaawadaaso *vai*
    TRAVEL AT NIGHT: niibaashkaa *vai*
    TRAVEL TO A CERTAIN PLACE: they
        travel in a group to a certain place
        inaawanidiwag /inaawanidi-/ *vai*
TRAVELLER
    TRAVELLER: bebaamaadizid *na-pt*
TRAVOIS
    TRAVOIS: niswaakodaabaan, -an *ni*
TREASURE
    TREASURE: treasure s.o. zaagi' *vta;* treasure
        s.t. zaagitoon *vti2*
TREASURED
    TREASURED: be treasured zaagichigaade,
        zaagichigaademagad *vii;* zaagichigaazo
        vai
TREAT
    TREAT WELL: treat s.o. well mino-doodaw
        vta
TREATY KETTLE
    TREATY KETTLE: okaadakik, -oog *na*
TREE
    TREE: mitig, -oog *na*
    BY A TREE: jiigaatig *pc*
    MANY TREES: there are many trees
        mitigokaa *vii*
TREETOP
    ON THE TREETOP: wanakong *pc*
TREMBLE
    TREMBLE: baapagishkaa *vai;*
        baapagishkaa, baapagishkaamagad *vii*
TREY
    TREY: nisoobii'igan, -ag *na*
TRICK
    PERFORM TRICKS: mamaandaagochige
        vai
TRICKSTER
    TRICKSTER: name of aadizookaan charac-
        ter viewed as culture hero and trickster
        Wenabozho *na,* also Nenabozho*
TRIM
    TRIM: agogwaajigan, -an *ni*
TRIP
    TRIP: bizozideshin *vai*
TROUBLE
    CAUSE TROUBLE: cause s.o. trouble
        aanimi' *vta*
TROUBLED
    TROUBLED: be troubled in one's mind
        mamiidaawendam *vai2*
TROUGH
    TROUGH: atoobaan, -an *ni*
    SUGARING TROUGH: naseyaawangwaan,
        -an *ni*

TRUCK
    TRUCK: aawadaasoowidaabaan, -ag *na;*
        ditibidaabaan, -ag *na*
    FIRE TRUCK: aate'ishkodawewidaabaan *na*
    MAIL TRUCK: mazina'iganiiwidaabaan, -ag
        na
TRUTH
    FIND OUT THE TRUTH: gwayakotam
        vai2
    TELL THE TRUTH: debwe *vai*
TRY
    TRY: gagwe- *pv4;* goji- *pv4;* goji'ewizi *vai;* try
        s.t. gagwejitoon *vti2;* try things
        gagwejichige *vai;* gojichige *vai*
    TRY ON: try on s.o. (e.g., clothes) gozikaw
        vta; try on s.t. (e.g., clothes) gozikan *vti*
    TRY TO DO: try to do s.t. wiikwajitoon *vti2*
    TRY TO GET: try to get s.o. to... gagweji' *vta*
    TRY TO GET FREE: wiikwaji'o *vai;* try to
        get free of s.t. wiikwajitoon *vti2*
TUB
    TUB: makakosag, -oon *ni*
TUBERCULOSIS
    TUBERCULOSIS: ozosodamwaapinewin *ni*
    HAVE TUBERCULOSIS:
        ozosodamwaapine *vai*
TUESDAY
    TUESDAY: be Tuesday niizho-giizhigad *vii*
TULLIBEE
    TULLIBEE: odoonibii, -g *na,* also
        odoonibiins, -ag
TURBULENT
    TURBULENT WATER: be turbulent water
        madaagamin /madaagami-/ *vii*
TURKEY
    TURKEY: mizise, -g *na*
TURN
    HER TURN: her turn *third person singular
        personal pronoun* wiinitam *pr*
    HIS TURN: his turn *third person singular
        personal pronoun* wiinitam *pr*
    MY TURN: my turn *first person singular
        personal pronoun* niinitam *pr*
    OUR TURN: our turn *first person exclusive
        plural personal pronoun* niinitamawind *pr;*
        our turn *first person inclusive personal
        pronoun* giinitamawind *pr*
    THEIR TURN: their turn *third person plural
        personal pronoun* wiinitamawaa *pr*
    YOUR TURN: your turn *second person plural
        personal pronoun* giinitamawaa *pr;* your
        turn *second person singular personal pronoun*
        giinitam *pr*
TURN
    TURN: turn (one's body) gwekitaa *vai;* turn
        s.o. biimiskon *vta;* turn s.t. biimiskonan
        vti
    TURN AND GO BACK: washki-giiwe *vai*
    TURN AND LOOK BACK: aabanaabi *vai;*
        turn and look back at s.o. aabanaabam
        vta; turn and look back at s.t.
        aabanaabandan *vti*

TURN AROUND WHILE SITTING:
gwekabi *vai*

TURN BY HAND: turn s.o. by hand **gwekin**
vta; turn s.t. by hand **gwekinan** *vti;* turn
things by hand **gwekinige** *vai*

TURN DRIVING: **gwekibizo** *vai*

TURN FACE DOWN: turn s.o. face down
animikon *vta;* turn s.t. face down
animikonan *vti*

TURN FACE UP: **aazhigijise** *vai;* **aazhigijise,
aazhigijisemagad** *vii*

TURN HEAD AROUND: turn one's head
around **gwekikweni** *vai*

TURN IN PLACE: **washkibagizo** *vai*

TURN INSIDE OUT: **aaboozikaa** *vai;*
aaboozikaa, aaboozikaamagad *vii;* turn
s.o. inside out **aaboodin** *vta;* turn s.t. inside out **aaboodinan** *vti*

TURN LYING IN PLACE: **gwekishin** *vai;*
gwekisin *vii*

TURN OVER: turn s.o. over (as something
sheet-like) **gwekiigin** *vta;* turn s.t. over (as
something sheet-like) **gwekiiginan** *vti*

TURN OVER BACKWARDS: **aazhigijise**
vai; **aazhigijise, aazhigijisemagad** *vii*

TURN QUICKLY: turn quickly, right self
gwekibagizo *vai*

TURN RUNNING: **gwekibatoo** *vai*

TURN STANDING: turn while standing
gwekigaabawi *vai;* **washkigaabawi** *vai*

TURN TO FACE BACKWARDS: turn s.o. to
face backwards **animikon** *vta;* turn s.t. to
face backwards **animikonan** *vti*

TURN WITH HANDS: turn s.o. with hands
gwekibizh /gwekibiN-/ *vta;* turn s.t. with
hands **gwekibidoon** *vti2*

TURN ON
TURN ON A LIGHT: turn s.t. on for a light
waazakonebidoon *vti2*

TURN OUT
TURN OUT: turn s.t. out (e.g., stove or lamp)
aatebidoon *vti2*

TURN OUT THAT
TURN OUT THAT: it turns out that
nangwana *pc, also* **ngwana, ingwana**

TURNED
PUT TURNED: put s.o. turned **gwekishim**
vta; put s.t. turned **gwekisidoon** *vti2*

TURNED FACE DOWN: be turned face
down **animikonigaade,
animikonigaademagad** *vii;*
animikonigaazo *vai*

TURNED TO FACE BACKWARDS: be
turned to face backwards **animikonigaade,
animikonigaademagad** *vii;*
animikonigaazo *vai*

TURTLE
PAINTED TURTLE: **miskwaadesi, -wag** *na*
SNAPPING TURTLE: **mikinaak, -wag** *na;*
mishiikenh, -yag *na*

TWELVE
TWELVE: **ashi-niizh** *nm;* **midaaswi ashi-niizh**
nm

TWELVE O'CLOCK: be twelve o'clock **ashi-
niizho-diba'iganed** *vii*

TWENTY
TWENTY: **niishtana** *nm*

TWENTY-TWO
TWENTY-TWO: twenty-two (gun)
niishtana-ashi-niizh *ni*

TWENTY-TWO BULLET: **anwiins, -an** *ni*

TWICE
TWICE: **niizhing** *pc*

TWILIGHT
TWILIGHT: be twilight
dibikaabaminaagwad *vii*

TWIN
TWIN: **niizhoodenh, -yag** *na*

TWINE
BALL OF TWINE OR YARN: **bikoojaan, -an**
ni

TWIST
TWIST: twist s.o. **biimiskon** *vta;* twist s.t.
biimiskonan *vti*

FALL AND TWIST ARM: fall and twist one's
arm **biimiskonikeshin** *vai*

TWISTED
TWISTED MOUTH: have a twisted mouth
(as from a stroke) **biimidoon** *vai*

TWO
TWO: **niizh** *nm;* **niizho-** *pv4;* they are two
niizhinoon /niizhin-/ *vii;* **niizhiwag
/niizhi-/** *vai;* two (card) **niizhoobii'igan,
-ag** *na*

AND TWO: **ashi-niizh** *nm;* **ashi-niizho-** *pv4*

TWO ACRES: **niizho-diba'igaans** *pc*

TWO DAYS: **niizho-giizhik** *pc;* **niizhogon** *pc;*
be two days **niizhogonagad** *vii*

TWO DAYS OLD: be two days old
niizhogonagizi *vai*

TWO DOLLARS: **niizhwaabik** *pc*

TWO EACH: **neniizh** *nm*

TWO FEET: **niizhozid** *pc*

TWO HOURS: **niizho-diba'igan** *pc*

TWO HUNDRED: **niizhwaak** *nm*

TWO INCHES: **niizhoninj** *pc*

TWO MILES: **niizho-diba'igan** *pc*

TWO MINUTES: **niizho-diba'igaans** *pc*

TWO MONTHS: **niizho-giizis** *pc*

TWO NIGHTS: **niizho-dibik** *pc*

TWO O'CLOCK: be two o'clock **niizho-
diba'iganed** *vii*

TWO PAIRS: **niizhwewaan** *pc*

TWO SETS: **niizhwewaan** *pc*

TWO THOUSAND: **niizhosagoons** *nm*

TWO TIMES: **niizhing** *pc*

TWO WEEKS: **niizho-anama'e-giizhik** *pc;* be
two weeks **niizho-anama'e-giizhigad** *pc*

TWO YEARS: **niizho-biboon** *pc;* be two years
niizho-biboonagad *vii*

TWO YEARS OLD: be two years old **niizho-
biboonagizi** *vai*

TYPE
TYPE: **mazinaabikiwebinige** *vai*

TYPEWRITER
TYPEWRITER: **bakite'ibii'igan, -an** *ni;*
mazinaabikiwebinigan, -an *ni*

U

UGLY
UGLY: be ugly **maanaadad** *vii;* **maanaadizi** *vai*

UMBILICAL CORD
UMBILICAL CORD: my umbilical cord **indis** */-disy-/ nid*

UMBRELLA
UMBRELLA: **agawaate'on, -an** *ni*

UNABLE
UNABLE TO DO: be unable to do s.t. **bwaanawitoon** *vti2;* be unable to do something **bwaanawi'o** *vai;* be unable to do something to s.o. **bwaanawi'** *vta;* be unable (to do something) **bwaanawichige** *vai*
UNABLE TO FIND A DRINK: be unable to find a drink **gwiinobii** *vai*
UNABLE TO MANAGE: be unable to manage s.o. **bwaanawi'** *vta;* be unable to manage s.t. **bwaanawitoon** *vti2*

UNCLE
UNCLE: my cross-uncle (mother's brother) **inzhishenh, -yag** */-zhisheny-/ nad;* my parallel uncle (father's brother) **nimishoome, -yag** */-mishoomey-/ nad*

UNCOMFORTABLY
LIE UNCOMFORTABLY: **maazhishin** *vai*
SIT UNCOMFORTABLY: **maanabi** *vai*
SLEEP UNCOMFORTABLY: **maazhingwaam** *vai*

UNCONNECTED
COME UNCONNECTED: come unconnected (as something string-like) **gidiskaabiigishkaa, gidiskaabiigishkaamagad** *vii*

UNCOVER
UNCOVER: uncover s.o. **baakin** *vta;* uncover s.t. **baakinan** *vti;* uncover (s.t.) for s.o. **baakinamaw** *vta;* uncover things **baakinige** *vai*

UNCOVERED
COME UNCOVERED: **baakise, baakisemagad** *vii*
LEAVE UNCOVERED: leave s.o. uncovered **baakoshim** *vta;* leave s.t. uncovered **baakosidoon** *vti2*
LIE UNCOVERED: **baakishin** *vai;* **baakisin** *vii;* **michishin** *vai;* **michisin** *vii*

UNDER
UNDER: **anaami-** *pn;* under it **anaamayi'ii** *pc*
UNDER A BOAT: **anaamoonag** *pc*
UNDER THE FLOOR: **anaamisag** *pc*
UNDER THE GROUND: **anaamakamig** *pc*
UNDER THE ICE: **anaamiskwam** *pc*
UNDER THE SNOW: **anaamaagon** *pc,* also **anaamaagonag**
UNDER WOOD: under wood (e.g., a tree or stick) **anaamaatig** *pc*

UNDERBRUSH
DENSE UNDERBRUSH: there is dense underbrush **zazagaa, zazagaamagad** *vii*

UNDERGROUND
UNDERGROUND: **anaamaki** *pc*

UNDERPANTS
UNDERPANTS: **biitoo-giboodiyegwaazon, -ag** *na*

UNDERSHIRT
UNDERSHIRT: **biitoo-babagiwayaan, -an** *ni*

UNDERSTAND
UNDERSTAND: **nisidotam** *vai2;* understand s.o. **nisidotaw** *vta;* understand s.t. **nisidotan** *vti;* they understand each other **nisidotaadiwag** */nisidotaadi-/ vai*
UNDERSTAND A CERTAIN WAY: **initam** *vai2;* understand s.o. a certain way **initaw** *vta;* understand s.t. a certain way **initan** *vti*

UNDERSTOOD
UNDERSTOOD: be understood **nisidotaagozi** *vai;* **nisidotaagwad** *vii*
UNDERSTOOD A CERTAIN WAY: be understood a certain way **initaagozi** *vai;* **initaagwad** *vii*

UNDERWATER
UNDERWATER: **anaamibiig** *pc*

UNDERWATER PANTHER
UNDERWATER PANTHER: **mishibizhii, -g** *na*

UNDERWEAR
UNDERWEAR: men's underwear **biitooshkigan, -an** *ni*

UNDO
UNDO: undo s.o. **aaba'** */aaba'w-/ vta;* undo s.t. **aaba'an** *vti;* undo (s.t.) for s.o. **aaba'amaw** *vta*
UNDO BY HAND: undo s.o. by hand **aabiskon** *vta;* undo s.t. by hand **aabiskonan** *vti*

UNDONE
UNDONE: be undone **aaba'igaade, aaba'igaademagad** *vii;* **aaba'igaazo** *vai*
COME UNDONE: **aabiskose** *vai;* **aabiskose, aabiskosemagad** *vii*

UNDRESS
UNDRESS: **giizikonaye** *vai;* undress s.o. **giizikonaye'** *vta*

UNFOLD
UNFOLD: unfold s.o. (as something sheet-like) **aabiskwegin** *vta;* unfold s.t. (as something sheet-like) **aabiskweginan** *vti*

UNITED STATES
UNITED STATES: **Gichi-mookomaan-aki** *ni*

UNIVERSITY
UNIVERSITY: **gabe-gikendaasoowigamig, -oon** *ni*

UNLOAD
UNLOAD A BOAT: **agwaanaaso** *vai*

UNLOCK
UNLOCK: unlock s.o. **aabaabika'** */aabaabika'w-/ vta;* unlock s.t.

aabaabika'an *vti;* unlock (s.t.) for s.o.
aabaabika'amaw *vta*

UNLOCKED
UNLOCKED: be unlocked
aabaabika'igaade,
aabaabika'igaademagad *vii*

UNMARRIED
UNMARRIED MAN: moozhaabe, -g *na*
UNMARRIED WOMAN: moozhikwe, -g *na*

UNRAVEL
UNRAVEL: aabiskose *vai;* aabiskose,
aabiskosemagad *vii;* unravel s.o. (as
something string-like) aabaabiigin *vta;* unravel s.t. (as something string-like)
aabaabiiginan *vti*

UNSATISFACTORY
FIND UNSATISFACTORY: find s.o. unsatisfactory aanawenim *vta;* find s.t. unsatisfactory aanawendan *vti;* find things unsatisfactory aanawenjige *vai*
FOUND UNSATISFACTORY: be found
unsatisfactory aanawendaagozi *vai;*
aanawendaagwad *vii*

UNSTEADY
FEEL UNSTEADY: giiwashkweyaabandam
vai2

UNTIE
UNTIE: untie s.o. aaba' /aaba'w-/ *vta;* untie
s.t. aaba'an *vti;* aaba'oodoon *vti2;* untie
(s.t.) for s.o. aaba'amaw *vta*
UNTIE WILD RICE: aaba'oodoo *vai*

UNTIED
UNTIED: be untied aaba'igaade,
aaba'igaademagad *vii;* aaba'igaazo *vai*

UNTIL
UNTIL: biinish *pc*

UNWIND
UNWIND: unwind s.o. (as something string-
like) aabaabiigin *vta;* unwind s.t. (as
something string-like) aabaabiiginan *vti*

UP TO
UP TO: biinish *pc*

UP TO YOU
IT'S UP TO YOU: booshke *pc, also* booshke
giniin

UPHILL
GO UPHILL: agidaakiiwe *vai*
RUN UPHILL: agidaakiiwebatoo *vai*

UPPER STORY
HAVE AN UPPER STORY:
ishpimisagokaade,
ishpimisagokaademagad *vii*

UPSET
UPSET BY HAND: upset s.o. by hand gawin
vta; upset s.t. by hand gawinan *vti*

UPSIDE DOWN
HANG UPSIDE DOWN: ajidagoode,
ajidagoodemagad *vii;* ajidagoojin *vai;*
hang s.o. upside down ajidagoozh
/ajidagooN-/ *vta;* hang s.t. upside down
ajidagoodoon *vti2*

HOLD UPSIDE DOWN: hold s.o. upside
down ajidin *vta;* hold s.t. upside down
ajidinan *vti*

UPSTAIRS
GO UPSTAIRS: akwaandawe *vai*

UPSTREAM
UPSTREAM: agidaajiwan *pc, also*
ogidaajiwan*, wagidaajiwan

UPWARDS
BLOWN UPWARDS: be blown upwards
ombaashi *vai;* ombaasin *vii*
FLY UPWARDS: ombibide,
ombibidemagad *vii;* ombibizo *vai*
GO UPWARDS: ombishkaa *vai;* ombishkaa,
ombishkaamagad *vii*
GO UPWARDS AS SMOKE: ombaabate *vii*
JUMP UPWARDS: ombigwaashkwani *vai*
SPEED UPWARDS: ombibide,
ombibidemagad *vii;* ombibizo *vai*
THROW UPWARDS: throw s.o. upwards
ombiwebin *vta;* throw s.t. upwards
ombiwebinan *vti*

URGE
URGE: urge s.o. gagaanzom *vta*
URGE TO COME: urge s.o. to come
wiizhaam *vta*

URINATE
URINATE: zhiishiigi *vai;* urinate on s.o.
zhigizh /zhigiN-/ *vta;* urinate on s.t.
zhigidan *vti;* urinate on oneself zhiginidizo
vai

US
US: us *first person exclusive plural pronoun*
niinawind *pr;* us *first person inclusive per-*
sonal pronoun giinawind *pr*

USE
USE: use s.o. aabaji' *vta;* use s.t. aabajitoon
vti2
GET GOOD USE: get good use of s.o.
minwaabaji' *vta;* get good use of s.t.
minwaabajitoon *vti2*
OF GOOD USE: be of good use
minwaabadad *vii;* minwaabadizi *vai*
USE A CERTAIN WAY: use s.o. a certain
way inaabaji' *vta;* use s.t. a certain way
inaabajitoon *vti2;* us_ things a certain way
inaabajichige *vai*

USE UP
USE UP: use s.o. up jaagaabaji' *vta;* use s.t.
up jaagaabajitoon *vti2;* use things up
jaaginige *vai*
USE UP AMMUNITION: use up all of the
ammunition jaaga'e *vai;* jaagizige *vai*
USE UP MONEY: use up all of the money
jaagizhooniyaaweshin *vai*

USED
USED: be used aabadad *vii;* aabadizi *vai*

USED TO
USED TO: be used to making s.o. nagaji' *vta;*
be used to making s.t. nagajitoon *vti2;* be
used to s.o. nagadenim *vta;* be used to s.t.
nagadendan *vti*

USED TO
USED TO: **iko** *pc*, *also* **ko**
USED UP
USED UP: be used up **jaaginigaade, jaaginigaademagad** *vii*
USEFUL
USEFUL: be useful **aabadad** *vii*; **aabadizi** *vai*; be very useful **minwaabadad** *vii*; **minwaabadizi** *vai*
USEFUL IN A CERTAIN WAY: be useful in a certain way **inaabadad** *vii*; **inaabadizi** *vai*

V

VAIN
IN VAIN: **aano-** *pv1*
VALLEY
VALLEY: be a valley **basadinaa, basadinaamagad** *vii*
VALUED
VALUED TO A CERTAIN EXTENT: be valued to a certain extent **apiitendaagozi** *vai*; **apiitendaagwad** *vii*
VAMP
MOCCASIN VAMP: moccasin vamp **apiingwe'igan, -an** *ni*
VAN
VAN: **aawazhiwewidaabaan, -ag** *na*
VARIEGATED
VARIEGATED: be variegated **gidagaa, gidagaamagad** *vii*; **gidagizi** *vai*; be variegated (as something sheet-like) **gidagiigad** *vii*; **gidagiigizi** *vai*
VARIETY
VARIETY OF THINGS: a variety of things **anooj gegoo** *pr*, *also* **anooji-gegoo**
VARIOUS
VARIOUS: **anooj** *pc*
VARIOUS THINGS: **anooj gegoo** *pr*, *also* **anooji-gegoo**
VEGETABLE
VEGETABLE: **gitigaanens, -an** *ni*
VEIN
VEIN: my vein **indiskweyaab, -iin** *nid*
VELVET
VELVET: **miishiigin, -oon** *ni*
VERY
VERY: **aapiji** *pc*; **gichi-** *pv4*, *also* **chi-**; **enda-** *pv4*
VESSEL
VESSEL: **naabikwaan, -an** *ni*
VEST
VEST: **gibide'ebizon, -an** *ni*
VETERAN'S HOME
VETERAN'S HOME: **zhimaaganishiiwigamig, -oon** *ni*

VETERAN'S HOSPITAL
VETERAN'S HOSPITAL: **zhimaaganishii-aakoziiwigamig, -oon** *ni*
VIEW
COME INTO VIEW: **bi-naagozi** *vai*; **bi-naagwad** *vii*
COME SUDDENLY INTO VIEW: come suddenly into view as from around a corner **zaagewe** *vai*
DRIVE SUDDENLY INTO VIEW: **zaagewebide, zaagewebidemagad** *vii*; **zaagewebizo** *vai*
PADDLE SUDDENLY INTO VIEW: **zaagewe'o** *vai*; **zaagewekwazhiwe** *vai*
RUN SUDDENLY INTO VIEW: **zaagewebatoo** *vai*
SPEED SUDDENLY INTO VIEW: **zaagewebide, zaagewebidemagad** *vii*; **zaagewebizo** *vai*
SWIM SUDDENLY INTO VIEW: swim as a fish suddenly into view **zaagewekwazhiwe** *vai*
VINE
VINE: **biimaakwad, -oon** *ni*
VINEGAR
VINEGAR: **zhiiwaaboo** *ni*
VIOLIN
VIOLIN: **naazhaabii'igan, -an** *ni*
VISIBLE
VISIBLE: be visible **naagozi** *vai*; **naagwad** *vii*
BARELY VISIBLE: be barely visible **naawinaagozi** *vai*; **naawinaagwad** *vii*
VISIBLE AT A DISTANCE: be visible at a distance **debaabaminaagozi** *vai*; **debaabaminaagwad** *vii*
VISION
VISION: have vision **waabi** *vai*
FAST FOR A VISION: **gii'igoshimo** *vai*
VISIT
VISIT: visit s.o. **mawadish /mawadiS-/** *vta*; **odish /odiS-/** *vta*; visit people **mawadishiwe** *vai*; **odishiwe** *vai*; they visit each other **mawadisidiwag /mawadisidi-/** *vai*
VISITOR
VISITOR: **biiwide, -g** *na*
VOICE
BAD VOICE: have a bad voice **maanowe** *vai*
GOOD VOICE: have a good voice **minogondaagan** *vai*; **minowe** *vai*
HAVE A SOFT VOICE: **bedowe** *vai*
HAVE DIFFICULTY WITH VOICE: have difficulty with one's voice **maazhigondaagan** *vai*
VOMIT
VOMIT: **zhigagowe** *vai*; keep vomiting **zhishigagowe** *vai*
VOTE
VOTE: **biinjwebinige** *vai*; vote for s.o. **biinjwebinigetamaw** *vta*
VULVA
VULVA: my vulva **nikidin /-kidin-/** *nad*

WADE
RUN ACROSS WADING:
aazhawagaaziibatoo *vai*
WADE ABOUT: **babaamaadagaazii** *vai*
WADE ACROSS: **aazhawagaazii** *vai*
WADE ALONG: **bimaadagaazii** *vai*
WADE AWAY: **animaadagaazii** *vai*
WADE FROM A CERTAIN PLACE:
ondaadagaazii *vai*
WADE HERE: **biidaadagaazii** *vai*
WADE TO A CERTAIN PLACE:
inaadagaazii *vai*

WAG
WAG TAIL: wag one's tail **wewebaanoweni**
vai

WAGON
WAGON: **ditibidaabaan, -ag** *na;* **odaabaan,
-ag** *na*
DRIVE ALONG IN A WAGON OR
SLEIGH: drive along quickly in a wagon
or sleigh **bimidaabiiba'igo** *vai*

WAIT
WAIT: **bii'o** *vai;* wait for s.o. **bii'** *vta;* wait for
s.t. **biitoon** *vti2;* wait! **bekaa** *pc*
KEEP WAITING: **baabii'o** *vai;* keep waiting
for s.o. **baabii'** *vta;* keep waiting for s.t.
baabiitoon *vti2*
TIRED OF WAITING: be tired of waiting
zhigajibii'o *vai;* be tired of waiting for s.o.
zhigajibii' *vta;* be tired of waiting for s.t.
zhigajibiitoon *vti2*
WAIT IN WATCH: **akawaabi** *vai;* wait in
watch for s.o. **akawaabam** *vta;* wait in
watch for s.t. **akawaabandan** *vti*

WAKE
WAKE: wake s.o. **amadin** *vta*
WAKE BY VOCAL NOISE: wake s.o. by vo-
cal noise **amajim** *vta*
WAKE FROM BEING COLD: **amadaji** *vai*
WAKE FROM PAIN: **amajine** *vai*
WAKE UP: **goshkozi** *vai*

WAKE
SIT UP WITH AT A WAKE: sit up with s.o.
(e.g., the deceased at a wake) **abiitaw** *vta*

WALK
ARRIVE WALKING: **bagamose** *vai*
HEARD WALKING: be heard walking on the
floor **madwesagishin** *vai*
HEARD WALKING ALONG: be heard
walking along **bimweweshin** *vai*
HEARD WALKING HERE: be heard walking
here **biidweweshin** *vai*
WALK A CERTAIN WAY: **inose** *vai*
WALK ABOUT: **babaamose** *vai;* **babimose**
vai
WALK ALONG: **bimose** *vai*
WALK ALONG ON THE ICE:
bimaadagaako *vai*

WALK ALONG SHORE TO A CERTAIN
PLACE: **inaazhagaame** *vai*
WALK ALONG THE SHORE:
jiigeweyaazhagaame *vai*
WALK AROUND: walk around s.o.
giiwitaashkaw *vta;* walk around s.t.
giiwitaashkan *vti;* walk around something
giiwitaawose *vai, also* **giiwitaa'ose**
WALK AROUND A LAKE:
giiwitaayaazhagaame *vai*
WALK AROUND THE EDGE:
giiwitaayaazhagaame *vai*
WALK AWAY: **animose** *vai*
WALK AWAY MAKING NOISE:
animwewetoo *vai*
WALK FROM A CERTAIN PLACE: **ondose**
vai
WALK HERE: **biidaasamose** *vai*
WALK SLOWLY: **bedose** *vai*
WALK TO CERTAIN PLACE: walk to a
certain place **inose** *vai*
WALK WITH: walk with s.o. **wiidosem** *vta*
WALK WITH DISCOMFORT: **maanose** *vai*

WALL
WALL: **aasamisag, -oon** *ni*
BY A WALL: **jiigaatig** *pc*

WALLEYE
WALLEYE: **ogaa, -wag** *na*

WANDER
WANDER ABOUT: **babaa-ayaa** *vai*

WANT
WANT: **misawendam** *vai2;* **nandawendam**
vai2; want s.o. **misawenim** *vta;* want s.o.
(to do...) **nandawenim** *vta;* want s.t.
misawendan *vti;* **nandawendan** *vti;* want
things **misawenjige** *vai*
WANT TO: **wii-** *pv1*

WAR
WAR: **miigaadiwin, -an** *ni*
GO TO WAR: go to war *archaic* **nandobani**
vai
SING WAR SONGS: **bwaanzhii-nagamo** *vai*

WAR CLUB
WAR CLUB: **bagamaagan, -an** *ni*

WAR DANCE
WAR DANCE: **bwaanzhii-niimi'idiwin, -an**
ni; dance a war dance **bwaanzhii-niimi** *vai;*
they dance a war dance **bwaanzhii-
niimi'idiwag /bwaanzhii-niimi'idi-/** *vai*

WAR WHOOP
GIVE WAR WHOOPS: **zaasaakwe** *vai*

WARM
WARM: be warm (as a liquid) **abaagamide,
abaagamidemagad** *vii;* warm s.t. (as a
liquid) **abaagamizan** *vti*
WARM AT THE FIRE: warm s.o. at the fire
abiz /abizw-/ *vta;* warm s.t. at the fire
abizan *vti;* warm (s.t.) for s.o. at the fire
abizamaw *vta*
WARM BACK: warm one's back
abaawiganezo *vai*
WARM BY THE FIRE: warm oneself by the
fire **awazo** *vai*
WARM FEET: warm one's feet **abizidezo** *vai*

WARM HANDS: warm one's hands
   abininjiizo *vai*
WARM UP: warm up in the sun **abaaso** *vai*
WARM WEATHER: be warm weather
   aabawaa, aabawaamagad *vii*
WEATHER WARMS UP: warm up (of the
   weather) **abaate, abaatemagad** *vii*
WRAPPED UP WARM: be wrapped up warm
   giizhoopizo *vai*
WARMLY
   DRESS WARMLY: **giizhoo'o** *vai*
WARMTH
   LIE IN WARMTH: **giizhooshin** *vai*
WARN
   WARN: warn s.o. **ayaangwaamim** *vta*
   WARN AGAINST: warn s.o. against (s.t.)
   gina'amaw *vta*
WARRIOR
   WARRIOR: **ogichidaa, -g** *na*
WART
   WART: **jiichiigom, -ag** *na*
WASH
   WASH: **giziibiigii** *vai;* wash s.o. by hand
   giziibiigin *vta;* wash s.o. using something
   giziibiiga' /**giziibiiga'w-**/ *vta;* wash s.t. us-
   ing something **giziibiiga'an** *vti;* wash s.t. by
   hand **giziibiiginan** *vti;* wash things
   giziibiiga'ige *vai*
   WASH CLOTHES: **giziibiiga'ige** *vai*
   WASH DISHES: **giziibiiginaagane** *vai*
   WASH FACE: wash one's face **giziibiigiingwe**
   vai
   WASH FLOORS: **giziibiigisaginige** *vai*
   WASH HAIR: wash one's hair **giziibiigindibe**
   vai
   WASH HANDS: wash one's hands
   giziibiigininjii *vai*
   WASH KETTLE: **giziibiiginakokwe** *vai*
   WASH PAIL: **giziibiiginakokwe** *vai*
WASH BASIN
   WASH BASIN: **giziibiigiingwewinaagan** *ni*
WASH UP
   WASH UP: **giziibiigazhe** *vai*
WASHBOARD
   WASHBOARD: **mimigwaakosijigan, -an** *ni*
WASHED
   WASHED: be washed **giziibiiginigaade,**
   giziibiiginigaademagad *vii*
WASHING MACHINE
   WASHING MACHINE: **giziibiiga'ige-**
   makak, -oon *ni*
WASHINGTON
   WASHINGTON: Washington, D.C.
   Waashtanong *place*
WASHTUB
   WASHTUB: **giziibiiga'ige-makak, -oon** *ni*
WASP
   WASP: **aamoo, -g** *na*
WASP NEST
   WASP NEST: **aamoo-wadiswan, -an** *ni*

WASTE
   WASTE: waste s.o. **nishwanaaji'** *vta;* waste s.t.
   nishwanaajitoon *vti2;* waste things
   nishwanaajichige *vai*
WATCH
   WATCH: **ganawaabi** *vai;* watch s.o.
   ganawaabam *vta;* watch s.t.
   ganawaabandan *vti;* watch things
   ganawaabanjige *vai;* they watch each
   other **ganawaabandiwag** /**ganawaabandi-**/
   vai
   WATCH CAREFULLY: watch s.o. carefully
   naanaagadawaabam *vta;* watch s.t. carefully **naanaagadawaabandan** *vti*
   WATCH OVER: watch over s.o. **gizhaazh**
   /**gizhaaN-**/ *vta;* watch over s.t. **gizhaadan**
   vti; watch over things **gizhaadige** *vai*
WATCH
   WATCH: **diba'igiiziswaanens, -ag** *na*
WATCHED
   WATCHED: be watched
   ganawaabanjigaade,
   ganawaabanjigaademagad *vii;*
   ganawaabanjigaazo *vai*
WATER
   WATER: **nibi** *ni;* water s.t. **ziiga'andan** *vti*
   AT THE WATER: **agamiing** *pc*
   BLOWN INTO THE WATER: be blown into
   the water **bakobiiyaashi** *vai;*
   bakobiiyaasin *vii*
   BY THE WATER: **jiigibiig** *pc*
   COLD WATER: **dakib** *ni*
   DRAG INTO THE WATER: drag s.o. into
   the water **bakobiidaabaazh**
   /**bakobiidaabaaN-**/ *vta;* drag s.t. into the
   water **bakobiidaabaadan** *vti*
   EMERGE FROM THE WATER: **mookibii**
   vai
   FALL INTO THE WATER: **bakobiise** *vai;*
   bakobiise, bakobiisemagad *vii*
   GET WATER: **nibinaadi** *vai;* get water for s.o.
   gwaaba'amaw *vta*
   GET WATER FROM A CERTAIN PLACE:
   onda'ibii *vai*
   GO AWAY FROM THE WATER: **gopii** *vai*
   GO DOWN INTO THE WATER: **bakobii**
   vai
   GO GET WATER: go get water or other
   liquid **naadoobii** *vai*
   IN THE DEPTHS OF A BODY OF
   WATER: **anaamiindim** *pc*
   JUMP INTO THE WATER:
   bakobiigwaashkwani *vai*
   MUCH WATER: be much water **nibiikaa,**
   nibiikaamagad *vii*
   ON THIS SIDE OF THE WATER:
   ondaasagaam *pc*
   ON TOP OF THE WATER: **agidibiig** *pc, also*
   ogidibiig*, wagidibiig
   OVER ACROSS THE WATER: **awasagaam**
   pc
   RUN INTO THE WATER: **bakobiibatoo** *vai*
   SUSPENDED IN WATER: be suspended in
   water **agomo** *vai;* **agonde** *vii*

THROW INTO THE WATER: throw s.o.
into the water **bakobiiwebin** *vta;* throw s.t.
into the water **bakobiiwebinan** *vti*
THROW OUT OF THE WATER: throw s.t.
out of the water **agwaawebinan** *vti;* throw
(s.t.) out of the water for s.o.
agwaawebinamaw *vta*
WATER SOURCE: **onda'ibaan, -an** *ni*

WATER PAIL
WATER PAIL: **nibiiwakik, -oog** *na*

WATERFALL
WATERFALL: be a waterfall **gakaamikijiwan**
vii; **gakijiwan** *vii*

WATERMELON
WATERMELON: **eshkandaming, -in** *ni-pt*

WATERY
WATERY: be watery **nibiiwan** *vii*

WAVE
WAVE: **digow, -ag** *na, also* **digo**
BIG WAVES: be big waves
mamaangaashkaa,
mamaangaashkaamagad *vii*
WAVES COME IN TO SHORE:
biidaashkaa, biidaashkaamagad *vii*

WAY
CERTAIN WAY: be a certain way **izhi-ayaa**
vai
IN A CERTAIN WAY: **izhi-** *pv3*
ON THE WAY: **ani-** *pv2, also* **ni-**; **bimi-** *pv2*
THIS WAY: **bi-** *pv2*

WAY OF LIFE
WAY OF LIFE: **inaadiziwin, -an** *ni*
CERTAIN WAY OF LIFE: have a certain way
of life **inaadizi** *vai*

WE
WE: we *first person exclusive plural pronoun*
niinawind *pr;* we *first person inclusive per-*
sonal pronoun **giinawind** *pr*

WEAK
WEAK: be weak **niinamad** *vii;* **niinamizi** *vai;*
be weak (as a liquid) **zhaagwaagamin**
/zhaagwaagami-/ *vii;* be weak in muscular
strength **zhaagwiiwii** *vai;* be weak in power
zhaagwaadad *vii;* **zhaagwaadizi** *vai*
CONSIDER WEAK: consider s.o. weak
zhaagwenim *vta;* consider s.t. weak
zhaagwendan *vti*
LOOK WEAK: **niinaminaagozi** *vai;*
niinaminaagwad *vii*

WEALTH
WEALTH: **daniwin** *ni*

WEAR
WEAR: wear s.o. **biizikaw** *vta;* wear s.t.
biizikan *vti*
WEAR A BRACELET: **jiiskinikebizo** *vai*
WEAR A COAT: **gigibabiinzikawaagane** *vai*
WEAR A SHIRT: **gigibabagiwayaane** *vai*
WEAR ACROSS THE SHOULDER: wear
s.t. across the shoulder **aazhooningwa'an**
vti
WEAR ARM GARTERS: **jiiskinikebizo** *vai*

WEAR AROUND NECK: wear s.o. around
one's neck **naabikaw** *vta;* wear s.t. around
one's neck **naabikan** *vti*
WEAR BLACK: **makadewi'o** *vai*
WEAR BLUE: **ozhaawashko'o** *vai*
WEAR BROWN: **ozaawi'o** *vai*
WEAR EARMUFFS: **giizhootawage'o** *vai*
WEAR GREEN: **ozhaawashko'o** *vai*
WEAR INSIDE OUT: wear s.o. inside out
aaboozikaw *vta;* wear s.t. inside out
aaboozikan *vti*
WEAR LAYERS: wear layers (as underwear)
biitookonaye *vai*
WEAR LEG GARTERS: **gashkidaasebizo** *vai*
WEAR MITTENS: **gigiminjikaawane** *vai*
WEAR NEW CLOTHES: **oshki'o** *vai*
WEAR OVERSHOES: **biitookizine** *vai*
WEAR PANTS: **gigigiboodiyegwaazone** *vai*
WEAR PATCHES: **bagwa'igaazo** *vai*
WEAR RED: **misko'o** *vai*
WEAR SOCKS: **gigazhigane** *vai*
WEAR THE WRONG WAY: wear s.o. the
wrong way **napaazikaw** *vta;* wear s.t. the
wrong way **napaazikan** *vti*
WEAR WHITE: **waabishki'o** *vai*
WEAR YELLOW: **ozaawi'o** *vai*

WEAR OUT
WEAR OUT IN OPERATION: **angobide,**
angobidemagad *vii;* **angobizo** *vai*
WEAR OUT WITH FOOT OR BODY: wear
s.o. out with foot or body (e.g., pants)
angoshkaw *vta;* wear s.t. out with foot or
body **angoshkan** *vti*

WEASEL
WEASEL: **zhingos, -ag** *na*

WEASEL SKIN
WEASEL SKIN: **zhingosiwayaan, -ag** *na*

WEATHER
BAD WEATHER: be bad weather **niiskaadad**
vii
CALM WEATHER: be calm weather
anwaatin *vii*
CERTAIN WEATHER CONDITION: be a
certain weather condition **izhiwebad** *vii*
COLD WEATHER: be cold (weather)
gisinaa, gisinaamagad *vii*
COOL WEATHER: be cool (weather)
dakaayaa, dakaayaamagad *vii, also* **daki-**
ayaa
GOOD WEATHER: be good weather
mizhakwad *vii*
HAVE GOOD TRAVELLING WEATHER:
mino-giizhiganishi *vai*
HOT WEATHER: be hot (weather) **gizhaate,**
gizhaatemagad *vii*
MILD WEATHER: be mild weather
aabawaa, aabawaamagad *vii*
WARM WEATHER: be warm weather
aabawaa, aabawaamagad *vii*
WEATHER WARMS UP: warm up (of the
weather) **abaate, abaatemagad** *vii*

WEAVE
WEAVE: weave s.t. **niibidoon** *vti2*

WEDGED
WEDGED IN TIGHTLY: be wedged in tightly (as something stick- or wood-like) **ziindaakoshin** *vai;* **ziindaakosin** *vii*

WEDNESDAY
WEDNESDAY: be Wednesday **aabitoose, aabitoosemagad** *vii*

WEED
WEED: weed s.t. **bashkwashkibidoon** *vti2;* weed things **bashkwashkibijige** *vai*

WEEK
CERTAIN DAY OF THE WEEK: be a certain day of the week **izhi-giizhigad** *vii*
CERTAIN NUMBER OF WEEKS: a certain number of weeks **daso-anama'e-giizhik** *pc;* be a certain number of weeks **daso-anama'e-giizhikwagad** *vii, also* **daswanama'e-giizhikwagad**

WEEP
WEEP: mawi *vai*

WEIGH
WEIGH: weigh s.o. **dibaabiishkoozh /dibaabiishkooN-/** *vta;* weigh s.t. **dibaabiishkoodoon** *vti2;* weigh things **dibaabiishkoojige** *vai*
WEIGH A CERTAIN AMOUNT: apiitinigozi *vai;* **apiitinigwad** *vii*

WELFARE OFFICE
WELFARE OFFICE: ashangewigamig, -oon *ni*

WELFARE WORKER
WELFARE WORKER: ashangewinini, -wag *na;* welfare worker (female) **ashangewikwe, -g** *na*

WELL
WELL: mino- *pv4;* **wawiinge** *pc;* be well **mino-ayaa** *vai*
BEHAVE WELL: mino-izhiwebizi *vai*
COOK WELL: minozekwe *vai;* cook s.o. well **minoz /minozw-/** *vta;* cook s.t. well **minozan** *vti*
DO WELL: do things well **minochige** *vai*
DRESS WELL: mino'o *vai*
EAT WELL: minwanjige *vai*
FIT WELL: minwashkine *vai;* **minwashkine, minwashkinemagad** *vii;* fit s.o. well (e.g., pants) **minokaw** *vta;* fit s.t. well **minokan** *vti*
GET ALONG WELL: minose *vai*
GO WELL: minose, minosemagad *vii;* have things go well for one **minose** *vai*
GROW WELL: minogi *vai;* **minogin** *vii*
LIVE WELL: mino-bimaadizi *vai*
MAKE WELL: make s.o. well **onizhishi'** *vta;* make s.t. well **onizhishitoon** *vti2*
RUN WELL: run well (as a machine) **minobide, minobidemagad** *vii;* **minobizo** *vai*
SEE WELL: minwaabi *vai*
SPEAK WELL: minowe *vai*
TREAT WELL: treat s.o. well **mino-doodaw** *vta*
WELL COOKED: be well cooked **minode, minodemagad** *vii;* **minozo** *vai*
WELL FILLED: be well filled **minwashkine** *vai;* **minwashkine, minwashkinemagad** *vii*

WELL
WELL: aanish *pc*
WELL HOW: well how? **aaniin danaa** *pc*
WELL NOW: aaniish *pc;* **aaniish naa** *pc*
WELL THEN: aanish *pc*
WELL WHY: well why? **aaniin danaa** *pc*

WELL
WATER WELL: onda'ibaan, -an *ni*

WEST
WEST: ningaabii'an *ni*
IN THE WEST: bangishimog in the west; *conjunct of:* **bangishimon /bangishimo-/** *vii* set as the sun

WET
WET: be wet **nibiiwan** *vii;* **nibiiwi** *vai*
GET WET: nisaabaawe *vai;* **nisaabaawe, nisaabaawemagad** *vii*
HEAVY WET SNOW: there is heavy wet snow falling **zhakipon /zhakipo-/** *vii*
WET GROUND: be wet ground **nibiiwakamigaa, nibiiwakamigaamagad** *vii*
WET ROAD: be wet (as a road or trail) **nibiiwadamon /nibiiwadamo-/** *vii*
WET THE BED: zhigingwaam *vai*
WET TRAIL: be wet (as a road or trail) **nibiiwadamon /nibiiwadamo-/** *vii*

WHAT
WHAT: what *inanimate interrogative* **wegonen, -an** *pr;* **awegonen, -an** *pr;* **wegonesh**
I DON'T KNOW WHAT: I don't know what *inanimate dubitative* **wegodogwen, -an** *pr*
I DON'T REMEMBER WHAT: ayi'ii, -n *pr*
I WONDER WHAT: I wonder what *inanimate dubitative* **wegodogwen, -an** *pr*

WHATEVER
WHATEVER: whatever *inanimate dubitative* **wegodogwen igo** *pr*

WHEEL
WHEEL: detibised *na-pt*

WHEEZE
WHEEZE: gaaskanaamo *vai*

WHEN
WHEN: apii *pc;* when? *interrogative* **aanapii** *pc, also* **aanapiish, aaniin apii, aaniin iw apii**
I DON'T KNOW WHEN: *dubitative* **amanj apii** *pc*
I WONDER WHEN: I wonder when *dubitative* **amanj apii** *pc*

WHENEVER
WHENEVER: *dubitative* **amanj igo apii** *pc*

WHERE
WHERE: where? *interrogative* **aandi** *pc, also* **aandish, aaniindi**
I DON'T KNOW WHERE: *dubitative* **dibi** *pc*
I WONDER WHERE: I wonder where *dubitative* **dibi** *pc*

WHEREVER
WHEREVER: *dubitative* **dibi go** *pc*

WHILE
WHILE: **eshkwaa** *pc;* **megwaa** *pc*
A LITTLE WHILE: **ajina** *pc*
EVERY LITTLE WHILE: **wewayiiba** *pc*

WHIP
WHIP: **bashanzhe'igan, -an** *ni;*
bashanzhe'ige *vai;* whip s.o.
bashanzhe' /**bashanzhe'w-/** *vta*

WHIRL
WHIRL: **gizhibaabide, gizhibaabidemagad**
vii; **gizhibaabise** *vai;* **gizhibaabise,**
gizhibaabisemagad *vii;* **gizhibaabizo** *vai*

WHIRLPOOL
WHIRLPOOL: be a whirlpool **maajijiwan** *vii*

WHIRLWIND
WHIRLWIND: be a whirlwind
gizhibaayaanimad *vii*

WHISKERS
WHITE WHISKERS: have white whiskers
waabishkawedoon *vai*

WHISPER
WHISPER: **gaaskanazo** *vai;* whisper to s.o.
gaaskanazootaw *vta*

WHISTLE
WHISTLE: **gwiishkoshi** *vai;*
noondaagochigan, -an *ni;* whistle to s.o.
gwiishkoshim *vta*
WHISTLE FROM BOILING:
gwiishkoshwewegamide,
gwiishkoshwewegamidemagad *vii;*
gwiishkoshwewegamizo *vai*

WHITE
WHITE: **waabishki-** *pv4;* be white
waabishkaa, waabishkaamagad *vii;*
waabishkizi *vai;* be white (as something
mineral) **waabishkaabikad** *vii;*
waabishkaabikizi *vai;* be white (as something sheet-like) **waabishkiigad** *vii;*
waabishkiigizi *vai;* be white (as something
stick- or wood-like) **waabishkaakozi** *vai;*
waabishkaakwad *vii;* be white (as something string-like) **waabishkaabiigad** *vii;*
waabishkaabiigizi *vai*
COLORED WHITE: be colored white
waabishkaande, waabishkaandemagad
vii; **waabishkaanzo** *vai*
WEAR WHITE: **waabishki'o** *vai*
WHITE CLOUDS: there are white clouds
waabishkaanakwad *vii*

WHITE ASH
WHITE ASH: white ash (tree)
baapaagimaak, -wag *na*

WHITE CEDAR
WHITE CEDAR: **giizhik, -ag** *na*

WHITE CLAY
WHITE CLAY: **waabaabigan** *na*

WHITE EARTH
WHITE EARTH: White Earth Reservation
Gaa-waabaabiganikaag *place*

WHITE HAIR
WHITE HAIR: have white hair
waabishkindibe *vai*

WHITE PERSON
WHITE PERSON: **gichi-mookomaan, -ag**
na; **wayaabishkiiwed** *na-pt;* be a white
person **waabishkiiwe** *vai*

WHITE PINE
WHITE PINE: **zhingwaak, -wag** *na*

WHITE SPOTS
WHITE SPOTS ON FINGERNAILS: have
white spots on fingernails **mindaweganzhii**
vai

WHITE SPRUCE
WHITE SPRUCE: **gaawaandag, -oog** *na*

WHITE WOMAN
WHITE WOMAN: **gichi-mookomaanikwe,**
-g *na*

WHITEFISH
WHITEFISH: **adikameg, -wag** *na*

WHITTLE
WHITTLE: **mookodaaso** *vai*

WHO
WHO: who? *animate interrogative* **awenen, -ag**
pr; **awenesh** *pr*
I DON'T KNOW WHO: I don't know who
animate dubitative **awegwen, -ag** *pr*
I DON'T REMEMBER WHO: **aya'aa, -g** *pr*
I WONDER WHO: I wonder who *animate*
dubitative **awegwen, -ag** *pr*
WHO THEN: who then *animate interrogative*
awenesh *pr*

WHOEVER
WHOEVER: whoever *animate dubitative*
awegwen igo *pr*

WHOLE
WHOLE: be whole **miziweyaa,**
miziweyaamagad *vii;* **miziwezi** *vai*
MAKE OF A WHOLE PIECE: make s.o. of a
whole piece **miziwe'** *vta;* make s.t. of a
whole piece **miziwetoon** *vti2*

WHOLE LOT
A WHOLE LOT: **neniibowa** *pc*

WHOOP
WHOOP: **zaasaakwe** *vai*

WHY
WHY: why? **aaniin** *pc;* **aaniish** *pc;* **aaniin dash**
pc
WHY NOT: why not? **aaniin danaa** *pc*

WIDE
WIDE: be wide **mangadeyaa,**
mangadeyaamagad *vii;* **mangadezi** *vai*
MAKE WIDE: make s.o. wide **mangade'** *vta;*
make s.t. wide **mangadetoon** *vti2*
SO WIDE: be so wide **inigokwadeyaa,**
inigokwadeyaamagad *vii;* **inigokwadezi**
vai; be so wide (as something mineral)
inigokwadeyaabikad *vii;*
inigokwadeyaabikizi *vai;* be so wide (as
something sheet-like) **inigokwadeyiigad**
vii; **inigokwadeyiigizi** *vai;* be so wide (as
something stick- or wood-like)
inigokwadeyaakozi *vai;*
inigokwadeyaakwad *vii;* be so wide (as
something string-like)

inigokwadeyaabiigad *vii;*
inigokwadeyaabiigizi *vai*
WIDE BOAT: be wide (as a boat)
mangadeyoonagad *vii*
WIDE RIVER: be wide (as a river)
mangitigweyaa, mangitigweyaamagad
vii
WIDE ROAD: be wide (as a road or trail)
mangademon /mangademo-/ *vii, also*
mangadademon
WIDE TRAIL: be wide (as a road or trail)
mangademon /mangademo-/ *vii, also*
mangadademon

WIDEN

WIDEN: widen s.o. mangade' *vta;* widen s.t.
mangadetoon *vti2*

WIDOW

WIDOW: zhiigaa, -g *na;* be a widow
zhiigaawi *vai*

WIDOWER

WIDOWER: zhiigaa, -g *na;* be a widower
zhiigaawi *vai*

WIDTH

CERTAIN WIDTH: be a certain width
inigokwadeyaa, inigokwadeyaamagad
vii; inigokwadezi *vai;* be a certain width
(as something mineral)
inigokwadeyaabikad *vii;*
inigokwadeyaabikizi *vai;* be a certain
width (as something sheet-like)
inigokwadeyiigad *vii;* inigokwadeyiigizi
vai; be a certain width (as something stick-
or wood-like) inigokwadeyaakozi *vai;*
inigokwadeyaakwad *vii;* be a certain
width (as something string-like)
inigokwadeyaabiigad *vii;*
inigokwadeyaabiigizi *vai*

WIFE

WIFE: my wife niwiidigemaagan, -ag
/-wiidigemaagan-/ *na;* niwiiw, -ag /-wiiw-/
nad

WIGOB

PEEL WIGOB: peel wigob (inner bark of
basswood) bisha'igobii *vai*

WIGWAM

WIGWAM: waaginogaan, -an *ni;* wiigiwaam,
-an *ni*
LIVE IN A WIGWAM: wiigiwaamige *vai*
MAKE A WIGWAM: wiigiwaamike *vai*

WIGWAM FRAME

WIGWAM FRAME: wiigiwaamaak, -oon *ni*

WIGWAM POLE

WIGWAM POLE: wiigiwaamaatig, -oon *ni*

WILD

WILD: bagwaji- *pv4*

WILD ANIMAL

WILD ANIMAL: awesiinh, -yag *na*

WILD POTATO

WILD POTATO: bagwajipin, -iig *na, also*
bagwaji-opin

WILD RICE

WILD RICE: manoomin *ni, also* anishinaabe-
manoomin

BARREL OR TUB USED IN THRESHING
WILD RICE: mimigoshkamwaagan, -an
ni
GREEN WILD RICE: ozhaawashko-
manoomin *ni*
HARVEST WILD RICE: bawa'am *vai2;*
manoominike *vai*
HAUL WILD RICE: aawajimine *vai*
KNOCK WILD RICE: bawa'am *vai2*
MUCH WILD RICE: there is much wild rice
manoominikaa, manoominikaamagad
vii
POPPED WILD RICE: gaapizigan, -an *ni*
TAKE WILD RICE INLAND: gopimine *vai*
THRESH WILD RICE: thresh something
mimigoshkam *vai2*
TIE WILD RICE: dakobidoo *vai*
TIED WILD RICE: dakobijigan, -an *ni*
UNTIE WILD RICE: aaba'oodoo *vai*

WILD RICE BROTH

WILD RICE BROTH: manoominaaboo *ni*

WILD RICE STALK

WILD RICE STALK: manoominaganzh, -iin
ni

WILDERNESS

IN THE WILDERNESS: bagwaj *pc*

WILL

WILL: will *future/desiderative verb prefix* wii-
pv1

WILLOW

WILLOW: oziisigobimizh, -iig *na*

WILLOW BASKET

WILLOW BASKET: oziisigobimizhii-makak,
-oon *ni*

WIN

WIN: gabenaage *vai;* mizhodam *vai2*
WIN IN A GAME: win from s.o. in a game
gabenaw *vta*
WIN OVER: win over s.o. bakinaw *vta;* win
over people bakinaage *vai*

WIND

WIND: there is a wind noodin *vii*
COLD WIND: be a cold wind dakaanimad *vii*
COME AS WIND FROM A CERTAIN
PLACE: come as wind from a certain
direction ondaanimad *vii*
COOLED BY THE WIND: be cooled by the
wind dakaashi *vai;* dakaasin *vii*
CREAK IN THE WIND: giziibweweyaashi
vai; giziibweweyaasin *vii*
EAST WIND: waabani-noodin *ni*
FAVORABLE WIND: there is a favorable
wind minwaanimad *vii*
HOT WIND: be a hot wind gizhaanimad *vii*
NORTH WIND: giiwedin *ni*
SOUTH WIND: zhaawani-noodin *na*
WIND BLOWS FAST: gizhiiyaanimad *vii*
WIND BLOWS WILDLY: aanimad *vii*
WIND COMES FROM A CERTAIN
DIRECTION: ondin *vii*
WIND COMES IN HARD: bagamaanimad
vii
WIND DIES DOWN: boonaanimad *vii;*
ishkwaayaanimad *vii*

WIND HAS A CERTAIN SPEED: the wind
  has a certain speed **apiitaanimad** *vii*
WIND LETS UP: **boonaanimad** *vii*
WIND PICKS UP: **maadaanimad** *vii*
WIND SHIFTS: **gwekaanimad** *vii*
WINDIGO
  WINDIGO: be a windigo **wiindigoowi** *vai;*
    windigo: winter cannibal monster
    wiindigoo, -g *na*
WINDLESS
  WINDLESS: be windless **awibaa,**
    awibaamagad *vii*
WINDOW
  WINDOW: **waasechigan, -an** *ni*
  LOOK THROUGH A WINDOW: **dapaabi**
    vai; look through a window at s.o.
    dapaabam *vta;* look through a window at
    s.t. **dapaabandan** *vti*
WINDOW GLASS
  WINDOW GLASS: **waasechiganaabik, -oon**
    ni
WINDOW PANE
  WINDOW PANE: **waasechiganaabik, -oon** *ni*
WINDOW SHADE
  WINDOW SHADE: **gibiiga'iganiigin, -oon** *ni*
WINDY
  WINDY: be windy **noodin** *vii*
  VERY WINDY: be very windy **gichi-noodin**
    vii
WINE
  WINE: **zhoominaaboo** *ni,* also
    zhawiminaaboo
WING
  WING: my wing **niningwiigan, -an**
    /-ningwiigan-/ *nid*
  SHAKE WINGS: shake one's wings
    bapawaangeni *vai*
WINK
  WINK: **jiibiingweni** *vai;* wink at s.o.
    jiibiingwetaw *vta;* **jiichiibiingwetaw** *vta*
WINNEBAGO
  WINNEBAGO: **wiinibiigoo, -g** *na*
WINNOW
  WINNOW: winnow s.t. (e.g., wild rice)
    nooshkaatoon *vti2;* winnow things (e.g.,
    wild rice) **nooshkaachige** *vai*
WINNOWED
  WINNOWED: be winnowed
    nooshkaachigaade,
    nooshkaachigaademagad *vii*
WINNOWING TRAY
  WINNOWING TRAY: **nooshkaachinaagan,**
    -an *ni*
WINTER
  WINTER: be a winter (year) **biboonagad** *vii;*
    be winter **biboon** *vii*
  LAST WINTER: **biboonong** *pc*
  LATE WINTER: be late winter **giiwe-biboon**
    vii
  SPEND THE WINTER: spend the winter
    somewhere **biboonishi** *vai*
  WINTER BEFORE LAST: **awas-biboonong**
    pc

WIPE
  WIPE: wipe s.o. by hand **giziin** *vta;* wipe s.t.
    by hand **giziinan** *vti*
  WIPE AFTER DEFECATING: wipe oneself
    after defecating **giziindime'o** *vai*
  WIPE DISHES: **gaasiinaagane** *vai*
  WIPE FACE: wipe one's face with something
    giziingwe'o *vai*
  WIPE HANDS: wipe one's hands **gaasiininjii**
    vai
  WIPE MOUTH: wipe one's mouth
    gaasiidoone'o *vai*
  WIPE USING SOMETHING: wipe s.o. using
    something **gaasii' /gaasii'w-/** *vta;* wipe s.t.
    using something **gaasii'an** *vti;* wipe things
    using something **gaasii'ige** *vai*
WIRE
  WIRE: **biiwaabikoons, -an** *ni*
  SNARE WIRE: **agoodwaaganeyaab, -iin** *ni;*
    nagwaaganeyaab, -iin *ni*
WISE
  WISE: be wise **nibwaakaa** *vai*
WISH
  WISH: **bagosendam** *vai2;* wish for s.o.
    agaawaazh /agaawaaN-/ *vta;* wish for s.t.
    agaawaadan *vti;* **bagosendan** *vti;* wish of
    s.o. **bagosenim** *vta*
  I WISH THAT: I wish that ... **apegish** *pc,* also
    ambegish*, ambesh*
WITH
  WITH: **wiiji-** *pv4;* be with s.o. **wiij'ayaaw** *vta,*
    also **wiiji-ayaaw**
  DANCE WITH: dance with s.o.
    wiijishimotaw *vta*
  EAT WITH: eat with s.o. **wiidoopam** *vta;* eat
    with people **wiidoopange** *vai*
  GO WITH: go with s.o. **wiijiiw** *vta;* go with
    people **wiijii'iwe** *vai;* they go with each
    other **wiijiindiwag /wiijiindi-/** *vai*
  IN A PLACE WITH: **dago-** *pv4'*
  PLAY WITH: play with s.o. **wiiji'** *vta*
  SHARE COVER WITH: share a cover with
    s.o. **wiidagwazhem** *vta*
  SIT WITH: sit with s.o. **wiidabim** *vta*
  SLEEP WITH: sleep with s.o. **wiipem** *vta;*
    sleep with s.t. **wiipendan** *vti;* they sleep
    with each other **wiipendiwag /wiipendi-/**
    vai
  SLEEP WITH CHILDREN PROTECTIVE-
    LY: **wiipemaawaso** *vai*
  STAY WITH: stay with s.o. **wiij'ayaaw** *vta,*
    also **wiiji-ayaaw**
  WALK WITH: walk with s.o. **wiidosem** *vta*
  WORK WITH: work with s.o. **wiidanokiim**
    vta; **wiij'anokiim** *vta,* also **wiiji-anokiim**
WITHOUT
  WITHOUT A DOUBT: **aapideg** *pc*
  WITHOUT PURPOSE: **anishaa** *pc*
  WITHOUT RESULT: **aano-** *pv1*
WITNESS
  WITNESS: be a witness **waabange** *vai*
WOLF
  WOLF: **ma'iingan, -ag** *na*

WOLF HIDE
    WOLF HIDE: **ma'iinganiwayaan, -ag** *na*
WOLVERINE
    WOLVERINE: **gwiingwa'aage, -g** *na*
WOMAN
    WOMAN: **ikwe, -wag** *na;* be a woman **ikwewi**
    vai
    DAKOTA WOMAN: **bwaanikwe, -g** *na*
    DRESSED-UP WOMAN: **zazegaa-ikwe,**
    -wag *na*
    INDIAN WOMAN: **anishinaabekwe, -g** *na;*
    be an Indian woman **anishinaabekwewi**
    vai
    OJIBWE WOMAN: **ojibwekwe, -g** *na*
    OLD WOMAN: **mindimooyenh, -yag** *na;* be
    an old woman **mindimooyenyiwi** *vai*
    UNMARRIED WOMAN: **moozhikwe, -g** *na*
    YOUNG WOMAN: **oshkiniigikwe, -g** *na;* be
    a young woman **oshkiniigikwewi** *vai*
WOMEN'S DANCE
    WOMEN'S DANCE: **ikwe-niimi'idiwin, -an**
    ni
    DANCE THE WOMEN'S DANCE: **ikwe-**
    niimi *vai;* they dance the women's dance
    ikwe-niimi'idiwag /ikwe-niimi'idi-/ *vai*
WONDER
    WONDER: wonder at s.o. **maamakaadenim**
    vta; wonder at s.t. **maamakaadendan** *vti*
    I WONDER HOW: I wonder how *dubitative*
    amanj *pc, also* **amanj iidog, namanj*,**
    namanj iidog*
    I WONDER WHAT: I wonder what *inanimate*
    dubitative **wegodogwen, -an** *pr*
    I WONDER WHEN: I wonder when *dubitative*
    amanj apii *pc*
    I WONDER WHERE: I wonder where
    dubitative **dibi** *pc*
    I WONDER WHO: I wonder who *animate*
    dubitative **awegwen, -ag** *pr*
WOOD
    DRY WOOD: **mishiiwaatig, -oon** *ni*
    PIECE OF WOOD: **mitig, -oon** *ni*
    PUT WOOD ON THE FIRE: **bagidinise** *vai*
    UNDER WOOD: under wood (e.g., a tree or
    stick) **anaamaatig** *pc*
WOOD TICK
    WOOD TICK: **ezigaa, -g** *na*
WOODCHUCK
    WOODCHUCK: **akakojiish, -ag** *na*
WOODPECKER
    WOODPECKER: **baapaase, -g** *na*
    RED-HEADED WOODPECKER: **meme, -g**
    na
WOODS
    BEYOND THE WOODS: **awasaakwaa** *pc*
    COME OUT OF THE WOODS:
    bapaakwa'am *vai2*
    DENSE WOODS: be dense woods
    zagaakwaa, zagaakwaamagad *vii*
    GO INTO THE WOODS: **jekaakwa'am** *vai2*
    IN THE WOODS: **megwaayaak** *pc;*
    noopiming *pc*
    MIDDLE OF THE WOODS: in the middle of
    the woods **naawaakwaa** *pc*

    NEAR WOODS: near the woods **jiigaakwaa** *pc*
    OVER ACROSS THE WOODS: **awasaakwaa**
    pc
    WOODS GO A CERTAIN DISTANCE:
    akwaakwaa, akwaakwaamagad *vii*
WORD
    WORD: **ikidowin, -an** *ni*
WORK
    WORK: **anokii** *vai;* **anokiiwin, -an** *ni;* work at
    s.o. **anokaazh /anokaaN-/** *vta;* work at s.t.
    anokaadan *vti;* work for s.o. **anokiitaw**
    vta; work for oneself **anokiitaazo** *vai;* work
    for people **anokiitaage** *vai*
    ABLE TO WORK: be able to work
    gashkanokii *vai*
    FINISH WORK: **giizhiitaa** *vai*
    KEPT BUSY IN WORK: be kept busy in
    work **ondamanokii** *vai*
    LOOK FOR WORK: **nanda-anokii** *vai*
    MAKE WORK: make s.o. work **anokii'** *vta*
    PRETEND TO WORK: **anokiikaazo** *vai*
    START TO WORK: **maadanoki** *vai;* start to
    work on s.o. **maadanokaazh**
    /maadanokaaN-/ *vta;* **maajiikaw** *vta;* start
    to work on s.t. **maadanokaadan** *vti;*
    maajiikan *vti*
    WORK A CERTAIN WAY: **inanokii** *vai*
    WORK IN A CERTAIN PLACE: **dananokii**
    vai
    WORK ON: work on s.o. **dazhiikaw** *vta;* work
    on s.t. **dazhiikan** *vti*
    WORK UNTIL DAWN: **waabananokii** *vai*
    WORK WITH: work with s.o. **wiidanokiim**
    vta; **wiij'anokiim** *vta, also* **wiiji-anokiim**
    WORK WITHOUT STOPPING:
    aabidanokii *vai*
WORKED
    SOMETHING WORKED ON: **anokaajigan,**
    -an *ni*
    WORKED ON: be worked on **dazhiikigaade,**
    dazhiikigaademagad *vii*
WORKER
    WORKER: **anokiiwinini, -wag** *na;* worker
    (female) **anokiiwikwe, -g** *na*
    GOOD WORKER: be a good worker
    gotaamigozi *vai*
WORKSHOP
    WORKSHOP: **anokiiwigamig, -oon** *ni*
WORLD
    ALL OVER THE WORLD: **miziwekamig** *pc*
WORM
    WORM: **moose, -g** *na*
WORRIED
    WORRIED: be worried **ondamendam** *vai2*
WORRY
    WORRY: **babaamendam** *vai2;*
    biingeyendam *vai2;* worry about s.o.
    babaamenim *vta;* **ondamenim** *vta;* worry
    about s.t. **babaamendan** *vti;*
    ondamendan *vti*
WORTHLESS
    WORTHLESS: be worthless **goopadizi** *vai*

CONSIDER WORTHLESS: consider s.o.
worthless **goopadenim** *vta;* consider s.t.
worthless **goopadendan** *vti*
WOULD
  WOULD: would *modal* **daa-** *pv1*
WOUND
  SHOOT AND WOUND: shoot and wound
  s.o. **maakinaw** *vta*
WRAP
  WRAP: wrap s.o. (as or as with something
  sheet-like) **wiiwegin** *vta;* wrap s.t. (as or as
  with something sheet-like) **wiiweginan** *vti*
  WRAP AND TIE IN A BUNDLE: wrap and
  tie s.o. in a bundle **gashkibizh**
  /gashkibiN-/ *vta;* wrap and tie s.t. in a
  bundle **gashkibidoon** *vti2;* wrap and tie
  things in bundle **gashkibijige** *vai*
WRAPPED
  WRAPPED AND TIED IN A BUNDLE: be
  wrapped and tied in a bundle **gashkibide,**
  gashkibidemagad *vii;* **gashkibijigaade,**
  gashkibijigaademagad *vii;*
  gashkibijigaazo *vai*
  WRAPPED UP WARM: be wrapped up warm
  giizhoopizo *vai*
WREN
  WREN: **anaamisagadaweshiinh, -yag** *na*
WRENCH
  WRENCH: **biimiskwa'igan, -an** *ni*
WRESTLE
  WRESTLE: they wrestle each other
  gagwejiiwaanidiwag /gagwejiiwaanidi-/
  vai; wrestle s.o. **gagwejiiwaazh**
  /gagwejiiwaaN-/ *vta*
WRESTLER
  WRESTLER: **gagwejiiwaazoowinini, -wag** *na*
WRING
  WRING: wring s.o. **ziinibizh /ziinibiN-/** *vta;*
  wring s.t. **ziinibidoon** *vti2*
  WRING NECK: wring s.o.'s neck
  bookogwebizh /bookogwebiN-/ *vta*
WRINKLE
  WRINKLE: wrinkle up **oziigishkaa** *vai;*
  oziigishkaa, oziigishkaamagad *vii*
WRINKLED
  WRINKLED: be wrinkled **oziigaa,**
  oziigaamagad *vii;* **oziigizi** *vai*
  WRINKLED FACE: have a wrinkled face
  oziigiingwe *vai*
WRITE
  WRITE: **ozhibii'ige** *vai;* write s.t. **ozhibii'an**
  vti; write (s.t.) for s.o. **ozhibii'amaw** *vta*
  MAKE A MISTAKE WRITING: **wanibii'ige**
  vai; make a mistake writing s.t. **wanibii'an**
  vti
  WRITE A CERTAIN WAY: write s.t. a certain way **izhibii'an** *vti;* write things a certain way **izhibii'ige** *vai*
  WRITE A LETTER: **maajiibii'ige** *vai;* write a
  letter to s.o. **maajiibii'amaw** *vta*
  WRITE ALL OVER: **miziwebii'ige** *vai;* write
  s.t. all over **miziwebii'an** *vti*

WRITE BACK: write (s.t.) back to s.o.
nakwebii'amaw *vta;* they write back to
each other **nakwebii'amaadiwag**
/nakwebii'amaadi-/ *vai*
WRITE CORRECTLY: **gwayakobii'ige** *vai;*
write s.t. correctly **gwayakobii'an** *vti*
WRITE DOWN: write s.o. down **ozhibii'**
/ozhibii'w-/ *vta;* write s.t. down **ozhibii'an**
vti
WRITE HERE: **biijibii'ige** *vai;* write (s.t.) here
to s.o. *inverse forms of:* **biijibii'amaw-** *vta*
WRITE IN ENGLISH:
zhaaganaashiiwibii'ige *vai;* write in English to s.o. **zhaaganaashiiwibii'amaw** *vta;*
write s.t. in English **zhaaganaashiiwibii'an**
vti
WRITE IN INDIAN: write in Indian (Ojibwe)
anishinaabewibii'ige *vai;* write s.t. in Indian (Ojibwe) **anishinaabewibii'an** *vti;* write
s.t. in Indian (Ojibwe) (e.g., a book)
anishinaabewisidoon *vti2;* write (s.t.) in
Indian (Ojibwe) to s.o.
anishinaabewibii'amaw *vta*
WRITE IN OJIBWE: write in Indian (Ojibwe)
anishinaabewibii'ige *vai;* write s.t. in
Indian (Ojibwe) **anishinaabewibii'an** *vti;*
write s.t. in Indian (Ojibwe) (e.g., a book)
anishinaabewisidoon *vti2;* write s.t. in
Ojibwe **ojibwewibii'an** *vti;* write (s.t.) in
Indian (Ojibwe) to s.o.
anishinaabewibii'amaw *vta;* write things
in Ojibwe **ojibwewibii'ige** *vai*
WRITE NUMBERS: **asigibii'ige** *vai*
WRITE ON: write on something **apibii'ige** *vai*
WRITE OVER: write s.t. over **aanjibii'an** *vti*
WRITING
  INDIAN WRITING: Indian (Ojibwe) writing
  anishinaabewibii'igan, -an *ni*
  OJIBWE WRITING: Indian (Ojibwe) writing
  anishinaabewibii'igan, -an *ni*
  WRITING SURFACE: **apibii'igan, -an** *ni*
WRITTEN
  WRITTEN: be written **ozhibii'igaade,**
  ozhibii'igaademagad *vii*
  SOMETHING WRITTEN: **ozhibii'igan, -an**
  ni
  SOMETHING WRITTEN IN INDIAN:
  something written in Indian (Ojibwe)
  anishinaabewibii'igan, -an *ni*
  WRITTEN A CERTAIN WAY: be written a
  certain way **izhibii'igaade,**
  izhibii'igaademagad *vii;* **izhisin** *vii*
  WRITTEN IN INDIAN: be written in Indian
  (Ojibwe) **anishinaabewibii'igaade,**
  anishinaabewibii'igaademagad *vii;* be
  written in Indian (Ojibwe) (e.g., a book or
  document) **anishinaabewisin** *vii*
  WRITTEN IN OJIBWE: be written in Indian
  (Ojibwe) **anishinaabewibii'igaade,**
  anishinaabewibii'igaademagad *vii;* be
  written in Indian (Ojibwe) (e.g., a book or
  document) **anishinaabewisin** *vii;* be
  written in Ojibwe **ojibwewibii'igaade,**
  ojibwewibii'igaademagad *vii;* be written
  in Ojibwe (e.g., a book) **ojibwewisin** *vii*

WRITTEN ON ALL OVER: be written on all over **miziwebii'igaade, miziwebii'igaademagad** *vii*

WRONG
GO WRONG: have things go wrong **maazhise** *vai*
MAKE WRONG: make s.o. wrong **maanaaji'** *vta;* make s.t. wrong **maanaajitoon** *vti2*
TAKE WRONG ONE: take s.o. who/that is the wrong one **wanin** *vta;* take s.t. that is the wrong one **waninan** *vti*
TOUCH WRONG ONE: touch s.o. who/that is the wrong one **wanin** *vta;* touch s.t. that is the wrong one **waninan** *vti*

X-RAY
GET X-RAY: get an x-ray **zhaabwaakizo** *vai*
X-RAY PLATE
X-RAY PLATE: **zhaabwaakizigan, -an** *ni*

YARDSTICK
YARDSTICK: **diba'aatigwaan, -an** *ni*
YARN
YARN: **miskogaadeyaab, -iin** *ni*
BALL OF TWINE OR YARN: **bikoojaan, -an** *ni*
YAWN
YAWN: **naanibaayawe** *vai*
YEAR
YEAR: **gikinoonowin** *ni*
CERTAIN NUMBER OF YEARS: a certain number of years **daso-biboon** *pc;* **daso-gikinoonowin** *pc;* be a certain number of years **daso-biboonagad** *vii*
CERTAIN NUMBER OF YEARS OLD: be a certain number of years old **daso-biboonagizi** *vai*
YEAR PASSES: a year passes **biboonagad** *vii;* **gikinoonowagad** *vii*
YELLOW
YELLOW: **ozaawi-** *pv4;* be yellow **ozaawaa, ozaawaamagad** *vii;* **ozaawizi** *vai;* be yellow (as something mineral) **ozaawaabikad** *vii;* **ozaawaabikizi** *vai;* be yellow (as something sheet-like) **ozaawegad** *vii;* **ozaawegizi** *vai;* be yellow (as something stick- or wood-like) **ozaawaakozi** *vai;* **ozaawaakwad** *vii;* be

yellow (as something string-like) **ozaawaabiigad** *vii;* **ozaawaabiigizi** *vai*
COLORED YELLOW: be colored yellow **ozaawaande, ozaawaandemagad** *vii;* **ozaawaanzo** *vai*
WEAR YELLOW: **ozaawi'o** *vai*
YELLOW BIRCH
YELLOW BIRCH: **wiinizik, -oog** *na*
YELLOW-SHAFTED FLICKER
YELLOW-SHAFTED FLICKER: **mooningwane, -g** *na*
YES
YES: **en'** *pc;* **enyan'** *pc, also* **en', eya';** **mii nange** *pc*
YES-NO QUESTION
YES-NO QUESTION: *yes-no question word* **ina** *pc, also* **na**
YESTERDAY
YESTERDAY: **bijiinaago** *pc*
DAY BEFORE YESTERDAY: **awasonaago** *pc*
YET
YET: **geyaabi** *pc*
NOT YET: **gaa mashi** *pc, also* **gaawiin mashi**
YOU
YOU: you *second person singular personal pronoun* **giin** *pr;* you *second person plural personal pronoun* **giinawaa** *pr*
YOU BET
YOU BET: sure! you bet! **enange** *pc*
YOU SEE
YOU SEE: **aaniish naa** *pc*
YOUNG
YOUNG: **oshki-** *pv4;* be young **oshkaya'aawi** *vai, also* **oshki-aya'aawi; oshkayi'iiwan** *vii;* **oshki-bimaadizi** *vai;* **oshkiniigi** *vai*
LOOK YOUNG: **oshkiinaagozi** *vai*
PROTECT YOUNG: protect one's young **gizhaawaso** *vai*
SOMEONE YOUNG: **oshkaya'aa, -g** *na, also* **oshki-aya'aa**
SOMETHING YOUNG: **oshkayi'ii, -n** *ni, also* **oshki-ayi'ii**
YOUNG MAN
YOUNG MAN: **oshki-inini, -wag** *na;* **oshkinawe, -g** *na;* be a young man **oshkinawewi** *vai*
YOUNG WOMAN
YOUNG WOMAN: **oshkiniigikwe, -g** *na;* be a young woman **oshkiniigikwewi** *vai*
YOUNGEST
YOUNGEST CHILD: **ishkwejaagan, -ag** *na*

ZIP
ZIP UP: zip oneself up **giboobinidizo** *vai*